Teacher's Edition

World History

by
Wayne E. King and Marcel Lewinski

 **Wieser Educational**

30281 Esperanza
Rancho Santa Margarita, CA 92688-2130
1 (800) 880-4433 ♦ Fax (800) 949-0209

www.wieser-ed.com ♦ Email info@wieser-ed.com

About the Authors

Wayne E. King is currently the Academic Dean at the Baltimore School for the Arts. He earned his Bachelor of Science and Master of Science degrees from The Johns Hopkins University. He has taught history and social studies at all educational levels. With extensive experience as a curriculum writer, he has served as a consultant to schools, museums, and federal agencies. He has lectured at numerous national and international conferences on the teaching of history and cultural studies.

Marcel Lewinski is an Assistant Adjunct Professor of History Education at Illinois State University. Previously, he was an award-winning high school social studies teacher. He taught a wide range of subjects including geography, world history, economics, political science, sociology, and contemporary problems. Lewinski is professionally active in many organizations and has given presentations at many state, regional, and national conferences. He has conducted numerous workshops for social studies teachers and has traveled all over the world. As author of several textbooks in the social studies, Mr. Lewinski acts as a consultant to school systems and has often contributed to educational publications.

Reading Consultant

Timothy Shanahan, Ph.D., Professor of Urban Education, Director of the Center for Literacy, University of Illinois at Chicago; Author, AMP Reading System

Reviewers

The publisher wishes to thank the following educators for their helpful comments during the review process for *World History*. Their assistance has been invaluable.

Lois Barnes (Content Reviewer), Assistant Superintendent of Curriculum and Instruction, Woodford County Board of Education, Versailles, KY; **Phyllis Berman,** Supervisor/Coordinator, Scott School Assistant Center, Toledo Public Schools, Toledo, OH; **Elizabeth Burley,** Itinerant Resource Teacher, Ager Road Center, Hyattsville, MD; **Anita Dearing,** Resource Teacher, Oak Ridge High School, Oak Ridge, TN; **Tom Ferrara,** Teacher/Education Coordinator, South Bend Juvenile Correctional Facility, South Bend, IN; **Debora Hartzell,** Lead Teacher for Special Education, Lakeside High School, Atlanta, GA; **Patricia Henry,** Instructional Specialist, Special Education Programs, Montgomery County Public Schools, Rockville, MD; **Anne Hoffman,** Teacher, Santana High School, Santana, CA; **Lenore Heino Hoyt,** Social Studies Teacher, Centennial High School, Circle Pines, MN; **Larry Manchester,** Lead Resource Teacher, St. Andrews School, St. Paul, MN; **Russell F. Maruna,** Supervisor of Social Studies, Cleveland Municipal School District, Cleveland, OH; **Debby Persky,** Teacher, City of Angels, Los Angeles, CA; **Alice Richardson,** Special Education Teacher, Central High School, Detroit, MI; **Carolyn Scott,** Special Education Coordinator, Terrebonne Parish Schools, Houma, LA; **Craig Viscardi,** Special Education Teacher, Pasadena High School, Pasadena, TX; **J. B. Whitten,** Exceptional Student Education Teacher, Lennard High School, Ruskin, FL

Acknowledgments appear on pages 858–860, which constitutes an extension of this copyright page.

Pearson AGS Globe™ is a trademark, in the U.S. and/or in other countries, of Pearson Education, Inc. or its affiliate(s).

ISBN-13: 978-0-7854-6406-8

ISBN-10:   0-7854-6406-9

4 5 6 7 8 9 10 V0CR 12 11 10

1-800-992-0244
www.agsglobe.com

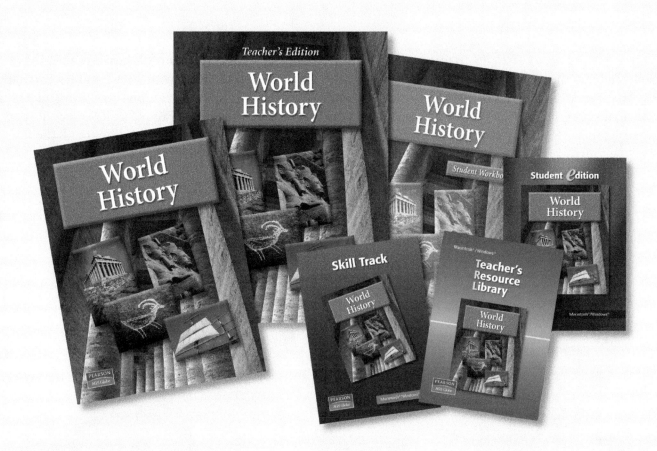

Understanding the world we live in should be important to everyone. Today, the people of the world are linked more closely than at any other time in history. As the global community becomes more interdependent culturally, economically, and politically, it is essential that students gain a better understanding of history. This text blends elements of both physical and human history. The text describes physical characteristics of each region of the world, including physical features and climate. It addresses the question of how the physical history of a place affects the people living there. Great attention is given to the people living in each region. Many aspects of culture including language, religion, customs, and problems are discussed. Special attention is focused on the challenges people of each region face in light of the many changes taking place in the world.

World History has been written with the student in mind. Written at a fourth-grade reading level, the text uses the latest research on how students learn. The text has been organized into an easy-to-understand format with many special features to aid students.

Each chapter has well-defined learning goals and each lesson has specific learning objectives. All headings are written in the form of questions to increase comprehension and establish a purpose for reading. The review sections after each lesson and at the end of each chapter help students and teachers assess learning. Critical-thinking questions and a variety of other question types are included.

Special features in the text enhance student learning. *Reading strategies* created by reading specialists help the student make sense of what they read. *Biographies* highlight people who have made a difference. *History in Your Life* relates history to current events. *Then and Now* highlights events and discoveries of the past that are still part of our lives. The *Document-Based Reading* feature presents original source documents for study. *Spotlight Stories* focus on both historical and current topics related to the content of the chapter. Writing skills are encouraged in the feature called *Writing About History*.

Enhance your social studies program with Pearson AGS Globe textbooks—an easy, effective way to teach students the practical skills they need. Each AGS Globe textbook meets your social studies curriculum needs. These exciting, full-color books use student-friendly text and real-world examples to show students the relevance of social studies in their daily lives. Each provides comprehensive coverage of skills and concepts. The short, concise lessons will motivate even your most reluctant students. With readabilities of all the texts at or below fourth-grade reading level, your students can concentrate on learning the content. AGS Globe is committed to making learning accessible to all students.

For more information on Pearson AGS Globe worktexts and textbooks:
call **1-800-328-2560**, visit our Web site at **www.agsglobe.com**,
or e-mail AGS Globe at **mail@agsglobe.com**

Skill Track monitors student progress and helps schools meet the demands of adequate yearly progress (AYP). Students using AGS Globe curriculum access multiple-choice assessments to see how well they understand the content of each textbook lesson and chapter. Skill Track is a tool available anytime. With timely and ongoing feedback from individual student and class reports, teachers can make informed instructional decisions. Administrators can use the reports to support teacher effectiveness and parents can keep up to date on what their students are learning.

Simple to use, Skill Track is secure and confidential. Students enter through two paths—lesson by lesson, or at the end of a chapter. Either way, mastery is assessed by a variety of multiple-choice items; parallel forms are available for chapter assessments. Hundreds of items cover the content and skills in each textbook. Students may retake any assessment as often as necessary and scores are reported for each attempt. Accordingly, teachers can identify areas in need of reinforcement and practice for individual learners as well as the class.

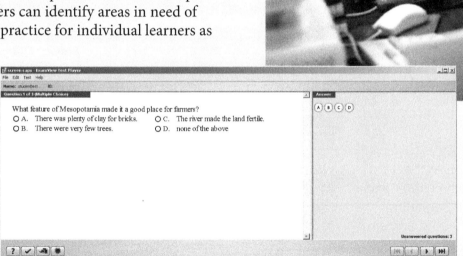

For more information about Skill Track:
call **1-800-328-2560** or visit our Web site at **www.agsglobe.com**

◆ Each lesson is clearly labeled to help students focus on the skill or concept to be learned.

◆ Maps, photos, illustrations, charts, and graphs provide visual representations of the content.

◆ Vocabulary terms are bold-faced and then defined in the margin on the page and in the glossary.

◆ Lesson Review questions allow students to check their understanding of key concepts presented in the text.

◆ Reading Strategy tips help students understand and make sense of what they read.

◆ Goals for Learning at the beginning of each chapter and Objectives at the beginning of each lesson identify learner outcomes.

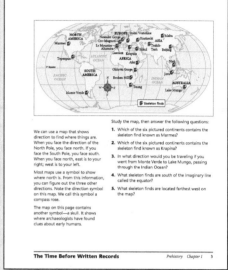

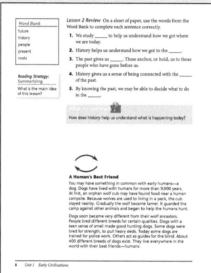

Neolithic Age

The age when people made polished stone tools; also called the New Stone Age

Nomad

A person who moves from place to place

Reading Strategy:
Summarizing

How does this lesson help you understand what you will be studying in this book?

Goals for Learning

◆ To define history and describe two kinds of sources of information

◆ To explain why we study history

◆ To describe artifacts and what historians learn from them

◆ To identify early hominids, the Stone Age, and the importance of farming

Objectives

◆ To describe how historians use artifacts to learn about the past

◆ To understand why there are different calendars

◆ To explain how radiocarbon dating is used

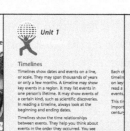
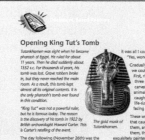

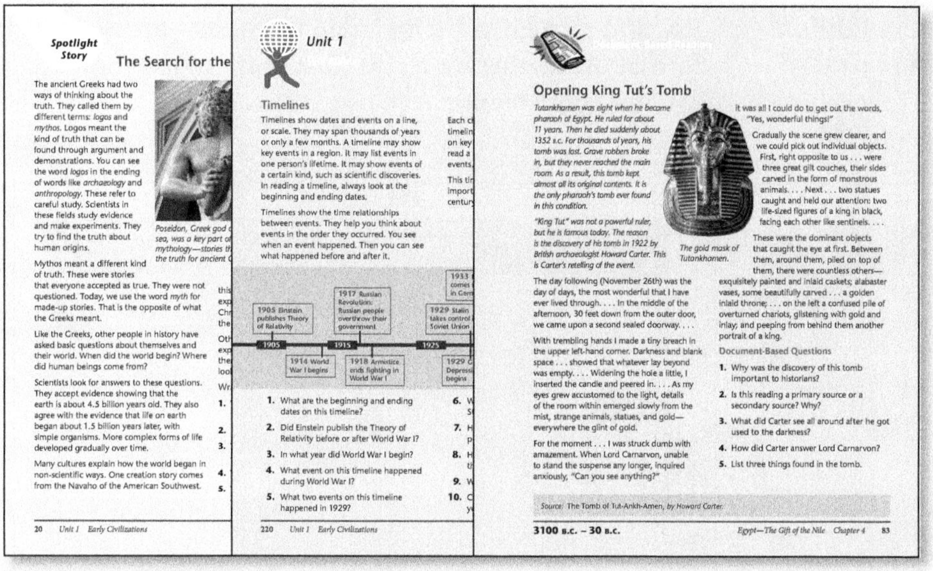

Spotlight Story — The Search for the...

The ancient Greeks had two ways of thinking about the truth. They called them by different terms: *logos* and *mythos*. Logos meant the kind of truth that can be found through argument and demonstrations. You can see the word *logos* in the ending of words like *archaeology* and *anthropology*. These refer to careful study. Scientists in these fields study evidence and make experiments. They try to find the truth about human origins.

Poseidon, Greek god of the sea, was a key part of mythology—stories that told the truth for ancient Greeks.

Mythos meant a different kind of truth. These were stories that everyone accepted as true. They were not questioned. Today, we use the word *myth* for made-up stories. That is the opposite of what the Greeks meant.

Like the Greeks, other people in history have asked basic questions about themselves and their world. When did the world begin? Where did human beings come from?

Scientists look for answers to these questions. They accept evidence showing that the earth is about 4.5 billion years old. They also agree with the evidence that life on earth began about 1.5 billion years later, with simple organisms. More complex forms of life developed gradually over time.

Many cultures explain how the world began in non-scientific ways. One creation story comes from the Navaho of the American Southwest.

20   *Unit 1 Early Civilizations*

Unit 1 — Timelines

Timelines show dates and events on a line, or scale. They may span thousands of years or only a few months. A timeline may show key events in a region. It may list events in one person's lifetime. It may show events of a certain kind, such as scientific discoveries. In reading a timeline, always look at the beginning and ending dates.

Timelines show the time relationships between events. They help you think about events in the order they occurred. You can see when an event happened. Then you can see what happened before and after it.

1. What are the beginning and ending dates on this timeline?
2. Did Einstein publish the Theory of Relativity before or after World War I?
3. In what year did World War I begin?
4. What event on this timeline happened during World War I?
5. What two events on this timeline happened in 1929?

220   *Unit 1 Early Civilizations*

Opening King Tut's Tomb

Tutankhamen was eight when he became pharaoh of Egypt. He ruled for about 11 years. Then he died suddenly about 1352 B.C. For thousands of years, his tomb was lost. Grave robbers broke in, but they never reached the main room. As a result, this tomb kept almost all its original contents. It is the only pharaoh's tomb ever found in this condition.

"King Tut" was not a powerful ruler, but he is famous today. The reason is the discovery of his tomb in 1922 by British archaeologist Howard Carter. This is Carter's retelling of the event.

The gold mask of Tutankhamen.

The day following (November 26th) was the day of days, the most wonderful that I have ever lived through.... In the middle of the afternoon, 30 feet down from the outer door, we came upon a second sealed doorway....

With trembling hands I made a tiny breach in the upper left-hand corner. Darkness and blank space . . . showed that whatever lay beyond was empty.... Widening the hole a little, I inserted the candle and peered in.... As my eyes grew accustomed to the light, details of the room within emerged slowly from the mist, strange animals, statues, and gold—everywhere the glint of gold.

For the moment . . . I was struck dumb with amazement. When Lord Carnarvon, unable to stand the suspense any longer, inquired anxiously, "Can you see anything?"

it was all I could do to get out the words, "Yes, wonderful things!"

Gradually the scene grew clearer, and we could pick out individual objects. First, right opposite to us . . . were three great gilt couches, their sides carved in the form of monstrous animals.... Next . . . two statues caught and held our attention two life-sized figures of a king in black, facing each other like sentinels....

These were the dominant objects that caught the eye at first. Between them, around them, piled on top of them, there were countless others—exquisitely painted and inlaid caskets; alabaster vases, some beautifully carved . . . a golden inlaid throne; . . . on the left a confused pile of overturned chariots, glistening with gold and inlay; and peeping from behind them another portrait of a king.

Document-Based Questions

1. Why was the discovery of this tomb important to historians?
2. Is this reading a primary source or a secondary source? Why?
3. What did Carter see all around after he got used to the darkness?
4. How did Carter answer Lord Carnarvon?
5. List three things found in the tomb.

Source: The Tomb of Tut-Ankh-Amen, by Howard Carter.

3100 B.C. – 30 B.C.   *Egypt—The Gift of the Nile Chapter 4*   83

Chapter 9 SUMMARY

- The first Americans arrived during the last Ice Age. They walked from Asia over the Bering Strait. Clues about how and when this happened are still being discovered.
- Bones found in Folsom, New Mexico, proved that American Indians had been living in the area for at least 9,000 years.
- The Clovis Point was more than 4,000 years older than the Folsom Point. Scientists believe that the Clovis people were the first Americans.
- The Hohokam civilization began about 300 B.C. in what is now Arizona. They built irrigation canals and created beautiful pottery and jewelry.
- Beginning about 200 B.C., the Mogollon lived in what is now southeastern Arizona and southern New Mexico. They created more artistic images than any other people in the world.
- The Anasazi are known as master builders. Their civilization began in about 100 A.D. They lived where Arizona, New Mexico, Utah, and Colorado meet.
- The Adena (beginning about 700 B.C.) and Hopewell (beginning about A.D. 100) were early Woodland cultures. They were both mound builders.
- Beginning around A.D. 1200, the Iroquois, a group of six different tribes,

were a powerful Woodland culture in Upper New York.
- The Plains Indians lived between the Mississippi River and the Rocky Mountains. They were Sioux, Cheyenne, Comanche, and Blackfoot Indians. The Mandans lived in what is now North Dakota.
- The Pacific Coast Indians lived in what is now Washington State. They were experts at fishing.
- Eskimos, or Inuits, lived a hard life in a frozen environment. They are known for their ivory and soapstone carvings.
- Mesoamerica is the land between North and South America. The Olmecs developed the first important civilization in this area around 1200 B.C.
- The Mayas developed an excellent written language. Their most important cultural and artistic achievements took place between A.D. 300 and 900.
- Around A.D. 900, the Toltecs moved into the Valley of Mexico. In this culture, warriors gained power.
- The Aztecs moved into the Valley of Mexico around A.D. 1200. In 1521, the Aztec Empire ended.
- The Inca Empire was in the Andes Mountains in South America. The empire lasted about 100 years, ending in 1532.

Prehistory – A.D. 1570   *Civilizations of the Americas: Prehistory – A.D. 1570 Chapter 9*   217

Unit 1 SUMMARY

- The discovery of fire and the beginning of farming were among the most important events in human history.
- The time before humans left written records is called prehistory.
- Civilizations began in Mesopotamia about 7,000 years ago.
- Sumerians invented a system of writing called cuneiform.
- The Assyrians were a warrior tribe in Mesopotamia.
- The teachings of Zoroaster influenced Judaism and Christianity.
- Egyptian civilizations developed in the valley of the Nile River in Africa.
- Pharaohs in Egypt built pyramids for tombs. People filled them with things the ruler would need in the afterlife.
- The first Indian civilization began in the Indus River Valley.
- Hinduism is based on castes, or classes. Everyone is born into a caste.
- Siddhartha Gautama became the Buddha. Buddhism spread from India into Asia.
- The Yangtze is the longer river in China; the first cities were built along this river about 2000 B.C.

- Socrates, Plato, and Aristotle were Greek philosophers during the "Golden Age" of Athens.
- In 60 B.C., Pompey, Julius Caesar, and Crassus ruled together as the First Triumvirate.
- Jesus was born in Palestine during the reign of Augustus. Followers of Jesus believed he was the Son of God.
- The Roman Empire fell in A.D. 476.
- Mesoamerica is the land between North and South America.
- The Olmecs developed the first system of writing in the Americas. They were mathematicians and astronomers.
- The Mayas are considered the most advanced culture in Mesoamerica. They influenced other great civilizations of Mesoamerica.
- The Aztecs moved into the Valley of Mexico about A.D. 900. Their capital was the magnificent city of Tenochtitlán.
- The Incan Empire grew up in the Peruvian Andes Mountains. It ended in A.D. 1532.

Prehistory – A.D. 1570   *Early Civilizations Unit 1*   221

Chapter 9 REVIEW

Word Bank
Anasazi
Aztec
Clovis
Hohokam
Incas
Inuit
Mayas
Mogollons
Olmecs
Toltecs

On a sheet of paper, use the words from the Word Bank to complete each sentence correctly.

1. Scientists think the _____ people were among the first Americans.
2. The _____ are known for their rock art—images of insects, fish, reptiles, birds, and mammals.
3. The _____ built cliff dwellings in the rock near where Arizona, New Mexico, Utah, and Colorado meet.
4. Because they lived in the desert, the _____ had to build irrigation canals to water their crops.
5. The _____ created the first system of writing in the Americas.
6. The _____ are known for their calendar, which was based on 400-year cycles.
7. By the early 1500s, the _____ people had become a harsh military power.
8. The _____ built more than 14,000 miles of roads to connect people in their large empire.
9. _____ civilization was different from others because of the importance of their military.
10. The _____, or Eskimo, people built shelters out of blocks of snow.

On a sheet of paper, write the letter of the answer that correctly completes each sentence.

11. The settlement of _____ was an important place for the Hohokam.
   A Clovis   B Folsom   C Snaketown   D Cahokia
12. Archaeologists named the _____ after the mountain ranges in which they lived.
   A Hohokam   B Mogollan   C Anasazi   D Adena

218   *Unit 1 Early Civilizations*

---

13. The _____ people created a very large earthen Snake Mound.
   A Hohokam   B Mogollan   C Iroquois   D Hopewell
14. The _____ culture was unusual because even though they were not farmers, they had the resources to build large earthen structures.
   A Anasazi   B Adena   C Poverty Point   D Cahokia
15. The _____ tribes lived in Puget Sound, a large body of water surrounded on three sides by land.
   A Pacific Coast   B Plains Indian   C Inuit   D Iroquois

On a sheet of paper, write the answer to each question. Use complete sentences.

16. Choose one of the cultures you have just studied. How did the environment determine what kinds of shelters they built and how they farmed?
17. How did George McJunkin know that the bones he discovered in 1908 were an important scientific discovery?
18. Besides water for their crops, how did the Hohokam use the water from their canals?

Critical Thinking On a sheet of paper, write your response to each question. Use complete sentences.

19. After the Incas conquered a tribe by military force, they asked the tribal leaders to become partners in their empire. How did this make the Incan Empire stronger?
20. Why do you think archaeologists have found so few artifacts from the earliest Americans?

> Try to answer all questions as completely as possible. When asked to explain your answer, do so in complete sentences.

Prehistory – A.D. 1570   *Civilizations of the Americas: Prehistory – A.D. 1570 Chapter 9*   219

- ◆ Many features reinforce and extend student learning beyond the lesson content.

- ◆ Summaries at the end of each chapter and unit highlight main ideas for students.

- ◆ Chapter Reviews allow students and teachers to check for skill mastery. These cover the objectives in the Goals for Learning at the beginning of each chapter and the Objectives at the beginning of each lesson.

- ◆ Test-Taking Tips at the end of each Chapter Review help reduce test anxiety and improve test scores.

The comprehensive, wraparound Teacher's Edition provides instructional strategies at point of use. Everything from preparation guidelines to teaching tips and strategies are included in an easy-to-use format. Activities are featured at point of use for teacher convenience.

1 Planning Guide — Early Civilizations

Chapter/Lesson	Title	Student Pages	Vocabulary	Lesson Review	Critical-Thinking Questions	Chapter Summary	Chapter Review	Reading Strategy	Map Study/Map Skills	Writing About History	Geography Note	Biography	History in Your Life	Communication In History	Technology Connection	Then and Now	Spotlight Story	Document-Based Reading	Background Information	Applications (Home, Cases, Community)	World Cultures	Study Skills	Online Connection	ELL/ESL Strategy	Auditory/Verbal	Visual/Spatial	Body/Kinesthetic	Interpersonal/Group Learning	Logical/Mathematical	Activities/Modified Activities	Workbook Activities	Self-Study Guide	Chapter Outline
Chapter 1	Prehistory	2–23	✔		✔	21	22	4	3							20	19					4	4			3						✔	✔
Lesson 1	The Meaning of History	5–6	✔	6	✔			✔											6	6							6			1	1		
Lesson 2	Why We Study History	7–8		8	✔			✔							8						8		8	8						2	2		
Lesson 3	The Way Historians Work	9–12	✔	12	✔			✔		11				11	10				11	10, 12	12		10							3	3		
Lesson 4	Prehistory	13–18	✔	18	✔			✔					14						16	15			17				15		16	4	4		
Chapter 2	Ancient Middle East	24–43	✔		✔	41	42	26	25							40	39							39									✔	✔
Lesson 1	The Sumerians	27–30	✔	30	✔			✔				29							29	30	28			30	29	28				5	5		
Lesson 2	The Akkadians and the Babylonians	31–34	✔	34	✔			✔	34	38						33			34			32								6	6		
Lesson 3	The Phoenicians and the Hebrews	35–38	✔	38	✔			✔	36			35	37								38		38	39	36		38	37		7	7		
Chapter 3	Middle Eastern Empires	44–63	✔		✔	61	62	46	45							60	59																✔	✔
Lesson 1	The Assyrians	47–50	✔	50	✔			✔	48										49	50	48	50	49		49	49				8	8		
Lesson 2	The Chaldeans	51–54	✔	54	✔			✔	51	53						53				54			53					52	54	9	9		
Lesson 3	The Persians	55–58	✔	58	✔			✔	56		57	58							58	58			57						56	10	10		

(Unit Planning Guide is continued on next page.)

Unit Activities

Student Text
Unit 1 Summary
Unit 1 Skill Builder

Teacher's Resource Library
Unit 1 Activities 1–2
Unit 1 Skills Activity

Assessment Options

Teacher's Resource Library
Chapter 1 Mastery Tests A and B
Chapter 2 Mastery Tests A and B
Chapter 3 Mastery Tests A and B
Chapter 4 Mastery Tests A and B
Chapter 5 Mastery Tests A and B
Chapter 6 Mastery Tests A and B
Chapter 7 Mastery Tests A and B
Chapter 8 Mastery Tests A and B
Chapter 9 Mastery Tests A and B
Unit 1 Mastery Test

TRL Activities

The Teacher's Resource Library (TRL) contains a set of lower-level worksheets called Modified Activities. These worksheets cover the same content as the standard Activities but are written at a lower reading level.

Skill Track

Use Skill Track for *World History* to monitor student progress and meet the demands of Adequate Yearly Progress (AYP). Make informed instructional decisions with individual student and class reports of lesson and chapter assessments. With immediate and ongoing feedback, students will also see what they have learned and where they need more reinforcement and practice.

xxxviA   xxxviB

Unit Planning Guides

◆ The Planning Guide saves valuable preparation time by organizing all materials for each unit.

◆ A complete listing of chapters and lessons allows you to preview each unit quickly.

◆ Assessment options are highlighted for easy reference. Options include:

  Lesson Reviews
  Chapter Reviews
  Chapter Mastery Tests, Forms A and B
  Midterm and Final Tests

◆ Page numbers of Student Text and Teacher's Edition features help customize lesson plans to your students.

◆ Many teaching strategies and learning styles are listed to support students with diverse needs.

◆ Activities for the Teacher's Resource Library are listed.

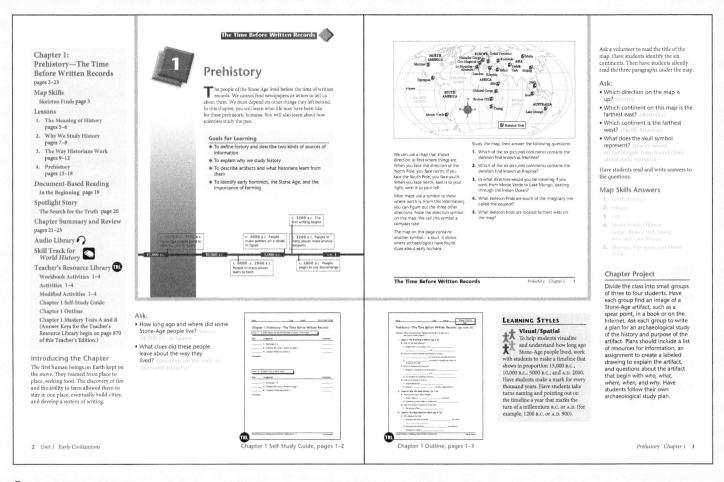

Lessons

◆ Quick overviews of chapters and lessons save planning time.

◆ Lesson objectives are listed for easy reference.

◆ Page references are provided for convenience.

◆ Easy-to-follow lesson plans in three steps save time: Warm-Up Activity, Teaching the Lesson, and Reinforce and Extend.

◆ Applications: Three areas of application—At Home, Career Connection, and In the Community—help students relate social studies to the world outside the classroom. Applications motivate students and make learning relevant.

◆ Online Connections list relevant Web sites.

◆ Learning Styles provide teaching strategies to help meet the needs of students with diverse ways of learning. Modalities include Auditory/ Verbal, Visual/Spatial, Body/Kinesthetic, Logical/ Mathematical, and Interpersonal/Group Learning.

Additional teaching activities are provided for ELL students in each lesson.

◆ Answers are provided in the Teacher's Edition for all reviews in the Student Text. Answers to the Teacher's Resource Library, and Student Workbook are provided at the back of this Teacher's Edition and on the TRL CD-ROM.

◆ Unit Activities, Unit Skills Activities, Unit Mastery Tests, Workbook Activities, Activities, Self-Study Guides, Chapter Outlines, and Chapter Mastery Test pages from the Teacher's Resource Library are shown at point of use in reduced form.

Increasing numbers of students learning English are among the students in most schools and classrooms. The purpose of the ELL/ESL Strategy feature in this Teacher's Edition is to incorporate the language and content needs of English Language Learners in a regular and explicit manner.

ELL/ESL Strategy activities promote English language acquisition in the context of content area learning. Students should not be separated or isolated for these activities and interaction with English-speaking peers is always encouraged.

The ELL/ESL Strategy helps the teacher scaffold the content and presentation in relation to students' language and skill proficiency. Each activity suggests to the teacher some ideas about how to adjust the presentation of content to meet the varying needs of diverse learners, including students learning English. *Scaffolding* refers to structuring the introduction of vocabulary, concepts, and skills by providing additional supports or modifications based on students' needs. Ideally, these supports become less necessary as students' language proficiency increases and their knowledge and skill level becomes more developed.

Each activity includes a language objective and strategy related to *listening, speaking, reading,* or *writing.* The language objective and activity relate to one or more content objectives listed in the Teacher's Edition under Lesson at a Glance.

Some examples of language objectives include: reading for meaning, understanding different styles or purposes of writing, identifying and practicing common grammar structures, learning vocabulary specific to the content area, preparing and giving a group presentation, speaking in front of a group, or discussing an assigned topic as a small group.

ELL/ESL STRATEGY

Language Objective:
To review and write newspaper articles

Have students examine the sections of a modern newspaper and note the titles of the sections and the kinds of articles that are found within them. Then ask each student to write an article that might have been published in ancient Sparta. Finally, have students organize their articles into a "daily Spartan newspaper."

Strategies That Support English Learners

- Identify and build on prior knowledge or experience; start with what's familiar and elaborate to include new content and new connections, personal associations, cultural context

- Use visuals and graphic organizers—illustrations, photos, charts, posters, graphs, maps, tables, webs, flowcharts, timelines, diagrams

- Use hands-on artifacts (realia) or manipulatives

- Provide *comprehensible input*—paraphrase content, give additional examples, elaborate on student background knowledge and responses; be aware of rate of speech, syntax, and language structure and adjust accordingly

- Begin with lower-level, fact recall questions and move to questions that require higher-order critical-thinking skills (application, hypothesis, prediction, analysis, synthesis, evaluation)

- Teach vocabulary—pronunciations, key words or phrases, multiple meanings, idioms/expressions, academic or content language

- Have students create word banks or word walls for content (academic) vocabulary

- Teach and model specific reading and writing strategies—advance organizers, main idea, meaning from context, preview, predict, make inferences, summarize, guided reading

- Support communication with gestures and body language

- Teach and practice functional language skills—negotiate meaning, ask for clarification, confirm information, argue persuasively

- Teach and practice study skills—structured note-taking, outlining, use of reference materials

- Use cooperative learning, peer tutoring, or other small group learning strategies

- Plan opportunities for student interaction—create a skit and act it out, drama, role play, storytelling

- Practice self-monitoring and self-evaluation—students reflect on their own comprehension or activity with self-checks

How Do AGS Globe Textbooks Support Students Learning English?

AGS Globe is committed to helping all students succeed. For this reason, AGS Globe textbooks and teaching materials incorporate research-based design elements and instructional methodologies configured to allow diverse students greater access to subject area content. Content access is facilitated by controlled reading level, coherent text, and vocabulary development. Effective instructional design is accomplished by applying research to lesson construction, learning activities, and assessments.

AGS Globe materials feature key elements that support the needs of students learning English in sheltered and immersion settings.

Lesson Preparation	◆ Content- and language-specific objectives
Building Background	◆ Warm-Up Activity ◆ Explicit vocabulary instruction and practice with multiple exposures to new words ◆ Background information; building on prior knowledge and experience
Comprehensible Input	◆ Controlled reading level in student text (Grades 3–4) ◆ Highlighted vocabulary terms with definitions ◆ Student glossary with pronunciations ◆ Clean graphic and visual support ◆ Content links to examples ◆ Sidebar notes to highlight and clarify content ◆ Audio text recordings (selected titles) ◆ Modified Activity pages (Grade 2 reading level)
Lesson Delivery	◆ Teaching the Lesson/3-Step Teaching Plan ◆ Short, skill- or content-specific lessons ◆ Orderly presentation of content with structural cues
Strategies	◆ ELL/ESL Strategy activities ◆ Learning Styles activities ◆ Writing prompts in student text ◆ Teaching Strategies Transparencies provide additional graphic organizers ◆ Study skills: Self-Study Guides, Chapter Outlines
Interaction	◆ Vocabulary-building activities ◆ Language-based ELL/ESL Strategy activities ◆ Learning Styles activities ◆ Reinforce and Extend activities
Practice/Application	◆ Skill practice or concept application in student text ◆ Reinforce and Extend activities ◆ Career, home, and community applications ◆ Student Workbook ◆ Multiple TRL activity pages
Review and Assessment	◆ Lesson reviews, chapter reviews, unit reviews ◆ Skill Track monitors student progress ◆ Chapter, Unit, Midterm, and Final Mastery Tests

For more information on these key elements, see Echevarria, J., Vogt, M., & Short, D. (2004). *Making content comprehensible for English language learners: The SIOP model* (2nd ed.). Boston, MA: Allyn & Bacon.

Differentiated instruction allows teachers to address the needs of diverse learners and the variety of ways students process and learn information. The Learning Styles activities in this Teacher's Edition provide additional teaching strategies to help students understand lesson content by teaching or expanding upon the content in a different way. The activities are designed to help teachers capitalize on students' individual strengths and learning styles.

The Learning Styles activities highlight individual learning styles and are classified based on Howard Gardner's theory of multiple intelligences: Auditory/Verbal, Body/Kinesthetic, Interpersonal/Group Learning, Logical/Mathematical, and Visual/Spatial. In addition, the various writing activities suggested in the Student Text are appropriate for students who fit Gardner's description of Verbal/Linguistic intelligence.

Following are examples of activities featured in the *World History* Teacher's Edition:

Body/Kinesthetic

Students learn from activities that include physical movement, manipulatives, or other tactile experiences.

LEARNING STYLES

Body/Kinesthetic
As a group project, have students construct a model of a ziggurat (a four-sided pyramid) using wood blocks or any materials of their choice. Encourage students to strive for detail and historical accuracy. They may find it helpful to do library or Internet research on the construction of ziggurats.

Auditory/Verbal

Students learn by listening to text read aloud or from an audio recording, and from other listening or speaking activities. Musical activities related to the content may help auditory learners.

LEARNING STYLES

Auditory/Verbal
Have students find a copy of the poem "Paul Revere's Ride" by Henry Wadsworth Longfellow. It should be relatively easy to find in the school library or on the Internet. Have students practice reading the poem more than once. Encourage students to recite the poem aloud, either as a class or by dividing the poem in sections and reciting in groups.

Interpersonal/Group Learning

Students learn from working with at least one other person or in a cooperative learning group on activities that involve a process and an end product.

LEARNING STYLES

Interpersonal/ Group Learning
Ask groups to pass around a log into which students will enter their observations about why the Chaldean Empire fell. The first student might write: "Nothing went well after Nebuchadnezzar died" and then give the log to another student. Students should continue to write short sentences and pass the log until the whole story has been told.

Logical/Mathematical

Students learn by using logical/mathematical thinking and problem solving in relation to the lesson content.

LEARNING STYLES

Logical/Mathematical
Have students make a timeline that shows the works of three writers—the English author Jonathan Swift, the French playwright Molière, and the American author Washington Irving. Research the works of each writer to find the common element in all of their work. Write a paragraph that explains what the three writers had in common.

Visual/Spatial

Students learn by viewing or creating illustrations, graphics, patterns, or additional visual demonstrations beyond what is in the text.

LEARNING STYLES

Visual/Spatial
To help students visualize and understand how long ago Stone-Age people lived, work with students to make a timeline that shows in proportion 15,000 b.c., 10,000 b.c., 5000 b.c., and a.d. 2000. Have students make a mark for every thousand years. Have students take turns naming and pointing out on the timeline a year that marks the turn of a millennium b.c. or a.d. (for example, 1200 b.c. or a.d. 900).

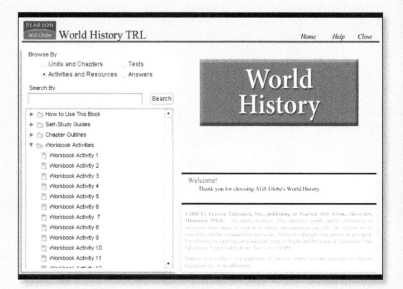

TRL All of the activities you'll need to reinforce and extend the text are conveniently located on the AGS Globe Teacher's Resource Library (TRL) CD-ROM. All of the reproducible activities pictured in the Teacher's Edition are ready to select, view, and print. You can also preview other materials by linking directly to the AGS Globe Web site.

Workbook Activities
Workbook Activities are available to reinforce and extend skills from each lesson of the textbook. A bound workbook format is also available.

Activities
Activities for each lesson give students additional skill practice. Unit activities help students further develop their critical-thinking skills.

Modified Activities
These activities cover the same content as the regular Activities but are written at a lower reading level.

Self-Study Guides/Chapter Outlines
An assignment guide provides teachers with the flexibility for individualized instruction or independent study.

Mastery Tests
Chapter, Unit, Midterm, and Final Mastery Tests are convenient assessment options. Critical-thinking items are included.

Answer Key
All answers to reproducible activities are included in the TRL and in the Teacher's Edition.

Unit Activities/Unit Skills Activities
The Unit Activities provide students with a project to work on throughout each unit. The Unit Skills Activities teach skills to support each unit.

Workbook Activities

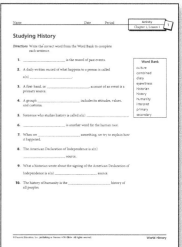

Activities

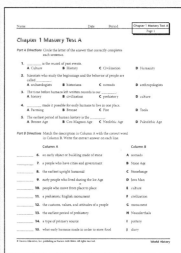

Unit Activities

Mastery Tests

Research-Based Principles	AGS Globe Textbooks	References
Standards Alignment		
Subject area instruction needs to be based on skills, concepts, and processes represented by common standards for that subject area.	◆ Textbook content and skills aligned with national standards and state grade-level or course-specific content standards, where available	Matlock, L., Fielder, K., & Walsh, D. (2001). Building the foundation for standards-based instruction for all students. *Teaching Exceptional Children, 33*(5), 68–72. Miller, S. P., & Mercer, C. D. (1997). Educational aspects of mathematics disabilities. *Journal of Learning Disabilities, 30*(1), 47–56. Reys, R., Reys, B., Lapan, R., Holliday, G. & Wasman, D. (2003). Assessing the impact of standards-based middle grades mathematics curriculum materials on student achievement. *Journal of Research in Mathematics Education, 34*(1), 74–95.
Readability		
Many students struggle to learn from core content-area textbooks that are written too high above their reading level. Students need access to textbooks written at a level they can read and understand, where the reading level is within the students' range of comprehension.	◆ Grade 4.0 or lower readability using the Spache formula ◆ Controlled vocabulary matched to student reading ability and use of synonyms to replace non-essential difficult words above grade 4 ◆ Simple sentence structures ◆ Limited sentence length	Allington, R. L. (2002). You can't learn mu Ch from books you can't read. *Educational Leadership, 60*(3), 16–19. Chall, J. S., & Conard, S. S. (1991). *Should textbooks challenge students? The case for easier or harder textbooks.* New York: Teachers College Press. *Readability calculations.* (2000). Dallas: Micro Power & Light Company.
Language Complexity and Sequence		
Students struggling with vocabulary and text comprehension need textbooks with accessible language.	◆ Simple, direct language using an active voice ◆ Clear organization to facilitate understanding ◆ Explicit language signals to show sequence of and links between concepts and ideas	Anderson, T. H., & Armbruster, B. B. (1984). Readable texts, or selecting a textbook is not like buying a pair of shoes. In R. C. Anderson, J. Osborne, & R. J. Tierney (Eds.), *Learning to read in American schools* (pp. 151–162). Hillsdale, NJ: Lawrence Erlbaum Associates, Inc. Curtis, M. E. (2002, May 20). *Adolescent reading: A synthesis of research.* Paper presented at the Practice Models for Adolescent Literacy Success Conference, U.S. Department of Education. Washington, DC: National Institute of Child Health and Human Development. Retrieved September 15, 2003, from http://216.26.160.105/conf/nichd/synthesis.asp McAlpine, L., & Weston, C. (1994). The attributes of instructional materials. *Performance Improvement Quarterly, 7*(1), 19–30. Seidenberg, P. L. (1989). Relating text-processing research to reading and writing instruction for learning disabled students. *Learning Disabilities Focus, 5*(1), 4–12.
Vocabulary Use and Development		
Students need content-related vocabulary instruction in the context of readable and meaningful text.	◆ New vocabulary boldfaced on first occurrence, used in context, and defined in a sidebar ◆ Glossary with pronunciation, definition, and relevant graphic illustrations for all vocabulary words ◆ Direct vocabulary instruction introduced in the Teacher's Edition and reinforced in context throughout ◆ Multiple exposures to new vocabulary in text and practice exercises	Ciborowski, J. (1992). *Textbooks and the students who can't read them: A guide to teaching content.* Cambridge, MA: Brookline. Kameenui, E. J., & Simmons, D. C. (1990). *Designing instructional strategies.* Columbus, OH: Merrill Publishing Company. Marzano, R. J. (1998). *A theory-based meta-analysis of research on instruction.* Aurora, CO: Mid-Continent Research for Education and Learning. Retrieved October 1, 2003, from http://www.mcrel.org/topics/productDetail/asp?productID=83 McAlpine, L., & Weston, C. (1994). The attributes of instructional materials. *Performance Improvement Quarterly, 7*(1), 19–30. National Reading Panel. (2000). *Teaching children to read: An evidence-based assessment of the scientific research literature on reading and its implications for reading instruction.* Reports of the subgroups. Washington, DC: National Institute of Child Health and Human Development. Taylor, S. E., Frackenpohl, H., White, C. E., Nieroroda, B. W., Browning, C. L., & Birsner, E. P. (1989). *EDL core vocabularies in reading, mathematics, science, and social studies.* Austin, TX: Steck-Vaughn.

Research-Based Principles	AGS Globe Textbooks	References
Text Organization: Presentation and Structure		

Text Organization: Presentation and Structure

Students need an uncluttered page layout, with easy-to-read print, that clearly directs the reader to main ideas, important information, examples, and comprehensive practice and review.

Reading comprehension is improved by structural features in the text that make it easier for learners to access the content.

Print characteristics and page layout:
- Serif font for body copy; sans serif font for boxed features, examples
- Maximum line length of 5" for ease of reading
- Unjustified (ragged) right margins
- Major/minor column page design presents primary instructional information in the major column and support content in the sidebar or in a box

Presentation characteristics:
- Lesson introductions, summaries
- Explicit lesson titles, headings, and subheadings label and organize main ideas
- Signals alert readers to important information, content connections, illustrations, graphics
- Cues (e.g., boldface type) highlight important information

Text structure:
- Lesson heads in question or statement format guide comprehension
- Text written to explicitly link facts and concepts within and across lessons; text cohesiveness
- Each skill or concept linked to direct practice and review

Armbruster, B. B., & Anderson, T. H. (1988). On selecting "considerate" content area textbooks. *Remedial and Special Education, 9*(1), 47–52.

Beck, I. L., McKeown, M. G., & Grommoll, E. W. (1989). Learning from social studies texts. *Cognition and Instruction, 6*(2), 99–158.

Chambliss, M. J. (1994). Evaluating the quality of textbooks for diverse learners. *Remedial and Special Education, 15*(5), 348–362.

Ciborowski, J. (1992). *Textbooks and the students who can't read them: A guide to teaching content.* Cambridge, MA: Brookline.

Dickson, S. V., Simmons, D. C., & Kameenui, E. J. (1995). *Text organization and its relation to reading comprehension: A synthesis of the research* (Technical Report No. 17) and *Text organization: Curricular and instructional implications for diverse learners* (Technical Report No. 18). National Center to Improve the Tools of Educators. Eugene, OR: University of Oregon. Retrieved January 26, 2000, from http://idea.uoregon.edu/~ncite/documents/techrep/tech17.html and http://idea.uoregon.edu/~ncite/documents/techrep/tech18.html

Dickson, S. V., Simmons, D. C., & Kameenui, E. J. (1998). Text organization: Research bases *and* Text organization: Instructional and curricular basics and implications. In D. C. Simmons & E. J. Kameenui (Eds.), *What reading research tells us about children with diverse learning needs: Bases and basics* (pp. 239–278; 279–294). Mahwah, NJ: Lawrence Erlbaum Associates, Inc.

Mansfield, J. S., Legge, G. E., & Bane, M. C. (1996). Psychophysics of reading. XV: Font effects in normal and low vision. *Investigative Ophthalmology and Vision Science, 37,* 1492–1501.

McAlpine, L., & Weston, C. (1994). The attributes of instructional materials. *Performance Improvement Quarterly, 7*(1), 19–30.

McNamara, D. S., Kintsche, E., Songer, N. B., & Kintsche, W. (1996). Are good texts always better? Interactions of text coherence, background knowledge, and levels of understanding in learning from text. *Cognition and Instruction, 14*(1), 1–43.

Tyree, R. B., Fiore, T. A., & Cook, R. A. (1994). Instructional materials for diverse learners: Features and considerations for textbook design. *Remedial and Special Education, 15*(6), 363–377.

Differentiated Instruction and Learning Styles

Student learning is more successful when tasks are aligned with academic skill levels and developmental stage, and adjustments are made to allow students multiple means to engage and express their learning strengths and styles at appropriate levels of challenge and support.

Differentiated instruction allows teachers to organize instruction to adjust for diverse learning needs within a classroom.

Learning activities that capitalize on students' learning styles can structure planning for individual differences based on multiple intelligences theory.

- Multiple features, including Learning Styles activities, help teachers mat Ch assignments to students' abilities and interests
- Variety of media to select from—print, audio, visual, software
- Step-by-step, part-by-part basic content and skill-level lessons in the Student and Teacher's Editions
- Alternative Activities written at a Grade 2 (Spache) readability in the Teacher's Resource Library
- Variety of review materials, activities, sidebars, and alternative readings
- Multiple assessments—lesson or chapter reviews, end-of-chapter tests, cumulative midterm/final mastery tests, alternative assessment items

Learning Styles activities include:
- Auditory/Verbal
- Body/Kinesthetic
- Interpersonal/Group Learning
- Logical/Mathematical
- Visual/Spatial

ELL/ESL Strategies provide support for students who are learning English and lesson content concurrently.

Allington, R. L. (2002). You can't learn mu Ch from books you can't read. *Educational Leadership, 60*(3), 16–19.

Carnine, D. (1994). Introduction to the mini-series: Diverse learners and prevailing, emerging, and research-based educational approaches and their tools. *School Psychology Review, 23*(3), 341–350.

Forsten, C., Grant, J., & Hollas, B. (2003). *Differentiating textbooks: Strategies to improve student comprehension and motivation.* Peterborough, NH: Crystal Springs Books.

Gardner, H. (1983). *Frames of mind: The theory of multiple intelligences.* New York: Harper and Row.

Gersten, R., & Baker, S. (2000). The professional knowledge base on instructional practices that support cognitive growth for English-language learners. In R. Gersten, E. P. Schiller, & S. Vaughn (Eds.), *Contemporary special education research: Syntheses of the knowledge base on critical instructional issues* (pp. 31–80). Mahwah, NJ: Lawrence Erlbaum Associates, Inc.

Hall, T. (2002, June). *Effective classroom practices report: Differentiated instruction.* Wakefield, NJ: National Center on Accessing the General Curriculum. Retrieved September 29, 2003, from http://www.cast. org/cac/index.cfm?i=2876

Lazear, D. (1999). *Eight ways of knowing: Teaching for multiple intelligences* (3rd ed.). Arlington Heights, IL: Skylight Training and Publishing.

Orlich, D. C., Harder, R. J., Callahan, R. C., & Gibson, H. W. (2001). *Teaching strategies: A guide to better instruction* (6th ed.). Boston: Houghton Mifflin Company.

Roderick, M. & Camburn, E. (1999). Risk and recovery from course failure in the early years of high school. *American Educational Research Journal, 36*(2), 303–343.

Tomlinson, C. A. (1999). *The differentiated classroom: Responding to the needs of all learners.* Alexandria, VA: Association for Supervision and Curriculum Development.

Research-Based Principles	AGS Globe Textbooks	References

Instructional Design: Lesson Structure and Learner Support Strategies

Instruction that includes the components of effective instruction, utilizes effective strategies and interventions to facilitate student learning, and aligns with standards improves learning for all students, especially diverse learners and students who are struggling.

Elements of effective instruction:

Step 1: Introduce the lesson and prepare students to learn
Step 2: Provide instruction and guided practice
Step 3: Provide opportunities for applied practice and generalization

Organizational tools:
Advance organizers
Graphic organizers

Instructional process techniques:
Cooperative learning
Student self-monitoring and questioning
Real-life examples
Mnemonics

Step 1: Introduce the lesson and prepare students to learn
In the Student Edition:
- ◆ "How to Use This Book" feature explicitly teaches text organization
- ◆ Chapter and lesson previews with graphic and visual organizers
- ◆ Goals for Learning
- ◆ Sidebar notes review skills and important facts and information

In the Teacher's Edition:
- ◆ Lesson objectives
- ◆ Explicit *3-Step Teaching Plan* begins with "Warm-Up Activity" to inform students of objectives, connect to previous learning and background knowledge, review skills, and motivate students to engage in learning

Step 2: Provide instruction and guided practice
In the Student Edition:
- ◆ Short, manageable lessons break content and skills into smaller, step-by-step, part-by-part pieces
- ◆ Systematic presentation of lesson concepts and skills
- ◆ Chapter and lesson headings presented as questions or statements
- ◆ Graphic organizers arrange content visually—charts, graphs, tables, diagrams, bulleted lists, arrows, graphics, mnemonics, illustrations, and captions
- ◆ Models or examples link directly to the explanation of the concept
- ◆ Multiple opportunities for direct practice throughout

In the Teacher's Edition:
- ◆ *3-Step Teaching Plan* for each lesson includes "Teaching the Lesson" with direct instruction, and helps teachers present and clarify lesson skills and concepts through guided practice and modeling of important ideas
- ◆ Supplemental strategies and activities, including hands-on modeling, transparencies, graphic organizers, visual aids, learning styles

Step 3: Provide opportunities for applied practice and generalization
In the Student Edition:
- ◆ Each skill or concept lesson is followed by direct practice or review questions
- ◆ Multiple exercises throughout
- ◆ Generalization and application activities in sidebars and lessons link content to real-life applications
- ◆ Chapter reviews and summaries highlight major points

---

llsopp, D. H. (1990). Using modeling, manipulatives, and mnemonics with eighth-grade math students. *Teaching Exceptional Children, 31*(2), 74–81.

Chambliss, M. J. (1994). Evaluating the quality of textbooks for diverse learners. *Remedial and Special Education, 15*(5), 348–362.

Ciborowski, J. (1992). *Textbooks and the students who can't read them: A guide to teaching content.* Cambridge, MA: Brookline.

Cole, R. W. (Ed.). (1995). *Educating everybody's children: Diverse teaching strategies for diverse learners.* Alexandria, VA: Association for Supervision and Curriculum Development.

Curtis, M. E. (2002, May 20). *Adolescent reading: A synthesis of research.* Paper presented at the Practice Models for Adolescent Literacy Success Conference, U.S. Department of Education. Washington, DC: National Institute of Child Health and Human Development. Retrieved September 15, 2003, from http://216.26.160.105/conf/nichd/synthesis.asp

Dickson, S. V., Simmons, D. C., & Kameenui, E. J. (1995). *Text organization: Curricular and instructional implications for diverse learners* (Technical Report No. 18). National Center to Improve the Tools of Educators. Eugene, OR: University of Oregon. Retrieved January 26, 2000, from http://idea.uoregon.edu/~ncite/documents/techrep/tech18.html

Dixon, R. C., Carnine, D. W., Lee, D., Wallin, J., & Chard, D. (1998). *Review of high quality experimental mathematics research: Report to the California State Board of Education.* Sacramento, CA: California State Board of Education.

Jarrett, D. (1999). *The inclusive classroom: Mathematics and science instruction for students with learning disabilities—It's just good teaching.* Portland, OR: Northwest Regional Educational Laboratory.

Johnson, D. W., Johnson, R. T., & Stanne, M. B. (2000, May). *Cooperative learning methods: A meta-analysis.* Minneapolis: The Cooperative Learning Center, University of Minnesota. Retrieved October 29, 2003, from http://www.cooplearn.org/pages/cl-methods.html

Kameenui, E. J., & Simmons, D. C. (1990). *Designing instructional strategies.* Columbus, OH: Merrill Publishing Company.

Lovitt, T. C., & Horton, S. V. (1994). Strategies for adapting science textbooks for youth with learning disabilities. *Remedial and Special Education, 15*(2), 105–116.

Marzano, R. J. (1998). *A theory-based meta-analysis of research on instruction.* Aurora, CO: Mid-Continent Research for Education and Learning. Retrieved October 1, 2003, from http://www.mcrel.org/topics/productDetail/asp?productID=83

Marzano, R. J., Pickering, D. J., & Pollock, J. E. (2001). *Classroom instruction that works: Research-based strategies for increasing student achievement.* Alexandria, VA: Association for Supervision and Curriculum Development.

Miller, S. P., & Mercer, C. D. (1993). Mnemonics: Enhancing the math performance of students with learning difficulties. *Intervention in School and Clinic, 29*(2), 78–82.

Montague, M. (1997). Cognitive strategy instruction in mathematics for students with learning disabilities. *Journal of Learning Disabilities, 30*(2), 164–177.

Reiser, R. A., & Dick, W. (1996). *Instructional planning: A guide for teachers* (2nd ed.). Boston: Allyn and Bacon.

Roderick, M., & Camburn, E. (1999). Risk and recovery from course failure in the early years of high school. *American Educational Research Journal, 36*(2), 303–343.

Steele, M. (2002). Strategies for helping students who have learning disabilities in mathematics. *Mathematics Teaching in the Middle School, 8*(3), 140–143.

Swanson, H. L. (2000). What instruction works for students with learning disabilities? Summarizing the results from a meta-analysis of intervention studies. In R. Gersten, E. P. Schiller, & S. Vaughn (Eds.), *Contemporary special education research: Syntheses of the knowledge base on critical instructional issues* (pp. 1–30). Mahwah, NJ: Lawrence Erlbaum Associates, Inc.

Tyree, R. B., Fiore, T. A., & Cook, R. A. (1994). Instructional materials for diverse learners: Features and considerations for textbook design. *Remedial and Special Education, 15*(6), 363–377.

Research-Based Principles	AGS Globe Textbooks	References

Instructional Design: Lesson Structure and Learner Support Strategies, *continued from previous page*

| | **Step 1: Introduce the lesson and prepare students to learn**
In the Student Edition:
◆ How to Use This Book" feature explicitly teaches text organization

◆ Chapter and lesson previews with graphic and visual organizers

◆ Goals for Learning

◆ Sidebar notes review skills and important facts and information

In the Teacher's Edition:
◆ Lesson objectives

◆ Explicit *3-Step Teaching Plan* begins with "Warm-Up Activity" to inform students of objectives, connect to previous learning and background knowledge, review skills, and motivate students to engage in learning | Armbruster, B. B., & Anderson, T. H. (1988). On selecting "considerate" content area textbooks. *Remedial and Special Education, 9*(1), 47–52.

Beck, I. L., McKeown, M. G., & Grommoll, E. W. (1989). Learning from social studies texts. *Cognition and Instruction, 6*(2), 99–158.

Chambliss, M. J. (1994). Evaluating the quality of textbooks for diverse learners. *Remedial and Special Education, 15*(5), 348–362.

Ciborowski, J. (1992). *Textbooks and the students who can't read them: A guide to teaching content.* Cambridge, MA: Brookline.

Dickson, S. V., Simmons, D. C., & Kameenui, E. J. (1995). *Text organization and its relation to reading comprehension: A synthesis of the research* (Technical Report No. 17) and *Text organization: Curricular and instructional implications for diverse learners* (Technical Report No. 18). National Center to Improve the Tools of Educators. Eugene, OR: University of Oregon. Retrieved January 26, 2000, from http://idea.uoregon.edu/~ncite/documents/techrep/tech17.html and http://idea.uoregon.edu/~ncite/documents/techrep/tech18.html

Dickson, S. V., Simmons, D. C., & Kameenui, E. J. (1998). Text |

Ongoing Assessment and Tracking Student Progress

| Textbooks can incorporate features to facilitate and support assessment of learning, allowing teachers to monitor student progress and provide information on mastery level and the need for instructional changes.

Assessment should measure student progress on learning goals over the course of a lesson, chapter, or content-area textbook.

Students and teachers need timely and ongoing feedback so instruction can focus on specific skill development. | ◆ Test-taking tips and strategies for students who benefit from explicit strategy instruction

◆ Lesson and chapter reviews check student understanding of content

◆ Workbook and reproducible lesson activities (Teacher's Resource Library) offer additional monitoring of student progress

◆ Discussion questions allow teachers to monitor student progress toward lesson objectives

◆ Self-Study Guides (Teacher's Resource Library) allow teacher and student to track individual assignments and progress

◆ Chapter assessment activities and curriculum-based assessment items correlate to chapter Goals for Learning:

• Chapter reviews
• End-of-chapter tests
• Cumulative midterm and final mastery tests
• Alternative chapter assessments
• Skill Track assesses and tracks individual student performance by lesson and chapter | Deshler, D. D., Ellis, E. S., & Lenz, B. K. (1996). *Teaching adolescents with learning disabilities: Strategies and methods* (2nd ed.). Denver, CO: Love Publishing Company.

Jarrett, D. (1999). *The inclusive classroom: Mathematics and science instruction for students with learning disabilities—It's just good teaching.* Portland, OR: Northwest Regional Educational Laboratory.

Reiser, R. A., & Dick, W. (1996). *Instructional planning: A guide for teachers* (2nd ed.). Boston: Allyn and Bacon.

Tyree, R. B., Fiore, T. A., & Cook, R. A. (1994). Instructional materials for diverse learners: Features and considerations for textbook design. *Remedial and Special Education, 15*(6), 363–377. |

For more information on the scientific research base for AGS Globe Textbooks, please go to www.agsglobe.com or call Customer Service at 1-800-328-2560 to request a research report.

World History Skills	How to Use This Book	Skills Hand-book	Unit 1 Ch. 1–9	Unit 2 Ch. 10–13	Unit 3 Ch. 14–18	Unit 4 Ch. 19–22	Unit 5 Ch. 23–24	Unit 6 Ch. 25–27	Unit 7 Ch. 28–31
Prehistory			1, 9						
Beginnings of Human Society			1, 2, 3, 4, 5, 6, 9						
Agricultural Revolution			1, 9						
Middle Eastern Civilizations			2, 3, 4						
Greek Civilizations			6						
Roman Civilizations			7, 8						
Major Religions			5	10, 11, 12	15				29
The Middle Ages				10, 11					
African Civilizations			4	12			24		
American Civilizations			9						
Asian Civilizations			5	13					
The Renaissance					14				
The Reformation					15				
Monarchies					18				
Explorations in Global Age					17				
Political Revolutions						20, 22		25, 26	28
The Age of Reason						19			
The Industrial Revolution						21			
Nationalism					18		23	26	
Imperialism					17		24		
World War I								25, 26	
Aftermath of World War I								25, 26	
World War II								27	
Aftermath of World War II								27, 28	
Contemporary Issues									30, 31

Social Studies Skills	How to Use This Book	Skills Hand-book	Unit 1 Ch. 1–9	Unit 2 Ch. 10–13	Unit 3 Ch. 14–18	Unit 4 Ch. 19–22	Unit 5 Ch. 23–24	Unit 6 Ch. 25–27	Unit 7 Ch. 28–31
Applications			1–9	10–13	14–18	19–22	23–24	25–27	28–31
Charts/Graphs		X			17	21			31
Communication			1, 4, 7	12, 13	14, 17	21, 22	23	27	31
Critical-Thinking		X	1–9	10–13	14–18	19–22	23–24	25–27	28–31
Document-Based Readings/ Questions			1–9	10–13	14–18	19–22	23–24	25–27	28–31
Economics			4, 7	10–13	14, 17, 18	20, 21, 22	23–24	25–27	28–31
Geography Notes			2, 9		17	20	23	27	28
Government/Civics			2–9	10–13	14–18	19–22	23–24	25–27	28–31
Maps		X	1–9	10–13	14–18	19–22	23–24	25–27	28–31
Reference Materials						U4			
Technology			5	11	16	21	23	25	28
Timelines			1–9	10–13	14–18	19–22	23–24	25–27	28–31
Writing			1–9	10–13	14–18	19–22	23–24	25–27	28–31

Study Skills	How to Use This Book	Skills Hand-book	Unit 1 Ch. 1–9	Unit 2 Ch. 10–13	Unit 3 Ch. 14–18	Unit 4 Ch. 19–22	Unit 5 Ch. 23–24	Unit 6 Ch. 25–27	Unit 7 Ch. 28–31
Note-Taking	X								
Outlines	X								
Test-Taking Tips	X		1–9	10–13	14–18	19–22	23–24	25–27	28–31
Vocabulary Development			1–9	10–13	14–18	19–22	23–24	25–27	28–31

Reading Skills	How to Use This Book	Skills Hand-book	Unit 1 Ch. 1–9	Unit 2 Ch. 10–13	Unit 3 Ch. 14–18	Unit 4 Ch. 19–22	Unit 5 Ch. 23–24	Unit 6 Ch. 25–27	Unit 7 Ch. 28–31
Summarizing		X	1, 8		15	22			29
Questioning		X	2, 9		16		23		30
Predicting		X	3	10	17		24		31
Text Structure		X	4	11	18			25	
Visualizing		X	5	12		19		26	
Inferencing		X	6	13		20		27	
Metacognition		X	7		14	21			28

World History

by
Wayne E. King and Marcel Lewinski

PEARSON
AGS Globe

Shoreview, Minnesota

About the Authors

Wayne E. King is currently the Academic Dean at the Baltimore School for the Arts. He earned his Bachelor of Science and Master of Science degrees from The Johns Hopkins University. He has taught history and social studies at all educational levels. With extensive experience as a curriculum writer, he has served as a consultant to schools, museums, and federal agencies. He has lectured at numerous national and international conferences on the teaching of history and cultural studies.

Marcel Lewinski is an Assistant Adjunct Professor of History Education at Illinois State University. Previously, he was an award-winning high school social studies teacher. He taught a wide range of subjects including geography, world history, economics, political science, sociology, and contemporary problems. Lewinski is professionally active in many organizations and has given presentations at many state, regional, and national conferences. He has conducted numerous workshops for social studies teachers and has traveled all over the world. As author of several textbooks in the social studies, Mr. Lewinski acts as a consultant to school systems and has often contributed to educational publications.

Reading Consultant

Timothy Shanahan, Ph.D., Professor of Urban Education, Director of the Center for Literacy, University of Illinois at Chicago; Author, AMP Reading System

Reviewers

The publisher wishes to thank the following educators for their helpful comments during the review process for *World History*. Their assistance has been invaluable.

Lois Barnes (Content Reviewer), Assistant Superintendent of Curriculum and Instruction, Woodford County Board of Education, Versailles, KY; **Phyllis Berman,** Supervisor/Coordinator, Scott School Assistant Center, Toledo Public Schools, Toledo, OH; **Elizabeth Burley,** Itinerant Resource Teacher, Ager Road Center, Hyattsville, MD; **Anita Dearing,** Resource Teacher, Oak Ridge High School, Oak Ridge, TN; **Tom Ferrara,** Teacher/Education Coordinator, South Bend Juvenile Correctional Facility, South Bend, IN; **Debora Hartzell,** Lead Teacher for Special Education, Lakeside High School, Atlanta, GA; **Patricia Henry,** Instructional Specialist, Special Education Programs, Montgomery County Public Schools, Rockville, MD; **Anne Hoffman,** Teacher, Santana High School, Santana, CA; **Lenore Heino Hoyt,** Social Studies Teacher, Centennial High School, Circle Pines, MN; **Larry Manchester,** Lead Resource Teacher, St. Andrews School, St. Paul, MN; **Russell F. Maruna,** Supervisor of Social Studies, Cleveland Municipal School District, Cleveland, OH; **Debby Persky,** Teacher, City of Angels, Los Angeles, CA; **Alice Richardson,** Special Education Teacher, Central High School, Detroit, MI; **Carolyn Scott,** Special Education Coordinator, Terrebonne Parish Schools, Houma, LA; **Craig Viscardi,** Special Education Teacher, Pasadena High School, Pasadena, TX; **J. B. Whitten,** Exceptional Student Education Teacher, Lennard High School, Ruskin, FL

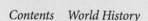

ISBN-13: 978-0-7854-6405-1

ISBN-10: 0-7854-6405-0

5 6 7 8 9 10   13 12 11 10 09

1-800-992-0244
www.agsglobe.com

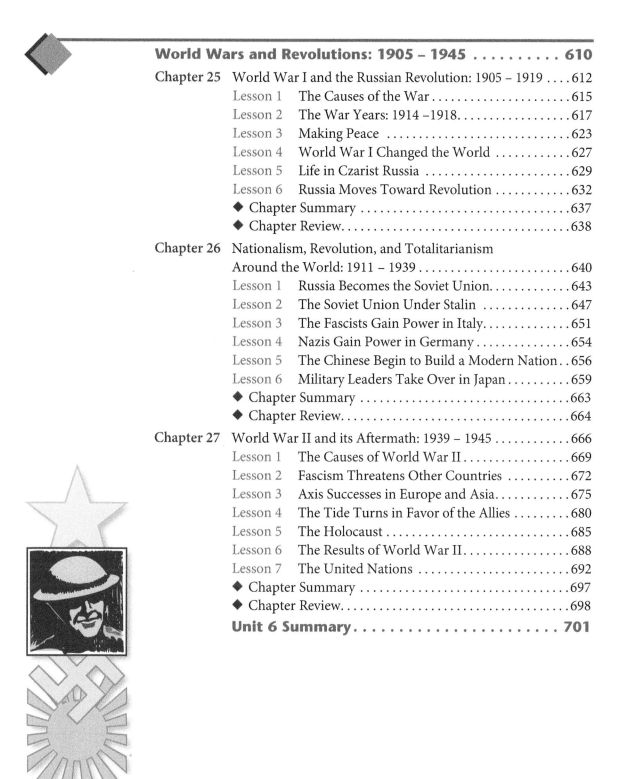

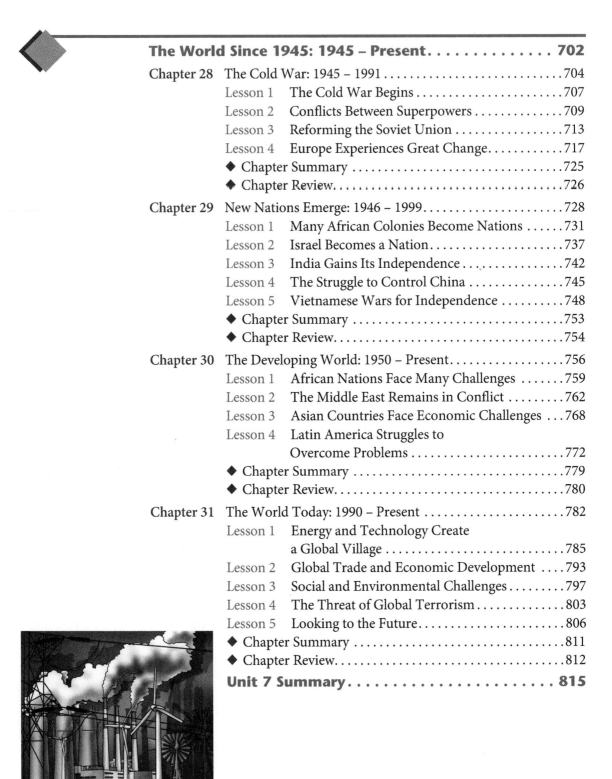

Biography

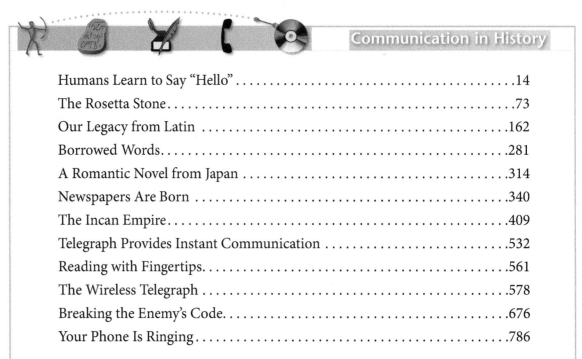

Writing About History

Spotlight Stories

Overview This portion of the book may be used to introduce the study of world history, to preview the book's features, and to review effective study skills.

Objectives

- To introduce the study of world history
- To preview the student textbook
- To review study skills

Student Pages xxii–xxix

Teacher's Resource Library
How to Use This Book 1–7

Introduction to the Book

Have volunteers read aloud the three paragraphs of the introduction. Discuss with students why studying geography is important and what kinds of things people can learn from it.

How to Study

Read aloud each bulleted statement, pausing to discuss with students why the suggestion is part of good study habits. Distribute copies of How to Use This Book 1, "Study Habits Survey." Read the directions together and then have students complete the survey. After they have scored their surveys, ask students to make a list of the study habits they plan to work on improving. After three or four weeks, have students complete the survey again to see if they have improved their study habits. Suggest that they keep the survey and review it every month or so to see whether they are maintaining and improving their study habits.

How to Use This Book: A Study Guide

Welcome to the study of world history. You may be asking yourself, "Why do I need to know about people, places, and events that happened a long time before I was even born?" When we study the past, we can have a better understanding of why some things happened the way they did. We can learn from the mistakes and the successes of the past. It is important that we know about our world and about the people who live in it. Everyone can help make the world a better place to live.

This book is a story about the world. As you read the units, chapters and lessons of this book, you will learn about some of the important people and events that shaped world history.

Before you start to read this book, it is important that you understand how to use it. It is also important that you know how to be successful in this course. Information in this first section can help you achieve these things.

How to Study

These tips can help you study more effectively:

- Plan a regular time to study.

- Choose a desk or table in a quiet place where you will not be distracted. Find a spot that has good lighting.

- Gather all the books, pencils, paper, and other equipment you will need to complete your assignments.

- Decide on a goal. For example: "I will finish reading and taking notes on Chapter 1, Lesson 1, by 8:00."

- Take a five- to ten-minute break every hour to keep alert.

- If you start to feel sleepy, take a break and get some fresh air.

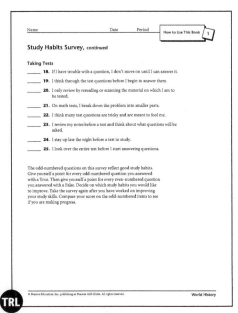

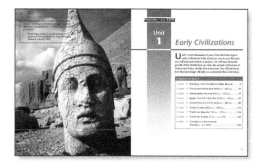

Before Beginning Each Unit

◆ Read the unit title and study the photograph. Do you recognize anything in the photo?

◆ Read the quotation.

◆ Read the opening paragraphs.

◆ Read the titles of the chapters in the unit.

◆ Read the Chapter Summaries and Unit Summary to help you identify key ideas.

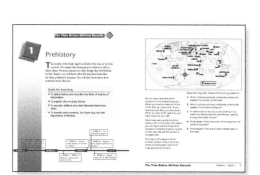

Before Beginning Each Chapter

◆ Read the chapter title and dates.

◆ Read the opening paragraphs.

◆ Study the Goals for Learning. The Chapter Review and tests will ask questions related to these goals.

◆ Study the timeline. These help you see when key events occurred. The timeline covers the years in the chapter title.

◆ Read the paragraph and bullets on the Reading Strategy page. The strategy will help you become a better reader. Reading Strategy Notes in each lesson will help you apply the strategy as you read.

◆ Read the words and definitions in the Key Vocabulary Words box. The words in this list are important vocabulary words in the chapter.

◆ Read the Chapter Summary to identify key issues.

◆ Look at the Chapter Review. The questions cover the most important information in the chapter.

How to Use This Book: A Study Guide   **xxiii**

Before Beginning Each Unit

When students begin their study of Unit 1, you may wish to have them read aloud and follow each bulleted suggestion on page xxiii. Actually trying the suggestions will help students understand what they are supposed to do and recognize how useful the suggestions are when previewing a unit. At the beginning of other units, refer students to page xxiii and encourage them to follow the suggestions. You may wish to continue to do this as a class each time or allow the students to work independently.

Before Beginning Each Chapter

When students begin their study of Chapter 1, you may wish to have them read aloud and follow each bulleted suggestion on page xxiii. Read aloud the first bulleted statement under "Before Beginning Each Chapter." Have students turn to page 2, and have a volunteer read aloud the title of Chapter 1. Read aloud the second bulleted statement and have volunteers take turns reading sentences from the opening paragraph of Chapter 1. Then read aloud the third bulleted statement and have volunteers take turns reading the Goals for Learning for Chapter 1. Discuss with students why knowing these goals can help them when they are studying the chapter. After reading aloud the remainder of the bulleted points, explain that all these tools—Reading Strategy, the Key Vocabulary Words, the Chapter Summary, and the Chapter Review—are there to help the students gain as much as they can from the chapter.

Unit and Chapter Introductions organize information into easy-to-read formats. To help students organize their time and work in an easy-to-read form, have them fill out How to Use This Book 2, "Weekly Schedule." Encourage them to keep the schedule in a notebook or folder where they can refer to it easily. Suggest that they review the schedule periodically and update it as necessary.

How to Use This Book 2

How to Use This Book   **xxiii**

Note These Features

Have students skim their textbooks and find one of each of the listed features. You may wish to remind students of a book feature that can help them with this activity—the Table of Contents. Ask volunteers to tell the page numbers of the features they have found. Have the other students check to see that the features do appear on those pages.

Note These Features

You can find complete listings of these features in this textbook's table of contents.

Biography
Highlights people who have played a part in the history of the world

History in Your Life
Relates history to the modern world

Writing About History
Provides history topics to write about in each chapter

Then and Now
Compares and contrasts something existing now to how it existed in the past

Technology Connection
Highlights inventions at the time that made life better or easier

Document-Based Reading
Presents primary- and secondary-source documents related to each chapter

Spotlight Story
Tells about an important part of history related to the content of the chapter

Skill Builder
Focuses on social studies skills

Before Beginning Each Lesson

Read the lesson title and restate it in the form of a question. example, write: *What is the meaning of history?*

Look over the entire lesson, noting the following:

◆ bold words
◆ text organization
◆ photos and illustrations
◆ maps
◆ graphs and charts
◆ Lesson Review questions

As You Read the Lesson

◆ Read the major headings.
◆ Read the subheads and paragraphs that follow.
◆ Study the maps, graphs, and charts.
◆ Before moving on to the next lesson, see if you understand the concepts you read. If you do not, reread the lesson. If you are still unsure, ask for help.
◆ Practice what you have learned by completing the Lesson Reviews.

Using the Bold Words

Knowing the meaning of all the boxed words in the left column will help you understand what you read.

History
The record of past events

These **vocabulary words** appear in **bold type** the first time they appear in the text and are often defined in the paragraph.

> **History** is the record of past events

All of the words in the left column are also defined in the **Glossary.**

> **History** (his´ tər ē) The record of past events (p. 5)

Before Beginning Each Lesson

Read through the information on page xxv with students. Then assign each of the three lessons in Chapter 2 (pp. 24–43) to a small group of students. Have them read each of the headings in their lesson. Then have students report on the specifics of what they expect to learn about in their lesson to the rest of the class.

As You Read the Lesson

Have students turn to page 5 in their textbooks. Read aloud the first bulleted point on page xxv and have a volunteer read aloud the first subhead in Lesson 1 of Chapter 1—"What Is the Meaning of History?" Then read the second bulleted comment and have volunteers read the paragraph under the subhead in the textbook. After reading the next two bulleted statements, ask students to answer the question in the subhead in their own words. You may wish to repeat this procedure using the other subheads in Lesson 1 of Chapter 1. Then read aloud the last bulleted statement and have students turn to Lesson 1 Review on page 6. Discuss how the questions in the subheads are related to the questions in the Lesson Review.

Using the Bold Words

Read aloud the information on page xxv. Make sure students understand what the terms bold type, vocabulary, and glossary mean. Then ask them to look at the boxed words on page 5. Have a volunteer read the first boxed word (history) and then find and read the sentence in the text in which that word appears in bold type. Have another volunteer read the second boxed word and then find and read the definition given in the text. Have another volunteer find and read the definition of this word in the Glossary at the back of the book.

Point out that boxed vocabulary words may appear on other pages in a lesson besides the first page. Have students turn to page 10 and look at the boxed word on that page. Explain that this word appears in a box here because it is used in the text on this page. Have a volunteer find and read the sentence in the text in which the vocabulary word on page 10 is used.

Word Study Tips

Have a volunteer read aloud the Word Study Tips on page xxvi. You may wish to demonstrate how to make a vocabulary card by filling out an index card for the word *history* and its definition (page 5). Point out that students can use words they list on How to Use This Book 3 to make their vocabulary cards.

Taking Notes in Class

Ask students why note taking is an important study skill. Encourage them to tell what method they use to take notes during class discussions or when reading. Then have volunteers read the information on page xxvi. Suggest that students who do not have a method for taking notes try one of the methods mentioned and see how it works for them.

Word Study Tips

◆ Start a vocabulary file with index cards to use for review.

◆ Write one term on the front of each card. Write the chapter number, lesson number, and definition on the back.

◆ You can use these cards as flash cards by yourself or with a study partner to test your knowledge.

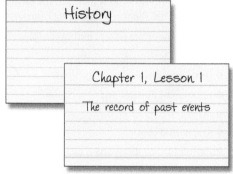

Taking Notes in Class

◆ Outline each lesson using the subheads as the main points.

◆ Always write the main ideas and supporting details.

◆ Keep your notes brief.

◆ Write down important information only.

◆ Use your own words.

◆ Do not be concerned about writing in complete sentences. Use phrases.

◆ Do not try to write everything the teacher says.

◆ Use the same method all the time. Then when you study for a test, you will know where to go to find the information you need to review.

◆ Review your notes to fill in possible gaps as soon as you can after class.

| Name | Date | Period | How to Use This Book 3 |

Writing About World History

Topic _____

World History

TRL

How to Use This Book 3

Using a Three-Column Chart

One good way to take notes is to use a three-column chart. Make your own three-column chart by dividing a sheet of notebook paper into three parts. In Column 1, write the topic you are reading about or studying. In Column 2, write what you learned about this topic as you read or listened to your teacher. In Column 3, write questions, observations, or opinions about the topic, or write a detail that will help you remember the topic. Here are some examples of different ways to take notes using the three-column chart.

The topic I am studying	What I learned from reading the text or class discussion	Questions, observations, or ideas I have about the topic
Information resources	• two sources of information • asks what, when, where, who, why	• This book contains both primary and secondary information • I wonder what primary sources are in this book

Vocabulary Word	Definition	Sentence with Vocabulary Word
Primary source	A first-hand account of a historical event	A primary source account of an event is told by someone who was there.

Topic	Facts	Page Number
the study of history	the past lives on in our culture (values, attitudes, customs)	p. 5
	different sources: primary: newspapers, diaries, letters secondary: books about events in the past	p. 6
	history as family tree of human race	p. 7

Using a Three-Column Chart

Have students read the information about making a three-column chart on page xxvii. Then demonstrate to students how to correctly divide the paper into thirds and to label each section. Ask students to create a three-column chart such as one of those on page xxvii and use it as they read and explore Chapter 1.

Explain to students that the three-column chart is one of many good organizational tools. Pass out the "How to Use This Book 4" worksheet and discuss with students certain ways this main idea chart could be used to organize information. Ask students for possible examples other than the one shown on the worksheet.

Using the Summaries

Have students turn to page 21. Point out that a Chapter Summary gives the main ideas covered in the chapter in the form of bulleted statements. Then read aloud the statements on page xxviii that suggest how to use the Chapter Summary when studying for a test.

Using the Reviews

Ask students to turn to page 22. Point out that a Chapter Review is intended to help them focus on and review the key facts and main ideas of a chapter before they are tested on the material. Suggest that they may want to complete the review after studying their notes, vocabulary lists, worksheets, and the Chapter Summary.

Preparing for Tests

Encourage students to offer their opinions about tests and their ideas on test-taking strategies. What do they do to study for a test? List their comments on the board. Then read the bulleted statements on page xxviii. Add these suggestions to the list on the board if they are not already there.

Suggest to students that they can use How to Use This Book 5 to help them review before a test. Distribute copies of How to Use This Book 5, "Organizing Information." Suggest that as they review a chapter, students fill it in with information covered in the chapter.

Using the Summaries

◆ Read each Chapter Summary to be sure you understand the chapter's main ideas.

◆ Review your notes and test yourself on vocabulary words and key ideas.

◆ Practice writing about some of the main events from the chapter.

◆ At the end of each unit, read the Unit Summary to be sure you understand the unit's main ideas.

Using the Reviews

◆ Answer the questions in the Lesson Reviews.

◆ In the Chapter Reviews, answer each fill-in-the-blank, multiple choice, short-answer question.

◆ Review the Test-Taking Tips.

Preparing for Tests

◆ Complete the Lesson Reviews and Chapter Reviews. Make up similar questions to practice what you have learned. You may want to do this with a classmate and share your questions.

◆ Review your answers to Lesson Reviews and Chapter Reviews.

◆ Reread the Chapter Summaries.

◆ Test yourself on vocabulary words and key ideas.

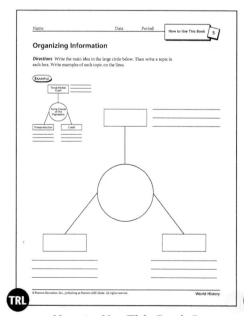

How to Use This Book 5

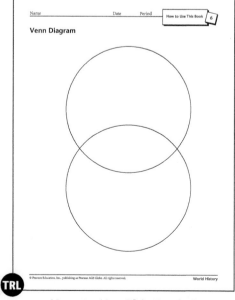

How to Use This Book 6

Reading Checklist

Good readers do not just read with their eyes. They read with their brains turned on. In other words, they are active readers. Good readers use strategies as they read to keep them on their toes. The following strategies will help you to check your understanding of what you read. A strategy appears at the beginning of each chapter of this book.

- **Summarizing** To summarize a text, stop often as you read. Notice these things: the topic, the main thing being said about the topic, important details that support the main idea. Try to sum up the author's message using your own words.

- **Questioning** Ask yourself questions about the text and read to answer them. Here are some useful questions to ask: Why did the author include this information? Is this like anything I have experienced? Am I learning what I hoped I would learn?

- **Predicting** As you read, think about what might come next. Add in what you already know about the topic. Predict what the text will say. Then, as you read, notice whether your prediction is right. If not, change your prediction.

- **Text Structure** Pay attention to how a text is organized. Find parts that stand out. They are probably the most important ideas or facts. Think about why the author organized ideas this way. Is the author showing a sequence of events? Is the author explaining a solution or the effect of something?

- **Visualizing** Picture what is happening in a text or what is being described. Make a movie out of it in your mind. If you can picture it clearly, then you know you understand it. Visualizing what you read will also help you remember it later.

- **Inferencing** The meaning of a text may not be stated. Instead, the author may give clues and hints. It is up to you to put them together with what you already know about the topic. Then you make an inference—you conclude what the author means.

- **Metacognition** Think about your thinking patterns as you read. Before reading a text, preview it. Think about what you can do to get the most out of it. Think about what you already know about the topic. Write down any questions you have. After you read, ask yourself: Did that make sense? If not, read it again.

Reading Checklist

Read the title and first paragraph on page xxix to students. Then ask a volunteer to read each of the reading strategies listed on the page. Go through each strategy one by one, making sure students understand the concepts behind each term. Then give examples of each strategy through the text. Have students participate. After reading a paragraph ask one volunteer for a summary. Ask another volunteer for a question that came from the reading. Ask another volunteer to make a prediction based on the text. Continue this way until all strategies are explained.

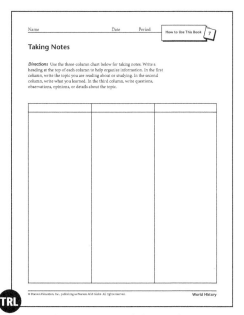

Using Globes and Maps

Present a globe for students to study. Explain that a globe accurately shows the geography of Earth. Then ask a volunteer to find the equator and the prime meridian. Ask another volunteer to find the international date line. Then ask students to find where you are on the globe. Ask them to find the closest lines of latitude and longitude.

Ask:

• **What advantages does a globe have over a map?** (Since both the globe and Earth are round, a globe accurately shows the shape of Earth and the size of physical features.)

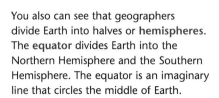

A globe is a model of Earth. Looking at the globe, you can see that Earth is round. You can see Earth's features and surfaces. A globe is the best way to show Earth. However, how do you show the round features of a globe on a flat page? You use a map.

You also can see that geographers divide Earth into halves or **hemispheres**. The **equator** divides Earth into the Northern Hemisphere and the Southern Hemisphere. The equator is an imaginary line that circles the middle of Earth.

The **prime meridian** and the **international date line** divide Earth into the Eastern Hemisphere and the Western Hemisphere. The prime meridian is an imaginary line that circles Earth from the North Pole to the South Pole. The international date line is on the side of Earth you cannot see here. It is directly opposite the prime meridian.

Geographers measure distances from the equator and the prime meridian. These distances are imaginary lines called **latitude** and **longitude**.

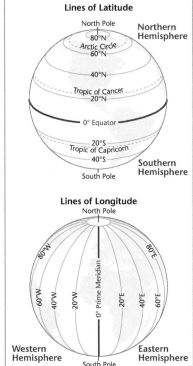

Lines of Latitude

North Pole
Northern Hemisphere
80°N
Arctic Circle
60°N
40°N
Tropic of Cancer
20°N
0° Equator
20°S
Tropic of Capricorn
40°S
South Pole
Southern Hemisphere

Lines of Longitude

North Pole
80°W
60°W
40°W
20°W
0° Prime Meridian
20°E
40°E
60°E
80°E
Western Hemisphere
South Pole
Eastern Hemisphere

Cartographers, or **mapmakers**, have created different map projections. Some of these map projections show the true size of a place, but distort, or change, the shape. Others show the true shape, but distort the size. All maps show some kind of distortion. Therefore, geographers must choose the best maps for their purposes.

A **Mercator projection** stretches the lines of latitude apart. It does not show the true size of landmasses. A Mercator projection does show true shape, however.

Landmasses in a **Robinson projection** are not as distorted as in a Mercator projection. However, there is some distortion in the size of the landmasses.

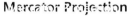

Mercator Projection

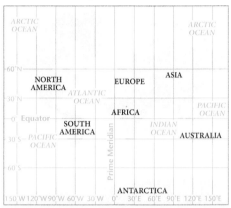

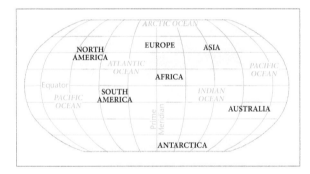

> **Critical Thinking**
> Why would a mapmaker choose to use a Robinson projection instead of a Mercator projection?

Skills Handbook **xxxi**

Using Globes and Maps

Explain that globes are not always available or detailed enough for a specific situation. In these cases, a map is a useful tool. Present a map of the world for students to study. Explain that it is impossible to correctly show both size and shape by using a map. Therefore, every map has some sort of distortion.

Ask students to identify the type of map you have displayed. (Answers will vary. Either Mercator projection or Robinson projection.)

Ask students to find your location on the map and pinpoint the latitude and longitude as closely as possible.

Critical Thinking

Answers will vary. Sample answer: A mapmaker might choose a Robinson projection over a Mercator projection if they were more interested in accurately showing the shape of the landmasses.

Reading a Map

Have students read page xxxii of the text. Explain that knowing how to read maps is an important skill in learning world history.

Ask:

- What are the main parts of a map? (a title, a key, a compass rose, and a scale)

Tell students to look at the political map of the Middle East on page xxxii.

Ask:

- How are the countries differentiated from one another? (borderlines and color)
- What country is directly west of Jordan? (Israel)
- What is the capital of Iran? (Tehran)

To understand geography, you need to know how to read maps. To read a map, you need to understand its parts. The main parts of a map are a title, a key, a compass rose, and a scale. Many of the maps you see are **general purpose maps**. These are political maps and physical maps. A **political map** shows features that people determine, such as country boundaries, cities, and capitals.

The **title** of a map tells the area the map covers.

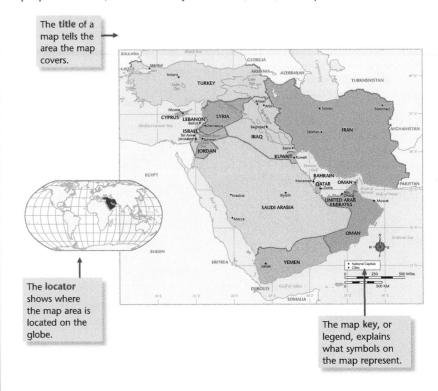

The **locator** shows where the map area is located on the globe.

The map **key**, or legend, explains what symbols on the map represent.

A **physical map** shows how high a landmass is. It also shows natural features such as rivers and oceans. Some of the maps you see show specific kinds of information. These maps are called **special purpose maps**. There are many types of special purpose maps. For example, a climate map is a special purpose map. It shows the typical weather in a place.

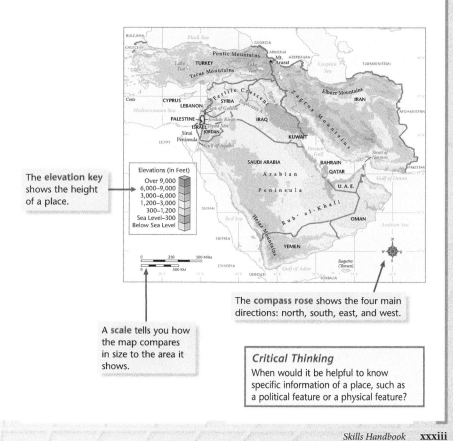

The **elevation key** shows the height of a place.

A **scale** tells you how the map compares in size to the area it shows.

The **compass rose** shows the four main directions: north, south, east, and west.

Critical Thinking
When would it be helpful to know specific information of a place, such as a political feature or a physical feature?

Reading a Map

Have a volunteer read the paragraph on page xxxiii. Then explain to students that a physical map, unlike a political map, shows elevation, or how high a landmass is. It also shows natural features, such as mountains, lakes, rivers, and oceans.

A special purpose map is designed to show one specific piece of information.

Ask:

- What are some possible topics for a special purpose map? (climate, resources, population, language, ethnicity)

Ask students which type of map would be most useful under the following circumstances:

- Discovering the highest region in America (physical map)
- Finding out the population density of Egypt (special purpose map)
- Finding the capital of the Philippines (political map)
- Discovering the natural resources of China (special purpose map)

Critical Thinking

Answers will vary. Sample answer: It would be helpful to know specifics when studying a region of the world. Learning from a map about physical features (such as deserts, mountains, or rivers) would help explain why the population size is low or high in a certain area.

Reading Graphs and Charts

Explain to students that graphs and charts are excellent ways to show information. Different graphs and charts can be used in different circumstances. Ask a volunteer to read the paragraph about circle graphs on page xxxiv.

Ask:

• What country is the single largest energy user in the world? (the United States)

Ask a second volunteer to read the paragraph about bar graphs at the bottom of page xxxiv.

Ask:

• Which country is larger: Canada or Brazil? (Canada)

Graphs and charts organize and present information in a visual way. There are different types of graphs and charts.

A **circle graph** is sometimes called a pie graph. It is a good way to show the sizes of parts as compared to a single whole. This single whole is represented as a circle. Each piece of the circle represents a part of the whole.

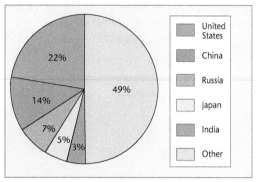

World's Top Energy Users

49% — United States
22%
14%
7%
5%
3%

United States
China
Russia
Japan
India
Other

A **bar graph** is a good way to show information visually. Each bar represents a set of facts. You can compare sets of facts by looking at the different sizes of the bars.

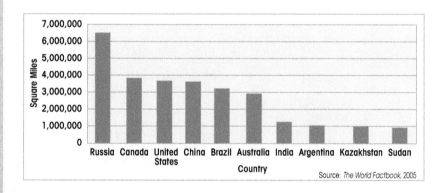

Square Miles

7,000,000
6,000,000
5,000,000
4,000,000
3,000,000
2,000,000
1,000,000
0

Russia Canada United States China Brazil Australia India Argentina Kazakhstan Sudan

Country

Source: *The World Factbook,* 2005

Fact	Place	Location	Size
Highest Mountain	Mount Everest	Nepal and China	29,035 feet high
Longest River	Nile	North and East Africa	4,160 miles long
Largest Island	Greenland	North Atlantic	840,000 square miles
Largest Body of Water	Pacific Ocean	From west of North and South America to east of Asia and Australia	63,800,000 square miles

A **chart** can also be called a table. Charts are organized into rows and columns. Charts can help you to compare information.

A **line graph** shows the relationship between two sets of information. A point is placed at the intersection of every fact. When all the points are on the graph, a line is drawn to connect them. You can get a quick idea as to the trend, or direction, of information by looking at the ups and downs of the line.

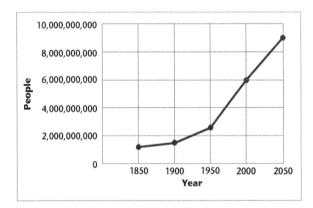

Critical Thinking
If you were to organize information about your classmates into categories such as age and gender, would you use a chart or a graph? Explain.

Reading Graphs and Charts

Ask a volunteer to read the paragraph about charts on page xxxv.

Ask:

• Where is Greenland, the world's largest island, located? (in the North Atlantic)

Ask a volunteer to read the paragraph about line graphs at the bottom of page xxxv.

Ask:

• Is the world's population expected to increase or decrease in the future? (increase)

Have students look over the graphs on pages xxxiv and xxxv. Then ask the following questions:

• Which is the best type of graph to use if you want to show a trend? (a line graph)

• Which is the best type of graph to use if you want to compare parts of a whole? (a circle graph)

Critical Thinking

It would be best to use a chart if I were organizing information about my classmates because a chart shows off multiple categories. I can create as many rows and columns as necessary to fit all the information I want to show. The other graphs are best for showing one piece of information.

Planning Guide
Early Civilizations

		Student Text Lesson					
		Student Pages	Vocabulary	Lesson Review	Critical-Thinking Questions	Chapter Summary	Chapter Review
Chapter 1	Prehistory	2–23	✔		✔	21	22
Lesson 1	The Meaning of History	5–6	✔	6	✔		
Lesson 2	Why We Study History	7–8		8	✔		
Lesson 3	The Way Historians Work	9–12	✔	12	✔		
Lesson 4	Prehistory	13–18	✔	18	✔		
Chapter 2	Ancient Middle East	24–43	✔		✔	41	42
Lesson 1	The Sumerians	27–30	✔	30	✔		
Lesson 2	The Akkadians and the Babylonians	31–34	✔	34	✔		
Lesson 3	The Phoenicians and the Hebrews	35–38	✔	38	✔		
Chapter 3	Middle Eastern Empires	44–63	✔		✔	61	62
Lesson 1	The Assyrians	47–50	✔	50	✔		
Lesson 2	The Chaldeans	51–54	✔	54	✔		
Lesson 3	The Persians	55-58	✔	58	✔		

(Unit Planning Guide is continued on next page.)

Unit Activities

Student Text
Unit 1 Summary
Unit 1 Skill Builder

Teacher's Resource Library
Unit 1 Activities 1–2
Unit 1 Skills Activity

Assessment Options

Teacher's Resource Library
Chapter 1 Mastery Tests A and B
Chapter 2 Mastery Tests A and B
Chapter 3 Mastery Tests A and B
Chapter 4 Mastery Tests A and B
Chapter 5 Mastery Tests A and B
Chapter 6 Mastery Tests A and B
Chapter 7 Mastery Tests A and B
Chapter 8 Mastery Tests A and B
Chapter 9 Mastery Tests A and B
Unit 1 Mastery Test

Reading Strategy	Map Study/Map Skills	Writing About History	Geography Note	Biography	History in Your Life	Communication In History	Technology Connection	Then and Now	Spotlight Story	Document-Based Reading	Background Information	Applications (Home, Career, Community)	World Cultures	Study Skills	Online Connection	ELL/ESL Strategy	Auditory/Verbal	Visual/Spatial	Body/Kinesthetic	Interpersonal/Group Learning	Logical/Mathematical	Activities/Modified Activities	Workbook Activities	Self-Study Guide	Chapter Outline
4	3								20	19				4	4			3						✔	✔
✔												6	6							6		1	1		
✔						8						8			8	8	8					2	2		
✔		11		11	10						11	10, 12		12		10						3	3		
✔			14								16	15				17			15		16	4	4		
26	25								40	39						39								✔	✔
✔				29							29	30		28		30		29	28			5	5		
✔	34	38					33					34				32						6	6		
✔	36		35	37									38		38	39	36			38	37	7	7		
46	45								60	59														✔	✔
✔	48										49	50		48	50	49	49	49				8	8		
✔	51	53					53					54				53			52	54		9	9		
✔	56		57	58							58	58				57					56	10	10		

TRL Activities

The Teacher's Resource Library (TRL) contains a set of lower-level worksheets called Modified Activities. These worksheets cover the same content as the standard Activities but are written at a lower reading level.

Skill Track

Use Skill Track for *World History* to monitor student progress and meet the demands of Adequate Yearly Progress (AYP). Make informed instructional decisions with individual student and class reports of lesson and chapter assessments. With immediate and ongoing feedback, students will also see what they have learned and where they need more reinforcement and practice.

Planning Guide
Early Civilizations
(continued)

		Student Pages	Vocabulary	Lesson Review	Critical-Thinking Questions	Chapter Summary	Chapter Review
Chapter 4	**Egypt - The Gift of the Nile**	64–87	✔		✔	85	86
Lesson 1	The Nile River	67–68	✔	68	✔		
Lesson 2	The Old Kingdom	69–73	✔	73	✔		
Lesson 3	The Middle Kingdom	74–75	✔	75	✔		
Lesson 4	The New Kingdom	76–79	✔	79	✔		
Lesson 5	Gifts from the Egyptians	80–82	✔	82	✔		
Chapter 5	**Ancient India and China**	88–115	✔		✔	113	114
Lesson 1	Ancient India	91–93	✔	93	✔		
Lesson 2	The History of Ancient India	94–96	✔	96	✔		
Lesson 3	Hinduism	97–99	✔	99	✔		
Lesson 4	Buddhism	100–102	✔	102	✔		
Lesson 5	China	103–105	✔	105	✔		
Lesson 6	The History of Ancient China	106–110	✔	110	✔		
Chapter 6	**Ancient Greece**	116–145	✔		✔	143	144
Lesson 1	Early Civilizations of the Aegean Sea	119–121	✔	121	✔		
Lesson 2	The Greek City-States	122–123	✔	123	✔		
Lesson 3	Athens	124–125	✔	125	✔		
Lesson 4	Sparta	126–127	✔	127	✔		
Lesson 5	War Tests the Greeks	128–131	✔	131	✔		
Lesson 6	Greek Cultural Contributions	132–136	✔	136	✔		
Lesson 7	Alexander the Great Spreads Greek Culture	137–140	✔	140	✔		

(Unit Planning Guide is continued on next page.)

Student Text Features											Teaching Strategies						Learning Styles					Teacher's Resource Library			
Reading Strategy	Map Study/Map Skills	Writing About History	Geography Note	Biography	History in Your Life	Communication in History	Technology Connection	Then and Now	Spotlight Story	Document-Based Reading	Background Information	Applications (Home, Career, Community)	World Cultures	Study Skills	Online Connection	ELL/ESL Strategy	Auditory/Verbal	Visual/Spatial	Body/Kinesthetic	Interpersonal/Group Learning	Logical/Mathematical	Activities/Modified Activities	Workbook Activities	Self-Study Guide	Chapter Outline
66	65								84	83							83							✔	✔
✔	68										68			68		68						11	11		
✔						73						71				72		70	73			12	12		
✔				75												75						13	13		
✔		78	76										78		79	77				79		14	14		
✔								82				82				81					81	15	15		
90	89								112	111					89, 112	111					90			✔	✔
✔	92	92													93	93				93		16	16		
✔	96										96					95		95				17	17		
✔												99	99			98	98					18	18		
✔								102			102			102		101						19	19		
✔					105						105	105				104						20	20		
✔	110		109				107									108			107	108		21	21		
118	117								142	141						118								✔	✔
✔														121		120						22	22		
✔																123						23	23		
✔												125				125						24	24		
✔		127														127						25	25		
✔	129			131												131					129	26	26		
✔					133	136					136	136	135			133	134	135		135		27	27		
✔	138				140						138					138			139			28	28		

Planning Guide

Early Civilizations
(continued)

		Student Text Lesson				
		Student Pages	Vocabulary	Lesson Review	Critical-Thinking Questions	Chapter Summary	Chapter Review
Chapter 7	The Roman Republic	146–167	✔		✔	165	166
Lesson 1	Early Rome	149–150	✔	150	✔		
Lesson 2	Rome Becomes a Republic	151–153	✔	153	✔		
Lesson 3	Rome Expands Its Boundaries	154–156	✔	156	✔		
Lesson 4	The Republic Faces Problems	157–159	✔	159	✔		
Lesson 5	The End of the Republic	160–162	✔	162	✔		
Chapter 8	The Roman Empire	168–191	✔		✔	189	190
Lesson 1	The Age of Augustus	171–173	✔	173	✔		
Lesson 2	Governing the Roman Empire	174–176	✔	176	✔		
Lesson 3	The Rise of Christianity	177–180	✔	180	✔		
Lesson 4	The Fall of the Roman Empire	181–182	✔	182	✔		
Lesson 5	Rome's Contributions to Civilization	183–186	✔	186	✔		
Chapter 9	Civilizations of the Americas	192–219	✔		✔	217	218
Lesson 1	In Search of the First Americans	195–197	✔	197	✔		
Lesson 2	Early Southwestern Cultures	198–201	✔	201	✔		
Lesson 3	Early Regional Cultures	202–207	✔	207	✔		
Lesson 4	Early Civilizations of Mesoamerica	208–214		214	✔		

Reading Strategy	Map Study/Map Skills	Writing About History	Geography Note	Biography	History in Your Life	Communication in History	Technology Connection	Then and Now	Spotlight Story	Document-Based Reading	Background Information	Applications (Home, Career, Community)	World Cultures	Study Skills	Online Connection	ELL/ESL Strategy	Auditory/Verbal	Visual/Spatial	Body/Kinesthetic	Interpersonal/Group Learning	Logical/Mathematical	Activities/Modified Activities	Workbook Activities	Self-Study Guide	Chapter Outline
148	147								164	163		148			163			147						✔	✔
✔	150															150			150			29	29		
✔		153					153				153	153				152				153		30	30		
✔	155				156									155		156	156				155	31	31		
✔	158											159				159						32	32		
✔				161		162							162	160		161						33	33		
170	169								188	187														✔	✔
✔				172	173										172	173						34	34		
✔	176	174										176		176		175		176				35	35		
✔	179															179	178		178		180	36	36		
✔																182				182		37	37		
✔								185			185	185	186			184						38	38		
194	193								216	215														✔	✔
✔		196										197				196		197				39	39		
✔				201								200, 201	200			199		199	200			40	40		
✔											205, 206		207	204	206	205	205		207		203	41	41		
✔	213			212			214				210		213	209	214	210				211	213	42	42		

"We archaeologists shine scientific flashlights into the past, throwing narrow beams of light hundreds, thousands, even millions of years back into remotest prehistory."

~ *Brian Fagan, professor of anthropology at U.C. Santa Barbara in his introduction to Time Detectives (Simon & Schuster, 1995)*

Other Resources

Books for Teachers

Atkinson, Austen. *Lost Civilizations: Rediscovering Ancient Sites Though New Technology.* New York: Watson-Guptill Publications, 2002.

McIntosh, Jane. *Ancient Mesopotamia: New Perspectives, Understanding Ancient Civilization Series.* Oxford: ABC-CLIO, 2005.

Van Tuerenhout, Dirk R. *The Aztecs: New Perspectives, Understanding Ancient Civilization Series.* Oxford: ABC-CLIO, 2005.

Books for Students

Constable, Nick. *Historical Atlas of Ancient Rome.* New York: Thalamus Publishing, 2005.

Gruber, Beth. *National Geographic Investigates: Ancient Inca.* National Geographic, 2006.

CD-ROM/Software

Fuedalism: Decisions, Decisions. Culver City, CA: Social Studies School Services (1-800-421-4246), 1997 (puts students in the position of a feudal lord who must decide how to command vassals)

Videos

Ancient Civilizations. (6 hours) Questar, 2002. (computer reconstructions and location footage recreate life in ancient Greece, Egypt, and Rome)

Ancient China. (50 minutes) Kultur, 2006. (computer recreation of Chinese civilization from its beginning through the Ming Dynasty)

Web Sites

www.agsglobewh.com/pagexxxvia (the art of ancient Egypt at the New York Metropolitan Museum of Art)

www.agsglobewh.com/pagexxxvib (multiple links for exploring the history, culture, and geography of ancient Greece)

Unit
1

Early Civilizations

Unit 1 covers thousands of years, from the Stone Age to early civilizations in the Americas. As you read this unit, you will learn how history is studied. You will read about the growth of the Middle East and Asia, the ancient civilizations of Greece and Rome, and the first Americans. You will also learn how this knowledge will help you understand the world today.

Chapters in Unit 1

1

Introducing the Unit

Tell students that Unit 1 introduces them to prehistoric and early people. Write the word *civilization* on the board. Have students brainstorm what the word means, such as settlement, people, language, farming, etc. List their ideas under the word. Read the title and paragraph on page 1 to the students. Then have them read through the list of chapters in Unit 1 as an overview of the civilizations they will study. Point out the abbreviations B.C. and A.D. Explain that Unit 1 covers civilizations from prehistoric times, ancient Greece and Rome to the Maya, Inca, and Aztec civilizations of the Americas.

Ask:

• **What is prehistory?** (a time before written history)

• **In what way does knowing about the past help us understand the world today?** (Answers will vary. Gives us the background and development of religions and cultures to help us understand them today.)

Read the quotation from anthropology professor Brian Fagan on page xxxvi to students, pausing to define unfamiliar words, such as *archaeologists, remotest*. Ask students to restate the quote in their own words. (Answers will vary. The work of archeologists provide an understanding of life long ago.)

Ask:

• **What do you think archaeologists might find at a site where prehistoric people once lived?** (answers will vary; students might say bones, fossil footprints, or cave paintings)

Presenting the Unit Activity

Assign Unit 1, Activity 1 to help students understand that though all early civilizations were unique, they shared similar characteristics. Encourage students to use the library and the Internet to do their research. Have students use Unit 1, Activity 2 to write a paragraph summarizing characteristics that are common to early civilizations.

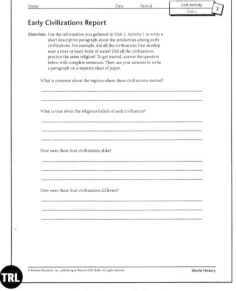

Unit 1, Activity 1   Unit 1, Activity 2

Introducing the Chapter

The first human beings on Earth kept on the move. They roamed from place to place, seeking food. The discovery of fire and the ability to farm allowed them to stay in one place, eventually build cities, and develop a system of writing.

Prehistory

The people of the Stone Age lived before the time of written records. We cannot find newspapers or letters to tell us about them. We must depend on other things they left behind. In this chapter, you will learn what life may have been like for these prehistoric humans. You will also learn about how scientists study the past.

Goals for Learning

◆ To define history and describe two kinds of sources of information

◆ To explain why we study history

◆ To describe artifacts and what historians learn from them

◆ To identify early hominids, the Stone Age, and the importance of farming

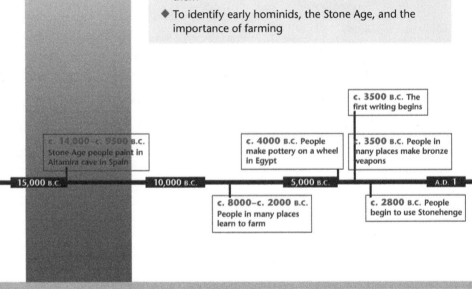

c. 3500 B.C. The first writing begins

c. 14,000–c. 9500 B.C. Stone-Age people paint in Altamira cave in Spain

c. 4000 B.C. People make pottery on a wheel in Egypt

c. 3500 B.C. People in many places make bronze weapons

15,000 B.C.   10,000 B.C.   5,000 B.C.   A.D. 1

c. 8000–c. 2000 B.C. People in many places learn to farm

c. 2800 B.C. People begin to use Stonehenge

Ask:

• How long ago and where did some Stone-Age people live? (about 14,000 B.C. in Spain)

• What clues did these people leave about the way they lived? (paintings on the walls of caves and artifacts)

Name   Date   Period   *SELF-STUDY GUIDE*

Chapter 1: Prehistory—The Time Before Written Records

Goal 1.1 To define history and describe two kinds of sources of information

Date	Assignment	Completed
	1. Read pages 2–6.	
	2. Complete the Lesson 1 Review on page 6.	
	3. Complete Workbook Activity 1.	

Comments:

Goal 1.2 To explain why we study history

Date	Assignment	Completed
	4. Read pages 7–8.	
	5. Complete the Lesson 2 Review on page 8.	
	6. Complete Workbook Activity 2.	

Comments:

TRL

World History

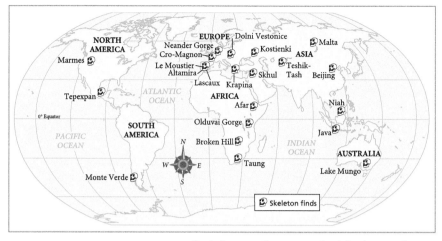

We can use a map that shows direction to find where things are. When you face the direction of the North Pole, you face north. If you face the South Pole, you face south. When you face north, east is to your right; west is to your left.

Most maps use a symbol to show where north is. From this information, you can figure out the three other directions. Note the direction symbol on this map. We call this symbol a compass rose.

The map on this page contains another symbol—a skull. It shows where archaeologists have found clues about early humans.

Study the map, then answer the following questions:

1. Which of the six pictured continents contains the skeleton find known as Marmes?

2. Which of the six pictured continents contains the skeleton find known as Krapina?

3. In what direction would you be traveling if you went from Monte Verde to Lake Mungo, passing through the Indian Ocean?

4. What skeleton finds are south of the imaginary line called the equator?

5. What skeleton finds are located farthest west on the map?

The Time Before Written Records

Ask a volunteer to read the title of the map. Have students identify the six continents. Then have students silently read the three paragraphs under the map.

Ask:

- Which direction on the map is up? (north)
- Which continent on this map is the farthest east? (Australia)
- Which continent is the farthest west? (North America)
- What does the skull symbol represent? (places where archaeologists have found clues about early humans)

Have students read and write answers to the questions.

Map Skills Answers

1. North America
2. Europe
3. east
4. Monte Verde, Olduvai Gorge, Broken Hill, Taung, Java, and Lake Mungo
5. Marmes, Tepexpan, and Monte Verde

Chapter Project

Divide the class into small groups of three to four students. Have each group find an image of a Stone-Age artifact, such as a spear point, in a book or on the Internet. Ask each group to write a plan for an archaeological study of the history and purpose of the artifact. Plans should include a list of resources for information, an assignment to create a labeled drawing to explain the artifact, and questions about the artifact that begin with *who, what, where, when,* and *why*. Have students follow their own archaeological study plan.

LEARNING STYLES

Visual/Spatial

To help students visualize and understand how long ago Stone-Age people lived, work with students to make a timeline that shows in proportion 15,000 B.C., 10,000 B.C., 5000 B.C., and A.D. 2000. Have students make a mark for every thousand years. Have students take turns naming and pointing out on the timeline a year that marks the turn of a millennium B.C. or A.D. (for example, 1200 B.C. or A.D. 900).

Summarizing

Explain to students that a chapter summary captures the general ideas presented in a chapter. Have students page through the chapter and make a list of the lesson headings, leaving several lines of space under each heading. Direct students to write a summary of each lesson under its heading after reading the lesson. Students can then use their lesson summaries to help them write a summary of the chapter.

Ask:

- Who or what is this chapter about? (how history is studied and prehistory)

- What is the main thing being said about this topic? (Answers will vary; The study of history connects the people of today with the past.)

- What details are important to the history of this chapter? (Answers will vary; how history is studied, information about the earliest people)

Key Vocabulary Words

Point out that these chapter words are presented in the order they appear in each lesson. They are also found in the Glossary. Have students brainstorm the different types of artifacts archeologists might find that help to explain the culture of a particular people.

Reading Strategy:
Summarizing

When readers summarize, they ask questions about what they are reading. As you read the text in this chapter, ask yourself the following questions:

- Who or what is this chapter about?
- What is the main thing being said about this topic?
- What details are important to the understanding of this chapter?

Key Vocabulary Words

Lesson 1

History The record of past events

Culture The values, attitudes, and customs of a group

Historian One who is an expert in history

Primary source A first-hand account of a historical event

Secondary source A second-hand account of a historical event; an account written by a person who was not there

Lesson 3

Archaeologist A scientist who finds and studies the things people left behind

Artifact An object made by a person for a practical purpose

Anthropologist A scientist who studies the beginnings and the behavior of people

Radiocarbon dating A way of measuring the radioactivity of historic artifacts to determine how old they are

Lesson 4

Prehistory The time before humans left written records

Hominids A group that includes humans and their closest relatives

Ice Age A period of time when much of Earth and Earth's water was frozen

Extinct No longer existing; died out

Cro-Magnon The hominid *Homo sapiens,* a direct ancestor of modern humans

Paleolithic Age The earliest period of human history; called the Old Stone Age

Neolithic Age The age when people made polished stone tools; also called the New Stone Age

Nomad A person who moves from place to place

Monument An object or building honoring a person or event, usually made of stone

Civilization A large group of people who have cities and government, and a high level of development as a group

---

ONLINE CONNECTION

Students can gain additional information by accessing the following Web sites:

www.agsglobewh.com/page4b (Several links on this Minnesota State University Web site take students to a variety of museum exhibits and maps on early civilizations in North and South America, Asia, and Europe.)

www.agsglobewh.com/page4a (This British site discusses the people, culture, and changes that occurred during the Bronze Age.)

www.agsglobewh.com/page4c (This is an excellent Web site for explaining how and where to access primary sources.)

STUDY SKILLS

Have students use the World Atlas on page 816 to find out the names of the nations in which archeologists found skeletons. Ask them to group the finds by continent. Then have them list the nations of each continent along with their respective archaeological discoveries.

Objectives

- ◆ To define history
- ◆ To identify the differences between primary and secondary sources
- ◆ To understand why people interpret history differently

History
The record of past events

Culture
The values, attitudes, and customs of a group

Historian
One who is an expert in history

Primary source
A first-hand account of a historical event

Secondary source
A second-hand account of a historical event

History is the record of past events. It is the story of people and what happened to them. Each group of people has its own history. In this book, you will learn about the combined history of all people—the history of humanity.

Why Do We Study History?

The people who lived before you learned many lessons they could share with you. Imagine knowing nothing about those people. You would have to learn all their lessons for yourself. If this happened, history would be dead. But happily, history is alive and well! It lives in our **culture,** or our values, attitudes, and customs. It can teach us its lessons.

What Are Primary Sources and Secondary Sources?

When writing history, **historians**—experts in history—ask themselves: *What* happened? *When* and *where* did it happen? *Who* was involved? *Why* did it happen? To find answers, they look for **primary sources.** These sources are first-hand, or eyewitness, accounts of the event. They also seek out **secondary sources,** or second-hand records of what happened. These accounts are written by a person who was not there.

Imagine an argument in the school cafeteria. It will show you the difference between these two sources. You see the argument, so you are an eyewitness. That makes you a primary source. You tell someone about the argument. That person is not an eyewitness. That person becomes a secondary source.

The American Declaration of Independence is a primary source.

The Time Before Written Records

Chapter 1: Lesson 1

Overview This lesson explains the meaning of history—what the written sources of history are and how historians interpret history.

Objectives

- ■ To define history
- ■ To identify the differences between primary and secondary sources
- ■ To understand why people interpret history differently

Student Pages pages 5–6

Teacher's Resource Library

  Workbook Activity 1

  Activity 1

  Modified Activity 1

Vocabulary

culture	primary source
historian	secondary source
history	

Read the terms listed on this page. Write the vocabulary words on the board. Read the definition of one of the terms and ask a volunteer to identify the word defined. Erase the word from the board and repeat.

1 Warm-Up Activity

Ask students to make a list of the different ways people study history. On the board write three headings: *Places, Resources, People.* Have students offer ideas from their lists. Place their ideas under the proper headings. (For example, museums for *Places*, books for *Resources*, and guest speakers for *People*) Discuss the value of oral histories. Have students write a short paragraph to summarize how people study history.

2 Teaching the Lesson

Invite students to share stories about events and people that are a part of history. Then have students read pages 5–6 to find out the sources of those stories and how historians evaluate the sources.

Name _____ Date _____ Period _____ | Workbook Activity | 1
| Chapter 1, Lesson 1 |

Do You Remember?

Directions Write the answers to these questions. Use complete sentences.

1. How have we learned about what happened to people in the past?

2. What is the difference between a primary and a secondary source? Give an example of each.

3. What are the five questions historians ask that begin with W?

4. Why might one person's account of an event be different from someone else's?

5. A group's culture is made up of many things. What are some of them?

Workbook Activity 1

Name _____ Date _____ Period _____ | Activity | 1
| Chapter 1, Lesson 1 |

Studying History

Directions Write the correct word from the Word Bank to complete each sentence.

1. _____ is the record of past events.

2. A daily written record of what happens to a person is called a(n) _____.

3. A first-hand, or _____, account of an event is a primary source.

4. A group's _____ includes its attitudes, values, and customs.

5. Someone who studies history is called a(n) _____.

6. _____ is another word for the human race.

7. When we _____ something, we try to explain how it happened.

8. The American Declaration of Independence is a(n) _____ source.

9. What a historian wrote about the signing of the American Declaration of Independence is a(n) _____ source.

10. The history of humanity is the _____ history of all peoples.

Word Bank
culture
combined
diary
eyewitness
historian
history
humanity
interpret
primary
secondary

Activity 1

Ask:

- What are some ways you could learn about people who lived in the Stone Age? (Answers will vary; students may suggest books, museum artifacts, or the Internet.)

- What is an example of a primary source? a secondary source? (Answers will vary; students may say an eyewitness account is a primary source; a newspaper story is a secondary source.)

Reading Strategy:
Summarizing

(Answers will vary. It helps us understand the many places information can be found and how that information is interpreted.)

 3 Reinforce and Extend

Reading Strategy:
Summarizing
___
How does this lesson help you understand what you will be studying in this book?

How Do Historians Use Sources?

A historian writing about the American Revolution would read what people living at the time wrote. These primary sources would include newspapers; diaries, or daily personal records; and letters.

The same historian would also read what recent historians have written about the war. Their books are secondary sources because these historians were not eyewitnesses.

You have used secondary sources ever since you started school. This textbook is a secondary source. But you are a primary source for what you actually see and hear each day.

How Do We Interpret History?

Individual people, like yourself, record history. Because people differ, what they record differs. You interpret, or explain, the cafeteria argument one way. Another eyewitness interprets it another way. Your two interpretations, or explanations of the meaning, differ. Secondary sources differ in their interpretations too.

This lesson of your history book is a secondary source. After reading it, each of your classmates will interpret it differently. Check out your various views.

Word Bank
___
culture
five
past
primary
secondary

 What do you think
___
Why do history books sometimes say different things about the same subject?

Lesson 1 Review On a sheet of paper, use the words from the Word bank to complete each sentence correctly.

1. History is the record of _____ events.

2. Historians ask _____ questions that begin with *W*.

3. _____ sources are second-hand accounts of what happened.

4. _____ sources might include what an eyewitness wrote in newspapers, diaries, and letters.

5. History lives in our _____ and our customs.

Lesson 1 Review Answers

1. past **2.** five **3.** Secondary
4. Primary **5.** culture

Answers will vary. History books differ because historians interpret historical events differently.

- ◆ To describe how the study of history connects you to the past
- ◆ To explain how you are part of the global community

Reading Strategy: Summarizing

This lesson summarizes the reasons for studying history. What does it tell you about the importance of learning about history?

History helps us remember our past. It also helps us understand how we got to the present. This knowledge helps us figure out what to do tomorrow.

What Can We Learn About People?

History tells us the story of all the people in every country of the world. We discover their new ideas. We realize that they did great things.

History helps us understand their problems. Remember that cafeteria argument? To really understand what caused it, we need to question each person involved. Then we discover all the things that caused the argument. The same is true with history.

How Does History Connect Us to the Past?

History connects us to all the people who have ever lived. Much happened before our lives began. Much will happen after our lives end. But the past gives us roots.

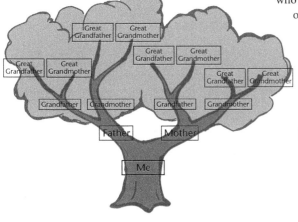

Roots anchor, or hold, a tree in the ground. A family tree helps you understand who you are. The family tree, or history, of the world helps you understand the human race. You are a part of the global community. The global community involves the whole world. It stretches back through time to the beginning of humanity.

The Time Before Written Records

Prehistory   Chapter 1   7

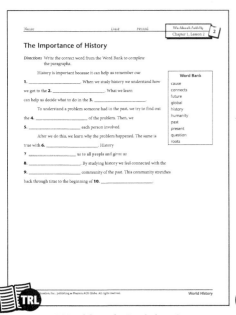

The Importance of History

Directions Write the correct word from the Word Bank to complete the paragraphs.

History is important because it can help us remember our

1. _____. When we study history we understand how we got to the 2. _____. What we learn can help us decide what to do in the 3. _____.

To understand a problem someone had in the past, we try to find out the 4. _____ of the problem. Then, we 5. _____ each person involved.

After we do this, we learn why the problems happened. The same is true with 6. _____. History 7. _____ us to all people and gives us 8. _____. By studying history we feel connected with the 9. _____ community of the past. This community stretches back through time to the beginning of 10. _____.

Word Bank
cause
connects
future
global
history
humanity
past
present
question
roots

Connecting with the Past

Directions People in your past made decisions that affect your life today. Make up five questions you might ask to help you understand one of those decisions. For example, you might ask what happened to cause your ancestors to move from one place to another.

1. What happened _____
2. When _____
3. Where _____
4. Who _____
5. Why _____

Chapter 1: Lesson 2

Overview This lesson describes how the study of history benefits people.

Objectives

- ■ To describe how the study of history connects you to the past
- ■ To explain how you are part of the global community

Student Pages pages 7–8

Teacher's Resource Library TRL

Workbook Activity 2
Activity 2
Modified Activity 2

1 Warm-Up Activity

Ask a volunteer to share an event from his or her past, such as a family move or success in a sporting event. Write the student's idea on the board. Then ask the student how this event affects what they do or how they think today. Write this idea on the board and draw a line connecting the past event with the present.

2 Teaching the Lesson

Ask students to suggest why they think it is worthwhile to study history. Then have them read page 7 to see if their ideas match those in the book.

Ask:

- What does history teach us about people? (what their ideas were; what they did; what problems they had)
- What does it mean to be part of a global community? (In some way, everyone throughout the world is connected.)

Reading Strategy: Summarizing

Remind students that summarizing uses general statements. (Answers will vary. Learning history helps us learn from and form connections with the past.)

3 Reinforce and Extend

ELL/ESL STRATEGY

Language Objective:
To explain and share individual family history

Students will create posters about their family's heritage. Provide students with poster board, markers, and glue. Show students an example of a simple family tree. Discuss how the family tree helps us see our connection with the people in our past. Have ELL students draw a family tree for their own family. Encourage them to use both English and their native language to label relationships in the family tree. Students should embellish their family tree posters with their own drawings, printed images from the Internet, or family photos. They might also add a map to their poster to show the country or countries of origin of their family. Ask students to present their posters to the class. ELL students might also want to wear or show traditional clothing, share traditional music, or display an important item from their family's native country as part of their presentation.

WORLD CULTURES

Information about cultures is shared much quicker today because of the ease of transportation and communication. The Internet, in particular, has created a readily accessible avenue for the sharing of information, understanding cultural ways, and for facilitating trade. As members of the global community, people throughout the world are both directly and indirectly affected by the political, social, economic, and environmental policies of other countries.

> **Word Bank**
> future
> history
> people
> present
> roots

Reading Strategy:
Summarizing

What is the main idea of this lesson?

Lesson 2 Review On a sheet of paper, use the words from the Word Bank to complete each sentence correctly.

1. We study _____ to help us understand how we got where we are today.

2. History helps us understand how we got to the _____.

3. The past gives us _____. These anchor, or hold, us to those people who have gone before us.

4. History gives us a sense of being connected with the _____ of the past.

5. By knowing the past, we may be able to decide what to do in the _____.

What do you think

How does history help us understand what is happening today?

A Human's Best Friend
You may have something in common with early humans—a dog. Dogs have lived with humans for more than 9,000 years. At first, an orphan wolf cub may have found food near a human campsite. Because wolves are used to living in a pack, the cub stayed nearby. Gradually the wolf became tamer. It guarded the camp against other animals and began to help the humans hunt.

Dogs soon became very different from their wolf ancestors. People bred different breeds for certain qualities. Dogs with a keen sense of smell made good hunting dogs. Some dogs were bred for strength, to pull heavy sleds. Today some dogs are trained for police work. Others act as guides for the blind. About 400 different breeds of dogs exist. They live everywhere in the world with their best friends—humans.

LEARNING STYLES

Auditory/Verbal
Have students work with a partner and take turns reading the questions and the paragraphs on pages 5–7. The listener should write the answer to the subhead question as his or her partner reads.

Lesson 2 Review Answers
1. history **2.** present **3.** roots
4. people **5.** future

Answers will vary. Many things, like revolutions, have happened in the past and continue to happen in the present. We use what we learn from those past events to help us understand the present ones.

Ask students who have dogs as pets to share photos and information about their dogs. Discuss the different roles dogs play in society, from companionship to entertainment to community police work. If possible, ask your local police canine unit to visit your class.

- To describe how historians use artifacts to learn about the past
- To understand why there are different calendars
- To explain how radiocarbon dating is used

Archaeologist
A scientist who finds and studies the things people left behind

Artifact
An object made by a person for a practical purpose

Anthropologist
A scientist who studies the beginnings and the behavior of people

Historians write about history. To do this, they study written sources that earlier people left behind. But early people did not write books, newspapers, or letters. What tells us about them?

Who Explores the Past?

Archaeologists are scientists who find and study things people left behind. These things are **artifacts,** or objects made for a practical purpose. They include tools, weapons, pottery, and jewelry.

Anthropologists are scientists who study the beginnings and the behavior of people. For example, they may study the garbage Americans throw out! The garbage tells them about the eating habits of Americans. It also tells them what Americans do for fun, what they read, and much more.

Why Are Dates Important?

Most students think that history is nothing but dates: 2186 B.C. and A.D. 1096. But dates help us measure time. Dates tell us when things happened. For example, a great earthquake shook India in 1897. By dating it, we know that this event happened over 100 years ago.

Archaeologists study things that are left behind from the past—even human remains.

The Time Before Written Records

Chapter 1: Lesson 3

Overview This lesson explains how archaeologists and anthropologists gather information about prehistoric people. Historians use this information as they try to piece together a picture of things that happened long ago.

Objectives

- To describe how historians use artifacts to learn about the past
- To understand why there are different calendars
- To explain how radiocarbon dating is used

Student Pages pages 9–12

Teacher's Resource Library **TRL**

Workbook Activity 3

Activity 3

Modified Activity 3

Vocabulary

anthropologist   artifact
archaeologist   radiocarbon

Have one student select a vocabulary word and read the definition for it. Ask another student to write the word defined on the board. Continue until all of the words are on the board.

PRONUNCIATION GUIDE

Use this list to help students pronounce difficult words in this lesson.

anno Domini   (an´ō dom´ ə nī)

Olduvai   (ōl dü vā´)

1 Warm-Up Activity

Tell the students that their task is to create a new calendar based on an event that is important to them. For example, the first day of their calendar might be their birthday or the first day of school. Have students determine how yearly, monthly, and daily time would be divided in their calendars. Then discuss the advantages and disadvantages of everyone having a different calendar for measuring time.

Exploring the Past

Directions Circle the word or phrase that correctly completes each sentence.

1. Prehistoric humans left behind objects such as tools, weapons, (books, letters, pottery), and jewelry.
2. (Archaeologists, Artifacts, Anthropologists) study the beginnings and the behavior of people.
3. Dates tell us (when, where, why) things happened.
4. (Archaeologists, Artifacts, Anthropologists) are things that earlier people made for a practical purpose and left behind.
5. (Archaeologists, Artifacts, Anthropologists) find and study the things people left behind.
6. (Carbon, Christians, Calendars) help us keep track of time.
7. The (Christian, Jewish, Muslim) calendar begins with the year God created the world.
8. Scientists use (calendars, dates, radiocarbon dating) to determine how old an artifact is.
9. For some periods of history, archaeologists have found few (artifacts, calendars, newspapers).
10. The (Christian, Jewish, Muslim) calendar has dates that contain the letters B.C. or A.D.
11. Archaeologists can tell a lot about early humans by looking closely at their (clothing, bones and teeth, fingerprints).
12. Anthropologists learn about people's diets by studying the (clothing, inventions, garbage) they throw away.
13. Collecting information about the past is like (collecting garbage, putting together a jigsaw puzzle, cleaning house).
14. The (Christian, Jewish, Muslim) calendar begins with the founding of the religion.
15. Archaeologists can sometimes tell where people came from because of an artifact's (size, weight, material).

Workbook Activity 3

Prehistory Puzzle

Part A Directions Write the correct word from the Word Bank to complete each sentence.

1. A scientist who finds and studies things people left behind is called a(n) _____.
2. Tools, weapons, pottery, jewelry, and other things people have left behind are called _____.
3. For historians, the past is like a(n) _____ puzzle.
4. Archaeologists figure out, or _____, how ancient people lived.
5. A scientist who might study the garbage that you throw out each day is a(n) _____.
6. A small number of _____ atoms in living things are radioactive.
7. The letters A.D. stand for the _____ *anno Domini*.
8. Radiocarbon _____ is a way of measuring the radioactivity of artifacts to figure out how old they are.
9. Based on historic events, _____ help us keep track of time.
10. Teeth and _____ can give clues about a person's diet.

Word Bank
anthropologist
archaeologist
artifacts
bones
calculate
calendars
carbon
dating
jigsaw
Latin

Activity 3, pages 1–2

2 Teaching the Lesson

Invite students to tell what they know about archaeologists and anthropologists and the work they do. Then have them read pages 9–12 to find out how scientists piece together information about people who lived before history began.

Ask:

• What do archaeologists do? anthropologists? (study artifacts like tools and pottery that prehistoric people left behind; study the behavior of people)

• What kinds of clues do historians use? (answers may include: dates A.D. and B.C., artifacts, and radiocarbon dating)

• How can articles found near an artifact help archaeologists decide how old the artifact is? (If they know how old articles near an artifact are, they may think the artifact is the same age.)

Reading Strategy: Summarizing

(calendars, radiocarbon dating; Students also may speculate on the special digging tools used by archaeologists and anthropologists.)

Other parts of the Iceman's remains, such as scalp hairs and tattoo-like markings, are clues scientists are using to learn more about the lifestyle of Stone-Age people who lived in Europe. Have students research the Iceman on the Internet or in the library to find out more about scientific studies on his remains.

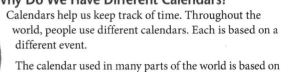

Why Do We Have Different Calendars?

Calendars help us keep track of time. Throughout the world, people use different calendars. Each is based on a different event.

The calendar used in many parts of the world is based on the birth of Jesus, who Christians believe is the "Christ." This kind of calendar lists some historical events as B.C., or "Before Christ." It lists other events as A.D. The letters A.D. stand for the Latin words *anno Domini*. This means "in the year of our Lord." So, A.D. 1776 is "in the year of our Lord 1776." The Jewish calendar begins with the year in which the Jews believe God created the world. Many Muslims use a calendar based on the date of Muhammad's flight from Mecca to Medina.

What Is Radiocarbon Dating?

All living things contain carbon. A small number of carbon atoms in living things are radioactive. Some of these atoms stay in animals and plants for thousands of years after they die. Scientists use **radiocarbon dating** to determine the age of an artifact. That is, they measure the radioactivity of historic artifacts to determine how old they are.

Radiocarbon dating

A way of measuring the radioactivity of historic artifacts to determine how old they are

---

Reading Strategy:
Summarizing

What tools do archaeologists and anthropologists use to determine the date of an object?

What Can You Learn from Bones?

A trained scientist would say you can learn a lot from bones. Scientists carefully study the bones and teeth of early humans. Bones are clues to diet, health, and lifestyles. The prehistoric man known as "the Iceman" was a Bronze-Age hiker. His 4,000-year-old frozen body was found in the Alps in 1991. The Iceman's worn-down teeth showed that he ate tough, raw foods. Scientists also analyze the chemicals in bones. Some experiments showed when early Americans stopped eating wild plants and began to eat corn. That meant they had become farmers.

Bones and teeth give other clues. They can show whether a person had a good diet or certain diseases. A fractured skull may mean that someone died violently. The long thigh bone is a good clue to a person's height. Measuring that bone can tell how tall or short people were in the past.

Biography

Louis Leakey: 1903–1972
Mary Leakey: 1913–1996

Louis and Mary Leakey made exciting discoveries about early humans. Louis Leakey believed that humankind had developed in Africa. The two British scientists worked in East Africa for about 40 years. They collected stone tools and pieces of bone, skulls, and teeth. These were clues to what early people were like. One major site was Olduvai Gorge, Tanzania. Mary Leakey found a large piece of skull there. Tests showed it was 1.75 million years old. That was much older than other human-type fossils. Later she found footprints more than 3 million years old. These showed that hominids (almost-humans) were walking upright that long ago.

How Else Do Archaeologists Date Artifacts?

Sometimes, archaeologists must guess the age of an object. They do this by studying where they found the object. For example, they might find one object near another one made of plastic. Plastic is a fairly new invention. So both objects are probably fairly new. In the same way, an archaeologist might find an object near ancient bones. Because the bones are old, the object probably is too.

Archaeologists must figure out how ancient people lived. To do this, they become detectives who use artifacts as clues. For example, an artifact is made of a certain material. We find this material in only a few areas of the world. The archaeologists can find out where the object may have been made. They may also be able to figure out where the people who used it came from.

Biography

Mary Leakey's 1948 discovery at Olduvai Gorge of a complete fossil skull and jaw of a primitive ape came after years of painstaking field study. To discover more about Mary and Louis Leakey's research and the contribution it has made to science, have students do research in the library or on the Internet. Students might organize their findings on a poster and use the poster as the basis for an oral report to the class.

Writing About History

Have students brainstorm about the job duties of an archeologist. Remind students that archeologists often work in remote regions of the world. Discoveries often take a very long time and require very meticulous work. Daily progress notes must be kept. Discuss the kinds of discoveries an archeologist might make. Have students look at the help-wanted section of a newspaper. Then have students work in pairs to create their help-wanted posters. Allow them to add drawings or pictures to their help-wanted ads. Display the ads in the classroom.

3 Reinforce and Extend

BACKGROUND INFORMATION

The Olduvai Gorge in Tanzania, Africa, is about 30 miles long and 295 miles deep. Objects found at the site range from 3 million to 15,000 years old. The area is distinguished by lava flows, volcanic-ash deposits, and other sediments. Fossils of the area show it was rich in plant life and give evidence of human life located along streambeds. Tools and animal bones and teeth are among the items that have been discovered.

Lesson 3 Review Answers

1. An archaeologist finds and studies the things humans left behind in the past. **2.** An anthropologist studies the beginnings of people and how they acted. **3.** An artifact is an object made by a human being. **4.** Dates help historians know when things happened. They also help historians relate the events to one another. **5.** B.C. tells us that an event took place before the birth of Jesus.

Answers will vary. Artifacts help archaeologists and historians put together a picture of the past. Each artifact is like a puzzle piece that fits into this picture.

How Is the Past Like a Jigsaw Puzzle?

For some periods of history, historians have few artifacts. That makes learning about people from the past hard. It is like a 1,000-piece jigsaw puzzle with no picture and only a few pieces. Historians can only guess what the finished puzzle of the past might look like.

But their guess can change. Sometimes, archaeologists discover new artifacts. They gather more missing pieces. Then their guess about the finished puzzle may change.

Lesson 3 Review On a sheet of paper, write the answer to each question. Use complete sentences.

1. What does an archaeologist do?
2. What does an anthropologist do?
3. What is an artifact?
4. Why are dates necessary to historians?
5. What does B.C. tell you about a date?

What do you think

How are artifacts like pieces in a jigsaw puzzle?

Objectives

- To identify early hominids, Neanderthals, and Cro-Magnons
- To describe the Old and New Stone Ages
- To understand the importance of farming
- To explain the Bronze Age

Prehistory

The time before humans left written records

Hominids

A group that includes humans and their closest relatives

Ice Age

A period of time when much of Earth and Earth's water was frozen

Extinct

No longer existing; died out

We know little about the earliest people who lived on Earth. Why? Because they left no written records. We have written records for only about the last 5,500 years. Scientists learned about prehistoric times by finding ancient bones and stone tools buried in the earth. The long, long time before humans left written records is our **prehistory.**

Who Was "Java Man"?

In 1891, on the island of Java in Asia, scientists discovered humanlike bones. It was determined that the bones were not those of a modern human. The bones of "Java Man" were thought to be around 2 million years old. "Java Man" was given the scientific name *Homo erectus,* meaning "upright man." Over the years, *Homo erectus* bones were found throughout Africa, Asia, and Europe. It is believed that *Homo erectus* was the first **hominid** to use fire. Hominids are a group that includes humans and their closest relatives. The bones of several hominids different from *Homo erectus* have also been discovered. These hominids were older in appearance and had smaller brains. They lived a million or more years before *Homo erectus.*

Who Were the Neanderthals?

In 1856, in Germany's Neander valley, the bones of a close relative to modern humans were discovered. Because of where the bones were found, it was given the name *Neanderthal.* Many more bones of the Neanderthals were found in Europe. Neanderthals appeared about 250,000 years ago. During this time, the climate changed from being mild to very cold. This cold period when much of Earth was frozen is called the **Ice Age.** Neanderthals were about 5 feet tall, stocky, and very strong. They had a large ridge of bone over their eyes. Their body shape helped them survive the harsh weather. They made different kinds of tools out of animal bones and stones. They skinned animals for clothing. They buried their dead. They may have been able to speak. Sometime between 20,000 and 30,000 years ago, the Neanderthals became **extinct,** or died out.

The Time Before Written Records

Chapter 1: Lesson 4

Overview This lesson explains what prehistory is. History began with the development of writing. Prehistoric people who lived before written records left tools, cave paintings, and other clues about the way they lived.

Objectives

- To identify early hominids, Neanderthals, and Cro-Magnons
- To describe the Old and New Stone Ages
- To understand the importance of farming
- To explain the Bronze Age

Student Pages pages 13–18

Teacher's Resource Library TRL

Workbook Activity 4

Activity 4

Modified Activity 4

Vocabulary

civilization	monument
Cro-Magnons	Neolithic Age
extinct	nomad
hominids	Paleolithic Age
Ice Age	prehistory

Have a student write one of the vocabulary words from the margins on pages 13–17 on the board. Have another student read the definition for it. Have a third student restate the definition in his or her own words and have a fourth student use it in a sentence. Continue until all vocabulary words are on the board. Have two volunteers carry on a brief impromptu conversation, using as many vocabulary words as they can as often as they can.

1 Warm-Up Activity

Ask students what they know about how early humans may have lived and what they looked like. If possible, find images of "Java Man," the Neanderthals, and Cro-Magnons to share with the class. Have students use the drawings to describe these early people.

Workbook Activity 4

Prehistory Match-Up

Directions Match the description in Column A with the correct terms in Column B for each set. Write the correct answer on each line.

Column A
1. helped early humans to store their food for later use
2. a person who moves from place to place
3. people or animals that have died out or no longer exist
4. a famous prehistoric monument made up of huge stones
5. another name for *Homo erectus*
6. a group of people with cities and government
7. another name for the Old Stone Age

Column B
A extinct
B Stonehenge
C nomad
D Paleolithic Age
E Java man
F pottery
G civilization

Column A
8. a hard metal of a blend of copper and tin
9. period during which much of Earth was frozen
10. another name for *Homo sapiens*
11. volcanic glass the Stone Age people used to make weapons
12. made it possible for humans to control their food supply
13. time when people made polished stone tools
14. the time before humans left written records
15. people who appeared about 250,000 years ago

Column B
H Cro-Magnons
I farming
J prehistory
K obsidian
L Ice Age
M Neanderthals
N Neolithic Age
O bronze

Activity 4

Descriptions and Developments in Prehistory

Part A Directions Write the letter of each description after the name of the human group it describes.

A lived during the Ice Age about 250,000 years ago
B had a spoken language
C first hominids to walk upright
D bones found in Africa, Asia, and Europe
E made tools out of animal bones and stones
F kept a simple calendar
G became extinct between 20,000 and 30,000 years ago
H painted pictures of animals on cave walls

Java Man _____ Neanderthals _____ Cro-Magnons _____

Part B Directions Write the letter of each discovery after the name of the age during which it was made.

I began planting seeds and growing food
J began making tools from copper and tin
K used fire to stay warm
L used pottery to protect food from insects and mice
M people settled into villages
N made tools out of obsidian
O hollowed out logs to allow travel on water

Paleolithic _____ Neolithic _____ Bronze _____

2 Teaching the Lesson

Tell students that they will be reading about Stone-Age and other prehistoric people. Have students read to learn details about the Stone Age and Bronze Age. Have students divide a sheet of paper into two columns. Title one column *Paleolithic Age* and the other column *Neolithic Age*. Ask students to fill in facts about each time period as they read.

Ask:

- **What happened during the Stone Age?** (People made tools and weapons from stone, discovered fire, built monuments like Stonehenge, made the dog a pet, and drew art on cave walls.)

- **What changes occurred during the Bronze Age?** (People learned to melt copper and tin together to make bronze; people made tougher tools and weapons from bronze; people made canoes.)

- **How did discovering how to grow food change the way people lived?** (They gave up nomadic ways and settled down in one place. Eventually, they built cities.)

Communication in History

Before students read this feature, ask them to suggest ways that people can communicate without speaking or writing. They may mention the use of gestures; icons on road signs that show, for example, where to find a telephone; or the sign language of the hearing impaired. Then have students read "Humans Learn to Say 'Hello'" to find out how anthropologists think human speech may have developed.

Cro-Magnon

The hominid *Homo sapiens,* a direct ancestor of modern humans

Paleolithic Age

The earliest period of human history; called the Old Stone Age

---

Who Were the Cro-Magnons?

Cro-Magnons, like all modern humans, are *Homo sapiens,* meaning "wise man." In 1868, five skeletons were found in a Cro-Magnon cave in France. The bones showed that the general body shape of these people was like that of modern humans. The Cro-Magnons appeared in Europe about 40,000 years ago. Unlike the Neanderthals, the Cro-Magnons are our direct ancestor. They had a spoken language. They were skillful hunters and toolmakers. On a piece of bone or stone, they kept count of the phases of the moon. This was a simple calendar. They were creative artists. They wore jewelry made of ivory and shells. On the walls of caves they painted colorful pictures of animals and simple figures of themselves.

What Are the Old and New Stone Ages?

We call the earliest period of human history the Old Stone Age, or **Paleolithic Age.** It is called the Old Stone Age because people made weapons and tools from stone. They shaped the earliest stone tools from obsidian, a volcanic glass. They also made hand axes and spears. People during the Paleolithic Age lived in small groups and moved frequently from place to place in search of food.

Communication in History

Humans Learn to Say "Hello"

What did early humans sound like? What language did they speak? No one can be sure. Anthropologists think that humans developed language over millions of years. Very early humans probably used a "call system." They made sounds with a certain meaning, like those that some animals use. Calls showed feelings. "Look out! There's a lion!" "I'm scared." "This plant tastes good."

Then life changed for early humans. For one thing, they began to walk upright on two feet. This freed their hands to make tools. People also began to live in larger groups. They worked together to find wild plants. Groups of hunters tracked animals. Now people needed a better way to share ideas. Hunters had to plan for the next day's hunt. A skillful potter needed to teach younger workers the craft. Humans also changed physically. Their brains and larynx, or voice box, developed. By about 100,000 years ago, some early humans were ready for complex human speech.

How Did Early Humans Use Fire?

The discovery of fire is one of the most important events in human history. Stone-Age humans knew that lightning caused fire. At some point, they learned that fire creates heat. With fire, they could warm themselves.

Much later, these early people learned how to move a fire inside a cave. They learned how to keep the embers, or glowing remains of the fire, burning. With these embers, they could start a new fire. Finally, they learned to cook with fire.

What Was the Neolithic Age?

About 10,000 years ago, the New Stone Age, or **Neolithic Age,** began. During this time, people made polished stone tools. They learned how to plant seeds and grow their own food. This allowed them to settle in one place. They also began to tame animals and raise them for food. The earliest humans were **nomads.** They moved from place to place to hunt and gather food. When people began to produce their own food, they were able to create settled communities. As time passed, these communities became villages and then cities. This important historical change is known as the agriculture, or farming, revolution. People lived in these farming communities for thousands of years. This would not change until the 1700s and 1800s, when the Industrial Revolution once again completely changed the way people lived.

How Did Early Humans Use Pottery?

Growing food created a new problem for these Stone-Age humans. They harvested crops once or twice a year. But how could they store the grains for later use?

Prehistoric humans solved their problem by making pottery. They made pottery jars out of clay from riverbeds. These pottery jars protected food from insects, mice, and dampness. Today, the broken parts of this pottery are like puzzle pieces. They help scholars calculate the dates a certain people lived.

Ask:

• What did the development of pottery make possible? (food storage)

Reading Strategy:
Summarizing

Ask students to revisit and finish adding details to the Paleolithic Age/Neolithic Age chart they started on page 13. Have students write one summary statement at the bottom of each column. Write the two column heads on the board and ask volunteers to read their summary statements aloud. Add this information under the correct column head on the board. Then have students read and answer the Reading Strategy: Summarizing question. (Growing food allowed humans to create settled communities.)

- What important invention did the workers who constructed the monument at Stonehenge not have? (the wheel)

Reading Strategy: Summarizing

Write students' ideas on the board. Then together as a class, write a short summary paragraph of their Stonehenge information. Read aloud the information on page 16 about Stonehenge, and then with students' help, revise the summary on the board. Ask students to answer the Reading Strategy: Summarizing question. (Answers will vary; Thinking about how important the invention of the wheel is helped me understand how difficult it must have been to build the monument.)

BACKGROUND INFORMATION

 Despite all the speculation about the purpose of the monumental stone configuration at Stonehenge, it remains a mystery. To compound the mystery, there are over 900 structures similar to Stonehenge in the British Isles alone. There is a field of knowledge devoted to the study of such structures. It is called *archaeoastronomy*. People in this field study archaeology, anthropology, astronomy, and mythology in an attempt to solve mysteries about ancient ruins, such as the purpose of Stonehenge.

Monument
An object or building honoring a person or event, usually made of stone

Reading Strategy: Summarizing
What do you already know about Stonehenge? Was it helpful in understanding these paragraphs?

What Art Did Early Humans Create?

Prehistoric humans left no written records. However, they did leave us some important artwork. In 1859, a young girl and her father explored a cave in northern Spain. They discovered beautiful pictures on the cave walls. The drawings pictured animals—deer, wild boar, horses, and bison, or buffalo.

Today, most scholars believe that Stone-Age artists painted these pictures. They probably used twigs or bits of moss for brushes. To make the paint, they mixed meat grease with colored clay and vegetable colorings.

What Is Stonehenge?

Stonehenge is a famous prehistoric **monument.** It stands near the city of Salisbury in England. It consists of a series of great stone circles. Over 30 huge stones make up the circles. Each stone weighs over 35 tons.

Scientists have discovered that the stones at Stonehenge came from as far away as 135 miles. About 250 workers would have had to move each stone that long distance. How could early humans do this before the invention of the wheel?

The piled-up bank of earth around Stonehenge had a ridge nearly six feet high. A ditch six feet deep lay outside it. Prehistoric people worked with simple tools. How many people worked to build this bank and this ditch? And for how long did they work? We do not know.

Stonehenge is a puzzling prehistoric monument near Salisbury, England. Today, experts can only guess what this ancient mass of huge stones was used for long ago.

LEARNING STYLES

 Logical/Mathematical
Challenge students to think about how massive an operation the building of Stonehenge must have been by doing some mathematics. Ask them to use the information in their text to calculate: the total miles the stones would have been dragged if each came from the likely maximum distance away (4,050 miles); the total approximate weight of the 30 stones (1,050 tons); and the total likely number of workers used if each worker helped move just one stone (7,500 workers).

Civilization

A large group of people who have cities and government, and a high level of development as a group

Stonehenge was in use for more than 1,700 years. Most scholars think prehistoric people honored their gods there. Or Stonehenge might have helped people guess when an eclipse, such as the moon hiding the sun, would happen.

How Did the Stone Age Become the Bronze Age?

Because stone tools broke easily, prehistoric humans looked for other materials for their tools. First, they used the metal copper. Later they discovered how to make bronze. Bronze is a harder metal made of an alloy, or blend, of copper and tin. It also holds a sharper cutting edge.

From about 3500 B.C., prehistoric people made their tools from bronze. They used it for the next 2,000 years. We call this time period the "Bronze Age."

How Did Bronze Change Life?

Bronze does not break easily. With it, ancient people invented many new tools. These made their lives easier. Bronze-Age people also invented a sled to carry things on land. They hollowed out logs and made canoes to carry things on water.

Where Does Prehistory Lead?

Prehistory is an exciting period of humanity's story. At first, humans were nomads. They moved from place to place to hunt and gather food. Then they learned to grow crops. They settled close to their fields and formed small groups.

Now prehistoric humans had a sure supply of food. Because of this, their population grew more quickly. This began a chain of fast changes. These changes brought about the first **civilizations,** in which people built cities and set up governments. People who belong to a civilization have a high level of development.

Ask:

- What two metals are melted together to make bronze? (copper and tin)

- What changes did civilization bring? (People built cities and formed governments.)

 3 **Reinforce and Extend**

ELL/ESL STRATEGY

 Language Objective:
To develop oral interaction skills

To help ELL students understand the basic concepts and chronological order of prehistory, prepare six cards with the dates and information found on the timeline on page 2. Include one card with the current date. Ask the students to shuffle the cards. Then have the students read and lay the cards out on a table in chronological order. Then ask students to create additional cards using information from Chapter 1. For example, dogs begin to live with humans 9,000 years ago, and Neanderthals lived in Europe 250,000 years ago.

Lesson 4 Review Answers

1. B **2.** A **3.** C **4.** C **5.** C

Answers will vary. The cave drawings and the Stonehenge monument tell us that prehistoric people were artistic and that they worshipped gods.

Chapter Project Follow-up

Divide a long piece of mural paper into sections, with one section for each student group working on the Chapter Project on page 3. Have each group draw or glue the image of its artifact in the group's assigned section of the mural. Under the artifact have the group post its study plan for the history and purpose of the artifact, and a written summary statement of what the group members learned though their planned study. Display the mural. As a class, compare and contrast the different plans with how an archeologist works. If possible, invite an archeologist or other scientist to speak to your class to talk about the discovery process.

Lesson 4 Review On a sheet of paper, write the letter of the answer that correctly completes each sentence.

1. The scientific name of "Java Man" is _____.

   A Neanderthal   **C** *Homo sapiens*

   B *Homo erectus*   **D** Neolithic Man

2. The discovery of _____ helped ancient people cook food and stay warm.

   A fire   **B** pottery   **C** painting   **D** monuments

3. Drawings in _____ tell us something about the life of prehistoric people.

   A riverbeds   **B** bronze   **C** caves   **D** tools

4. Because they learned to _____, early people stopped being nomads.

   A make drawings   **C** farm

   B make bronze   **D** make pottery

5. Bronze is a mixture of copper and _____.

   A obsidian   **B** clay   **C** stone   **D** tin

What do you think

What do cave drawings and Stonehenge tell you about prehistoric people?

"In the Beginning . . ."

The Bible (this name comes from the Greek word meaning "book") is a special book of Jews and Christians. It is a collection of smaller books written over many years. Most existed as spoken stories before they were written down. They were written down over a period of more than 1,000 years.

The Jewish Bible is mostly about the history of the Hebrew, or Jewish, people in the Middle East. Most of it is set in Palestine or Israel. Christians usually call the Jewish Bible the Old Testament.

What Christians call the New Testament is about the teaching of Jesus and his followers, who started the Christian church. It was mostly written between A.D. 50 and A.D. 100.

The Bible was not written in English. It was written in the Hebrew, Aramaic, and Greek languages. It has been translated into many other languages. The following reading is from the first book, Genesis. That name means "beginning." In a poetic way Genesis describes the creation of the world. Read the excerpt below. Then answer the questions that follow.

In the beginning when God created the heavens and the earth, the earth was a formless void. . . . And God said, "Let there be light"; and there was light. God called the light Day and the darkness he called Night. . . .

And God said, "Let the waters under the heavens be gathered together into one place, and let the dry land appear." And it was so. God called the dry land Earth and the waters . . . he called Seas. . . . And God said, "Let the earth put forth vegetation . . . and fruit trees." . . . And it was so. . . .

"Let there be light . . . to separate the day from the night; and let them be for signs and for seasons and for days and years. . . ." And it was so. . . .

So God created . . . every living creature that moves, of every kind, with which the waters swarm, and every winged bird. . . .

Then God said, "Let us make humankind in our image, according to our likeness; and let them have dominion over . . . every creeping thing that creeps upon the earth." . . . God saw everything that he had made, and indeed, it was very good. . . .

And on the seventh day God finished the work that he had done, and he rested on the seventh day from all the work that he had done.

Document-Based Questions

1. What two religions consider the Bible a very special book?

2. What names did God give the waters and the dry land?

3. What do you think were the "lights" that separated day from night?

4. What do you think is meant by "dominion" (power) over "every creeping thing"?

5. According to Genesis, what happened on the seventh day?

Source: Quotes are from New Revised Standard Version.

The Time Before Written Records

Call attention to the title. Some students may be unfamiliar with the use of ellipses. Explain that ellipses, or three dots, are used to indicate that some copy from the original source has been deleted. Point out that, in some places, there is a fourth dot. This indicates a period at the end of a sentence before the ellipses.

Read the two introductory paragraphs to students. Explain that many religions have sacred writings. For Jews, some of those writings are the books of the Torah, and for Christians, they are the books of the Bible. Tell students that they will read the beginning of the first book in the Jewish Torah, which is also the first book in the Christian Bible.

Call attention to the photo and discuss it. Then have students read to find out how God created the world, according to the book of Genesis, and answer the questions.

Answers to Document-Based Questions:

1. Judaism and Christianity consider the Bible a special book.

2. He named the waters Seas and dry land Earth.

3. The lights may have been the sun, the moon, and the stars.

4. God planned for humans to have power over all other living things, and to care for them.

5. God ended his work and rested.

Have a volunteer read the title. Then read the first three paragraphs to students. Remind them that the beginning of Genesis is for many people a special story that speaks the truth—it explains how God created the world and from where human beings came.

Have students look at the photo and ask a volunteer to read the caption. Then have students complete the reading to learn scientists' answers to questions such as how the world began. Tell students to answer the questions when they complete the reading.

Answers to Spotlight Story Wrap-Up:

1. They used argument and demonstrations.

2. Mythos was a kind of truth that no one questioned; logos could be proved.

3. Scientists collect evidence, study it, and make experiments.

4. Chinese myth uses yin and yang.

5. Genesis describes the creation.

The Search for the Truth

The ancient Greeks had two ways of thinking about the truth. They called them by different terms: *logos* and *mythos*. Logos meant the kind of truth that can be found through argument and demonstrations. You can see the word *logos* in the ending of words like *archaeology* and *anthropology*. These refer to careful study. Scientists in these fields study evidence and make experiments. They try to find the truth about human origins.

Mythos meant a different kind of truth. These were stories that everyone accepted as true. They were not questioned. Today, we use the word *myth* for made-up stories. That is the opposite of what the Greeks meant.

Like the Greeks, other people in history have asked basic questions about themselves and their world. When did the world begin? Where did human beings come from?

Scientists look for answers to these questions. They accept evidence showing that the earth is about 4.5 billion years old. They also agree with the evidence that life on earth began about 1.5 billion years later, with simple organisms. More complex forms of life developed gradually over time.

Many cultures explain how the world began in non-scientific ways. One creation story comes from the Navaho of the American Southwest.

Poseidon, Greek god of the sea, was a key part of Greek mythology—stories that spoke the truth for ancient Greeks.

It says there were once smaller worlds inside the earth. The story tells how people escaped to the earth's surface by climbing up a reed.

The Chinese have another story. It begins with a great void, or emptiness. Yin and yang were opposing forces in the void. Yin is the force of stillness. Yang is the force of action. Yin and yang combined and created the world.

In the Bible, the book of Genesis describes how God created the world and all life in six days. Because of this account, some Christians reject scientific explanations for human origins. Other Christians accept both scientific evidence and the biblical story.

Other peoples in other places have other explanations. Humans still seek the truth about themselves. In different ways, they will go on looking for answers to important questions.

Wrap-Up

1. What methods did the ancient Greeks use to find the truth of "logos?"

2. How was "mythos" different from "logos?"

3. What methods do scientists use to determine the truth?

4. What were the two forces in Chinese myth?

5. What book of the Bible describes the creation?

Chapter 1 SUMMARY

- Human history is a record of events that have happened to people everywhere.

- Historians ask five questions about an event: *What* happened? *When* did it happen? *Where* did it happen? *Who* was involved? *Why* did it happen?

- Primary sources, such as letters and newspapers, give a first-hand account of events. Secondary sources report events as they were seen by others.

- History helps connect us to people of the past. It helps us understand what caused events. It helps us see how we got where we are today. It helps us make decisions about the future.

- Archaeologists are scientists who study tools and other things people have made. These objects are called artifacts.

- Anthropologists are scientists who study people's customs and behavior.

- Using dates is a way to measure time. Americans and Europeans commonly use a calendar based on what is believed to be the birth of Jesus. The abbreviations B.C. and A.D. refer to years before and after that date.

- Scientists use radiocarbon dating to find the age of once-living things. This method measures the number of radioactive atoms left in an artifact.

- The time before humans left written records is called prehistory.

- *Homo erectus* was an early hominid.

- The Cro-Magnons and Neanderthals lived during the Ice Age.

- We call the earliest period of human prehistory the Old Stone Age, or Paleolithic Age.

- About 10,000 years ago, the New Stone Age, or Neolithic Age, began.

- Learning to use fire was a major step forward in human history.

- The earliest humans were nomads. They hunted and gathered wild food. When humans began to farm and grow crops, they settled in one place. To store food, they learned to make pottery.

- Early humans created art. They made cave paintings and built large monuments such as Stonehenge.

- From about 3500 B.C. prehistoric people made tools and other objects from bronze (a mix of tin and copper). This time period is called the Bronze Age. It lasted about 2,000 years.

- Farming gave prehistoric people a sure supply of food. As the number of people increased, they built cities and set up governments. This marked the beginning of civilization.

Using the Chapter Summary

Have students read the Chapter Summary on page 21 to review the main ideas presented in Chapter 1.

Ask:

- **What are the questions historians ask when they write history?** (what happened, when and where did events occur, who was there, and why did events happen)

- **What is alike and different about primary and secondary sources?** (Both give an interpretation of history; primary sources are first-person accounts of events; secondary sources depend on the reports of other people.)

- **Why is it important to study history?** (It helps us understand our world today and figure out what we should do in the future.)

- **What do archaeologists and anthropologists do?** (Archaeologists study artifacts people leave behind; anthropologists study what people do—their culture and behavior.)

- **How does the calendar that most Americans and Europeans use divide dates in history?** (by B.C., or before Jesus's birth, and A.D., or in the year of our Lord)

- **What is one tool scientists use to date artifacts?** (radiocarbon dating)

- **What two names are given to the earliest period of human history?** (the Old Stone-Age and the Paleolithic Age)

- **What did Stone-Age humans discover besides how to make stone tools and weapons?** (how to use fire)

- **What process ended the Stone Age?** (making bronze by mixing tin and copper)

- **What made it possible for humans to settle down in one place?** (learning to grow crops)

- **What made it possible for history to begin?** (writing)

- **What marked the beginning of civilization?** (the creation of cities and governments)

Chapter 1 Review

Use the Chapter Review to prepare students for tests and to reteach content from the chapter.

Chapter 1 Mastery Test

The Teacher's Resource Library includes two forms of the Chapter 1 Mastery Test. Each test covers the chapter Goals for Learning. An optional third page of additional critical-thinking items is included for each test. The difficulty level of the two forms is equivalent.

Chapter 1 Review Answers

1. History
2. primary
3. secondary
4. archaeologist
5. anthropologist
6. bronze
7. artifact
8. prehistory
9. Cro-Magnons
10. Neanderthals
11. B
12. C
13. B

Chapter 1   REVIEW

Word Bank
anthropologist
archaeologist
artifact
bronze
Cro-Magnons
history
Neanderthals
prehistory
primary
secondary

On a sheet of paper, use the words from the Word Bank to complete each sentence correctly.

1. _____ is the record of conditions and events in the past.

2. A personal diary is an example of a(n) _____ source.

3. A book written today about events 1,000 years ago is a(n) _____ source.

4. A(n) _____ is a scientist who finds and studies the things people left behind.

5. A(n) _____ is a scientist who studies the beginnings and behavior of people.

6. Prehistoric humans learned to blend copper and tin together to make _____.

7. A(n) _____ is something made by a human being.

8. We call the period before written records our _____.

9. _____ are the direct ancestors of modern humans.

10. _____ had a large ridge of bone over their eyes.

On a sheet of paper, write the letter of the answer that correctly completes each sentence.

11. Among primary sources are _____.

   A newspapers   **C** letters
   B diaries   **D** all of the above

12. Tools, weapons, pottery, and jewelry are examples of _____.

   A bronze   **C** artifacts
   B secondary sources   **D** radiocarbon dating

13. For archaeologists, the past is like a _____.

   A cave   **C** bronze pot
   B jigsaw puzzle   **D** matchstick

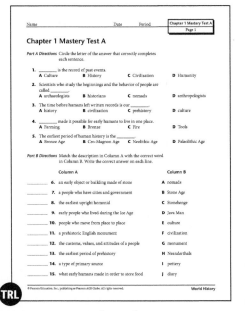

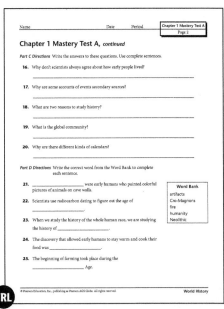

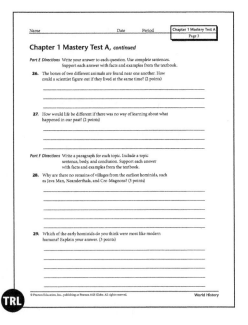

Chapter 1 Mastery Test A, pages 1–3

14. Prehistoric people were nomads who moved from place to place searching for _____.

   A food   **C** primary sources

   B artifacts   **D** bronze

15. The making of _____ helped prehistoric people store food.

   A fire   **C** pottery

   B bronze   **D** Stonehenge

On a sheet of paper, write the answer to each question. Use complete sentences.

16. Why was the discovery of fire important?

17. Why were bronze tools and weapons better than those made of stone?

18. Why are historians lucky that early humans left trash behind?

Critical Thinking On a sheet of paper, write your response to each question. Use complete sentences.

19. Stone-Age people were very different from modern people. Do you agree or disagree? Explain your answer.

20. Why do you think schools often make history a required subject?

Always read directions more than once. Then try to say them in your own words. That way, you can make sure you know how to answer the questions.

The Time Before Written Records

14. A

15. C

16. Fire helped people cook food, protect themselves from animals, and stay warm.

17. Bronze tools lasted longer and did not break as easily as those made of stone.

18. Answers will vary. Students may say that trash helps the historians learn many things about these people.

Critical Thinking

19. Answers will vary. Students may say that Stone-Age people are like us because they did many of the things we do. However, they are unlike us in that they did not have any modern technology, permanent buildings, or a written language.

20. Answers will vary. Students may say that schools require us to study history so that we will learn from it. History can help us understand the present and plan for the future.

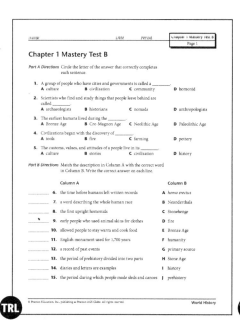

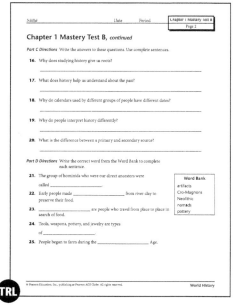

Chapter 1 Mastery Test B, pages 1–3

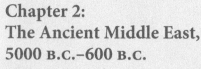

Chapter 2:
The Ancient Middle East, 5000 B.C.–600 B.C.
pages 24–43

Introducing the Chapter

Some of the earliest civilizations developed in the Middle East about 7,000 years ago. These civilizations made many important contributions to architecture, language, law, and religion. Have students make a list of factors that are necessary for civilizations to develop. (Answers may include fertile land for farming, written language to record information, and natural resources to build shelter.)

The Ancient Middle East

As early as 7,000 years ago, civilization began to develop in the Middle East. Many people settled along the Tigris and the Euphrates Rivers there. We call this area Mesopotamia, a word that means "land between the rivers." Mesopotamia and the land to its east form the "Fertile Crescent." In this chapter, you will learn about the people who lived along the Fertile Crescent. You will also discover the gifts they gave to us.

Goals for Learning

◆ To describe life in Sumer and identify the Sumerians' contributions to the world

◆ To describe Akkadian and Babylonian civilizations in Mesopotamia and analyze the rule of Hammurabi

◆ To evaluate the role of the Phoenicians and the Hebrews in world civilization

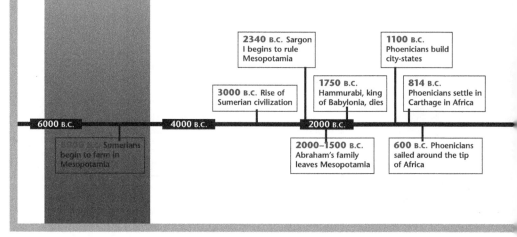

| 3000 B.C. Rise of Sumerian civilization | 2340 B.C. Sargon I begins to rule Mesopotamia | 1750 B.C. Hammurabi, king of Babylonia, dies | 1100 B.C. Phoenicians build city-states | 814 B.C. Phoenicians settle in Carthage in Africa |

6000 B.C.   4000 B.C.   2000 B.C.

5000 B.C. Sumerians begin to farm in Mesopotamia

2000–1500 B.C. Abraham's family leaves Mesopotamia

600 B.C. Phoenicians sailed around the tip of Africa

Have students add to or change their lists as they read this chapter.

Ask:

• Where and when did the Sumerians first begin farming? (Mesopotamia, about 5000 B.C.)

• Who was the king of Babylonia and when did he die? (Hammurabi, 1750 B.C.)

• What were three major accomplishments of the Phoenicians? (They built great cities, they traveled to new places and founded colonies there, they mapped sea routes, they developed an alphabet, and they spread their culture around the world.)

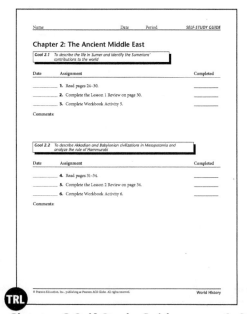

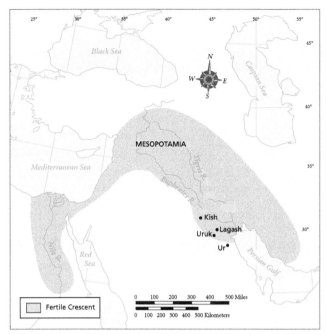

MESOPOTAMIA

Fertile Crescent

0 100 200 300 400 500 Miles
0 100 200 300 400 500 Kilometers

We have given Mesopotamia, the "land between the rivers," many names. Since the first great civilizations developed there, we called it "the cradle of civilization." We also called it the "Fertile Crescent." Why? Because Mesopotamia and the land to its west is shaped like a crescent, or quarter, moon. Also, it is fertile, or able to provide plentiful crops.

Because of the oil in this area, the Fertile Crescent is important to the whole world today.

Study the map, then answer the following questions:

1. What are the names of the five seas shown on the map?

2. What four cities appear on the map?

3. What two great rivers flow in Mesopotamia?

4. About how many miles long is the Fertile Crescent?

5. In what direction is Mesopotamia from the Mediterranean Sea?

Have students study the map and silently read the two paragraphs under the map. Have students read and write answers to the Map Skills questions.

Ask:

• **Where is Mesopotamia located?** (between the Tigris and Euphrates rivers)

• **Why is Mesopotamia called the "Fertile Crescent"?** (It is shaped like a crescent moon and its land is able to provide plentiful crops.)

• **Why is the Fertile Crescent important today?** (Much of the world's oil comes from this area.)

Map Skills Answers

1. Mediterranean Sea, Black Sea, Caspian Sea, Persian Gulf, Red Sea

2. Kish, Lagash, Uruk, and Ur

3. the Tigris and Euphrates rivers

4. about 1,200 miles

5. east

Chapter Project

Have students research Hammurabi's code of laws and write a report. In the report, students should describe the code of laws in general, telling what the laws cover. They should also choose one or two laws to discuss in greater detail. Reports should also describe punishments or consequences if a person breaks the described laws.

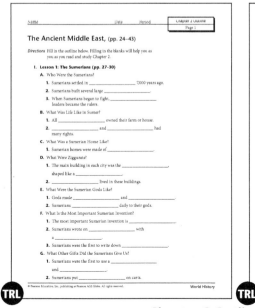

Chapter 2 Outline, pages 1–3

Questioning

Introduce the reading skill *questioning*. Explain that when you ask questions about something you are reading, you are making connections between what you have just read and what you are about to read. Asking questions can also lead to predictions.

Have students read the two opening paragraphs on page 27.

Ask:

- **What questions can you ask about the first paragraph?** (Students may ask where the Tigris and Euphrates Rivers are located. They may ask what modern countries have replaced Mesopotamia.)

- **What questions can you ask about the second paragraph?** (What makes flooded land fertile? Why did few trees grow there? What materials did the Sumerians use to build their houses if there was little wood or stone?)

- Point out to students that when they ask questions about what they are reading, they can look forward to finding out the answers to their questions in the paragraphs to come. This feeling of anticipation makes reading exciting.

Key Vocabulary Words

The vocabulary words on this page are important terms students will encounter in Chapter 2. Have students work in pairs to practice learning the words and definitions.

Reading Strategy:
Questioning

Asking questions as you read will help you understand and remember more of the information. Questioning the text will also help you to be a more active reader. As you read, ask yourself:

- ◆ What is my reason for reading this text?
- ◆ What decisions can I make about the facts and details in this text?
- ◆ What connections can I make between this text and my own life?

Key Vocabulary Words

Lesson 1

City-state A city surrounded by smaller villages

Military Having to do with the army

Temple A place in which to honor gods

Worship To honor and praise a god

Priest A religious leader

Cuneiform The writing invented by Sumerians

Lesson 2

Translate To change the words of one language into those of another

Reign To rule; the period of time a king or queen rules

Lesson 3

Fertile Crescent The area in the Middle East shaped like a quarter moon (crescent) where one of the earliest civilizations developed

Bible The Hebrew and Christian book that is thought to be holy

Famine A time when crops do not grow and there is no food

Commandment A rule, or a way to act

Judaism The religion of the Hebrews that Jews practice today

Covenant An agreement

- To describe life in Sumer
- To identify four things the Sumerians added to world civilization

City-state

A city surrounded by smaller villages

Military

Having to do with the army

Reading Strategy:
Questioning

What do you think you will learn about by reading this lesson?

About 7,000 years ago, several groups of people settled between the Tigris and the Euphrates Rivers. The place where they settled is called Mesopotamia. Mesopotamia means "the land between the rivers."

Every spring the rivers flooded their banks and made the land fertile. The rivers helped people raise crops and care for their goats, cows, and sheep. Few trees grew there, and there was little stone for building. Yet in this place, an unusual people—the Sumerians—began to build a great civilization. Their civilization is called Sumer.

Who Were the Sumerians?

At first, the Sumerians lived in the hills northeast of Mesopotamia. Gradually they moved into the river valleys. The Sumerians shared a common language and religion. They were one of many different tribes that lived in this area.

The Sumerians built several large **city-states,** or cities surrounded by smaller villages. More than 20,000 people lived in the largest cities. They built strong, protective walls around the cities. They also built canals and dikes—banks of earth that keep out water. Then they drained the nearby water-soaked land and irrigated the farmlands.

Each city had its own government. In the beginning, the people chose their leader. But then the city-states began to fight with each other. Leaders of the **military,** or army, became their rulers.

5000 B.C. – 600 B.C.

The Ancient Middle East   Chapter 2   **27**

Chapter 2: Lesson 1

Overview This lesson describes the Sumerians, the first great civilization to develop in Mesopotamia. Students will learn about Sumerian government, law, home life, religion, and inventions.

Objectives

- To describe life in Sumer
- To identify four things the Sumerians added to world civilization

Student Pages pages 27–30

Teacher's Resource Library **TRL**

Workbook Activity 5

Activity 5

Modified Activity 5

Vocabulary

city-state	priest
cuneiform	temple
military	worship

Have each student make flashcards for these vocabulary words. On the front of each card, they should write a vocabulary word. The back of each card should contain the correct definition. Give students a few minutes to review silently the definitions on their flashcards. Then have pairs of students quiz each other.

1 Warm-Up Activity

Review with students the work of archaeologists and how they learn about ancient civilizations. Have students identify some of the things archaeologists may have discovered in the Fertile Crescent that told them how the Sumerians lived. Describe a dig in which archaeologists uncover the ruins of buildings and entire villages. Show students photographs of Sumerian dwellings that have been discovered.

Reading Strategy:
Questioning

(Students should recognize from the titles and subtitles that they will learn about the Sumerians.)

Workbook Activity 5

Activity 5, pages 1–2

The Ancient Middle East   Chapter 2   **27**

Use this list to help students pronounce difficult words in this lesson.

Mesopotamia   (mes´ ə pə tā mē ə)

Sumerians   (sü mir´ ē ənz)

ziggurat   (zig´ u rat)

 Teaching the Lesson

On a sheet of paper, have each student make a chart with two columns and five rows. The heading for the first column should be *Sumer*, and the heading for the second column should be *Modern America*. The headings for the rows should be *Cities, Government, Rights of Women and Children, Religion,* and *Inventions*. As students read the lesson, they should list one or two key facts for each row under the *Sumer* column. Then, drawing on their own observations, students should list one or two facts for each row under the *Modern America* column. After all students have completed the chart, lead a discussion on the similarities and differences between life in Sumer and life in America as students know it.

Ask:

• Why do you think a ziggurat was the most important building in a Sumerian city? (Answers may vary; students may say that religion was important to the Sumerians.)

LEARNING STYLES

Body/Kinesthetic
As a group project, have students construct a model of a ziggurat (a four-sided pyramid) using wood blocks or any materials of their choice. Encourage students to strive for detail and historical accuracy. They may find it helpful to do library or Internet research on the construction of ziggurats.

Temple
A place in which to honor gods

Worship
To honor and praise a god

Priest
A religious leader

What Was Life Like in Sumer?

Sumerians lived far better than prehistoric humans had. Even the poorest citizens owned their own farm or house. Women had many legal, or lawful, rights. They could own property and run a business. Sumerian slaves could set up a business, borrow money, and buy their freedom. Children had to obey. If they disobeyed, their parents could sell them into slavery! In school, teachers could beat children who made mistakes. The children's parents chose whom they would marry.

What Was a Sumerian Home Like?

The Sumerians learned to make bricks by putting clay in molds. Then they baked the bricks in the hot sun. They used these clay bricks to build one-story houses. Each had several rooms surrounding an open patio.

People with more money built larger, two-story houses. They coated the walls with a mixture of water, sand, and perhaps other materials. Then they painted the inside and the outside of their house white.

What Were Ziggurats?

The main building in each Sumerian city was its **temple.** There, the people **worshiped,** or honored, their gods. Each temple was in a ziggurat, or pyramid, shape with four sides. A temple ziggurat was up to six or seven stories high.

Inside the temple, the Sumerians built rooms for their **priests,** or religious leaders. The priests made sure that the workers built the ziggurat correctly. Building was expensive, so the priests asked for and received a part of each farmer's crop.

The ziggurat was the main part of every Sumerian city. It was a temple with rooms inside for priests and worship. Some ziggurats are still standing today.

STUDY SKILLS

 Outlining is a useful way for students to organize a large amount of information. Review proper outlining techniques with students and then have them outline Lesson 1 of this chapter. You might encourage them to use the subhead questions as the titles for each Roman numeral in their outline. Remind students that outlines should not contain every piece of information. Rather, they should contain main points and some key details.

What Were the Sumerian Gods Like?

Like most people at that time, the Sumerians believed in gods who had human feelings. They believed that when the gods became angry, they punished the Sumerians. They made rivers flood and crops fail.

To keep their many gods happy, the Sumerians built ziggurats in which to worship them. They kept statues of the gods in these temples. They also sacrificed animals daily to their gods.

What Is the Most Important Sumerian Invention?

The Sumerians invented writing. We call their writing **cuneiform.** Writing probably began when the priests started to keep records. Later, the Sumerians made cuneiform more simple by creating a different symbol for each sound or word. They created about 600 characters, or symbols.

The Sumerians had no paper. They wrote on soft clay tablets with a sharp, pointed tool called a stylus. Then they baked the tablets to make them hard.

The Story of Gilgamesh

The story of Gilgamesh is the world's oldest known written literature. It is a long poem, or epic, that tells Sumerian myths. It is on clay tablets written about 4,000 years ago. The story itself is even older. Gilgamesh was a real person. He probably ruled Uruk, a city in Mesopotamia, before 2500 B.C. The myth makes him a hero king. He is part god and part human. The poem centers on his hunt for a way to live forever. There are battles with spirits and divine animals. Enkidu is another character. He lived in the forest with animals.

Gilgamesh beat him in a fight. Then Enkidu became his friend and companion.

Some stories in the Gilgamesh epic are similar to those in the Bible. One story tells about a great flood in Mesopotamia. A man tells Gilgamesh how he built a boat and lived through the flood. This is similar to the story of Noah and the Great Flood from the Bible.

5000 B.C. – 600 B.C.

Ask:

• How were Sumerians able to write without using paper? (They used a stylus to make marks on clay tablets.)

BACKGROUND INFORMATION

 The Sumerians are credited with inventing cuneiform. Later civilizations—including the Akkadians, Babylonians, and Persians—made important improvements while continuing to use it. At first, cuneiform was written in columns that were read from right to left. Columns were later changed to lines that were read from left to right. In addition, the symbols were turned 90 degrees so that they appeared horizontally rather than vertically. These changes enabled a person to write cuneiform more quickly and easily. Archaeologist Sir Henry Creswicke Rawlinson started deciphering cuneiform texts in the 19th century, and the work continues to this day.

LEARNING STYLES

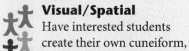 **Visual/Spatial**
Have interested students create their own cuneiform, or symbolic language, by selecting five to ten common words (possibilities include *school, car, love,* or *family*) and creating a symbol that represents each word. Students should draw their symbols and write the corresponding words on a piece of paper or poster board, which may be displayed in the classroom or in the hallway. Simple sentences can be written.

Tell students that all cultures have their own myths or stories that are passed down from generation to generation. These stories are called folklore. An example of American folklore is the story of Johnny Appleseed. Ask students if they know any folklore from their own cultural background. If they cannot think of any, encourage them to ask parents or grandparents.

Ask:

- **What were some of the Sumerians' inventions?** (writing, plow, sailboat, wheeled carts, potter's wheel, arches, ramps)

Reading Strategy:
Questioning

Students can judge whether or not they understood the material in each subsection by answering the questions in the subheads. If they cannot answer the questions correctly, have them read the material again, either aloud or with a partner.

ELL/ESL STRATEGY

Language Objective:
To describe how Sumerian inventions made life easier

Have each ELL student choose a device that Sumerians invented and give a class presentation to show and describe how the invention works and what it looks like. Students may draw pictures or show magazine pictures of the device and tell how it is used in their native country. Class presentations should include a description of how the device made life easier and better for the Sumerian people. For example, the invention of the plow enabled people to cultivate land more easily so that people could grow more food and be better nourished.

3 **Reinforce and Extend**

AT HOME

In Sumer and in some cultures today, marriages were arranged. Ask students whether they think parents should choose who their child marries. Encourage students to ask their parents the same question. Have students share the results of the interview with parents in class discussion.

Archaeologists have found many of these tablets. Most of them are legal and business records. About 5,000 of them, however, contain our oldest known writings—hymns, stories, and poems. Some tablets list the names of cities, trees, insects, and many other things. This means the Sumerians were the first people to write down history.

What Other Gifts Did the Sumerians Give Us?
The Sumerians may have been the first people to use a plow and a sailboat. They were the first to put wheels on carts. They also invented the potter's wheel. On this wheel, they could make more useful pottery shapes.

Sumerians created arches and ramps. These curved openings and smooth stairways helped them build taller and stronger buildings. To do this, they needed to know arithmetic. They based their arithmetic on the number 60. Even today, we use this number to measure time. For example, we have a 60-second minute and a 60-minute hour.

Reading Strategy:
Questioning

Ask yourself: "Did I understand what I just read about the Sumerians?" If not, read the material again.

Word Bank

bricks
cuneiform
Sumerians
temple
20,000

Lesson 1 Review On a sheet of paper, use the words from the Word Bank to complete each sentence correctly.

1. The _____ were one of many different tribes that lived in the Middle East.

2. The largest Sumerian cities had more than _____ people.

3. A ziggurat is the name for a Sumerian _____.

4. The Sumerians built with _____.

5. The Sumerians invented writing called _____.

What do you think

What do you think was the most important invention of the Sumerians? Why do you think this?

IN THE COMMUNITY

Have students observe the buildings that have ramps in their community. Tell students that in 1990, the United States Congress passed a law called the Americans with Disabilities Act, which stated that public buildings, such as businesses, schools, and government agencies, must be made accessible to people with physical disabilities. To accomplish this, ramps for people in wheelchairs were often built. Ask students whether they think all buildings should be required to have ramps.

Lesson 1 Review Answers
1. Summerians **2.** 20,000 **3.** temple
4. bricks **5.** cuneiform

Answers will vary. Students may suggest that writing has influenced every culture since the time of the Sumerians. Students may also suggest that arches and ramps have made more styles of buildings possible.

Objectives

◆ To describe how
the Akkadian and
Babylonian
civilizations
became powerful
◆ To identify Sargon I
◆ To identify the
system of laws that
Hammurabi
created

Translate

To change the words
of one language into
those of another

Years after the Sumerians built their city-states in
Mesopotamia, Sargon I united them. He ruled a kingdom north
of the Sumerians called Akkad. Because his Akkadian army
used bronze weapons, they were stronger than other armies.

In time, Sargon's kingdom spread from the shores of the
Mediterranean Sea eastward. It covered all of the Tigris and
Euphrates River Valleys to the Persian Gulf. For the first time
in history, one person ruled all this land. He ruled for about 35
years, from around 2340 B.C. to 2305 B.C.

What Did Sargon I Borrow from the Sumerians?

Sargon I borrowed many ideas from the Sumerians. The most
important was their way of writing. The Akkadians had their
own language, but they used the Sumerian cuneiform to make
written records.

Scribes **translated** many Sumerian writings. That is, they
changed the Sumerian words into their own Akkadian ones.
In this way, the Akkadians discovered many of Sumer's ideas
about religion and government.

Sargon I was a strong leader. He repaired dikes and made the
irrigation systems longer. His army protected important trade
routes. Sargon I died in 2305 B.C.

Chapter 2: Lesson 2

Overview This lesson describes
the rise and fall of two powerful
kingdoms in Mesopotamia—the
Akkadians and the Babylonians.
Each made important contributions,
especially in the area of written law.

Objectives

■ To describe how the Akkadian
and Babylonian civilizations
became powerful

■ To identify Sargon I

■ To identify the system of laws
that Hammurabi created

Student Pages pages 31–34

Teacher's Resource Library

Workbook Activity 6

Activity 6

Modified Activity 6

Vocabulary

reign   **translate**

Have students fill in each blank with the
correct vocabulary word. Then, have
students write a new sentence using each
vocabulary word.

1. The _____ of Sargon lasted about
35 years. (reign)

2. Who can _____ this book from
English to Spanish? (translate)

1 Warm-Up Activity

Have students work in pairs to create a
word-find puzzle using the five words
in the pronunciation guide on page 32:
*Akkad, Akkadians, Sargon, Babylon,
Hammurabi.*

Encourage students to arrange their
puzzle with letters in 10 columns and
10 rows. The five words can be placed
in the puzzle horizontally, vertically, or
diagonally. For a challenge, have students
give a definition for each word instead of
listing the words to find. Students should
exchange their completed puzzles with a
classmate and solve each other's puzzle
by finding and circling the five words.

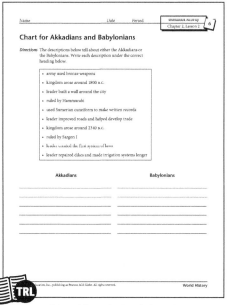

Workbook Activity 6   **Activity 6, pages 1–2**   *The Ancient Middle East   Chapter 2*   **31**

PRONUNCIATION GUIDE

Use this list to help students pronounce difficult words in this lesson.

Akkad	(äk´ äd)
Akkadians	(ə kā´ dē ənz)
Sargon	(sär´ gän)
Babylon	(bab´ ə lən)
Hammurabi	(häm´ u rä´ bē)

2 Teaching the Lesson

Have students offer their opinions about what characteristics a powerful leader should have. Then have students read pages 31–33 to learn what Sargon and Hammurabi did to become such powerful leaders.

Ask:

- Why was Sargon's army stronger than other armies? (It used bronze weapons.)

- What were two of Sargon's major accomplishments? (He repaired dikes, made irrigation systems longer, and had important trade routes protected.)

- Who was Hammurabi, and when did his reign begin? (Hammurabi was the king of Babylon, who ruled from about 1800 B.C.)

Reading Strategy: Questioning

Students should recognize that the purpose of this text is to give them information about world history. Form students into groups. Have each group suggest one relevant question for each subtitled section. Write the questions on the board. Have each group write the answers to all the questions as a way of checking whether they have found out the correct information from the lesson.

Think about the purpose of this text. Ask yourself: "Am I finding out the information I expected to when I began reading?"

Who Were the Babylonians?

Around 1800 B.C., a new city-state called Babylon arose. People feared its powerful army. Hammurabi, the king of Babylon, fought both the Akkadians and the Sumerians and won. His kingdom stretched from the Persian Gulf northward through Mesopotamia.

This memorial made of marble shows the Babylonian king (left) and the Lord Mayor of Babylon (right). Above them are cuneiform symbols of different gods.

Hammurabi built a giant ziggurat to honor the god Marduk. He also built a wall around Babylon to protect it. The wall was 11 miles long and nearly 80 feet wide. He improved roads and helped develop trade. Merchants, or traders, from as far away as India and China came to Babylon to do business.

---

32 *Unit 1 Early Civilizations*

ELL/ESL STRATEGY

Language Objective:
To use a graphic organizer to compare the kings Sargon I and Hammurabi

Ask ELL students to review pages 31–33 and make a two-column chart that compares the reigns of Sargon I and Hammurabi. Charts should include the following information.

- the length of each king's rule

- the size of their kingdoms
- each king's construction projects
- each king's contributions to civilization

Charts should be organized with one column for each king. Comparative information, such as length of rule, should be lined up in rows across the chart. Encourage students to use their completed charts as a study tool for this lesson.

"An Eye for an Eye"

Hammurabi's Code shows what life in Babylonia was like.
Property was important. Ordinary people were valued less
than nobles. Harming a common person brought a small fine.
Harming a noble meant harsh punishment. This code was
important because the laws were written out. Written laws were
fairer because people knew what the law was. A ruler could not
change laws without telling people. Laws were the same from
case to case. People could defend themselves.

Today nearly every modern country has a written code of laws.
Ideas about the laws have changed over time, though. In
general, penalties for small crimes are not harsh like those in
Hammurabi's Code.

Why Do We Remember Hammurabi?

People today remember Hammurabi because he created the
first system of laws. We call these laws "Hammurabi's Code."
He looked at the laws of all the lands he ruled. Then he
collected what he thought were the best ones. Hammurabi put
these into a code, or group of laws. He expected everyone in
his kingdom to obey them. He also expected his government
to carry out these laws.

Hammurabi ruled, or **reigned,** for almost 40 years. He was
proud of all he had done during that time. Near the end of his
reign, he ordered a scribe to carve his record on a large block
of stone. In this way everyone knew his laws. The scribe carved
nearly 300 laws on the stone. Archaeologists found it buried in
the sands of Iran in 1902.

We call Hammurabi's reign the Golden Age of Babylon. After
his death in 1750 B.C., the Babylonians lost their power. Then
Mesopotamia was again divided into small city-states.

CAREER CONNECTION

 Akkadian scribes had to be fluent in two languages— Sumerian and Akkadian—if they were to translate Sumerian writings into Akkadian. Today, people who are fluent in two or more languages can work as translators. In this age of increasing globalization, the demand for translators is high. Nowhere is that more apparent than on the Internet. Companies that want to sell products on the Internet must hire translators to translate their Web sites into other languages. This allows people around the world to view the site in their own language so they can purchase the products. Use this opportunity to stress the usefulness of learning other languages. Encourage interested students to research the career opportunities available for translators.

Review with students how to use scales on maps. Have them measure the distances, in miles and kilometers, between different geographical features. Then have students answer the questions in the caption. (The three kingdoms shown are Sumer, Akkad, and Babylonia. The oldest is Sumer. The largest is Akkad.)

Lesson 2 Review Answers

1. Sargon I **2.** Akkadians
3. Babylon **4.** Hammurabi **5.** code

Answers will vary. Sargon had the skills to unite people and to recognize their gifts and use them. Hammurabi had the skill to appreciate good laws and to declare them.

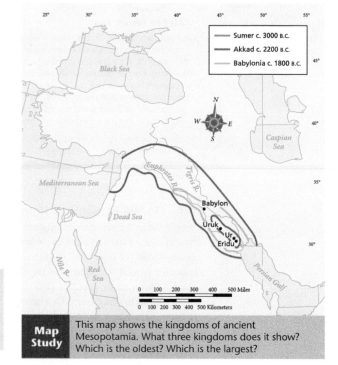

Sumer c. 3000 B.C.
Akkad c. 2200 B.C.
Babylonia c. 1800 B.C.

Map Study This map shows the kingdoms of ancient Mesopotamia. What three kingdoms does it show? Which is the oldest? Which is the largest?

What do you think

What made Sargon I and Hammurabi great leaders?

Word Bank

Akkadians
Babylon
code
Hammurabi
Sargon I

Lesson 2 Review On a sheet of paper, use the words from the Word Bank to complete each sentence correctly.

1. The first ruler to unite the city-states of Mesopotamia was _____.

2. He was the leader of the _____.

3. Around 1800 B.C. a new city-state called _____ came to power.

4. One of its great leaders was _____.

5. He collected laws from many groups of people and put them into a _____.

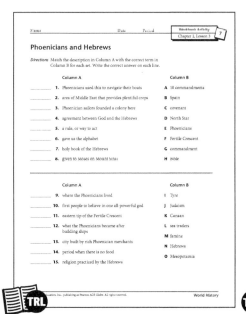

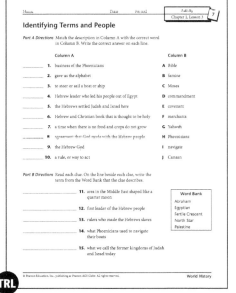

Objectives

♦ To identify some advancements made by the Phoenicians

♦ To understand what led to the birth of the Jewish religion

Fertile Crescent

The area in the Middle East shaped like a quarter moon (crescent) where one of the earliest civilizations developed

Geography Note

The rich soil in the Fertile Crescent provided those who lived there with foods such as wild wheat, barley, and nuts. Gazelle were among the wild animals available for food.

The **Fertile Crescent** is a part of the Middle East where one of the earliest civilizations developed. It is shaped like a quarter moon, or crescent, and it provides plentiful crops. Historians call its western tip Canaan and its eastern end Mesopotamia.

Why Did the Phoenicians Become Sailors?

Around 1100 B.C., a people we call the Phoenicians built a number of city-states in Canaan. Phoenicia was a narrow civilization squeezed between the mountains and the Mediterranean Sea. It had little land for farming.

The Phoenicians did, however, live in an area with many tall cedar trees. The Phoenicians used these to build ships. Soon they became sea traders. The merchants and traders became rich and built the great cities of Tyre and Sidon.

These traders sold cloth, glass, wood, and beautiful metal objects to people in other lands. Phoenician sailors carried this cargo in their ships. Then they sailed back home with ivory, metals, weapons, slaves, and wine.

Where Did the Phoenician Sailors Travel?

Phoenician sailors traveled to places no one else had been. They sailed to England in search of tin and copper. They traveled to Africa to trade for ivory. During their travels, they founded colonies in places such as France and Spain.

About 814 B.C., some Phoenicians settled in Carthage in northern Africa. Around 600 B.C., Phoenician sailors may have sailed around the tip of Africa. Some historians believe they even sailed across the ocean to America!

Phoenicians sailed in ships with a single sail. Many sailors pushed and pulled the oars that moved the ship forward. Phoenician sailors could sail far and wide because they mapped sea routes. They also used the North Star to navigate, or steer, their boats. They were the first sailors to do this.

5000 B.C. – 600 B.C.

Chapter 2: Lesson 3

Overview This lesson describes the development of two groups in the western tip of the Fertile Crescent—the Phoenicians and the Hebrews—and the contributions they made to civilization.

Objectives

■ To identify some advancements made by the Phoenicians

■ To understand what led to the birth of the Jewish religion

Student Pages pages 35–38

Teacher's Resource Library TRL

Workbook Activity 7

Activity 7

Modified Activity 7

Vocabulary

Bible	famine
commandment	Fertile Crescent
covenant	Judaism

Read each vocabulary word aloud. After you read each word, have students look up its definition in the Glossary and have a volunteer read the definition aloud. After all words are read, ask students to close their books. Repeat the vocabulary words aloud, encouraging students to recall the definitions from memory.

1   Warm-Up Activity

Guide a discussion about whether students would prefer to live in a small, independent city-state or in a large kingdom ruled by a king. Have them justify their opinions. Ask if there is anything in the United States today that might be similar to a city-state. (No; federal and state laws govern everyone.)

PRONUNCIATION GUIDE

Use this list to help students pronounce difficult words in this lesson.

Canaan	(kā´ nən)
Phoenicians	(fə nish´ ənz)
Yahweh	(yä´ wā)

Workbook Activity 7

Activity 7

2 Teaching the Lesson

The Phoenicians and the Hebrews both moved from place to place. As students read the lesson, ask them to list the different places these groups moved to and the reasons for their movements. Use a modern map of the Middle East to help students.

Ask:

- What five things did the Phoenicians bring back from other lands? (ivory, metals, weapons, slaves, and wine)
- What did the Phoenicians use to build their boats? (tall cedar trees)
- Where did the Phoenician sailors travel? (England, Africa, France, Spain, and possibly America)

Geography Note

Although agriculture is believed to have originated in the rich soils of the Fertile Crescent, the Phoenicians lived farther to the west. In Canaan, the area in which they lived, the soil was poor and few food crops could be grown. The Phoenicians turned to shipbuilding and trade as a way of life.

After students study the map on page 36, have them answer the questions in the caption. (Judah is the farthest south. The Jordan River is important to these kingdoms. Israel is north and northeast from Judah.) Have students use a world map to place the Middle East in perspective. They should notice how small the area discussed in this chapter is compared with the rest of the world. Have them use the map to answer the following questions.

Ask:

- What four countries are now located on the sites of Phoenicia, Philistia, and the Hebrew kingdoms? (Syria, Lebanon, Israel, and Jordan)
- What does the English language owe to the Phoenicians? (its alphabet)

Bible
The Hebrew and Christian book that is thought to be holy

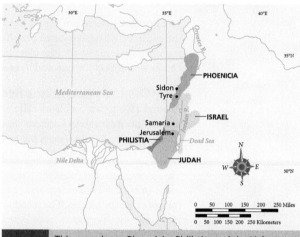

Map Study This map shows Phoenicia, Philistia, and the Hebrew kingdoms. Which kingdom is farthest south? What river is important to these kingdoms? In what direction is Israel from Judah?

Reading Strategy: Questioning

Think beyond the text. Consider your own thoughts and experiences as you read about the Phoenicians.

What Gifts Did the Phoenicians Give Us?

We remember the Phoenicians for two important reasons: First, they developed a simple alphabet of 22 letters. These few letters took the place of the nearly 600 letters of the cuneiform alphabet. The Greeks and Romans used this alphabet to build their own. The English and Spanish languages also use it. Second, the Phoenicians spread the culture and the products of the Middle East to many places. They did this through their trade and their colonies. Because of this, important ideas spread around the world.

What Is the Holy Book of the Hebrews?

The Hebrews are another Middle Eastern people. For many centuries, Hebrew scribes wrote books to tell their story. These books have been collected into one large book that we call the **Bible.** Jews and Christians believe the Bible is holy. We find the story of the Hebrew people in the first part of Christian Bibles.

- How was the Phoenician alphabet different from cuneiform? (The Phoenician alphabet had only 22 letters; cuneiform had about 600 symbols.)

Reading Strategy: Questioning

Students may have experienced a situation where they had to make use of the materials at hand. For example, they may have had to substitute an ingredient in a recipe and discovered how good the modified recipe was.

LEARNING STYLES

Auditory/Verbal
Ask students to listen for specific information about the contributions of the Phoenicians. Then ask a volunteer to read aloud the paragraph titled "What Gifts Did the Phoenicians Give Us?" Then ask volunteers to describe the Phoenician's gifts. (a simple alphabet; the spread of ideas, culture, and products of the Middle East)

Where Did the Hebrews Come From?

Abraham was the first leader of the Hebrew people. The Hebrew part of the Bible says that God called Abraham's family out of Mesopotamia. With his family and relatives, he was to go to a new country. Historians think that this happened sometime between 2000 and 1500 B.C.

For many years, they wandered the deserts as nomads. During a **famine**—a time when crops do not grow and there is no food—they traveled to Egypt. Years passed, and the Hebrews grew large in number. The Egyptian rulers made them slaves.

Who Led the Hebrew People Out of Slavery?

A Hebrew leader named Moses led his people out of Egypt sometime between 1300 and 1200 B.C. According to the Bible, the people wandered in the desert to the east of Egypt. There Moses climbed Mount Sinai to pray.

There, the Hebrew god—Yahweh—gave Moses the Ten Commandments. These rules told the Hebrews what to do to live peacefully with God, themselves, and other people. The **commandments** became the roots of the religion of the Hebrews. Today, we call this religion **Judaism.** We now call the Hebrew people Jews.

Biography

Solomon: Ruled c. Mid–900s B.C.

Solomon was the son of King David and the greatest king of ancient Israel. According to the Bible, he ruled for 40 years. Solomon became a famous ruler.

To keep the throne, Solomon had his enemies killed. Then he made Israel a rich empire. His ships traded with other countries for gold and silver. The king had new cities built in the lands he ruled. His most famous building was the magnificent temple in Jerusalem. Thousands of workers cut cedar wood for it. They brought huge blocks of stones. The temple was richly carved and covered with gold.

5000 B.C. – 600 B.C.

The Ancient Middle East   Chapter 2   **37**

Famine

A time when crops do not grow and there is no food

Commandment

A rule, or a way to act

Judaism

The religion of the Hebrews that Jews practice today

Reading Strategy:
Questioning

What details are important to understanding what this lesson is about?

Ask:

- Who was the first leader of the Hebrew people? (Abraham)
- During what period of time did Moses lead his people out of Egypt? (1300–1200 B.C.)

Biography

According to biblical accounts, King Solomon had 700 wives and 300 mistresses. Point this out, and tell students that in some cultures today, it is acceptable to have more than one spouse. This practice is called polygamy. Ask students whether they think polygamy should be allowed today and who they think should make that decision.

Reading Strategy:
Questioning

(Students may suggest that the details about where the Phoenicians lived are important to understanding why they became sailors. Learning details about the early history of the Hebrews and why they moved from place to place is important to understanding the Jewish religion and the Bible.)

LEARNING STYLES

Logical/Mathematical
Some students may have difficulty understanding chronology in the B.C. era. To check their understanding, ask which year was earlier: 814 B.C. or 600 B.C.; 1200 B.C. or 2000 B.C. (814 B.C.; 2000 B.C.) To help students visualize this concept, refer them to the timeline on page 24.

 Writing About History

Have students survey other students, teachers, and administrators to ask what they feel are the biggest problems in the school. Then, have students make a list of the 10 biggest problems. Have them brainstorm laws that would help solve each problem.

- What two kingdoms did the Hebrews settle and what is this land called today? (Judah and Israel; today it is called Palestine)

3 Reinforce and Extend

Covenant
An agreement

Writing About History

Think about ancient laws, such as Hammurabi's Code and the Ten Commandments. Then write a code of laws for your school. In your notebook, list ten laws to govern people's behavior.

What do you think?

Why did the Phoenicians turn to the sea to make a living?

What Covenant Did the Hebrews Make?

The Hebrew people believed that their god had made a **covenant,** or agreement, with them. They promised to honor Yahweh's commandments and worship him alone. In return, God promised to protect the Jews. The land of Canaan would belong to them forever.

After many years of wandering, the Hebrews came to Canaan. There they fought the people who lived in Philistia, along the coast of the Mediterranean Sea. In time, the Hebrews settled two kingdoms in Canaan—Judah and Israel. Later, invading armies destroyed both kingdoms. Today, we call this land Palestine. A large part of Palestine is the Jewish state of Israel.

What Gifts Did the Hebrews Give Us?

The Hebrews were the first people to believe in one all-powerful god. They set a high standard of behavior toward others. The Ten Commandments still influence many people.

Lesson 3 Review On a sheet of paper, write the letter of the answer that correctly completes each sentence.

1. The Phoenicians lived in _____.

   A Egypt   **B** Sumer   **C** Babylon   **D** Canaan

2. The Phoenicians became famous as _____.

   A sailors   **B** soldiers   **C** painters   **D** lawyers

3. The Phoenicians were the first people to use the _____ to help them navigate.

   A North Star   **B** compass   **C** astrolabe   **D** Orion

4. The holy book of the Hebrew people is called the _____.

   A Vegas   **B** Bible   **C** Ziggurat   **D** Cedar

5. The Hebrews differed from other ancient people because they believed in one _____.

   A commandment   **C** god
   B Marduk   **D** Sanskrit

Lesson 3 Review Answers

1. D **2.** A **3.** A **4.** B **5.** C

Answers will vary. Students may suggest that the Phoenicians had trees for building ships or that there was little land for farming. Students may also suggest that the Mediterranean Sea to their west must have beckoned them to sail for adventure and profit.

Chapter Project Follow-up

Student reports about Hammurabi's Code should describe the type of laws in general, then describe one or two laws in greater detail and in the student's own words. Punishment for breaking these laws should be cited. If you prefer not to have students choose which laws to describe, you can assign specific laws so that students as a class cover a wider range of laws. Student reports can be displayed in the classroom.

Hammurabi's Code

Hammurabi was very concerned about justice. Having a written code of laws was fairer to his people. The laws applied to everyone. They dealt with all parts of daily life. Some laws set rules for business and trade. Others listed punishments for crimes. Still others protected women's rights. Hammurabi's Code was an important step forward in government. Many systems of laws that came later were based on Hammurabi's Code.

1. If a man destroys the eye of another man, they shall destroy his eye.

2. If he breaks a man's bone, they shall break his bone.

3. If he destroys the eye of a common man or breaks a bone of a common man, he shall pay one mina of silver.

4. If a man knocks out a tooth of a man of his own rank, they shall knock out his tooth.

5. If he knocks out a tooth of a common man, he shall pay one-third mina of silver.

6. If a house falls in and kills the owner's son, the son of the builder shall be put to death.

7. If a man strikes his father, they shall cut off his hand.

8. If a man is robbed and the robber is not caught, the governor of the city shall give the victim the value of the stolen goods.

9. If a man has stolen goods from a temple or house, he shall be put to death.

10. If a man has broken into a house, he shall be killed in front of the place where he broke through and buried there.

11. If a man wishes to divorce his wife who did not bear him children, he shall return to her the dowry [the property a woman brings to the husband at marriage] that she brought from her father's house and then he may divorce her.

Document-Based Questions

1. Compare the third law with the first and second. How were laws different for ordinary people and people of high rank?

2. Think about the saying "an eye for an eye, a tooth for a tooth." How do these laws fit with Hammurabi's Code?

3. What did Babylonians seem to value more—human life or property? Explain.

4. How was a careless builder punished? Do you think this punishment fits the crime?

5. How was a childless woman protected in a divorce?

Explain to students that Babylonian society was divided into three classes. The upper class was made up of political and religious leaders. Next were the shopkeepers, merchants, and artisans, who were considered commoners. The lowest class consisted of slaves. According to Hammurabi's Code, the punishment a person received depended on the victim's social class.

Select a student to read aloud the introductory paragraph. Then ask for volunteers to read aloud the 11 laws of Hammurabi's Code.

Finally, have students answer the questions. After considering question 1, ask students whether they think that different laws should apply to people of different classes or that the same laws should apply to everyone regardless of class. Conclude with a discussion of the remaining questions.

Answers to Document-Based Questions:

1. Someone who harmed a high-ranking person was punished more severely than if he or she hurt an ordinary person.

2. The expression fits Hammurabi's Code because some of the laws punish a criminal by doing the same action to him or her, such as knocking out a tooth or breaking a bone.

3. They thought property was more important, because laws put people to death for stealing from a temple or house.

4. If a defective house killed the owner's son, the builder's son would be put to death. Answers will vary about whether this punishment fits the crime, but some students may respond that it is not a fair law because the builder did not plan to kill the owner's son.

5. Her husband had to return her dowry.

ELL/ESL STRATEGY

Language Objective: *To learn the definitions of unfamiliar words in the Document-Based Reading*

Students may encounter several unfamiliar words in the Document-Based Reading on page 39. Have small groups of 3 to 4 students work together to compile a list of unfamiliar words. Then using a dictionary, students should write a definition for each word. Have group members take turns quizzing each other by having one student read a word from the list, a second student say the definition, and a third student find the word and read the sentence in which it appears in the document on page 39.

Encourage students to reread the Document-Based Reading when their lists are complete, using the lists as a comprehension guide.

Have students read "Technology Moves Ahead." Ask them to imagine that they are historians 2,000 years into the future, looking back on human civilization in the 20th and 21st centuries. Ask students what discoveries and inventions historians in the future will consider important. (Answers may include automobiles, airplanes, computers, or the Internet.) Then ask if these inventions and discoveries are more or less important than the use of iron by the Hittites and the development of sailing by the Phoenicians. Be sure students explain and defend their opinions. Finally, have students answer the Wrap-Up questions.

If students encounter any unfamiliar words in the Spotlight Story, have them make lists of the words. Using a dictionary, students should write a definition for each unfamiliar word.

Answers to Spotlight Story Wrap-Up:

1. Iron was stronger than bronze and could be hammered to have a sharper edge.

2. Iron was melted (or smelted) out of rock, heated to high temperatures, and then hammered into shape.

3. The Hittites were the first people in the Middle East to work with iron.

4. The Phoenicians made wooden ships that depended on a single sail and human rowers. This enabled them to sail greater distances.

5. Answers will vary. Students may say that trade encouraged inventions. It brought people with new ideas and new materials together. It also spread new technology.

Technology Moves Ahead

Technology is the use of knowledge to solve practical problems. Before 1500 B.C., technology was moving ahead in the ancient Middle East. People learned to control floods. They built impressive buildings. Clever, curious people have always made inventions and discoveries.

One giant step was learning to work with iron. Much earlier, people had mixed copper and tin to make bronze. Iron, however, was stronger than bronze. It made better knives and tools. Iron swords had a sharper edge. But it was harder to work with, too. It took a very hot fire to melt, or smelt, iron out of the rock. Then a worker called a smith hammered it into shape while it was red-hot.

We know little about the Hittites. Their craftsmen, however, were the first in the Middle East to work with iron. Hittites probably came from central Europe to what is now Turkey. Iron swords and horse-drawn war chariots helped them conquer their neighbors. The Hittite empire fell about 1200 B.C. After that, the secret of iron spread to others. Iron could then be used for new purposes. In Israel, farmers had iron-tipped plows. They used iron sickles to harvest grain. Carpenters had sharper iron tools.

Trade also encouraged the development of new technology for better transportation. For example, tin was scarce. People had to travel long distances to find it. Trading ships of the time had both a sail and oars. Most of the time, human crews rowed the ship. Large crews, however, were not practical for long trips. Then the Phoenicians turned a problem into an advantage.

They did not have much good farmland, but they did have tall cedar trees. Phoenicians used them to make sturdy wooden ships. Instead of rowers, their ships had one large, square sail. The Phoenicians had developed the technology to sail long distances.

In the 1300s B.C., traders sailed all over the eastern Mediterranean Sea. Usually they stayed within sight of land, the stars their only navigation tools. Traders from different cultures exchanged goods. Caravans brought goods to the coast from far inland. Hardwoods and gold came from Africa. Amber came from the Baltic Sea. Traders might bring a new ship into a region. Then others would copy it, further spreading the technology.

Wrap-Up

1. Why was iron more useful than bronze?

2. Describe how iron tools were made.

3. What people in the Middle East were the first to work with iron?

4. How did Phoenicians change the way ships were made? Why?

5. Describe how trade and technology worked together.

Chapter 2 SUMMARY

- Civilization developed in Mesopotamia about 7,000 years ago. People settled the land between two rivers—the Tigris and the Euphrates. Floods made the land good for farming. People built canals and dikes to control the water.

- The Sumerians were a tribe in Mesopotamia. They built walled city-states. Most people in Sumer could own property. Women and slaves had legal rights. Sumerians built houses out of baked clay bricks.

- Sumerians feared their gods. A ziggurat, or temple, was the most important building in a city. Their buildings had ramps and arches.

- Sumerian inventions included a writing system called cuneiform. They used a stylus to make symbols on clay tablets. They were the first to use the wheel on carts. Their counting system was based on the number 60.

- Sargon I was the ruler of Akkad in about 2340 B.C. He made the Sumerian city-states part of his lands. The Akkadians learned cuneiform.

- Hammurabi ruled the city-state of Babylon from about 1800 B.C. to his death in 1750 B.C. He organized his laws into a system, or code. They applied everywhere in the kingdom. This time is called the Golden Age of Babylon.

- The term "Fertile Crescent" refers to an area in the Middle East. It is a crescent-shaped area of land from Mesopotamia to the Mediterranean Sea.

- The Phoenicians built city-states in Canaan. They became shipbuilders and sea traders. Their main cities were Sidon and Tyre. Phoenicians also built the city of Carthage in North Africa. They made maps of the seas. They used the North Star for navigation.

- The Phoenicians developed a 22-letter alphabet. It is the ancestor of the alphabet we use today. They took ideas from the Middle East to many places.

- The first books of the Bible tell the history of the Hebrews. Their first great leader was Abraham. He led them out of Mesopotamia, probably between 2000 and 1500 B.C.

- The Hebrews were desert nomads for many years. Then they became slaves in Egypt. A leader named Moses led them out of Egypt.

- The Hebrews settled in Canaan. They believed God had promised them this land. They divided it into the kingdoms of Judah and Israel.

5000 B.C. – 600 B.C.

TEACHER'S RESOURCE

The AGS Globe Teaching Strategies in Social Studies Transparencies may be used with this chapter. The transparencies add an interactive dimension to expand and enhance the *World History* program content.

- What happened to the Hebrews when they were in Egypt? (They became slaves.)

- Why did the Hebrews settle in Canaan? (They believed God had promised them this land.)

Using the Chapter Summary

Have students read the Chapter Summary on page 41 to review the main ideas presented in Chapter 2.

Ask:

- Why did people settle the lands between the Tigris and Euphrates rivers? (Floods made the land good for farming.)

- How was life in Sumer an improvement over life in earlier civilizations? (People could own property, women and slaves had legal rights, and walled cities offered protection.)

- What was the most important building in a Sumerian city? What was it used for? (The ziggurat or temple was used for worshipping gods.)

- What were some of the Sumerians' inventions? (the cuneiform writing system, wheeled carts, a counting system)

- Who ruled Akkad? How did he form his kingdom? (Sargon I took over the Sumerian city-states and made them into his kingdom.)

- What is Hammurabi most famous for? (his system of laws, called Hammurabi's Code)

- What is the name given to the curved area of land from Mesopotamia to the Mediterranean Sea? Why was it given this name? (The Fertile Crescent was named for its crescent shape and its rich soil.)

- What were some of the contributions of the Phoenicians? (They built cities and new kinds of ships, made maps of the seas, and developed a system of navigation using the North Star.)

- What is important about the Phoenician's alphabet? (It had only 22 letters and is the ancestor of our modern alphabet.)

- Who was Abraham? What is he known for? (Abraham was the first great leader of the Hebrews. He led the Hebrews out of Mesopotamia.)

Chapter 2 Review

Use the Chapter Review to prepare students for tests and to reteach content from the chapter.

Chapter 2 Mastery Test

The Teacher's Resource Library includes two forms of the Chapter 2 Mastery Test. Each test addresses the chapter Goals for Learning. An optional third page of additional critical-thinking items is included for each test. The difficulty level of the two forms is equivalent.

Chapter 2 Review Answers

1. ziggurats
2. Mesopotamia
3. Sargon I
4. Hammurabi
5. Phoenicians
6. Hebrews
7. Sumerians
8. Marduk
9. Yahweh
10. wheels
11. A
12. A
13. D

Chapter 2 R E V I E W

Word Bank

Hammurabi
Hebrews
Marduk
Mesopotamia
Phoenicians
Sargon I
Sumerians
wheels
Yahweh
ziggurats

On a sheet of paper, use the words from the Word Bank to complete each sentence correctly.

1. The Sumerians built _____, which were pyramid-shaped buildings.
2. We call the region between the Tigris and the Euphrates rivers _____.
3. _____, the king of Akkad, united the city-states of the Middle East.
4. _____ developed the first code of law.
5. The _____ were the first great sailors and traders.
6. The _____ were the first people to believe in one all-powerful god.
7. The _____ invented writing.
8. The name of the chief Babylonian god was _____.
9. The name of the Hebrew god was _____.
10. The Sumerians were the first people to put _____ on carts.

On a sheet of paper, write the letter of the answer that correctly completes each sentence.

11. The Sumerians built _____.

   A city-states   **C** the Bible
   B boats   **D** a code

12. The Akkadians _____ Sumerian writings into their own language.

   A translated   **C** stylus
   B cuneiform   **D** painted

13. The Babylonian king Hammurabi collected laws into a _____.

   A Bible   **C** ziggurat
   B Vedas   **D** code

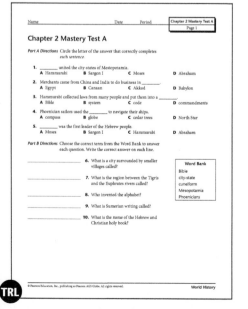

Chapter 2 Mastery Test A, pages 1–3

14. The Phoenicians built boats of _____.

    A jade   **C** clay
    B marble   **D** cedar

15. The Hebrews became slaves in _____.

    A Egypt   **C** Phoenicia
    B Canaan   **D** Palestine

On a sheet of paper, write the answer to each question. Use complete sentences.

16. What gifts did the Sumerians give us?

17. Why do we remember Hammurabi?

18. In what way did the Hebrew people differ from other ancient people?

Critical Thinking On a sheet of paper, write your response to each question. Use complete sentences.

19. Which country or group of people in the ancient Middle East gave us the greatest gifts? Explain your answer.

20. Why is the invention of writing an important step in world civilization?

14. D

15. A

16. They gave us the gift of writing, the pottery wheel, wheels on carts, arches, ramps, arithmetic based on the number 60, and possibly the plow and the sailboat.

17. Hammurabi collected the laws of all the people he ruled and made a code of all the best laws. He applied these laws to both the people and his government.

18. Unlike the other people of their time, the Hebrews believed in only one god.

Critical Thinking

19. Answers will vary. Students may say that the Sumerians gave us writing, a great contribution. The Hebrews started the belief in one god, which has influenced much of Western civilization. The Phoenicians spread culture and learning around the known world.

20. Answers will vary. Students may say that writing enabled people to keep records and write stories, poems, histories, geographies, myths, and all the literature that tells us about a people.

When a teacher announces a test, listen carefully. Write down the lessons that will be included. Write down any specific topics the teacher says to review.

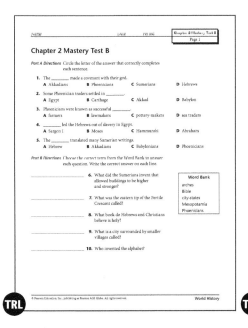

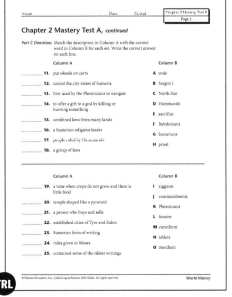

Chapter 2 Mastery Test B, pages 1–3   *The Ancient Middle East*   *Chapter 2*   **43**

Chapter 3: Middle Eastern Empires, 800 B.C.–330 B.C.

Introducing the Chapter

Three major empires fought and conquered each other in the Middle East. They brought devastation to the land, its inhabitants, and their cities. However, each empire made valuable contributions: ideas, architecture, and technology. Many of these contributions are still with us today. Have students study the timeline, which shows the reigns of the three major empires.

Middle Eastern Empires

The Middle East was home to many city-states and kingdoms. For hundreds of years, they made war against each other. Finally, one group—the Assyrians—controlled most of the area. In fact, they controlled so much land that they became an empire. This chapter introduces you to the Assyrian Empire and to the Chaldean and Persian Empires that followed it. One by one, these empires controlled much of the Middle East.

Goals for Learning

◆ To describe the life, army, and government of the Assyrians

◆ To describe the life, army, and government of the Chaldeans

◆ To explain the ways the Persians unified their great empire and describe Zoroastrianism

586 B.C. Nebuchadnezzar, king of the Chaldeans, captures Jerusalem

800 B.C. Assyrian Empire expands in Mesopotamia

612 B.C. Nineveh, the capital of Assyria, is destroyed

570 B.C. Zoroaster preaches a new religion in Persia

530–330 B.C. Persian Empire dominates Middle East

650 B.C. King Assurbanipal builds Nineveh

562 B.C. Nebuchadnezzar dies

800 B.C.   600 B.C.   400 B.C.

Ask:
- What three empires are identified on the timeline? (Assyrian, Chaldean, Persian)
- In what year did Nebuchadnezzar capture Jerusalem? (586 B.C.)
- How long after he captured Jerusalem did Nebuchadnezzar die? (24 years)

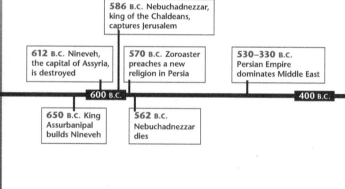

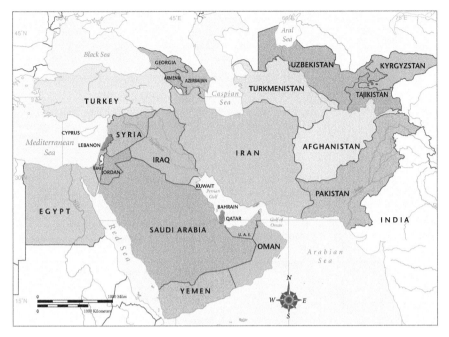

Many seas touch the shores of the Middle East. Many rivers flow through it. Deserts stretch for miles, and mountains stand tall. This geography has helped to shape the cultural and political history of the region.

Study the map, then answer the following questions:

1. What Egyptian river empties into the Mediterranean Sea?

2. What are the names of three countries that border the Mediterranean Sea?

3. What body of water separates Iran from Saudi Arabia?

4. Which country is farther south—Yemen or Egypt?

5. Which country is farther east—Iraq or Iran?

800 B.C. – 330 B.C.

Middle Eastern Empires   Chapter 3   45

Refer students to the map on page 45.

Ask:

- What large bodies of water are shown on the map? (Black Sea, Caspian Sea, Mediterranean Sea, Red Sea, Persian Gulf, Gulf of Oman, Arabian Sea)

- Which rivers are shown on the map? (Nile, Tigris, Euphrates)

Have students read and write answers to the Map Skills questions.

Map Skills Answers

1. Nile River
2. Turkey, Syria, Lebanon, Israel, and Egypt all border the Mediterranean Sea.
3. Persian Gulf
4. Yemen
5. Iran

Chapter Project

As students read Chapter 3, have them keep a diary describing one week in each of the lives of an Assyrian, a Chaldean, and a Persian. Diary entries should be dated and might include job descriptions, observations of daily life, thoughts on the government, or eyewitness accounts of historical events.

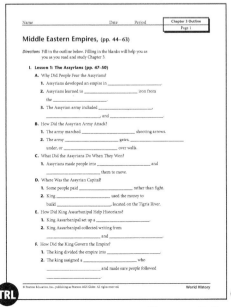

Chapter 3 Outline, pages 1–3

Predicting

Introduce the reading skill *predicting*. Explain that when you make a prediction, you add new details to what you already know about a subject. This process allows you to make an "educated guess" about what will happen next. Stopping to make predictions as you read will make you a more attentive reader and help you to better analyze what you are reading.

Ask:

- How can you predict whether you will have a quiz on this chapter on Friday? (Students may already know that they always have a quiz the day after they finish studying a chapter.)

Point out to students that when they predict they will have a quiz on this chapter on Friday, they are using prior knowledge because they know that they always have a quiz the day after finishing a chapter. Adding the new detail that they will finish a chapter on Thursday allows you to make an educated guess about a quiz. Stress to students that when they make a prediction, they make a logical assumption about what will happen in the future.

Key Vocabulary Words

Ask for volunteers to read each word and definition in the Key Vocabulary Words list. Then tell students to focus on the words from Lesson 1. Ask students to predict what the lesson will be about. (Students may say the lesson will be about one group ruling another.)

Reading Strategy:
Predicting

Previewing a text helps readers think about what they already know about a subject. It also prepares readers to look for new information—to predict what will come next. Keep this in mind as you make predictions:

- ◆ Make your best guess about what might happen next.
- ◆ Add details about what you think will happen.
- ◆ Check your predictions. You may have to change your predictions as you learn more information.

Key Vocabulary Words

Lesson 1 ——————————
Empire A large area of land ruled by one person

Dominate To control

Artisan A person who works with his or her hands to create something

Chariot A two-wheeled, horse-drawn carriage

Cavalry Soldiers on horseback

Archer A soldier who fights with a bow and arrows

Tribute A payment given by a weaker ruler or nation to a stronger ruler or nation

Capital The city from which a ruler, or emperor, rules

Govern To rule

Province An area, such as a state, that is part of a larger country

Rebel To disobey or fight against

Alliance An agreement to help one another

Lesson 2 ——————————
Terraced Going upward like steps

Astronomer A person who keeps track of the sun, the planets, and the stars

Lesson 3 ——————————
Inspector A person who looks at how things are being done

Unify To bring together as one

Objectives

♦ To identify why the Assyrian army was so feared

♦ To describe the way the Assyrians treated conquered peoples

Reading Strategy:
Predicting

Read the heading of the next section. What do you think you'll find out about the Assyrians?

Empire
A large area of land ruled by one person

Dominate
To control

Artisan
A person who works with his or her hands to create something

Chariot
A two-wheeled, horse-drawn carriage

Cavalry
Soldiers on horseback

Archer
A soldier who fights with a bow and arrows

Between 900 B.C. and 700 B.C., the Assyrian **Empire** began to develop in Mesopotamia. An empire is a large area of land ruled by one person. It developed on the eastern side of the Fertile Crescent in the Tigris River Valley. The Assyrians were a fierce tribe of warriors. Their enemies hated and feared them. For several hundred years, they **dominated,** or controlled, the cities and trading routes of Mesopotamia.

Why Did People Fear the Assyrians?

Assyrian soldiers had iron weapons. The Assyrians had learned to smelt iron from the people known as the Hittites. The smelting process required three steps. First, the **artisan,** or person who works with his or her hands, heated the iron until it was red hot. Second, the artisan hammered the iron to remove unwanted materials. Third, the artisan quickly cooled the iron. Then the iron was shaped into weapons. These were harder and stronger than the copper and bronze weapons other armies used.

The Assyrian army divided itself into groups. Some became charioteers who drove **chariots**—two-wheeled, horse-drawn carriages. The army also had a **cavalry.** These soldiers on horseback were the first of their kind. The most feared soldiers were the **archers,** who fought with bows and arrows.

How Did the Assyrian Army Attack?

With its iron weapons, the Assyrian army became a fighting machine. On the field of battle, the soldiers marched forward shoulder to shoulder. Then they let fly a shower of iron-tipped arrows. These killed and wounded the enemy.

Next, the cavalry and the charioteers attacked. They wore iron helmets and breast plates; they carried iron spears and swords. Their weapons and their skill forced the enemy to run back into the city and hide behind its walls.

Walls did not stop the Assyrians. They battered down the gates with a thick iron-tipped tree trunk! Sometimes they tunneled under the walls or climbed over them on ladders.

800 B.C. – 330 B.C.

Chapter 3: Lesson 1

Overview This lesson explains why the Assyrian army was so successful in battle. The lesson describes the cultural contributions of the Assyrians.

Objectives

■ To identify why the Assyrian army was so feared

■ To describe the way the Assyrians treated conquered peoples

Student Pages pages 47–50

Teacher's Resource Library TRL

Workbook Activity 8

Activity 8

Modified Activity 8

Vocabulary

alliance	cavalry	govern
archer	chariot	province
artisan	dominate	rebel
capital	empire	tribute

Remind students that the vocabulary terms are defined in the Glossary, which is organized alphabetically. Encourage students to become more familiar with lesson vocabulary by creating their own method of organizing the terms. For example, they can list terms by numbers of syllables or according to whether the terms are nouns, verbs, or adjectives. Have students write their newly-organized lists on a sheet of paper.

1 Warm-Up Activity

Ask students why they think the Assyrians needed to destroy their enemies and the cities where their enemies lived. (Students may suggest that the Assyrians feared their enemies would rebel if they were left alive.) Discuss ways that conquerors could and should treat conquered people. Ask students what conquerors could do to ensure that those they have conquered do not rebel. Ask students how they would want to be treated to ensure they did not rebel if they were a conquered people.

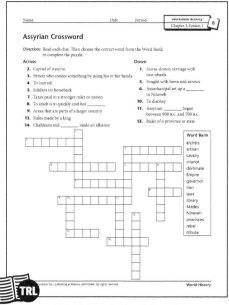

Workbook Activity 8

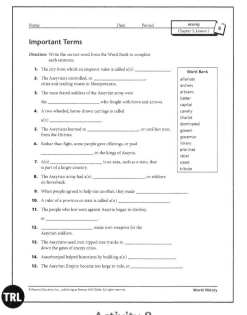

Activity 8

PRONUNCIATION GUIDE

Use this list to help students pronounce difficult words in this lesson.

Assyria	(ə sir´ ē ə)
Nineveh	(nin´ ə v ə)
Assurbanipal	(äsh´ ur bän´ ē päl)

2 **Teaching the Lesson**

As students read the section, have them think about why the Assyrians were so successful and what factors led to their downfall.

Ask:

• **What factors were responsible for the success of the Assyrian Empire?** (Students will probably mention that the powerful army was equipped with iron weapons, cavalry, and chariots. Division of the territory into provinces, the ability of governors to collect taxes and enforce laws, and a system of good roads were also factors.)

• **How did the Hittite people unknowingly help the Assyrian army conquer Mesopotamia?** (The Assyrians learned to smelt iron from the Hittites. The Assyrians used this process to make iron weapons that were superior to those of their enemies.)

• **Imagine that you had lived in an area near the Assyrian Empire and the Assyrian army threatened to invade the area. Would you have fought or paid tribute?** (Answers will vary; students may say they would have paid tribute because the Assyrians had better weapons and were cruel to the people they conquered.)

Reading Strategy:
Predicting

(Students have read that the Assyrian army became a fighting machine and used iron spears and swords. They may predict correctly that the Assyrians would not be kind to the people they conquered.)

Reading Strategy:
Predicting

Based on what you have read about the Assyrians, how do you predict they behaved after they won?

Tribute

A payment given to a stronger ruler or nation

Capital

The city from which a ruler, or emperor, rules

What Did the Assyrians Do When They Won?

After beating their enemies, the Assyrians burned some alive or cut their heads off. They made others into slaves. Then they forced them to move to lands far from home. Next, the Assyrians stole everything they wanted. Finally, they burned the captured city to the ground.

Where Was the Assyrian Capital?

Everyone in Mesopotamia feared the Assyrians. Who could win against them? Some paid **tribute** rather than fight. That is, they gave a payment to the kings of Assyria. This tribute, the loot won in war, and taxes made the Assyrian kings rich. One of these kings used this money to build a mighty **capital**. From this city, he ruled his empire.

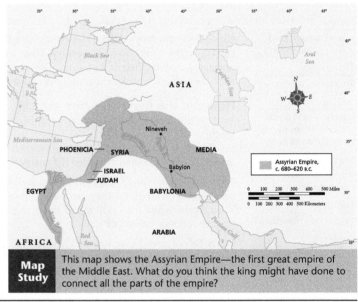

Map Study This map shows the Assyrian Empire—the first great empire of the Middle East. What do you think the king might have done to connect all the parts of the empire?

STUDY SKILLS

 Have students summarize how everyday life changed for the people in Mesopotamia after they were conquered by the Assyrians.

Have students compare the map on page 48 with the map on page 45. Ask them to name the modern countries that were once part of the Assyrian Empire. (Egypt, Israel, Lebanon, Syria, Jordan, Iraq, Turkey) Then, have students answer the question in the caption. (Answers will vary. Students may respond that the king might have divided up the empire or built transportation systems, such as roads, to connect the parts.)

Nineveh, on the Tigris River, was the largest city of its day. In 650 B.C., King Assurbanipal made it the showplace of the ancient world. Assurbanipal was one of the most powerful kings on earth. He boasted "I am Assurbanipal, the Great King, the Mighty King . . . King of Kings." He had a scribe carve these words on stone.

How Did King Assurbanipal Help Historians?

At his palace in Nineveh, Assurbanipal set up a library. There he collected and saved the ancient writings from the old Mesopotamian kingdoms of Sumer and Akkad. Hundreds of years later, in A.D. 1852, an archaeologist uncovered what was left of this library. He found 22,000 clay tablets!

These tablets contained dictionaries, which gave the same words in different languages. Some listed names of kings and important events in the ancient world. Still others contained songs and stories about the past. These tablets helped historians learn about life in the ancient Middle East.

Assurbanipal (shooting the bow) was the last great Assyrian king. Assyrians were mighty fighters and were the first to use cavalry.

Ask:

• What do you think was Assurbanipal's greatest accomplishment? (Answers will vary; students may mention his library, the building of Nineveh, or the road system he built.)

ELL/ESL STRATEGY

Language Objective: *To identify and build on prior knowledge of libraries*

Have ELL students make a list of some of the functions of a library and the activities that might take place there, such as casual reading, researching, or studying. Also, ask students to identify the people who work in a library. Encourage students to name library books they have read, and to tell about things they have done in their school or public library. If possible, visit the library and have ELL students find examples of nonfiction history books, fiction, audio materials, reference material including a dictionary, and magazines. Ask students if there was anything like these materials in King Assurbanipal's library. (Yes, his library contained dictionaries, history, songs, and stories.) Students might also draw a diagram of a library to show the location of these types of library materials.

LEARNING STYLES

Visual/Spatial
To help visually-oriented students understand the flow of events during the time of the Assyrian Empire, have them construct a timeline that shows the major events discussed in this lesson.

BACKGROUND INFORMATION

Assurbanipal's father, King Esarhaddon, appointed him crown prince of Assyria in 672 B.C. When Esarhaddon died in December, 669 B.C., Assurbanipal became king. He was an accomplished athlete and enjoyed hunting, archery, and riding horses. Assurbanipal had much more education than most of the previous kings. He studied history and literature and could read Sumerian and other languages. The library at Nineveh contained dictionaries of other languages as well as copies of religious and other texts.

LEARNING STYLES

Auditory/Verbal
Have a small group of students create a skit, with students playing an Assyrian provincial governor, a Mede, and a Babylonian at tax collection time. Other students might act as narrators by introducing the scenes, providing the time and place of the scenes, and explaining the characters. In the skit, have the Mede and the Babylonian discuss the tax collection and what they think they might do about it with the Assyrian governor.

Ask:

- What factors contributed to the downfall of the Assyrian Empire? *(The Empire got too big to be governed effectively. The Chaldeans from Babylon and the Medes from Persia made an alliance to fight the Assyrians together.)*

Reading Strategy:
Predicting

(Students may respond that they will learn what the Assyrian king did to help or hurt the empire.)

 3 Reinforce and Extend

CAREER CONNECTION

 The practice of making maps is called cartography. The oldest maps that have been found were drawn by the Babylonians on clay tablets in 2300 B.C. The ancient Greeks realized Earth was round long before Columbus arrived in the New World and are said to have made a globe in 150 B.C. Today, cartographers rely largely on aerial photography and satellite imagery. Have students research the skills needed to become a cartographer.

ONLINE CONNECTION

 The Web site www. agsglobewh.com/page50 contains an article from *Archaeology* magazine that describes an Assyrian king's palace in modern-day Iraq and efforts to preserve it. The palace, one of only two restored Assyrian palaces in the world, was destroyed in 612 B.C. when the Medes army captured the city of Nineveh. Many photographs are included in the article.

Govern
To rule

Province
An area, such as a state, that is part of a larger country

Rebel
To disobey or fight against

Alliance
An agreement to help one another

How Did the King Govern the Empire?

The Assyrian Empire included all of Mesopotamia, the Fertile Crescent, and Egypt. To help **govern**, or rule, all this land, the Assyrian king divided it into **provinces**. (Provinces are areas similar to states.) Then he chose a governor for each province. This governor collected taxes and made sure that everyone obeyed the king's laws.

The king needed to control his empire and keep it connected. The Assyrians built a road system. They made all the roads level so that chariots traveled easily on them. Because of these roads, merchants and soldiers moved quickly from Nineveh to the provinces.

Why Did the Assyrian Empire Fall?

The Assyrian Empire became too large to govern. The people who had lost wars against the Assyrians began to **rebel**, or disobey, them. Fighting began. Soon the Chaldeans from Babylon and the Medes from Persia made an **alliance**. They agreed to help one another fight the Assyrians.

In 612 B.C., the Babylonians, Medes, and other armies captured the city of Nineveh and destroyed it. People throughout the empire celebrated!

Lesson 1 Review On a sheet of paper, write the answer to each question. Use complete sentences.

1. How did the Assyrians make their weapons?
2. What was the cavalry?
3. Why was Nineveh important to the Assyrians?
4. How did the Assyrians connect their empire?
5. What happened that destroyed the Assyrian Empire?

 What do you think

Why is the library of Assurbanipal important to historians?

Lesson 1 Review Answers

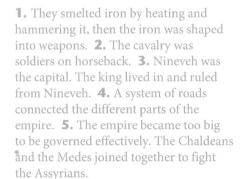 **1.** They smelted iron by heating and hammering it, then the iron was shaped into weapons. **2.** The cavalry was soldiers on horseback. **3.** Nineveh was the capital. The king lived in and ruled from Nineveh. **4.** A system of roads connected the different parts of the empire. **5.** The empire became too big to be governed effectively. The Chaldeans and the Medes joined together to fight the Assyrians.

Answers will vary. Students may say that the clay tablets in this library tell us about the ancient Assyrians and how they lived. The library also contains dictionaries that reveal the languages of ancient peoples. Because these contain the same words in different languages, we can now translate the writings of people who were not Assyrians.

◆ To describe the beauty of the city of Babylon

◆ To explain the fall of the Chaldean Empire

Like the Assyrians, the Chaldeans defeated many different peoples. After destroying Nineveh, they became the leading Middle Eastern empire. We often call their society Neo-Babylonia or the new Babylonia. Their ancestors were the people Hammurabi ruled hundreds of years before.

Who Did King Nebuchadnezzar Defeat?

One of the greatest Chaldean kings was Nebuchadnezzar. Under his rule, the Chaldean empire grew as far west as Syria and Canaan.

Nebuchadnezzar defeated the army of Egypt when it tried to take over Syria and Phoenicia. He ruled the Hebrew, or Jewish, people too. After years of warfare, his armies defeated the Jews in 586 B.C. The soldiers destroyed Jerusalem and its temple. They marched 15,000 Jews to Babylon as slaves.

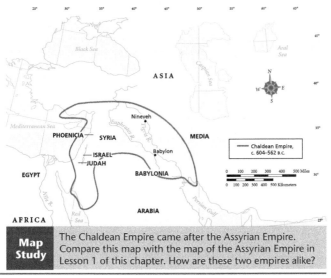

Map Study The Chaldean Empire came after the Assyrian Empire. Compare this map with the map of the Assyrian Empire in Lesson 1 of this chapter. How are these two empires alike?

800 B.C. – 330 B.C.

Middle Eastern Empires   Chapter 3   51

Chapter 3: Lesson 2

Overview The Chaldeans conquered the Assyrians and other peoples by force, but they were not quite as cruel as the Assyrians had been. The Chaldeans made important contributions to architecture, art, and science.

Objectives

■ To describe the beauty of the city of Babylon

■ To explain the fall of the Chaldean Empire

Student Pages pages 51–54

Teacher's Resource Library TRL

Workbook Activity 9

Activity 9

Modified Activity 9

Vocabulary

astronomer   **terraced**

Remind students that these vocabulary terms are as much a part of modern vocabulary as they are a way to describe events in ancient history. Have students brainstorm modern uses for each term. For example, "The rock garden in the backyard was terraced" and "Astronomers recently decided that Pluto is not a planet."

1 Warm-Up Activity

Have students examine some of the constellations shown on star charts or a celestial globe. They should note how early astronomers drew imaginary lines between stars to make constellations. Give each student a diagram showing a group of stars. Have students connect the stars to form a picture. Point out that student pictures will differ according to what each student imagines, just as the Chaldean astronomers once did.

Workbook Activity 9   **Activity 9**   *Middle Eastern Empires   Chapter 3*   **51**

Refer students to the map on page 51. Have them use the scale of kilometers to estimate the maximum distances of the Chaldean Empire from east to west and north to south. (east to west, 1,200 kilometers; north to south, 1,100 kilometers) Have students answer the question in the caption. (The maps show that the Chaldean and Assyrian empires were about the same size and shape, with some differences in territory.)

2 Teaching the Lesson

Remind students that the historical events described in this lesson were current events 2,500 years ago. Today's current events will be history for future generations. As students read pages 51–54, ask them to consider parallels between the past and what is happening in the world today.

Reading Strategy: Predicting

(Students may predict that some of the beautiful features of Babylon, such as gardens and statues, will be mentioned. Have students make a list of some of the features that make their town or city beautiful.)

Ask:

• Why was Nebuchadnezzar able to develop Babylon into a trading and learning center? (During his reign, it was relatively peaceful. The people didn't have to spend time on war.)

• How were the Hanging Gardens similar to a modern garden? (Answers will vary; students may say that the gardens had a system for delivering water to plants, as do modern gardens.)

Reading Strategy: Predicting

What kinds of things do you predict will be mentioned in the next paragraphs?

Terraced

Going upward like steps

Reading Strategy: Predicting

Think about your prediction. Were you accurate?

Bulls and dragons decorate the Ishtar gate in Babylon, the city Nebuchadnezzar made beautiful.

What Made Babylon Beautiful?

Nebuchadnezzar made the city of Babylon the most beautiful city in the ancient Middle East. In A.D. 1899, a German archaeologist found ancient Babylon. He discovered that a long wall—300 feet high and 80 feet wide—surrounded the city! The wall was so wide that a chariot with four horses could turn around on top of it! From its 250 towers, soldiers watched for the enemy. People and chariots entered the city through several bronze gates.

A broad street ran down the center of Babylon. At one end stood a beautiful gate of bricks coated with a blue glaze, or shiny polish. This gate is called the Ishtar gate. Animal sculptures, or carvings from stone, decorated the gate. Red-brick sidewalks ran down both sides of this long street. Carved into each brick was the message "I am Nebuchadnezzar, king of Babylon, who made this."

What Were the Hanging Gardens?

Nebuchadnezzar's palace had walls covered with brightly colored tiles. The most famous part of the palace was the Hanging Gardens. Some say that Nebuchadnezzar built the gardens for a queen who had lived in a mountainous country.

The king built **terraced,** or stepped, gardens, which rose upward like a mountain. In them, he planted the flowers and bushes of the queen's homeland. He had well water pumped up to the terraces to water the plants.

---

52 Unit 1 Early Civilizations

Reading Strategy: Predicting

(Students' predictions will be accurate if they suggested that gardens full of flowers and bushes, beautiful bronze gates, and the royal palace with the Hanging Gardens would be described.)

Astronomer

A person who keeps track of the sun, the planets, and the stars

How Did Priests Use the Ziggurat of Babylon?

The highest building in Babylon was a 300-foot-high ziggurat. From the top of this great temple, the Chaldean priests studied the night sky. These early **astronomers** mapped the heavens and tracked the sun, the planets, and the stars.

Some groups of stars brought pictures to the astronomers' minds. They called these star pictures constellations. In fact, they saw 12 constellations evenly spaced across the sky. These became the zodiac. The astronomers believed that the stars told the future. They thought that stars had power over a person's life.

For many years the Chaldean priests viewed the night sky. They broke time into seven-day weeks. They also figured out the length of the year.

Why Did the Chaldean Empire Fall?

While Nebuchadnezzar ruled, the city of Babylon was a great trading and learning center. But after he died in 562 B.C., war broke out. The Chaldeans and the people they had defeated did not like the kings who followed Nebuchadnezzar.

Reading Signs in the Stars

People today read their horoscopes for clues to the future. This idea goes back to ancient Babylonia. There, priests were also astronomers. They studied the movements of the sun, moon, and stars. During a year, the sun seemed to circle through 12 constellations. The priests named these star patterns mostly after animals, such as the goat (Capricornus).

Using the sun and stars, priests predicted natural events. They also set the times for holidays. About the 6th century B.C., Chaldean priests began to make horoscopes. They told the future for rulers and nobles. A horoscope was based on the time of birth and the sun's position. Later the Greeks conquered Babylon. They gave the 12 star signs the names we use today. They named this circle of constellations the "zodiac."

Writing About History

Imagine you are a reporter for the *Mesopotamian Times.* In your notebook, write an article. Tell about an event in this chapter, such as the building of the Hanging Gardens.

---

800 B.C. – 330 B.C.

Middle Eastern Empires Chapter 3 **53**

Ask:

- **What factor led to the eventual downfall of the Chaldean Empire?** (The kings who followed Nebuchadnezzar were not as well-liked, so the Persians were able to defeat them.)

Have students read the Then and Now feature on page 53. Ask them to find the horoscope section in a newspaper and determine their astrological sign. Then have students research and write a brief report that details the characteristics of their sign. Student reports should include a drawing of their sign's constellation.

Writing About History

Have students choose a topic before they begin to write. Then, have them write just the first sentence of their story. Explain that many readers don't read the rest of a story if the first sentence doesn't grab their attention. The opening sentence or two should tell what the story is about. Depending on the subject, it can also be dramatic (Thirty thousand slaves labored . . .), humorous (Would you build a garden in the sky . . .), or inspiring. Have students share their opening sentences. Then have them write the rest of their story in their notebooks. Tell students to be sure to address *Who, What, When, Where,* and *Why* questions.

ELL/ESL STRATEGY

Language Objective:
To become familiar with the names of the zodiac

ELL students may not be the only ones unfamiliar with the names of the zodiac since the 12 sign names are in Latin. Even many native English speakers do not know the English translations for the zodiac signs. Write these Latin names and the English translations on the board. Help students as necessary to pronounce the Latin names and read the English translations.

Aries (Ram)
Taurus (Bull)
Gemini (Twins)
Cancer (Crab)
Leo (Lion)
Virgo (Virgin)
Libra (Balance)
Scorpius (Scorpion)
Sagittarius (Archer)
Capricorn (Goat)
Aquarius (Water Bearer)
Pisces (Fish)

Ask:

- Which book of the Bible describes the destruction of Babylon? (the Book of Daniel)

 3 Reinforce and Extend

AT HOME

 Nebuchadnezzar decorated the city of Babylon to reflect his personal tastes. Art and architecture can often reveal something about a person's personality and interests. Ask a student to describe his or her home or the type of home he or she eventually would like to have and personal art objects he or she owns. Then, have another student summarize what the descriptions say about the first student's personal style.

Lesson 2 Review Answers

1. Chaldean Empire
2. Babylon **3.** Hanging Gardens
4. Nebuchadnezzar **5.** astronomers

Answers will vary. Students may think that he was proud of his city and wanted people to know that he was the person who had planned it and saw that the plan was carried out.

Few written accounts of the fall of Babylon exist. One source, the Book of Daniel, offers one description. The Book of Daniel in the Hebrew Bible describes how, in 538 B.C., King Belshazzar held a great feast. Suddenly, a strange hand appeared and wrote mysterious words on the wall. No one except Daniel, a young Hebrew, could interpret the writing. Daniel told the king what the words meant: His days were coming to an end, and the Persian army would defeat his empire.

That night the Persians killed Belshazzar. Cyrus the Great, king of Persia, captured Babylon. The Chaldean Empire then became part of the great Persian Empire.

Lesson 2 Review On a sheet of paper, use the words from the Word Bank to complete each sentence correctly.

Word Bank
astronomers
Babylon
Chaldean Empire
Hanging Gardens
Nebuchadnezzar

1. The Middle Eastern empire that Nebuchadnezzar ruled was the _____.
2. The capital of his empire was _____.
3. One of the wonders of this capital was its _____.
4. _____ died in 562 B.C.
5. The Chaldean priests became _____, for they mapped the night skies.

What do you think

Why did Nebuchadnezzar carve his name on the red bricks of Babylon's sidewalks?

Objectives

◆ To explain how the Persians' system of roads helped them
◆ To identify the two forces that Zoroaster said existed in the world

Inspector
A person who looks at how things are being done

Unify
To bring together as one

In 538 B.C., Cyrus the Great, king of Persia, defeated the Chaldeans. In a few years, he conquered all his neighbors. Under later kings, the Persian Empire stretched more than 3,000 miles—from the Nile River of Egypt to the Indus River of India.

Because the Persian Empire was large, Darius I, another king, divided it into 20 provinces. A governor ruled each province. To keep an eye on his governors, he hired government **inspectors.** These people looked at how things were being done. They became "the eyes and ears of the king." Traveling around the empire, they reported back to the king.

How Did the Persians Keep Their Empire Together?

To hold their empire together, the Persians built a great system of roads. One road stretched for more than 1,600 miles! It took merchants three months to go from one end to the other. Messages from the king went faster than this.

Horseback riders carried these messages across the empire. They could stop at 100 different places to change horses. The Persians could relay, or pass along, messages in one week, not three months! Another way to **unify,** or bring together, the empire was to use the same weights and measures throughout the land. Because of this, doing business was easier.

How Did Coins Help Traders?

From a people called the Lydians, the Persians got the idea of using metal coins. Then two people no longer had to barter, or trade things. The problem with bartering is that both people must want to trade something of equal worth. Money took care of this problem.

800 B.C. – 330 B.C.

Middle Eastern Empires   Chapter 3   55

Chapter 3: Lesson 3

Overview Like their predecessors, the Persians defeated their neighbors. They also had slaves but were more open-minded about the diverse religions, languages, and cultures of the people they ruled.

Objectives

■ To explain how the Persians' system of roads helped them
■ To identify the two forces that Zoroaster said existed in the world

Student Pages pages 55–58

Teacher's Resource Library TRL

Workbook Activity 10
Activity 10
Modified Activity 10

Vocabulary

inspector   **unify**

Have students read the vocabulary words and definitions in this lesson. Ask students for examples of an inspector and examples of what it means to unify in today's world. Then have students write a sentence using each word. Students should check the accuracy of their modern word use by comparing their sentences with the definitions in the Glossary.

1 Warm-Up Activity

Help students understand the system of bartering by giving each student a picture of a common object with its approximate price. Provide pictures of appliances, computers, and small items, such as pencils and food items, from magazines or advertising circulars. Examples should include a wide value range. Ask students to circulate and find a classmate willing to barter for, or trade, objects. Discuss whether trading objects would be easier or more difficult if students used money instead of bartering with objects.

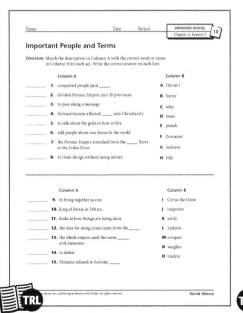

Workbook Activity 10   **Activity 10, pages 1–2**   *Middle Eastern Empires   Chapter 3   55*

PRONUNCIATION GUIDE

Use this list to help students pronounce difficult words in this lesson.

Lydians	(lid´ ē ənz)
Zoroaster	(zôr´ ō as´ tər)
Ahura Mazda	(ə hur´ ə maz´ də)
Ahriman	(är´ i mən)

2 Teaching the Lesson

Tell students to keep in mind the chapter goals of comparing how the Assyrians, Chaldeans, and Persians treated the people they conquered.

Ask:

- How did the Persians make it easier to do business? (They established one system of weights and measures for everyone and used metal coins.)

- How did the Persians demonstrate their tolerance of other people? (Conquered people could keep their own religion and language and follow their own laws.)

Reading Strategy: Predicting

(Students have learned that the Persians Empire was well-governed. A good road network, a system of governors and inspectors to keep the king informed, and a money system that made doing business easier were introduced. Students may predict correctly that the Persians would treat the people they conquered fairly.)

Have students compare the map on this page with the map on page 45. What modern countries would the Royal Road pass through if it existed today? (Turkey, Syria, Iraq, Iran)

Have students answer the question in the caption. (The Persian Empire is largest of the three empires. It was so large because it included the former Assyrian and Chaldean empires, plus the lands already in Persia's possession.)

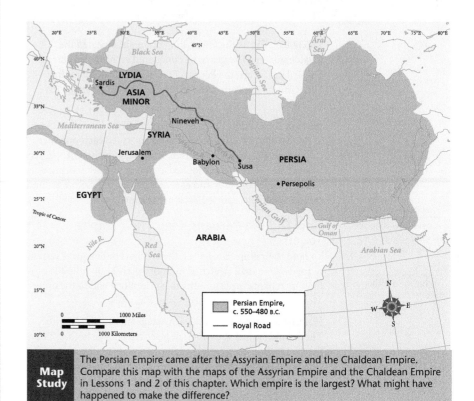

Map Study

The Persian Empire came after the Assyrian Empire and the Chaldean Empire. Compare this map with the maps of the Assyrian Empire and the Chaldean Empire in Lessons 1 and 2 of this chapter. Which empire is the largest? What might have happened to make the difference?

Reading Strategy: Predicting

Think about what you just read. What do you predict you will learn about how Persians treated others?

How Did the Persians Treat Others?

The Persians treated other people fairly. They did not destroy a city when they conquered it. They also did not loot from the people they defeated. They let conquered people keep their own language and religion. They even allowed some groups to follow their own laws. The Persians did ask everyone to pay taxes. But the taxes were small.

56   Unit 1   Early Civilizations

LEARNING STYLES

Logical/Mathematical

The Royal Road was 1,600 miles long. Riders made 100 stops in the seven days needed to travel the entire road. How many miles did the riders travel between stops? (16) If riders were able to rest six hours out of twenty-four, about how many miles did they ride each day? (about 229 miles) About how many miles per hour did they ride? (about 13)

Reading Strategy:
Predicting

Think about your earlier prediction. Were you correct, or do you need to revise your prediction?

How Did the Persians Live?

The art of Persia tells us how people lived. It shows rich men on horseback. Slaves carried others on litters, or stretchers. The men often had long beards and wore makeup on their faces and eyelids.

Women were not allowed much freedom. They lived apart from the men. Girls were taught to be good wives and mothers. Boys were taught to ride horses, use the bow and arrow, and speak the truth.

The Persians protected merchants, but they refused to become traders. Why? They thought that buying or selling made people selfish. It made them lie and cheat other people. Instead, Persians became soldiers, farmers, or shepherds.

Who Was Zoroaster?

The Persians worshipped many gods. Then, in about 570 B.C., a religious leader called Zoroaster began to preach. He talked about the gods and told people how to live. He told people that there were two forces in the world. One force was goodness and light; the other, evil and dark. Zoroastrianism had a strong effect on other religions, especially Judaism and Christianity. Both religions share the idea of life after death and a final reward or punishment.

Biography

Zoroaster: c. 628–551 B.C.

Zoroaster grew up in the Persian countryside, where people were herders. This religious teacher was probably a priest. He taught that the world was a fight between good and evil. The highest god was Ahura Mazda, the Wise Lord. He stood for light and truth. The evil spirit of darkness was Ahriman. Zoroaster taught that good would win in the end. His followers called him a great prophet. Others saw him as a healer and magician. Zoroaster's teachings became the official religion of Persia.

Biography

Some beliefs of major religions today originated with the thinking of the founder of the Zoroastrian religion. These include the concepts of heaven and hell and of angels. The Zoroastrian religion today has spread throughout the world. Followers try to walk a threefold path: think good thoughts, speak good words, and do good deeds.

Ask:

- Which group of people had the most freedom in ancient Persia? (free men)
- How were women treated in Persia? (They had little freedom and lived apart from men.)

Reading Strategy:
Predicting

(Students have read that the Persian kings were progressive and that they treated the people fairly. If students have understood this information, their predictions will be correct. Students will learn on page 57 how important religion was to the people and how it influenced the way they lived.)

ELL/ESL Strategy

Language Objective: *To teach and model gaining meaning from and paraphrasing context*

Have ELL students read, or read aloud to them, the three paragraphs under the subhead "How Did the Persians Live?" Pause at the end of the first paragraph and model how to use your own words to paraphrase the information about the difference in classes. Pause at the end of the second paragraph, and with student input, together paraphrase the information about the differences in the way males and females were treated. Then pause at the end of the third paragraph and encourage students to tell in their own words about the Persians' choice of jobs. Finally, ask students to give examples to the question in the subhead: How Did the Persians Live?

WORLD CULTURES

Today, the Middle East is rich in cultural diversity and is home to people of many different religions and languages. Have students select two countries from the map on page 45. Have them research the countries and make a chart that compares the ethnic groups, languages, and religions of the two countries.

IN THE COMMUNITY

The ancient Persians were relatively tolerant rulers. Have students give examples of tolerance in their own modern community. Then have them suggest contemporary situations in which people need to be more tolerant.

Lesson 3 Review Answers

1. D **2.** C **3.** A **4.** D **5.** A

Answers will vary. Students may suggest that if measures such as pounds, quarts, and meters are the same, then trading will be easier and people will not argue over them when buying and selling.

Chapter Project Follow-up

Have students share parts of their diaries with the class. Students may also wish to record their diaries for playback to the class. Diaries should be assessed with respect to historical accuracy. Dates should be accurate, and described events should be realistic.

Lesson 3 Review On a sheet of paper, write the letter of the answer that correctly completes each sentence.

1. One great king of the Persian Empire was _____.

  A Hammurabi   **C** Daniel
  B Nebuchadnezzar   **D** Cyrus the Great

2. The Persian Empire stretched from Egypt to _____.

  A China   **C** India
  B England   **D** Phoenicia

3. The Persian Empire had _____ provinces.

  A 20   **B** 100   **C** 1,600   **D** 3,000

4. The Persians built a system of _____.

  A dikes   **B** litters   **C** canals   **D** roads

5. To trade things without using money is to _____.

  A barter   **B** govern   **C** litter   **D** tribute

What do you think

How would a system of weights and measures help to unify a country?

A Few Words from the "Great King"

Darius I and an attendant are pictured in this carving.

Two Persian kings (Cyrus and Darius) are known as "the Great." Starting in about 550 B.C., Cyrus the Great built the Persian Empire. It became the largest empire ever known in the region. Cyrus died in battle about 529 B.C. His son became king, but others fought for the throne.

Darius, a general, became king in 522 B.C. He was an outstanding leader. The empire grew. Darius found ways to run the huge empire efficiently. Darius wanted to make sure he was remembered as "the Great." He planned a great tomb for himself. Then he wrote what he wanted carved on it. The excerpt below is part of what he wrote.

A great god is Ahura Mazda, who created this earth, who created yonder sky, who created man, who created happiness for man, who made Darius king, one king of many, one lord of many.

I am Darius the great King, king of kings, king of countries containing all kinds of men, king in this great earth far and wide: . . .

Saith Darius the King: By the Favor of Ahura Mazda these are the countries which I seized outside Persia, I ruled over them; they bore tribute to me; what was said to them by me, that they did; my law—that held them firm:

Media, Elam, Parthia, Aria, Bactria, Sogdiana, Chorasmia, Drangiana, Arachosia, Sattagydia, Gandara, Amyrgian, Sind, Scythians with pointed caps, Babylonia, Assyria, Arabia, Egypt, Armenia, Cappadocia, Sardis, Ionia, Scythians who are across the sea, Skudra, petasos-wearing Ionians, Libyans, Ethiopians, men of Maka, Carians.

Saith Darius the King: Much which was ill-done, that I made good. Provinces were in commotion; one man was smiting another. The following I brought about by the favor of Ahura Mazda, that the one does not smite the other at all, each one has his place. My law—of that they feel fear, so that the stronger does not smite nor destroy the weak.

Saith Darius the King: By the favor of Ahura Mazda, much handiwork which previously had been put out of its place, that I put in its place . . . .

Saith Darius the King: May Ahura Mazda, together with the gods protect me and my royal house, and what has been inscribed by me.

Document-Based Questions

1. Who is Ahura Mazda?

2. According to Darius, who gave him the right to rule as king?

3. What titles does Darius give himself?

4. What did Darius require people in conquered countries to do?

5. List two things of which Darius is proud.

Read aloud the title and the introduction to the Document-Based Reading, "A Few Words from the 'Great King.'" Call attention to the photo. Ask a student to read the caption. Then have students read the selection. Ask volunteers to read the paragraphs aloud as if they were Darius speaking. Then ask students what kind of a person they think Darius was. (They may say confident, proud, religious, or boastful.) Students should then answer the Document-Based Questions.

Answers to Document-Based Questions:

1. Ahura Mazda is a great god and creator of the world and man.

2. Ahura Mazda gave Darius the right to be king.

3. Darius calls himself the great King, king of kings, king of countries containing all kinds of men, and king in this great earth far and wide.

4. Darius demanded that conquered peoples pay tribute to him, follow his orders, and obey his laws.

5. Answers will vary. Students may say that Darius was proud of conquering so many countries, of bringing order to areas that were in disorder, and of protecting weaker people through his laws.

Spotlight
Story

The Babylonian Captivity

The Bible tells us a lot about Middle Eastern history. Several books are about the history of the Jews. They tell about the Jewish kingdoms. The Bible also talks about neighboring rulers. In the 6th century B.C., the Chaldeans of Babylonia conquered the Jewish kingdom. But the Jews rebelled against their rule. The Bible tells how the king of Babylon put down the rebels. Nebuchadnezzar's soldiers attacked Jerusalem. His soldiers captured the Jewish king and his family. They were taken to Babylon as prisoners. So were thousands of skilled craftsworkers. Strong men were taken for the army. These Jews were kept in Babylon for many years. This period is known as the Babylonian Captivity.

Meanwhile, the Jews rebelled again a few years later in 586 B.C. Again the Babylonians attacked Jerusalem. They burned the Great Temple. They destroyed the city. They took away most of the city's people. Only poor people and farmers were left in the country. The Babylonians also took gold and silver from the temple.

The Jews suffered greatly in Babylon. Psalm 137 tells how sad they were. "By the rivers of Babylon, . . . we wept, when we remembered our Zion. . . ." (*Zion* is another name for Jerusalem.) The Babylonian Captivity was an important time in Jewish history. It tested the strength of the Jews' faith. They were in a strange place with different customs. There was pressure to change their religion and culture. Through many years away from home, they never lost their faith. Their leaders set up houses of worship, or synagogues.

Jewish houses of worship are called synagogues. This ancient synagogue is at Capernaum.

People observed the Sabbath and religious holidays. Their communities stayed strong.

At the same time, the Jewish people learned new skills in Babylon. They learned to be traders. They learned about banking. They slowly gave up farming in favor of business.

In 538 B.C., Persian armies led by Cyrus the Great conquered Babylon. The next year, Cyrus sent the Jews home to Jerusalem. In the Bible, Cyrus is praised for his actions. He gave the Jews money to rebuild the temple.

Wrap-Up

1. Why did Nebuchadnezzar attack Jerusalem?

2. What was the Babylonian Captivity?

3. What did the Jews do to keep their religion in Babylon?

4. What did the Jews learn from the Babylonians?

5. What events ended the Babylonian Captivity?

Chapter 3   S U M M A R Y

- The Assyrians were a warrior tribe in Mesopotamia. They built an empire between 900 and 700 B.C. People feared the Assyrian armies. They had iron weapons. Other armies only had bronze weapons. The Assyrian army also had archers, war chariots, and cavalry. The Assyrians were cruel to defeated peoples.

- Nineveh was the capital of Assyria. Assurbanipal was king in 650 B.C. He built a huge library. It included writings from earlier kingdoms in Mesopotamia.

- Assyrian kings divided their empire into provinces. They built roads to link its parts. Then the empire got too large to rule. Conquered peoples banded together against Assyria. They captured Nineveh in 612 B.C.

- The Chaldeans were next. Their capital was Babylon. Nebuchadnezzar made it beautiful. One feature was its Hanging Gardens.

- Nebuchadnezzar expanded the Chaldean Empire. He defeated Egypt and the Jews. He brought the Jews to Babylon as slaves.

- Chaldean priests were astronomers. They studied the stars. They named the constellations of the zodiac. They set up a seven-day week.

- Nebuchadnezzar died in 562 B.C. Then wars broke out. In 538 B.C., the Persians captured Babylon.

- Cyrus the Great was king of Persia. He conquered the peoples around him. At its largest, the Persian Empire stretched from Egypt to India. King Darius divided it into 20 provinces. His inspectors kept track of governors. Good roads connected all parts of the empire. Relays of messengers on horseback carried news quickly.

- Persian rulers treated other people well. They could keep their own language and religion.

- The Persians were not merchants. They did, however, encourage trade. Metal coins were used throughout the empire. Everyone used the same weights and measures for trade.

- Men and women lived separately in Persian society. Men had more freedom.

- Zoroaster brought a new religion to Persia. He saw life as a fight between good and evil. His teachings influenced Judaism and Christianity.

TEACHER'S RESOURCE

The AGS Globe Teaching Strategies in Social Studies Transparencies may be used with this chapter. The transparencies add an interactive dimension to expand and enhance the *World History* program content.

- Who had more freedom in Persian society, men or women? (men)
- Why was Zoroaster important? (He brought a new religion to Persia, and his teachings influenced Judaism and Christianity.)

Using the Chapter Summary

Have students read the Chapter Summary on page 61 to review the main ideas presented in Chapter 3.

Ask:

- Why did people fear the Assyrian armies? (The Assyrian armies had iron weapons, archers, war chariots, and cavalry.)

- What material did Assurbanipal keep in his library? (The library contained writings from earlier kingdoms in Mesopotamia.)

- What happened to the Assyrian Empire in 612 B.C.? (Nineveh, the capital, was captured by conquered peoples who united to defeat the Assyrians.)

- Who was Nebuchadnezzar, and how did he make Babylon beautiful? (Nebuchadnezzar was the leader of the Chaldeans. He built the Hanging Gardens in Babylon.

- What did Nebuchadnezzar do after defeating Egypt and the Jews? (He brought the Jews to Babylon as slaves.)

- Name two achievements of Chaldean priests. (They named the constellations of the zodiac and they set up a seven-day week.)

- What happened after Nebuchadnezzar died? (Wars broke out and the Persians captured Babylon.)

- Who were the two great Persian kings, and what were some of their accomplishments? (Cyrus the Great and King Darius enlarged the Persian Empire, divided it into provinces that could be governed effectively by inspectors and governors, and built good roads.)

- How did Persian rulers treat other people? (They treated the people well, allowing them to keep their own language and religion.)

- What did the Persian rulers do to make trade easier? (They introduced metal coins and a uniform system of weights and measures.)

Chapter 3 Review

Use the Chapter Review to prepare students for tests and to reteach content from the chapter.

Chapter 3 Mastery Test

The Teacher's Resource Library includes two forms of the Chapter 3 Mastery Test. Each test addresses the chapter Goals for Learning. An optional third page of additional critical-thinking items is included for each test. The difficulty level of the two forms is equivalent.

Chapter 3 Review Answers

1. iron
2. cavalry
3. chariots
4. provinces
5. alliance
6. terraced
7. astronomers
8. zodiac
9. barter
10. litters
11. A
12. C
13. B
14. A
15. B
16. Having iron to use in their weapons and armor helped the Assyrian armies defeat their enemies. Also, they developed a cavalry, charioteers, and skillful archers.

Word Bank
alliance
astronomers
barter
cavalry
chariots
iron
litters
provinces
terraced
zodiac

On a sheet of paper, use the words from the Word Bank to complete each sentence correctly.

1. Everyone feared the Assyrian army because it had weapons made of _____.

2. The Assyrian army was the first to use a(n) _____ with its soldiers riding war horses.

3. Some Assyrian soldiers drove horse-drawn _____.

4. Both the Assyrians and the Persian kings divided their kingdoms into _____, or smaller areas.

5. The Chaldeans and the Medes formed a(n) _____ and agreed to help one another defeat the Assyrians.

6. Nebuchadnezzar, the king of the Chaldeans, built a(n) _____, or stepped, garden for his queen.

7. The Chaldean priests became the first _____, for they mapped the night sky.

8. These priests saw 12 constellations, or star pictures in the night sky, which would later become the _____.

9. People in the Persian Empire had coins, so they no longer needed to _____, or trade things without money.

10. From Persian art, we learn that slaves sometimes carried Persian men on _____, or stretchers.

On a sheet of paper, write the letter of the answer that correctly completes each sentence.

11. The first great empire of the Middle East was the _____.

    A Assyrian   **B** Chaldean   **C** Persian   **D** Hebrew

12. The largest city of the Assyrian Empire was _____.

    A Babylon   **B** Jerusalem   **C** Nineveh   **D** Canaan

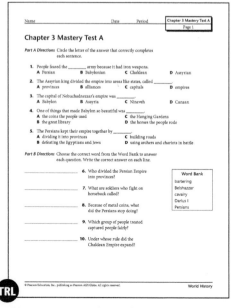

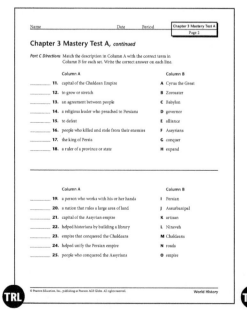

13. One powerful king of Assyria was _____.

   A Hammurabi   **C** Nebuchadnezzar

   B Assurbanipal   **D** Cyrus the Great

14. One powerful king of the Chaldeans was _____.

   A Nebuchadnezzar   **C** Cyrus

   B Daniel   **D** Darius

15. One powerful king of the Persians was _____.

   A Daniel   **B** Cyrus   **C** Moses   **D** Zoroaster

On a sheet of paper, write the answer to each question. Use complete sentences.

16. What helped the Assyrians become a war machine?

17. What was the difference between the way the Assyrians treated defeated people and the way the Persians did?

Critical Thinking On a sheet of paper, write your response to each question. Use complete sentences.

18. Why do you think so many people in the Assyrian Empire were happy when the Chaldeans captured and destroyed Nineveh?

19. Think about the Persian religion of Zoroastrianism. What influence might it have had on the way Persians treated the people they conquered?

20. Which of the Middle Eastern peoples described in this chapter have influenced the course of world history the most? Explain your opinion.

Schedule short study periods that are easy to manage. Take breaks between study periods.

17. The Assyrians were cruel to the people they conquered. They killed or enslaved them and destroyed their cities. The Persians treated people more fairly. They did not destroy the conquered cities, nor did they force people to give up their gods or language.

Critical Thinking

18. Answers will vary. Students may suggest that the Assyrians were cruel leaders. People feared them and were happy when the Chaldeans defeated them.

19. Answers will vary. Students may say that Zoroastrianism taught that there were two forces in the world—a good force and an evil one. It also taught that people were rewarded for doing good and punished for doing evil. Perhaps the Persians treated conquered people more fairly because they wanted to do good and to gain entry to heaven.

20. Answers will vary. Students may say that the Assyrians left behind important clay tablets that told future generations the history, languages, and literature of the ancient Middle East. The priest-astronomers of the Chaldeans gave us the zodiac, the seven-day week, and the length of our year. The Persian leader Zoroaster gave us a religion based on good and evil and this influenced both Judaism and Christianity.

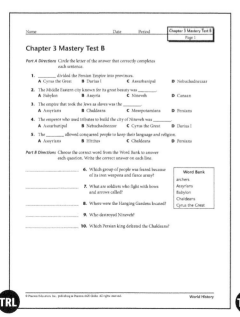

Chapter 3 Mastery Test B, pages 1–3

Introducing the Chapter

In ancient Egypt, many people lived along the fertile Nile River. They built cities and established a civilization that lasted for thousands of years.

Egypt—The Gift of the Nile

You have read about some of the people of the ancient Middle East. These people lived in an area known as the Fertile Crescent. Their city-states did not last long. However, the Egyptian civilization, which grew along the Nile River, lasted for more than 3,000 years! In this chapter, you will learn about the three kingdoms of the Egyptians: the Old Kingdom, the Middle Kingdom, and the New Kingdom.

Goals for Learning

◆ To explain why Egypt is "the gift of the Nile"

◆ To describe how Egypt was united in the Old Kingdom and explain how and why the pyramids were built

◆ To identify differences between the Old and the Middle Kingdoms

◆ To compare the New Kingdom with earlier periods of Egyptian history

◆ To list key contributions Egypt has made to world civilization

3100 B.C. Upper and Lower Egypt unite; Old Kingdom begins

2040 B.C. Middle Kingdom begins

1600 B.C. New Kingdom begins

30 B.C. Cleopatra dies

3000 B.C. — 2000 B.C. — 1000 B.C. — A.D. 1

Egyptians build great pyramids

1630 B.C. Hyksos invade Egypt

332 B.C. Alexander the Great conquers Egypt

Ask:

• When were both Upper and Lower Egypt brought under unified rule? (3100 B.C.)

• What year marked the beginning of the Middle Kingdom? (2040 B.C.)

• When did the New Kingdom begin? (1600 B.C.)

• When did Hyksos invade Egypt? (1630 B.C.)

Name _____ Date _____ Period _____ *SELF-STUDY GUIDE*

Chapter 4: Egypt—The Gift of the Nile

Goal 4.1   To explain why Egypt is "the gift of the Nile"

Date	Assignment	Completed
	1. Read pages 64–68.	_____
	2. Complete the Lesson 1 Review on page 68.	_____
	3. Complete Workbook Activity 11.	_____

Comments:

Goal 4.2   To describe how Egypt was united in the Old Kingdom and explain how and why the pyramids were built

Date	Assignment	Completed
	4. Read pages 69–73.	_____
	5. Complete the Lesson 2 Review on page 73.	_____
	6. Complete Workbook Activity 12.	_____

Comments:

Goal 4.3   To identify differences between the Old and the Middle Kingdoms

Date	Assignment	Completed
	7. Read pages 74–75.	_____
	8. Complete the Lesson 3 Review on page 75.	_____
	9. Complete Workbook Activity 13.	_____

Comments:

© Pearson Education, Inc., publishing as Pearson AGS Globe. All rights reserved.   World History

TRL

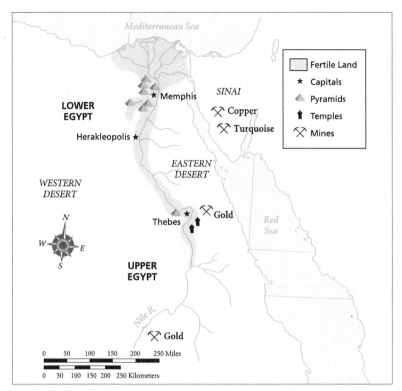

The Nile River dominates the geography of Egypt. Since ancient times, the river has provided water for irrigation. It also serves as a highway that unified Upper and Lower Egypt. The ancient Egyptians built their main cities and temples in the Nile Valley.

Study the map carefully, then answer the following questions:

1. Upper Egypt is in what direction from Lower Egypt?
2. What two deserts protected Egypt from invaders?
3. What are the names of the three Egyptian capitals shown on the map?
4. About how far is Thebes from Memphis?
5. What sea lies to the north of Lower Egypt?

3100 B.C. – 30 B.C.

Egypt—The Gift of the Nile Chapter 4 **65**

Ask a volunteer to read the title of the map and call attention to the dates when the map was accurate. Have students study the map. Then have students read the paragraph under the Map Skills heading.

Ask:

- Which direction is north on this map? (up)
- How is fertile land shown on this map? (shaded green) capital cities? (star) pyramids? (pyramid) temples? (tower) mining areas? (tools)
- The beginning, or source, of the Nile River is near gold mines within the continent of Africa. Into which large body of water does the Nile River flow? (Mediterranean Sea)

Have students write answers to the questions.

Map Skills Answers

1. south
2. the Western Desert and the Eastern Desert
3. Memphis, Herakleopolis, and Thebes
4. about 250 miles, or about 375 kilometers
5. Mediterranean Sea

Chapter Project

Have students work in groups of three or four. Have each group choose a specific pyramid and research how it was constructed. Then have students use available materials to make a model of the pyramid they studied. At the end of the chapter, students will give a brief presentation about their pyramid.

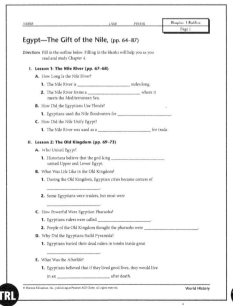

Chapter 4 Outline, pages 1–3

Egypt—The Gift of the Nile Chapter 4 **65**

Text Structure

Introduce the reading skill of text structure. Draw students' attention to the definition. Tell students that using the structure, or organization, of a text can help them figure out which pieces of information are the most important. Stress the importance of reading the headings in text, and looking at the photographs, captions, charts, and illustrations that accompany the text.

Explain that the headings in a text will often provide a hint about the most important information in a section of text. Sometimes the headings are written as questions. After reading the text, students should be able to answer the question.

Ask:

• Why are the events on page 64 organized in a timeline? (Those are important events in ancient Egypt, and the author wants us to remember them in the order that they happened.)

Encourage students to preview the remaining pages in Chapter 4 to look for the text structure. After reading Chapter 4, have students identify the organizational structures that helped them understand the chapter.

Key Vocabulary Words

Explain that the list of words here is a glossary of the Key Vocabulary they will read in Chapter 4. Call on volunteers to read aloud the words and their definitions.

Ask:

• Which term means a kind of picture writing? (hieroglyphics)
• Which word is a unit of measurement? (cubit)
• How are the words *papyrus* and *scroll* related? (Papyrus is a reed used to make paper and a scroll is a roll of papyrus paper.)

Reading Strategy:
Text Structure

Understanding how text is organized helps readers decide which information is most important. Before you begin reading this chapter, look at how it is organized.

◆ Look at the title, headings, boldfaced words, and photographs.
◆ Ask yourself: Is the text a problem and solution, description, or sequence? Is it compare and contrast or cause and effect?
◆ Summarize the text by thinking about its structure.

Key Vocabulary Words

Lesson 1 —————————————
Delta An area of fertile land at the mouth of a river

Silt A rich layer of soil left behind after a flood

Lesson 2 —————————————
Unite To bring together as one

Caravan A group of traders traveling together, often through deserts

Pharaoh An Egyptian ruler

Abundant More than enough

Civil war Fighting between people within their own country

Economy The system of making and trading things

Lesson 3 —————————————
Mummify To wrap a dead body in strips of cloth to keep the body from decaying

Armor A strong metal covering that protects the body in battle

Lesson 4 —————————————
Annex To take over; to add a piece of land to one's country

Obelisk A tall, pointed stone pillar

Hieroglyphics A kind of picture writing in Egypt

Lesson 5 —————————————
Papyrus A reed from the Nile River used to make paper

Scroll A roll of papyrus

Cubit A measurement that is the length of an arm from the end of the middle finger to the elbow

The Egyptian civilization, like earlier civilizations, developed in a river valley. Historians call Egypt "the gift of the Nile." The Nile River is the longest in the world. It begins in the mountains of central Africa. Then it flows northward to the Mediterranean Sea.

Objectives

◆ To identify some facts about the Nile River

◆ To describe the way Egyptians used floodwaters from the Nile

How Long Is the Nile River?

For most of its 4,000 miles, the Nile cuts through desert. It seldom branches out, but this changes just before it reaches the Mediterranean. There, it forms a triangular-shaped area of fertile land. We call such an area at the mouth of a river a **delta.**

How Did the Egyptians Use Floods?

Every spring, snow melts in the mountains of eastern Africa. Rain falls. Then the Nile floods. Most people think that floods are disasters. However, the ancient Egyptians used these floodwaters to irrigate their fields. When the floodwater went down, it left behind a rich layer of **silt.** Because of this, the Egyptians harvested two, and sometimes three, crops a year.

Along the banks of the Nile, Egyptian farmers grew wheat, barley, and many other crops. They had more than enough food for themselves. They traded their extra food for the things they did not have.

How Did the Nile Unify Egypt?

The Nile became an excellent "highway" for trade. Going north on it was easy because the Nile flows north. To go south, the Egyptians put large sails on their boats. These sails caught the winds that blew from north to south. Egyptian traders, government workers, and the rulers easily traveled up and down the river.

Delta

An area of fertile land at the mouth of a river

Silt

A rich layer of soil left behind after a flood

Reading Strategy:
Text Structure

Preview this lesson. Notice the headings, features, and boldfaced words.

Overview Students will learn how the Nile River, with its fertile soil and consistent pattern of flooding, made development of civilization along its banks successful.

Objectives

■ To identify some facts about the Nile River

■ To describe the way Egyptians used floodwaters from the Nile

Student Pages pages 67–68

Teacher's Resource Library (TRL)

Workbook Activity 11

Activity 11

Modified Activity 11

Vocabulary

delta   **silt**

Have students look up the word *delta* in a dictionary. Encourage a volunteer to read the definition aloud. Point out that the geometric shape of a delta resembles a triangle. Then ask how silt and delta may be related.

 1 Warm-Up Activity

Give each student a calculator. Explain that the Nile River is about 4,000 miles long. Have students figure out the length in feet. One mile = 5,280 feet, so students should multiply 5,280 by 4,000 to find the length of the Nile River in feet. (21,120,000 feet)

 2 Teaching the Lesson

Have students read page 67 and view the map on page 68 to learn about the Nile River and its importance to the Egyptians.

Ask:

• Which area of the Nile River had the most fertile land? (the delta at the mouth of the river)

• What types of activities did people engage in along the Nile River? (farming and trade)

3100 B.C. – 30 B.C.

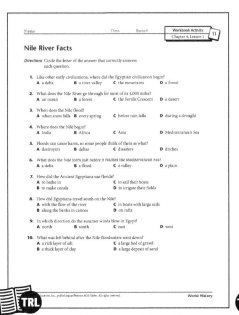

Some students may have difficulty understanding how the Egyptians used flooding along the Nile River to their benefit. Point out that the Nile is surrounded by desert, which is difficult to use for farming. However, flooding provides much needed water to grow crops, and the areas where the river floods has very fertile land that was good for farming.

Point out on the map on page 68 that the Nile River flows northward. This may be different than what students are used to seeing. Tell students that the Nile originates in the mountains to the south. The water flows downhill from the mountains to the Mediterranean Sea in the north. Discuss how people made the trip upstream, in the opposite direction of the current.

 3 Reinforce and Extend

STUDY SKILLS

Have students use the Internet to find a map of modern Egypt. Have students list the countries that share a border with Egypt. (Sudan, Libya, Israel) Have students point out some of the geographical features found in Egypt.

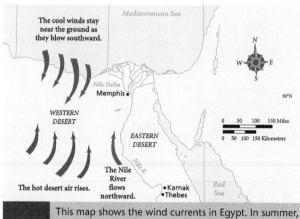

The cool winds stay near the ground as they blow southward.

Mediterranean Sea

Nile Delta
Memphis

WESTERN DESERT

EASTERN DESERT

The hot desert air rises.

The Nile River flows northward.

•Karnak
•Thebes

Red Sea

N
W—E
S

30°N

0   50   100   150 Miles
0   50   100 150 Kilometers

Map Study This map shows the wind currents in Egypt. In summer, the wind blows southward. Why do you think the Egyptians used sails when traveling upstream? How do you think they traveled downstream toward the sea?

What do you think
Why do you think historians call Egypt "the gift of the Nile"?

Lesson 1 Review On a sheet of paper, write the letter of the answer that correctly completes each sentence.

1. Like other ancient people, the Egyptians settled in _____ valleys.

   A desert   **B** dry   **C** river   **D** warm

2. The Nile River is about _____ miles long.

   A 2,000   **B** 4,000   **C** 6,000   **D** 6,500

3. Each year the Nile River floods, and this _____ the farmers.

   A surprises   **B** helps   **C** harms   **D** saddened

4. For traveling _____ on the Nile, the Egyptians put sails on their boats.

   A North   **B** South   **C** East   **D** West

5. The Nile River empties into the _____ Sea.

   A Black   **B** Mediterranean   **C** Red   **D** Dead

68   *Unit 1   Early Civilizations*

Lesson 1 Review Answers
1. C **2.** B **3.** B **4.** B **5.** B

Answers will vary. Students may say that the Nile River, with its yearly floods and rich silt, has made the fertile land that helped farmers produce enough food for all of Egypt. This river also enabled traders to travel up and down the country, keeping it united.

Objectives

◆ To identify two important gods that ancient Egyptians worshiped

◆ To describe why the Old Kingdom ended

Unite

To bring together as one

Caravan

A group of traders traveling together, often through deserts

At first, the ancient Egyptians lived in small villages. The people of the north, or Lower Egypt, lived near the Nile delta. Swampy marshland cut them off from one another.

The Egyptians living in the south, or Upper Egypt, began big irrigation projects. To finish these projects, they needed to work together. Upper Egypt was already unified around 3400 B.C.

Who United Egypt?

We do not know who **united,** or brought together, Upper and Lower Egypt. One story says that a god-king named Menes conquered Lower Egypt around 3100 B.C. He built his capital where Upper Egypt and Lower Egypt meet and called it Memphis. It is near Egypt's present capital—Cairo.

Menes wanted to show that Egypt was now united. He put the red crown of Lower Egypt and the white crown of Upper Egypt together into one crown. Pictures often show the later rulers of Egypt wearing this double crown.

We do not know if Menes was a real person. But Menes and the kings who followed him made up the first dynasty of Egypt. During the following 2,500 years, Egypt had 30 different dynasties!

What Was Life Like in the Old Kingdom?

Historians call the time from about 3100 B.C. to 2186 B.C. the Old Kingdom. During this time, Egyptian cities became centers of business. Groups of traders, called **caravans,** traveled together to Sumer to trade things. They also traveled to parts of Africa and the Mediterranean to trade.

Some Egyptians were traders, but most were farmers. They lived in mud-brick houses in small villages. They built their homes on the highest land. This protected them from the yearly floods. Because of the heat, people often slept on the roof.

3100 B.C. – 30 B.C.

Chapter 4: Lesson 2

Overview In this lesson, students will learn what happened as the result of the consolidation of power over Upper and Lower Egypt by the god-king Menes. Students will also read about the widespread trade and building of pyramids.

Objectives

■ To identify two important gods that ancient Egyptians worshipped

■ To describe why the Old Kingdom ended

Student Pages pages 69–73

Teacher's Resource Library

Workbook Activity 12

Activity 12

Modified Activity 12

Vocabulary

abundant	economy
caravans	pharaohs
civil war	united

Have students read aloud the definitions for the vocabulary words. Ask a volunteer to name the word you defined and write it on the board. Continue until all of the words are listed.

PRONUNCIATION GUIDE

Use this list to help students pronounce difficult words in this lesson.

Cairo	(kī´ rō)
Champollion	(chä pol yo)
Giza	(ge´ zə)
Menes	(mē´ nēz)
Pharaoh	(fer´ ō)

1 Warm-Up Activity

Have you ever traded belongings with a friend? Maybe you traded baseball cards with a friend when you were younger. Trading involves both parties giving something up in order to get something they want or need. Trading was used often in ancient Egypt instead of money.

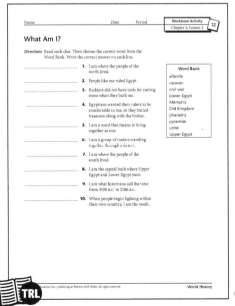

Workbook Activity 12

Activity 12

2 Teaching the Lesson

Have students refer back to the timeline on page 64. Have them locate the date for the unification of Upper Egypt (3400 B.C.) and the end of the Old Kingdom (2100 B.C.). Explain that they will be reading about what life was like during the years that the Old Kingdom was successful.

Ask:

- Why do you think historians are not absolutely sure about who united Egypt? (Answers will vary. This happened thousands of years ago, and people were not able to keep records of exactly what happened like they can today.)

- Who is believed to have united Upper and Lower Egypt? (the god-king Menes)

- What was the most common job among the Egyptian people? (Most were farmers.)

- How did the Egyptian people feel about their kings? (They thought their kings were gods.)

- What did the Egyptian people build to honor their pharaohs? (pyramids)

Reading Strategy:
Text Structure

Words like *next, during,* and *after* are called transition words. A transition is a change from one thing to the next. Transitions make writing flow more smoothly.

LEARNING STYLES

Visual/Spatial
Have students copy a map of the Nile River that shows major cities and the places and names of ancient monuments found along its banks. Students may look into reference sources in the library or on the Internet for locations of major monuments. Have students make a key for their map, using the key on the map on page 65 as an example.

Pharaoh
An Egyptian ruler

One of the most well-known monuments of the Old Kingdom is the stone Sphinx at Giza, Egypt. It was built about 2500 B.C.

How Powerful Were Egyptian Pharaohs?

The Egyptian rulers were called **pharaohs.** They were both kings and priests. In Mesopotamia, the kings spoke for the gods. In Egypt, the people thought the kings were gods.

The pharaoh of the Old Kingdom controlled the lives of his people. He owned all the land and water. The Egyptians believed that he even made the waters of the Nile rise and fall. Because life depended on the Nile, who would turn against this god-king? No one.

Reading Strategy:
Text Structure

As you read, look for words like *next, during,* and *after.* These words will help you understand the order of events in the text.

Why Did the Egyptians Build Pyramids?

The Egyptians believed that pharaohs continued to rule even after they died. They built great tombs, or places to bury the dead rulers. They were in the shape of a pyramid. To make these tombs last forever, the Egyptians built with stone. About 75 pyramids still stand in the Egyptian desert. The three most famous are in an area called Giza, outside modern Cairo.

Building the pyramids was hard work. The builders had no iron tools to cut the stone. They had no wheels or work animals to carry the huge stone blocks, which weighed about 5,000 pounds each. It took thousands of skilled workers many years to build a pyramid.

Reading Strategy:
Text Structure

As you read this lesson, notice the instructions on how to build a pyramid. What is the purpose of this feature?

How to Build a Pyramid

◆ Work 20,000 men for 20 years; feed them.
◆ Have 10,000 workers make about 26 million mud bricks for the inside of the pyramid.
◆ Have the other 10,000 workers cut huge stone blocks.
◆ Transport these blocks—about 12,600 of them—up the river to the building site.
◆ Dig a canal to connect the site to the river.
◆ Find a rock base, clear it of sand, and make it level.
◆ Make the sides of the stone blocks smooth; polish them.
◆ Build ramps upon which to haul the stone blocks higher and higher.
◆ Remove the building ramps as you work back downward.
◆ Build a funeral temple, the surrounding walls, a valley temple, and smaller pyramids for family members.

What Was the Afterlife?

The ancient Egyptians had two important gods. They called the sun god Ra and the river god Hapi. These gods were important because the Egyptians knew that the sun and the flooding of the Nile River provided their **abundant** food crops. This meant that they had more than enough to eat. This allowed most Egyptians to live well.

The Egyptians also believed that there was life after death. If people had led good lives before they died, they lived happily in an afterlife forever. They thought that if they had lived bad lives, a monster would eat them. The Egyptians wanted their dead pharaohs to be comfortable in the afterlife. They filled their tombs with treasure: food, clothing, jewelry, furniture, and beautiful art.

The Egyptians painted pictures of the king's friends and servants on the walls. They thought that the pharaoh would want these people with him in the afterlife. They believed everything pictured on the walls would magically come alive.

Ask:

• Why did it take so long to build a pyramid? (The workers did not have any tools. They had to move very heavy stone blocks into place.)

• Why did the people paint pictures on the walls of a pharaoh's tomb? (They thought that everything pictured on the walls would come to life.)

• What did the people think would be the reward for living a good life? (They believed they would live happily in an afterlife.)

Reading Strategy:
Text Structure

(Answers will vary. The purpose of this feature is to organize in a list all the steps involved in creating a pyramid.)

CAREER CONNECTION

 The modern counterpart to stone construction such as that of the Egyptian pyramids is masonry. Masonry involves building with stone or brick and carving from stone. Students interested in a career that involves building with stone or brick and mortar should contact their school counselor to find out how to prepare themselves for a career in masonry.

Ask:

- What did the Egyptians do in an attempt to protect their dead pharaohs? (They buried them in rooms deep within the pyramid and sealed the rooms with huge stone blocks.)

- What information has helped archaeologists learn about ancient Egypt? (the wall paintings inside pyramids)

- What happened to Egypt's economy at the end of the Old Kingdom? (the economy collapsed)

Reading Strategy:
Text Structure

(Students might say that they are unable to answer the heading question because no one knows exactly what caused the Old Kingdom to fall.)

ELL/ESL STRATEGY

Language Objective:
To prepare and give a group presentation

Divide the class into groups, preferably in groups of seven students, incorporating ELL students into each group. Have each student in the group choose a section from the lesson to reread. The students should reread their section, then write an answer to the question heading. Students should read their answers to their group members and work together to correct any factual errors. Each group should come up with a list of facts they learned from reading the lesson.

Then each group will give a presentation to the class. Each student in the group will present the information about their section, and the whole group should talk about what they learned at the end.

Civil war
Fighting between people within their own country

Economy
The system of making and trading things

The towering pyramids at Giza are amazing examples of Egyptian architecture.

How Did the Egyptians Protect Pharaohs?

The Egyptians buried the dead pharaoh in rooms deep within a pyramid. Then they sealed the rooms with huge stone blocks. However, robbers broke into the tombs and stole the treasures there. Even though the treasures are gone, archaeologists can still learn from a pyramid. Its wall paintings tell us much of what we know about ancient Egypt.

Reading Strategy:
Text Structure

Notice that the section headings are written as questions. Are you able to answer the question in the last section heading? Why or why not?

Why Did the Old Kingdom Fall?

Around the year 2186 B.C., the Old Kingdom ended. The pharaohs had lost power and government officials had become more powerful. The city leaders began to fight each other. Then **civil war** broke out as the people within Egypt began to fight each other.

Some historians believe that natural disasters may have caused the troubles in Egypt. Perhaps little rain fell for many years. Perhaps the people then began to doubt that the pharaoh controlled the rain. Egypt's **economy,** or system of making and trading things, collapsed.

Word Bank

afterlife
farmers
Hapi
Menes
pyramids

Lesson 2 Review On a sheet of paper, use the words from the Word Bank to complete each sentence correctly.

1. According to an old story, _____ united Upper and Lower Egypt.

2. Most Egyptians in the Old Kingdom were _____.

3. The Egyptians believed in a(n) _____ that was like the life they lived on earth.

4. Ra and _____ were two important gods.

5. The Egyptians built wonderful tombs, or _____, for their pharaohs.

How does the building of pyramids show that the pharaohs had money and power?

Communication in History

The Rosetta Stone

Scribes in ancient Egypt wrote with picture symbols. This writing system is called hieroglyphics. The term comes from the Greek words for "sacred carving." As time passed, though, people could no longer read them. Centuries later, the key to hieroglyphics was found. It was a stone tablet we now call the Rosetta Stone.

In 1799 Napoleon's army was in Egypt. French engineers were working near the Nile River. They dug up a tablet carved with three kinds of writing. One was Greek. One was a newer form of Egyptian writing. The third was hieroglyphics.

Jean François Champollion, a French scholar, knew many languages. He found that the inscriptions in Greek and the new Egyptian writing were the same. Then he compared the hieroglyphics with the Greek. After a long time, Champollion could read many of the symbols. The Rosetta Stone opened the door to learning about ancient Egypt.

---

3   Reinforce and Extend

LEARNING STYLES

Body/Kinesthetic

Have students who learn well through tactile experiences make a model of an Egyptian burial chamber. Their model should include miniature replicas of artifacts that were typically buried with pharaohs in their tombs. Encourage students to write brief explanations of some of the artifacts they include. Have them report to the class about their work, explaining how they did their research about what to include in their models.

Lesson 2 Review Answers

1. Menes   2. farmers   3. afterlife
4. Hapi   5. pyramids

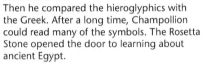

Answers will vary. Students may say that the pyramids took many years to build. During that time, the pharaohs had to provide food and housing for the 20,000 men who were working. This required money. It took a lot of power to get the farmers to leave their fields and come work on building the pyramids.

Communication in History

Champollion learned Greek, Latin, and about six ancient east Asian languages while in his teens. Deciphering the Rosetta Stone was his most important piece of work. He figured out that the symbols on the Rosetta Stone represented letters, syllables, and ideas. Beginning in 1821, he published scholarly papers based on the deciphering of the Rosetta Stone.

Chapter 4: Lesson 3

Overview In this lesson, students will read about the differences between the Old and the Middle Kingdoms. Students will also learn about the accomplishments of the Middle Kingdom.

Objectives

- To identify ways that the Egyptians changed their surroundings
- To describe the nomads from Asia who invaded Egypt

Student Pages pages 74–75

Teacher's Resource Library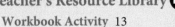

Workbook Activity 13

Activity 13

Modified Activity 13

....

Vocabulary

armor   **mummify**

Have students read the definition of each word and write a sentence in their own words. Ask volunteers to share their sentences with the class.

....

PRONUNCIATION GUIDE

Use this list to help students pronounce difficult words in this lesson.

Hyksos   (hik´ sōs)

Thebes   (thēbz)

1 Warm-Up Activity

Ask students to think of a situation in which they have decision-making power. For example, while babysitting, they have to make decisions. Ask students to discuss situations in which they have to share power, such as when they are with a group of friends deciding what to do on a Friday night. Explain that a change in power came along with the Middle Kingdom in Egypt.

Reading Strategy:
Text Structure

(the word "differ" tells us)

Objectives

- To identify ways that the Egyptians changed their surroundings
- To describe the nomads from Asia who invaded Egypt

Reading Strategy:
Text Structure

Read the next heading. How do you know the section will contrast two different things?

Mummify

To wrap a dead body in strips of cloth to keep the body from decaying

Around 2040 B.C., a new dynasty of powerful pharaohs reunited Egypt. This was the beginning of the Middle Kingdom. Its capital was Thebes.

Once again, traders sold artifacts and other products in faraway places. To help trade and transportation, the Egyptians dug a long canal. It joined the Nile River with business centers near the Red Sea.

They also emptied out many swampy marshes to create vast areas of farmable land. The water they drew from these swamps flowed to a large natural basin. In this bowl-like place, they kept the water from the swamp. During dry months, farmers used it for irrigation. Once again, the Egyptians had more than enough food for everyone.

How Did the Two Kingdoms Differ?

The Old Kingdom and the Middle Kingdom differed in three ways. First, the Old Kingdom Egyptians thought their pharaohs were gods. People of the Middle Kingdom still thought this, but their pharaohs no longer had complete power. They had to share their power with other officials.

Second, the people of the Old Kingdom thought that only the pharaoh would live forever. However, the Middle Kingdom Egyptians thought that *all* people would live forever. They **mummified** everyone after death. They wrapped the dead body in strips of cloth to keep it from decaying.

Third, the Egyptians buried the Old Kingdom pharaohs in pyramids. However, they buried later pharaohs in tombs cut into cliffs near Thebes.

Who Invaded Egypt?

About 1630 B.C., nomads from Asia known as the Hyksos invaded Egypt. The Egyptians knew medicine and arithmetic, but the Hyksos knew war. They had horse-drawn chariots,

---

About the Middle Kingdom

Directions Write the answers to these questions. Use complete sentences.

1. What marked the beginning of the Middle Kingdom?

2. How did Egyptians in the Middle Kingdom change the Nile River?

3. Describe the natural basin built by Egyptians during the Middle Kingdom.

4. What is one difference between the Old Kingdom and the Middle Kingdom?

5. Who were the Hyksos?

Workbook Activity 13

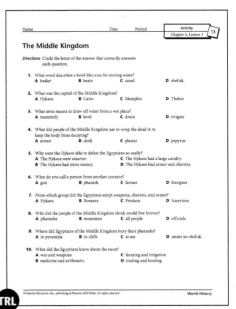

The Middle Kingdom

Directions Circle the letter of the answer that correctly answers each question.

1. What word describes a bowl-like area for storing water?
   A basket   B basin   C canal   D obelisk

2. What was the capital of the Middle Kingdom?
   A Hyksos   B Cairo   C Memphis   D Thebes

3. What term means to draw off water from a wet place?
   A mummify   B level   C drain   D irrigate

4. What did people of the Middle Kingdom use to wrap the dead in to keep the body from decaying?
   A armor   B cloth   C plaster   D papyrus

5. Why were the Hyksos able to defeat the Egyptians so easily?
   A The Hyksos were smarter.   C The Hyksos had a large cavalry.
   B The Hyksos had more money.   D The Hyksos had armor and chariots.

6. What do you call a person from another country?
   A god   B pharaoh   C farmer   D foreigner

7. From which group did the Egyptians adopt weapons, chariots, and armor?
   A Hyksos   B Romans   C Persians   D Assyrians

8. Who did the people of the Middle Kingdom think would live forever?
   A pharaohs   B mummies   C all people   D officials

9. Where did Egyptians of the Middle Kingdom bury their pharaohs?
   A in pyramids   B in cliffs   C at sea   D under an obelisk

10. What did the Egyptians know about the most?
    A war and weapons   C farming and irrigation
    B medicine and arithmetic   D trading and boating

Activity 13

bronze and iron weapons, and **armor.** This strong covering of metal protected their bodies. Because of all this, the Hyksos easily defeated the Egyptians. For the first time in Egypt's history, foreigners, or people from another country, ruled.

How Long Did the Hyksos Rule?

The Hyksos were mean rulers. They buried some Egyptian cities and destroyed temples. The Egyptians were not happy with their new rulers. However, they learned a lot from the Hyksos, such as how to make bronze, new weapons, chariots, and armor, and how to weave. Meanwhile, the Egyptians began to use the weapons, chariots, and armor of the Hyksos. In 1570 B.C., the Egyptians drove out the foreign invaders.

Why do you think the Egyptians took so long to drive out the Hyksos?

Lesson 3 Review On a sheet of paper, write the answer to each question. Use complete sentences.

1. What did Middle Kingdom pharaohs do with swamps and canals?

2. How did Middle Kingdom pharaohs help traders?

3. What are three differences between the Old Kingdom and the Middle Kingdom?

4. Why were the Hyksos able to conquer Egypt?

5. What did the Egyptians learn from the Hyksos?

Farming Along the Nile

Egypt's success depended on thousands of peasants. But raising good crops depended on the Nile flooding every year. These floodwaters covered the land along its banks, making a strip of rich farmland. The rich soil came from farther up the river. The Nile also provided water for irrigation. The rest of Egypt was desert.

Men and women worked in the fields during the day. They grew grains such as wheat and barley. The flour from these grains was mixed with honey to make sweet bread. Farmers grew grapevines and picked dates too. Other peasants tended herds of sheep, goats, or cattle. They also hunted deer and water birds.

Besides food crops, Egyptian farmers grew cotton and flax, a plant that was used for its fibers. They spun the fibers to make cotton and linen cloth. Most farmwork was done by hand. Tomb paintings show farmers using metal tools to cut grain. Oxen were used for heavy work, such as turning water wheels.

3100 B.C. – 30 B.C.

Have students locate the beginning date for the Middle Kingdom on the timeline on page 64. (2040 B.C.) Then have them locate the beginning of the New Kingdom. (1600 B.C.) Explain that they will read about the important events that occurred during the time of the Middle Kingdom.

Ask:

- What accomplishments did the Egyptians make during the Middle Kingdom? (trade of products, draining of swamps, building of a canal to the Red Sea)

- How was the Middle Kingdom different from the Old Kingdom? (The belief about the power of pharaohs changed from complete power to shared power. The old belief that only pharaohs went on to an afterlife changed to all people. Instead of burying the pharaohs in pyramids, the people of the Middle Kingdom buried the pharaohs in cliffs.)

- For how long did the Hyksos rule? (from 1630 B.C. until 1570 B.C.; about 60 years)

ELL/ESL STRATEGY

Language Objective: *To compare and contrast two different periods in time*

After reading the lesson, make a Venn Diagram on the board. The three headings for this graphic organizer should be *Ancient Egypt, Both,* and *Today.* Explain that in the text, the Old Kingdom and the Middle Kingdom are compared. Students can also compare and contrast life today with life in ancient Egypt. Model for students how to use the Venn Diagram. Encourage volunteers to come up with other ways to compare and contrast ancient Egypt and today. Write their ideas on the Venn Diagram.

 Reinforce and Extend

Lesson 3 Review Answers

1. The Middle Kingdom pharaohs emptied the swamps and then dug a 300-foot wide canal in their place. **2.** They built a canal connecting the Nile with business centers near the Red Sea. **3.** The pharaohs of the Middle Kingdom did not have complete power as the Old Kingdom pharaohs had. The Middle Kingdom people thought they would all live forever. The Old Kingdom Egyptians buried their leaders inside pyramids; the Middle Kingdom Egyptians buried their pharaohs inside cliffs. **4.** The Hyksos were skilled at war. They had bronze and iron weapons, horse-drawn chariots, and armor. **5.** The Egyptians learned to fight like the Hyksos using chariots, weapons, and armor.

Answers will vary. Students may say that the Egyptians needed time to build up their supply of weapons. They also needed the time to learn how to fight.

Several of the agricultural methods used in ancient Egypt are still used in Egypt today. Have students research modern Egyptian agriculture in library reference sources or on the Internet. Find out which farming methods have not changed since the time of the pharaohs.

Chapter 4: Lesson 4

Overview This lesson covers events and accomplishments and describes some of the ways in which people lived during the New Kingdom era.

Objectives

- To explain accomplishments of the New Kingdom
- To describe why Egyptians lost control of Egypt

Student Pages pages 76–79

Teacher's Resource Library **TRL**

Workbook Activity 14

Activity 14

Modified Activity 14

....

Vocabulary

annexed   **obelisks**
hieroglyphics

Have a student write one of the vocabulary words on the board. Have another student read the definition for it. Have a third student restate the definition in his or her own words. Continue until all vocabulary words are on the board. Have two volunteers carry on a brief conversation, using all three vocabulary words.

....

▸ Pronunciation Guide

Use this list to help students pronounce difficult words in this lesson.

Hatshepsut	(hat shep′ sŭt)
Ikhnaton	(ok′ not′ ən)
Nefertiti	(nef′ ər tē′ tē)
Ramses	(ram′ sēz)

❶ Warm-Up Activity

Ask students to think about monuments they have seen. Have students describe the monuments to the class and explain who is honored by each monument. Lead students in a discussion about why people throughout history have found it important to construct monuments to various people.

Objectives

- To explain accomplishments of the New Kingdom
- To describe why Egyptians lost control of Egypt

Annex

To take over; to add a piece of land to one's country

In about 1600 B.C., the New Kingdom began. During that time, strong pharaohs ruled Egypt. Like the pharaohs of the Old Kingdom, they controlled the people of Egypt.

Who Was the First Woman Pharaoh?

With its strong army, Egypt began to expand. It **annexed,** or took over, lands next to the upper Nile and along the eastern Mediterranean. Hatshepsut—the first woman pharaoh—spread the influence of Egypt down into the heart of Africa. From there, traders got products such as beautiful wood, animal skins, and feathers.

What Pharaoh Was a Great Conqueror?

When Hatshepsut died, Thutmose III became pharaoh. He spread Egypt's influence all the way to the Euphrates River. Almost every year for 20 years, his soldiers won victories in Asia. As they did so, he built army bases in all the lands he controlled. He also organized, or set up, a navy to conquer the cities along the eastern Mediterranean.

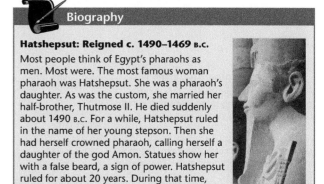

Biography

Hatshepsut: Reigned c. 1490–1469 B.C.
Most people think of Egypt's pharaohs as men. Most were. The most famous woman pharaoh was Hatshepsut. She was a pharaoh's daughter. As was the custom, she married her half-brother, Thutmose II. He died suddenly about 1490 B.C. For a while, Hatshepsut ruled in the name of her young stepson. Then she had herself crowned pharaoh, calling herself a daughter of the god Amon. Statues show her with a false beard, a sign of power. Hatshepsut ruled for about 20 years. During that time, Egypt had a long period of peace. She had many great temples and monuments built.

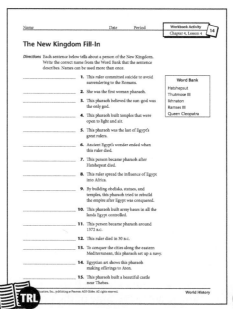

Workbook Activity 14

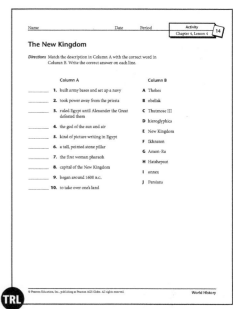

Activity 14

Obelisk

A tall, pointed stone pillar

Hieroglyphics

A kind of picture writing in Egypt

Under Thutmose, Egypt's empire stretched far and wide. For this reason, historians sometimes call the period of the New Kingdom the "empire age." The many people the Egyptians conquered paid tribute, or taxes, to the pharaohs. The rulers and the nobles became rich.

What Did the New Kingdom Pharaohs Build?

The rulers and nobles of the New Kingdom used their money to build temples, palaces, and statues. Hatshepsut built a beautiful temple near Thebes, the capital of the New Kingdom. Artists painted and carved the story of Egypt's victories on the temple's walls.

Thutmose III used slaves to build great palaces and to rebuild temples. Tall, pointed stone pillars called **obelisks** were also built. Artists carved **hieroglyphics,** or picture writing, on the sides of these pillars.

The Egyptians honored their pharaohs by building giant statues, which stood many stories high. With its beautiful palaces and temples, Thebes became the most wonderful city in the ancient world.

Where Did Egyptian Children Go to School?

The Egyptians built great temples to honor their gods. These were both religious centers and schools. In them, the children of Egyptian nobles and those from conquered lands learned what Egyptians believed. The pharaohs hoped that these schools would make the children faithful to Egypt when they got older. The schools trained boys as young as five years old to be scribes. These scribes kept important records and wrote down religious laws.

Obelisks are tall pillars carved from a single stone. This one is from the ancient Egyptian village of Karnak.

Reading Strategy:
Text Structure

Read the next heading. How do you know that Egyptian children went to school?

Teaching the Lesson

Ask:

- **What do we know about Hatshepsut?** (the first female pharaoh, expanded empire along Mediterranean, expanded trade routes to Africa) **Thutmose?** (conquered territory in Asia, organized a navy to conquer cities along the Mediterranean) **Ramses?** (built many great obelisks, rebuilt the empire, was the last great pharaoh of Egypt)

Biography

One reason Hatshepsut remained in power was that she had influential officials who were loyal to her. Among the architectural accomplishments of Hatshepsut was the restoration of buildings damaged during the rule of the Hyksos. What became of Hatshepsut when Thutmose III became pharaoh is unknown. She may have died a natural death or she may have been murdered.

Ask:

- **Why was the time of Thutmose known as the "empire age"?** (During his reign, Egypt ruled in many places. They collected taxes from the people, so the rulers became rich.)

- **What monuments were built during the New Kingdom?** (obelisks, giant statues, and temples)

- **What do we know about the education of Egyptian children?** (Children went to school at the temples. The purpose of this was to make children faithful to Egypt. Boys were trained to be scribes so they could keep records.)

Reading Strategy:
Text Structure

(The heading asks where the children went to school. That makes it apparent that the children went to school.)

ELL/ESL STRATEGY

Language Objective:
To practice common grammar structure

Have students look closely at the photo of the obelisk on page 77. If possible, display other photos of obelisks, including the Washington Monument in Washington, D.C. Have students generate a list of adjectives to describe the obelisks. Write the list on the board. Some adjectives might include: *tall, hard, beautiful, pointed, strong,* and *heavy.*

Then write sentence frames on the board using the adjectives. For example: I think the obelisk is tall because _____. Have a volunteer come to the board, read the sentence frame, and complete the sentence. For example: I think the obelisk is tall because it looks bigger than the rocks that surround it.

Ask:

- How did Ikhnaton change the way people worshipped their gods? (He chose one god to be the only one worshipped, and he closed the temples to all of the other gods. He also built temples that were completely open to light and air.)

- What distracted Ikhnaton from paying attention to the success of the empire? (People did not like having only one god. The priests began to fight with the pharaoh, taking up his time and attention.)

- What event caused the end of ancient Egypt? When? (the death of Queen Cleopatra in 30 B.C.)

Writing About History

Remind students that letters and diaries are important primary sources for historians studying a particular era. Vivid, detailed letters and diaries are especially helpful. Ask students to keep this in mind as they read Writing About History and as they write their letter to a friend.

 3 **Reinforce and Extend**

WORLD CULTURES

The mythical sphinx is a symbol often associated with ancient Egypt. Some nations today adopt real animals as national symbols. For the United States, the national symbol is the bald eagle. Have students use the World Atlas to find modern nations located near the eastern end of the Mediterranean Sea. Then have students research the animals that are the national symbols of these countries. Have students display the symbols on an area map showing the nations they researched.

 Writing About History

A time machine has taken you to ancient Egypt. You can go anywhere and see anything. What impresses you most? In your notebook, write a letter to a friend. Tell about your visit to Egypt.

Reading Strategy:
Text Structure

As you read the next section, make a list of causes and effects as Egypt lost its power.

How Did Ikhnaton Change the Egyptian Religion?

The people of Thebes worshiped many gods. Sometimes they combined gods. That is, they put them together into one. For instance, they combined Amon, the god of the wind, with Ra, the sun god. The two became one. In fact, Amon-Ra became the most powerful god of all. He had power over both the sun and the air.

Around 1372 B.C., Amonhotep IV became pharaoh. He believed that the sun god, now called Aton, was the only god. To honor Aton, he changed his name to *Ikhnaton*, which means, "It is well with Aton." The new pharaoh closed the temples of the other gods. He took power away from the priests.

Ikhnaton built new temples that were completely open to the light and air. Often, Egyptian art shows this pharaoh and his wife, Nefertiti, giving gifts to Aton. The rays of the sun god beam down on them.

How Did Egypt Lose Its Power?

Many Egyptians did not like the new religion with its one god. The priests became angry and jealous because they had lost power. Soon they began to fight with the pharaoh. When that happened, he could not pay as much attention to the empire. The conquered people in many parts of the empire began to rebel against Egypt.

A later pharaoh, Ramses III, rebuilt the empire, but the weakened Egypt never became as powerful as it had once been. He built many obelisks, giant statues, and beautiful temples. He was the last great ruler of Egypt.

Who Conquered Egypt in 332 B.C.?

Egypt could no longer defend itself. Over the years, many people invaded the land—Ethiopians from farther south in Africa; Babylonians; Assyrians; and, Persians.

The Persians ruled Egypt until Alexander the Great defeated them in 332 B.C. Many years later, in 30 B.C., Queen Cleopatra killed herself to avoid surrendering Egypt to the Romans. The wonder of ancient Egypt ended with her death.

Lesson 4 Review On a sheet of paper, write the letter of the answer that correctly completes each sentence.

1. The first woman pharaoh was _____.

  A Cleopatra   **C** Ramses III
  B Hatshepsut   **D** Ikhnaton

2. The capital of the New Kingdom was _____.

  A Memphis   **B** Cairo   **C** Thebes   **D** Persia

3. Thutmose III organized a _____ to help him conquer other lands.

  A caravan   **B** obelisk   **C** navy   **D** religion

4. The name of the one god worshiped by Ikhnaton was _____.

  A Aton   **B** Ra   **C** Amon   **D** Amon-Ra

5. The glory of ancient Egypt ended in _____ B.C.

  A 1600   **B** 1372   **C** 332   **D** 30

Why do you think Ikhnaton's new religion was unpopular?

Chapter 4: Lesson 5

Overview This lesson includes some of the important contributions the Egyptians made to civilization in the areas of medicine, mathematics, the arts, and science.

Objectives

- To describe the way Egyptians advanced medicine, building, and artwork
- To identify the counting system that the Egyptians invented

Student Pages pages 80–82

Teacher's Resource Library

Workbook Activity 15

Activity 15

Modified Activity 15

Vocabulary

cubit   **scroll**
papyrus

Let students study the vocabulary words and definitions in the margins on page 80. Then tape a card with a definition or a vocabulary word on the back of a volunteer. Have the volunteer let class members read what is on the card. Then let the volunteer ask questions of students that can be answered with "yes" or "no" about the word until the student is able to identify what is written on the card they wear. Continue until all words and definitions are used.

 Warm-Up Activity

Ask students to take out a sheet of paper and a pen. Give each student a rock found outside. (You can return them outside later.) Have students write their name on the sheet of paper using the pen. Then have students write their name on the rock with the same pen. Have students tell which was the easiest to write on, paper or rock, and describe why.

Reading Strategy:
Text Structure

Notice the title of this lesson. What do you expect to learn in the lesson?

Objectives

- To describe the way Egyptians advanced medicine, building, and artwork
- To identify the counting system that the Egyptians invented

Papyrus
A reed from the Nile River used to make paper

Scroll
A roll of papyrus

Cubit
A measurement that is the length of an arm from the end of the middle finger to the elbow

Egyptian civilization has given many gifts to the modern world. As early as 3000 B.C., the Egyptians learned how to use **papyrus,** a reed from the Nile River, to make paper. (The English word *paper* comes from the word *papyrus.*) Their paper was so well made that even today we can still read the writing on it!

This invention was important because writing on paper is much easier than writing on stone. Of course, in order to write on paper, they also had to invent ink.

What Did the Egyptians Know About Medicine?

The Egyptians made papyrus **scrolls,** or rolls. Archaeologists have discovered some of these in Egyptian tombs. One of the most famous papyrus scrolls shows the Egyptians' interest in medicine. The scroll describes how to set broken bones, how to check for a heartbeat, and how to deal with fevers and accidents. People who lived at later times learned much of their medicine from these ancient Egyptians.

What Were Egyptian Temples Like?

The Egyptians were skilled builders. Some of their statues, temples, and pyramids stood several stories high! People from all over the world still come to see their size and beauty. However, most of the great temples that the Egyptians built are in ruins today.

How Much Arithmetic Did the Egyptians Know?

The Egyptians invented a system of counting based on ten. This helped them add and subtract. They used this system to collect taxes. They also invented a system for measurement and weights. They measured things in **cubits**—the length of an arm from the end of the middle finger to the elbow. They used geometry to survey, or measure, land.

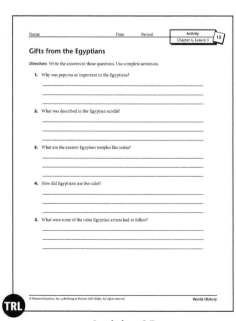

Workbook Activity 15

Activity 15

What Artwork Did Egyptian Artists Produce?

Egyptian artists carved huge statues from stone. Many had heads about twelve feet high, with ears three feet long! They made small figures of people and animals from wood, bronze, or copper.

These same artists decorated temples with many drawings. We can still see much of their beautifully colored artwork today. Archaeologists have also found beautiful jewelry, pottery, and furniture in the pharaohs' tombs.

Egyptian pectoral jewelry, such as this "Sacred Animals of Thot" pectoral, was worn on the wearer's chest.

There were strict rules for Egyptian artists to follow. One rule was that important people had to be the largest figures in a piece of art. For example, a pharaoh would appear larger than a lesser god. Another rule said that figures in paintings and sculpture should be facing forward. However, the arms and legs of a figure should be turned to the side so they would be easier to see. The style of art in Egypt stayed this way for thousands of years.

Egyptian figures such as this one of the goddess, Isus, and her child, Horus, show that Egyptians were talented artisans.

---

2 Teaching the Lesson

Students may not be familiar with what a papyrus plant looks like, or even with what a reed is. If possible, find pictures on the Internet of a papyrus plant and print them out to share with the class.

Ask:

- Which invention from the Egyptians do you use in school every day? (paper)

- What clue tells us that the Egyptians were interested in medicine? (They wrote about it in a scroll.)

- Describe the system of measurement developed by the Egyptians. (The system involved cubits. A cubit was the distance from the end of the middle finger to the elbow.)

- What were the rules for artwork that the Egyptian artists had to follow? (Important people had to be the largest figures in a piece of art. Figures in paintings and sculptures should face forward, but the arms and legs should be turned to the side.)

ELL/ESL STRATEGY

Language Objective:
To read for meaning

Divide the class into pairs. Have students reread the section of the lesson that is about artwork. Ask students to make a numbered list of the rules for Egyptian artists. Stress that each rule should be written as a complete sentence. Have students read their sentences to another pair of students, and have all four students work together to make corrections as needed.

Then have each student pair create a drawing that follows the rules established for Egyptian artists. Have pairs share their drawings with the class and explain how their drawing follows the artistic rules.

LEARNING STYLES

Logical/Mathematical

Have students work in groups to design a cubit stick to use as a measuring tool. They can use their own forearm and hand as a standard for the cubit. The cubit stick should be long enough to measure three or four cubits with each cubit divided in halves, thirds, or fourths. Students can measure their classmates and inform them of their height in cubits. Point out to students that cubits will be slightly different among people because the length from the middle finger to the elbow is different for each person.

3 Reinforce and Extend

IN THE COMMUNITY

As a way to compare the complexity of today's society with that of the Egyptians, have students look up physicians in a local telephone book. Have them count the number of listings. Then have students list the different types of physicians and look up what these types of doctors do. Students might want to present a skit with a partner, one playing an ancient Egyptian brought forward in a time machine to the present and the other a modern person explaining where the ancient Egyptian could call for medical help, depending on the medical complaint.

Lesson 5 Review Answers

1. papyrus **2.** statues **3.** scroll
4. drawings **5.** geometry

Answers will vary. Students may say that a cubit is really not a standard unit of measurement because one person's forearm may be smaller than another person's. The dimensions could be off in measuring things. However, most people do have a forearm to measure with, making measurement easy and convenient.

Ask students if they have heard of a sundial, and show pictures of sundials. Explain that a sundial was used long ago to measure the passage of time throughout a day. Different cultures use different calendars to measure the months in a year today, but every culture agrees that there are 24 hours in a day.

Word Bank

drawings
geometry
papyrus
scroll
statues

Lesson 5 Review On a sheet of paper, use the words from the Word Bank to complete each sentence correctly.

1. The Egyptians made paper from a reed called _____.

2. The Egyptians built tall _____, temples, and pyramids.

3. An ancient _____ describes the Egyptians' interest in medicine.

4. The Egyptians decorated their temples with _____.

5. The Egyptians used _____ to survey their land.

What do you think

What is good and what is bad about measuring something in cubits?

The First Solar Calendar

Ancient Egyptians carefully watched the regular rise and fall of the Nile River. It stood for the cycle of birth and death. It also gave people a way to measure time. Egyptians discovered that the time between floods averaged about 365 days. So, nearly 5,000 years ago, they developed a calendar. It had 12 months, each 30 days long. An extra five days were added at the end of the year as holidays. This calendar was almost perfectly in tune with the solar year. That's the time it takes the earth to circle the sun—365 1/4 days. Today's calendar is a solar calendar, too. It has 12 months and 365 days, except in leap year.

Chapter Project Follow-up

Have students present their pyramid models to the class. Students should give details about how the pyramids were built by the Egyptians. They should explain why the pyramid they chose was originally built. Each group should also talk about how historians have used the information obtained from their pyramid to learn about Egyptian history.

Opening King Tut's Tomb

Tutankhamen was eight when he became pharaoh of Egypt. He ruled for about 11 years. Then he died suddenly about 1352 B.C. For thousands of years, his tomb was lost. Grave robbers broke in, but they never reached the main room. As a result, this tomb kept almost all its original contents. It is the only pharaoh's tomb ever found in this condition.

"King Tut" was not a powerful ruler, but he is famous today. The reason is the discovery of his tomb in 1922 by British archaeologist Howard Carter. This is Carter's retelling of the event.

The gold mask of Tutankhamen.

The day following (November 26th) was the day of days, the most wonderful that I have ever lived through. . . . In the middle of the afternoon, 30 feet down from the outer door, we came upon a second sealed doorway. . . .

With trembling hands I made a tiny breach in the upper left-hand corner. Darkness and blank space . . . showed that whatever lay beyond was empty. . . . Widening the hole a little, I inserted the candle and peered in. . . . As my eyes grew accustomed to the light, details of the room within emerged slowly from the mist, strange animals, statues, and gold—everywhere the glint of gold.

For the moment . . . I was struck dumb with amazement. When Lord Carnarvon, unable to stand the suspense any longer, inquired anxiously, "Can you see anything?"

it was all I could do to get out the words, "Yes, wonderful things!"

Gradually the scene grew clearer, and we could pick out individual objects. First, right opposite to us . . . were three great gilt couches, their sides carved in the form of monstrous animals. . . . Next . . . two statues caught and held our attention: two life-sized figures of a king in black, facing each other like sentinels. . . .

These were the dominant objects that caught the eye at first. Between them, around them, piled on top of them, there were countless others—exquisitely painted and inlaid caskets; alabaster vases, some beautifully carved . . . a golden inlaid throne; . . . on the left a confused pile of overturned chariots, glistening with gold and inlay; and peeping from behind them another portrait of a king.

Document-Based Questions

1. Why was the discovery of this tomb important to historians?

2. Is this reading a primary source or a secondary source? Why?

3. What did Carter see all around after he got used to the darkness?

4. How did Carter answer Lord Carnarvon?

5. List three things found in the tomb.

Source: The Tomb of Tut-Ankh-Amen, *by Howard Carter.*

After several years of searching for Tutankhamen's tomb, Howard Carter came very close to giving up the hunt. His sponsors were running out of patience, and Carter ran out of money. He pleaded for his sponsors to pay for one more season of searching. Within days of starting, he found the tomb. Many of the treasures found in Tutankhamen's tomb have been displayed for all to see at museums around the world.

To read this document, you may wish to have students read aloud. Encourage volunteers to each read a paragraph. Provide assistance with unfamiliar words as needed. Encourage students who are reading Howard Carter's retelling to imagine his excitement about his discovery and read with expression.

Answers to Document-Based Questions:

1. Answers will vary. Students may say that since the tomb was almost completely intact, it showed what a royal tomb was really like. The contents could tell a lot about ancient Egypt.

2. This reading is a primary source because Carter is telling what happened when he found the tomb.

3. He saw the glint of gold.

4. Carter said, "Yes, wonderful things!"

5. In the tomb, there were carved gilt couches, life-sized statues of kings, painted and inlaid caskets, alabaster vases, beds, carved chairs, a golden inlaid throne, chariots, and a portrait of a king.

LEARNING STYLES

Auditory/Verbal
Have students read Carter's account into an audio recorder. While students shut their eyes, play back the audio so they can listen to the words and visualize what Carter says he saw. Then play the audio again and have students read along as they listen.

Explain that most people have rituals for burying the dead and that today that practice often includes embalming or chemical preparation of the body for burial. Many of the rituals for burial are related to the religious beliefs of the relatives of the person who has died. Have a volunteer read the title, "Burying the Dead." Call attention to the photo and read the caption. Then ask students to say what they think of when they hear the word *mummy*. (Students may mention Egyptian pharaohs or horror movies.) Ask students to complete the reading with a partner and answer the questions.

Answers to Spotlight Story Wrap-Up:

1. They thought the pharaoh was the human form of a god.

2. They thought that there was an afterlife much like life on Earth.

3. If a person's body decayed, a person could not enjoy the afterlife.

4. The dead person would need them in the afterlife.

5. They can learn about the lives and health of ancient Egyptians.

Burying the Dead

The people of ancient Egypt saw their pharaohs as god-kings. They believed that each pharaoh was the human form of a god. Egyptians also believed in an afterlife. It was much like life on earth. After death, a pharaoh would continue to rule in the next life.

The Egyptians believed that a dead person's body must not decay. Otherwise a person could not enjoy the afterlife. To protect the body, Egyptians used a process called embalming.

Embalming took time. First, the embalmers removed all the internal organs. The heart and other important organs were put in small jars. These are called canopic jars. Then the body was put in a pine box. It was covered with a salty liquid called natron. The natron removed most of the water in the body, making it shrink. That took about 70 days. Then the body was wrapped with bandages of wax-covered cloth. The wrapped body was now a mummy. It was placed in a decorated coffin and put in a tomb.

The tombs of the pharaohs were meant to last forever. They were decorated like a palace. The tombs were filled with things the dead might need in the next life. That would include food, furniture, jewels, and cosmetics. A ruler needed servants, too. Early in Egypt's history, servants were buried with the ruler. They were probably smothered or given poison. The pharaoh Djer ruled Egypt around 2900 B.C. When he died, about 580 members of the court may have been buried with him. Later, Egyptians buried small pottery figures in tombs to act as servants, instead of killing actual servants.

Mummies were prepared with great care. This one is an Egyptian priestess from about 100 B.C., with the original wood coffin.

Ancient embalmers were very skillful. Thousands of years later, many mummies are well preserved. You can see some in museums. Today scientists are also interested in mummies. They examine their bones, hair, and other parts. Research on mummies can discover much about the lives and health of ancient Egyptians.

Wrap-Up

1. What did the ancient Egyptians think of their pharaoh?

2. What did the Egyptians believe happened after death?

3. Why did the Egyptians not want the body to decay?

4. Why were things like food and furniture placed in a tomb?

5. What can scientists learn from mummies?

Chapter 4 SUMMARY

- Egyptian civilization developed in the valley of the Nile River. The river runs north from central Africa. The Nile's yearly floods made the soil rich. Farmers could grow many crops in a year. The river was also a good route for trade.

- Upper Egypt, in the south, was unified by about 3400 B.C. Stories say that Menes, a god-king, conquered Lower Egypt about 3100 B.C. He unified Upper and Lower Egypt. The symbol for this new Egypt was the double crown. Its capital was Memphis. His rule began Egypt's first dynasty.

- The Old Kingdom in Egypt began about 3100 B.C. The rulers were called pharaohs. They were all-powerful. People believed they were gods. Trade became important.

- Egyptians believed in an afterlife that was much like life on earth. Pharaohs built pyramids for tombs. People filled them with things the ruler would need in the afterlife.

- The pharaohs lost power. Then civil war broke out. The economy collapsed. As a result, the Old Kingdom ended about 2100 B.C.

- Egypt was reunited about 2040 B.C. The Middle Kingdom began. Its capital was at Thebes. The pharaohs had less power than in the Old Kingdom.

- Beliefs about the afterlife changed in the Middle Kingdom. Pharaohs were buried in tombs cut into cliffs. Ordinary people could share the afterlife.

- Egyptians had many gods. Ra was the sun-god. Hapi was the river god.

- The Hyksos from Asia ended the Middle Kingdom about 1630 B.C. They had iron weapons and metal armor. They ruled until 1570 B.C.

- The New Kingdom began about 1600 B.C. Egypt took over more land. Hatshepsut, the first woman pharaoh, encouraged trade. Thutmose III made the empire much larger.

- The pharaoh Amonhotep IV tried to change Egypt's religion. He believed in only one god. The fight over religion that followed made Egypt weak. Other peoples invaded it. Persia ruled Egypt until 332 B.C.

- The ancient Egyptians made paper from the papyrus reed.

- Egyptian doctors were skillful. They knew how to set broken bones and deal with fevers.

- Egyptian artists carved huge statues. They created jewelry, pottery, and artwork. They invented a counting system based on 10. They used geometry.

3100 B.C. – 30 B.C.

Egypt—The Gift of the Nile Chapter 4 **85**

Using the Chapter Summary

Have students read the Chapter Summary on page 85 to review the main ideas presented in Chapter 4.

Ask:

- How did the Nile River make it possible for civilization to flourish along its banks? (It allowed farmers to grow many crops during a year, allowing them to feed a great many people.)

- Who were two of the gods of the Egyptians? (the sun-god Ra and the river god Hapi)

- When was Upper Egypt unified? (3400 B.C.) Upper and Lower Egypt? (3100 B.C.)

- Why did the pharaohs command the respect and loyalty of all the Egyptians? (Egyptians thought the pharaohs were gods.)

- What did Egyptians believe about the afterlife? (It would be much like life on Earth. They filled the pharaohs' tombs with things that would be needed in the afterlife.)

- What caused the downfall of the Old Kingdom? (Pharaohs lost power; there was civil war.)

- When Egypt was reunited in the Middle Kingdom, where was the capital? (Thebes)

- What caused the downfall of the Middle Kingdom? (the Hyksos invaded)

- During which kingdom did the first female pharaoh rule? (New Kingdom)

- What change did Ikhnaton try to make in the Egyptian religion? (He wanted worship of only one god.)

- What were some of the accomplishments of the ancient Egyptians? (invented paper; doctors practiced medicine; created statues and other forms of art, for example, jewelry; created a number system)

Chapter 4 Review

Use the Chapter Review to prepare students for tests and to reteach content from the chapter.

Chapter 4 Mastery Test

The Teacher's Resource Library includes two forms of the Chapter 4 Mastery Test. Each test addresses the chapter Goals for Learning. An optional third page of additional critical-thinking items is included for each test. The difficulty level of the two forms is equivalent.

Chapter 4 Review Answers

1. papyrus
2. mummy
3. hieroglyphics
4. pharaoh
5. Menes
6. Ra
7. Hatshepsut
8. Thutmose III
9. Ramses III
10. Ikhnaton
11. C
12. A
13. B
14. D
15. D
16. The flooding of the Nile each year made rich farmland. Also, the Nile was a "highway" on which traders, government officials, and the pharaoh could travel and keep the country united.

Word Bank

Hatshepsut
hieroglyphics
Ikhnaton
Menes
mummy
papyrus
pharaoh
Ra
Ramses III
Thutmose III

On a sheet of paper, use the words from the Word Bank to complete each sentence correctly.

1. The reed from which the Egyptians made paper is _____.

2. The Egyptians made a _____ by wrapping a dead body in cloth strips to keep it from decaying.

3. The Egyptians used _____, which is a kind of picture writing.

4. The Egyptians called their king or ruler a _____.

5. _____ was the god-king who unified Upper and Lower Egypt and began the Old Kingdom.

6. _____ was the Egyptian sun-god.

7. _____ was the first woman pharaoh.

8. _____ was the pharaoh who enlarged the Egyptian empire to its greatest size.

9. _____ was the last great ruler of Egypt.

10. The Egyptian pharaoh _____ believed in only one god.

On a sheet of paper, write the letter of the answer that correctly completes each sentence.

11. Upper Egypt was the _____ part of Egypt.

   A northern   C southern
   B eastern   D western

12. Lower Egypt was the _____ part of Egypt.

   A northern   C southern
   B eastern   D western

13. The Egyptians thought their rulers were _____.

   A children   C wind
   B gods   D sun

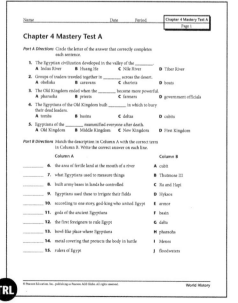

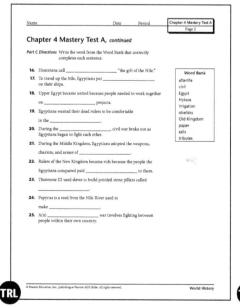

Chapter 4 Mastery Test A, pages 1–3

14. Building a pyramid took about _____ years.

A 3   **C** 13

B 7   **D** 20

15. The _____ invaded Egypt in 1630 B.C.

A Persians   **C** Assyrians

B Babylonians   **D** Hyksos

On a sheet of paper, write the answer to each question. Use complete sentences.

16. Why was the Nile River so important to the Egyptians?

17. How did the three kingdoms of Egypt differ?

18. Why were the Hyksos and later invaders able to defeat the Egyptians?

Critical Thinking On a sheet of paper, write your response to each question. Use complete sentences.

19. The Egyptians buried treasures with pharaohs when they died. We learn about the Egyptian society from this treasure. Think of things that would tell other people about our society. What five things from our society would you choose to put in your tomb? Explain your choices.

20. What gift from the ancient Egyptians do you think is best? Why do you think so?

Organize a study group to study a subject. Each person can share his or her notes on a different part of the subject.

3100 B.C. – 30 B.C.

17. In the Old Kingdom, the pharaoh had complete power and the people built pyramids in which to bury him. Only he would enjoy an afterlife. Also, Memphis was the capital and the people worshipped many gods. In the Middle Kingdom, the pharaoh had less power, all people were to enjoy an afterlife, and the pharaohs were buried in cliff tombs. Also, Thebes was the capital. In the New Kingdom, the pharaohs once again had total power as in the Old Kingdom. Their capital was Thebes as it had been in the Middle Kingdom. The building projects were temples, palaces, and statues instead of the pyramids of the Old Kingdom.

18. Sometimes the Egyptians did not have the weaponry of war. At other times, the pharaoh, nobles, and priests were involved in a struggle for power. This kept them from taking care of the needs of Egypt.

Critical Thinking

19. Answers will vary. Students may say that many things represent our society today—computers, video games, credit cards, cars and car keys, televisions, mp3 players, cell phones, plastic objects, human-made fibers and fabrics.

20. Answers will vary. Students may mention things such as paper, medicine, math, and art that the Egyptians have left us.

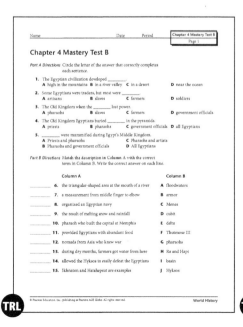

Chapter 4 Mastery Test B, pages 1–3

Chapter 5:
Ancient India and China, 6000 B.C.–A.D. 220

pages 88–115

Teacher's Resource Library **TRL**

Introducing the Chapter

As early as 6000 B.C., great civilizations
grew in India and China. Before students
begin reading this chapter, have the class
brainstorm a list of everything that comes

---

5 Ancient India and China

Thousands of years ago, civilization developed in India
and China. In India, villages grew into cities in the Indus
River Valley. In China, small towns grew large in the Yangtze
River and the Huang He Valleys. In this chapter, you will learn
that ancient people in India planned their two large cities and
that the Chinese people became great builders and artisans.
You will also learn about Hinduism and Buddhism, two
religions that developed.

Goals for Learning

◆ To explain the importance of geography in the history
of civilization

◆ To describe India's first civilization

◆ To describe Hinduism and castes

◆ To compare Hinduism and Buddhism and describe the
four noble truths of Buddhism.

◆ To explain two wonders of ancient China

◆ To describe the Shang, Qin, and Han dynasties

6000 B.C. Farming begins along Huang He in China

1600 B.C. Shang dynasty begins in China

563 B.C. Buddha is born

202 B.C. Han dynasty begins

6000 B.C.   **4000 B.C.**   **2000 B.C.**   **1 B.C.**

3700 B.C. Farming begins in Indus River Valley in India

1122 B.C. Zhou dynasty begins

221 B.C. Qin dynasty begins

A.D. 220 Han dynasty ends

to mind when they think of India and
China. Write the following categories
on the board: *Geography, Culture and
History, Government.* Ask students to
provide ideas for what can be placed
under each category. Have students copy
the categories into their notebooks and
add information as they read the chapter.

Ask:

• What geographical feature was
needed to begin farming in China
and India? (rivers)

• When did the Shang dynasty
begin? (1600 B.C.)

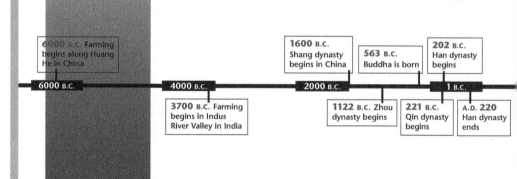

TRL

Ask a volunteer to read the title of the map. Have students identify the countries shown on the map. Then have students silently read the paragraph under the map.

Ask:

- **What body of water is east of India?** (Bay of Bengal)
- **What is the name of the mountain range in the southwest part of China?** (Himalaya Mountains)
- **What ocean is east of China?** (Pacific Ocean)

Have students read and write answers to the questions.

Map Skills Answers

1. Gobi Desert
2. the Yangtze River and the Huang He
3. the Indus River or the Ganges River
4. China
5. Students may respond that the mountains have isolated China from the cultures of the West.

Civilization began thousands of years ago along the river valleys of Asia. Geography, or the land and the weather, was important in the history of India and China. Both countries are large. Mountains cut them off from other countries. The people get water from the rivers and use them for travel.

Study the map, then answer the following questions:

1. Name the large desert in Mongolia.
2. Name two rivers in China.
3. Name one river in India.
4. What country is directly south of Mongolia?
5. Mountains separate China from the West. How do you think this has affected China's history?

Have students identify the Huang He and Indus River Valley, noted on the timeline on page 88 and the map on page 89. Have them make a general statement about the spread of civilizations in the East.

Chapter Project

Divide the class into two. One group will study Sanskrit. One group will study Chinese characters. Ask students to research the historical context of when the writing was invented, create a visual presentation, and prepare a written or oral report.

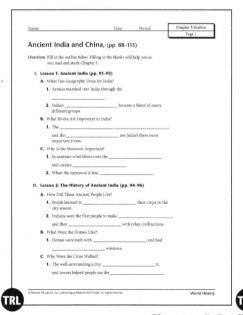

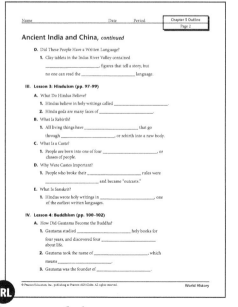

Chapter 5 Outline, pages 1–4

Visualizing

Introduce the reading strategy of visualizing. Draw students' attention to the definition. Tell students that visualizing helps readers remember what they read by creating pictures in their mind about the topic.

Explain that students should also use drawings, maps, and photographs to help them visualize what is described in the text. Encourage students to pay close attention to the graphics in the chapter to further their understanding of the ancient civilizations in India and China.

Ask:

• How can looking at maps help you understand how the geography affected ancient civilizations? (There were physical advantages, such as locations of rivers, and disadvantages, such as proximity of mountains or deserts, that influenced development of civilizations.)

Point out to students that visualizing as they read helps them understand how and where the people of ancient India and China lived.

Key Vocabulary Words

Point out that these chapter words are presented in the order they appear in each lesson. They are also found in the Glossary. Point out particular words, such as *peninsula, irrigate, canal, invade,* or *symbol.* Have students read the definition, visualize the term, and explain what the word means to them.

Ask:

• When you think of the word *irrigate* what pictures come to mind? (farming, crops growing, water running between rows)

• How can visualizing help you remember what these terms mean? (Answers will vary. Creating a picture in my mind gives detail to the term.)

Reading Strategy:
Visualizing

Visualizing is another strategy that helps readers understand what they are reading. It is like creating a movie in your mind. Use the following ways to visualize a text:

◆ Look at the photographs, illustrations, and descriptive words.

◆ Think about experiences in your own life that may add to the images.

◆ Notice the order in which things are happening and what you think might happen next.

Key Vocabulary Words

Lesson 1
Geography The science that deals with land, weather, bodies of water, and plant and animal life

Peninsula A piece of land surrounded on three sides by water

Subcontinent A large landmass that is somewhat smaller than a continent

Monsoon A seasonal wind

Lesson 2
Irrigate To bring water to crops

Pictogram A figure that tells a story

Lesson 3
Hinduism The main religion of India, which stresses the belief in the Vedas

Reincarnation The rebirth of the soul into a new body

Cycle The events that keep happening, one after another

Caste A class of people in India

Lesson 4
Buddha A name meaning the "Enlightened One"; the name given to Siddhartha Gautama, the founder of Buddhism

Enlightened Knowing the truth

Desire To wish for something

Nirvana A condition of complete emptiness in which a person's soul finds perfect peace

Soul A person's spirit

Lesson 5
Isolate To keep apart or away from others

Plateau A flat area that rises above the land close by

Canal A waterway made by humans

Invade To attack or march into another country

Lesson 6
Dynasty A family that rules a country over a long period of time

Noble A person of high birth

Artisan A person who makes beautiful objects for everyday use

Symbol Something that stands for something else

Scribe A person from ancient times who could read and write

Society A group of people whose members live together for the good of all

90   *Unit 1   Early Civilizations*

Lesson 1 — Ancient India

The civilization of India is one of the oldest in the world. **Geography**—land, weather, bodies of water, plant and animal life—shapes all civilizations. India has a very interesting geography. It is a **peninsula** surrounded on three sides by water. India is often called a **subcontinent** because it is so large. From north to south, India extends about 2,000 miles. It has the world's highest mountains, called the Himalayas. The Ganges and Indus are two great rivers. Great seasonal winds called monsoons are very important to life in India.

What Has Geography Done for India?

Most of the time, geography has protected India. However, many armies have marched into India over the past 4,000 years. These armies reached India through passes, or openings, in the mountains. The best known passage into India is the Khyber Pass.

The people who came through these passes changed India's history. Each group brought new ideas. The newcomers sometimes married the people who had come before. Indian culture became a blend of many different groups.

What Rivers Are Important to India?

The Indian subcontinent has many rivers. The three most important are the Ganges, the Brahmaputra, and the Indus Rivers. The Ganges River is so important to the Indians that they call it "Mother Ganges."

Objectives

◆ To describe why ancient towns formed along river valleys
◆ To describe the climate of India

Geography
The science that deals with land, weather, bodies of water, and plant and animal life

Peninsula
A piece of land surrounded on three sides by water

Subcontinent
A large landmass that is somewhat smaller than a continent

Chapter 5: Lesson 1

Overview This lesson describes the significant role geography has played in the development of civilization in India.

Objectives

■ To describe why ancient towns formed along river valleys
■ To describe the climate of India

Student Pages pages 91–93

Teacher's Resource Library TRL

Workbook Activity 16

Activity 16

Modified Activity 16

Vocabulary

geography	peninsula
monsoon	subcontinent

On a sheet of graph paper, have students create a crossword puzzle using these four vocabulary words. Encourage students to invent clues that are not simply copied directly from the text. Have students exchange puzzles.

PRONUNCIATION GUIDE

Use this list to help students pronounce difficult words in this lesson.

Himalayas	(him´ ə lā´ əz)
Hindu Kush	(hin´ dü kush´)
Khyber	(kī´ bər)
Ganges	(gan´ jēz)
Indus	(in´ dəs)

1   Warm-Up Activity

Help students identify the Himalayas and the Hindu Kush mountain ranges on a map. Have students search the library or Internet for images of the Khyber Pass. Discuss its physical features and location, and ask students to speculate on the advantages of a pass in a mountain range. Ask students to visualize the difficulty people may have had in moving through the Khyber Pass.

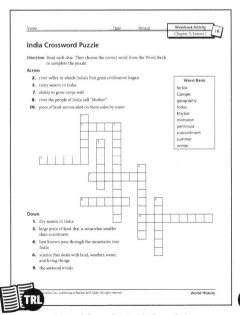

Workbook Activity 16

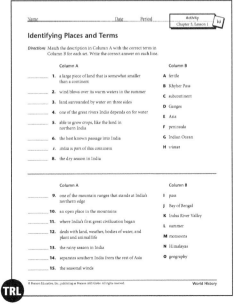

Activity 16

2 Teaching the Lesson

Have students read pages 91–93 to learn about India's geography.

Ask:

- **Why is India called a subcontinent?** (It is a large piece of land, but not as large as a continent.)

- **How did armies make it through the mountains?** (They marched through low points, or passes.)

- **How much of India's yearly rain comes from the monsoon?** (90 percent)

- **What are India's two seasons like?** (Summer is rainy; winter is dry.)

Reading Strategy:
Visualizing

(Words include winds, land, rain falls, monsoons, hot, freezing)

- **What do you think of when you read the word *monsoons*?** (wind, large amount of rain, flooding)

- **What picture comes to mind when you think of the word *freezing*?** (snow, ice, people wearing heavy coats)

Review with students the three continents shown on this map. Then have them answer the questions in the caption. (The Nile civilization is farthest west; the Huang He civilization is farthest east; none of them were in Europe; civilizations began on any two of the following rivers: Nile, Tigris, Euphrates, Indus, or Huang He.)

Writing About History

Before students begin writing, have them brainstorm a list of all the geographical features in their area. In addition to landforms and bodies of water, have students consider the climate and the types of plants and animals native to your area. What is the temperature like? How much rain or snow falls? Does the weather change or stay the same? Next, ask them to write one way in which each geographical feature has affected how people live. Once their lists are complete, students may begin writing their essays.

Writing About History

Geography influenced ancient India and China. What is the land like where you live? In your notebook, write an essay. Tell how rivers, mountains, or other features have affected the way people live in your area.

Monsoon
A seasonal wind

Reading Strategy:
Visualizing

What words in this paragraph help you visualize the geography of India?

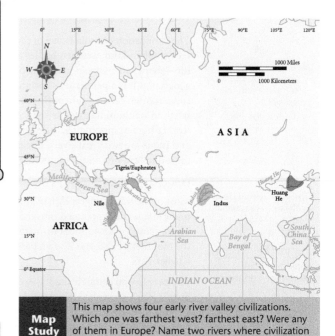

Map Study This map shows four early river valley civilizations. Which one was farthest west? farthest east? Were any of them in Europe? Name two rivers where civilization began.

Why Is the Monsoon Important?

Life in India depends on seasonal winds called **monsoons.** In the summer, wind blows over the warm waters of the Indian Ocean. When this air reaches land, rain falls. Sometimes rain pours down for weeks. In fact, 90 percent of India's yearly rain comes from the summer monsoon. Sometimes the monsoon is late or little rain falls. Then crops fail, and many people go hungry.

India is hot most of the year. The temperature usually stays above freezing. Its two seasons depend on the rain. Summer is the rainy season; winter is the dry season.

Word Bank

geography

Indus

Khyber Pass

monsoon

subcontinent

Lesson 1 Review On a sheet of paper, use the words from the Word Bank to complete each sentence correctly.

1. We sometimes call India a _____.

2. Two important rivers in India are the Ganges and the _____.

3. A _____ is a seasonal wind that brings rain to India.

4. Armies marched into India through the _____.

5. _____ is the study of how land, bodies of water, weather, plants, and animals change people's lives.

In what ways has its geography helped or hurt the people of India?

The Indus River is an important river in India.

6000 B.C. – A.D. 220   *Ancient India and China   Chapter 5*   **93**

Lesson 1 Review Answers

1. subcontinent **2.** Indus **3.** monsoon
4. Khyber Pass **5.** geography

Answers will vary. Students may say that the mountains probably kept out invaders for centuries. The rivers helped civilizations grow.

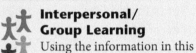

Ancient India and China   Chapter 5   **93**

Chapter 5: Lesson 2

Overview This lesson describes India's first civilization, known for its achievements in city planning, farming, trading, and written language. Mysteriously, this ancient civilization came to a sudden end for reasons that still baffle historians.

Objectives

- To describe the farming, art, homes, and writing of the civilization
- To explain possible reasons why this civilization suddenly ended

Student Pages pages 94–96

Teacher's Resource Library **TRL**

Workbook Activity 17

Activity 17

Modified Activity 17

Vocabulary

irrigate   **pictogram**

Have volunteers take turns reading the words and their definitions. Then challenge all students to write original sentences that correctly use each word. Ask volunteers to share their sentences with the class.

PRONUNCIATION GUIDE

Use this list to help students pronounce difficult words in this lesson.

Harappa   (hə rap′ ə)

Mohenjo-Daro   (mō hen′ jō där′ ō)

1 Warm-Up Activity

Ask students to describe, and if possible draw, the icons, or picture symbols used on computers and in the business world. Discuss how each small icon or visual carries a meaning. Direct students' attention to the pictograms on page 95. Explain that these pictograms also had specific meaning to the people of ancient India, although archeologists are not

Objectives

- To describe the farming, art, homes, and writing of the civilization
- To explain possible reasons why this civilization suddenly ended

Irrigate

To bring water to crops

Reading Strategy: Visualizing

How could this paragraph be written differently to create a stronger picture of these homes in your mind?

India's first civilization developed in the Indus River Valley. This river begins in the Himalayas. When the snow melts, the river floods. Later, the water retreats and leaves silt, or a rich layer of soil, behind. Because this silt makes the soil fertile, people settled along the Indus River.

Two cities, Harappa and Mohenjo-Daro, looked like modern, planned cities. Their streets were wide and straight. The people built with clay bricks, which were all exactly the same.

How Did These Ancient People Live?

The people of the Indus River Valley raised grains and vegetables in their rich soil. They learned how to **irrigate,** or bring water to, their fields during the dry season.

The farmers grew enough food to feed everyone. Because of this, the city people could make pottery, cloth, jewelry, and metal tools. How do we know? Because archaeologists have dug up beautifully painted pottery, stone carvings, and gold and silver jewelry. We also know that Indians made the first cotton cloth.

Archaeologists have also found things from faraway in the ruins of ancient India. This early civilization traded goods with other civilizations.

What Were the Homes Like?

In the cities, people's homes were sometimes two stories high. Most had a patio, or rooms open to the sky. Stairs led up to the roof. The people built alabaster windows. This marblelike stone allowed light to shine through. Some homes had indoor bathrooms and toilets. Dirty water drained away through clay pipes.

sure what they mean. Have each student design a pictogram that tells something about him or her. Share and discuss their pictograms.

2 Teaching the Lesson

As students read this lesson, have them create a list of all the natural resources the Indus Valley civilization used to lead comfortable and prosperous lives. (Answers include silt, clay, alabaster, metals, and cotton.)

Ask:

- What is silt and why did it cause people to settle in the Indus River Valley? (rich dirt; It helped people grow crops.)

- How do we know that the Indus River Valley cities had strong governments? (Everything was alike, such as bricks and buildings.)

- What are four possible reasons why this civilization ended? (Possible answers: trading became difficult, the monsoons failed, natural disasters struck, and disease wiped them out, farmers could not grow enough crops, or armies invaded)

Why Were the Cities Walled?

A great wall surrounded each city and protected it. Towers were built into the walls. From these towers, people could see any enemy. In the center of the city was another walled area. Behind the wall stood a fort, a place to store food, and a large bath. The people may have used this area as a place to honor their gods.

Did These People Have a Written Language?

Archaeologists have discovered many clay tablets in the Indus River Valley. On them are **pictograms**—figures that tell a story. They have also found hundreds of small carved markers. Did business people use these to stamp the things they sold? We do not know because at this time no one can read the Harappan language.

What Caused This Ancient Civilization to End?

About 1500 B.C. this civilization suddenly ended. Perhaps the coastline changed so trading became harder. Maybe the monsoon failed. Maybe disease, an earthquake, or a flood struck. Perhaps farmers could no longer grow enough food. Or maybe armies from central Asia invaded.

It is not known what these pictograms mean. No one can read the writing of the Indus Valley civilization.

ELL/ESL STRATEGY

Language Objective:
To classify vocabulary relative to different aspects of daily life

Have ELL students make a booklet of words using the following categories: *Farming, Inside the Home, Architecture, Business,* and *City Life*. Have students use words from the lesson and their own knowledge to make a word bank for each category. Each word bank should have words and a drawing or photo related to each word. For example, a word bank for the business category might have words and photos of different kinds of stores, such as grocery store, clothing store, computer shop, coffee shop, etc. Encourage students to add a sentence for each word and accompanying image.

LEARNING STYLES

Visual/Spatial

As an extra challenge, invite interested students to create a "pocket travel guide." The purpose of the guide is to persuade tourists to visit Harappa and Mohenjo-Daro on their next vacation. Encourage students to include plenty of pictures with captions. Remind students that this is not a report. Instead, it is a visual presentation intended to convince people of the beauty and attractions of these ancient Indian cities.

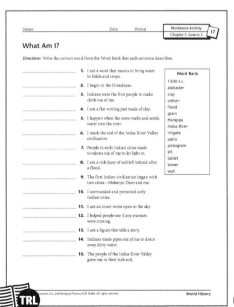

Workbook Activity 17　　　　　　**Activity 17**

Some students may have difficulty understanding how to use a map key. Help them to understand that the shaded area represents the Indus Valley civilization and the arrows represent the movements of Aryan invaders. Then have students study the map and answer the questions in the caption. (The map covers from about 2500 B.C. to 1500 B.C. Armies invaded through the Khyber Pass and the Bolan Pass. Both passes are in the Hindu Kush Mountains. The Himalaya Mountains are to the east of the Indus River Valley civilization.)

3 Reinforce and Extend

AT HOME

The pottery, carvings, and jewelry that archaeologists have dug up in the Indus River Valley are called artifacts. Artifacts are objects that tell us how people lived. Have students collect a set of artifacts from their homes that historians in the future would study to find out about American life in the early 21st century. Students might wish to put them in a shoe box and label it with the date and place where they live. Have students explain to the class why they included certain artifacts. Remind students that it is probably not a good idea to bring valuable items to school.

Lesson 2 Review Answers
1. Indus **2.** silt **3.** Harappa
4. alabaster **5.** pictograms

Answers will vary. Students may say that the cities seem planned because they have certain areas set aside for business and living. Also, the streets are straight.

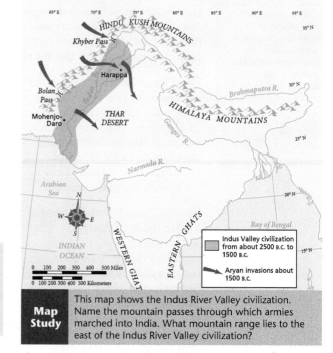

What do you think

Why do you think we call Harappa and Mohenjo-Daro "planned cities"?

Word Bank
alabaster
Harappa
Indus
pictograms
silt

Map Study This map shows the Indus River Valley civilization. Name the mountain passes through which armies marched into India. What mountain range lies to the east of the Indus River Valley civilization?

Lesson 2 Review On a sheet of paper, use the words from the Word Bank to complete each sentence correctly.

1. The first civilization in India grew up along the _____ River Valley.

2. This happened because of the rich _____ that the spring floods left behind in the valley.

3. The two great cities of this civilization were _____ and Mohenjo-Daro.

4. People in these cities built _____ windows to let in light.

5. In this valley, archaeologists have discovered clay pads with _____, or pictures, on them.

Objectives

♦ To identify the major features of Hinduism

♦ To understand the importance of Sanskrit to India

♦ To explain the purpose of castes

Hinduism

The main religion of India that stresses the belief in the Vedas

Reincarnation

The rebirth of the soul into a new body

Cycle

The events that keep happening, one after another

Reading Strategy:
Visualizing

What words in this paragraph help you understand what you are reading?

For the next 500 years, people fought wars in the Indus River Valley. Many soldiers wandered into India. They fought with each other and with the people who came before them. Over hundreds of years, these people married one another. Eventually, they developed a new set of beliefs and practices called **Hinduism.** Hinduism is the main religion of modern India.

What Do Hindus Believe?

The Hindus, or the people who practice Hinduism, believe that everything is God, or Brahman. The Vedas, their holy writings, explain "Brahman is one, and yet expresses itself as many." The word *Vedas* means "books of knowledge." Hindus believe that Brahman, Vishnu, and Shiva are different faces of God. Brahma creates, or makes, life. Vishnu preserves life, and Shiva destroys it. Hindus believe that these three faces express the main powers of God.

The Hindu god Vishnu preserves life.

What Is Rebirth?

Hindus believe that all living things—weeds, water, insects, animals, and people—have souls. Hindus believe in **reincarnation,** or the rebirth of the soul into a new body. The **cycle** of birth, death, and rebirth keeps happening until a soul becomes perfect. Then the cycle ends, and a soul becomes one with Brahman. Hindus do not kill animals. They believe that cows are especially holy.

Overview This lesson describes the Vedas, the beliefs and practices of Hinduism, and the origins and importance of Sanskrit.

Objectives

■ To identify the major features of Hinduism

■ To understand the importance of Sanskrit to India

■ To explain the purpose of castes

Student Pages pages 97–99

Teacher's Resource Library TRL

Workbook Activity 18

Activity 18

Modified Activity 18

Vocabulary

caste	**Hinduism**
cycle	**reincarnation**

Have students write each word and its definition on the top half of a sheet of paper. On the bottom half, students should write original sentences with the correct use of each word. Invite volunteers to share their sentences.

PRONUNCIATION GUIDE

Use this list to help students pronounce difficult words in this lesson.

Shiva	(shē´ və)
Vedas	(vā´ dəz)
Vishnu	(vish´ nü)

1 **Warm-Up Activity**

Have students discuss the different social groups in American society. Discuss how economic opportunity and education play important roles in determining an individual's social group. Lead a discussion on how individual choice also plays a role. Explain that religion played a major role in determining social groups in ancient civilizations.

Workbook Activity 18

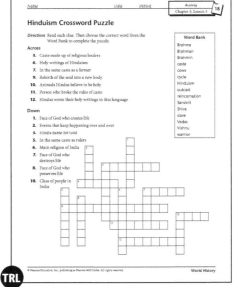

Activity 18

2 Teaching the Lesson

Have students create a graphic organizer for Hinduism. Suggest that the word *Hinduism* be at the center, with different aspects of Hinduism branching off from the center. Remind students that a graphic organizer may take any shape as long as it presents the information in a clear and organized way.

Reading Strategy:
Visualizing

Words such as *rebirth, perfect, cycle* and *holy* are helpful in understanding the paragraph. (Answers will vary; rebirth, perfect, cycle, holy)

Ask:

- **What does the Vedas contain?** (the legends and religious beliefs of the ancient Indians)

- **Why are Hindus against killing animals?** (They believe each animal has a human soul and is part of Brahman.)

- **What are the four main castes?** (the Brahmin, made up of religious leaders; the ruler and warrior caste; the shopkeeper, landowner, and skilled-worker caste; the farmer, unskilled worker, servant, and slave caste)

- **How does a Hindu become part of a caste?** (He or she is born into it.)

Reading Strategy:
Visualizing

Ask students to describe the lives of the people of these different castes and where the people lived. (Answers will vary; I was able to visualize the work these individuals do, what they wore, and where they lived.)

LEARNING STYLES

Auditory/Verbal

Ask a volunteer to verbally summarize the information presented about reincarnation. Ask other volunteers to do the same for the caste system and Sanskrit. This exercise will make it easier for auditory/verbal learners to process this information.

Reading Strategy:
Visualizing

Draw a picture to help you visualize what this paragraph is about. How does this image help you remember the four main castes?

Caste

A class of people in India

What Is a Caste?

Hinduism teaches that people are born into **castes,** or classes of people. Hindus have four main castes:

1. the Brahmin caste made up of religious leaders
2. the ruler and warrior caste
3. the shopkeeper, landowner, and skilled-worker caste
4. the farmer, unskilled worker, servant, and slave caste

The Brahmin caste is the highest; the fourth caste listed is the lowest. Over thousands of years, the Hindus have divided their four main castes into smaller and smaller groups. They divide according to work, money, skin color, and religious beliefs.

There are many religious temples in India. This is the Vimal Vasahi Temple at Mount Abu, India. It is from the Jainist religion, which uses parts of Hinduism.

ELL/ESL STRATEGY

Language Objective:
To identify words that bridge different languages

Have ELL students make a list of words in their native language that are commonly used, such as words for mother, father, brother, dog, cat, house, etc. Have students list these words on the board. Have a classmate write the English words that have the same meaning. As a class, compare the spelling and pronunciation of the same word in two or more languages. Discuss other words from other languages that are used in the English language but have a similar spelling, meaning, and perhaps a different pronunciation.

Why Were Castes Important?

The members of each caste remained in the caste for life and followed its rules. For example, a person could marry only within the same caste. Another rule was that all the people in a caste did the same kind of work. When people broke these rules, they were thrown out from the caste. People called them "outcaste," because they are outside any caste.

What Is Sanskrit?

Sanskrit was the language of ancient India. It is one of the oldest languages in the Indo-European family. Latin, English, German, Spanish, Greek, and Persian are also in this language family. The languages have many words in common. For example, *mata* is the Sanskrit word for "mother."

Lesson 3 Review On a sheet of paper, write the answer to each question. Use complete sentences.

1. What are the Vedas?
2. What does the saying "Brahman is One, and yet expresses itself as many" mean?
3. Why do some Hindus not kill animals?
4. What is an Indian caste?
5. What does Sanskrit have to do with the English language?

What can the Hindu religion teach us?

Answers will vary. Students may say that the Hindu religion could teach us to respect animals and treat them humanely. It could also teach us to look for the face of God in everyone we meet and in everything that happens to us.

Ancient India and China   *Chapter 5*   **99**

Ask:

- How long does a Hindu remain part of a caste? (for life)

3   Reinforce and Extend

IN THE COMMUNITY

If there is a Hindu population in your community, invite a practicing Hindu to speak to the class about the religious and cultural aspects of Hinduism. If there are Hindu students in the class or in the school, you may wish to invite them instead of an outside community member.

WORLD CULTURES

Hindu religious festivals can be traced back to ancient times and are still practiced today. They take many different forms, including religious ceremonies, worship, prayer, music, dances, eating and drinking, and feeding the poor. During the New Year festival, objects representing the impurities of the previous year are thrown into a bonfire. These festivals usually include the entire community and can last for several days.

Lesson 3 Review Answers

1. It is the earliest written record about life in India. It also contains the legends and religious beliefs of the ancient Indians. **2.** The Hindus believe that everything is God, so God is one. The powers of the one God are expressed in many different beings, or gods. **3.** Hindus believe that some people are reborn as animals, so animals have human souls and should not be killed. **4.** A caste is a class of people. **5.** Sanskrit is the base language for English.

Chapter 5: Lesson 4

Overview This lesson describes the Buddha, Siddhartha Gautama, and the beliefs and practices of Buddhism. The lesson also compares and contrasts Buddhism with Hinduism.

Objectives

- To explain how Siddhartha Gautama founded Buddhism
- To explain how and where Buddhism spread

Student Pages pages 100–102

Teacher's Resource Library TRL

Workbook Activity 19

Activity 19

Modified Activity 19

Vocabulary

Buddha	**nirvana**
desire	**soul**
enlightened	

Write the word *nirvana* on the board. Ask students to explain the meaning and generate synonyms for the word. (blessedness, bliss) Repeat the activity for the word *soul*. (spirit, being, life) Explain that these two concepts are central to Buddhism.

PRONUNCIATION GUIDE

Use this list to help students pronounce difficult words in this lesson.

Siddhartha
Gautama   (sid där´ tə gô´ tə mə)

1 Warm-Up Activity

Have students draw a picture of nirvana, or complete emptiness. Then have students add the concept of a soul to their drawing of nirvana. Reinforce that these are abstract terms that mean different things to different people. Have students share their drawing and meanings. Have students consider how religion might have affected the lives of the people of ancient India.

Objectives

- To explain how Siddhartha Gautama founded Buddhism
- To explain how and where Buddhism spread

Buddha

A name meaning the "Enlightened One"; the name given to Siddhartha Gautama, the founder of Buddhism

Enlightened

The state of knowing the truth

Hinduism developed over a long period of time. Later in India, a man named Siddhartha Gautama began to question Hindu beliefs. He explained his beliefs to others. These beliefs are the basis of Buddhism.

How Did Gautama Become the Buddha?

Gautama was born around 563 B.C. His family was very rich. As a young man he began to feel sorry for the poor people in India. According to an old story, Gautama left his palace one day with his servant. They saw a crippled man, a sick man, a dead man, and a holy man. His servant said, "Such is the way of life, to that we must all come." This led Gautama to realize that birth, old age, sickness, and death come to everyone. The next day Gautama left his wife and newborn son. For several years, he walked the countryside and studied the Hindu holy books.

One day, while sitting under a giant tree, Gautama discovered four noble truths about life. From then on, he was known as the **Buddha,** or the "**Enlightened** One." To be enlightened is to know the truth.

What Are the Four Noble Truths Buddha Discovered?

For the rest of his life, Buddha taught and preached. He walked from village to village, dressed in a yellow robe. He trusted others to give him the food and shelter he needed.

Many statues and sculptures honor Buddha. This one is from the second or third century B.C.

Buddha preached four "Noble Truths" about the meaning of life:

1. Our life is full of suffering.

2. Our own selfish wishes cause this suffering.

3. We stop suffering when we stop being jealous, greedy, and selfish.

4. We can stop wishing for, or desiring, more.

To stop wanting more and more, Buddha said that people must follow the "Eightfold Path." To stop wanting so much a person must believe, think, speak, wish, enjoy, act, try, and live in the right way. When all **desires** finally end, a person enters the spiritual place called **nirvana.** In nirvana, a person's **soul,** or spirit, finds perfect peace.

How Are Buddhism and Hinduism Alike and Different?

Gautama was born a Hindu, so many Buddhist beliefs are the same as those of Hinduism. Both religions believe that life is sad and evil. Both believe in reincarnation. Many followers of both religions refuse to kill an animal or eat meat.

A big difference between the two religions is that Buddhists do not believe in the caste system. Buddha treated all people the same. He believed that when people follow the Eightfold Path, they reach nirvana in their own lifetime.

Where Did Buddhism Spread?

Buddha founded several groups of monks. These holy men lived in monasteries that became important centers of learning. Buddhism spread from India into Burma, Thailand, Southeast Asia, China, Korea, and Japan.

Reading Strategy:
Visualizing

What clues on this page help you visualize the four "Noble Truths"?

Desire

To wish for something

Nirvana

A condition of complete emptiness in which a person's soul finds perfect peace

Soul

A person's spirit

Reading Strategy:
Visualizing

Create a graphic organizer to show how Buddhism and Hinduism are alike and different.

ELL/ESL STRATEGY

Language Objective:
To improve listening, speaking, and summarizing skills

Pair an ELL student with a native speaker to give students practice in listening, speaking, and summarizing skills. Have the native speaker read the first paragraph of Lesson 4 to the ELL student. Then have the ELL student dictate a sentence that restates the paragraph. Have the native speaker write the sentence. Instruct the student to make and point out any needed corrections to grammar or phrasing. Continue the activity through the end of page 101 so that the end result is a one or two paragraph summary of the lesson. Then have the ELL student read aloud the summary paragraph created by his or her sentences.

 Teaching the Lesson

Have students read the lesson. Discuss the main features of Buddhism and how it differs from Hinduism. Have students create a Venn diagram with two interlocking circles, labeling one circle *Buddhism* and the other *Hinduism*. In the overlapping portion of the two circles, have students note what is similar about both religions. In the two sections that do not overlap, have students list the main features of Buddhism and Hinduism.

Ask:

- **Who was Gautama?** (A young man who left all he had to live according to the four noble truths about life and become the Buddha, or Enlightened One)

- **What are the four noble truths?** (life is full of suffering; selfish wishes cause this suffering; suffering ends when people stop being jealous, greedy, and selfish; people can stop wishing for more)

Reading Strategy:
Visualizing

(Students may say that the numbered list helped them visualize.)

- **Why is a caste system not part of Buddhism?** (Buddha taught that all people are alike.)

Reading Strategy:
Visualizing

Have students review the Venn diagrams they made earlier in this lesson. Explain that a Venn diagram is a good way to compare and contrast information, but is not the only way. Have students use the information in their Venn diagrams to create another graphic organizer, such as a two-column chart, to compare Buddhism and Hinduism. (Answers will vary.)

Ask:

- Who was Ashoka?
(the third emperor of the Maurya who changed from being a warrior to one who ruled with justice and wisdom)

- What does the text mean when it says Ashoka had a "change of heart"? (Ashoka changed from a warrior to a peaceful person who ruled with justice and wisdom.)

Have students read the Then and Now feature on page 102. Have pairs of students work together to research the beliefs of Buddhism. Ask interested students to prepare a skit about a young Buddhist entering the United States. Have the Buddhist explain his or her beliefs to an American, non-Buddhist family.

3 Reinforce and Extend

STUDY SKILLS

Outlining is an excellent technique for sorting and remembering important information. Work together with students to outline Lesson 4. Have students change each question to a statement before outlining the lesson section.

BACKGROUND INFORMATION

A key belief of Buddhism is the concept of Karma, or a belief that all actions have consequences. Accordingly, the lives of people are affected by their past actions. Everyone is responsible for their actions and the effects of those actions. Every individual is responsible for his or her life, and thus the joy or pain imposed on others. Through reincarnation, Karma becomes a force that extends from all past lives and affects future lives. Some people today use the term "karma" figuratively to mean bad attitude or negative experiences.

Who Was Ashoka?

The first Indian empire, the Maurya, was created in 321 B.C. Ashoka was its third emperor. At first, Ashoka fought wars to expand his empire. In one military victory, more than 100,000 people died. Seeing this, he realized the evil of war. He became *shoka,* or powerful. He accepted the teachings of Buddhism. Because of his change of heart, he was called "without sorrow," or *ashoka.* Ashoka is remembered as an emperor who tried to rule with justice and wisdom.

Lesson 4 Review On a sheet of paper, write the letter of the answer that correctly completes each sentence.

Why do you think that some Hindus became Buddhists?

1. Siddhartha Gautama was born _____.

   A rich   **B** poor   **C** small   **D** large

2. Another name for the Buddha is _____ One.

   A Channa   **B** Allah   **C** Enlightened   **D** Nirvana

3. Gautama preached _____ "Noble Truths."

   A two   **B** four   **C** six   **D** eight

4. Buddhists give up _____ when they reach nirvana.

   A desire   **B** religion   **C** food   **D** labor

5. Some Buddhist beliefs are similar to _____ beliefs.

   A Christian   **B** Muslim   **C** Orthodox   **D** Hindu

Buddhism, Yesterday and Today

Buddhism spread quickly throughout Asia. Buddhism started in India, but it has nearly disappeared there today. Worldwide, there are about 353 million Buddhists.

Buddhism has split into three main groups: Tibetan, Pure Land, and Zen.

The major difference among them has to do with how a person can reach enlightenment.

Buddhism spread to America in the 1900s. Why? Partly because many people from Asia moved to the United States. Also, Buddhism appealed to some Americans who were looking for a new kind of religious experience and expression.

BACKGROUND INFORMATION

All Buddha art has similar attributes of symmetry and a sense of peace. Images of Buddha transition from man to god. The entire work of art is in perfect proportion. Sculptures of Buddha during the 3rd century B.C. show the influence of Greek culture in the use of flowing robes. Some art shows the Buddha in the yoga position, hiding the lower part of the body but portraying an upper body of strength in perfect harmony.

Lesson 4 Review Answers

1. A **2.** C **3.** B **4.** A **5.** D

Answers will vary. Students may say that the two religions are similar in beliefs, but that Buddhism appealed to some because it did not limit or discriminate against people by placing them into a lifelong caste.

Lesson 5 — Ancient China

People have lived in China for thousands of years. Its geography made China a safe and productive place to live. In fact, farming began there more than 1,000 years ago. These farm villages eventually grew into cities. The first Chinese cities began near the Huang He about 2000 B.C. The ancient Chinese were also great builders.

What Is China's Geography?

China is huge. In ancient times, its geography **isolated** or kept it away from other peoples. The enormous Gobi Desert lies to the north. The Tibetan mountain **plateau**—a flat area that rises above the land close by—stretches toward the west. The mighty Himalayas rise in the southwest. The sea guards the east and south.

What Keeps the Yangtze from Flooding?

The Yangtze is the longest and most important river in China. Because it is deep and runs swiftly, it hardly ever floods. In fact, it is the world's deepest river. Large ships travel inland on it as far as 600 miles. The Yangtze flows through southern China. It has been one of China's main trade routes since ancient times.

Isolate

To keep apart or away from others

Plateau

A flat area that rises above the land close by

Why Does the Huang He Flood?

The Huang He flows across northern China. Because the river is shallow, it often floods. Throughout the years, it has destroyed both cities and farms. Since 600 B.C., it has flooded more than 1,500 times. Hunger, disease, and death follow. For this reason, it is sometimes called "China's Sorrow."

The Huang He in China is about 3,000 miles long. The first Chinese civilization began near the Yellow River in about 2000 B.C.

6000 B.C. – A.D. 220

Ancient India and China Chapter 5 **103**

Workbook Activity 20

Activity 20

Chapter 5: Lesson 5

Overview This lesson describes China's sprawling geography and the ancient Chinese efforts to overcome the challenges it presented.

Objectives

■ To describe the geography of China

■ To explain how the Yangtze River and Huang He have influenced life in China

Student Pages pages 103–105

Teacher's Resource Library

Workbook Activity 20

Activity 20

Modified Activity 20

Vocabulary

canal   isolate
invade   plateau

Have students complete each sentence with the correct vocabulary word.

1. To prevent nomads from _____, the Chinese built the Great Wall. (invading)

2. The Grand _____ connected the Huang He and Yangtze River. (Canal)

3. To the west of China stretches a _____, a flat area that rises above the surrounding land. (plateau)

4. Because of its geography, ancient China was _____ from other peoples. (isolated)

1 Warm-Up Activity

On a small piece of paper, have each student write one advantage of settlement along a river. Have students fold and place their paper in a cup. Then have each student pull out a folded paper and read the river settlement advantage. Form groups of students that have chosen same or similar advantages and have group members work together to report on the ways the advantage applies to the Yangtze River or Huang He.

Ancient India and China Chapter 5 **103**

PRONUNCIATION GUIDE

Use this list to help students pronounce difficult words in this lesson.

Yangtze   (yang´ sē)

2 Teaching the Lesson

After students read the lesson, lead a discussion on whether the benefits of the Grand Canal and the Great Wall were worth the lives lost in building them.

Ask:

- How many people worked on the Grand Canal and how many died, became ill, or ran away? (more than five million; two million)

- Why did Chinese rulers build the Great Wall? (to keep out invaders)

- How many people died working on the Great Wall? (400,000)

- Compare the Great Wall to the Grand Canal. How were they alike? How were they different?
(Answers will vary; students may say both were like a road—people and goods could move along them; they may say the canal was built to connect rivers while the wall was built to keep invaders out.)

Reading Strategy:
Visualizing

(words include: five million people, men, worked, army, guards, beat, beheaded)

Canal

A waterway made by humans

Invade

To attack or march into another country

Reading Strategy:
Visualizing

What words in this paragraph help you visualize the building of a canal?

Why Did the Chinese Build a Grand Canal?

A great wonder of the ancient world was the Grand **Canal**. Most of China's rivers flow from west to east. The Chinese rulers built a 1,100-mile canal, or waterway, that flowed north and south. It joined the Huang He and the Yangtze River.

The Chinese used the canal to transport grain and other supplies from the fertile south to the north.

Who Built the Canal?

The Chinese rulers began the canal more than 2,400 years ago. More than 5 million people worked on it. In some areas, the rulers forced all men between the ages of 15 and 50 to work on the canal. An army of 50,000 guards beat and sometimes beheaded those who refused to work.

One person in every five families had to supply and prepare food for the workers and guards. During the building of the canal, 2 million workers died, became ill, or ran away.

Why Did the Chinese Build a Great Wall?

In ancient times, nomads **invaded,** or attacked, China on its northern and western frontier. Rulers built walls to keep them out. Two rulers joined all the walls together and created the Great Wall of China. It is another wonder of the ancient world.

How Big Is the Great Wall?

Builders started work on the wall over 2,000 years ago. It stretches nearly 1,500 miles from the Yellow Sea westward. It is really a collection of short walls. In some places, it stands about 35 feet high. Its base was 15 to 30 feet thick. The workers built towers along the wall. From these, guards looked far to the north and to the west. They watched for signs of invaders.

An ancient Chinese historian says 300,000 workers built the Great Wall of China. Others believe that 1 million people worked on it and that 400,000 of them died while building the wall.

ELL/ESL STRATEGY

Language Objective:
To understand the meaning and use of idioms

Draw attention to the term *sweet and sour* in the History in Your Life feature. Ask for an example of a food that is sweet and an example of a food that tastes sour. Explain that the term "sweet and sour" can apply to food, but as a saying, *sweet and sour* can also apply to things in life that are good and those that are bad. Present the following idioms: *bitter sweet, bad hair day, blue in the face, egg on your face,* and *come to mind.* Write the idioms on the board. Form groups of ELL students with native English speakers. Have each group make a drawing and write a sentence for five idioms. Have the groups share their drawings and sentences.

Lesson 5 Review On a sheet of paper, write the letter of the answer that correctly completes each sentence.

1. For nearly 1,000 years China was nearly cut off from the rest of the world because of _____.

   A the Gobi Desert   **C** the Himalayan Mountains
   B the Tibetan plateau   **D** all of the above

2. The _____ River is the deepest river in China and in the world.

   A Yangtze   **B** Huang   **C** Ganges   **D** Indus

3. The _____ joins together the Yangtze River and the Huang He.

   A Great Wall of China   **C** Gobi Desert
   B Grand Canal   **D** Tibetan mountain plateau

4. The Great Wall protected the Chinese from invaders from the north and the _____.

   A east   **B** west   **C** south   **D** all of the above

5. "China's Sorrow" is another name for the _____.

   A Great Wall of China   **C** Huang He
   B Grand Canal   **D** Yangtze River

Why do people think that the Great Wall of China is a wonder?

The Huang He, Sweet and Sour

Many popular Chinese dishes mix sweet and sour flavors. China's Huang He has "sweet and sour" traits too. This river flows out of the western mountains across the flat North China Plain. For farmers, the river can be "sweet." It waters the fields. It also brings loess, a rich yellow soil, from the mountains. The yellow mud gave the river its Western name. It also makes the soil the most fertile in China.

Sometimes, though, the river turns "sour." It overflows its banks and floods the plains. Then it becomes deadly. More than 1,500 floods have been recorded in the past 3,000 years. One terrible flood in 1887 killed almost a million people. The Chinese people have built dikes and dams to control the river. Even today, the floodwaters of the Huang He can be a "sour" threat.

CAREER CONNECTION

Today, people who plan and supervise the construction of canals are called civil engineers. Civil engineers work on other major construction projects as well, including bridges, dams, tunnels, airports, highways, sewer systems, and railroads. Encourage interested students to research the training needed to become a civil engineer and the job opportunities that are available in their area.

BACKGROUND INFORMATION

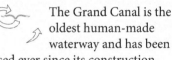

The Grand Canal is the oldest human-made waterway and has been used ever since its construction. Between 1958 and 1964, workers made the canal straighter and wider, giving it the capability of carrying much bigger ships, and even added an entirely new section 40 miles in length. Ask students if they can think of other famous canals in the world (possibilities include the Erie Canal, the Suez Canal, and the Panama Canal).

Lesson 5 Review Answers

1. D **2.** A **3.** B **4.** B **5.** C

Answers will vary. Students should say that the wonder is how people at that time, without modern machinery, could have built such a long, high, and thick wall. It wanders up and down over hills and valleys for about 1,500 miles. That in itself is a wonder. (It is also the only human-made structure that astronauts have seen from space.)

After reading the History in Your Life feature, ask students to think of other things in nature that also have sweet and sour traits. Possibilities include snowfall (pretty during the holiday season, yet troublesome for drivers), the sun (supplies energy needed for life, yet too much exposure can cause damage to skin and eyes), or spiders (eat pests that destroy gardens, yet capable of delivering dangerous venom to people).

Chapter 5: Lesson 6

Overview This lesson describes the rise and fall of China's first dynasty, the Shang. This dynasty made key contributions in cities, farming, crafts, writing, and religion.

Objectives

- To describe what life was like during the Shang dynasty
- To explain why the Shang dynasty might have collapsed
- To identify China's first golden age

Student Pages pages 106–110

Teacher's Resource Library **TRL**

Workbook Activity 21

Activity 21

Modified Activity 21

....

Vocabulary

dynasty   society
noble   symbol
scribe

Ask a volunteer to read aloud the definition of a vocabulary word. Then ask the class to identify which word corresponds to the definition. Repeat until all definitions and words have been read.

....

PRONUNCIATION GUIDE

Use this list to help students pronounce difficult words in this lesson.

Anyang   (an´ yäng´)
Zhou   (jō´)

1 **Warm-Up Activity**

Explain that in this lesson, students will learn about the three dynasties that ruled ancient China. Divide the class into three groups, or dynasties. Allow each group to name its dynasty. Explain that their dynasty has absolute power and that it rules a country the size of China with a population of millions. Have the groups share their approaches to ruling. Then compare and discuss students' ideas.

Objectives

- To describe what life was like during the Shang dynasty
- To explain why the Shang dynasty might have collapsed
- To identify China's first golden age

Dynasty
A family that rules a country over a long period of time

Noble
A person of high birth

Symbol
Something that stands for something else

Reading Strategy: **Visualizing**

Create a symbol that has two parts, like a Chinese character. How does this help you visualize a Chinese character?

In ancient times in the valley of the Huang He, many rulers fought one another. Around 1600 B.C., one powerful ruling family took over the whole plain. This family ruled for many years. A family that rules a country for a long period of time is called a **dynasty.** We call China's first dynasty the Shang.

What Was a Shang City Like?

Like the people of ancient India, the ancient Chinese built cities. The people of the Indus River Valley in India built brick homes. However, the people of the Yellow River Valley in China built wooden ones.

Archaeologists have discovered over 130 Shang villages and cities. Among the most important was Anyang, which was carved out of a forest. A palace and a temple stood in its center.

Near these important buildings, the **nobles**—people of high birth—lived. Their homes were large rectangles. Anyang had a business area with shops and government buildings.

What Is a Chinese Character?

During the Shang dynasty, the Chinese developed writing. At first, they wrote pictograms. Later they included **symbols.** These figures stood for something else. It was a difficult language with over 3,000 characters, or symbols.

Each Chinese character includes two parts. One gives the meaning of the character. The other tells how to pronounce it. The language of modern China still uses the same characters the Shang dynasty used.

The Shang made beautiful things out of bronze, such as this kettle.

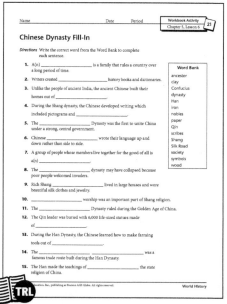

Workbook Activity 21

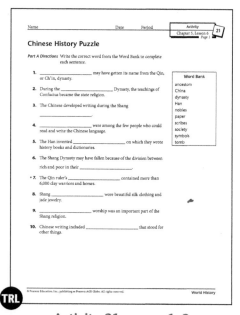

Activity 21, pages 1–2

Scribe

A person from ancient times who could read and write

Society

A group of people whose members live together for the good of all

Who Were the Scribes?

The written language of the Shang dynasty was difficult. Only a few people could read and write. We call these people **scribes.** Shang scribes wrote on long, narrow bamboo strips. Scribes wrote the characters up and down the strip rather than across.

What Is Ancestor Worship?

The Shang people believed that the gods controlled all things. They believed that the spirits of nature gave their rulers power. Among these spirits were the spirits of dead ancestors. When bad things happened, families thought that dead ancestors were not pleased with them. Ancestor worship was an important part of the Shang religion.

Why Did the Shang Decline?

The Shang dynasty lasted over 500 years. Then in 1122 B.C., the Zhou people captured the city of Anyang. The Shang **society** was sharply divided into rich and poor people. A society is a group of people whose members live together for the good of all.

The rich nobles lived in large houses in the cities. They owned bronze weapons. They were proud of their beautiful silk clothes and jade jewelry. But the poor lived in small huts or in caves. They owned no land. They could only work the land the nobles owned. When invaders came, the poor may have welcomed them. Perhaps because of this, the Shang dynasty fell apart.

 Early Earthquake Detection

A man named Zhang Heng thought he could predict that an earthquake was about to occur. In about A.D. 132, he created what is believed to be the world's first earthquake detector.

Zhang Heng's instrument was shaped like a large vase. Its copper-domed top featured eight dragons' heads around its edge. Each of these heads held a bronze ball.

A pendulum under the dome would swing if the earth shook. As the pendulum swung, it caused a ball to drop from a dragon's mouth into the mouth of a bronze toad beneath it.

The loud sound of the falling ball warned of an impending earthquake. The position of the dragon showed the direction of the earthquake's epicenter. The epicenter is the point where an earthquake begins.

Ask:

- What was the most important Shang city? (Anyang)
- What did most common people in China do? (farming)
- The Shang dynasty lasted for more than 500 years. What factors may have contributed to the Shang dynasty's long rule? (Answers will vary; students may suggest their well-built cities, abundant crops, written language, or religion.)

Reading Strategy:
Visualizing

Have students work with a partner or a small group to share their symbols. Ask students to describe how the symbols help them visualize Chinese characters. (Answers will vary.)

LEARNING STYLES

Body/Kinesthetic
Have interested students simulate the work of a Chinese scribe. Instead of bamboo strips, suggest cutting long and narrow strips of construction paper and attaching them to form a strip several feet in length. Then have them select a short poem or their favorite saying to write on the strip. Remind students that scribes wrote the characters up and down, so students may wish to do the same with letters. Encourage them to be creative and decorative—the work of scribes was, and still remains, an art as well as a form of communication.

Have students read the Technology Connection on page 107. Explain that the coastline of China is part of the Pacific Ring of Fire where most of Earth's major earthquakes occur. This made Zhang Heng's invention especially valuable. To help students visualize this invention, have them draw it as you read the feature aloud.

Ask:

- **What were four accomplishments of the Qin Dynasty?** (writing became more uniform, a system of laws was created, roads and canals were built, the Great Wall of China was built)

- **What was very different about the Qin dynasty?** (It united China under a strong central government.)

- **What was the Golden Age of China?** (China expanded in land; trade expanded along the Silk Road; Buddhism came to China; several inventions; government followed teachings of Confucius)

What Were the Accomplishments of the Qin Dynasty?

The Qin dynasty ruled China for only a short time, from 221 to 206 B.C. It was the first to unite China with a strong central government. *Qin* is pronounced as Ch'in. This may be why the land is called China. Before the Qin dynasty took control, there was no central ruler of China. The Qin leader, Shi Huangdi, named himself First Emperor. For 2,000 years after Shi Huangdi, Chinese rulers took the title of Emperor. The First Emperor is known for many accomplishments. Writing became more uniform. This allowed people in different areas to better communicate. The same system of laws was created throughout the land. New roads and canals were built. Nearly 2000 miles of the Great Wall of China was built to protect the country from northern enemies.

However, the Qin Dynasty did not last long. When the First Emperor died, he was buried in a tomb beneath a huge mound of earth. Buried near the tomb in a large pit were more than 6,000 life-size clay statues of warriors and horses. When the First Emperor died, his son became the Second Emperor. At this time, the peasants were unhappy with high taxes and harsh treatment by the Qin rulers. The peasants rebelled. In 206 B.C., Liu Bang, a peasant, who became the Prince of Han, defeated the Emperor's army. Under the Han Dynasty, China entered its first Golden Age.

Why Is the Han Dynasty Known as the First Golden Age of China?

The Han Dynasty changed China in important ways. Beginning in 206 B.C., the Han military expanded China's empire by conquering Vietnam, Korea, and much of what is now western China. The Han created a trade route called the Silk Road. It increased trade with central Asia, western Asia, Africa, and, later, Europe. The Silk Road brought China a new religion called Buddhism. Buddhism began in India. It taught how to escape the hardships of life. Many Chinese became Buddhist.

Besides military conquest and economic progress, the Han Dynasty had many other achievements. The Han learned how to make paper out of wood pulp. Chinese writers wrote history books and dictionaries printed on paper. They learned how to mass produce iron and steel farming tools. They invented sundials, water clocks, wheelbarrows, and compasses.

Before the Han Dynasty, government workers were selected by the influence of family and friends. Under the Han Dynasty, government workers were selected for their knowledge and skills. They had to be honest and respectable. It was thought that this would make the government more stable. Each worker had to pass an examination based on the teachings of Confucius, a very important Chinese philosopher.

He taught that a ruler should govern by good example. Confucius thought that if a ruler used force to govern, the ruler had failed. The teachings of Confucius were so important that they became the state religion of China.

The Han dynasty ended in A.D. 220, but the influence of the Han can still be seen in the culture and people of China. Today, more than 90 percent of the Chinese people identify themselves as the "People of the Han."

Biography

Confucius: c. 551–479 B.C.

Confucius was China's greatest teacher. (In Chinese, he was called "Master Kung.") Confucius did not teach religion, but he advised local rulers. His students later wrote down his sayings.

China was in great disorder when Confucius was alive. He hoped his ideas would bring back order. Confucius thought each person had a place in society. People owed respect to a superior, such as a ruler or a father. They should obey him or her. In turn, that person should set a good example. Confucius also taught his students to be loyal and honest. Culture and polite behavior were important too.

Ask:

• **Why was the invention of paper important?** (It allowed Chinese writers to create a paper history and dictionaries.)

Biography

Confucius was the most important philosopher in Chinese history. His emphasis on character and morals greatly influenced China and surrounding countries, including Japan, Korea, and Vietnam. Have students interpret these famous words of wisdom:

- Confucius said, "[A good man] does not worry about not being known by others but rather worries about not knowing them."
- Confucius said, "If one's acts are motivated by profit, he will have many enemies."
- Confucius said, "The superior man is ashamed that his words exceed his deeds."

3 Reinforce and Extend

Remind students that Huang He is the Chinese name for this river. After students study the map, have them answer the questions in the caption. (The Gobi Desert is north of the Huang He. The Yangtze River crosses the southern part of China. These mountain ranges are to the west of China: Altai, Tien Shan, Kunlun, and the Himalayas.)

Lesson 6 Review Answers

1. dynasty **2.** Shang **3.** characters
4. Qin **5.** Han

Answers will vary. Students may say that when the poor are left behind economically, they feel this is unfair. If the rich do not share with them, the poor may revolt.

Chapter Project Follow-up

Ask each group to present what it learned about Sanskrit or Chinese characters. Provide materials and allow time for the class to enjoy writing characters from both languages. If you have ELL students in class who write Arabic, Hebrew, Russian, or other languages, have them share their written language with the class. Make a classroom display of Sanskrit, Chinese characters, and as many other written languages as possible.

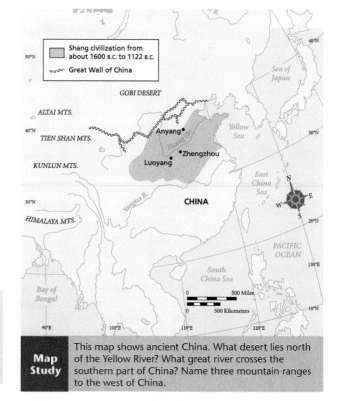

Map Study This map shows ancient China. What desert lies north of the Yellow River? What great river crosses the southern part of China? Name three mountain ranges to the west of China.

What do you think?

Why would the division of society into the rich and the poor cause problems?

Word Bank

characters
dynasty
Han
Qin
Shang

Lesson 6 Review On a sheet of paper, use the words from the Word Bank to complete each sentence correctly.

1. A _____ is a family that rules a country over a long period of time.

2. The _____ was the first dynasty in China.

3. In their writing, the Chinese use _____.

4. The _____ dynasty was the first to unite China with a strong central government.

5. The _____ invented paper out of wood pulp.

The Bhagavad Gita

Hinduism is the major religion of India. Over 80 percent of India's more than one billion people follow it. Hinduism is one of the oldest of the great world religions. It is different from the others in several ways. Hinduism is not based on the teachings of one person. It grew slowly over hundreds of years. It also does not have one holy book, such as the Bible or the Qur'an. Instead, there are many religious hymns and poems.

In Hinduism, there are many hymns and poems in the Vedas. This drawing shows Vishnu, one of the three main faces of Brahman.

This excerpt is from the Bhagavad Gita. The name means "Song of the Lord." This poem was probably written about A.D. 100. It is part of an older epic, or long poem. In it, the god Krishna teaches lessons about life and death.

What is work? What is beyond work? Even some seers [wise men] see this [incorrectly]. I will teach thee the truth of pure work, and this truth shall make thee free.

He whose undertakings are free from anxious desire and fanciful thought, whose work is made pure in the fire of wisdom: he is called wise by those who see. In whatever work he does such a man in truth has peace: he expects nothing, he relies on nothing, and ever has fullness of joy.

He has no vain hopes, he is the master of his soul, he surrenders all he has, only his body works: he is free from sin. He is glad with whatever God [the eternal spirit] gives him, and he has risen beyond the two contraries here below; he is without jealousy, and in success or in failure he is one: his works bind him not.

He has attained liberation: he is free from all bonds, his mind has found peace in wisdom, and his work is a holy sacrifice. The work of such a man is pure.

Greater is thine own work, even if this be humble, than the work of another, even if this be great. When a man does the work God gives him, no sin can touch this man.

And a man should not abandon his work, even if he cannot achieve it in full perfection; because in all work there may be imperfection, even as in all fire there is smoke.

Document-Based Questions

1. What does the speaker want to teach?

2. Who is a wise man?

3. Why should a person do his or her own work?

4. Should a person give up a job if he or she is not good at it? Why or why not?

5. How does the advice in this reading relate to the caste system?

Remind students that brackets in document-based readings are used to enclose words that are not part of the original source. Explain that ancient texts, such as the Bhagavad Gita, are open to different interpretations. That is, people may explain the same text in different ways. Inform students that ever since it was written, philosophers and historians have written many essays and books trying to interpret the meaning of the Bhagavad Gita. One of the best modern interpretations was written by Mahatma Gandhi, the respected leader who freed India from British rule in 1947. Ask students what this excerpt means to them. Encourage students to come up with their own unique interpretations.

Answers to Document-Based Questions:

1. The speaker wants to teach the truth of pure work.

2. He is someone who works without worrying too much or expecting anything.

3. Each person should do his or her own work because God gave it to him or her.

4. A person should not give up a job if he or she is not good at it because every kind of work has some faults in it.

5. The caste system teaches that each person has a duty that depends on his or her caste. This advice reinforces that idea.

ELL/ESL Strategy

Language Objective: *To summarize the main points presented in a primary document*

ELL students may have difficulty understanding this excerpt from the Bhagavad Gita. Assign ELL students to groups of three or four, making sure each group has a mix of ELL students and native English speakers. Collaborating with their group, have each student write a one or two sentence summary of each of the six paragraphs in this excerpt. The summaries should capture the main idea in each paragraph and should be written in clear, everyday language.

After reading the Spotlight Story, "Family Ties—The Ties That Bind," and answering the questions that follow, lead a discussion on the importance of respecting older people in society.

Ask:

- What do older people have to offer that younger people do not have?
- How should we treat older people?
- On the whole, how do you think American society treats its older people?

You might have students write a short essay comparing the treatment of older people in ancient China and in the contemporary United States.

Answers to Spotlight Story Wrap-Up:

1. The family is the backbone of Chinese society.

2. They gave them food and drink and cared for their graves.

3. They were used in the Shang dynasty to answer people's questions about the future.

4. They respected old age.

5. A father had authority over his children and wife. Men were considered better than women.

Family Ties—The Ties That Bind

The family has always been the backbone of Chinese society. In ancient China, people thought that the dead were still part of the family. Living family members honored those who had died. People offered them food and drink. They took care of family graves. These ancestors were seen as powerful spirits. Families hoped their ancestors could help them gain the gods' approval. That would bring good luck.

During the Shang dynasty, ancestors had a special role. People asked their help before making decisions. Even rulers asked their advice. People would go to a priest and ask him a question. To answer, priests used animal bones or tortoise shells. These were called oracle bones. The priest scratched a question on a bone. Next, he touched it with a red-hot bronze rod. The heat made cracks in the bone. These lines were the ancestors' answer. The priest studied the shape of the cracks. Then he explained what they meant.

Traditional Chinese families were very close. The family made sure every member was taken care of. It provided work, especially in farming areas. In turn, people were loyal to their families. A person's actions affected his or her whole family. If one member did wrong, it would shame them all.

The Chinese had great respect for old age. Children were expected to care for aging parents and grandparents. Older members of the family also had the most power. The teachings of Confucius made such relationships very important. A father had authority over his children and wife. Men were seen as better than women.

In the past, families arranged marriages for their children. Often the groom and bride met for the first time at their wedding!

Chinese society has changed a lot in recent times. In general, families are smaller. The government makes some decisions that families used to make. But even in modern times, Chinese family ties remain strong.

Wrap-Up

1. What is the backbone of Chinese society?

2. How did the ancient Chinese people show respect for their ancestors?

3. How were oracle bones used?

4. In general, what did the Chinese think of older family members?

5. How did Confucius affect beliefs about the family?

STUDY SKILLS

Discuss with students the strategies they use to answer questions about readings, such as the Spotlight Story Wrap-Up questions. Suggest that a useful strategy is to identify a key word in the question, such as the word *backbone* in question 1, and to quickly scan the reading until you locate that key word. To come up with the correct answer, students can reread the question and the portion of the reading surrounding the key word. The ability to locate answers with speed and accuracy will particularly benefit students on the reading comprehension component of standardized tests.

Chapter 5 SUMMARY

- India is a large peninsula in south Asia. The world's highest mountains are in the north.

- India gets water from the Ganges and Indus rivers. Seasonal storms called monsoons also bring rain.

- The first Indian civilization began in the Indus River Valley. The largest cities were Harappa and Mohenjo-Daro.

- Harappa and Mohenjo-Daro were walled cities. The careful planning of these cities shows their people knew mathematics.

- People in the Indus River Valley irrigated crops. They made pottery and cotton cloth. They traded with other peoples and wrote pictograms on clay tablets. The civilization ended suddenly about 1500 B.C.

- A set of religious beliefs and practices called Hinduism developed. The Vedas contains some of its holy writings.

- The Hindus believe that everything is god, or Brahman. Hindus believe in a cycle of birth, death, and rebirth (reincarnation).

- Hindus developed a spoken and written language called Sanskrit. It belongs to the same language family as many European languages.

- Hinduism is based on castes, or classes. Everyone is born into a caste. A person's job and way of life depend on this.

- The Indian Siddhartha Gautama became the Buddha. He taught the four "Noble Truths." He said that people should follow the "Eightfold Path" to reach nirvana.

- Buddhism shares some beliefs with Hinduism, but not the caste system. Buddhism spread from India into other parts of Asia.

- China is a huge region. A desert, mountains, and oceans kept it isolated. Chinese rulers built the Great Wall to keep out invaders.

- The Yangtze, in southern China, is its longest river. The Huang He (the Yellow River), in northern China, often floods. The first cities were built along this river about 2000 B.C.

- The Shang was China's first dynasty. It began about 1600 B.C. Its center was in the Huang He Valley.

- Shang society was sharply divided between rich and poor.

- The Shang developed a written language. Only scribes could read and write it. It is still used today.

- Ancestor worship was an important part of the Shang religion.

- The Qin dynasty was the first to unite China with a strong central government.

- The Han dynasty is known as the first golden age of China.

TEACHER'S RESOURCE

The AGS Globe Teaching Strategies in Social Studies Transparencies may be used with this chapter. The transparencies add an interactive dimension to expand and enhance the *World History* program content.

Using the Chapter Summary

Have students read the Chapter Summary on page 113 to review the main ideas presented in Chapter 5.

Ask:

- What are monsoons and how often do they occur? (storms that bring rain; once a year)

- What can we learn about the ancient Indians by studying the cities of Harappa and Mohenjo-Daro? (They knew mathematics and they had a strong government.)

- What is the name of the text containing Hinduism's legends and religious beliefs? (the Vedas)

- What is reincarnation? (Hindu belief in the cycle of birth, death, and rebirth)

- Who was Siddhartha Gautama and what did he teach? (He was the Buddha. He taught the Four Noble Truths.)

- Why did Chinese rulers build the Great Wall? (to keep out invaders)

- Where were the first cities in China built? (near the Huang He)

- When and where did the Shang dynasty begin? (1600 B.C.; Huang He Valley)

- Which group of people could read and write in the Shang dynasty? (scribes)

- Which dynasty is known as the first Golden Age of China? (Han Dynasty)

Chapter 5 Review

Use the Chapter Review to prepare students for tests and to reteach content from the chapter.

Chapter 5 Mastery Test

The Teacher's Resource Library includes two forms of the Chapter 5 Mastery Test. Each test addresses the chapter Goals for Learning. An optional third page of additional critical-thinking items is included for each test. The difficulty level of the two forms is equivalent.

Chapter 5 Review Answers

1. Sanskrit
2. Harappa
3. monsoons
4. planned
5. Hinduism
6. Vedas
7. Yangtze
8. Grand Canal
9. Han
10. Shang
11. B
12. D
13. B
14. B
15. C

Word Bank

Grand Canal
Han
Harappa
Hinduism
monsoons
planned
Sanskrit
Shang
Vedas
Yangtze

On a sheet of paper, use the words from the Word Bank to complete each sentence correctly.

1. The ancient language of India is _____.

2. _____ was one of the two big cities of the Indus River Valley civilization.

3. Farming in India depends on the _____, or seasonal winds.

4. Mohenjo-Daro in the Indus River Valley is a _____ city.

5. One religion practiced in India is _____.

6. The earliest written record in India comes from the _____ or "books of knowledge."

7. The two most important rivers in China are the Huang He and the _____.

8. The two great wonders of ancient China are its Great Wall and its _____.

9. Under the _____ dynasty, government workers were selected for their knowledge and skills.

10. The first dynasty, or ruling family, in China was the _____.

On a sheet of paper, write the letter of the answer that correctly completes each sentence.

11. The _____ are in the northern part of India.

   A Huang He and Yangtze Rivers
   B Himalayan Mountains
   C Sahara and Gobi desert
   D all of the above

12. Civilizations developed along rivers because _____.

   A people can travel on them to other places
   B people can send objects and food on them to other places
   C they connect the villages and cities of the country
   D all of the above

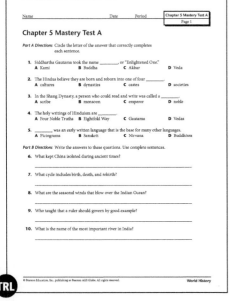

13. When rivers flood and the water retreats, they leave behind rich dirt called _____.

   A bronze   **B** silt   **C** jade   **D** monsoon

14. The first villages in India and China grew up around _____.

   A deserts   **C** oceans
   B river valleys   **D** mountains

15. The Hindus believe that they are born or reborn into one of _____ castes.

   A two   **B** three   **C** four   **D** five

On a sheet of paper, write the answer to each question. Use complete sentences.

16. Why did ancient civilizations all start in river valleys?

17. Why is geography important to history? (Hint: Use the geography of China and India to explain your answer.)

18. What are three facts about Hinduism?

Critical Thinking On a sheet of paper, write your response to each question. Use complete sentences.

19. What does the saying "the monsoon means life or death to the Indian people" mean?

20. What was the same about life in ancient India and life in ancient China? What was different? (Hint: You might think about where the cities grew up, city life, and religion.)

Study test material with a partner. Take turns quizzing each other on the material.

6000 B.C. – A.D. 220

Ancient India and China   *Chapter 5*   **115**

---

16. River valleys had fertile land where people could farm and settle down together. These settlements became villages and then cities. Artisans in the cities could create objects that made life easier and more beautiful for everyone.

17. Geography helps people in many ways. Rivers provide fertile soil for farming. Monsoons in India help farmers by providing necessary rain for growing crops. Mountains can keep out invading armies.

18. Answers will vary. Students may say that Hindus believe in the many faces of God. They see God in all people and animals and in all human events. They believe that human souls return again and again to Earth until they are perfected. Then they become one with Brahman.

Critical Thinking

19. Answers will vary. Students may say that without the monsoon, the Indian people cannot grow crops. Without food to eat, they die.

20. Answers will vary. Students may say that in both places, early settlements were built in river valleys. The Indians built houses of brick; the Chinese built wooden ones. The Indians worshipped one God, Brahman, who has many faces. The Chinese worshipped their ancestors.

Chapter 5 Mastery Test B, pages 1–3

Ancient India and China   *Chapter 5*   **115**

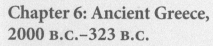

Chapter 6: Ancient Greece, 2000 B.C.–323 B.C.

pages 116–145

Map Skills

Lessons

Document-Based Reading

Spotlight Story

Chapter Summary and Review

Audio Library 🎧

Skill Track for *World History* 🖱

Teacher's Resource Library **TRL**

Workbook Activities 22–28

Activities 22–28

Modified Activities 22–28

Chapter 6 Self-Study Guide

Chapter 6 Outline

Chapter 6 Mastery Tests A and B
(Answer Keys for the Teacher's Resource Library begin on page 870 of this Teacher's Edition.)

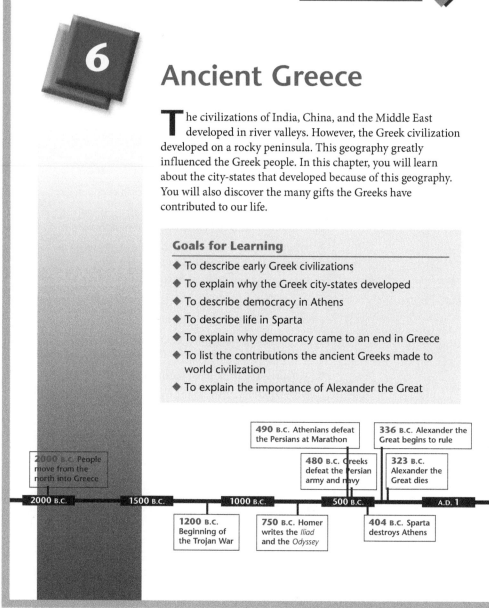

6

Ancient Greece

The civilizations of India, China, and the Middle East developed in river valleys. However, the Greek civilization developed on a rocky peninsula. This geography greatly influenced the Greek people. In this chapter, you will learn about the city-states that developed because of this geography. You will also discover the many gifts the Greeks have contributed to our life.

Goals for Learning

◆ To describe early Greek civilizations

◆ To explain why the Greek city-states developed

◆ To describe democracy in Athens

◆ To describe life in Sparta

◆ To explain why democracy came to an end in Greece

◆ To list the contributions the ancient Greeks made to world civilization

◆ To explain the importance of Alexander the Great

490 B.C. Athenians defeat the Persians at Marathon

336 B.C. Alexander the Great begins to rule

480 B.C. Greeks defeat the Persian army and navy

323 B.C. Alexander the Great dies

2000 B.C. People move from the north into Greece

| 2000 B.C. | 1500 B.C. | 1000 B.C. | 500 B.C. | A.D. 1 |

1200 B.C. Beginning of the Trojan War

750 B.C. Homer writes the *Iliad* and the *Odyssey*

404 B.C. Sparta destroys Athens

Introducing the Chapter

Ask students to describe how we use the word *marathon* today. Tell students that this popular long-distance race is like one that was run in ancient Greece. Then have students study the timeline and note the dates of events in ancient Greece.

Ask:

- How is the word *marathon* used in the timeline? (It is the site of a battle.)

- Who won the war between Athens and Sparta? (Sparta)

- How many years passed between the beginning of Alexander the Great's rule and his death? (13 years)

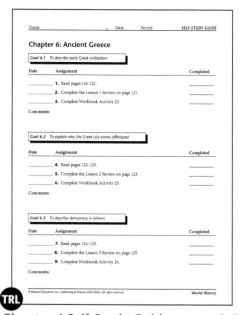

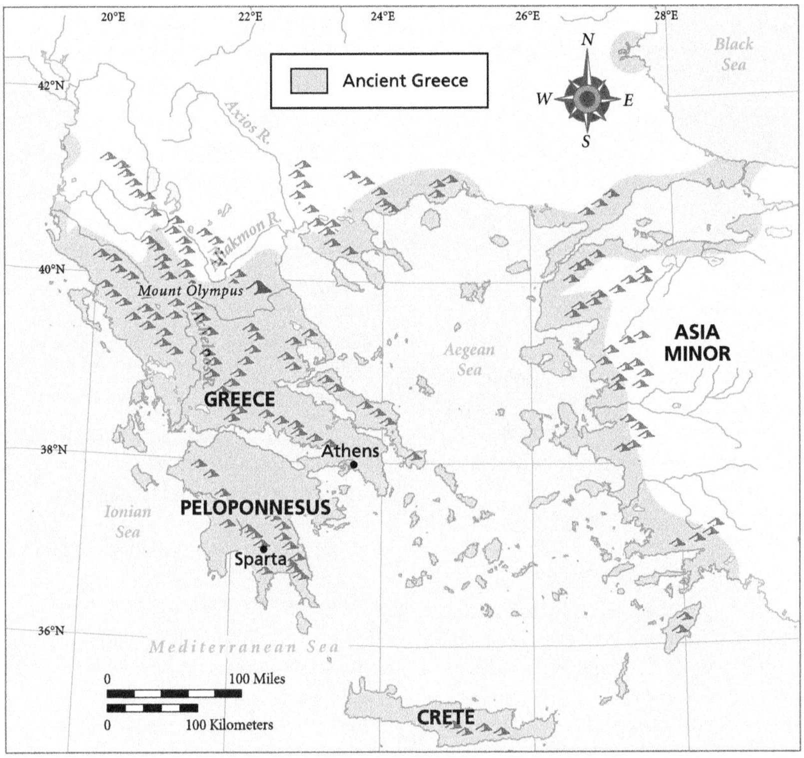

The geography of Greece has had an effect on its growth and its history. Its mountains made traveling by land hard. The Greeks took to the seas, which surrounded them on three sides, and became sailors. The geography of Greece helps us understand how each city-state developed its own culture.

Study the map, then answer the following questions:

1. What Greek city-state is located closest to the Aegean Sea?
2. Many islands surround Greece. What is the name of the largest island that lies near Greece?
3. What three seas surround Greece?
4. What tall mountain stands in the north of Greece?
5. What city-state is located in Peloponnesus?

Have a volunteer read the title of the map, "Ancient Greece." Have students infer from the timeline what date this map of Greece represents. Then have students read the paragraph below the map.

Ask:

- What does the shaded area represent? (ancient Greece)
- What direction from Greece is Asia Minor? (east)
- In miles and kilometers, what is the approximate distance between the southern tip of Peloponnesus and the western tip of Crete? (about 80 miles, or 120 kilometers)

Have students read and write answers to the questions.

Map Skills Answers

1. Athens
2. Crete
3. Ionian Sea, Mediterranean Sea, and the Aegean Sea
4. Mount Olympus
5. Sparta

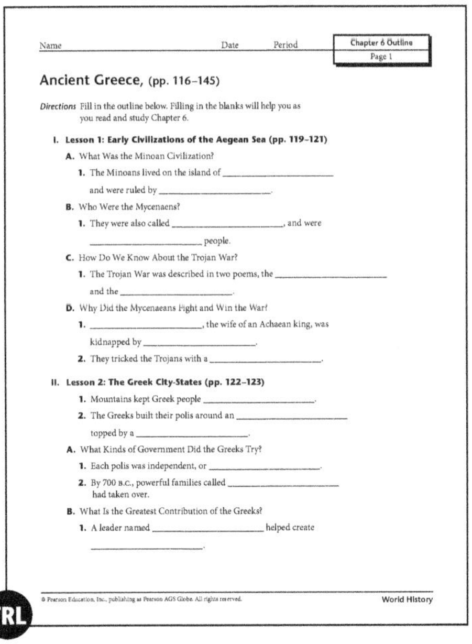
Name ______ Date ______ Period ______ | Chapter 6 Outline, Page 1

Ancient Greece, (pp. 116–145)

Directions Fill in the outline below. Filling in the blanks will help you as you read and study Chapter 6.

I. **Lesson 1: Early Civilizations of the Aegean Sea (pp. 119–121)**
   A. What Was the Minoan Civilization?
      1. The Minoans lived on the island of ______ and were ruled by ______.
   B. Who Were the Mycenaens?
      1. They were also called ______, and were ______ people.
   C. How Do We Know About the Trojan War?
      1. The Trojan War was described in two poems, the ______ and the ______.
   D. Why Did the Mycenaeans Fight and Win the War?
      1. ______, the wife of an Achaean king, was kidnapped by ______.
      2. They tricked the Trojans with a ______.

II. **Lesson 2: The Greek City-States (pp. 122–123)**
   1. Mountains kept Greek people ______.
   2. The Greeks built their polis around an ______ topped by a ______.
   A. What Kinds of Government Did the Greeks Try?
      1. Each polis was independent, or ______.
      2. By 700 B.C., powerful families called ______ had taken over.
   B. What Is the Greatest Contribution of the Greeks?
      1. A leader named ______ helped create ______.

© Pearson Education, Inc., publishing as Pearson AGS Globe. All rights reserved. World History

TRL

Chapter 6 Outline, pages 1–4

Chapter Project

Students may work individually or in small groups on a topic of their choosing from the list below. Suggest different types of final products, such as reports, skits, videos, songs, and so on.

- Art of Ancient Greece (How are the designs of Minoan and Mycenaean art alike? How are they different? What feelings do they impart?)
- Geography of Ancient Greece (Use salt dough or modeling clay to construct a scale relief map of the Aegean area. Label surrounding seas and note trade routes and ship routes used in war.)
- Architecture Photo-Journal (Survey your community or a nearby town for buildings whose design was influenced by ancient Greek architecture.)
- Greek Theater (Prepare and present a skit of a Greek comedy or a Greek tragedy performed with a Greek chorus.)

Inferencing

Students intuitively know how to make inferences in everyday situations. They make inferences based on the physical appearance, actions, speech, facial expressions, and body language of people with whom they come in contact. Have two students role-play different situations, while other students make inferences based on the volunteers' facial expressions, body language, and speech patterns. Have students describe how they used clues to infer meaning. Discuss methods which students can use to transfer this strategy to their interactions with text. To draw upon prior knowledge, ask students to volunteer anything they might know about the saying "...the face that sank a thousand ships" that was used to describe Helen of Troy. Display a picture of the Trojan Horse, and ask if any students recognize it. If so, ask them to make inferences about the horse based on its size.

Key Vocabulary Words

Point out that these words are presented in the order they appear in each lesson. They are also found in the Glossary. Explain that students should be aware of inferencing as they read new words and information presented in Chapter 6. Explain that as students come across these words in the lessons, they will infer the full meaning of vocabulary words based on what they already know. Point out that words, such as *lottery*, may have more than one meaning.

Ask:

• **What do you think of when I say** *lottery?* (Answers will vary; I think of tickets, choosing numbers, winning money.)

Reading Strategy:
Inferencing

Sometimes the meaning of a text is not directly stated. You have to make an inference to figure out what the text means.

◆ What You Know + What You Read = Inference

◆ To make inferences, you have to think "beyond the text." Predicting what will happen next and explaining cause and effect are helpful strategies for making inferences.

Key Vocabulary Words

Lesson 1
Heroic Being brave and bold

Lesson 2
Polis The Greek name for a city-state

Acropolis A hill on which the people in a Greek city built their main temple

Aristocrat A member of the powerful ruling class

Tyrant A leader who rules by force and not by law

Democracy The rule by the people

Lesson 3
Direct democracy A type of government in which each citizen votes on everything

Assembly A meeting

Lottery A system of picking names from a container so that each person has an equal chance of being chosen

Jury A group who listens to court cases and decides the outcome

Lesson 4
Architecture The art of building

Enslave To force people to become slaves

Helot A slave in Sparta

Patriotic Being loyal toward one's country

Lesson 5
Fleet A group of ships

Independence Being free; being able to govern one's self

Maneuver To move around easily

Lesson 6
Goddess A female god

Column A tall post used to support a building

Philosopher A person who tries to find truth by asking questions

Astronomy The study of the stars

Biology The study of living things

Ethics The study of what is right and wrong

Logic The science of thinking

Physics The science of matter and energy

Politics The work of government

Lesson 7
Hellenism The blend of Western and Eastern cultures made possible by Alexander the Great

Geometry The study of the measurement of flat and round things

Hellenistic Age The time between 323 B.C. and 31 B.C., when Greek culture influenced the world

ONLINE CONNECTION

Students can gain additional information by accessing the following Web sites:

www.agsglobewh.com/page118a (The Web site of the British Museum features interactive activities under the categories "Story," "Explore," and "Challenge." Activities involve students in 10 different topics related to life in ancient Greece. The home page has a good map of the Aegean region, and displays examples of period art and sculpture.)

www.agsglobewh.com/page118b (The Metropolitan Museum of Art offers a wealth of thematic essays on ancient Greece, all of which contain photographs of works of art produced during the period.)

Objectives

♦ To describe the Minoan and Mycenaean civilizations

♦ To explain how the Mycenaeans won the Trojan War

Heroic

Being brave and bold

Reading Strategy:
Inferencing

What do you already know about the Trojan War?

Unlike Mesopotamia, Egypt, India, and China, the Greek civilization did not develop around river valleys. Greece is a peninsula. Its mainland reaches out into the Mediterranean Sea like the fingers of a hand. One ancient Greek teacher said that the Greeks lived on the shores of the sea "like frogs around a pond."

What Was the Minoan Civilization?

The first people to develop a civilization in this area lived on the island of Crete. In 1900, Sir Arthur Evans discovered the ruins of this island civilization. One town he dug up was Knossos. It probably had a population of 100,000 people in ancient times. Evans named this island civilization Minoan because a legend said that a king named Minos once ruled it.

Who Were the Mycenaeans?

The Greek civilization came after the Minoan. About 2000 B.C., people from the north moved southward into the peninsula of Greece. Historians call these people the Achaeans. They built walled cities in the southern part of Greece. Warrior kings ruled these cities. Their most important city was Mycenae. Because of this city, historians call the Achaeans by a second name—the Mycenaeans.

These warlike people sailed to other cities around the Aegean Sea and suddenly attacked them. Their most famous attack was on the city of Troy around 1200 B.C. Hundreds of years later, Greeks saw this time in their history as an age of heroes. The Trojan War became a symbol of **heroic,** or brave and bold, actions.

2000 B.C. – 323 B.C.

Ancient Greece Chapter 6 119

Chapter 6: Lesson 1

Overview This lesson describes the development of two early civilizations, the Minoans and the Mycenaeans, and tells the story of the Trojan War.

Objectives

■ To describe the Minoan and Mycenaean civilizations

■ To explain how the Mycenaeans won the Trojan War

Student Pages pages 119–121

Teacher's Resource Library TRL

Workbook Activity 22

Activity 22

Modified Activity 22

Vocabulary

heroic

Ask a volunteer to read the definition of this word aloud. Then have each student write three original sentences that correctly use the word. Ask volunteers to share their sentences with the class.

PRONUNCIATION GUIDE

Use this list to help students pronounce difficult words in this lesson.

Achaeans	(ə kē´ ənz)
Knossos	(nos´ əs)
Mycenae	(mī sē´ nē)

1 Warm-Up Activity

Have each student interview three adult family and/or community members to ask: "During your lifetime, for what reasons has your country gone to war?" Tell students to record the answers. During class, work with students in small groups on ways to combine and classify the responses they collected. For example, categories of response could include fighting to protect life, property, land, beliefs, or values, and so on. Combine the results of all groups into a class chart. Refer to this information when discussing the reasons for the Trojan War.

Do You Remember?

Directions Write the answers to these questions. Use complete sentences.

1. Where did the Minoan civilization begin?

2. How did the Greek civilization develop?

3. What kind of people were the Mycenaeans? What did they do?

4. How do we know about the Trojan War?

5. What trick did the Mycenaean warriors use to win the Trojan War?

Workbook Activity 22

Early Civilizations of the Aegean Sea

Directions Read each clue. Then choose the correct word from the Word Bank to complete the puzzle.

Across

6. body of water on which Greece is located
7. location of Minoan civilization
8. poem that tells us about the Trojan War
9. geographic shape of Greece

Down

1. nature of the Mycenaean people
2. being brave and bold
3. trick used by the Mycenaeans to win the war
4. Trojan War was fought over this woman
5. Minoan town dug up by Sir Arthur Evans
6. most important city in Achaean civilization

Word Bank
Crete
Helen
heroic
horse
Iliad
Knossos
Mediterranean
Mycenae
peninsula
warlike

Activity 22

Have students describe what they know about the different ways of learning about the past. Then have them read pages 119–121 to discover how we know about the Minoans, Mycenaeans, and the Trojan War.

Ask:

• Why did Sir Arthur Evans name the island civilization he discovered Minoan? (According to a legend, a king named Minos once ruled the island.)

Reading Strategy:
Inferencing

Have volunteers describe what they already knew about the Trojan War before reading the material. After reading, ask if this knowledge added to what they just read by providing details about the setting, or providing explanations for events presented in the text?

• Where and when did the Mycenaeans' most famous attack take place? (Troy; about 1200 B.C.)

• Explain how the Mycenaeans tricked the Trojans to win the war. (Mycenaean warriors hid inside a wooden horse, which the Trojans brought inside Troy's gates; then the Mycenaeans left the horse, opened the gates, and allowed the Mycenaean army to enter and destroy the city.)

• Who was Helen? (the beautiful wife of an Achaean king)

• According to Homer, why did the Achaeans fight the Trojan War? (to win back Helen, who had been taken by Paris, the son of the king of Troy)

The Lion's Gate at Mycenae and similar ruins show what Mycenaean buildings were like.

How Do We Know About the Trojan War?

We remember the Trojan War because of two long poems—the *Iliad* and the *Odyssey*. A blind poet named Homer probably wrote them about 500 years after the war ended. He spoke or sang the stories. For centuries, the Greeks continued to sing these poems. In this way, they remembered the story of the war. Then, many years after Homer died, someone wrote them down.

Why Did the Mycenaeans Fight the War?

According to Homer, the Mycenaeans fought the Trojans because of a beautiful woman named Helen. She was the wife of the Achaean king. Paris, a son of the king of Troy, took her back to Troy. The Mycenaeans fought the Trojan War to win Helen back.

ELL/ESL STRATEGY

Language Objective:
To write for a variety of purposes: to express feelings, ideas, and opinions

Discuss the meaning of the word *heroic* in the reading. Ask students if they can think of a situation other than a military battle in which a person can be heroic. Have students meet in small groups and describe to each other someone in their lives who they think is heroic. Have them ask each other, "What are the characteristics of this person?" and "Describe one thing that this person has done that you consider heroic." Each student should write a short essay describing the person and his or her heroic qualities. Have volunteers share their essays with the class.

How Did the Mycenaeans Win the War?

The two sides fought for 10 years. Finally, the Mycenaeans defeated Troy with a clever trick. They pretended to sail away from Troy. But they left behind a giant wooden horse. The Trojans thought that they had won the war and that the Mycenaeans had left behind a victory gift. They opened their gates and brought the wooden horse within the city's thick, protective walls. Then they closed their gates. They thought they had locked the enemy out. Instead, they had locked the enemy in! Mycenaean warriors hid inside the wooden horse! During the night, these warriors silently left the horse and opened the gates of Troy. The rest of the Mycenaean army poured into the city and destroyed it.

Lesson 1 Review On a sheet of paper, use the words from the Word Bank to complete each sentence correctly.

Word Bank
Crete
Helen
Mycenaean
Odyssey
Trojan War

1. The _____ civilization came after the Minoan civilization.

2. The Minoan civilization was located on the island of _____.

3. The Mycenaeans fought a 10-year war called the _____.

4. They fought the war because Paris, a son of the king of Troy, had stolen the beautiful _____.

5. We can read the story of the Trojan War in the *Iliad* and the _____.

Do you think the Mycenaeans won the Trojan War fairly?

STUDY SKILLS

Discuss the concept of a main idea. Read several short paragraphs from a local newspaper, stopping after each one to have a student identify the main idea. Then have students write a single sentence about the main idea of each paragraph in Lesson 1. Tell students that their sentences should answer the subhead questions.

Lesson 1 Review Answers

1. Mycenaean 2. Crete *Odyssey*
3. Trojan War 4. Helen 5. Bible

Answers will vary. Some students will think that the Mycenaeans were clever in their trick. Other students may think that the Mycenaeans did not act in a fair manner. This can lead to a discussion about what is fair in war.

Chapter 6: Lesson 2

Overview This lesson describes the development of Greek city-states and the different forms of government they tried.

Objectives

- To identify early forms of government in Greece
- To understand the meaning of democracy and why it developed in Athens

Student Pages pages 122–123

Teacher's Resource Library

Workbook Activity 23

Activity 23

Modified Activity 23

Vocabulary

acropolis   polis
aristocrat   tyrant
democracy

Have students create a crossword puzzle on graph paper using these vocabulary words. Suggest using the definitions or fill-in-the-blank sentences as clues. Allow students to exchange and solve the puzzles.

PRONUNCIATION GUIDE

Use this list to help students pronounce difficult words in this lesson.

Solon   (sō´ lən)

1 Warm-Up Activity

Before beginning this lesson, assign each student to a country, and have them find a copy of the country's pledge of allegiance to its flag. Begin the lesson with the class reciting the pledge of allegiance to the American flag. Discuss the set of values articulated in the United States pledge of allegiance. Then ask volunteers to read aloud the the pledges they found for other countries. (Students are apt to find very few; most countries do not have a pledge to their flag.)

Objectives

- To identify early forms of government in Greece
- To understand the meaning of democracy and why it developed in Athens

Polis

The Greek name for a city-state

Acropolis

A hill on which the people in a Greek city built their main temple

Aristocrat

A member of the powerful ruling class

Tyrant

A leader who rules by force and not by law

Greece is rocky and mountainous. In ancient times, the mountains kept the people isolated from one another. So the Greeks had many small settlements or city-states. They called each city-state a "**polis**." Each polis was independent, or self-governing. A Greek was a citizen of the polis, or city-state.

The Greeks built their polis around a hill called an **acropolis**. On this high ground stood their main temple. Below the acropolis, they built homes and a marketplace. They also built theaters where they enjoyed plays and meeting places for the government.

What Kinds of Government Did the Greeks Try?

Over a period of time, the Greek city-states tried several different forms of government. In 800 B.C., kings ruled and passed their power to their sons. By 700 B.C., a small group of families with large amounts of land had taken over. We call members of these powerful families **aristocrats**. They also passed the right to rule from father to son. In about 600 B.C., strong leaders began to use force to take over the government of several city-states. We call such a person a **tyrant**. At first, tyrants kept the peace and passed fair laws. They also helped trade grow. Then some tyrants became cruel and unjust. Today, the word *tyrant* means anyone who uses power in a cruel and unfair way.

The acropolis was a hill overlooking the city where temples were built. This photo shows the acropolis at Athens—the most magnificent of all in the Greek city-states.

---

2 Teaching the Lesson

Have students read pages 122–123 to learn about the four types of government the Greeks tried. Have students name the type of government ruled by a king (a monarchy), by a small group of wealthy people (an aristocracy), by a tyrant (a dictatorship), and by the people (a democracy).

Write these terms and their definitions on the board. Ask students which type of government they find most desirable and least desirable. Have them explain and defend their answers.

Ask:

- What was a polis? (an independent city-state)

- Name three types of people that ruled Greek city-states before Solon helped create democracy. (kings, aristocrats, and tyrants)

Democracy

The rule by the people

Reading Strategy:
Inferencing

After reading this section, what inference can you make about the importance of Greek civilization to our world today?

Word Bank

acropolis
Athenians
democracy
polis
Solon

What Is the Greatest Contribution of the Greeks?

A leader named Solon helped create **democracy,** or rule by the people, in Athens. In 594 B.C., the Athenian leaders were fighting among themselves. Solon set out to improve the government. Because of his improvements, the average citizens of Athens had political power for the first time. Democracy has become the most important contribution the ancient Greeks made to civilization.

Lesson 2 Review On a sheet of paper, use the words from the Word Bank to complete each sentence correctly.

1. A _____ is a Greek city-state.

2. On the _____ in each city-state, the people built their main temple.

3. The form of government known as _____ is the most important contribution the ancient Greeks made to civilization.

4. The _____ were the first Greeks to develop a democratic government.

5. A leader named _____ helped to create the democratic form of government.

Why do you think the Greek people built their main temple on a hill in each city-state?

- What form of government did Solon seek to improve? (democracy)

- What was the most important contribution the ancient Greeks made to civilization? (democracy)

Reading Strategy:
Inferencing

Ask students to refer to the reading to identify the most important contribution ancient Greeks made to civilization. Then have them draw a conclusion from this related to our world today.

ELL/ESL STRATEGY

Language Objective: *To compare, contrast, and role-play two different forms of government*

Have students work in small groups, discuss the meanings of *rule by tyrant* and *rule by democracy*, and consult reference materials to find examples of tyrannical behavior in leaders. Each group should then choose a scenario from everyday life and work together to write two short skits to present to the class. One skit will illustrate how this scenario would look under a tyrant's rule, and the other how it would look in a democracy.

3 Reinforce and Extend

Lesson 2 Review Answers

1. polis 2. acropolis 3. democracy 4. Athenians 5. Solon

Answers will vary. Example: Perhaps they wanted to be able to see their temple from far away. Or perhaps they felt closer to the gods when they were higher up.

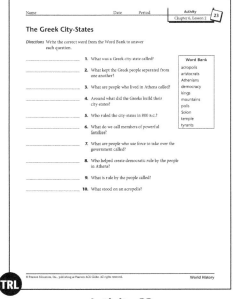

Chapter 6: Lesson 3

Overview This lesson describes Athenian democracy, the responsibilities of Athenian citizens, and the reasons why people came to Athens.

Objectives

- To define direct democracy
- To explain who could be a citizen
- To describe the responsibilities of citizenship

Student Pages pages 124–125

Teacher's Resource Library (TRL)

Workbook Activity 24

Activity 24

Modified Activity 24

Vocabulary

assembly   jury
direct democracy   lottery

Have students create flashcards using the vocabulary words and their definitions. Allow students to quiz each other in pairs.

 Warm-Up Activity

Begin the class by announcing that today, all girls with brown eyes (or all girls wearing a certain color, or all girls with another characteristic) will have certain privileges that no one else in the class will have. Describe several of these privileges. (Choose privileges that are highly favored by students in your school.) Do not give a reason for this action. If students ask for an explanation, tell them that they will understand it as they complete the lesson.

 Teaching the Lesson

Have students work in small groups to read the lesson. Tell students that as they read they should make an inference about the fairness of democracy in Athens.

Objectives

- To define direct democracy
- To explain who could be a citizen
- To describe the responsibilities of citizenship

Direct democracy
A type of government in which each citizen votes on everything

Assembly
A meeting

Lottery
A system of picking names from a container so that each person has an equal chance of being chosen

Reading Strategy:
Inferencing

After reading this section, what inference can you make about the fairness of democracy in Athens?

Athenian democracy meant rule by only some people, not all. Only 40,000 of the 300,000 Athenians had the right to vote, or choose leaders and pass laws. Only citizens had this right, and only Athenian men could be citizens. Women, the more than 100,000 slaves, and Greeks from other city-states could not be citizens.

An Athenian leader expected three things of each citizen. He had to be loyal to Athens. He had to take part in the government. He also had to defend the city when necessary.

Why Did the Athenians Change Their Direct Democracy?

At first, each Athenian citizen voted on every law. We call this type of government a **direct democracy.** Soon, however, the number of citizens at the city **assembly,** or meeting, became too large. The government created a council of 500 citizens.

The government chose the members of this council by **lottery.** That is, they picked names from a container. In that way, each citizen had an equal chance of being chosen. The council members served for one year. During that time, they carried out the day-to-day business of Athens.

A Greek legend says that the goddess Athena named Athens after herself. This is the "Contemplating Athena" sculpture.

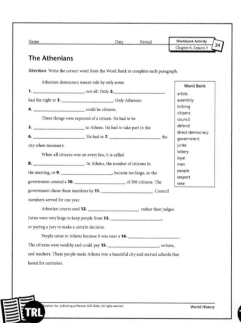

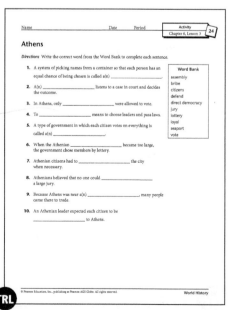

How Large Was an Athenian Jury?

Athenian courts did not use judges, but they did use large **juries.** A jury is a group who listens to a case in court and decides the outcome. Each year, the Athenians chose 6,000 citizens by lottery to serve on juries.

Between 201 and 501 people made up each jury. (In the United States, juries usually have 12 members.) When a court case was serious, 1,000 citizens might serve on the jury. Athenians believed that no one could bribe, or pay, a large jury to make a certain decision.

Why Did People Come to Athens?

Athens was near a seaport. Its sea trade helped this city-state grow in wealth and power. Because the citizens had money to pay artists, writers, and teachers, many of them came to Athens. They created beautiful art and built beautiful buildings. They started schools that lasted for centuries.

Lesson 3 Review On a sheet of paper, write the answer to each question. Use complete sentences.

1. How many slaves lived in ancient Athens?
2. Which people were not allowed to vote in Athens?
3. What is a direct democracy?
4. Why did the Athenian citizens begin to use a lottery for their government meetings?
5. How did Athenian juries differ from American juries?

Do you think large juries are better than small ones? Why or why not?

Jury
A group who listens to court cases and decides the outcome

Reading Strategy:
Inferencing

After reading this lesson, what inference can you make about the people of ancient Athens? What words helped you make your inference?

Lesson 3 Review Answers

1. There were at least 60,000 more slaves than citizens. **2.** Women, slaves, and Greeks from other city-states could not vote in Athens. **3.** A direct democracy is a government in which each citizen votes for each law. **4.** The governmental meetings became too large so they used a lottery to choose council members. **5.** American juries usually have 12 members. Athenian juries had as many as 1,000.

Answers will vary. A small jury can probably reach an agreement easier. A large jury may represent many points of view.

Have them use this to formulate an opinion about whether the United States is a direct democracy. Then lead a discussion on whether the United States is a direct democracy. (The United States is not a direct democracy because we elect leaders to make decisions for us; this is called representative democracy.)

Reading Strategy:
Inferencing

Remind students that in making an inference about the fairness of democracy in Athens, they are using their own point of view in formulating an interpretation of the text.

Ask:

- Who could be a citizen in Athens? (men who were not slaves)
- Why did the Athenian government abandon direct democracy? (The number of citizens at the city assembly became too large.)
- Why did Athenian juries have up to 1,000 people on them? (No one could bribe a large jury to make a certain decision.)
- Why did artists, writers, and teachers come to Athens? (Athenian citizens had enough money to pay them.)

Reading Strategy:
Inferencing

Have students identify information given in the reading that will help them form a conclusion about the people of ancient Athens.

3 **Reinforce and Extend**

Chapter 6: Lesson 4

Overview This lesson describes the city-state of Sparta, known for its strong soldiers and large slave population.

Objectives

- To describe how men, women, children, and slaves were treated in Sparta
- To identify how Sparta is different from Athens

Student Pages pages 126–127

Teacher's Resource Library TRL

Workbook Activity 25

Activity 25

Modified Activity 25

Vocabulary

architecture	helot
enslave	patriotic

Write the vocabulary words on the board. Read aloud a definition and have students identify and write down the correct word. Repeat until all definitions have been read. Then discuss the correct answers.

1 Warm-Up Activity

Distribute copies of an excerpt from "Ender's Game" by Orson Scott Card. In this excerpt, the government takes away children from their families. Have students work in small groups to read, analyze, and describe what they think is happening and why. Each group should write a position statement describing their conclusion. Have a representative from each group read their statement to the class. Discuss their conclusions, and ask students if they support the right of the government to take children in this way.

Lesson 4 Sparta

Objectives

◆ To describe how men, women, children, and slaves were treated in Sparta
◆ To identify how Sparta is different from Athens

Enslave
To force people to become slaves

Helot
A slave in Sparta

Sparta, another city-state, was located on a peninsula in southern Greece called the Peloponnesus. Around 1100 B.C., people settled in the area. They built the city of Sparta and became known as Spartans. They **enslaved** the farmers who already lived there. That is, they forced the farmers to become slaves. They called these new slaves **helots.** The helots farmed the land surrounding the city.

What Was Sparta's "Wall of Men"?

For every Spartan, there were seven helots. This many slaves was a danger to the Spartans. What if the helots rebelled? Yet the leaders built no protective wall around their city. They thought that their military skills would protect them. According to one leader, they had a wall of men instead of bricks.

About 600 B.C., the helots did rebel. The Spartans defeated them, but the event frightened the Spartans. They sent people to spy on the helots. They also killed any helot who started to make trouble.

What Was Life Like for a Spartan Man?

In Sparta, government officials examined each newborn baby. They left sick children on hills to die. When a boy was seven, the government took him from his parents. It kept him hungry and expected him to steal food. But if he got caught, he was punished severely. At the age of 20, he became a citizen. At 30, he married. Until age 60, he lived in a military camp with all the other soldiers.

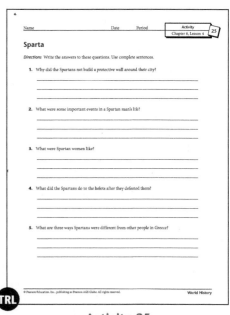

Sparta Puzzle

Part A Directions Write the correct word from the Word Bank to complete each sentence.

1. Sparta was a(n) _____.
2. Art or _____ did not interest the Spartans.
3. Sparta was located on a(n) _____ in southern Greece.
4. Spartan women were independent and _____, or loyal to their city-state.
5. The Spartans forced the farmers to become slaves they called _____.
6. The Spartans were known as the best _____ in Greece and the whole world.
7. Spartan wives told their husbands to come home as a(n) _____ carrying your shield.
8. The Spartans thought their _____ skills would protect them if the slaves rebelled.
9. People who built the city of Sparta _____ the farmers who already lived there.
10. Boy babies were taken from their parents and were expected to _____ food.

Word Bank
architecture
city-state
enslaved
helots
military
patriotic
peninsula
soldiers
steal
victor

Sparta

Directions Write the answers to these questions. Use complete sentences.

1. Why did the Spartans not build a protective wall around their city?

2. What were some important events in a Spartan man's life?

3. What were Spartan women like?

4. What did the Spartans do to the helots after they defeated them?

5. What are three ways Spartans were different from other people in Greece?

Patriotic

Being loyal toward one's country

Architecture

The art of building

Writing About History

Imagine that you are an Athenian visiting Sparta or a Spartan visiting Athens. In your notebook, write a letter home. Describe what you have seen. Tell what you think of this city-state.

Reading Strategy: Inferencing

After reading this lesson, what can you infer about the Spartans' attitude toward life? What words helped you make your inference?

What Did Spartan Women Say to the Men?

Spartan women were independent and **patriotic,** or loyal, to their city-state. When a husband went off to war, his wife told him two things: Come home as a victor carrying your shield, or come home dead, being carried on your shield. He was to do one or the other, nothing else.

What Price Did the Spartans Pay for Being Warriors?

Art or **architecture,** which is the art of building, did not interest the Spartans. They did not trade with others, and they feared new ideas. Yet many people thought that they were the best soldiers in Greece and maybe in the whole world!

Lesson 4 Review On a sheet of paper, write the letter of the answer that correctly completes each sentence.

1. Sparta was located on the _____ peninsula.

   A Athenian   **B** Indian   **C** Sinai   **D** Peloponnesus

2. The helots were Spartan _____.

   A citizens   **B** slaves   **C** traders   **D** officials

3. For every Spartan citizen there were _____ helots.

   A 7   **B** 10   **C** 20   **D** 100

4. Spartan boys began training to be soldiers at the age of _____.

   A 7   **B** 20   **C** 30   **D** 60

5. A Spartan woman wanted her warrior husband to come home carrying his _____ or to be carried home on it.

   A horse   **B** shield   **C** spear   **D** chariot

Why do you think the Spartans wanted boys to steal and then punished them if they got caught?

Have students look up the word *spartan* in the dictionary. They will likely find a definition similar to "a person of great courage and self-discipline." Have students read pages 126–127 to find out why the word has taken on that meaning.

Ask:

- After the helots rebelled, how did the Spartans treat them? (They sent people to spy on them and they killed any helot who started to make trouble.)

- Where did Spartan men live until age 60? (They lived in a military camp with all the other soldiers.)

- What two things did a Spartan woman say to her husband as he went off to war? (Come home as a victor carrying your shield; or come home dead, being carried on your shield.)

- What was the one thing Spartans feared? (new ideas)

Reading Strategy: Inferencing

Discuss the meanings of the words that students identify as giving them information about the Spartans. Have them explain how they can use the meanings of these words in to infer the attitude of the Spartans toward life.

 Writing About History

Before students begin writing, have them create a list of facts about either Sparta or Athens. Encourage students to make the lists as detailed as possible. You might suggest that their letter be divided into two paragraphs. First, they should describe what they have seen. Second, they should explain their opinion of this city-state.

 Reinforce and Extend

ELL/ESL STRATEGY

Language Objective:
To review and write newspaper articles

Have students examine the sections of a modern newspaper and note the titles of the sections and the kinds of articles that are found within them. Then ask each student to write an article that might have been published in ancient Sparta. Finally, have students organize their articles into a "daily Spartan newspaper."

Lesson 4 Review Answers

1. D **2.** B **3.** A **4.** A **5.** B

Answers will vary. The Spartan leaders probably felt that being able to steal showed that a boy would be able to do all that a soldier had to do to win battles. If the boy got caught, he might not become a good soldier.

Chapter 6: Lesson 5

Overview This lesson describes three wars fought by the Greeks between 500 B.C. and 400 B.C.

Objectives

- To describe the battles at Marathon, Thermopylae, and Salamis
- To explain the causes and results of the Peloponnesian War

Student Pages pages 128–131

Teacher's Resource Library TRL

Workbook Activity 26

Activity 26

Modified Activity 26

Vocabulary

fleet   **maneuver**
independence

Review the definitions of these words. Then ask volunteers to come up with original sentences that correctly use each word. As an extra challenge, ask students to use all four words in a single sentence.

PRONUNCIATION GUIDE

Use this list to help students pronounce difficult words in this lesson.

Herodotus	(hə rod´ ə təs)
Macedon	(mas´ ə don)
Peloponnesian	(pel´ ə pə nē´ zhən)
Pheidippides	(fī dip´ ə dēz´)
Thermopylae	(thər mop´ ə lē)

1 Warm-Up Activity

Have students work in small groups to develop plans to find out who thought of the name "Nike" for sneakers. Monitor the groups as they are working, and when plans are approved by the teacher, have the groups put their plans into action. Later, have each group describe its plan and the results. Read the lesson to find out which groups have the correct answer.

Objectives

- To describe the battles at Marathon, Thermopylae, and Salamis
- To explain the causes and results of the Peloponnesian War

Fleet
A group of ships

Between 500 and 400 B.C., the Greeks fought several wars. They fought the first two against the huge and powerful Persian Empire. It lay to the east of Greece. These wars united the city-states and made the Greeks proud. In the next war, the city-states of Athens and Sparta battled. We call this the Peloponnesian War. It lasted for 27 years.

Why Did the Persians Invade Greece?

Around 545 B.C., the Persians conquered a group of people called the Ionian Greeks who lived in Asia Minor. Forty-six years later, in 499 B.C., they asked the mainland Greeks to help them remove the Persians. Athens sent warships, but the Ionian Greeks could not win their freedom.

All this made King Darius of Persia angry. He wanted to punish Athens. In 490 B.C., Darius sent 600 ships and thousands of soldiers to invade Greece. According to legend, Athens sent the runner Pheidippides to ask the Spartans for help. He ran 150 miles in two days. When he arrived, the Spartans were celebrating a religious feast and refused to help until the next full moon.

Who Won the Battle of Marathon?

The Persian **fleet,** or group of ships, landed at the Bay of Marathon, about 25 miles northeast of Athens. The Persian army had more soldiers and weapons than the Athenians. The Athenians had no one to help them.

The Persians decided to attack Athens by sea. While they were loading their ships, the Athenians attacked and defeated them. A Greek legend says that Pheidippides ran 25 miles from Marathon to Athens to announce the victory. When he arrived, he yelled, "Nike!" or victory. Then he fell dead, worn out by his run. Today, we remember what Pheidippides did in the modern-day 26-mile marathon run. The Battle of Marathon may be the most important battle in Greek history.

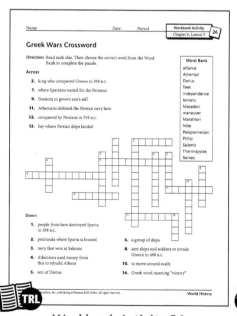

Workbook Activity 26

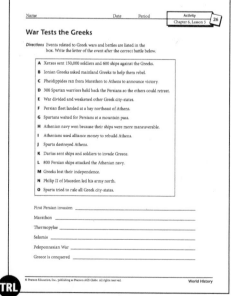

Activity 26

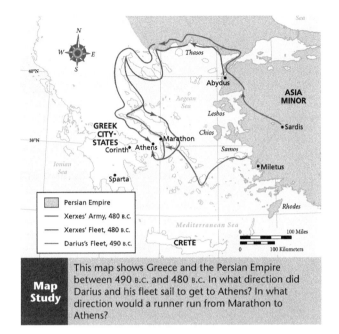

This map shows Greece and the Persian Empire between 490 B.C. and 480 B.C. In what direction did Darius and his fleet sail to get to Athens? In what direction would a runner run from Marathon to Athens?

Map Study

What Happened at Thermopylae?

Ten years later in 480 B.C., Xerxes, the son of Darius, sent 150,000 soldiers and nearly 600 ships against the Greeks. This time, 31 Greek city-states joined together to meet the Persian invaders. The Spartans took charge of the army; Athens supplied the navy.

The great Persian army had little trouble as it moved through northern Greece. Then it came to a narrow mountain pass called Thermopylae. There, 7,000 Spartans waited for the Persians. For several days, they stopped the Persian army from moving forward.

Then a Greek traitor led the Persians behind the Greek army. The Spartan soldiers began to retreat to their ships. As the Persians marched forward, 300 Spartan warriors faced them. To protect the retreat of the others, they gave up their lives.

2000 B.C. – 323 B.C.

Have students draw three columns on a sheet of paper. The headings should read *First War Against Persia, Second War Against Persia,* and *Peloponnesian War.* As they read this lesson, have students write down key facts in each column, including dates, names, battles, and who won.

Ask:

- According to a Greek legend, what did Pheidippides do? (He ran 25 miles from Marathon to Athens to announce the Athenian victory over the Persians, yelled "Nike!" and fell dead from exhaustion.)

- What did the Greeks do when Xerxes and his soldiers invaded? (Thirty-one Greek city-states joined together to meet the Persian invaders.)

- What did the 300 Spartan warriors do to protect the retreat of the other Spartan warriors? (they gave up their lives)

Ask a volunteer to read the title of the map and to explain, using the key, what the shaded area and the different lines represent. Then have students answer the questions in the caption. (Darius's fleet sailed west. A runner would travel southwest from Marathon to Athens.)

LEARNING STYLES

Logical/Mathematical
To help students understand what the Spartan soldiers faced at Thermopylae, challenge them to solve this mathematical problem:

Suppose that all 200,000 Persian soldiers marched to Thermopylae. For every one Spartan soldier, how many Persian soldiers were there? (about 28 Persian soldiers)

Ask:

- **What was Salamis?** (a small island near Athens)

- **How did the Athenians defeat the Persians at Salamis?** (Their small ships destroyed Persia's large ships, which had difficulty maneuvering in the water.)

- **How did Athens use the alliance money, and how did the other city-states feel about it?** (They used the money to rebuild Athens; the other city-states became angry, leading to the Peloponnesian War.)

- **How long did the Peloponnesian War last?** (27 years)

- **Who won the Peloponnesian War?** (Sparta)

- **Why did the Greeks lose their independence?** (They were conquered by King Philip II of Macedon in 338 B.C.)

Reading Strategy:
Inferencing

Have students identify information given in the reading that they can use as clues to make an inference about the Greeks' attitude toward war. Ask what specific words they can use and why.

Biography

Although Herodotus was not the first historian, he made the study of history what it is today. By traveling throughout the Middle East, Herodotus was the first to make research the starting point of historical investigation. Today, when a historian wants to find out about something, he or she does research by visiting foreign lands and interviewing people, just as Herodotus did. Tell students that the word *history* actually comes from the Greek word for investigation.

Maneuver
To move around easily

Independence
Being free; being able to govern one's self

Reading Strategy:
Inferencing

After reading this lesson, what inference can you make about the Greeks' attitude toward war?

Spartan soldiers were trained to be fighters from a very early age.

Who Won at Salamis?

The Persians marched almost 100 miles south and destroyed Athens. The Athenians had already moved to Salamis, a small island nearby. Hundreds of Persian ships attacked the Athenian navy near this island. Yet the Athenians defeated the powerful empire. How? The large Persian ships could not **maneuver,** or move around easily, in the water. The smaller Greek ships destroyed them by poking holes in them with their battering rams. Historians call this one of history's great sea battles. Defeated, King Xerxes returned to Persia. The Greeks had won the battle with a wooden wall of Athenian ships.

What Caused the Peloponnesian War?

In 477 B.C., more than 100 Greek city-states formed a military alliance called the Delian League. Each city-state agreed to give money or ships to be used to defend all of them. Athens led the alliance. During the next 30 years, the Athenians used the alliance money to rebuild Athens. As Athens became rich and powerful, Sparta and other city-states became jealous and angry.

In 431 B.C., war broke out between Athens and Sparta. We call it the Peloponnesian War because Sparta was located on the Peloponnesian peninsula. Sparta had the stronger army, but Athens had the better navy. The war lasted 27 years and ended in 404 B.C. Sparta destroyed Athens. The war divided and weakened the other Greek city-states. They were unable to form a new alliance. Sparta tried to rule all of them.

The Peloponnesian War weakened all the city-states. They were no longer as rich and powerful. In 338 B.C., King Philip II of Macedon, a small kingdom just north of Greece, led his army from the north and conquered Greece. His dream was to control all of Greece. The Greeks lost their **independence,** or freedom. They no longer governed themselves. However, their ideas continued to influence the world.

Herodotus: c. 480–430 B.C.

The Greek writer Herodotus was born in Asia Minor. He had enough money to travel widely, so he toured Egypt and the Middle East. He is known as "the father of history" because he wrote the first history of the ancient world. Herodotus wrote about events he saw. He also included stories and legends.

His book *History* has two main parts. The first describes the people of the huge Persian Empire. It is a travel guide to customs and geography. The other part tells about the wars between Persia and Greece. Much of what we know about this period comes from his books.

Lesson 5 Review On a sheet of paper, write the answer to each question. Use complete sentences.

1. Who were the Ionian Greeks?

2. What was the Battle of Marathon?

3. What did Xerxes do?

4. How did the Greeks win at Salamis?

5. Why did Athens and Sparta fight the Peloponnesian War?

Why do you think the Spartans won the Peloponnesian War?

ELL/ESL STRATEGY

Language Objective:
To use description to explain characteristics of a familiar place

Discuss Herodotus, "the father of history," who wrote about events that he saw, and whose history of the Persian Empire is a travel guide to customs and geography. Have students create a "travel" brochure or "history" about the events that they have seen in their school, neighborhood, or community. The brochure or history can be printed or role-played, and students should be encouraged to include art, poetry, music, or dance in their descriptions of customs and geography.

Lesson 5 Review Answers

1. The Ionian Greeks were a group who lived in Asia Minor and were conquered by the Persians. **2.** The Battle of Marathon was a sea battle between Athens and Persia. **3.** Xerxes led the Persians in an attack on the Greeks at Thermopylae. **4.** The Greeks won by destroying the large Persian ships. **5.** They fought because Sparta became jealous of the wealth and power Athens had.

Answers will vary. The Spartans trained all their lives to become soldiers. The Athenians seemed more interested in art, architecture, and government. So, from a military standpoint, the Spartans were more prepared.

Chapter 6: Lesson 6

Overview This lesson describes ancient Greek contributions to architecture, sculpture, theater, and philosophy.

Objectives

- To describe the features of the Parthenon
- To explain the two types of Greek plays
- To describe the teachings and writings of Socrates, Plato, and Aristotle

Student Pages pages 132–136

Teacher's Resource Library TRL

Workbook Activity 27

Activity 27

Modified Activity 27

Vocabulary

astronomy	logic
biology	philosopher
column	physics
ethics	politics
goddess	

Write the vocabulary words on the board and ask volunteers to provide their own definition for each. Then have students read each definition from the text and compare it to those on the board.

1 Warm-Up Activity

Some personality inventories note that people use either their "thinking (logic)" or "feeling" tendencies when making decisions. Present a current social or school issue to the class. Have students meet in small groups to discuss the issue. After all groups have met, discuss the decision-making process that ensued in each group. It is likely that there were disagreements between the "thinkers" and "feelers." When reading about Plato later in the lesson, ask students how this experience influenced their thoughts about Plato's plan for what type of people should be the rulers.

Objectives

- To describe the features of the Parthenon
- To explain the two types of Greek plays
- To describe the teachings and writings of Socrates, Plato, and Aristotle

Reading Strategy: Inferencing

What do you already know about the beautiful things the Greeks built?

Goddess

A female god

Column

A tall post used to support a building

On the Athenian acropolis stand the ruins of a temple to Athena—a female god, or **goddess.** We call the temple the Parthenon. Many people think it is one of the most beautiful buildings ever built. The Athenians built it after the Persian Wars ended. We call this period of time the "Golden Age of Athens."

Their love of beauty led the Greeks to create beautiful works of art. Besides making beautiful things with their hands, they used their minds. They asked questions about nature, society, and themselves. Their art and their search for truth are two of Greece's greatest contributions to civilization.

How Did Greek Architecture Please the Eye?

The Athenians built many beautiful public buildings and decorated them with fine works of art. Their Parthenon has 46 **columns,** or tall posts used for support. It is 237 feet long and 110 feet wide. The builders knew that columns seem to bend when seen from a distance. They made each column curve a little. Because of this, the columns seem to be perfectly straight when someone sees them from a distance.

The Parthenon, built in the 400s B.C. in Athens, is considered by many to be the most perfect building ever made.

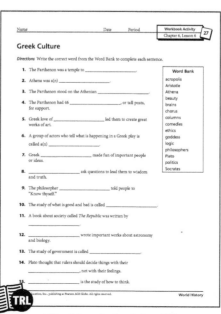

Workbook Activity 27

Activity 27

What Are the Two Kinds of Greek Plays?

The Greeks were the first people to perform plays in outdoor theaters. A group of actors, called the chorus, stood on stage and talked about what was happening in the play. Only men could act in a Greek play.

Greek play writers wrote tragedies and comedies. In a tragedy, the gods defeat the hero. The hero is always smart and he always has courage. He also has too much pride. He tries to achieve more than the gods want him to. After seeing a tragedy, the Greeks felt both sad and happy. They were sad because the hero met defeat. They were happy because the hero had shown courage and strength.

Greek comedies made fun of important people or ideas. A writer named Aristophanes wrote many famous comedies. In his play *The Clouds,* he made fun of Socrates, a famous **philosopher.** Philosophers try to understand the basic nature of knowledge and reality.

A Gift from the Muses

Ancient Greeks believed music was a gift from the gods. Their word for music meant "arts of the Muses." The Muses were nine goddesses. They looked after music (songs and dances), poetry, history, drama, and astronomy. Musical instruments also came from the gods. The lyre and the pipes were two popular instruments. A lyre is a small stringed instrument.

Some special humans also had the gift of music. The most famous was Orpheus. It was believed that even wild animals stopped to hear him play and sing.

Early Greek poets sang or chanted their verses. They played along on the lyre. Music was part of most special occasions. Some poets wrote lyrics for a chorus to sing. These songs often honored winners of athletic games. Music and dancing went with them. Greek drama used music, too. A chorus danced and sang between scenes in a play.

After students read "A Gift From the Muses," ask them what the Greek word for music meant. (arts of the Muses) Then share with students the names and arts of all nine Muses:

Calliope: Muse of heroic poetry

Clio: Muse of history

Erato: Muse of love poetry

Euterpe: Muse of music

Melpomene: Muse of tragedy

Polymnia: Muse of sacred poetry

Terpsichore: Muse of dancing

Thalia: Muse of comedy

Urania: Muse of astronomy

ELL/ESL STRATEGY

Language Objective:
To participate in dramatic speaking
Have students work in a small group to prepare and present a skit of an excerpt from a Greek comedy or a Greek tragedy. Encourage students to use facial expressions and to speak loudly and clearly.

PRONUNCIATION GUIDE

Use this list to help students pronounce difficult words in this lesson.

Aristotle	(ar´ ə stot´ l)
Athena	(ə thē´ nə)
Parthenon	(pär´ thə non)
Plato	(plā´ tō)
Socrates	(sok´ rə tēz)

 2 Teaching the Lesson

As students read this lesson, have them keep a running list of the great contributions the ancient Greeks made to world civilization. Then have students identify what great contributions, if any, the United States has made to world civilization.

Reading Strategy:
Inferencing

During the teaching of this chapter, you have probably had pictures and/or artifacts of ancient Greek life displayed in the classroom. Call students' attention to the beauty of these things. Ask students to describe what these images bring to mind in terms of other beautiful things built by the Greeks.

Ask:

- How did Greek sculptors show the human body? (perfect; without any flaws)

- In a Greek tragedy, what happens to the hero? (the gods defeat him)

- Where did the Greeks perform their plays? (in outdoor theaters)

- What is the purpose of a Greek comedy? (to make fun of important people or ideas)

- What do philosophers want to find, and how do they try to find it? (the truth; by asking questions)

- What happened to Socrates after the jury found him guilty of hurting the young people of Athens? (He was put to death.)

- Do you believe Socrates' death sentence was a fair punishment? (Students may agree or say that Socrates should be given a lighter punishment.)

- Why did Socrates refuse to escape when he had the chance? (He chose to obey the law that condemned him to death.)

- If you were Socrates, would you have escaped, or would you have obeyed the law and accepted your death sentence? (Students' answers will vary. Those who understand Socrates' ethics will say that they would do as Socrates had done.)

LEARNING STYLES

Auditory/Verbal

Lead a discussion on how the Athenians treated Socrates. First, ask students why they think the Athenians did not trust Socrates. (Answers will vary; students may say that the Athenians felt threatened because Socrates questioned their way of life or that they believed asking questions was unpatriotic.)

Some ancient Greek theaters are still standing today. Greek plays were performed outdoors.

What Do Philosophers Want to Prove?

In Greek, the word *philosopher* means "a lover of wisdom." Most philosophers ask questions to lead them to wisdom. They want to find truth. In fact, they want proof of the truth. They do not stop asking questions until they have this proof. Greece produced three of the greatest philosophers in history: Socrates, Plato, and Aristotle.

Why Did the Athenians Want to Get Rid of Socrates?

By asking questions, the philosopher Socrates forced people to examine what they believed. This great teacher always said, "Know thyself." He meant that people need to know why and what they believe. They need to look at why they think something is true, beautiful, just, or good.

Socrates questioned everything, even Athenian democracy. Many Athenians did not trust him. They had just lost the Peloponnesian War, and they thought that anyone who asked questions was unpatriotic.

Astronomy
The study of the stars

Biology
The study of living things

Ethics
The study of what is right and wrong

Logic
The science of thinking

Physics
The science of matter and energy

Politics
The work of government

Reading Strategy:
Inferencing

After reading this lesson, what can you infer about the teachings of Greek philosophers?

In 399 B.C., when Socrates was 70 years old, the Athenian citizens spoke out against him. They said that his teachings hurt the young people of Athens. More than half of the 501 members of the jury voted against him. They said that he must kill himself by drinking poison. His friends and pupils arranged for his escape from Athens, but Socrates refused. He chose to obey the Athenian law, and was put to death.

What Was Plato's Republic?

Plato, a pupil of Socrates, was 28 years old when his teacher died. What the Athenians had done upset Plato. He wrote a book called *The Republic* about a made-up society. It was perfect, orderly, and just. In this society, three classes of people lived: workers, soldiers, and philosophers.

Plato's make-believe society was not a democracy. He thought that only the wisest men and women—philosophers—should rule. Why? Because they would decide things with their brains, not with their feelings. A fine teacher, Plato began a school in Greece that lasted for 900 years. We still study his ideas today.

What Did Aristotle Write About?

Plato's most famous pupil was Aristotle. He wrote important works on **astronomy** (the study of the stars); **biology** (the study of living things); **ethics** (the study of what is right and wrong); **logic** (the science of thinking); **physics** (the science of matter and energy); and **politics** (the work of government).

In his book *Politics,* Aristotle wrote about different kinds of governments. He said that no government was perfect. Just as we still study Plato's writings today, so we study what Aristotle had to say about government.

Today, we can only imagine what the death of Socrates looked like. This is one artist's version.

2000 B.C. – 323 B.C.

WORLD CULTURES

The ancient Greek emphasis on education can be seen in modern Greece, where nine out of ten adults can read and write. All children between the ages of six and fifteen must attend school. Free public schools are available at all levels, including the college level, where enrollment has increased significantly in recent decades.

Ask:

- Why did Plato believe that only philosophers should rule? (They would decide things with their brains, not with their feelings.)
- Name six things Aristotle studied. (astronomy, biology, ethics, logic, physics, and politics)

Reading Strategy:
Inferencing

Discuss with students how some aspects of making inferences focus on identifying motivations. Then ask them what motivation led the philosophers to engage in their teachings.

3 **Reinforce and Extend**

LEARNING STYLES

Visual/Spatial
Have students study the painting of the death of Socrates. Ask them to list details that make the scene seem authentic.

LEARNING STYLES

Interpersonal/ Group Learning
Review with students Plato's ideas for a perfect society and ask them whether they agree or disagree with those ideas. Then divide the class into groups of three or four students and have each group create their own plan for a "perfect society." Encourage students to make detailed plans. When all groups have finished, have a representative from each group share the group's plan with the rest of the class. After each group has shared, ask students which group's society they would most want to live in and why.

Invite students to create a poster that compares the events of the ancient Olympics with the events of the modern Olympic Games. It might show which events have been dropped, which have been added, and which have remained the same. You might wish to display posters in the classroom or hallway.

Lesson 6 Review Answers

1. Parthenon **2.** Aristophanes **3.** Socrates **4.** Plato **5.** Aristotle

Answers will vary. Philosophers are often wise and so may make wise decisions. The question is, however, are they practical? Can they compromise? Are they energetic? Leadership often requires all three qualities.

The Olympic Games

Today's Olympic Games come from ancient Greece. The Greeks loved sports. At that time, sporting contests were part of religious festivals. The Olympic Games began about 776 B.C. They were held at Olympia, a place sacred to the god Zeus.

Ancient Olympic athletes hoped to win glory for themselves and their city. Contests included foot races, boxing, the broad jump, and the discus throw. Unlike now, women could not compete. Nor were there any team sports.

The first modern Olympics took place in 1896 in Athens, Greece. They were the idea of a Frenchman, Pierre de Coubertin. Today, there are Olympic Games every two years. The winter games alternate with the summer games. They take place in different countries. The games include many new sports.

Word Bank
Aristophanes
Aristotle
Parthenon
Plato
Socrates

Lesson 6 Review On a sheet of paper, use the words from the Word Bank to complete each sentence correctly.

1. The _____ was built for the goddess Athena.

2. One Athenian writer of comedies was _____.

3. The philosopher _____ had to drink poison because the Athenians thought he was unpatriotic.

4. The philosopher _____ wrote a book about a government ruled by philosophers.

5. The philosopher _____ thought that no government was perfect.

What do you think

Do you think philosophers would make the best leaders of a country? Why or why not?

Aristotle's most famous pupil was Alexander, the son of Philip II of Macedon. After Philip II conquered the Greeks in 338 B.C., he planned to conquer Persia too. He died before he could make that happen, so his son set out to conquer the world. Soon people would call him Alexander the Great.

What Did Alexander Conquer?

When Philip II died in 336 B.C., Alexander was 20. Two years later, Alexander marched eastward with 35,000 soldiers. They quickly conquered Asia Minor. At the eastern end of the Mediterranean, they defeated the armies of Darius III, the Persian king. Swinging south, Alexander freed Egypt from Persian rule. At the mouth of the Nile River, he built the city of Alexandria.

Reading Strategy:
Inferencing

What can you infer about Alexander's abilities as a leader?

How Far Did Alexander's Army March?

Next, Alexander moved east again and conquered Babylon. He continued to move eastward, deeper into the Persian Empire. By 330 B.C., Alexander had defeated all the Persian armies. He was now king of Persia and dreamed of uniting the known world under one government.

world under one government.

For four more years, Alexander's tired army moved eastward. They went as far as the Indus River. For the Greeks, this was the end of the known world. Alexander wanted to push on, but his men begged him to turn back.

In 323 B.C., Alexander developed a fever in Babylon. Within a few days, the 32-year-old leader was dead. For 13 years, Alexander ruled. During that time he had changed the world.

Alexander the Great conquered many lands at a very young age.

Objectives at left:
- To identify the lands that Alexander the Great conquered
- To identify the Hellenistic Age

2000 B.C. – 323 B.C.

Ancient Greece   *Chapter 6*   **137**

Chapter 6: Lesson 7

Overview This lesson describes Alexander the Great's empire and the spreading of Greek culture that resulted from his conquests.

Objectives

- To identify the lands that Alexander the Great conquered
- To identify the Hellenistic Age

Student Pages pages 137–140

Teacher's Resource Library TRL

Workbook Activity 28

Activity 28

Modified Activity 28

Vocabulary

geometry   **Hellenistic Age**
Hellenism

Have students write original sentences using each word or phrase. Have volunteers write their sentences on the board.

PRONUNCIATION GUIDE

Use this list to help students pronounce difficult words in this lesson.

Euclid   (yü´ klid)

1 Warm-Up Activity

Distribute copies of a modern map of the region formerly occupied by Alexander's empire. Have students work in small groups to make a list of the countries that now occupy the area. Point out that Alexander's army began its march in Macedonia and traveled eastward into India. Using the map's scale, have students calculate the number of miles that the army marched before they returned to Babylon (over 11,000 miles).

Workbook Activity 28

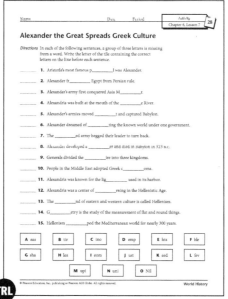

Activity 28

② Teaching the Lesson

Have students read the lesson to find out whether Alexander was successful at conquering the world and what influence his conquests had on civilization.

Reading Strategy:
Inferencing

Ask students to identify facts presented in the text that can help them form a conclusion about Alexander's abilities as a leader.

Ask:

- **What was Alexander's goal?** (to conquer the world)

- **What happened as Greek culture spread?** (It blended with other cultures; this blend is called Hellenism.)

- **Name three ways Middle Eastern people adopted Greek culture.** (They spoke Greek; they built buildings as the Greeks did; they gave themselves Greek names.)

Have students study the map on page 138. Alexander's empire covered parts of three continents. Have students use maps in the World Atlas to determine the three continents. (Africa, Asia, and Europe) Then have them answer the questions in the caption. (Many of the cities include the name "Alexandria." His army passed by the Caspian Sea in northern Persia. Anatolia, or Asia Minor, is south of the Black Sea. Persepolis is east of Athens.)

Have students study the map on page 138.

ELL/ESL STRATEGY

Language Objective:
To role-play a scene from a historical event
Have a group of students role-play a scene in which the men of Alexander's army beg him to turn back after they had marched as far as India. More proficient students can write the skit themselves, giving reasons for their pleas. Less proficient students can act in a skit written by the teacher or other students.

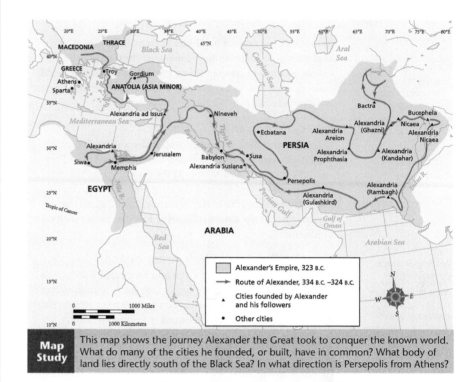

Map Study This map shows the journey Alexander the Great took to conquer the known world. What do many of the cities he founded, or built, have in common? What body of land lies directly south of the Black Sea? In what direction is Persepolis from Athens?

What Is the Hellenistic Culture?

Hellenism
The blend of Western and Eastern cultures made possible by Alexander the Great

Alexander's huge empire fell apart after his death. His three generals divided the empire into three kingdoms—Macedon, Egypt, and Syria. These three kingdoms often fought each other. But one thing held them together—their Greek culture.

Throughout the Middle East, people adopted Greek customs. They spoke Greek, they built their buildings as the Greeks did, and they gave themselves Greek names. At the same time, many Greeks married Persian women. Some began to dress like the Persians. Some Persians joined the Greek army. Soon Greek culture and Persian culture blended into what is called **Hellenism.**

138   *Unit 1   Early Civilizations*

AT HOME

Students who come from immigrant families may have personal experiences in the blending of two cultures. Have them create a list of things from home that represent a blend of their own culture and American culture. Possibilities may include clothing, art objects, and food. Use this activity to help students understand Hellenism, which was a blending of Eastern and Western cultures following Alexander's conquests.

Hellenistic Age

The time between 323 B.C. and 31 B.C., when Greek culture influenced the world

Geometry

The study of the measurement of flat and round things

Reading Strategy:
Inferencing

After reading this section, what can you infer about the people who were influenced by Greek culture?

What Made Alexandria Famous?

The **Hellenistic Age** was the time between 323 and 31 B.C., when Greek culture influenced the world. The people built great cities. Antioch, in Syria, had lighted streets, which the builders paved to make them smooth and level. However, Alexandria in Egypt was the greatest city in the Hellenistic Age. Its harbor had ships from every Mediterranean country. It had a lighthouse 35 feet tall. It had wide streets with many statues. It also had a museum, a zoo, and an art gallery. More than 500,000 people lived in this center of learning. Its library had nearly 500,000 works for them to read.

What Did the Hellenistic Age Contribute to Civilization?

During this time, Euclid of Alexandria put together everything people knew about **geometry.** It's the study of the measurement of flat and round things. Some schools in the 20th century still used his book. Archimedes was Euclid's student. He used mathematics to explain how to lift heavy things with levers and pulleys. (A pulley is a wheel for a rope to pass over.) Archimedes said, "Give me a place to stand, and a lever long enough, and I will move the Earth."

Other important people during the Hellenistic Age included Eratosthenes and Hippocrates. The scientist Eratosthenes is thought to be the first man to calculate the distance around the earth. Hippocrates was a great physician during this time. He is known as the founder of medicine.

Hellenistic culture influenced the Mediterranean world for nearly 300 years. However, Alexander's dream did not come true during this time. He hoped to create an empire ruled by one government. The Greeks did not do this, but the Romans did. Their homeland lay to the northwest of Greece.

2000 B.C. – 323 B.C.

Ancient Greece Chapter 6 **139**

Ask:

- What was the greatest city in the Hellenistic Age? (Alexandria in Egypt)

- What are some features of Hellenistic cities that match those of modern cities? (Answers will vary; students may say streetlights, paved streets, and a library.)

- Does Alexander deserve the name "Alexander the Great"? (Answers will vary; students may say yes, because he took over so much of the world.)

- What school subject uses Euclid's teachings? (mathematics/geometry)

Reading Strategy:
Inferencing

First, review the Greek influences and write them on the board. Then ask students to discuss with a partner and make inferences about those people influenced by Greek culture.

 3 **Reinforce and Extend**

LEARNING STYLES

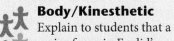 **Body/Kinesthetic**
Explain to students that a major focus in Euclid's geometry is the triangle. Have students figure out where the triangle might fit into the design of objects in their classroom. For example, a rectangle, such as the board or a window, is made up of triangles. Ask students to work with a partner and examine areas of the classroom for places triangles would fit. Then have them make a list of 10 areas that they found.

Lesson 7 Review Answers

1. Alexander marched his army to the Indus River in India. **2.** He built the city of Alexandria. **3.** He ruled for 13 years. **4.** The word *Hellenism* describes the blend of Eastern and Western cultures after Alexander's death. **5.** He organized what people knew about geometry.

Answers will vary. As he conquered the known world, Alexander brought to the conquered people Greek ideas about art, architecture, and government.

Have students read the feature "Math—and Music Too" and list Pythagoras' accomplishments and beliefs. Have a volunteer explain the Pythagorean Theorem on the board, and ask a student who plays an instrument to demonstrate musical ratios. Discuss the quotation, "There is geometry in the humming of the strings . . . there is music in the spacing of the spheres."

Chapter Project Follow-up

Student presentations of the chapter projects may begin during the teaching of this lesson. Schedule presentation topics as near to the times of related chapter study as possible. Encourage students to plan some class-participation activities within their presentations. Display student products from the projects in the classroom throughout the teaching of the chapter.

Lesson 7 Review On a sheet of paper, write the answer to each question. Use complete sentences.

1. How far eastward did the empire of Alexander the Great go?

2. What city did Alexander build in Egypt?

3. For how many years did Alexander rule the known world?

4. What word describes the blend of Eastern and Western cultures after Alexander's death?

5. What mathematical information did Euclid organize?

What do you think

How did Alexander help Greek culture spread far and wide?

Math—and Music, Too

The famous scholar Pythagoras was born on the Greek island of Samos in 580 B.C.

He is best known for his study of math. Pythagoras found that a diagonal line through a square was longer than any side of the square. He and his followers created formulas for this and other math questions. Pythagoras also believed that people could use numbers to understand everything in the world. This would include many sciences, even astronomy.

Pythagoras experimented with strings, bells, and hammers to learn about music. He used numbers to explain changes in musical tones. He created scales and the idea of the octave in music. Many people feel that his work was the basis for music as we know it today. After Pythagoras' death in about 500 B.C., his many students continued his work.

Pericles Praises Athens

Pericles was a great leader of Athens. In about 431 B.C., he made a famous speech. It honored Athenians who had died in the war with Sparta. It is known as "Pericles' Funeral Oration." In the speech, Pericles explains why Athens is great.

Thucydides was the greatest Athenian historian. This speech is in his History of the Peloponnesian War. Thucydides probably heard Pericles give the speech. This is the way Thucydides remembered it.

Pericles: c. 495–425 B.C.

Our form of government does not enter into rivalry with the institutions of others. We do not copy our neighbors, but are an example to them. It is true that we are called a democracy, for government is in the hands of the many and not of the few. But while the law secures equal justice to all alike in their private disputes, the claim of excellence is also recognized; and when a citizen is in any way distinguished, he is elected to the public service, not as a matter of privilege, but as the reward of merit. Neither is poverty a bar, but a man may benefit his country whatever may be the obscurity of his condition.

And we have not forgotten to provide for our weary spirits many relaxations from toil; we have regular games and sacrifices throughout the year; at home the style of our life is refined; and the delight which we daily feel in all these things helps to banish melancholy. Because of the greatness of our city, the fruits of the whole earth flow in upon us, so that we enjoy the goods of other countries as freely as of our own.

And in the matter of education, whereas the Spartans from early youth are always undergoing laborious exercises which are to make them brave, we live at ease, and yet are equally ready to face the perils which they face.

. . . For we are lovers of the beautiful, yet simple in our tastes, and we cultivate the mind without loss of manliness. . . . An Athenian citizen does not neglect the state because he takes care of his own household; and even those of us who are engaged in business have a very fair idea of politics. We alone regard a man who takes no interest in public affairs, not as a harmless, but as a useless character. . . .

Document-Based Questions

1. According to Pericles, why is Athens a democracy?

2. Why is a person elected to public service?

3. How do Athenians relax?

4. According to Pericles, how are the Athenians different from the Spartans?

5. How important are public affairs to Athenians? How can you tell this from the speech you just read?

Read aloud the two introductory paragraphs of the Document-Based Reading. Ask students to read what Pericles said. Then ask volunteers to read the paragraphs aloud as if they were giving a speech. You can record the readings and play back the presentations. Then have students answer the questions.

Answers to Document-Based Questions:

1. It is a democracy because government is in the hands of the many and not of the few.

2. A citizen is elected as a reward for excellence or merit.

3. They have games and sacrifices; they have a pleasant home life.

4. Spartans are always undergoing laborious exercises to make them brave. Athenians have an easy life but are still ready to fight if necessary.

5. Athenians think that a man who isn't interested in public affairs is a useless person.

Have volunteers read the title: "Greek Mythology." Then read the first two paragraphs to students. Ask them to name heroes of myths they know. Ask students to complete the reading, listing the Greek gods as they do so. After students have read the Spotlight Story, explain that ancient Greeks held different opinions about myths. Some people believed that they were true stories. Other people did not believe that these stories actually happened, but they tried to understand the lessons the stories contained. Still others rejected the stories altogether. Ask students what they think about the Greek myths. (Answers will vary; students may say we can learn lessons from them or that they are just stories.)

Answers to Spotlight Story Wrap-Up:

1. A myth is a story that tries to explain a natural event.

2. They lived on Mount Olympus.

3. Zeus was the father of the gods.

4. Atlas had to hold the world on his shoulders forever.

5. Two heroes are Achilles and Odysseus.

Greek Mythology

Have you ever admired the strength of Hercules? He is a famous person in Greek mythology. Myths are stories that try to answer questions about natural events. Why does the sun move across the sky? Why do the seasons change? What causes thunder and lightning?

The Greeks believed in many gods. The chief family included twelve gods and goddesses. They lived on Mount Olympus. These gods were powerful, but not perfect. They acted like the Greeks themselves. They had quarrels. They got angry. Often they took part in people's lives. Many Greek poems and plays retold myths about the gods.

Zeus was the father of the gods. He was lord of the sky. When he was angry, he threw lightning bolts. His brother, Poseidon, ruled the sea. His other brother, Hades, ruled the underworld. One of his sons was Apollo, god of the sun. The Greeks believed that every morning he drove his fiery chariot across the sky. Apollo was also the god of music and medicine. Artemis was his twin sister. She was the goddess of the moon. Artemis protected the young, wild animals, and women. Zeus's favorite child was Athena. She protected city life, especially Athens.

Myths also tell about giants and heroes. Atlas was a giant. He and other giants went to war against the Olympians. They lost. Zeus punished Atlas harshly. He would have to hold the world on his shoulders forever. A book of maps, an atlas, gets its name from this giant.

Some Greek heroes were part god. Others were human beings with special gifts. The greatest hero was Hercules. He was brave and strong. He also had a quick temper. One story

tells how he had to perform 12 difficult tasks. Then he would be forgiven for a terrible crime.

The story of the Trojan War has many heroes. Achilles was the greatest Greek warrior. When he was a child, his mother dipped him in a magic river. Its water would always protect him. She did not notice that the heel she held stayed dry. His "Achilles' heel" was the one place where he could be hurt. At Troy an arrow struck his heel, and he died.

The hero Odysseus was both brave and clever. He thought of the idea for the Trojan horse. That trick helped the Greeks capture Troy. After the war, it took him many years to get home. Homer's *Odyssey* tells of his adventures on the way.

Wrap-Up

1. What is a myth?

2. Where did the main Greek gods live?

3. Who was the father of the gods?

4. What was Atlas's punishment?

5. Who are two heroes of the Trojan War?

Chapter 6 SUMMARY

- Greece is on a hilly peninsula in the Mediterranean Sea. The Minoan civilization started on the island of Crete. About 2000 B.C., the Achaeans built walled cities in southern Greece. Their main city was Mycenae.

- The Mycenaeans fought a 10-year war with Troy. Two long poems by Homer, the *Iliad* and the *Odyssey*, tell about heroes of the Trojan War.

- The Greeks lived in small city-states. Each was a polis. At the center was a hill, or acropolis, and a temple.

- The city-state of Athens began the first democracy. Its citizens ran the government. Only Athenian men were citizens. Women, slaves, and foreign residents were not citizens.

- Sparta was a city-state on a peninsula called the Peloponnesus. Slaves called helots farmed the land.

- Spartan men were soldiers all their lives. Spartan women expected them to fight heroically. Unlike Athenians, Spartans did not care about trade or the arts.

- The Greek city-states united to fight the Persian Empire twice. In 490 B.C., King Darius of Persia tried to invade Greece. The Greeks defeated the Persians at Marathon.

- Persians under Xerxes invaded Greece again in 480 B.C. Spartan soldiers held off the Persians at Thermopylae. The Athenian navy defeated them at Salamis.

- In 431 B.C., Athens and Sparta went to war against each other. This was the Peloponnesian War. Sparta won. The war weakened all the city-states. In 338 B.C., Philip II of Macedon conquered Greece.

- The "Golden Age" of Athens followed the Persian Wars. Greek writers invented two kinds of drama—tragedy and comedy. Socrates, Plato, and Aristotle were Greek philosophers who explored ideas.

- Alexander the Great was the son of Philip II of Macedon. Alexander had studied with Aristotle. He became ruler of Greece in 336 B.C. Alexander's army conquered the Persian Empire.

- Alexander died in 323 B.C. His conquests helped spread Greek culture. A new culture, Hellenism, began. Alexandria, Egypt, was a center of Hellenistic culture.

2000 B.C. – 323 B.C.

Using the Chapter Summary

Have students read the Chapter Summary on page 143 to review the main ideas presented in Chapter 6.

Ask:

- How do we know about the heroes of the Trojan War? (from Homer's poems the *Iliad* and the *Odyssey*)

- Where was the first democracy? (Athens)

- How were Spartans different from Athenians? (They did not care about trade or the arts.)

- How many times did the Greek city-states unite to fight the Persian Empire, and who won the fights? (twice; the Greeks)

- Who fought in the Peloponnesian War and who won? (Athens and Sparta; Sparta)

- Name three Greek philosophers. (Socrates, Plato, and Aristotle)

- What empire did Alexander the Great conquer? (the Persian Empire)

- What is the name given to the mix of Greek culture and other cultures that formed as a result of Alexander the Great's conquests? (Hellenism)

TEACHER'S RESOURCE

The AGS Globe Teaching Strategies in Social Studies Transparencies may be used with this chapter. The transparencies add an interactive dimension to expand and enhance the *World History* program content.

Chapter 6 Review

Use the Chapter Review to prepare students for tests and to reteach content from the chapter.

Chapter 6 Mastery Test

The Teacher's Resource Library includes two forms of the Chapter 6 Mastery Test. Each test addresses the chapter Goals for Learning. An optional third page of additional critical-thinking items is included for each test. The difficulty level of the two forms is equivalent.

Chapter 6 Review Answers

1. Minos
2. Homer
3. Xerxes
4. Aristophanes
5. Parthenon
6. Socrates
7. Plato
8. Aristotle
9. Philip II
10. Alexander
11. C
12. D
13. B

Word Bank

Alexander
Aristophanes
Aristotle
Homer
Minos
Parthenon
Philip II
Plato
Socrates
Xerxes

On a sheet of paper, use the words from the Word Bank to complete each sentence correctly.

1. The Minoan civilization is named after King _____.
2. _____ was a blind poet who wrote the *Iliad*.
3. In 480 B.C., the Greeks defeated the Persian Army of King _____.
4. _____ wrote a play called *The Clouds*, which made fun of the philosopher Socrates.
5. The name of the temple of Athena in Athens is the _____.
6. In 399 B.C., the Athenians found the philosopher _____ guilty of teaching things that hurt the young people of Athens.
7. The philosopher _____ wrote *The Republic* about a perfect society.
8. The philosopher _____ wrote a book about the different kinds of governments.
9. Alexander the Great was the son of _____ of Macedon.
10. The conquering army of _____ spread Greek culture into Asia.

On a sheet of paper, write the letter of the answer that correctly completes each sentence.

11. The Greek city-state that trained all its citizens to be soldiers was _____.

    A Persia   **C** Sparta
    B Athens   **D** Alexandria

12. The philosopher Aristotle wrote books on _____.

    A ethics   **C** astronomy
    B biology   **D** all of the above

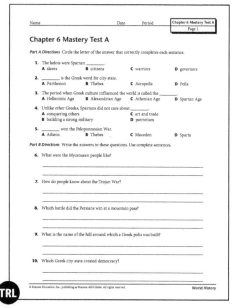

13. The Athenians defeated the Persian fleet at the battle of _____ in 480 B.C.

A Marathon   **C** Thermopylae
B Salamis   **D** Babylon

14. Alexander the Great's army fought against the _____ Empire.

A Persian   **C** Mycenaean
B Roman   **D** Minoan

15. The _____ civilization developed on the island of Crete.

A Mycenaean **B** Persian **C** Minoan **D** Greek

On a sheet of paper, write the answer to each question. Use complete sentences.

16. Greece is on a peninsula and has many rocky mountains. What effect did this geography have on its history?

17. Why did the Greeks want to defeat the Persian Empire?

18. What are three contributions the Greek civilization made to the world? Give three details of each contribution.

Critical Thinking On a sheet of paper, write your response to each question. Use complete sentences.

19. Which ancient Greek city-state would you want to live in—Athens or Sparta? Give three reasons why.

20. Does Alexander deserve to be called "the Great"? Why or why not?

Do not wait until the night before a test to study. Plan your study time so that you can get a good night's sleep the night before a test.

14. A

15. C

16. Because of mountains, the Greek people were isolated from one another, so they built separate city-states. Because the Athenians lived on a peninsula, they became sailors and traders.

17. The Persians, under Darius, had invaded Greece. The Greeks did not want to lose their independence, so they fought back.

18. The Greeks made many contributions including democracy, beautiful architecture and sculptures, the writings of philosophers and mathematicians, and beautiful cities. Answers will vary about the details of each.

Critical Thinking

19. Answers will vary. Sparta was a place of order. The people of Athens loved beauty and beautiful things. They welcomed new ideas and philosophies. The Athenian citizens could afford to support artists.

20. Answers will vary. From the Persian point of view, Alexander probably was not great, because he defeated them. From the point of view of historians, his 13-year journey through the known world with his large army was a wonderful feat.

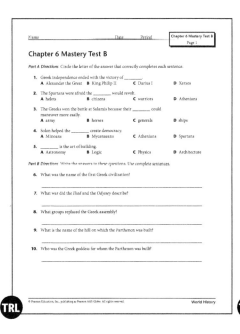

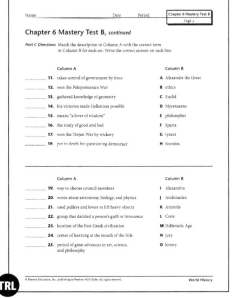

Chapter 6 Mastery Test B, pages 1–3

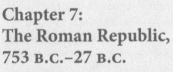

Chapter 7:
The Roman Republic,
753 B.C.–27 B.C.

pages 146–167

Audio Library

Skill Track for
World History

Teacher's Resource Library **TRL**

Workbook Activities 29–33

Activities 29–33

Modified Activities 29–33

Chapter 7 Self-Study Guide

Chapter 7 Outline

Chapter 7 Mastery Tests A and B
(Answer Keys for the Teacher's
Resource Library begin on page 870
of this Teacher's Edition.)

Introducing the Chapter

From the legendary founding of the city
of Rome through the centuries of the
Roman Republic and the Punic Wars
to the reign of Octavian, this chapter
chronicles Roman contributions to
civilization.

The Roman Republic

The ancient Romans had a legend that twin brothers named
Romulus and Remus founded Rome in 753 B.C. Cruel
leaders ruled the Romans until 509 B.C. In that year, the people
rebelled and created a republic. In this chapter, you will learn
about the patricians who ruled this republic. You will also
learn about the plebeians who fought as citizen-soldiers for the
republic. Finally, you will learn what happened to bring the
Roman Republic to an end.

Goals for Learning

◆ To describe the early history of the Roman peninsula

◆ To define the term *republic* and explain the
organization of the Roman republican form of
government

◆ To explain the causes of the Punic Wars

◆ To explain how Rome lost its republican form of
government

◆ To identify Julius Caesar and Octavian and explain
their importance to Roman history

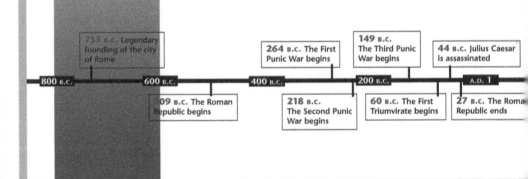

753 B.C. Legendary founding of the city of Rome

264 B.C. The First Punic War begins

149 B.C. The Third Punic War begins

44 B.C. Julius Caesar is assassinated

800 B.C.   600 B.C.   400 B.C.   200 B.C.   A.D. 1

509 B.C. The Roman Republic begins

218 B.C. The Second Punic War begins

60 B.C. The First Triumvirate begins

27 B.C. The Roman Republic ends

Ask:

• What date is given for the
legendary founding of Rome?
(753 B.C.)

• What are the dates for the
beginning and ending of the
Roman Republic? (509 B.C. and
27 B.C.)

• What name is given to the three
wars fought by the Roman
Republic? (the First, Second, and
Third Punic wars)

• Who was assassinated in 44 B.C.?
(Julius Caesar)

Name	Date	Period	SELF-STUDY GUIDE

Chapter 7: The Roman Republic

Goal 7.1 To describe the early history of the Roman peninsula

Date	Assignment		Completed
	1. Read pages 146–150.		
	2. Complete the Lesson 1 Review on page 150.		
	3. Complete Workbook Activity 29.		

Comments:

Goal 7.2 To define the term republic and explain the organization of the Roman republican form of government

Date	Assignment		Completed
	4. Read pages 151–153.		
	5. Complete the Lesson 2 Review on page 153.		
	6. Complete Workbook Activity 30.		

Comments:

Goal 7.3 To explain the causes of the Punic Wars

Date	Assignment		Completed
	7. Read pages 154–156.		
	8. Complete the Lesson 3 Review on page 156.		
	9. Complete Workbook Activity 31.		

Comments:

TRL

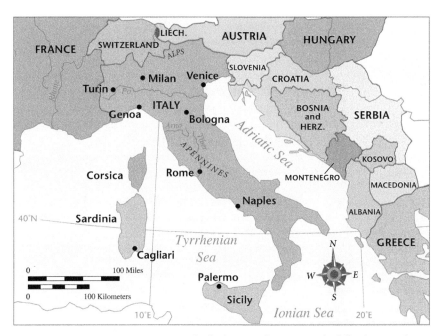

Italy is a boot-shaped peninsula in southern Europe. It has two mountain ranges. One of these—the Alps— forms the northern border of Italy. This is an important natural barrier, or wall, between Italy and other nations. Three important rivers flow through Italy. Its capital city sits next to one of them—the Tiber.

Study the map, then answer the following questions:

1. What is the name of the mountain range that lies northeast of the city of Rome?

2. What are the names of three rivers in Italy?

3. What is the name of the large island that lies near the southern tip of Italy?

4. What is the name of the sea along Italy's east coast?

5. What European country lies to the far northwest of Italy?

Have students study the map of modern Italy. Ask students to read the paragraph beneath the map, then answer the questions using information from the map and the paragraph.

Ask:

• Which two islands are part of Italy? (Sardinia and Sicily)

• Which countries touch its northern border? which mountains? (France, Switzerland, Lichtenstein, Austria, and Slovenia; the Alps)

• Which seas surround Italy? (the Tyrrhenian, Ionian, and Adriatic seas)

Have students read the paragraph under the map and answer the questions.

Map Skills Answers

1. Apennines Mountains

2. Arno River, Po River, and the Tiber River

3. Sicily

4. Adriatic Sea

5. France

Chapter Project

Divide the class into groups of 3 to 4 students. Assign each group a leader related to the Roman Republic, such as Hannibal, Scipio, Marius, Lucius Sulla, Julius Caesar, Octavian, Mark Antony, or Marcus Lepidus. Have each group use this textbook, library materials, and the Internet to research their assigned leader. Presentations should include a biography and explain the leader's importance to Roman history. Each group should prepare a multi-media presentation to share their information with the class.

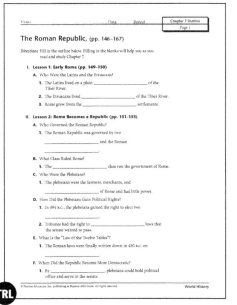

LEARNING STYLES

Visual/Spatial

To help students learn about the geography of Italy, have them trace the map on this page, including the national boundaries, Italy's two mountain ranges, and its three major rivers. Have students color the map and label the mountain ranges, rivers, and surrounding bodies of water. Then have students make a list of the other place names—names of islands, cities, and countries that are shown on the map. Students should cut out these names and place them in the correct locations.

Chapter 7 Outline, pages 1–3

Metacognition

Introduce the reading strategy *metacognition*. Explain to students that when we think about our thoughts as we read, we are using metacognition. Tell students that when they read, it can be helpful to picture, or visualize, the information in their mind. Explain that it is also helpful to think of questions about the text and organize the information as they read. Read the bulleted list on page 148 aloud with students. Have students use the ideas presented to preview the text in the chapter.

Have students look at the heading on page 149, "Who Were the Latins and the Etruscans?"

Ask:

- What information do you think you will learn in this section of Lesson 1? (who the Latins and the Etruscans were)

Direct students' attention to the map on page 150.

- How do you think the map on page 150 can help you understand the Latins and the Etruscans? (Responses will vary. Some students may say that the map will help them understand how close the two groups lived to each other.)

Key Vocabulary Words

Explain that the list of words here is a glossary of the Key Vocabulary students will encounter in Chapter 7. Call on volunteers to read aloud the words and the definitions.

Ask:

- Which term is defined as "a Roman who owned land and helped a ruler govern"? (patrician)
- What does *veto* mean? (to say no to a decision)
- How are a dictator and an emperor similar? (both have control over the government)

Reading Strategy:
Metacognition

Metacognition means "thinking about your thinking." Use metacognition to become a better reader:

- ◆ Preview the text.
- ◆ Make predictions and ask yourself what you already know about the topic.
- ◆ Write the main idea, details, and any questions you have.
- ◆ Visualize what is happening in the text. If something does not make sense, go back and read it again.
- ◆ Summarize what you have read and make inferences about the meaning.

Key Vocabulary Words

Lesson 1 ————————
Founded To have begun a country or city

Advanced Beyond the beginning stage

Senate A governing body

Patrician A Roman who owned land and helped a ruler govern

Lesson 2 ————————
Republic A type of government with no king in which a few people represent, or speak for, everyone

Representative A person who speaks and governs for others

Consul A Roman leader who served a one-year term in the government

Veto To say no to a decision

Dictator A leader who has full control of laws and rules with force

Laborer A person who does hard work with his or her hands

Plebeian A common person in Rome who was not wealthy

Tribune A representative who protected the rights of the plebeian class

Political Having to do with governing

Lesson 3 ————————
Ally A friend; a country or person who helps another

Lesson 4 ————————
Senator A member of a senate

Reform To make something better through change

Politician A government leader

Triumvirate Rule by three people

Lesson 5 ————————
Assassinate To kill someone important

Retire To give up one's job

Emperor A person who is ruler of an empire

IN THE COMMUNITY

Have students find out the story behind the founding of their community. The library, local historical society, or a community Web site might have this information. Then have students write a report that details the historical events. Be sure they include their sources of information in their reports.

- To tell the legend of how Rome was founded
- To describe how the Etruscans governed Rome

Reading Strategy:
Metacognition

Before you read the rest of this lesson, think about what you can do that will help you understand the Latins and Etruscans.

Founded
To have begun a country or city

Advanced
Beyond the beginning stage

Senate
A governing body

Patrician
A Roman who owned land and helped a ruler govern

Rome sits on the western side of the boot-shaped peninsula of Italy. It is 20 miles inland on the Tiber River. No one really knows how or when Rome began. An ancient legend says that the twin brothers Romulus and Remus **founded,** or began, the city in 753 B.C. According to this legend, the baby twins were left to die on the banks of the Tiber River. A she-wolf found them and cared for them. Then a shepherd killed the wolf and raised the twins as his sons. As men, Romulus and Remus built a city. They fought over who should rule. Romulus killed his brother, became king, and named the city Rome.

Who Were the Latins and the Etruscans?

A group of people called Latins lived on a plain called Latium. This plain was located south of the Tiber River. This tribe spoke Latin. Because they could not write, they have left us no written records. However, they did build small villages on hills near the Tiber. Rome grew from these settlements.

People from Greece built several city-states on the southern coast of the Italian peninsula. They brought their Greek culture with them. The Latin people learned many things from their Greek neighbors.

The Etruscans were a tribe of people who lived north of the Tiber. Like the Greeks, they were **advanced,** or beyond the beginning stage. They had a written language and made pottery and fine clothing. They were also expert sailors and traded throughout the Mediterranean. By 600 B.C., the Etruscans had conquered Rome and the plain of Latium. They drained the marshes around Rome to create more living space.

Etruscan kings ruled the Romans for more than a century. The king appointed men to a **senate.** This governing body helped him make decisions. The senate members, or **patricians,** also controlled large amounts of land. Since *patrician* is related to *pater,* the Latin word for father, they were thought to be the "fathers of the state."

Chapter 7: Lesson 1

Overview This lesson covers the development of Rome prior to the beginning of the Roman Republic. It contains the story of Rome's founding and information about its inhabitants both north and south of the Tiber River and its first rulers, the Etruscans.

Objectives
- To tell the legend of how Rome was founded
- To describe how the Etruscans governed Rome

Student Pages pages 149–150

Teacher's Resource Library

Workbook Activity 29

Activity 29

Modified Activity 29

Vocabulary

advanced	patrician
founded	senate

Have students study the vocabulary words and their definitions. Ask them to write each vocabulary word on an index card. Then, read the definitions randomly and have students hold up the card with the correct vocabulary word. Continue until students respond without hesitation.

1 **Warm-Up Activity**

Explain to students that a legend is a story that is passed down through the generations to explain why an event happened. Sometimes parts of a legend are true, and sometimes the entire legend is made up. Tell students that they will be reading a legend about the founding of Rome. Ask students to share legends that other people have passed down to them.

Workbook Activity 29

What Am I?

Directions Write the correct word from the Word Bank that each sentence describes.

___ **1.** I am a plain south of the Tiber River.

___ **2.** Romulus and I founded Rome in 753 B.C.

___ **3.** I am an advanced tribe of people who lived north of the Tiber River.

___ **4.** I am a word that means "to have begun a country or city."

___ **5.** In Rome, I was a person who owned land and helped govern.

___ **6.** To help him make decisions, the king appointed men to me.

___ **7.** I am a boot-shaped peninsula.

___ **8.** I am a word that means "beyond the beginning stage."

___ **9.** I am the river on which Rome is located.

___ **10.** I am a group of people from Latium.

Word Bank
advanced
Etruscans
founded
Italy
Latins
Latium
patrician
Remus
senate
Tiber

Activity 29

Early Rome

Directions Write the answers to these questions. Use complete sentences.

1. What is the legend used to explain how Rome was founded?

2. Who were the Latins?

3. Who were the Etruscans?

4. How were the Etruscans different from the Latins?

5. What kind of government did the Etruscans set up in Rome?

Workbook Activity 29   **Activity 29**   *The Roman Republic   Chapter 7*   **149**

2 Teaching the Lesson

Ask students to recall what they read on page 146 about the founding of Rome. Then have students read page 149 for a more detailed account of the legend, and of the life in and near Rome before the founding of the republic.

Ask:

- According to the legend, which twin, Romulus or Remus, killed his brother and became ruler of Rome? (Romulus)
- Which two groups of people lived in Rome? (Latins and Greeks)
- The kings of which tribe ruled Rome for more than a century? (the Etruscans)

Reading Strategy:
Metacognition

(Students may say that they can create a chart that has a column for facts about the Etruscans and a column for facts about the Latins. They can record information about each group as they read.)

Have students look at the map of ancient Italy and locate areas where the Latins, Greeks, Etruscans, and Phoenicians lived. Then have students read the caption and answer the questions orally. (The Latins and the Phoenicians also lived in Italy. The Phoenicians settled in northern Africa.) Ask students to answer the questions below the caption.

3 Reinforce and Extend

LEARNING STYLES

Body/Kinesthetic
Have students use butcher paper to make an enlarged version of the timeline on page 146. Have them draw time segments carefully so that each century is the same length. Students can then add important events that occurred during each century as they read this chapter about the Roman Republic.

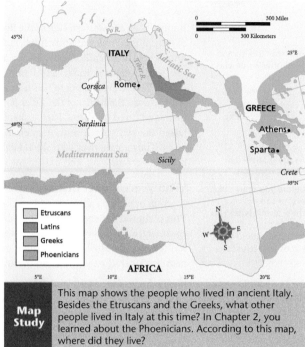

| Etruscans |
| Latins |
| Greeks |
| Phoenicians |

Map Study This map shows the people who lived in ancient Italy. Besides the Etruscans and the Greeks, what other people lived in Italy at this time? In Chapter 2, you learned about the Phoenicians. According to this map, where did they live?

Do you think the legend about Romulus and Remus is at all true? Why or why not?

Lesson 1 Review On a sheet of paper, write the answer to each question. Use complete sentences.

1. According to Roman legend, who founded Rome?
2. What tribe lived to the south of the Tiber River and built settlements on the surrounding hills?
3. What people ruled the Romans for a century?
4. What does the word *patrician* mean in Latin?
5. Why did the Romans call wealthy landowners patricians?

ELL/ESL STRATEGY

Language Objective:
To understand different purposes for writing
Divide the class into pairs. Ask each pair to choose a paragraph to reread from page 149. Have students discuss what they think the purpose was for writing that paragraph. Then ask each pair to read the caption for the map on page 150. Have them discuss the purpose for writing. Finally, ask the pairs to read the vocabulary on page 149 and discuss the purpose for that writing.

Lesson 1 Review Answers

1. The twin brothers Romulus and Remus founded Rome. 2. The Latins lived to the south of the Tiber River. 3. The Etruscans ruled Rome for a century. 4. The word *patrician* means "father." 5. They thought the patricians were the "fathers of the state."

Answers will vary. Some students may say that the legend of Romulus and Remus is not true because it seems very unlikely that the babies would have survived and been raised in the wild.

Objectives

◆ To compare the patrician and plebeian classes
◆ To identify the Law of the Twelve Tables

Republic
A type of government with no king in which a few people represent everyone

Representative
A person who speaks and governs for others

Consul
A Roman leader who served a one-year term in the government

Veto
To say no to a decision

Dictator
A leader who has full control of laws and rules with force

In 509 B.C., the patricians rebelled against the cruel Etruscan king. They defeated the king and set up a different kind of government—a republic. In a **republic,** citizens vote to elect **representatives,** or people who will speak and govern for them. (In a republic, rule does not pass from parent to child.) This Roman Republic lasted from 509 B.C. to 27 B.C.—almost 500 years.

Who Governed the Roman Republic?

The Romans replaced the Etruscan king with two **consuls.** These leaders served the government for a one-year term. Each consul could **veto,** or say no to, a decision by the other consul. Serving only one year and the threat of the veto kept the consuls from becoming too powerful.

The Roman senate, made up of 300 patricians, helped the consuls rule. It had the power to pass laws. In times of war, it could choose a **dictator** for six months. This kind of leader had full control of laws and ruled with force.

What Class Ruled Rome?

The Roman Republic was not a democracy, because it allowed only patricians to vote. They were from the oldest and the richest families in Rome. This wealthy patrician class made up only 10 percent of the population, or all the people, of Rome. Yet patricians ran government. They thought of themselves as the ruling class.

The Roman senate was made up of 300 patricians.

Overview After overthrowing the Etruscans in 509 B.C., the Romans began an almost 500-year experiment with representative government. This lesson explains how the Romans instituted a republic and how all citizens used their political power.

Objectives

■ To compare the patrician and plebian classes
■ To identify the Law of the Twelve Tables

Student Pages pages 151–153

Teacher's Resource Library TRL

Workbook Activity 30
Activity 30
Modified Activity 30

....

Vocabulary

consul	representative
dictator	republic
laborer	tribune
plebeian	veto
political	

Give students an opportunity to study the vocabulary words and definitions listed throughout this lesson. Then write a vocabulary word on the board and ask someone to define it. If class members agree that the definition given is correct, have the individual who defined the word write the next word to be defined on the board. Continue until all the words have been defined.

....

1 Warm-Up Activity

Tell students that the Romans formed a republic. Encourage them to think about today's republican governments. On the board, list charateristics of these governments. Then, as students read, have them compare the list with what they learn about the Roman Republic.

Read pages 151–153 with students to find out how Rome became a republic. Explain that although the republic of Rome was quite different than the United States government is today, one thing they have in common is that most of the population is made up of hard-working people.

Ask:

- **How long did the Roman Republic last?** (almost 500 years)

- **Who were the patricians? the plebeians?** (the wealthy Romans who ran the government; the workers, or common people who paid taxes and served in the army)

- **Why did the patricians need the plebeians? How did this help the plebeians gain some political power?** (The patricians needed the plebeians to fight in the wars to defend Rome. In order to keep the plebeians fighting, the patricians gave them the right to elect tribunes to represent them in government.)

- **How did the tribunes defend the rights of the plebeians?** (by sitting outside the door of the senate and shouting "veto" when they did not like a law)

- **What did the Romans do so that all of the people would know what the laws were?** (they wrote them on twelve bronze tablets and placed the tablets in the marketplace; children had to learn the laws)

Reading Strategy:
Metacognition

(Students may say that the main idea of the lesson is that the Romans set up a republic form of government. The details should support the main idea.)

After each section, students should write a summary that is only a few sentences long and highlights the most important ideas.

Laborer

A person who does hard work with his or her hands

Plebeian

A common person in Rome who was not wealthy

Tribune

A representative who protected the rights of the plebeian class

Reading Strategy:
Metacognition

Note the main idea and important details of this lesson. After each section, summarize what you have read.

Who Were the Plebeians?

Most Romans were not wealthy. They were small farmers, merchants, and **laborers**—people who did hard work with their hands. Yet they were citizens of Rome. The Romans called them **plebeians,** which means "from the common people."

As citizens, the plebeians paid taxes and served in the army. They could not marry out of their class. Also, the patricians could sell plebeians into slavery if they did not pay their debts. They had little power alone, but as a group they were powerful. There were more plebeians than there were patricians. The upper classes tried to keep the plebeians happy with "bread and circuses." In other words, the plebeians were given food and entertainment.

How Did the Plebeians Gain Political Rights?

The plebeians had one important power. They were citizen-soldiers. The patricians needed them to defend Rome against its enemies. In 494 B.C., the Roman Republic gave the plebeians the right to elect, or choose by voting, two **tribunes.** These two representatives protected the rights of the plebeian class.

As time passed, the number of tribunes increased from two to ten. They sat outside the door of the senate and shouted "Veto!" when they did not like a law that a patrician wanted. By 350 B.C., the senate could pass only those laws to which the tribunes said yes.

What Is the "Law of the Twelve Tables"?

In the beginning of the republic, the senate did not write down the laws it passed. The plebeians were not sure what the laws were. As a result, patrician judges were unfair to plebeians. Soon, they demanded that the senate write the laws down. Around 450 B.C., the senate wrote their laws on 12 bronze tablets. Then they put them in the marketplace. Every school child had to learn these laws.

ELL/ESL STRATEGY

 Language Objective:
To learn specific content vocabulary

Have pairs of students write each vocabulary word from Lesson 2 on an index card. Then have them write the definition for each word on a separate index card. Have pairs place the word cards and the definition cards facedown randomly on a table. Students can play a memory game by turning over two cards and trying to match a word with the correct definition. As students find a match, they must read the word and definition aloud to their partner. Students keep the pairs of cards that match. If they do not get a match, they will turn the cards facedown again in the same spot. The student with the most pairs when all word and definition cards are matched is the winner.

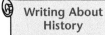
When Did the Republic Become More Democratic?

By 280 B.C., Rome had become more democratic. Plebeians could hold **political**, or governing, offices. They could also serve in the senate. In fact, one consul could come from the plebeian class. Still, problems continued between the patricians and the plebeians. This struggle became an important part of Roman history for several centuries.

Word Bank

Etruscan
patricians
plebeians
republic
tribune

Lesson 2 Review On a sheet of paper, use the words from the Word Bank to complete each sentence correctly.

1. In 509 B.C. some Romans rebelled against the _____ king.

2. After defeating him, they set up a _____, or representative form of government.

3. At first, only _____ sat in the senate and made laws.

4. As time passed, the _____, or common people, got some power in the Roman government.

5. A _____ was a person who represented the plebeians in the Roman Republic.

What can happen when laws are not written down?

Echoes of Roman Rule

At one time, Rome ruled most of Western Europe. Many modern governments have taken ideas from Rome. For instance, in 509 B.C. the Romans rebelled against their kings. They set up a republic. In a republic, the people elect others to represent them. For example, the United States is a republic.

The senate was the main governing body in ancient Rome. The word comes from *senex*, or "old." The United States also has a law-making group called the Senate, but senators are elected. Some Roman officials could *veto* a law. This Latin word means "I forbid." Today, the American president has veto power.

Writing About History

You are running for the office of tribune in the Roman Republic. In your notebook, write a speech. In it, tell the plebeians what you will do for them. Explain why they should choose you.

Writing About History

Before students begin, have them brainstorm a list of issues and/or complaints plebeians might have had. For example, they were the only ones who had to do hard work. Then have them read the Writing About History feature and record their ideas.

3 **Reinforce and Extend**

CAREER CONNECTION

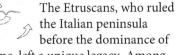

The Romans valued rule by law. Today the law is a focus for a variety of professionals, including paralegals. Paralegals have opportunities for work in law firms and government agencies. They may also work for public-interest groups, such as environmental and civil rights organizations. Candidates for paralegal training must have a college degree and demonstrate proficiency in word processing. To qualify for work as a paralegal, candidates complete a postgraduate course of study.

Lesson 2 Review Answers

1. Etruscan **2.** republic
3. patricians **4.** plebeians **5.** tribune

Answers will vary. Students may say that when laws are not written down, people will forget about them or will not interpret them correctly.

After students read the Then and Now feature, have them investigate how the United States Senate and House of Representatives can override a presidential veto. Have students share their findings with the class. It may help them to know that this information is found in the Constitution of the United States. (It requires a vote of two-thirds of both houses to override a veto.)

BACKGROUND INFORMATION

The Etruscans, who ruled the Italian peninsula before the dominance of Rome, left a unique legacy. Among their gifts to civilization is the Doric column, an architectural feature used in buildings to this day. They also invented a loose-fitting draped garment worn by the ancient Romans called a toga. In ancient Rome, one could often tell a person's status by his toga. Senators wore white. Other colors denoted free-born adolescent boys, free men, and people in mourning.

LEARNING STYLES

Interpersonal/ Group Learning

Have small groups prepare a campaign for plebeian rights. Members should agree on a plan for the group to follow. For example, individuals in a group might prepare speeches, write leaflets, or design posters demanding rights—or the group as a whole might design and make a mural to get their point across.

Chapter 7: Lesson 3

Overview This lesson describes the three Punic Wars and the roles of the people involved that resulted in the expansion of Roman influence.

Objectives

- To describe the three Punic Wars
- To describe the expansion of Rome

Student Pages pages 154–156

Teacher's Resource Library

Workbook Activity 31

Activity 31

Modified Activity 31

Vocabulary

ally

Ask students to use a dictionary to look up the definition for *ally*. Then tell them to write a definition in their own words. Next, ask students to write a paragraph about someone whom they consider a personal ally. Students should describe what makes this person their ally. Have students share their paragraphs with the class.

① Warm-Up Activity

Ask students to consider the part geography might play in a war. Then have them look at the map of Carthage on page 155. Point out the Pyrenees and Alps mountain ranges and the Mediterranean Sea. Ask students how the mountains and sea might protect Rome during a time of war. Students should keep in mind that the Romans did not have the sophisticated military or communications equipment that we have today. Have students discuss their ideas in small groups.

Lesson 3 — Rome Expands Its Boundaries

Objectives

- To describe the three Punic Wars
- To describe the expansion of Rome

During the years of the republic, Rome was often at war with its neighbors. First, the Romans defeated the Etruscans to the north. By 275 B.C., they had conquered the Greeks in southern Italy.

What Caused the Punic Wars?

To the south of Rome, on the northern coast of Africa, lay Carthage. The Phoenicians had settled Carthage, and it had a powerful navy. It controlled Northern Africa, Spain, and several islands close to Italy. Then in 264 B.C., Carthage tried to take control of all of Sicily, an island at the southern tip of Italy. This led to war. In fact, Rome and Carthage fought three wars that lasted over 100 years. The Romans called them the Punic Wars, because *Punici* is the Latin word for "Phoenician."

How Did the Romans Win the First Punic War?

The First Punic War lasted 23 years—from 264 B.C. to 241 B.C. Carthage had a mighty, or powerful, navy. Also, its population of 250,000 was three times the size of Rome. Rome had a fine army, but no navy. How could Rome defeat Carthage?

The Romans added a plank, or long, wide, flat piece of wood, to their ships. When they got close enough to a Carthaginian ship, the plank hooked it and linked the two ships together. Then Roman soldiers ran across the plank and jumped down into their enemy's ship. In this clever way, the Roman army defeated the Carthaginian navy. In 241 B.C., Carthage asked for peace. Rome took control of Sicily and the other islands off its coast.

What Did Hannibal Do in the Second Punic War?

In 218 B.C., Hannibal, a great Carthaginian soldier, planned a bold attack on Rome. His army of 60,000 soldiers, 38 elephants, and many horses marched across Spain, over the Pyrenees, to the foot of the Alps. The Romans thought that these mountains would protect them from attack.

Hannibal's bold attack on Rome surprised the Romans.

154 *Unit 1 Early Civilizations*

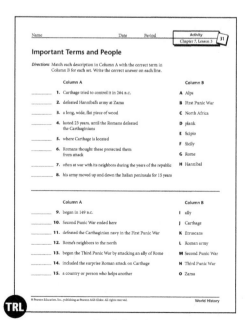

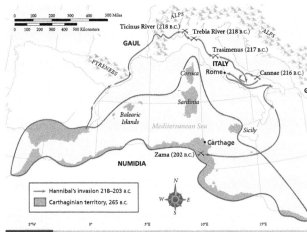

This map shows Carthaginian territory in 265 B.C. and the route of Hannibal's invasion of Rome in 218 B.C. What two mountain ranges did he cross to get to Italy? Name one battle fought in Italy. How far is Carthage from Rome?

2 Teaching the Lesson

Have students look back at the map on page 150 to recall which groups were neighbors of ancient Rome. Then have students read the lesson to find out how Rome and their neighbors solved their differences.

Ask:

• Where does the word *Punic* come from? (Punici is the Latin word for Phoenician.)

• With whom did the Romans fight the Punic Wars? Where did these people live? (the Phoenicians; they lived in Carthage)

• What was Hannibal's role in the Punic Wars? (He was a famous Carthaginian soldier whose army won many battles against the Romans.)

• How did Hannibal surprise the Romans? (He came into Italy from the north, over the Alps.)

Reading Strategy:
Metacognition

Questions that students ask themselves will vary. For example, students may ask, "Who was Hannibal?" Their response might be that Hannibal was a powerful soldier from Carthage.

Reading Strategy:
Metacognition

Remember to ask yourself questions as you read. This will help you make sure that you understand what you are reading.

For two weeks, his soldiers, elephants, and horses moved through narrow, snow-covered mountain paths. They faced snowstorms and bitter cold. Half of his men and most of the elephants died.

Finally, Hannibal's army came down onto the northern plain of Italy. It attacked and defeated the surprised Romans. In less than two years, Hannibal defeated three more Roman armies. Filled with fear, the Romans retreated behind the strong walls of Rome. Even Hannibal could not knock them down.

For 15 years, Hannibal's army moved up and down the Italian peninsula. It destroyed towns and farmland. Then, in a surprise move, the Romans crossed the Mediterranean and attacked Carthage in North Africa. Hannibal had to rush home to defend the city.

---

753 B.C. – 27 B.C.   *The Roman Republic   Chapter 7*   **155**

Ask students what the shaded area on the map represents. (territory dominated by the Phoenicians) Have students trace the route traveled by Hannibal from Carthage to Roman territory, beginning in 218 B.C. Then ask them to read the caption and answer the questions. (He crossed the Alps and the Pyrenees Mountains. Possible battles include: Ticinus River, Trebia River, Trasimenus, and Cannae. Rome is about 400 miles, or about 645 kilometers, from Carthage.)

Language Objective:
To ask for clarification of text

Choose a section of text from Lesson 3 that ELL students might be struggling to understand. Using that text, think aloud about how to ask for clarification of text. For example, have students turn to page 156. Say: "I don't understand what the word *invaded* means in the sentence 'Rome then invaded Carthage.' I can do a few different things to figure out the meaning. I can look at the sentences around it to see if I can figure out what *invaded* means. If that doesn't work, I can look up *invaded* in the dictionary. I can also ask a classmate or my teacher to explain the meaning to me in a different way." Then have students try these strategies with sections of text in the lesson that they do not understand.

Learning Styles

Auditory/Verbal
Make a separate audio recording for the descriptions of the three Punic Wars on pages 154–156. Give students who learn best by listening the opportunity to use the recordings as they fill in their charts of the Punic Wars.

Ask:

• What caused many Carthaginians to starve to death? (Romans invaded Carthage and cut off the food supply to the city.)

• Who was the final victor in the Punic Wars? (Rome)

Ally
A friend; a country or person who helps another

Word Bank
Carthage
Punic
Romans
Second
Zama

What do you think

Do you think Hannibal was a great general? Why or why not?

In 202 B.C., the Roman general Scipio defeated Hannibal's army at Zama. This ended the Second Punic War. Rome forced Carthage to destroy most of its navy and took control of Spain.

What Happened in the Third Punic War?

The Third Punic War began in 149 B.C. Carthage attacked an **ally**, or friend, of Rome. Rome then invaded Carthage. When the Romans cut off food supplies to the city, many Carthaginians starved to death. The Romans burned Carthage to the ground and sold its people into slavery. A legend says that the Romans covered the farmland outside the city with salt so that nothing would grow. Carthage was no more.

Lesson 3 Review On a sheet of paper, use the words from the Word Bank to complete each sentence correctly.

1. The _____ Wars were fought between Rome and Carthage.

2. The _____ won the First Punic War.

3. Hannibal fought the Romans in the _____ Punic War.

4. Hannibal lost the war at the battle of _____.

5. The Romans destroyed _____ around 150 B.C. and won the Third Punic War.

What Year Is It?

What year is it? That depends on when you start to count. Julius Caesar set up the Julian calendar about 46 B.C. It had a 365-day year of 12 months, plus a leap year. For the Romans, Year One was the legendary founding of Rome. By our counting, that was 753 B.C. (What year is it now by the Roman calendar?)

There were small errors in the Julian calendar. Pope Gregory XIII, therefore, set up a new one in 1582. His calendar starts on the date that people thought Jesus was born. Countries gradually began to use it. Today most people in the world use the Gregorian calendar, at least for business.

Some calendars count in still other ways. The Chinese calendar begins at 2637 B.C. on our calendar. The Hebrew calendar starts 3,760 years earlier than the Gregorian. That is considered by the Hebrews as the date of the creation of Earth.

  Reinforce and Extend

Lesson 3 Review Answers

1. Punic **2.** Romans **3.** Second
4. Zama **5.** Carthage

Answers will vary. Many students will respond that Hannibal was a great general because he had to travel a great distance over rough terrain to attack the Romans, and he fought successfully very far from home.

Ask a volunteer to read aloud the History in Your Life feature on page 156 titled "What Year Is It?" Challenge students to answer the question at the end of the first paragraph: What year is it now by the Roman calendar? (to answer this question, add 753 to the current year; for example, if the current year is 2008, the year is 2761 according to the Roman calendar)

Objectives

◆ To explain problems of the poor in early Rome

◆ To describe a triumvirate

Senator

A member of a senate, a governing body

By 133 B.C., Rome controlled the Greek city-states and Asia Minor. It was the most powerful state in the Mediterranean area. The Romans even called this sea *Mare Nostrum,* which means "Our Sea."

Why Did the Roman Poor Grow Poorer?

The early Roman Republic depended on its soldiers, who were free citizens. These citizen-soldiers worked as farmers, laborers, and merchants when they were not fighting a war. Before Rome expanded, its citizen-soldiers fought only in Italy. When a battle ended, they returned home.

But as Rome grew more powerful, it had more territory to defend. Soldiers traveled overseas for long periods of time to fight. Citizens had to pay taxes to support the government. Many soldiers returned home to nothing, because the government had sold their farms for unpaid taxes.

Having no land, the farmers moved to the city. Jobs were hard to find because slaves were doing most of them. With no land and no jobs, many plebeians lost hope. To get a little money, they sold their votes to people running for political office. In this way, the rich became richer; the poor became poorer.

Reading Strategy:
Metacognition

Remember to look at the photographs, illustrations, and maps. Note the descriptive words. This will help you visualize what you are reading.

What Happened to Those Who Helped the Poor?

In 134 B.C., a tribune named Tiberius Gracchus tried to give public land to the poor. He said that soldiers, who fought to protect the wealthy, got nothing in return. The plebeians liked Gracchus, but the patrician **senators,** or members of the senate, feared him. They started a riot, and Gracchus and his followers were killed.

One third of the Roman population were slaves.

Chapter 7: Lesson 4

Overview This lesson describes the rebellions of the plebeian people, the rise of the Roman military to power, and the rule of the First Triumvirate.

Objectives

■ To explain problems of the poor in early Rome

■ To describe a triumvirate

Student Pages pages 157–159

Teacher's Resource Library TRL

Workbook Activity 32

Activity 32

Modified Activity 32

....

Vocabulary

politician	senator
reform	triumvirate

Have students work with a partner to find each vocabulary word and definition, its use in the text, and the Glossary entry for it. Have partners make a chart that displays these three uses of each word—in the margin, in text, and in the Glossary.

....

PRONUNCIATION GUIDE

Use this list to help students pronounce difficult words in this lesson.

Tiberius
Gracchus   (tī bir´ ē əs grak´əs)

Gaius Gracchus   (gā´ əs grak´ əs)

1 Warm-Up Activity

Explain to students that they will read about some people during the Roman era who tried to help the poor citizens. Ask students how people who are in need are helped today. Discuss what students can do to help people who are less fortunate than they. Ask a volunteer to list students' suggestions on the board. Have students use the Internet to find ways they can put their ideas into action in the local community.

The Roman Republic   Chapter 7   **157**

2 Teaching the Lesson

Discuss the reasons why many of the Roman people became poorer as the empire expanded and became more powerful. Ask students to think about what the Roman government could have done differently to avoid this problem. (They could have waived taxes while the farmers were fighting. They could have given soldiers new plots of land after the wars were over.)

Ask:

- What happened to the land of citizen soldiers when they went to fight during the wars? (The government sold the land because the citizens did not pay their taxes.)

- Who tried to give public land to the poor? (a tribune named Tiberius Gracchus)

Reading Strategy: Metacognition

Tell students that the photos, illustrations, maps, and charts in the lesson often contain information to further explain the text. Remind students to also read the captions.

Have students use the scale to figure out how far Roman rule extended north, south, east, and west from Rome. (north about 400 miles, or 600 kilometers; south about 500 miles, or 770 kilometers; east about 1,000 miles, or 1,500 kilometers; west about 1,200 miles, or 1,800 kilometers)

Then have them read the caption and answer the questions. (Rome controls all of the Italian peninsula. Rome also controls Greece to the east. Rome also controls Carthage.)

Reading Strategy: Metacognition

Students may say that they can take notes about each military leader and write what each leader did in their own words.

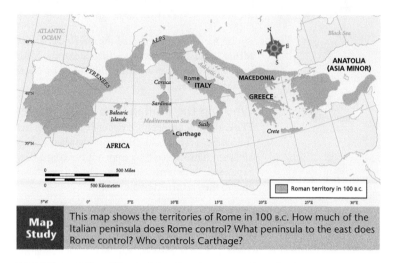

Map Study This map shows the territories of Rome in 100 B.C. How much of the Italian peninsula does Rome control? What peninsula to the east does Rome control? Who controls Carthage?

Reading Strategy: Metacognition

Before you read the next section, think about what you can do that will help you understand more about military leaders in Rome.

Reform

To make something better through change

When Tiberius's brother Gaius was elected tribune in 123 B.C., he too helped the poor plebeians. He was able to lower the price of grain for the poor. He also helped more people in Italy become citizens. But once again, the patrician senators stopped the **reform** movement. They did not want change that would make things better for the plebeians. Gaius Gracchus and several thousand of his followers were killed.

How Did Military Leaders Gain Power?

The plebeians and the tribunes wanted reform. The patrician senators hated it. What happened? Military generals took power. In 110 B.C., Marius, a popular army general, formed an army from the poor who had no land. He promised them a share of the money made from conquering other people. His army won victories in North Africa and Gaul. His soldiers were more loyal to him than to the republic.

In 88 B.C., Lucius Sulla, another powerful general, challenged the power of Marius. War between followers of the two men began. Thousands of people died before Sulla defeated Marius and made himself dictator.

Ask:

- What did Gaius Gracchus do to help the poor people of Rome? (He helped people become citizens; he got the price of grain lowered.)

- How was the general Marius able to win the loyalty of landless soldiers? (He promised them a share of the money made in their conquests.)

- How did Lucius Sulla become a dictator? (He challenged the leadership of a popular general and started a civil war. Then he got rid of a rule that said that dictators could only rule for six months.)

Politician

A government leader

Triumvirate

Rule by three people

By law, dictators had power for only six months. Sulla threw out this law so he could rule longer. Military generals continued to rule Rome until 27 B.C.

What Was the First Triumvirate?

In 60 B.C., three men agreed to rule Rome together: Crassus, a wealthy **politician,** or government leader, and two generals—Pompey the Great and Julius Caesar. Caesar was elected consul. We call the rule by these men the First **Triumvirate.** It lasted less than 10 years.

Lesson 4 Review On a sheet of paper, write the letter of the answer that correctly completes each sentence.

1. The Roman Republic depended on its _____.

A navy   **C** citizen-soldiers

B dictators   **D** enemies

2. A tribune named _____ tried to give land to the poor.

A Pompey the Great   **C** Tiberius Gracchus

B Julius Caesar   **D** Crassus

3. The citizen-soldiers became loyal to _____.

A senators   **C** laws

B Carthaginians   **D** generals

4. _____, a military general, threw out the Roman law that allowed a dictator for only six months.

A Tiberius Gracchus   **C** Marius

B Gaius Gracchus   **D** Lucius Sulla

5. We call the rule of three Romans in 60 B.C. the _____.

A Mare Nostrum   **C** senate

B tax   **D** First Triumvirate

Imagine that you are a citizen of a republic. Why would selling your vote to someone hurt the republic?

Ask:

• What was the First Triumvirate?
(rule of Rome by three men—Crassus, Pompey the Great, and Julius Caesar)

ELL/ESL Strategy

Language Objective:
To understand how prefixes and suffixes affect word meaning

In this lesson, students are exposed to vocabulary words that have prefixes or suffixes. Write the words *reform* and *senator* on the board. Explain to students that the word *reform* is made up of the prefix *re-* plus the root word *form*. Explain that *form* means "to put together" and *re-* means "to do again." Therefore, *reform* means "to put together again." The word *senator* is made up of the root word *senate* and the suffix *-or*. A *senate* is "a governing body." The suffix *-or* is "a condition or activity." So, a *senator* is a person who is part of a governing body.

3 Reinforce and Extend

At Home

Suggest that students talk to family members, read newspapers, and watch news reports on television about current political leaders in the news today. Have students write a paragraph explaining what they have learned or discussed about those leaders, and how they would handle those leadership positions.

Lesson 4 Review Answers

1. C **2.** C **3.** D **4.** D **5.** D

Answers will vary. Selling votes hurts the republic because unworthy people who couldn't otherwise get elected can take over control of the senate. The people who could afford to pay the most for votes would be the people elected.

Chapter 7: Lesson 5

Overview This lesson covers events beginning with the rule of the First Triumvirate and ending with the beginning of the Roman Empire.

Objectives

- To explain how Julius Caesar used his power
- To identify who assassinated Julius Caesar
- To explain how Octavian became Rome's first emperor

Student Pages pages 160–162

Teacher's Resource Library

Workbook Activity 33

Activity 33

Modified Activity 33

Vocabulary

assassinate   **retire**

emperor

Have students read the definition for each vocabulary word. Then have them write a short paragraph using each word correctly.

---

1 Warm-Up Activity

Tell students that there have been important political and social figures in the United States who have been assassinated, including Presidents John F. Kennedy and Abraham Lincoln, and civil rights leader Martin Luther King, Jr. Share brief biographies about these leaders and then elicit students' ideas on how the assassinations of these people may have affected how they are remembered in American history.

STUDY SKILLS

 Have students make a vertical timeline to illustrate the rulers of Rome from the First Triumvirate through the beginning of the empire. Include the names of rulers and the dates of their rule.

---

160 *Unit 1   Early Civilizations*

Objectives

- To explain how Julius Caesar used his power
- To identify who assassinated Julius Caesar
- To explain how Octavian became Rome's first emperor

Assassinate

To kill someone important

Reading Strategy:
Metacognition

Notice the structure of this lesson. Look at the titles, headings, and boldfaced words.

Pompey feared Julius Caesar. He got the senate to limit Caesar's power. In 49 B.C., the senate ordered Caesar to return to Rome without his army. He challenged their power by marching his army to the Rubicon River between Gaul and Italy, crossing it, and marching on to Rome. Pompey fled. Caesar's army defeated Pompey's troops in Greece, Spain, and Egypt. Caesar had broken Roman law, but he had won power.

How Did Caesar Use His Power?

Now Caesar had more power than the senate. He gave jobs to the poor. He told the rich to stop wearing pearls and other signs of their wealth. He passed tougher laws against crime. He also forgave his old enemies and made them government officials. He also made the Roman calendar more accurate, or correct. People in Europe used his calendar for the next 1,500 years.

Who Assassinated Julius Caesar?

In 44 B.C., the senate made Caesar a dictator for life. Many artists carved statues of him, and people could see these everywhere in Rome. The government even stamped his face on Roman coins. Because of all this, some senators feared that they would lose their power. This would end the republic. Some senators **assassinated,** or killed, him on March 15, 44 B.C. These senators, some of them his friends, said that they had killed Caesar to save the republic.

Julius Caesar ruled for a short time before he was assassinated.

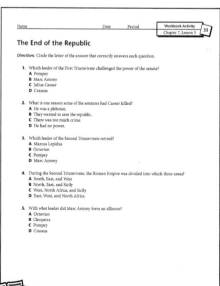

The End of the Republic

Directions Circle the letter of the answer that correctly answers each question.

1. Which leader of the First Triumvirate challenged the power of the senate?
   - A Pompey
   - B Marc Antony
   - C Julius Caesar
   - D Crassus

2. What is one reason some of the senators had Caesar killed?
   - A He was a plebeian.
   - B They wanted to save the republic.
   - C There was too much crime.
   - D He had no power.

3. Which leader of the Second Triumvirate retired?
   - A Marcus Lepidus
   - B Octavian
   - C Pompey
   - D Marc Antony

4. During the Second Triumvirate, the Roman Empire was divided into which three areas?
   - A South, East, and West
   - B North, East, and Sicily
   - C West, North Africa, and Sicily
   - D East, West, and North Africa

5. With what leader did Marc Antony form an alliance?
   - A Octavian
   - B Cleopatra
   - C Pompey
   - D Crassus

Workbook Activity 33

The End of the Republic

Directions Circle the letter of the answer that correctly answers each question.

1. What leader marched his army into Rome, breaking Roman law?
   - A Pompey
   - B Julius Caesar
   - C Octavian
   - D Mark Antony

2. What Egyptian leader had an alliance with Mark Antony?
   - A Marcus Lepidus
   - B Octavian
   - C Pompey
   - D Cleopatra

3. What did Octavian, Mark Antony, and Marcus Lepidus form?
   - A the Roman senate
   - B the Rome/Egypt alliance
   - C the First Triumvirate
   - D the Second Triumvirate

4. What type of leader ruled Rome after the Roman Republic ended in 27 B.C.?
   - A an emperor
   - B a tribune
   - C a dictator
   - D a king

5. What was the result of the battle of Actium?
   - A Octavian was assassinated.
   - B Marcus Lepidus retired.
   - C The Roman Republic ended.
   - D Rome and Egypt formed an alliance.

Activity 33

Retire
To give up one's job

Emperor
A person who is ruler of an empire

Reading Strategy:
Metacognition

Note the main idea and important details of this lesson. After each section, summarize what you have read to make sure you understand how the Roman Republic ended.

Who Formed the Second Triumvirate?

After Caesar's death, fighting broke out. His 19-year-old son, Octavian, and two of his supporters—Mark Antony and Marcus Lepidus—formed the Second Triumvirate. They divided the Roman Empire into three areas. Octavian ruled the West; Antony ruled the East; and Lepidus ruled North Africa. Each shared power over Italy. After Lepidus **retired,** or gave up his job, Octavian and Mark Antony fought for complete power.

How Did Octavian Become Rome's First Emperor?

Mark Antony formed an alliance with Cleopatra, the queen of Egypt. This upset Octavian, because he feared that Antony and Cleopatra would create their own empire. Octavian asked the senate to take away Antony's power. Then Octavian declared war on Antony and Cleopatra. In 31 B.C., at the battle of Actium, the Romans defeated the Egyptians. After learning of their defeat, Antony and Cleopatra killed themselves.

Four years later, in 27 B.C., the Roman Republic ended. The senate made Octavian the **emperor.** For the next 500 years, emperors ruled Rome.

Biography

Cleopatra: 69–30 B.C.

Cleopatra is famous for her charm. She was also brave and ambitious. She became queen of Egypt at age 17. Her family was Greek. They had ruled Egypt for almost 300 years.

Cleopatra and her brother were at war. Julius Caesar helped her win. After his death, she turned to Mark Antony, a Roman general. He helped her keep Egypt independent. They married and had three children.

Then Rome declared war on Antony and Cleopatra. Octavian's fleet defeated them, so Antony killed himself. Cleopatra could not bear to be Octavian's prisoner, so she also killed herself. She and Antony were buried together.

753 B.C. – 27 B.C.

The Roman Republic   Chapter 7   **161**

ELL/ESL Strategy

Language Objective:
To read text for meaning and to speak in front of a group

Divide the class into groups of four students. Have each group work together to reread pages 160–161. Have each student in the group choose one of the heading questions and write it on an index card. Each student in the group should choose a different question.

Students should silently reread the text under the heading that he or she chose and write an answer to the question on the back of their index card.

Have each student share their questions and answers orally with the other members of their group. Students should talk about the answers to determine whether or not they are correct and revise if necessary.

---

2 Teaching the Lesson

Have students read pages 160–162 with a partner to find out how Rome finally became an empire.

Reading Strategy:
Metacognition

Remind students that after they read each section in the lesson, they should be able to answer the question posed in the section heading. Have students make sure they understand the definition of each vocabulary word before reading the section.

Ask:

- Why did the senators say they assassinated Caesar? (to save the republic)

- Who formed the Second Triumvirate? (Octavian, Mark Antony, and Marcus Lepidus)

- Who became the first emperor of Rome? (Octavian)

- Who declared Octavian the emperor? (the Roman senate)

Reading Strategy:
Metacognition

Students should write a few sentences to summarize each section. Sentences should focus on how the Roman Republic ended.

Biography

Throughout her life, Cleopatra schemed to maintain power. When Julius Caesar arrived in Egypt with his strong army, she pursued him romantically in order to further her own interests. After Caesar's assassination, she pursued Mark Antony and ultimately married him. Mark Antony was already married to his rival Octavian's sister at the time of this marriage. Octavian was infuriated by Mark Antony's marriage to Cleopatra, which was invalid according to Roman law. This disregard for Roman law unified the Romans against Mark Antony and prepared them for backing Octavian's conquest of Egypt, during which Antony and Cleopatra committed suicide.

The Roman Republic   Chapter 7   **161**

WORLD CULTURES

 For the Romans, the toga served as a type of uniform. They could tell a man's social class and, in the case of senators, his occupation by the style of his toga. Today we can often tell what people do for a living or for recreation by their uniforms. Brainstorm a list of uniforms people wear today. Sort the uniforms into categories. Examples might include uniforms for sports teams, public servants, hospital workers, and the military.

Lesson 5 Review Answers

1. Caesar disobeyed when he continued marching with his army after the senate told him to return to Rome alone.
2. Senators were afraid of Caesar and said they assassinated him to save the republic. **3.** The Second Triumvirate was made up of Octavian, Mark Antony, and Marcus Lepidus. **4.** She was the queen of Egypt who made an alliance with Mark Antony. **5.** Octavian was the first emperor of Rome.

Answers will vary. It is possible that some high-minded senators may have assassinated Caesar because they feared that he would bring about the end of the republic. Perhaps some simply did not like the fact that he had more power than they did.

Communication in History

Have students read "Our Legacy from Latin." Ask them what happened in 1066 to cause more French words to be added to the English language. (the Normans from France conquered England) Explain that the invention of computers and other technology caused new words to enter the English language. Have students brainstorm a list of terms, such as *Web site*, that are additions to our vocabulary due to the invention of computers.

Lesson 5 Review On a sheet of paper, write the answer to each question. Use complete sentences.

1. How did Julius Caesar disobey the senate?
2. Why was Caesar assassinated?
3. What was the Second Triumvirate?
4. Who was Cleopatra?
5. Who became the first emperor of Rome?

What do you think

Do you think the senators who assassinated Julius Caesar did so for the good of the republic? Why or why not?

Communication in History

Our Legacy from Latin

Is Latin a "dead language"? Has anyone used it since the ancient Romans? In fact, Latin lives on. For many years, educated people in Europe learned it. Scientists still use Latin for plant and animal names. The French, Spanish, and Romanian languages are partly based on Latin.

The English language has two main sources. One is German. The other is Latin. In fact, the word language comes from the Latin word *lingua*. School, library, table—all of these words have Latin roots.

Latin came into English in two ways. At first, many people in England spoke the language of the Angles, Saxons, and Jutes. These were Germanic languages. Then, in 1066, Normans from France conquered England. They added many French words to the language. Other Latin words came from scholars and scientists. For a while, ordinary people used Saxon words. People of higher rank used Latin-based words. Over time, the two blended to form our modern English language.

162   *Unit 1   Early Civilizations*

Chapter Project Follow-up

Have student groups present their multi-media presentations about a leader during the Roman Republic to the class. Assess the accuracy of their information, how well they present the most important facts, and their ability to hold the interest of their audience.

How to Get Elected in Rome

Ancient Rome was a republic. It did not have a king, and it was not a democracy. Only patricians held office. For many years, ordinary people tried to get some voice in government. They won some rights, but power stayed with just a few.

However, Roman officials did need the people's support. Like modern politicians, they tried different ways to get it. This reading is from a letter written in 63 B.C. In it, Quintus Cicero tells his brother how to get elected.

Whoever gives any sign of liking you, or regularly visits your house, you must put down in the category of friends. . . . You must take great pains that these men should love you and desire your highest honor as, for example, your tribesmen, neighbors, clients, and finally your freedmen, yes even your slaves; for nearly all the gossip that forms public opinion emanates from your own servants' quarters.

In a word, you must secure friends of every class, magistrates, consuls and their tribunes to win you the vote of the centuries [that elect the consuls]: men of wide popular influence. . . .

So you see that you will have the votes of all the centuries secured for you by the number and variety of your friends. . . . After that, review the entire city, all guilds, districts, neighborhoods. If you can attach yourself to the leading men in these, you will by their means easily keep a hold upon the multitude.

And you should be strenuous in seeing as many people as possible every day of every possible class and order, for from the mere numbers of these who greet you, you can make a guess of the amount of support you will get on the balloting. It often happens that people, when they visit a number of candidates, and observe the one that pays special heed to their attentions, leave off visiting the others, and little by little become real supporters of the man.

Document-Based Questions

1. Whom does Cicero say a candidate should consider as friends?

2. Why should a candidate make sure that his servants think highly of him?

3. How can a candidate get support throughout Rome?

4. Why do people often vote for a candidate?

5. Would Cicero's advice be useful to someone running for political office today? Why or why not?

Discuss with students public offices they know of that are filled by election. (They may say president, governor, or mayor.) Have a volunteer read the title of the document. Then read the first two paragraphs of "How to Get Elected in Rome" aloud. Remind students the rest of the reading is from a letter. As they read, have them list the suggestions that Quintus Cicero gives his brother. Have students compare their lists and then answer the questions.

Answers to Document-Based Questions:

1. He thinks that a candidate's friends are people who often visit or seem to like a candidate; he also mentions tribesmen, neighbors, clients, and servants.

2. Servants' gossip often affects public opinion.

3. He should get to know and become friends with the leading men in all the city neighborhoods.

4. They notice that he is paying special attention to their interests.

5. Answers will vary. Politicians today need the support of influential people, and they try to get voters' support by paying attention to what they want. Politicians also spend a lot of time meeting all kinds of possible voters.

ONLINE CONNECTION

Cicero was well-known for his many writings on a variety of topics. There are many Web sites that contain excerpts of his writings. Students can also learn more about Cicero's life on Web sites such as the Internet Encyclopedia of Philosophy at www.agsglobewh.com/page163.

Point out the title and the illustration.
Ask students to describe what is
going on in the illustration. Then
read the first two paragraphs aloud.
Encourage students to think about
how the life the Romans led is like
their own life today as they read
the rest of "Life in Rome," and then
answer the questions.

Answers to Spotlight Story Wrap-Up:

1. You would see temples, theaters,
   markets, public baths, arenas, private
   townhouses, and apartment buildings.

2. They went to the public baths. They
   also watched chariot races and
   gladiator fights.

3. They lived in small apartments in
   wooden apartment buildings.

4. He made family decisions and
   conducted worship of the household
   gods. He also directed his sons'
   education.

5. Men wore a knee-length tunic.
   Citizens sometimes wore togas.
   Women wore longer tunics and robes.

Life in Rome

Rome was the largest city in the Roman
Empire. By about A.D. 100, it had nearly
one million people. The city was busy and
crowded. At the heart of Rome was the
Forum. It had great temples, theaters, and
markets. The public baths were also important
buildings. They were popular meeting places.

Romans also loved games and races. The
city had several huge public arenas. People
watched chariot races in the huge Circus
Maximus. Gladiators and wild animals fought
in the Colosseum. (You can still see the ruins of
this stadium in present-day Rome.)

In town, wealthy patricians lived in
comfortable townhouses. They had gardens
and fountains. These nobles also owned large
country homes called *villas*. Most ordinary
Romans rented small apartments in buildings
with four or five floors. Small shops took up
the first floor. These wooden buildings were
dark and crowded. Fire was a constant danger.

Crime was also a problem in Rome. Wealthy
people avoided certain parts of the city. They
might walk there only with armed slaves.

The family was the center of Roman life.
In early Rome, the father had total control
over his household. Later, fathers became less
strict. They still made major family decisions.
They held religious ceremonies to honor
household gods. The goddess Vesta was the
spirit of the hearth. The god Janus guarded the
doorway. Each family also had its own spirits
to protect it.

A Roman father took charge of his sons'
education. Tutors were often Greek slaves.
Young boys learned to read, write, and do
arithmetic. Later they studied Greek and Latin
literature. Public speaking was also important.
Girls were taught cooking and sewing at
home. Young women in patrician families
got more education. They learned literature,
music, and dance. Poorer women often
worked in a shop or laundry.

Like people today, Romans cared about
their looks. They wore jewelry. Women had
elaborate hairstyles. Men wore a simple
short-sleeved garment that fell to the knees.
Women wore a similar, but longer, tunic.
Their robes were wool, linen, or silk. Men who
were Roman citizens could wear a toga. This
was a long piece of cloth that was wrapped
around the body. Different styles of togas had
special meaning. Senators, for example, wore
white togas with a purple border. It was hard
to move while wearing a toga. Workers and
soldiers usually wore just the tunic.

Wrap-Up

1. What kinds of buildings would you see in
   ancient Rome?

2. What did Romans do for fun?

3. Where did most ordinary Romans live?

4. What was the father's role in the Roman
   family?

5. What was Roman clothing like?

Chapter 7 SUMMARY

- Legends say that Romulus and Remus founded Rome in 753 B.C.

- The Latins lived on the plains south of the Tiber River. Greek settlers lived in city-states nearby. The Latins learned from the Greeks.

- The Etruscans lived north of the Tiber River. They were more advanced than the Latins. By about 600 B.C., they conquered Rome. Etruscan kings ruled Rome. Wealthy landowners, called patricians, ran the government.

- In 509 B.C., the Romans overthrew the Etruscan kings. They set up a republic. Two officials called consuls ran the republic. A senate of patricians made laws.

- Most ordinary Romans were plebeians. They paid taxes and served as soldiers. The plebeians wanted political power. Two officials—tribunes—were named to represent them. Tribunes and consuls could veto laws.

- In about 450 B.C., Roman laws were written down on 12 bronze tablets. Plebeians gradually got more power.

- The Roman Republic fought its neighbors. Rome's land and power grew. Three wars were fought with Carthage, a powerful Phoenician city. The First Punic War lasted 23 years, from 264 to 241 B.C. Rome won. In the Second Punic

War, Hannibal crossed the Alps. He invaded Rome itself. A Roman general finally defeated him at Zama in 202 B.C. Rome won the Third Punic War as well. The Romans destroyed Carthage about 149 B.C.

- By 133 B.C., Rome ruled the Mediterranean. But the plebeians were getting poorer. Two brothers named Gracchus tried to help. Both were killed along with many followers.

- Military leaders took power in Rome. Two popular generals were Marius and Sulla. In 60 B.C., three leaders agreed to rule together as the First Triumvirate. Two were generals—Pompey and Julius Caesar. The other was a wealthy politician, Crassus.

- The senate made Caesar dictator for life. Some senators thought that would end the Republic, so they killed Caesar in 44 B.C.

- The Second Triumvirate formed. It included Caesar's adopted son, Octavian, and another general, Mark Antony. A third man, Lepidus, retired. Antony made an alliance with Cleopatra, queen of Egypt. Octavian declared war on them and defeated them. The Senate named him emperor.

753 B.C. – 27 B.C.

The Roman Republic Chapter 7 **165**

Using the Chapter Summary

Have students read the Chapter Summary on page 165 to review the main ideas presented in Chapter 7.

Ask:

- From what culture did the early Romans learn? (Greek culture)

- What kind of government did the Romans set up after they overthrew the Etruscans? (a republic led by two consuls; the senate made the laws)

- Which class of people were soldiers who paid taxes, and who represented them in the senate? (plebeians, tribunes)

- How were the laws made known to all the people? (on bronze tablets)

- What was the final result of the wars with Carthage? (Carthage was defeated.)

- As Rome extended its territory, what happened to the plebeians? (They got poorer.)

- Who ruled in the First Triumvirate? (Pompey, Caesar, and Crassus)

- After Caesar was assassinated, a Second Triumvirate formed. Which of these three rulers was declared emperor by the senate? (Octavian)

Chapter 7 Review

Use the Chapter Review to prepare students for tests and to reteach content from the chapter.

Chapter 7 Mastery Test

The Teacher's Resource Library includes two forms of the Chapter 7 Mastery Test. Each test addresses the chapter Goals for Learning. An optional third page of additional critical-thinking items is included for each test. The difficulty level of the two forms is equivalent.

Chapter 7 Review Answers

1. Scipio
2. Lucius Sulla
3. Hannibal
4. Tiberius Gracchus
5. Pompey the Great
6. Julius Caesar
7. Cleopatra
8. Mark Antony
9. Octavian
10. Gaius Gracchus
11. C
12. D
13. A
14. C
15. A
16. Having two consuls kept one person from having total control. The senate had many different representatives of the people in it. Having a senate kept the two consuls from having total control. The veto kept either of the two consuls from gaining too much power. It also allowed the tribunes to keep the patricians from passing laws that would hurt the plebeians. The tribunes represented the plebeians and were able to help them in a senate that was made up only of the patrician class. The Law of the Twelve Tables made all the laws accessible to all the people.

Chapter 7   R E V I E W

Word Bank

Cleopatra
Gaius Gracchus
Hannibal
Julius Caesar
Lucius Sulla
Mark Antony
Octavian
Pompey the Great
Scipio
Tiberius Gracchus

On a sheet of paper, use the words from the Word Bank to complete each sentence correctly.

1. _____ defeated Hannibal at Carthage.

2. _____ got rid of the law about dictators governing only six months.

3. _____, a great general from Carthage, won many victories against the Romans.

4. As a tribune, _____ gave land to poor plebeians.

5. Along with Crassus and Julius Caesar, _____ was a member of the First Triumvirate.

6. _____ took power by disobeying the Roman senate and marching his army across the Rubicon River.

7. As queen of Egypt, _____ formed an alliance against Rome with Mark Antony.

8. Along with Octavian and Marcus Lepidus, _____ was a member of the Second Triumvirate.

9. _____, the adopted son of Julius Caesar, became the first emperor of Rome.

10. As a tribune, _____ was able to lower the price of grain so that the poor could buy it.

On a sheet of paper, write the letter of the answer that correctly completes each sentence.

11. The word _____ comes from the Latin word for father.

   A plebeian   **C** patrician
   B senate   **D** republic

12. A _____ is a form of government in which citizens elect representatives to govern them.

   A dictatorship   **C** patrician
   B senate   **D** republic

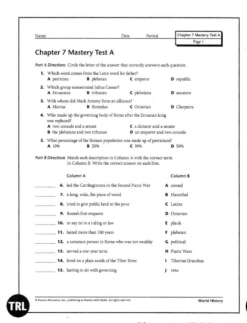

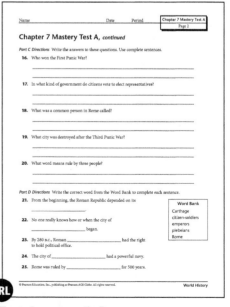

Chapter 7 Mastery Test A, pages 1–3

13. To _____ something is to say no to it.

A veto   **C** term
B accurate   **D** elect

14. In times of war, the Romans would appoint a _____ to rule for six months.

A senate   **C** dictator
B senator   **D** emperor

15. _____ means "from the common people."

A Plebeian   **C** Senate
B Patrician   **D** Triumvirate

On a sheet of paper, write the answer to each question. Use complete sentences.

16. Explain how each of the following was important for the Roman Republic: two consuls; the senate; the veto; the tribunes; the Law of the Twelve Tables.

17. What was one difference between the patricians and the plebeians?

18. Why did the Roman patricians need the Roman plebeians?

Critical Thinking On a sheet of paper, write your response to each question. Use complete sentences.

19. The Roman Republic lasted 500 years. Why do you think it lasted so long?

20. Why do you think the Roman Republic finally ended?

Look over a test before you begin answering questions. See how many parts there are. See what you are being asked to do on each part.

---

17. The patricians were wealthy landowners, probably descended from the Etruscans. The plebeians were common, probably descended from the Latins. They were often poor laborers, merchants, tradesmen, and farmers. The patricians had much more power than the plebeians.

18. The patricians needed the plebeians to fight Roman wars.

Critical Thinking

19. Answers will vary. It lasted so long because the people were devoted to spreading power among many. The two consuls and the senate shared power. The Romans seemed to be devoted to law. There seemed to be some patricians throughout these years who were fair-minded and made changes that helped the poor.

20. Answers will vary. It ended because of the constant quarreling between the patricians and the plebeians. The distance between these two classes became so great that military leaders stepped in and took over. The step from three leaders to one took less than 10 years. The step from one to dictator took a shorter time. Then the Romans grew weary of the power struggle and gave all the power to one person—an emperor.

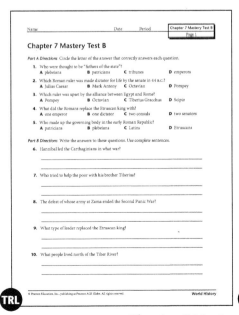

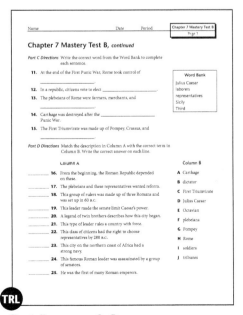

Chapter 7 Mastery Test B, pages 1–3

Introducing the Chapter

Led by both good and bad emperors, the Roman Empire lasted 500 years and grew to a population of nearly 100 million people before its fall in A.D. 476. During this period, one of the world's great religions was born.

---

8 The Roman Empire

In 27 B.C., Rome began the second great period of its history. It became an empire that lasted for 500 years. People of different races, customs, and religions lived in the Roman Empire. In this chapter, you will learn about the Pax Romana, which Octavian began. You will also learn about the rise of Christianity and about the fall of the Roman Empire in A.D. 476.

Goals for Learning

- To describe the reign of Octavian, who was known as Augustus Caesar
- To distinguish between Rome's good and bad emperors
- To describe the rise of Christianity and the conflicts between Rome and Christianity
- To list at least three reasons for the fall of the Roman Empire
- To recognize the practical gifts of the Romans to world civilization

27 B.C. Augustus Caesar becomes first emperor of Rome

A.D. 14 Tiberius becomes emperor

A.D. 161 Marcus Aurelius becomes emperor

A.D. 375 Huns invade Europe

125 B.C. — A.D. 125 — A.D. 250 — A.D. 375

A.D. 1 Traditional date for the birth of Jesus

A.D. 117 Hadrian becomes emperor

A.D. 306 Constantine becomes emperor

A.D. 476 The German Odoacer takes control of Rome; fall of Rome in the West

Ask:

- Who was the first emperor of Rome? (Augustus Caesar)
- What event represents the dividing line between B.C. and A.D.? (the birth of Jesus)
- When did the Huns invade Europe? (A.D. 375)
- What caused the fall of Rome? (the German Odoacer took control)

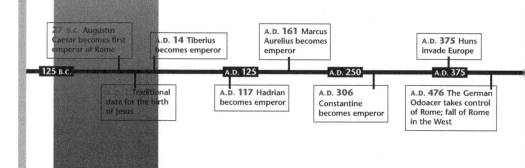

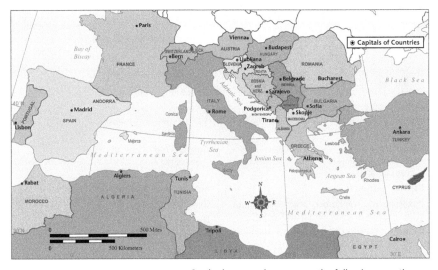

By 27 B.C., Rome controlled most of the known world. The Roman Empire was very large. Much of the empire included what we now call the Mediterranean Region. The Romans called the Mediterranean Sea *Mare Nostrum*. This means "Our Sea."

Study the map, then answer the following questions:

1. What is the capital of Greece?
2. Which country lies directly west of Italy and what is its capital?
3. What countries in northern Africa lie to the south of Italy?
4. What sea touches the coastline of Italy on its east?
5. How many miles does the Mediterranean Sea stretch from east to west?

27 B.C. – A.D. 476

Have a volunteer read aloud the title of the map and the paragraph underneath.

Ask:

- What do we now call the region controlled by the Roman Empire? (the Mediterranean Region)
- What did the Romans call the Mediterranean Sea? (Mare Nostrum, or "Our Sea")
- On which continents did the Roman Empire have territory? (Africa, Europe, Asia)

Have students read and answer the questions.

Map Skills Answers

1. Athens
2. Spain; Madrid
3. Egypt, Libya, Algeria, Tunisia, and Morocco
4. Adriatic Sea
5. about 2,400 miles

Chapter Project

Students will use political candidate debates as a model for a debate among emperors of Rome, who ruled between 125 B.C. and 476 A.D. Divide students into groups of 4 or 5 students. Each group will have the responsibility for preparing one component of the debate (for example, stage scenery, props, and costumes), preparing a panel to ask the questions during the debate, preparing students who will portray the Roman emperors, and preparing students to role-play citizens, who will evaluate, judge, and vote for best emperor.

Chapter 8 Outline, pages 1–3

Summarizing

Introduce the reading strategy *summarizing*. Assign students to work in small groups and provide each group with a newspaper. Ask each group to choose an interesting article to read and summarize for the class. As each group describes their article, write the *Who?*, *What?*, *When?*, *Where?*, *Why?*, and *How?* information on the board.

Explain that questioning words such as *Who?*, *What?*, and *Why?* can help students identify the main ideas that are important in summarizing. Alert readers to ask themselves these questions as they read.

As students read each lesson, encourage them to take notes of important details. After each lesson, ask a volunteer to give a verbal summary of the lesson. Stress to students that summarizing as they read helps them identify and put together main ideas, which will help them understand and remember what they read.

Key Vocabulary Words

Point out that these chapter words are presented in the order that they appear in each lesson. They are also found in the Glossary. Write the following word pairs on the board and ask students how the words in each pair might be related: *plague, sanitation; messiah, disciple; Christianity, Gospel; civilized, homeland.*

Reading Strategy:
Summarizing

As you read the text in this chapter, you will want to ask yourself questions to help you understand what you read.

◆ What is the chapter about?

◆ What new ideas am I being introduced to?

◆ Why is it important that I remember these ideas?

Key Vocabulary Words

Lesson 1

Aqueduct A structure that carries water from far away

Eternal Lasting forever

Pax Romana The Roman peace that began during the reign of Augustus Caesar

Civilized Having good government and the things that make life easier

Lesson 2

Decline To lose power

Plague A disease that spreads from person to person and kills many people

Lesson 3

Christianity The religion based on the teachings of Jesus Christ

Prophet A person who speaks for God

Homeland The land that belongs to a people

Messiah A person sent by God to save people

Gospel One of four books of the New Testament part of the Bible; a word that means "good news"

Betray To stop being loyal to someone

Crucify To hang someone on a cross to die

Disciple A follower of someone

Gentile A non-Jew

Lesson 4

Co-emperor A person who rules part of an empire while another person rules the other part

Lesson 5

Vaulted A ceiling that is high, arched, and covers a large space

Sanitation The act of keeping something clean and free from disease

Imperfection Something that makes an object or person less than perfect

◆ To explain why Augustus Caesar's reign is called the "Golden Age of Rome"

◆ To describe the Pax Romana

Aqueduct

A structure that carries water from far away

Eternal

Lasting forever

Augustus Caesar

In 27 B.C., Octavian, now known as Augustus Caesar, began the second great period of Roman history. Rome was no longer a republic; it had become an empire. This empire lasted for 500 years—from 27 B.C. to A.D. 476.

The empire stretched northwest to Britain and as far north as the Rhine and Danube Rivers. Rome controlled the Mediterranean Sea, much of North Africa, and Egypt. It reached the Euphrates River in the East and the Atlantic Ocean in the West. Nearly 100 million people lived under its rule.

Who Ruled During Rome's Golden Age?

We call Augustus Caesar's 41-year reign the "Golden Age of Rome." He wanted to bring back the old customs of the republic. He slept on a plain bed and wore the same clothes that common people wore. Augustus brought new things to the empire too.

Augustus built new temples, theaters, public buildings, and roads. He also built a large **aqueduct**—a structure that carried water to Rome. He said, "I found Rome a city of brick and left it a city of marble." The Romans were proud of their beautiful city, which was hundreds of years old. They thought it would last forever; it was the "**eternal** city."

More than 50,000 people could attend sporting events in the Roman Colosseum. It was completed in A.D. 80.

27 B.C. – A.D. 476

The Roman Empire Chapter 8 **171**

Chapter 8: Lesson 1

Overview The topic of this lesson is the reign of Augustus Caesar, the first emperor of the Roman Empire. Augustus's leadership brought 200 years of peace and order to the Roman Empire.

Objectives

■ To explain why Augustus Caesar's reign is called the "Golden Age of Rome"

■ To describe the Pax Romana

Student Pages pages 171–173

Teacher's Resource Library TRL

Workbook Activity 34

Activity 34

Modified Activity 34

Vocabulary

aqueduct	eternal
civilized	Pax Romana

Have each student write a fill-in-the-blank sentence for each vocabulary word. Ask volunteers to write their sentences on the board. Have other students come to the board to fill in the blanks with the correct words.

1 **Warm-Up Activity**

Distribute pieces of brick and of white marble to students in small groups. Ask students to record their observations about the color, texture, and beauty of the two substances (brick is darker in color, coarse texture, and of average beauty; marble is shiny and light in color, smooth texture, and beautiful).

After reading the lesson, ask students if they think that Augustus's comment on page 171, "I found Rome a city of brick and left it a city of marble" applied only to building materials. Have them explain their reasoning.

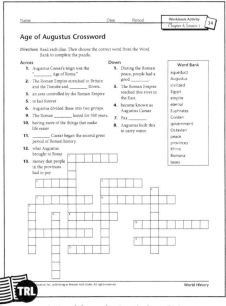

Workbook Activity 34

Activity 34

The Roman Empire Chapter 8 **171**

Use this list to help students pronounce difficult words in this lesson.

Danube   (Dan´ yüb)

Rhine   (rīn)

2 Teaching the Lesson

Before students read the lesson, ask them to think about what it would be like to be the ruler of a large area with millions of people. What do they think would be the most effective ways to control such a large area? Then have them read pages 171–173 to discover how Augustus Caesar brought peace and order that lasted 200 years to the Roman Empire.

Ask:

- About how many people lived under the rule of the Roman Empire? (nearly 100 million)

- What new things did Augustus Caesar build? (temples, theaters, public buildings, roads, and an aqueduct)

- Why was Augustus Caesar's reign called the "Golden Age of Rome"? (Answers will vary. Students may say this is because he built new temples, theaters, public buildings, roads, and an aqueduct.)

- What were the responsibilities of the two government officials in each province? (one official handled military and government affairs; the other took care of money)

Reading Strategy: Summarizing

(The process is governing.)

Have students identify details in this section to help them summarize the information.

- What was the Pax Romana and how long did it last? (the Roman peace; 200 years)

Reading Strategy:
Summarizing

What process is this section about?

Pax Romana

The Roman peace that began during the reign of Augustus Caesar

Civilized

Having good government and the things that make life easier

What Kept Government Officials Honest?

The Romans called the lands outside of Italy the provinces. The people in these provinces paid heavy taxes. But some officials were not honest. Much of this money never reached Rome. What could Augustus do to change this?

He divided the provinces into two groups. The senate controlled the older provinces. The emperor controlled the newer provinces on the frontier. Two government officials took care of the business of each province. One official took care of military and governmental things. The other official took care of everything that had to do with money. Each official watched the other. This kept them honest.

What Is the Pax Romana?

With these changes, Augustus brought peace to Rome and order to the empire. This period of peace lasted for 200 years—from 27 B.C. to A.D. 180. We call it the **Pax Romana,** or the Roman peace. During this time, each province could trade with every other province, and the people lived **civilized** lives. That is, the people had good government and the things that make life easier and more beautiful.

 Biography

Claudius Ptolemy: c. A.D. 100–165

Ptolemy was a famous scientist. He lived and worked in Alexandria, Egypt. We know little else about his life.

Ptolemy observed the sun and stars. He studied Greek geometry. His writings on these topics are in 13 books. They are called the *Almagest.* That means "the greatest." Ptolemy said the earth was the center of the universe. It stood still. The sun and stars moved around it. For about 1,400 years, almost everyone believed this. Ptolemy was also a geographer. In his *Geography,* he corrected the mistakes of earlier geographers. He drew a map of the world that everyone accepted.

Biography

Inform students that while Claudius Ptolemy's map of the world was widely accepted, it contained many errors. For example, the equator was too far north, the circumference of the earth was too small, and Asia extended too far east. Ptolemy's map is historically important, however, because Christopher Columbus used it to show that Asia could be reached by sailing west. However, we all know what Columbus really found when he sailed west!

3 Reinforce and Extend

ONLINE CONNECTION

Students can gain additional information by accessing the following Web site: www.agsglobewh.com/page172.

They will find history and fun facts about Rome on this Web site from the United Kingdom.

Reading Strategy:
Summarizing

What did you learn
about Rome's Golden
Age in this lesson?

Lesson 1 Review On a sheet of paper, write the answer to each
question. Use complete sentences.

1. What do we call the reign of Augustus Caesar?

2. About how many people lived under the rule of the Roman
   Empire?

3. How did Augustus change the city of Rome?

4. Why did Romans call their city the "eternal city"?

5. What do we call the period of peace that began during the
   reign of Augustus?

How could having two government officials in each province
keep them both honest?

The Buried City of Pompeii

The year was A.D. 79. The day was August 24,
a day just like any other day in the Roman
city of Pompeii. Then the volcano Mount
Vesuvius exploded! Fiery lava, or hot melted
rock, lit the sky. Ash and cinders—small
pieces of burnt rock—rained down on
everyone and everything. They made the
sky dark as night for three days.

Thousands of frightened people tried to
run from the city. They tied pillows on their
heads for protection from the rain of fire.
Within days, 30 feet of ash and cinders
buried Pompeii. Poison gas killed the people
who had not gotten away. Some fell dead in
the streets; others died in their homes. One
merchant died next to a stack of coins. Pets
died with their masters.

Then the rain of fire ended. Only the tops
of walls and a few columns stood above
the blanket of ash and cinders. The city of
Pompeii had disappeared! Over time, it was
completely buried and forgotten. Then in
1748, a man hit a wall while digging one day.
He had discovered Pompeii after more than
1,600 years!

For many years, archaeologists have been
digging up the ruins of Pompeii. They
have discovered that mud had covered and
hardened on many dead bodies. When the
bodies decayed, they left their shape, or
mold, behind in the hardened mud.

The archaeologists have also discovered nuts,
bread, figs, eggs on dinner tables, furniture,
and children's toys that still work! Today,
visitors can see the Pompeii of 1,900 years
ago. Its ruins stand frozen in time.

Challenge students to write a 20 to
30-word statement summarizing
information about Rome's Golden Age.

Lesson 1 Review Answers

1. We call it the Golden Age of
Rome. **2.** Nearly 100 million people
lived under the rule of the Roman
Empire. **3.** Augustus built new temples,
theaters, public buildings, roads, and
a large aqueduct. **4.** The Romans
thought their city was so beautiful and
it had lasted for over 500 years, so they
thought it would go on forever. **5.** We
call this 200-year period of peace the Pax
Romana, or the Roman peace.

Answers will vary. Neither official would
want the other to become more well
known. Each official would probably spy
on the other so as to have things to report
to the emperor.

Inform students that the first excavations
at Pompeii were made by people hunting
for valuable treasures. As a result, they
were conducted in a disorganized way,
with little effort to preserve the ruins. In
1860, archaeologist Giuseppe Fiorelli
began an organized excavation, carefully
mapping out the area and recording
every discovery. Modern archaeologists
are racing to complete their studies of the
excavated area of Pompeii because
weathering and root damage from
vegetation have put the ruins in danger of
being lost.

ELL/ESL STRATEGY

Language Objective:
*To understand and orally
describe a historical
event*

Have students read, or read aloud to
them, "History in Your Life—The
Buried City of Pompeii" on page 173.
Discuss what it might have been like
for people in the city on the days that
Mt. Vesuvius exploded and Pompeii
was destroyed.

Have an ELL student work with other
students to role-play the experience
of a Roman family living their normal
life, then realizing that the mountain
was erupting, and finally trying to run
from the city during the destruction.
Encourage students to describe the
situation and narrate the action, either
with their own words, or by reading
aloud parts of the text in "History in
Your Life."

Chapter 8: Lesson 2

Overview This lesson describes the good and bad Roman emperors and the reasons why the empire declined.

Objectives

- To list three good and three bad Roman emperors
- To identify at least three reasons why the Roman Empire began to decline

Student Pages pages 174–176

Teacher's Resource Library TRL

Workbook Activity 35

Activity 35

Modified Activity 35

Vocabulary

decline   **plague**

Have students write the vocabulary words on index cards. As you read each definition, have students hold up the card with the correct word. Check that each student is holding up the correct card. Read the definitions several times in random order to ensure that students master the meanings of the words.

1 Warm-Up Activity

Hold a class discussion about good and bad leaders. Include not only world leaders, but leaders of companies, groups, and teams. Have students describe characteristics of good and bad leaders. Write these on the board. Then tell students they will read about Roman leaders in this lesson.

2 Teaching the Lesson

As students read pages 174–176, ask them to create a list of all the Roman emperors discussed in this lesson. Have students create a second list of the emperors, ranked from best to worst according to their opinion. Discuss the rankings with students explaining and defending their reasoning.

Objectives

- To list three good and three bad Roman emperors
- To identify at least three reasons why the Roman Empire began to decline

Writing About History

Augustus Caesar had the Latin poet Virgil write a poem about Rome's greatness. Think about what you have read about the Roman Empire. In your notebook, write a poem about ancient Rome.

Augustus did good things for the people in his empire. After his death in A.D. 14, however, some emperors did well, while others did poorly. Because these emperors served for life, people had to accept them. Sometimes, when citizens did not want to accept the bad emperors, they murdered them! Between A.D. 180 and 284, there were 29 emperors; 25 of them were murdered.

Who Were Some Bad Emperors?

After the death of Augustus in A.D. 14, his son, Tiberius, became Rome's second emperor. He knew how to lead, but he was not popular. He was intelligent, but he suffered from depression. In his last years, he became a cruel tyrant.

In A.D. 37, Caligula became emperor. He was mentally ill. Some say he made his favorite horse a senator and demanded that people call him a god. He spent all the government's money on foolish things. Because of this, his own guards killed him.

How Did Claudius Become Emperor?

After Caligula's death, the senate tried to decide who should be the next emperor. While they talked about this problem, the guards picked Claudius, the 50-year-old uncle of Caligula. Most senators thought he was a fool. However, Claudius surprised everyone by becoming a fine ruler.

Claudius helped Rome to be orderly and peaceful. In A.D. 54, his second wife poisoned him. Nero, her 16-year-old son from another marriage, became emperor.

What Kind of Emperor Was Nero?

Most historians think that Nero was one of Rome's worst emperors. He sang and played the lyre, a small musical instrument with strings. People were forced to listen to him. Even the senators and the soldiers thought he played poorly.

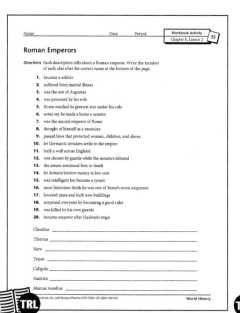

Workbook Activity 35

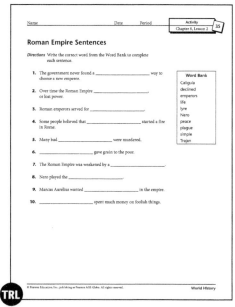

Activity 35

Decline
To lose power

Plague
A disease that spreads from person to person and kills many people

In A.D. 64, a fire lasting nine days destroyed half of Rome. Some said that Nero not only started the fire, he played his lyre while Rome burned! In A.D. 68, some powerful army generals rebelled against Nero. The senate sentenced him to death. Rather than be executed by the government, Nero took his own life.

How Did Good Leaders Improve the Empire?

For 80 years—from A.D. 98 to 180—three good leaders ruled Rome. Under Trajan, the first of the three, Rome reached its greatest size. He gave grain to the poor and let farmers borrow money at low cost.

Hadrian, who followed Trajan as emperor, passed laws that protected women, children, and slaves. He built new buildings, lowered taxes, and built a wall across England.

Marcus Aurelius, the last of the three, took direct command of the Roman army. He did this because Germanic tribes from the north wanted to settle within the empire.

As the empire grew, Rome needed many soldiers to defend and protect it. All these soldiers cost the government a lot of money. Aurelius wanted peace. Rather than fight the Germanic invaders, he let them settle inside the borders of the empire. The empire lasted for another 300 years, but it had already started to **decline,** or lose its power. A Roman historian wrote that Rome had changed "from a kingdom of gold to one of iron and rust."

Marcus Aurelius spent much of his time as emperor in the field with soldiers.

Reading Strategy:
Summarizing

What event is this section about?

Why Did the Empire Decline?

The Roman Empire began to weaken for several reasons. First, its government never found a simple way to choose a new emperor. Too often when an emperor died, civil war broke out. Often, military generals fought each other for power. Sometimes, as with Claudius, soldiers chose the new leader.

Second, because of its wars, taxes were high. The government had little money. Third, a **plague,** a deadly disease that spreads from person to person, hit. All this weakened the empire.

ELL/ESL STRATEGY

Language Objective:
To understand and appreciate that English words have origins in other languages

Include ELL students in work groups of three to four students. Tell students that they are going to prepare for a language contest. Students will use a regular or etymology dictionary (one is available online at www.agsglobewh.com/page175)

as a resource for finding English words that are derived from Latin. Each group will write and perform a 2-minute skit about the Roman Empire, using as many Latin-to-English derivations as possible in the script. The winner of the contest will be the group that has used the largest number of these words correctly. Award extra points for the use of any English words derived from languages of the students who are learning English.

PRONUNCIATION GUIDE

Use this list to help students pronounce difficult words in this lesson.

Aurelius	(ô rē´ lē əs)
Caligula	(kə lig´ yə lə)
Hadrian	(hā´ drē ən)
Nero	(nir´ ō)
Pompeii	(pom pā´)
Ptolemy	(tol´ ə mē)
Trajan	(trā´ jən)

 Writing About History

Suggest to students that they write their poem from the point of view of a specific person. Possibilities include a Roman emperor, an average citizen, a slave, or a person living in a province. Discuss with students how your view of Rome would depend on who you are.

Ask:

• Who killed Caligula? (his own guards)

• Who poisoned Claudius? (his wife)

• What did Nero do to avoid being killed? (He took his own life.)

• Under which emperor did Rome reach its greatest size? (Trajan)

• List four of Hadrian's accomplishments. (He passed laws protecting women, children, and slaves; built new buildings; lowered taxes; and built a wall across England.)

• What did Marcus Aurelius want? (peace)

• What did Rome need as the empire grew larger? (more soldiers to defend and protect it)

Reading Strategy:
Summarizing

(the fall of the Roman Empire)

• Identify three things that caused the Roman Empire to decline.
(inability to choose new leaders; wars drained the government's money; and a plague hit the empire)

LEARNING STYLES

Visual/Spatial
Have students create diagrams that show the three reasons the Roman Empire declined. You might suggest that "Decline of the Roman Empire" be at the center with each of the three reasons forming branches.

Have students study the map of the Roman Empire on page 176. Ask them to measure the distance, in miles and kilometers, between Rome and Hadrian's Wall. (about 1,200 miles; about 1,800 kilometers) Then have students answer the questions in the caption. (The wall is Hadrian's Wall. The Romans built other walls near the Danube and Rhine rivers. A person going from Rome to Alexandria would be traveling southeast.)

3 Reinforce and Extend

STUDY SKILLS

Review proper outlining techniques with students and then have them outline Lesson 2 of this chapter. You might encourage them to change the subhead questions to statements. Remind students that outlines should contain main points and some key details.

Lesson 2 Review Answers

1. The guards chose Claudius. **2.** Trajan gave grain to the poor and let farmers borrow money. **3.** Hadrian passed laws to protect women, children, and slaves. **4.** He wanted peace instead of fighting. **5.** The empire declined because the government could not find a way to choose an emperor, the taxes were high, and a plague hit.

Answers will vary. A plague kills almost everyone. This means there is no one left to produce food, govern, fight wars, solve problems, or entertain people.

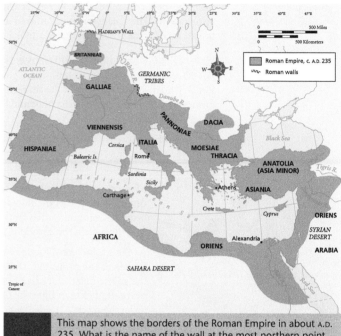

Map Study This map shows the borders of the Roman Empire in about A.D. 235. What is the name of the wall at the most northern point of the empire? Near what rivers did the Romans build other protective walls? What direction would someone travel when going from Rome to Alexandria?

Lesson 2 Review On a sheet of paper, write the answer to each question. Use complete sentences.

1. Who chose Claudius to be emperor?
2. How did Trajan help the empire?
3. What did Hadrian do to help people?
4. Why did Marcus Aurelius allow German invaders to settle inside the empire?
5. What were three reasons the Roman Empire declined?

What do you think

How would a plague weaken a country or an empire?

CAREER CONNECTION

The cause of the plague that hit the Roman Empire was a mystery. The plague resulted in a death rate high enough to contribute to the empire's decline. Today, scientists who study the causes of a disease and try to limit its spread are called epidemiologists. To become an epidemiologist, students must complete an advanced degree program. Encourage interested students to research the high school and college courses that would best prepare them for a career in epidemiology.

AT HOME

Rome spent more money defending its empire than it took in through taxes. This drained the treasury. To this day, governments strive for balanced budgets—collecting at least as much money as they spend. Ask students to clip articles that deal with the national budget of the United States or of some other country from newspapers or magazines. Have them write a summary of the article and bring the clipping to class. Invite students to share their findings.

- To explain who Jesus of Nazareth was and what he did to spread Christianity
- To identify the major conflicts between Rome and Christians

Christianity

The religion based on the teachings of Jesus Christ

Prophet

A person who speaks for God

Homeland

The land that belongs to a people

Messiah

A king sent by God to save people

Gospel

One of four books of the New Testament part of the Bible; a word that means "good news"

While Augustus Caesar was emperor, Jesus of Nazareth was born. His home was in the far eastern section of the Roman Empire called Judea, part of Palestine. Jesus preached a new message to the poor. Out of his preaching grew a new religion—**Christianity.** It changed the Roman Empire and became one of the world's great religions.

Why Did the Jewish People Want a Messiah?

Rome allowed the people in its empire to believe in their own gods. However, the Jews did not have political freedom. For centuries their **prophets**—people who speak for God—said that the Jews would one day rule their own **homeland.** (Homeland is the land that belongs to a people.) Palestine was their homeland. They felt it belonged to them, not to Rome. The Jews believed that their god would send a **messiah,** or savior, to lead them to political freedom. Some people thought that Jesus of Nazareth was this messiah.

What Did Jesus of Nazareth Teach?

Four books called the **Gospels** tell about Jesus. *Gospel* means "good news." The Gospels are the first four books of the New Testament of the Bible. Jesus' followers wrote these books after his death.

Jesus grew up as a Jew in the small town of Nazareth. He earned his living as a carpenter. When he was 30, he began to preach a new message—God loved all people equally. Jesus asked his followers to love all people, just as God did. They were to show this love through service. Finally, he asked them to love even their enemies. Jesus showed a special interest in people others thought were less important: sick people, women, and foreigners.

27 B.C. – A.D. 476 *The Roman Empire* Chapter 8 **177**

Chapter 8: Lesson 3

Overview This lesson describes the rise of Christianity and the Roman Empire's changing attitude toward the growing religion.

Objectives

- To explain who Jesus of Nazareth was and what he did to spread Christianity
- To identify the major conflicts between Rome and Christians

Student Pages pages 177–180

Teacher's Resource Library (TRL)

Workbook Activity 36

Activity 36

Modified Activity 36

Vocabulary

betray	Gospel
Christianity	homeland
crucify	Messiah
disciple	prophet
gentile	

On a blank sheet of paper, have students draw two columns. In the left-hand column, students should write the vocabulary words. In the right-hand column, they should write the definitions in random order. Have students exchange papers and draw lines to match the words and their definitions.

1 Warm-Up Activity

Have half of the class bring in information gathered from newspapers, magazines, television, or the Internet about what Palestine is like today. Have the other half consult reference materials to find out what Palestine was like during Jesus's time. Have students meet in small groups of three to four students with their materials to prepare an analysis of how modern Palestine is alike and different from ancient Palestine. Have students post their findings on chart paper for class discussion.

Workbook Activity 36 | **Activity 36**

PRONUNCIATION GUIDE

Use this list to help students pronounce difficult words in this lesson.

Palestine   (pal´ ə stīn)

Pontius Pilate   (pon´ shəs pī´ lət)

② Teaching the Lesson

Invite students to share what they already know about the Christian religion. Then have students read pages 177–180 to learn about the birth of Christianity and how the Roman Empire reacted to the spread of this new religion.

Ask:

• What new message did Jesus begin to preach when he was 30? (that God loved all people equally)

• Why did many poor people like the Christian message? (They saw it as an answer to their problems.)

Reading Strategy: Summarizing

(Details of teachings include that Jesus's followers should love all people, show love through service, and love their enemies.)

• Name two miracles that Jesus performed according to the Gospels. (He healed the sick and gave sight to the blind.)

• Why did some Jewish leaders turn against Jesus? (They feared his followers would turn against Rome and cause Roman soldiers to kill Jews.)

• What happened when Jesus was betrayed? (One of Jesus's followers turned Jesus over to his enemies.)

• Who was the Roman governor who charged Jesus with being a rebel? (Pontius Pilate)

• What were Jesus's followers called? (disciples)

• What caused Saul to take the name Paul and become a follower of Jesus? (He had a religious experience in which he believed that the risen Jesus had spoken to him.)

Reading Strategy: Summarizing

What details help you understand the teachings of Jesus?

Betray
To stop being loyal to someone

Crucify
To hang someone on a cross to die

Disciple
A follower of someone

Gentile
A non-Jew

Jesus said that God had sent him to preach this good news to the poor. The poor in Palestine liked his message. Large crowds gathered to hear him speak. The Gospels report that he healed the sick, gave sight to the blind, and performed other miracles. Because of this, many people began to follow him.

Why Did Some People Fear Jesus of Nazareth?

For three years, Jesus preached God's love. Then some Jewish leaders turned against him. They feared that his followers would rebel against Rome. Then one of the followers of Jesus **betrayed** Jesus, or stopped being loyal to him. He turned Jesus over to his enemies. Roman soldiers arrested Jesus. Pontius Pilate, the Roman governor, charged him with being a rebel. Then soldiers **crucified** Jesus, or hung him on a cross to die.

Why Did His Followers Call Jesus, the Christ?

The New Testament says the followers of Jesus believed that God raised him from the dead. They also believed that Jesus was the son of God and that he had returned to his father in heaven. These followers, or **disciples,** carried on his teachings. They called him the Christ, or *Christos,* which is the Greek word for "messiah." Those who believed he had risen from the dead became known as Christians, or followers of Christ.

How Did the Gospel Spread?

At first, Jesus' disciples preached their good news only to Jews. Then Saul, who now took the Roman name Paul, became a follower of Jesus. For 30 years, he traveled from Palestine to Greece to Italy. He preached that God had raised Jesus from the dead, and people should love and serve others. He preached to Jews and **gentiles,** or non-Jews. He helped Christianity take its first steps in becoming a world religion.

• What two things did Paul preach? (God had raised Jesus from the dead, and people should love and serve others.)

LEARNING STYLES

Auditory/Verbal

Some students may benefit from explaining the birth of Christianity in their own words. Have them record their explanations and use it later to review this material.

LEARNING STYLES

Body/Kinesthetic

Have students create a poster titled "The Path to a Christian Roman Empire." The poster should trace the development of Christianity from before Jesus's birth to A.D. 395 when Theodosius I made Christianity the official religion of the Roman Empire. Posters should describe key figures, dates, and events. Encourage students to be creative and to include plenty of illustrations.

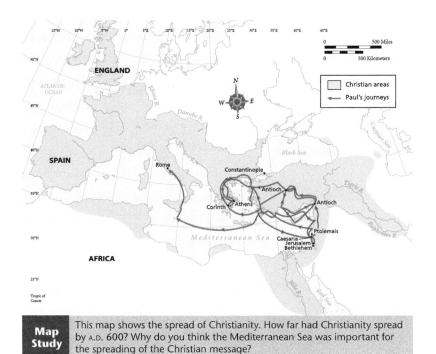

Map Study This map shows the spread of Christianity. How far had Christianity spread by A.D. 600? Why do you think the Mediterranean Sea was important for the spreading of the Christian message?

Reading Strategy:
Summarizing

What process does this section describe?

How Did Christianity Affect Rome?

Roman law said that everyone must honor the emperor as a god. Christians refused to follow this law. Because of this and some other Christian beliefs, the Romans killed many of them.

Over the next three centuries, the Roman Empire grew weaker, but Christianity grew stronger. Many people, especially the poor, saw Christianity as an answer to their problems. Jesus had preached that God loved all people equally. He had promised eternal life to those who believed in him. By A.D. 337, Rome had its first Christian emperor—Constantine. In A.D. 395, the emperor Theodosius I made Christianity the official religion of the Roman Empire.

Ask a volunteer to read the title of the map on page 179 and to explain what the shaded area and arrows represent.

Ask:

- How many years does this map cover? (about 365)
- Parts of which continents are on the map? (Africa, Asia, Europe)

Then have students answer the questions in the caption. (Christianity had spread as far as Spain in the west, England in the north, Africa in the south, and the Tigris/Euphrates rivers in the east. The Mediterranean helped spread the Christian message, because Christians could sail across it to get to other civilizations.)

Ask:

- Who was Rome's first Christian emperor? (Constantine)

Reading Strategy:
Summarizing

(the process of the development of Christianity into Rome)

ELL/ESL STRATEGY

Language Objective:
To visually organize events

Incorporate ELL students into class groups whose purpose will be to write and illustrate a "mindmap" of the stages of life and death of Jesus and of the growth of Christianity until A.D. 395. Have each group put the mindmap on chart paper or butcher paper with the name *Jesus* written or illustrated at the left, and *Christianity* at the right. Have students write Jesus's name in English as well as in the languages of the students whose native language is not English. Stages of the life and death of Jesus and of the growth of Christianity should be illustrated in whatever way the group decides, moving from left to right. The progression should show the flow of events throughout Jesus's life and death, and the ultimate rise of Christianity. Hang the mindmap on the wall for a class presentation.

3   Reinforce and Extend

Lesson 3 Review Answers

1. Gospels   **2.** Messiah   **3.** Saul
4. gentiles   **5.** Constantine

Answers will vary. Christianity preached that God loved all people equally. So, all people were equal. In the Roman Empire that was not true at all. Also, the Romans demanded that people obey the emperor because they thought he was a god. Christians would not do this, so they broke the law. When too many people break the law, a government can fall apart.

LEARNING STYLES

Logical/Mathematical
After students have read Lesson 3, check their understanding of the development of Christianity. Write the following phrases on the board:

- Paul spreads the Gospel.

- Jesus is born.

- Christianity becomes the official religion of the Roman Empire.

- Jesus begins preaching a new message.

- Peter and Paul are put to death.

- Roman soldiers crucify Jesus.

Have students place these six events in the correct chronological sequence. (Jesus is born, Jesus begins preaching a new message, Roman soldiers crucify Jesus, Paul spreads the Gospel, Peter and Paul are put to death, Christianity becomes the official religion of the Roman Empire)

Word Bank
Constantine
gentiles
Gospels
messiah
Saul

Lesson 3 Review On a sheet of paper, use the words from the Word Bank to complete each sentence correctly.

1. We learn about Jesus of Nazareth from the four _____ that his followers wrote.

2. Many Jews believed Jesus was the _____.

3. Another follower of Jesus was _____, who later became known as Paul.

4. Paul preached to Jews and _____.

5. The first Christian emperor was _____.

What do you think

Why do you think the Roman Empire feared Christianity and its message?

- To explain why Diocletian divided the Roman Empire
- To identify the Huns and Visigoths

Co-emperor

A person who rules part of an empire while another person rules the other part

Reading Strategy:
Summarizing

What groups of people are being introduced in this section?

In A.D. 284, Diocletian, a general, became the Roman emperor. He thought that the empire was too large for one person to govern, so he divided it into two parts. The dividing line between the two parts lay west of Greece. Diocletian ruled the eastern part. Another person ruled the western part. This person was the **co-emperor,** or person who ruled one part of an empire while another person ruled the other part.

Who Moved the Capital to Byzantium?

In A.D. 306, Constantine became emperor. By this time, the western part of the empire—the part in which Rome was located—was weak. Constantine moved the capital to Byzantium. This old Greek city stood on the western edge of Asia Minor. He named his new capital Constantinople after himself.

Who Were the Huns and Visigoths?

For hundreds of years, German tribes had fought the Roman army. In battle, they were skilled warriors. By A.D. 200, many Germans lived within the empire. Some of them even became Roman soldiers.

Around A.D. 375, a non-Germanic tribe called the Huns invaded Eastern Europe. They came from central Asia and were expert horsemen and fierce warriors. Their most famous leader was Attila the Hun.

For many years, the Huns rode across Europe, defeating every tribe they met in battle. One German tribe, the Visigoths, feared them. Rome let the Visigoths move within the Roman Empire. The Visigoths promised not to bring weapons with them. Rome promised to give them land. Neither side kept its promise.

As king of the Huns, Attila led his warriors on several raids on the Roman Empire.

Chapter 8: Lesson 4

Overview This lesson describes the struggle between Germanic tribes and the Romans.

Objectives
- To explain why Diocletian divided the Roman Empire
- To identify the Huns and Visigoths

Student Pages pages 181–182

Teacher's Resource Library

Workbook Activity 37

Activity 37

Modified Activity 37

Vocabulary

co-emperor

Review with students the definition of this vocabulary word. Then have them write sentences that use the word correctly.

PRONUNCIATION GUIDE

Use this list to help students pronounce difficult words in this lesson.

Adrianople	(ā´ drē ə nō´ pəl)
Attila	(ə til´ ə)
Byzantium	(bi zan´ tē əm)
Constantine	(kon´ stən tēn)
Odoacer	(ō´ dō ā´ sər)

 Warm-Up Activity

"If it were easy to be a chieftan, everyone would be one."

-Attila the Hun (A.D. 375)

"We are about to embark upon the Great Crusade, toward which we have striven these many months."

-General Dwight Eisenhowser (1944)

Write the quotes on the board and explain the role of General Eisenhower in leading the D-Day invasion. Define *chieftan*. Then ask the students how his tasks as a chieftan were similar to and different from that of Attila the Hun.

---

2 Teaching the Lesson

Ask students to predict why the Roman Empire collapsed. Then have them read pages 181–182 to find out whether their predictions are accurate.

Reading Strategy:
Summarizing

(the non-Germanic Huns and the Germanic Visigoths)

Ask:

• From which direction did the invading Visigoths come into the Roman Empire? (the north)

• Where were the Huns from? (central Asia)

• When did a leader from outside of the Roman Empire take control of Rome? (A.D. 476)

• Name the two Germanic tribes that destroyed Rome. (the Visigoths and the Vandals)

• What happened to the eastern part of the Roman Empire? (it survived)

Reading Strategy:
Summarizing

(the Visigoths defeat Romans at the Battle of Adrianople and loot Rome, Vandals destroy much of Rome's beauty, a German leader takes control of Rome)

3 Reinforce and Extend

What Year Did the Roman Empire Fall?

The Visigoths began to attack Roman towns. In A.D. 378, Rome sent an army against them. But the Visigoths defeated the Romans at the Battle of Adrianople. This was one of the most important events in world history. For the first time in hundreds of years, Rome could not defend itself!

In A.D. 410, the Visigoths sacked Rome. In A.D. 455, another German tribe, the Vandals, came into Rome and destroyed much of its beauty. (To this day, we call people who destroy property vandals.)

Reading Strategy:
Summarizing

What are some important details that help you understand the fall of the Roman Empire?

Then in A.D. 476, Odoacer, a German leader, took control of Rome. Roman rule—as a republic and as an empire—had lasted for 1,000 years, but now it was no more. The western part of the empire had collapsed. However, the eastern part survived.

Lesson 4 Review On a sheet of paper, write the letter of the answer that correctly completes each sentence.

1. Emperor _____ divided the Roman Empire into two parts.

   A Marcus Aurelius   **C** Diocletian
   B Constantine   **D** Visigoth

2. Emperor _____ moved the capital of the empire from Rome to Byzantium.

   A Marcus Aurelius   **C** Diocletian
   B Constantine   **D** Attila

3. The name of the new capital was _____.

   A Adrianople   **C** Odoacer
   B Hun   **D** Constantinople

4. The best known leader of the Huns was _____.

   A Attila   **C** Diocletian
   B Odoacer   **D** Visigoth

5. Historians give the date of A.D. _____ for the fall of Rome.

   A 378   **B** 410   **C** 455   **D** 476

How do you think the Germanic tribes were able to take over the Roman Empire?

Lesson 4 Review Answers

1. C **2.** B **3.** D **4.** A **5.** D

Answers will vary. The Romans had grown weak. They had run out of money. Governments need money to function. Also, the Germanic tribes were greedy for the settled land and cities of the empire and for its culture and beauty. The Romans may have also grown too self-confident, and gradually, the Germanic tribes were able to take over.

- ◆ To describe Roman law
- ◆ To describe Roman buildings, art, and science

Vaulted

A ceiling that is high, arched, and covers a large space

Reading Strategy:
Summarizing

What is the main idea of this paragraph?

The fall of Rome did not end its influence. Roman culture influenced the German invaders. Its influence continues to this day, because Rome gave many gifts to world civilization. These gifts were useful for the Romans, who were a practical people. They liked useful things.

Why Is Roman Law a Gift to Civilization?

In many ways, Roman law made the empire a success for a thousand years. Romans respected the law. They thought that a law should be fair, just, and reasonable. They thought that law should do two things. First, it should protect people's lives and property. Second, it should punish those who do wrong. Law codes based on Roman ideas are still used in some countries of Europe. Roman law stated that all people are equal before the law.

What Useful Things Did the Romans Build?

The Romans became the greatest road builders before modern times. (People in some countries still use Roman-built roads today!) They also built fine bridges and large aqueducts.

The Romans developed a kind of concrete with which to build. (Concrete is a mixture of sand, water, and other materials. It hardens to become rocklike.) To add beauty to their concrete buildings, they covered them with thin, flat, wide pieces of marble. To make the buildings larger, they built high **vaulted** ceilings. A vaulted ceiling has an arch to it and can support a roof that covers a large space.

Chapter 8: Lesson 5

Overview This lesson describes Rome's contributions to law, road building, architecture, art, and public health.

Objectives
- ■ To describe Roman law
- ■ To describe Roman buildings, art, and science

Student Pages pages 183–186

Teacher's Resource Library **TRL**

Workbook Activity 38

Activity 38

Modified Activity 38

Vocabulary

imperfection   vaulted
sanitation

Have students read each vocabulary word and definition aloud. Then have students work in pairs and do a vocabulary mime. One student should act out the word while the other student tries to guess.

PRONUNCIATION GUIDE

Use this list to help students pronounce difficult words in this lesson.

Galen   (gā′ lən)
Pantheon   (pan′ thē on)

1 Warm-Up Activity

Display a photograph of a statue of Lady Justice in modern day United States and the Roman Goddess of Justice. Explain to students that the statue in the United States was derived from the Roman Goddess of Justice. Guide students to notice that both hold scales as a symbol of balanced judgment.

Workbook Activity 38

Name _____ Date _____ Period _____ | Workbook Activity 38 Chapter 8, Lesson 5

Rome's Contributions

Directions Match each description in Column A with the correct term in Column B for each set. Write the correct answer on each line.

Column A	Column B
___ 1. high and arched ceiling	A vaulted
___ 2. protected lives and property	B practical
___ 3. thought law should be fair and just	C Romans
___ 4. people such as the Romans who like useful things	D the Pantheon
___ 5. keeping something clean and free from disease	E sanitation
___ 6. allowed the poor to have medical care	F imperfections
___ 7. temple for all the Roman gods	G health-care system
___ 8. Roman statues had these	H laws

Column A	Column B
___ 9. transported water above ground	I the Colosseum
___ 10. held 50,000 people	J marble
___ 11. practiced medicine around A.D. 180	K Hadrian
___ 12. covered Roman buildings in flat, wide pieces	L German invaders
___ 13. built the Pantheon	M Galen
___ 14. mixture of sand, water, and other materials	N concrete
___ 15. influenced by Roman culture	O aqueducts

World History

Activity 38

Name _____ Date _____ Period _____ | Activity 38 Chapter 8, Lesson 5

Roman Culture

Directions Write the correct word from the Word Bank to complete each sentence.

1. The Romans thought that laws should be _____, just, and reasonable.

2. Roman _____ had imperfections.

3. The fall of Rome did not end its _____.

4. Galen wrote a book about _____.

5. The Pantheon had a high, _____ ceiling.

6. The Romans built sewers to improve public _____.

7. The _____ is still standing today.

8. The Romans _____ the law.

9. Roman builders made fine roads, _____, and aqueducts.

10. The Colosseum was a center for _____.

Word Bank
art
bridges
entertainment
fair
influence
medicine
Pantheon
respected
sanitation
vaulted

World History

2 Teaching the Lesson

Discuss the meaning of the word *practical* with students. Have volunteers give examples of things in their life that they consider "practical" and "not practical." Then have them read pages 183–186 to learn about the practical contributions Rome made to world civilization.

Ask:

- **What two things did the Romans think the law should do?** (protect people's lives and property and punish those who do wrong)

- **How did the Romans make concrete buildings more beautiful?** (They covered them with pieces of marble.)

- **What is concrete?** (a mixture of sand, water, and other materials that hardens to become rocklike)

- **What is the advantage of a vaulted ceiling?** (Its arch can support a roof over a very large area.)

Reading Strategy:
Summarizing

(Romans were great builders.)

- **How were Greek statues different from Roman statues?**
(Greek statues were perfect; Roman statues showed imperfections, such as broken noses and wrinkles.)

Reading Strategy:
Summarizing

(The Pantheon still stands, the Colosseum could seat 50,000 people, aqueducts transported water, and art was not intended to be perfect.)

Imperfection
Something that makes an object or person less than perfect

Reading Strategy:
Summarizing

What important details help you understand the wonders of Roman art and architecture?

What Is the Pantheon?

Emperor Hadrian built the Pantheon, which is still standing today. It is a temple for all the Roman gods. With its vaulted ceiling, the Pantheon is 142 feet wide. Some Roman buildings could hold 3,000 people. In fact, the Colosseum, where the Romans went for entertainment, could seat 50,000 people! The practical Romans built their roads and their buildings to last. People still use a few of them today.

How Were Roman Art and Science Practical?

The Romans wanted to find a good use for art and science. This made them different from the Greeks, who wanted perfect beauty and knowledge. For example, Greeks made their statues perfect. Roman artists showed **imperfections**, such as broken noses and wrinkles. These imperfections made an object or person more realistic.

One practical thing the Romans did was build aqueducts like this one. These were used to transport water.

ELL/ESL STRATEGY

Language Objective:
To draw on prior knowledge and experience when constructing meaning

Tell students that Romans thought that law should (1) protect people's lives and property, and (2) punish those who do wrong. Have students look in magazines and newspapers for photographs, articles, or other illustrations of these two things happening in our country today.

In addition, or as an alternative, suggest that students take their own photos or make their own drawings or cartoons to illustrate the two categories of law. Then ask students to work together in small groups to organize and display their illustrations using the two legal categories. Students might use poster board or chart paper to display their illustrations and use headings that describe the two categories. Display students' work for use in a class discussion.

Sanitation

The act of keeping something clean and free from disease

Romans also used their knowledge of science in a practical way. They set up the first health-care system. Government doctors cared for the poor. The Romans built sewers to improve public **sanitation.** Sewers, which are usually underground pipes, carry away dirty water and human waste. This helps sanitation. That is, it helps keep people clean and free from disease.

Galen, who was a Greek, practiced medicine in Rome around A.D. 180. He wrote a book in which he wrote down everything anyone knew about medicine. We now know that the book has many mistakes. Still, it influenced medicine for more than a thousand years.

Roman Technology

Roman engineers could build large structures. Two advances helped them. One was the round arch. The arch was not new. The Greeks, for example, had built arched gates. The Romans learned how to use it in new ways, however. The Roman arch was a half circle. Side columns supported it. It could hold up heavy loads. The Romans built arched stone bridges across rivers. They also used round arches to build great aqueducts. They brought freshwater to Roman cities everywhere. The Romans also built arched roofs over large indoor spaces.

The other advance was concrete. Concrete was a Roman invention. It let them build strong walls and arched roofs. Concrete also made Roman roads strong and lasting. Modern builders still use this Roman technology.

Ask:

- **How do sewers help keep disease from spreading?** (they carry away dirty water and human waste)

- **What type of book did Galen write?** (a book containing everything anyone knew about medicine)

Have students read the Then and Now feature on page 185, titled "Roman Technology." Then have them create a chart that shows how one of the Romans' technological advances led to the development of others. (Their charts might begin with concrete, which led to the development of roads and buildings, or the vaulted ceiling, which led to the development of bridges, aqueducts, and roofs over large spaces.) Check each student's chart to ensure that they understand the connections between these Roman advances.

3   Reinforce and Extend

BACKGROUND INFORMATION

 The Roman aqueducts were built over a 500-year period, bringing fresh water to Rome from 57 miles away. Most people imagine the aqueducts as sitting high atop stone arches. In fact, only 30 miles of the total 260-mile system were above the ground. The rest lay underground. The Romans built aqueducts throughout their empire in Greece, Italy, France, Spain, North Africa, and Asia Minor. Unfortunately, when the Roman Empire collapsed, so did much of the aqueduct system.

Modern aqueducts are much longer and can carry more water than ancient ones. For example, New York City relies on a system that carries nearly 2 billion gallons of water a day from 120 miles away. A project is in the works to build an aqueduct from northern California 600 miles south to the Mexican border!

IN THE COMMUNITY

 Before sewage is dumped into rivers or lakes, it undergoes a special treatment process to clean it. Encourage interested students to visit the sewage treatment facility in their community to learn more about how sewage treatment works. If time permits, you might wish to take the class on a field trip. It is important for students to realize how this Roman advancement keeps us clean and healthy today.

Under the emperor Trajan, Romans enjoyed free entertainment. While it might not be free anymore, the tradition of entertainment remains strong in modern Rome. The city is home to several major orchestras and the world's oldest music academies. Romans also enjoy plays, musical theater, and operas, which in the summer months are performed outdoors at the ruins of ancient public baths.

Lesson 5 Review Answers

1. They thought laws should protect people's lives and property and punish those who do wrong. **2.** All people are equal before the law. **3.** Hadrian built the Pantheon to honor the Roman gods. **4.** Roman art was more realistic and had more imperfections. **5.** Possible answers: Romans wrote fair and reasonable laws, developed concrete, created useful art, set up a health-care system, and built sewers to improve sanitation.

Answers will vary. It probably did help people because it held truth as well as error. It collected together what was known at the time and made all this knowledge available to people practicing medicine. They could not have found all this out on their own.

Chapter Project Follow-up

Allow enough in-class time so that students, with some homework time, will be able to complete their debate project work by Lesson 4. Schedule the debates for before the Chapter 8 Review, if possible, so that students will have the benefit of using information gained from the presentations during the chapter wrap-up.

Lesson 5 Review On a sheet of paper, write the answer to each question. Use complete sentences.

1. What did the Romans believe laws should do?
2. What was the basic principle of Roman law?
3. Why did Emperor Hadrian build the Pantheon?
4. How did Roman art differ from Greek art?
5. Describe three contributions the Romans made to civilization.

What do you think

The book of medicine that Galen wrote had mistakes in it. Do you think it still helped people after his time? Why or why not?

The Battle of Adrianople

Ammianus Marcellinus was a professional Greek soldier. He was born about 330; the date of his death is not known. He wrote a history of the Roman Empire that includes a description of the Battle of Adrianople, which happened in A.D. 378. This battle is considered to be a turning point in Roman history. Marcellinus was living at the time of the battle, but he was not there. He refers to written sources and also talked to people who were there. The following excerpt gives us an idea of how horrible the war was.

By this time such great clouds of dust arose that it was hardly possible to see the sky. The air resounded with terrible cries. The darts, which brought death on every side, reached their mark and fell with deadly effect, for no one could see them quickly enough to place himself on guard. The barbarians, rushing on with their enormous army, beat down our horses and men and gave us no open spaces where we could fall back to operate. They were so closely packed that it became impossible for us to escape by forcing a path through them. Our men finally began to despise the thought of death and, again taking their swords, slew all they encountered. Helmets and breastplates were smashed in pieces by mutual blows of battle-axes. . . .

The plain was covered with corpses, showing the mutual ruin of the combatants. The groans of the dying, or of men horribly wounded, were intense and caused much dismay on all sides. Amidst all this great tumult and confusion, our infantry were exhausted by toil and danger, until at last they had neither the strength left to fight nor the spirit to plan anything. Their spears were broken by the frequent collisions, so that they were forced to content themselves with their drawn swords, which they thrust into the dense battalions of the enemy, disregarding their own safety, and seeing that every possibility of escape was cut off. . . .

Document-Based Questions

1. What details does Marcellinus give that make it sound like he fought in the battle?

2. How did his experience as a soldier help him write this account of the battle?

3. Later historians thought his descriptions of the battle were accurate. Do you think it is possible for a writer to give a balanced report of an event?

4. This work was written to be read in public. What details might Marcellinus have added just to make the account more interesting?

5. How do you think he felt about war?

The outcome of the Battle of Adrianople was so momentous and disastrous that Marcellinus called it "the beginning of evils for the Roman Empire then and thereafter." The Emperor Valens was killed and his army lost to an army of Goths. Valens, who had been informed that the Goths numbered no more than 10,000, thought that his troops could defeat that number, and led the Roman army into battle. In the midst of the battle, an additional contingent of Gothic troops arrived, outnumbering the Roman troops, and Gothic victory was assured.

Describe this scenario to the class and ask a student to draw a diagram on the board of how these movements may have looked. Have students read the selection in pairs; then, because the work was written to be read in public, ask two students to prepare a shared dramatic reading to present to the class.

Answers to Document-Based Questions:

1. He gives details about the sights and sounds of the battle.

2. His experience helped him know how it felt to see, hear, and feel soldiers fighting, being wounded, and dying.

3. Answers will vary, but should include reasons why reports might be balanced or unbalanced.

4. Details added to make the account more interesting might be those with vivid imagery.

5. Answers will vary, but might include indications that Marcellinus was horrified and appalled at the events of which he is writing.

Spotlight Story

Have students read the title "Women in Greek and Roman History." Then ask students what they think women's contributions to the history of Greece and Rome were. Then ask volunteers to take turns reading paragraphs of the Spotlight Story aloud. Instruct students to number a sheet of paper 1–5, leaving about three lines between numbers. Working in pairs, have students identify the main point of each paragraph and summarize it in a single sentence. Invite students to share their sentences with the class.

Answers to Spotlight Story Wrap-Up:

1. She wrote poems about feelings and friendship.

2. They were all men.

3. She encouraged artists and thinkers; she ruled while her son was at war.

4. They ruled the Byzantine Empire.

5. She refused to run away from riots; she convinced her husband to stay.

Spotlight Story

Women in Greek and Roman History

Women in ancient Greece and Rome led limited lives. Few got an education. Still, we know of some women who did influence history.

Sappho was a Greek poet. She was born around 630 B.C. She married and had a daughter, Cleis. One of her poems says, "I have a beautiful child who looks like golden flowers." Sappho wrote many poems about feelings and friendship. Only one complete poem exists today. Others have only a few lines.

All Roman emperors were men. But sometimes the real rulers were their wives or mothers. Julia Domna was the wife of the emperor about A.D. 200. She was known as Julia the Philosopher. She invited scholars and artists to court. They discussed art and ideas. Julia's son Caracalla became emperor in A.D. 211. While he went to war, she ruled the empire. A few years later, in A.D. 222, the teenage Alexander Severus became emperor. His mother, Julia Mamaea, ruled the empire for 13 years.

In the early 300s A.D., Constantine became emperor of the eastern part of the Roman Empire. The most powerful woman in this empire was Empress Theodora (A.D. 497–548). Her family was poor. Her father worked in a circus. She was an actress. Then she met and married Justinian, the emperor's nephew. Justinian became emperor in A.D. 527. She became empress and co-ruler.

Empress Theodora and her court.

Theodora was smart and ambitious. She was also brave. In A.D. 532, the rulers faced dangerous riots. Justinian was ready to flee. Theodora changed his mind. She spoke to his advisers. "I'll never see the day," she said, "when I am not hailed as Empress. Caesar [Justinian's title], if you wish to flee, well and good. You have the money. The ships are ready. The sea is clear. But I shall stay!" Justinian stayed. Then the riots ended.

Wrap-Up

1. For what was Sappho famous?

2. What did all Roman emperors have in common?

3. How did Julia Domna influence Rome?

4. Where did Justinian and Theodora rule?

5. How did Theodora show she was brave?

Chapter 8 SUMMARY

- Rome became a great empire during the reign of Augustus Caesar. The empire lasted from 27 B.C. to A.D. 476.

- Augustus ruled for 41 years. This time is called the Golden Age. He built many new buildings in Rome. He reformed government in the provinces. Roman rule brought peace and order to the empire. Pax Romana, the Roman peace, lasted from 27 B.C. to A.D. 180.

- Good and bad emperors followed Augustus. His stepson Tiberius ruled cruelly. The next emperor, Caligula, was insane. The imperial guards killed him. They then picked Claudius to be emperor. He ruled well, but was poisoned by his wife. Her son Nero became emperor. In A.D. 64, while Nero ruled, a fire destroyed much of Rome.

- From A.D. 98 to 180, Rome had three good emperors. They were Trajan, Hadrian, and Marcus Aurelius. To avoid war, Aurelius let German tribes settle inside the empire.

- The Roman Empire began to decline. Soldiers fought over who would become emperor. Diseases and the cost of wars made the empire weak.

- Jesus was born in Palestine during the reign of Augustus. Jews had religious freedom under Roman rule. Jesus preached about God's love. He made enemies among both Jewish leaders and Romans. He was crucified under Roman law. After his death, his followers wrote the Gospels to tell about his life and work.

- Followers of Jesus believed he was the son of God. His disciples, called Christians, spread his teachings. Paul helped spread Christianity.

- Some Roman rulers harmed Christians. In A.D. 337, however, Emperor Constantine became a Christian. Christianity later became the official religion.

- Emperor Diocletian wanted to make the empire easier to rule. He divided it into eastern and western parts.

- In A.D. 306, Emperor Constantine moved the capital to Byzantium. He renamed the city Constantinople.

- The Huns invaded Eastern Europe around A.D. 375. The Visigoths feared the Huns, so they moved into the Roman Empire. Then they attacked Roman towns. They beat a Roman army at Adrianople. The Visigoths and the Vandals attacked Rome. The western empire fell in A.D. 476. Odoacer, a German, took control.

- Roman law was one important Roman contribution. Other gifts were in art, building, language, and medicine.

Using the Chapter Summary

Have students read the Chapter Summary on page 189 to review the main ideas presented in Chapter 8.

Ask:

- How long did Augustus Caesar rule and what was this period called? (41 years; the Golden Age)

- Name three bad emperors and three good emperors who followed Augustus. (bad emperors were Tiberius, Caligula, and Nero; good emperors were Claudius, Trajan, Hadrian, and Marcus Aurelius)

- What happened as the result of diseases and the cost of wars? (the empire became weak)

- What did Jesus's followers do after his death? (wrote the Gospels to tell about his life and work)

- What were Jesus's disciples called? (Christians)

- What did Diocletian do to make the empire easier to rule? (divided it into eastern and western parts)

- Why did the Visigoths move into the Roman Empire and what did they do after they got there? (to escape the Huns; attacked Roman towns and defeated a Roman army at Adrianople)

- What were some Roman contributions? (law, art, building, language, and medicine)

TEACHER'S RESOURCE

The AGS Globe Teaching Strategies in Social Studies Transparencies may be used with this chapter. The transparencies add an interactive dimension to expand and enhance the *World History* program content.

Chapter 8 Review

Use the Chapter Review to prepare students for tests and to reteach content from the chapter.

Chapter 8 Mastery Test

The Teacher's Resource Library includes two forms of the Chapter 8 Mastery Test. Each test addresses the chapter Goals for Learning. An optional third page of additional critical-thinking items is included for each test. The difficulty level of the two forms is equivalent.

Chapter 8 Review Answers

1. Augustus Caesar
2. Jesus
3. Paul
4. Christianity
5. Visigoths
6. Attila
7. Diocletian
8. Constantine
9. Theodosius I
10. Odoacer
11. C
12. B
13. B
14. D
15. A

Chapter 8 R E V I E W

Word Bank

Attila
Augustus Caesar
Christianity
Constantine
Diocletian
Jesus
Odoacer
Paul
Theodosius I
Visigoths

On a sheet of paper, use the words from the Word Bank to complete each sentence correctly.

1. Historians call the reign of _____ the "Golden Age of Rome."

2. When _____ was 30 years old, he began to preach good news to the poor in Palestine.

3. _____ was a follower of Jesus who preached to Jews and gentiles.

4. The new religion that came from Jesus's teaching was called _____.

5. Rome could not defend itself for the first time in history when the _____ attacked.

6. _____, king of the Huns, led his tribe of warriors across Europe.

7. Emperor _____ divided the Roman Empire into two parts.

8. _____ was the first Christian emperor.

9. _____ made Christianity the official religion of the Roman Empire.

10. A German leader, _____, took control of Rome in A.D. 476 and ended the Roman Empire.

On a sheet of paper, write the letter of the answer that correctly completes each sentence.

11. The Pax Romana was a period of peace in Rome that lasted for _____ years.

   A 41   **B** 100   **C** 200   **D** 1,000

12. _____ was an unpopular emperor because in his last years, he was a cruel tyrant.

   A Augustus Caesar   **C** Caligula
   B Tiberius   **D** Claudius

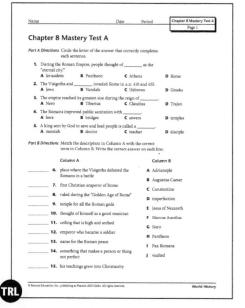

Chapter 8 Mastery Test A, pages 1–3

13. The Romans gave Jewish people _____ freedom.

   A political   **C** worldwide

   B religious   **D** none of the above

14. The Roman Empire declined because of _____.

   A a plague

   B lack of money

   C no system to pick an emperor

   D all of the above

15. The _____ and the Vandals invaded Rome in A.D. 410 and 455.

   A Visigoths   **C** Carthaginians

   B Huns   **D** Greeks

On a sheet of paper, write the answer to each question. Use complete sentences.

16. In what ways were the Romans a practical people?

17. Why did the Roman Empire decline and then fall?

18. In what ways did Augustus Caesar make Rome better?

Critical Thinking On a sheet of paper, write your response to each question. Use complete sentences.

19. Rome never found a good way to pick a new emperor. What happened because of this?

20. Why do you think Christianity spread easily throughout Europe?

16. The Romans were practical in the things they built: roads to get them places, vaulted ceilings to make bigger buildings, and aqueducts to carry water to their cities.

17. The Roman Empire declined for several reasons. A plague killed many people and the government did not have enough money to support the army. (It needed a big army to protect its large empire.) Finally, the government never found a peaceful way to choose a successor when an emperor died.

18. Augustus Caesar made Rome better by building new temples, theaters, and roads.

Critical Thinking

19. Answers will vary. That is part of the reason why the empire declined and fell. It also led to civil war that must have hurt all the people.

20. Answers will vary. Students may say that Christianity spread easily because many people were poor and liked the promises of Jesus's word.

On the day of the test, try to arrive at class early. Sometimes teachers give helpful information about the test at that time.

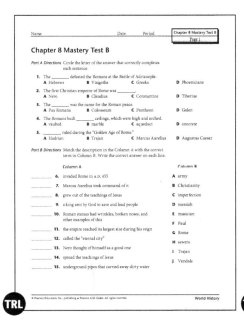

Chapter 8 Mastery Test B, pages 1–3

Introducing the Chapter

While civilizations thrived in Europe and Asia, early American civilizations began to develop in the North American Southwest. American Indian cultures reached their highest level of development in Mesoamerica, the land between North and South America. The

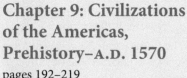

Civilizations of the Americas

The first Stone Age humans set foot in what is now the Americas as early as 20,000 B.C. They had no idea that they were the first people to walk on this land. They did not know that the land consisted of two huge continents that we call North and South America. Within these two regions lies a cultural region we call Mesoamerica. It is made up of Mexico and Central America. Some of the earliest civilizations in the Americas developed here.

Goals for Learning

◆ To explain how the first Americans may have come to the Americas

◆ To identify three important early Southwestern cultures

◆ To explain characteristics of four regional Indian cultures

◆ To identify the cultures of early Mesoamerica and South America

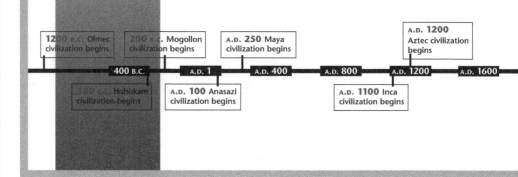

1200 B.C. Olmec civilization begins

200 B.C. Mogollon civilization begins

A.D. 250 Maya civilization begins

A.D. 1200 Aztec civilization begins

400 B.C. A.D. 1 A.D. 400 A.D. 800 A.D. 1200 A.D. 1600

Hohokam civilization begins

A.D. 100 Anasazi civilization begins

A.D. 1100 Inca civilization begins

Incan civilization in South America arose last.

Ask:

● What civilization on the timeline developed first? (the Olmec civilization, about 1200 B.C.)

● Which American Indian civilization on the timeline developed the most recently? (the Aztec civilization, about A.D. 1200)

TRL

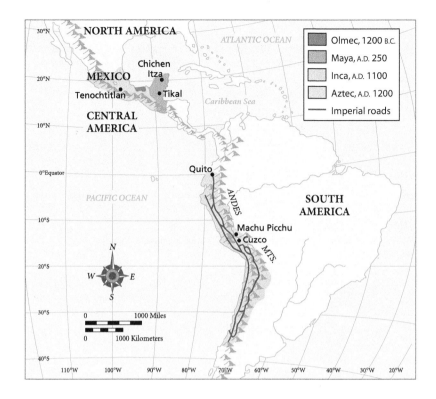

The land that connects the continents of North America and South America is called Mesoamerica. It is made up of Mexico and Central America.

This map shows four early American empires—the Olmecs, the Mayas, the Aztecs, and the Incas. The dates show about when those empires began. It also shows the roads in the Incan Empire.

Study the map, then answer the following questions:

1. Why did the Incan roads run mostly north and south instead of east and west?

2. Which empire seems to have been the biggest?

3. Which empire was the smallest?

4. What mountain range runs along the west coast of South America, within the Incan empire?

5. Which empire is the oldest?

Have students study the map of the early American empires. Tell them that a piece of land surrounded by water on three sides is called a peninsula. Point out that the Maya lived on a peninsula, called the Yucatán Peninsula, in the Gulf of Mexico. Have students read the paragraph under the map and answer the questions.

Ask:

- **Where did the Incas live in relation to the Aztecs?** (southeast)
- **On what land did the Olmecs live?** (Central America, also called Mesoamerica)
- **What people built the cities of Machu Picchu and Cuzco?** (the Incan people)

Map Skills Answers

1. Most likely, the roads ran north and south because the Andes Mountains prevented roads from running east and west.
2. the Incan empire
3. the Olmec empire
4. the Andes Mountains
5. the Olmec Empire

Chapter Project

Have students research the Maya calendar system and write a report. The Maya used several calendars simultaneously to keep track of long and short periods of time. The Long Count calendar identifies a date by counting the number of days from August 11, 3114 B.C. Students should describe in general how the calendar works and how Maya life revolved around the calendar. Diagrams will help to clarify the system. Student reports may discuss the significance of December 21, 2012, a date predicted by the calendar as being the end of the world.

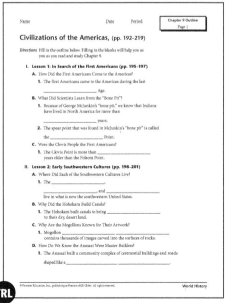

Chapter 9 Outline, pages 1–3

Questioning

Introduce the reading skill *questioning*. Explain that when you ask questions about something you are reading, you are making connections between what you have just read and what you are about to read. Asking questions can also lead to predictions.

Have students read the first paragraph on page 195.

Ask:

• **What questions can you ask about the information in the paragraph?** (Students may ask what kind of artifacts archaeologists found. They may also ask where the first Americans came from.)

Point out to students that when they ask questions about what they are reading, they can look forward to finding the answers to their questions in the paragraphs to come. This feeling of anticipation makes reading exciting.

....

Key Vocabulary Words

Explain that the list of words here is a glossary of the key vocabulary students will read in Chapter 9. Call on volunteers to read aloud the words and the definitions.

....

Ask:

• **Which term is defined as "a small underground building used for ceremonies"?** (kiva)

• **What is a palisade?** (a wooden fence)

Reading Strategy:
Questioning

As you read, ask yourself questions. This will help you understand more of the information. You'll also become a more active reader. Questioning the text will also help you to be a more active reader. Ask yourself:

◆ What do I hope to learn from this text?

◆ What do the facts and details in this text tell me?

◆ Are there any people or situations in this text that make connections with my life?

Key Vocabulary Words

Lesson 1 ————————————
Glacier a thick sheet of ice

Lesson 2 ————————————
Kiva a small underground building used for ceremonies

Geometric Having simple designs made up of straight lines and circles

Lesson 3 ————————————
Palisade a wooden fence

Objectives

- To explain how people may have first come to the Americas
- To describe an important discovery in New Mexico
- To explain the importance of the Folsom Point and the Clovis Point

Reading Strategy:
Questioning

What details are important to understanding the first Americans?

Glacier

A thick sheet of ice

Archaeologists want to learn when the first Americans reached the Americas. They also want to learn where the people came from and what their lives were like. These people lived so long ago that archaeologists have found only a few artifacts. Archaeologists will continue to search for new evidence to help them better understand these people.

How Did the First Americans Come to the Americas?

The first Americans came to the Americas during the last Ice Age. Thick sheets of ice called **glaciers** covered the upper third of North America. Life during the Ice Age was hard, bitter cold, and very dangerous. People were nomads, surviving by hunting. A nomad is a person who moves from place to place. Eventually, they walked from Asia over a frozen body of water now called the Bering Strait. In search of food, they probably were following herds of animals. Others would follow them over thousands of years. When the Ice Age ended, the land grew warmer. Slowly, the people we now call American Indians settled in communities all over North and South America. They created different cultures. Some created ways of living that were simple. Other cultures created complex societies like those in Europe, Asia, and Africa.

How Long Have Indians Lived in North America?

At one time, scientists thought that American Indians had lived in North America for no more than 4,000 years. Then, in 1908, George McJunkin, an African American cowboy, made a discovery. He was riding his horse in Folsom, New Mexico. Heavy rain had flooded the area. McJunkin noticed that the floodwaters had washed away many layers of dirt. The water had uncovered many very large animal bones. He called it his "bone pit." He knew that the bones were important because of how big they were and how deep they were buried.

Chapter 9: Lesson 1

Overview This lesson describes the first Americans and their probable origins. Students will learn about the artifacts that helped archaeologists determine how long Indians have lived in North America.

Objectives

- To explain why nomads probably came to America
- To describe an important discovery in New Mexico
- To explain the importance of the Folsom Point and the Clovis Point

Student Pages   pages 195–197

Teacher's Resource Library

Workbook Activity 39

Activity 39

Modified Activity 39

Vocabulary

glacier   **nomad**

Have students work with a partner to write a short paragraph using the vocabulary words. Each vocabulary word should be underlined for emphasis, and the words should be connected in a meaningful way. Ask student pairs to read their paragraphs aloud.

1 Warm-Up Activity

Have students examine a globe or world map. Point out how close Asia and North America are in the vicinity of the Bering Strait. Ask students how ancient people might have moved from Siberia into North America. (Elicit the response that the strait was covered with ice during much of the year.) Ask why these people probably had no boats. (Few trees for boat building grew in the ice-covered region.)

First Americans Fill-In

Directions Write the correct word from the Word Bank that each sentence describes.

_____ 1. These people move from place to place and survive by hunting.

_____ 2. These are human-made objects from people who lived long ago.

_____ 3. This was McJunkin's major scientific discovery.

_____ 4. These are thick sheets of ice.

_____ 5. This spear point was stuck in the rib bones of an ancient buffalo.

_____ 6. This spear point was found in New Mexico in the 1930s.

_____ 7. The first Americans came to the Americas during this time.

_____ 8. After the Ice Age ended, these people settled in communities all over North America and South America.

_____ 9. This African American cowboy discovered a "bone pit."

_____ 10. Nomads walked from Asia to the Americas over this frozen body of water.

Word Bank
American Indians
artifacts
Bering Strait
bone pit
Clovis Point
Folsom Point
George McJunkin
glaciers
Ice Age
nomads

Workbook Activity 39

The First Americans

Directions Write the answers to these questions. Use complete sentences.

1. How did the first Americans get to the Americas?

2. What happened after the Ice Age ended?

3. Who was George McJunkin and what did he find?

4. Why was the "bone pit" important?

5. How long ago do scientists think the Clovis people entered the Americas?

Activity 39

2 Teaching the Lesson

Ask students to imagine that they are nomads living in eastern Asia about 13,000 years ago. Point out that food is scarce and life is hard during the Ice Age. Have students write a diary in which they describe daily life including descriptions of weather, land, travel, animals, hunting tools, and food. Suggest that students take one nomad's viewpoint to describe how these people might have reached North America.

Ask:

- Do you think the nomads of eastern Asia knew that they were entering a new continent? Explain. (Answers may vary; students will probably say that there were no maps or other ways for the nomads to know where they were.)

Reading Strategy:
Questioning

(Students may suggest that it is important to know where the first Americans came from, and how and when they arrived. Knowing where they went is important to understanding the relationships among the different groups of American Indians.)

- How does the work of archaeologists help us know about the first Americans? (Archaeologists search for clues of past life. Radiocarbon dating helps them know when the people lived and bones and tools tell about their way of life.)

- Why was the Folsom Point evidence that people lived in New Mexico 9,000 years ago? (The spear point was stuck in buffalo bones that were radiocarbon dated to 9,000 years ago. The animal and the spear point had to have existed at the same time.)

Reading Strategy:
Questioning

Have students write a short paragraph telling what they would have done to get scientists to take notice of a discovery if they were George McJunkin. If students have ever had a personal experience in which they thought they discovered

Reading Strategy:
Questioning

Think beyond the text. Consider your own thoughts and experiences as you read about important discoveries.

Writing About History

Imagine you have just made a discovery like the one George McJunkin made. Write two paragraphs in your notebook describing the first thing you would do.

something important but people weren't interested, they should describe this experience in their paragraphs.

 Writing About History

Before students write their paragraphs, explain that George McJunkin was a former slave, probably uneducated, and lived on a remote ranch. Then have students write their paragraphs. Discuss how the reaction to their discovery may have differed from McJunkin's.

Although self taught, McJunkin had collected ancient bones, rocks, minerals, and old arrowheads. He owned books on geology and natural history. McJunkin wrote to scientists asking them to come and see what he had discovered. At first, scientists were not interested. It was only after McJunkin died in 1922 that scientists decided to take his advice and examine his "bone pit."

What Did Scientists Learn from the "Bone Pit"?

In 1926, the animal bones were dug up and brought to the Colorado Museum of Natural History. They turned out to be important evidence about how long American Indians had lived in North America. The bones were those of ancient buffaloes. Radiocarbon dating of the bones showed them to be about 9,000 years old. Scientists also discovered a piece of flint stuck in the ribs of one of the animals. It had been shaped by a human into a sharp spear point. Scientists named the sharpened flint piece the Folsom Point. The Folsom Point had been buried at the same time as the bones. That meant that American Indians had been living in the New Mexico area for at least 9,000 years. George McJunkin had made a major scientific discovery. Anthropologists now wondered if those who made the Folsom Point were really the oldest people. Were there even more ancient people who lived before the makers of the Folsom Point?

The Clovis Point was found in Clovis, New Mexico, in the 1930s.

Were the Clovis People the First Americans?

In Clovis, New Mexico, a new spear point was found in the 1930s. The Clovis Point was more than 4,000 years older than the spear point found in Folsom. Many anthropologists believe that the Clovis people entered the Americas about 13,000 years ago. For many years, anthropologists thought that the Clovis people were the first Americans. However, new evidence changed that belief. It is now thought that other groups entered the Americas at about the same time.

Lesson 1 Review On a sheet of paper, write the answer to each question. Use complete sentences.

1. How do we think the first people got to the Americas? Why did they come here?

2. What was George McJunkin's discovery?

3. How did scientists determine the age of the bones in the pit?

4. Why are the Folsom Point and the Clovis Point important?

5. Why did many anthropologists think that the Clovis people were the first Americans?

George McJunkin knew that his discovery was important. Why do you think that scientists were not interested in it until after he died?

Answers will vary. Students may suggest that scientists did not take him seriously because he was not a scientist and was not educated. Students may also suggest that McJunkin lived in an isolated area that was hard to get to.

 3   **Reinforce and Extend**

CAREER CONNECTION

 Radiocarbon dating is a technique used to determine the absolute age of a once-living thing. It measures the amount of radioactive carbon remaining in the specimen since death occurred. The number of radiocarbon dating labs worldwide has grown; today there are more than 100 labs. Trained lab personnel perform radiocarbon assays for anthropologists, archeologists, and other scientists. As the need for these assays increases, the demand for lab workers increases. Encourage interested students to research the work of and the career opportunities available for radiocarbon technicians and technologists.

LEARNING STYLES

Visual/Spatial

Have interested students research the Clovis Point on the Internet. Have them make a poster with a drawing showing what the point looks like and how it was attached to a spear. Labels can be added to indicate the material it is made of and its special features. Students may want to include information about how many Clovis Points have been found, where they were found, and where they are now. Encourage students to display their posters.

Lesson 1 Review Answers

1. They came across the frozen Bering Strait in search of food. **2.** McJunkin's discovery was a bone pit containing animal remains and spear points. **3.** Radiocarbon dating is used to determine the age of bones. **4.** They represent the time when the first American Indians arrived in North America. **5.** No earlier artifacts had been found.

Chapter 9: Lesson 2

Overview This lesson describes three early groups of American Indians in southwestern United States—the Hohokam, the Mogollons, and the Anasazi. Each lived in a different environment and developed in a unique way.

Objectives

- To identify the cultures of the Hohokam, the Mogollon, and the Anasazi
- To explain the environment in which each of these cultures lived

Student Pages pages 198–201

Teacher's Resource Library

Workbook Activity 40

Activity 40

Modified Activity 40

Vocabulary

geometric   **kiva**

Have students define each vocabulary word in his or her own words. Then, have students write sentences using each word.

1   Warm-Up Activity

Tell students that three groups of early American Indians lived in different environments. Discuss the ways life would have been different in a dry desert area, in a river valley surrounded by tree-covered mountains, and in canyons and flat-topped mesas. (Students should know that water would have to be brought to a dry desert. They might suggest that trees from mountains were used to build structures in river valleys, and that buildings could be built into the canyon and mesa walls.)

Objectives

- To identify the cultures of the Hohokam, the Mogollon, and the Anasazi
- To explain the environment in which each of these cultures lived

Reading Strategy:
Questioning

What do you think you will learn about early Southwestern cultures?

In what is now the Southwestern United States, archaeologists discovered the remains of three important societies of ancient Indians. These Indians—the Hohokam, the Mogollon, and the Anasazi—shared a similar background. Each had changed from hunting and gathering their food to growing their food. However, the environments where they lived were very different.

Where Did Each of the Southwestern Cultures Live?

The Hohokam lived in a dry desert area in what is now Arizona. The Mogollon lived among tree-lined mountain ranges and a river valley in southeastern Arizona and southern New Mexico. The Anasazi lived in the canyons and the flat-topped mesas where Arizona, New Mexico, Utah, and Colorado meet. Because of the different environments, the cultures developed different methods of farming, building shelters, and showing their artistic ideas.

Why Did the Hohokam Build Canals?

Anthropologists believe that the Hohokam developed from a combination of local people in Arizona and Mesoamericans who had moved from the south. Their civilization began about 300 B.C. The Hohokam lived in a desert area. They had to figure out how to bring water to their land. Their solution was to build irrigation canals using simple hand tools. From A.D. 800 until 1000, they built hundreds of miles of canals. The network of canals provided the Hohokam with more than just water for their crops. The canals provided water for drinking, cooking, and washing. The Hohokam grew cotton that was woven into cloth. They used canal water to create painted pottery. The Hohokam also made beautiful jewelry using seashells.

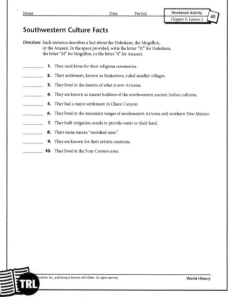

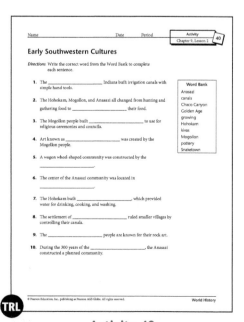

What Was Snaketown?

Snaketown was an important place for the Hohokam. This settlement ruled smaller villages by controlling their canals. The Hohokam built ball courts in Snaketown for sports and rituals. Mounds found within the remains of Hohokam villages may have been dance platforms or places where their leaders lived. By about 1450, most people had abandoned the Hohokam area. This most likely was caused by a lack of water and a failed irrigation system. The Pima Indians later lived in the same area. They named the earlier people *Hohokam,* meaning "the vanished ones."

Why Are the Mogollons Known for Their Artwork?

We do not know what ancient peoples called themselves. For example, Mogollons were given their name by anthropologists because they lived among the Mogollon mountain ranges. These mountains where named after Don Juan Mogollon, a Spanish governor of New Mexico in the early 1700s. It is believed that the Mogollon people began farming this area about 200 B.C. The Mogollon created shelters both on high ground and underground. These unusual **kivas,** or small underground buildings, were used for religious ceremonies and councils.

The Mogollon people are especially known for their artwork. They created a new form of pottery. Between A.D. 900 and 1200, they created beautiful clay bowls. These had black and white **geometric** designs and animal images. Geometric designs are created with circles and straight lines. The most important art that the Mogollons are known for is their rock art. Over a wide geographic area, the Mogollon people carved thousands of mysterious images into the surfaces of rocks. There are images of insects, fish, reptiles, birds, and mammals. There are also human faces and masks. No other people anywhere in the world created so many artistic images.

Kiva

A small underground building used for ceremonies

Geometric

Having simple designs made up of straight lines and circles

ELL/ESL STRATEGY

Language Objective:
To describe the unique pottery of the Mogollons

Have ELL students locate some of the many photographs of Mogollon art. Then ask them to make an oral presentation in which they describe the Mogollon art found on pottery and rocks. Students might also compare the Mogollon designs with designs from their native countries. Suggest that students bring in examples, illustrations, or drawings of their native art to show the class.

LEARNING STYLES

Visual/Spatial
Have interested students find a collection of different geometric designs. Point out and have students trace the circles, diagonal lines, zigzags, and arcs that are commonly found in geometric designs. Then encourage students to create a geometric design of their own.

 Teaching the Lesson

Ask students what a canal is. (a human-made channel for moving water) Ask what it can be used for. (moving water for growing crops and for drinking, cooking, and washing) Then have students read Lesson 2 on pages 198–201 to learn about the canals that played an important part in the lives of the Hohokam, the art left behind by the Mogollons, and the planned communities and pueblos of the Anasazi.

Reading Strategy:
Questioning

(Answers will vary. Students may examine the subheads and correctly think they will learn where the Southwestern cultures lived, why they had to build canals, what their cities were, what kind of artwork they made, and what the Anasazi built.)

Ask:

• **What was Snaketown?** (a Hohokam settlement that ruled smaller villages by controlling their canals)

• **What does the word *Hohokam* mean?** (vanished ones) **Why was this name given to this group of early people?** (Hohokam abandoned the area due to lack of water and failed irrigation systems.)

• **Which early American Indian culture is known for their rock art?** (the Mogollons)

• **For what are the Anasazi noted?** (building a planned community with cliff dwellings and a road system)

• **What were kivas used for?** (for religious ceremonies and councils)

Ask:

- **What is a planned community?** (a city or town in which each building and road is placed in a specific place rather than being built in a haphazard arrangement)

- **What was the Chaco Canyon Anasazi settlement known for?** (trade, crafts, religious ceremonies, and astronomy)

 3 **Reinforce and Extend**

IN THE COMMUNITY

 The Hohokam people built canals to bring water from its source to where they lived in the dry desert. Have students find out where their water supply comes from. They can get this information from their local water company or from city government offices. Students who live in rural areas might have wells. Ask students to find out if their water supply is treated to make it safe for drinking and how this is done.

STUDY SKILLS

 Have students skim through the material on page 200 to find the main ideas. The main ideas should answer the question in the subhead for this section of the text. Finding main ideas is a useful study tool. Encourage students to read a page or a short section and then write down the main ideas for each lesson. When they have finished a chapter, they will have a review guide.

How Do We Know the Anasazi Were Master Builders?

The Anasazi are known as the master builders of the Southwestern ancient Indian cultures. Their "Golden Age" was between A.D. 850 and 1150. During these 300 years, the Anasazi constructed a planned community. This community contained a massive complex of ceremonial buildings and roads. This building project was shaped like a wagon wheel (which the ancient Indian people did not use). The center of the "wheel" was in Chaco Canyon in New Mexico. It was here that huge ceremonial buildings, known as great houses or cliff dwellings, were built. The style of the stone buildings is called pueblo.

It is estimated that more than 100,000 pieces of timber had to be carried from the mountains to create floors and roofs. They had no work animals, such as horses, to help them. The timber had to be carried about 50 miles on the backs of workers. Roads were built from the center like the spokes of a wheel. The roads led to villages lying along the rim of the wheel. The villages

could be as far as 10 miles away from the center. The leaders of the Anasazi communicated from the central great houses to these villages with signal fires. They used obsidian glass like a mirror to reflect the message being signaled by the firelight.

This is an example of Anasazi petroglyphs, or rock art.

LEARNING STYLES

 Interpersonal/ Group Learning
Have students working in groups of three or four research Anasazi cliff dwellings and create a model of a simple dwelling. They can use modeling clay, small cardboard boxes, or other material of their choice. Students can build small ladders out of toothpicks or drinking straws to show how the people reached the dwellings, which were built in hollows in cliff faces. Have each group present both their model and a report to the class to share their findings.

What Was the Chaco Canyon Settlement?

There may have been more than 100,000 people living in the Chaco Canyon Anasazi settlement. It became a major center for trade, crafts, and religious ceremonies. There is evidence that it was also a place to carefully study the stars and planets. It was a place of wealth and power. Eventually, around A.D. 1150, the "Golden Age" ended. The people left the area for unknown reasons. Maybe there was not enough rain. There may have been too many people and not enough resources. Leaders may have lost their ability to lead such a complex community.

Word Bank

Anasazi

Chaco Canyon

Hohokam

Mogollon

Snaketown

Lesson 2 Review On a sheet of paper, use the words from the Word Bank to complete each sentence correctly.

1. The _____ built canals to bring water to their land.

2. The _____ were known as "master builders" because of their buildings and roads.

3. The _____ were known for their beautiful pottery.

4. The _____ settlement ruled the canals of smaller villages.

5. The _____ planned settlement became a major center for trade.

Why do you think the Chaco Canyon settlement disappeared?

Visiting Anasazi Treasures

Explorers of the 2000s are lucky to be able to visit places built by the Anasazis.

Archaeologists have found the ruins of numerous Anasazi creations. Most of these can be found in the Four Corners area, where Colorado, Utah, Arizona, and New Mexico meet.

Mesa Verde National Park and the nearby Ute Mountain Tribal Park are located in southwestern Colorado. Both parks feature Anasazi cliff dwellings and rock art. Mesa Verde Park features Cliff Palace, the largest known cliff home. Other attractions include mesa-top pueblos and pit houses.

Chapter 9: Lesson 3

Overview This lesson divides the cultures of regional American Indians into four groups depending on where they lived. The cultures and contributions of Woodland, Mississippian, Great Plains, and Pacific Northwest Indians are described.

Objectives

■ To describe where the Woodland Indians lived

■ To describe Mississippian civilizations

■ To describe a Plains Indian settlement

■ To explain one way the Indians of the Pacific Northwest were different from other cultures

Student Pages pages 202–207

Teacher's Resource Library

Workbook Activity 41

Activity 41

Modified Activity 41

Vocabulary

palisade

Discuss the vocabulary word and its definition. Ask students if they have used the word before. Then ask them to suggest terms that we might use today that mean almost the same thing. Write the list on the board. (fence, posts, stakes, barrier, etc.)

1 **Warm-Up Activity**

Obtain copies of the poem *The Song of Hiawatha* by Henry Wadsworth Longfellow. Explain that Hiawatha was a famous Iroquois leader. Have students read aloud passages from the poem. Guide a discussion about Hiawatha's life. Ask students if the poem helps them to develop mental images of Iroquois life.

Reading Strategy:
Questioning

What do you think you will learn about by reading this lesson?

Objectives

◆ To describe where the Woodland Indians lived

◆ To describe Mississippian civilizations

◆ To describe a Plains Indian settlement

◆ To explain one way the Indians of the Pacific Northwest were different from other cultures

Indian cultures differ from one region to another. Anthropologists divide these cultures into four basic groups. These groups are Woodland, Mississippi River (Mississippian), Great Plains, and Pacific Northwest. Adena and Hopewell were early Woodland cultures. Mississippian Indian settlements were in what is now the Midwestern and Southeastern states in the United States. The Indians of the Great Plains lived west of the Mississippi River. Their way of life was very different from the Woodland and Mississippian Indians. On the West Coast, the Indians of the Pacific Northwest had a way of life different from all the others.

What Is Known About the Woodland Indians and the Adena Burial Mounds?

Woodland Indians lived east of the Mississippi River. They could be found on the East Coast and around the Great Lakes. They lived in forest areas near streams and lakes. The Adena and Hopewell were Woodland Indians. They were also hunter-gatherers and mound builders. In Ohio, on private property called Adena, burial mounds were discovered. The Adena burial mounds measured 300 feet wide. Inside the burial mounds were small log rooms in which the dead were buried. The burial rooms also contained tobacco and pipes. Adena pipes were beautifully made and are considered works of art. The Adena people lived in villages of less than 500 people. This culture survived from 700 B.C. to A.D. 100.

What Was the Hopewell People's Snake Mound?

The Hopewell people followed the Adena in the Ohio area. Hopewell mounds were found in the 1840s on the Hopewell farm in Ohio. The largest mound was over 30 feet high. By A.D. 100, the Hopewell people had become farmers. They planted barley, sunflowers, and squash. By concentrating on farming, they took an important step to control their food supply.

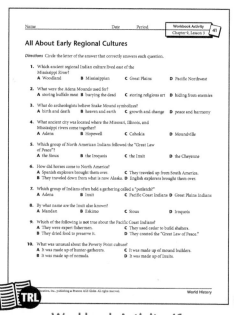

Workbook Activity 41

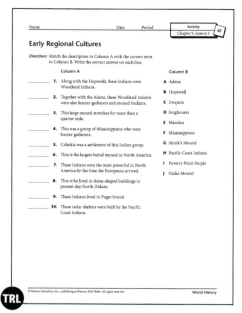

Activity 41

One of the most interesting creations in this area is a very large earthen Snake Mound. The jaw of the Snake Mound is 17 feet long. Its mouth is swallowing a huge egg. The Snake Mound curves over the land for more than a quarter mile. Some archaeologists believe the Snake Mound is an Indian symbol of growth and change. There is evidence that Indian cultures believed this because snakes grow and change by shedding their skin.

Reading Strategy:
Questioning

As you read, notice the details in the text. What questions can you ask yourself about these early cultures?

Where Was the Poverty Point Culture?

In the 1950s, archaeologists discovered an old aerial photograph of what looked like a 19th-century Louisiana cotton plantation. The plantation, named Poverty Point, was located in the lower Mississippi River Valley. The photograph showed the outlines of a large earthwork made by humans. It was more than 4,000 years old. This great structure is evidence of the existence of another highly developed ancient American Indian culture. This group of Mississippians was named the Poverty Point people.

The Poverty Point culture was unusual because it appeared to be made up of hunter-gatherers, not farmers. Hunter-gatherers must get their food by hunting, fishing, and gathering wild plants. They move from place to place. This way of life does not usually produce extra food for workers. It took many workers hundreds of years to create and enlarge the earthwork. It was completed around 1000 B.C. After that, the Poverty Point culture declined and eventually ended.

Where Was the City of Cahokia?

The city of Cahokia was located in the present state of Illinois. By 1200, the city of Cahokia had a population of more than 20,000 people. At the time it was the largest settlement of Mississippians in North America, covering six square miles. Cahokia was located where three rivers come together: the Missouri, Illinois, and Mississippi Rivers.

PRONUNCIATION GUIDE

Use this list to help students pronounce difficult words in this lesson.

Cahokia	(kə hō′ kē ə)
Inuit	(in′ ə wət)
Iroquois	(ir′ ə kwoi)
Sioux	(sū)

 Teaching the Lesson

Have students copy the timeline on page 192. As they read about each group of American Indians in this lesson, ask them to place these American Indian cultures on the timeline: Poverty Point 2000 B.C., Adena 700 B.C., Cahokia A.D. 1200, Iroquois A.D. 1200, Plains A.D. 1800. Discuss which cultural beginnings overlapped with Central and South American civilizations.

Reading Strategy:
Questioning

(Students will probably look at the lesson title and subtitles and respond that they will learn about early American Indian cultures.)

Ask:

- Which civilization developed first— the Adena or the Iroquois? (the Adena)

- Why did the Adena build mounds? (to bury their dead)

- What was unusual about the Poverty Point culture? (They appeared to be hunter-gatherers rather than farmers.)

- What was an advantage of farming over hunting and gathering? (The food supply could be controlled and stocked for bad times. Farming also ensured that all people would be fed, not just those that gathered food.)

LEARNING STYLES

Logical/Mathematical
Cahokia was six square miles in area. Have students find out the area of their town or city from their local government. If students live in a rural area, have them find out the area of an average farm. Have students make a bar graph comparing the areas of Cahokia, their town or city, and some other well-known cities. This information is available on the Internet.

Reading Strategy:
Questioning

(Answers will vary. Students may ask themselves why people were buried in mounds rather than below ground, why the mounds were divided into rooms, and why pipes and tobacco were found in the mounds. Other questions might be why the Poverty Point people did not farm and how the Pacific Coast Indians lived.)

- What might have been the purpose of the palisade around Cahokia? (Students will probably suggest that it protected Cahokia against attack by enemies or wild animals.)

- Where was the city of Moundville located? (in Alabama)

ONLINE CONNECTION

The Web site, www. agsglobewh.com/page204 from the University of Alabama Museums, contains photographs, history, and detailed descriptions of the Moundville Archeological Park. Within the park is an Indian Village and craft pavilions. Photos of each house in the village depict the daily lives of the people who once lived in Moundville.

Palisade
A wooden fence

Cahokia was a planned city with many public buildings. A wooden fence called a **palisade** surrounded the city. The people of Cahokia were also mound builders. They built 120 mounds. One mound, called Monk's Mound, is the largest mound in North America. Monk's Mound was named after a French monk who found it in the early 1800s. Over the years, the population of the city declined. It is not known why this happened. It could be because the weather changed and they were unable to produce enough food. Disease may have played a part, or wars may have caused a decline. By 1500, the people of Cahokia had vanished.

Where Was the City of Moundville?

The city of Moundville was located in present-day Alabama. Second only to Cahokia, it had the largest population between 1000 and 1400. This Mississippian settlement was built on a high bluff overlooking the Black Warrior River. In the center of the settlement were 26 earthen mounds located on a large plaza. A major agricultural center, Moundville had large supplies of Indian maize, or corn. The people of Moundville were known for their artistic achievements. They made excellent pottery, copper pieces, and stonework. By 1350, Moundville began to decline. By the 1500s, it had been abandoned.

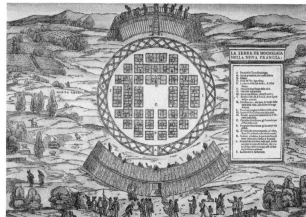

Iroquois Village

Why Were the Iroquois Important?

Between 1200 and 1400, a powerful Woodland culture in Upper New York developed. These people are believed to have descended from the Mississippian Indians. Six tribes called the Iroquois created a peace treaty called the "Great Law of Peace." They organized themselves into a democracy. Their great leaders, Hiawatha and Seneca, are still remembered today for their important speeches. When Europeans arrived, the Iroquois were the most powerful Indians in North America.

What Was the Culture of the Great Plains Indians Like?

The Great Plains is an area located between the Mississippi River and the Rocky Mountains. The Great Plains is a place of flat grasslands, rivers, streams and a few mountains. There are not many trees. Summers are hot and dry, and winters are very cold. The Plains Indian tribes living in the 1800s were the Sioux, Cheyenne, Comanche, and Blackfoot. These Indians rode horses while hunting buffalo. But their way of life was not always like this. Before the 1500s, there were no horses in the Americas. The horse arrived later, with Spanish explorers.

Indian settlements before the 1500s were mostly found on the borders of the Great Plains near rivers and streams. From about 850, settlements grew up along the Missouri River. The Mandan tribe lived along this river in present-day North Dakota. Each Mandan village contained only a few hundred people. They lived in dome-shaped buildings. This type of building was made of large logs covered with earth and straw. These Indians were farmers.

Ask:

- Where did early Plains Indian settlements grow up? (along the Missouri River)

- What were four tribes of Great Plains Indians of the 1800s? (Sioux, Cheyenne, Comanche, and Blackfoot)

- What kind of houses did the Mandan tribe live in? (in dome-shaped buildings made of logs and covered with earth and straw)

LEARNING STYLES

Auditory/Verbal
Have a student volunteer pretend he or she is an Iroquois leader such as Hiawatha or Seneca. Have the student choose a topic that would be important to the tribe and give a speech to the class. The speech should try to persuade students to agree with the orator's viewpoint.

BACKGROUND INFORMATION

In the 1600s, the Spanish in the American Southwest had Indian slaves and workers who learned how to train and ride horses. When the Spanish were forced out of the Southwest during the Pueblo Rebellion of 1680, they left behind many horses. The Navaho and Pueblo Indians traded the horses and the knowledge to handle and ride them to the Plains Indians. The Plains Indians soon recognized the advantages of hunting buffalo from horseback.

Ask:

- Why was the way of life of the Pacific Coast Indians different from that of the Plains Indians? (The Pacific Coast region had abundant food, water, and cedar trees. Also, the winters were mild.)

- Where do the Inuit live? (in present-day Alaska)

 3 **Reinforce and Extend**

BACKGROUND INFORMATION

 Pacific Coast Indian potlatches were given to establish or retain a host's social status in society. They were held to celebrate special occasions, such as a child's birth, a special birthday or anniversary, or the marriage of a son. Potlatches differed from feasts in that the guests at a potlatch were given large amounts of gifts, food, or money to take home. A potlatch might take a year of planning and cost large amounts of money, and they are still held today by the Pacific Coast Indian people.

How Were the Pacific Coast Indians Different from the Plains Indians?

The abundant supply of many natural resources made the way of life of the Pacific Coast Indians different from that of the Plains Indians. The Pacific Coast Indians lived in Puget Sound in what is now Washington State. Puget Sound is a large body of water surrounded on three sides by land. It is an area rich in seafood, especially salmon. The Indians were experts at fishing. Besides an endless supply of seafood, the woods were filled with wildlife, nuts, berries, and root vegetables.

Even in winter there was enough food. In winter, they ate stored food that they had preserved by drying. The woods were filled with cedar trees. The Indians used cedar to build their shelters. These buildings were called longhouses, because they could be up to 100 feet long. They shaped cedar into shoes, clothing, rope, and mats. They carved it into tools and shaped it into bows and arrows. Even their canoes were made of cedar.

The Pacific Coast Indians showed their wealth with a custom called a potlatch. The word *potlatch* means "to throw through the air." The host of the potlatch gave the guests many gifts. The potlatch custom appears to be something only the Pacific Coast Indians did.

Who Are the Inuit?

In the Arctic in present-day Alaska and northern Canada, north of the Pacific Northwest Indians, live the people that others call Eskimo. The word *Eskimo* means "eaters of raw meat." They call themselves *Inuit,* meaning "real people." Their lives were hard. They lived in a harsh, frozen environment for most of the year. They built shelters out of blocks of snow. The shelter is called an igloo, which means "home." They hunted sea mammals and caribou for food. Their possessions were simple. They are known for their delicate carvings of ivory and soapstone.

Lesson 3 Review On a sheet of paper, write the letter of the answer that correctly completes each sentence.

1. The Adena and _____ were early Woodland cultures.

   A Hopewell   **C** Poverty Point
   B Seneca   **D** Cahokia

2. Mound builders buried _____ in the mounds along with people who had died.

   A weapons   **C** tobacco and pipes
   B extra food   **D** barley, sunflowers, and squash

3. The _____ culture was probably made up of hunter-gatherers, not farmers.

   A Hopewell   **C** Poverty Point
   B Seneca   **D** Cahokia

4. Plains Indians of the Mandan tribe lived in _____ buildings

   A low, flat   **C** square
   B dome-shaped   **D** log

5. The abundant supply of seafood, wildlife, nuts, berries, and vegetables made the lives of the _____ Indians unusual.

   A Woodland   **C** Great Plains
   B Mississippian   **D** Pacific Northwest

Great leaders of this time, such as Hiawatha and Seneca, are remembered for their speeches. Who do you think will be remembered for their speeches 100 years from now?

Chapter 9: Lesson 4

Overview This lesson describes five civilizations that developed in Central and South America—the Olmecs, the Maya, the Toltecs, the Aztecs, and the Incas.

Objectives

■ To identify the area known as Mesoamerica

■ To identify five cultures of Mesoamerica and South America

Student Pages pages 208–214

Teacher's Resource Library TRL

Workbook Activity 42

Activity 42

Modified Activity 42

Vocabulary

Although there are no boldface vocabulary words in this lesson, there still may be words that students struggle with. Have students go through the lesson and make a list of words whose meaning they are not sure about. Ask them to find the definitions of these words in a dictionary. Then distribute index cards to students and have them make a flash card for each word. The word should be written on one side of the card and the definition on the other side.

1 Warm-Up Activity

Refer students to the map of Early American Empires on page 193. Ask them to identify Mesoamerica on the map. Ask what lines of latitude form the northern and southern boundaries of Mesoamerica. (from 30°N to just south of 10°N) Have students note that Central America runs almost east and west, rather than north and south as many people believe.

Objectives

◆ To identify the area known as Mesoamerica

◆ To identify five cultures of Mesoamerica and South America

Reading Strategy: Questioning

Study the photographs and artwork in this lesson. Ask yourself how they relate to what you are reading.

More than 10,000 years ago, in a valley in what is now Mexico, an ancient hunter walked in the mud for 30 feet. In 2006, archaeologists discovered 13 of his footprints preserved in solid rock. Today, we call the area where he walked Mesoamerica. *Mesoamerica* means "middle America." It is the name given to the land between the continents of North and South America. It is in Mesoamerica that American Indians reached their highest level of cultural development. The Olmecs, the Mayas, the Toltecs, and the Aztecs created these advanced Mesoamerican civilizations. The Inca Empire on the continent of South America is another important example of a highly advanced civilization in the Americas.

What Were the Cultural Contributions of the Olmecs?

The Olmecs were ancient people living in the heart of Mesoamerica between 1200 B.C. and 400 B.C. During this time, the Olmecs developed the first important civilization in this area. The Olmecs created the first system of writing in America. They were good mathematicians and astronomers. They used the zero many centuries before the Greeks. They developed a calendar of 365 days and a special 260-day religious calendar. The best example of Olmec art is 10-foot-tall stone heads. The purpose of the giant stone heads is a mystery.

What Were Olmec Settlements Like?

Olmec settlements contained up to 1,000 people. They lived in a rich agricultural area and grew maize, squash, and beans. Around 900 B.C. they built a very tall earthen mound shaped like a pyramid with a flat top. Some anthropologists believe that the Olmecs were the "mother culture" of Mesoamerica. This means that the Olmecs' cultural developments laid the foundation for the achievements of the Mayas, the Toltecs, and the Aztecs.

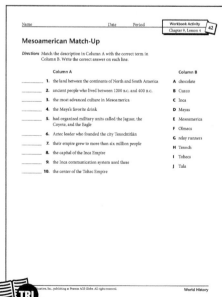

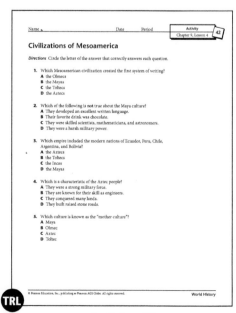

Workbook Activity 42

Activity 42

Reading Strategy:
Questioning

What do you already
know about the
Mayas?

Why Are the Mayas Considered the Most Advanced Culture in Mesoamerica?

Maya civilization is considered the most advanced in Mesoamerica. It started around A.D. 250. The Mayas developed an excellent written language. It equaled the complex written languages of the Europeans and Chinese. The Mayas were scientists, master mathematicians, and excellent astronomers. These skills allowed them to keep track of time in the past and into the future. The Maya calendar began in 3114 B.C. It was based on 13 cycles of 400 years each. The Mayas thought that this calendar would end in 2012. After this date, a brand-new calendar cycle would begin.

Maya civilization was a complex agricultural society. The Mayas farmed an area for up to five years. Then they planted nothing there for five to 10 years, allowing the soil to recover. Their favorite drink was chocolate. Chocolate was so special it was reserved for political and religious leaders.

A large, stone temple stood in the center of each Maya city. This photo shows the temple and surrounding areas of the Maya city of Chichén Itzá in Yucatán, Mexico.

Prehistory – A.D. 1570   *Civilizations of the Americas: Prehistory – A.D. 1570   Chapter 9*   **209**

 2 Teaching the Lesson

Have students again study the map on page 193 to find where the Olmecs, Maya, Aztecs, and Incas were located. Then have students read this lesson to learn about the cultures of these Central and South American civilizations and the gifts they gave us.

Ask:

- When did the Olmec people live? (between 1200 B.C. and 400 B.C.)

Reading Strategy:
Questioning

Ask students what they know about the Mayas. Write their information on the board. Have students write a short paragraph in which they ask additional questions about the Mayas. Then have students read aloud the two sections on pages 209 and 210 about the Mayas.

- What were some contributions of the Mayas? (a written language, a calendar, the practice of allowing farmland to recover, chocolate)

- What was a result of Maya science skills? (an accurate calendar based on astronomy)

STUDY SKILLS

 Comparing and contrasting is a useful way for students to study different cultures. Have students read about each culture in this lesson. As they read, they should make a chart with a column for each culture and rows for time period, location, cities, leaders, kind of society, and contributions. The chart will serve as a visual tool for comparing and contrasting the cultures.

The Mayas were skilled engineers. They cleared jungles and built large cities throughout the area. These cities contained impressive buildings and boulevards. The Mayas were also known for their beautiful artwork, especially their colorful murals. Ancient artists in other cultures were not identified. However, Maya artists added their names to their art work. Today, the descendants of the Mayas still live in the land of their ancestors.

What Kind of Political System Did the Mayas Have?

A king ruled the Mayas. A central council headed by the king ruled on very important matters. There was a court system with local judges. Taxes were paid to tax collectors. To keep expanding their teritory, the Mayas had a well-organized army. The army conquered other people who were then brought into the Maya civilization.

How Was the Toltec Civilization Different from the Olmecs and Mayas?

Around A.D. 900, the Toltecs moved into the Valley of Mexico. There they found a city called Tula. The city of Tula became the center of a great Toltec Empire. The Toltec culture was different from the Olmecs and the Mayas. Political and religious leaders were most important in those cultures. But in the Toltec culture, a special class of warriors gained power. Warriors of the Jaguar, the Coyote, and the Eagle were names for organized military units. For 200 years, the Toltecs' military might made them the strongest culture in Mesoamerica. By A.D. 1200, a less advanced invader destroyed the Toltec Empire. Eventually the city of Tula was destroyed. However, for another 200 years, Toltec influence could be seen throughout the area. The ideas and achievements of the Toltecs heavily influenced the Aztec civilization.

What Caused the Aztecs to Settle on an Island in Mexico?

Around A.D. 1200, the Aztecs began moving into the Valley of Mexico. Their culture was a simple one. They were not a powerful people. In fact, other groups looked down upon them. At this time, the Aztecs had no written records. But they told a story of how, around A.D. 1300, a god spoke to their leader. The god told their leader, Tenoch, to take his people to an island in Lake Texcoco. On the island he should look for an eagle eating a snake. The eagle would be sitting on a cactus growing from a rock. It was on that spot that Tenoch was told to build a great city. They named the city *Tenochtitlán,* or "the city of Tenoch." The island was not a good building site. Large buildings gradually sank into the wet land. The Aztecs kept building new buildings on top of those that sank below ground. Eventually, the wet land was filled in. Tenochtitlán became a magnificent city. To connect the island to the mainland, the Aztecs built raised stone roads.

How Did the Aztecs Become an Empire?

In 1376, they selected their first emperor. Their leader's ancestors were the Toltecs. The Aztecs sought to recreate the influential Toltec civilization. Like the Toltecs, the Aztecs began to conquer other groups by military force. They forced these conquered people to pay part of their food or other valuables to them. By the early 1500s, the Aztecs had built a large empire and had become a harsh military power.

This is a sun stone or a calendar from the temple at Tenochtitlán, the Aztec capital city.

Ask:

- Why did the city of Tenochtitlán gradually sink? (The land was on an island and was wet and unsuitable for buildings.)

- How did the Aztecs become a strong empire? (They copied the earlier Toltecs and began to conquer other groups by military force.)

LEARNING STYLES

Interpersonal/ Group Learning

Have small groups of students work together to write a page of a Maya, an Aztec, an Olmec, or an Incan newspaper. Suggest that their pages might include a sports section, a weather report, a local news item, and an advertisement. Encourage groups to use the information in this lesson. In addition, students will have to do some research on the daily life of the culture they choose.

Ask:

- What was the Inca's capital city? (Cuzco)

- What five modern countries were once parts of the Inca Empire? (Ecuador, Peru, Chile, Argentina, and Bolivia)

- How were the Incas able to govern such a large empire? (They divided the empire into four areas, asked conquered people to become partners in the government, and built a system of roads for communicating with the various parts of the empire.)

Reading Strategy:
Questioning

(Answers will vary. Students may suggest that it is important to know some of the problems the Incas had and how they solved them. Knowing how a culture solves problems tells the reader a lot about the culture. Students may also suggest that it is important to know if the rulers were fair or cruel, whether the people were loyal to the rulers, what everyday life was like for common people, and whether times were peaceful.)

Biography

Provide students with this additional background material about Pachacutec, the 9th Inca emperor. Pachacutec, followed by his son, conquered so many peoples that within three generations the Inca Empire had spread to almost all of civilized South America. He reformed his empire by founding towns and building temples. He built storehouses and filled them with food to be used when crops were poor.

Who Were the Incas?

The empire of the Inca was located in the valleys of the Andes Mountains in South America. Their capital city of Cuzco was built high in the mountains of what is now Peru. Around A.D. 1100, the Incas began conquering tribes from the surrounding lands. By 1453, the Inca Empire covered a large area containing more than six million people. The Inca Empire included parts of five modern nations: Ecuador, Peru, Chile, Argentina, and Bolivia. It was the largest empire in North and South America.

The Inca Empire faced more difficult problems than the empires in Mesoamerica. One of the problems was how to govern such a large area with so many different kinds of people. First, the Incas divided the empire into four geographic areas. They call their empire the "Land of the Four Quarters." *Inca* was the name they gave their emperor. Second, once a tribe was conquered by military force, they asked the tribal leaders to become partners in the empire. The Incas set up rules that the tribal leaders had to follow. In this way, local leaders could make many decisions for their own tribes but still remain loyal to the Inca Empire.

 Biography

Pachacutec Inca Yupanqui: died 1471

The year of Pachacutec's birth is not known. His name means "he who changes the world." He became emperor of the Inca people in 1438. Pachacutec proved himself to be a brave warrior and a good ruler. He also served as the religious leader of his empire. During his rule, Inca territory expanded, and the Incas built a system of roads. He developed an effective government and economy. Pachacutec was responsible for many building projects. It is thought that he built Machu Picchu as a place to go to relax. Machu Picchu, also known as the "Lost City," is high in the Andes Mountains. Many historians consider Pachacutec to be one of the greatest rulers of all time.

• What did the Incas do to connect their vast empire? (They built a network of roads.)

• How did different parts of the Inca Empire communicate with each other? (They used relay runners to carry messages along the roads.)

Why Were Roads So Important to the Incas?

The empire covered about 2,500 miles from the northern to the southern end. Cuzco was the capital city. From Cuzco, the Inca emperor needed to communicate with the rest of the empire. The Incas were skilled engineers. They built more than 14,000 miles of roads. The network of roads connected the coastal areas and the valleys. In the mountains, roads rose to heights of 5,000 feet. Using the network of roads, the Incas created a fast communication system by using relay runners along the roads. There were rest areas that contained food and water.

Writing About History

Imagine that you are visiting one of the Olmec, Maya, Incan, or Aztec cities. Research the architecture and layout of such a place. In your notebook, describe it. Include a drawing.

Machu Picchu, in Peru, is an important archaeological site.

Writing About History

Ask students where they might find additional information about Olmec, Maya, Incan, or Aztec cities. (encyclopedias, books, the Internet) After students select a civilization to write about, have them locate resources in the library and record their research in note form. Have students use their notes to write their descriptions.

LEARNING STYLES

Logical/Mathematical
The Incan Empire stretched about 2,500 miles from north to south. The Incas built more than 14,000 miles of road. If these roads were stretched out from north to south in a single straight line, how many times could they go through the empire? (between five and six times)

3 **Reinforce and Extend**

WORLD CULTURES

Maya people still live in the Yucatán Peninsula and surrounding areas. Most Maya groups live on farms that surround a central village area. They grow corn, beans, and squash. Some Maya people raise pigs and chickens. Most Maya people consider themselves Roman Catholic, though in practice, their religion is a blend of Christianity and traditional Maya rituals.

ONLINE CONNECTION

The Field Museum of Chicago's Web site at www.agsglobewh.com/page214 contains a wealth of information about chocolate. It discusses the history of chocolate and how it spread to Europe. Many of the links explore how chocolate drinks were used by the Maya and Aztecs.

Lesson 4 Review Answers

1. Mesoamerica is the land that connects North and South America. **2.** It was a complex agricultural society, but there were also many scientists, mathematicians, engineers, and astronomers. **3.** Many Olmec practices were part of later cultures. **4.** They were told of a story in which a god described a place on an island where they should build the city. **5.** The Incas built roads to connect the parts of their vast empire.

Answers will vary. Make sure students give details from the chapter in their responses.

Ask a volunteer to describe the court, equipment, and rules of modern basketball. Then have students read the feature on page 214. Have students compare and contrast the Maya game with modern basketball. In what ways are the two games similar? In what ways are they different?

Chapter Project Follow-up

Student reports about Maya calendars should describe the way the calendar worked and what it looked like. Reports should give some information about Maya life, how life was determined by the calendar, and the importance of astrology and astronomy in the calendar system. Student reports can be displayed in the classroom.

How About a Game of Basketball?

In the center of Maya cities near the temples and palaces, you might have found a large court. Its shape was like today's basketball court. Tall stone walls stood on the two long sides of the court.

High in the middle of each wall was a stone ring, or hoop. Often, it was 30 feet above the ground! The Mayas put the hoop straight up and down instead of parallel to the ground. The Mayas used the court to play a game with a ball made of solid rubber. The ball weighed about five pounds. Players were not allowed to use their hands or feet to get the ball through the hoop. They passed the ball back and forth with their hips, knees, and forearms.

Some people believe that for the Mayas, the game represented the battle between life and death. The rubber ball may have been a symbol of the sun. What do you think the game of basketball represents today?

Lesson 4 Review On a sheet of paper, write the answer to each question. Use complete sentences.

1. What is Mesoamerica?

2. What was the culture of the Mayas like?

3. Why do some anthropologists think that the Olmecs may be the "mother culture" of Mesoamerica?

4. Why did the Aztecs build their city on an island in a lake in Mexico?

5. Why did the Incas build so many miles of roads?

What do you think

What is the most important thing you have learned by studying these ancient Mesoamerican cultures?

Knighthood for the Incas

In the Inca empire, it was a great honor for a boy to become a knight. He had to be over 16 years old to take part in this test. His whole family shared his honor—or his disgrace, if he failed. Here is an account of the difficult test faced by one group.

The candidates were required to observe a very strict fast for six days, receiving only a handful of raw sara (their corn) apiece and a jug of plain water, without anything else. . . .

Such a rigorous fast was not usually permitted for more than three days, but this period was doubled for the initiates undergoing their ordeal, in order to show if they were men enough to suffer any hunger or thirst to which they might be exposed in time of war. The fathers, brothers, and other close relatives of the candidates underwent a less rigorous, but none the less strictly observed, fast, praying their father the Sun to strengthen and encourage the youths so that they might come through the ordeal with honor. Anyone who showed weakness or distress or asked for more food was failed and eliminated from the test. After the fast they were allowed some victuals

[food] to restore their strength and then tried for bodily agility. As a test they were made to run from the hill called Huanacauri, which they regarded as sacred, to the fortress of the city . . . at the fortress a pennant or banner was set up as a finishing post, and whoever reached it first was elected captain over the rest. Those who arrived second, third, fourth, and down to the tenth fastest were also held in great honor, while those who flagged or fainted on the course were disgraced and eliminated. . . .

The next day they were divided into two equal bands . . . and they were required to fight one against the other . . . so that they could all display their agility and skill . . . In such struggles the weapons were blunted so that they were less formidable than in real warfare; nevertheless there were severe casualties which were sometimes fatal. . . .

Document-Based Questions

1. How do you know that this event is important in the lives of young men in Peru?

2. Why do you think that family members of the candidates also fasted?

3. Why is showing hunger or thirst considered a sign of weakness?

4. Do you think that this custom is a fair test of a man's strength? Explain.

5. From the last sentence, how do you know that this custom could be very dangerous?

Source: Royal Commentaries of the Incas and General History of Peru, by Garcilaso de la Vega, El Inca.

Prehistory – A.D. 1570 *Civilizations of the Americas: Prehistory – A.D. 1570 Chapter 9* **215**

Explain to students that the initiation ceremony into knighthood was called the *huarachico ceremony.* It celebrated the passage of a boy of Inca aristocracy into adulthood. There were three stages to the initiation: the ritual stage, which involved fasting and praying to the gods, the warrior stage in which the boys fought one against the other, and the festive or war dance stage. At the end, an Inca boy who passed all the tests had his ears pierced and received his first breechcloth, which ensured him Inca citizenship and his eligibility for marriage and war. The ultimate goal of the ceremony was for a boy to convince the powerful Inca leaders that he qualified to become a great warrior.

Select a student to read aloud the introductory paragraph of the Document-Based Reading. Have students think about initiation rites and ceremonies in other cultures they may be familiar with. Discuss why a culture had these ceremonies. Ask if females also had ceremonies for entering adulthood. Continue reading the selection. Finally, have students answer the Document-Based Questions.

Answers to Document-Based Questions:

1. Becoming a knight was a great honor that was shared by his whole family. If a boy failed, both he and his family were disgraced.

2. Family members hoped that their father, the Sun, would listen to their prayers and would strengthen and encourage the youth. Fasting was a part of praying.

3. Knights might have to endure hunger and thirst in time of war. They had to show that they were men enough for this.

4. Answers will vary. Students may suggest that the custom is meant to show the kind of endurance needed for warfare in ancient times. It overlooks other forms of strength and character.

5. There were severe casualties and some youths died.

Have students read "The Lady of the Lines." Tell them that the Nasca Lines are an example of a geoglyph, a carving in rock or sand. Write the word on the board and break it down into parts: *geo*, meaning "earth" and *glyph*, meaning "writing." Many geoglyphs worldwide have disappeared over the years, stolen or worn away by wind and water. However, the Nasca Lines are located in a place that is ideal for preserving such markings. The Nasca Desert receives rain for about 20 minutes a year.

In 1968, a study by the National Geographic Society determined that, while some of the Nasca Lines did point to the positions of celestial bodies, it was no more than could be expected by mere chance. Other scientists have come to the same conclusion. Some people insist that the Lines are landing strips for spaceships!

Distribute small, simple drawings that you have cut from magazines. Have students draw a grid on the drawings. Then have them draw a grid on a larger piece of paper and reproduce the drawing in the same way Marie Reiche believed the Nasca Lines were made.

Answers to Spotlight Story Wrap-Up:

1. She was curious about their origin and meaning.

2. They thought she was crazy and didn't understand her passion for her work.

3. Answers will vary. Students may suggest that her idea of making a grid to enlarge a drawing was mathematical.

4. The Nasca people left no records or writings about why they made the drawings.

5. Answers will vary. Students may say that preserving historical sites is important because they help us to understand early civilizations.

The Lady of the Lines

Before the Great Incan Empire existed, the Nascan people lived near Peru's southern coast from 200 B.C. to A.D. 650. Today, because of the work of Maria Reiche, we now know that the Nascans created mysterious, gigantic drawings in one of the world's driest deserts. Nasca means a "hard place to live." Each of the more than 70 drawings was created by a single line. The drawings are known as the Nasca Lines of Peru.

Maria Reiche was born in Germany in 1903. In 1940, although a mathematician, she became an assistant to an archaeologist studying the Nasca Lines. Most of the drawings are of animals or geometric designs. They are so large that they can be seen only from an aircraft. What one can see on the ground are straight paths with dark rocks lining the sides.

Maria made the study of the Nasca Lines her life's work. The work was physically difficult. The wind continually covered the lines with pebbles. She had to sweep the pebbles away. The people in the area called her the "crazy woman sweeping the desert." Maria said, "What compelled me on this quest was my curiosity."

Maria Reiche especially wanted to know how and why the drawings were made. She thought that the Nascans created the drawings by first drawing crisscrossed parallel lines, called a grid, on cloth. They then drew a picture on the grid to use as a model. Next, they drew a larger grid on the desert floor. They then copied the smaller cloth drawing onto the larger desert grid. By doing this they were able to create enormous drawings.

Maria noticed that at different times of the year many of the lines directly pointed to the rising and setting of the sun and the moon. She thought the Nascans used the drawings to determine when to plant seeds to assure a good harvest. The drawings, she thought, were a sky calendar.

Maria Reiche, the Lady of the Lines, died at age 95. She said that the Nasca Lines "should be treated like a very fragile manuscript that is guarded in a special room in a library." Because of her work, in 1995 the United Nations declared that the location of the Nasca Lines was a World Heritage Site.

Wrap-Up

1. Why did Maria Reiche want to study the Nasca Lines?

2. What did the people in the area think of her?

3. How could her background as a mathematician help Reiche in her study of the Nasca Lines?

4. Why don't we know exactly why the ancient society in Peru created the Nasca Lines?

5. Why is it important to preserve historical sites like this one?

Chapter 9 S U M M A R Y

- The first Americans arrived during the last Ice Age. They walked from Asia over the Bering Strait. Clues about how and when this happened are still being discovered.

- Bones found in Folsom, New Mexico, proved that American Indians had been living in the area for at least 9,000 years.

- The Clovis Point was more than 4,000 years older than the Folsom Point. Scientists believe that the Clovis people were the first Americans.

- The Hohokam civilization began about 300 B.C. in what is now Arizona. They built irrigation canals and created beautiful pottery and jewelry.

- Beginning about 200 B.C., the Mogollon lived in what is now southeastern Arizona and southern New Mexico. They created more artistic images than any other people in the world.

- The Anasazi are known as master builders. Their civilization began in about 100 A.D. They lived where Arizona, New Mexico, Utah, and Colorado meet.

- The Adena (beginning about 700 B.C.) and Hopewell (beginning about A.D. 100) were early Woodland cultures. They were both mound builders.

- Beginning around A.D. 1200, the Iroquois, a group of six different tribes, were a powerful Woodland culture in Upper New York.

- The Plains Indians lived between the Mississippi River and the Rocky Mountains. They were Sioux, Cheyenne, Comanche, and Blackfoot Indians. The Mandans lived in what is now North Dakota.

- The Pacific Coast Indians lived in what is now Washington State. They were experts at fishing.

- Eskimos, or Inuits, lived a hard life in a frozen environment. They are known for their ivory and soapstone carvings.

- Mesoamerica is the land between North and South America. The Olmecs developed the first important civilization in this area around 1200 B.C.

- The Mayas developed an excellent written language. Their most important cultural and artistic achievements took place between A.D. 300 and 900.

- Around A.D. 900, the Toltecs moved into the Valley of Mexico. In this culture, warriors gained power.

- The Aztecs moved into the Valley of Mexico around A.D. 1200. In 1521, the Aztec Empire ended.

- The Inca Empire was in the Andes Mountains in South America. The empire lasted about 100 years, ending in 1532.

TEACHER'S RESOURCE

The AGS Globe Teaching Strategies in Social Studies Transparencies may be used with this chapter. The transparencies add an interactive dimension to expand and enhance the *World History* program content.

Using the Chapter Summary

Have students read the Chapter Summary on page 217 to review the main ideas presented in Chapter 9.

Ask:

- How did the first Americans get to North America? (They walked across the frozen Bering Strait.)

- What did bones found in Folsom, New Mexico prove? (that people had lived there for at least 9,000 years)

- Who are now believed to have been the first Americans? (the Clovis people)

- What were the Hohokam people noted for? (irrigation canals, pottery, and jewelry)

- What did the Mogollon people excel at? (They made large numbers of artistic images.)

- What culture is known as master builders? What did they build? (the Anasazi; cliff dwellings)

- Which two cultures were mound builders? (Adena and Hopewell)

- How many tribes made up the Iroquois and where did they live? (Six tribes of Iroquois lived in Upper New York.)

- Where did the Plains Indians live? (between the Mississippi River and the Rocky Mountains)

- What were the Pacific Coast Indians noted for? (They were experts at fishing.)

- Why did the Inuits have a hard life? (They lived in a frozen environment where finding food was hard.)

- What is Mesoamerica? (the land between North and South America)

- What are the Maya best known for? (They developed a complex written language.)

- Who were the most powerful in the Toltec culture? (warriors)

- Between what years did the Aztec Empire exist? (between about A.D. 1200 and 1521)

- Where did the Incas live? (in the Andes Mountains in South America)

Chapter 9 Review

Use the Chapter Review to prepare students for tests and to reteach content from the chapter.

Chapter 9 Mastery Test

The Teacher's Resource Library includes two forms of the Chapter 9 Mastery Test. Each test covers the chapter Goals for Learning. An optional third page of additional critical-thinking items is included for each test. The difficulty level of the two forms is equivalent.

Chapter 9 Review Answers

1. Clovis
2. Mogollons
3. Anasazi
4. Hohokam
5. Olmecs
6. Maya
7. Aztec
8. Incas
9. Toltecs
10. Inuit
11. C
12. B

Word Bank

Anasazi
Aztec
Clovis
Hohokam
Incas
Inuit
Mayas
Mogollons
Olmecs
Toltecs

On a sheet of paper, use the words from the Word Bank to complete each sentence correctly.

1. Scientists think the _____ people were among the first Americans.

2. The _____ are known for their rock art—images of insects, fish, reptiles, birds, and mammals.

3. The _____ built cliff dwellings in the rock near where Arizona, New Mexico, Utah, and Colorado meet.

4. Because they lived in the desert, the _____ had to build irrigation canals to water their crops.

5. The _____ created the first system of writing in the Americas.

6. The _____ are known for their calendar, which was based on 400-year cycles.

7. By the early 1500s, the _____ people had become a harsh military power.

8. The _____ built more than 14,000 miles of roads to connect people in their large empire.

9. _____ civilization was different from others because of the importance of their military.

10. The _____, or Eskimo, people built shelters out of blocks of snow.

On a sheet of paper, write the letter of the answer that correctly completes each sentence.

11. The settlement of _____ was an important place for the Hohokam.

    A Clovis   **B** Folsom   **C** Snaketown   **D** Cahokia

12. Archaeologists named the _____ after the mountain ranges in which they lived.

    A Hohokam   **B** Mogollan   **C** Anasazi   **D** Adena

Name _____ Date _____ Period _____ | Chapter 9 Mastery Test A / Page 1

Chapter 9 Mastery Test A

Part A Directions Circle the letter of the answer that correctly answers each question.

1. Which group were probably the first Americans?
   A priests   B nomads   C farmers   D astronomers

2. What kind of evidence did the "bone pit" bones provide?
   A how long American Indians had lived in North America
   B how the first Americans set up their communities
   C how American Indians farmed their land
   D how the first Americans reached North America

3. Which early southwestern culture was known for its artwork?
   A Hohokam   B Inca   C Anasazi   D Mogollon

4. Which early regional cultural group rode horses while hunting buffalo?
   A Great Plains   B Mississippian   C Woodland   D Aztec

5. Which Mesoamerican civilization created the first system of writing?
   A Maya   B Aztec   C Inca   D Olmec

Part B Directions Match the description in Column A with the correct term in Column B. Write the correct answer on each line.

Column A	Column B
_____ 6. thick sheets of ice	A Anasazi
_____ 7. entered the Americas about 13,000 years ago	B Cahokia
_____ 8. small underground building built by the Mogollon	C Clovis people
_____ 9. built a "wagon wheel" community	D glaciers
_____ 10. largest Mississippian settlement in A.D. 1200	E Hiawatha
_____ 11. a great Iroquois leader	F Inca Empire
_____ 12. American Indians who hunt sea mammals and caribou	G Inuit
_____ 13. considered the most advanced Mesoamerican culture	H kiva
_____ 14. referred to by some as the "mother culture" of Mesoamerica	I Maya
_____ 15. also called the "Land of the Four Quarters"	J Olmec

---

Name _____ Date _____ Period _____ | Chapter 9 Mastery Test A / Page 2

Chapter 9 Mastery Test A, *continued*

Part C Directions Write the answers to these questions. Use complete sentences.

16. What item became George McJunkin's major scientific discovery?
    _____

17. What did the Hohokam build to bring water to their land?
    _____

18. From which early regional culture did the Iroquois descend?
    _____

19. Which civilization did the Aztecs try to recreate?
    _____

20. Which Mesoamerican empire included parts of Ecuador, Peru, Chile, Argentina, and Bolivia?
    _____

Part D Directions Write the correct word from the Word Bank to complete each sentence.

21. The _____ built canals to provide water for crops and for drinking.

22. _____ was a major Anasazi settlement.

23. The Adena and Hopewell were hunter-gatherers and _____ builders.

24. The Poverty Point People were part of the _____ culture.

25. The _____ lived in dome-shaped buildings made of large logs covered with earth and straw.

Word Bank
Chaco Canyon
Hohokam
Mandan
Mississippian
mound

Name _____ Date _____ Period _____ | Chapter 9 Mastery Test A / Page 3

Chapter 9 Mastery Test A, *continued*

Part E Directions Write your answer to each question. Use complete sentences. Support each answer with facts and examples from the textbook.

26. Who were the first Americans and where did they come from? (2 points)
    _____
    _____

27. Name one of the early Southwestern cultures and one of its major contributions. (2 points)
    _____
    _____

Part F Directions Write a paragraph for each topic. Include a topic sentence, body, and conclusion. Support each answer with facts and examples from the textbook.

28. Describe the "wagon wheel" construction of the Anasazi community. (3 points)
    _____
    _____
    _____
    _____

29. Compare and contrast the Olmec, Maya, and Toltec civilizations. (3 points)
    _____
    _____
    _____
    _____

Chapter 9 Mastery Test A, pages 1–3

13. The _____ people created a very large earthen Snake Mound.

A Hohokam **B** Mogollan **C** Iroquois **D** Hopewell

14. The _____ culture was unusual because even though they were not farmers, they had the resources to build large earthen structures.

A Anasazi **B** Adena **C** Poverty Point **D** Cahokia

15. The _____ tribes lived in Puget Sound, a large body of water surrounded on three sides by land.

A Pacific Coast **C** Inuit
B Plains Indian **D** Iroquois

On a sheet of paper, write the answer to each question. Use complete sentences.

16. Choose one of the cultures you have just studied. How did the environment determine what kinds of shelters they built and how they farmed?

17. How did George McJunkin know that the bones he discovered in 1908 were an important scientific discovery?

18. Besides water for their crops, how did the Hohokam use the water from their canals?

Critical Thinking On a sheet of paper, write your response to each question. Use complete sentences.

19. After the Incas conquered a tribe by military force, they asked the tribal leaders to become partners in their empire. How did this make the Incan Empire stronger?

20. Why do you think archaeologists have found so few artifacts from the earliest Americans?

Try to answer all questions as completely as possible. When asked to explain your answer, do so in complete sentences.

13. D

14. C

15. A

16. Answers will vary depending on the culture chosen. Sample answer: The Hohokam lived in a desert area. In order to raise food, they had to dig a system of canals to bring water to their crops. They lived in small villages that could be sustained by smaller amounts of crops.

17. He knew his discovery was important because the bones were very large and deeply buried.

18. The canals provided water for drinking, cooking, washing, and making pottery.

Critical Thinking

19. Answers will vary. Students may say that the tribal leaders could make many decisions for their own tribes. By making them feel like they were part of the empire, they were less likely to rebel.

20. Answers will vary. Students may suggest that many artifacts have been removed from sites or that the early civilizations did not leave much behind since they were primitive people. They may also think that artifacts have been lost to erosion or been destroyed since the earliest Americans lived so long ago.

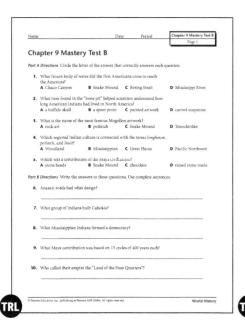

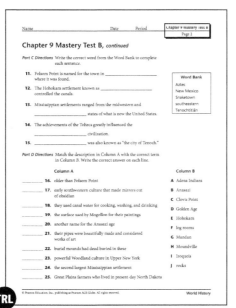

Chapter 9 Mastery Test B, pages 1–3 *Civilizations of the Americas Chapter 9* **219**

Display several timelines—both horizontal and vertical. You may find samples in newspapers, magazines, or books.

Ask:

• What is the purpose of the timelines? *(Timelines show the chronological, or time, order of events.)*

Have students read the Skills Lesson on page 220 and answer the questions.

Unit 1 Skill Builder Answers

1. 1905 and 1945
2. before World War I
3. 1914
4. Russian Revolution
5. Stalin takes control in Soviet Union; Great Depression begins.
6. Stalin
7. 6 years
8. 2 years
9. 1945
10. Events shown in chronological order on a timeline will vary.

Unit Skills Activity

Distribute copies of the Unit 1 Skills Activity. Briefly discuss the types of events that students might include on their personal timelines. In addition to dates important to their personal lives, such as birthdays, first day of school, a vacation, etc., they might include local, state, and national events that took place during their lifetimes, such as the championship of a local team or the passage of a new law.

Unit 1
Skill Builder

Timelines

Timelines show dates and events on a line, or scale. They may span thousands of years or only a few months. A timeline may show key events in a region. It may list events in one person's lifetime. It may show events of a certain kind, such as scientific discoveries. In reading a timeline, always look at the beginning and ending dates.

Timelines show the time relationships between events. They help you think about events in the order they occurred. You see when an event happened. Then you can see what happened before and after it.

Each chapter in this book begins with a timeline. Those timelines will help you focus on key events and ideas in the chapter. As you read a chapter, create your own timeline of events. That will help you study those events.

This timeline gives the dates of some important events in the first half of the 20th century. Study it. Then answer the questions.

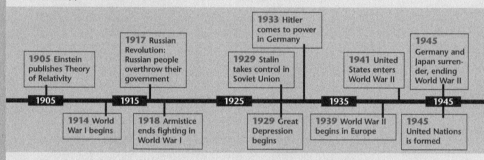

1. What are the beginning and ending dates on this timeline?
2. Did Einstein publish the Theory of Relativity before or after World War I?
3. In what year did World War I begin?
4. What event on this timeline happened during World War I?
5. What two events on this timeline happened in 1929?
6. Who came to power first—Hitler or Stalin?
7. How many years after Hitler came to power did World War II begin?
8. How long did World War II go on before the United States entered the war?
9. When was the United Nations formed?
10. Create a timeline showing key events in your life during the last school year.

Unit Skills Activity

Unit 1 SUMMARY

- The discovery of fire and the beginning of farming were among the most important events in human history.

- The time before humans left written records is called prehistory.

- Civilizations began in Mesopotamia about 7,000 years ago.

- Sumerians invented a system of writing called cuneiform.

- The Assyrians were a warrior tribe in Mesopotamia.

- The teachings of Zoroaster influenced Judaism and Christianity.

- Egyptian civilizations developed in the valley of the Nile River in Africa.

- Pharaohs in Egypt built pyramids for tombs. People filled them with things the ruler would need in the afterlife.

- The first Indian civilization began in the Indus River Valley.

- Hinduism is based on castes, or classes. Everyone is born into a caste.

- Siddhartha Gautama became the Buddha. Buddhism spread from India into Asia.

- The Yangtze is the longest river in China; the first cities were built along this river about 2000 B.C.

- Socrates, Plato, and Aristotle were Greek philosophers during the "Golden Age" of Athens.

- In 60 B.C., Pompey, Julius Caesar, and Crassus ruled together as the First Triumvirate.

- Jesus was born in Palestine during the reign of Augustus. Followers of Jesus believed he was the Son of God.

- The Roman Empire fell in A.D. 476.

- Mesoamerica is the land between North and South America.

- The Olmecs developed the first system of writing in the Americas. They were mathematicians and astronomers.

- The Mayas are considered the most advanced culture in Mesoamerica. They influenced other great civilizations of Mesoamerica.

- The Aztecs moved into the Valley of Mexico about A.D. 900. Their capitol was the magnificent city of Tenochtitlán.

- The Incan Empire grew up in the Peruvian Andes Mountains. It ended in A.D. 1532.

Prehistory – A.D. 1570

Early Civilizations   Unit 1   **221**

Using the Unit Summary

Read and discuss the Unit 1 Summary statements on page 221 with students.

Ask:

- Why were fire and farming among the most important events in history? (provided warmth, food, and allowed people to live in one place)

- How important were river valleys to early civilizations? (provided fertile land for farming and an avenue for trade)

- What was cuneiform? (a system of writing invented by the Sumerians)

- What role did religion play in early civilizations? (Answers will vary. Students should explain how religion helped to structure each civilization.)

- Who were three Greek philosophers of the "Golden Age"? (Socrates, Plato, Aristotle)

- Where is Mesoamerica? (between North and South America)

- Why is the Maya civilization considered the most advanced culture of Mesoamerica? (The Maya had a written language and advanced agricultural methods.)

Unit 1 Mastery Test

The Teacher's Resource Library includes a two-page Unit Mastery Test. An optional third page of additional critical-thinking items is included for each test. The Unit 1 Mastery Test is pictured on page 861 of this Teacher's Edition.

Unit Activity Follow-Up

Discuss with students characteristics that are common to all civilizations. (settlement near water, religion, some form of government, and the division of work) Have students share what they have learned about early civilizations.

- To evaluate student performance, consider the following questions:

- Did students complete Unit 1 Activity 1 and Unit 1 Activity 2?

- Did students identify characteristics that are common to all civilizations?

- Were student paragraphs organized and complete?

Planning Guide
Regional Civilizations

		Student Pages	Vocabulary	Lesson Review	Critical-Thinking Questions	Chapter Summary	Chapter Review
Chapter 10	The High and Late Middle Ages	224–247	✔		✔	245	246
Lesson 1	The Church during the Middle Ages	227–231	✔	231	✔		
Lesson 2	Feudalism	232–234	✔	234	✔		
Lesson 3	The Manor	235–238	✔	238	✔		
Lesson 4	Culture in the Middle Ages	239–242	✔	242	✔		
Chapter 11	The Byzantine Empire, Russia, and E. Europe	248–269	✔			267	268
Lesson 1	The Byzantine Empire	251–254	✔	254	✔		
Lesson 2	The Russians	255–259	✔	259	✔		
Lesson 3	Europe During the Middle Ages	260–264	✔	264	✔		
Chapter 12	Africa and the Spread of Islam	270–293	✔			291	292
Lesson 1	The Rise of Islam	273–276	✔	276	✔		
Lesson 2	Islamic Civilization	277–281	✔	281	✔		
Lesson 3	African Kingdoms	282–288	✔	288	✔		
Chapter 13	The Spread of Civilization in E. and SE Asia	294–321			✔	319	320
Lesson 1	India	297–300	✔	300	✔		
Lesson 2	China	301–304	✔	304	✔		
Lesson 3	The Mongols Conquer China	305–306	✔	306	✔		
Lesson 4	Japan	307–309	✔	309	✔		
Lesson 5	Japan Develops Its Own Culture	310–314	✔	314	✔		
Lesson 6	The Tokugawa Unify Japan	315–316	✔	316	✔		

Unit Activities

Student Text
Unit 2 Summary
Unit 2 Skill Builder

Teacher's Resource Library
Unit 2 Activities 1–2
Unit 2 Skills Activity

Assessment Options

Teacher's Resource Library
Chapter 10 Mastery Tests A and B
Chapter 11 Mastery Tests A and B
Chapter 12 Mastery Tests A and B
Chapter 13 Mastery Tests A and B
Unit 2 Mastery Test

Student Text Features											Teaching Strategies						Learning Styles					Teacher's Resource Library			
Reading Strategy	Map Study/Map Skills	Writing About History	Geography Note	Biography	History in Your Life	Communication in History	Technology Connection	Then and Now	Spotlight Story	Document-Based Reading	Background Information	Applications (Home, Career, Community)	World Cultures	Study Skills	Online Connection	ELL/ESL Strategy	Auditory/Verbal	Visual/Spatial	Body/Kinesthetic	Interpersonal/Group Learning	Logical/Mathematical	Activities/Modified Activities	Workbook Activities	Self-Study Guide	Chapter Outline
226	225								244	243				226, 244										✔	✔
✔				231								228		230	229	229	230					43	43		
✔													234			233			234			44	44		
✔		238					238				238					237					236	45	45		
✔			242									241		244		241		240		240		46	46		
250	249								266	265				250			265							✔	✔
✔	253										254	253, 254		252				254	253			47	47		
✔	256			257	259							259, 263			257	256				257	258	48	48		
✔	262	263					264	261								261						49	49		
272	271								290	289	290													✔	✔
✔															276	275	274					50	50		
✔	277					281					280					278			280			51	51		
	286	279		287	284						287		287			283, 285			283	288	285	52	52		
296	295								318	317									295					✔	✔
✔	299											299, 300		298	299	298						53	53		
✔				302	304							303	304			302		303				54	54		
✔																306				306		55	55		
✔	309										308					308						56	56		
✔	310				314										312	312	313					57	57		
✔											316					316				316		58	58		

TRL Activities

The Teacher's Resource Library (TRL) contains a set of lower-level worksheets called Modified Activities. These worksheets cover the same content as the standard Activities but are written at a lower reading level.

Skill Track

Use Skill Track for *World History* to monitor student progress and meet the demands of Adequate Yearly Progress (AYP). Make informed instructional decisions with individual student and class reports of lesson and chapter assessments. With immediate and ongoing feedback, students will also see what they have learned and where they need more reinforcement and practice.

Other Resources

Books for Teachers

Cantor, Norman. *The Civilization of the Middle Ages: A Completely Revised and Expanded Edition of Medieval History.* New York: HarperCollins, 1994. (a classic history of the Middle Ages)

Holmes, George (ed). *The Oxford History of Medieval Europe.* Oxford University Press, USA, 2002.

Shahar, Shulamit. *Fourth Estate: A History of Women in the Middle Ages.* Routledge, 2003.

Books for Students

Fry, Plantagenet Somerset. *History of the World.* London: Dorling Kindersley Limited, 2005. (a visual chronology of world history with photographs of real artifacts, tools, and art)

Parsons, Jayne. *Crusades.* London: DK Children, 2001. (a well-illustrated history of the Crusades)

CD-ROM/Software

The Middle Ages. Culver City, CA: Social Studies School Services (1-800-421-4246), 1994. (this interactive CD-ROM correlates history, literature, art, and music.)

Videos

Hildegard. DVD, Vision Video, 2006. (the story of Hildegard of Bingen, a remarkable woman of the Middle Ages)

Maghreb: Back in Middle Ages. DVD, CustomFlix, 2007. (visits the city of Fes dating from the 9th century)

Web Sites

www.agsglobewh.com/page222a (Internet Medieval Sourcebook from Fordham University; has links to maps, speeches, and historic writings related to the Middle Ages)

www.agsglobewh.com/page222b (from NOVA Online; contains links to virtual activities and an account of life in a medieval castle)

Unit 2

Regional Civilizations

By A.D. 500, the Roman Empire had fallen apart. Historians call the 1,000 years following the fall of Rome the Middle Ages. These years are in the middle between the fall of Rome and the rebirth of learning in Europe in the 1500s.

In this unit you will learn about the lives of serfs, peasants, and knights. You will visit a castle of the Middle Ages, learn about Gothic architecture, and go on the Crusades. You will meet Muhammad and journey to Ghana and Mali. Then you will sail back to India to meet Buddha, follow Genghis Khan into China, and travel into Japan.

223

Introducing the Unit

Have a student volunteer read aloud the quotation by Taizong, emperor of China. Ask students to study the picture on page 222. Tell students that the building was built in the 1400s in Venice, Italy. Tell them that in this unit, they will learn about what happened in Europe, Africa, and Asia during the Middle Ages and what part religion played in many of these events. Ask a student volunteer to read aloud the unit introduction on page 223.

Ask:

• Does the design of this building remind you of anything? (answers will vary)

• What years are covered in Unit 2? (320 to 1630)

• What historical event marks the beginning of the Middle Ages? (the fall of the Roman Empire)

• How long did the Middle Ages last? (about 1,000 years)

Presenting the Unit Activity

Students will find, record, and use information about eight noted leaders in the Middle Ages for a quiz game. Assign four students to each team. Make sure there is an even number of teams. These teams will work together in both phases of the Unit Activity. Distribute copies of Unit 2, Activities 1 and 2. Have students read the directions on Activity 1 and then meet in their groups to choose the leaders they will research. Students can fill out their charts in one class session or during the course of Unit 2. Check to make sure students have completed their charts.

When students have finished Unit 2, assign pairs of teams to play the Powerful Leaders Game.

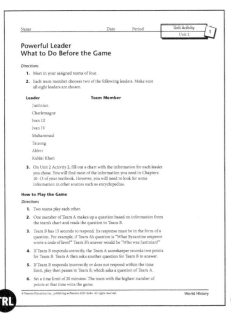

Unit 2, Activity 1

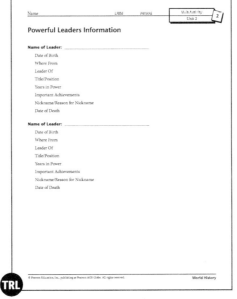

Unit 2, Activity 2

Introducing the Chapter

The fall of the Roman Empire in the West resulted in the formation of small governments and new conflicts. The Roman Catholic Church filled much of the cultural and religious void, while feudalism formed the basis for a new type of government based on land ownership.

The High and Late Middle Ages

After the Roman Empire fell, the Germanic tribes made war on one another for many years. During this time, the monks and nuns of the Roman Catholic Church tried to keep learning alive. Some members of the church also tried to take control of the Holy Land. In this chapter, you will join the Crusades and travel to Palestine. Then you will return to your castle and the manor and learn about the life of a serf, a peasant, a page, a squire, a knight, a vassal, and a lord. While doing this, you will learn about feudalism.

Goals for Learning

◆ To explain the role of the Roman Catholic Church in the Middle Ages in Europe and recognize the causes and effects of the Crusades

◆ To describe European feudalism

◆ To describe life on a manor

◆ To describe improvements in culture during the Middle Ages

1066 Normans conquer England

1154 Henry II begins to rule in England

1291 Muslims conquer the last Christian city in the Holy Land; Crusades to Holy Land end

1000   **1250**   **1500**

1095 Pope Urban II calls for the First Crusade

1348 Plague breaks out in Europe

Ask:

• When did Henry II begin to rule in England? (1154)

• What two groups fought against one another in the crusades? (Muslims and Christians)

• How many years passed between the first and last crusades? (196 years)

| Name | Date | Period | SELF-STUDY GUIDE |

Chapter 10: The High and Late Middle Ages

Goal 10.1 To explain the role of the Roman Catholic Church in the Middle Ages in Europe and recognize the causes and effects of the Crusades

Date	Assignment	Completed
	1. Read pages 224–231.	
	2. Complete the Lesson 1 Review on page 231.	
	3. Complete Workbook Activity 43.	

Comments:

Goal 10.2 To describe European feudalism

Date	Assignment	Completed
	4. Read pages 232–234.	
	5. Complete the Lesson 2 Review on page 234.	
	6. Complete Workbook Activity 44.	

Comments:

© Pearson Education, Inc., publishing as Pearson AGS Globe. All rights reserved.   World History

TRL

Chapter 10 Self-Study Guide, pages 1–2

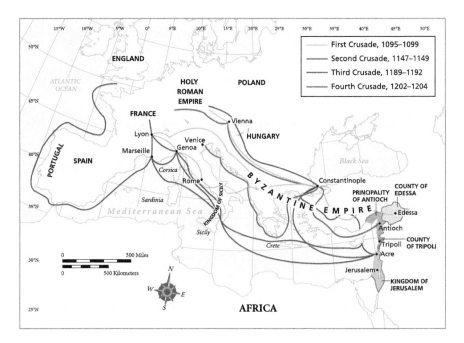

In A.D. 1095, the Europeans of the western world began a series of military journeys called the Crusades. They traveled to Palestine, which they called the Holy Land because Jesus had lived there. But by 1095, people of the Muslim faith lived in Palestine. The Europeans thought that God wanted them to rescue the Holy Land from the Muslims. For almost 200 years, European Christians went on the Crusades to win back Palestine.

Trace the routes these Christian warriors took, then answer the following questions:

1. From what countries did the four biggest Crusades begin?

2. On which crusade did Europeans go by land from Constantinople to Jerusalem?

3. Which crusade went to the Holy Land by a water route only?

4. In which crusade did the English take part?

5. Why do you think that each of these four Crusades took so long?

Ask a volunteer to read aloud the title of the map, "The Crusades," the information in the map key, and the paragraph below.

Ask:

- What do the different color lines represent? (the four crusades)
- Which of the four crusades involved the most travel? (the Third Crusade)
- In which direction did the crusaders generally go, east to west or west to east? (west to east)

Have students work in small groups to answer the questions.

Map Skills Answers

1. The First, Second, and Fourth crusades began in the Holy Roman Empire and France. The Third Crusade began in England.
2. the First Crusade
3. the Third Crusade
4. the Third Crusade
5. Answers will vary. Students should suggest that the crusades took a long time because they had to travel great distances with poor means of transportation and they had to stop and start in between battles.

Chapter Project

Explain that the Middle Ages has been used as the setting for many works of fiction. Have students work in groups to learn more about the life and livelihood of one type of people of the Middle Ages: serf, peasant, page, squire, knight, vassal, or lord. Have each group research their topic to learn as many details as possible about their category. Tell students that their research will culminate in a class literary work.

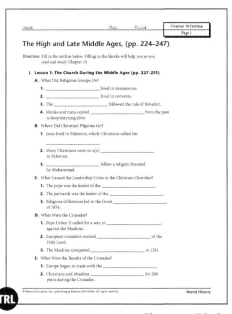

Chapter 10 Outline, pages 1–3

Predicting

Introduce the reading strategy *predicting*. Draw students' attention to the definition. Tell students that predicting is a valuable reading skill to apply when reading fiction, such as stories about adventures of knights in the Middle Ages. Predicting is also valuable when reading nonfiction because predicting as they read could help them focus on details that will help them better analyze events in history.

Ask:

- What details in the morning sky help you predict the weather for the day? (Answers will vary; clouds may indicate it will rain or snow, or a prediction for a rain-free day can be made if there is a lack of clouds.)

- How does setting, such as a castle, help you predict what will happen in a story or historical event? (provides background, draws the reader's attention to detail, gives a sense of excitement or other emotion)

Point out to students that predicting involves using prior knowledge and making logical assumptions.

Key Vocabulary Words

Point out that these chapter words are presented in the order they appear in each lesson. They are also found in the Glossary. Explain that when reading about events, certain words allow the reader to predict what might happen, based on what they know about the topic. Read the following key vocabulary words, *vassal, blacksmith, serf,* and *pilgrim,* and ask students to use the definitions provided to predict what might happen in a fictional story. Repeat the activity using a second set of four vocabulary words.

Reading Strategy:
Predicting

As you read a text, you can make predictions about what will happen next. It helps to preview the text and think about what you already know about the topic. As you make predictions, keep these things in mind.

- Make your best guess about what happens next.
- Use what you know to predict what will be next.
- Check your predictions. As you learn more information, you may find you need to change your predictions.

Key Vocabulary Words

Lesson 1

Holy Land Palestine; the area where Jesus of Nazareth lived

Pilgrim A person who travels to visit a holy place

Muslim A follower of Islam, the religion that Muhammad founded in Arabia in the seventh century

Schism A permanent separation

Crusade Any of the military journeys taken by Christians to win the Holy Land from the Muslims

Lesson 2

Feudalism A political and military system based on the holding of land

Lord A king or a noble who gave land to someone else

Vassal A person who received land from a king or noble

Fief The land and peasants who farmed it, which a lord gave to a vassal

Page A young noble who learned certain behaviors to become a knight

Squire A 15-year-old page who learned how to ride a horse and use weapons to become a knight

Knighted To be made a knight

Lesson 3

Manor The part of a fief that peasants farm to support the lord's family

Blacksmith A person who works with iron and makes tools and weapons

Serf A peasant who was bound to the land and whose life was controlled by the lord of the manor

Moat A dug-out area filled with water that circles a castle

Drawbridge A bridge that can be raised or lowered over a moat

Courtyard A large open area inside the castle walls

Joust A contest between two knights carrying lances and riding horses

Lesson 4

Bishop A priest who is in charge of other priests and a number of churches

Romanesque A style of building that was like what the Romans built with thick walls and arches

Gothic A style of architecture with thin walls, pointed arches, many windows, and flying buttresses

Parliament The English council or lawmaking assembly

STUDY SKILLS

Explain that organizing words into categories is a good way to understand and remember the meaning of words. Write the following categories on the board: *People, Places, Architecture,* and *Events.* Have students read through the Key Vocabulary Words and place each word into an appropriate category, giving an example or reason for the placement. Have students copy the word charts into their notebooks.

Objectives

◆ To identify the Benedictines
◆ To explain why Christian pilgrims traveled to Palestine
◆ To describe those who joined the Crusades

The Roman Empire fell apart in A.D. 476. Soon Europe broke up into hundreds of small governments. But the Church remained strong. Its officials did things that the Roman government had done before. For example, the church set up courts and collected taxes.

By the year 1050, Western Europe had settled down. For years, Germanic tribes had fought wars. Now farming and trade expanded again. We call the years from 1050 to about 1500 the late Middle Ages. The word *medieval* refers to this period between ancient and modern times.

What Did Religious Groups Do?

Some Christian men left the world behind and became monks.

Some Christian women also gave up material things and became nuns. Both monks and nuns joined together in religious groups to serve God.

The monks lived and worked in monasteries; the nuns lived in convents. In the early sixth century, a monk named Benedict wrote a rule for monks and nuns. They promised never to marry, never to own property, and never to disobey the head of the monastery or convent.

The Benedictines spent their lives praying and working. Some took care of the sick and the homeless. Some learned new things about farming and taught the farmers who lived nearby. Some welcomed travelers. (They had no place else to stay because there were no hotels at this time.) Religious groups also supplied teachers to the new towns that were springing up.

Mont St. Michel is a famous old monastery in Normandy, France.

1050 – 1500   *The High and Late Middle Ages*   *Chapter 10*   **227**

Chapter 10: Lesson 1

Overview This lesson describes the role of religion in preserving civilization after the Roman Empire and explains about the crusades, a series of wars between Christians and Muslims.

Objectives

■ To identify the Benedictines
■ To explain why Christian pilgrims traveled to Palestine
■ To describe those who joined the Crusades

Student Pages pages 227–231

Teacher's Resource Library

Workbook Activity 43

Activity 43

Modified Activity 43

Vocabulary

crusade	pilgrim
Holy Land	schism
Muslim	

Have students write fill-in-the-blank sentences for each of the vocabulary words. Then invite students to exchange papers and complete each other's sentences with the correct words.

1   Warm-Up Activity

Have students turn to the map on page 225. Explain that thousands of men took part in the Crusades. Ask students to predict the kinds of difficulties the crusaders might have had during their travels on land and at sea. Also have them predict the reception the crusaders received as they invaded foreign lands. Next, have students write three words they think of when they hear the word *crusade*. Finally, ask students to explain their three words.

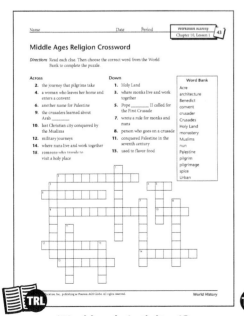

Workbook Activity 43

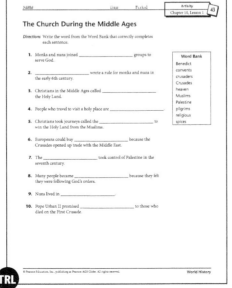

Activity 43

PRONUNCIATION GUIDE

Use this list to help students pronounce
difficult words in this lesson.

Acre	(äk´ ər)
Benedict	(ben´ ə dikt)
Saladin	(sal´ ə dən)

2 Teaching the Lesson

Ask students to predict how Europe might
be different after the fall of the Roman
Empire. Then have them read pages
227–231 to find out what changes took
place in Europe during the Middle Ages.

Ask:

• **What promises did monks and nuns
make?** (never to marry, never to
own property, and never to disobey
the head of the monastery or
convent)

**Reading Strategy:
Predicting**

(Answers will vary. They wrote books,
kept diaries, and saved important
books and documents.)

• **At the end of the Crusades, which
group controlled Palestine?**
(the Muslims)

• **Why did Christians call Palestine
the Holy Land?** (because Jesus of
Nazareth had lived there)

• **Who was the leader of the Roman
Catholic Church in the West?**
(the pope)

**Reading Strategy:
Predicting**

(Answers will vary. They copied
books by hand, decorated books
using bright colors and pictures, and
monasteries and convents became
centers for learning.)

**Reading Strategy:
Predicting**

Read the title of the
next section. What do
you think the people
of the church did to
advance learning?

Holy Land

Palestine; the area
where Jesus of
Nazareth lived

Pilgrim

A person who travels
to visit a holy place

Muslim

A follower of
the religion that
Muhammad founded
in Arabia in the 7th
century

**Reading Strategy:
Predicting**

Think about your
prediction. What
details can you now
add to make your
prediction more
specific?

How Did the Church Keep Learning Alive?

Monks and nuns copied books from the past by hand. No
one in Europe had invented a machine to copy words. They
decorated these books with bright colors and pictures. Over
time, the largest monasteries and convents became centers
of learning. They kept alive the learning from ancient Greek
and Rome.

Where Did Christian Pilgrims Go?

During the Middle Ages, Christians called Palestine the
Holy Land because Jesus of Nazareth had lived there. Many
Christians traveled there to see places that Jesus had visited.
We call such a trip a pilgrimage. People who go on a pilgrimage
are **pilgrims.**

In the 7th century, **Muslims** conquered Palestine. (The
Muslims were members of a religion founded by a man named
Muhammad.) For nearly 400 years, the Muslims let Christian
pilgrims visit the Holy Land. Then another group of Muslims
took control of Palestine. According to some reports, this group
killed Christians and destroyed churches.

What Caused the Leadership Crisis in the Christian Churches?

At about the same time, the Christian church faced a leadership
crisis. For many centuries the Christian church had been
divided into the Western and Eastern Churches. In the West,
in the city of Rome, the pope was the leader of the Roman
Catholic Church. There was a different leader in the East,
nearly 900 miles away, in the city of Constantinople. Here, the
patriarch was the leader of the Greek Orthodox Church. The
two churches developed different beliefs and practices. Latin,
not Greek, was the language of the Roman Catholic Church.
Unlike the Roman Catholic Church, the Greek Orthodox
Church allowed priests to marry. (*Orthodox* refers to religious
groups who follow well-known customs and traditions.)

CAREER CONNECTION

The monks and nuns who
decorated books with bright
colors and pictures may
have been the first graphic
artists. Today, graphic artists rely on
sophisticated equipment to create
advertisements in newspapers and
magazines. Graphic artists also work
in art reproduction, computer game
design, bookmaking, and fashion
design. Encourage artistic students to
research the education and training
needed to become a graphic artist.

AT HOME

Have students interview
older relatives or friends
who are war veterans.
Students should find out
why the veteran joined the armed
forces and fought in a war. Are any
of these reasons the same reasons the
crusaders fought? Are any reasons
different? Students may discover that
in many cases veterans did not
choose to fight but were drafted,
while others, like the crusaders,
chose to join the military. Have
students record their findings and
report them to the class.

Schism

A permanent separation

Crusade

Any of the military journeys taken by Christians to win the Holy Land from the Muslims

There were differences in the celebration of holy days. The pope asserted that he alone was leader of all Christians. In 1054, religious differences led to a **schism,** or permanent separation, between the Greek Orthodox and the Roman Catholic Church. This is known as the Great Schism of 1054.

What Were the Crusades?

In 1095, Pope Urban II, the head of the Roman Catholic Church, called for a **crusade,** or war, against the Muslims. He wanted to free Palestine from their control. The pope promised heaven to those who died on the crusade. Historians believe that about 5,000 men on horseback, and 25,000 foot soldiers, fought in this First Crusade. A large number of common people also joined the crusade. We call all these people crusaders.

Why Did People Volunteer for the Crusades?

Many people became crusaders. Some felt that they were following God's orders. Others wanted adventure. Still others wanted to escape hard work at home. Kings and nobles joined the Crusades to get more power. The pope encouraged them to do this by forgiving their debts and by letting them pay fewer taxes.

For almost 200 years—from 1096 to 1291—European crusaders went to the Holy Land. They fought four big Crusades and many small ones. But they did not get control of the Holy Land. In 1291, the Muslims conquered Acre, the last Christian city. After that, the Muslims controlled Palestine until modern times.

Ask:

- Why did Pope Urban II call for a crusade against the Muslims? (He wanted to free Palestine from Muslim control.)

- List three reasons why people became crusaders. (Some believed they were following God's orders, some wanted adventure, some wanted to escape hard work at home, and some wanted more power.)

3 Reinforce and Extend

ELL/ESL Strategy

Language Objective: *To summarize using sentences*

Have students work in small groups of three students. Include ELL students in each group. List the following questions on the board:

Who is this lesson about?
What is this lesson about?
Where do these events take place?
When did these events take place?
Why did these events take place?

Tell students to use the information in Lesson 1 to write one sentence in response to each question. Have students in each group, including ELL students, share information by reading their sentences aloud.

Online Connection

Students can gain additional information by accessing the following Web sites:

www.agsglobewh.com/page229a (This interactive site allows students to view the Metropolitan Museum of Art's arms and armor collection.)

www.agsglobewh.com/page229b (This Internet Medieval Sourcebook of Fordham University Center for Medieval Studies has several primary documents related to the Crusades.)

Ask:

- What was one result of the Crusades? (exploration of Africa, Asia, and America; religious killings; split between the Roman Catholic Church and the Eastern Orthodox Church)

- What did the crusaders learn from the Arabs? (art, architecture, medicine, and mathematics)

- How did the crusades cause interest in exploring Africa, Asia, and America? (The experience of crusaders in Palestine stimulated a desire to explore other faraway lands.)

LEARNING STYLES

Auditory/Verbal
Have students summarize the results of the Crusades in their own words. They might wish to prepare a note sheet for themselves that they may refer to as they speak.

STUDY SKILLS

Have small groups of students write three cause-and-effect statements based on this lesson. For example, because Pope Urban II wanted to free Palestine from Muslim control, he started a crusade against the Muslims. On a different sheet of paper, have groups write only the causes. Have students exchange papers with other groups, who will fill in the effects.

What Were the Results of the Crusades?

The Crusades did not win control of the Holy Land for Christians. However, the pope and European kings ended up with more power. Also, because Europe began to trade with the Middle East, Europeans could buy things like sugar, lemons, and spices. The crusaders also learned about Arab art, architecture, medicine, and mathematics. The Crusades brought other changes too. During the Crusades, Europeans traveled to Palestine, which was far away from their homeland. When they returned home, their small villages in Europe seemed less interesting. They wanted to see more faraway lands. Many people began to explore Africa, Asia, and America.

Many bad things happened during the Crusades, too. Christians began to kill Jews simply because they were not Christians. During the 200 years of the Crusades, Muslims

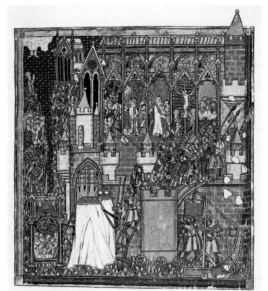

killed thousands of Christians, and Christians killed thousands of Muslims. In fact, some European Christians killed eastern Christians simply because they dressed like the Muslims. Before the Crusades, most Muslims had accepted Christians. After all the killing and violence, they thought Christians were uncivilized. They viewed the Christians as enemies.

This painting shows crusaders storming Jerusalem during the Crusades.

Biography

Saladin: 1138–1193

Saladin was a Muslim leader. He became the ruler of Egypt and Syria. Saladin built schools and mosques there. He was so brave and honorable that even crusaders admired him.

For years, the crusaders held Palestine. Saladin wanted those Muslim lands back. He united Muslims against the crusaders. His forces captured Jerusalem in 1187. Then they took back most of Palestine.

As a result, the Third Crusade began. It ended Saladin's two-year siege of the crusaders at Acre. But they never won back Jerusalem. Finally, Saladin and crusade leader Richard the Lion-hearted met. Their truce let Christian pilgrims visit Jerusalem.

Lesson 1 Review On a sheet of paper, write the answer to each question. Use complete sentences.

1. According to Benedict, how were monks and nuns supposed to live?

2. Why did monks and nuns copy books?

3. What was the Holy Land?

4. Why did Pope Urban II start the First Crusade?

5. Describe one good and one bad outcome of the Crusades.

Were the Crusades good or bad for the people of Europe and the Middle East? Explain your answer.

Biography

Although Saladin is remembered most for resisting Christian crusaders, his other accomplishments should not be overlooked. Saladin made Egypt the most powerful empire in the Muslim world. Under his firm leadership, education grew, population increased, Egypt became financially stable, and culture flourished. He was also known for his generosity. At his death, Saladin did not even leave enough money to pay for his own grave.

Lesson 1 Review Answers

1. They should never marry, never own property, and never disobey the head of the monastery or convent. **2.** By copying books, they kept alive the learning from the past. **3.** Palestine was called The Holy Land because Jesus of Nazareth had lived there. **4.** He wanted to free Palestine from Muslim control. **5.** One good outcome of the Crusades was an understanding and spread of Arab art, architecture, medicine, and mathematics; one bad outcome of the Crusades was the killing of thousands of people.

Answers will vary. The Crusades introduced new products to Europeans, gave them adventure, and made them want to explore more faraway places. However they also ended the life of many crusaders and led to hatred of the Jews. For the people of the Middle East, the Crusades also led to death. Both Europe and the Middle East poured money into the Crusades that could have been spent for other things, such as helping the poor, education, and art.

Chapter 10: Lesson 2

Overview This lesson describes feudalism, a new system of government in the Middle Ages based on the holding of land, and the training and responsibilities of knights.

Objectives

- To explain why the feudal system started
- To describe what it took to become a knight

Student Pages pages 232–234

Teacher's Resource Library **TRL**

Workbook Activity 44

Activity 44

Modified Activity 44

....

Vocabulary

feudalism	**page**
fief	**squire**
knighted	**vassal**
lord	

Have students create flashcards for the vocabulary words, placing the words on one side of the cards and the definitions on the other. Allow a few minutes for students to study their cards. Then have them quiz each other in pairs.

....

1 Warm-Up Activity

Introduce students to the idea of land division. Give one student a paper square. Tell the student that he or she is a lord and the paper represents a land holding. Have the student divide the "land" by tearing or cutting the paper and giving a piece to one or more vassals. Then have the vassals repeat the activity by further dividing the land among other vassals. Tell students that vassals are loyal to higher vassals, who are loyal to the lord.

Objectives

- To explain why the feudal system started
- To describe what it took to become a knight

Feudalism
A political and military system based on holding land

Lord
A king or a noble who gave land to someone

Vassal
A noble who received land from a king or noble

Fief
The land and peasants to farm it

Page
A young noble who learned to become a knight

Squire
A 15-year-old page who learned to ride a horse and use weapons to become a knight

The Roman Empire had laws to govern people and armies to protect them. But during the Middle Ages, there was no one power in Europe. A new political and military system arose. We call this system **feudalism.** It was based on the holding of land.

How Did Feudalism Work?

Under the feudal system, the king owned all the land. But he needed loyal nobles to serve him. How could he win their loyalty? He could give them land. The nobles could then give land to other people and ask for their loyalty.

What Were the Titles of the Nobles?

We call the powerful kings and nobles who gave land **lords.** We call the nobles who received land **vassals.** When lords gave land, they did so in a special ceremony. The vassal knelt down before the lord and promised loyalty. He would serve the lord and help him in battle.

In return, the lord gave the vassal a **fief,** or piece of land, and peasants to farm it. To protect his fief, each vassal needed his own soldiers. He had much land, but little money. He offered land to men who agreed to be his vassals. The lords and vassals kept dividing the land into smaller and smaller pieces.

How Many Years Did Someone Train to Become a Knight?

The Middle Ages was a time of thousands of small wars. Knights, or soldiers who fought for a lord, did most of the fighting. Only the son of a noble could become a knight. A young noble started training to be a knight by first becoming a **page.** He learned religion, manners, obedience, and loyalty. When he was about 15 years old, the page became a **squire.** Then he learned to ride a horse and use weapons. At age 21, most squires became knights.

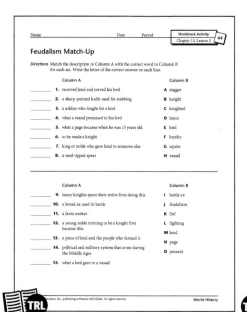

Workbook Activity 44

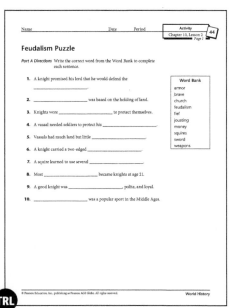

Activity 44, pages 1–2

During the Middle Ages, knights fought each other for sport on horseback.

Armor of the Middle Ages

During the Middle Ages, knights, lords, and even kings rode to their many battles in armor. Armor changed as weapons and ways of fighting changed.

In 1066, when William the Conqueror invaded England, his knights wore simple cone-shaped helmets and suits of mail. To make this mail, an iron worker heated and then hammered out a small iron bar. When it was long and thin, he wound it around another rod. Next, he cut rings from the thinned iron. Finally, he linked them together so that they overlapped, or partly covered, one another. He spent many months making a complete mail suit. It looked like a mesh suit of iron.

The knights wore padded coats underneath the mail. Because the sun makes metal hot, the knights often wore a loose-fitting cloth coat over their mail suit.

By the 1200s, knights wore a helmet that covered their face. As time passed, they began to protect their whole body with armor. A breast plate protected their chest. Other pieces of armor protected their shoulders, hands, and legs. The knight wore spurs on his armored heels. He used these spiked wheels to make his horse obey.

On his clothes, each knight painted his coat of arms. This was a design in the shape of a shield. Each man wore a different coat of arms. It showed everyone who he was. Some coats of arms were simple. Others contained trees, birds, and animals.

1050 – 1500

The High and Late Middle Ages Chapter 10 **233**

 ## 2 Teaching the Lesson

After they read this lesson, have students draw a pyramid showing the power structure in the feudal system. Tell them to write the most powerful group of people at the top of the pyramid, the next most powerful in the middle, and the least powerful group at the base. (at the top should be lords, followed by vassals, and peasants at the base)

Ask:

- Under the feudal system, who owned all the land? (the king)
- Who could become a knight? (the son of a noble)
- What promise did a knight make? (to defend the church, be loyal to the lord, protect the weak, and be polite to women)
- What did William the Conqueror's knights wear? (cone-shaped helmets and suits of mail)
- Why did a knight wear a cloth coat over his mail suit? (to prevent the metal suit from becoming hot in the sun)
- Why did a knight wear spurs on his heels? (to make his horse obey)
- What did a knight wear to show who he was? (a coat of arms painted on his clothes)

ELL/ESL STRATEGY

Language Objective: *To use transition words to define a sequence of events*

With student help, make a list on the board of transition words such as *then, after, until, before, finally, first, second,* and similar words that define time or sequence. Have ELL students each work with a native speaker to use the transition words to explain how land is divided between the lord and vassals. To begin, ask native speakers to use the transition words in sample sentences. Then have the ELL student describe how feudalism worked. For example, *first,* the lord divides the land among vassals, *then* the vassals divided the land to other vassals. *Later,* those vassals divided the land. *Finally,* the vassals gave land to knights who agreed to protect him.

High/Late Middle Ages Chapter 10 **233**

(Answers may vary. The knight will be expected to be loyal to the vassal, to be brave and a good warrior, and to be a strong leader.)

Ask:

• Why did many knights never become lords? (They spent their entire lives fighting wars.)

LEARNING STYLES

Body/Kinesthetic

Invite several students to perform a simulation of a knighting ceremony. One student should play the role of a lord and the others should play the roles of squires. Have the lord explain his or her expectations to the future knights and have the squires recite their promises. Then have the lord officially pronounce them knights.

 Reinforce and Extend

WORLD CULTURES

The tradition of knights lives on in modern Great Britain. The British government recommends a person of high achievement or service to the Queen. Then the Queen officially selects the person to be knighted. Male knights adopt the title "Sir" and their wives are called "Lady." Women who receive the honor adopt the title "Dame." These titles carry no responsibility; they are purely honorary.

Lesson 2 Review Answers

1. feudalism **2.** lord **3.** fief
4. peasant **5.** knight

Answers will vary. One good thing about being a knight is the adventure and importance associated with the lifelong role of protecting a vassal. One bad thing about being a knight is the uncertainty of war and the risk of being killed.

Based on what you just read about the training of a knight, what do you predict will be expected of him?

Knighted

To be made a knight

Word Bank

feudalism

fief

knight

lord

peasant

What Did Lords Expect from Their Knights?

A lord **knighted** a squire, or made him a knight, in a special ceremony. The lord commanded the new knight to be brave, polite, and loyal. The knight promised to defend the church, be loyal to the lord, protect the weak, and be polite to women.

Each knight had to be strong. He wore heavy armor and carried a lance, or steel-tipped spear; a two-edged sword; a dagger, or sharp-pointed knife; and a broad ax called a battle ax. His armor and weapons could weigh as much as 100 pounds.

Every knight hoped to become a lord and have a great amount of land to give to vassals some day. However, many knights never became lords. They spent their entire lives fighting one war after another.

Lesson 2 Review On a sheet of paper, use the words from the Word Bank to complete each sentence correctly.

1. The _____ of the Middle Ages was a political and military system based on the holding of land.

2. A _____ gave land to a vassal and asked for his loyalty.

3. A _____ is the name of the land the vassal received.

4. A _____, or poor farmer, worked the land.

5. A _____ was a soldier who was loyal to a noble and fought for him.

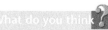
What do you think

What would be one good thing and one bad thing about being a knight?

Objectives

◆ To explain changes in farming

◆ To explain why nobles built castles and what life was like in them

Manor

The part of a fief that peasants farm to support the lord's family

Blacksmith

A person who works with iron and makes tools and weapons

Serf

A peasant who was bound to the land and whose life was controlled by the lord of the manor

The whole feudal system was based on the control of land. A **manor** was that part of the fief that peasants farmed to support a lord's family.

What Made the Manor Self-Sufficient?

A manor was self-sufficient because the people who lived on it grew, raised, or made nearly everything that they needed without help. They made clothing from the wool of the sheep they raised. They cut wood for building from the manor's forests. They grew or raised all the food they ate. The **blacksmith** worked with iron to make tools and weapons. The lord of the manor bought only a few things—like salt and iron—from the outside world.

Who Were Serfs?

About 90 percent of the people who lived during the Middle Ages were peasants. A few peasants were free, but most were **serfs.** They had to stay on the manor on which they had been born. A serf's life was controlled by the lord of the manor.

Serfs worked on the manor farms from early in the morning until late at night. They did the farmwork, cut wood, and built fences. Women serfs worked in the fields, cooked, made clothing, and cared for the house. About 60 percent of what each serf raised went to the lord of the manor and to the church.

Women of the Middle Ages spent much of their time spinning wool and weaving cloth.

Chapter 10: Lesson 3

Overview This lesson describes everyday life for peasants on a manor and the much different life of nobles in a castle.

Objectives

■ To explain changes in farming

■ To explain why nobles built castles and what life was like in them

Student Pages pages 235–238

Teacher's Resource Library

Workbook Activity 45

Activity 45

Modified Activity 45

Vocabulary

blacksmith	**manor**
courtyard	**moat**
drawbridge	**serf**
joust	

Write the vocabulary words on the board. Then read aloud a definition and ask students to identify the word that matches the definition. Repeat this process with the remaining definitions in random order.

1　Warm-Up Activity

Have students write the name of an invention on a piece of paper, fold the paper, and put it into a cup. Then have each student choose one slip of paper, read it, and give an idea of how the invention has benefited society. Write the inventions and students' ideas about the invention on the board. Explain that in this lesson students will read about inventions of the Middle Ages and how they benefited the people.

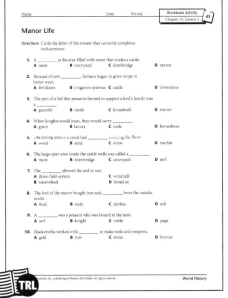

Manor Life

Directions Circle the letter of the answer that correctly completes each sentence.

1. A _____ is the area filled with water that circles a castle.
   A moat　B courtyard　C drawbridge　D manor

2. Because of new _____, farmers began to grow crops in better ways.
   A fertilizers　B irrigation systems　C cattle　D inventions

3. The part of a fief that peasants farmed to support a lord's family was a _____.
   A gauntlet　B castle　C household　D manor

4. When knights would joust, they would carry _____.
   A grain　B lances　C tools　D horseshoes

5. The dining area in a castle had _____ covering the floor.
   A wood　B sand　C straw　D marble

6. The large open area inside the castle walls was called a _____.
   A moat　B drawbridge　C courtyard　D serf

7. The _____ allowed the soil to rest.
   A three-field system　C windmill
   B waterwheel　D broad ax

8. The lord of the manor bought iron and _____ from the outside world.
   A food　B tools　C clothes　D salt

9. A _____ was a peasant who was bound to the land.
   A serf　B knight　C noble　D page

10. Blacksmiths worked with _____ to make tools and weapons.
    A gold　B iron　C stone　D bronze

Workbook Activity 45

The Manor

Directions Write the answers to these questions. Use complete sentences.

1. What jobs did serfs have?

2. How was a manor self-sufficient?

3. How did the three-field system improve farming?

4. What was in a courtyard?

5. Why did better farming lead to a rebirth of learning?

Activity 45

2 Teaching the Lesson

Some students may already know about life on a manor from books, television, computer games, or movies. Before they read this lesson, have students brainstorm anything that comes to mind. (Answers will vary; students may mention castles, moats, drawbridges, kings, or queens.) Write their ideas on the board. After they read the lesson, lead a discussion on whether books, television, and movies give an accurate picture of life on a manor. If not, what are the inaccuracies? (answers will vary)

Ask:

- Who were serfs? (peasant farmers who had to stay and work on the manor on which they had been born)

- List the five inventions that changed farming in the Middle Ages. (the three-field system, the horseshoe, a better plow, the waterwheel, and the windmill)

Reading Strategy:
Predicting

Discuss the benefits of each of the five inventions (three-field system, horseshoe, better plow, waterwheel, windmill) mentioned on page 236. Then have them answer the question. (Answers will vary. The inventions made farming more efficient and easier.)

- How did the new farming inventions affect the population? (Answers will vary; students may say that the new inventions allowed farmers to produce more food, causing the population to triple in 300 years.)

- Why did nobles build high walls and moats around their castles? (to protect themselves from their enemies)

- Why did nobles build their castles on hilltops or by river bends? (to make the castle easier to protect and defend)

Moat
A dug-out area filled with water that circles a castle

Drawbridge
A bridge that can be raised or lowered over a moat

Reading Strategy:
Predicting

How do you think these improvements in farming affected the farmers in the Middle Ages?

What Improved Farming?

During the Middle Ages, farming changed because of five inventions: the three-field system, the horseshoe, a better plow, the waterwheel, and the windmill.

Under the three-field system, a lord left one-third of his fields unplanted each year. This allowed the soil to rest. Then the field produced more food when the serfs planted it a year later. Up to this time, people had used the slow-moving ox to do heavy work. With horseshoes, they could plow with the faster-moving horse.

With a better plow, a tool used to dig up soil before planting seeds, serfs could farm the heavy soil of northern Europe. The newly invented waterwheel used the power of running water to make more power. With this new power, serfs could grind grain, like wheat, into flour. Windmills, invented in Holland around 1170, used wind power for the same purpose.

How Did Better Farming Change the Population?

Because of these new inventions, farmers began to grow their crops in better ways. This meant that they produced more food. More food meant that the population grew. In 300 years—from 1000 to 1300—the number of people living in Western Europe got three times as big. Because they had more food than they needed, some people had time to do other things. This led to a rebirth of learning.

Why Did Nobles Build Castles?

Many nobles lived in huge stone castles to protect themselves from their enemies. Most castles had high walls. A **moat,** or dug-out area filled with water, made a circle around the castle. To enter the castle, visitors crossed the moat by using a **drawbridge.** The people inside the castle lowered and raised it over the moat.

The nobles often built their castles on hilltops or by river bends. This made the castle easier to protect and defend. Some castles were big enough to include the noble's house and his household—all the people who lived and worked inside the

---

LEARNING STYLES

LOGICAL/MATHEMATICAL
After students read about the three-field system, have them solve this problem:

Suppose three fields can produce 900 pounds of food each year. Under the three-field system, how many years would it take to produce 3,000 pounds of food? (Because only two-thirds of the fields are planted at a time, 600 pounds of food would be produced each year; it would therefore take five years to produce 3,000 pounds of food.)

---

castle. The fields and the homes of the serfs were outside the castle walls. In times of war, they moved inside the walls for protection.

Inside the castle walls was a large open area called a **courtyard.** In good weather, the lord held his court there. The courtyard also contained many small buildings and sheds: the blacksmith's workshop; the bakery; the kitchen; the stable for the knight's horses; and rooms to store weapons and extra food. An attack against the castle could last many months. The lord of the manor had to store plenty of weapons and food.

Castles were designed for protection. This castle is from 15th century France.

What Was Life Like in a Castle?

Castles were dark, damp, and cold. Their tiny windows let in little light. Straw covered the floor of the dining area. The straw was usually dirty because the lord and his household threw garbage on the floor for the dogs to eat! The serfs cooked the food in the courtyard. It was often cold by the time the lord and his family ate it.

But not everything was dull in a castle. During the long winter nights, the lord and his guests drank and sang. They played board games like chess and backgammon. In better weather, the nobles held tournaments, or contests between knights. In these tournaments, two knights in armor would **joust.** They would carry lances and ride horses toward each other at full speed. Each would try to knock the other off his horse!

Writing About History

Before writing, you might suggest that students create an hour-by-hour schedule of activities that reflects a typical day in the life of lord, lady, peasant, serf, page, or knight. Have students use this schedule to write their essay. Remind them that their essay should not simply repeat their schedule, but should expand on it with added details and reflections.

Ask students if any of them know how to play chess. Have them demonstrate the rules of the game to the class. Inform students that scientists have created a computer program that can defeat even the greatest chess player. Ask students if they think it is fair for a computer to compete against a human, or if computers have an advantage.

3 Reinforce and Extend

BACKGROUND INFORMATION

Before 1100, castles were made of wood and mud. Castle builders switched to stone in the 1100s to better protect against enemy invaders, fire, and weather. In some cases, the stone walls could be as wide as 33 feet. While stone provided better protection, it also had its disadvantages. Stone walls became cold and wet, and they failed to protect inhabitants from the cold drafts of harsh European winters.

Lesson 3 Review Answers

1. A **2.** B **3.** D **4.** C **5.** D

Answers will vary. If fields produce more food with less work, then the peasant's family has more time to study and learn. Also, the peasant might sell some of the extra food and make money. With this money, he might be able to hire a tutor or provide other education for his children.

Writing About History

Imagine that you live on a feudal manor. Be the lord or lady of the manor, a peasant, a serf, a page, or a knight. In your notebook, write about your daily life.

Chess, the Game of Kings

Have you ever played chess? It was a popular game in the Middle Ages, too. Even then, it was centuries old. Like silk and spices, it came to Europe from the East. It was played in Asia as early as 550 B.C. The Arabs brought it to Spain in the 700s.

Chess pieces changed during the Middle Ages to reflect life at that time. Kings, queens, knights, and bishops moved around the board. There were even foot-soldiers (pawns) and castles (rooks). As in medieval warfare, pawns had the least value. In the language of the game, players "capture" pieces, such as castles. The object of the game is to capture your opponent's king. Playing chess is indeed like looking back into the Middle Ages.

Lesson 3 Review On a sheet of paper, write the letter of the answer that correctly completes each sentence.

1. Most of the peasants were _____.

   A serfs   **B** free   **C** knights   **D** slaves

2. Serfs gave _____ percent of what they raised to the lord of the manor and to the church.

   A 30   **B** 60   **C** 90   **D** 100

3. Farming improved during the Middle Ages because of the invention of the _____.

   A three-field system   **C** horseshoe
   B waterwheel   **D** all of the above

4. A _____, which was a dug-out area filled with water, made a circle around a castle.

   A manor   **B** fief   **C** moat   **D** drawbridge

5. Castles were _____.

   A dark   **B** damp   **C** cold   **D** all of the above

What do you think

How does having more food lead to more time to learn?

Reading Strategy:
Predicting

Preview the lesson title. Predict what you will learn about culture in the Middle Ages.

When the Roman Empire fell, education stopped. But then monasteries opened schools to prepare boys to become monks or priests. From about 1000 to 1100, **bishops** set up schools in their cathedrals. Bishops are priests who are in charge of other priests and a number of churches. A cathedral is the church where the bishop is the main priest. These cathedral schools were located in towns that later became centers of learning.

What Did Students Study?

Classes at cathedral schools lasted 10 hours a day. In addition to religion, they studied seven subjects: Latin; rhetoric (speaking and writing correctly); arithmetic; geometry; astronomy; logic (figuring things out); and music. The teachers often beat lazy students. As years passed, the number of subjects increased. This led to the first universities.

What Did Art Teach the People?

Artists and artisans during the Middle Ages built beautiful churches and cathedrals. They made beautiful windows out of colored glass. They carved life-like statues and created colorful wall paintings to show the life of Jesus, the saints, and people from the Bible. Most people did not know how to read or write. They learned about Christianity from these windows and statues and paintings.

◆ To identify changes in education, art, architecture, literature, and law
◆ To describe the influence of the Church in each area of culture

Bishop

A priest who is in charge of other priests and a number of churches

The first schools in the Middle Ages were set up to prepare boys to become monks or priests.

Chapter 10: Lesson 4

Overview This lesson describes how religion influenced culture in the Middle Ages.

Objectives

■ To identify changes in education, art, architecture, literature, and law

■ To describe the influence of the Church in each area of culture

Student Pages pages 239–242

Teacher's Resource Library TRL

Workbook Activity 46

Activity 46

Modified Activity 46

Vocabulary

bishop	**Parliament**
Gothic	**Romanesque**

Have students create a crossword puzzle using the vocabulary words. You might suggest using definitions or fill-in-the-blank sentences as clues. Invite students to exchange and solve each other's puzzles.

1 Warm-Up Activity

Share images of well-known cathedrals with your students. A good Web site for reference is www.agsglobewh.com/page239. Ask students to compare and contrast the cathedrals, noting designs that are similar and those that are different. Ask an art teacher or architect to visit the classroom to talk about Gothic art and architecture, in particular the structure and purpose of a flying buttress. An interested student may wish to design a cathedral.

Reading Strategy:
Predicting

(Answers will vary. I will learn about the customs, religion, and way of life of people in the Middle Ages.)

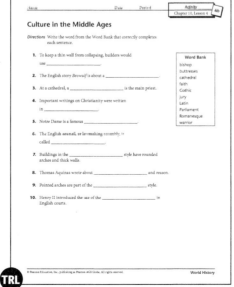

Workbook Activity 46   **Activity 46**   *High/Late Middle Ages* Chapter 10 **239**

Use this list to help students pronounce difficult words in this lesson.

Aquinas	(a kwī′ nəs)
Beowulf	(bā′ ə′ wúlf)
buttresses	(but′ ris əz)
Charlemagne	(shär′ lə mān)
Nibelungenlied	(nē′ bə lùng′ ən lēt′)
Notre Dame	(nōt′ rə däm′)
rhetoric	(ret′ ər ik)

2 Teaching the Lesson

Tell students that the Middle Ages are often thought of as a time when no significant contributions were made to world civilization. After students read the lesson, have them challenge that idea by listing the contributions made in the Middle Ages that are an important part of life today. (Answers will vary; students may say universities, religious art, or juries.)

Ask:

• What seven subjects did students study in the Middle Ages? (Latin, rhetoric, arithmetic, geometry, astronomy, logic, and music)

• How did people who did not know how to read or write learn about Christianity? (They looked at windows, statues, and paintings that showed Biblical stories.)

• When did church builders begin building in the Gothic style? (around 1200)

• What did builders use to hold up the thin walls of Gothic churches? (buttresses)

• How long did the cathedral of Notre Dame take to finish and how many people can it hold? (150 years; 9,000 people)

Romanesque
A style of building that was like what the Romans built with thick walls and arches

Gothic
A style of architecture with thin walls, pointed arches, many windows, and flying buttresses

What Is Gothic Architecture?

Until about 1100, most churches looked like Roman buildings. We call this style of architecture **Romanesque.** The churches had rounded arches. To hold up the heavy roof, the builders built thick walls with narrow openings for windows. Because of this, Romanesque churches were dark and gloomy.

Around 1200, church builders began building in a new style. We call it **Gothic.** Narrow, heavy ribs of stone supported the roof. To keep these thin walls from collapsing, the builders used flying buttresses. The buttresses held up the thin walls. Finally, they used pointed arches, which drew the eyes upward.

Artists and artisans built hundreds of churches and cathedrals in the Gothic style. Some were so large that builders worked on them for many years. For example, the beautiful cathedral of Notre Dame in Paris took 150 years to finish. It can hold 9,000 people.

What Was Literature Like in the Middle Ages?

People wrote two kinds of literature in the Middle Ages. Some wrote in Latin. Others wrote in the language of the common people.

The Latin works included important writings on Christianity. Thomas Aquinas wrote a book called *Summa Theologica*. In it, he explained that faith and reason are both gifts from God. He tried to bring the two together. He helped to keep alive much of the learning of the ancient world.

This gothic church is Rheims Cathedral in France.

LEARNING STYLES

Interpersonal/ Group Learning

Have groups of three or four students create poster projects comparing Romanesque and Gothic architecture. They might find photographs or illustrations in architecture books or on the Internet. Their posters should contain visuals and text highlighting the similarities and differences between these two styles. Encourage groups to assign a different task to each group member.

LEARNING STYLES

Visual/Spatial

Visual learners will benefit from noticing details of a Gothic church. Have them study the photograph of Rheims Cathedral on page 240 and identify the following features: thin walls, buttresses, and pointed arches. Have the students identify how similar features are duplicated in the design of the cathedral. Discuss how the cathedral's design features give a sense of importance and spirituality. Talk about the size of the cathedral in comparison to the buildings behind it.

Reading Strategy:
Predicting

Predict what trials might have been like at this time in history.

Some people wrote stories in the language of the common people. They usually retold an old story. People had passed these stories down in song. Storytellers had told them long before anyone wrote them down.

One well-known story was the *Song of Roland*. It is the oldest and greatest French medieval poem. The *Nibelungenlied* puts together several German legends. The first great work in English is *Beowulf*. Like the two other stories, it tells about the heroic deeds of a warrior.

What Changes Took Place in Law?

Important developments in law took place during the Middle Ages. Henry II, an English king who ruled from 1154 to 1189, introduced the use of the jury in English courts.

The English jury was a group of 12 people who helped the judge. The jury asked questions to discover the truth. Then it could decide whether a person accused of doing something wrong was guilty or innocent. Today, we call this a grand jury.

If the jury thought that a crime might have been committed, a judge held a trial with another jury. This jury examined all the information and the facts in court. The jury decided if the person had done wrong. Today, we call this a petit jury.

What Is a Parliament?

During the Middle Ages, kings began to ask nobles for ideas about government. Soon councils of nobles and church leaders formed in most of Western Europe. The English called their council, or lawmaking assembly, **Parliament.** The French called their council the Estates General. Nobles organized assemblies in other countries during the Middle Ages, but these rarely lasted.

Ask:

• Name four important pieces of literature from the Middle Ages. (*Summa Theologica, Song of Roland, Nibelungenlied,* and *Beowulf*)

• How many people sat on an English jury? (12 people)

Reading Strategy:
Predicting

Have students discuss who might have sat on a jury in 12th century England. Then have students answer the question. (Answers will vary; students may predict that the trial system encouraged fairness in English courts, especially for those unjustly accused.)

• What did the English call their council? What did the French call theirs? (Parliament; the Estates General)

 3 **Reinforce and Extend**

ELL/ESL STRATEGY

 Language Objective:
To retell a story

Explain to students that each language and culture has its own stories that are passed down. Have students whose first language is not English share examples of stories from their native language. If the story is in print, have them bring a copy to class. If the story has been passed down orally, have them recite it in their native language. Then have them explain what the story is about in English.

IN THE COMMUNITY

 Invite students interested in the criminal justice system to attend a jury trial or watch one on cable television. Trials are generally open to the public. Have students record what they see, compare their observations to the information on this page, and present their findings to the class in an oral report.

Lesson 4 Review Answers

1. In the cathedral schools, students studied Latin, rhetoric, arithmetic, geometry, astronomy, logic, and music. **2.** The stained-glass windows, statues, and wall paintings of Jesus, the saints, and people in the Bible taught the worshippers even though many could not read or write. **3.** Romanesque architecture has rounded arches and thick walls. Gothic architecture has pointed arches and thin walls held up with flying buttresses. **4.** Each of these stories is about the deeds of a heroic warrior. **5.** Henry II introduced the 12-member jury.

Answers will vary. Some students might like the appeal of studying the unusual subjects of the Middle Ages classroom, but many would not like the harsh discipline and learning conditions.

Inform students that many words in English and the Romance languages, which include Spanish, French, and Italian, are derived from Latin. Share this chart with students and have them explain how the root and the example are related. Challenge students to think of other words that come from these Latin roots.

Latin Root	Definition	Example
annus	year	annual
dormire	to sleep	dormitory
flectere	to bend	flexible
putare	to think	computer
urbs	city	urban
vita	life	vitamin

Lesson 4 Review On a sheet of paper, write the answer to each question. Use complete sentences.

1. What were the seven subjects studied in the cathedral schools of the Middle Ages?

2. How did church buildings help the people of the Middle Ages learn about their faith?

3. What are two differences between Romanesque and Gothic architecture?

4. What is one thing that is the same about the *Song of Roland*, the *Nibelungenlied*, and *Beowulf*?

5. What changes did Henry II introduce into English law during the Middle Ages?

 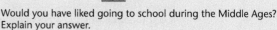

What do you think?

Would you have liked going to school during the Middle Ages? Explain your answer.

Learning the Latin Language

Why could educated people from different lands understand each other during the early Middle Ages? They spoke Latin. It was the international language of Europe. Knowledge from the past was written in Latin. Any new learning or information, such as a law, would also be in Latin.

But Latin was a foreign language. It was different than what students spoke every day. In English, you say, "I know" but "he knows." The -s is a verb ending. In Latin, there is a different ending for each person— *I, he, we, you, they*. Other kinds of words, such as nouns and adjectives, also have endings. Take, for example, the words *boys*, *ball*, *big*, and *hit*. In Latin, endings would tell if the sentence meant:

The big boys hit the ball or *The big ball hit the boys.*

Latin was the key to knowledge. Grammar schools, therefore, became very important.

Chapter Project Follow-up

Have the groups share details they learned about the lives and livelihoods of people in different levels of society during the Middle Ages. Ask a volunteer to record student ideas. Together as a class, create a story line for a class literary work on the Middle Ages. Have each group add interesting details to the story based on what they learned in their group research. Students might also create illustrations for the story. Have interested students publish the story using a computer publishing program that inputs text and images.

A Crusader's Letter

Thousands of people joined the First Crusade in 1096. Many were princes and nobles. Much of what we know about the Crusades comes from letters. This letter is from Stephen, count of Blois in France. His wife, Adele, was the daughter of William the Conqueror.

Count Stephen to Adele, his . . . wife, to his dear children, and to all his vassals of all ranks—his greeting and blessing:

You may be very sure, dearest, that the messenger whom I sent to you left me before Antioch safe and unharmed and, through God's grace, in the greatest prosperity. And already at that time, together with all the chosen army of Christ . . . , we had been continuously advancing for twenty-three weeks toward the home of our Lord Jesus. You may know for certain, my beloved, that of gold, silver, and many other kinds of riches, I now have twice as much as you, my love, supposed me to have when I left you. For all our princes, with the common consent of the whole army, though against my own wishes, have made me, up to the present time, the leader, chief, and director of their whole expedition.

You have . . . heard that after the capture of the city of Nicaea we fought a great battle with the Turks and, by God's aid, conquered them. Next we conquered for the Lord all Romania. . . .

We besieged it [Antioch] and had many conflicts there with the Turks. Seven times we fought with the citizens of Antioch and with the troops coming to their aid; we rushed to meet them and we fought with the fiercest courage under the leadership of Christ; and in all these seven battles, by the aid of the Lord God, we conquered, and . . . killed . . . [many] of them. In those battles, indeed, and in very many attacks made upon the city, many of our followers were killed, and their souls were borne to the joys of paradise. . . .

I can write to you only a few, dearest, of the many things which we have done. Although I am not able to tell you all that is in my mind, I trust that all is going well with you, and urge you to watch over your possessions and to treat as you ought your children and your vassals. You will certainly see me as soon as I can possibly return to you. Farewell.

Document-Based Questions

1. What is the "army of Christ"?

2. When Stephen sent the messenger to Adele, how long had he been away?

3. What honor did the other nobles give Stephen?

4. Name two cities where Stephen fought in battles.

5. Reread the advice Stephen gave Adele. What can you tell about her duties at home?

Read aloud the title, "A Crusader's Letter," and the introductory paragraph of the Document-Based Reading. Then have volunteers take turns reading aloud the rest of the selection. After each paragraph is read, have students write down one or two main ideas in their own words. Invite students to share what they wrote. Before moving on to the next paragraph, ensure that all students understand the main ideas. After all paragraphs have been read and discussed, have students read and answer the questions.

Answers to Document-Based Questions:

1. Stephen means the army of crusaders.

2. He had been traveling for 23 weeks.

3. They had made him the leader and director of the whole expedition.

4. He mentioned Nicaea and Antioch.

5. Answers will vary. She is in charge of running the manor, taking care of the children, and handling relations with vassals.

Have students silently read the
Spotlight Story, titled "Unlucky
King John and the Magna Carta,"
and write down any words that are
unfamiliar to them. Ask each student
to share his or her list of words.
Compile a master list of unfamiliar
words on the board. Ask volunteers
to define words they do know and
write the correct definitions on the
board next to the words. Then define
any remaining unfamiliar words.
Have students reread the story and
answer the Wrap-Up questions.

Answers to Spotlight Story Wrap-Up:

1. He was an extremely unpopular ruler,
so no one wanted to use his name.

2. John tried to seize the throne while
Richard was on the Third Crusade.

3. He lost a war, he lost English lands in
France, he had a quarrel with the pope,
and he imposed new duties on his
vassals and new taxes on the Church.

4. Laws apply to the king as well as to
ordinary people.

5. At first, it protected mainly the
rights of nobles, but it gradually was
extended to protect everyone.

STUDY SKILLS

Have students access
the Magna Carta to
compare details found
in the primary source document
with the concepts presented in the
Spotlight Story. The Magna Carta
can be found online at
www.agsglobewh.com/page244.

Unlucky King John and the Magna Carta

In all of English history, there has been only one King John. He was so unpopular that no other English king has used the name. John was not just unpopular. He was unlucky too.

John's older brother was Richard I, the Lion-hearted. Richard was a well-loved hero. While he was on the Third Crusade, John tried to make himself king. When Richard came home in 1199, he banished his brother from England.

After Richard died in 1199, John became king. He was actually able and clever, but things never went right. The French beat him in a war. That defeat cost him money and influence. He lost English lands in France, too. Next, John had a serious disagreement with the pope. The pope cut him off from the Church. John had to agree to be the pope's vassal.

Then the king demanded more services from his vassals. He placed new taxes on the Church. Both the nobles and church leaders got angry at John. Many members from both groups felt that the king had too much power. By the spring of 1215, there was a war going on inside England. Some nobles backed John. Some wanted to get rid of him. A large army marched toward London.

To avoid losing his throne, John gave the rebel leaders new rights. The event took place on June 15, 1215, in a large open field called Runnymede. The leaders and churchmen met King John. They told him the terms that they wanted him to sign, and John agreed to them. Then he put his royal seal on the document that Church leaders had written.

The paper that King John signed is called the Magna Carta, or Great Charter. It gave specific rights to the feudal nobles and to the towns. It also promised church leaders some freedoms. Most importantly, the Magna Carta meant that even the king had to obey the law.

King John signing the Magna Carta in 1215.

At first, the Magna Carta protected mainly the rights of nobles. Gradually these rights were extended. Finally, every Englishman would claim them. English settlers brought these ideas to America.

Wrap-Up

1. Why has there only been one King John in English history?

2. What caused John's disagreement with his brother Richard?

3. What actions made leaders angry with John?

4. What is the most important principle in the Magna Carta?

5. How has the importance of the Magna Carta changed since 1215?

Chapter 10 SUMMARY

- After 1050, Western Europe was again at peace. Farming and trade began to grow again.

- The Catholic Church was important in the Middle Ages. Monks and nuns were members of religious groups. Some cared for the sick or studied farming methods. Others taught students and supplied places for travelers to stay. The Catholic Church kept learning alive.

- Christian pilgrims visited Palestine, or the Holy Land. In about 1095, one group of Muslims stopped pilgrimages. The pope then called for a holy war, or crusade, to regain control of Palestine.

- Europeans fought four major Crusades between 1096 and 1291. Both nobles and common people were crusaders. In the end, Muslims kept control of Palestine.

- The Crusades had three results. These included increased trade with the Middle East and curiosity about distant lands. Unfortunately, they were also the beginning of harsh treatment toward Jews and Orthodox Christians.

- Feudalism began in Europe in the Middle Ages because there was no central government. It was based on an exchange of a lord's land for a vassal's service.

- Knights were medieval soldiers who came from noble families. They trained for knighthood first as pages and then as squires.

- Feudal manors were self-sufficient. Most people were peasants; some were serfs who could not leave the land.

- Five inventions changed farming. They were the three-field system, the horseshoe, an improved plow, the waterwheel, and the windmill. With better crops and more food, the population of Europe grew larger.

- Nobles built strong castles for protection. Sometimes knights practiced their skills in tournaments on castle grounds.

- In the Middle Ages, boys began attending school in monasteries and cathedral schools. Classes were conducted in Latin.

- Early medieval churches were Romanesque. They had thick walls with rounded arches. The later Gothic style had pointed arches and tall, thin walls. The stained glass windows taught people religious stories.

- There were two kinds of medieval literature. Religious works were written in Latin and traditional stories in local languages.

- English law introduced the jury system and Parliament.

1050 – 1500

The High and Late Middle Ages Chapter 10   245

Using the Chapter Summary

Have students read the Chapter Summary on page 245 to review the main ideas presented in Chapter 10.

Ask:

- **How did the Church keep learning alive during the Middle Ages?** (Religious orders supplied teachers to new towns; monks and nuns copied books from the past by hand.)

- **Identify three results of the crusades.** (Answers will vary; students may say that the Muslims controlled Palestine, the pope and European kings had more power, Europe traded with the Middle East, crusaders learned about Arab culture and science, or that Europeans gained an interest in exploration.)

- **What was feudalism?** (a new political and military system based on the holding of land)

- **Describe the steps the son of a noble needed to take to become a knight.** (First, he learned religion, manners, obedience, and loyalty and became a page. Next, he learned to ride a horse and use weapons and became a squire. Then at age 21, he became a knight.)

- **Who worked on a manor and what did they do?** (Serfs; they worked on the farm.)

- **Why did nobles build castles?** (to protect themselves from their enemies)

- **Name two architectural styles of medieval churches.** (Romanesque and Gothic)

- **Name two changes that took place in law in the Middle Ages.** (King Henry II introduced the use of the jury in English courts. Councils of nobles and church leaders were formed in England and France.)

TEACHER'S RESOURCE

The AGS Globe Teaching Strategies in Social Studies Transparencies may be used with this chapter. The transparencies add an interactive dimension to expand and enhance the *World History* program content.

Chapter 10 Review

Use the Chapter Review to prepare students for tests and to reteach content from the chapter.

Chapter 10 Mastery Test

The Teacher's Resource Library includes two forms of the Chapter 10 Mastery Test. Each test covers the chapter Goals for Learning. An optional third page of additional critical-thinking items is included for each test. The difficulty level of the two forms is equivalent.

Chapter 10 Review Answers

1. fief
2. page
3. serf
4. convent
5. pilgrim
6. lance
7. moat
8. manor
9. lord
10. knight
11. C
12. B
13. D
14. D
15. A

Word Bank

convent
fief
knight
lance
lord
manor
moat
page
pilgrim
serf

On a sheet of paper, use the words from the Word Bank to complete each sentence correctly.

1. The land given to a vassal by his lord is a _____.
2. A _____ was a young nobleman training to be a knight.
3. A _____ was a peasant bound to the land on which he or she was born.
4. Nuns live in a _____.
5. A _____ visited the Holy Land to see the place where Jesus had lived.
6. A _____ is a steel-tipped spear.
7. A _____ is a dug-out place filled with water that circles a castle.
8. A _____ is a self-sufficient area of land on which the peasants grew or raised almost everything that the lord and they needed.
9. A _____ is a king or noble who gives land to someone else in return for loyalty.
10. A _____ is a soldier who gives loyalty to his lord.

On a sheet of paper, write the letter of the answer that correctly completes each sentence.

11. The military journeys to the Holy Land that lasted for nearly 200 years are the _____.

    A Muslims   **C** Crusades
    B Vassals   **D** Romanesque

12. _____ was a political and military system used in the Middle Ages that was based on the holding of land.

    A Gothic   **C** Monastery
    B Feudalism   **D** Buttress

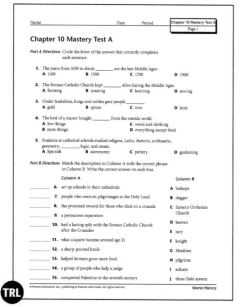

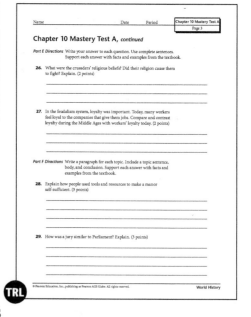

Chapter 10 Mastery Test A, pages 1–3

13. Gothic architecture had _____.

   A pointed arches   **C** flying buttresses

   B thin walls   **D** all of the above

14. Many castles had _____.

   A courtyards   **C** drawbridges

   B moats   **D** all of the above

15. The oldest and greatest French medieval poem is the _____.

   A *Song of Roland*   **C** *Beowulf*

   B *Nibelungenlied*   **D** none of the above

On a sheet of paper, write the answer to each question. Use complete sentences.

16. What is one good thing and one bad thing that resulted from the Crusades?

17. What was feudalism?

18. What did the church have to do with education, art, and architecture during the Middle Ages?

Critical Thinking On a sheet of paper, write your response to each question. Use complete sentences.

19. Why do you think the people living on manors welcomed travelers, actors, and musicians? Describe how this tells about what life was like living on a manor.

20. If you were a crusader, what reasons would you give for being one? List at least three reasons.

After you have completed a test, reread each question and answer. Ask yourself: Have I answered the question that I was asked? Have I answered it completely?

16. The Crusades introduced new foods and products into Europe as the Europeans began to trade with the Middle East. The Crusades also made people want to explore and introduced them to art, architecture, medicine, and mathematics from other cultures. But many people died fighting the Crusades, and increased hatred for Jews developed.

17. Feudalism was a political and military system based on the holding of land.

18. The church opened the first schools after the fall of the Roman Empire. It also hired artists and architects to design and decorate beautiful church buildings.

Critical Thinking

19. Answers will vary. Manor life could become somewhat boring because people did not travel far from home. So the lord and his household would always welcome strangers who could sing, dance, and entertain.

20. Students might mention that they went on a crusade to see faraway lands and meet people from other places; to eat different food; to fight people who didn't worship God the same way they did; and to find adventure.

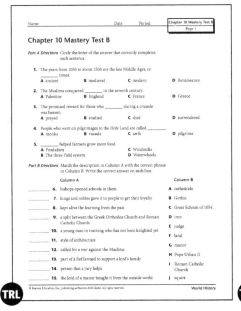

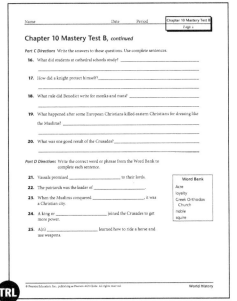

Chapter 10 Mastery Test B, pages 1–3

Introducing the Chapter

Europe's Middle Ages cover roughly a
millennium, or 1,000 years—from A.D.
500 to A.D. 1500. This chapter describes
important events that occurred during
this time.

When you think about a period of
1,000 years of history, such as the
Middle Ages, it is helpful to consider
the centuries in which events occurred.

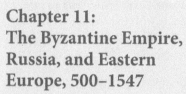

500 – 1547

11 The Byzantine Empire, Russia, and Eastern Europe

During the Middle Ages, the eastern part of the old
Roman Empire grew strong. But the western part broke
into many parts and fell into decay. In this chapter, you will
learn about the Byzantine Empire and its greatest emperor. You
will discover the ways this empire influenced the Slavic people
of Eastern Europe. You will follow the Germanic tribes as they
invade Western Europe. You will sail with the Vikings and
find new lands! Finally, you will witness a battle that changed
England forever.

Goals for Learning

◆ To compare the Byzantine and the Roman Empires

◆ To describe the influence of the Byzantine Empire on
the people of Eastern Europe, especially Russia

◆ To list several reasons why some historians call this
period the "Dark Ages" and explain the importance of
Charlemagne to European history

527 Justinian becomes emperor
of the Byzantine Empire

862 The founding of Russia

1066 Normans
conquer England

1240 The Mongols
destroy Kiev

1547 Ivan the
Terrible becomes
first czar of Russia

| 500 | 750 | 1000 | 1250 | 1500 |

800 Charlemagne is
crowned emperor

1016 Canute, a
Viking, becomes
ruler of England

1453 Turks take control of
Constantinople and change
its name to Istanbul

1462 Ivan
the Great rules
Russia

We know that an event that happened
in 1999 was in the 20th century. We
usually think of the year A.D. 2000 as
the beginning of the 21st century. Life
can change dramatically over the course
of 1,000 years. With each new century
in a millennium come new inventions,
advances, and challenges.

Ask:

• What are the five dates in the
center strip of the timeline? (500,
750, 1000, 1250, and 1500)

• Why do you think those dates are
marked on the timeline? (Possible
response: to give the reader a
frame of reference for when those
events occurred in the history of
the world)

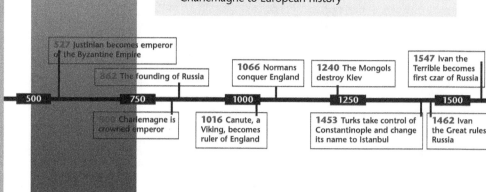

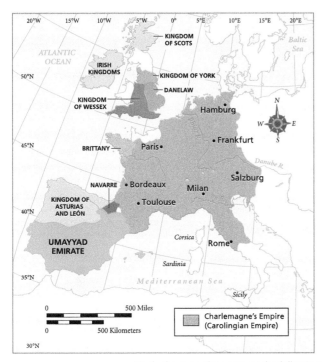

After the fall of the Roman Empire in A.D. 476, Europe broke into many small kingdoms. Cities disappeared. More than 300 years passed before a strong king united all of Western Europe again. His name was Charlemagne, or Charles the Great. This map shows his empire. It was located where the countries of France, Italy, Spain, Switzerland, Austria, the Czech Republic, and Germany are now located.

Study the map, then answer the following questions:

1. What are the names of three rivers in Charlemagne's empire?

2. What are the names of five cities in his empire?

3. What sea lies to the south of the empire?

4. How many miles did this empire stretch from east to west at its widest point? from north to south at its widest point?

5. Between what two lines of latitude was much of Charlemagne's empire?

Have students study the map of Charlemagne's empire. Read the title of the map and the paragraph below it with students.

Ask:

- Which body of water lies to the north and east of Charlemagne's empire? (Baltic Sea)

- Which part of Europe did Charlemagne rule? (Western Europe)

- Which mountain range divides northern parts of Charlemagne's empire from southern parts of the empire? (the Alps)

Have students read and answer the questions about the map and the text.

Map Skills Answers

1. the Rhine, the Danube, and the Po

2. Possible cities include Toulouse, Paris, Hamburg, Frankfurt, Salzburg, Milan, and Bordeaux.

3. the Mediterranean Sea

4. It was about 800 miles wide and about 850 miles from north to south.

5. Much of it was between 40 and 55 degrees north latitude.

Chapter Project

Divide the class into groups of 3 or 4 students. Ask each group to choose one of the leaders discussed in the chapter. Have students use library or Internet resources to research their chosen leader's life. Assign groups to compile their research into a one-minute webcast on the leader's life, accomplishments, and role in history. Remind students that when writing for their webcast, they must be concise and focus on the important information.

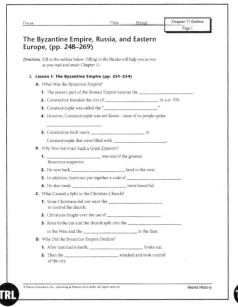

Chapter 11 Outline, pages 1–3

Text Structure

Introduce the reading strategy *text structure*. Explain that text is often organized in a way that will help the reader understand and remember what he or she is reading. Text structure helps the reader focus on the important information in the text. Read the bulleted questions on page 250 aloud to students. Have students determine if description or sequence is used in Lesson 1. Then have them determine if Lesson 1 uses compare and contrast or cause and effect as a text structure.

Have students read the headings on page 251.

Ask:

• Do you think those sections are structured using description or sequence? (description)

• Do they use compare and contrast or cause and effect? (compare and contrast) Why? (The headings indicate that the Byzantine empire and Constantinople will be described. Also, the Byzantine empire is being compared to Rome, and Constantinople is being contrasted with Rome.)

Key Vocabulary Words

Explain that the list of words shown here is a glossary of the Key Vocabulary students will read in Chapter 11. Call on volunteers to read the words and their definitions aloud.

Ask:

• What term is used to describe something that is very old, and that also has something to do with God? (relic)

• What is a patriarch? (a church leader)

• What was the title of the ruler of Russia? (czar)

Reading Strategy:
Text Structure

Before you begin reading this chapter, look at how it is organized. Look at the title, headings, boldfaced words, and photographs. Ask yourself:

◆ Is the text a description or sequence?

◆ Is it compare and contrast or cause and effect?

Key Vocabulary Words

Lesson 1 ————————
Relic A holy object

Saint A person who follows God's ways

Barbaric Not civilized

Patriarch A leader of the church

Icon A small picture of a saint or Jesus

Lesson 2 ————————
Monk A member of a religious order

Cyrillic alphabet The alphabet invented by Cyril and Methodius and used to translate the Bible into Slavic languages

Boyar A Russian noble who owned land

Veche The Russian assembly that represented all free, adult male citizens

Kremlin The center of the Russian church and the Russian government

Czar The ruler of Russia; a Russian title that means "caesar"

Lesson 3 ————————
Literature The written works that have lasting influence

Pope The head of the Roman Catholic Church

STUDY SKILLS

Tell students that they will be reading about many people who influenced the history of Europe during the Middle Ages. Suggest that they use index cards to track these individuals. On each card they should put a person's name, a date or dates given in the text, and the reason why the individual is important. They can keep the cards in chronological order. Students can review the information on these cards as they prepare for the chapter review and test.

Objectives

- ◆ To list the accomplishments of the Byzantine Empire
- ◆ To identify the greatest Byzantine emperor
- ◆ To explain the disagreement that divided Christians

Reading Strategy:
Text Structure

Preview the first two headings. How do you know that they will compare and contrast two things?

Relic

A holy object from the past

Saint

A person who follows God's ways

Remember when Emperor Diocletian divided the Roman Empire into two parts in A.D. 284? The eastern part became the Byzantine Empire. Constantine founded the city of Constantinople there in A.D. 330. He made his new city the capital of the Byzantine Empire.

How Was the Byzantine Empire Like Rome?

Constantine called his capital city the "new Rome." He built as the emperors had in Rome. One building—the Hippodrome—was like Rome's Colosseum. Constantine held chariot races in it.

An army of officials helped the emperor rule. They took charge of building and repairing roads. As in Rome, there was a senate, but the emperor held all the power. He organized the army along Roman lines. In the early years of the empire, all the Byzantine emperors were Roman and spoke Latin.

But Constantinople was not Rome. Most of its people were Greek and spoke the Greek language. Many had come there from other lands. Constantinople was located on one of the most important trade routes between Asia and Europe. Jews, Turks, Persians, Slavs, and Italians lived there.

How Did Rome and Constantinople Differ?

Constantinople was a Christian city. Emperor Constantine built many beautiful Christian churches there. Often, these churches were the most beautiful buildings in the city. He collected **relics** for them. These relics were holy objects from the past. That is, they had something to do with God or with **saints**—people who followed God's ways. People came from all parts of the empire to pray in these churches.

Chapter 11: Lesson 1

Overview This lesson presents a comparison of the Byzantine and Roman empires and outlines important Byzantine contributions in the areas of law and architecture. It also provides an explanation of the disagreement that divided the Christian world.

Objectives

- ■ To list the accomplishments of the Byzantine Empire
- ■ To identify the greatest Byzantine emperor
- ■ To explain the disagreement that divided Christians

Student Pages pages 251–254

Teacher's Resource Library (TRL)

Workbook Activity 47

Activity 47

Modified Activity 47

....

Vocabulary

barbaric	relic
icon	saint
patriarch	

Have students work in pairs to create a crossword puzzle that uses the vocabulary words. They can use the definitions in their books or write their own. Give students an opportunity to work with their partner to solve other students' puzzles.

....

1 **Warm-Up Activity**

Explain to students that in this lesson, they will read about the code of laws that Justinian, a Byzantine emperor, put into action. Have students work in small groups to come up with a list of current "laws" or rules at your school. As a class, discuss these laws. Encourage students to consider what their school experience might be like without the laws or rules. Have students discuss how reasonable laws help a society to function effectively.

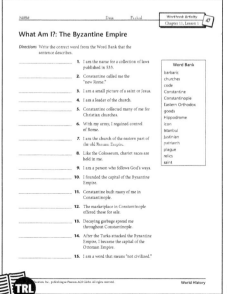

Workbook Activity 47

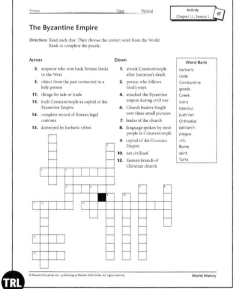

Activity 47

2 Teaching the Lesson

Ask students to brainstorm outstanding features and accomplishments of the Roman Empire. Then have them read pages 251–254 to find out about the empire that followed Rome.

ELL/ESL STRATEGY

Language Objective:
To learn content-area vocabulary

List the vocabulary words from Lesson 1 on the board. Say each word aloud as you point to it. Have students repeat each word after you. Then write the definition for each word next to the word on the board. If possible, act out the meaning of each word as you say it aloud. For example, have a student trade a pencil for a pen with you to act out the word *trade*. Start a word wall for the chapter by adding the words and definitions to a large sheet of butcher paper. Attach this to the board, and add more words to it as needed throughout the rest of the chapter.

Ask:

• How was the Byzantine Empire like the Roman Empire? How was it different? (Responses will vary. Possible responses: similarities—had army, built roads; differences—the language, the place of religion; the ethnic backgrounds of the people)

Reading Strategy:
Text Structure

(Answers will vary. Students may say that the headings each mention two different things; Rome and the Byzantine Empire, or Rome and Constantinople. The first heading uses the word "like," and the second heading uses the word "differ," which are both clues that tell you things are being compared and contrasted.)

Barbaric
Not civilized

Reading Strategy:
Text Structure

Notice that the section headings are written as questions. After you read each section, try to answer the question asked in the heading.

Ask:

• Which tribes were invading Rome? (Germanic)

• How did Justinian preserve the laws of the Roman Empire? (Responses will vary. Students may say he had scholars organize the laws into a single code.)

• Why is Justinian's code of laws important today? (It has shaped laws in Europe and the United States.)

Who Was the Greatest of the Byzantine Emperors?

In 527, a man named Justinian became emperor. Most historians call him the greatest of the Byzantine emperors. We remember him for three reasons. First, he tried to win back the Roman lands in the West. Second, he put together a code of laws. Third, he made Constantinople more beautiful.

What Land Did Justinian Win Back?

Justinian tried to win back all the western lands that Rome had lost the century before. One of his armies won back much of Italy and North Africa. Another army threw back the Persians. During this time, several different Germanic tribes took over Rome. Finally, Justinian's armies won control of Rome. But the **barbaric** tribes, which were not civilized, had left it in ruins.

What Was Good About Justinian's Code of Laws?

Justinian asked a group of Greek and Latin scholars to collect and organize the laws of his empire. They published their code of laws in 533. Historians call this the greatest thing Justinian did.

Justinian (center) is considered to be one of the best emperors of the Byzantine Empire.

The code was a complete record of Roman legal customs. It listed the rights that the empire gave to each person. For 900 years, this code was the basis for Byzantine law. The main ideas of the code later shaped the legal systems of Europe and the United States.

How Did Justinian Make Constantinople More Beautiful?

Justinian built a government building in which 20,000 people worked. Across from it, he built one of the world's most beautiful churches—the Hagia Sophia. Its ceiling rises 180 feet

Reading Strategy:
Text Structure

Have students work together to answer each section question on page 252. (According to the text, the greatest Byzantine Emperor was Justinian. Justinian won back Italy, North Africa, and Persia. The good thing about Justinian's code of laws was that it shaped future legal systems because it was written down. Justinian made Constantinople more beautiful by building beautiful buildings.)

Patriarch

A leader of the church

Icon

A small picture of a saint or Jesus

from the floor. He used beautifully colored marble for the walls, floors, and pillars. Justinian also built three walls to protect Constantinople. A marketplace on its main street offered goods from Africa, Asia, and Europe.

What Caused a Split in the Christian Church?

Justinian's motto was "one empire, one church, one law." He became the head of the church within the lands he controlled. Priests and **patriarchs,** or leaders of the church, became government officials. But some Christians did not want an emperor to control the church. They fought over this.

They also fought over the use of **icons**—small pictures of the saints and Jesus. Several emperors wanted to get rid of them. They thought people were worshipping the icons instead of God.

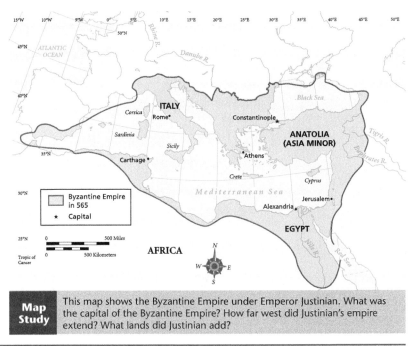

Map Study This map shows the Byzantine Empire under Emperor Justinian. What was the capital of the Byzantine Empire? How far west did Justinian's empire extend? What lands did Justinian add?

Have a volunteer read the title of the map: "Byzantine Empire Under Justinian." Ask students to compare this map of the Byzantine Empire with that of Charlemagne's empire on page 249.

Ask:

- Which empire is farthest east? farthest north? (east—Byzantine; north—Charlemagne's)

- Have students read the caption under the map and answer the questions. (Constantinople was the capital of the Byzantine Empire; his empire went as far west as the Atlantic Ocean in Western Europe; Justinian added parts of northern Africa, Italy, Sardinia, Corsica, Sicily, and lands east of Italy.)

Ask:

- In addition to beautifying Constantinople, why did Justinian build three walls in the city? (to protect it against invaders)

- Why were some Christians upset about the use of icons? (They thought people were worshipping the icons instead of God.)

- What issue divided Rome and Constantinople? (religion/the use of icons)

WORLD CULTURES

The painting of icons, or iconography, is sometimes thought of as Russia's national art. It was very popular for about 300 years. In the 15th century, Russians gradually changed the images on their icons. Until then, icons had reflected Byzantine culture. But Russians began to paint backgrounds that more closely matched their own surroundings. For example, they drew locally-seen vegetation and churches like the ones in which they worshipped. By the 17th century, outside cultural influences impacted Russian artists and changed the character of the icons.

LEARNING STYLES

Body/Kinesthetic

Have students research the architecture of the Hagia Sophia. Have them read about the unique combination of features that causes it to be recognized today as one of the world's most beautiful structures. Have students create drawings or clay models to illustrate each of these features, and write on an index card what the feature contributed to the total design. Students can use these cards as prompts when they report to the class what they discovered about the architecture of the Hagia Sophia.

3 Reinforce and Extend

BACKGROUND INFORMATION

 Istanbul, in Turkey, is unique. It stands on two continents—Europe and Asia. A waterway called the Bosporus separates the Asian side from the European side of the city. Today, two bridges span the Bosporus, linking Asia and Europe.The Bosporus is on a major trade route, connecting the Black Sea with the Sea of Marmara, eventually leading to the Mediterranean. Istanbul has a blend of Muslim and Christian cultures, with nearly 500 mosques and 25 historic Byzantine churches.

LEARNING STYLES

 Visual/Spatial
Have students follow these instructions to create a map: Place a piece of tracing paper over a map of Turkey and surrounding countries, with Istanbul in the center. Trace the outline of the city, the land, and the seas. Write the names of bodies of water, countries, and major cities, including Istanbul, on the map. Then, draw long double-headed arrows indicating land and sea trade routes that go through the city of Istanbul, linking Europe to Asia and the Black Sea to the Sea of Marmara and eventually to the eastern and western ends of the Mediterranean Sea. Label the map "Major Trade Routes Through Istanbul."

Soon, riots broke out. Christians in the eastern part of the old Roman Empire and Christians in the western part began to think differently. This caused a split in the church. In 1054, the church in the West became known as the Roman Catholic Church. The church in the East became the Eastern Orthodox Church.

Why Did the Byzantine Empire Decline?

The death of Justinian in 565 marked the beginning of the end for the Byzantine Empire. Garbage filled Constantinople's narrow streets. Civil war broke out. People fought to decide who should become the next emperor. In the centuries after Justinian, the empire faced attacks by Persians, Slavs, Vikings, Mongols, and Turks. In 1453, the Turks took control of Constantinople and changed its name to Istanbul. It became the capital of the Ottoman Empire.

Word Bank
Hagia Sophia
Hippodrome
Jesus
Justinian
Rome

Lesson 1 Review On a sheet of paper, use the words from the Word Bank to complete each sentence correctly.

1. Constantine tried to build his capital like _____.

2. The _____ was like Rome's Colosseum.

3. Historians think that _____ was the greatest emperor of the Byzantine Empire.

4. Justinian built the beautiful church known as the _____.

5. People in the Byzantine Empire began to fight over the use of icons, or small pictures of saints and _____.

What do you think ?

A plague weakened both the western Roman Empire and the eastern Byzantine Empire. Why do you think that the people at that time had such trouble with plagues?

CAREER CONNECTION

 Modern nations rely on the military to defend their interests, just as Justinian did. In the United States, the branches of the military are the Army, the Air Force, the Marines, and the Navy. There are many avenues to a military career today. Students interested in learning more about military careers can research their options in the library or on the Internet.

Lesson 1 Review Answers

1. Rome **2.** Hippodrome
3. Justinian **4.** Hagia Sophia **5.** Jesus

Responses will vary. The people did not have good sanitation, nor modern vaccines and antibiotics. Also, they did not know about germs.

The Byzantine Empire greatly influenced the people of Eastern Europe. We call these people Slavs. They moved from central Asia into the countries we now call Russia, Ukraine, Slovakia, Bulgaria, the Czech Republic, Slovenia, Croatia, and Poland.

The Slavs included many groups. Each group had its own culture and language, but they were alike in some ways. The largest group was the Russians.

What Happened When the Slavs Became Christians?

The Slavs admired the Byzantine civilization. Around 900, two **monks,** or members of a religious group, began to preach to the Slavs. Cyril and Methodius helped many Slavs give up their old religions and become Christians.

The Slavs had no written language. The monks invented an alphabet for their spoken language. We call this the **Cyrillic alphabet.** Some Slavic countries still use it today. Then the monks translated the church's Bible, songs, and ceremonies into Slavic languages. Because of this, the Slavs could read the Bible and understand the songs and ceremonies.

Two monks named Cyril and Methodius helped Slavs become Christians.

To explain the relationship between Russia and the Byzantine Empire

To describe the formation of an independent Russia

Monk
A member of a religious order

Cyrillic alphabet
The alphabet invented by Cyril and Methodius and used to translate the Bible into Slavic languages

---

500 – 1547   *The Byzantine Empire, Russia, and Eastern Europe*   Chapter 11   255

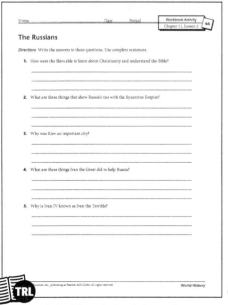

Workbook Activity 48

Activity 48

Chapter 11: Lesson 2

Overview This lesson explains the rising importance of Russia. This includes its adoption of Christianity, the development of Kiev as a major trading center, and the ultimate dominance of Moscow that led to the structures that mark modern Russia.

Objectives

- To explain the relationship between Russia and the Byzantine Empire
- To describe the formation of an independent Russia

Student Pages pages 255–259

Teacher's Resource Library TRL

Workbook Activity 48

Activity 48

Modified Activity 48

Vocabulary

boyar	Kremlin
Cyrillic alphabet	monk
czar	Veche

Give students an opportunity to study the vocabulary words and definitions listed on the pages in this lesson. Then write a vocabulary word on the board and ask someone to give a definition using their own words. If class members agree that the definition given is correct, have the individual who defined the word write the next word to be defined on the board. Continue until all the words have been defined.

1 Warm-Up Activity

Tell students that they will be reading about many changes in Eastern Europe in this lesson. Explain that even within the last century, there have been many changes in the political divisions of Eastern Europe. Lead a discussion about these recent changes in the region. Then have students read to find out about the beginning of Russia.

PRONUNCIATION GUIDE

Use this list to help students pronounce difficult words in this lesson.

Cyril	(sir′ əl)
Methodius	(mi thō′ de əs)
Neva	(nē′ və)
Rurik	(rú r′ ik)

2 Teaching the Lesson

As students read the lesson, have them make a list of factors that helped Russia become a strong country. Student lists might include unified religious beliefs, strong leaders, and a good location along trade routes. Discuss with students why the items on their lists were a factor in strengthening Russia.

Ask:

• Who invented the Cyrillic alphabet?
(Cyril and Methodius)

• What event made Russians feel closer to the Byzantine Empire?
(when Eastern Orthodoxy became the official religion)

Reading Strategy:
Text Structure

(Students may respond that Russia was tied to the Byzantine Empire because they had the same official religion. An early Russian king married the sister of the Byzantine emperor. They had churches that looked alike.)

Have students study the map and the map key. Then have students answer the questions in the caption. (traders used the Dnieper River; Kiev was a capital and a trade center)

Ask:

• On which continent is Kiev?
(Europe)

• What direction is Russia from the Byzantine Empire? (north)

• What direction is Kiev from Constantinople? (north)

Byzantine Christianity helped unite the people of Eastern Europe. The Slavs accepted the Eastern Orthodox Church. However, most of the rest of Europe belonged to the Roman Catholic Church. This difference isolated the Slavs. For nearly 300 years, they knew little of the discoveries and inventions that were changing civilization in Western Europe.

Reading Strategy:
Text Structure

Notice that the section headings are written as questions. After you read this section, answer the question asked in the heading.

What Ties Did Russia Have with the Byzantine Empire?

In 989, Eastern Orthodoxy became the official religion of Russia. Now Russians felt closer to the Byzantine Empire. For example, Vladimir, an early Russian king, married the sister of the Byzantine emperor. The empire and Russia traded with one another. Also, the Russians built their churches to look like the ones in the Byzantine Empire. The beautiful church of Saint Sophia in Kiev is one example of this. By 1050, Russian civilization was the most advanced in Europe.

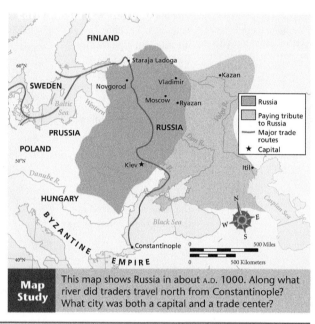

Map Study This map shows Russia in about A.D. 1000. Along what river did traders travel north from Constantinople? What city was both a capital and a trade center?

ELL/ESL STRATEGY

Language Objective:
To compare and contrast
After reading pages 255–256, divide the class into two groups. Give each group a sheet of butcher paper or chart paper and a marker. Tell each group to choose one member to act as its writer. Then ask one group to write everything they know about the Byzantines, and ask the other group to write everything they know about the Russians. Suggest that both groups write this information in a bulleted list. When both groups have

finished, display the two sheets next to each other on a wall. Explain that the first thing you will do is to compare the Byzantines and the Russians—that is, you will figure out how they are alike. Circle all of the listed items that show how the two are alike. Then tell students that you are going to contrast the two. Remind students that this means you will see how the Byzantines and Russians are different. Underline the items that show how the two are different.

Olga: c. A.D. 890–969

Olga, Grand Princess of Kiev, was Russia's first woman ruler. Her husband, Prince Igor, was murdered in 945. In response to this, Olga had hundreds of people executed. Since her son was young, Olga ruled Kiev for him. Then the young prince came of age. But he was more interested in war than in ruling. While he was away, Olga ruled Kiev.

Most people in Kiev still worshiped the old gods. Olga, however, became a Christian in 957. She went to Constantinople and invited Byzantine missionaries to Russia. Kiev became Christian under her grandson Vladimir.

Boyar

A Russian noble who owned land

Veche

The Russian assembly that represented all free, adult male citizens

What Made Kiev So Important?

Historians give 862 as the date Russia was founded. In that year, Prince Rurik became ruler. His capital was Kiev. It is located on the Dnieper River—one of the main north-south water trade routes. Whoever controlled Kiev controlled Russia's trade with Constantinople.

Kiev was also at the center of two other trading routes: one between Europe and Asia and one between Scandinavia and the Middle East. By 1000, Kiev was the biggest city in Europe. It was larger than London or Paris.

At this time, Russia was a group of small territories. The Grand Prince of Kiev ruled these territories. He shared power with other princes and with **boyars**—Russian nobles who owned land. A **Veche,** or assembly, represented all free, adult male citizens. It could accept or remove a prince. It also handled business and government.

Why Did Kiev Fall?

Kievan Russia reached its peak between 1000 and 1050. Its ruler unified Russia. However, when he died, his sons fought each other for control. This weakened the kingdom. Trade with Constantinople was cut off. In 1240, fierce Mongol armies from central Asia completely destroyed Kiev.

500 – 1547   *The Byzantine Empire, Russia, and Eastern Europe*   Chapter 11   **257**

ONLINE CONNECTION

Have students do some research that focuses on the rise and fall of Kievan Russia. Students may find valuable information at: www. agsglobewh.com/page257 among other Web sites. Have students use this information to write a one-page report on Kiev.

The historical account of the founding of the Russian royal family by the Viking Rurik around A.D. 880 is told in a chronicle. It was compiled about 300 years after the founding. Needless to say, some historians are skeptical of the validity of this chronicle. Grand Princess Olga married Rurik's son Igor. Some historians think that Igor, who founded Kiev as a principality, is the real founder of Russia's royal family.

Ask:

• Which city became a trading center around the year A.D. 1000? (Kiev)

• Around the year A.D. 1000, Kiev's Grand Prince shared power with other princes and landowners. How do you think Grand Princess Olga would have liked sharing her power with others? (Responses will vary. Students may say she was a very strong ruler and might not have liked to share power.)

LEARNING STYLES

Interpersonal/ Group Learning

Have a group of six or more students plan five or six tableaus to illustrate action from the fall of Kiev. Student groups will need to do some additional research to prepare each tableau. In each tableau, the actors freeze in position at a certain point in the story while a narrator reads a description of what is happening at that point. Once the group decides which scenes to dramatize, they can divide tasks. One group can write brief descriptions of the scenes; the other group can plan the tableaus. The actors might use props to help interpret a scene. Ask the group to perform their dramatizations with narration for the class.

Ask:

- Which two things were centered in the Kremlin? (the church and the government)
- Where did Ivan the Terrible get the title "czar"? (from the Roman title "caesar")

Reading Strategy:
Text Structure

(Possible response: Because the heading says he was called Ivan the Terrible, it tells me that he was a mean, cruel person.)

Kremlin

The center of the Russian church and the Russian government

Czar

The ruler of Russia; a Russian title that means "caesar"

Reading Strategy:
Text Structure

Read the heading of the next section. What does it tell you about the rule of Ivan IV?

When Did Moscow Become Important?

To escape the invaders, many Russians headed north. In that same year, Alexander, a Russian prince, defeated the Swedes at the Neva River. The Swedes had tried to force the Russians to become Catholics. The Russians gave Alexander the title *Nevsky* or "of the Neva."

In 1294, Nevsky's youngest son, Daniel, became ruler of Muscovy, or Moscow. (It is the capital of Russia today.) At that time, Moscow was a small, rich town located on an important trade route. Later, the princes of Moscow took the title, or name, of "Grand Prince of All Russia."

Who Was the Founder of Modern Russia?

By the late 1400s, Moscow was the most powerful city in Russia. It became the center of the Russian church. Historians call Ivan III, or Ivan the Great, the founder of modern Russia. He ruled from 1462 to 1505. This great leader freed Russia from foreign rule and set up a government.

Ivan's wife, Sophia, was related to the last Byzantine emperor. She got him to adopt the double-headed eagle as his symbol. (It had been the symbol of Byzantine emperors.) Sophia also encouraged Ivan to take complete power of both the church and the government. Ivan the Great rebuilt the **Kremlin.** It became the center of the Russian church and the Russian government.

Who Was Ivan the Terrible?

In 1533, Ivan IV, just three years old, became the ruler of Russia. He was the grandson of Ivan the Great. Ivan IV began to govern when he was 14. During his reign, he made the kingdom three times larger. He believed that the Roman emperor Augustus Caesar was one of his ancestors. So in 1547, he crowned himself the first **czar** of Russia. This title means the same as the Roman title "caesar."

Ivan IV was a good military leader, but he was also cruel. He ordered thousands of Russians and enemy soldiers killed. Because he was so cruel, historians call him Ivan the Terrible.

Lesson 2 Review On a sheet of paper, use the words from the Word Bank to complete each sentence correctly.

Word Bank

Cyril

Kremlin

Nevsky

Rurik

Vladimir

1. Methodius and _____, both monks, created an alphabet for the Slavic languages and used it to translate the Bible.

2. _____, an early Russian king, married the sister of the Byzantine emperor.

3. Historians date the founding of Russia to A.D. 862 when Prince _____ became ruler.

4. Prince Alexander became a hero to the Russians, and they called him _____ because of where he won a great battle.

5. Ivan the Great rebuilt the _____ as the center for church and government.

Would creating an alphabet for a spoken language be hard? Explain your answer.

The Kremlin

The Kremlin is more than the center of Russian government. It contains beautiful churches and palaces. They stand inside a walled area more than a mile around. Impressive brick towers guard the entrance gates.

The first Kremlin was a wooden fort on the Moscow River. The Mongols burned it several times. By the late 1400s, however, Moscow was the most powerful city in Russia. Its ruler, Ivan the Great, hired Italian and Russian architects to build a new Kremlin. Inside its thick walls, they built three beautiful cathedrals with gold domes. Rulers were crowned in one church. They married in another. Their funerals were in the third. Later rulers added palaces and other buildings.

Today some buildings in the Kremlin are museums. There you can see the czars' crown jewels and other treasures.

Lesson 2 Review Answers

1. Cyril **2.** Vladimir **3.** Rurik **4.** Nevsky **5.** Kremlin

Answers will vary. Finding symbols for sounds might be easy. However, the letter *a* in the English alphabet has several sounds. So, does the inventor make a different letter for each sound? Or does one letter stand for several? And how does the inventor determine the spelling of each spoken word? These problems make inventing an alphabet difficult.

Before students read "The Kremlin," explain that there are no longer czars ruling in Russia. There is evidence that the entire Russian royal family may have been secretly executed during the Russian revolution. However, the Kremlin still exists and is a site often visited by tourists.

IN THE COMMUNITY

Have students work in small groups to map the locations of two types of places in their community: government offices and places of worship. Have them share their maps. Help them to conclude whether the pattern reflects the separation of "church and state," a fundamental principle in the United States Constitution. Ask them to compare this design with that of the Kremlin. (In the Kremlin, churches and palaces of the ruling czars were built very near each other.)

Chapter 11: Lesson 3

Overview This lesson explains what was going on in Western Europe during the Middle Ages: the brief union of Germanic tribes under Charlemagne, the effects of the Viking raids, and the influence of Norman rule on England.

Objectives

■ To describe some Germanic tribal kingdoms that replaced the Roman Empire

■ To identify some groups that invaded Britain and influenced its language and culture

Student Pages pages 260–264

Teacher's Resource Library

Workbook Activity 49

Activity 49

Modified Activity 49

....

Vocabulary

literature   **pope**

Have students read the definition for each word independently. Then ask students to use the definitions given in the lesson to write a sentence for each word. Have students trade sentences with a partner, read that student's sentences, and approve the way the word is used or recommend changes.

....

1 **Warm-Up Activity**

Explain to students that the Middle Ages in Europe are sometimes called the "Dark Ages" because life was very hard for everyone. Many bad things happened, and people had to work hard just to survive. Have students imagine that they are living 1,000 years from now and looking back in time to the current date. Have students work in small groups to come up with a name for this period in history, the "___ Ages." Have each group share their name with the class and explain how they came up with that name.

Objectives

◆ To describe some Germanic tribal kingdoms that replaced the Roman Empire

◆ To identify some groups that invaded Britain and influenced its language and culture

Literature
The written works that have lasting influence

Reading Strategy:
Text Structure

As you read the next section, notice the sequence of events that led to the Dark Ages.

The fall of Rome brought important changes to Western Europe. Germanic tribes slowly moved south and took over Roman lands. People did not obey Roman laws any longer. Roman soldiers could not keep order.

For 500 years there had been one Roman Empire. Now hundreds of little kingdoms took its place. These kingdoms had no system for collecting taxes. Rulers had little money for a government.

What Happened in Europe During the Middle Ages?

These little kingdoms were always at war with one another. This made doing business almost impossible. Also, along each road, robbers waited to attack travelers. Merchants were afraid to take their goods from city to city. There were no governments to repair roads and bridges. These fell into ruin. Towns and villages did, too.

As time passed, people lost interest in learning. Many useful books and artwork were lost in wars. People no longer learned about art, architecture, and **literature**, or written works that have lasting influence. The schools closed and the people had only enough time to take care of their day-to-day needs. Civilization lost its knowledge of the past.

Think of what life was like then. All the tribes fought, people were afraid to travel, they had no schools, few could read or write—the world was falling down around them. Historians call this period of history the "Dark Ages." The early Middle Ages was a difficult time for people in Western Europe.

Workbook Activity 49, pages 1–2

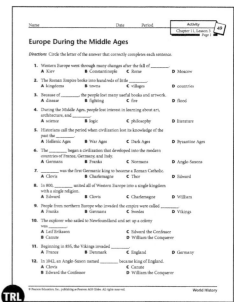

Activity 49, pages 1–2

Pope
The head of the Roman Catholic Church

Who Were the Franks?

The Franks were one of the largest of the German tribes. They began a civilization that later developed into the modern countries of France, Germany, and Italy. In 481, a warrior named Clovis united the Franks and became their king. He made Paris his capital. He was the first Germanic king to become a Roman Catholic.

Clovis united the Franks. He ruled for more than 20 years.

Who United All of Western Europe?

In 800, one king became strong enough to unite all of Western Europe. His name was Charlemagne, or Charles the Great. First, Charlemagne defeated the other Germanic tribes. Then he united them into one kingdom, with one religion—Roman Catholic. Next, Charlemagne fought against the enemies of the Roman Catholic Church. **Pope** Leo III, the head of the Roman Catholic Church, crowned him "Emperor of the Romans."

I Didn't Know There Was a God Named Tuesday

Have you ever wondered where the names for the days of the week come from? At one time, they were all named for Roman gods. Then Germanic peoples invaded Western Europe and beat the Romans. This fact may surprise you, but the English language comes from theirs. As a result, most English names for days honor Germanic gods.

Woden was the chief Germanic god. His son Thor's magic hammer made the sound of thunder. Tiw was god of war. Tuesday (Tiw), Wednesday (Woden), and Thursday (Thor) are named after them. Friday belongs to Frigg. She was the goddess of love. What about the other days? Sunday and Monday belong to the sun and moon. Saturday is named after the Roman god Saturn.

PRONUNCIATION GUIDE

Use this list to help students pronounce difficult words in this lesson.

Clovis	(klō´ vis)
Vinland	(vin´ lənd)

 Teaching the Lesson

As you read this lesson with students, point out the importance of a strong government to any society. Talk about what happened when there was no government in Western Europe. Point out that the environment was very chaotic. Then explain that when Charlemagne gained control of the area, law and order returned.

Ask:

- **What was the effect of the Dark Ages on children?** (Schools were closed, so children were not being educated.)
- **Who was Clovis?** (a king of the Franks; the first Germanic king to become a Roman Catholic)

Have students read "I Didn't Know There Was a God Named Tuesday" with a partner.

Ask:

- **Where did names for the days of the week come from?** (the names of Germanic gods)

Then have students research mythology in the library or on the Internet to find the names of Greek and Roman gods. Have them list modern names for things that borrow the names of Greek or Roman gods. (Saturn and Mercury automobiles, Venus's-flytrap, Mars and other heavenly bodies, Apollo space program, and so on)

ELL/ESL STRATEGY

Language Objective:
To describe events

After students read about the Dark Ages, have them work with a partner to find words and phrases in the text that describe this period. Tell students to write the words and phrases they find on paper. Explain to students that these words and phrases will help them understand what it was like to live during the Dark Ages. When all of the pairs have finished, bring the class together as a group. Make a list on the board of the words and phrases that students found. Read the entire list with students. Then have student volunteers think of adjectives that can be used to describe how the people must have felt during the Dark Ages.

Read the map title to students. Ask them to study the map and name the point farthest east, west, and south of the Vikings' journeys. Then have them read the caption under the map and follow the directions. (Sample answers; Dublin, Bordeaux, Lisbon, Seville, Pisa, Constantinople, among others)

Reading Strategy:
Text Structure

(Possible response: The map shows all of the different paths the Vikings traveled. You can use the distances shown in the scale at the bottom of the map to figure out how long each path is.)

Ask:

• Which tribes did Charlemagne unite? Which crown did he wear? (Germanic; that of emperor of the Romans)

• What was Charlemagne able to return to Western Europe? (law and order)

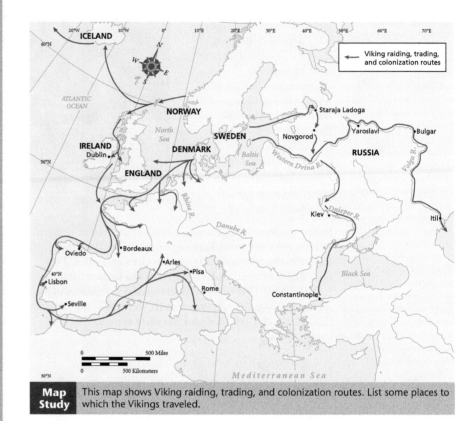

| Map Study | This map shows Viking raiding, trading, and colonization routes. List some places to which the Vikings traveled. |

Reading Strategy:
Text Structure

Study the map on this page. How does it help you understand how widely the Vikings traveled?

Charlemagne's rule brought law and order back to Western Europe. However, less than 30 years after his death, his empire broke apart. Civil war began. New invaders threatened his kingdom.

Writing About History

Imagine you are a news reporter. You have been assigned to report on the Viking voyages. In your notebook, write what you would say in your report.

How Far Did the Vikings Travel?

One group of invaders that attacked Charlemagne's empire was the Vikings. They came from Northern Europe—from the present-day countries of Denmark, Sweden, and Norway. The Vikings were fine sailors who built excellent ships. They could sail them on shallow rivers and in deep oceans. These ships had both sails and long oars. The largest ship held up to 100 men, but as few as 15 men could sail a Viking ship.

Viking explorers traveled to Russia, all across Europe, and to America. They set up colonies on the islands of Iceland and Greenland. A Viking named Leif Eriksson landed on an island on the northeast coast of North America. He called it Vinland. Today, we call this area Newfoundland. It is part of Canada.

What Viking Became King of England?

After the Romans left Britain in the fifth century, different Germanic tribes invaded the island. Historians know little about the tribes called Angles, Saxons, and Jutes. What they do know is that they destroyed as they invaded. Beginning in 835 and continuing for over 100 years, the Vikings invaded Britain too. In 1016, a Viking named Canute became the ruler of England. In 1042, Edward the Confessor, an Anglo-Saxon, became king.

How Did the Normans Begin to Rule England?

When Edward died, his brother-in-law Harold was chosen to rule. William, Duke of Normandy, also claimed the throne. (Normandy is a peninsula in present-day France.) At the Battle of Hastings in 1066, William defeated Harold. William the Conqueror, as he was now known, became king of England. The year 1066 is an important date in English history. William's victory meant that the Normans, rather than the Anglo-Saxons, would rule England. This has had a lasting influence on the English language and on the culture of England.

500 – 1547   *The Byzantine Empire, Russia, and Eastern Europe*   Chapter 11   **263**

Explain that effective reporters prepare before going on an assignment. Students have prepared for this writing assignment by learning about the Vikings. To complete their preparation, have them list some questions they might ask a Viking. Suggest that students write their questions on the board. Then have students read Writing About History and do the assignment.

Ask:

- **Which areas did the Vikings explore?** (Responses will vary. Students may say Russia, Europe, Iceland, Greenland, North America.)

- **Which language did the Normans speak? What lasting influence did they have on England?** (French; they influenced the English language)

- **In which battle did the Normans defeat the Anglo-Saxons and take control of England?** (the Battle of Hastings)

3 Reinforce and Extend

AT HOME

Have students find out the history of languages used in their family. They should ask how many generations before theirs, if any, spoke English and which other language or languages were spoken. Ask students who are bilingual to discuss the advantages of knowing a second language well. Have them share what influence another language has on their English. (Students might mention it causes them to speak with an accent different from that of other students or it helps them to learn new words.)

Lesson 3 Review Answers

1. D **2.** C **3.** A **4.** D **5.** C

Answers will vary. Without any learning, we would have to depend on one another to pass on what we know. But without books, the Internet, movies, and encyclopedias, people would begin to forget all the facts, dates, and names in history. We, too, might plunge into a dark age.

Have a volunteer read the Technology Connection aloud. Then invite observations about the features that made the dromon so effective. (For example, a tower in the center of the ship was a place from which warriors could fire arrows or hurl spears. Warriors were able to use catapults and rams on the large flat deck below.) Discuss why a faster, lighter ship would be more effective in war.

Chapter Project Follow-up

Have students perform their webcasts for the class. If the technology is available, record the students during their webcasts and post them on a class Web site or burn them onto a CD that students can watch later. All students in a group should be responsible for reading a part of the one-minute webcast to the class. Evaluate students based on the quality of their research as well as their performance delivery.

Lesson 3 Review On a sheet of paper, write the letter of the answer that correctly completes each sentence.

1. Historians call the period of time after the fall of Rome the "Dark Ages" because _____.

A there were no governments in Western Europe
B schools closed
C the people lost the learning of the past
D all of the above

2. _____ brought the Franks together and made Paris his capital.

A Charlemagne   **C** Clovis
B William of Normandy   **D** Leif Eriksson

3. In 800, Pope Leo III named _____ as the "Emperor of the Romans."

A Charlemagne   **C** Clovis
B William of Normandy   **D** Leif Eriksson

4. The Vikings visited _____.

A Iceland   **C** Newfoundland
B Greenland   **D** all of the above

5. The Battle of _____ took place in 1066.

A Charlemagne   **C** Hastings
B Normandy   **D** Newfoundland

What do you think

What would the world be like today if we lost all books and Internet learning from the past?

The Byzantine Dromon

Byzantine craftspeople of around A.D. 500 believed they could build a better ship. They improved upon the Greek galley most commonly used up until that time. The dromon was a faster, lighter ship used for war as well as for the ample trade within the Byzantine Empire.

Dromons used as warships were built with a tower in the center. From this tower, warriors could fire arrows or hurl spears at enemies. From the large flat deck below, others could use catapults or rams during sea battles. Dromons used for trade provided faster delivery of goods. Dromons were powered by rowers and by sail. They could carry large amounts of cargo or up to 300 passengers.

Life Among the Germans

Tacitus was a Roman historian. He did not like the way that Romans lived during his lifetime—he thought people lived in sin. Tacitus served as an official in several parts of the empire. As a result, he learned about different barbarians—people who were not Romans.

Many Germanic tribes lived on the northern borders of the empire. Tacitus admired their strength and simple life. He thought the Germans stood for an older, simpler way of life. After Rome fell, Germanic tribes conquered much of the empire. They soon controlled Europe.

This reading comes from Tacitus's history of the German tribes. He wrote it in A.D. 98.

The same make and form is found in all [men], eyes stern and blue, yellow hair, huge bodies, but vigorous only in the first onset. Of pains and labour they are not equally patient, nor can they at all endure thirst and heat. To bear hunger and cold they are hardened by their climate and soil. . . .

Their lands . . . consist of gloomy Forests, or nasty Marshes; . . . very apt to bear Grain, but altogether unkindly to fruit Trees; abounding in Flocks and Herds, but generally small of growth. . . .

They who live more remote are more primitive and simple in their dealings . . . The money which they like is the old and long known . . .

that impressed with a chariot and two horses. Silver too is what they seek more than gold . . . because small silver pieces are more ready in purchasing things cheap and common.

In the choice of Kings they are determined by the splendor of their race, in that of Generals by their bravery . . . their Generals procure obedience not so much by the force of their authority, as by that of their example. . . .

The moment they rise from sleep, which they generally prolong till late in the day, they bathe, most frequently in warm water, as in a country where the Winter is very long and severe. From bathing they sit down to meat, every man apart, upon a particular seat, and at a separate table.

Upon the funeral pile they accumulate neither apparel nor perfumes. Into the fire are always thrown the arms of the dead, and sometimes his horse.

This is what in general we have learnt of the original and customs of the whole people of Germany.

Document-Based Questions

1. What did Tacitus think were Germanic weaknesses?

2. How did the Germans choose their rulers and generals?

3. How did the Germans govern themselves?

4. Where did Germans eat? Why might this seem odd to Romans?

5. Describe a typical day for German men.

Discuss with students how words said or stories written about other people can make a person have positive or negative feelings about those people. Then read the title, "Life Among the Germans," and the three introductory paragraphs to students. Continue through the reading, paragraph by paragraph, having students read along silently and then discussing whether the writing of Tacitus was positive or negative. Students should then read and answer the questions.

LEARNING STYLES

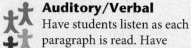

Auditory/Verbal

Have students listen as each paragraph is read. Have listeners give a thumbs-up if they heard a positive comment in the paragraph or a thumbs-down if what they heard was a negative comment. Encourage students to discuss their differences of opinion.

Answers to Document-Based Questions:

1. Germans did not like anything that required work or effort.

2. The Germans chose their rulers on the basis of who their ancestors were and their generals for their bravery.

3. They let chiefs decide minor matters, but in important affairs, all the people were consulted.

4. Germans ate at a particular seat at a table separate from others. This might have seemed unfriendly to Romans.

5. They slept late and took a bath when they got up. They ate separately. They might spend all day and night drinking and quarreling.

Explain to students that during the Middle Ages in Europe it was common practice for a ruler to convert to a new religion and expect all of his or her people to do the same. Promote a discussion of how this contrasts with religious freedom in the United States. (People do not have to be of the same religion of any of their elected officials.) Call attention to the title, "How the Russians Became Christians," and read it out loud. Then read the first paragraph to students. Have students continue reading the paragraphs alternately with a partner. Then have them read and answer the Wrap-Up questions independently.

Answers to Spotlight Story Wrap-Up:

1. They worshipped the old Slavic gods.

2. Grand Princess Olga was the first Christian Russian ruler.

3. He rejected the Muslims because Islam forbids drinking, and drinking was important to the Russians. He felt that the Jewish god had not protected his people.

4. Its beauty overwhelmed them.

5. The Russians could use their own language, not Latin. The head of the Byzantine Church was an emperor, not the pope in Rome. No one would be able to tell him what to do.

How the Russians Became Christians

The early Russian state was a mixture of two cultures. It was both Slavic and Viking. Rurik was the first ruler. He was probably a Viking chief and trader from Scandinavia. The people were mostly Slavs. They worshipped the old Slavic gods. In about 900, some people became Christians. Missionaries from the Byzantine Empire came to Kiev around 950. Olga, the Grand Princess, became a Christian in 957. Her grandson, Vladimir I, made Russia a Christian country.

St. George and the Dragon is the oldest religious icon in Russia.

An old Russian document says that several religions sent groups to Vladimir. He was still a pagan. Each pointed out the advantages of their faith. A group of Muslims came from Bulgaria. Vladimir rejected them because Muslims may not drink wine. "Drink," said Vladimir, "is the joy of the Russians." He also rejected the Jews. He saw that Jews were scattered throughout the world. Vladimir felt that their god had not protected them.

Vladimir still had two choices to consider. There was the Roman Catholic Church, the Christian church in the West. In addition, there was the Byzantine Church, the Christian church in the East.

Vladimir then sent his own men to investigate. They watched people worshipping. From Germany, they wrote, "We beheld no glory there!" German Catholic churches seemed too simple and plain. Another group went to Constantinople. That city was the center of the Byzantine Church. They visited the beautiful cathedral of Hagia Sophia. They were amazed. The church had mosaics of gold. Thousands of candles lit the soaring interior. They wrote, "We knew not whether we were in heaven or on earth. . . . We know only that God dwells there among men."

Two other things about the Byzantine Church appealed to Vladimir. First, the Russians could use their own language in church. He preferred this choice. In contrast, the Western Christian Church insisted that people worship in Latin. Second, the emperor was the head of the Byzantine Church. He had some control over it. The pope in Rome was head of the Western Church. In matters relating to religious faith, the pope could tell rulers what to do. Vladimir kept his independence. He chose the Byzantine Church. He ordered his people to be baptized. It was several hundred years, however, before most Russians accepted this new religion.

Wrap-Up

1. What religion did most Russians follow before 900?

2. Who was the first Christian Russian ruler?

3. Why did Vladimir reject the Muslims? the Jews?

4. How did Vladimir's team feel about Hagia Sophia?

5. For what other reasons did Vladimir join the Byzantine Church?

266 *Unit 2 Regional Civilzations*

Chapter 11 SUMMARY

- Constantine founded the Byzantine capital Constantinople in 330. It was a beautiful Christian city with many churches.

- Justinian, the greatest Byzantine emperor, began to rule in 527. He won back Roman lands from the Germans and made a code of laws. He also built the Church of Hagia Sophia.

- The Byzantine emperor was head of the church. Church leaders ran the government. People disagreed over church rule and the use of icons. In 1054, the Christian church split in two. It became the Eastern Orthodox Church and the Roman Catholic Church.

- The Byzantine Empire declined and civil war broke out. In 1453, Turks captured Constantinople and changed its name to Istanbul.

- Many people in Eastern Europe were Slavs. The Russians were the largest Slavic group. Byzantine missionaries converted many Slavs to Christianity. To be able to write Slavic languages, two monks invented the Cyrillic alphabet.

- The Russian state began about 862 in Kiev, a trading center. Kiev was ruled by a Grand Prince and nobles, the boyars. Byzantine culture influenced early Russia.

- Mongols from Asia destroyed Kiev in 1240. Swedes also invaded Russia, but were held off by Alexander Nevsky. Power then shifted to the princes of Moscow.

- Ivan the Great founded modern Russia. He rebuilt the Kremlin, a walled city of palaces and churches. Ivan the Terrible, his grandson, made Russia larger. He became the "czar."

- The period after the fall of Rome is called the "Dark Ages." Western Europe split into many kingdoms and wars were frequent. Learning also declined.

- The Franks were a Germanic tribe. They lived in what are now France, Germany, and Italy. Clovis became their king in 481, and he made Paris their capital.

- A Frankish king, Charlemagne, united Western Europe in 800. The Pope crowned him "Emperor of the Romans." However, his empire collapsed after his death.

- Vikings attacked various parts of Europe. They also established colonies in Iceland and North America.

- Germanic tribes—Angles, Saxons, Jutes—settled in Britain. Vikings also invaded it. In 1066, William of Normandy invaded and conquered Britain, bringing French influence to England.

Using the Chapter Summary

Have students read the Chapter Summary on page 267 to review the main ideas presented in Chapter 11.

Ask:

- Who was the first Byzantine emperor? (Constantine)

- Over which visual symbol did the Christians in Rome and Constantinople argue? (icons)

- In what year did the Turks take control of the capital of the Byzantine Empire? What did they name it? (1453; Istanbul)

- Which Russian city first became important as a trading center? Which city later became important? (Kiev; Moscow)

- What type of buildings were built within the Kremlin walls? (churches and palaces)

- What activity declined during the Middle Ages in Europe? (learning)

- Which leader made Paris the capital of the Franks? Which leader united all of Western Europe? (Clovis; Charlemagne)

- In addition to Europe, where else did the Vikings make settlements? (Iceland and North America)

- In what year did French influence come to England? (1066)

TEACHER'S RESOURCE

The AGS Globe Teaching Strategies in Social Studies Transparencies may be used with this chapter. The transparencies add an interactive dimension to expand and enhance the *World History* program content.

Chapter 11 Review

Use the Chapter Review to prepare students for tests and to reteach content from the chapter.

Chapter 11 Mastery Test

The Teacher's Resource Library includes two forms of the Chapter 11 Mastery Test. Each test covers the chapter Goals for Learning. An optional third page of additional critical-thinking items is included for each test. The difficulty level of the two forms is equivalent.

Chapter 11 Review Answers

1. Constantine
2. Justinian
3. Methodius
4. Hagia Sophia
5. Rurik
6. Ivan the Great
7. Franks
8. Charlemagne
9. Leo III
10. Vikings
11. C
12. A
13. D
14. B
15. A
16. Constantine called his capital the "new Rome" because he built it as the emperors had built Rome. He had a senate. He organized his army along Roman lines. Also, in the early years of the empire, all the Byzantine emperors were Roman and spoke Latin just as the emperors had in Rome.

Word Bank

Charlemagne
Constantine
Franks
Hagia Sophia
Ivan the Great
Justinian
Leo III
Methodius
Rurik
Vikings

On a sheet of paper, use the words from the Word Bank to complete each sentence correctly.

1. _____, Rome's first Christian emperor, built Constantinople.

2. The Byzantine emperor _____ ordered a code of all Roman laws.

3. Cyril and _____, both monks, invented an alphabet so that the Slavic people could read the Bible.

4. Justinian built a great church called the _____.

5. Russia was founded in 862, which was the year that Prince _____ became ruler.

6. _____ of Russia rebuilt the Kremlin.

7. The _____ were one of the largest of the German tribes.

8. In 800, _____ united all of Western Europe.

9. Pope _____ crowned Charlemagne "Emperor of the Romans."

10. The _____, who were excellent sailors, came from northern Europe.

On a sheet of paper, write the letter of the answer that correctly completes each sentence.

11. The name for the leaders of the Russian church is _____.

   A relic   C patriarchs
   B icons   D boyars

12. A _____ is a holy object from the past that has something to do with God or the saints.

   A relic   C Veche
   B patriarch   D czar

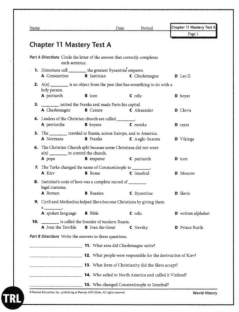

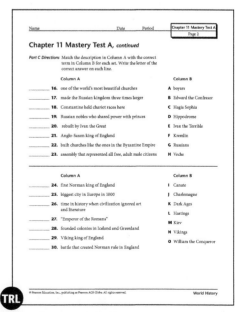

Chapter 11 Mastery Test A, pages 1–3

13. The nobles in Russia who owned land are _____.

A icons   **C** czars
B patriarchs   **D** boyars

14. Small religious pictures of saints and Jesus are _____.

A relics   **C** boyars
B icons   **D** titles

15. _____ is written works that have a lasting influence.

A Literature   **C** Principle
B Ceremony   **D** Icons

On a sheet of paper, write the answer to each question. Use complete sentences.

16. Why did Constantine call Constantinople the "new Rome"?

17. Why was the development of the Cyrillic alphabet important to the Slavic people?

18. Give three reasons why some historians call the Middle Ages in Europe the "Dark Ages."

Critical Thinking On a sheet of paper, write your response to each question. Use complete sentences.

19. Charlemagne's empire fell apart 30 years after his death. How might world history be different if his empire had stayed together until the present time?

20. Imagine that you are a Viking. Describe the ship you travel on. Name and describe the foreign lands you visit. Describe what you like best about your life.

> Wear a watch to the test and use it to pace yourself as you work through the test questions.

17. The Cyrillic alphabet was important to the Slavs because now they could be taught to read and write. Also, Cyril and Methodius translated the Bible and church songs and ceremonies into their written language. This allowed them to read the Bible and understand the words of the songs they sang at their ceremonies. They could also write down their own stories and history.

18. Some historians call the Middle Ages in Europe the "Dark Ages" because all the tribes were at war, schools closed, knowledge of the past was lost, and no governments existed to repair and build roads and public buildings.

Critical Thinking

19. Answers will vary. If Charlemagne's kingdom had stayed together, we would not have two separate countries called France and Germany. These two countries went to war in World War I and World War II.

20. Answers will vary. The Vikings traveled on long ships with oars. The ships could hold 100 sailors using the oars to move through the water. The sails flapped in the wind as they traveled westward to lands across the Atlantic Ocean. The Vikings visited many lands. A Viking warrior might like many things about his life: traveling beneath the light of the moon and stars, meeting new people, weathering wind and rain, taking loot, seeing great cities, and buying goods from many faraway places.

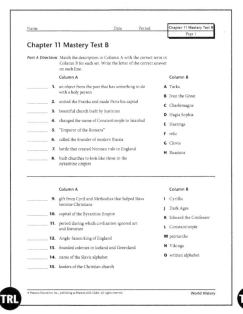

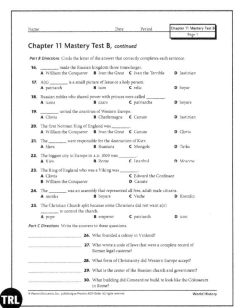

Chapter 11 Mastery Test B, pages 1–3

Introducing the Chapter

Civilizations thrived elsewhere in the
world between 400 and 1596 at a time
when no single power dominated
Europe. This period witnessed the rise
of Islam as a major world religion and
the development of great civilizations in
Africa and the Americas.

Africa and the Spread of Islam

Things changed in Europe between 500 and 1500.
Things also changed in Africa. In Arabia, the prophet
Muhammad founded a new religion called Islam. From
about 1150 to 1200, the Islamic world was the center of world
civilization. In Africa, powerful kingdoms arose during the
"Golden Age." In this chapter, you will travel and trade with the
people of Arabia, Ghana, Mali, and Songhai.

Goals for Learning

◆ To recognize that Islam is one of the great religions of
the world

◆ To identify contributions Arabs have made in science,
mathematics, and literature

◆ To compare three West African civilizations

400 Ghana
is founded

622 Muhammad
flees Mecca

1240 Mali
becomes a great
empire

1596 Songhai
falls

400   **800**   **1200**   **1600**

570 Muhammad
is born

632 Muhammad
dies and Islam
begins to spread

1465 Songhai
becomes a great
empire

Ask:

• Which civilization on the timeline
developed the earliest? (the
civilization in Ghana)

• How old was Muhammad when he
died? (62 years old)

• What African civilization on the
timeline was the last to fall?
(Songhai)

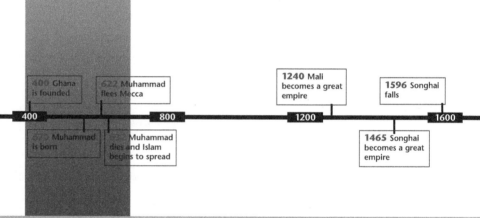

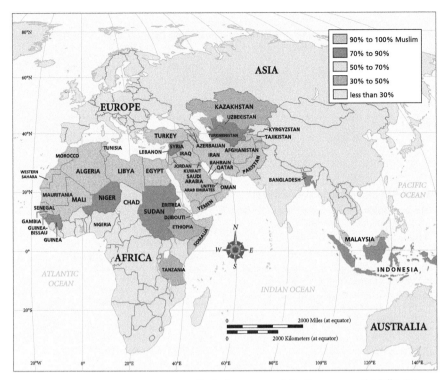

This map shows the percentage of Muslims in Africa and Asia today. About one in every five people on the earth today is of the Islam faith. More than 50 countries have populations with a majority of Muslims. Most Muslims are Sunnis. About 10 to 15 percent are Shi'ites.

Study the map carefully, then answer the following questions:

1. Which part of Africa, north or south, has the most Muslims?

2. What percent of Muslims is there in Chad?

3. What percent of Muslims is there in Tanzania?

4. Name three countries that are 90 to 100 percent Muslim.

5. Name three countries that are between 70 and 90 percent Muslim.

Africa and the Spread of Islam Chapter 12 271

Tell students that maps are used for more than simply locating places. They can show all kinds of information. Ask students what kind of information is shown on the map "Where Muslims Live." (the percentage of Muslims in the populations of some African and Asian countries today) Ask students to think of other kinds of information that maps can show. (Answers will vary. Students may mention weather, roads and highways, or the movement of people or armies.) Then have students read the Map Skills questions and write their answers.

Map Skills Answers

1. North Africa has the most Muslims.

2. Chad has 50–70 percent Muslims.

3. Tanzania has 30–50 percent Muslims.

4. Countries that are 90–100 percent Muslim include Somalia, Egypt, Libya, Senegal, Mali, Mauritania, Morocco, Algeria, Tunisia, Turkey, Iraq, Jordan, Iran, Saudi Arabia, Oman, Qatar, Yemen, United Arab Emirates, Afghanistan, Pakistan, and Malaysia.

5. Countries that are 70–90 percent Muslim include Sudan, Niger, Guinea, Syria, Lebanon, Bangladesh, Turkmenistan, and Indonesia.

Chapter Project

Have student groups research the contributions Arabs have made in science, mathematics, and literature. Ask each group to choose one contribution and write a report describing it. Student reports should explain why the contribution has been important to world civilizations. Students may wish to build a model of their contribution or illustrate their report with pictures showing how the contribution is used.

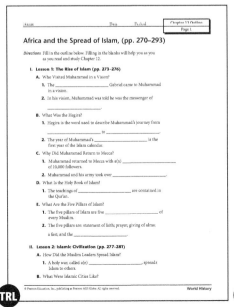

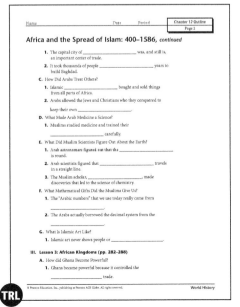

Chapter 12 Outline, pages 1–3

Africa and Islam Chapter 12 271

Visualizing

Introduce the reading skill *visualizing*. Explain that when you look at the illustrations and read the captions in a text, you are finding out more about the subject. Point out that thinking about experiences in your own life may add additional information about the subject.

Have students look at the photograph and read the caption on page 274.

Ask:

- In which direction is Mecca in the photograph? (toward the left)

- How do you know this? (The people are kneeling and facing toward the left.)

- How many times a day must Muslims pray? (five times a day)

- Can you tell from the photograph whether men and women pray together? (The photograph appears to show only men.)

Ask if any students have experiences in their own lives that can contribute information about the subject of the photograph.

Key Vocabulary Words

Have students work in pairs or small groups to create a crossword puzzle using the vocabulary words. Students should use definitions for clues. Suggest to students that they begin with the two words that contain the letter *J*. When puzzles are complete, have groups exchange and solve them.

Reading Strategy:
Visualizing

Visualizing is like creating a movie in your mind. It will help you understand what you are reading. Use the following ways to visualize a text:

- ◆ Think about the order in which things are happening. That may be a clue to what will happen next.

- ◆ Look at the photographs, illustrations, and descriptive words.

- ◆ Think about experiences in your own life that may add to the images.

Key Vocabulary Words

Lesson 1
Fast To give up eating food for a while
Hegira Muhammad's journey from Mecca to Medina; his flight from danger
Vision A visit from God's angel
Idol A statue of a god that people worship
Qur'an The holy book of the Muslims that contains the teachings of Islam
Alms The money or care that one gives to the poor and needy

Hajj The pilgrimage to Mecca that is a religious duty of all Muslims

Lesson 2
Jihad A holy war fought by Muslims to spread Muhammad's teachings
Mosque A Muslim place of worship

Lesson 3
Infidel One who does not believe in the religion of another person

Objectives

◆ To describe how the prophet Muhammad founded and spread Islam

◆ To list the five basic duties each Muslim must accept

Fast

To give up eating food for a while

Vision

A visit from God's angel

Hegira

Muhammad's journey from Mecca to Medina; his flight from danger

In 570, a man named Muhammad was born in Mecca in Arabia. When he was young, he saw nomads fighting and suffering as they moved from one oasis to another.

Who Visited Muhammad in a Vision?

Once a year, Muhammad went to a desert cave to pray and to **fast,** or give up eating food for a while. One year, the angel Gabriel came to him in this cave. Gabriel said, "O, Muhammad, you are the messenger of Allah." Muhammad was to be God's prophet.

In the beginning, Muhammad told only a few people about his **vision,** or visit from God's angel. Soon, he began to preach, but he had little success. The people of Mecca worshipped hundreds of gods. They did not like the idea of only one god— Allah. Life became dangerous for Muhammad and his followers in Mecca, so they had to flee the city.

What Was the Hegira?

In 622, the people in Yathrib invited Muhammad to come and preach. They accepted his teachings and renamed their city Medina to honor Muhammad. (Medina means "City of the Prophet.") Historians call Muhammad's journey from Mecca to Medina the **Hegira.** This word means a journey, or flight, from danger.

Muhammad's teachings started a new religion—Islam. This Arabic word means to give oneself to God. Those who surrender themselves to Allah are Muslims. The Hegira, or Muhammad's flight, is an important event for Muslims. The year of his journey is the first year of the Islamic calendar.

Overview This lesson describes the life of Muhammad and the fundamental beliefs of Islam.

Objectives

■ To describe how the prophet Muhammad founded and spread Islam

■ To list the five basic duties each Muslim must accept

Student Pages pages 273–276

Teacher's Resource Library **TRL**

Workbook Activity 50

Activity 50

Modified Activity 50

Vocabulary

alms	**idol**
fast	**Koran**
Hajj	**vision**
Hegira	

Write the vocabulary words in a column on the board. In a second column, write the definitions in random order. Have students copy the columns onto a sheet of paper and draw lines matching the words to their definitions. Check each student's paper to ensure that he or she has correctly matched the words and definitions.

1 Warm-Up Activity

Review with students the basic beliefs of Judaism and Christianity. Have students make a chart with three columns labeled *Judaism, Christianity,* and *Islam.* Ask students to list some of the basic beliefs of Judaism and Christianity in the first two columns. As they read the lesson, students should fill in the third column about Islam.

Workbook Activity 50   **Activity 50**   *Africa and Islam Chapter 12* **273**

2 Teaching the Lesson

Have students locate Mecca on a world map. Tell them that this is the city where Muhammad, the founder of Islam, was born. Then have them read pages 273–276 to find out about Muhammad's life and the beliefs of Islam.

Ask:

• What did the angel Gabriel tell Muhammad? (that Muhammad was Allah's messenger, or prophet)

• To where did Muhammad and his army return in A.D. 630? (Mecca)

• What is the holy book of the Muslims? (the Qur'an)

• What do Muslims believe about Judaism and Christianity? (They recognize the teachings of these religions because they believe that God spoke to Jewish and Christian prophets as well as to the prophet Muhammad.)

LEARNING STYLES

Auditory/Verbal
Students may benefit from hearing the audio recording of Lesson 1. Play the recording of this lesson and have students follow along in the book. Encourage students to write down main ideas and key words as they listen.

Idol
A statue of a god that people worship

Qur'an
The holy book of the Muslims that contains the teachings of Islam

Why Did Muhammad Return to Mecca?

Muhammad began to gather around him an army of 10,000 followers. In 630, he returned to Mecca with his army and took over the city. He went to the center of the city. In a temple there, called the Kaaba, people of Mecca worshipped statues, or **idols,** of their many gods. Muhammad destroyed these idols and told the people, "There is but one God, and Allah is his name."

What Is the Holy Book of Islam?

Do you remember that the Bible contains the holy teachings of the Jews and Christians? The holy book of the Muslims is the **Qur'an** (also spelled *Koran*). It contains the teachings of Islam. That is, it contains the words God spoke to Muhammad through the angel Gabriel.

The Qur'an says that God spoke to earlier prophets of the Jews and the Christians. Muslims recognize the teachings of Judaism and Christianity. They believe that Jesus was born of the spirit of God and did many wonderful things.

Muslims must pray five times a day, no matter where they are. They kneel and face toward Mecca, their holy city.

The angel Gabriel gave the Qur'an to the prophet Muhammad in the Arabic language. Because of this, Muslims always study their holy book in Arabic. Translations could be wrong or the reader might not understand them. As Islam spread across the world, so did the Arabic language. Muslims still use Arabic for their religious services, even in non-Arab countries.

What Are the Five Pillars of Islam?

The Qur'an lists five duties, or pillars, for each Muslim. The first pillar is the statement of faith. A person becomes a Muslim by announcing, "There is no God but Allah, and Muhammad is His Prophet."

The second pillar is prayer. Muslims must pray five times a day wherever they are—in a field, at home, or in an office. As they begin to pray, they face Mecca, their holy city. Then they go through the motions of washing their heads, hands, and feet. To show their surrender to God, they kneel, bow, and touch their foreheads to the ground.

The third pillar of Islam is the giving of **alms.** That is, Muslims are expected to help the poor and needy by giving money to them or by caring for them.

The fourth pillar includes a fast. During the holy month of Ramadan, healthy adult Muslims stop eating and drinking from sunrise to sunset. At the end of Ramadan, they celebrate with a large meal and then give presents.

The fifth pillar of Islam is the **Hajj,** or the pilgrimage to Mecca. At least once in their lifetime, all Muslims who are able to travel must visit Mecca. It is their religious duty. Visiting Mecca, the birthplace of Muhammad, is often the high point of a devout Muslim's life. All the pilgrims to Mecca wear the same simple clothes. This shows their belief that all people are the same before God, whether rich or poor. The pilgrims follow special rules about what to do and say. Those who make the trip add the title "hajji" to their name. This means "someone who will go to heaven when he or she dies."

Ask:

- In what language did Gabriel give the Qur'an to Muhammad? (Arabic)
- What are the five pillars of Islam? (the statement of faith, prayer, the giving of alms, fasting during Ramadan, and the Hajj, or pilgrimage to Mecca)
- How many times must Muslims pray each day? (five)
- How do Muslims celebrate the end of Ramadan? (with a large meal and presents)

Reading Strategy:
Visualizing

Ask students what type of graphic organizer would be best to help them visualize the Five Pillars. (A spider diagram or word web would be best.) Ask what information should be placed in the organizer? (a few words explaining each pillar) Then, have students create their graphic organizer.

ELL/ESL STRATEGY

Language Objective:
To explain the meaning of the word fast

Some students may not know the meaning of the word *fast.* Explain that when people fast, they do not eat food for a certain period of time. Usually the fasting period is 24 hours or less. In some cases, people may refrain from eating only some kinds of foods, such as meat or sweets. Ask students whether their cultural or religious traditions require fasting. Ask if fasting in their culture includes any special traditions, such as special times for eating and for fasting, or special foods that are eaten to break a fast.

Reinforce and Extend

ONLINE CONNECTION

 The Web site at www.
agsglobewh.com/page276
and its links from
University of Southern
California show small segments of
the Qur'an written in Arabic. The
site has a link to each chapter in the
Qur'an, so students can select a
chapter to read. The Web site also
contains links to explanations of the
various beliefs of Islam. A link to
misconceptions about Islam may be
interesting to students, and can lead
to a class discussion about
misconceptions students may have.

Lesson 1 Review Answers

1. Muhammad was the founder of Islam.
He received a message and the Qur'an
from the angel Gabriel. **2.** Mecca is
the birthplace of Muhammad and is
considered a holy city. **3.** The Qur'an
is the holy book of Islam. It contains the
teachings of Islam. **4.** The angel Gabriel
gave Muhammad the Qur'an written
in Arabic. **5.** Pillars of Islam include a
statement of faith, prayer, giving of alms,
fasting during Ramadan, and making a
hajj to Mecca.

Answers will vary. To see the place where
Muhammad walked, talked, preached,
and had his vision would inspire a
Muslim and deepen his or her faith. All
their lives, Muslims face Mecca when
they pray. When they journey there, they
see the place that they have gazed upon
from afar.

Lesson 1 Review On a sheet of paper, write the answer to each
question. Use complete sentences.

1. Who was Muhammad?

2. Why is Mecca an important city to Muslims?

3. What is the Qur'an?

4. Why is the Qur'an written in Arabic?

5. Identify three of the five pillars of Islam.

What do you think

Why do you think that visiting Mecca is the high point of a
Muslim's life?

Objective

- To identify the two groups of Muslims
- To describe life in Islamic cities
- To explain how Arabs treated conquered peoples of different religions

Muhammad died in 632. His death raised the question of who should succeed him. Different answers to that question led to the creation of two groups of Muslims—the Sunnis and the Shia. The Sunnis believe that Muhammad did not appoint a successor. Therefore, a new religious leader could be chosen by a vote. The new leader did not have to be a relative of Muhammad. Shi'ites believe that Muhammad appointed Ali as his successor. Ali was married to Muhammed's daughter. Shi'ites believe that a new religious leader should be related to Muhammad. Eventually, these two groups developed different laws and religious practices. Today, it's believed that about 90% of Muslims are Sunnis.

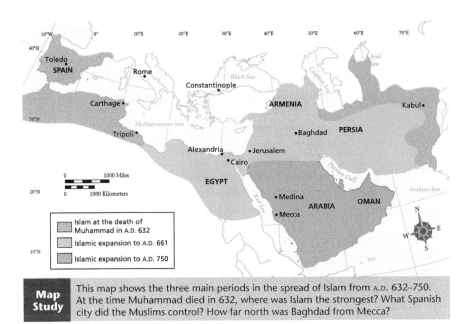

Map Study This map shows the three main periods in the spread of Islam from A.D. 632–750. At the time Muhammad died in 632, where was Islam the strongest? What Spanish city did the Muslims control? How far north was Baghdad from Mecca?

400 – 1596

Africa and the Spread of Islam Chapter 12 **277**

Chapter 12: Lesson 2

Overview This lesson describes the spread of Islam following Muhammad's death in 632. Muslims made significant contributions in science, mathematics, art, and literature.

Objectives

- To identify the two groups of Muslims
- To describe life in Islamic cities
- To explain how Arabs treated conquered peoples of different religions

Student Pages pages 277–281

Teacher's Resource Library TRL

Workbook Activity 51

Activity 51

Modified Activity 51

Vocabulary

jihad   **mosque**

Write the syllables of each vocabulary word on separate index cards. Mix up the cards and display them on the board. Read aloud a definition and invite a volunteer to come up to the board, select the correct cards, and arrange them so they form the word that matches the definition. Repeat until all words have been arranged.

1   Warm-Up Activity

Tell students that Arab artists did not portray animals or people in their works of art. Instead, they created art using Arabic writing. Locate some examples of Arabic writing. Distribute copies to students and have them create a piece of art incorporating Arabic writing. Students should use a different color pen or crayon to outline the part of the art based on writing. Completed art can be displayed for the school to view.

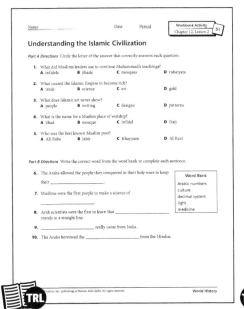

Workbook Activity 51

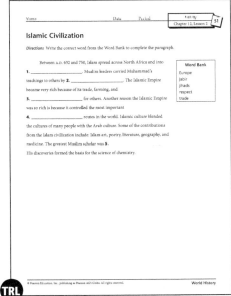

Activity 51

2 Teaching the Lesson

After students read this lesson, have
them select what they consider the
most significant contribution Islamic
civilization has made to the world. Have
students explain and defend their choices.

Have students study the map titled
"Spread of Islam (A.D. 632–750)" on page
277 and identify the three continents
onto which Islam spread during this
period. (Asia, Africa, and Europe) Then
have students answer the questions in the
caption. (Islam was strongest in Arabia in
632. The Muslims controlled Toledo,
Spain. Baghdad was about 1,900 miles, or
2,900 kilometers, north of Mecca.)

Ask:

• How did Muslim leaders spread
Muhammad's teachings after his
death? (by engaging in jihads)

• What was the city of Baghdad like?
(It had many large libraries and
hospitals, and beautiful gardens.)

Reading Strategy:
Visualizing

(Answers will vary. Students may
suggest that the words *many large
public buildings, libraries, hospitals,*
and *gardens* help them to visualize
what Baghdad looked like.)

• How did Arabs treat the people
they conquered? (They respected
their cultures.)

Jihad
A holy war fought
by Muslims to
spread Muhammad's
teachings

Reading Strategy:
Visualizing

What words in this
paragraph help you
visualize what you are
reading?

How Did the Muslim Leaders Spread Islam?

Muslim leaders carried Muhammad's teachings to others by
means of holy wars, or **jihads.** Islam spread across North Africa
and into Europe. West and northward, it spread across the
Persian Empire and the Byzantine Empire to parts of India,
Southeast Asia, and China.

What Were Islamic Cities Like?

In 750, the Abbasid dynasty became rulers of the Arabian
Empire. The rulers built a new capital—Baghdad—on the
banks of the Tigris River. It became, and still is, an important
center of trade. Thousands of people worked for four years to
build Baghdad. It had many large public buildings, including
libraries, hospitals, and gardens.

How Did Arabs Treat Others?

The Islamic Empire became rich because of its trade, farming,
and respect for others. It controlled the most important trade
routes in the world. These routes linked together Africa,
Europe, and Asia. Islamic traders bought and sold things from
all parts of Africa, China, India, and Russia. Arab artisans
made many things to sell to people in other places.

The Muslims improved farming. The lands of Mesopotamia and
the Nile Valley produced more than enough food. Farmers were
able to feed the people who lived in the many large Arab cities.

Arabs respected the cultures of people they conquered in their
holy wars. They allowed Jews and Christians to keep their own
religions. Islamic culture blended the cultures of many people
with the Arab culture.

ELL/ESL STRATEGY

Language Objective:
To identify main ideas

Have ELL students read
the three paragraphs
under "How Did the Arabs Treat
Others?" Have students write down
the main ideas of the paragraphs
as they read. Ask students to name
the three ways the Islamic Empire
became rich. (trade, farming, and
respect for others) Have students
explain how and why each way could
make the Empire rich. Ask students
to suggest another subtitle for this
short section.

What Made Arab Medicine a Science?

The Muslims built hospitals to care for the sick. In these hospitals, doctors studied why people got sick. Muslims became the first people to make a science of medicine. They studied it carefully and they trained their doctors carefully. From their study, they discovered that some sicknesses are able to spread from one person to another.

One Arab doctor named Al-Razi wrote books about two diseases—smallpox and measles. He also wrote a set of 25 books about medicine. Students in both the East and the West used these until the 1400s. Al-Razi may have been the first doctor to sew up cuts and to put casts on broken arms and legs.

What Did Muslim Scientists Figure Out About the Earth?

Arab astronomers figured out that the earth is round. They correctly guessed that it was about 25,000 miles around. An Arab geographer was the first to put a map on a ball to show the right shape of the earth.

Other Arab scientists studied light and were the first to learn that it travels in a straight line. They also learned that the curving of a lens makes things appear larger. The greatest Muslim scholar was an Arab named Jabir. His discoveries led to the science of chemistry. Chemists study the makeup of substances. He may have been the first person to carefully record the results of an experiment. Other Arab scientists invented much of the equipment we use today in chemistry.

Reading Strategy:
Visualizing

How could this paragraph be written differently to create a stronger picture in your mind?

Writing About History

Some amazing discoveries are described here. Research one of them--how light travels, why a curved lens makes things appear larger, different kinds of chemistry equipment--or something else that is mentioned in this section--and draw it in your notebook. Be sure to label parts of the item you are drawing.

Africa and the Spread of Islam   Chapter 12   **279**

- What major discovery did Muslim doctors make about some diseases? (that they are contagious)
- What is Al-Razi known for? (He wrote 25 books about medicine, and may have developed the practices of sewing up cuts and putting casts on broken bones.)

Reading Strategy:
Visualizing

(Answers will vary. Students may suggest that visualization would be enhanced if the last sentence about Al-Razi putting casts on broken limbs and sewing up cuts were placed first in the paragraph. Also, more examples of his work would help to create a stronger picture of Al-Razi as a doctor.)

- What did Arab geographers figure out about the earth? (that it is round)
- Name the Arab scientist whose discoveries led to chemistry. (Jabir)

BACKGROUND INFORMATION

Al-Razi wrote many books on medicine, including a comprehensive medical encyclopedia called *Al-Hawi*. The encyclopedia included Al-Razi's commentary on all the available medical knowledge from the Greeks and Arabs. Al-Razi was the first person to use certain foods to cure disease and to make the connection between mental and physical health. He also was the first person to test the effects of new medicines on animals and to use opium as an anesthetic during surgery.

Writing About History

Ask students to use Internet or library resources to find out more about the discoveries of Al-Razi, Jabir, or other early Arab scientists, astronomers, or doctors. The students should draw a simple illustration in their notebooks of an early map, light passing through a curved lens, an early example of equipment used in chemistry, or some other experiment or device. Have them label parts of their drawing. Then discuss why these discoveries are so amazing, given the tools and resources the people had.

Africa and Islam   Chapter 12   **279**

Ask:

- What mathematical tool did the Arabs get from the Hindus? (the decimal system)

- What did Muslim mathematicians borrow from India? from the Hindus? (the nine Arabic numbers we use today; the decimal system based on the number 10)

 3 Reinforce and Extend

Mosque
A Muslim place of worship

What Mathematical Gifts Did the Muslims Give Us?

In mathematics, Muslim scholars expanded on what they learned from other people. From India, they borrowed the nine numbers that we still use today. We call these "Arabic numbers" even though they came from India.

From the Hindus, the Arabs borrowed the decimal system. This is a number system based on the number 10. It includes the idea of zero. This was a good system because it was much easier to use than the Babylonian system based on 60.

What Is Islamic Art Like?

Islamic art never shows people or animals. Artists decorate **mosques,** or Muslim places of worship, with beautiful designs and writing. Islamic art also appears on their world-famous rugs, on leather goods, and on swords.

Many Arab artists wrote poems about the beauty of nature and love. The best known Muslim poet was Omar Khayyam, who wrote *The Rubaiyat.* Westerners know another collection of Arab stories called the *Arabian Nights.* In it are the stories "Ali Baba and the Forty Thieves" and "Aladdin and His Lamp."

Muslim scholars studied medicine, the heavens, chemistry, and mathematics.

---

280   *Unit 2   Regional Civilzations*

Lesson 2 Review On a sheet of paper, use the words from the Word Bank to complete each sentence correctly.

Word Bank

Al-Razi

Baghdad

Jabir

jihads

Khayyam

1. The Arabs spread their religion through a series of _____, or holy wars.

2. The Abbasid dynasty ruled the Islamic Empire in A.D. 750 and built the city of _____.

3. _____ may have been the first doctor to put casts on broken arms and legs.

4. The greatest Arab scholar was _____, whose work led to the science of chemistry.

5. Omar _____ wrote the poem *The Rubaiyat,* which is about love and nature.

What do you think is the best gift the Arab people of the Middle Ages gave the world? Explain your answer.

Communication in History

Borrowed Words

Have you eaten *sherbet?* Are you studying *algebra?* We borrowed these words from the Arabic language. We got some from the Muslims who lived in Spain. Others were

the names of products from the Middle East—*sugar, alcohol,* and *syrup.* Traders also brought the *lime, orange,* and *artichoke* to Europe. *Mohair* and *cotton* are Arabic, too.

Muslim scholars studied chemistry and astronomy. The words *alkali* and *zenith* resulted from their knowledge. They gave us the names for stars, such as *Aldebaran.* From Arab mathematicians came *tariff* and *zero.* We use Arab words that describe how people live or the world around us. People sit on a *sofa.* A *sultan* and a *sheik* are kinds of rulers. The commander of a fleet is an *admiral.* English is indeed a richer language because of these Arabic words.

Lesson 2 Review Answers

1. jihads　2. Baghdad　3. Al-Razi　4. Jabir　5. Khayyam

Answers will vary. The Arab people of the Middle Ages have given us many wonderful gifts. In science, they gave us books on medicine, studies on light and lenses, chemistry, and the globe. In mathematics, they gave us Arabic numbers and zero and the decimal system we use today. In literature, they gave us beautiful poems about nature and love and wonderful adventure stories from the *Arabian Nights*. In art, they gave us beautiful designs that we see in their mosques, rugs, leather goods, and swords.

Communication in History

Write the word *etymology* on the board. Inform students that an etymology tells you the history of a word. Have students read the Communication in History feature "Borrowed Words" on page 281. Then, have them select two or three of the words mentioned in the feature and look them up in a dictionary. Help them find where the word's etymology is located in the entry.

Chapter 12: Lesson 3

Overview This lesson describes three powerful empires that developed in West Africa between A.D. 1000 and 1600—Ghana, Mali, and Songhai.

Objectives

- To compare the civilizations of Ghana, Mali, and Songhai
- To identify important leaders in these civilizations

Student Pages pages 282–288

Teacher's Resource Library

Workbook Activity 52

Activity 52

Modified Activity 52

Vocabulary

infidel

Discuss the word and its definition. Then review the difference between a noun (a person, place, or thing) and a verb (an action). Ask students whether *infidel* is a noun or a verb. (noun)

◆1 Warm-Up Activity

Have students examine a globe to find the Sudan, the Senegal River, Ghana, and the region of North Africa. Explain that trade was a vital activity because each civilization rarely had everything it needed to live. Guide a discussion about what commodities students might need if they had lived in Ghana during A.D. 800. Ask them where and how they would get these items. (Students may say that they need food and water, wool or cotton to make clothing, and animals such as camels for transportation.)

Objectives

◆ To compare the civilizations of Ghana, Mali, and Songhai
◆ To identify important leaders in these civilizations

The crusaders first set out to capture the Holy Land in 1095. About that time, a series of empires developed in West Africa. Arab geographers called this grassland area the Sudan. It is very different from the dry Sahara to the north and the wet tropical rain forest to the south.

How Did Ghana Become Powerful?

Ghana was founded about 400. Within 400 years, it had become an important center of trade. In fact, Ghana controlled all the important trade routes from the Sudan to North Africa.

Early stories about Ghana call it "the land of gold." Ghana never owned any gold fields, but it controlled the trade in gold. With gold came power.

The gold came from a region near the Senegal River. People there had much gold, but no salt, and they needed salt to live. Arab traders on camel caravans carried their goods to the people near the Senegal River in the south. Then they traded salt for gold. Next, the caravan turned north again to trade with their gold. On both trips, they traveled through Kumbi, the largest city in Ghana. The government of Ghana taxed the caravan each way. Both the Arabs from the north and the forest people from the south paid tribute to the king of Ghana.

How Did Ghana's Army Create Peace?

By 1070, Ghana was one of the most powerful empires in the world. Taxes from trade filled the king's treasury. With all this money, he could keep as many as 200,000 warriors. (At this same time, William the Conqueror could raise an army of only 15,000 soldiers to invade England.)

Ghana's large army gave it great power. With this power, Ghana created peace in West Africa and made trade safe. Ghana could easily have conquered its weaker neighbors, but it did not. Instead, it took tribute from these neighbors.

---

282 *Unit 2 Regional Civilzations*

Workbook Activity 52

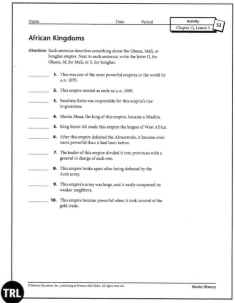

Activity 52

What Made Ghana Fall?

The kings of Ghana invited Muslim teachers to begin schools in Kumbi and other cities. The rulers of Ghana did not become Muslims, but many of the people of Ghana did. This helped improve the connection between the two areas and brought money to the empire.

In 1076, Arabs from North Africa, called Almoravids, invaded Ghana. They began a holy war against the **infidels,** or non-Muslims, of Ghana. (An infidel does not believe in the religion of another person.) They destroyed Kumbi. During this time, people stopped paying tribute to Ghana. In time, Ghana defeated the Almoravids. However, the country was never again as powerful as it had once been.

How Did Mali Become Powerful?

Mali existed as early as 1000. When Ghana lost its power, Mali was able to form a new empire. It, too, took control of the trade routes.

Timbuktu was a great center of learning and trade in West Africa.

The man most responsible for Mali's rise to greatness was Sundiata Keita. He took control of the gold fields. His armies swept across Africa, and his empire included large areas of the Sahara. Keita divided his kingdom into provinces. Then he put one general in charge of each province. Each general was responsible for keeping law and order in his province.

ELL/ESL Strategy

Language Objective:
To describe the city of Timbuktu from a picture
Pair an English language student with a student proficient in English. Have student pairs examine the picture of Timbuktu on page 283. Have a few hand lenses available so students can see the tiny details in the picure.

Each ELL student should describe the city to his or her partner and suggest which parts of the picture are clues that the city was a great center of learning and trade. (Students may notice several large buildings that are too large to be dwellings. They may suggest that these buildings are schools or other public buildings.)

Use this list to help students pronounce difficult words in this lesson.

Almoravids	(al mȯr´ ə vidz)
Mansa Musa	(män´ sä mü sä´)
Songhai	(song gī´)
Sundiata Keita	(sùn jät´ ä kē āt´ ə)
Sonni Ali	(sȯn ē´ ä lē´)

 2 Teaching the Lesson

Ask students to think of the things an empire would need to have to become powerful. (Answers will vary; students may mention a strong leader, a large army, or wealth.) Then have them read pages 282–287 to find out how the empires of Ghana, Mali, and Songhai became powerful.

Ask:

• How did the government of Ghana make money from the gold and salt trade? (by taxing caravans that passed through)

• What was the result of the war between the Almoravids and Ghana? (Ghana defeated the Almoravids, but lost much of its power.)

• Which empire rose after Ghana lost its power? (Mali)

LEARNING STYLES

 Body/Kinesthetic
Divide the class into four groups. Group 1 will be people from the Senegal River region who have gold, Group 2 will be people from the north who have salt, Group 3 are Arab traders, and Group 4 are representatives of Ghana. Place Group 1 at one end of the room, Group 2 at the opposite end, and Group 4 in the middle. Group 3 will transport gold and salt back and forth between Groups 1 and 2. Each time they pass through Ghana, Group 3 must pay a tax to Group 4. Use this simulation to show students how Ghana was able to gain wealth by controlling trade.

- Who was the most powerful leader of the Mali Empire? (Mansa Musa)

- What made Mali's king Mansa Musa different from Ghana's rulers? (He became a Muslim.)

- What city in Mali became a great center of Islamic learning? (Timbuktu)

- What three things was Mansa Musa noted for? (building a university, being a Muslim, and visiting the holy city of Mecca)

Tell students that historians often refer to periods in ancient history according to the most important resource of the time, such as the Stone Age and the Bronze Age. Tools were often made from that resource. Have students speculate on what historians living 1,000 years from now will name our time. (Answers will vary; students may say "The Computer Age" or "The Transportation Age.") Have students read the History in Your Life feature, titled "African Metalworking," on page 284 to find out about minerals used in African art and crafts.

Which Famous Mali King Became a Muslim?

Mansa Musa was king of Mali when it was most powerful. Unlike the rulers of Ghana, Mansa Musa became a Muslim. He brought many Arab scholars to his capital. He set up a great center of Islamic learning in Timbuktu. Scholars came from all over the world to study there.

Mansa Musa ran his kingdom well. Arab visitors wrote about the peace and safety of Mali. The visitors saw how the people of Mali obeyed the Five Pillars of Islam. In fact, one writer said that Mali parents wanted their children to learn the Qur'an by heart. If the children did not do this, they were put in chains until they memorized the holy book.

What Was Mansa Musa's Pilgrimage?

Mansa Musa was famous for building a university, being a Muslim, and visiting the holy city of Mecca. Some historians think that 60,000 people made the pilgrimage with Mansa Musa. (About 12,000 of them were his servants.) They loaded 80 camels with bags of gold dust to pay for the 3,000-mile trip from Mali to Mecca. Imagine all the food and supplies 60,000 people would need!

African Metalworking

Learning to work with iron was a big step forward in technology. Iron made stronger farming tools and weapons. Ironworking in Africa probably began at Meroë, in the kingdom of Kush along the Nile. Artisans in Kush began to work with iron about 500 B.C. Iron ore came from local mines. Forests supplied wood for hot fires. These craftspeople worked with gold, too.

Another tribe, the Nok, lived in West Africa. They worked with iron, gold, and tin. The Bantu people learned these skills. Then the Bantu moved south. They carried this knowledge to others.

Africa was rich in many metals, such as copper. This beautiful metal was used for jewelry and pots. People combined copper with other metals to make bronze. The kingdom of Benin was famous for its bronze sculptures. Artists made them by pouring melted bronze into molds.

The pilgrimage began in 1324 and took more than a year. Everywhere Mansa Musa went he gave away gold to rulers and government officials. When he reached Mecca, Mansa Musa gave that city gold, too.

Mansa Musa's gifts of gold made news even in Europe. In 1375, someone in Spain drew a map that shows Mansa Musa. He holds a large gold ball in his hand. The artist wrote on the map. The writing says that Mansa Musa has so much gold that "he is the richest and most noble king of all the land."

After Mansa Musa died, civil war broke out in Mali. Within 150 years, the great empire fell. Then the last great empire of this golden age arose—Songhai.

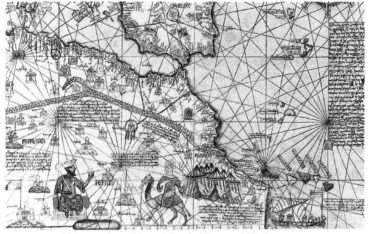

This map shows Mansa Musa holding a gold ball.

• What advantage did Morocco's army have over Songhai? (It had guns.)

LEARNING STYLES

Logical/Mathematical
Point out to students that 12,000 of the 60,000 people who made the pilgrimage with Mansa Musa were servants. Ask students to calculate the percentage of pilgrims who were servants. (To calculate the percentage, students should divide 12,000 by 60,000; the correct answer is 0.20, or 20 percent.)

ELL/ESL STRATEGY

Language Objective:
To use vocabulary to answer questions

Have students read the material on page 285. Discuss the meaning of the word *pilgrimage* with ELL students. Then write these questions on the board and have students write the answers:

• How many people made the pilgrimage with Mansa Musa? (about 60,000)

• What did Mansa Musa and the other pilgrims use to pay for their trip from Mali to Mecca? (gold dust)

• How long did the pilgrimage take? (more than a year)

• Why did the Spanish artist draw Mansa Musa holding a large gold ball? (because Mansa Musa had much gold, and gave it away everywhere he went)

Ask:

- What was the last of the great West African empires? (Songhai)
- When did the Songhai Empire become powerful? (in the 1400s)

Ask students to study the map titled "Early Kingdoms of Africa" on page 286.

Ask:

- Which empire was located the farthest east? (Songhai)
- Which two empires were nearest to the Atlantic Ocean? (Mali and Ghana)

Have students answer the questions in the caption. (Mali was largest. Cities that were part of the three empires include Kumbi, Gao, and Timbuktu.)

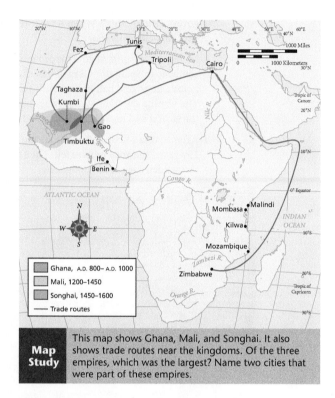

Map Study

This map shows Ghana, Mali, and Songhai. It also shows trade routes near the kingdoms. Of the three empires, which was the largest? Name two cities that were part of these empires.

How Did Songhai Become Powerful?

The third and last of the great empires of West Africa was Songhai. Songhai already existed in the 800s, but it did not become powerful until the 1400s. Like Ghana and Mali before it, Songhai grew powerful by controlling the gold and salt trade.

Songhai's greatest king was Sonni Ali. From 1464 until 1492, he never lost a battle. King Sonni Ali made Songhai the largest empire that West Africa ever had. His army captured the university city of Timbuktu. Ali's empire stretched from the Atlantic Ocean eastward nearly 1,800 miles.

Ali divided Songhai into provinces. Then he chose officials to carry out the laws. He also made sure that all weights and measures were the same in his empire.

Other countries wanted Songhai's riches and attacked it. At first, Songhai's army easily defeated its neighbors. Then, in 1590, the Arab ruler of Morocco in North Africa sent an army to conquer Songhai. The Arab army had only 2,000 soldiers, but it had a new, powerful weapon—the gun. In 1596, Songhai fell. The empire broke apart, and West Africa was never united again.

Biography

Sonni Ali: died 1492

King Sonni Ali made Songhai a powerful empire. He took lands from the old Mali empire. It was weak when he became king in 1464. First, he captured Timbuktu in 1468. It was a center of Muslim learning. Later, he captured Jenne, a wealthy trade center. Sonni Ali won many victories partly because he used cavalry well.

Sonni Ali was a harsh ruler, however. He had scholars in Timbuktu killed. He executed many people, even close friends. His death in 1492 was a mystery. Some stories said he drowned. Others said he was murdered.

Ask:

- Who was Songhai's greatest king? (Sonni Ali)

- Who conquered Songhai? (an army from Morocco)

Biography

King Sonni Ali did not come to Timbuktu as an uninvited guest. In fact, Muslim leaders in the city asked Sonni Ali to come to help them get rid of a desert tribe that had invaded the city. Sonni Ali helped them remove the tribe, but he did not stop there. He also looted the city and murdered many of its inhabitants. Invite students to discuss what they have learned about Sonni Ali. Have them vote on whether it was a good idea for Muslim leaders to invite him to Timbuktu.

3 Reinforce and Extend

AT HOME

Have students ask their families to pretend with them that they have just heard news that Sonni Ali is planning to come to their town or city. Have them discuss what they will do, whether they will stay at home or leave, and how they will act toward the king if they should meet him. They should also discuss what kind of a ruler they think he will be based on his reputation. Invite students to share their families' reactions to the news.

WORLD CULTURES

African cultures today are known for their art. Much of this art is made with a specific function in mind. Hair ornaments, face masks, bowls, knives, and textiles may be decorated with geometric designs or with figures of animals or humans. Much of the art is abstract. Figures of people may be elongated or stretched to make them look less realistic. In fact, several 20th-century artists, such as Picasso, Matisse, Van Gogh, and Modigliani, were aware of African art and were influenced by it.

Interpersonal/ Group Learning
Have student pairs work together to compare Mansa Musa and Sonni Ali. They should compare the men's effectiveness as rulers and how they treated their subjects. Students should write a report telling which ruler they would rather live under and why. Encourage students to visit the library to do research to supplement what they have learned in this lesson. Have each pair of students present a report to the class in which they share their findings.

Lesson 3 Review Answers

1. A **2.** D **3.** D **4.** B **5.** B

Answers will vary. Traders carry their goods along a trade route and pay taxes or tolls to the cities along the route. If a country controls the trade route, the government makes a lot of money. Also, the artisans in the cities along the trade route have a ready market among the traders. So this brings in additional money.

Chapter Project Follow-up

Student reports about Arab contributions should describe the contribution and explain why it was important to world civilizations. Assess the accuracy of the information in the report. If students have made a model of their contribution, display the models or have students give presentations to the class. Set up an area in your school in which student projects are displayed.

Lesson 3 Review On a sheet of paper, write the letter of the answer that correctly completes each sentence.

1. The first empire to develop in West Africa was _____.

   A Ghana   **C** Songhai
   B Mali   **D** Timbuktu

2. King Mansa Musa of Mali founded a university at _____.

   A Kumbi   **C** Paris
   B Songhai   **D** Timbuktu

3. _____ controlled trade in West Africa.

   A Ghana   **C** Songhai
   B Mali   **D** all of the above

4. Traders from the north brought _____ to trade for gold.

   A horses   **C** guns
   B salt   **D** fish

5. The Arab ruler of Morocco defeated the last great empire of West Africa because he had _____.

   A camels   **C** gold
   B guns   **D** a large army

What do you think?

Why does control of a trade route lead to power?

The Qur'an

The Qur'an (also spelled Koran) is the holy book of Islam. It contains 114 chapters, which are divided into verses. Muslims believe that the Qur'an is the word of God as given to Muhammad. The following excerpt tells Muslims how to be righteous and faithful.

It is not righteousness
That ye turn your faces
Towards East or West;
But it is righteousness–
To believe in Allah
And the Last Day,
And the Angels,
And the Book,
And the Messengers;
To spend of your substance,
Out of love for Him,
For your kin,
For orphans,
For the needy,
For the wayfarer,
For those who ask,
And for the ransom of slaves;
To be steadfast in prayer,
And practice regular charity,
To fulfil the contracts
Which ye have made;
And to be firm and patient,
In pain (or suffering)
And adversity,
And throughout
All periods of panic.
Such are the people
Of truth, the God-fearing.
2:177

Document-Based Questions

1. What is righteousness?

2. What should believers do for the needy?

3. What other behavior should a righteous person have?

4. To which Pillars of Islam does this excerpt refer?

5. What should Muslims do when they are suffering?

Explain to students that Muslims believe that the Qur'an was handed down to Muhammad over a period of 23 years. According to Islamic belief, Allah revealed the Qur'an to Muhammad, who recited it to his companions. They memorized many of the verses Muhammad recited, and wrote down others on stones, bark, or whatever else was available.

Tell students that the Qur'an contains 114 chapters arranged in order by length from longest to shortest. It was thought that this arrangement makes oral memorization easier. Each chapter has several verses. There are more than 6,200 verses in the entire Qur'an.

Point out the semicolons between phrases in the passage from the Document-Based Reading. Tell students that each idea is separated from the next by the semicolons. Read aloud the entire passage so students can hear the rhythm of the words. Then have student volunteers read each segment between semicolons. Discuss the meaning of each segment. Then have students answer the questions.

Answers to Document-Based Questions:

1. Righteousness is believing in Allah and all the commandments in the Qur'an.

2. Believers should give money to the needy.

3. A righteous person should pray earnestly, practice regular charity, fulfill contracts that he or she has made, and be firm and patient in pain or suffering.

4. It refers to the pillar of giving alms to the poor.

5. They should be firm and patient.

Have students read the Spotlight Story, "Farming in Africa and Oceania." If they encounter any unfamiliar words in the Spotlight Story, have them make lists of the words. Using a dictionary, students should write a definition for each unfamiliar word. Then have students draw a vertical line down the center of a piece of paper. They should title the left-hand column "Farming in Africa" and the right-hand column "Farming in the Pacific Islands." Have students reread the story and list key facts, including crops, animals, and tools, in each column. Finally, have students answer the questions.

Answers to Spotlight Story Wrap-Up:

1. Both places have warm climates and palm trees; people grow yams and taro.

2. They planted fields of grain.

3. The development of iron tools made farming easier.

4. The Polynesians settled Hawaii between A.D. 300 and 500; they arrived in New Zealand by about A.D. 1000.

5. They grew yams, taro, sweet potatoes, flax, coconut palms, bananas, and breadfruit.

IN THE COMMUNITY

After reading the Spotlight Story, students should recognize that their diets are made up of foods from around the world. Ask students to categorize the restaurants in their community according to the national or ethnic origin of the food. Possible categories include Mexican, Greek, Italian, Chinese, and so on. Have students share their results with the class.

Spotlight Story — Farming in Africa and Oceania

Most early societies depended on farming. People ate whatever they could grow. They also fished or hunted. Bringing food from other places was not practical. In Africa south of the Sahara, the economy has always centered on farming. That is also true of the islands in the Pacific Ocean. Both those places have warm climates. They grow some of the same foods. The history of their economies is quite different, though.

Africa is a huge continent. Farming varies greatly from place to place. In the rain forests, people grow small gardens. For thousands of years, yams have been a favorite crop. So has palm oil. Some of its oils are used in cooking. Others make soaps and other products. People also grow several kinds of nuts, including peanuts. Plantains are another popular food.

The grasslands areas of Africa are drier. People here planted fields of grain. These grains can be pounded or ground into flour. Flour is used in porridges, puddings, and flat breads. About 2,000 years ago, people began using iron tools. Iron hoes and knives made farming easier. Farming villages became more stable.

Farming in the Pacific Islands has a different history. In Africa, people have farmed for about 7,000 years. The Pacific Islands were settled only recently. Polynesians reached the islands of Hawaii between about A.D. 300 and 500. By about A.D. 1000, they had settled New Zealand. The first settlers brought yams, taro, and sweet potatoes. They also brought pigs, dogs, and chickens. They grew flax to make cloth. In some places, they built terraces or ponds to grow taro. People eat the starchy root of this plant. Islanders also planted coconut palms, bananas, and breadfruit trees. These trees grew around fields and gardens.

People used the coconut palm tree in many ways. They ate its meat and drank the liquid inside. The hard shell became a cup or bowl. Palm leaves could be woven into baskets. They were also used for roofs.

Farming is still important in Africa and the Pacific. Some crops have changed, though. Trade brought new foods to Africa. From the Americas came sweet potatoes, chili peppers, and tomatoes. From Asia came taro. Europeans also took new crops to the Pacific Islands when they settled there.

Wrap-Up

1. How is farming in Africa and in the Pacific Islands similar?

2. What kinds of crops did people plant in Africa's grasslands?

3. What major change in technology influenced farming in Africa?

4. Who first settled Hawaii and New Zealand? About when did they arrive?

5. What crops were grown in the Pacific Islands?

Chapter 12 SUMMARY

- Muhammad was born in Arabia in 570. He preached a new religion, Islam, with one god, Allah. Its followers are called Muslims.

- In 622, Muhammad and his followers fled from Mecca to Medina. This event is called the Hegira.

- Muhammad died in 632. After his death, two branches of Islam developed—the Sunnis and the Shi'ites. They have different laws and religious practices.

- The holy book of Islam is the Qur'an, written in the Arabic language. Muslims regard Muhammad as God's prophet. They also recognize Jewish and Christian prophets.

- Islam has five duties, or pillars. They must state their faith, pray five times a day, give alms, and fast. If possible, they make a pilgrimage, or Hajj, to Mecca.

- Holy wars, or jihads, helped Islam grow. It spread across North Africa, into Europe, and to parts of Asia.

- The Abbasid dynasty began in 750. Its capital was Baghdad. The Islamic Empire excelled in trade and farming. It let Jews and Christians keep their customs.

- Muslims made important advances in medicine; science, especially chemistry; and mathematics. Islamic art shows beautiful patterns, not people or animals.

- Ghana became rich by taxing the trade in gold and salt. By 1070, Ghana had built a powerful army to keep peace. Muslim Arabs from North Africa invaded it in 1076.

- Mali followed Ghana as the most powerful empire. Its king Sundiata Keita made Mali great. Another king, Mansa Musa, became a Muslim. He made Timbuktu a center for Islamic scholars.

- The greatest king of Songhai was Sonni Ali. His empire fell to an Arab army armed with guns in 1596.

400 – 1596

Africa and the Spread of Islam *Chapter 12* **291**

TEACHER'S RESOURCE

The AGS Globe Teaching Strategies in Social Studies Transparencies may be used with this chapter. The transparencies add an interactive dimension to expand and enhance the *World History* program content.

Using the Chapter Summary

Have students read the Chapter Summary on page 291 to review the main ideas presented in Chapter 12.

Ask:

- What is the name of the religion founded by Muhammad, and what are its followers called? (Islam; Muslims)

- What is the Hegira? (the event that occurred when Muhammad and his followers fled from Mecca to Medina)

- What happened to Islam after Muhammad died? (Two branches of Islam, Shi'ite and Sunni, developed with different laws and religious practices.)

- Who do Muslims believe is Allah's prophet? Do Muslims recognize Jewish and Christian prophets also? (Muhammad is Allah's prophet; Muslims also recognize Jewish and Christian prophets.)

- What are the Five Pillars of Islam? (statement of faith, praying five times a day, giving alms, fasting, and making a pilgrimage to Mecca if possible)

- How did Islam spread across North Africa, Europe, and parts of Asia? (through a series of holy wars, or jihads)

- What was the Abbasid dynasty? (an Islamic empire that excelled in trade and farming; its capital was Baghdad)

- In what fields were some important Muslim advances made? (medicine, chemistry and other sciences, mathematics, art)

- How did Ghana become rich and powerful? (The government taxed the trade in gold and salt.)

- Who were two powerful Mali kings and what were they noted for? (Sundiata Keita made Mali a great empire. Mansa Musa became a Muslim and made Timbuktu a center for Islamic scholars.)

- Who was Songhai's greatest king? When did his empire fall? (Sonni Ali's empire fell to an Arab army with guns in 1596.)

Chapter 12 Review

Use the Chapter Review to prepare students for tests and to reteach content from the chapter.

Chapter 12 Mastery Test

The Teacher's Resource Library includes two forms of the Chapter 12 Mastery Test. Each test addresses the chapter Goals for Learning. An optional third page of additional critical-thinking items is included for each test. The difficulty level of the two forms is equivalent.

Chapter 12 Review Answers

1. Muhammad
2. Islam
3. Allah
4. Medina
5. Abbasid
6. Al-Razi
7. Jabir
8. Ghana
9. Mansa Musa
10. Songhai
11. B
12. C
13. A
14. D
15. C
16. Muslims must announce their belief in Allah, pray five times a day, give alms, fast during the holy month of Ramadan, and make a pilgrimage to Mecca.

Chapter 12   R E V I E W

Word Bank

Abbasid
Allah
Al-Razi
Ghana
Islam
Jabir
Mansa Musa
Medina
Muhammad
Songhai

On a sheet of paper, use the words from the Word Bank to complete each sentence correctly.

1. The prophet _____ was born in 570.
2. He started a religion known as _____.
3. The Muslims call God _____.
4. People in the city of Yathrib renamed their city _____ in 622.
5. In 750, the _____ dynasty ruled the Arabian Empire.
6. The Arab doctor _____ wrote many books about medicine.
7. The greatest Arab scholar was _____.
8. People called _____ "the land of gold."
9. The ruler _____ founded a university in Mali.
10. People from Morocco attacked the empire of _____ with guns.

On a sheet of paper, write the letter of the answer that correctly completes each sentence.

11. Islam was spread through holy wars, or _____.

    A mosques   **C** causeways
    B jihads   **D** infidels

12. Muslims accept five duties, or _____, of their religion.

    A languages   **C** pillars
    B visions   **D** caravans

13. The holy book of the Muslims is the _____.

    A Qur'an   **C** *Rubaiyat*
    B *Arabian Nights*   **D** *Song of Roland*

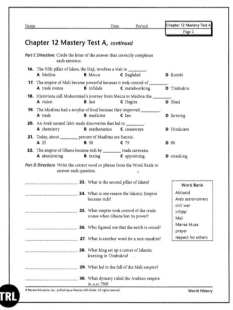

Chapter 12 Mastery Test A, pages 1–3

14. _____ grew powerful because of trade.

A Ghana   **C** Songhai
B Mali   **D** all of the above

15. Mansa Musa's pilgrimage took him from Mali to _____.

A Timbuktu   **C** Mecca
B South Africa   **D** all of the above

On a sheet of paper, write the answer to each question. Use complete sentences.

16. What are the five basic duties each Muslim must accept?

17. What was the key to power for the three empires of West Africa?

18. Why did the religion of Islam break into two groups, the Sunnis and the Shi'ites?

Critical Thinking On a sheet of paper, write your response to each question. Use complete sentences.

19. Which one of the following people would you like to have met and why? Sundiata Keita, Mansa Musa, Sonni Ali

20. In this chapter, you learned about many wonderful cities— Mecca, Medina, Baghdad, Kumbi, Timbuktu. Which one of these cities would you like to have visited and why?

When studying for a test, use the titles and subtitles in the chapter to help you recall information.

400 – 1586

Africa and the Spread of Islam   Chapter 12   293

---

17. The key to power for the three empires of West Africa was control of the trade routes.

18. After Muhammad died, questions arose about who should succeed him. The Muslims split into two groups: the Sunnis, who believed that a new religious leader could be chosen by vote since Muhammad had not appointed a successor; and the Shi'ites, who believed that a successor had been named by Muhammad.

Critical Thinking

19. Answers will vary. All these people might be interesting to meet for different reasons: Sundiata Keita extended the boundaries of Mali and was very powerful; Mansa Musa built a university, and when he went on a pilgrimage to Mecca, he took 60,000 people with him; Sonni Ali of Songhai never lost a battle but was a harsh ruler.

20. Answers will vary. All these places are interesting, depending on the background and interests of the students. Mecca is the home of Muhammad and the center of the Muslim religion. Medina is the place that welcomed Muhammad on his Hegira. Baghdad was a beautiful city with libraries, hospitals, and gardens. Kumbi was the capital of Ghana and an important trade center. Timbuktu was a university town.

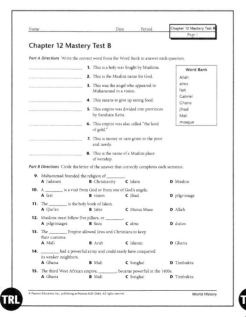

Chapter 12 Mastery Test B, pages 1–3

Africa and Islam   Chapter 12   **293**

Audio Library 🎧

Skill Track for
World History 🖱

Teacher's Resource Library **TRL**

Workbook Activities 53–58

Activities 53–58

Modified Activities 53–58

Chapter 13 Self-Study Guide

Chapter 13 Outline

Chapter 13 Mastery Tests A and B
(Answer Keys for the Teacher's Resource Library begin on page 870 of this Teacher's Edition.)

Introducing the Chapter

The Middle Ages in India, China, and Japan saw the birth and adoption of new religions, a flowering of inventions, and momentous political changes.

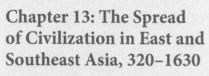

The Spread of Civilization in East and Southeast Asia

he continent of Asia also experienced many changes. In this chapter, you will learn about India and the Mongol invaders. Then you will find out about China and its many wonderful inventions. Finally, you will discover the religion called Shintoism that was born in Japan. In all these places, you will meet rulers and scholars, scientists and artists, inventors and warriors.

Goals for Learning

◆ To identify some inventions that made ancient China the richest and most powerful country in the world

◆ To describe life in China under Mongol rule

◆ To explain how geography has influenced Japan's history

◆ To explain why the Shinto religion is unique

◆ To compare Japanese and European feudalism

◆ To list the reasons why Japan and China turned to isolationism

320 The Golden Age of India begins

960 Sung dynasty begins to rule China

1279 Kublai Khan rules China

1525 Babur sets up Mogul Empire in India

A.D. 1   A.D. 1000   A.D. 1300   A.D. 1600

T'ang dynasty begins to rule China

1206 Genghis Khan, Mongol leader, begins to conquer Asia

1368 Mongol dynasty falls in China; a 250-year isolation begins

1630 Japan begins 200-year isolation

Ask:

• What happened in India in 1525?
(Babur set up the Moghul Empire)

• Which Khan became important in Asia first? Which ruled China?
(Genghis Khan; Kublai Khan)

• What happened to the Mongols in 1368? (Mongol dynasty fell)

• When did Japan's period of isolation begin? (1630)

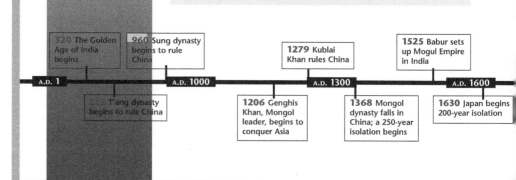

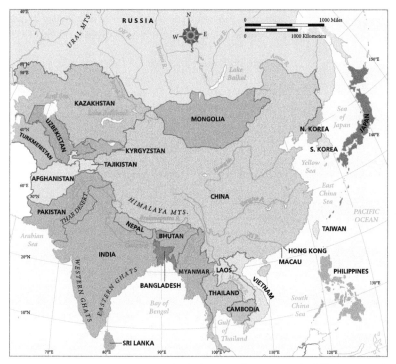

Study the map, then answer the following questions:

Asia is the largest of the world's continents. China and India—Asia's two largest countries—have a population of well over two billion people. Out of every five people on the earth, two are either Chinese or Indian. Both in population and in land area, Japan is smaller than China and India. But it has many people for its size.

1. Which of the three nations—Japan, China, or India—is located farthest south?

2. Which of the three is an island nation?

3. Find the mouth of the Yangtze River at the East China Sea. Then find the mouth of the Indus River at the Arabian Sea. What is the distance—by the most direct route—from one river mouth to the other?

4. What mountains separate India, Nepal, and Bhutan from China?

5. In what direction is Vietnam from China? from India? from Japan?

Have students read the title of the map, "Three Asian Giants—China, India, and Japan." Then have them identify the countries on the map.

Ask:

• Why do you think China, India, and Japan are called "Asian Giants"? (Answers will vary; students may say that these are the most powerful countries in Asia.)

Read the paragraph below the map to students. Then have them read and answer the questions.

Map Skills Answers

1. India

2. Japan

3. about 3,400 miles, or about 5,200 kilometers

4. the Himalayas

5. Vietnam is southeast of China, east of India, and southwest of Japan.

LEARNING STYLES

 Body/Kinesthetic
Have students use salt clay or a similar material to make a three-dimensional topographical map of the area covered by the map on this page. Explain to them that their map will illustrate the greatest rise in elevation on Earth—from sea level to the tops of the Himalayan Mountains. If possible, have an art teacher join your class to demonstrate how to work with the salt clay to create a three-dimensional map.

Chapter Project

Students will work in groups to research inventions made in India, China, or Japan in the period between 320 and 1630. Organize the class into three groups and assign each to one of the three civilizations. Each group should use library and Internet resources to gather information, and then create a visual display on their findings. Displays should showcase at least two inventions. Examples of displays may include a hands-on display, scale model, or role-play.

Chapter 13 Outline, pages 1–3

Civilization in E/SE Asia   Chapter 13   **295**

Inferencing

Introduce the reading strategy *inferencing*. Draw students' attention to the definition. Tell students that making inferences allows them to use information they already know to help them understand new information and concepts. For example, by having an understanding of feudalism in Europe, students will be able to use inferences to better understand Japanese feudalism. Explain that inference is used not only with what is read, but also with visuals, such as artwork.

Ask:

- How might inferencing help you understand the artwork on page 297? (Answers will vary; knowing about the culture of India will help in understanding the meaning of the images presented in the artwork.)

- What inference can you make about trade in China by first thinking about the importance of the Silk Road? (Answers will vary; China became an important center of trade for traders from many other countries.)

- How does having an understanding of different religions help in learning about new cultures? (Answers will vary; by knowing about different religions, I can infer the importance of religion in a culture I'm just beginning to study.)

Key Vocabulary Words

Point out that these chapter words are presented in the order they appear in each lesson. They are also found in the Glossary. Explain that students should be aware of making inferences as they read new words and information presented in Chapter 13.

Use the following key vocabulary words: *masterpiece* and *shogun*. Explain that as students come across these words in the lessons, they will infer the full meaning of these words based on what they already know.

Reading Strategy:
Inferencing

Sometimes you have to make an inference to figure out what the text means. You have to make an inference because the meaning of a text is not directly stated.

◆ What You Know + What You Read = Inference

You can make inferences by thinking "beyond the text." Add what you already know to what you read in the text. This is a helpful strategy for making inferences.

Key Vocabulary Words

Lesson 1 ————————
Stupa A large building in which a monk is buried

Civilian A person who is not in the military

Civil service A system of government run by civilians

Lesson 2 ————————
Abacus A tool that helps people add and do other things with numbers

Masterpiece A piece of art that seems almost perfect

Lesson 3 ————————
Barbarian An uncivilized person

Lesson 4 ————————
Shinto The Japanese religion that involves a love of nature and worship of spirits

Kami Spirits of the Shinto religion

Lesson 5 ————————
Shogun A Japanese word that means "great general"; a military dictator

Daimyo The highest nobles next to the shogun

Estate A large piece of land with a house on it

Samurai A Japanese warrior who received land from a daimyo and fought for him

Calligraphy The art of beautiful handwriting

Bushido The Samurai code of honor in Japan

Hari-kari The act of killing oneself with a knife

Lesson 6 ————————
Ikebana One Japanese art of arranging flowers

Noh drama A Japanese play with only two actors

Kabuki A Japanese play with exaggerated actions

Ask:

- What do you think of when I say *masterpiece*? (Answers will vary; I think of something beautiful, like a painting by a famous artist.)

- What inference can you make about a Japanese work of art if I told you it was a masterpiece? (Answers will vary; the artwork would be very beautiful, perhaps with a lot of color, and highly valued.)

- How can inferences be used to understand the importance of a shogun? (Answers will vary; I think about the importance of lords and vassals in Europe. This gives me an idea of how important a shogun might have been in Japan.)

- To describe India's Golden Age
- To explain what happened during the Mogul Empire and what led up to it

Stupa

A large building in which a monk is buried

The Golden Age of India lasted from 320 to 535. The Gupta dynasty ruled India at this time. The Gupta rulers and most Indian people were Hindus, not Buddhists. The four major castes of Hinduism had divided into smaller groups. In time, nearly 3,000 castes developed.

How Was Indian Art Unique?

Most Indian art during this time had something to do with religion. Indian artists decorated large, rounded buildings called **stupas,** in which monks were buried. They also decorated temples with carved animals, flowers, and pictures of the Hindu gods.

For centuries, Greek art influenced Indian artists. During the Golden Age, Indian art became unique. It was like no other art anywhere. Wall drawings in the Ajanta caves tell us about ancient India. These colorful paintings show hunting parties, dancing women, and the life of Indian nobles.

Some of the oldest Indian art can be seen at the Ajanta caves in central India.

Chapter 13: Lesson 1

Overview This lesson discusses the accomplishments of the Gupta dynasty, the Mongol raids of the 14th century, and the Mogul Empire.

Objectives

- To describe India's Golden Age
- To explain what happened during the Mogul Empire and what led up to it

Student Pages pages 297–300

Teacher's Resource Library

  Workbook Activity 53

  Activity 53

  Modified Activity 53

Vocabulary

civilian   stupa
civil service

Have students make a crossword puzzle from the vocabulary words. They can use the definitions in the book or write their own as clues. Then have students trade puzzles and solve them.

PRONUNCIATION GUIDE

Use this list to help students pronounce difficult words in this lesson.

Ajanta	(ə jun´ tə)
Tamerlane	(tam´ ər lān)
Shah Jahan	(shä ā hän´)
Timur	(tē´ mür)

1 **Warm-Up Activity**

Have students turn to the map on page 299. Explain that the area in green shows the extent of a long-standing empire, called the Mogul Empire. Have students use the map and their knowledge of India and empires in general to make inferences about the Mogul Empire. Then tell students they will be reading about an amazing time in the history of India.

---

2 Teaching the Lesson

Ask students to think about what the term "Golden Age" means and what might be accomplished during a Golden Age. Then have them read pages 297–300 about the Golden Age of India and some of the events that followed it.

Ask:

- What period of Indian art do the wall drawings on the Ajanta caves tell us about? (the Golden Age)
- We rely on a system of numbers based on 10. Who first developed this system? (Indian scientists)
- Who led the first Mongol invasion of India? (Timur the Lame, or Tamerlane)

Reading Strategy:
Inferencing

Discuss the medical and mathematical advances of Indian doctors and scientists. Draw a connection between the importance of these discoveries and life today. Have students read and answer the question. (Answers will vary; the Indian doctors and scientists were very creative, intelligent, and dedicated to making life better for Indians.)

STUDY SKILLS

Since students will read about many inventions made by Asians, have them organize this knowledge by creating a chart titled "Asian Inventions." They should set up three columns headed *Invention*, *Date*, and *Place of Discovery*. Have students add information to the chart as they read the chapter.

What Did Indian Scientists Discover?

During the Golden Age, scientists in India made many discoveries. They figured out the size of the moon. They also understood gravity many years before Europeans did.

Indian mathematicians made important discoveries too. They were the first people to use a system of numbers based on 10. We still use their symbols for 1 to 9. They were also among the first mathematicians to use zero. The Arabs later adopted the Indian decimal and number system.

Reading Strategy:
Inferencing

After reading about Indian doctors and scientists, what can you infer about the abilities of some Indians at this time?

What Were Indian Doctors Able to Do?

Indian doctors learned to inoculate people against disease. They put a small amount of the disease into a person's body to keep the person from getting the disease. (Europeans first tried inoculations about 1,000 years later.) These doctors performed many different types of surgery. The Indians invented hundreds of different medical tools. They set broken bones and made medicine from plants.

What Happened to the Gupta Empire?

The Huns—nomads from central Asia—attacked the Gupta Empire. The empire slowly got smaller until it disappeared during the 600s. From 600 until 1300, India became a land of small kingdoms. Warriors invaded it again and again. The Indian Muslims and Hindus also fought one another.

Who Were the Mongols?

In 1398, the Mongols invaded India. These fierce warriors had already conquered Persia and Mesopotamia. Their leader's name was Timur the Lame. (Later, he became known as Tamerlane.) Timur and his armies attacked India, killing thousands of Hindus and Muslims. When he marched away from a conquered village, Tamerlane left behind pyramids of human skulls.

ELL/ESL STRATEGY

Language Objective:
To correctly pronounce numbers

Remind students that long ago Indian mathematicians developed the system of numbers based on 10. Write the numerals 1–10 on the board in a column with number words next to each numeral. Ask ELL students to share number words from their native languages. Continue to add number word columns for the native language of each ELL student in the class. Compare the words across for the same number. Have ELL students use the English number words in sentences, such as "I listened to three new songs today." Then have English speaking students repeat the same sentence but exchange the English number word with a number word from another language shown on the board.

How Did Akbar Keep Peace?

In 1525, another conqueror from central Asia named Babur attacked India. Babur set up the Mogul Empire there. (The name *Mogul* probably comes from the word *Mongol*.) The most famous Mogul ruler was Babur's grandson, Akbar. He ruled the empire from 1556 to 1605. Some of his soldiers rode elephants. More than 12,000 soldiers rode horses. His army helped Akbar add new lands to his empire.

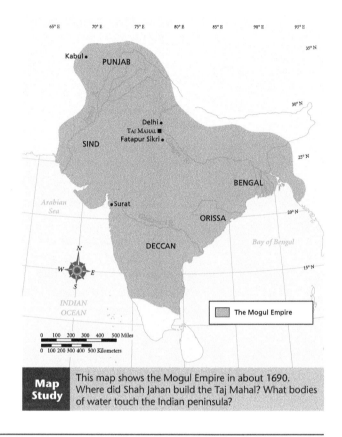

 Map Study This map shows the Mogul Empire in about 1690. Where did Shah Jahan build the Taj Mahal? What bodies of water touch the Indian peninsula?

Ask:

- **What empire did Babur set up in India?** (the Mogul Empire)
- **Who was the most famous Mogul ruler?** (Akbar)
- **What did Akbar's army help him do?** (add new lands to Akbar's empire)

Read the map title, "The Mogul Empire (c. 1690)," to students. Then ask students to name three rivers in the Mogul Empire. (Indus River, Ganges River, Godavan River)

Then have students read the paragraph under the map and answer the questions. (The Taj Mahal was built near the cities of Delhi and Fatehpur Sikri, west of the Ganges River in India. The Arabian Sea, Indian Ocean, and the Bay of Bengal touch the peninsula.)

ONLINE CONNECTION

Students can gain additional information by accessing the following Web sites:

www.agsglobewh.com/299a (Students are able to easily access links for short biographies on India's early rulers, including Babur and Akbar.)

www.agsglobewh.com/299b (This short history of the Gupta Empire provides students with a concise understanding of this time period.)

www.agsglobewh.com/page299c (Students can read a detailed history of the Mogul Empire by accessing this Web site.)

IN THE COMMUNITY

Brainstorm with students on how Akbar's army cared for so many horses and elephants as they moved from place to place. Discuss the need for food and water. Have students learn about their local animal shelter. If possible, ask the local animal shelter director to visit your class. Discuss community efforts to adopt sheltered animals, and house and feed them.

Ask:

- Who did Akbar appoint to help him govern his vast empire? (civilian officials)

- What did Akbar do that made him a fair ruler? (Answers will vary; students may say he taxed fairly and tried to give everyone religious freedom.)

Reading Strategy:
Inferencing

(Answers will vary; he valued peace and respected the religious beliefs of others.)

3 Reinforce and Extend

CAREER CONNECTION

In the United States, many people have careers in the civil service of the state or federal government. Applicants take tests and are appointed to their jobs on the basis of test results. Students can find out about eligibility for federal civil service jobs and how to apply for them through the Internet or by asking officials at their local post office. State governments similarly provide information on state civil service jobs and careers.

Lesson 1 Review Answers

1. Hindus **2.** Huns **3.** Mongols
4. Tamerlane **5.** Akbar

Answers will vary. Alexander the Great had gotten as far as the Indus River when he tried to conquer the world, so Greek ideas and art had come to India at that time and stayed to influence Indian artists.

Civilian

A person who is not in the military

Civil service

A system of government run by civilians

Reading Strategy:
Inferencing

After reading this section, what can you infer about the kind of person Akbar was?

Word Bank

Akbar
Hindus
Huns
Mongols
Tamerlane

Akbar divided his empire into 12 provinces. He appointed nonmilitary, or **civilian,** officials to run the day-to-day business of each province. This system is called **civil service** because civilians run the government. These officials figured out how much food each province should produce. Then Akbar used their findings to work out fair taxes.

Like all the Mogul rulers, Akbar was a Muslim. To keep peace, he married a Hindu princess and appointed Hindus to important positions in the government. He tried to give everyone religious freedom and to treat them all fairly.

What Did the Mogul Leaders Build?

Akbar and the Moguls who came after him built beautiful buildings. Shah Jahan built the beautiful Taj Mahal as a tomb for his favorite wife. In addition, Mogul rulers built three royal palaces that contained thousands of jewels from all over Asia. The Red Fort in Agra had ceilings of solid gold. Even today, visitors say that no words can describe the beauty of these buildings.

Lesson 1 Review On a sheet of paper, use the words from the Word Bank to complete each sentence correctly.

1. The Gupta rulers during India's Golden Age were _____.

2. Toward the end of this Golden Age, the _____ invaded the Gupta Empire.

3. In 1398, the _____ invaded India.

4. _____, the leader of the Mongols, left behind skull pyramids as he marched through India.

5. _____, who ruled India from 1556 to 1605, was a great ruler.

What do you think

Why do you think that Greek ideas influenced Indian artists? (Hint: Remember Chapter 6 and Alexander the Great.)

Objectives

♦ To describe accomplishments of the T'ang and Sung dynasties

♦ To explain what it meant to be educated in the T'ang dynasty

From 618 to 907, the T'ang dynasty ruled China. During this period, China became the richest and most powerful country in the world. Civil servants governed T'ang China. They got their jobs after taking difficult tests on law, mathematics, and events happening in the world. Any Chinese man could take the test. However, those who passed it always had a good education. China soon had a ruling class of scholars.

With Whom Did T'ang China Trade?

T'ang China welcomed traders from other lands. These traders brought goods into China from Persia, the Middle East, Korea, and Southeast Asia. They carried silk and porcelain out of China to the Middle East and the West. This exchange of goods also led to an exchange of ideas. A large number of foreigners worked side-by-side with the Chinese within the capital city.

What Could Educated People Do in T'ang China?

Every educated person in T'ang China could read, write, and create poems. (During this time, someone said that "whoever was a gentleman was a poet.") Chinese poems were about nature or about the problems ordinary people face in everyday life. During the T'ang dynasty, the artists painted mostly in black and a few other colors. Usually their paintings were about nature.

Why Was the Invention of Printing Important?

Reading Strategy:
Inferencing

What do you already know about inventions in China during this time?

Around 1040, the Chinese invented printing. An artisan carved Chinese characters on a block of wood. Then a printer covered the wooden surface with ink and pressed sheets of paper against it. (The Chinese began printing books nearly 400 years before Europeans.)

Before the development of printing, people copied books by hand. Copying took time, so there were few books. But a printer could make more books faster. Since people learn by reading, printing led to the spread of knowledge.

320 – 1630   *The Spread of Civilization in East and Southeast Asia   Chapter 13*   301

Chapter 13: Lesson 2

Overview This lesson presents the political organization and accomplishments of two dynasties in China—the T'ang dynasty and the Sung dynasty.

Objectives

■ To describe accomplishments of the T'ang and Sung dynasties

■ To explain what it meant to be educated in the T'ang dynasty

Student Pages pages 301–304

Teacher's Resource Library

Workbook Activity 54

Activity 54

Modified Activity 54

....

Vocabulary

abacus   **masterpiece**

Have students work with a partner to make flash cards for the vocabulary words. Then have them use the cards to quiz their partners on the meanings of the words.

....

1 Warm-Up Activity

Show a compass to the class. Explain that the needle of the compass always points north. Tell students that the compass was invented by the Chinese. Have students speculate on how the compass affected Chinese sea travel, trade, and an exchange of ideas between cultures. Explain that they will read about other Chinese inventions that had a great impact on the Chinese culture.

Reading Strategy:
Inferencing

(Answers will vary; students may mention Chinese characters, the canal, or the Great Wall of China.)

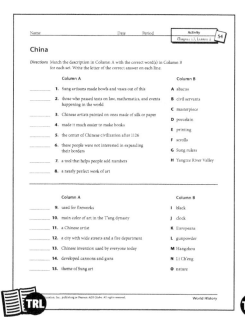

Workbook Activity 54

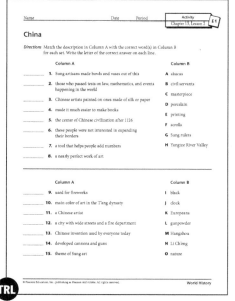

Activity 54

2 Teaching the Lesson

Explain that the word *dynasty* is used rather loosely in modern times, especially in sports where a *dynasty* of a particular team may last only as many as five years. Dynasties actually last much longer—perhaps hundreds of years. Explain that many powerful dynasties ruled ancient China. Have them read pages 301–304 to find out about two of these dynasties.

Ask:

- What important invention of the T'ang dynasty made it easier to produce books? (printing)
- To what location did the capital move during the Sung dynasty? (The capital was Hangzhou, in the Yangtze River Valley.)
- What were some of the features of the capital city of Hangzhou that made it like a modern city? (Students may mention that it had wide streets, streetlights, and a fire department.)
- What effect did gunpowder have on warfare? (Students may suggest that smaller armies could defeat larger armies; walls and castles could no longer keep out invading armies.)

Reading Strategy:
Inferencing

(Answers will vary; life was very organized and orderly.)

Biography

Emperor Taizong capitalized on the invention of printing by publishing standard editions of literary classics.

Ask:

- Taizong is remembered as one of China's greatest emperors. What do you think was his greatest accomplishment? (Answers will vary; students may mention setting up schools or civil service.)
- How might history have been different if Taizong had not taken control of important trade routes? (Answers will vary; students may say that Taizong wouldn't have had the resources to do all the things he did.)

302   *Unit 2   Regional Civilizations*

Biography

Taizong: 600–649

Emperor Taizong made the T'ang dynasty great. He helped his father Kao-tsu defeat the Sui dynasty. In 626, Taizong became emperor.

Years of civil war had destroyed most local government. Taizong restored it. He set up local schools. There, students studied the teachings of Confucius. Interested students could take civil service exams. Until then, nobles had held most government jobs. Over time, civil servants took power away from the nobles.

Taizong also fought off the Turks. He also began to gain control over many other kingdoms by controlling trade routes.

Reading Strategy:
Inferencing

After reading this section, what inference can you make about life in the Sung dynasty?

What Was the Sung Dynasty?

The Sung dynasty ruled China from 960 to 1279. After 1126, the center of Chinese civilization shifted south, from the Huang He Valley to the Yangtze River Valley.

Sung China was rich. Its capital city, Hangzhou, was one of the most modern cities of the world. At this time, European cities had dirty, dark, narrow, and crowded streets. Hangzhou had wide streets with streetlights. People cleaned these streets every day. Hangzhou even had a fire department.

What Things Did Sung China Create?

The Chinese invented many things that helped change world history. By the 800s, they had invented gunpowder. At first, they used it only for fireworks. Some think they may have used it later as a weapon.

An Arab trader in China learned how to make gunpowder and introduced it to Europe. Sung rulers were not interested in expanding their borders, so they made little use of gunpowder. However, Europeans developed guns and cannons. This changed the way soldiers fought wars.

302   *Unit 2   Regional Civilizations*

ELL/ESL STRATEGY

Language Objective:
To describe different features of nature

Invite a student who enjoys drawing to step up to the board. Have students mention a feature in nature, such as a tree, flower, or hill. Have the art student draw and label the feature on the board. Have ELL students provide the spelling for the same word in their native languages. Continue the activity until a nature picture has been complete on the board, or until students have exhausted ideas to add to the drawing. Have each ELL student describe the nature drawing created by the class.

Abacus

A tool that helps people add and do other things with numbers

Masterpiece

A piece of art that seems almost perfect

Someone in the Sung dynasty also invented the compass. This is a tool for finding direction by the use of a magnet. The magnetic needle of this compass always points north-south. The compass allowed Chinese ships to travel far away.

The Chinese invented the **abacus.** This tool helps people add and do other things with numbers. They also invented the clock and a machine to detect, or discover, earthquakes.

What Did Sung Artisans Create?

The artists of Sung China painted pictures that people today call **masterpieces.** That is, the paintings seem almost perfect. Sung artists painted on paper or silk scrolls. Most Sung artists tried to show the mood of what they saw. Their paintings show people as small and unimportant. Nature—trees, mountains, and water—are most important.

Nature was often the theme for Sung artists. This scroll painting shows a temple in front of mountain peaks.

• What mood do you think Chinese painters were trying to express in their paintings? (Students may say peacefulness or simplicity, especially of nature.)

 3 Reinforce and Extend

AT HOME

 Ask your family to pretend a Chinese artist will visit your home. Make up a list of questions you might ask about how his or her paintings were made and the meaning they were meant to convey. Share the questions your family had with the class, and compare them with other students' questions. Encourage students to volunteer any answers they may know.

LEARNING STYLES

Visual/Spatial

Encourage students to make a visual guide of the religions covered in this chapter. For each religion, suggest that students draw a trunk of a tree and label it with the name of the religion. Have students add branches to each tree with facts they already know. As students learn more about the religion, have them add additional branches with facts. Additional branches may grow from the trunk or from other branches.

WORLD CULTURES

The fine porcelain pottery of China inspired potters in other countries to make their own form of fine china. The English especially excelled at adapting the Chinese porcelain formula. In the 18th century, two firms, Spode and Wedgewood, began manufacturing china that still can be found in homes all over the world.

Have students read the History in Your Life feature to find out about the invention of gunpowder. When students finish, have them think about how a traveler who had been to China and witnessed fireworks might have explained the sight to Europeans who had not even heard about gunpowder. Remind students that words such as *explosive, explosion, gunpowder, cannon, gun,* and *bomb* had not yet been invented. Invite students to role-play this encounter.

Lesson 2 Review Answers

1. Scholars governed T'ang China.
2. Trading led to the exchange of ideas with other peoples. **3.** Printing produced many more books than copying did, so more people could read and learn from books. **4.** Hangzhou, the capital of Sung China, had wide streets with streetlights and a fire department. It was a modern city for its time. **5.** Three important inventions of Sung China are gunpowder, the magnetic compass, and the abacus. (Students might also mention clocks and machines to detect earthquakes.)

Answers will vary. China was a vast land and perhaps that made the artists think of nature as huge and people as small. Also, nature may have seemed powerful or spiritual to the Chinese.

Gunpowder

It is the Fourth of July. You watch as brilliant fireworks burst in the sky. Whom can you thank for these exciting displays? The chemists of ancient China.

Fireworks are made mainly of gunpowder. Other materials add color. About 1,000 years ago, the Chinese discovered the formula for gunpowder. It was the first explosive. Gunpowder has three ingredients: charcoal, sulfur, and saltpeter. Charcoal is made from burned wood. Sulfur and saltpeter are mined.

In the 1200s, Muslim armies learned the secret of gunpowder from the Chinese. This knowledge reached Europe in the 1300s. Explosives changed warfare and history. Medieval castles could no longer protect the people inside. Bombs and cannons could knock down their walls.

Artisans of Sung China created beautiful porcelain. This is a shiny pottery made from a baked white clay. Sung artisans made thin porcelain bowls and vases. When Europeans came to China, they studied the making of porcelain. They used the word *china* to describe the beautiful porcelain.

Lesson 2 Review On a sheet of paper, write the answer to each question. Use complete sentences.

1. Who governed T'ang China?
2. What did trading lead to in T'ang China?
3. Why was the invention of printing important?
4. What was the capital of Sung China like?
5. What are three important inventions of Sung China?

What do you think

Why do you think artisans of the Sung period showed human beings as small and nature as large?

304   *Unit 2   Regional Civilizations*

Objectives

◆ To describe life in China under Mongol rule

◆ To explain the results of China's isolation after Mongol rule fell

The Mongols rode out of central Asia and conquered Russia, India, and China. Their greatest leader was Genghis Khan. Between 1206 and 1227, he conquered most of Asia.

What Did Kublai Khan Build?

In 1279, Kublai Khan, a grandson of Genghis Khan, conquered China. He adopted the Chinese name Yuan for his dynasty. Kublai Khan spent almost all his life in China. In time, the Mongol rulers adopted many Chinese ways. Kublai Khan built a new Chinese capital city. (Today we call this city Beijing.) At its center was his palace. It was the largest empire the world had ever seen.

How Did the Mongol Rulers Make Trade Easier?

The Mongol rulers built great highways and protected merchants and travelers. Travel and trade increased. Traders from the Middle East, Russia, and Europe came to China. Some Chinese and Mongols settled in Russia and Europe.

All this was important to world history. The Arabs and the Europeans learned from the Chinese. The Europeans got paper, porcelain, printing, gunpowder, and other inventions from the Chinese. The Chinese got glass, clothes, cotton, silver, carpets, honey, and slaves in return.

How Did Chinese Opera Begin?

Mongol rulers did not allow the Chinese to become high government officials. They gave these jobs to Mongols or to foreigners. Chinese scholars who had been officials began to write plays and operas. (An opera is a play in which people sing all the words.) The actors, who were all men, acted, sang, and danced while the musicians sat on stage and played music.

Kublai Khan (center), grandson of Genghis Khan, was a Mongol who ruled China under the Yuan dynasty.

320 – 1630   *The Spread of Civilization in East and Southeast Asia*   *Chapter 13*   **305**

Chapter 13: Lesson 3

Overview This lesson details the Mongol domination of China.

Objectives

■ To describe life in China under Mongol rule

■ To explain the results of China's isolation after Mongol rule fell

Student Pages pages 305–306

Teacher's Resource Library (TRL)

Workbook Activity 55

Activity 55

Modified Activity 55

Vocabulary

barbarian

Have students generate synonyms for the word *barbarian*. Write the words on the board. Then have students create sentences interchanging the word *barbarian* with its synonyms. Discuss how the meaning of the sentence changes slightly when different synonyms are used.

1   Warm-Up Activity

Explain that, though it had flourished for hundreds of years, China isolated itself from the outside world for 250 years after the Mongol dynasty fell. Divide the class into small groups, and tell each group to discuss what life would be like if their community isolated itself from all other communities. Have each group make a list of the consequences of isolation. Then have the groups share their ideas with the class.

Workbook Activity 55   **Activity 55**   *Civilization in E/SE Asia*   *Chapter 13*   **305**

2 Teaching the Lesson

Ask students to tell what they already know about Genghis Khan or Kublai Khan. Have them read pages 305–306 to find out the influence these rulers had on China.

Ask:

* Which Mongol leader led the invasion of China? (Ghenghis Khan)

* What do we call the city to which Kublai Khan moved the capital? (Beijing)

* Why did the Ming dynasty decide to isolate China? (The Ming emperors thought people who lived in other countries were barbarians.)

* What effect did isolation have? (It limited trading or traveling, and kept the Chinese from learning new things happening in other places.)

Reading Strategy:
Inferencing

Ask students to write an answer to the question. Allow time for students to share and discuss their inferences. (Answers will vary; people lived the same way for more than 200 years with little economic or social progress.)

LEARNING STYLES

Interpersonal/ Group Learning

Have a small group of students research on the Internet or in the library the travels of Marco Polo. Encourage them to make a creative poster highlighting some of the information Marco Polo brought back to Europe about the court of Kublai Khan. Students might also include a map to show where Marco Polo traveled.

Barbarian
An uncivilized person

Reading Strategy:
Inferencing

After reading this section, what can you infer about life in China during this time?

Why Did China Begin to Isolate Itself?

In 1368, the Mongol dynasty fell. Afterward, the Chinese did not see as many foreigners. The Ming emperors gained power. They thought the people who lived in all other countries were **barbarians,** or uncivilized. In the 1500s, these emperors began to isolate China from other countries. They kept foreigners out and the Chinese in.

Isolation kept the Chinese from learning the exciting new things happening elsewhere. For the next 250 years, the Chinese did little trading or traveling, so China changed. It had been ahead of other civilizations, but isolation caused it to fall behind.

Lesson 3 Review On a sheet of paper, write the answer to each question. Use complete sentences.

1. Who was Kublai Khan?

2. What was the capital of the Yuan dynasty?

3. What are two ways the Mongol rulers protected travelers and merchants?

4. Why was Chinese trade important to the Europeans?

5. Why did the Chinese begin to write operas?

What do you think

Why did the Ming dynasty begin to isolate China?

---

3 Reinforce and Extend

ELL/ESL STRATEGY

Language Objective:
To be able write a short summary given a specific set of facts

Divide the class into small groups, making sure to include ELL students in each. Have students reread the section "What Did Kublai Khan Build?" Assign each group to list facts from the paragraph, and then use this to write a short summary. Have each group read its summary of facts to the rest of the class.

Lesson 3 Review Answers

1. Kubai Khan conquered China and created the largest empire the world had seen. **2.** The capital city was Beijing. **3.** They built highways and protected merchants. **4.** Europeans got paper, porcelain, printing, gunpowder, and other inventions from the Chinese. **5.** Mongol rulers did not allow Chinese to be government officials so the scholars began writing plays and operas.

Answers will vary. The Ming dynasty thought that people from other countries were barbarians. They may have thought that if these "uncivilized" people came to China, the Chinese people would become uncivilized too.

Chapter 13: Lesson 4

Overview This lesson covers the history and development of culture in ancient Japan.

Objectives

■ To explain how geography has shaped Japan's history

■ To explain why the Shinto religion is like no other

Student Pages pages 307–309

Teacher's Resource Library **TRL**

Workbook Activity 56

Activity 56

Modified Activity 56

Objectives

◆ To explain how geography has shaped Japan's history

◆ To explain why the Shinto religion is like no other

Shinto

The Japanese religion that involves a love of nature and worship of spirits

Kami

The spirits of the Shinto religion

Reading Strategy:
Inferencing

Based on what you just read, what can you infer about the importance of geography to Japan?

Japan is a country spread over more than 3,000 islands. The islands stretch for more than 1,200 miles. People have lived on them for thousands of years, perhaps as far back as 30,000 B.C. These Stone-Age people probably came from nearby China and Korea.

How Has Geography Shaped Japan's History?

The waters that surround Japan have protected it from invaders. Unlike China and India, Japan has never been conquered by foreign armies. Yet these same waters brought ideas to Japan from Korea and China. The Japanese changed these ideas to fit their own way of life. This resulted in a unique Japanese culture.

For example, the Japanese adopted the Chinese system of writing. This allowed them to read Chinese books about medicine, mathematics, and science. The Japanese copied Chinese art and literature, wore Chinese clothing, and used the Chinese calendar. For a time, the Japanese adopted the Chinese civil service. Later, they changed this system so that nobles, rather than scholars, ran the government.

What Makes the Shinto Religion Unique?

The religion born in Japan is **Shinto.** Historians do not know who founded it. It has no holy books like the Vedas, the Bible, or the Qur'an. Shinto followers love nature and worship **kami,** or spirits. They believe that these kami control the forces of nature.

The word *Shinto* means "the way of the gods." The Japanese people worship thousands of gods and spirits. The goddess of the sun is the most important Shinto god. In fact, the Japanese call their country Nippon, which means "source of the sun."

Vocabulary

kami **shinto**

After students study the vocabulary words and their definitions, have students draw a circle and label it *Shinto.* Then have students write the word *kami* inside the circle. Discuss how the spirits of the Shinto religion are part of it. Have students think about other words that could be placed inside the Shinto circle.

1 **Warm-Up Activity**

Have students turn to the map on page 309. Have students speculate on different cultural features brought to Japan from other countries, including foods, religion, customs, and inventions. Talk about how the cultures of other countries may have influenced Japan's culture. Discuss the image on page 308. Ask students to think about the importance of the Shinto sun goddess on the culture of Japan.

2 Teaching the Lesson

Explain to students that among the places they study in this chapter, Japan is geographically unique. Have them read pages 307–309 to find out why Japan geographically is like none of the other places they have read about in this chapter.

Ask:

- How has the geography of Japan shaped its history? (Answers will vary; students may say it is an island isolated and protected from the influence of other cultures.)

- What religion was born in Japan? (the Shinto religion)

- Which Japanese people first learned about Buddhism? (students sent by the emperor to study in China)

- How did Buddhism first come to Japan? (Answers will vary; students may say that the Japanese who had studied abroad brought it with them when they returned home.)

Reading Strategy:
Inferencing

(Answers will vary; Japan's geography has allowed for trade and protected the country from invaders.)

ELL/ESL STRATEGY

Language Objective:
To use placement words in descriptions
Placement words and phrases include *next to, over there, under, to the east, beside,* and other words. Create a drawing of the school and surrounding streets and homes or businesses on the board. Then make a list of placement words on the board. Have ELL and English-speaking students use placement words to explain where buildings and streets are in relation to each other. Then tell students to turn to the map of Asia on page 823 in the back of this book. Repeat the activity by noting the placement of countries and landforms in relation to each other.

The royal family of Japan traces its ancestors back to Jimmu. According to myth, Jimmu was the founder of Japan. The Japanese believe that he was connected in some way to the sun goddess. Until the end of World War II, they thought that their emperor was a god.

In 600, a Japanese prince sent a large group of young men to China to study. Many became Buddhists. Later, they returned to Japan. There they tried to get the Japanese to change their religion from Shintoism to Buddhism.

Buddhist missionaries came to Japan from Korea. Soon, Japanese rulers and warriors accepted many Buddhist ideas. Many artists and writers became Buddhist monks.

This image shows Amaterasu, the Shinto sun goddess.

3 Reinforce and Extend

BACKGROUND INFORMATION

Shinto is still practiced in many parts of the world. Shintoism is rooted in the customs and beliefs of ancient Japan. According to Shinto myth, Japan became an island when one Shinto god dipped his spear into the waters below. The geography of Japan is closely tied to the many gods of the Shinto religion.

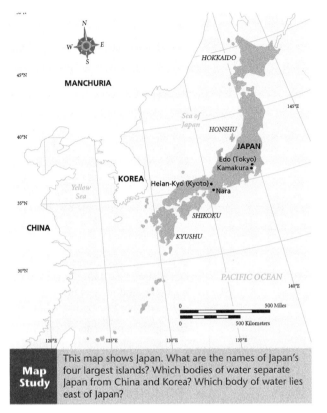

HOKKAIDO

MANCHURIA

45°N

145°E

Sea of Japan

HONSHU

40°N

JAPAN

Edo (Tokyo)
Kamakura •

KOREA

Heian-Kyo (Kyoto) •
• Nara

35°N

Yellow Sea

SHIKOKU

CHINA

KYUSHU

30°N

PACIFIC OCEAN

140°E

0   500 Miles

0   500 Kilometers

120°E   125°E   130°E   135°E

Map Study

This map shows Japan. What are the names of Japan's four largest islands? Which bodies of water separate Japan from China and Korea? Which body of water lies east of Japan?

Lesson 4 Review On a sheet of paper, write the answer to each question. Use complete sentences.

1. Why did no one invade Japan during its Middle Ages?

2. What did Japan borrow from China?

3. What does the word *Shinto* mean?

4. What is unique about the Shinto religion?

5. From what two countries did Buddhism come to Japan?

Why do you think the Japanese call their country Nippon, or the "source of the sun"?

Call attention to the map, titled "Japan (c. 1200–1600)," and the scale of miles.

Ask:

• What is the distance from the northernmost point to the southernmost point on the islands that make up Japan? (approximately 1,270 miles or 2,044 kilometers)

Have students read the paragraph next to the map and answer the questions. (The four largest islands are Kyushu, Shikoku, Honshu, and Hokkaido. The Sea of Japan and the Yellow Sea separate these countries. The Pacific Ocean is east of Japan.)

Lesson 4 Review Answers

1. Japan was made up of islands that were between two seas and the Pacific Ocean. No one had the ships to invade by water. **2.** Japan adopted the Chinese system of writing. **3.** The word *Shinto* means "the way of the gods." **4.** Shintoism is unique because it is based on the concept of worshipping nature. The founder of this religion is not known, which also makes it unique. **5.** Buddhism came to Japan from China and Korea.

Answers will vary. Since the sun first rises on a new day in Japan, that may have had something to do with the name. Another reason is that the Japanese worshipped the sun god.

Chapter 13: Lesson 5

Overview This lesson describes the culture that developed in Japan during the 400-year period beginning in A.D. 800.

Objectives

- To describe the culture that developed in Japan during the Heian era
- To compare the feudal systems of Japan and Europe

Student Pages pages 310–314

Teacher's Resource Library

Workbook Activity 57

Activity 57

Modified Activity 57

Vocabulary

bushido	hari-kari
calligraphy	samurai
daimyos	shogun
estate	

Ask students to write their own definitions after studying the definitions provided in the text. Have them trade papers with another student. Students will then read each other's definitions and agree with or suggest corrections for their partner's definitions.

 Warm-Up Activity

Have students recall what they know about European feudalism. Create a graphic organizer on the board as students offer details about the structure of European feudalism. Explain that in this lesson, students will learn about and be able to compare European feudalism with Japanese feudalism. Have students copy the graphic organizer into their notebooks for later comparison with the graphic organizer on page 312 and the information on page 313.

Objectives

- To describe the culture that developed in Japan during the Heian era
- To compare the feudal systems of Japan and Europe

Shogun
A Japanese word that means "great general"; a military dictator

Writing About History
Using what you have just learned about haiku and tanka, write your own haiku or tanka in your notebook. Remember, these poems usually show a mood or a feeling, and haiku is often about nature.

Japan had borrowed from the Chinese and Korean cultures. Then between 800 and 1200, it began to develop its own culture. This period of Japanese history is called the Heian era. The life of the Japanese ruling class was different from that of the common people. The common people were mostly farmers and fishermen who lived in small villages. The ruling class was made up of nobles who stayed in the cities.

The nobles played music and games and wrote poetry, especially the tanka and the haiku. The tanka is a five-line poem with 31 syllables. The three-line haiku has 17 syllables. It has five in its first line, seven in its second, and five in its third. Haiku is often about nature. Both poems usually show a mood or a feeling. The nobles wrote them for special times and put them in letters.

What Was Japanese Feudalism?

During this time, the emperor was the head of the government. But noble families held the real power. Because they refused to pay taxes, they grew rich and bought much land.

To keep their power, these lords gave away some of their land to other people. These people promised to be loyal to the lords. Soon Japan was divided into many pieces of land by different nobles.

In the late 1100s, one noble family grew more powerful than any other. The leader of this family forced the emperor to appoint him **shogun.** This word means "great general." For the next 700 years, powerful shoguns governed Japan. They said that they ruled in the emperor's name. In fact, the shogun was a military dictator who controlled officials, judges, and armies.

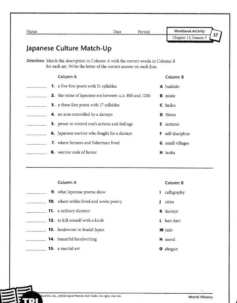

Workbook Activity 57

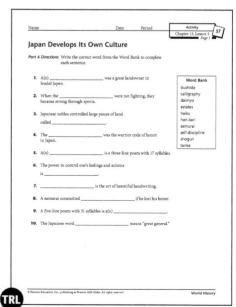

Activity 57, pages 1–2

Daimyos

The highest nobles next to the shogun

Estate

A large piece of land with a house on it

Samurai

A Japanese warrior who received land from a daimyo and fought for him

Calligraphy

The art of beautiful handwriting

Bushido

The Samurai code of honor in Japan

Hari-kari

The act of killing oneself with a knife

Reading Strategy:
Inferencing

After reading this section, what inference can you make about the samurai? What words helped you make your inference?

The highest nobles next to the shogun were the **daimyos.** They controlled large **estates.** An estate is a large piece of land with a house. An army of warriors fought for each daimyo. The daimyos gave land to these warriors who were known as **samurai,** which means "one who serves." The samurai were fearless soldiers who carried sharp swords. They believed that to die in battle was an honor.

When the samurai were not fighting, they developed strength through sports. They practiced judo and karate, which are martial arts. These are ways of fighting or defending oneself. Sumo wrestling was also popular.

The samurai were also artists. They painted beautiful scroll pictures, wrote poetry, and perfected the Japanese tea ceremony. When they were not using swords, the samurai used brushes to do **calligraphy**—the art of beautiful handwriting.

What Was Bushido?

A samurai had a code of honor called **bushido.** It demanded that he be brave and loyal to his lord. He had to obey orders and practice self-discipline, or control over one's feelings and actions. Honor was the most important thing in his life. If he lost his honor, a samurai committed **hari-kari,** or *seppuku*. That is, he killed himself with a knife. The nobles believed that hari-kari brought back honor.

This is what a Samurai warrior looked like.

 2 Teaching the Lesson

Tell students that the Japanese borrowed ideas from China, but that during one 400-year period, they developed a distinct culture. Then have students read pages 310–313 to find out about the Heian era.

Ask:

- **What is an example of an accomplishment of the Heian era?** (Answers will vary; students may say poetry such as the tanka and haiku.)

- **How did the Japanese nobles become more powerful than the emperor?** (Nobles owned large sections of land, refused to pay taxes, and had many loyal followers.)

- **Who were the daimyos?** (the highest nobles except for the shogun)

- **Which martial arts did the samurai practice?** (judo and karate)

Reading Strategy:
Inferencing

Call attention to the image of the Samurai warrior. Discuss how the image portrays the qualities of a Samurai warrior. Have students answer the question. (Answers will vary; a Samurai warrior believed in honor above everything else.)

 Writing About History

After students read the Writing About History feature, have them work with a partner to write a tanka or haiku.

Ask:

- What is one way in which Japanese feudalism differed from European feudalism? (Answers will vary; students may say the samurai valued education and the European knights did not, the samurai obeyed because of morality and European knights obeyed because of the law, a daimyo chose the son to leave his land to and a vassal's oldest son received his land, or European knights and Japanese samurai treated women differently.)

How Did Japanese and European Feudalism Differ?

Japanese and European feudalism differed in four ways. First, the connection between the European lord and his vassal was a kind of legal arrangement. However, the Japanese based their connection on morality instead of law. A samurai obeyed because he believed that his daimyo had the right to rule.

Second, when a vassal died in Europe, his property was given to the oldest son. Or it was divided among all his sons. This often led to civil war. In Japan, a man chose the son who could best take care of the land. If a daimyo had no son, he adopted one.

FEUDAL SOCIETY IN JAPAN

EMPEROR
Held the highest rank in society, but had no political power

↑

SHOGUN
Actual ruler

↑

DAIMYOS
Great landowners

↑

VASSALS AND SAMURAI SOLDIERS
Held land granted by daimyo or shogun

↑

LANDLESS SAMURAI SOLDIERS
Fought for daimyo, but held no land

↑

PEASANTS AND ARTISANS
Provided food and weapons for samurai class

↑

MERCHANTS
Held low social status, but gradually gained influence

Reading Strategy:
Inferencing

After reading this section, what can you infer about the effect of feudalism in Japan and Europe?

Third, in Europe, lords and vassals thought women were not equal to men, but they still respected women. Japanese warriors expected women to be tough and self-disciplined. They had to accept bad times—even death or hari-kari—without complaining.

Fourth, a European knight did not think that education was important. However, a Japanese samurai took pride in his poetry and calligraphy.

Anyone for Tea?

The Japanese began to practice tea ceremonies in the 1400s. Since then, they have made rules about how to prepare and serve tea. The ceremony takes place in a small room with a water container, flowers, and a hanging scroll.

To begin the ceremony, the host carefully prepares the tea. Then the host places the tea bowl in front of the most honored guest. The guest takes a sip and praises the tea maker on the flavor of the tea. Next, the guest takes another sip or two and passes the bowl.

This continues until the bowl comes back to the host. The tea maker carefully wipes the rim of the bowl with a special piece of paper.

Four things are important in a tea ceremony: harmony, respect, purity, and peace. Harmony comes from the plain tools the host uses in making the tea, the sounds of the wind and water, and the flowers. The host respects the guests; the guests respect the host. Their minds are pure and clear. When the ceremony is over, the tea maker and the guests are at peace with themselves and nature.

Ask:

• In Japan, which son inherited his father's land? (the son the father chose)

• Which skills were marks of the samurai's education? (calligraphy, poetry)

Reading Strategy:
Inferencing

Discuss the division of land and power in Japan. Then have students answer the question. (Answers will vary; feudalism created a very ordered society in Japan.)

• What does a guest do after first tasting the tea? (praises the tea maker)

• What four things are important in a tea ceremony? (harmony, respect, purity or clearness, peace)

LEARNING STYLES

Auditory/Verbal

Students who learn best by auditory activities will enjoy discussing the planning that would go into a Japanese tea party. Have the class brainstorm phrases of praise that could be said during the tea party. Divide the class into groups of four. Have each group reenact a tea party, verbalizing the actions during the reenactment. Encourage each group to incorporate words of praise into their reenactments. Reconvene as a group and discuss what students enjoyed most about the tea parties.

3 Reinforce and Extend

Lesson 5 Review Answers

1. haiku **2.** tanka **3.** shogun
4. daimyos **5.** samurai

Answers will vary. To write poems that develop a mood and that can be only a certain number of lines and syllables is hard work. To do this, the samurai must focus his mind; this takes emotional and mental discipline. To develop beautiful calligraphy also takes hard work. To do this, the samurai must have a steady hand; this takes physical control.

Communication in History

Have a volunteer read the title "A Romantic Novel from Japan." Explain that romantic novels are very popular in the United States today. Have students read to find out about the first romantic novel ever written. When they finish reading, ask what new way of writing developed around A.D. 1000 (kana) and why it was developed (to express sounds in the Japanese language).

Word Bank

daimyos
haiku
samurai
shogun
tanka

Lesson 5 Review On a sheet of paper, use the words from the Word Bank to complete each sentence correctly.

1. A _____ is a three-line poem with 17 syllables.

2. A _____ is a five-line poem with 31 syllables.

3. The military dictator of Japan was the _____.

4. The great landowners of Japan were the _____.

5. The _____ were Japanese warriors.

What do you think

How did calligraphy and poetry help the samurai win control of his feelings and actions?

Communication in History

A Romantic Novel from Japan

Literature was important in Heian Japan. Many women at court kept diaries. They described their elegant life. One lady of the court wrote the world's first novel. We know only her court name, Murasaki Shikibu. She came from a noble family. She married and had a daughter. A few years later, her husband died. Lady Murasaki then went to court to serve the empress. Her novel grew out of her diary of court life.

Her novel is called *The Tale of Genji*. Its hero is Prince Genji, the "shining Prince." Genji has many adventures and romances.

The Japanese used many Chinese characters in their writing. There were, however, some Japanese sounds that these characters could not express. As a result, a new way of writing Japanese developed around 1000. It is called kana. *The Tale of Genji* is written in kana.

Objectives

◆ To explain how geography helped Japan become isolated

◆ To describe some arts of Japan

Reading Strategy:
Inferencing

After reading this section, what can you infer about the power of shoguns in Japan?

In 1603, the Tokugawa family took control of Japan. The shogun forced the daimyos to move to Edo, a small town on the coast. He could keep his eye on them there. (Today, Edo is the city of Tokyo, one of the world's largest cities.) A daimyo could visit his estate only if he left his wife and oldest son in Edo.

Why Did Japan Isolate Itself?

In the 1600s, many foreigners—merchants and missionaries—visited Japan. But the shoguns thought that Western influence could hurt their power. Beginning in 1623, they began to isolate Japan. They killed all foreign missionaries or forced them to leave. In 1614, the shogun said that no one could be a Christian. In the next 20 years, thousands of Christian Japanese were killed.

The Japanese could not leave Japan. If they did, they could not return. By 1639, only the city of Nagasaki was open to foreigners. The shogun let some Chinese and Dutch traders live there. For the next 200 years, Japan shut itself off from the world.

The Japanese still have beautiful gardens, as they had hundreds of years ago.

What Arts Did Japan Develop?

Japanese paintings usually show the beauty of Japan. Some samurai painters drew pictures of war. The most famous painter of ancient Japan was Sesshu, a Buddhist monk. In the late 1400s, he painted a beautiful silk scroll that is 52 feet long. It shows the land of Japan as it changes over the four seasons of the year.

In their gardens, the Japanese copy nature in a small way. They carefully choose and place rocks in the garden. They also make hills and ponds that look natural.

Chapter 13: Lesson 6

Overview This lesson describes how the Tokugawa family brought unity to Japan.

Objectives

■ To explain how geography helped Japan become isolated

■ To describe some arts of Japan

Student Pages pages 315–316

Teacher's Resource Library TRL

Workbook Activity 58

Activity 58

Modified Activity 58

Vocabulary

ikebana	Noh drama
kabuki	

Have students write three sentences, using each of the vocabulary words once. Encourage volunteers to read their sentences aloud.

PRONUNCIATION GUIDE

Use this list to help students pronounce difficult words in this lesson.

Edo	(ed′ ō)
Sesshu	(se′ shü)
Tokugawa	(tō ku gä′ wə)

 Warm-Up Activity

Draw students' attention to the photo on page 315. Discuss how the garden creates a sense of peace and harmony. Encourage students to create drawings that in some way show peace and harmony. Display the drawings for others to view.

 Teaching the Lesson

Ask students to suggest the advantages of a people developing their own ways of doing things. Then have them read pages 315–316 to find out what happened when the Japanese sealed themselves off from the rest of the world.

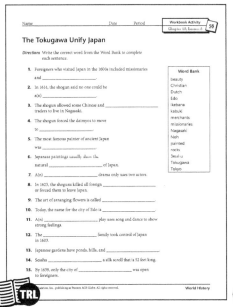

Workbook Activity 58   **Activity 58**

Ask:

- What did the shogun force the daimyo to do? (move to Edo)
- Today, what do we call the city where the daimyo moved? (Tokyo)

Reading Strategy:
Inferencing

Tell students to make a list of the different actions of the shoguns. Then have students answer the question. (Answers will vary; the shoguns selfishly used their power to protect their position in Japanese society.)

- What is one form of artistic expression that developed during Japan's isolation? (Answers will vary; students may say kabuki, Noh dramas, or ikebana.)
- When did Noh dramas begin? (1325)

3 **Reinforce and Extend**

Ikebana
One Japanese art of arranging flowers

Noh drama
A Japanese play with only two actors

Kabuki
A Japanese play with exaggerated actions

Japan still developed a rich culture. Among its arts are arranging flowers, writing and acting in plays, painting, and gardening. The Japanese call one art of arranging flowers **ikebana.** This art uses only a few flowers.

Noh dramas began in 1325. A Noh play uses only two actors, who wear masks. A storyteller tells the story while musicians play and the two actors act. In 1586, **kabuki** developed. A kabuki play uses song and dance to show strong feelings. Actors tell the story with exaggerated movements that are larger than in real life.

Lesson 6 Review On a sheet of paper, write the letter of the answer that correctly completes each sentence.

1. The Tokugawa shogun moved the capital of Japan to _____.

   A Edo   **C** Hangzhou
   B Beijing   **D** Nagasaki

2. Noh dramas use only _____ actors.

   A five   **B** four   **C** three   **D** two

3. Kabuki plays developed _____ Noh plays.

   A earlier than   **C** at the same time as
   B later than   **D** 200 years later than

4. The Japanese call one art of flower arranging _____.

   A shogun   **C** ikebana
   B exaggerate   **D** hari-kari

5. _____ was the name of the family that began to isolate Japan.

   A Shogun   **C** Samurai
   B Daimyo   **D** Tokugawa

What do you think

What do you like best about the Japanese arts discussed in this lesson? Explain your answer.

Lesson 6 Review Answers
1. A **2.** D **3.** B **4.** C **5.** D

Answers will vary. Students should refer to ikebana, kabuki, Noh dramas, or Japanese gardens in their answers.

Document-Based Reading

Marco Polo in China

Marco Polo wrote a book about China in the late 1200s.

Marco Polo's father and uncle were merchants in Venice, Italy. In 1271, they left Venice for the court of Kublai Khan in China. Marco Polo was 17 years old.

Polo worked as an official for the Khan. When he returned to Europe in 1295, he wrote The Travels of Marco Polo. *This reading from that book describes the Khan's palace.*

For three months every year Kublai Khan lives in the capital of Cathay . . . where he has a great palace. It is surrounded by a square wall, each side of which is a mile long. The wall is very thick and ten paces high. . . . At each of the four corners of the square there is a splendid and beautiful palace where the Great Khan's arms are stored. Halfway along each side of the square there is another similar palace, making eight in all. Every palace houses different equipment. For example, in one there is harness for the horses; in another there are bows, ropes, arrows, quivers and all the implements for archery; in a third there are breastplates and armour made of boiled leather; and so it goes on.

There are five gates in the south side of the wall. The central one is only opened for the Great Khan himself. Two small gates on either side of the main gate and two large ones near the corners of the wall are for citizens and other people.

Inside this wall is another one, slightly longer than it is wide. . . .

Within the second wall is the Great Khan's palace—the biggest palace ever to be seen. It abuts onto the northern wall, but to the south is a wide open space where barons and soldiers parade. It is built on only one floor, with a very high roof. . . .

The walls inside are covered with silver and gold and there are paintings of horsemen, dragons, and every kind of bird and animal. The vaulted ceiling is also entirely covered with paintings and gold ornamentation. The main reception room can seat more than 6,000 people. There is an overwhelming number of rooms; no architect in the world could have designed the palace better. The roof is beautifully painted in many colors—vermilion, green, blue, yellow, and so forth—so that it shines like a jewel and can be seen from afar. . . .

Document-Based Questions

1. The Khan's palace was well protected. Describe the area around it.

2. How were the eight palaces on the outer wall used?

3. Why was the central gate special?

4. How were the palace walls and ceilings decorated?

5. How many people could the main reception room hold?

Read the title, "Marco Polo in China," to students. Explain that people have loved the stories of Marco Polo for generations. In this section, the reader gets a firsthand glimpse of the inner workings of the court of Kublai Khan. Have students read the two introductory paragraphs silently.

Ask:

- Where did Marco Polo's journey begin? (Venice)
- How many years was Marco Polo gone? How old was he when he returned? (24 years; 41 years old)

Have students read about Marco Polo's adventure and answer the questions.

Answers to Document-Based Questions:

1. It was on a piece of land a mile square, surrounded by two thick walls, which had palaces and gates built into them.

2. They stored military equipment, such as harnesses for horses, implements for archery, and armor.

3. It was only opened for Khan.

4. The walls and ceiling were covered with silver and gold. They were decorated with paintings of horsemen, dragons, birds, and animals.

5. The hall could seat 6,000 people.

Chapter Project Follow-up

Put aside one day for groups to present their studies and explain their displays on inventions from India, China, or Japan. Invite other members of the school staff to enjoy the displays. Have a student who has an interest in photography take photos for the school newspaper. Videotape the displays for student portfolios.

Ask students if they have ever seen pictures of the Taj Mahal or heard about it. Have them read the story, "The Taj Mahal—A Monument of Love," with a partner, alternating reading the paragraphs. When they have finished, ask students if they think the story of the building of the Taj Mahal would make a good plot for a romantic novel. Let them express their views on how the story could be enhanced, if at all, to appeal to popular tastes. Then have them read and answer the Wrap-Up questions on their own.

Answers to Spotlight Story Wrap-Up:

1. It is a memorial of love for his favorite wife.

2. It is made of white marble.

3. It took 22 years to build.

4. It was decorated with a carved marble screen, a blanket of pearls, gold, silver, and jeweled flowers.

5. He planned a matching tomb of black marble, but he lost power and never built it. Shah Jahan was buried next to his wife in the Taj Mahal.

Spotlight Story

The Taj Mahal— A Monument of Love

The Taj Mahal is one of the most beautiful buildings in the world. It is also a love story in stone.

Shah Jahan was one of the last Mogul emperors. He was the grandson of Akbar. In 1631, Shah Jahan's favorite wife died. They had been close companions for 19 years of marriage. The broken-hearted shah built this tomb to show their great love. The queen's name was Mumtaz Mahal. It means "Chosen One of the Palace." The building's name comes from her name.

Workers brought materials from all over Asia. White marble was brought up the Jumna River to the town of Agra. More than 20,000 workers worked for 22 years to complete it.

The Taj Mahal itself is a four-sided marble building. It sits on a raised square platform. Each side has a huge central arch and small domes. Both the inside and outside walls are delicately carved. At each corner stands a slender tower, or minaret. Gardens surround the tomb. Nearby are a mosque and other buildings.

Here is one visitor's reaction: "With its minarets rising at each corner, its dome and tapering spire, it creates a sense of airy, almost floating lightness. Looking at it, I decided [that] I had never known what perfect proportions were before."

The burial room is eight-sided, with a marble screen around it. The screen is carved so delicately that it looks like lace. At first it was decorated with jewels. A blanket of pearls covered the queen's coffin. Gold and silver decorated the walls. Blue sapphires and red

The Taj Mahal was built for Shah Jahan's favorite wife.

rubies gave color to carved marble flowers. Over time, the pearls and other treasures were stolen.

Shah Jahan planned to build a copy of the Taj Mahal for himself. It would be in black marble. A bridge of silver would join the two tombs. The black tomb, however, was never built. Shah Jahan lost power in 1658. He died in 1666. He was buried next to his beloved queen in the Taj Mahal.

Wrap-Up

1. Why did Shah Jahan build the Taj Mahal?

2. What material was used for the Taj Mahal?

3. How long did the construction take?

4. How was the inside of the building decorated?

5. What were Shah Jahan's plans for his own burial? What happened?

---

318   *Unit 2   Regional Civilizations*

Chapter 13　S U M M A R Y

- The Gupta dynasty ruled India during its Golden Age (320 to 535). Indian religious artists developed a unique style. Scientists made many discoveries. Mathematicians used zero and the numerals 1 through 9.

- In 1398, Mongols led by Tamerlane attacked India. In 1525, another Mongol leader began the Mogul empire. Akbar was its best-known ruler. Mogul architects built beautiful buildings.

- China was rich and powerful during the T'ang dynasty (618 to 907). Scholars ran the government, and trading brought foreign visitors and new ideas.

- In the Sung dynasty (960 to 1279), the center of culture shifted south to the Yangtze River Valley. Chinese inventions included gunpowder, the compass, the abacus, the clock, and porcelain.

- In the 1200s, Mongols conquered China, India, and Russia. Later, Kublai Khan established the Yuan dynasty. Mongol rulers encouraged trade with the Arabs and Europeans. Scholars wrote and performed in plays and operas.

- After the fall of the Mongols in 1368, China began to isolate itself.

- The Japanese adapted many ideas from Korea and China. Japan's native religion, Shinto, worships many nature spirits. Many Japanese also became Buddhists.

- During the Heian era (800 to 1200), Japanese nobles wrote haiku and tanka poetry. Noble families took power from the emperor. The shoguns were the real rulers.

- In Japan's feudal system, the daimyos were powerful lords. Samurai were warrior knights. The samurai practiced martial arts and were artists. They followed a code of honor called bushido. Women were also expected to be brave.

- Shoguns from the Tokugawa family took control of Japan in 1603. They moved the capital to Edo. They tried to end foreign influence, including Christianity.

- Flower-arranging, plays, painting, and gardening are important arts in Japanese culture. Noh and kabuki are forms of drama.

TEACHER'S RESOURCE

The AGS Globe Teaching Strategies in Social Studies Transparencies may be used with this chapter. The transparencies add an interactive dimension to expand and enhance the *World History* program content.

Using the Chapter Summary

Have students read the Chapter Summary on page 319 to review the main ideas presented in Chapter 13.

Ask:

- Which dynasty ruled India during its Golden Age? (the Gupta dynasty)

- Which Mongol leader is remembered as an invader of India? as the best-known ruler of India's Moghul Empire? (Tamerlane; Akbar)

- Which Chinese dynasty brought in foreign visitors? Which shifted the center of culture south? (the T'ang; the Sung)

- Under which Mongol ruler were strong trade ties established between China and lands to the west? (Kublai Kahn)

- After the fall of which people did China begin to isolate itself? (the Mongols)

- From which people did Japan adopt many ideas? Which religion originated in Japan? (the Chinese; Shinto)

- Which individuals dominated Japan's feudal system? (the daimyos)

- Which powerful family took control of Japan from the daimyo? (the Tokugawa family)

- What is an example of an art form that flourished during the Tokugawa period? (answers include ikebana, Noh dramas, and kabuki theater)

Chapter 13 Review

Use the Chapter Review to prepare students for tests and to reteach content from the chapter.

Chapter 13 Mastery Test

The Teacher's Resource Library includes two forms of the Chapter 13 Mastery Test. Each test covers the chapter Goals for Learning. An optional third page of additional critical-thinking items is included for each test. The difficulty level of the two forms is equivalent.

Chapter 13 Review Answers

1. Ajanta
2. Gupta
3. Mongols
4. T'ang
5. Sung
6. Genghis Khan
7. Shinto
8. Shoguns
9. Tokugawa
10. Sesshu
11. A
12. C
13. D
14. A
15. D

Word Bank

Ajanta
Genghis Khan
Gupta
Mongols
Sesshu
Shinto
Shoguns
Sung
T'ang
Tokugawa

On a sheet of paper, use the words from the Word Bank to complete each sentence correctly.

1. Wall drawings in the _____ caves tell us about life in ancient India.

2. The _____ dynasty ruled India during its Golden Age.

3. The _____ invaded India in 1398.

4. In the _____ dynasty, scholars ruled China.

5. The artists of the _____ dynasty painted masterpieces.

6. The greatest Mongol conqueror was _____.

7. _____ is the religion born in Japan.

8. _____ ruled Japan in the name of the emperor.

9. The _____ shoguns isolated Japan from the rest of the world.

10. _____ was the most famous painter of ancient Japan.

On a sheet of paper, write the letter of the answer that correctly completes each sentence.

11. During the Golden Age, scientists in India figured out the _____ of the moon.

   A size
   B shape
   C craters
   D weight

12. Indian doctors learned about _____ 1,000 years before Europeans did.

   A Shinto
   B compass
   C inoculation
   D abacus

13. The Chinese invented _____.

   A gunpowder
   B compasses
   C clocks
   D all of the above

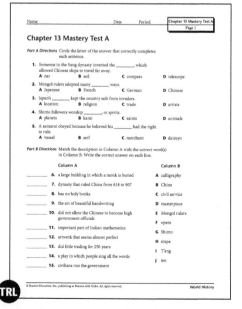

Chapter 13 Mastery Test A, pages 1–3

14. The real ruler of Japan during the Heian era was the _____.

  A shogun   **C** samurai
  B daimyo   **D** tanka

15. The Japanese wrote _____.

  A haiku   **C** kabuki
  B tanka   **D** all of the above

On a sheet of paper, write the answer to each question. Use complete sentences.

16. What is one gift India has given to world civilization?

17. What is one gift China has given to world civilization?

18. What is one thing that is the same and one thing that is different between Japanese and European feudalism?

Critical Thinking On a sheet of paper, write your response to each question. Use complete sentences.

19. Imagine that you are a European merchant in the Middle Ages. Which country would you choose to visit: India, China, or Japan? Explain why.

20. Chinese and Japanese artists usually paint nature—trees, mountains, and flowers. Western artists often draw people. What does this tell you about the different cultures?

Save tests and quizzes you take. Use them to study for future tests.

16. Among India's gifts are: Hinduism, Buddhism, knowledge about the size of the moon and gravity, the number system based on 10, the concept of zero, our decimal system, inoculation, and tools and understanding of medicine.

17. Among China's gifts are: a type of poetry, the invention of printing, gunpowder, the magnetic compass, clocks, a machine to detect earthquakes, a style of painting, and porcelain.

18. Both Japan and Europe based feudalism on land. Both had men in varied positions of power: king/shogun; vassal/daimyo; knight/samurai. But they differed in that European feudalism was a kind of legal agreement between the knight and the lord, whereas in Japan, the warriors felt that it was the right of the daimyo to rule.

Critical Thinking

19. Answers will vary. Students should use details from the chapter in their responses.

20. Answers will vary. Perhaps the Chinese and Japanese find nature mysterious and boundless, while Western artists are intrigued with the power and wonder of human beings.

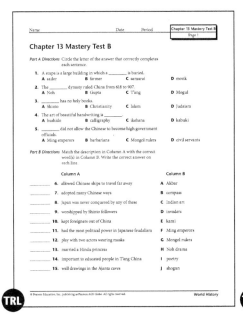

Chapter 13 Mastery Test B, pages 1–3   *Civilization in E/SE Asia   Chapter 13*   **321**

Write the following two statements on the board:

> Charlemagne was a Frankish king. (fact)
>
> Charlemagne was not a very good king. (opinion)

Read the statements aloud and ask students which statement gives a fact and which gives an opinion. Ask students how they know which is which. (They may suggest that the first statement can be verified in a reference book, but the second cannot.) Write "fact" and "opinion" above the appropriate statements and have students offer additional examples of each.

Then have students read the Skill Builder on page 322 and answer the questions.

Ask:

- **What is an opinion?** (An opinion is someone's judgment or belief about something.)

- **Would you expect to find facts or opinions in a reference book?** (facts)

Unit 2 Skill Builder Answers

1. Fact—The existence of a law code can be proved; opinion—The words *wise* and *able* express opinions about Justinian as a ruler.

2. Opinion—The word *great* states an opinion about the importance of William's victory; fact—It can be proved that William became king because he had defeated all other claimants to the throne.

3. Fact—It can be proved that the pope made such a demand; opinion—*Necessary* states an opinion. It was what the pope thought, but not everyone agreed.

4. Fact—It can be verified that Muslim teachers started schools at the invitation of the kings; opinion—The word *improve* states an opinion about the schools' role in changing the connection between areas.

5. Answers will vary. Sample fact: Feudalism was based on the ownership of land; sample opinion: Living on a manor was comfortable.

Unit 2
Skill Builder

Fact and Opinion

As you study history, you will read many facts. Sometimes people write books about history in which they state their opinions. You need to be able to tell the difference between fact and opinion.

A fact can be proved true or false.

> Mansa Musa ruled Mali in the 1300s.

An opinion is someone's judgment, belief, or way of thinking about something. To identify an opinion, look for words that tell how someone felt. An opinion is more than just a fact.

> Mansa Musa was a rich and noble ruler.
>
> Mansa Musa was generous to everyone.

Read each pair of sentences in items 1–4. Decide which sentence in each pair is fact and which is opinion. Explain your answer.

1. Justinian had Roman laws collected and organized into a code. Justinian was a wise and able ruler.

2. William the Conqueror's victory was a great step in English history. William the Conqueror's victory made him king of England.

3. The pope called for the First Crusade to free Palestine. The crusades were necessary to defend Christianity.

4. The kings of Ghana invited Muslim teachers to begin schools in Kumbi. This helped improve the connection between the two areas.

5. Write a fact and an opinion about the Middle Ages.

Unit Skills Activity

Cut out a letter to the editor from a local newspaper to read to students. Try to find one that would be of interest to students. First, read aloud a sentence from the letter and ask students to identify it as a fact or an opinion. (Choose sentences that clearly state either facts or opinions.) Continue until students have identified several facts and opinions. Then have them listen as you read the entire letter. Ask whether they think the writer makes a persuasive argument, and if so, why. After the discussion, distribute copies of the Unit 2 Skill Builder for students to complete.

| Name | Date | Period | **Unit Skills Activity** Unit 2 |

In My Opinion, As a Matter of Fact

Part A Directions Read the following opinion and reasons why the writer thinks you should agree with that opinion. Check the box on the right to show whether each reason is a fact or an opinion. Then explain how you know the reason is a fact or an opinion.

Opinion: I believe our government should devote more money to the exploration of Mars.

Reasons:	Fact	Opinion
1. The Pathfinder mission showed that we can successfully place equipment on Mars.	☐	☐
2. Space exploration has led to many advances in medicine and industry.	☐	☐
3. The information that space probes send back is very valuable.	☐	☐
4. All of society benefits from the wonderful knowledge we get from space experiments.	☐	☐

Part B Directions You can read people's opinions every day in the letters to the editor section of a newspaper. By writing a letter to the editor, people try to persuade others to think as they do. Choose one of the following subjects for a letter to the editor.

- Whether or not families should be required to recycle as part of the local trash pickup program
- Whether or not teenagers should have a citywide curfew

Before you begin writing your letter, write your opinion at the top of a sheet of paper. Then list as many reasons as you can think of that support your opinion. Circle the reasons that are facts. These are your strongest reasons. Be sure to use them. Write your letter to the editor on a separate sheet of paper.

World History

TRL

Unit 2 SUMMARY

- Farming and trade revived in the late Middle Ages. Between 1095 and 1291, Europeans went on Crusades to take Palestine from the Muslims.

- Under feudalism, a lord granted land to a vassal in exchange for service. Knights fought frequent wars. Peasants and serfs worked the farm on a manor.

- Romanesque churches were dark and heavy with rounded arches. Gothic buildings had pointed arches; tall, thin walls; and stained-glass windows.

- The eastern Roman Empire became the Byzantine Empire. Its greatest ruler, Justinian, organized a code of laws. The empire fell to the Turks, however, in 1453.

- In 1054, the Christian Church split into Roman Catholic and Eastern Orthodox.

- Russia began in Kiev about 862. Then power shifted to Moscow. Modern Russia began in the 1400s when Ivan the Great drove out Mongol invaders.

- Charlemagne, a Frankish king, united Western Europe in 800. Later, Vikings attacked parts of Europe. William of Normandy invaded Britain in 1066.

- Muhammad was born in Arabia in 570. He preached a new religion, Islam, with one god, Allah. Its followers are called Muslims.

- The holy book of Islam is the Qur'an, written in Arabic. Muslims regard Muhammad as God's prophet.

- Muslims have five duties, or pillars. They must state their faith, pray five times a day, give alms, and fast. If possible, they make a pilgrimage, or Hajj, to Mecca.

- Ghana, Mali, and Songhai were great trading kingdoms in West Africa. Their wealth came from the gold-salt trade.

- The Gupta dynasty (320 to 535) brought a Golden Age to India. Mathematicians invented zero and the numerals 1 through 9. The Mogul empire in India began in 1525.

- China was rich and powerful in the T'ang and Sung dynasties. Trade was important. Chinese inventions included printing, gunpowder, the compass, and porcelain. Mongols led by Genghis Khan conquered China, India, and Russia in the 1200s.

- The Heian era (800 to 1200) was important in Japanese culture.

- In Japan's feudal system, the daimyos were land-owning lords. Samurai, or warrior knights, followed a code of honor and discipline. Military leaders, called shoguns, ruled Japan instead of the emperor. After 1603, the Tokugawa shoguns ended foreign influence.

Using the Unit Summary

Read and discuss the Unit Summary statements on page 323 with students.

Ask:

- **What was the purpose of the crusades?** (The Roman Catholic Church wanted to take Palestine from the Muslims.)

- **What was the role of each of the following under feudalism: lord, vassal, knight, and serf?** (Lords owned the land, vassals received the land in exchange for loyalty to the lord, knights fought for the lord, and serfs did the physical work on the manor.)

- **What are some of the characteristics of Gothic architecture?** (Gothic buildings have pointed arches; tall, thin walls; and stained glass windows)

- **What event marked the beginning of Modern Russia? When did it take place?** (Ivan the Great drove out Mongol invaders in the 1400s.)

- **What was Charlemagne noted for?** (He united the countries of Western Europe in 800.)

- **What are the five pillars, or duties, of Islam?** (Muslims must state their faith, pray five times a day, give alms, fast, and make a pilgrimage to Mecca if possible.)

- **Who was Genghis Khan?** (Genghis Khan was the leader of the Mongols, who conquered China, India, and Russia in the 1200s.)

- **How was the Japanese feudal system organized?** (The shoguns were the military leaders that ruled the country, the daimyos were land-owning lords, and the samurai were the warrior knights.)

Unit Activity Follow-Up

After all of the student teams have played the Powerful Leaders Game, discuss the experience with them. Students may want to collect information on other leaders and play the game again.

Unit 2 Mastery Test

The Teacher's Resource Library includes a two-page Unit Mastery Test. An optional third page of additional critical-thinking items is included for each test. The Unit 2 Mastery Test is pictured on page 861 of this Teacher's Edition.

Planning Guide
Early Modern Times

		Student Text Lesson					
		Student Pages	Vocabulary	Lesson Review	Critical-Thinking Questions	Chapter Summary	Chapter Review
Chapter 14	The Renaissance	326–349	✔		✔	347	348
Lesson 1	The Troubled 14th Century	329–330	✔	330	✔		
Lesson 2	The Spirit of the Renaissance	331–333	✔	333	✔		
Lesson 3	The Renaissance Begins in Italy	334–337	✔	337	✔		
Lesson 4	Renaissance Literature	338–340	✔	340	✔		
Lesson 5	Great Renaissance Artists	341–344	✔	344	✔		
Chapter 15	The Reformation	350–373	✔		✔	371	372
Lesson 1	People Challenge the Church's Authority	353–354	✔	354	✔		
Lesson 2	Martin Luther Leads the Reformation	355–357	✔	357	✔		
Lesson 3	Luther Starts His Own Church	358–359	✔	359	✔		
Lesson 4	Protestant Ideas Spread to England	360–362	✔	362	✔		
Lesson 5	John Calvin Organizes a New Religion	363–365	✔	365	✔		
Lesson 6	The Counter-Reformation	366–368	✔	368	✔		
Chapter 16	The New Science	374–395			✔	393	394
Lesson 1	The Development of Modern Science	377–378	✔	378	✔		
Lesson 2	Copernicus	379–381	✔	381	✔		
Lesson 3	Galileo	382–384	✔	384	✔		
Lesson 4	Isaac Newton	385–386	✔	386	✔		
Lesson 5	Other Early Scientists	387–390	✔	390	✔		

(Unit Planning Guide is continued on next page.)

Unit Activities

Student Text
Unit 3 Summary
Unit 3 Skill Builder

Teacher's Resource Library
Unit 3 Activities 1–2
Unit 3 Skills Activity

Assessment Options

Teacher's Resource Library
Chapter 14 Mastery Tests A and B
Chapter 15 Mastery Tests A and B
Chapter 16 Mastery Tests A and B
Chapter 17 Mastery Tests A and B
Chapter 18 Mastery Tests A and B
Unit 3 Mastery Test

Reading Strategy	Map Study/Map Skills	Writing About History	Geography Note	Biography	History in Your Life	Communication in History	Technology Connection	Then and Now	Spotlight Story	Document-Based Reading	Background Information	Applications (Home, Career, Community)	World Cultures	Study Skills	Online Connection	ELL/ESL Strategy	Auditory/Verbal	Visual/Spatial	Body/Kinesthetic	Interpersonal/Group Learning	Logical/Mathematical	Activities/Modified Activities	Workbook Activities	Self-Study Guide	Chapter Outline
328	327								346	345		345												✔	✔
✔					330											330						59	59		
✔		332	333													332				332	333	60	60		
✔	336											335	337			335			336			61	61		
✔						340	339					340				340	339					62	62		
✔											344			342		343		342				63	63		
352	351								370	369														✔	✔
✔														354				354				64	64		
✔					357		356					357				356						65	65		
✔		359																		359		66	66		
✔															362	362			362		361	67	67		
✔											365		365			364						68	68		
✔				368								368				367	367					69	69		
376	375								392	391														✔	✔
✔								378								378				378		70	70		
✔							381				381	381			381	380					380	71	71		
✔		382										383		384		383						72	72		
				386												386			386			73	73		
✔					390						388	389		389		389			388			74	74		

Student Text Features

Teaching Strategies

Learning Styles

Teacher's Resource Library

TRL Activities

The Teacher's Resource Library (TRL) contains a set of lower-level worksheets called Modified Activities. These worksheets cover the same content as the standard Activities but are written at a lower reading level.

Skill Track

Use Skill Track for *World History* to monitor student progress and meet the demands of Adequate Yearly Progress (AYP). Make informed instructional decisions with individual student and class reports of lesson and chapter assessments. With immediate and ongoing feedback, students will also see what they have learned and where they need more reinforcement and practice.

3

Planning Guide
Early Modern Times

(continued)

		Student Text Lesson					
		Student Pages	Vocabulary	Lesson Review	Critical-Thinking Questions	Chapter Summary	Chapter Review
Chapter 17	**Beginnings of Our Global Age**	396–425	✔		✔	423	424
Lesson 1	Europeans Search for New Trade Routes	399–400	✔	400	✔		
Lesson 2	Exploring New Lands	401–405	✔	405	✔		
Lesson 3	The Spanish Conquer Two Empires in America	406–409	✔	409	✔		
Lesson 4	Spain Establishes Colonies in America	410–412	✔	412	✔		
Lesson 5	The Growth of the Slave Trade	413–415	✔	415	✔		
Lesson 6	The Results of Exploring and Establishing Colonies	416–420	✔	420	✔		
Chapter 18	**The Age of Kings**	426–455	✔		✔	453	454
Lesson 1	The Rise of Nations	429–431	✔	431	✔		
Lesson 2	The Rise and Fall of Spain	432–436	✔	436	✔		
Lesson 3	English Monarchs Struggle for Power	437–438	✔	438	✔		
Lesson 4	England Rejects Absolute Monarchy	439–443	✔	443	✔		
Lesson 5	Absolute Monarchy in France	444–447	✔	447	✔		
Lesson 6	Russia and Prussia Produce Strong Monarchs	448–450	✔	450	✔		

Reading Strategy	Map Study/Map Skills	Writing About History	Geography Note	Biography	History in Your Life	Communication in History	Technology Connection	Then and Now	Spotlight Story	Document-Based Reading	Background Information	Applications (Home, Career, Community)	World Cultures	Study Skills	Online Connection	ELL/ESL Strategy	Auditory/Verbal	Visual/Spatial	Body/Kinesthetic	Interpersonal/Group Learning	Logical/Mathematical	Activities/Modified Activities	Workbook Activities	Self-Study Guide	Chapter Outline
398	397								422	421		422												✔	✔
✔																				400		75	75		
✔	402			403		405								402	402	403, 405					404	76	76		
✔		406	407			409					409		408			408						77	77		
												412				411		412				78	78		
✔	415															414	414					79	79		
✔	419		418								420					417			418			80	80		
428	427								452	451														✔	✔
✔						431						430		431	431	431				430		81	81		
✔	434		436									435	436			436		433	435			82	82		
✔												438				438						83	83		
✔	440															442	443					84	84		
✔			447								445					446					446	85	85		
✔		449														450						86	86		

Other Resources

Books for Teachers

MacCulloch, Diarmaid. *The Reformation.*
New York: Viking Penguin, 2005. (an
authoritative account of the Reformation
arranged in chronological order)

Turner, Richard N. *Renaissance Florence:
The Invention of a New Art.* Englewood
Cliffs, NJ: Prentice Hall Press, 2005. (an
introduction to life among the artists in
14th and 15th century Florence)

Books for Students

Kramer, S.A. *Who Was Ferdinand
Magellan?* New York: Grosset & Dunlap,
2004. (describes Magellan's life and
voyage; includes a timeline to put
Magellan's voyage into historical context)

Panchyk, Richard. *Galileo for Kids:
His Life and Ideas.* Chicago Review
Press, 2005. (describes Galileo's life and
the people and events that influenced
him; contains 25 hands-on activities
designed to explain Galileo's ideas)

CD-ROM/Software

The Renaissance of Florence. E.M.M.E.
Interactive (203-869-8144). (this
interactive CD-ROM narrates the story
of the early Renaissance in architecture,
sculpture, and paintings)

Videos

Christopher Columbus. (95 minutes)
DVD, Vision Video, 2005. (the story of
Christopher Columbus's journey to the
New World; originally a 1949 classic
movie, starring Frederic March)

In the Footsteps of Martin Luther. DVD,
Vision Video, 2006. (traces the most
important stages of Luther's life through
the ten German towns in which he lived)

Web Sites

www.agsglobewh.com/page324a (official
Web site of the British Monarchy)

www.agsglobewh.com/page324b
(The Mariners' Museum in Newport
News, Virginia, hosts an online
exhibition that retraces the steps of great
marine explorers.)

Unit 3

Early Modern Times

After the Middle Ages in Europe, change began to creep across the land. In this unit, you will settle in Rome, where great artists create masterpieces. You will be there for the Renaissance, or rebirth of learning. You will travel to Germany and learn about the Reformation. Then you will journey to many parts of Europe to see how scientists used the new scientific method to question old beliefs.

Later in the unit, you will meet kings and queens, explorers and conquistadors, emperors and warriors as you sail back and forth across the Atlantic Ocean.

Chapters in Unit 3

325

Introducing the Unit

Read aloud the quotation by Sir Isaac Newton. Ask students to study the picture of Queen Elizabeth I on page 324. Then have volunteers read aloud the introductory paragraphs on page 325.

Ask:

- What is another word for renaissance? (rebirth)
- Which religion dominated European culture in the Middle Ages? (Christianity)
- In which country did Martin Luther begin teaching? (Germany)
- What was the Spanish Armada? (a large fleet of warships that was sent by Philip II of Spain to attack England)

Presenting the Unit Activity

Romeo and Juliet, written by William Shakespeare, is one of the greatest plays ever written. Students will read and explain the meaning of the 14 lines of the play's introduction, the prologue. Distribute copies of Unit 3, Activity 1. Explain that the 14 lines on the activity sheet are the play's prologue. They are read to the audience by an actor or chorus at the beginning of the play. Add that the prologue is also a sonnet. Then be sure students understand the instructions.

In Unit 3, Activity 2, students will have the opportunity to express their opinions about the meaning of the prologue. Activities 1–2 are provided here to give students some exposure to Shakespeare, whose life and works are discussed in Chapter 14.

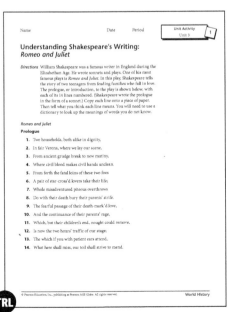

Name _____ Date _____ Period _____ | Unit Activity Unit 3 | 1

Understanding Shakespeare's Writing:
Romeo and Juliet

Directions William Shakespeare was a famous writer in England during the Elizabethan Age. He wrote sonnets and plays. One of his most famous plays is *Romeo and Juliet*. In this play, Shakespeare tells the story of two teenagers from feuding families who fall in love. The prologue, or introduction, to the play is shown below, with each of its 14 lines numbered. (Shakespeare wrote the prologue in the form of a sonnet.) Copy each line onto a piece of paper. Then tell what you think each line means. You will need to use a dictionary to look up the meanings of words you do not know.

Romeo and Juliet
Prologue

1. Two households, both alike in dignity,
2. In fair Verona, where we lay our scene,
3. From ancient grudge break to new mutiny,
4. Where civil blood makes civil hands unclean.
5. From forth the fatal loins of these two foes
6. A pair of star-cross'd lovers take their life;
7. Whole misadventured piteous overthrows
8. Do with their death bury their parents' strife.
9. The fearful passage of their death-mark'd love,
10. And the continuance of their parents' rage,
11. Which, but their children's end, nought could remove,
12. Is now the two hours' traffic of our stage;
13. The which if you with patient ears attend,
14. What here shall miss, our toil shall strive to mend.

World History

Unit 3, Activity 1

Name _____ Date _____ Period _____ | Unit Activity Unit 3 | 2

Expressing Opinions

Directions When *Romeo and Juliet* is performed, a single actor or a chorus of actors recites the prologue to the audience. Read each question below and then write your opinion.

1. The prologue to *Romeo and Juliet* is the first part of the play that the audience hears. Why do you think Shakespeare began his play with a prologue?

2. Practice reading aloud one or two lines of the prologue. Is the language hard to get used to? How do you think the actors who perform Shakespeare's plays today might prepare for their roles?

3. What mood, or feeling, does the prologue give? Look at the words Shakespeare uses. What mood do you think Shakespeare was trying to create? Why?

4. You may have seen a performance of *Romeo and Juliet* or another of Shakespeare's plays. Perhaps the play was presented as a feature film or a musical. What do you think Shakespeare might say about the modern films, musical productions, and other interpretations of his play, *Romeo and Juliet*?

5. Some people think Shakespeare is one of the greatest writers in the English language. Do you agree or disagree? Write at least three reasons for your opinion of Shakespeare.

World History

Unit 3, Activity 2

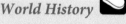
Introducing the Chapter

In the middle of the 14th century, the Middle Ages in Europe were brought to an end by the Black Death. A new interest in creativity and learning emerged, producing great artists, writers, and thinkers. We call this period the Renaissance.

326 *Unit 3 Regional Civilizations*

The Renaissance

Between the years 1348 and 1600, change came to Europe. During this period, people questioned old beliefs. They also took a new interest in learning, creativity, and independent thinking. Historians call this the Renaissance. It ended the Middle Ages. In this chapter, you will see how the Black Death affected Europe. You will travel to Florence and visit Lorenzo the Magnificent. Then you will journey to England to meet the playwright William Shakespeare. Finally, you will sail back to Italy and watch Leonardo da Vinci, Michelangelo, and Raphael create art masterpieces.

Goals for Learning

◆ To describe the changes the Black Death brought to Europe and explain why historians use the term *renaissance* for this period

◆ To describe the beliefs of humanism

◆ To describe the beginning of the Renaissance in Italy

◆ To list some Renaissance writers and their works

◆ To describe the work of Renaissance artists

1348 Black Death comes to Europe

1455 Gutenberg prints Bible

1506 Leonardo da Vinci paints the Mona Lisa

1558 Queen Elizabeth begins to rule England

1350   1450   1550   1650

Renaissance begins in northern Italy

1469 Lorenzo de Medici comes to power in Florence

1508 Michelangelo begins Sistine Chapel

Ask:

• Where did the Renaissance begin? (northern Italy)

• Who painted the Mona Lisa? (Leonardo da Vinci)

• In what century did Michelangelo begin painting the Sistine Chapel? (16th century)

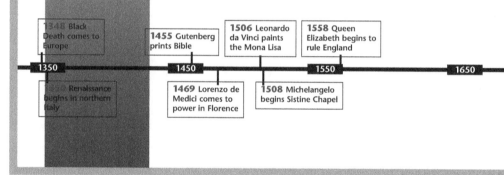

Chapter 14 Self-Study Guide, pages 1–2

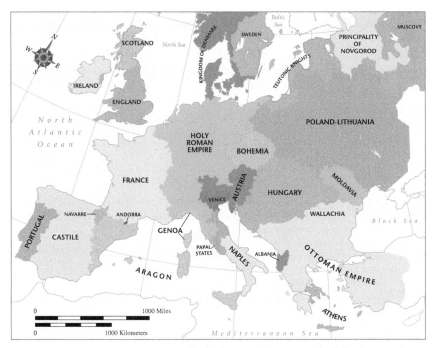

During the Renaissance, many of today's nations began to develop. As you look at the map, you will see names you know, such as England, France, and Sweden. However, two large empires existed during this period that no longer exist now. In addition, the city-states and kingdoms of Italy during the Renaissance took nearly four centuries to unite.

Study the map, then answer the following questions:

1. What sea separates England from the Kingdom of Denmark?

2. What sea is northeast of the Holy Roman Empire?

3. What country borders Castile on the west?

4. In what direction are the Papal States from England?

5. What country borders the Holy Roman Empire on the west?

1348 – 1600

The Renaissance   Chapter 14   **327**

Have a volunteer read aloud the title of the map, "Renaissance Europe." Encourage students to spend a few moments studying the map. Then have students read the Map Skills paragraph below the map and answer the questions.

Ask:

• In addition to England, France, and Sweden, what other names of countries do you see on this map that you recognize? (answers will vary; students may mention Denmark, Ireland, Scotland, Portugal, Poland, Hungary, or Austria)

• Name the two large empires shown on this map that no longer exist. (the Holy Roman Empire and the Ottoman Empire)

Map Skills Answers

1. the North Sea
2. the Baltic Sea
3. Portugal
4. southeast
5. France

Chapter Project

Organize the class into pairs. Have each pair of students select one artist, writer, leader, or historian from the Renaissance to research. (To avoid having multiple reports on the same individual, make sure each pair of students chooses a different historical figure.) Tell students to use reliable Internet and library sources to gather information on their chosen individual. Then have each student pair prepare a five-minute presentation on their findings. Presentations should include visual aids such as photographs or illustrations, and should add to the knowledge presented in the textbook about the individual.

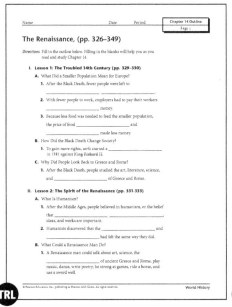

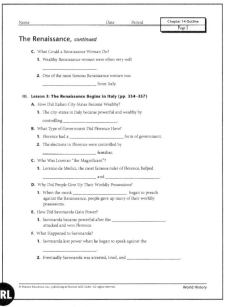

Chapter 14 Outline, pages 1–3

The Renaissance   Chapter 14   **327**

Metacognition

Introduce the reading strategy *metacognition*. Explain that when you read something, you often make a picture of the information in your mind. You might also think of questions about the text as you read. Furthermore, your mind tries to organize the information as you read. When you think about how you learn as you read, you are using metacognition. Have students read the title of Lesson 1 on page 329.

Ask:

• **What do you predict this lesson is about?** (problems that occurred during the 14th century)

• **Why?** (The heading describes the century as "troubled.")

Read the bulleted list on page 328 out loud. Encourage students to use these ideas as they read each lesson in Chapter 14.

Key Vocabulary Words

Explain that the list of words here is a glossary of the key vocabulary students will read in Chapter 14. Call on volunteers to read aloud the words and their definitions.

Ask:

• **What is the meaning of the word *renaissance*?** (rebirth)

• **What is a person who teaches one student at a time called?** (a tutor)

• **Who is someone who carves statues?** (a sculptor)

• **What is a portrait?** (a drawing of a person)

Reading Strategy: Metacognition

Metacognition means being aware of the way you learn. Use metacognition to become a better reader.

◆ Write the main idea, details, and any questions you have.

◆ Make predictions and ask yourself what you already know about the topic.

◆ Visualize what is happening in the text. If something doesn't make sense, go back and read it again.

◆ Summarize what you have read and make inferences about the meaning.

Key Vocabulary Words

Lesson 1
Clergy Leaders of religious groups

Rebellion A fight by people against a government; a struggle for change

Renaissance Rebirth; a period in European history that focused on being an individual and expanding creative thoughts and ideas

Lesson 2
Humanism A belief that human actions, ideas, and works are important

Tutor A teacher who teaches one person at a time

Lesson 3
Architect A person who draws plans for buildings

Sculptor A person who carves statues

Worldly Having nothing to do with religion

Lesson 4
Drama A story that is acted out on stage

Sonnet A 14-line poem about one idea

Lesson 5
Portrait A drawing of a person

Fresco A painting done in wet plaster on a wall

Patron A person who supports an artist with money

Chapel A small church

Vatican The home of the pope

♦ To describe the effects of the Black Death on Europe
♦ To explain why people looked to Greece and Rome for ideas

Clergy

Leaders of religious groups

During the 1300s, troubled times came to Western Europe. Workers had little money, and the cost of food was high. Early in the century, when many people had no food, nearly 10 percent of them died.

Then, in 1348, a plague hit Western Europe. This deadly disease made ugly black spots on people's skin, so they called it the Black Death. People got this disease from fleas. These small, wingless insects live on the bodies of people and animals. In the 1300s, the fleas on sick rats spread the Black Death from one person to the next. Between 1348 and 1400, millions of people died. England alone lost nearly one-third of its population.

What Did a Smaller Population Mean for Europe?

When the Black Death attacked Europe, people left the towns and cities and fled to the country. Millions died. Because fewer people were left alive to pay taxes, governments had less money. Fewer people were left to work, so employers had to pay their workers more money. Also, less food was needed for a smaller population. The price of food dropped, and farmers made less money. Because of this, many serfs wanted to leave the manor farms and work somewhere else.

The Black Death killed millions of people in Europe. This image shows the burying of plague victims in Tournai, Belgium.

How Did the Black Death Change Society?

During the Middle Ages, nobles and **clergy**—the leaders of religious groups—stood at the top of society. At the bottom stood peasants, or serfs. The law did not let them leave the land on which they worked. But as death marched through Europe, some peasants demanded change.

1348 – 1600

The Renaissance Chapter 14 **329**

Chapter 14: Lesson 1

Overview In this lesson, students will read about the Black Death and its affect on Europe at the end of the Middle Ages. Students will also be introduced to the Renaissance.

Objectives

■ To describe the effects of the Black Death on Europe
■ To explain why people looked to Greece and Rome for ideas

Student Pages pages 329–330

Teacher's Resource Library

Workbook Activity 59

Activity 59

Modified Activity 59

Vocabulary

| clergy | Renaissance |
| rebellion | |

Have students work in pairs. One student should read the definition of a vocabulary word and the other student should identify the word that matches the definition. After all words are identified, have students reverse roles and repeat this process. Students should eventually be able to match vocabulary words and definitions without using the text.

1 Warm-Up Activity

Tell students that a plague killed millions of people in Europe in the 14th century. Explain that in England, nearly one third of the people died. At the board, write the number of students in your school. Also write the number of faculty and staff at your school. Help students figure out how many students, faculty, and staff would remain at the school if one third of them suddenly moved away. Discuss with students how this sudden reduction could change the everyday operations of the school. Students should discuss the effects on class size, how classes are organized, and how athletics and clubs would be affected.

---

2 Teaching the Lesson

Have students read pages 329–330 with a partner. Students may struggle to understand how the Black Death affected everyone. Explain that when a society loses such a large number of people very quickly, it loses many people who do important jobs that keep society working properly. Also, there are not as many people to buy goods and services. This causes prices to drop, and the people who make the goods cannot make enough money to survive.

Reading Strategy:
Metacognition

Students may respond that they can make a cause-and-effect chart that lists the Black Death as the cause, and then lists all of the effects that stemmed from it.

Ask:

- How was Black Death spread? (It was spread by fleas who carried it from one person to another.)

- How did the decrease in population affect farmers? (Less food was needed and prices dropped, so farmers made less money.)

- Why was the new creative period called the Renaissance? (The word means rebirth; the focus was on humans expanding creative thoughts and ideas.)

3 Reinforce and Extend

Lesson 1 Review Answers

1. The Black Death was a plague that killed millions in Europe in the 14th century. **2.** Fewer people paid taxes or were able to work. Employers had to pay higher wages and the price of food dropped. **3.** They wanted to leave manor farms and find other work. **4.** The Black Death was also called the Bubonic Plague. **5.** The period after the Black Death was called the Renaissance.

Answers will vary. Some students may say that the people may have thought the country was safer than the city because there were fewer people in the country.

Rebellion
A fight by people against a government; a struggle for change

Renaissance
Rebirth; a period in European history that focused on being an individual and expanding on creative thoughts and ideas

What do you think

Why did people leave the cities and flee to the country when the Black Death attacked Europe?

These peasants began to question old beliefs. In 1381, English peasants started a **rebellion** against King Richard II. They began to fight for their rights. The king and his nobles stopped it. But the rebellion was a clear warning: change marched with the Black Death!

Why Did People Look Back to Greece and Rome?

Now people wanted to use their imaginations to make things. They looked back to ancient Greece and Rome where people had done this. They studied the art, literature, science, and philosophy of Greece and Rome.

Historians call this new creative period the **Renaissance.** This French word means "rebirth." This period focused on being an individual and expanding on creative thoughts and ideas. With the beginning of the Renaissance, the Middle Ages in Europe ended.

Lesson 1 Review On a sheet of paper, write the answer to each question. Use complete sentences.

1. What was the Black Death?
2. How did the Black Death affect Europe's population?
3. How did the Black Death affect the peasants?
4. What was another name for the Black Death?
5. What is the period after the Black Death called?

The Bubonic Plague

The first recorded cases of the Black Death were on the Black Sea in Russia. Starting in 1347, the Black Death, or bubonic plague, spread west along trade routes. It attacked seaports, then inland cities, and finally rural areas. At first, people thought poisoned air or water caused the Black Death. They fled from areas where others were sick.

The Black Death spread very easily. It spread by infected fleas on rats, coughing, and sneezing. By fleeing from the disease, people protected themselves somewhat. As of 1352, the plague had killed over 25 million people in Europe. Over the next 300 years, the sickness broke out over and over again.

The last great outbreak of the Black Death took place in China in 1894. There were two small outbreaks in India in 1994. Modern medicine can control the disease. Today, finding and treating the sickness quickly can save 90 to 95 percent of its victims.

Ask students to read "The Bubonic Plague" silently. Inform them that vaccines can now protect people from many diseases. A vaccine is a weakened form of a disease that is injected into a person's body, causing the body to be immune to, or not get, the disease in the future. British doctor Edward Jenner developed the first vaccine in 1798 to protect against cowpox. Since then, vaccinations have successfully controlled smallpox, polio, measles, chicken pox, and other devastating diseases. Scientists are working on vaccines that, in the future, may prevent some forms of cancer.

ELL/ESL STRATEGY

Language Objective:
To describe information from text

Divide the class into groups of 3–4 students. Have each group work together to research the symptoms of the plague, or Black Death. Then have groups make a list of the symptoms on butcher paper. Each group should find or make illustrations that will help them describe the symptoms. Then have students describe what they think would happen if a plague started to spread around the world today.

Objectives

◆ To explain what people during the Renaissance thought of people in the Middle Ages

◆ To list the qualities of Renaissance men and women

The Renaissance dominated Europe for 250 years. It began around 1350 in a few city-states in northern Italy and spread to other countries.

Renaissance people thought that the people of the Middle Ages were ignorant, meaning they had little knowledge or education. One Renaissance writer called the Middle Ages the "Dark Ages." He thought that the "light of learning" had gone out in Europe when Rome fell in A.D. 476. Renaissance people believed that progress in art, literature, and science had stopped in the Middle Ages.

What Is Humanism?

Humanism

A belief that human actions, ideas, and works are important

The Renaissance produced **humanism.** It is the belief that human actions, ideas, and works are important. During the Middle Ages, people wanted to get ready for life after death. That was their reason for living. They believed that happiness came only after death. Humanists said that people should be happy while alive.

Reading Strategy: Metacognition

Remember to ask yourself questions as you read. This will help you make sure that you understand the Renaissance period in history.

Humanists discovered that the Greeks and Romans had felt the same way they did. They searched libraries and monasteries for writings from ancient Greece and Rome. Then they studied the Greek and Latin languages to read these writings. All this led to a rebirth, or renaissance, of learning.

What Could a Renaissance Man Do?

Renaissance thinkers loved learning. They wanted to know many different things. A Renaissance man could read and talk about the writings of ancient Greece and Rome. Art and science interested him, too. However, book learning was not enough. He had to have fine manners and be interesting and funny when he talked. He had to play music, dance, and write poetry. He had to be strong and good at games. He also had to ride a horse and use a sword well.

Overview This lesson describes the beliefs of humanism and the qualities of Renaissance men and women.

Objectives

■ To explain what people during the Renaissance thought of people in the Middle Ages

■ To list the qualities of Renaissance men and women

Student Pages pages 331–333

Teacher's Resource Library

Workbook Activity 60

Activity 60

Modified Activity 60

Vocabulary

humanism   **tutor**

On the board, write each vocabulary word with the letters scrambled. Have a volunteer read a definition aloud and ask another volunteer to unscramble the letters of the matching word. Continue until both words have been unscrambled.

1 Warm-Up Activity

Explain to students that the Renaissance was a time when Europeans realized that humans had a lot to offer to the world. This made Europeans want to learn as much as possible about the world around them. Have students make a list of different learning opportunities available to them today. Explain that learning opportunities include more than just school. They can include athletics, art, music, and other activities and interests. From the lists they made, have students to choose one learning opportunity that they have never tried before. Then have students explain why they are interested in that learning opportunity.

Reading Strategy: Metacognition

Have students share some of the questions they asked themselves as they read that helped them understand the text.

Renaissance Ideas

Directions Write the correct word from the Word Bank to complete each sentence.

1. A(n) _____ is a teacher who teaches one person at a(n)

2. _____ had political power and became the ruler of Mantua, Italy.

3. A person who believes that people should be happy while alive is a(n) _____

4. The _____ began around 1350 in northern Italy.

5. Humanists searched libraries for writing from ancient Rome and _____

6. Renaissance people thought the people of the Middle Ages were _____

7. To learn about ancient Greece and Rome, people of the Renaissance studied _____

8. _____ is the belief that human actions, ideas, and works are important.

9. The Renaissance was a rebirth of _____

10. One Renaissance writer called the _____ the "Dark Ages."

Word Bank
Greece
humanism
humanist
ignorant
Isabella d'Este
Latin
learning
Middle Ages
Renaissance
tutor

Workbook Activity 60

The Spirit of the Renaissance

Directions Match the description in Column A with the correct term in Column B. Write the correct answer on each line.

	Column A	Column B
___ 1.	a belief that was produced by the Renaissance	A "Dark Ages"
___ 2.	began around 1350 and dominated Europe for 250 years	B humanism
___ 3.	another word for renaissance	C humanists
___ 4.	taught Renaissance women	D Isabella d'Este
___ 5.	famous Italian Renaissance woman	E Mantua
___ 6.	territory ruled by Isabella d'Este	F Niccolò Machiavelli
___ 7.	wrote *The Prince*	G rebirth
___ 8.	another term for the "Middle Ages"	H Renaissance man
___ 9.	well-read, fine manners, interesting, funny, and skilled in music, dance, writing, poetry, and games	I the Renaissance
___ 10.	believed that people should be happy while alive	J tutors

Activity 60

2 Teaching the Lesson

Have students read pages 331–333 to learn about humanism and the qualities of Renaissance men and women. Then ask students whether they can think of someone they know who excels at a variety of intellectual, creative, and physical tasks. Tell students that this type of person could be considered a modern-day Renaissance man or woman.

Ask:

• **What did humanists believe?** (that human actions, ideas, and works are important and that people should be happy while alive)

• **Identify three characteristics of a Renaissance man.** (Answers will vary; students may mention an interest in art and science, fine manners, and physical strength.)

• **What happened after Isabella d'Este's husband was captured in a war?** (She became the ruler of Mantua.)

• **How did many wealthy women gain education during the Renaissance?** (They were taught by tutors who came to their homes.)

ELL/ESL Strategy

Language Objective:
To learn about suffixes
Explain to students that a suffix is an ending that is added to the end of a word to give the word a new meaning. On page 331, the word *humanism* is introduced. Write *humanism* on the board. Then write *human* + *ism* on the board. Then write a definition for *human* on the board, such as "A human is a person." Write a definition for *–ism* on the board, such as, "An –ism is an attitude or a belief." Explain that when you put *human* and *–ism* together, you get a new word that means, "A belief that human actions, ideas, and works are important." Have students think of other suffixes that are added to the ends of words. Discuss how those suffixes change the meanings of the root words.

Tutor
A teacher who teaches one person at a time

Writing About History
Renaissance people had a special way of living and behaving. How does a well-mannered person act in today's world? In your notebook, list five good manners.

What Could a Renaissance Woman Do?

During the Renaissance, many women from wealthy families were also well educated. **Tutors,** teachers who taught one person at a time, came to their homes to teach these women. One of the most famous women during the Italian Renaissance was Isabella d'Este. Isabella was born in 1474. When she grew up, she married a wealthy man. Later, however, an enemy captured her husband in a war. Isabella then became the ruler of Mantua, a small territory in Italy.

Isabella d'Este had political power. She was also a well-educated woman. She studied Greek and Latin, and she collected many books for her home. She also sang beautifully and gave money to artists who created great works. At the time, some called her "the first lady to the world."

Isabella d'Este was a Renaissance woman of many talents and interests.

 Writing About History

To help students brainstorm lists of good manners, have them think of situations in which good manners are especially important. For example, job interviews, fancy restaurants, meeting someone for the first time, and so on. Ask students to create a list of all the manners that are required in these situations. Then have them select the five that they believe are the most important.

LEARNING STYLES

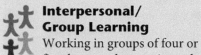

Interpersonal/ Group Learning
Working in groups of four or five, have students write and perform skits to showcase the lifestyle of Renaissance men or Renaissance women, or both. Give students time to prepare dialogue and acquire or make necessary props. Tell students that their skits should have well-defined characters and a plot. Encourage the use of humor. Each student in the group should have a speaking role in the skit. Have groups take turns performing their skits for the class.

Biography

Niccolò Machiavelli: 1469–1527

Machiavelli was a famous writer and historian. He had a job as secretary to a government council that traveled throughout Italy. During these trips, Machiavelli met many rulers. He wondered how they got and kept power. As a result, he watched how they acted.

Based on what he saw, Machiavelli set up his own ideas about how to rule. He stated them in his book *The Prince*. He believed that for a ruler, the end justifies the means. He said that the usual rules for behavior do not apply to rulers. He believed they should focus on power and success.

Word Bank

Greece

Humanism

Italy

Mantua

Renaissance

Lesson 2 Review On a sheet of paper, use the words from the Word Bank to complete each sentence correctly.

1. _____ is the belief that human actions, ideas, and works are important.

2. The Renaissance began in northern _____.

3. People of the Renaissance studied the writings of ancient Rome and _____.

4. A _____ man was interested in learning to do many things well.

5. Isabella d'Este became the ruler of _____, Italy.

Who do you think had better ideas about the way to live life—the people of the Middle Ages or the people of the Renaissance? Explain your answer.

Have students read about Niccolò Machiavelli on page 333. Then have them look up the word *Machiavellian* in a dictionary. They should encounter a definition similar to "cunning and lacking morals." Ask students why they think the word has taken on that meaning. (Answers will vary; students may say that Machiavelli believed a ruler should do whatever it takes to maintain power, even if his actions are dangerous and morally wrong.)

Ask:

• How did Machiavelli gain the opportunity to study the actions of rulers? (He worked as a secretary to a government council.)

 3 **Reinforce and Extend**

LEARNING STYLES

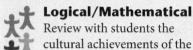

Logical/Mathematical
Review with students the cultural achievements of the Middle Ages discussed in Chapter 10. Then have students evaluate the claim that the "light of learning" had gone out in Europe when Rome fell in A.D. 476. Does the evidence in Chapter 10 support or refute that claim? Is it accurate to describe this period immediately following the Middle Ages as a renaissance, or rebirth? (Answers will vary; students may say that the term *renaissance*, or rebirth, is inaccurate because learning never stopped during the Middle Ages.)

Lesson 2 Review Answers

1. Humanism **2.** Italy **3.** Greece
4. Renaissance **5.** Mantua

Answers will vary. The people of the Middle Ages put more stress on the spiritual world and less on the physical world. Of course, their lives were so hard that the spiritual world gave them something to look forward to. But as life changed, the people in the Renaissance had a little more leisure to enjoy life.

Overview This lesson describes the Italian city-state of Florence, which symbolized the spirit of the Renaissance.

Objectives

- To describe Florence's rise as a Renaissance city
- To explain why Savonarola gained power and what he represented

Student Pages pages 334–337

Teacher's Resource Library TRL

Workbook Activity 61

Activity 61

Modified Activity 61

Vocabulary

architect   worldly
sculptor

Have students write the vocabulary words on index cards. Read a definition aloud and have students hold up the matching card. Continue until all definitions have been read.

---

1 Warm-Up Activity

In this lesson, students will explore the early days of the Renaissance in Florence, Italy. Italy was more financially successful than many other cities because it produced wool cloth. Ask students to think about what it takes for a city today to be financially secure. Have students work in small groups to list their ideas. Then have each group share their ideas with the class.

PRONUNCIATION GUIDE

Use this list to help students pronounce difficult words in this lesson.

Medici   (med´ ə chē)

Savonarola   (sav´ ə nə rō´ lə)

Objectives

- To describe Florence's rise as a Renaissance city
- To explain why Savonarola gained power and what he represented

Reading Strategy:
Metacognition

Notice the structure of this lesson. Look at the headings, captions, and boldfaced words.

At the beginning of the Renaissance, Italy was made up of more than 200 separate city-states. Many of these city-states had less than 10,000 people. However, as time passed, several cities in northern Italy grew to a population of 100,000. Outside Italy, only Paris had more people.

How Did Italian City-States Become Wealthy?

These city-states grew wealthy and powerful by controlling trade. Most of the trade routes from the East passed through the eastern end of the Mediterranean Sea. Goods then went to the northern Italian city-states of Venice, Milan, Florence, and Genoa.

Because northern Italy was not united, each city-state had its own ruler. At times, these city-states fought each other. In the 14th century, Venice defeated Genoa and gained control of Mediterranean trade. Because Venice was by the Adriatic Sea, people called it the "Queen of the Adriatic."

What Type of Government Did Florence Have?

The city-state of Florence showed the creative spirit of the Renaissance. The city became wealthy because it produced wool cloth. As many as 30,000 workers made this cloth.

Florence was an exciting city during the Renaissance. Scholars and artists came to this city from all over Europe.

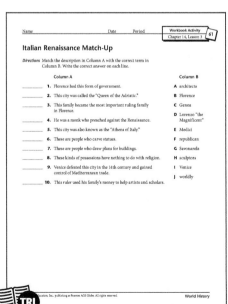

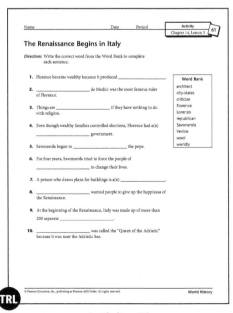

Architect
A person who draws plans for buildings

Sculptor
A person who carves statues

Florence had a republican form of government. However, several hundred wealthy families controlled the election of government leaders. These leaders were usually bankers and merchants. One of the most important of these ruling families in Florence was the Medici.

Who Was Lorenzo the Magnificent?

In 1469, the most famous ruler of Florence came to power. His name was Lorenzo de Medici. He used his family's wealth to help artists and scholars. Florence came alive with new ideas, holidays, and beautiful art. **Architects**—people who draw plans for buildings—built wonderful buildings. **Sculptors** carved statues and put them outside so everyone could enjoy them.

Every year on the birthday of the Greek philosopher Plato, Lorenzo held a party. The best scholars in Italy came to it. They ate, drank, listened to music, and talked about new ideas. The ancient Athenians had done this, too. With his yearly party and his support for the arts, Lorenzo made Florence the "Athens of Italy."

Because of all this, people called Lorenzo "the Magnificent." He died in 1492, the year Christopher Columbus sailed west into unknown waters. The king and queen of Spain wanted him to find a new trade route to the East. If Columbus could find this route, the Italian city-states would no longer control trade with the East. Spain would.

Lorenzo de Medici was called Lorenzo "the Magnificent" for his leadership in Florence.

1348 – 1600

The Renaissance   Chapter 14   **335**

IN THE COMMUNITY

In Florence, sculptors and artists displayed their work in public for everyone to enjoy. Working individually or with a partner, have students go on an "art treasure hunt," searching for examples of art in their community. Possibilities include sculptures, murals, carvings, and so on. If possible, invite students to photograph what they find and organize the photos into a presentation. Otherwise, students might wish to write a description of the art and note its location in the community. Have students share their findings with the class.

2 Teaching the Lesson

Have students read pages 334–337 to find out what Florence was like under the Medici family and how it changed when Savonarola came to power.

Reading Strategy:
Metacognition

Students should notice that the lesson is structured with questions for headings. After reading each section of text, students should be able to answer the question posed in its heading.

Ask:

- Who was the most important ruling family in Florence? (the Medici family)
- Who was the most famous ruler of Florence? (Lorenzo de Medici)
- What took place in Florence every year on the day of Plato's birth? (Lorenzo de Medici held a party where scholars ate, drank, listened to music, and discussed new ideas.)
- What did the people of Florence call Lorenzo? ("the Magnificent")

ELL/ESL STRATEGY

Language Objective:
To learn to read for meaning
At the high school level, a very important component of reading text for meaning includes the ability to take notes effectively. Many students learning English struggle with taking notes. To help students with this skill, you can model how to take good notes. Read each section of the lesson aloud with students. After each section, think aloud about how you would take notes. Model taking notes on an overhead, board, or computer projection screen. Have students copy your notes as you write them. Then model for students ways that you would use those notes when studying for a test about the chapter.

Have students study the map, titled "Trade Routes from Asia to Italy," on page 336.

Ask:

- What ocean is Calicut near? (Indian Ocean)

- What were four important trading cities in Europe? (Milan, Genoa, Florence, and Venice)

- How was the route from Beijing to Constantinople different from the route from Calicut to Alexandria? (This first route was over land; the second route was mainly over water.)

Have students read the caption and answer the questions. (Goods went west from Beijing to Constantinople. Alexandria was in Africa.)

Ask:

- What happened to Florence's economy near the end of Lorenzo's life? (It declined as people grew poorer and food became scarce.)

- Why did Savonarola preach against the Renaissance? (He believed that the people of Florence thought too much about themselves and not enough about their souls.)

- How did Italian religious leaders feel about nonreligious books, artwork, and beautiful clothing? (that they were dangerous and should be thrown into a bonfire)

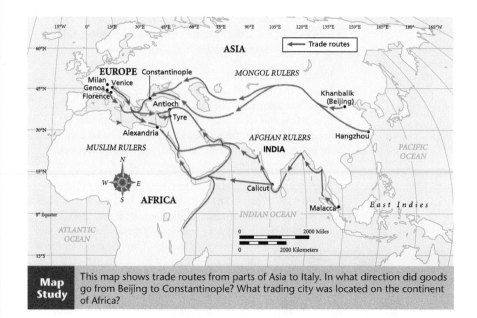

| Map Study | This map shows trade routes from parts of Asia to Italy. In what direction did goods go from Beijing to Constantinople? What trading city was located on the continent of Africa? |

Why Did People Give Up Their Worldly Possessions?

Worldly
Having nothing to do with religion

Near the end of Lorenzo's life, the economy of Florence began to decline. People grew poorer. Food was scarce. Then a monk named Savonarola began to preach against the Renaissance. He said that the people of Florence thought too much about themselves and not enough about religion.

All over Italy, religious leaders warned people about the dangers of dancing, poetry, and nonreligious music. They asked everyone to throw their nonreligious books, artwork, beautiful clothing, and other goods into a bonfire. All these possessions were **worldly**. That is, they had nothing to do with religion.

How Did Savonarola Gain Power?

Savonarola called Lorenzo Medici a tyrant. Then in 1494, the French attacked Florence. The Medici family gave up the city without a fight. When this happened, the people of Florence thought Savonarola had been right. They forced the Medici family out of power. Then Savonarola became the leader of Florence.

What Happened to Savonarola?

Reading Strategy:
Metacognition

Before you read this section, make a prediction about what will happen to Savonarola. Check your prediction as you continue reading.

For four years, Savonarola tried to force the people of Florence to change their lives. But soon the people of Florence became tired of Savonarola and his hard ways. Then he began to say bad things about the pope. The people did not like this. They arrested him and put him on trial. Then they executed him in the city square.

Florence continued to decline. However, it remained a powerful symbol of the spirit of the Renaissance.

Lesson 3 Review On a sheet of paper, write the answer to each question. Use complete sentences.

1. Where did the Renaissance begin?

2. Who was Lorenzo the Magnificent?

3. Which city-state was called the "Athens of Italy"?

4. Why did the spirit of the Renaissance upset some religious leaders?

5. What religious leader gained political power in Florence?

Why do you think the people of Florence tired of Savonarola's hard ways?

Reading Strategy:
Metacognition

(Student predictions will vary. Some students may predict that Savonarola went on to conquer new lands. Other students may predict that Savonarola lost power to a new leader.)

Ask:

- Why was Savonarola executed? (for criticizing the pope)

 Reinforce and Extend

WORLD CULTURES

 Today, Florence thrives on its Renaissance past and remains one of the world's leading cultural centers. Students come to the city to study at the University of Florence, the Academy of Fine Arts, or the Conservatory of Music. Native Florentines and tourists alike enjoy operas in the city's famous opera houses. Florence is also home to the Biblioteca Laurenziana, a library that dates back over 400 years and contains many important ancient texts. Many Florentines do the same work people did during the Renaissance—making and selling handicrafts such as pottery, straw products, and jewelry.

Lesson 3 Review Answers

1. The Renaissance began in northern Italy. 2. He was a popular ruler of Florence during the Renaissance. 3. Florence was called the "Athens of Italy." 4. Some religious leaders thought that people were not paying enough attention to the spiritual world. Also, the Renaissance was taking some power away from the Church's clergy. 5. The monk Savonarola gained political power in Florence.

Answers will vary. People probably enjoyed having artwork and reading literature. They did not want someone telling them how to conduct their personal lives.

Chapter 14: Lesson 4

Overview This lesson describes the work of Renaissance writers, several of whom are considered geniuses and are still admired.

Objectives

- To identify the language writers used during the Renaissance
- To identify great writers from Italy, England, and Spain
- To explain who printed the first book in Europe

Student Pages pages 338–340

Teacher's Resource Library TRL

Workbook Activity 62

Activity 62

Modified Activity 62

Vocabulary

drama   **sonnet**

Write a sentence on the board that uses one of the vocabulary words, but write a blank in place of the vocabulary word. Have a volunteer read the sentence aloud and determine which word, *drama* or *sonnet*, belongs in the sentence. Have another student explain how they know that the word chosen was correct or incorrect.

1 Warm-Up Activity

In this lesson, students will learn about some of the famous writers who lived and worked during the Renaissance. To introduce students to some of these writers, gather samples of work by Chaucer, Shakespeare, Cervantes, and Dante from your school library. Introduce students to Renaissance literature by reading excerpts from a few of their works that you think your students will find interesting.

Objectives

- To identify the language writers used during the Renaissance
- To identify great writers from Italy, England, and Spain
- To explain who printed the first book in Europe

Drama
A story that is acted out on stage

Sonnet
A 14-line poem about one idea

Reading Strategy:
Metacognition

Before you read this lesson, think about what you can do that will help you understand the text.

During most of the Middle Ages, people wrote books in Latin—the language of educated people. Then, near the end of the Middle Ages, writers and poets began to write in their own languages. The great Italian poets Petrarch and Dante wrote in Italian. In England, Geoffrey Chaucer wrote stories in Old English. Even today, people still read the works of these great writers.

Who Was a Great Writer of the Elizabethan Age?

Between 1558 and 1603, Queen Elizabeth I ruled England. She was one of England's greatest rulers. Today, historians call the time of her reign the Elizabethan Age. During these years, England gained new political power and economic wealth.

The Elizabethan Age produced some of the finest writers in English history. William Shakespeare, one of the greatest writers in the English language, lived during this time. Between 1590 and 1613, he wrote many works, including **dramas,** or stories acted out on stage. He also wrote beautiful **sonnets.** This type of poem is 14 lines about one idea.

Who Was a Great Renaissance Writer from Spain?

Another leading writer of the Renaissance was Miguel de Cervantes, a Spanish writer. He created the wonderful character of Don Quixote. Cervantes published the first part of his novel, *Don Quixote de la Mancha*, in 1605.

Quixote sees himself as a knight who must right the wrongs of the world. With his servant, Sancho Panza, he rides throughout Spain. They have one adventure after another. Don Quixote is a funny character. People have loved Don Quixote for over 400 years.

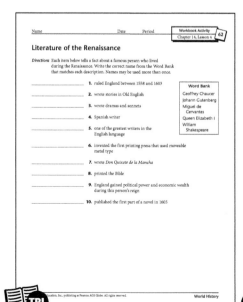

Workbook Activity 62

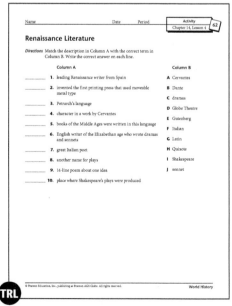

Activity 62

What Was the First Book Printed in Europe?

You already learned that in 1040 the Chinese invented a printing press that used wood blocks. Historians believe that in the 1400s, Johann Gutenberg from Germany invented the first printing press that used moveable metal type.

In 1455, Gutenberg printed a Bible. The Gutenberg Bible was one of the first books printed in Europe. Soon printers were printing books in Italy, France, England, and 15 other countries. By the 1500s, they had printed thousands of books. Learning began to spread as books became part of education.

William Shakespeare

William Shakespeare (1564–1616) wrote 39 plays. *Romeo and Juliet* is about two teenagers from warring families who fall in love. In *Macbeth*, the main character is too ambitious. *Hamlet* is the story of a prince who seeks revenge for his father's murder. Although his plays are over 400 years old, many are still performed today. Perhaps you have seen one done as a movie.

Many of Shakespeare's plays were first produced in London's Globe Theatre. It has been rebuilt and once again his plays are being performed there. Works by Shakespeare are often seen in major London and New York theaters, too. There are also many Shakespeare festivals. Stratford-upon-Avon, his birthplace, has hosted such an event since 1769.

1348 – 1600   *The Renaissance   Chapter 14*   **339**

Have students read "William Shakespeare." Ask them whether they have read any of Shakespeare's plays or have seen them performed on stage or in a movie. Provide students with this background information: In Shakespeare's time, only men were allowed to act in plays. As a result, female roles were performed by young men or boys. Have students discuss why they think plays are performed today with both male and female actors.

LEARNING STYLES

 Auditory/Verbal
Locate a book of Shakespeare's sonnets in your school library. Select two or three sonnets and read them to the class. You might wish to distribute printed copies of the sonnets so students can follow along. Challenge students to explain in their own words what Shakespeare was expressing in these sonnets.

PRONUNCIATION GUIDE

Use this list to help students pronounce difficult words in this lesson.

Cervantes	(sər van´ tēz´)
Chaucer	(chȯ´ sər)
Dante	(dän´ tā)
Don Quixote	(don ki hō´ tē)
Donatello	(don´ ə tel´ ō)
Petrarch	(pe´ trärk)

 2   Teaching the Lesson

Have students read pages 338–340 to find out about some great writers of the Renaissance.

Reading Strategy:
Metacognition

Ask students to share their ideas for understanding the text. Some students may say that they can write down questions that they have as they are reading, and try to answer those questions later on.

Ask:

- In what way were Renaissance writers different from writers in the Middle Ages? (Renaissance writers wrote in their own languages; writers in the Middle Ages wrote in Latin.)

- For what types of writing is William Shakespeare most famous? (dramas and sonnets)

- What famous character did Spanish author Miguel de Cervantes create? (Don Quixote)

- How would you describe Don Quixote? (Answers will vary; students might say he is a comic character who sees himself as a knight who must right the wrongs of the world.)

- What did Johann Gutenburg invent and why was it important? (the printing press; printers throughout Europe began manufacturing books, which contributed to the spread of learning)

Give students time to silently read "Newspapers Are Born." Then ask a volunteer to read it aloud.

Ask:

- What invention made printing easier and cheaper? (movable metal type)

- What were early newspapers like? (one page in length; published weekly)

- Where and when did the first known newspaper start? (Germany; 1609)

- What kind of information did the *Boston News-Letter* contain? (financial and foreign news, births, deaths, and social events)

3 Reinforce and Extend

AT HOME

Have students compare the contents of early newspapers to those of modern newspapers. At home, have them examine a newspaper and list its different content features. (Possibilities include local, national, and international news, sports, comics, weather, classified ads, horoscopes, and so on.) Which features also appeared in early newspapers? (news) Ask students why they think today's newspapers contain so many different features. (Answers will vary. Students may say that newspaper publishers want to appeal to as many people as possible so they can sell more newspapers.)

Lesson 4 Review Answers

1. D 2. D 3. C 4. A 5. C

Answers will vary. In order to read a book in another language, a person has to learn the language. That can make learning doubly difficult, even if a person does have the money to buy a book.

Newspapers Are Born

When Gutenberg invented movable metal type in the 15th century, printing became easier and cheaper. As a result, newspapers were born. Their purpose was to report news and information to people.

Early newspapers were small, usually one page. They looked like newsletters. They were published weekly, not daily.

The first known newspaper started in Germany in 1609. It told about events in other countries. The first London paper began in 1622. Then in 1665, *The London News Gazette* started. It was published on a regular basis in newspaper format. *The Boston News-Letter* was the first continuously published American newspaper. It began in 1704. Like papers today, it had financial and

Gutenberg's press allowed people to publish books and newspapers for the first time.

foreign news. It also recorded births, deaths, and social events.

Lesson 4 Review On a sheet of paper, write the letter of the answer that correctly completes each sentence.

1. During most of the Middle Ages, people wrote books in the _____ language.

   A English   **B** Italian   **C** French   **D** Latin

2. One of the greatest English writers of plays and sonnets was _____.

   A Petrarch   **B** Dante   **C** Chaucer   **D** Shakespeare

3. The English writer _____ wrote stories in the English language.

   A Petrarch   **B** Dante   **C** Chaucer   **D** Shakespeare

What do you think?

Why would having books in one's own language lead to more learning?

4. The Italian poet _____ wrote in his country's language.

   A Dante   **B** Chaucer   **C** Gutenberg   **D** de Cervantes

5. The first book that _____ printed was the Bible.

   A Dante   **B** Chaucer   **C** Gutenberg   **D** de Cervantes

---

ELL/ESL STRATEGY

Language Objective: *To compare and contrast different writing purposes*

Students who are learning English may find it very challenging to read and understand writing done for different purposes. For example, the purpose of the writing in the textbook is to provide information. A play, such as *Romeo and Juliet* by William Shakespeare, is written to provide entertainment. Help students understand the purpose for writing different kinds of texts by asking some simple questions. For example, you might ask: Did you learn anything new from the text? Did the text give facts? Did the text include charts, graphs, or maps? Point out that if they answered *yes* to these, the purpose of the writing was probably to provide information. Explain that texts written to entertain the reader usually are not full of facts. Also, they often are written in the form of a story that includes characters as well as a problem and a solution.

Objectives

◆ To describe Leonardo da Vinci's achievements as an artist

◆ To list Michelangelo's and Raphael's achievements in art

◆ To describe the challenges Michelangelo faced as he painted the ceiling of the Sistine Chapel

During the Renaissance, artists wanted to make their paintings and sculptures look just as good as those of Greek artists. In fact, someone once heard the great Renaissance sculptor Donatello say to one of his sculptures, "Speak then! Why will you not speak!"

But artists also wanted the people in their paintings and sculptures to look even better than they did in real life. By doing this—with paint, bronze, and marble—they created masterpieces. During the Renaissance, people called a gifted artist a genius. That is, the artist had been born with special skills and was different from ordinary people. Many artists produced important works of art during the Renaissance. However, few of them produced masterpieces like those of da Vinci, Michelangelo, and Raphael Santi.

What Is Leonardo da Vinci Remembered For?

Portrait

A drawing of a person

Reading Strategy:
Metacognition

Remember to look at the photographs and illustrations, and to note the descriptive words. This will help you visualize Renaissance art.

Leonardo da Vinci was a true Renaissance man. Born in the small Italian village of Vinci in 1452, he had many interests and much skill. His curiosity drove him to explore many fields of study. Leonardo was an artist, a scientist, an engineer, and a clever inventor.

Leonardo left us only a few paintings. He completed his most famous painting in 1503. It is the **portrait,** or drawing, of a 24-year-old woman from Florence.

Leonardo da Vinci was a very skilled Renaissance man. This drawing is a self-portrait.

1348 – 1600

The Renaissance Chapter 14 **341**

Chapter 14: Lesson 5

Overview This lesson describes the work of the famous Renaissance man da Vinci, as well as that of Michelangelo and Raphael.

Objectives

■ To describe Leonardo da Vinci's achievements as an artist

■ To list Michelangelo's and Raphael's achievements in art

■ To describe the challenges Michelangelo faced as he painted the ceiling of the Sistine Chapel

Student Pages pages 341–344

Teacher's Resource Library TRL

Workbook Activity 63

Activity 63

Modified Activity 63

Vocabulary

chapel	portrait
fresco	Vatican
patron	

Have students draw two columns on a sheet of paper. In the left-hand column, they should write the vocabulary words. In the right-hand column, they should write the definitions in random order. Have students exchange papers and match each word to its definition.

1 Warm-Up Activity

In this lesson, students will learn about the outstanding works of Leonardo da Vinci, Michelangelo, and Raphael. To introduce students to some of the works of these three men, borrow some art books from a local library. Show these works to students and have them discuss the similarities and differences between them. Point out that all of these artists wanted the people featured in their work to look realistic.

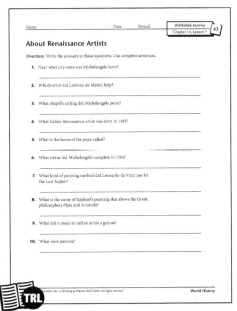

Workbook Activity 63

Activity 63

PRONUNCIATION GUIDE

Use this list to help students pronounce difficult words in this lesson.

da Vinci   (də vin´chē)

2   Teaching the Lesson

Ask students who invented the airplane and when it was invented. (the Wright brothers; early 1900s) Students may be surprised to learn that the idea for the airplane actually dates back to the Renaissance. Have students read pages 341–344 to find out about the achievements and ideas of a true Renaissance man, Leonardo da Vinci.

Reading Strategy: Metacognition

Students may say that all of the art shown includes people. This indicates the importance of showing humans in the artwork of the Renaissance period.

Ask:

- During the Renaissance, what was a gifted artist called? (a genius)

- What did artists do during the Renaissance to make the people who were their subjects look better than they did in real life? (They used paint, bronze, and marble to create masterpieces.)

- What other things did Leonardo da Vinci do besides paint? (He was a scientist, engineer, and inventor.)

- Identify two famous paintings by Leonardo. (the *Mona Lisa* and the *Last Supper*)

- Why did Leonardo need patrons? (They supported him financially.)

- Who helped Michelangelo with his studies? (Lorenzo de Medici)

The *Mona Lisa is one of da Vinci's most famous portraits.*

Fresco

A painting done in wet plaster on a wall

Patron

A person who supports an artist with money

She looks at us with a mysterious smile. The painting, called the *Mona Lisa,* is one of the most famous paintings in the world.

Another important painting of Leonardo's is the *Last Supper.* It shows Jesus of Nazareth eating with his disciples on the night before he died. Leonardo painted it in wet plaster on a wall. Plaster is a mixture of sand, water, and lime. It gives a smooth finish to a wall. Leonardo used his own way of doing this **fresco.**

Like all Renaissance artists, Leonardo needed **patrons.** These people supported artists by giving them money. One of Leonardo's patrons was Beatrice d'Este, the wife of the duke of Milan. Another was the king of France, Francis I. Leonardo's work in France helped spread Renaissance ideas to countries beyond Italy. Leonardo da Vinci died in 1519 at the age of 67.

What Are Two Sculptures by Michelangelo?

Michelangelo was born near Florence in 1475. As a young man, he wanted to be a sculptor, and Lorenzo de Medici helped him in his studies. At the age of 23, Michelangelo became famous for carving the Pietà, which means "pity." The sculpture shows Mary, the mother of Jesus, holding his dead body. In 1504, Michelangelo completed a statue of David. (In a Bible story, David killed the giant Goliath with a stone thrown from a slingshot.) Michelangelo loved being a sculptor. But he also became famous as a painter.

Michelangelo was an artistic genius. He thought of himself as a sculptor, but he was also a painter.

LEARNING STYLES

Visual/Spatial

Explain that Leonardo da Vinci often drew sketches of his ideas for new inventions. Invite students who enjoy drawing to sketch ideas for new inventions in the same way that Leonardo did. You might suggest that they label the parts of the invention and provide a brief written explanation of its purpose. Ask volunteers to show their sketches to the class.

STUDY SKILLS

Have students use reference sources such as books, encyclopedias, and the Internet to find information about one of these people from the Renaissance:

- Shakespeare
- Michelangelo
- Donatello
- Leonardo
- Cervantes
- Raphael

Ask students to write down three facts that are not mentioned in this chapter about the work of the person they chose. Then compile a master list of all the facts about each person. Discuss similarities and differences between each artist.

Chapel
A small church

Vatican
The home of the pope

Michelangelo painted this fresco in the Sistine Chapel. It is titled The Last Judgement.

Reading Strategy:
Metacognition

Note the important details about Michelangelo. Summarize what you have read about him.

What Ceiling Did Michelangelo Paint?

In 1508, Pope Julius II asked 33-year-old Michelangelo to come to Rome. The pope wanted him to paint frescoes on the ceiling of the Sistine **Chapel** in the **Vatican.** The chapel was a small church in the Vatican. The Vatican is the home of the pope.

Michelangelo did not want the job. He insisted that he was a sculptor and not a painter. But the pope held firm, and Michelangelo finally accepted.

The pope told Michelangelo that he could paint what he wanted. So on the wet plaster of the ceiling, Michelangelo painted pictures from Bible stories. He started with the creation, or the making of the world, and ended with the great flood.

Ask:

• Why didn't Michelangelo want to paint the ceiling of the Sistine Chapel at first? (He considered himself a sculptor, not a painter.)

• What types of scenes did Michelangelo choose to paint? (scenes from Bible stories)

Reading Strategy:
Metacognition

(Summaries may vary. Summaries should include that Michelangelo was a sculptor and a painter. One of his most famous works was the painting of the Sistine Chapel in the Vatican.)

ELL/ESL STRATEGY

Language Objective:
To summarize information in texts

Explain to students that one of the best ways to remember the information in text is to summarize it. Many students learning English may not be familiar with the idea of summarizing. Explain that summarizing means to tell the most important ideas about something you know. You can demonstrate how to summarize text by using the text on pages 343 and 344 about Michelangelo and the Sistine Chapel. First, read this text aloud. After each paragraph, pause and think aloud about the most important information in the paragraph. Then, write that information on the board. After reading all of the paragraphs, write a short summary on the board. Point out to students that the summary includes only the most important information from the paragraphs.

Ask:

- How long did it take Michelangelo to paint the ceiling of the Sistine Chapel? (four years)
- What two Greek philosophers are shown in Raphael's *School of Athens*? (Plato and Aristotle)

 3 Reinforce and Extend

BACKGROUND INFORMATION

 Over the course of 500 years, a layer of soot and grime accumulated on the ceiling of the Sistine Chapel. Michelangelo's colorful frescoes were reduced to drab grays, obscuring many details of the paintings. In the early 1980s, the Vatican began what would become a 10-year restoration project. Sitting atop of scaffolding that reached all the way to the ceiling, conservators carefully applied a special cleaning paste. After the paste dried and the powder was brushed off, the fine details and bright colors that Michelangelo had painted were revealed.

Lesson 5 Review Answers

1. Leonardo's most famous painting is the *Mona Lisa*. **2.** The artists needed patrons so they had money to continue their work. **3.** Michelangelo carved the Pietà and the statue of David.
4. Working on the Sistine Chapel was hard because Michelangelo had to lie on his back, 80 feet above the floor.
5. The *School of Athens* showed Greek influence on Renaissance culture.

Answers will vary. Perhaps he liked to work with marble, bronze, and wood. They are more tactile than paint. Also, he may have liked to work in three dimensions instead of just one.

Raphael Santi painted mostly religious paintings during the Renaissance.

For four years, Michelangelo painted the ceiling while lying on his back, 80 feet above the floor. Paint dropped into his eyes. At night he painted by candlelight. He felt tired, gloomy, and anxious. Only his genius and physical strength enabled Michelangelo to complete the ceiling. He painted more than 300 people and pictures on that ceiling! Some were ten feet tall. Most historians think that the ceiling of the Sistine Chapel is one of the greatest masterpieces in the history of art. Michelangelo died in 1564.

What Is Raphael Remembered For?

Raphael Santi was born in Italy in 1483. He painted mostly religious pictures. People remember him for his paintings of Mary and the baby Jesus. Art historians call these his Madonna paintings. (*Madonna* is Italian for "my lady.") One of Raphael's most famous paintings is the *School of Athens*. At the center of the painting, Raphael placed the Greek philosophers Plato and Aristotle. He surrounded them with other Greek scholars. The painting shows that the learning and culture of ancient Greece influenced the Renaissance. Raphael, another genius of the Renaissance, died in 1520 at the age of 37.

Lesson 5 Review On a sheet of paper, write the answer to each question. Use complete sentences.

1. What is the name of Leonardo's most famous painting?
2. Why did Renaissance artists need patrons?
3. What are two statues Michelangelo carved?
4. Why was working on the Sistine Chapel hard for Michelangelo?
5. What painting of Raphael's showed the Renaissance interest in ancient Greek culture?

What do you think?

Why do you think being a sculptor was more important to Michelangelo than being a painter?

Chapter Project Follow-up

Have each student pair give its presentation about a historical figure of the Renaissance. Assess students on the quality of their research by having students turn in a list of sources. Evaluate student presentations in terms of the quality of the delivery, visual aids, and enthusiasm of the students.

The Making of a Renaissance Gentleman

In 1528, Baldassare Castiglione published The Book of the Courtier. *A courtier was a person who visited a royal court. This book told young gentlemen what the rules were for visiting the court. Gentlemen followed its rules for several centuries.*

Besides his noble birth, then I would have the Courtier [show] a certain grace and (as we say) air that shall make him at first sight pleasing and agreeable to all who see him. . . .

[The Courtier should] know how to swim, to leap, to run, to throw stones, for besides the use that may be made of this in war, a man often has occasion to show what he can do in such matters; whence good esteem is to be won, especially with the multitude. . . . Another admirable exercise, and one very befitting at court, is the game of tennis. . . .

I would have him more than passably accomplished in letters, at least in those studies that are called the humanities. . . . Let him be versed in the poets, and not less in the orators and historians, and also proficient in writing verse and prose, especially in [speech] . . . for besides the enjoyment he will find in it, he will by this means never lack agreeable

entertainment with ladies, who are usually fond of such things. . . .

I am not content with the Courtier unless he be also a musician and unless, besides understanding and being able to read notes, he can play . . . instruments. For if we consider rightly, there is to be found no rest from toil or medicine for the troubled spirit more becoming and praiseworthy in time of leisure, than this; and especially in courts, where . . . many things are done to please the ladies, whose tender and gentle spirit is easily penetrated by harmony and filled with sweetness. . . .

When dancing in the presence of many and in a place full of people, it seems to me that he should preserve a certain dignity, . . . and airy grace of movement.

Document-Based Questions

1. What is a courtier?

2. Why was *The Book of the Courtier* written?

3. What athletic abilities should a courtier have?

4. According to the author, in what two ways may a courtier please the ladies?

5. How may the knowledge of music help a courtier in his personal life?

CAREER CONNECTION

Much of what we know about history comes from art. Unfortunately, great pieces of art—such as the Sistine Chapel ceiling—can suffer damage over time. Restoring art to its original beauty and protecting it from future damage are the important tasks of conservators. To become a conservator, students should take courses in science, humanities, and studio art in college. Science is important for understanding the effects of different cleaning solutions on the art work. Then they can enroll in a graduate program and earn a Master's degree or certificate in conservation. Students usually spend their final year of study as interns working for experienced conservators.

The Hundred Years' War

Ask students to read "The Hundred Years' War" silently, keeping a tally sheet with one mark to represent each battle. Then have volunteers take turns reading parts of the selection aloud. Instruct students to create a timeline of the war in their notebooks, beginning with the year 1337 and ending with 1453. Their timelines should contain all of the key events discussed in this story. You might suggest that they write a one-sentence description of each event. Their timelines will serve as useful study guides when students review this chapter.

The Hundred Years' War extended over the reigns of five English and five French kings. From 1337 to 1453, they fought for control of France. This struggle was actually a series of battles broken by truces and treaties.

The war had several causes. The French kings wanted to control the English province of Gascony in southwest France. Gascony was a valuable wine-producing region. The French supported the Scots against the English. These actions angered the English. English and French sailors and fishermen fought over rights in the English Channel. The wool trade in Flanders was also a point of disagreement. In addition, in 1337, the English king, Edward III, claimed the throne of France. His uncle, the French king, had died without a male heir. When Edward III landed an army in Normandy, the Hundred Years' War began.

In the fighting that followed, the English won many battles. But the French won the war. The French had three times the resources—soldiers, supplies, and wealth—of the English. Several events also hindered the warfare. The Black Death, the deadliest plague ever known, killed millions of people. There was also a peasant revolt in England.

During the war, new military tactics developed. English archers used the newly developed longbow. With that weapon, they won the war's greatest victory in the Battle of Crecy (1346). The English also won the Battle of Poitiers (1356). Then the Treaty of Bretigny in 1360 began a brief period of peace. Henry V of England renewed the fighting, though. He won the Battle of Agincourt (1415). The Treaty of Troyes in 1420 gave him the French crown.

The Battle of Crecy.

The peace was short-lived, however. Henry V died in 1422 and the French reclaimed the throne. War flared up again. By 1428, the English controlled northern France. They laid siege to Orléans, an important city in central France. Then Joan of Arc, an unknown peasant girl, led a French army to save Orléans. She claimed to have had visions from heaven. In them, saints told her to lead a French army against the English. Joan was victorious in Orléans, Patay, and Reims. Later, the English took her prisoner and burned her as a witch.

The French kept winning battles and the English retreated. At the end of the war in 1453, they controlled only the city of Calais. The French took over this port in 1558.

Wrap-Up

1. What two countries fought the Hundred Years' War?

2. What were five causes of the war?

3. Why did England's Edward III claim a right to the French throne?

4. What problems inside France and England interrupted the war?

5. Who was a French hero during the war?

Answers to Spotlight Story Wrap-Up:

1. England and France fought the Hundred Years' War.

2. Causes of the war include: 1. French desire to control the English province of Gascony; 2. French support for the Scots; 3. quarrels over sailing and fishing rights in the English Channel; 4. disagreements about the wool trade in Flanders; and 5. Edward III's claim to the French throne.

3. The French king had died without a male heir and Edward III was his nephew.

4. The Black Death killed millions of people and there was a peasant revolt in England.

5. Joan of Arc was a French hero during the war.

Chapter 14 SUMMARY

- A deadly plague, the Black Death, struck Europe in 1348. Millions of people died. As a result, society changed. There were fewer workers, so workers and serfs could demand more rights.

- The Renaissance began about 1350, ending the Middle Ages. It was a time of creativity and learning. People studied the classical learning of ancient Greece and Rome.

- Men and women of the Renaissance valued education, art, and science. They also valued good manners and skills such as music, dance, and swordplay.

- The Renaissance began in the city-states of Italy. City-states such as Venice, Milan, Florence, and Genoa grew rich from trade with the East. Each had its own ruler. In the 1300s, Venice, on the Adriatic Sea, defeated Genoa. It gained control of trade in the Mediterranean.

- The Medici were the leaders of Florence, the "Athens of Italy." Lorenzo de Medici encouraged artists and scholars.

- Florence began to decline in the late 1400s. The monk Savonarola led a religious movement against the Renaissance. The Medicis lost power. Savonarola tried to establish a more religious way of life in Florence. After a few years, people rebelled against him.

- Renaissance artists made lifelike paintings and sculptures. Artists depended on wealthy patrons, such as Isabella d'Este and the pope.

- Late medieval writers wrote in their native languages, not Latin. Renaissance writers also used local languages. In England, Shakespeare wrote plays and sonnets. In Spain, Cervantes created the character Don Quixote. In Germany, Gutenberg used moveable metal type to print a Bible in 1455. Printed books spread learning.

- Leonardo da Vinci was an artist, scientist, and inventor. His most famous paintings are the *Mona Lisa* and the *Last Supper*. When Leonardo worked in France for King Francis I, Renaissance ideas spread.

- Michelangelo was a sculptor in Florence. He is famous for statues, such as *David*. He also painted the ceiling of the Sistine Chapel.

- Raphael made many religious paintings. He was influenced by the learning and culture of ancient Greece.

1348 – 1600

The Renaissance *Chapter 14* **347**

Using the Chapter Summary

Have students read the Chapter Summary on page 347 to review the main ideas presented in Chapter 14.

Ask:

- How did the Black Death change European society? (There were fewer workers, so workers and serfs could demand more rights.)

- When and where did the Renaissance begin? (about 1350; city-states of Italy)

- What was the Renaissance? What did people study during the Renaissance? (a time of creativity and learning; people studied the ancient Greek and Roman texts)

- Which family led Florence? (the Medici)

- Why did the Medici lose power? (Savonarola led a religious movement against the Renaissance and took control of the city.)

- How did Renaissance artists earn a living? (They depended on wealthy patrons.)

- Name two Renaissance writers. (Shakespeare and Cervantes)

- Why was the invention of moveable metal type important? (It allowed books to be printed, which spread learning.)

- Identify Leonardo da Vinci's most famous paintings. (the *Mona Lisa* and the *Last Supper*)

- What is Michelangelo famous for? (Answers will vary; students may say the statue David or painting the ceiling of the Sistine Chapel.)

TEACHER'S RESOURCE

The AGS Globe Teaching Strategies in Social Studies Transparencies may be used with this chapter. The transparencies add an interactive dimension to expand and enhance the *World History* program content.

Chapter 14 Review

Use the Chapter Review to prepare students for tests and to reteach content from the chapter.

Chapter 14 Mastery Test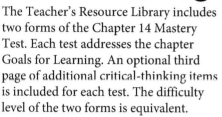

The Teacher's Resource Library includes two forms of the Chapter 14 Mastery Test. Each test addresses the chapter Goals for Learning. An optional third page of additional critical-thinking items is included for each test. The difficulty level of the two forms is equivalent.

Chapter 14 Review Answers

1. Lorenzo de Medici
2. Savonarola
3. Isabella d'Este
4. Shakespeare
5. Cervantes
6. Gutenberg
7. Leonardo da Vinci
8. Michelangelo
9. Raphael
10. Beatrice d'Este
11. C
12. D
13. A
14. B
15. A

Word Bank

Beatrice d'Este
Cervantes
Gutenberg
Isabella d'Este
Leonardo da Vinci
Lorenzo de Medici
Michelangelo
Raphael
Savonarola
Shakespeare

On a sheet of paper, use the words from the Word Bank to complete each sentence correctly.

1. People called _____ "the Magnificent" because he worked to make Florence into a great city.

2. The monk _____ criticized the people of Florence because they liked worldly possessions.

3. _____, the ruler of Mantua, was a true Renaissance woman.

4. People call _____ one of the greatest writers in the English language.

5. _____ wrote a funny novel about a Spaniard who wanted to be a knight so he could right the wrongs of the world.

6. _____ invented the first printing press to use moveable metal type.

7. _____ was an artist, scientist, engineer, and inventor.

8. _____ painted the ceiling of the Sistine Chapel.

9. People remember _____ for his paintings of the Madonna.

10. One of Leonardo da Vinci's patrons was _____.

On a sheet of paper, write the letter of the answer that correctly completes each sentence.

11. During the Renaissance, many people believed in _____, which said that the actions, ideas, and works of human beings were important.

   A architect   **C** humanism
   B sculptor   **D** philosophy

12. It is the job of _____ to design buildings and other structures.

   A philosophers   **C** humanists
   B frescoes   **D** architects

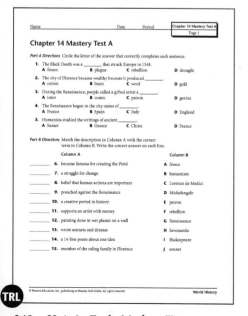

Chapter 14 Mastery Test A, pages 1–3

13. A 14-line poem is a(n) _____.

   A sonnet   **C** tanka
   B haiku   **D** opera

14. A _____ is a person who supports an artist.

   A portrait   **C** sonnet
   B patron   **D** tutor

15. A _____ is a drawing of a person.

   A portrait   **C** plaster
   B patron   **D** sonnet

On a sheet of paper, write the answer to each question. Use complete sentences.

16. How did the Black Death change Europe?

17. Why was Leonardo da Vinci a Renaissance man?

18. Renaissance men and women were skilled and smart. What would a Renaissance person be like today? Write down three people living today who could be called "renaissance" people.

Critical Thinking On a sheet of paper, write your response to each question. Use complete sentences.

19. During the Renaissance, some religious leaders asked people to give up their worldly possessions. Imagine that these leaders are alive today. What possessions might they want you to give up?

20. Before the Renaissance, writers wrote in Latin. But few people could read this language. Describe your life if all web sites, books, television shows, and movies were in a language you did not know or understand.

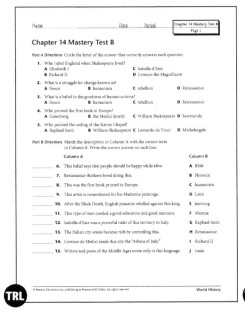

For open-book tests, write short summaries of every chapter or section.

1348 – 1600

---

16. The Black Death killed so many people that many changes came to Europe. Fewer people paid taxes, so governments had less money. Less food was needed for the smaller population, so farm prices went down.

17. Leonardo was a Renaissance man because he could do so many things well. He was an artist, a scientist, an engineer, and an inventor. He had the lively curiosity and the genius of a true Renaissance person.

18. Answers will vary. A Renaissance person today would probably know a great deal about computers, Wall Street, the political scene, movies and theater, great literature, and sports.

Critical Thinking

19. Answers will vary. Reincarnated Renaissance religious leaders might ask us to throw away our televisions, our cars, our computers and the Internet.

20. Answers will vary. If books, Web sites, movies, or television were all in another language, we would have to learn that language or we would have to learn by using tutors who could teach us without books and other media.

Chapter 14 Mastery Test B, pages 1–3

Audio Library

Skill Track for *World History*

Teacher's Resource Library ⓉⓇⓁ

Workbook Activities 64–69

Activities 64–69

Modified Activities 64–69

Chapter 15 Self-Study Guide

Chapter 15 Outline

Chapter 15 Mastery Tests A and B
(Answer Keys for the Teacher's
Resource Library begin on page 870
of this Teacher's Edition.)

The Reformation

In Chapter 14, you read about the Renaissance. Much of this took place in Italy. This chapter takes you north to Germany. There you will see how a monk named Luther began the religious reform movement. From Germany, you will cross the English Channel and meet Henry VIII, who also led reform. Next, you will travel to Geneva to learn about John Calvin and his beliefs. Finally, you will journey back to Italy. There you will see how the Catholic Church decided to fight the other reformers—the Protestants.

Goals for Learning

◆ To define the term *Reformation*

◆ To explain the importance of Martin Luther in the Reformation

◆ To list the three basic reforms Martin Luther made

◆ To explain how the Anglican Church was founded

◆ To describe the beliefs of Calvinism

◆ To describe the Catholic Reformation

1415 Catholic Church burns John Huss at the stake

1534 Henry VIII begins Anglican Church

1545 The Council of Trent begins

| 1450 | 1500 | 1550 | 1600 |

1517 Luther writes his 95 theses and starts the Reformation

1536 Calvin publishes *Institutes of the Christian Religion*, begins Calvinist Church

1572 French Catholics kill Huguenots in St. Bartholomew's Day Massacre

Introducing the Chapter

During the late 14th and 15th centuries, Europe experienced turbulent changes in religious thought. The demand for changes in the Catholic Church led to wars, new political alliances, and the formation of new churches.

Ask:

• **What happened in 1415?** (In 1415, John Huss was burned at the stake for criticizing the church.)

• **When did Luther write his 95 theses? When did Calvin write his Institutes?** (1517; 1536)

| Name | Date | Period | SELF-STUDY GUIDE |

Chapter 15: The Reformation

Goal 15.1 To define the term Reformation

Date	Assignment	Completed
	1. Read pages 350–354.	
	2. Complete the Lesson 1 Review on page 354.	
	3. Complete Workbook Activity 64.	

Comments:

Goal 15.2 To explain the importance of Martin Luther in the Reformation

Date	Assignment	Completed
	4. Read pages 355–357.	
	5. Complete the Lesson 2 Review on page 357.	
	6. Complete Workbook Activity 65.	

Comments:

Goal 15.3 To list the three basic reforms Martin Luther made

Date	Assignment	Completed
	7. Read pages 358–359.	
	8. Complete the Lesson 3 Review on page 359.	
	9. Complete Workbook Activity 66.	

Comments:

© Pearson Education, Inc., publishing as Pearson AGS Globe. All rights reserved.   World History

ⓉⓇⓁ

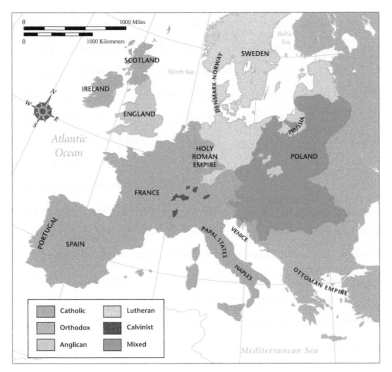

Before the Protestant Reformation, the Catholic Church had great power in most of Western Europe. However, people began to challenge this power. New religions began. This map shows where different religions had developed by 1550.

Study the map, then answer the following questions:

1. What religion was practiced in England at this time?

2. What religions were practiced in the Holy Roman Empire?

3. Where was the Catholic religion still practiced?

4. Where did the Calvinist religion develop?

5. What religion dominated Western Europe at this time?

Read the map title, "Reformation Europe (1550)," to students and ask students to notice the different religions in Western Europe in 1550.

Ask:

• In which countries did the Catholic Church have great power? (Spain, Portugal, France, Italy, Ireland, and Scotland)

• In what direction is England from the Papal states? (northwest) Sweden? (north) France? (northwest)

Have students silently read the paragraph under the map and then read and answer the questions.

Map Skills Answers

1. Anglican

2. Catholic and Lutheran

3. The Catholic religion was still practiced throughout much of Western Europe, from the Holy Roman Empire to Portugal.

4. The Calvinist religion was developed in France and south of the Holy Roman Empire.

5. The Catholic religion dominated Western Europe during this time.

Chapter Project

Have students choose one reformer from Chapter 15 to study in depth. They might choose John Wycliffe, John Huss, Martin Luther, King Henry VIII, or John Calvin. Ask students to write a letter from the point of view of the reformer to a trusted friend explaining why they are unhappy with the practices of the Catholic Church. In the letter, students should describe their disagreements with the Church and tell what they think should be done to remedy the situation. Remind students that the Church was powerful and disagreeing with its practices could be dangerous.

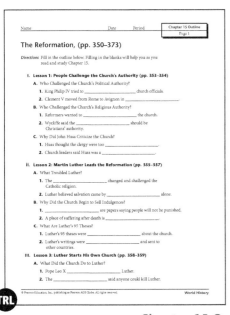

Chapter 15 Outline, pages 1–3

Summarizing

Introduce the reading skill *summarizing*. Draw students' attention to the definition. Tell students that the strategy of summarizing is an ongoing strategy that can be used as students read. Ask a volunteer to read the three bullet point questions in the Reading Strategy. Point out to students that summarizing as they read will help them understand and review what they have read.

Key Vocabulary Words

Have students read the vocabulary words and their definitions. Ask them to write sentences, each using more than one vocabulary word in the correct context. Students should write as many sentences as necessary to use all the words at least once. (Words can be used more than once.) Challenge students to use as many vocabulary words in a single sentence as possible.

Reading Strategy:
Summarizing

When you summarize, you ask questions about what you are reading. That way you can review what you have just read. As you read the text in this chapter, ask yourself these questions:

◆ What details are most important to the person or period in history?

◆ What is the main thing being said about the person?

◆ What events are pointed out about this period in history?

Key Vocabulary Words

Lesson 1
Authority Power
Reformer A person who tries to change something
Heretic A person who holds a belief that a religious authority thinks is false

Lesson 2
Reformation A movement that challenged and changed the Catholic religion in Europe
Salvation Eternal happiness for one's soul
Indulgence A church paper that says that a person will not be punished after death for their sins
Purgatory A place of suffering after death
Thesis A statement that people argue about or try to prove

Lesson 3
Excommunicate To say that someone can no longer be a member of a church
Lutheran Church The church established by Martin Luther
Minister A person who can lead a religious ceremony in a Lutheran church
Ritual A ceremony
Baptism A ritual by which a person becomes a Christian
Communion A ritual by which Christians grow in their faith
Protestant A reformer who protested against the Catholic Church

Lesson 4
Annul To announce that a marriage never existed between two people
Archbishop The top religious leader in a church province
Anglican Church The Church of England
Compromise An agreement in which both sides give up something
Puritan An English Protestant who wanted to purify the Anglican Church
Purify To make clean

Lesson 5
Calvinism The religious movement founded by John Calvin
Elect A Calvinist term for those whom God has chosen to save
Elder An experienced, older person
Huguenot A French Calvinist
Massacre The act of killing many people who are often defenseless

Lesson 6
Catholic Reformation The Catholic Church's reforms that attempted to fight Protestant beliefs
Censor To prevent someone from reading or viewing something
Roman Inquisition A Catholic court that inquired into people's religious beliefs
Jesuit A member of the Catholic religious order known as the Society of Jesus

Objectives

- To describe how the king of France challenged the pope and Rome
- To define the word *reformer* as used in this chapter
- To understand the threat that the reformers posed to the Catholic Church

Authority
Power

Reformer
A person who tries to change something

In Unit 2, you studied the Middle Ages. Historians also call this period the Age of Faith. The Catholic Church had great religious and political power. In fact, the pope could command kings. Beginning in the 1300s, some people challenged the **authority,** or power, of the church.

Who Challenged the Church's Political Authority?

In 1294, King Philip IV of France tried to tax church officials. The pope told the French clergy not to pay the tax. In 1303, the king arrested Pope Boniface VIII, an Italian. Six years later, the king helped to elect a French pope, Clement V. The new pope moved from the Vatican in Rome to Avignon in France.

Seventy years passed before a pope lived in Rome again. But problems continued. At different times, more than one person claimed to be pope. Some church leaders suggested that a council should take the place of the pope. All this weakened the church's power.

Who Challenged the Church's Religious Authority?

Other people challenged the religious authority of the church. We call them **reformers** because they believed that the church needed to be reformed, or changed, for the better.

One reformer in the 1300s was the Englishman John Wycliffe. He said that the church had too much power and wealth. He also said that the Bible, and not leaders of the church, should be the authority for Christians. To allow people to read the Bible, Wycliffe translated the Latin Bible into English.

John Wycliffe was an early church reformer.

1415 – 1650

The Reformation Chapter 15 **353**

Chapter 15: Lesson 1

Overview This lesson describes how reformers challenged the authority of the pope and the Roman Catholic Church.

Objectives

- To describe how the king of France challenged the pope and Rome
- To define the word *reformer* as used in this chapter
- To understand the threat that the reformers posed to the Catholic Church

Student Pages pages 353–354

Teacher's Resource Library

  Workbook Activity 64

  Activity 64

  Modified Activity 64

Vocabulary

authority   **reformer**
heretic

Have students write a fill-in-the-blank sentence for each vocabulary word. Ask volunteers to write their sentences on the board. Have other students come to the board to fill in the blanks with the correct words.

1 Warm-Up Activity

Ask students for their ideas of what life might have been like in France 700 years ago in the early 14th century. Ask them for ideas about who might have been more powerful, a pope or a king. Encourage them to consider the ideas of protest and reform and if these ideas had a place in the early 14th century. Write students' ideas on the board and revisit and revise their ideas after reading Lesson 1.

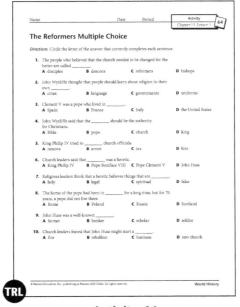

Workbook Activity 64   **Activity 64**

PRONUNCIATION GUIDE

Use this list to help students pronounce difficult words in this lesson.

Avignon	(a vē nyôn´)
Boniface	(bon´ ə fəs)
Huss	(hus)
Wycliffe	(wik´ lif)

2 Teaching the Lesson

Help students recall the structure of the Christian Church in Western Europe during the Middle Ages before the Renaissance. (The pope in Rome was head of the only church.)

Ask:

- Why did King Philip IV of France arrest Pope Boniface VIII? (Answers may vary; students may suggest that the king was angry because the pope told the clergy not to pay taxes to the king.)

- What were people who challenged the religious authority of the Catholic Church called? (reformers)

- Why did John Wycliffe want to translate the Latin Bible into English? (so people could read it in their own language)

- Why did the church punish John Huss? (Answers may vary; students may suggest that he criticized the church. Church leaders wanted to prevent a rebellion.)

Reading Strategy: Summarizing

(Students may suggest that the church was getting involved in non-religious activities or that the country needed the taxes from the clergy.)

STUDY SKILLS

Have students make a chart to keep track of each reformer as they read this chapter. They can name their chart "Important Reformers," and title the column heads *Name, Action, Place, Year,* and *Result*.

Heretic

A person who holds a belief that a religious authority thinks is false

Reading Strategy: Summarizing

What are some important details that help you understand why people challenged the church?

Word Bank

Avignon
Bible
Huss
King Philip IV
Wycliffe

People called Wycliffe's followers the "Poor Preachers." They had no interest in money. All they wanted to do was to teach religion to people in their own language instead of in Latin.

Why Did John Huss Criticize the Church?

The ideas of John Wycliffe influenced John Huss. He was a well-known scholar at the University of Prague in Bohemia. (Bohemia was part of the Holy Roman Empire. It is now part of the Czech Republic.) Huss thought that the church's clergy were too worldly and that the church should remove them from office.

When Huss and his followers criticized the church, both religious and political leaders feared a rebellion. Church leaders said that Huss was a **heretic.** A heretic teaches a belief that a religious authority thinks is false. In 1415, they arrested Huss and burned him at the stake.

Lesson 1 Review On a sheet of paper, use the words from the Word Bank to complete each sentence correctly.

1. _____ of France challenged the authority of the pope in 1294.

2. In 1309, Pope Clement V moved from the Vatican to _____.

3. John _____ said that the church had too much money and power.

4. Wycliffe translated the _____ from Latin to English.

5. The church burned John _____ as a heretic.

What do you think

Why did the church not want to lose its political and religious authority?

---

3 Reinforce and Extend

LEARNING STYLES

Visual/Spatial

Have students design and make an icon to represent the authority of the Catholic Church and the pope. Then have students trace an outline map of Europe. Have them place Avignon and Rome in the center, labeling both cities with their icon. Students can use their map to explain what happened when the French king tried to control the Catholic Church.

Lesson 1 Review Answers

1. King Philip IV **2.** Avignon
3. Wycliffe **4.** Bible **5.** Huss

Answers will vary. Most people and institutions want to be powerful. The Catholic Church was probably no different. Also, the church may have felt responsible for its members and may have felt that the church needed to be powerful.

- To explain Martin Luther's disagreements with the Catholic Church
- To describe the way Luther spread the word about his disagreements

Reformation

A movement that challenged and changed the Catholic religion in Europe

Salvation

Eternal happiness for one's soul

Indulgence

A church paper that says that a person will not be punished after death for their sins

Reading Strategy:
Summarizing

What reformer is being introduced in this lesson?

Just over 100 years after Huss was executed, Martin Luther challenged the church's religious authority. What he did began a new period of European history—the **Reformation.** This movement challenged and changed Christianity in Europe.

What Troubled Luther?

Martin Luther was born in Germany in 1483. His father wanted him to become a lawyer. But when Luther studied law, he did not like it. Then, in 1505, Luther was caught in a summer storm and lightning nearly hit him. Fearing for his life, Luther promised to become a monk if he lived. In 1507, he kept his promise.

In 1512, Luther began to teach religion at the University of Wittenberg in Saxony. Questions about **salvation,** or eternal happiness for his soul, troubled him. How, he asked, should he act to save his soul? Luther struggled for a long time with this problem. Then, while reading the Bible, he found his answer.

Luther came to believe that he could win salvation by faith alone. He said that fasting, prayer, and religious ceremonies could not guarantee, or promise, salvation. But the Catholic Church said that people needed to do these good works to save their souls. Luther said that his discovery made him feel as though he were "born again."

Why Did the Church Begin to Sell Indulgences?

In 1517, Luther and the church leadership began to struggle with one another because Pope Leo X started to sell **indulgences.** These are papers the church gives people that say they will not be punished after death for their sins. People bought indulgences for themselves and for loved ones who were already dead. The church said that doing this was a good deed. The pope sold indulgences because he needed more money to build St. Peter's Church, a big church in Rome.

Chapter 15: Lesson 2

Overview This lesson describes how Martin Luther's personal questions about the Catholic Church became seeds for the Reformation.

Objectives

- To explain Martin Luther's disagreements with the Catholic Church
- To describe the way Luther spread the word about his disagreements

Student Pages pages 355–357

Teacher's Resource Library TRL

Workbook Activity 65

Activity 65

Modified Activity 65

Vocabulary

indulgence   salvation
purgatory   thesis
Reformation

Have students study the definitions in the lesson. Ask them to write a sentence for each vocabulary word, replacing the vocabulary word with a blank. Then, have students trade papers with a partner and fill in the answers on their partner's paper.

PRONUNCIATION GUIDE

Use this list to help students pronounce difficult words in this lesson.

Tetzel   (tet´ səl)

Warm-Up Activity

Have students think about what they would do if leaders of a church or synagogue began doing things with which the members did not approve or agree. Ask how much they might be willing to accept before they objected. Ask what form their objections would take.

Workbook Activity 65   **Activity 65, pages 1–2**

2 Teaching the Lesson

In this lesson, another reformer challenges the authority of the Catholic Church. Have students read pages 355–357 to find out about that challenge.

Ask:

- What did Martin Luther think was the one way a person could win eternal happiness? (by faith)

- What did the Catholic Church do to ensure that people alive and dead would receive eternal happiness? (They sold indulgences.)

Reading Strategy: Summarizing

(Students will recognize from the lesson head and subheads that the lesson is about Martin Luther.)

Have students summarize details of Luther's life.

- How did John Tetzel raise money to send to Rome? (by selling indulgences)

- Why did Luther think that buying indulgences was wrong? (Answers may vary; students may suggest that Luther believed you couldn't buy forgiveness for their sins.)

- What did Luther's 95 theses criticize? (Answers will vary; students may suggest that they criticized the Catholic Church or the indulgences.)

- Why did the church lose money when people started reading Luther's 95 theses? (Answers may vary; students may suggest that people stopped buying the indulgences when they found out that Luther was against them.)

After students have read the Then and Now feature, "Origins of the Lutheran and Presbyterian Churches," challenge them to make a list of the different denominations of churches and synagogues that are found in their community.

Purgatory
A place of suffering after death

Thesis
A statement that people argue about or try to prove

In 1517, a monk named John Tetzel began selling indulgences near Luther's university. Tetzel told people to buy an indulgence to free a friend's soul from **purgatory.** This is what is believed to be a place of suffering after death. Tetzel said that the person who bought the indulgence could be sure of salvation. He raised a great deal of money and sent it back to Rome for St. Peter's Church.

What Are Luther's 95 Theses?

Someone asked Luther what he thought about the selling of indulgences. He said that it was wrong because people could not buy forgiveness for sins. On hearing this, Tetzel criticized Luther.

Martin Luther started the Reformation by disagreeing with the Catholic Church.

Luther began to write a series of 95 **theses,** or statements, against indulgences and other actions of the church. He nailed these statements on the door of a church. He wanted to argue the theses with church officials. On October 31, 1517, he let other people read his ideas. Printers printed Luther's 95 statements. People sent them to other countries. Because of this, the sale of indulgences went down, and the church lost money. The church decided to take steps to stop Luther's influence in Europe.

Origins of the Lutheran and Presbyterian Churches

Many Protestant churches began during the Reformation. Martin Luther formed the Lutheran Church and John Calvin's ideas shaped the Presbyterian Church. Both churches rejected the power of the pope and stressed the authority of the Bible. Their members believed in the importance of individual faith.

Both churches are still thriving today in the United States. The Evangelical Lutheran Church has just over 5 million members. The Presbyterian Church has almost 4 million members. There are many other Protestant churches as well.

ELL/ESL STRATEGY

Language Objective:
To learn lesson-related vocabulary

Have ELL students choose a school or class rule that they do not think is fair. Possible examples could be no chewing gum in class, having to wear a school uniform, or not carrying a cell phone. Have students write a few theses, or statements of their thoughts, about the rule they chose. Post the theses on the board or on chart paper. Then use the students' statements to involve the ELL students in a short class discussion in which arguments for and against the rule are presented. Check for student understanding of the content vocabulary, such as *thesis, statement, ideas,* and *argue.*

Disks for the Eyes

When were eyeglasses invented? The Chinese claim to have used them before A.D. 300. Marco Polo wrote in 1275 that he saw many Chinese wearing glasses. The scientist Roger Bacon mentioned eyeglasses in his writings in 1268. History, however, has no record of their invention.

We do know that by the 1300s, eyeglasses were popular among Europe's upper classes. However, people could use them only for seeing at a distance. What about glasses for seeing objects that were close? It took another hundred years to learn how to make them.

Venice became the chief producer of eyeglasses. However, people did not call them glasses. They called them "disks for the eyes."

In the 1500s, the demand for eyeglasses increased. The printing presses were producing more books and more people were reading. Some scholars needed glasses to be able to read.

Do you think that Luther had trouble with more than just indulgences? Explain your answer.

Lesson 2 Review On a sheet of paper, write the letter of the answer that correctly completes each sentence.

1. Martin Luther was born in _____.

   A England   **C** Italy
   B Germany   **D** France

2. As a monk and teacher, Luther struggled with the idea of _____.

   A salvation   **C** confrontations
   B vows   **D** translations

3. Luther believed that people could be saved by _____ alone.

   A the Bible   **C** faith
   B good works   **D** indulgences

4. Pope Leo X began to sell _____ to pay for the building of St. Peter's Church.

   A theses   **C** frescoes
   B portraits   **D** indulgences

5. Luther wrote _____ theses, or statements, about church actions that he did not agree with.

   A 85   **B** 95   **C** 105   **D** 1500

Lesson 2 Review Answers

1. B 2. A 3. C 4. D 5. B

Answers will vary. If Luther had trouble with only indulgences, he probably would not have written as many as 95 theses against the Catholic Church.

Have students speculate about where eyeglasses may have been invented. Then have them read "Disks for the Eyes" to find out how and where glasses were invented.

Ask:

• What choices of eyewear do people have today? (Answers will vary; students may mention both sunglasses and contact lenses.)

• Is there a place in your community where eyeglasses can be taken for recycling? (Answers will vary; students may mention that some stores and doctor's offices collect eyeglasses for recycling. They may also know that some service organizations, such as the Lions Club, collect eyeglasses and donate them to those who cannot afford to buy them.)

3 **Reinforce and Extend**

AT·HOME

Explain that churches and other charities today sometimes raise money by sending letters asking for donations. Ask students to check the mail at home for several days. Have them list the groups that send letters asking for donations. Have students bring their lists to class and compare them with those of their classmates.

CAREER CONNECTION

In the 16th century, the Catholic Church raised money by selling indulgences. Today, nonprofit organizations, such as churches, often hire professional fundraisers to help them raise money to pay for expenses. Have students research how someone might prepare for a career in fundraising.

Chapter 15: Lesson 3

Overview This lesson describes Luther's excommunication from the Catholic Church, how he founded his own church, and what some German princes did in response.

Objectives

- To explain how the Lutheran Church was founded
- To explain why many German princes became Lutherans

Student Pages pages 358–359

Teacher's Resource Library TRL

Workbook Activity 66

Activity 66

Modified Activity 66

Vocabulary

Baptism	minister
Communion	Protestant
excommunicate	ritual
Lutheran Church	

Have students create a crossword puzzle that uses the vocabulary words and their definitions. Then have students exchange puzzles and solve them.

1 Warm-Up Activity

Ask students for synonyms for the word *freedom*. (liberty, independence) Tell students that Martin Luther wrote a letter to Pope Leo called "The Freedom of the Christian" in which Luther outlined his ideas. Ask students what they think Luther might have meant by *freedom*. (Students may suggest that Luther meant the right to interpret the Bible for themselves or the ability to worship as they choose.) Encourage students to develop a definition of Martin Luther's *freedom* as they read Lesson 3.

2 Teaching the Lesson

Have students recall what Martin Luther did to anger the Catholic Church. Then have students read pages 358–359 to find out what the church did in response.

Objectives

- To explain how the Lutheran Church was founded
- To explain why many German princes became Lutherans

Excommunicate

To say that someone can no longer be a member of a church

Lutheran Church

The church established by Martin Luther

Minister

A person who can lead a religious ceremony in a Lutheran church

Ritual

A ceremony

Baptism

A ritual by which a person becomes a Christian

Communion

A ritual by which Christians grow in their faith

When Luther called for reform, the church ordered him to stop. Luther said he could not go against his beliefs. He said, "Here I stand. I cannot do otherwise."

What Did the Church Do to Luther?

In 1521, Pope Leo X said that Luther's beliefs were wrong and **excommunicated** him. That is, the pope said that Luther was no longer a member of the Catholic Church. The ruler of the Holy Roman Empire—a Catholic—signed the Edict of Worms. This decree said that anyone could kill Luther without being punished. But several German princes protected Luther from this.

What Did Luther Want to Change?

Luther called for three reforms. First, he said that only faith in Jesus Christ could save people. Good works alone would not save them. Second, he taught that religious truth came from the Bible. People should read the Bible and decide for themselves what it meant. Third, Luther said that people did not need the clergy to tell them what the Bible means. To help people read the Bible, Luther translated it into German.

What Church Did Luther Begin?

In the beginning, Martin Luther did not want to break away from the Catholic Church. All he wanted was to debate his 95 theses and reform the church. However, in time, he started the **Lutheran Church.** His church had some differences from the Catholic Church. Catholic priests were not allowed to marry, but Lutheran **ministers** could. (Ministers are the leaders of religious ceremonies.) The job of a minister was to help people find or strengthen their faith in Jesus Christ.

Luther also got rid of some of the **rituals,** or ceremonies, of the Catholic Church. Luther did, however, keep two rituals—**Baptism,** by which people become Christians, and **Communion,** by which Christians grow in their faith.

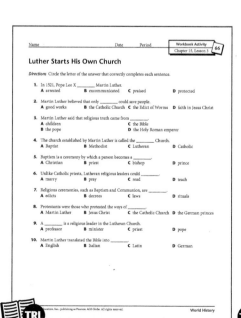

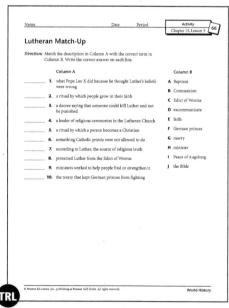

Protestant

A reformer who protested against the Catholic Church

 Writing About History

Pretend you are Martin Luther. Explain what you meant when you said, "Here I stand. I cannot do otherwise." In your notebook, write two or three sentences about this.

Reading Strategy:
Summarizing

In your own words, summarize the three reforms that Luther called for.

Why Did German Princes Become Lutherans?

Many German princes liked Luther's ideas. They began to protest the ways of the Catholic Church. Because of this, people called them **Protestants.** In the 1530s, war broke out between the armies of the Protestant Lutheran princes and Charles V, a Catholic ruler.

In 1546, Martin Luther died. Nine years after his death, a treaty was signed to stop the fighting. According to this treaty, each German prince could pick his own church. All the people in his area had to follow his religion. Called the Peace of Augsburg, the treaty kept the German princes from fighting for more than 50 years.

Lesson 3 Review On a sheet of paper, write the answer to each question. Use complete sentences.

1. What does the term *excommunication* mean?

2. Why did the Catholic Church excommunicate Martin Luther?

3. According to Luther, where could people find religious truth?

4. What is one difference between a Catholic priest and a Lutheran minister?

5. Why did people call religious reformers Protestants?

What might have kept Luther from starting a new church?

Ask:

- How did the Catholic Church punish Luther? (The church excommunicated him.)

- What did Luther do in response? (He started his own church.)

- Why did many German princes become Lutherans? (Answers will vary; students may say the princes liked Luther's views.)

- If you had been living on land owned by a German prince, would you have been a Lutheran or a Catholic? (You would have had to belong to the same church the prince belonged to.)

Reading Strategy:
Summarizing

(Only faith in Jesus Christ could save people. Religious truth came from the Bible. People did not need clergy to tell them what the Bible meant.)

 Writing About History

Have students brainstorm present-day issues about which they feel strongly and the reasons why they feel as they do. (Some may suggest racial or religious intolerance, or pollution.) Remind students before reading the feature that the Catholic Church was very powerful, and Luther took a great risk in voicing his beliefs.

 Reinforce and Extend

Lesson 3 Review Answers

1. The term *excommunication* means that someone can no longer be a member of a church group. 2. The Catholic Church thought that Luther's beliefs were wrong. 3. People could find religious truth in the Bible. 4. A minister can marry; a priest cannot. 5. Protestants protested Catholic beliefs.

Answers will vary. Luther might have stayed within the Catholic Church if the church officials had been willing to examine his beliefs objectively.

LEARNING STYLES

 Interpersonal/ Group Learning
Discuss with students the treaty called the Peace of Augsburg. Then give students an opportunity to discuss the pros and cons of the treaty through debate. Ask for volunteers to represent each side of the argument, or divide the class in half according to their views.

Chapter 15: Lesson 4

Overview This lesson outlines the conflict between the Catholic Church and the Crown in England, which resulted in the establishment of the Anglican Church.

Objectives

- To explain how a political problem started the Reformation in England
- To describe the influence of Queen Mary and Queen Elizabeth I on the church

Student Pages pages 360–362

Teacher's Resource Library TRL

Workbook Activity 67

Activity 67

Modified Activity 67

Vocabulary

Anglican Church	compromise
annul	purify
archbishop	Puritan

Read the definitions from the book one at a time in random order. Have students match the word or term to the definition and say it aloud as in a chorus. Students may want to take turns saying a vocabulary word or term while other students provide its definition. Continue until students show familiarity with the vocabulary list.

1 Warm-Up Activity

Have students create a large flow diagram showing the formation of new religions during the Reformation. At the top of the chart should be the Catholic Church. Lutheran, Protestant, Anglican, Puritan, and Presbyterian Churches should be shown as labeled arrows that come off the Catholic Church. When students read the remaining lessons in the chapter, they can add Calvinists and Huguenots to their charts.

360   *Unit 3   Early Modern Times*

Objectives

- To explain how a political problem started the Reformation in England
- To describe the influence of Queen Mary and Queen Elizabeth I on the church

Reading Strategy:
Summarizing

What important person is introduced in this section?

Annul

To announce that a marriage never existed between two people

Luther's religious reform movement quickly spread beyond Germany. By 1534, it reached England, where Henry VIII ruled. Just 13 years before, Henry had attacked Luther's ideas. To thank him, Pope Leo X called the king "Defender of the Faith."

Why Did Henry VIII Break with the Pope?

A political problem started the Reformation in England. Henry VIII became king there in 1509. He married a Spanish princess, Catherine of Aragon. They had a daughter named Mary. In 1527, Henry VIII tried to end his marriage to Catherine. He wanted a son, but Catherine could not have more children. However, the Catholic Church did not allow divorce. Henry asked Pope Clement VII to **annul** the marriage. That is, to announce that the marriage had never existed.

Catherine refused to accept this. She asked her nephew, Charles V, who was the Holy Roman emperor, to influence the pope's decision. Charles had an army in Italy, so Catherine won the pope's support. He refused to annul the marriage. But by then, Henry had secretly married another woman, Anne Boleyn.

King Henry VIII of England was a powerful ruler who helped start the Anglican Church.

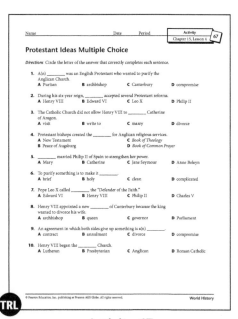

Protestant Ideas Spread to England

Directions Write the answers to these questions. Use complete sentences.

1. Had Henry VIII always agreed with Luther's ideas? Explain your answer.

2. How did the Reformation in England begin?

3. Why did Henry VIII appoint a new archbishop of Canterbury?

4. How did many Anglican rituals become a blend of Catholic and Protestant ceremonies?

5. Who were the Puritans?

Protestant Ideas Multiple Choice

Directions Circle the letter of the answer that correctly completes each sentence.

1. A(n) _____ was an English Protestant who wanted to purify the Anglican Church.
   A Puritan   B archbishop   C Canterbury   D compromise

2. During his six-year reign, _____ accepted several Protestant reforms.
   A Henry VIII   B Edward VI   C Leo X   D Philip II

3. The Catholic Church did not allow Henry VIII to _____ Catherine of Aragon.
   A visit   B write to   C marry   D divorce

4. Protestant bishops created the _____ for Anglican religious services.
   A New Testament   C Book of Theology
   B Peace of Augsburg   D Book of Common Prayer

5. _____ married Philip II of Spain to strengthen her power.
   A Mary   B Catherine   C Jane Seymour   D Anne Boleyn

6. To purify something is to make it _____.
   A brief   B holy   C clean   D complicated

7. Pope Leo X called _____ the "Defender of the Faith."
   A Edward VI   B Henry VIII   C Philip II   D Charles V

8. Henry VIII appointed a new _____ of Canterbury because the king wanted to divorce his wife.
   A archbishop   B queen   C governor   D Parliament

9. An agreement in which both sides give up something is a(n) _____.
   A contract   B annulment   C divorce   D compromise

10. Henry VIII began the _____ Church.
    A Lutheran   B Presbyterian   C Anglican   D Roman Catholic

Archbishop

The top religious leader in a church province

Anglican Church

The Church of England

Reading Strategy:
Summarizing

What are some important details that help you understand Henry VIII?

What Was the Name of Henry's New Church?

In order to divorce Catherine, Henry VIII appointed a new **archbishop** of Canterbury. An archbishop is the top religious leader in a church province. This archbishop said that Henry's marriage to Catherine was not legal. In 1534, Parliament made the king the head of the Church of England, or **Anglican Church.** Henry took control of all lands the Catholic Church owned in England.

What Did Edward Do as King?

Henry and Anne had a daughter they named Elizabeth. But three years after their marriage, Henry said that Anne was not faithful to him and executed her. Then he married Jane Seymour and they had a son named Edward. When Henry died in 1547, his nine-year-old son became King Edward VI. The young king accepted several Protestant reforms. During his reign, Protestant bishops created the *Book of Common Prayer* for Anglican religious services.

Who Tried to Change the Protestant Reforms?

Edward ruled for only six years and died in 1553. Then Mary—Henry's first child—became queen of England. She was a Catholic and used her power to make England a Catholic nation once again. To strengthen her power, she married the Catholic king of Spain, Philip II. But the English Protestants hated Mary and refused to become Catholics again.

---

2 Teaching the Lesson

Explain that the church the Protestants formed in England was called the Anglican Church. Have students read pages 360–362 to find out how the Anglican Church was formed.

Reading Strategy:
Summarizing

(Students will probably say that Henry VIII is introduced, although Queens Mary and Elizabeth I, King Edward VI, and Pope Clement VII are also important to history.)

Ask:

- Which king left the Catholic Church to begin another church? (Henry VIII)

- How did Henry VIII have his divorce from Catherine made legal? (He appointed his own archbishop.)

- During King Edward's reign, what did the Protestant bishops do? (They created the *Book of Common Prayer*.)

- Which Queen tried to make England Catholic again? (Mary)

Reading Strategy:
Summarizing

(Students should note that wanting to have a son to succeed him to the throne is in important detail in understanding Henry VIII's motivation.)

Ask:

• How did Elizabeth I try to make Catholics and Protestants happy in the Anglican Church? (Answers will vary; students may say she tried to reach a compromise to make both groups happy.)

ELL/ESL STRATEGY

Language Objective: *To compare and contrast to organize and understand factual information*

Have ELL students read the section on page 362 subtitled "What Compromise Did Elizabeth Make?" or read the section aloud. Help the students to make two lists of the terms of the compromise for the formation of the Anglican Church. Each list should have two columns. Head the two columns of the first list "What the Catholics Gave Up" and "What the Catholics Kept." Head the two columns of the second list "What the Protestants Gave Up" and "What the Protestants Kept." Guide ELL students to put information from the section into the correct list and correct column. (List 1 Col 1: The Catholics gave up heading the church in England. Col 2: They retained many rituals and ceremonies. List 2 Col. 1: The Protestants gave up some rituals. Col. 2: They gained the right to run the day-to-day church business.)

3 Reinforce and Extend

LEARNING STYLES

Body/Kinesthetic
Have students make a diorama showing the Puritans about to leave England by ship for North America. Students could write a paragraph to accompany the diorama, which explains why the Puritans left England.

Compromise
An agreement in which both sides give up something to stop an argument

Puritan
An English Protestant who wanted to purify the Anglican Church

Purify
To make clean

Word Bank
Anglican
Edward VI
Elizabeth I
Henry VIII
Puritans

ONLINE CONNECTION

This Web site www.agsglobewh.com/page362 is based on a series of programs about Henry VIII and his six wives shown on public television. Included are biography and background material on each wife and links to lesson plans and activities suitable for grades 1 through 12.

What Compromise Did Elizabeth Make?

When Mary died in 1558, her half-sister became Queen Elizabeth I. She tried to join together the Protestants and Catholics into the Anglican Church. The king or queen of England was still the head of the Anglican Church. But Anglican bishops ran the day-to-day church business. Many Anglican rituals became a blend of Catholic and Protestant ceremonies.

Not all Protestants liked this **compromise,** or agreement in which both sides give up something to stop an argument. Some wanted to rid the Anglican Church of Catholic rituals. Historians call this group of English Protestants the **Puritans** because they wanted to **purify** the church, or make it clean. In the 1600s, some Puritans left England and settled in North America.

Lesson 4 Review On a sheet of paper, use the words from the Word Bank to complete each sentence correctly.

1. Pope Leo X gave _____ the name "Defender of the Faith."

2. Henry VIII of England began the _____ Church.

3. During the reign of _____, the Anglican clergy produced the *Book of Common Prayer*.

4. _____ tried to work out a compromise between the English Protestants and Catholics.

5. The _____ were English Protestants who did not like the compromise and wanted to purify the church.

What do you think

What do you think Charles V's army might have done if the pope had let Henry divorce Catherine of Aragon?

Lesson 4 Review Answers

1. Henry VIII **2.** Anglican
3. Edward VI **4.** Elizabeth I **5.** Puritans

Answers will vary. Students may suggest that Charles V's army might have attacked the Vatican and taken the pope and his home hostage.

Lesson 5 · John Calvin Organizes a New Religion

Objectives

◆ To explain the effect John Calvin had on the Protestant Reformation

◆ To describe what happened on St. Bartholomew's Day

Calvinism

The religious movement founded by John Calvin

Elect

A Calvinist term for those whom God has chosen to save

Elder

An experienced, older person

Reading Strategy: Summarizing

What religious movement is being described in this lesson?

Martin Luther had sparked the religious Reformation in 1517. Almost 20 years later, another man created an organized set of Protestant beliefs. Because his name was John Calvin, we call his religious movement **Calvinism.** He greatly influenced the Protestant Reformation.

What Did Calvin Teach?

John Calvin was born in France in 1509. During his life, his body was weak, but his will was strong. In 1536, he published his most important book—*Institutes of the Christian Religion.* This book contained what he thought each person should believe about religious questions.

First, Calvin taught that people are full of sin when they are born. Next, he said that few people would be saved from sin. Finally, Calvin told his followers that God had already chosen who would be saved. He called these special people the **"elect."** Calvin believed that the elect of God had a political mission. They were to rule Christian society.

Why was Calvin's book important? Because for the first time, the Protestant movement had a fully organized set of beliefs. However, not all Protestants accepted Calvin's ideas. In fact, the Lutherans in northern Germany accepted none of his ideas. The Anglicans in England accepted some and refused to accept others.

How Big Was Calvin's Religious Community?

John Calvin's teaching quickly spread. In 1541, the city officials of Geneva, Switzerland, asked him to organize their city into a religious community. (Geneva's population was 20,000.) Calvin started a school there to train ministers. Then he set up a council of 12 **elders.** These men were older and experienced.

1415 – 1650

The Reformation   Chapter 15   363

Chapter 15: Lesson 5

Overview This lesson features the life, work, and influence of John Calvin.

Objectives

■ To explain the effect John Calvin had on the Protestant Reformation

■ To describe what happened on St. Bartholomew's Day

Student Pages pages 363–365

Teacher's Resource Library TRL

Workbook Activity 68

Activity 68

Modified Activity 68

Vocabulary

Calvinism   Huguenot
elder   massacre
elect

Read the definitions in random order and have volunteers write the matching words on the board. Ask students to suggest ways to use each word in context.

PRONUNCIATION GUIDE

Use this list to help students pronounce difficult words in this lesson.

Nantes   (nants)

---

1 **Warm-Up Activity**

Tell students that most religions tell their members what is right and what is wrong, what proper behavior is, and what sinful behavior is. Have students imagine that they are forming a new religion. Have them make a list of what they would include as sinful behavior. Then have students read the lesson to find out what John Calvin considered to be sinful behavior. Have students compare their lists with the text.

The Reformation   Chapter 15   363

2 Teaching the Lesson

Explain to students that the views of the next reformer they will read about, John Calvin, would have a lasting effect on the formation of Protestant churches. Have students read pages 363–365 to find out what Calvin's views were.

Ask:

- **Why was John Calvin's writing important?** (Answers will vary; students may say he was the first reformer to write a book that told people what they should believe about religious questions.)

- **In what city and country was Calvin asked to form a religious community?** (Geneva, Switzerland)

Reading Strategy: Summarizing

(John Calvin and the rise of Calvinism)

- **How did the Calvinists check on the behavior of church members?** (Answers will vary; students may suggest that the Calvinist leaders visited people's homes to make sure they were leading good lives.)

- **What were French Calvinists called, and how were they treated by French Catholics?** (French Calvinists, called Huguenots, were persecuted by French Catholics.)

- **What do you think was the cause of the hatred between French Catholics and Huguenots?** (Answers will vary; students may say that the peoples' beliefs were affected by their church leaders.)

John Calvin started his own Protestant religion called Calvinism. This religion was the first Protestant religion with a fully organized set of beliefs. Calvin lived from 1509 to 1564.

Huguenot
A French Calvinist

Massacre
The act of killing many people who are often defenseless

Next, Calvin gave these elders the power to make laws that said what was right and what was wrong. The elders said that playing cards, betting money on something, drinking alcohol, singing, and dancing were wrong, or sinful.

Finally, Calvin said that citizens had to go to church services several times a week. Members of the council even visited people's homes once a year to make sure that people were leading good lives. The council put people in prison if they did not live the Calvinist way. Sometimes, the council forced people to leave the city. In time, Calvinists began to call Geneva a "city of saints."

What Happened on St. Bartholomew's Day?

Calvinism soon spread to the Catholic country of France. By 1560, about 15 percent of the French population was Calvinist. These French Calvinists became known as **Huguenots**. Many Catholics and Huguenots hated one another.

On August 24, 1572, the hate exploded. On that day, the Catholic Church was celebrating St. Bartholomew's Day. At daybreak, in the city of Paris, Catholics began attacking and killing Huguenots. Historians call the attack the St. Bartholomew's Day **Massacre**. A massacre is the act of killing many people who are often defenseless.

ELL/ESL STRATEGY

Language Objective:
To use a timeline to organize factual information

After all students have read the lesson, help them organize the factual information by making a simple timeline on the board. Use the dates 1560, 1572, 1598, and 1685 on the timeline. Have students fill in the important event for each date. (1560—French Calvinists become known as Huguenots; 1572—Catholics attack Huguenots in St. Bartholomew's Day Massacre; 1598—Edict of Nantes; 1685—Protestantism illegal in France, thousands flee.) Then ask ELL students to compare the religious conflicts between French Catholics and Huguenots with their own knowledge of religious or racial conflicts in their native countries. Add these events to the timeline.

For a month, in the towns and cities of France, Catholics murdered Protestants. More than 12,000 Huguenots lost their lives. But people still continued to become Calvinists. Finally in 1598, the king of France issued the Edict of Nantes. This gave the Protestant Huguenots more political and religious rights. It also protected Catholics by discouraging the building of Protestant churches in Catholic areas. Tension continued between Catholics and Protestants. In 1685, King Louis XIV ended the Edict of Nantes by making Protestantism illegal in France. Hundreds of thousands of Protestants fled France. The loss of so many skilled workers hurt the economy of France for many years.

Lesson 5 Review On a sheet of paper, write the letter of the answer that correctly completes each sentence.

1. John Calvin organized a set of _____ beliefs.

   A Catholic   **C** Protestant
   B Anglican   **D** Lutheran

2. Calvin taught that people are born _____.

   A sinful   **C** educated
   B holy   **D** strong

3. The city of _____ was organized into a religious community.

   A Paris   **C** Canterbury
   B Rome   **D** Geneva

4. Calvin gave the _____ power to make laws.

   A kings   **C** peasants
   B elders   **D** elect

5. St. _____ Day Massacre led to the death of many Huguenots.

   A Peter's   **C** Luther's
   B Bartholomew's   **D** John's

Calvin said that people are sinful and that God has already chosen those to be saved. Why do you think so many people accepted these ideas?

Lesson 5 Review Answers

1. C 2. A 3. D 4. B 5. B

Answers will vary. Perhaps the people who became Calvinists thought that they were all among "the elect." That is, God had already chosen them to be saved.

Ask:

• What did the Edict of Nantes do?

(It gave the French Huguenots more political and religious rights and protected Catholics by discouraging the building of Protestant churches in Catholic areas.)

3 Reinforce and Extend

WORLD CULTURES

Geneva, the city in Switzerland that asked John Calvin to come and form a religious community in its midst, has a tradition of welcoming the world. Many international agreements—such as the Geneva Conventions that regulate the treatment of the wounded, prisoners, and noncombatants during war—were written in the city. Geneva by tradition is an international city. It was home to the League of Nations that emerged after World War I. Today, Geneva is the home base for the International Red Cross, the European headquarters of the United Nations, the International Labor Organization, and the World Council of Churches.

BACKGROUND INFORMATION

Soon after 1517 and the beginning of the Protestant Reformation in Germany, the ideas of religious reform spread to France. French Protestants, called Huguenots, immediately were persecuted by the Catholic majority. In 1523, Jean Valliere was burned at the stake in Paris. He became the Huguenot's first martyr. Some Huguenots fled the persecution, many going to Strasbourg in Germany, which had been named a free city under the Holy Roman Empire. Among the Huguenot refugees in Strasbourg was John Calvin. Huguenot-Catholic conflicts continued until the French Revolution of 1789, when the National Assembly declared the principle of religious liberty.

Chapter 15: Lesson 6

Overview This lesson explains the Catholic Reformation, the means by which the Catholic Church chose to fight the Protestant Reformation.

Objectives

- To describe the purpose of the Council of Trent
- To identify Ignatius of Loyola and his work

Student Pages pages 366–368

Teacher's Resource Library **TRL**

Workbook Activity 69

Activity 69

Modified Activity 69

Vocabulary

Catholic Reformation
censor
Jesuit
Roman Inquisition

Have students study the definitions in the lesson. Ask students to create questions that can be answered by the vocabulary words. Then have them work with a partner to take turns asking and answering questions. Allow students to work with different partners until they feel comfortable with the definitions.

PRONUNCIATION GUIDE

Use this list to help students pronounce difficult words in this lesson.

Ignatius   (ig nā´ shəs)

1 Warm-Up Activity

Now that students have learned about a number of reformers, have them play a game of Twenty Questions. Have a volunteer think of a reformer. The other students should ask up to 20 questions that can be answered by *yes* or *no* to determine who the reformer is. Challenge students to ask specific questions so they can guess the reformer after only two or three questions.

Objectives

- To describe the purpose of the Council of Trent
- To identify Ignatius of Loyola and his work

Catholic Reformation

The Catholic Church's reforms that attempted to fight Protestant beliefs

Censor

To prevent someone from reading or viewing something

Roman Inquisition

A Catholic court that inquired into people's religious beliefs

In the mid-1500s, the Catholic Church began its own reform—the **Catholic Reformation.** (This is sometimes called the Counter-Reformation.) It had three goals. The first was to reform the church itself. The second was to convert non-Christians into Catholics. The third goal was to stop the spread of Protestant beliefs.

What Did the Catholic Church Do First?

Popes Paul III and Paul IV tried to fix problems within the church itself. They appointed new church officials who were well educated. They also began to **censor** books. That is, they prevented people from reading certain books. Finally, they set up a special court—the **Roman Inquisition.** It looked into the religious beliefs of people. It could execute heretics.

What Did the Council of Trent Do?

In 1545, the church called for a council of church officials to meet at the Italian city of Trent. This council lasted 18 years. It wrote down the most important beliefs of the Catholic Church and stopped the sale of indulgences. It refused to accept the teachings of Luther and Calvin on salvation. The council said that people found salvation only through the Catholic Church.

The council also said that to be saved people had to go to church and do good deeds. They also had to accept the pope as the only leader of the Christian Church. Finally, Catholics had to agree with the church's interpretation of the Bible. To counter Protestant translations of the Bible, the council ordered its own new translation.

Who Were the Jesuits?

Ignatius of Loyola was born in Spain in 1491. He played a big part in the Counter-Reformation. Like Luther and Calvin, he asked questions about salvation. But his answers were different from theirs. Ignatius thought that self-discipline and good actions saved people.

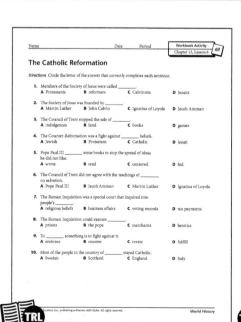

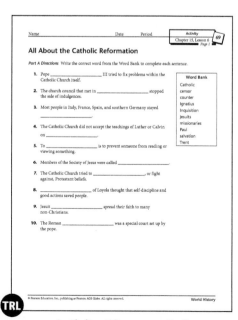

Jesuit

A member of the Catholic religious order known as the Society of Jesus

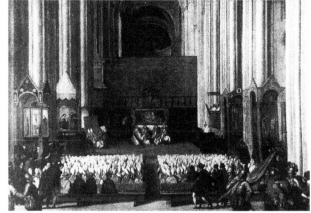

The Council of Trent wrote down the most important beliefs of the Catholic Church.

Ignatius created a new Catholic religious order called the Society of Jesus. Members of this order are called **Jesuits.** They had to be smart, strong, and holy, because they wanted to help Catholics stay in the Catholic Church. They also wanted to help Protestants return to it. Over the next 200 years, Jesuit missionaries spread their faith to non-Christians in Africa, Asia, and North and South America.

Reading Strategy:
Summarizing

What process is this lesson about?

What Countries Stayed Catholic?

Europe now had two groups of Christian churches—Catholic and Protestant. Many people in northern Germany, Norway, Sweden, the Netherlands, Switzerland, England, and Scotland became Protestants. Most of the people in Italy, France, Spain, and southern Germany stayed Catholic. Soon these different religious beliefs caused wars. Between 1550 and 1650, Europeans fought over their different religious beliefs.

Ask students to share their understanding of censorship and then read pages 366–368 to find out what measures the Catholic Church took to counter the Protestant Reformation.

Ask:

• How did Popes Paul III and Paul IV let people know which books were acceptable to read? (They censored the books they found objectionable.)

• Which fundraising practice was stopped by the Council of Trent? (the selling of indulgences)

• Which European countries were considered Catholic countries during the 15th and 16th centuries? (Italy, France, Spain, southern Germany)

• Which European countries were considered Protestant countries during this time? (northern Germany, Norway, Sweden, the Netherlands, Switzerland, England, Scotland)

Reading Strategy:
Summarizing

(Students may suggest that this lesson is about countering, the process of fighting against something. In this case, the "something" is Protestant beliefs.)

LEARNING STYLES

 Auditory/Verbal
Have a class debate about whether the Catholic Church and its Council of Trent were right to censor books and to force people to accept the Church's teachings. Encourage students to discuss the positive actions of the Council of Trent in their arguments.

ELL/ESL STRATEGY

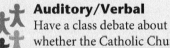 **Language Objective:**
To identify main ideas
Invite ELL students to imagine themselves in the role of Ignatius of Loyola. Have them write a letter to Catholic Church officials at the Council of Trent. The letter should state that they want to create a new Catholic religious order

called the Society of Jesus. They should explain the purpose of the Society, its beliefs, some of its goals, and its importance to the Church. Tell students that they should make the letter as convincing as possible so the pope will give his approval to the plan. Have students underline the main idea or main ideas in their letter.

3 Reinforce and Extend

IN THE COMMUNITY

Censorship is sometimes experienced at a community level. Have students interview or research comments by school and public librarians, bookstore owners, local newspaper editors, and radio and TV managers about any experiences they have had with censorship issues. These might range from actual censorship of a book by a library or school board to responses to community pressure regarding the handling of news, display of magazines and books, or choices in programming. Give students an opportunity to report their findings.

Biography

Provide students with the following background material about the Amish people in the United States:

• The first Amish farm communities were established in eastern Pennsylvania.

• Today there are Amish communities in Pennsylvania, Ohio, Indiana, Iowa, Illinois, and Kansas.

• Amish clothing epitomizes a commitment to a plain lifestyle. Clothes are fastened with hooks and eyes instead of buttons or zippers. Women wear bonnets and long dresses in dark, solid colors. They do not wear jewelry. Men wear broad-brimmed black hats.

• Amish religious services are conducted in a mixture of German and English known as Pennsylvania Dutch. The Amish people are sometimes called Pennsylvania Dutch.

Lesson 6 Review On a sheet of paper, write the answer to each question. Use complete sentences.

1. What did the Catholic Reformation try to do?

2. What was the name of the court that Pope Paul III created to inquire into people's beliefs?

3. What council wrote down the most important beliefs of the Catholic Church?

4. What religious group did Ignatius of Loyola start?

5. What were the two jobs of Jesuits?

What do you think

What kind of books do you think Pope Paul III censored during the Catholic Reformation?

Biography

Jacob Amman: late 17th century

Jacob Amman was a Swiss man who belonged to a Protestant group called Mennonites. However, he and others disagreed with some of the church's practices. They thought the church rules were not strict enough. Amman led a group away from the church in the 1690s. They became known as the Amish. Following his directions, they shunned, or completely avoided, excommunicated members.

The Amish first came to America in the 1720s. Today they still live in farm communities. They teach separation from the world. Members must not go to war, swear oaths, or hold public office. Their personal life must be simple. They do not use electricity or telephones. They limit education to the eighth grade.

368   Unit 3   Early Modern Times

Lesson 6 Review Answers

1. Answers may vary. The Catholic Church tried to reform itself and counter Protestantism. **2.** Pope Paul III created the Roman Inquisition. **3.** The Council of Trent wrote down the most important beliefs of the Catholic Church. **4.** Ignatius of Loyola began the Society of Jesus. **5.** The Jesuits tried to keep Catholics from leaving the Catholic Church and to persuade Protestants to return to it.

Answers will vary. The pope probably banned books that had Protestant beliefs, especially about salvation, in them.

Chapter Project Follow-up

Student letters from the point-of-view of a reformer during the Reformation should be dated during the correct time period. Letters should accurately express the reformer's dissatisfaction with the Church's practices and explain the changes he wants to make. Letters should also reflect the writer's caution and awareness that disagreeing with Church authorities could be dangerous. Post students' letters in the classroom.

John Calvin's Strict Code of Conduct

John Calvin believed in a very strict moral code of conduct. He published his beliefs in the Institutes of the Christian Religion in 1536. Later, this code was called puritanical. The English who settled in Plymouth, Massachusetts, in 1620 followed Calvin's rules. They were called Puritans.

Whoever shall have blasphemed, swearing by the body or by the blood of our Lord, or in similar manner, he shall be made to kiss the earth for the first offense; for the second to pay five sous, and for third six sous, and for the last offense be put in the pillory for one hour.

If anyone sings immoral, dissolute, or outrageous songs, or dances the virollet or other dance, he shall be put in prison for three days and then sent to the consistory [church court].

That no one shall take upon interest or profit more than five percent upon penalty of confiscation of the principal and of being condemned to make restitution, as the case may demand.

That no one shall play at any game whatsoever it may be, neither for gold nor silver nor for any excessive stake, upon penalty of five sous and forfeiture of stake played for.

No one who wishes to be thought religious dares simply deny predestination, by which God adopts some to hope of life and sentences others to eternal death. When we attribute foreknowledge to God, we mean that all things always were, and perpetually remain, under his eyes, so that to his knowledge there is nothing future or past but all things are present. Therefore, as any man has been created to one or the other of these ends, we speak of him as predestined to life or to death.

He has appointed duties for every man in his particular way of life. And that no one may thoughtlessly transgress his limits, he has named these various kinds of living "callings." Therefore each individual has his own kind of living assigned to him by the Lord as a sort of sentry post, so that he may not heedlessly wander about throughout life.

Document-Based Questions

1. What was the punishment for singing outrageous songs?

2. How much profit should a person be allowed to earn?

3. What is Calvin's position on gambling?

4. What does the term *predestination* mean?

5. In your opinion, what parts of the moral code would help business people be successful?

Read the title, "John Calvin's Strict Code of Conduct," to students and have them read the first paragraph to find out which religious group brought Calvin's moral code to North America. (the Puritans)

Have students write the column headings *Sin* and *Punishment* on a sheet of paper. Then, as they read the next four paragraphs, have them write down one sin and its punishment mentioned in each paragraph. Give students an opportunity to share their opinions about this code of conduct.

Explain that Calvin believed that God had decided certain things about people before they entered this world. He called this belief *predestination*. Have students finish the reading to find out more about Calvin's idea of predestination and then have them read and answer the questions.

Answers to Document-Based Questions:

1. For singing outrageous songs, a person was sent to prison for three days and then sent to the church court.

2. A person could earn up to five percent interest.

3. Anyone caught gambling pays a fine of five sous and also loses the prize he or she was playing for.

4. Answers will vary. Students should say that *predestination* means that God knows everything that was and ever will be. When a person is born, God has already decided if he or she is going to heaven or hell.

5. Answers will vary. Business people knew that they could charge up to five percent interest. God has assigned each person an occupation. If a person seems to be successful, then they know what God wants for them, and they can be sure they will do well in business.

Have students look back through the pages of this chapter and brainstorm a list of jobs that the people mentioned in the chapter had. Then explain that most Europeans who lived in the 15th and 16th centuries farmed the land and were extremely poor. Ask a volunteer to read the title "The Harsh Life of the German Peasants." Then have students read the selection to find out how hard life was for most of the people.

When students finish the reading, they should read and answer the questions.

Answers to Spotlight Story Wrap-Up:

1. They were protesting the poor conditions under which they lived.

2. He told peasants to obey their nobles.

3. Answers will vary. More than 100,000 peasants were killed. Children lost their parents. Property was destroyed. People starved and died of disease. There was no law or order.

4. Answers will vary. They had to give the Church part of their crops and animals. They had to give the lord of the manor part of their crops, and they had to work for him for two months every year. Even if there wasn't enough food, they could not hunt in the manor woods.

5. Answers will vary. Many students will respond that he was wrong, and that he should have helped people who were having such a hard time.

The Harsh Life of the German Peasants

In 1524, German peasants revolted against the princes who ruled them. Peasants were protesting the poor conditions in which they lived. They expected Martin Luther to support their rebellion. Luther had challenged the authority of the Catholic Church. To them, their revolt against the nobles seemed similar to his.

As the revolt spread, however, Luther sided with the German princes. He feared the mob violence that it had caused. Luther condemned the revolt. He wrote, "Let every soul be subject unto the higher powers. Peasants should be obedient." Because of Luther's actions, he lost peasant support.

The Peasants' War, as the revolt is known, was a bloody event. More than 100,000 peasants were killed. Homes and farmlands were destroyed. People starved. Disease spread from one area to another. Children wandered the countryside. They had no parents or means to take care of themselves. Bands of soldiers attacked defenseless villages. Bandits roamed about, attacking the weak and helpless.

Before the revolt, some peasants worked in towns as paid laborers. Some were skilled craftsmen. Serfs, however, could not leave a noble's land. By the 1500s, some peasants were free, but many still worked the nobles' lands. Many were heavily in debt to the landowners.

During the Reformation, the life of a peasant was harsh. Peasants were not allowed to keep or sell all of the crops they raised. The church, for example, got 10 percent of their crops. This rule also applied to their farm animals. Twice a year, a percentage of their crops went to the lord of the manor. In addition, they

had to work for him for two months a year. A landowner could use peasants any way he wished.

Food was often in short supply. Peasants sometimes risked hunting animals, or poaching, in the manor woods. This activity was strictly forbidden. Peasants caught poaching were severely punished.

Peasants could not even get married without permission from their lords. In addition, they had to pay a marriage tax.

Wrap-Up

1. Why did German peasants revolt in 1524?

2. What did Martin Luther say about this revolt?

3. How did the Peasants' War affect the common people in Germany?

4. What are two examples of the harsh conditions in which German peasants lived?

5. Do you agree or disagree with the position that Luther took on the revolt? Why?

Chapter 15 SUMMARY

- Beginning in the 1300s, reformers challenged the authority of the Catholic Church. Wycliffe translated the Bible into English so ordinary people could read it. John Huss in Bohemia criticized the clergy.

- Martin Luther, a German monk, questioned Church teachings about salvation. In 1517, he wrote 95 theses, or statements. His actions led to the Reformation.

- The pope punished Luther with excommunication. The Holy Roman Emperor agreed that he could be killed. However, some German princes protected Luther.

- Luther taught that people could be saved only by faith. He also translated the Bible into German.

- Luther eventually started his own church. The Lutheran Church kept two Catholic rituals—baptism and communion. Unlike priests, Lutheran ministers could marry.

- Some German princes agreed with Luther. They were called Protestants. In the 1530s, war broke out between Catholic and Protestant rulers. A peace treaty let each prince decide the religion in his lands.

- King Henry VIII of England wanted to divorce Catherine of Aragon. The pope refused to allow a divorce, so Henry broke with the church and started a new church, the Anglican Church.

- Henry VIII married several more wives. He had three children: Mary, Elizabeth, and Edward VI. During Edward's reign, Anglican bishops wrote the *Book of Common Prayer*.

- As queen, Mary tried to make England Catholic again. After her death in 1558, Elizabeth became queen. She compromised with some Catholic beliefs. But strict Protestants, called Puritans, wanted to rid the church of all Catholic rituals.

- John Calvin wrote a book organizing Protestant beliefs. He taught that God had already chosen those who would be saved. Angry Catholics killed French Calvinists, or Huguenots, in the St. Bartholomew's Day Massacre of 1572.

- The Catholic Church began the Catholic Reformation. The pope reformed the clergy. He began the Roman Inquisition. The Council of Trent restated Catholic beliefs.

- Ignatius of Loyola began the Society of Jesus to strengthen the church.

- The Reformation split Europe into Catholic and Protestant areas. Wars of religion went on between 1550 and 1650.

1415 – 1650

The Reformation   Chapter 15   **371**

TEACHER'S RESOURCE

The AGS Globe Teaching Strategies in Social Studies Transparencies may be used with this chapter. The transparencies add an interactive dimension to expand and enhance the *World History* program content.

- What was the Catholic Church's response to the Protestant Reformation? (It reformed the clergy, began the Inquisition, and formed the Council of Trent. These changes were called the Counter-Reformation.)

- Who was Ignatius of Loyola? (the man who founded the Society of Jesus)

- What was the result of the Protestant Reformation? (Europe was split into Catholic and Protestant areas.)

Using the Chapter Summary

Have students read the Chapter Summary on page 371 to review the main ideas presented in Chapter 15.

Ask:

- What movement called for changes in the Catholic Church and resulted in the formation of new churches? (the Reformation or Protestant Reformation)

- How did Martin Luther's actions lead to the Reformation? (He questioned Church beliefs about salvation and wrote 95 theses criticizing the Catholic Church.)

- How did the pope punish Luther? (He excommunicated Luther.)

- What did Luther teach people? (Answers will vary; students may say that people could be saved only by faith.)

- What are examples of changes Luther made in Catholic ritual and ritual that he kept? (Changes: Lutheran ministers could marry, but priests could not. Kept: baptism and communion)

- Were the German princes Catholic or Protestant? How was the religion of an area decided? (The princes could choose to be Catholic or Protestant; the peasants took on the beliefs of the prince they worked for.)

- Why did Henry VIII break with the Catholic Church? (The pope would not grant him a divorce from Catherine of Aragon, so Henry started the Anglican Church.)

- What was accomplished during Edward VI's reign? (Anglican bishops wrote the *Book of Common Prayer*.)

- Which English queen tried to make England Catholic again? Which English queen tried to get Protestants and Catholics to compromise? (Mary; Elizabeth I)

- What was the St. Bartholomew's Day Massacre? (an uprising when angry French Catholics killed many Huguenots)

Chapter 15 Review

Use the Chapter Review to prepare students for tests and to reteach content from the chapter.

Chapter 15 Mastery Test

The Teacher's Resource Library includes two forms of the Chapter 15 Mastery Test. Each test addresses the chapter Goals for Learning. An optional third page of additional critical-thinking items is included for each test. The difficulty level of the two forms is equivalent.

Chapter 15 Review Answers

1. Wycliffe
2. Huss
3. Pope Leo X
4. Luther
5. Henry VIII
6. Mary
7. Elizabeth I
8. Calvin
9. Pope Paul III
10. Ignatius of Loyola
11. D
12. A

Chapter 15 REVIEW

On a sheet of paper, use the words from the Word Bank to complete each sentence correctly.

1. The "Poor Preachers" were the religious followers of _____.

2. The Catholic Church burned _____ at the stake in 1415 for his religious beliefs.

3. _____ ordered the Catholic Church to sell indulgences to help build St. Peter's Church.

4. _____ wrote 95 theses to show what he thought about the sale of indulgences.

5. Pope Leo X called _____ the "Defender of the Faith."

6. _____ tried to make England a Catholic nation again.

7. _____ of England tried to talk Catholics and Protestants into a compromise.

8. _____ believed that God had already chosen the people who would be saved.

9. _____ tried to reform the Catholic Church and called a special council to do this.

10. _____ began the Jesuit order to help in the Catholic Reformation.

On a sheet of paper, write the letter of the answer that correctly completes each sentence.

11. A(n) _____ is a person who teaches a belief that a religious authority thinks is false.

   A elder   **C** thesis
   B salvation   **D** heretic

12. A(n) _____ is a member of the Society of Jesus.

   A Jesuit   **C** Anglican
   B Calvinist **D** Lutheran

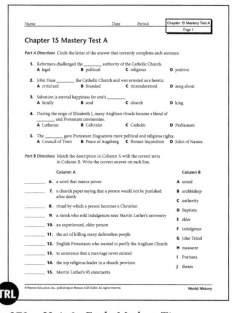

Chapter 15 Mastery Test A, pages 1–3

13. _____ were French Calvinists.

   A Jesuits   **C** Huguenots

   B Archbishops   **D** Censors

14. The _____ were Anglicans who wanted to purify their church.

   A Jesuits   **C** Huguenots

   B Puritans   **D** Calvinists

15. The Catholic Church sold _____ that were supposed to take away punishment for sins.

   A indulgences   **C** salvation

   B heretics   **D** theses

On a sheet of paper, write the answer to each question. Use complete sentences.

16. What was one cause of the Reformation?

17. How did Calvin's reforms differ from Luther's and King Henry VIII's?

18. What was one thing the Catholic Church did during the Catholic Reformation?

Critical Thinking On a sheet of paper, write your response to each question. Use complete sentences.

19. What part do you think the printing press played in the Reformation?

20. Luther, Calvin, and Ignatius of Loyola all asked questions about salvation. Which of their answers do you like best and why?

Look for multiple-choice answers that are opposites. Often, one of them is correct.

1415 – 1650

The Reformation   *Chapter 15*   **373**

---

13. C

14. B

15. A

16. The immediate cause of the Reformation was the pope's selling of indulgences to raise money to build St. Peter's Church. However, people were also protesting the great religious and political powers that the Catholic Church had by the 16th century.

17. Calvin wrote down an organized set of beliefs in a book. Both Luther and Henry VIII kept some Roman Catholic ideas and were not as organized as Calvin was.

18. The Catholic Church tried to reform itself by educating its clergy better. It also began to censor books so that Catholics did not get to read Protestant ideas. It set up a court to try heretics. Finally, it called the Council of Trent to set down its religious beliefs.

Critical Thinking

19. Answers will vary. Without the printing press, the ideas of Luther and Calvin would not have spread throughout Europe so quickly.

20. Answers will vary. Luther stressed the Bible and faith. Calvin stressed sin and being among the elect. Ignatius of Loyola stressed good works and self-discipline.

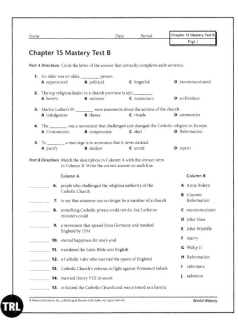

Chapter 15 Mastery Test B, pages 1–3

The Reformation   *Chapter 15*   **373**

The New Science

During the 1500s and 1600s, a new method of learning about the physical world developed. Scientists challenged beliefs from the past. Instead, they began to use experiments to find truth for themselves. In this chapter, you will meet many of these scientists, and you will learn what they studied.

Goals for Learning
◆ To list the five steps of the scientific method
◆ To describe early theories of the universe
◆ To describe Galileo's discoveries about the universe and gravity
◆ To describe the role Isaac Newton played in the history of science
◆ To list the inventions and contributions of a number of early scientists

1543 Copernicus develops new theory of the universe

1609 Galileo builds telescope

1628 Harvey publishes work on blood circulation

1687 Newton publishes work on gravity

| 1550 | 1600 | 1650 | 1750 |

Vesalius publishes book on human anatomy

1616 The Roman Catholic Church rules that Copernicus's theory is wrong

1674 Leeuwenhoek makes better microscope

Introducing the Chapter

Starting in the 16th century, scientists began to look for new methods of learning about the physical world. The use of experiments represented the birth of modern science.

Ask:
• Name two scientists who studied the stars and planets. (Copernicus and Galileo)

• Who challenged Copernicus? (The Roman Catholic Church)

• Name two scientists who studied the human body. (Versalius and Harvey)

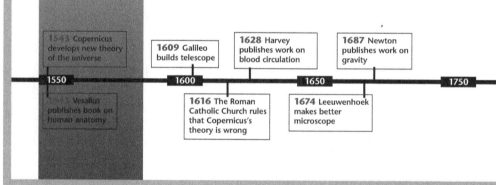

Name   Date   Period   *SELF-STUDY GUIDE*

Chapter 16: The New Science

Goal 16.1   To list the five steps of the scientific method

Date	Assignment	Completed
	1. Read pages 374–378.	
	2. Complete the Lesson 1 Review on page 378.	
	3. Complete Workbook Activity 70.	

Comments:

Goal 16.2   To describe early theories of the universe

Date	Assignment	Completed
	4. Read pages 379–381.	
	5. Complete the Lesson 2 Review on page 381.	
	6. Complete Workbook Activity 71.	

Comments:

Goal 16.3   To describe Galileo's discoveries about the universe and gravity

Date	Assignment	Completed
	7. Read pages 382–384.	
	8. Complete the Lesson 3 Review on page 384.	
	9. Complete Workbook Activity 72.	

Comments:

© Pearson Education, Inc., publishing as Pearson AGS Globe. All rights reserved.   World History

TRL

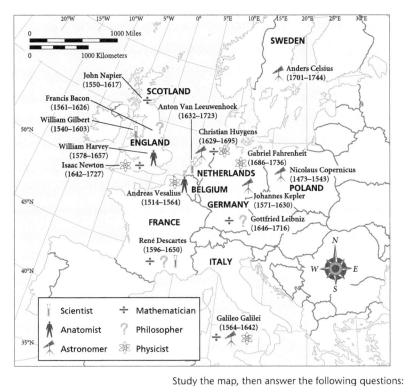

A great number of scientists of all kinds worked in Europe during the 1500s, 1600s, and early 1700s. Some of them invented new ways to solve mathematical problems. Others looked at the sky above them. Some made discoveries about the physical world. This was an exciting time, but a frightening one as well. These scientists found that many things that people had believed for centuries were wrong.

Study the map, then answer the following questions:

1. In what country did Galileo work?
2. How long did Francis Bacon live?
3. In what country did Andreas Vesalius do his work?
4. How many great scientists does the map show in England during this time?
5. What is the name of the French mathematician, scientist, and philosopher from this period?

Ask a volunteer to read aloud the title of the map, "Early Scientists (1540–1720)," and the paragraph that follows. Remind students that 16th century refers to the 1500s, 17th century refers to the 1600s, and so on.

Ask:

- During which centuries did the scientists on the map live? (16th, 17th, and 18th)
- Name three things scientists studied. (mathematical problems, the sky, and the physical world)
- Why was this a frightening time? (because scientists disproved many things that people had believed for centuries)

Have students read and write answers to the questions.

Map Skills Answers

1. Galileo worked in Italy.
2. Bacon lived to about age 65.
3. Vesalius worked in Belgium.
4. Four great scientists lived in England.
5. René Descartes was a French mathematician, scientist, and philosopher.

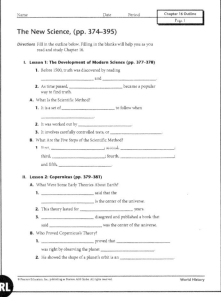

Chapter Project

Have students choose an invention or a new or altered scientific theory from those highlighted in Chapter 16. Explain that students will use library and Internet resources to research their chosen topic.
Tell students to focus their research on the following questions:

- Who was the scientist?
- What was invented or what theory was established or altered?

- What was the design of the invention or the details of the new theory?
- How did society respond to the invention or the new theory?
- How did the invention or the new theory change history?

Tell students to record their information on study cards.
Explain that students will pool their research as the class progresses through the chapter.

Questioning

Explain that questioning while reading helps to establish a purpose for reading and improves our understanding of what we have read. Point out that the two subheadings on page 377 are each in the form of a question. Have students read the two subheadings. Then have a volunteer change the first question into a statement.

Ask:

- **What statement can be made from the first subheading on page 377?** (The scientific method is a set of steps scientists follow for studying things.)

- **In what way did changing the question into a statement assist in your understanding?** (Answers will vary; It helped me learn the meaning of the term scientific method.)

- **What statement can be made from the second subheading on page 377?** (There are five steps in the scientific method.)

- **How does questioning help you with understanding what you read?** (Answers will vary; Questioning makes me look for facts or ideas needed to answer the question.)

Key Vocabulary Words

Point out that these chapter words are presented in the order they appear in each lesson. They are also found in the Glossary. Explain that students can develop a question using a vocabulary word as a way to better understand the word.

Ask:

- **What question could you ask using the vocabulary word *hypothesis*?** (What is a hypothesis?)

- **What question could you ask using the vocabulary word *prism*?** (Answers will vary; How does a prism work?)

- **What question could you ask using the vocabulary word *amber*?** (Answers will vary; Is amber a type of volcanic rock?)

Reading Strategy:
Questioning

Ask yourself questions as you read. Questioning the text will help you to be a more active reader. You will remember more of what you read if you do this. As you read, ask yourself:

- ◆ Why am I reading this text?

- ◆ What connections can I make between this text and my own life?

- ◆ What decisions can I make about the facts and details in this text?

Key Vocabulary Words

Lesson 1 ————————————
Scientific method A set of steps scientists follow for study

Hypothesis An educated guess based on what a scientist already knows

Conclusion An answer; a decision reached through step-by-step thinking

Lesson 2 ————————————
Revolve To move around something

Theory A statement that explains why or how something happens

Universe All the planets and stars that exist in space

Conclude To decide by using facts

Ellipse The shape of an egg

Lesson 3 ————————————
Experimental science The science that begins with and depends on careful experiments and measurements

Lesson 4 ————————————
Prism A three-sided object that can be seen through and separates white light into colors

Attract To pull something toward oneself

Scientific law A pattern in nature that someone can predict

Lesson 5 ————————————
Community A group of people with something in common

Anatomy The structure of a human or animal body

Core The center of something

Amber The hard, yellowish remains of a liquid that comes out of trees

Static electricity The electricity that builds up in something and is produced when one object rubs up against another

Objectives

◆ To describe how people learned about the natural world before the scientific method was developed

◆ To identify who worked out the scientific method

Scientific method

A set of steps scientists follow for study

Hypothesis

An educated guess based on what a scientist already knows

Conclusion

An answer; a decision reached through step-by-step thinking

Reading Strategy:
Questioning

Ask yourself: Did I understand the five steps of the Scientific Method? If not, read the section again.

Before 1500, most scholars decided what was true or false in two ways: they read the Bible and they read ancient Greek and Roman writers. During the Middle Ages, they believed that the writings of Aristotle were true. Only the Bible was a higher authority than this great Greek philosopher. The word *science* comes from a Latin word that means "to know." As time passed, science became a popular way to find truth.

What Is the Scientific Method?

During the 1500s and 1600s, a new way of learning about the natural world developed. Scientists based their new way of doing things on a few important steps. They called these steps the **scientific method.**

At the heart of the scientific method is the experiment. When scientists experiment, they carefully control a test. The test helps them discover truth for themselves. They no longer depend on authorities who say that something is true or false. Leonardo da Vinci wrote that science should be "born from experiment, the mother of all certainty." In the 1500s, this idea was new.

What Are the Five Steps of the Scientific Method?

In the 1620s, Francis Bacon, an Englishman, worked out the five steps of the scientific method. First, a scientist picks a problem or question. Second, the scientist makes a guess about the answer. This is an educated guess, based on what he or she already knows. We call such a guess a **hypothesis.** Third, the scientist does an experiment and carefully controls it. Fourth, the scientist observes what is happening during the experiment and makes notes. Fifth, the scientist draws a **conclusion,** or answer, from these notes. Then the scientist decides if the hypothesis was right.

Bacon's five steps still influence science today. Scientists still conduct experiments using these ideas.

Chapter 16: Lesson 1

Overview This lesson describes the development of the scientific method and details its five steps.

Objectives

■ To describe how people learned about the natural world before the scientific method was developed

■ To identify who worked out the scientific method

Student Pages pages 377–378

Teacher's Resource Library TRL

Workbook Activity 70

Activity 70

Modified Activity 70

Vocabulary

conclusion   scientific method
hypothesis

Have students work with a partner to write a paragraph that describes what they think they will learn about the scientific method, using and underlining each vocabulary word. Invite students to read their paragraphs aloud.

1 Warm-Up Activity

Show the students two identical plants. Have the students think about some ways in which the plants could be used to determine how light affects plant growth. Discuss the need for controls, proper recording of results, and the importance of asking a question that can be answered by the experiment. Have students think about the kind of questions 16th-century scientists might have been interested in answering.

---

2 Teaching the Lesson

Ask students who have taken science classes to describe the steps they go through before, during, and after performing an experiment. Then have students read pages 377–378 to find out the five steps of the scientific method.

Ask:

- Where does the word *science* come from? (a Latin word that means "to know")

- How did scholars decide what was true or false before 1500? (They read the Bible and they read Greek and Roman writers.)

- What are the five steps of the scientific method? (pick a problem or question, make a hypothesis, do an experiment, observe the experiment and make notes, and draw a conclusion)

Reading Strategy: Questioning

Have students list the five steps in the scientific method. Tell them to write one question about each step. Then have students answer the Reading Strategy question. (Answers will vary; Yes, I understand the five steps of the scientific method.)

Some of the instruments that are available to scientists today can perform truly mind-boggling tasks. Invite interested students to research a modern scientific instrument, such as the electron microscope or the Hubble telescope, and write a brief report. Have them present their findings to the class.

3 Reinforce and Extend

Lesson 1 Review Answers
1. A 2. B 3. A 4. B 5. C

Answers will vary. An experiment provides real data, which could be different than what the hypothesis states.

The Scientific Method

The scientific method is a well-defined series of steps. Accurate measurement is very important at each step. Scientists began to use this method in the 1500s. However, they did not have today's instruments and techniques.

New technologies have changed what scientists can do. Computers quickly count and compare data. In the past it would take people years to do the same jobs. More powerful microscopes see much smaller objects. Telescopes look farther. Unlike in the 1500s, scientists can look inside living beings and materials.

Today there is also an increasing number of highly trained scientists. In the 1500s, one person might investigate a problem. Today an army of scientists attacks an issue. There has been a tremendous growth in scientific knowledge in the last 100 years.

Lesson 1 Review On a sheet of paper, write the letter of the answer that correctly completes each sentence.

1. Before the 1500s, scholars often decided what was true or false by reading _____.

   A the Bible   C ancient French writers
   B ancient German writers   D the Vedas

2. The name of the steps that scientists use to discover the truth is the _____.

   A experiment   C hypothesis
   B scientific method   D conclusion

3. At the heart of the scientific method is the _____.

   A experiment   C tool
   B Bible   D Aristotle's teaching

4. The _____ is an educated guess in the scientific method.

   A experiment   C mathematics
   B hypothesis   D note

5. The scientific method has _____ steps.

   A three   B four   C five   D six

What do you think

How could an experiment prove that a hypothesis is wrong? Explain your answer.

LEARNING STYLES

Interpersonal/ Group Learning

To help students understand the scientific method, divide the class into small groups. Ask each group to design an experiment to determine whether a bean plant grows better in water, sand, or potting soil. Remind students to follow the five steps of the scientific method. Have students compare and discuss how each experimental design uses the five-step method.

ELL/ESL STRATEGY

Language Objective: *To write scientific terms*

Include ELL students in the Learning Styles activity on this page by including them in groups with English speakers. ELL students should list the following words on a sheet of paper: *problem, hypothesis, procedure, results, conclusion.* Each ELL student should write down in English the group's proposed experiment—describing the problem, hypothesis, and procedure. Then have each ELL student explain why the results and conclusion must be left blank.

- To describe Copernicus's new theory of the universe
- To explain why many people thought Copernicus was wrong

Revolve
To move around something

Theory
A statement that explains why or how something happens

Universe
All the planets and stars that exist in space

Reading Strategy:
Questioning

What do the details about these theories tell you about their outcome?

For thousands of years, humans have looked up at the night sky. They have wondered about the movement of the stars and planets. In the daylight hours, they watched as the sun climbed slowly into the eastern sky, traveled overhead, then disappeared into the west. People could see all of this, but they could not explain it. One question they asked was "Does the sun **revolve,** or move around, a nonmoving Earth?" Most people thought the answer was yes.

What Were Some Early Theories About Earth?

About 150, Ptolemy, an Egyptian scientist, developed a **theory** about heavenly movement. A theory is a statement that explains why or how something happens. His theory said that the earth is the center of the **universe.** The universe is all the planets and stars that exist in space. Ptolemy believed that the sun and the five known planets revolved around the earth. This theory lasted for 1,400 years.

Nicolaus Copernicus was the first to think that the earth traveled around the sun.

Overview This lesson describes Copernicus's theory about the earth, planets, and stars. His theory was controversial because it challenged beliefs that had been held for over a thousand years.

Objectives

- To describe Copernicus's new theory of the universe
- To explain why many people thought Copernicus was wrong

Student Pages pages 379–381

Teacher's Resource Library TRL

Workbook Activity 71

Activity 71

Modified Activity 71

......

Vocabulary

conclude	theory
ellipse	universe
revolve	

Have students create a crossword puzzle using the vocabulary words. Suggest that they use the definitions or fill-in-the-blank sentences as clues. Have students exchange and solve each other's puzzles.

......

PRONUNCIATION GUIDE

Use this list to help students pronounce difficult words in this lesson.

Ptolemy   (tol′ ə mē)

 Warm-Up Activity

Ask a student to stand in the center of an area in the room. Have other students form a circle around the center student. Explain that the students forming the circle represent planets and the sun, while the student in the center represents the earth. Have the student representing the earth remain stationary while the students in the circle revolve around him or her. Explain that long ago, scientists believed that the sun and planets revolved around the earth. Allow time for comments and discussion.

2 Teaching the Lesson

Ask students to imagine that they are living 2,000 years ago. Unaware of what we now know, have students come up with theories to explain why the sun rises and sets every 24 hours. Then have them read pages 379–381 to find out about Ptolemy's and Copernicus's different answers to this question.

Ask:

• **What was Ptolemy's theory?** (The earth is the center of the universe and the sun and the planets revolve around the earth.)

Reading Strategy: Questioning

(Answers will vary; students may conclude that through scientific observation and an understanding of fact, old theories were replaced by new theories.)

• **How did Copernicus explain the rising and setting of the sun?** (He said that the earth spun like a top.)

• **What did Kepler conclude by observing the planet Mars?** (The earth and the other planets did move around the sun, just as Copernicus had said.)

• **What did Kepler prove about a planet's orbit around the sun?** (It orbits in an ellipse.)

• **Why did Aristotle believe that all movement in the heavens had to be in a circle?** (A circle is perfect, and the heavens were a perfect place.)

Conclude
To decide by using facts

Ellipse
The shape of an egg

A Polish churchman named Nicolaus Copernicus did not accept Ptolemy's theory. In 1543, he published a book that said that the sun was the center of the universe. The earth, he said, traveled around the sun. His theory was a simple explanation for what he saw happening in the skies.

How did he explain the rising and the setting of the sun? Copernicus said that the earth spun like a top. Many people laughed at this idea. They asked why things did not fly off into space if the earth spins. Later, Isaac Newton, another scientist, answered that question. He was the first to outline the laws of gravity.

Johannes Kepler proved that Copernicus was right—the earth does orbit the sun.

Who Proved Copernicus's Theory?

Johannes Kepler proved that Copernicus was right. In the early 1600s, Kepler carefully observed the planet Mars. He **concluded,** or decided by using facts, that the earth and other planets did move around the sun.

Using mathematics, Kepler even showed the shape of a planet's orbit around the sun. He proved that a planet did not orbit in a circle. It orbited in an **ellipse,** which is the shape of an egg. With this discovery, Kepler proved Aristotle wrong too. Almost 1,900 years before, Aristotle had written that all movement in the heavens had to be in a circle. A circle is perfect, and the heavens were a perfect place.

LEARNING STYLES

Logical/Mathematical
Challenge students to use information presented later in this chapter to answer the question, "If the earth spins, why don't things fly off the earth into space?" (Students should point to Newton's theory of gravity, which states that everything in the universe is attracted to every other thing; therefore, things don't fly off the earth because gravity holds them on the surface.)

ELL/ESL STRATEGY

Language Objective:
To describe theories
Divide the class into small groups. Have each group discuss the theories of Ptolemy, Copernicus, and Kepler. As students discuss each theory, have them make a drawing of it on study cards. Have students label their drawings with the words *universe, sun, Earth, planets, ellipse,* and *revolve.* Under each drawing have students write the word *Theory* and provide a summary statement of each scientist's theory.

Word Bank

Aristotle
Copernicus
Kepler
Newton
Ptolemy

Lesson 2 Review On a sheet of paper, use the words from the Word Bank to complete each sentence correctly.

1. In 1543, _____ said that the sun was at the center of the universe.

2. _____ concluded that the earth's orbit around the sun was in the shape of an ellipse.

3. _____ was the Egyptian scientist who developed a theory about heavenly movement that was accepted for 1,400 years.

4. The new discoveries about the planets challenged _____'s theories.

5. The Law of Gravity was _____'s most important discovery.

Why would a person need courage to announce a new scientific theory at this time?

 The Men Who Made Temperatures

Gabriel Fahrenheit was a German physicist. He invented the alcohol thermometer in 1709. Then in 1714 he introduced the mercury thermometer, the same type in use today. He developed the Fahrenheit temperature scale. Water boils at 212 degrees and freezes at 32 degrees. Anders Celsius, a Swedish inventor and astronomer, presented the Celsius, or centigrade scale, in 1742. On the Celsius scale, water boils at 100 degrees and freezes at 0 degrees.

Lesson 2 Review Answers

1. Copernicus 2. Kepler 3. Ptolemy
4. Aristotle 5. Newton

Answers will vary. Most of the people at the time put all their faith in the Bible and in the writings of ancient Greece and Rome. Yet some of these new theories went against these sources. In addition, the Catholic Church could censor someone who had a theory that went against the Bible.

WORLD CULTURES

The impact of science on society can be tremendous. In New Mexico, for example, an entire city was built around science. In 1942, the United States government chose Los Alamos as the site for the Atomic Research Laboratory. The laboratory uses more than 300 buildings and sits on a 77-square-mile (199-square-kilometer) area. In 1957, the government built an entire city to accommodate the laboratory's employees and their families. Today, Los Alamos boasts a population of more than 18,000 people.

Chapter 16: Lesson 3

Overview This lesson describes Galileo's discoveries, his condemnation by the Roman Catholic Church, and his use of experiments to learn about gravity.

Objectives

■ To explain why the Roman Catholic Church condemned the teachings of Galileo

■ To describe why Galileo is called the father of experimental science

Student Pages pages 382–384

Teacher's Resource Library TRL

Workbook Activity 72

Activity 72

Modified Activity 72

....

Vocabulary

experimental science

Write the vocabulary word on the board. Have students generate ideas about different types of experimental science, such as stem-cell research or pharmaceutical testing. Write the ideas on the board. Discuss why careful experiments and measurements are important in experimental science.

....

PRONUNCIATION GUIDE

Use this list to help students pronounce difficult words in this lesson.

Galileo   (gal´ ə lā´ ō)

Padua   (paj´ ü ə)

1 Warm-Up Activity

Ask a science teacher to visit the class to talk about the use and design of telescopes. Divide the class into small groups. Have each group research the Hubble Telescope by accessing www.agsglobewh.com/page382 and similar Web sites. Provide time for each group to create a collage of photos taken by the Hubble Telescope. Talk about the importance of discoveries made by telescopes.

Objectives

◆ To explain why the Roman Catholic Church condemned the teachings of Galileo

◆ To describe why Galileo is called the father of experimental science

Writing About History

Galileo conducted an experiment with a one-pound and a ten-pound ball. Do a similar experiment with a tennis ball and a basketball. Drop them from a high place and time their falls. Then write about what you observed.

Galileo Galilei became the most important supporter of Copernicus's theory of a sun-centered universe. He was born in Italy in 1564. When he was a young man, a Dutch lens maker put glass lenses at the ends of a tube to make a simple telescope. This new tool excited Galileo. In 1609, he greatly improved the telescope and used it to look at the night sky.

What Did Galileo Galilei Discover with a Telescope?

Galileo Galilei was born in Italy in 1564. He was a mathematics teacher at the University of Padua until 1610. He became the most important supporter of Copernicus's theory of a sun-centered universe. Galileo used the telescope to look at the heavens. He saw the rough surface of the moon and that the moon reflected light from the sun. He discovered the dark spots on the sun and the four moons of Jupiter. From his observations, Galileo concluded that Copernicus was right. The earth was not the center of the universe; the sun was.

Why Did Galileo's Work Cause Problems?

Many scholars and church officials refused to accept Galileo's discoveries. The Catholic Church said that this theory challenged the Bible. The church even censored Copernicus's work. They said that people could not read it.

However, Galileo did not give up. In 1632, he published a book to debate the theories of the universe. Church authorities said Galileo's book was an attack on Catholic teachings and put him on trial for heresy. He was forced to admit he was wrong. He was ordered to stop writing about the theory of Copernicus.

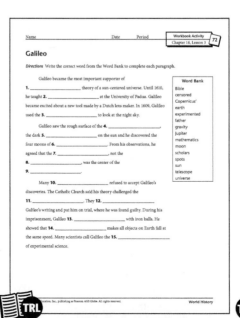

Workbook Activity 72

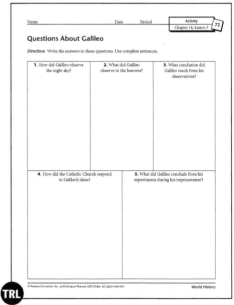

Activity 72

The Roman Inquisition found Galileo guilty of heresy. He was then imprisoned in his own home, but he continued his work.

During his imprisonment, Galileo wrote about his earlier discoveries. By experimenting and measuring with iron balls, he found that the ten-pound ball fell at the same rate of speed as the one-pound ball. His findings contradicted, or went against, the teachings of Aristotle. Galileo showed that gravity makes all objects on the earth fall at the same rate of speed. Today, many scientists call Galileo the father of **experimental science.** That is, he started the science that begins with careful experiments and measurements.

Experimental science

The science that begins with and depends on careful experiments and measurements

After students read pages 382–384, set up a modern-day reenactment of Galileo's trial in front of the Roman Inquisition. Possible roles include Galileo, his lawyer, representatives from the Roman Catholic Church, lawyers for the Church, a judge, a jury, and television reporters.

Ask:

- What new tool did Galileo use to make discoveries? (telescope)
- Did Galileo agree or disagree with Copernicus's theory? (He agreed.)
- Why did Church authorities put Galileo on trial? (They saw his book as an attack on Catholic teachings.)
- Why is Galileo known as the father of experimental science? (He founded the science that begins with careful experiments and measurements.)

Reading Strategy:
Questioning

(Answers will vary; students may suggest questions about how Galileo set up his experiments, how he conducted his experiments, or how he actually measured the rate of speed.)

 Writing About History

Before students perform their experiment, have them write down a hypothesis, or educated guess, on what they think the results will be. After the experiment, students should determine whether their hypothesis was proven true or false. In addition to writing what they observed, you might instruct students to include their hypothesis and conclusion in their reports.

ELL/ESL STRATEGY

 Language Objective:
To define words from the lesson
Tell students to find the terms *universe* and *heavens* in the lesson. Then have them write sentences that correctly use the words. Have students trade papers with another student and discuss the definitions. Then have students again exchange papers and discuss the definitions. Have papers returned to their owners. Invite students to read their sentences aloud. Talk about the different definitions offered by students.

IN THE COMMUNITY

 Have students research different scientific institutions in their community. Some institutions, such as universities and hospitals, focus on scientific research. Others focus on applied science, or science that has practical value for the community. Examples include water filtration plants and landfills. Have students select an institution that uses applied science and write a report describing its purpose and methods. Students may wish to visit the institution and interview scientists who work there.

3 ⬥ Reinforce and Extend

Lesson 3 Review Answers

1. Galileo used a telescope to prove Copernicus's theory. **2.** The Catholic Church said Galileo's support of Copernicus's theory challenged the Bible. **3.** Galileo wrote a book to debate the theories of the universe. **4.** The church held a trial where Galileo was force to admit he was wrong. **5.** Galileo discovered that objects, even of different weights, fall at the same rate of speed.

Answers will vary. Galileo looked at the moon and planets. He also published a book about the universe even when he knew it could get him into trouble. Also, he continued doing experiments while he was imprisoned in his home.

Lesson 3 Review On a sheet of paper, write the answer to each question. Use complete sentences.

1. What instrument did Galileo use to prove Copernicus's theory?

2. Why did Galileo's scientific discoveries cause problems for the Roman Catholic Church?

3. What were some of Galileo's discoveries?

4. How did the church punish Galileo for his support of Copernicus's theory?

5. What discovery did Galileo make concerning falling objects?

What do you think

What things did Galileo do that show he was a great scientist?

◆ To describe Newton's explanation for why objects appear in certain colors

◆ To explain Newton's Universal Law of Gravitation

Prism

A three-sided object that can be seen through

Attract

To pull something toward oneself

What Discoveries Did Isaac Newton Make?

When Isaac Newton was a 23-year-old mathematician at Cambridge University, a plague broke out in London. Newton left Cambridge to protect his health. In the next two years, he made important discoveries.

First, Newton discovered that white sunlight is a mixture of all colors. Second, Newton discovered why objects appear to be a certain color. He said that a red object appears red because it reflects red light and absorbs all the other colors in sunlight. When an object reflects a color, the other sunlight colors bounce off the object. When the object absorbs colors, it soaks them up so that they disappear from our sight. Newton proved this with an experiment. He passed light through a **prism,** or a three-sided object that can be seen through.

What Was Newton's Most Important Discovery?

Newton built on the work of Copernicus, Kepler, and Galileo. They showed that the planets orbit the sun. Now Newton began to think that Galileo's idea of gravity went as far as the orbit of the moon.

Newton used a falling apple to explain his theory. He said that because of gravity, the earth **attracts** a falling apple. (That is, earth pulls a falling object toward itself.) Then he said that a force exists in the universe. This force causes everything in the universe to attract every other thing. This force is gravity. It increases as objects move close to each other. Big objects have a greater attractive force than smaller objects. Newton said that the sun's strong gravity kept planets traveling in their orbits.

Isaac Newton used a falling apple to explain gravity.

1540 – 1750

Chapter 16: Lesson 4

Overview This lesson describes Isaac Newton's important discoveries on the nature of light and gravity.

Objectives

■ To describe Newton's explanation for why objects appear in certain colors

■ To explain Newton's Universal Law of Gravitation

Student Pages pages 385–386

Teacher's Resource Library

Workbook Activity 73

Activity 73

Modified Activity 73

Vocabulary

attract	**scientific law**
prism	

Have students write sentences that correctly use the vocabulary words. Invite students to write their sentences on the board.

1 Warm-Up Activity

Drop a tennis ball. Ask students why the ball fell to the floor. Have students share their knowledge of the force of gravity. Then ask students to speculate on what life would be like in a weightless environment, such as what astronauts experience in space.

2 Teaching the Lesson

Ask students to read pages 385–386 to find out about Isaac Newton's discoveries.

Ask:

• What did Newton discover about white light? (It is a mixture of all colors.)

• According to Newton, why does a red object appear red? (It reflects red light and absorbs all other colors.)

Workbook Activity 73   Activity 73

Ask:

- What did Newton say kept planets in their orbits and held people and objects to the spinning earth? (gravity)

- What did Newton's Universal Law of Gravitation prove? (The laws of gravity apply to both the earth and the heavens.)

- How did Newton's work influence other scientists? (They began to look for other scientific laws.)

Scientific law

A pattern in nature that someone can predict

Newton showed that we can predict the pattern for all objects in the universe. We call a predictable pattern a **scientific law.** Historians call Newton's discovery the Universal Law of Gravitation. (Universal means that his law about gravity applies to the whole universe.)

In 1687, Newton published a book about his work. His ideas excited scientists. His law showed that the universe was orderly and logical. Scientists began to look for other natural laws. Mathematics, the scientific method, and human reason became powerful tools for unlocking nature's secrets.

Lesson 4 Review On a sheet of paper, write the answers to the following questions. Use complete sentences.

1. What two discoveries did Newton make when he was a young man?

2. What did Newton prove by using a prism?

3. What was the force Newton discovered that keeps planets in orbit around the sun?

4. What did Newton call the predictable pattern for all objects in the universe? What did it show?

5. How did the book Newton published in 1687 affect other scientists?

What do you think

Do you think Newton was a genius? Explain your answer.

The Original Mother Goose

Isaac Newton's work affected people's lives. Charles Perrault's did, too, but in a different way.

Perrault became a lawyer in 1651, but the work bored him. He became a French government official, but that was not satisfying. Then he found work that gave him pleasure. He recorded fairy tales that he was fond of telling to his children.

In 1697, Perrault published a book called *Histories or Tales of Times Passed with Morals.* Its stories were timeless tales that most of us have heard many times. They included "Little Red Riding Hood," "Sleeping Beauty," "Puss in Boots," and "Cinderella." Perrault wrote them in a simple, charming style.

On the front of the book was a picture of an old woman sitting by a fireplace. A sign on the wall read: "Tales of Mother Goose." For this reason, some people believe Perrault was the original Mother Goose.

3 ▶ Reinforce and Extend

Objectives
- To explain what is meant by *scientific community*
- To describe how advances in mathematics and tools helped scientists

Community
A group of people with something in common

Anatomy
The structure of a human or animal body

Reading Strategy:
Questioning
What do you think you will learn about by reading this lesson?

During this period, scientists developed new ways of doing mathematics. They also invented new scientific tools. By the end of the 1600s, a scientific **community** had developed. A community is a group of people with something in common. This community studied science. Isaac Newton had said that all scientists were friends because they were all seeking truth.

What Did Vesalius Study?
Andreas Vesalius, a Belgian doctor, studied the **anatomy,** or structure, of the human body. Up to his time, people knew little about anatomy. What they did know, they had learned from studying animals and from reading Galen, an ancient Greek doctor. Vesalius wanted more than this. He wanted to see for himself.

The Catholic Church said that cutting up the human body was wrong. Vesalius went against church law and began to study the anatomy of dead human bodies. In 1543, he published his findings. His book contained thousands of careful drawings of the parts of the human body.

Many of Vesalius's drawings showed that Galen was wrong. (For example, Vesalius discovered that the heart had no bone in it.) Today, historians call Vesalius's work the beginning of the modern study of anatomy.

What Did Harvey Describe?
In the early 1600s, William Harvey, an English doctor, also studied human anatomy. He performed many experiments on the hearts and blood vessels of animals. A blood vessel is a tube in the body through which blood passes. He discovered that the heart works as a pump. It circulates, or moves in a pattern, blood through the vessels of the body. (At that time, doctors thought that the blood did not move.) Harvey published his findings in 1628.

Chapter 16: Lesson 5

Overview This lesson describes the achievements of other early scientists who made important contributions in a variety of scientific disciplines.

Objectives
- To explain what is meant by *scientific community*
- To describe how advances in mathematics and tools helped scientists

Student Pages pages 387–390

Teacher's Resource Library

  Workbook Activity 74

  Activity 74

  Modified Activity 74

Vocabulary

amber	core
anatomy	static electricity
community	

Read the definitions in random order and have students identify the word that belongs with each definition. Then have students write sentences that correctly use each word.

---

1 Warm-Up Activity

Visit the science lab to have a science teacher explain the design and use of microscopes. Have students view prepared slides under the microscope. Ask students to draw pictures of what they see. Then have students share and explain their drawings. Discuss the scientific benefits of the microscope.

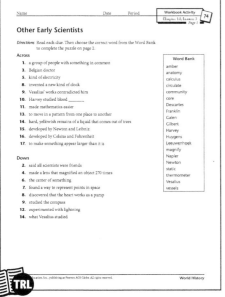

Workbook Activity 74, pages 1–2   **Activity 74**   *The New Science Chapter 16* **387**

2 Teaching the Lesson

Tell students that they will learn about other important scientists in this lesson. Then have them read pages 387–390.

Reading Strategy:
Questioning

(Students should speculate that they will be learning about early scientific discoveries.)

Ask:

• What did Vesalius's book contain? (thousands of careful drawings of the parts of the human body)

• What did Harvey discover about the heart? (It works as a pump, circulating blood through the vessels of the body.)

• Why does the needle of a compass always point north? (because the earth is a large magnet, and the needle points to the magnetic core of the earth)

• What important invention was a result of Franklin's electricity experiments? (the lightning rod)

Reading Strategy:
Questioning

Page through the lesson with students. Discuss each photograph or artwork. Then have students answer the question. (Answers will vary; The photograph and artwork help me connect what I am reading to a real person or object.)

Core
The center of something

Amber
The hard, yellowish remains of a liquid that comes out of trees

Static electricity
The electricity that builds up in something and is produced when one object rubs up against another

Reading Strategy:
Questioning

Study the photographs and artwork in the lesson. Ask yourself how they relate to what you are reading.

What Did Gilbert Study?

William Gilbert, another Englishman, studied the compass. He wanted to know why a compass needle always points north. After much study, he explained that the earth is a large magnet. A compass needle points to the magnetic **core,** or center, of the earth.

Next, Gilbert explored **amber**—the hard, yellowish remains of a liquid that comes out of trees. Like the ancient Greeks, he wondered why amber attracted other objects when he rubbed it. Gilbert experimented and discovered that glass behaved in the same way. Gilbert called these objects "electric." He got the word from the Greek word *elektron,* which means "amber."

What Did Franklin Prove?

Gilbert's work became the basis for the study of electricity. In 1752, American Benjamin Franklin proved that lightning was a form of **static electricity.** Static electricity builds up in something. When one object rubs up against another, the static electricity escapes. To prove this, Franklin did a dangerous experiment. He tied a metal key to a kite and flew it in a thunderstorm. Lightning struck the kite and traveled down the string. This made the metal key spark. Franklin proved his theory, but he was lucky that he was not harmed from his experiment. His work led to the invention of the lightning rod to protect buildings and tall trees from lightning.

Early microscopes looked different from those used today. This one is from the 1600s.

What Advances in Mathematics Helped Scientists?

New scientific tools and advances in mathematics helped early scientists make important discoveries about nature. One advance was the use of symbols to represent addition (+), subtraction (−), multiplication (×), division (÷), and equality (=). In Scotland, John Napier discovered a way to make mathematics easier. He turned multiplication and division problems into addition and subtraction problems. René Descartes, a great French mathematician, found a way to represent points in space. We call his discovery analytic geometry. Both Isaac Newton in England and Gottfried Leibniz in Germany developed a new way to calculate forces that change all the time. We call their method calculus.

What New Tools Helped Scientists?

Early in the 1590s, a Dutch maker of eyeglasses invented the microscope. In 1674, Anton van Leeuwenhoek, also from the Netherlands, made a lens that magnified an object 270 times. The object appeared much larger than it really was.

Looking at water, Leeuwenhoek was the first person to see one-celled animals. He proved that fleas and flies hatch from eggs. (At the time, people thought that fleas came from sand and flies from spoiled meat.)

Three scientists who gave us scientific tools that we use in our homes were Christian Huygens, Gabriel Fahrenheit, and Anders Celsius. In 1656, Huygens gave us a new kind of clock. Fahrenheit and Celsius gave us the thermometer.

In many ways, the modern world began with the investigations of scientists in the 1500s and 1600s. The scientific method became the way to search for truth.

1540 – 1750

Ask:

- What did Leeuwenhoek prove by looking at one-celled animals? (that fleas and flies hatch from eggs)
- Identify four new tools that helped scientists. (the telescope, the microscope, a new kind of clock, and the thermometer)

ELL/ESL STRATEGY

Language Objective:
To describe a scientific event

Pair up each ELL student with an English-speaking student. Have each ELL student review Lesson 5 and choose one scientific event to describe. Ask the English-speaking student to read aloud the scientific event chosen by the ELL student. Then have the ELL student describe the event that was just read to him or her.

3 Reinforce and Extend

AT HOME

The thermometer and the clock are examples of scientific tools that we commonly use in our homes. Ask students to make a list of other scientific tools that they have in their homes. (possibilities include a smoke alarm, light bulb, egg timer, burners on a stove, etc.) If students have a particularly unusual tool in their home, ask them to bring it to class and share how it is used.

STUDY SKILLS

Have students create a chart with two columns. In the left-hand column, students should list all the scientists discussed in this section. In the right-hand column, they should write down each scientist's discoveries. You might suggest listing scientists discussed previously in this chapter as well. The charts will serve as useful study guides when students review this chapter.

Biography

In addition to writing a biography of her husband, Margaret Cavendish also wrote an autobiography, one of the first known autobiographies of a woman. In it, she criticizes marriage and expresses strong feminist views. She also wrote science fiction works in which she speculates about the possibility of tiny worlds within our own—"a world in an ear-ring worn by some lady quite unconscious of her responsibility." Despite harsh criticism, Cavendish continued to write, publishing 22 works in her life.

Lesson 5 Review Answers

1. Vesalius studied human anatomy.
2. Harvey discovered the circulation of blood through the body. **3.** He said that the core of the earth is magnetic and that the compass needle points to the magnetic core of the earth. **4.** The term electric comes from the Greek word for amber. **5.** Mathematicians found new ways of doing multiplication and division. They also invented symbols for the various mathematical functions. They found ways to represent points in space (analytic geometry) and a way to calculate forces that change all the time (calculus).

Answers will vary. New discoveries were being made and announced all the time. It was an age of curiosity in which the scientists built their theories on the work of other scientists.

Chapter Project Follow-up

Group students according to the scientists they researched and have them pool their information. Then have each group work cooperatively to create a skit, video, or PowerPoint presentation on their chosen scientist. Stress that each production should be informative and creative.

Biography

Margaret Cavendish: 1623–1673

When you look at Margaret Cavendish's background, she seems like any English noblewoman. She was educated by tutors. She married a noble—William Cavendish, Duke of Newcastle. But Cavendish was an unusual woman. For one thing, she was one of the first females to write a biography. It was about her husband. For another, she was not afraid to speak her mind in the company of men.

Her brother-in-law Charles was a scientist and a member of the Newcastle Circle. She spent many hours in discussion with these scientists and philosophers. She argued in person and in books.

Lesson 5 Review On a sheet of paper, write the answer to each question. Use complete sentences.

1. What did the scientist Andreas Vesalius study?
2. Which English scientist discovered that the blood circulates through the body?
3. How did William Gilbert answer the question of why a compass needle always points north?
4. Where did the term *electric* come from?
5. What were some advances in mathematics that helped scientists study the natural world?

What do you think

Why would it be exciting to be a scientist during the 1500s and 1600s?

True Directions Concerning the Interpretation of Nature

In 1620, Francis Bacon set down the scientific method. It told scientists what they should do to discover how nature worked. Bacon said to ignore all existing ideas on a topic. Scientists should experiment and observe the results. As they worked, scientists should carefully record what they did and saw. New ideas should only come from what they observed. These principles are in his Novum Organum, or True Directions Concerning the Interpretation of Nature. *The following is a passage from that writing.*

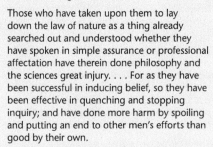

Francis Bacon

Those who have taken upon them to lay down the law of nature as a thing already searched out and understood whether they have spoken in simple assurance or professional affectation have therein done philosophy and the sciences great injury. . . . For as they have been successful in inducing belief, so they have been effective in quenching and stopping inquiry; and have done more harm by spoiling and putting an end to other men's efforts than good by their own.

Now my method, though hard to practice, is easy to explain. I propose to establish progressive stages of certainty. . . . I open and lay out a new and certain path for the mind to proceed in, starting directly from the simple . . . perception. . . . Namely, that the entire work of the understanding be commenced afresh, and the mind itself be from the very outset not left to take its own course, but guided at every step; and the business be done as if by machinery.

[First there is] simple experience, which, if taken as it comes, is called an accident. If [experience] is sought for, [it is called] an experiment. [A good] experiment [is like] lighting a candle. Then by means of the candle, [it] lights the way [to the truth about nature.]

Let men, therefore, cease to wonder that the course of science is not yet wholly run [its course]. The [scientific] method rightly ordered leads by an unbroken route through the woods of experience to the open ground of [natural laws].

And therefore there are [some] things which [scientists] should be warned [against]. First then, . . . [fancy writing], let it be utterly dismissed. [Next,] all superstitious stories and experiments of ceremonial magic should be altogether rejected.

Document-Based Questions

1. According to the reading, what was Bacon's main contribution to science?

2. What does Bacon think his system can do?

3. In your opinion, why did Bacon call simple experience an accident?

4. Why does Bacon compare a good experiment to a candle?

5. According to Bacon, what should scientists do with superstitions and magic?

1540 – 1750

Read aloud the title, "True Directions Concerning the Interpretation of Nature." Then read the introductory paragraph to students. Explain that the language used by Francis Bacon is old-fashioned. If spoken, it would sound unnatural to our ears.

Write the following sentence beginnings and endings on the board in two columns.

Sentence Beginnings

1. People who think we already know the law of nature (d)

2. My method is to establish a certain path (a)

3. A simple experience (e)

4. The scientific method will lead to (b)

5. Be warned against (c)

Sentence Endings

a. and follow it.

b. the natural laws.

c. superstitions.

d. stop other men from trying to learn.

e. just happens; it is not planned like an experiment.

Have students read one paragraph at a time. Then have them select and write the sentence beginning and ending that explains what the author says in the paragraph. Finally, have students read and answer the Document-Based Questions.

Answers to Document-Based Questions:

1. He developed the scientific method.

2. It can establish small steps that eventually lead to certainty.

3. Answers will vary. Experiences are things that happen without planning, so they cannot be measured scientifically or proven true.

4. Answers will vary. Bacon is comparing the lack of knowledge to darkness. Candles bring light to darkness and show how to get somewhere. A good experiment produces knowledge and maybe shows the answer to a problem.

5. Scientists should reject superstitions and magic.

Spotlight Story

Ask students to think of things that require precision timing in order to work smoothly. (Answers will vary; students may say public buses, trains, commercial airlines, television and radio programming, traffic signals, and so on.) Then invite students to imagine what life would be like without precise clocks. How would we know when to wake up? How would we know when school begins and ends? How would we know when to meet our friends? As preparation for reading "The Importance of the Clock," have students read the Wrap-Up questions. Then have them read the selection, watching for answers to the questions. Finally, have students reread and write answers to the questions.

Answers to Spotlight Story Wrap-Up:

1. Answers will vary. He suggested that the universe was orderly, and therefore, it was possible to find a way to measure time exactly.

2. It was compared to a clock.

3. The sundial (or shadow clock), the water clock, and the sand glass were three early methods of telling time.

4. Christian Huygens invented the pendulum clock in 1656.

5. Answers will vary. Since time could be measured to the minute, people could be expected to be somewhere at a precise time.

Spotlight Story

The Importance of the Clock

The work of Newton and other scientists showed that the universe was very orderly. People began to think that there were rules to explain everything in nature. In the 1700s, it seemed that the universe operated like a giant mechanical clock. The idea that the universe was like a machine was very powerful. The idea lasted into the 1900s.

Why did people living in the 1700s compare the world to a clock? For them, the clock was a marvelous device. Before its invention, people used many methods to tell time. None of them were very accurate, however.

The ancient Egyptians, Greeks, and Romans used sundials, or "shadow clocks." A sundial was a flat surface with a standing piece of wood or metal. As the sun traveled through the sky, it cast a shadow off this piece. The shadow's length told the time. At night or on cloudy days, water clocks were popular. They had two parts—a large bucket and a pan with measurement lines. Water dripped through a tiny hole in the bucket into the pan. By checking the level of the water in the pan, people could tell the time. Sand glasses were also popular with the Romans. They looked like the egg timers we use today. Sand flowed through a small hole in the top container into the bottom one.

The first mechanical clocks were so large they needed to be in towers. They worked by allowing gravity to gradually pull heavy weights connected to ropes to the ground. These weights were hooked up to a device that struck the hour.

Then in the early 1500s, there was a new development. A German locksmith built a small clock that used a tightened spring. The spring gradually released its energy to turn an hour hand. In 1656, Christian Huygens

This clock is from the 1660s England.

invented the pendulum clock. It stood upright and had hour and second hands. Falling weights drove the pendulum. In time, this type of clock became the famous grandfather clock.

The mechanical clock changed our concept of time. It became very precise. Now, people could ask the time in the late afternoon. They would get an exact answer, such as "ten minutes after four." The mechanical clock changed people's relationship to each other and to their work. For the first time in history, being "on time" was measured to the minute!

Wrap-Up

1. What role did Newton play in improving the measurement of time?

2. In the 1700s, what was the universe compared to?

3. What were three early methods of telling time?

4. Who invented the pendulum clock? When?

5. How did the mechanical clock change people's idea of time?

Chapter 16   SUMMARY

- During the 1500s and 1600s, scholars no longer accepted answers given by the Bible or ancient writers. They used experiments to investigate the natural world.

- In the 1620s, Francis Bacon worked out the five steps of the scientific method. It begins with a problem and an educated guess, or hypothesis, about its answer. The next steps are to experiment, to observe, and to make conclusions. Scientists still follow this method.

- From ancient times, most people thought Earth was the center of the universe. Ptolemy wrote that the sun and planets revolve around the earth.

- In 1543, Copernicus published a new theory. He said that the earth traveled around the sun. Kepler used mathematics to prove the theory of a sun-centered universe. He showed that planets travel in elliptical, or egg-shaped, orbits, not circles.

- Galileo, an Italian scientist, built a telescope to study the sky. He discovered the moons of Jupiter. He concluded that Copernicus was right about a sun-centered universe. The Catholic Church tried to stop Galileo's work. They forced him to say he was wrong.

- Isaac Newton was an English mathematician of the late 1600s. He studied light and color. He also demonstrated the earth's gravity and how gravity keeps the planets in orbit. He showed that the Universal Law of Gravitation applies throughout the universe.

- By the end of the 1600s, a community of scientists was at work in Europe.

- Belgian Andreas Vesalius studied human anatomy. His work showed that Galen, an ancient Greek doctor, was wrong. William Harvey, an English doctor, showed how blood circulates in the body.

- William Gilbert showed that the earth acts like a magnet. He also discovered electricity. Benjamin Franklin, an American, showed that lightning is a form of electricity.

- Mathematics was an important tool of the new science. Napier made multiplication and division easier. Descartes discovered analytic geometry. Newton and Leibniz developed calculus.

- New scientific tools included the microscope and the thermometer. Leeuwenhoek used magnifying lenses to observe one-celled animals.

Using the Chapter Summary

Have students read the Chapter Summary on page 393 to review the main ideas presented in Chapter 16.

Ask:

- How did people's way of thinking change during the 1500s and 1600s? (They no longer accepted the answers given by the Bible and ancient writers; they used experiments to find answers instead.)

- Who worked out the five steps of the scientific method? (Francis Bacon)

- What was Ptolemy's theory of the universe? Copernicus's? (The sun and planets revolve around the earth; the earth travels around the sun.)

- Why was Galileo's work controversial? (It went against the teachings of the Catholic Church.)

- Which scientist was responsible for discovering the Universal Law of Gravitation? (Isaac Newton)

- What is William Harvey remembered for? (showing how blood circulates)

- What did Benjamin Franklin discover about lightning? (It is a form of electricity.)

- Name three tools of the new science. (mathematics, the microscope, and the thermometer)

TEACHER'S RESOURCE

The AGS Globe Teaching Strategies in Social Studies Transparencies may be used with this chapter. The transparencies add an interactive dimension to expand and enhance the *World History* program content.

Chapter 16 Review

Use the Chapter Review to prepare students for tests and to reteach content from the chapter.

Chapter 16 Mastery Test

The Teacher's Resource Library includes two forms of the Chapter 16 Mastery Test. Each test addresses the chapter Goals for Learning. An optional third page of additional critical-thinking items is included for each test. The difficulty level of the two forms is equivalent.

Chapter 16 Review Answers

1. Bacon
2. Copernicus
3. Kepler
4. Galileo
5. Newton
6. Vesalius
7. Harvey
8. Gilbert
9. Napier
10. Leeuwenhoek
11. A
12. C
13. D
14. B
15. A

Chapter 16 REVIEW

Word Bank

Bacon
Copernicus
Galileo
Gilbert
Harvey
Kepler
Leeuwenhoek
Napier
Newton
Vesalius

On a sheet of paper, use the words from the Word Bank to complete each sentence correctly.

1. _____ worked out the basic steps of the scientific method.

2. In 1543, a book by _____ challenged the belief that the sun travels around the earth.

3. Using mathematics, _____ discovered that the planets revolve around the sun in an orbit shaped like an ellipse.

4. The Catholic Church put _____ on trial because he said that the earth travels around the sun.

5. _____ discovered the Law of Universal Gravitation.

6. In 1543, _____ wrote a book about human anatomy.

7. After many experiments, _____ discovered that the heart was a pump.

8. _____ used the new word *electric* to describe materials, like amber, that attract feathers and bits of dust.

9. Thanks to _____, multiplying and dividing numbers is easier today.

10. _____ invented a powerful microscope to see one-celled animals for the first time.

On a sheet of paper, write the letter of the answer that correctly completes each sentence.

11. To _____ something is to make it appear larger than it really is.

   A magnify   **C** theory
   B revolve   **D** hypothesis

12. The _____ is a set of steps scientists follow for study.

   A theory   **C** scientific method
   B hypothesis   **D** prism

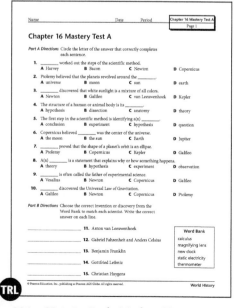

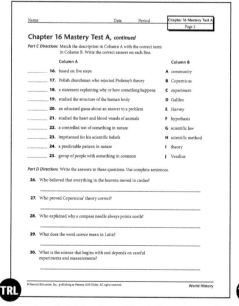

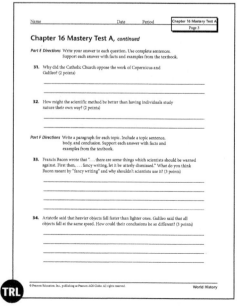

Chapter 16 Mastery Test A, pages 1–3

13. A _____ is an educated guess.

A theory   **C** method
B basic   **D** hypothesis

14. A _____ is a statement that explains how or why something happens.

A logical   **B** theory   **C** univers   **D** heresy

15. Benjamin Franklin proved that lightning is a form of _____.

A static electricity   **C** steam
B amber   **D** gravity

On a sheet of paper, write the answer to each question. Use complete sentences.

16. What are the five steps of the scientific method?

17. Before Copernicus, what did most scholars believe about the earth and the heavens?

18. How did Newton build on the work of Copernicus, Kepler, and Galileo?

Critical Thinking On a sheet of paper, write your response to each question. Use complete sentences.

19. You read in Chapter 14 about the rebirth of learning during the Renaissance. Why do you think the scientists in this chapter went against some of that learning?

20. Isaac Newton said, "I seem to have been only like a boy playing on the seashore . . . finding a smoother pebble . . . whilst the great ocean of truth lay all undiscovered before me." In your own words, explain what Newton meant.

> If an essay question asks for facts, give facts and not opinions.

1540 – 1750

The New Science   Chapter 16   395

---

16. The five steps of the scientific method are as follows: First, a scientist picks a problem or question. Second, the scientist makes a hypothesis. Third, the scientist does an experiment and carefully controls it. Fourth, the scientist observes what is happening during the experiment and makes notes. Fifth, the scientist draws a conclusion from these notes and decides if the hypothesis was right.

17. Before Copernicus, most scholars believed that the earth was the center of the universe.

18. Newton took all this learning and began to do his own experiments to develop the Universal Law of Gravitation. He showed how gravity kept the planets in orbit around the sun.

Critical Thinking

19. Scientists went against some learning as they gathered more facts and were able to develop better tools to use in experiments.

20. Answers will vary. Newton realized that the world was very complex and large (like the ocean), and he had only begun to find out some of the truths with a childlike wonder and appreciation (like a child playing on the seashore).

Chapter 16 Mastery Test B, pages 1–3

The New Science   Chapter 16   395

Audio Library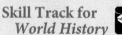

Skill Track for
World History

Teacher's Resource Library TRL

Workbook Activities 75–80

Activities 75–80

Modified Activities 75–80

Chapter 17 Self-Study Guide

Chapter 17 Outline

Chapter 17 Mastery Tests A and B
(Answer Keys for the Teacher's Resource Library begin on page 870 of this Teacher's Edition.)

Beginnings of Our Global Age

In the 1400s, European explorers set sail to find a water route to China and India. Portugal began the search, but soon explorers from other countries took to the seas. In this chapter, you will learn about Columbus and other explorers. You will witness how cruel Europeans were to the native people they found. Then you will study the African slave trade. All of this was part of the settling of the Americas by the Europeans.

Goals for Learning

- ◆ To explain why some European nations searched for an all-water route to China and India
- ◆ To list three reasons why Spaniards came to the Americas
- ◆ To describe what Spanish conquest did to the American Indian population
- ◆ To describe how Spain established colonies in America
- ◆ To explain why Portugal introduced African slavery into the New World
- ◆ To describe the growth of European colonies in the Americas

1487 Bartholomeu Dias sails around the tip of Africa

1518 Portuguese bring African slaves to the Americas

1607 English settle Jamestown in Virginia

1620 Pilgrims settle Plymouth in Massachusetts

1425 1525 1625

...98 Vasco da Gama sails around Africa to India

1532 Francisco Pizarro conquers Incas in Peru

1608 Champlain settles Quebec in Canada

Introducing the Chapter

From the mid-1400s to the mid-1600s, explorers from Europe searching for trade routes sailed around the southern tips of Africa and South America and across the Atlantic, Pacific, and Indian Oceans. By the early part of the 17th century, European colonies had been established in the New World.

Ask:

- • In which three centuries were these discoveries made? (15th, 16th, and 17th centuries)
- • Which two explorers sailed around the southern tip of Africa during these years? (Bartholomeu Dias and Vasco da Gama)

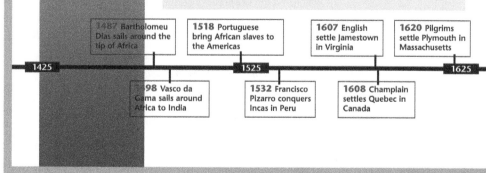

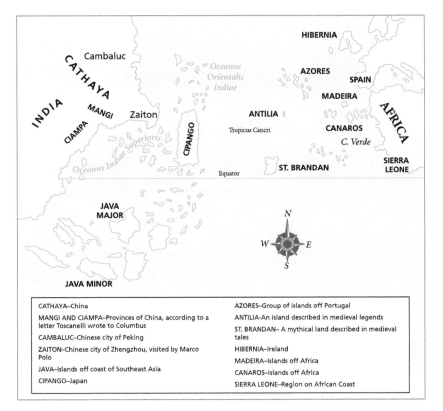

CATHAYA–China
MANGI AND CIAMPA–Provinces of China, according to a letter Toscanelli wrote to Columbus
CAMBALUC–Chinese city of Peking
ZAITON–Chinese city of Zhengzhou, visited by Marco Polo
JAVA–Islands off coast of Southeast Asia
CIPANGO–Japan

AZORES–Group of islands off Portugal
ANTILIA–An island described in medieval legends
ST. BRANDAN– A mythical land described in medieval tales
HIBERNIA–Ireland
MADEIRA–Islands off Africa
CANAROS–Islands off Africa
SIERRA LEONE–Region on African Coast

Paolo Toscanelli made a map similar to the above map in 1474. Christopher Columbus used a copy to find a water route to China. As the map shows, a good sailor could do this by sailing west. Clearly, Toscanelli did not know about North or South America!

Study the map, then answer the following questions:

1. Near what continent are the Madeira Islands?
2. What is the name of a group of islands that lie north of the equator and west of Spain?
3. What was Ireland's name during Columbus's time?
4. On what continent do you find Sierra Leone?
5. Cipango is another name for what country?

Beginnings of Our Global Age Chapter 17   397

Have a volunteer read aloud the title of the map, "Toscanelli's Map, 1474." Encourage students to spend a few moments studying the map and reading the information provided about each location on the map. Then have students read the Map Skills paragraph below the map and answer the questions.

Ask:

- Which parts of this map look similar to the way they look on modern maps? Why do you think this is true? (answers will vary—students may say Europe and the land that is close to Europe; answers will vary—students may say because people knew more about Europe and lands close to it in 1474 than they knew about other parts of the world)
- On this map, what is the name given to the country we call China? (Cathaya)
- According to this map, in which direction would you sail to go from Africa to what is now China? (west)
- What are the names of the islands south of the equator? (Java Major and Java Minor)

Map Skills Answers

1. Africa
2. Azores
3. Hibernia
4. Africa
5. Japan

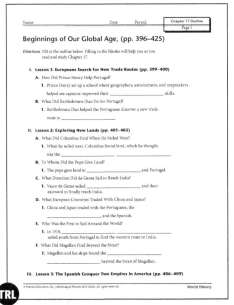

Chapter 17 Outline, pages 1–3

Chapter Project

Make a list of all of the explorers mentioned in this chapter. Divide the class into groups of three or four students, and have each group choose a different explorer from the list to research. Students should use the Internet and library resources to research their explorer and each expedition the explorer undertook.

Point out that students should do enough research to answer *who, what, when, where, why,* and *how* questions. Have each group prepare a large display poster about its explorer that answers these questions. Posters also should include illustrations and route maps.

Beginnings of Global Age Chapter 17   **397**

Predicting

Introduce the reading strategy *predicting*. Explain that before you read a text, you can make predictions about what you will read. These predictions are based on the things you already know about a subject. As you read, you can watch for information that is new to you so that you can predict what will happen next. Have students preview the text in Lesson 1. Invite students to make predictions about what they will read, and share those predictions with the class. After reading the lesson, students can share whether or not their predictions were correct.

Ask:

- **What do you predict this lesson is about?** (people searching for new trade routes)

- **Why did you predict this?** (It is mentioned in the lesson title.)

- **What do you already know about this subject?** (Answers will vary. Students may say that they know Columbus accidentally landed in the New World while looking for a trade route.)

Key Vocabulary Words

Explain that the list of words here is a glossary of the key vocabulary they will read in Chapter 17. Call on volunteers to read the words and their definitions aloud.

Ask:

- **Which word is related to planning and directing the journey of a ship?** (navigation)

- **What is a *viceroy*?** (an official who governs land for the king or queen)

- **What are you doing when you *abolish* something?** (getting rid of it)

- **Who agreed to the Mayflower Compact?** (the Pilgrims)

Reading Strategy: Predicting

Preview the text. Think about what you already know about a subject. Look for new information. These things will help you predict what will happen next.

Check your predictions as you read. As you learn more information, you may find you need to change your predictions.

Key Vocabulary Words

Lesson 1
Navigation The science of planning and directing a ship's journey

Lesson 2
Exploration The act of looking around some unknown place

Strait A narrow strip of water that connects two bigger bodies of water

Lesson 3
Conquistador A Spanish conqueror

Lesson 4
Viceroy An official who governs land for the king or queen

Plantation A large area of farmland

Encomienda The Spanish system of forced physical labor

Lesson 5
Slavery The owning of human beings as property

Abolish To get rid of something

Lesson 6
Colonist A person who settles in a new place

Majority More than half of a group of people or group of things

Mayflower Compact The agreement made by the Pilgrims that set up a form of government for their new colony

Economic Having to do with money

◆ To explain why Portugal sought a new route to China and India

◆ To identify a technical advance that helped sailors improve their travel

Navigation

The science of planning and directing a ship's journey

Reading Strategy: **Predicting**

Preview the lesson title. Predict what you will learn about trade routes in this lesson.

During the 1300s and 1400s, Arab merchants bought goods like silks and spices in China and India. (People wanted spices because they helped preserve food. They also covered up the taste and smell of spoiled food.) Then they carried these goods overland to the eastern end of the Mediterranean Sea. There, they loaded the goods on Italian ships and took them to the Italian city-states.

The overland journey was slow and hard. But once on the sea, the journey was fast and easy. Soon, the goods arrived in the Italian city-states. Then Italian merchants sold the goods at high prices to other European states. Italian city-states like Venice grew wealthy from this eastern trade.

For many years, these city-states controlled the trade routes to the East. Other countries wanted to become wealthy too. They began to look for new trade routes. During the 1400s, Portugal began its search for a new route to the East.

How Did Prince Henry Help Portugal?

Prince Henry the Navigator helped the Portuguese prepare for their search. Around 1416, he established a school where geographers, astronomers, and mapmakers helped sea captains improve their **navigation.** That is, they learned how to plan and direct a ship's journey.

Prince Henry the Navigator established a school in Portugal to teach sea captains navigation and other skills.

Chapter 17: Lesson 1

Overview This lesson focuses on the efforts of leaders from Portugal to find a new trade route to China and India by exploring the coast of Africa.

Objectives

■ To explain why Portugal sought a new route to China and India

■ To identify a technical advance that helped sailors improve their travel

Student Pages pages 399–400

Teacher's Resource Library **TRL**

Workbook Activity 75

Activity 75

Modified Activity 75

Vocabulary

navigation

Have students look up the word *navigation* in the dictionary and write down other words that begin with the same three letters that have to do with the sea, such as *navy, navigable,* and *navigator.* Have students write several sentences using both *navigation* and one or more of these other words.

1 Warm-Up Activity

Have students think of different ways that products such as fresh fruit are transported from where they are grown to your local store. Make a list of students' ideas on the board. Some of these ideas should include transport by ship, train, truck, or airplane. Then have students think about how products had to be transported before these vehicles were invented.

PRONUNCIATION GUIDE

Use this list to help students pronounce difficult words in this lesson.

Bartholomeu Dias

(bär´ tü lü mā´ ü dē´ äsh)

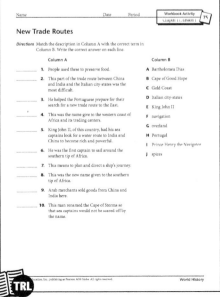

Workbook Activity 75

New Trade Routes

Directions Match the description in Column A with the correct term in Column B. Write the correct answer on each line.

Column A

1. People used these to preserve food.
2. This part of the trade route between China and India and the Italian city-states was the most difficult.
3. He helped the Portuguese prepare for their search for a new trade route to the East.
4. This was the name give to the western coast of Africa and its trading centers.
5. King John II, of this country, had his sea captains look for a water route to India and China to become rich and powerful.
6. He was the first captain to sail around the southern tip of Africa.
7. This means to plan and direct a ship's journey.
8. This was the new name given to the southern tip of Africa.
9. Arab merchants sold goods from China and India here.
10. This man renamed the Cape of Storms so that sea captains would not be scared off by the name.

Column B

A Bartholomeu Dias
B Cape of Good Hope
C Gold Coast
D Italian city-states
E King John II
F navigation
G overland
H Portugal
I Prince Henry the Navigator
J spices

Activity 75

Europeans Search for New Trade Routes

Directions Write the correct term from the Word Bank to complete each sentence.

1. Between the 1300s and 1400s, Italian city-states grew wealthy and controlled trade routes from the _____.

2. During the 1400s, _____ wanted to find a new trade route.

3. _____ skills help a sea captain plan and direct a ship's journey.

4. Portuguese captains traded _____ and ivory with African merchants.

5. Dias was the first to sail around the southern tip of _____.

6. The king of Portugal wanted to find a water route to _____ and China.

7. The southern tip of Africa was first called the _____.

8. King John II renamed Africa's tip the _____.

9. The Portuguese set up trading centers on the western coast of Africa, which became known as the _____.

10. _____ bought goods in China and India to sell to the Italian city-states.

Word Bank

Africa
Arab merchants
Cape of Good Hope
Cape of Storms
East
gold
Gold Coast
India
navigation
Portugal

2 Teaching the Lesson

As they read page 399, some students may not be aware of what geographers, astronomers, and mapmakers do. Explain the job of each of these professionals to students. Have students read pages 399–400 to learn about the new trade route that Portugal sought.

Reading Strategy: Predicting

Have students share what they think they will learn about trade routes. For example, students may say that they think they will learn about who was responsible for finding a new trade route.

Ask:

- Who controlled the land routes to China and India in the 1300s and 1400s? Where did they sell goods from these places? (Arab merchants; Italian city-states)

- What did Prince Henry the Navigator of Portugal do to improve the skills of sea captains? (Answers will vary; students may say he set up a school to show them how to do a better job of planning a journey by sea.)

- Which European explorer first sailed around the tip of Africa? What country was this explorer from? (Bartholomeu Dias; Portugal)

- During which years did the Chinese send out ships to explore the seas? Which areas did they explore? (1405–1433; the Indian Ocean and the east coast of Africa)

- Why did the Chinese find exploring so expensive? (Answers will vary. Students may say that because the Chinese wanted to impress the people they visited with their wealth, they gave them beautiful gifts.)

Why Didn't the Chinese "Discover" Europe?

Between 1405 and 1433, China sent fleets of up to 300 ships out into the seas to explore. These huge ships visited the lands in the Indian Ocean and traveled down the east coast of Africa.

The last Chinese journey lasted two years and ended in 1433. The Chinese emperor called an end to these journeys because they were too expensive. Since the Chinese already had the things they wanted, Chinese explorers gave the people they visited beautiful gifts and treasures to show their wealth. So the more lands the Chinese explorers visited, the more wealth flowed out of the Chinese treasury. If the Chinese had "discovered" Europe, their discovery might have cost them a fortune!

Word Bank

Africa
Bartholomeu Dias
Italian city-states
Prince Henry
western

What do you think

Why do you think King John of Portugal did not want sea captains to be scared by the name "Cape of Storms"?

With this learning, Portuguese captains sailed south to explore the western coast of Africa. There the Portuguese set up trading centers. Merchants in Africa traded gold and ivory for goods from Portugal. Soon, people began calling the western coast of Africa the Gold Coast.

What Did Bartholomeu Dias Do for Portugal?

In 1481, King John II of Portugal had his sea captains begin to look for a water route to India and China. Such a route would make Portugal rich and powerful. They carefully sailed south along the western coast of Africa. Each captain went a little farther south. Then mapmakers made maps of the coastline.

In 1487, Bartholomeu Dias sailed around the southern tip of Africa. If the Portuguese could do that, they could also sail eastward to India and China. The weather at the tip of Africa was bad. Dias named it the Cape of Storms. But King John II renamed it the Cape of Good Hope. He did not want the other sea captains to be scared off by the name.

Lesson 1 Review On a sheet of paper, use the words from the Word Bank to complete each sentence correctly.

1. _____ controlled the trade routes to India and China during the 1300s.

2. _____ established a school for sailors in Portugal.

3. Portuguese sailors first explored the _____ coast of Africa.

4. The Portuguese were the first Europeans to sail around the southern tip of _____.

5. _____ named the southern tip of Africa the Cape of Storms.

---

3 Reinforce and Extend

LEARNING STYLES

Interpersonal/ Group Learning
Have small groups of students brainstorm a list of supplies, equipment, and staff Prince Henry would have needed to set up his navigation school in Portugal. Students should record the ideas. Then students should research maps that were made for exploration in the 1400s and 1500s. Have them collaborate on a report about how the maps changed and then share their list and report with the class.

Lesson 1 Review Answers

1. Italian city-states 2. Prince Henry 3. western 4. Africa 5. Bartholomeu Dias

Answers will vary. He did not want sea captains to be frightened because they might not want to sail in that direction for Portugal.

Objectives

◆ To describe the journeys of Columbus, da Gama, and Magellan

◆ To explain how the pope controlled exploration

There were two problems in trying to reach India and China by sailing around Africa. First, the weather at the southern tip of Africa made the voyage dangerous. Second, reaching the southern tip of Africa took a long time. Sailing on to India took even longer.

Christopher Columbus thought that he had a better way to reach the East. He would sail west across the Atlantic Ocean. At the time, his idea seemed strange. How could a sailor reach the Indies by sailing west?

What Did Columbus Find When He Sailed West?

For many years, Columbus tried to get an important person interested in his idea. Then, in 1492, he convinced Queen Isabella of Spain to provide the money for his voyage. On August 3, 1492, Columbus, his officers, and his crew sailed from Spain. They sailed in three ships: the *Niña*, the *Pinta*, and the *Santa Maria*.

First, the ships headed south. Then they caught a wind that blew them west into the unknown waters of the Atlantic Ocean. Early on the morning of October 12, 1492, a sailor sighted land! Columbus thought that he had reached the islands of the East Indies, so he called the people he met "Indians." He was sure that China and Japan were nearby.

In 1493, Columbus returned to Spain. He made three more voyages across the Atlantic Ocean. In 1506, Columbus died, still believing that he had discovered a new route to Asia.

Columbus convinced Queen Isabella of Spain to pay for his voyage across the Atlantic.

1450 – 1650

Beginnings of Our Global Age Chapter 17 401

Chapter 17: Lesson 2

Overview This lesson describes how Spain and Portugal financed expeditions by Columbus, da Gama, and Magellan in an effort to compete for trade with China and India.

Objectives

■ To describe the journeys of Columbus, da Gama, and Magellan

■ To explain how the pope controlled exploration

Student Pages pages 401–405

Teacher's Resource Library

Workbook Activity 76

Activity 76

Modified Activity 76

Vocabulary

exploration   **strait**

Have students look up the word *strait* in the dictionary. Then have them use a world map or an atlas to find examples of straits around the world. Have students look up the word *exploration* and write a definition in their own words. Then have students write a paragraph describing how they think someone would explore a strait for the first time.

1 Warm-Up Activity

The idea of the exploration of new lands may be difficult for students to relate to, because most areas of the earth's surface have now been explored by humans. Have students think about what it would be like to go somewhere that nobody had ever seen before. Have students work in small groups and make a list of supplies they would need for survival in unknown terrain and weather conditions. Have each student in the group write a paragraph describing how they would feel about the expedition before they left.

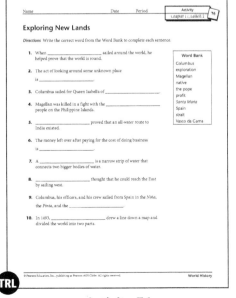

Workbook Activity 76   **Activity 76**

As students read, explain the importance of having money for the voyages of Columbus, da Gama, and Magellan. Just like the United States' space program today, none of these voyages would have been possible without government funding.

Ask:

- Who financed Columbus's voyage? (Queen Isabella)

- Why did Columbus call the people he encountered on his journey "Indians"? (He thought he had reached the East Indies.)

- Who drew a line that divided land that was yet to be explored between Spain and Portugal? (the pope)

- When the pope divided the world between Spain and Portugal, who controlled all new land east of the line? West of the line? (Portugal controlled the east; Spain controlled the west)

Read the title of the map, "Early European Explorers," aloud. Have students study the map independently. Instruct them to trace one of the routes from start to finish. Then ask students to answer the questions in the caption. (Drake traveled west; Drake went farther north in the Pacific.)

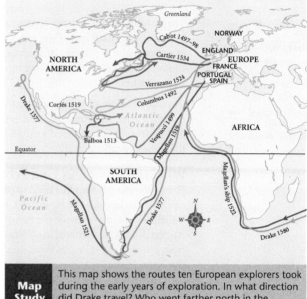

Map Study
This map shows the routes ten European explorers took during the early years of exploration. In what direction did Drake travel? Who went farther north in the Pacific—Magellan or Drake?

Exploration
The act of looking around some unknown place

To Whom Did the Pope Give Land?

As early as the 1450s, the pope gave Portugal control over all African trade and **exploration.** Exploration is the act of looking around some unknown place. Then, 30 years later, the pope gave Portugal the right to explore and trade as far as the East Indies. After the first journey by Columbus, Spain asked the pope what non-Christian areas it might claim.

In 1493, the pope drew a line down a map and divided the world into two parts. He said that Spain could control all new land discovered west of the line. Portugal could control all new land east of the line: Africa and India. But Portugal did not like this decision. In 1494, officials from Spain and Portugal met to settle the problem. They agreed to move the line farther west. This let Portugal control Brazil in the Americas.

ONLINE CONNECTION

 One area of the earth that is difficult to explore due to extreme weather conditions is the Antarctic. Within about the last 100 years, governments from various countries have set up observation posts in the Antarctic. Today, people live and work there year round. Students can learn about the work being done in the Antarctic and see current pictures by visiting the U.S. Antarctic Program Web site: www. agsglobewh.com/page402.

STUDY SKILLS

 Have students set up a separate sheet for notes about each group of people, set of city-states, and countries mentioned in this chapter. Students may want to set up their notes in a three-column chart. As they read the chapter, ask students to make notes about the role each played in this age of exploration.

Reading Strategy:
Predicting

Predict what da
Gama will find on this
voyage.

What Direction Did da Gama Sail to Reach India?

Columbus reached land by sailing west. The Portuguese still wanted to reach India by sailing south and then eastward. In the summer of 1497, Vasco da Gama left Portugal with four ships. Three months later, he rounded the Cape of Good Hope. In May 1498, da Gama reached Calicut, India.

Da Gama and his men returned to Portugal in September 1499. He proved that an all-water route to India existed. Now the Italian city-states would no longer control trade with India and China.

Da Gama's ships came back to Portugal with spices like pepper and cinnamon, along with jewels and other goods. When they sold this cargo, it brought 60 times the cost of the trip! That was an enormous profit. But of the 170 men who left with da Gama, only 54 were left alive to return to Portugal.

Pass the Pepper, Please

Why did European explorers try so hard to reach the Indies? One answer is in your kitchen—pepper. Ordinary black pepper was not ordinary at all in Europe. Meat was often eaten half-spoiled. Pepper made it taste better. Sailors on long voyages even carried small sacks of peppercorns. But pepper grew only in India and Java.

Italian merchants got rich importing spices, which they sold to the rest of Europe. Then, about 1300, the Turks cut off trade to these eastern lands. So explorers looked for new routes to Asia. Some went south around Africa. Others sailed west . . . and found the Americas.

Europeans did not find the black pepper they were looking for in the Americas. Rather, a new kind of pepper grew there. In 1493, Columbus brought red peppers from Haiti to Spain. Their spicy taste quickly became popular. The use of red pepper then spread to Africa and Asia.

Reading Strategy:
Predicting

(Answers will vary. Some students may say that da Gama will find India by traveling strictly by water.)

Ask:

- How many ships did Vasco da Gama have when he left Portugal? (four) How many ships made it around the world? (two)
- Who sponsored da Gama's journey to India? What route did he take? (Portugal; around Africa and then eastward)

Ask students to think of some of their favorite meals. Encourage them to think about how many of those foods are seasoned with red or black pepper. Then have students silently read "Pass the Pepper, Please" to find out about the importance of pepper and the discovery of a new source.

ELL/ESL STRATEGY

Language Objective:
To practice common grammar structures
Remind students that in order for a sentence to be complete, it must contain a verb. The verb tells the action in the sentence. Tell students that verbs can be written in the past tense, present tense, or future tense. If you are writing about something that happened in the past, you should use a past-tense verb. Explain that most of the text in the students' *World History* book is written using past-tense verbs because the book describes events that happened in the past. On the board, write two sentences (each using a past-tense verb) from page 403. Have a volunteer circle the past-tense verb in each sentence. After students have read the lesson, have them choose two sentences from the lesson, write them on paper, and circle the past-tense verbs in each sentence.

Ask:

- **What advantage did Portugal have during most of the 1500s?** (controlled the spice trade in the East Indies)

- **Which other European people established trade in Asia? Where did they trade?** (the Spanish and the Dutch; Canton, China)

Reading Strategy: Predicting

(Answers will vary. Some students may predict that Magellan finds a quick, easy route across the Pacific Ocean.)

- **Into which ocean did Magellan sail after passing through the strait at the tip of South America?** (Pacific)

- **Where was Magellan killed?** (the Philippines)

 3 Reinforce and Extend

LEARNING STYLES

Logical/Mathematical

Remind students that degrees of longitude begin with 0° at Greenwich, England, and become greater as one travels east or west. In addition, starting with 0° at the equator, latitude degrees become greater as one travels north or south from the equator. Have students examine a map and determine the approximate degrees of latitude and longitude for a ship entering the Pacific Ocean from the Atlantic Ocean through the Strait of Magellan (70°W longitude, 51°S latitude). Have students then calculate the same information for the modern shortcut from the Pacific to Atlantic oceans—through the Panama Canal (83°W longitude, 10°N latitude). Students should draw maps to illustrate their findings and share them with the class.

Strait

A narrow strip of water that connects two bigger bodies of water

Reading Strategy: Predicting

Based on what you have just read, predict what Magellan finds.

What European Countries Traded With China and Japan?

For most of the 1500s, the Portuguese controlled the spice trade in the East Indies. As the years passed, their ships reached China and Japan too. The Chinese and Japanese did not trust Europeans, so the Chinese allowed the Portuguese to trade only in one off-shore island, Macau. Later the Chinese allowed the Dutch and the Spanish to open a trading center in the city of Canton.

Who Was the First to Sail Around the World?

In September 1519, Ferdinand Magellan, a Portuguese captain, set sail from Spain with five ships and about 265 crewmen. King Charles I of Spain asked him to find the western route to India that Columbus had failed to find.

First, Magellan sailed south. Then he turned westward and explored the coast of South America. The trip was so long that some sailors rebelled, and Magellan lost one ship. The four remaining ships slowly moved through a **strait** at the tip of South America. A strait is a narrow strip of water that connects two bigger bodies of water. This strait connected the Atlantic Ocean with the Pacific Ocean, but Magellan did not know that. (Geographers now call it the Strait of Magellan.)

What Did Magellan Find Beyond the Strait?

After passing through the strait, the three remaining ships reached the calm, open water of the Pacific Ocean. But as they journeyed for three months across this peaceful ocean, conditions for the crew worsened. They had to eat wormy food, rats, and cooked leather. Their water turned yellow and tasted bad.

Finally the three ships reached the Philippine Islands. Here, in a fight with the native people, Magellan was killed. (A native is someone who was born in a particular place.) Soon, two more ships were lost. All alone, the last ship sailed across the Indian Ocean, down the eastern coast of Africa, around the Cape of Good Hope, and up the western coast of Africa.

In September 1522—three years after leaving Spain—this one ship, with 18 sailors, reached home port. The voyage covered about 44,000 miles. It had sailed around the world and proved two things: First, the world is round. Second, the earth contains much more water than land.

Lesson 2 Review On a sheet of paper, write the answer to each question. Use complete sentences.

1. What was one problem that sailors faced in traveling around the southern tip of Africa?

2. Who thought that he could reach the East by sailing across the Atlantic Ocean?

3. Who was the first European to reach India by sailing around Africa?

4. What are the names of three countries that sent ships to China to trade?

5. Who led the expedition that proved the world was round?

Navigating at Sea

How did sailors long ago know where they were? On a clear night, they could spot the North Star. The sun's position was also a guide. But the compass was the first navigational instrument. Its magnetized needle points north.

By the 1400s, sailors were making longer voyages and needed better tools. One such tool was the astrolabe. It could measure the angle of the sun or the North Star with the horizon. From that, a navigator could determine latitude, or the distance north or south of the equator.

Today's instruments would amaze Columbus! The newest method is GPS, or global positioning system. It uses signals from 24 satellites orbiting the earth to determine position. Ships, planes, and cars can use GPS. It has made travel much easier.

How do you think the Arab and Italian merchants felt when Vasco da Gama's ships sailed into Calicut? Explain your answer.

ELL/ESL Strategy

Language Objective:
To read for meaning
In this lesson, students have read about the voyages of Columbus, da Gama, and Magellan. Give each student three large index cards, and have them make fact cards about each of the three explorers. On the lined side of the card, have students write facts about where the explorer was from, where he sailed, the reason for the voyage, and what he found. On the blank side of the card, have students sketch a map that shows the route or routes followed by the explorer. Have students read their fact cards with a partner. Explain to students that these fact cards can be used to study for the chapter test.

Lesson 2 Review Answers

1. The weather was bad at the tip. The trip to the southern tip of Africa also took a long time. **2.** Columbus had this plan. **3.** Vasco da Gama was the first to reach India by sailing around Africa. **4.** The Portuguese, Dutch, and Spanish sent ships to China. **5.** Magellan led the three-year expedition that proved the world was round.

Answers will vary. The Arab and Italian merchants must have been angry. A trip by sea would cost less than by land, so the Portuguese had now taken the upper hand away from the Arab and Italian merchants who used an overland route to India.

Have a volunteer read the title: "Navigating at Sea." Then have students read the feature with a partner to discover the contrast in navigation tools available to sailors in the 1400s and today. When they finish, ask them to work together to write a paragraph explaining what they think is the most important advantage today's sailors have over sailors in the 1400s. Give volunteers an opportunity to read their paragraphs to the class.

Chapter 17: Lesson 3

Overview This lesson discusses the motivation the Spanish had for taking over the New World, the conquest of the Aztecs by Cortés, and the conquest of the Incas by Pizarro.

Objectives

- To identify Montezuma and the mistakes he made
- To describe how small groups of Spaniards conquered two large empires

Student Pages pages 406–409

Teacher's Resource Library TRL

Workbook Activity 77

Activity 77

Modified Activity 77

. . . .

Vocabulary

conquistador

Have one student read the definition for the vocabulary word, and another student write the word on the board. Then ask volunteers to use the word in a sentence. Classmates should either say that the sentence is OK or suggest a way to change the sentence to make the usage correct.

. . . .

1 Warm-Up Activity

Throughout history, legends, or stories passed down from one generation to the next, have had a huge impact on people's actions. Explain to students that a legend had an impact on how the Aztecs treated the conquistadors. Ask students to share a legend that they have heard. Have students discuss the impact one of those legends could have on the way people treat each other.

Objectives

- To identify Montezuma and the mistakes he made
- To describe how small groups of Spaniards conquered two large empires

Conquistador

A Spanish conqueror

Reading Strategy: Predicting

Preview the lesson title. Predict what empires the Spanish conquer.

Writing About History

What did the Spaniards and the Aztecs say on meeting for the very first time? In your notebook, write a conversation that happened then. One person is a Spanish soldier. The other is an Aztec.

Some Spaniards liked to explore and discover new places. Others—the **conquistadores,** or conquerors—wanted gold and glory. Jesuit missionaries wanted the Indians to change their religion and become Catholics. These missionaries and the conquistadores came to Central and South America for "God, Gold, and Glory."

What Aztec Legend Helped Cortés?

In 1519 Hernando Cortés sailed with 11 ships to the coast of Mexico. Some 500 soldiers and 16 horses sailed with him. The fleet landed on the Mexican coast in an area that the Aztecs ruled.

Before this time, the Aztecs had conquered other tribes in the area to create an empire. Montezuma was the Aztec ruler. When he heard that Cortés had landed, the emperor thought of an ancient Aztec legend. According to this legend, the Aztec god Quetzalcoatl had sailed from Mexico toward the East. The legend said that the great feathered god would one day return. According to the legend, Quetzalcoatl was to return in 1519! The Aztecs at first believed that Cortéz and his men were gods.

Why Did Montezuma Send Cortés Gifts?

Montezuma had more than 200,000 warriors, but he did not march against the Spanish invaders. Thinking they were gods, he sent golden gifts to them. This was a mistake. The gifts made the Spanish want more gold.

Soon, Cortés met a woman who spoke several native languages. She helped Cortés speak with the other tribes that the Aztecs had conquered. Many of these tribes hated their Aztec rulers, so they became allies of Cortés.

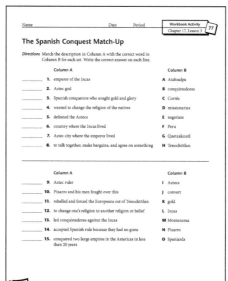

Workbook Activity 77

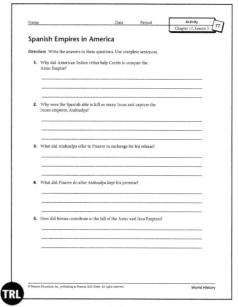

Activity 77

How Did the Spanish Treat Montezuma?

Cortés and his 500 men marched to Tenochtitlan, the Aztec city where the emperor lived. When they reached it, Montezuma allowed them to enter. That was his second mistake. Once inside the city, Cortés made Montezuma a prisoner. The Aztecs quickly rebelled and forced the Europeans out of Tenochtitlan. At that point, Cortés asked his Indian allies for help. With the Spaniards, they surrounded the city for three months. Finally, the Aztecs surrendered. Spain had broken the power of the Aztec Empire.

What Did the Conquistadores Do to the Incas?

To the south of Mexico, in the mountains of Peru, the Spanish conquered another empire, the Incas. In 1532, fewer than 200 Spanish conquistadores landed in South America. Francisco Pizarro led them. King Charles V of Spain had told him to conquer South America.

Pizarro and his men marched toward the Inca capital. They came at a time when Atahualpa, the Inca emperor, was fighting a civil war with his brother. Atahualpa heard that the Spanish were coming, so he went out to meet them with many of his people. When they met, Pizarro and his men attacked. The Incas carried no weapons, so the Spanish killed many of them and captured Atahualpa.

The Inca emperor offered to fill a large room with gold if Pizarro would release him. Pizarro agreed. From all parts of the Incan Empire, gold poured into the room until it was full.

Geography Note

Ask a volunteer to read the Geography Note. Point out that the climate and geography of the coast of Chile determine what kinds of plants and animals can live there. Discuss how fog can provide the moisture that allows life in the desert.

PRONUNCIATION GUIDE

Use this list to help students pronounce difficult words in this lesson.

Quetzalcoatl	(ket säl´ kō ät´ l)
Tenochtitlan	(tä nòch tē´ tlän´)
Atahualpa	(ä tə wäl´ pə)

 2 Teaching the Lesson

Have students create a Venn diagram to use as they read this lesson. One circle should list the characteristics of the conquistadors, and the other should list the characteristics of the Aztecs and Incas. The middle should list what the groups had in common.

Reading Strategy:
Predicting

After reading the section headings, the students may predict that the Spanish conquered the Aztecs and the Incas.

Ask:

- Why was Montezuma in awe of Cortés? (He thought Cortés was a god.)

- Why did people in tribes side with Cortés against the Aztecs and the Incas? (because they did not like them)

- What did the Inca emperor do to secure his release? (filled a room with gold)

- Even though the Aztec leader Montezuma agreed to accept rule by the king of Spain, what happened to him? (He was killed.)

- Where was the Inca Empire? (in the mountains of Peru)

 Writing About History

Before students read this feature, ask them to discuss the challenges they face when trying to communicate with someone who speaks a different language. Then have students read Writing About History and write their conversation between a Spanish soldier and an Aztec or Inca in their notebook.

Ask:

- How did Pizarro die? (His men killed him in an argument over gold.)

- How long did it take the Spanish to conquer the Aztecs and the Incas? (less than 20 years)

Reading Strategy:
Predicting

(Answers will vary. Students may add the detail that the Spanish conquered the large empires because of the Aztecs' belief in a legend and because of the willingness of other tribes to fight against the Aztecs and Incas.)

 Reinforce and Extend

WORLD CULTURES

 When the Europeans first came to what is now known as Latin America, the population consisted of Indian groups such as the Aztecs, Incas, and Maya. Today, the people of Latin America have a varied ancestry. Throughout Latin America there are Indians, whites, and blacks, as well as people of mixed ancestry. People of mixed Indian and white descent are called *mestizos*.

Atahualpa was emperor of the Incas in 1532. Pizarro captured and executed him. The Spanish then took control of the Inca Empire.

Reading Strategy:
Predicting

Think about your prediction. What details can you now add to make your prediction more specific?

How Did Pizarro Treat the Inca Emperor?

The emperor had kept his promise. Now the time had come for Pizarro to keep his. But Pizarro had heard an untrue story that Inca warriors were going to attack. He put Atahualpa on trial and executed him.

The Inca emperor was dead, and his warriors had no guns and no will to fight, so they accepted Spanish rule. By 1535, the Spanish controlled much of the Incan Empire. In time, Pizarro and his men argued over the gold, and they killed him.

Why Did the Empires in the Americas Fall?

In less than 20 years, small groups of Spaniards conquered two large empires in the Americas. How was this possible? Historians give five reasons.

First, they came at the right time. Montezuma believed an Aztec legend was coming true. Pizarro arrived when a civil war was going on. Second, tribes that did not like the Aztecs or Incas joined the Spanish to fight against them. Third, the Spanish had cannons and guns. The American Indians had never seen weapons like these. Fourth, the Spanish had horses. They were new too. At first, the Indians thought that each horse and its rider was a two-headed god. When a rider got off his horse, the god seemed to divide itself into two parts. Fifth, the Spanish brought smallpox and measles to the Americas. The Indians had no natural protection against these diseases. This killed millions of Indians.

The Incan Empire

One problem facing the Incan Empire was that it stretched thousands of miles through the rugged Andes Mountains. At the time, communication was difficult over such a distance. However, to connect its different parts, the Incas built an excellent system of roads. Some ran along the coast. Others crossed the mountains. Woven bridges allowed people to cross rivers and canyons. These roads allowed merchants and officials to travel safely throughout the empire. In addition, they enabled relays of runners to quickly deliver messages.

The Incan Empire faced two other communications problems. Its people spoke several different languages, and there was no system of writing. As a result, the Incas developed an unusual way to keep records—the quipu. It was a long cord that had other strings tied to it. The cords were knotted in different ways. Knots and spaces represented different numbers—ones, tens, hundreds. The colors of the cords represented different items. One color meant taxes. Another was used to keep track of food in storehouses.

Word Bank
Atahualpa
Aztecs
God
Montezuma
Pizarro

Lesson 3 Review On a sheet of paper, use the words from the Word Bank to complete each sentence correctly.

1. Many Spaniards came to the Americas in the 1500s for _____, Gold, and Glory.

2. The _____ built a great civilization in present-day Mexico.

3. The Aztec ruler _____ thought that Cortés was a god.

4. _____ was the leader of the Inca Empire in Peru.

5. _____ put the Inca emperor on trial and executed him.

Could the Incas and the Aztecs have defeated the Spaniards? Explain your answer.

After students read "The Incan Empire," have them compile a list of the methods of communication available today. Then challenge students to say how they would explain each of these technologies to Pizarro, who would know nothing about them. For instance, students would have to explain telephones and computers in order to explain e-mail, cell phones, and text messaging.

Lesson 3 Review Answers

1. God **2.** Aztecs **3.** Montezuma
4. Atahualpa **5.** Pizarro

Answers will vary. The Incas and the Aztecs greatly outnumbered the Spanish. But the Spanish weapons were far superior, and the Spanish were also able to use allies.

BACKGROUND INFORMATION

 Francisco Pizarro's attack on the Incas in 1532 coincided with a civil war between Atahualpa and his brother Huáscar. The civil war began at the time of their father's death. Huáscar was the designated heir to the kingdom, but Atahualpa rose up against him using his large army to take control of the empire. While victorious, Atahualpa's army had been severely weakened by the war. They were more easily overcome by Pizarro's troops than they might have been at any other time.

Chapter 17: Lesson 4

Overview This lesson explains how Spain governed its lands in the Americas and how Spanish landowners obtained the necessary labor to run their plantations and silver mines.

Objectives

- To explain how Spain governed its colonial lands in the Americas
- To describe the relationship between Spanish landowners and the people who worked for them

Student Pages pages 410–412

Teacher's Resource Library **TRL**

Workbook Activity 78

Activity 78

Modified Activity 78

Vocabulary

encomienda   **viceroy**
plantation

Have students work in pairs to study the vocabulary definitions. Students should then each write sentences using the vocabulary words. When they finish, have them check their partner's work. If students think word usage is not correct, have them offer corrections that will make it correct.

1   Warm-Up Activity

During the time when Spain was establishing colonies in the New World, many of the American Indians struggled to survive. Explain to students that in trying to help, one man solved the problem by actually creating another one. Have students think of a time when they accidentally created a new problem as they tried to solve another problem. Ask volunteers to share their experiences with the class.

Objectives

- To explain how Spain governed its colonial lands in the Americas
- To describe the relationship between Spanish landowners and the people who worked for them

Viceroy

An official who governs land for the king or queen

Plantation

A large area of farmland

Encomienda

The Spanish system of forced physical labor

For many years, the Spanish explored the Americas. Hernando de Soto—one of Pizarro's men—went north and explored Florida. Then he turned west. By 1541, he reached the Mississippi River. Another Spaniard, Francisco de Coronado, led an expedition into the southwest of North America. Spain claimed control of this area in 1560 and called it "New Mexico."

Who Ruled New Spain?

Spain also had a name for the land that had once been the Aztec and Inca Empires. These became New Spain. Soon the king of Spain created five provinces in New Spain and sent a **viceroy,** or official, to govern each province. To encourage Spanish settlement, the king gave large areas of land to Spanish conquistadores. Their descendants formed a class of wealthy landowners.

Why Did the Encomienda Lead to Death?

Spain had a lot of land in the Americas. Spanish landowners wanted to make money on it. To do that, they needed millions of farmworkers. They also needed miners for the silver mines in Mexico. Bringing millions of workers from Spain was not practical. The Spanish forced the native people to work for them. The Spanish landowners were cruel to these workers.

Often a Spanish landowner forced a whole village of natives to work on **plantations,** or large areas of farmland. The Spanish called this system of forced physical labor the **encomienda.** Under this system, a Spanish landowner had two duties. First, he had to care for the needs of the natives. Second, he wanted to change their religion so that they became Catholics. Often, the landowner paid little attention to the first duty.

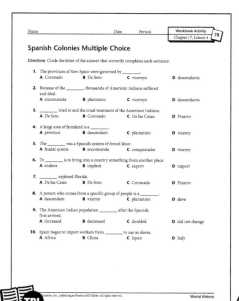

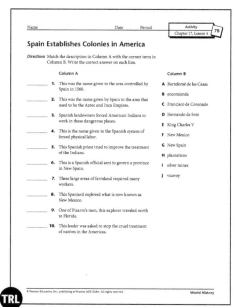

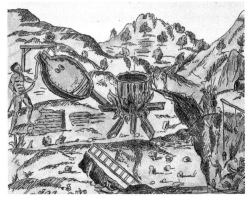

The Spanish forced American Indians to work in silver mines. This dangerous work killed many Indians.

Because of the encomienda, thousands of native people suffered and died. More than 25 million lived in Latin America when the Spanish first came there. Within 100 years, the native population was down to 4 million because of European diseases and hard, dangerous work in the silver mines. The Spanish refused to allow them to practice their customs and traditions. They had to accept new and strange ways of doing things. Because of all this, many native people lost hope.

How Did las Casas Try to Help?

A Spanish priest named Bartolomé de las Casas tried to end the cruel treatment of the natives by the Spanish. He wrote to King Charles V and explained that the natives were dying in great numbers. Something had to be done.

But the plantation owners needed workers, so las Casas suggested that Spain use African workers. Soon Spain began to import Africans to the Americas. Las Casas quickly felt sorry that he had ever suggested this. He had solved one problem, but caused another.

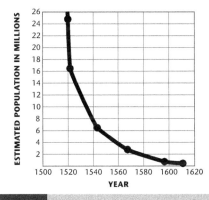

Graph Study About how many Indians were there in Central America in 1520? in 1560? in 1600?

PRONUNCIATION GUIDE

Use this list to help students pronounce difficult words in this lesson.

Bartolomé de las Casas
(bär´ tō lō mā´ dā läs käs´ äs)

2 Teaching the Lesson

As students read the lesson, have them take notes on what happened to the American Indians who lived in the area during this time. Have students discuss how the lives of the Indians changed.

Ask:

- What name did Spain give its new land in the Americas? (New Spain)
- What did the king of Spain do to encourage settlement? (He gave large areas of land to the conquistadores.)
- Who was Bartolomé de las Casas? (Spanish priest who tried to help the American Indians)
- What did he say should be done to solve the problem related to cruel treatment of workers? (He said that Spain should use African workers instead of American Indians.)

ELL/ESL STRATEGY

Language Objective: *To understand different purposes for writing*

As students read the text on page 411, have them focus on the graph that shows the changes in the native population in Central America. Point out the title. Point out the information given on the x axis and on the y axis. Explain that writers will often put the information they have, called data, into a graph so it is easier to read. Read the graph data aloud with students. Have students write a few sentences explaining the information provided in this graph. Their sentences should also include a conclusion that they can draw from the data, such as that since the native population was decreasing, it probably continued to decrease after 1620.

Have students study the graph, "Changes in Native Population of Central America (1519–1605)." Ask a volunteer to read the labels for the vertical axis (millions of people) and horizontal axis (year). Invite another volunteer to choose a year and state how many millions of Indians were alive at that time. Then have students answer the questions under the graph. (There were about 25 million Indians in Central America in 1520, about 4 million in 1560, and about a million in 1600.)

3 Reinforce and Extend

LEARNING STYLES

Visual/Spatial

Some students may find that it is easier to understand the meaning behind a series of numbers if they can visualize the relationship between them. Have students create a bar graph illustrating the number of American Indians in Latin America before the arrival of the Spaniards. On the same graph, have them represent the number of American Indians in Latin America 100 years later. The chart should illustrate that in 1519 there were 20 million Indians, but by 1619 there were only 4 million.

AT HOME

Ask students to remember a time when they had to be explorers themselves, and write a few paragraphs about how they felt during their adventures. Experiences could be based on their first day in a new country, city, neighborhood, or school. Ask students to question family members about having similar experiences. Then encourage volunteers to share their stories with the rest of the class.

Lesson 4 Review Answers

1. B **2.** A **3.** D **4.** C **5.** C

Answers will vary. The Spaniards had no appreciation of the cultures and civilizations they had destroyed. Perhaps the needs of the Indians were not important to them. Perhaps the Spanish simply had the upper hand and enjoyed their power. Perhaps some of them were just cruel whenever they could be.

Lesson 4 Review On a sheet of paper, write the letter of the answer that correctly completes each sentence.

1. For the Spanish, the former Aztec and Inca Empires became _____.

  A New Mexico   **C** India
  B New Spain   **D** China

2. The Spanish explorer _____ traveled as far west as the Mississippi River.

  A Hernando de Soto   **C** Cortés
  B Francisco de Coronado   **D** Pizarro

3. _____ was a Spanish priest who tried to help the native people.

  A Hernando de Soto   **C** Francisco de Coronado
  B Pizarro   **D** Bartolomé de las Casas

4. Bartolomé de las Casas suggested to the Spanish king that _____ workers could take the place of the native workers.

  A Spanish   **C** African
  B Italian   **D** Chinese

5. The Spanish used a system of forced physical labor that they called the _____.

  A viceroy   **C** encomienda
  B plantation   **D** conquistador

What do you think?

Why did the Spanish treat the Indians in such a cruel way?

Lesson 5: The Growth of the Slave Trade

Objectives

♦ To explain why African slavery was introduced into the New World

♦ To describe how slaves were brought to the Americas

Slavery
The owning of human beings as property

Reading Strategy:
Predicting
Preview the lesson title. Predict what you will learn about the beginning of slavery.

A slave is a person who is forced to work without pay or rights and is treated as property. Slaves built the Egyptian pyramids. Slaves labored in Greece and Rome. In the ancient world, people became slaves in different ways. Many were captured in wars. Others may not have been able to pay a debt, so they became property of the person they owed.

What European Country Began to Buy and Sell Slaves?

In a small way, **slavery,** or the owning of human beings as property, had existed in Africa for many centuries. But in Africa, slaves had rights. The owner was not allowed to overwork them. The owner had to let slaves earn money. The slaves could then buy their freedom.

In the 1440s, the Portuguese started buying slaves. They set up slave trading centers along the Gold Coast of Africa and the Gulf of Guinea. In 1518, Spain let Portugal bring African slaves to the Americas. This solved the Spanish labor problem in their American colonies.

What Was the Journey to the Americas Like for Slaves?

Europeans took away the rights the slaves had in Africa. European slave traders and owners were cruel. The traders packed African men and women into dirty ships and locked them in chains. The chained slaves spent most of the voyage to the Americas below deck. Their food was unfit to eat, they never had enough water, and slave traders whipped them.

Why Did the Slave Trade Grow?

For over 300 years, slave traders captured and sold into slavery more than 20 million Africans. Of these, 5 million, or one-fourth, never reached the Americas. They died on ship, and the slave traders threw their bodies into the sea.

1450 – 1650   *Beginnings of Our Global Age* Chapter 17   413

Chapter 17: Lesson 5

Overview This lesson explains how the slave trade was born from the need for workers in the newly colonized Americas.

Objectives

■ To explain why African slavery was introduced into the New World

■ To describe how slaves were brought to the Americas

Student Pages pages 413–415

Teacher's Resource Library

Workbook Activity 79

Activity 79

Modified Activity 79

Vocabulary

abolish   **slavery**

Have students look up the word *abolish* in the dictionary. Ask them to list other forms of the word *abolish* and to identify the word that means getting rid of slavery. (*abolition*) Have students identify the word that means a person who called for the end of slavery. (*abolitionist*) Call on volunteers to write sentences on the board using the vocabulary words.

1 Warm-Up Activity

Explain to students that the slave trade began with the European settlement of the New World. Have students share what they have already learned about the slave trade during that time period. Have students brainstorm viable alternatives to slavery that might have worked for the colonies.

2 Teaching the Lesson

Some students may have difficulty understanding why the slave trade became such a popular way of gaining workers in the New World. As students read the lesson, explain why land owners found it cheaper to bring over slaves than it was to bring workers from their native countries.

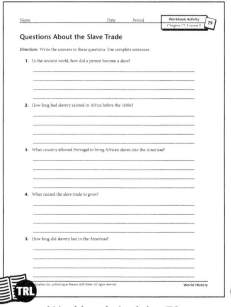

Workbook Activity 79

Name _____ Date _____ Period _____ Workbook Activity 79
Chapter 17, Lesson 5

Questions About the Slave Trade

Directions Write the answers to these questions. Use complete sentences.

1. In the ancient world, how did a person become a slave?

2. How long had slavery existed in Africa before the 1400s?

3. What country allowed Portugal to bring African slaves into the Americas?

4. What caused the slave trade to grow?

5. How long did slavery last in the Americas?

Activity 79

Name _____ Date _____ Period _____ Activity 79
Chapter 17, Lesson 5

The Growth of the Slave Trade

Directions Circle the letter of the answer that correctly completes each sentence.

1. Spain let _____ bring African slaves to the Americas.
   A Greece   B Portugal   C France   D the Netherlands

2. Of the 20 million Africans captured by slave traders, _____ never reached the Americas.
   A one-fourth   B one-third   C two-thirds   D three-fourths

3. As Europe settled more colonies, the slave trade _____.
   A decreased   B increased   C stayed the same   D ended

4. To _____ is to say that something is no longer legal.
   A convert   B enslave   C navigate   D abolish

5. The English forced slaves to work in the colonies of _____.
   A North America B Brazil   C Africa   D France

6. Slavery in the Americas lasted for almost _____ years.
   A 100   B 400   C 600   D 800

7. Slaves in _____ led a successful rebellion in the 1790s.
   A Cuba   B Brazil   C North America D Haiti

8. In _____, slaves had rights.
   A North America B Portugal   C Spain   D Africa

9. The Portuguese set up slave trading centers along the _____.
   A Gold Coast   B Cape of Good Hope C northern Africa coast D coast of Peru

10. In _____, slaves built pyramids.
    A Haiti   B Cuba   C Egypt   D Greece

Beginnings of Global Age Chapter 17   413

(Answers will vary. Students may predict that buying slaves from Africa started because it was cheaper than hiring workers and there were plenty of slaves available.)

Ask:

- Was there any way for a slave in the Americas to become free again? a slave in Africa? (no; in Africa, slaves could earn their freedom)

- In what year did Portugal begin to bring African slaves to the Spanish colonies? (1518)

- Where were the sugar plantations that employed slaves during this time? (Cuba, Haiti, and Brazil)

- When did England take control of the slave trade from Spain? (1713)

- What crops did slaves raise on southern plantations? (rice, tobacco, and cotton)

- How many years did slavery last in the Americas? (almost 400 years)

- When did the slave trade end in all of the Americas? (1888)

LEARNING STYLES

Auditory/Verbal
Have students listen to the recording of this lesson, "The Growth of the Slave Trade." Ask students to make notes as they listen. Remind them that they should listen for and write the main points only. While listening to the recording a second time, they can check their notes and fill in any information they missed the first time.

The slave trade became popular when colonization began in the Americas. For hundreds of years, African slaves were taken to the Americas. Many died on the way; those who survived had to endure harsh treatment.

Abolish
To get rid of something

Soon European colonies expanded from South and Central America to North America. As Europe settled more colonies, the slave trade grew. Slaves worked the Spanish sugar plantations in the Caribbean Islands of Cuba and Haiti. They also worked the Portuguese sugar plantations in Brazil.

The English forced slaves to work in the colonies of North America. (In 1713, England took control of the slave trade from Spain.) On southern plantations, slaves worked long hours to raise rice, tobacco, and cotton for their owners. In all these places, slaves had no freedom. Cruel owners sometimes beat and killed them.

How Long Did Slavery Last in the Americas?

Slavery in the Americas lasted for almost 400 years. During that time, a number of slaves rebelled. Most of these rebellions failed, but some slaves did gain freedom.

In the 1790s, slaves on the island of Haiti led a successful rebellion. Haiti had the first government in the Americas led by the free Africans. Many years passed before the United States **abolished,** or got rid of, slavery. This happened in 1865, after a civil war. In 1888, slavery ended in all of the Americas. In that year, Brazil abolished it.

414   *Unit 3   Early Modern Times*

ELL/ESL STRATEGY

Language Objective:
To summarize information from text
In Lesson 5, students will read about slavery in the Americas. This lesson contains many pieces of information about slavery that the students will need to be able to remember for a test. Organize students into four small groups—one group for each section of text in the lesson. Give each group a sheet of butcher paper and a marker, and assign them a section of text. Have the groups read their sections together. Ask them to write a list of the most important facts on their butcher paper. Then bring the entire class together and have groups share their information in the same order as it appears in the text. As students share, model how to take each piece of information and incorporate it into a summary for the lesson on a new sheet of butcher paper.

NORTH AMERICA

Charleston
AMERICAN COLONIES

West Indies

CENTRAL AMERICA

PACIFIC OCEAN

BRAZIL

SOUTH AMERICA

ATLANTIC OCEAN

WEST AFRICA

SONGHAI
DAHOMEY
ASANTE BENIN

AFRICA

CENTRAL AFRICA
KONGO

EAST AFRICA

30°N

0° Equator

30°S

120°W   90°W   60°W   30°W   0°   30°E   60°E

Map Study This map shows different slave trading routes. From which area of Africa—West or Central—did the slave traders take most of the slaves? What city in the North American colonies was a slave port?

Lesson 5 Review On a sheet of paper, write the answer to each question. Use complete sentences.

1. Who were the first Europeans to begin buying and selling African slaves?

2. How did the lives of slaves in Africa and in Europe differ?

3. Over a period of almost 300 years, how many African men and women did traders capture?

4. Who took control of the slave trade in 1713?

5. What was the first country in the Americas in which African slaves rebelled and won their freedom?

Why did slave traders begin to buy and sell slaves?

3 Reinforce and Extend

Read the title of the map aloud: "African Slave Trades." Ask student volunteers to explain the main reason for bringing slaves to the Americas from West Africa rather than from East Africa. (easier passage, direct route) Then ask students to read the caption and answer the questions. (They took most of the slaves from West Africa. They also sold slaves in Central America and in North American colonies. Charleston was a slave port.)

Lesson 5 Review Answers

1. The Portuguese first bought and sold slaves. **2.** In Africa, slaves had rights and could earn money to buy their freedom. In Europe, slaves became the property of their owner. **3.** Traders captured over 20 million Africans. **4.** England took control of the slave trade in 1713. **5.** Slaves first rebelled and won their freedom in Haiti.

Answers will vary. Trading in slaves was profitable, as workers were needed in the Americas.

Chapter 17: Lesson 6

Overview This lesson describes the first colonies established in North America, and how discoveries made in these colonies benefited Europeans.

Objectives

- To identify the first English colony in North America
- To list the plants grown in the Americas that affected the lives of people around the world

Student Pages pages 416–420

Teacher's Resource Library

Workbook Activity 80

Activity 80

Modified Activity 80

Vocabulary

colonist   Mayflower
economic   Compact
majority

Have students study the definitions of the vocabulary words. Students will create a class story that includes these words. Have students write a vocabulary word of their choice on an index card. Then ask for a volunteer to use the word in a sentence. Another volunteer will use his or her word to continue the story. Proceed in this way until all of the students have had a chance to use their word in the class story.

1 Warm-Up Activity

Students may remember many things about the Pilgrims and other early settlers in North America from their studies in earlier years. As a class, make a K-W-L chart and write what students already know in the "Know" column. Have students generate questions for the "Want to Know" column. Leave the chart on display so information can be added to the "Learned" as the class reads the lesson.

Objectives

- To identify the first English colony in North America
- To list the plants grown in the Americas that affected the lives of people around the world

Colonist

A person who settles in a new place

Majority

More than half of a group of people or group of things

Spain, Portugal, the Netherlands, England, and France explored and set up colonies in the Americas. They brought change with them. Some changes were good. Other change destroyed whole civilizations in the Americas. In Africa, the slave trade destroyed African life and cultures.

What Was the First English Colony in North America?

Spain was the first country to send explorers to the Americas. It also set up colonies. Then England and France did the same. In 1585, Sir Walter Raleigh established an English colony on Roanoke Island, off the coast of North Carolina. Within three years, all the **colonists**—the people who had settled in this new place—disappeared. No one knows what happened to them.

In 1607, the English established another colony in Virginia. They named it Jamestown after King James I. It became the first permanent English colony in America.

Who Helped the English Pilgrims?

In 1620, the Pilgrims, who wanted religious freedom, came to North America on the *Mayflower*. On board ship, they agreed to base their government on the rule of the **majority** of men settlers. A majority means

The Mayflower Compact was based on the idea of rule by the majority. It was the beginning of democracy in America.

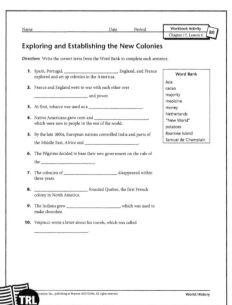

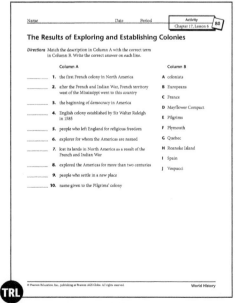

that more than half of them had to agree on something to make it a law. Historians call the agreement made by the Pilgrims the **Mayflower Compact.** The Pilgrims named their colony Plymouth.

Half of the Plymouth colonists died during the first winter. However, American Indians helped them, and the Pilgrims soon did well in their new settlement, or colony. In time, English settlements grew. By 1733, there were 13 English colonies on the Atlantic coast of North America.

Where Did the French Settle?

French fishing boats sailed off the Newfoundland coast. In 1535 Jacques Cartier claimed for France the land that is now eastern Canada. The first French colony in North America was Quebec, in present-day Canada. Samuel de Champlain founded it in 1608. The French also founded settlements along the Great Lakes and the Mississippi River. (The French mostly trapped animals and traded their furs.) In the 1680s, the French claimed Louisiana in the lower Mississippi Valley. They named this rich land after King Louis XIV. Like the Spanish, the French gave their land in North America a name—New France.

European trade ships brought goods to and from the Americas and Europe.

---

 2 Teaching the Lesson

Some students may have difficulty understanding why the Mayflower Compact was necessary, since the Pilgrims were still under the rule of England. Explain that at that time it took months for information to be sent back and forth between the colony and England by ship. Because of this, the Pilgrims needed some rules they could follow on an everyday basis.

Ask:

- Which European country was the first to send explorers to the New World? (Spain)
- What happened to the first English colony on Roanoke Island? (Nobody knows; the people just disappeared.)
- Why did the Pilgrims come to North America? (for religious freedom)
- What document was an agreement among the Pilgrims about how they would be governed? (the Mayflower Compact)
- Where was the first French colony in North America? (in Quebec, in what today is Canada)

ELL/ESL STRATEGY

 Language Objective: *To explain content-area vocabulary*

In this lesson, one of the vocabulary terms students are reading about is the *Mayflower Compact.* Explain to students that when two people or two groups of people enter into an agreement, they are entering into a compact. This particular agreement, or compact, was named after the ship on which the Pilgrims sailed. Have students do research about the Mayflower Compact on the Internet or in the library. Then tell students to think about how they would explain the Mayflower Compact to someone who has never read about it. Have students write an explanation of the Mayflower Compact. Ask volunteers to read their explanations to the class.

Biography

Read the title, "Amerigo Vespucci: 1454–1512," to students. Then have students read the biography independently. Explain to students that many countries, cities, and bodies of water were named after early explorers. Challenge students to look at a world map and find as many of these places as they can.

Reading Strategy:
Predicting

(Answers will vary. Students may predict that corn and potatoes were the plants that were new to the Europeans.)

Ask:

• Which plants native to the Americas changed the diets of Europeans? (corn and potatoes)

• Which crop native to the Americas became an important cash crop in Maryland and Virginia? (tobacco)

LEARNING STYLES

Body/Kinesthetic
Have students work with a partner to make two mobiles from pictures cut out of magazines. On one of them, include plants and animals from the Americas that were new to Europeans; on the other, include plants and animals from Europe that were new to American Indians. Students might do some research in the library or on the Internet to find examples other than those mentioned in this lesson. Each mobile should have a title, such as "What's New to Europe" and "What's New to the Americas." Display the mobiles when students finish. Give students an opportunity to report the results of their research to the class.

Biography

Amerigo Vespucci: 1454–1512

Amerigo Vespucci was not the first European to find the Americas. Still, these continents are named for him.

In 1491, this Italian worked for a bank in Spain. It lent money for voyages of exploration. Later, Vespucci became a navigator. He made several voyages, including two that reached and explored Brazil.

Unlike Columbus, Vespucci thought he had seen a new continent. Around 1503, he wrote a letter about his travels. It was published under the title "New World." Many people read it, including a German mapmaker. He then named these new lands "America" on his maps.

France and England tried to outdo one another in North America. Both wanted money and power. After a number of wars, France lost its lands in North America. The French and Indian War was a nine-year war between France and England. When it ended in 1763, French lands in Canada went to Britain. French territory west of the Mississippi River went to Spain.

Reading Strategy:
Predicting

Preview the title of the next section. Predict what plants will be new to the Europeans.

How Did Plants from the Americas Help Others?
When European ships came to the Americas, they carried animals, plants, and goods. The American Indians had never seen horses, pigs, and chickens. They had never grown plants like wheat, oats, rice, apples, bananas, coffee, and sugar cane.

These same ships carried corn and potatoes back to Europe. These became important foods for the whole world. Corn and potatoes were easy to grow. With more food to eat, fewer Europeans starved, and the population grew.

The Indians grew other crops that were new to people in the rest of the world. Some of these were tomatoes; cacao, for making chocolate; lima beans; and tobacco. Indians were the first to use tobacco, smoking it in pipes. At first, the Europeans used tobacco as medicine. Then they also began to smoke it.

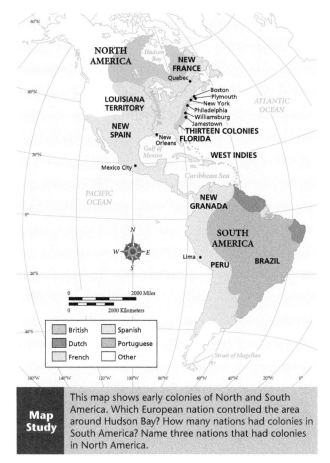

British		Spanish
Dutch		Portuguese
French		Other

Have a volunteer read the map's title, "European Colonies in the Americas." Encourage students to study the map using the key and read the caption. Have students answer the questions in the caption. (The British controlled the area around the Hudson Bay. Four nations had colonies in South America. Three nations with colonies in North America include Spain, France, and England or Britain.)

Ask:

- Which part of North America was not under European control? (western)
- Which part of South America was not under European control? (southern)

Map Study This map shows early colonies of North and South America. Which European nation controlled the area around Hudson Bay? How many nations had colonies in South America? Name three nations that had colonies in North America.

In 1612, John Rolfe planted tobacco in Jamestown. Englishmen were willing to pay high prices for it. Tobacco became an important cash crop for colonists in Virginia and Maryland.

Ask:

- In addition to the Americas, what other parts of the world did Europeans control by the late 1800s? (India, parts of the Middle East, and most of Africa and Asia)

- What does it mean when one country has economic control over another country? (It means that one country has control of the government and money matters in the other country.)

3 Reinforce and Extend

Lesson 6 Review Answers

1. Corn and potatoes became important food for the world. **2.** Jamestown was the first permanent English colony. **3.** The Mayflower Compact was an agreement the Pilgrims made among themselves. They agreed to base their government on majority rule. **4.** The French established colonies in Canada and in the lower Mississippi Valley. **5.** By 1763, England came to dominate half of the North American continent.

Answers will vary. Perhaps all the people died from a cold winter, starvation, or an illness they had brought with them from England. Perhaps some died and the others could not manage alone and joined an American Indian tribe. Perhaps they were all killed by American Indians.

IN THE COMMUNITY

Ask students to take a notebook to the grocery store and list items for sale that are from continents other than North America. Students should list both the name of an item and the continent it is from. Give students time to compare their lists with those of other students. Have students discuss how those items are delivered to North America.

Economic
Having to do with money

Who Controlled the World at the End of the 1800s?

The Europeans explored the Americas for more than two centuries. During this time, they took control of the rich lands of North America and Latin America. The Spanish, Dutch, English, and French set up colonies in North America. As the years passed, European power grew stronger throughout the world. By the late 1800s, European nations had gained political and **economic** control of India, parts of the Middle East, and most of Africa and Asia. That is, Europe controlled the government and money matters in these places.

Lesson 6 Review On a sheet of paper, write the answer to each question. Use complete sentences.

1. What two American vegetables became an important food for the world?

2. What English colony became the first permanent English colony in North America?

3. What was the Mayflower Compact?

4. Where did the French establish colonies in North America?

5. Which European nation came to dominate half of the North American continent by 1763?

What do you think

What do you think happened to the "Lost Colony" at Roanoke?

Chapter Project Follow-up

Have student groups complete final preparations of their explorer display posters. Remind students to make sure they have answered *who, what, when, where, why,* and *how* questions about their explorer and his expeditions. The poster should also contain at least one map showing the route or routes their explorer followed. Have students display their posters in the classroom and give a brief presentation to the class using their posters.

A Warm Welcome for Cortés

Spanish settlers in the Americas treated the natives cruelly. One of these conquistadores was Hernando Cortés. In search of riches, Cortés sailed to the coast of Mexico. When the Aztec emperor Montezuma (here spelled Moctezuma) heard of the arrival, he thought that Cortés and his men were gods. In this excerpt, Moctezuma welcomes Cortés to Tenochtitlán, the capital of the Aztec empire. Within months of the meeting, Cortés killed Montezuma and destroyed the Aztec Empire.

Then Cortés addressed Moctezuma: "Is this indeed you? Are you not Moctezuma?"

"Yes," Moctezuma answered; "I am he."

On this, he rose, to stand facing Cortés. He bowed deeply, drew him close, and stood firmly. Then he said,

"O our lord, you have tired yourself; you are weary. At last you have come to earth; you have come to govern your city of Mexico, to take your position of authority, which for a short time I have been keeping and guarding for you. Your former deputy governors have departed—the rulers Itzcoatl, Moctezuma the Elder, Axayacatl, Tizoc, Auizotl, who also had come to keep watch, to govern the city of

Cortés and Montezuma meet in peace in 1519.

Mexico for you a short time ago and keep your people under their protection. Do the former rulers know what is happening in their absence? O that any of them might see, might wonder at what has befallen me—at what I am seeing now that they have gone. For I cannot be dreaming.

"For some time now I have been afflicted; I have gazed at the clouds, the mists, out of which you have come. And now this has come to pass. The departed rulers said as they left us that you would revisit your city, would return to your position of authority, and now it has so happened. You have come; you have tired yourself; you are weary. Rest yourself. Go into the palace; rest. Peace be with our lords."

Document-Based Questions

1. Why did Cortés go to Mexico?

2. Why did Montezuma think that Cortés was a god?

3. Why do you think Montezuma is so friendly toward Cortés when they first meet?

4. What does Montezuma tell Cortés to do?

5. The word *afflicted* means "worried." Why was Montezuma worried?

Source: The War of Conquest: How It Was Waged Here in Mexico, by Arthur J. O. Anderson and Charles E. Dibble.

1450 – 1650

Beginnings of Our Global Age Chapter 17 **421**

Read aloud the title to "A Warm Welcome for Cortés." Then read aloud the introductory paragraph. Next, have students read aloud the text with a partner. You may wish to have one student read the parts of Cortés and the narrator, and the other student read the part of Montezuma. Have students discuss how Montezuma might have felt as he looked upon the faces of people he believed to be gods.

Have students work independently to answer the Document-Based Questions.

Answers to Document-Based Questions:

1. He went to Mexico in search of riches.

2. The former rulers told stories about the gods returning to the city, so Montezuma thought these strangers were those gods.

3. Montezuma thinks Cortés is a god.

4. He tells Cortés to go inside the palace and rest.

5. Answers will vary. Students may say that Montezuma was worried that the gods would never return.

Spotlight Story

Have a volunteer read the title, "Diseases in Human History." Ask students to raise their hands if they have ever had the chickenpox, measles, or flu. After students have read the feature silently, ask for volunteers to read the story aloud. Then have students answer the Wrap-Up questions.

Answers to Spotlight Story Wrap-Up:

1. American Indians died from cruel treatment and hard work, but mainly from new diseases that came from Europe.

2. They can become immune by getting a disease and recovering from it or by inheriting some immunity.

3. They brought smallpox, chickenpox, measles, and mumps.

4. An epidemic is a disease that spreads rapidly through a group of people, affecting almost everyone.

5. He devised a vaccination for it, using the cowpox virus.

CAREER CONNECTION

Since Edward Jenner's development of a smallpox vaccination in 1790, many people have worked to prevent the spread of disease. Across the country, workers in public health facilities treat people with health problems, provide vaccinations to prevent some diseases, and educate the public about ways to stay healthy. Have students research local colleges to find out about their public health curriculum and requirements for admission to classes. Students might also interview public health professionals to find out what they do in their jobs and how they trained for their work.

Diseases in Human History

Cortés and his army came to Mexico in 1519. At that time, about 11 million natives lived in central Mexico. By about 1650, fewer than 2 million remained. Cruel treatment and hard work had killed some. But diseases from Europe had been the main killer.

In Europe, diseases such as measles were common. Over time, many Europeans had built up a natural immunity, or resistance, to these illnesses. To understand how immunity develops, take a look at measles. For centuries, people in Europe caught measles when they were young. There were no modern medicines. Some children died. Many survived, though. They were now immune to measles. Mothers passed on some of their immunity to their children. They might get measles, but they would recover. This happened generation after generation. Finally, fewer people died from measles.

What made smallpox, chickenpox, measles, and mumps so deadly in America? The native people had never been exposed to them. They, therefore, had no immunity.

Epidemics of these diseases broke out among the native people. An epidemic is a sickness that spreads quickly through a group of people. It affects most of them. The first smallpox epidemic in Mexico began in 1520. It helped the Spaniards defeat the Aztecs. Other smallpox epidemics happened later in the 1500s. Measles and flu were also serious. These diseases swept through villages, killing people of all ages. When adults died, there were fewer people to bear children. The native population fell each year. Whole cultures disappeared. Later, the same thing happened to natives in North America.

Today, modern medicine can make people immune to some diseases. In the 1700s, smallpox was a dangerous disease. About 20 percent of those who caught it died. Smallpox also left bad scars on people's skin. About 1790, Edward Jenner, a British physician, noticed that milkmaids did not get smallpox. They got a similar, milder illness called cowpox. Jenner made a vaccine using the cowpox virus and gave it to a boy. When tested, the boy was immune to smallpox. Soon many doctors were giving vaccinations or "shots." In 1980, world health officials said that smallpox had been wiped out everywhere.

Scientists have since made vaccines against other diseases. These include measles, mumps, chicken pox, and polio. Most children in the United States now get these shots and others. Many developing countries do not have these health services for their children.

Wrap-Up

1. Why did the native population in Mexico fall after 1519?

2. How do people become naturally immune to a disease?

3. What diseases did Europeans bring to the Americas?

4. What is an epidemic?

5. How did Edward Jenner help wipe out smallpox?

Chapter 17 SUMMARY

- Arab merchants and Italian city-states traded in spices and other goods from Asia. In the 1400s, other countries looked for new trade routes.

- Prince Henry of Portugal began a school that taught navigation. In 1487, Dias sailed around the tip of Africa, the Cape of Good Hope.

- Columbus believed he could reach Asia by sailing west. Queen Isabella of Spain provided money for his voyage in 1492.

- In 1493, the pope said that newly discovered eastern lands belonged to Portugal and western ones to Spain.

- Da Gama sailed around Africa to reach India in 1498. Eventually, the Portuguese, Spanish, and Dutch traded at certain ports in China.

- Magellan's expedition sailed west around the world in 1519–1522, exploring the Pacific Ocean. The trip proved that the world is round and that the earth contains more water than land.

- Cortés conquered the Aztecs of Mexico in 1519. In 1532, Pizarro's men defeated the Incan Empire.

- Guns and horses gave the Spanish an advantage over the native people. Many were also killed by European diseases.

- De Soto explored Florida and reached the Mississippi River. Coronado explored the American Southwest.

- Aztec and Inca lands became the colony of New Spain. Under the encomienda system, Spanish landowners used native workers.

- Spanish landowners in the Americas began to use African slaves instead of the native people. The slave trade was cruel and inhuman. Millions of Africans died. African slaves worked in the Caribbean, Brazil, and the English colonies in North America. Slaves in Haiti rebelled successfully in the 1790s.

- England and France wanted colonies in North America. The English settled Jamestown, Virginia, in 1607. In 1620, English Pilgrims settled Plymouth colony. They signed the Mayflower Compact.

- Champlain founded Quebec in 1608. The French had fur-trading posts around the Great Lakes. They claimed Louisiana of the lower Mississippi valley. France lost its North American lands in 1763.

- Europeans brought new plants and animals, such as horses, to the Americas. Corn, potatoes, tomatoes, chocolate, and other products from the Americas were introduced to Europe.

1450 – 1650

Beginnings of Our Global Age Chapter 17 **423**

Using the Chapter Summary

Have students read the Chapter Summary on page 423 to review the main ideas presented in Chapter 17.

Ask:

- Which European country was the first to search for new trade routes to India and China? (Portugal)

- Who was the first explorer to sail around the southern tip of Africa? (Bartholomeu Dias)

- When Columbus discovered the New World, where did he think he had landed? (the East Indies or Asia)

- Which explorer was first to sail to India? (Vasco da Gama)

- A ship from which explorer's expedition was first to sail around the world? (Ferdinand Magellan's)

- Who worked for the Spaniards before the African slave trade began? (American Indians)

- What was the first permanent English settlement in North America? (Jamestown)

- Where did the French settle first in North America? (Quebec)

TEACHER'S RESOURCE

The AGS Globe Teaching Strategies in Social Studies Transparencies may be used with this chapter. The transparencies add an interactive dimension to expand and enhance the *World History* program content.

Chapter 17 Review

Use the Chapter Review to prepare students for tests and to reteach content from the chapter.

Chapter 17 Mastery Test

The Teacher's Resource Library includes two forms of the Chapter 17 Mastery Test. Each test addresses the chapter Goals for Learning. An optional third page of additional critical-thinking items is included for each test. The difficulty level of the two forms is equivalent.

Chapter 17 Review Answers

1. Prince Henry
2. Dias
3. Columbus
4. da Gama
5. Magellan
6. Cortés
7. Montezuma
8. Pizarro
9. Las Casas
10. Sir Walter Raleigh
11. D
12. A
13. C
14. D
15. C
16. The overland trade routes to India and China had made the Italian city-states wealthy. Portugal and Spain wanted money, too, so they looked for a water route to the East.

Word Bank

Columbus
Cortés
da Gama
Dias
Las Casas
Magellan
Montezuma
Pizarro
Prince Henry
Sir Walter Raleigh

On a sheet of paper, use the words from the Word Bank to complete each sentence correctly.

1. _____ established a school in Portugal to help sea captains get better at navigation.

2. In 1487, _____ sailed around the tip of Africa.

3. In 1492, _____ sailed west across the Atlantic Ocean to reach Asia.

4. In 1498, _____ left Portugal with four ships and reached India.

5. In 1519, _____ began a three-year trip around the world.

6. In 1519, _____ sailed to Mexico and conquered the Aztec Empire.

7. _____ led the Aztec Empire when the Spanish landed in Mexico.

8. In 1532, _____ marched up the mountains of Peru and conquered the Incan Empire.

9. _____ was a priest who tried to help American Indians in New Spain.

10. In 1585, _____ established an English colony that later disappeared.

On a sheet of paper, write the letter of the answer that correctly completes each sentence.

11. Europeans from _____ explored the Americas.

    A Spain   C France
    B England   D all of the above

12. The first French settlement in North America was _____.

    A Quebec   C Jamestown
    B Roanoke   D Plymouth

Chapter 17 Mastery Test A

Part A Directions Circle the letter of the answer that correctly completes each sentence.

1. Hernando Cortés conquered the _____.
   A Aztecs   B Incas   C Portuguese   D French

2. The _____ set up a form of government for the Pilgrims.
   A Mayflower Rule   B Majority Rule   C Bill of Rights   D Mayflower Compact

3. After Europeans came to the Americas, the native population _____.
   A increased   B decreased   C stayed the same   D left the Americas

4. England and _____ fought over the colonies in North America.
   A Spain   B France   C Portugal   D Brazil

5. The United States _____ slavery after the Civil War.
   A accepted   B annexed   C adopted   D abolished

Part B Directions Write the correct name from the Word Bank to complete each sentence.

6. _____ established a school of navigation.

7. In 1487, _____ sailed around the southern tip of Africa.

8. Portuguese captain _____ was killed by Philippine natives.

9. _____ led conquistadores in the defeat of the Incas.

10. Spanish priest _____ tried to help the native Americans.

11. _____ convinced the queen of Spain to finance his voyage.

12. In 1585, _____ established a colony on Roanoke Island.

13. _____ founded Quebec in 1608.

14. Spaniard _____ explored Florida.

15. _____ was an Aztec god.

Word Bank
Columbus
de Champlain
de las Casas
de Soto
Dias
Magellan
Pizarro
Prince Henry
Quetzalcoatl
Raleigh

World History

Chapter 17 Mastery Test A, continued

Part C Directions Match the description in Column A with the correct word in Column B. Write the correct answer on each line.

Column A	Column B
16. official who governs land for the king or queen	A colonist
17. born in a particular place	B descendant
18. having to do with money	C economic
19. narrow strip of water	D exploration
20. science of planning and directing the route of a ship	E import
21. looking around some unknown place	F native
22. someone who comes from a specific group of people	G navigation
23. settles a colony	H settlement
24. a colony	I strait
25. to bring into a country	J viceroy

Part D Directions Write the correct term from the Word Bank to complete each sentence.

26. Another name for _____ is conqueror.

27. Because of the _____, thousands of Native Americans suffered and died.

28. Christopher Columbus thought he had reached the _____.

29. The _____ defeated the Aztecs and the Incas with guns, cannons, and horses.

30. The _____ came to North America for religious freedom.

Word Bank
conquistador
East Indies
encomienda
Pilgrims
Spanish

World History

Chapter 17 Mastery Test A, continued

Part E Directions Write your answer to each question. Use complete sentences. Support each answer with facts and examples from the textbook.

31. Why did Portugal want to find a water route to India and China? (2 points)

32. How did African slavery begin in the New World? (2 points)

Part F Directions Write a short paragraph for each topic. Include a topic sentence, body, and conclusion. Support each answer with facts and examples from the textbook.

33. Discuss how the conquest of the Aztec and Inca Empires affected the American Indians. (3 points)

34. Explain how the colonization of Europeans in North America began. (3 points)

World History

Chapter 17 Mastery Test A, pages 1–3

13. The English Pilgrims settled at _____.

   A Roanoke   **C** Plymouth
   B Jamestown   **D** Quebec

14. In 100 years, the American Indian population went from 20 million to _____ million.

   A 10   **B** 8   **C** 6   **D** 4

15. In 300 years, traders captured and sold into slavery more than _____ million Africans.

   A 60   **B** 40   **C** 20   **D** 1

On a sheet of paper, write the answer to each question. Use complete sentences.

16. Why did Portugal and Spain want to find a water route to China and India?

17. Why did so many native people die under Spanish rule?

18. What new plants did the Europeans find in the Americas and how did these change European civilization?

Critical Thinking On a sheet of paper, write your response to each question. Use complete sentences.

19. Historians give five reasons why the Spanish defeated the Aztecs and the Incas. Which of these reasons seems the most important to you and why?

20. The Spanish conquistadores said they came to the Americas for "God, Glory, and Gold." Which of these do you think was the most important to them? Explain your answer.

Write your answers neatly on essay questions. Neat papers are easier for the teacher to read and grade.

1450 – 1650   *Beginnings of Our Global Age*   Chapter 17   **425**

17. American Indians died because the Spanish landowners and mine owners were cruel and mistreated them. Also, the conquistadores brought disease with them. American Indians had no immunities to these diseases, so they died.

18. American Indians introduced Europeans to corn, potatoes, tomatoes, cacao, lima beans, and tobacco. Growing corn and potatoes was easy, so people had more to eat and the population increased.

Critical Thinking

19. Answers will vary. The five reasons historians give for the Spanish defeat of the Aztecs and the Incas are as follows: First, they came at the right time. Second, tribes that did not like the Aztecs or Incas joined the Spanish to fight against them. Third, the Spanish had cannons and guns. Fourth, the Spanish had horses. Fifth, the Spanish brought smallpox and measles to the Americas. Students should explain why their choice seems important.

20. Answers will vary. From the way the Spanish conquistadores treated the American Indians, gold seems to be the primary reason they came to the Americas. Their actions do not bring them much glory. Nor do their actions glorify God.

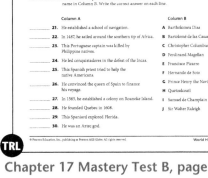

Chapter 17 Mastery Test B, pages 1–3   *Beginnings of Global Age*   Chapter 17   **425**

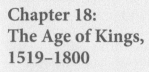
Introducing the Chapter

Europe in the 16th century made progress toward more modern political structures with the development of

---

18

The Age of Kings

In Chapter 10, you read about feudalism. It was the political organization of the Middle Ages. Now you will learn about nationalism. As you watch nations develop, you will study many different kings and queens. Some thought that God gave them the right to rule. Many thought that everything revolved around them.

You will do more than learn about kings and queens in this chapter. You will sail in an armada, learn about a beautiful capital in St. Petersburg, Russia, and see a civil war in England. You will also learn about Prussia and Russia.

Goals for Learning

◆ To explain nationalism and explain how nations developed

◆ To describe the rise and fall of Spain as a powerful nation

◆ To explain rule by "divine right"

◆ To describe England's constitutional monarchy

◆ To explain how Louis XIV help France become powerful

◆ To explain why historians call two Russian monarchs "Great" and explain how Prussia became powerful

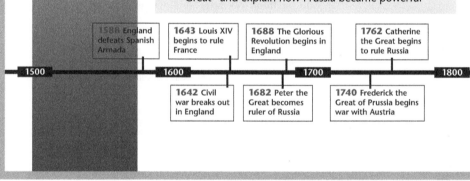

1588 England defeats Spanish Armada

1643 Louis XIV begins to rule France

1688 The Glorious Revolution begins in England

1762 Catherine the Great begins to rule Russia

1500   1600   1700   1800

1642 Civil war breaks out in England

1682 Peter the Great becomes ruler of Russia

1740 Frederick the Great of Prussia begins war with Austria

---

nationalism. As nations formed, royal hopefuls and monarchs entered into a series of wars to increase their treasuries and territories. Throughout the 15th and 16th centuries, rulers and subjects struggled with the limits of power.

Ask:

• In what year did England defeat the Spanish Armada? (1588)

• What event occurred in 1642?
  (Civil war starts in England)

• Who emerged in 1682 as ruler of Russia? (Peter the Great)

• Who began a war with Austria in 1740? (Frederick the Great)

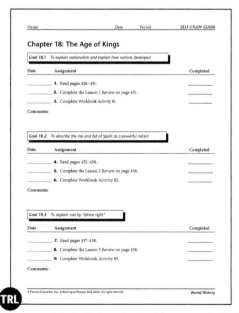

Have a volunteer read the title of the map, "Spain," and count and name the large bodies of water that touch Spain's shores. (three—Bay of Biscay, Atlantic Ocean, Mediterranean Sea)

Ask:

- In which part of Spain is Seville? (southwestern part)
- Which continent lies south of Spain? (Africa)

Have students read the paragraph below the map and then read and answer the questions.

Map Skills Answers

1. the Strait of Gibraltar
2. the Pyrenees
3. Bay of Biscay
4. the Guadalquivir River
5. Cartagena and Barcelona

Chapter Project

Divide the class into small groups of four to five students. Ask each group to choose a historical personality from one of the five European countries in this chapter. Tell students that they will role-play their character in an illustrated "Living Timeline." Groups will use resource materials and the Internet to obtain information about the personalities, such as political philosophies, physical characteristics, quotes, mannerisms, clothing, and attitudes of the characters. Have each group prepare illustrations of the time period and/or location of the personality to hang on the wall around the room as background for the presentations.

Spain became the most powerful nation in Europe during the 1500s. During this time, Spain sent explorers to the Americas. This brought money into the Spanish treasury. Spain used some of this money to build a great navy. Its navy brought Spain more power. Madrid, located in central Spain, was its capital city.

Study the map carefully, then answer the following questions:

1. What strait do ships pass through to get from the Mediterranean Sea to the Atlantic Ocean?

2. What mountains separate Spain from France?

3. What bay is directly north of Spain?

4. What river flows through Seville?

5. What are the names of two seaports in Spain?

1519 – 1800

The Age of Kings Chapter 18   427

Chapter 18 Outline, pages 1–3

The Age of Kings Chapter 18   **427**

Text Structure

Introduce the reading strategy of thinking about *text structure*. Tell students that recognizing common text structures found in expository texts can help them monitor their reading comprehension. Structures that authors choose for organizing information for readers include:

- Description/List Structure
- Cause/Effect Structure
- Comparison/Contrast Structure
- Order/Sequence Structure
- Problem/Solution Structure

Students experience a variety of text structures in their everyday lives. To use these experiences to introduce the concept of text structure, distribute or display copies of a comic strip, a restaurant menu, and a page from an instruction manual.

Ask:

- What kind of information is organized in this framework?
(comic strip: order/sequence; menu: description; manual: description in a list of directions)

Have students look at and read aloud the lesson titles, headings, boldface words, and illustrations on pages 429–449 of Chapter 18. Encourage them to ask the questions that will help them recognize the text structures in each lesson.

Key Vocabulary Words

Point out that these chapter words are presented in the order that they appear in each lesson. They are also found in the Glossary. Have students explain what they think the chapter will be about based on the vocabulary words.

Reading Strategy:
Text Structure

Understanding how text is organized helps you decide which information is most important. Before you begin reading this chapter, do these things:

- ◆ Look at how it is organized.
- ◆ Look at the title, headings, boldfaced words, and photographs.
- ◆ Ask yourself: Is the text a problem and solution, description, or sequence? Is it compare and contrast or cause and effect?
- ◆ Summarize the text by thinking about its structure.

Key Vocabulary Words

Lesson 1
Nationalism Loyalty to one's country or nation
Boundary Dividing line
Tradition A custom, idea, or belief handed down from one person to the next
Monarch A king or a queen
Absolute monarch A king or queen who had complete and unlimited power over his or her people

Lesson 2
Inherit To receive money, land, or a title from someone who has died
Armada A large fleet of warships
Formation A shape or pattern

Lesson 3
Divine right The belief that God chooses the ruler of a nation
Petition of Right An English document that brought about more democracy
Resolution A formal statement that a governmental body writes
Treason The act of turning against the laws and people of your own country

Lesson 4
Cavalier A person who fought for the king in the English Civil War

Roundhead A Puritan who fought for Parliament in the English Civil War
Restoration The period that saw monarchy return to England in 1660
Habeas Corpus A law that says that the government has to charge someone with a crime before putting the person in prison
Tory A person who supported a strong monarchy in England
Whig A person who supported the English Parliament
Glorious Revolution The overthrow of James II and the crowning of William and Mary as monarchs of England
Constitutional monarchy A form of government in which a king or queen rules, but there are laws of a democracy to protect the people

Lesson 5
Cardinal A high official of the Roman Catholic Church
Advisor A person who gives advice

Lesson 6
Constitution A body of laws that states the rights of the people and the power of the government
Military state A place in which a leader rules through the military

---

The Renaissance, the Reformation, and new scientific discoveries brought great change to European societies. Each challenged the way people had lived since the Middle Ages. Another challenge came when Europe began to develop into nations.

What Is Nationalism?

Feudalism was a political and military system based on the holding of land. In the feudal system, many people might share the same language and customs. But they were loyal to different nobles, because the nobles controlled the land they lived on. People did not think of themselves as English, French, or Spanish. When did they begin to think of themselves that way? When **nationalism**—loyalty to one's country—developed.

Nationalism began in Europe in the 11th century when England became a nation. France soon followed. People in these new countries shared the same geographic **boundaries,** or dividing lines.

In these new nations, people shared the same language and history. They also shared the same **traditions,** or customs, ideas, and beliefs that had been handed down from one person to the next. The nation became part of who a person was. When someone asked "Who are you?" a person could answer: "I am English" or "I am French." (Nationalism continues to be an important force today.)

What Is Absolute Power?

All new nations had to answer one question: what form of government shall we have? Different groups wanted power— city governments, the nobility, church officials. The English philosopher Thomas Hobbes wrote in the 1600s that a powerful **monarch,** or king or queen, was the best way to unify a nation. Gradually, some monarchs in Europe gained great power.

Objectives (sidebar)

- To compare feudalism and nationalism
- To identify what "absolute power" meant during this time

Nationalism
Loyalty to one's country or nation

Boundary
Dividing line

Tradition
A custom, idea, or belief handed down from one person to the next

Monarch
A king or a queen

Reading Strategy:
Text Structure

Preview this lesson. Notice the headings, features, and boldfaced words.

Chapter 18: Lesson 1

Overview This lesson describes how European nations emerged from the chaos of feudalism with the development of nations, identity for people, and power for monarchs.

Objectives

- To compare feudalism and nationalism
- To identify what "absolute power" meant during this time

Student Pages pages 429–431

Teacher's Resource Library

Workbook Activity 81

Activity 81

Modified Activity 81

Vocabulary

absolute monarch	nationalism
boundary	tradition
monarch	

Have volunteers read a word and its definition and then pause to give their classmates time to write the word in a sentence. Continue until all the words have been read. Have students work in groups of three to peer-edit their sentences.

1 Warm-Up Activity

The U.S. national anthem, "The Star-Spangled Banner," was written by Francis Scott Key after he watched the bombardment of Fort McHenry during the War of 1812. The national anthem of France, "La Marseillaise," was composed in one night during the French Revolution in 1792. Distribute copies of the lyrics of these anthems (music and translation of the French is available on the Internet) and play these anthems for the class. Discuss the connection between national anthems and feelings of nationalism.

Workbook Activity 81

Nations Fill-In

Directions Write the correct word from the Word Bank to complete the paragraphs.

People have not always thought of themselves as loyal to their country. During feudalism, people were loyal to

1. _____. England became a nation in the 11th century in Europe, and 2. _____ began. Nationalism is loyalty to one's 3. _____. The people in the new nations of Europe shared geographic 4. _____. They spoke the same 5. _____, shared the same history, and shared the same 6. _____.

Each new nation needed a form of 7. _____. Philosopher Thomas 8. _____ believed that a powerful 9. _____, or king or queen, would best 10. _____ a nation. Some of these people had so much 11. _____ that historians call them 12. _____ monarchs. The time in which they ruled is known as the 13. _____.

Philip III was the king of 14. _____ in the early 1600s. His servants let fire burn him because they did not want to 15. _____ his royal orders.

Word Bank
absolute
Age of Kings
boundaries
country
disobey
government
Hobbes
language
monarch
nationalism
nobles
power
Spain
traditions
unify

Activity 81

The Rise of Nations

Directions Circle the letter of the answer that correctly completes each sentence.

1. _____ began in Europe in the 11th century and continues to be an important force today.
   A Tradition   B Religion   C Nationalism   D Government

2. Historians call one kind of ruler a(n) _____ monarch because the ruler had complete, unlimited power over his or her people.
   A absolute   B wealthy   C noble   D smart

3. People in countries share geographic _____, or dividing lines.
   A clothing   B boundaries   C products   D leaders

4. A _____ is a shared idea, custom, or belief handed down from one person to the next.
   A system   B fable   C tradition   D tool

5. Groups such as city governments, the wealthy class, and _____ officials all wanted power.
   A sports   B arts   C tribe   D church

6. _____ wrote in the 1600s that a powerful monarch was the best way to unify a nation.
   A Martin Luther   B Thomas Hobbes   C Philip III   D Anne Boleyn

7. A monarch is a king or _____.
   A senator   B princess   C governor   D queen

8. The period when monarchs ruled is called the _____ of Kings.
   A Age   B Ceremony   C Election   D Finding

9. Philip III was the king of _____.
   A England   B Spain   C France   D Italy

10. Philip III ordered that only one person could move his _____.
   A horse   B armies   C books   D chair

Workbook Activity 81   **Activity 81**   *The Age of Kings*   *Chapter 18*   **429**

Teaching the Lesson

Ask students to share what they have heard, seen, or read about kings and queens. Have themread pages 429–431 to find out how European nations were formed and how monarchies came to power in Europe.

Reading Strategy:
Text Structure

Discuss the organization of the text as it is indicated by the headings, features, and boldfaced words. Guide students to see that the text is descriptive.

Ask:

- To whom were people loyal in the feudal system? (nobles)
- When did the first European nation form? What nation was it? (11th century; England)
- What term do historians use to describe monarchs whose power is limitless? (absolute monarch)

 3

Reinforce and Extend

At Home

 Invite students to discuss with family members what countries their ancestors have lived in. Ask them to find out if these nations had a king or a queen or some other form of royalty when their ancestors lived there. Students with American Indian heritage might ask their parents what they know about the ruling structure of their tribe.

Louis XIV was a powerful French monarch. This painting shows him unveiling a statue in France.

Absolute Monarch

A king or queen who had complete and unlimited power over his or her people

For some rulers, this power was so great that it had no limits. These monarchs had so much power that historians call them **absolute monarchs.** An absolute monarch had complete, unlimited power over his or her people.

But why give all this power to one person? Doing this was one early answer to the question of how to govern a new nation. Historians call this period of absolute monarchs the Age of Kings.

How Absolute Was a Monarch's Power?

How powerful did these monarchs become? There was a humorous story told about Philip III, for example. Early in the 1600s, Philip III, the king of Spain, fell asleep before a blazing fire. Earlier the king had ordered that only one person could move his chair. But this one person was no longer in the room. Seeing that the fire was going to burn the king, his servants searched the castle. No one found the man who had permission to move the king's chair, so the servants stood there and did nothing. They let the fire burn the king! If they had moved the chair, they would have gone against a royal order. That is absolute power! The story, however, is not true.

430 *Unit 3 Early Modern Times*

Learning Styles

 Interpersonal/ Group Learning
Have students work in small groups to research and plan a presentation for the class about the dress and decoration of royalty—crowns, thrones, scepters, castles, jewels, titles, and so on. These items will vary between nations over hundreds of years. Students may want to organize the project by having each group concentrate on a different country over a given period of time. Encourage students to be creative in their presentations.

Modern Monarchs

Rulers had absolute, or total, power in the Age of Kings. People often believed this power came from God. Such a monarch ruled by "divine right." During the 1700s and 1800s, some people rebelled against their rulers. World War I ended other monarchies.

Some countries, however, still have a king or queen. They include Great Britain, Spain, Holland, and Sweden. Present-day monarchs wear rich robes and jeweled crowns for important events. They live in castles and their children inherit the throne. But today's monarchs are only symbols. They stand for a country's tradition and history. In all these countries, a constitution severely limits a monarch's powers. The parliament and prime minister actually make the laws.

Lesson 1 Review On a sheet of paper, write the letter of the answer that correctly completes each sentence.

1. _____ is rule by a king or queen.

   A Crusades   **C** Feudalism
   B Nationalism   **D** Monarchy

2. During the Age of Kings, _____, or loyalty to one's country, developed.

   A nationalism   **C** monarchy
   B feudalism   **D** none of the above

3. _____ developed into a nation before France did.

   A The United States   **C** North America
   B Italy   **D** England

4. During this period many monarchs had absolute, or _____, power.

   A limited   **C** little
   B unlimited   **D** some

5. Philip III of _____ was a king with absolute power.

   A France   **C** Spain
   B England   **D** Italy

What might happen to someone who questioned a monarch's absolute power?

For information about the events between 1493 and 1600, which culminated in the dominance of Spain in the New World and on the high seas, go to www.agsglobewh.com/page431a.

For information on the history of Parliament in the United Kingdom explore this official Web site: www.agsglobewh.com/page431b.

For photographs and background information about the Palace of Versailles, go to www.agsglobewh.com/page431c.

STUDY SKILLS

Have students write in their own words one key fact that is the main idea for each paragraph in Lesson 1. Then have students share their facts. Encourage them to write down other students' facts when they hear one they think would be helpful when reviewing Lesson 1.

ELL/ESL STRATEGY

Language Objective:
To compare and contrast through group work and presentation

Have students work in small groups and include ELL students in the group. Assign students to gather information and compare a U.S. national holiday, such as the Fourth of July, with a national holiday of another country. Students should organize their information using a two-column graphic organizer. Each column head will be name of one of the countries and the holiday. Rows should be labeled *Activities, Traditional Foods, Music and Dance,* and other categories suggested by the group.

Then encourage all students to participate in a presentation to the class. The presentation may include photos, role-plays of celebrations, or performances of music or dance.

Explain that people who lived under the rule of monarchs considered themselves subjects of the crown, meaning the king or queen. A subject is one who is loyal to and is protected by a monarch. Have students read the Then and Now feature, "Modern Monarchs." Ask them to write a few sentences to explain the importance of tradition and history in countries that have constitutional monarchies.

Lesson 1 Review Answers

1. D **2.** A **3.** D **4.** B **5.** C

Answers will vary. Monarchs with absolute power could do whatever they liked to a person—have the person put to death, have the person made a noble, or have the person imprisoned for life.

Chapter 18: Lesson 2

Overview This lesson describes how Spain became the most powerful nation in the world and how it abruptly lost that dominant position.

Objectives

- To identify the city the Moors built in Spain
- To name the kind and queen who first unified Spain

Student Pages pages 432–436

Teacher's Resource Library TRL

Workbook Activity 82

Activity 82

Modified Activity 82

....

Vocabulary

armada **inherit**
formation

Have students write brief paragraphs that use the three vocabulary words correctly. Have volunteers read their paragraphs, humming a different tone in place of pronouncing each vocabulary word. Students can be creative in expressing the tone as a clue to the word. Have classmates suggest which word should replace each tone.

....

1 Warm-Up Activity

Display these items or pictures: oatmeal, sugar, onions, lettuce, peaches, pears, watermelon, citrus fruit, rye bread, bananas; and pictures of horses, cattle, pigs, sheep, chickens, and honeybees. Tell students that these items have something in common. Then play a game of 20 questions, with students asking the teacher questions that can be answered *yes* or *no*, to deduce what the items have in common. Guide students to discover that these things were brought to America from Europe after Columbus's first voyage.

Objectives

- To identify the city the Moors built in Spain
- To name the king and queen who first unified Spain

Reading Strategy:
Text Structure

Notice that the section headings are written as questions. After you read each section, try to answer the question asked in the heading.

Reading Strategy:
Text Structure

As you read, look for words like *first, then, next, afterward,* and *finally.* These words will help you understand the order of the events in the rise and fall of Spain.

Both England and France became nations before Spain. However, Spain was the first to become truly powerful. During most of the 1500s, its political and economic power was much greater than that of England and France. Spain's story begins with the Moors.

Where Did the Moors Settle?

The Moors were nomads in northern Africa. In the eighth century, they accepted Islam—the religion of Muhammad. They invaded Spain and brought with them their new religion. The Moors pushed through Spain and over the Pyrenees Mountains to Tours. The Franks defeated them there in 732. The Moors settled in southern Spain. There, they built a civilization that lasted for almost 800 years.

What Was the City of Córdoba Like?

At that time, civilization was in decline in Europe. But the Moors in Spain built Córdoba. More than a million people lived there. Lamps lit the streets. The library contained thousands of books from all over the world. In fact, the Moors helped to reintroduce ancient Greek and Roman learning into Europe. They studied geometry, astronomy, medicine, and philosophy. Christian scholars came from all over Europe to study in Moorish Spain.

How Did Spain Become a Nation?

Slowly, four Christian kingdoms developed in Spain. Castile and Aragon were the strongest. In 1469, Ferdinand, the king of Aragon, married Isabella of Castile. Their marriage united much of Spain under two strong rulers. They forced Spanish nobles to accept their rule. Ferdinand said that he should make all important decisions because "one head is better than a thousand."

Queen Isabella and her husband, King Ferdinand, united Spain, and made the nation Catholic. They paid for Christopher Columbus's voyages to the Americas.

Why Did Isabella Go to War?

Isabella wanted to make all of Spain into a Catholic nation. In 1482, she went to war against Granada—the last Moorish kingdom in Spain. In 1492, Granada surrendered. Then Isabella said everyone in Spain had to be Catholic. Any Moor or Jew who refused to become a Catholic had to leave Spain. A few months after conquering Granada, the two rulers provided Christopher Columbus with three ships. He sailed west and found great wealth in the Americas.

What Empire Did Charles V Rule?

King Ferdinand died in 1516. Then his grandson Charles became the second king of Spain. Charles I was also the grandson of the Holy Roman Emperor. When the emperor died in 1519, Charles became Charles V, emperor of the Holy Roman Empire. He was only 19, but he ruled one of the largest empires in history and was the most powerful king in Europe.

Inherit

To receive money, land, or a title from someone who has died

What Countries Made Up Charles V's Empire?

Charles V was a member of the powerful Hapsburg family. It held power for more than 700 years—from the 1200s to 1918. Charles V **inherited** lands in France from his father. To inherit is to receive money, land, or a title from someone who has died. Through his grandfather, he became ruler of Austria. He also ruled half of Italy and all of the Netherlands, Germany, and Belgium. Charles also controlled all the lands that Columbus and other Spanish explorers discovered. The gold and silver from the Americas made Charles's empire rich.

1519 – 1800

The Age of Kings   Chapter 18   **433**

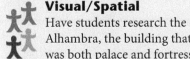
 ## Teaching the Lesson

Invite students to share what they know about King Ferdinand and Queen Isabella of Spain. Then have them read pages 432–436 to learn about the events that brought Spain to the brink of world power.

Reading Strategy:
Text Structure

Have students write answers to the questions in the heads in Lesson 2. The answer to the first heading question is the Moors settled in southern Spain.

Ask:

• Who developed great institutions of learning in Spain? What was their faith? Where were they from originally? (the Moors; Islam; Africa)

Reading Strategy:
Text Structure

The rise of Spain began in 1469, with the marriage of Ferdinand and Isabella. Have students make a list of events in chronological order using words such as *first, next, afterward,* and *finally.*

• How did Isabella make all of Spain Catholic? (She forced anyone who refused to become a Catholic to leave Spain.)

• Who succeeded Ferdinand as king of Spain? (Charles I)

• Which empire did Charles V rule? (the Holy Roman Empire)

• How old was Charles V when he was named emperor of the Holy Roman Empire? (19)

Have students read the title, "Hapsburg Land (c. 1560)." After they have studied the map, ask students what c. means in the title. (approximately) Ask a volunteer what the map shows. (land owned by the Hapsburgs)

Ask:

- In what century did the Hapsburgs own the land shown on the map? (16th century)
- Of which continent did the Hapsburgs control a major portion? (Europe)

Have students read the caption under the map and answer the questions. (The Austrian Hapsburgs controlled Bohemia. Spain was the largest area controlled by the Spanish Hapsburgs. The Spanish Hapsburgs controlled the Netherlands.)

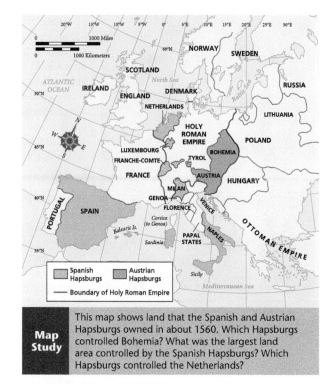

Map Study

This map shows land that the Spanish and Austrian Hapsburgs owned in about 1560. Which Hapsburgs controlled Bohemia? What was the largest land area controlled by the Spanish Hapsburgs? Which Hapsburgs controlled the Netherlands?

Why Did Charles V Retire?

Charles V was one of the most powerful rulers in history. His large empire kept him busy. He fought religious wars in Germany. He fought against France over lands in Italy. In fact, Charles spent most of his life traveling throughout his empire fighting one enemy after another.

Armada

A large fleet of warships

Finally, when he was 56, Charles V had had enough. In 1556, he gave up his power. He gave control of the Holy Roman Empire to his brother, Ferdinand I. He gave his lands in Italy, the Netherlands, and Spain to his son, Philip II. Afterward, Charles went to a monastery and stayed there until his death.

Why Did Philip II Build an Armada?

As a Roman Catholic, Philip II wanted to stop the spread of Protestantism. Elizabeth I of England had made her country into a leading Protestant nation. Philip II wanted to defeat Elizabeth I and England. He thought that Europe would then become Catholic again.

Philip II decided to invade England. To do this, he built a naval **armada,** or large fleet of warships. In the spring of 1588, the Spanish Armada of 130 ships sailed for England with 1,100 cannons and 30,000 soldiers.

The English navy defeated the Spanish Armada in 1588. Only half of the Spanish Armada ships made it back to Spain. The loss put an end to Spain's status as a sea power.

1519 – 1800

The Age of Kings Chapter 18 **435**

Have students write two headings on a sheet of paper: "The Galleon" and "The Caravel." As students read the History in Your Life feature, "Sailing Ships," have them write down the main points about each type of ship under the appropriate heading. When students complete their work, have them share and compare their lists.

Sailing Ships

Explorers in the 1400s used the new full-rigged ships. They had three masts and multiple sails. Such a ship moved under sail power. It did not rely on rowers. The Portuguese developed a full-rigged ship called a caravel to explore the African coast. It was small and very fast. Explorers used it to explore other places too.

In comparison, galleons were heavier and larger. They were first built in the 1500s.

They could carry bulky cargoes or heavy guns. Spanish galleons, for example, brought gold and silver from the Americas to Spain. About one-third of the Spanish Armada in 1588 were galleons. These craft relied on boarding an enemy ship and using soldiers to capture it. English galleons, however, were faster and easier to maneuver. They relied on firepower, which could disable an enemy ship from a distance. This ability defeated the Spanish Armada

Formation
A shape or pattern

How Did England Defeat the Armada?

The Spanish fleet sailed north and anchored off the coast of England. Next, the captains put the ships into a protective **formation**, or shape. But then they broke their formation. The English captains sent three burning ships into the Spanish fleet. This scattered all the Spanish ships.

The Spanish Armada ships also had a weakness: they were too big and too slow. The smaller and faster English ships attacked the scattered Spanish ships. One by one, they sank.

Knowing that the English had defeated them, the Spanish captains tried to sail home. A sudden storm sank many more of their ships. Only half of them returned to Spain. In 1598, Philip II died. In the next two centuries, England and France replaced Spain as the most powerful nations in Europe.

Lesson 2 Review On a sheet of paper, write the answer to each question. Use complete sentences.

1. From what area of Africa did the Moors come?

2. What important city did the Moors build in Spain?

3. What are the names of the king and queen who first unified Spain?

4. In 1519, who became the most powerful ruler in Europe?

5. What country defeated the Spanish Armada?

What do you think?

Where do you think Philip II got the money to build the Spanish Armada?

Lesson 2 Review Answers

1. The Moors came from northern Africa. **2.** The Moors built Córdoba. **3.** King Ferdinand of Aragon and Queen Isabella of Castile united Spain. **4.** In 1519, Charles V—the Holy Roman Emperor and the king of Spain—became the most powerful ruler in Europe. **5.** England defeated the Spanish Armada.

Answers will vary. Philip II probably got the money from all the minerals and other things that Spanish explorers were bringing back to Spain from the Americas.

Objectives

- To explain how King James I used his power
- To identify the "Petition of Right"

Divine Right
The belief that God chooses the ruler of a nation

Petition of Right
An English document that brought about more democracy

Reading Strategy:
Text Structure

This lesson tells about a problem and the solution. Ask yourself: What is the problem? What is the solution?

Elizabeth I was a strong monarch in England. She shared power with the English Parliament. For example, Elizabeth took care of business with other countries. Parliament made laws and taxed people.

What Is Divine Right?

When Elizabeth died in 1603, King James of Scotland became James I of England and Scotland. He refused to share power with Parliament. Instead, he said that he ruled by **divine right.** That is, James thought that God had chosen him to rule. He thought no one had the right to question him and his decisions.

A simple story shows how divine right worked. In 1603, a man accused of stealing was brought before James. James ordered that the man be hanged without a trial. He believed that, as king, he was both judge and jury.

What Made Parliament and the People Angry?

James I died in 1625. His son, Charles I, also believed in divine right. But Parliament did not. Soon after becoming king, Charles asked Parliament for money to fight a war with Spain. Parliament said no. Because of this, the king did not have money to pay for a place for his soldiers to stay. Charles forced people to house the soldiers. The people and Parliament did not like this. They decided to do something to limit the king's power.

When Did Parliament Limit the King's Power?

In 1628, the king again asked Parliament for money. Once again, Parliament refused. Parliament said that it would give money only if the king signed the **Petition of Right**. This important paper was a big step in the growth of English democracy. By signing it, the king agreed to three things.

Overview This lesson covers the beginning of the struggle for power in England between the king and Parliament.

Objectives

- To explain how King James I used his power
- To identify the "Petition of Right"

Student Pages pages 437–438

Teacher's Resource Library TRL

Workbook Activity 83

Activity 83

Modified Activity 83

Vocabulary

divine right	resolution
Petition of Right	treason

Invite students to create a fill-in-the-blank game to play with other students. Have them study the definitions before writing a sentence that includes each vocabulary word. Students will substitute a blank line for the word. Then have them exchange papers with a partner and write the correct words in the blanks.

1 Warm-Up Activity

Read aloud the two paragraphs under the heading "What is Divine Right?" Then ask volunteers to create a short skit showing how divine right would look in a school situation (for example a student is accused of cheating, or a person in authority writes a new school rule). After the skit, ask the class for suggestions for alternatives for handling the same situation, such as a trial by peers, or public input into the decision to make a new rule.

2 Teaching the Lesson

Have students describe rights that all people have. Then have them read pages 437–438 to find out about a right that some English kings thought they had.

Workbook Activity 83

Activity 83

Have students identify the problems associated with King James, King Charles I, and the people and government of England.

Ask:

- Who did King James think had chosen him to rule? (God)

- What right did James I say that he had as king? What did that mean? (divine right; God chose him to rule, and no one could question his decisions.)

- What happened when Charles I tried to exercise the same rights as James I had? (Parliament did not do what he wanted and decided to limit his power.)

- What document did Parliament make Charles I sign before it would give him any money? (the Petition of Right)

- What three important ideas did the king agree to? (only Parliament could collect taxes; the king could not send a person to prison without a trial; no one could be forced to house soldiers)

3   Reinforce and Extend

IN THE COMMUNITY

Some English kings thought they ruled by divine right—they believed that God gave them the power to rule without any interference. In the United States, the power is vested in the people. Ask students to name persons of authority in their community or state. For example, students might mention the chief of police, mayor, or state senator. Have students list five state or local government figures and, in a few sentences, explain how their power ultimately comes from the people.

King James I believed that God had given him the right to rule England as he pleased.

Resolution

A formal statement that a governmental body writes

Treason

The act of turning against the laws and people of your own country

1. Only Parliament can collect taxes.

2. The king can send no one to prison without a trial.

3. No one, not even the king, can force citizens to house soldiers unless these citizens want to.

The next year, Charles again asked for money. This time, Parliament passed a **resolution,** or formal statement, that said three things.

1. The king cannot change English Protestantism.

2. The king cannot tax the English people unless Parliament says he can.

3. If the king does these things, he commits the crime of **treason.** That is, he turns on his country and its laws.

Charles was forced to accept these limits. Slowly, power shifted from monarchs to Parliament.

Lesson 3 Review On a sheet of paper, write the answer to each question. Use complete sentences.

1. In England, which government group makes the laws?

2. How did James I rule England?

3. How did Charles I anger Parliament?

4. What was the Petition of Right?

5. What are two things Parliament said in its resolution?

What do you think

Should Parliament have limited the power of Charles I? Explain your answer.

Lesson 3 Review Answers

1. Parliament makes the laws. **2.** James I ruled by divine right. **3.** Charles I angered Parliament when he forced people to house soldiers. **4.** The Petition of Right was a document that helped democracy grow. **5.** Answers will vary. The king cannot change Protestantism. The king cannot tax without Parliament's approval. If a king does these, he commits treason.

Answers will vary. People who want kings to have absolute power would not want to limit the power of Charles I. But people concerned about their own rights and the power of the government would welcome a limit to a king's power.

ELL/ESL STRATEGY

Language Objective:
To research the history of a holiday

Have students work in small groups to find out what "Guy Fawkes Day" is. Each group will create a poster of a political cartoon, a jingle that they will sing, or a skit to perform. Tell students that Guy Fawkes was an English conspirator in the Gunpowder plot to assassinate James I and blow up the Parliament in 1605. He was arrested in the cellar beneath Parliament and executed. The event has been celebrated in Britain each November 5 ever since.

◆ To describe the period known as the Restoration

◆ To explain how political groups brought about the Glorious Revolution

Reading Strategy:
Text Structure

Study the map on page 440. How does it help you understand the causes of the civil war in England?

What Led to Civil War in England?

In 1639, Charles was again out of money. He needed it to put down a rebellion in Scotland. The people of Scotland refused to become members of the Church of England.

Once again Charles asked Parliament for money. And once again, Parliament worked to limit the king's power. Then, in 1642, the king tried to arrest the leaders of Parliament. This was too much for the English people. They became so angry that Charles had to leave London. Civil war broke out between two groups: the people who supported the king and the people who supported Parliament.

The English Parliament (above) and the Puritans fought the king and his supporters in the English Civil War.

Chapter 18: Lesson 4

Overview This lesson describes further struggles between the kings of England and Parliament that resulted in a constitutional monarchy.

Objectives

■ To describe the period known as the Restoration

■ To explain how political groups brought about the Glorious Revolution

Student Pages pages 439–443

Teacher's Resource Library

Workbook Activity 84

Activity 84

Modified Activity 84

Vocabulary

cavalier	Habeas Corpus
constitutional monarchy	Restoration Roundhead
Glorious Revolution	Tory Whig

Have students study the words and definitions. Then have small groups hold "vocabulary bees" in which a leader reads a definition at random and students give the correct word. Students take turns answering until they give an incorrect response. Continue until one student is left or all the definitions have been answered correctly at least twice.

 Warm-Up Activity

Display pictures of people dressed in different types of clothing (socialites, outdoorsmen, athletes, businessmen, teenagers, etc.). Discuss whether or not the clothing provides information about each person's ideas and values. Then display pictures of a Cavalier and a Puritan and ask students if this clothing gives them information about the person. Discuss whether the clothing tells them which person belonged to the group that prohibited theater, sports, and dancing events. (Plain clothing is associated with disapproval of "worldly pleasures.")

Workbook Activity 84

What Am I?

Directions Read each clue. Then choose the correct word or name from the Word Bank to match each clue. Write the correct answer on each line.

_____ **1.** I fought for the king in the English Civil War.

_____ **2.** During the Restoration, I was brought back to England.

_____ **3.** I was James II's older daughter, and I became queen.

_____ **4.** I am a form of government that includes both a democracy and a king or queen.

_____ **5.** I supported a strong monarchy in England.

_____ **6.** As a Puritan, I fought for Parliament in the English Civil War.

_____ **7.** I gave members of Parliament the right to speak freely.

_____ **8.** In Latin, I mean "you should have the body."

_____ **9.** I supported the English Parliament.

_____ **10.** I am what historians call the period in England when James II was overthrown.

_____ **11.** My wife was Mary, and I signed the English Bill of Rights.

_____ **12.** My army of Roundheads defeated the Cavaliers.

_____ **13.** I was beheaded in 1649.

_____ **14.** I am the name of the 25-year reign of Charles II.

_____ **15.** I am a word that means having respect for the beliefs of others.

Word Bank
Cavalier
Charles I
constitutional monarchy
English Bill of Rights
Glorious Revolution
habeas corpus
Mary
monarchy
Oliver Cromwell
Restoration
tolerant
Tory
Whig
William

Activity 84

England Rejects Absolute Monarchy

Part A Directions Write the correct term from the Word Bank to complete each sentence.

1. The period that saw monarchy return to England is called the _____.

2. The _____ Act said that a person must be charged with a crime before going to prison.

3. The _____ fought for the king and wore fancy clothes.

4. A _____ was a person who supported a strong monarchy.

5. _____ and Mary became the king and queen of England and Scotland.

6. The _____ were Puritans led by Oliver Cromwell.

7. A government with both a monarch and laws of democracy is a _____ monarchy.

8. A _____ was a person who supported the English Parliament.

9. Neither the Tories nor the Whigs wanted a _____ king.

10. In 1642, civil war broke out in _____.

Word Bank
Catholic
Cavaliers
constitutional
England
Habeas Corpus
Restoration
Roundheads
Tory
Whig
William

2 Teaching the Lesson

Have students recall the strategy Parliament used to make the king sign the Petition of Right. (It would not give him any money.) Then have students read pages 439–443 to learn about the continued struggle for power between Parliament and the monarchy.

Ask:

- In the English Civil War, which side supported the king? Which side opposed the king? (Cavaliers; Puritans, or Roundheads)

- What group of people were known as the Cavaliers? (They were mostly rich Anglicans or Catholics.)

Have students study the map: "The English Civil War." Ask volunteers to explain what a map of this type intends to show. (Answers will vary; students may say that showing areas controlled by both sides gives a physical perspective of the war.)

Ask:

- Where is England in relation to Scotland? (south)

Have students read the sentences below the map and answer the questions. (Parliament controlled London. Parliament controlled the land by the English Channel. Possible battle sites include: Naseby, Edgehill, Worcester, Lostwithiel, Nantwich, Preston, Marston Moor, Philiphaugh, Dunbar, Tippermuir, Antrim, Drogheda, and Wexford.)

Reading Strategy:
Text Structure

Guide students through an analysis of the areas of the map controlled by Parliament and compare them to the areas controlled by the king.

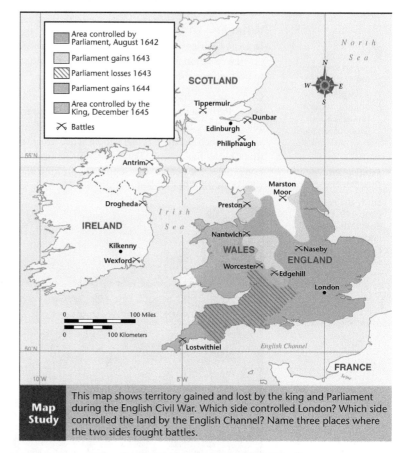

Map Study This map shows territory gained and lost by the king and Parliament during the English Civil War. Which side controlled London? Which side controlled the land by the English Channel? Name three places where the two sides fought battles.

Who Fought the English Civil War?

Cavalier

A person who fought for the king in the English Civil War

The two groups who fought the war were different. They had different religions and they dressed differently. **Cavaliers** fought for the king. They were mostly Anglicans or Catholics. They dressed in fancy clothes and wore wigs with long curls.

Roundhead

A person who fought for Parliament in the English Civil War

Restoration

The period that saw monarchy return to England in 1660

Reading Strategy:
Text Structure

As you read the lesson, use a graphic organizer to compare and contrast the Cavaliers and the Roundheads.

Puritans fought for Parliament. They were English Protestants who wanted to purify the Anglican Church. The Puritans dressed simply. Because they wore their hair so short, people called them **Roundheads.** Oliver Cromwell led the Roundheads. His army was better than the king's Cavaliers. In 1643, the Roundheads defeated the Cavaliers.

What Did the Puritans Do to Charles I?

The Roundheads put King Charles I on trial. They found him guilty of treason. That is, he had turned against England and its laws. Charles was then beheaded in 1649. Never before had a king been put on trial and then put to death before a crowd of people.

What happened next? In 1653, Cromwell took control of the English government. He became a military dictator. The Puritans began to change English society. They closed the theaters; they said no one could play sports. All this lasted until Cromwell's death in 1658.

What Is the Restoration?

The English grew tired of Puritan rule. In 1659, Parliament voted to bring back the monarchy to England. In the spring of 1660, the oldest son of Charles I returned to England. He was crowned Charles II. Historians call his 25-year reign the **Restoration.**

Charles II rejected the idea of the divine right of kings. He tried to avoid religious problems by asking Catholics and Puritans to be tolerant toward one another. That is, they should respect one another's beliefs and customs.

Oliver Cromwell led the Roundheads during the English Civil War. He ruled England after defeating the king in the war.

Ask:

- Which religion did the Puritans support? (Protestant)
- What action did Oliver Cromwell's Roundheads take against the king? (They put him on trial for treason.)
- For how long was Oliver Cromwell a military dictator? (five years)

Reading Strategy:
Text Structure

Suggest that students use a two-column graphic organizer to compare and contrast the Cavaliers and the Roundheads.

- When the English Parliament brought Charles I's oldest son to the throne, he ruled for 25 years. What do historians call that period? (the Restoration)

Ask:

- Why did the English people call Charles II the "Merry Monarch"? (He encouraged theater, sports, and other entertainment, which the Puritans had banned.)

- Which law, passed by Parliament, required a person to be charged with a crime before putting the person in prison? (Habeas Corpus Act)

- Which English political party supported the monarchy? Which party supported Parliament? (Tories; Whigs)

- Who did the Tories and the Whigs agree should become the Protestant rulers of England? (William and Mary)

ELL/ESL STRATEGY

Language Objective:
To use a graphic organizer to show cause and effect

Have students use a graphic organizer such as an outline, list, or chart to show the cause and effect of events in England between 1639 and 1660. Demonstrate how to use the date, a cause statement, and an effect statement to fill in the organizer. Guide students through the process of organizing the first two entries:

Date	Cause	Effect
1639	Charles I of England needed money because Scotland threatened to attack.	Parliament refused him.
1642	The king tried to arrest the leaders of Parliament.	Civil war broke out between the people who supported the king and those who supported Parliament.

Have students work on their own to search for events and causes and effects of the events in Lesson 4 and write the information into a graphic organizer.

Habeas Corpus
A law that says that the government has to charge someone with a crime before putting the person in prison

Tory
A person who supported a strong monarchy in England

Whig
A person who supported the English Parliament

Glorious Revolution
The overthrow of James II and the crowning of William and Mary as monarchs of England

The English people liked Charles II. He encouraged the theater, sports, and other entertainment. He loved to have fun, so people called him the "Merry Monarch."

What New Law Did Parliament Pass?

In 1679, Parliament passed the **Habeas Corpus** Act. This law said that the government has to charge someone with a crime before putting the person in prison. *Habeas corpus* is Latin for "you should have the body." The Habeas Corpus Act is an important protection of a citizen's rights. Now, not even the king could take away a person's freedom without a trial.

What Is the Glorious Revolution?

When Charles II died in 1685, his brother, James, became king. Like Charles, James II was a Catholic. But James wanted the monarchy to have more power.

At the time, two political groups held power in England. The **Tories** supported a strong monarchy; the **Whigs** supported a strong Parliament. Both sides agreed on one thing—they did not want a Catholic king. However, James was old and his two daughters were Protestant. The Tories and the Whigs believed that after the king's death, they would have a Protestant ruler. Then, in 1688, James II's wife gave birth to a son.

This son would grow up and become a Catholic king. The Tories and the Whigs joined together. They said that Mary, who was James II's older daughter, should become queen. In the fall of 1688, Mary and her husband, William, left the Netherlands and arrived in England with an army.

James II had no support, so he fled to France. Parliament then said that William and Mary were the king and queen of England and Scotland. The English had rebelled against their king without anyone being killed. Historians call this the **Glorious Revolution.**

What Is a Constitutional Monarchy?

Before William and Mary could become monarchs, they had to sign the English Bill of Rights. This document said that only Parliament can make laws. It also said that the king must obey the laws Parliament passes.

The document also gave the members of Parliament freedom of speech. Now the king could not arrest them if he did not like what they said.

Between 1628 and 1689, Parliament passed the Petition of Right, the Habeas Corpus Act, and the English Bill of Rights. These documents showed that England did not want an absolute monarch.

England wanted both a democracy and a king. We call this form of government a **constitutional monarchy.** That is, England has a monarchy, plus a body of laws and elected officials to protect the rights of the people.

Lesson 4 Review On a sheet of paper, use the words from the Word Bank to complete each sentence correctly.

1. _____ was the king of England when civil war broke out.

2. A _____ was a person who supported the king in the civil war.

3. A _____ was a person who supported Parliament in the civil war.

4. _____ was the leader of the group that fought against the king.

5. _____ were the first English monarchs who ruled under a form of government called a constitutional monarchy.

Why did the English get tired of Puritan rule?

Constitutional monarchy

A form of government in which a king or queen rules, but there are laws of a democracy to protect the people

Word Bank

Cavalier
Charles I
Cromwell
Roundhead
William and Mary

- What did William and Mary sign before they became king and queen of England and Scotland? (the English Bill of Rights)

- What were the two main points of the English Bill of Rights? (Only Parliament can make laws and the king must obey these laws.)

- What is a constitutional monarchy? (a government that has laws created by elected officials, and a monarchy)

3 Reinforce and Extend

LEARNING STYLES

Auditory/Verbal

To help students better understand the events of this chapter, have them listen to the audio recording. As they do, have them write down notes about important details. Students can fill in any missing information when they replay the recording. Encourage the students to study their notes as they prepare for completing the chapter review.

Lesson 4 Review Answers

1. Charles I **2.** Cavalier **3.** Roundhead **4.** Cromwell **5.** William and Mary

Answers will vary. Puritans did not let the English people do what they wanted, so the English got tired of them.

Chapter 18: Lesson 5

Overview This lesson focuses on France and what happened when a five-year-old child ascended to the throne.

Objectives

- To explain the problems that Louis XIV faced
- To describe how his love of beautiful things caused a problem

Student Pages pages 444–447

Teacher's Resource Library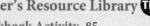

Workbook Activity 85

Activity 85

Modified Activity 85

Vocabulary

advisor   **cardinal**

Write the vocabulary words on the board and discuss their meanings. Ask a volunteer to choose a word and make up a sentence that is a clue to one of the words. Classmates should try to guess the word from the clue. Continue until both the words have been guessed and all students who wish to volunteer have had an opportunity to do so.

 Warm-Up Activity

Display a photograph of the Grand Stables at Versailles. Tell students that after a long drive into the grounds at Versailles, this building comes into view. Ask students to speculate what the building is and what it is used for. (Many people think the Grand Stables at Versailles is the palace.) After identifying the building as the stables, discuss why the stables might be mistaken for something else, and why a king might have such a grand building for horses.

Objectives

- To explain the problems that Louis XIV faced
- To describe how his love of beautiful things caused a problem

Cardinal

A high official of the Roman Catholic Church

Advisor

A person who gives advice

Reading Strategy: Text Structure

As you read, look for the words *but, that is,* and *however.* These words often introduce important information to help you understand what you are reading.

Much was happening in England during the seventeenth century. But much was also happening across the English Channel in France. In 1643, Louis XIII of France died. His son, who was only five, then became king. He ruled as Louis XIV.

Who Helped the Young King Rule?

Louis XIII had been a weak king. He had turned over much of his power to a **cardinal,** or high official, in the Catholic Church. From 1624 to 1642, Cardinal Richelieu served as the king's **advisor.** That is, he gave advice to the king. Richelieu was against any form of democratic government.

By the time Louis XIV became king, the French monarchy had a lot of power. For many years, however, Louis XIV was too young to make decisions. Another church official, Cardinal Mazarin, really ruled France. Under the leadership of these two cardinals, France became the strongest nation in Europe.

When Cardinal Mazarin died, people wanted to know who would be the king's next advisor. Louis was now 23. He decided then and there that he alone would rule France. He ruled France alone for 54 years. Louis became one of the most powerful monarchs in history.

Louis XIV faced many problems when he decided to rule France alone, but he soon became a powerful king.

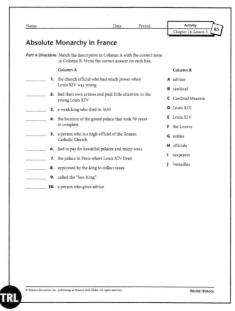

Workbook Activity 85   Activity 85

Reading Strategy:
Text Structure

Notice that the section headings are questions. After you read each section, try to answer the question.

What Problems Did Louis XIV Face?

Louis wanted to rule France alone. But many problems stood in his way. The nobles often paid little attention to what he wanted. He had a hard time collecting taxes. Each noble had his own army, but he had no national army that he could control. Sometimes the nobles and their armies fought against him.

How Did Louis XIV Centralize France's Government?

All these problems existed because France had no central, or main, government that was more powerful than the nobles. Louis wanted to force these nobles to obey his wishes. He thought that he alone should decide what was best for the people of France, so he began to centralize the government.

Louis XIV built a grand palace at Versailles as a symbol of his power. Some historians estimate that he spent $100 million to build it.

1519 – 1800

The Age of Kings Chapter 18 **445**

LEARNING STYLES

Logical/Mathematical

The building of the palace at Versailles was an extravagant undertaking. Among the most famous rooms in the palace is the Hall of Mirrors, which reflected the light from enormous windows and chandeliers. Ask students to imagine that their job is to supply mirrors and windows for a room. Suppose one wall of mirrors faces another wall of windows. Each wall is 80 feet long and each window and mirror is 5 feet wide. How many windows and mirrors would it take to completely cover the two walls? (80 divided by 5 equals 16, so 16 mirrors will complete one wall, and 16 windows will complete the other wall)

ELL/ESL STRATEGY

Language Objective: *To speak or write to express feelings, ideas, and opinions*

Have students work in small groups to respond to the following hypothetical scenario: a government official used $100 million of government money to build a palatial second home. Meanwhile, government budgets to fund education, medical, and welfare programs have been severely cut.

Have students in the group discuss the scenario. From their group discussion, they should form an opinion about the situation and decide how they will react to the official's action of spending government money while cutting benefits for the people. Then have the students form their response as a newspaper article or editorial with headline, an illustrated billboard advertisement, a role-play interview with a panel of citizens and government officials, or another presentation of their choice.

First, Louis XIV appointed officials to collect taxes. They ruled over different areas of France in the name of the king. Next, Louis reorganized the French army. He gave uniforms to the soldiers to show that they belonged to his army. Then he increased the size of the army from 100,000 to 400,000. This large army made Louis XIV powerful.

What Other Things Did Louis XIV Do As King?

Louis XIV lived in a palace in Paris called the Louvre. He built a second great palace at Versailles, which was 10 miles away. Versailles took 30 years to complete. More than 30,000 people worked to build this dream palace. His love of beautiful things was a problem for the French taxpayers. They had to pay for all of this. They also had to pay for the wars Louis XIV fought. Between 1667 to 1714, he fought many wars to get more land. These wars drained the French treasury. At the end of his life, Louis XIV was sorry that he had fought so much. Before he died in 1715, he advised his grandson, the future king, to keep peace. Louis said, "I have been too fond of war."

The long reign of Louis XIV was a great time for France. Beautiful churches and palaces were built. Art and music spread. The French nobility was weakened. People called Louis XIV the "Sun King" because all of France seemed to revolve around him like planets around the sun.

Lesson 5 Review On a sheet of paper, write the answer to each question. Use complete sentences.

1. What two cardinals advised Louis XIII and Louis XIV of France?

2. What are five problems Louis XIV faced when he decided to rule alone?

3. What steps did Louis XIV take to improve the army of France?

4. Where did Louis XIV build his second great palace?

5. What advice did Louis XIV give his grandson?

What could happen to a country like France if an absolute monarch puts too great a burden on the people?

Biography

Cardinal Richelieu: 1585–1642

Armand Richelieu was often called the true power behind the throne of King Louis XIII. He started studying religion when he was a teenager. In 1622, he was made a cardinal in the Roman Catholic Church. He advised the king on government matters from 1624 to 1642.

Henry IV had issued the Edict of Nantes in 1598 to give religious freedom to the Huguenots. Richelieu was against participation in state affairs by any Huguenots. He wanted to make the monarchy stronger. After King Louis died, Richelieu changed the Edict of Nantes to limit the Huguenots' freedoms.

Richelieu chose Cardinal Mazarin to take his place when he died. During the reign of Louis XIV, Mazarin continued to work toward a stronger monarchy.

1519 – 1800

The Age of Kings Chapter 18 **447**

Lesson 5 Review Answers

1. Cardinal Richelieu advised Louis XIII; Cardinal Mazarin advised Louis XIV. **2.** Five of the problems Louis XIV faced include: the nobles often paid little attention to what he wanted; he had a hard time collecting taxes; each noble had his own army; he had no national army that he could control; sometimes the nobles and their armies fought against him. **3.** He gave uniforms to the soldiers to show that they were a national army. He also increased the size of the army from 100,000 to 400,000. **4.** He built it at Versailles. **5.** Louis XIV told his grandson to keep peace and avoid war.

Answers will vary. Usually, people will take only so much abuse, then they will rebel.

Biography

Tell students that in 1627, Cardinal Richelieu set out to secure the authority of the king through force and political repression. List his three ideas of how society should function on the board.

- The king had divine right.

- The nobility with arms should be under the control of the king.

- The common people should be obedient.

Chapter 18: Lesson 6

Overview This lesson describes development of two powerful nations in Eastern Europe—Prussia and Russia.

Objectives

- To describe what Peter the Great did for Russia
- To describe what Catherine the Great did for Russia
- To explain how Prussia expanded its territory

Student Pages pages 448–450

Teacher's Resource Library

Workbook Activity 86

Activity 86

Modified Activity 86

Vocabulary

constitution   **military state**

Have students study the definitions for the vocabulary words. Have students look up the words *constitution, military*, and *state* in the dictionary. Ask them to list the alternative meanings provided for *constitution* and *state* and the different grammatical ways *military* can be used in a sentence.

1 Warm-Up Activity

Write the word *serf* on the board. Tell students that unlike serfs elsewhere, Russian serfs were treated like slaves, forced to give unpaid labor, and could be bought and sold. Tell students that one group of peasants never gave in to serfdom—the Cossacks, who lived along the Don and Dnieper Rivers. Play some stirring music of the Don Cossack Choir and ask students to write and share one sentence about how the music expresses the spirit of these people.

Objectives

- To describe what Peter the Great did for Russia
- To describe what Catherine the Great did for Russia
- To explain how Prussia expanded its territory

Reading Strategy:
Text Structure

As you read this lesson, use a graphic organizer to keep track of facts about the two countries Russia and Prussia.

Russia and Prussia also had strong absolute monarchs. In 1613, a young noble was chosen to lead Russia. His name was Mikhail Romanov. His family ruled Russia for the next 300 years, until the Russian Revolution of 1917. One of Russia's most powerful leaders was his grandson, Peter the Great. He became king in 1682 and believed in his absolute power.

What Was Peter's "Window on the Sea"?

Peter the Great wanted to make Russia into a modern nation. To improve his nation's culture, he invited scholars and artists to his country. He also wanted to increase trade with the nations in Western Europe. Russia's ports were frozen during the winter, so he went to war to gain warm water seaports.

To do this, Peter fought to gain control of Swedish territory on the Baltic Sea to the north and Turkish territory on the Black Sea to the south. Peter wanted these ports to give his nation a "window on the sea." On the Baltic Sea, Peter built a new, modern capital called St. Petersburg. He said that it was the perfect "window for Russia to look at Europe."

What Did Catherine the Great Do for Russia?

In 1762, Catherine the Great became queen of Russia. She was a strong leader. She improved education and allowed more religious freedom in Russia. In 1767, she tried to have a **constitution** written for her nation. A constitution is a body of laws that states the rights of the people and the power of the government. However, this effort failed.

For a time, Catherine favored freedom for Russian serfs. When the serfs rebelled against the nobles, she no longer supported the idea.

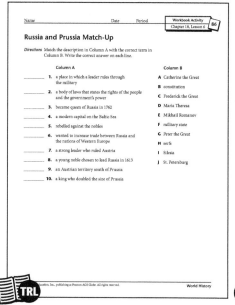

Workbook Activity 86

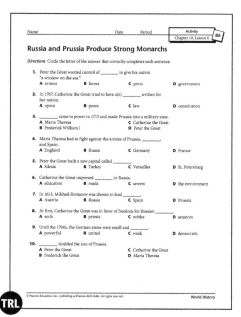

Activity 86

When Did Prussia Become a Military State?

Until the late 1600s, the German states were small and weak. This changed with the rise to power of Prussia—one of the German states. Frederick William came to power as an absolute ruler in 1713. He increased the size of the Prussian army and made Prussia into a **military state.** A military state is one in which a leader rules through the military.

How Did Prussia Expand Its Territory?

In 1740, Frederick William's great-grandson became Frederick II. He wanted to increase the size and power of Prussia. He invaded the Austrian territory of Silesia, which was south of Prussia.

At that time, Maria Theresa—a strong leader—ruled Austria. She decided to fight the Prussian army. But she had to battle more than one army. Both France and Spain wanted more power too. They invaded Austria. Then England, the Netherlands, and Russia entered the war and supported Maria Theresa. The war lasted on and off for many years.

When all the fighting ended, Maria Theresa lost Silesia to Prussia, which doubled its size. Because of his success, the Prussian people called their king Frederick the Great. By the 1790s, Prussia had become a powerful military force in Europe.

Catherine the Great of Russia was a strong ruler. She improved education and granted more religious freedom to her people.

Writing About History

Research a monarch named in this chapter. How would this ruler describe what ruling in the Age of Kings was like? In your notebook, write the monarch's response as a speech.

1519 – 1800

The Age of Kings   Chapter 18   **449**

---

2 **Teaching the Lesson**

Have students read pages 448–450 to find out how two emerging powers gained strength in Eastern Europe.

Reading Strategy:
Text Structure

Demonstrate the structure of a two-column graphic organizer and monitor student activity to check that they are using it correctly.

Ask:

- How did Peter the Great improve Russia's chances of developing trade with the world? (He built St. Petersburg on the Baltic Sea, which provides access to the Atlantic Ocean.)

- What were some ways Catherine the Great tried to make Russia more modern? (Answers will vary; students may say she improved education, allowed more religious freedom, tried to have a constitution written, and tried to give the serfs more freedom.)

- How did Frederick II try to expand Prussia's boundaries? (by invading Silesia)

- Who opposed Prussia's invasion of Silesia? Of what country was Silesia a territory? (Maria Theresa; Austria)

- Which nations sided with Frederick II against Maria Theresa's Austria? (Spain and France)

- Which nations supported Austria? (England and Russia)

- After he gained Silesia by defeating Austria, what did the Prussians call their popular king? (Frederick the Great)

- What kind of a state did Prussia become? How does the leader of such a state rule? (military state; the leader rules by using the military)

Writing About History

Have students submit a one-page research plan outlining ways that they might find out more about one of the monarchs mentioned in this chapter. Encourage them to include various library and Internet research strategies. Then have students read the Writing About History feature and write their responses in their notebooks.

Students can practice reading maps and understand Peter the Great's point of view by illustrating the routes Russian ships took to reach European countries. Give students individual blank maps, or have a group use a large classroom map. Instruct students to label or point to Russia, St. Petersburg, and the bodies of water that touch Russia. Then have students trace with their fingers or highlight with a pen the routes from the Baltic Sea to the Atlantic Ocean and from the Black Sea to the Mediterranean Sea. Ask students to explain what Peter the Great meant by calling St. Petersburg "a window for Russia to look at Europe."

3 **Reinforce and Extend**

Lesson 6 Review Answers

1. A **2.** B **3.** A **4.** D **5.** C

Answers will vary. They probably did not want Spain and France to get any more land or power.

Chapter Project Follow-up

Ways to organize the historical personality "Living Timeline" might include having each group perform in front of the timeline illustration of the time period or location for their characters, or having groups perform without identification in random order and asking the class to decide who they are and in what time period or location they belong. Assessment can be based upon a rubric of objectives distributed at the start of the project.

Lesson 6 Review On a sheet of paper, write the letter of the answer that correctly completes each sentence.

1. Peter the Great built the new Russian capital _____.

  A St. Petersburg   **C** Prussia
  B Romanov   **D** Silesia

2. _____ wanted to have warm water seaports so (s)he could trade with other European nations.

  A Catherine the Great   **C** Maria Theresa
  B Peter the Great   **D** Frederick II

3. For a while, _____ wanted to free the serfs.

  A Catherine the Great   **C** Peter the Great
  B Frederick William I   **D** Frederick II

4. _____ invaded the Austrian territory of Silesia.

  A Catherine the Great   **C** Maria Theresa
  B Peter the Great   **D** Frederick II

5. Austria's monarch, _____, had a long reign marked by many wars.

  A Frederick William I   **C** Maria Theresa
  B Frederick II   **D** Peter the Great

What do you think

Why did England and Russia support Maria Theresa in her war with Prussia and Spain?

The English Bill of Rights

As you read in Lesson 4 of this chapter, the English Parliament passed the English Bill of Rights in 1689. It gave members of Parliament more authority than kings and queens. It also said that Roman Catholics could not become kings or queens. In addition, it said that the people of England also had rights. The ideas in the English Bill of Rights spread to the colonies. These ideas helped to shape the Constitution of the United States. Here are some excerpts.

[Members of Parliament declared]

That the pretended [claimed] power of dispensing with [setting aside of] laws or the execution of laws by regal authority, as it hath been assumed and exercised of late, is illegal;

That levying [collecting] money for or to the use of the Crown by pretence of prerogative [power] without grant of Parliament, for longer time or in other manner than the same is or shall be granted, is illegal;

That it is the right of the subject to petition [request from] the king, and all commitments and prosecutions for such petitioning are illegal;

That the raising or keeping a standing army within the kingdom in time of peace, unless it be with consent of Parliament, is against law;

That election of members of Parliament ought to be free;

That the freedom of speech and debates or proceedings in Parliament ought not to be impeached [doubted] or questioned in any court or place out of Parliament;

That excessive bail ought not to be required, nor excessive fines imposed, or cruel and unusual punishments inflicted; . . .

And that, for redress [setting right] of all grievances and for the amending, strengthening, and preserving of the laws, Parliaments ought to be held frequently.

Document-Based Questions

1. How did kings and queens rule before the English Bill of Rights was passed?

2. The Magna Carta, written in 1215, limited the power of kings and queens. Why do you think the kings and queens ignored it?

3. What is one way the United States Declaration of Independence was like the English Bill of Rights?

4. Do you think that the rights demanded in the English Bill of Rights were reasonable? Why or why not?

5. Why is a document identifying the rights of its citizens important to a country?

The writers of the English Bill of Rights begin with this grievance: "Whereas the late King James the Second, by the assistance of divers evil counsellors . . . did endeavor to subvert and extirpate the Protestant religion and the laws and liberties of this kingdom. . . ." This document then continues to make Parliament stronger than the monarch. The English Bill of Rights also protects the rights of individuals by guaranteeing trial by jury for anyone accused of a crime, outlawing cruel and unusual punishment, and limiting the amount of bail that could be imposed upon an individual. The English Bill of Rights does not, however, guarantee a democratic society. At the time of the English Bill of Rights, few people had the right to vote since most members of Parliament were not paid, only the wealthy could afford to take office, and only Protestants had freedom to worship.

Have students work in pairs to rewrite the points in the English Bill of Rights in their own words.

Answers to Document-Based Questions:

1. Before the English Bill of Rights was passed, kings and queens ruled by divine right.

2. Answers will vary, but may include the ideas that the original purpose of the Magna Carta was to protect the rights and property of the nobility, and the majority of the English population did not have the voice or power to demand protection.

3. Answers will vary, but may include the ideas of the protection of individual freedoms and that no man is above the law.

4. Answers will vary, but explanations should support students' answers.

5. Answers will vary, but may include the idea that such a document provides laws to protect the rights of citizens.

Students may be unfamiliar with the way that the word *fool* is used in this reading. *Fool*, in contemporary usage, is a derogatory word. Explain that the fools discussed in "Playing the Fool" were comedians. They possessed the ability to speak freely—a valuable privilege. Have students read the Spotlight Story silently. When they finish, ask them to name some of today's fools. (Answers will vary; students may suggest late-night–variety-show hosts or comedic actors.) Also ask how they feel about the way current comedians sometimes make fun of important people. (Answers will vary; students may say it is OK because jokes are meant to make light of serious things.)

Answers to Spotlight Story Wrap-Up:

1. There were jesters at the time of the Egyptian pharaohs and ancient Romans.

2. He might be treated almost as a member by sharing meals and celebrations, playing with the children, and hearing family secrets.

3. He wore a multicolored checked coat with bells, bright-colored hose, a tight jacket with a peaked hood, and pointed shoes.

4. They amused people and sometimes pointed out unwise actions.

5. People made fun of the Catholic Church, its official, and its ceremonies.

Playing the Fool

Clowns make us laugh. So do other comic actors. They poke fun at people. They get away with pointing out people's faults. Historically, that has been their job.

Playing the fool has a long history. In earlier times, clowns were called fools or jesters. The pharaohs of ancient Egypt had fools, as did the ancient Romans.

Fools were very popular from the Middle Ages to the 1600s. Often they lived at the court of a ruler or wealthy noble. A jester sometimes seemed like a family member. He shared meals and celebrations, played with the children, and heard family secrets.

The jester's costume was a checked coat of many colors. A fool wore bright-colored hose, pointed shoes, and a tight jacket with a pointed hood. Bells jingled on his toes and coat.

Most court jesters acted silly and foolish. They danced and tumbled. They also made up clever songs and verses. They used their wit and sharp tongues to tease.

Jesters held a special place at court. They could say almost anything. Sometimes their purpose was amusement. At other times, they pointed out unwise actions. Fools could have a lot of influence. Richard Tarlton was a famous English comic actor. He was also a jester for Queen Elizabeth I. He was the only person who could criticize her. Louis XIV's court jester was called L'Angely. Nobles were afraid of his sharp wit.

Archie Armstrong was the fool for King James I of England. He was known as Count Archie. The king sent him to Spain with his ambassadors and he insulted the Spanish. Then Archie wrote the king to tell him what a good job he had done. Eventually, this jester went too far. He insulted church officials and had to leave the court, but he was already wealthy.

Even the powerful Catholic Church could not avoid foolishness. The Feast of Fools was a popular holiday, especially in France. People chose a mock pope or bishop and made fun of church ceremonies.

Court jesters lost their popularity in the 1700s. Today, clowns are only entertainers, but some comedians still carry on the jester's tradition. They say what no one else dares.

Wrap-Up

1. How long have there been jesters?

2. How was a jester like a part of a noble family?

3. What did a court jester usually wear?

4. What has been the role of court jesters and fools in history?

5. What used to happen on the Feast of Fools?

Chapter 18   SUMMARY

- As European nations developed, nationalist feelings grew. Absolute monarchs had total power over their subjects.

- Moors from North Africa occupied southern Spain in the 700s. They made Córdoba a center for learning.

- Christian kingdoms in Spain fought the Moors. Ferdinand of Aragon and Isabella of Castile united Spain. By 1492, they had conquered Granada, the last Moorish kingdom. Jews and Moors had to become Catholic or leave Spain.

- In the 1500s, Spain was more powerful than England or France. King Charles I of Spain, a Hapsburg, became the Holy Roman Emperor Charles V. This family ruled large parts of Europe. Charles defended the Catholic faith.

- Philip II, the son of Charles V, ruled Spain, part of Italy, and the Netherlands. In 1588, he sent the Spanish Armada against England to make it Catholic again. Philip failed when fast English ships and a storm sank Spanish ships.

- King James of Scotland followed Elizabeth I as England's ruler and ruled by divine right. His son Charles I fought with Parliament over money and power. Parliament made Charles sign the Petition of Right.

- Civil war broke out in England. The Cavaliers, on the king's side, were mostly Anglican or Catholic. Puritans, or "Roundheads," were Protestant. Their leader was Oliver Cromwell.

- The Puritans won the English Civil War in 1643. Charles I was tried for treason and beheaded. Cromwell set up a strict military government. In 1659, Parliament voted to restore the monarchy under King Charles II.

- In the Glorious Revolution (1688), Parliament rebelled against James II, a Catholic king. His Protestant daughter Mary and her husband, William, ruled next. They agreed to a Bill of Rights.

- Louis XIV of France became Europe's most powerful ruler. Louis fought many wars and made the central government stronger.

- Peter the Great wanted to make Russia more like Europe. He built a new capital at St. Petersburg. Later, Catherine the Great supported education and the idea of a constitution.

- Prussia, in Germany, became a military state. Its ruler Frederick II went to war against Maria Theresa, the ruler of Austria. Prussia became a powerful military force in Europe.

Using the Chapter Summary

Have students read the Chapter Summary on page 453 to review the main ideas presented in Chapter 18.

Ask:

- What form of political organization replaced feudalism after the Middle Ages? (nationalism)

- What city did the Moors build as a center for learning? (Córdoba)

- Who were the leaders in nationalist Europe? (kings, queens, and other royalty)

- In the 1500s, what country was more powerful than England or France? (Spain)

- Which event marked the beginning of Spain's decline? (its failed attack on England in 1588)

- Whose power did the English Parliament seek to control? (the king's)

- Who was the leader of the Roundheads? (Oliver Cromwell)

- What happened in the Glorious Revolution of 1688? (Parliament rebelled against James II.)

- What nation did Peter the Great rule? (Russia)

TEACHER'S RESOURCE

The AGS Globe Teaching Strategies in Social Studies Transparencies may be used with this chapter. The transparencies add an interactive dimension to expand and enhance the *World History* program content.

Chapter 18 Review

Use the Chapter Review to prepare students for tests and to reteach content from the chapter.

Chapter 18 Mastery Test

The Teacher's Resource Library includes two forms of the Chapter 18 Mastery Test. Each test addresses the chapter Goals for Learning. An optional third page of additional critical-thinking items is included for each test. The difficulty level of the two forms is equivalent.

Chapters 1–18 Midterm Mastery Test TRL

The Teacher's Resource Library includes the Midterm Mastery Test. This test is pictured on page 865 of this Teacher's Edition. The Midterm Mastery Test assesses the major learning objectives for Chapters 1–18.

Chapter 18 Review Answers

1. Hobbes
2. Isabella
3. Charles V
4. Philip II
5. James I
6. Cromwell
7. Charles I
8. Louis XIV
9. Peter
10. Catherine
11. A
12. C

Word Bank

Catherine
Charles I
Charles V
Cromwell
Hobbes
Isabella
James I
Louis XIV
Peter
Philip II

On a sheet of paper, use the words from the Word Bank to complete each sentence correctly.

1. _____ was a philosopher who believed that a powerful king should rule a nation.

2. The marriage of Ferdinand and _____ united Spain into one kingdom.

3. _____, a powerful emperor and the king of Spain, gave up his power and went to live in a monastery.

4. _____ sent a powerful Armada to invade England in 1588.

5. The English king from Scotland who believed that he ruled by divine right was _____.

6. During the English Civil War, _____ led the Roundheads.

7. _____ was the first English king to be put to death by his own people.

8. The French called _____ the "Sun King."

9. _____ the Great tried to improve his country's culture by inviting artists and scholars to Russia.

10. _____ the Great tried to have a constitution written for Russia.

On a sheet of paper, write the letter of the answer that correctly completes each sentence.

11. During the English Civil War, the _____ supported the king.

   A Cavaliers   C Parliament
   B Roundheads   D Whigs

12. During the Glorious Revolution, the _____ supported a strong Parliament.

   A Cavaliers   C Whigs
   B Roundheads   D Tories

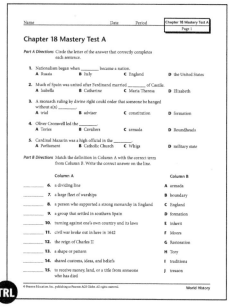

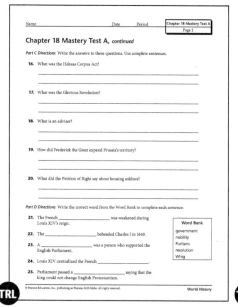

13. The _____ caused problems for Louis XIV of France.

  A nobles with armies   **C** lack of a national army
  B collection of taxes   **D** all of the above

14. Prussia doubled its territory under the leadership of _____.

  A Peter the Great   **C** Catherine the Great
  B Frederick the Great   **D** Isabella of Castile

15. The queen of Austria when Prussia attacked was _____.

  A Maria Theresa   **C** Isabella of Castile
  B Catherine the Great   **D** Elizabeth I

On a sheet of paper, write the answer to each question. Use complete sentences.

16. What is the difference between feudalism and nationalism?

17. What does ruling by "divine right" mean?

18. What is the difference between an absolute monarchy and a constitutional monarchy?

Critical Thinking On a sheet of paper, write your response to each question. Use complete sentences.

19. Do you think that the name "Sun King" was a good description of King Louis XIV? Explain your answer.

20. King Philip II said, "When Spain stirs, the earth trembles." After the defeat of his navy in 1588, what do you think Queen Elizabeth I might have said about his boast?

Pace yourself. If you are unsure about a question, put a check next to it and move on. If you have time left, go back and try to answer the checked questions.

1519 – 1800

The Age of Kings   *Chapter 18* **455**

---

13. D

14. B

15. A

16. With feudalism, people are tied to the land. They give their loyalty to nobles. With nationalism, people give their loyalty to a country.

17. To rule by divine right means to believe that God made you the ruler. God gave you the right to rule.

18. An absolute monarchy is a type of rule in which the king or queen holds unlimited power. A constitutional monarchy is a type of rule in which a nation has a king or a queen, but it also has a body of laws. These laws protect the rights of the citizens, and state the powers of the government.

Critical Thinking

19. Answers will vary. Because Louis XIV had absolute power, everything did, indeed, have to revolve around him like the planets around the sun. He believed in his divine right to rule, so people who went against him were in trouble.

20. Answers will vary. Queen Elizabeth I might have laughed in his face!

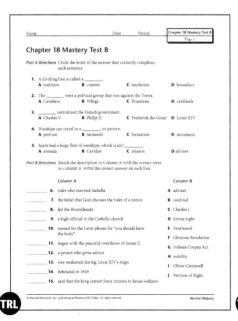

Chapter 18 Mastery Test B, pages 1–3

The Age of Kings   *Chapter 18* **455**

Demonstrate several examples of cause and effect, as follows.

- Remove a doorstop and allow the door to close.
- Place a book too close to the edge of a desk and let the book fall off the desk.
- Feel the soil around a potted plant, remark that the soil is dry, and water the plant.

As you perform one of the above demonstrations, state what you are doing as a cause and an effect. For example, "Because I removed the doorstop, the door closed. The cause was removing the doorstop; the effect was the door closing."

Ask:

- Was the falling book a cause or an effect? (an effect)
- The plant received water. Was this a cause or an effect? (an effect)
- Why did the plant receive water? (the soil was dry) Is this a cause or an effect? (a cause)

Have students read the Skill Builder on page 456 and then copy and label the sentences as *cause* or *effect* in each part.

Unit 3 Skill Builder Answers

1. first part: cause; second part: effect
2. first part: effect; second part: cause
3. first part: cause; second part: effect
4. first part: effect; second part: cause
5. first part: effect; second part: cause

Unit Skills Activity

Write the words *Cause* and *Effect* on the board and draw an arrow pointing from *Cause* to *Effect*. Then ask a volunteer to write a pair of cause-and-effect sentences on the board, putting each sentence under the appropriate label. Review with students why one sentence is a cause and the other is an effect. Then distribute copies of the Unit 3 Skill Builder for students to complete.

Unit 3

Skill Builder

Cause and Effect

Looking for causes and effects will help you better understand what you read. An effect is something that happens as a result of a cause. One cause may have several effects. To determine causes and effects, ask these questions:

> Why did the event happen? (cause)
>
> What made the event happen? (cause)
>
> What triggered an event? (cause)
>
> What happened as a result of the event? (effect)
>
> What happened because of that event? (effect)

Here is an example of one cause and effect related to the Hundred Years' War:

Cause: The French wanted control of the English province of Gascony.

Effect: The English fought to keep their control of Gascony.

In the next column are more causes and effects related to the Hundred Years' War. Read each pair of sentences. Decide which statement is the cause and which is the effect. Rewrite each sentence on your paper. Label it with "cause" or "effect."

1. France's king died without a male heir.

   Edward III of England was the French king's nephew. He thought the French throne should go to him.

2. Edward III landed an army in Normandy. It was part of his plan to get the French throne.

   Edward III decided to take the French throne by force.

3. The English developed the longbow.

   The English beat the French in battle.

4. Joan of Arc beat the English at Orléans, Patay, and Reims.

   Joan of Arc said that she saw visions from heaven. They told her to lead the French against the English. French soldiers believed what she told them.

5. England had to give up all its land in France except for Calais.

   The French won many battles and the Hundred Years' War.

Name _____ Date _____ Period _____ | **Unit Skills Activity** Unit 3

Cause and Effect

Directions Read the following paragraphs about the Renaissance. Note the causes and effects. Then fill out the cause-and-effect charts below. If a cause is given in the chart, write its effect. If an effect is given, write its cause.

In the 14th century, Western Europe struggled through hard times. Workers were paid low wages and food was expensive. People who did not get enough food often died. In the early 1300s, almost 10 percent of Western Europeans died. To make things worse, the Bubonic Plague hit Western Europe in 1348. Millions of Europeans died because of the plague called the Black Death.

Europe's population was greatly decreased. Fewer people in the work force meant that employers had to pay their workers more money. It also meant that less food was needed to feed the smaller population, so the price of food dropped. Many farmers left the country to find work somewhere else.

These peasant farmers did not like the laws of their society. They began to demand changes and question old beliefs. In 1381, some English peasants rebelled against King Richard II. This was the beginning of a great change of thinking in Europe. People wanted to be more creative and independent. They studied the art, literature, science, and philosophy of ancient Greece and Rome. This period of new learning is called the Renaissance. It ended the Middle Ages in Europe.

Cause	Effect
1. Food was expensive in the 1300s in Western Europe.	
2.	Millions of Europeans died, and Europe's population greatly decreased.
3. The price of food dropped.	
4.	They rebelled against King Richard II.
5.	The Middle Ages in Europe ended.

© Pearson Education, Inc., publishing as Pearson AGS Globe. All rights reserved. | **World History**

Unit Skills Activity

Unit 3   S U M M A R Y

- The Renaissance began about 1350. It was a time of creativity and learning.

- Education, art, and science were important during the Renaissance.

- Great Renaissance writers include Shakespeare and Cervantes. Important artists include da Vinci, Michelangelo, and Raphael.

- The Protestant Reformation began in the 1400s.

- Martin Luther questioned the teachings of the church. His actions led to the Reformation. Luther started the Lutheran Church in about 1530.

- King Henry VIII of England began the Anglican Church after the pope refused to allow his divorce.

- The Catholic Church began a Catholic Reformation, which led to the Roman Inquisition.

- The Reformation split Europe into Catholic and Protestant areas.

- During the 1500s, scholars began to investigate the natural world. Francis Bacon worked out the scientific method in the 1620s.

- In 1543, Copernicus said the earth traveled around the sun. Galileo built a telescope and concluded that Copernicus was right. The Catholic Church tried to stop Galileo's work.

- Isaac Newton studied light and color; he also discovered how gravity works.

- Advances were made in the study of the human body. Magnetism and electricity were discovered.

- Mathematics, geometry, and calculus, along with the microscope and thermometer, were important scientific tools.

- In the 1400s, explorers from many European countries began to look for new trade routes.

- Columbus and da Gama tried to reach Asia. Magellan proved that the world is round during his trip of 1519 to 1522.

- Cortés and Pizzaro destroyed Indian empires in Mexico and South America. The land became the colony of New Spain.

- The English founded the colonies of Jamestown in 1607 and Plymouth in 1620. Champlain founded Quebec in 1608.

- In the 1500s, Spain was more powerful than England or France.

- Civil war broke out between the Catholics and Protestant Puritans in England; the Puritans won in 1643.

- In France, Louis XIV became Europe's most powerful ruler.

1348 – 1800

Early Modern Times   Unit 3   457

Using the Unit Summary

Read and discuss the Unit Summary statements on page 457 with students.

Ask:

- **What subjects were important during the Renaissance?** (education, art, science)

- **Whose actions led to the Protestant Reformation?** (Martin Luther) **What did he do?** (He questioned the teachings of the Catholic Church. He started the Lutheran Church.)

- **What decision by the Pope led to the formation of the Anglican Church in England?** (The Pope refused to give King Henry VIII a divorce.)

- **What was the result of the Reformation and Counter-Reformation?** (Europe was split into Catholic countries and Protestant countries.)

- **Who were three scientists of the 16th and 17th centuries? What were their ideas?** (Copernicus believed that Earth traveled around the sun. Galileo concluded that Copernicus was right. Newton made discoveries about light, color, and gravity.)

- **What were Columbus, da Gama, and Magellan looking for?** (new trade routes to Asia) **What did they find?** (the New World)

- **What two American colonies were begun by the English?** (Jamestown and Plymouth)

- **What two groups fought each other in the English civil war?** (Catholics fought the Protestant Puritans.)

Unit 3 Mastery Test

The Teacher's Resource Library includes a two-page Unit Mastery Test. An optional third page of additional critical-thinking items is included for each test. The Unit 3 Mastery Test is pictured on page 862 of this Teacher's Edition.

Unit Activity Follow-Up

Follow up on Unit 3, Activity 1 by asking students to read their interpretations of the prologue sentences from *Romeo and Juliet*. Follow up on Unit 3, Activity 2 by asking students to explain whether or not they think Shakespeare was one of the greatest writers ever born. Students should give reasons for their opinions.

Planning Guide
Enlightenment and Revolution

	Student Text Lesson					
	Student Pages	Vocabulary	Lesson Review	Critical-Thinking Questions	Chapter Summary	Chapter Review
Chapter 19 The Age of Reason	460–481	✔		✔	479	480
Lesson 1 In Search of Natural Laws	463–464	✔	464	✔		
Lesson 2 New Theories on Government	465–468	✔	468	✔		
Lesson 3 The Influence of Enlightened Thinkers	469–473	✔	473	✔		
Lesson 4 Enlightenment Ideas Influence Artists	474–476	✔	476	✔		
Chapter 20 Revolutions and Napoleon	482–511	✔		✔	509	510
Lesson 1 Revolution in the American Colonies	485–487	✔	487	✔		
Lesson 2 The American Revolutionary War	488–492	✔	492	✔		
Lesson 3 The French Revolution	493–495	✔	495	✔		
Lesson 4 Revolutionary Reforms and Terror in France	496–499	✔	499	✔		
Lesson 5 Napoleon and the French Empire	500–506	✔	506	✔		
Chapter 21 The Industrial Revolution Begins	512–539	✔		✔	537	538
Lesson 1 The Industrial Revolution Begins in England	515–518	✔	518	✔		
Lesson 2 The Growth of the First Modern Industries	519–523	✔	523	✔		
Lesson 3 Transportation Improves	524–528	✔	528	✔		
Lesson 4 Industry Brings Changes and Problems	529–534	✔	534	✔		
Chapter 22 Revolutions in Europe and Latin America	540–567	✔		✔	565	566
Lesson 1 The Congress of Vienna Meets	543–545	✔	545	✔		
Lesson 2 Nationalism Becomes Powerful	546–547	✔	547	✔		
Lesson 3 Wars for Independence in Latin America	548–552	✔	552	✔		
Lesson 4 New Revolution and Reform in Europe	553–556	✔	556	✔		
Lesson 5 The Year of Revolutions—1848	557–562	✔	562	✔		

Unit Activities

Student Text
Unit 4 Summary
Unit 4 Skill Builder

Teacher's Resource Library
Unit 4 Activities 1–2
Unit 4 Skills Activity

Assessment Options

Teacher's Resource Library
Chapter 19 Mastery Tests A and B
Chapter 20 Mastery Tests A and B
Chapter 21 Mastery Tests A and B
Chapter 22 Mastery Tests A and B
Unit 4 Mastery Test

	Student Text Features											Teaching Strategies						Learning Styles					Teacher's Resource Library			
Reading Strategy	Map Study/Map Skills	Writing About History	Geography Note	Biography	History in Your Life	Communication in History	Technology Connection	Then and Now	Spotlight Story	Document-Based Reading	Background Information	Applications (Home, Career, Community)	World Cultures	Study Skills	Online Connection	ELL/ESL Strategy	Auditory/Verbal	Visual/Spatial	Body/Kinesthetic	Interpersonal/Group Learning	Logical/Mathematical	Activities/Modified Activities	Workbook Activities	Self-Study Guide	Chapter Outline
---	---	---	---	---	---	---	---	---	---	---	---	---	---	---	---	---	---	---	---	---	---	---	---	---	---
462	461								478	477														✔	✔
✔				464												464						87	87		
✔							468					466		467	466	468						88	88		
✔		471	472									470	472	473		471		472	470			89	89		
✔												476		475		475	475				476	90	90		
484	483								508	507									508					✔	✔
✔			485	487								487		486		486						91	91		
✔	490				492							489			492	491	489	490				92	92		
✔												494				495					495	93	93		
✔													499			497						94	94		
✔	504	505		501							505					501				503		95	95		
514	513								536	535														✔	✔
✔	516		517			518									518	517	516					96	96		
✔												521		520		521			523	522		97	97		
✔	525				528						526					527		525				98	98		
✔		531	530	532								530, 532	531			534					533	99	99		
542	541								564	563						541								✔	✔
✔	544	545										545				544		545				100	100		
✔				547							547		547									101	101		
✔	551		550												552	550			552	549	550	102	102		
✔					556							556		554		555	555					103	103		
✔				561							558	562		559		558		560				104	104		

TRL Activities

The Teacher's Resource Library (TRL) contains a set of lower-level worksheets called Modified Activities. These worksheets cover the same content as the standard Activities but are written at a lower reading level.

Skill Track

Use Skill Track for *World History* to monitor student progress and meet the demands of Adequate Yearly Progress (AYP). Make informed instructional decisions with individual student and class reports of lesson and chapter assessments. With immediate and ongoing feedback, students will also see what they have learned and where they need more reinforcement and practice.

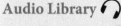

"You cannot hope to build a better world without improving the individuals. To that end each of us must work for his own improvement, and . . . share a general responsibility for all humanity, our particular duty being to aid those to whom we think we can be most useful."

~ *Marie Curie, from her* Autobiographical Notes, *1891*

Other Resources

Books for Teachers

Mozart, Wolfgang Amadeus. Rose, M. and P. Washington, ed. *Letters.* New York: Alfred A Knopf, 2007.

Nelson, Craig. *Thomas Paine: Enlightenment, Revolution, and the Birth of Modern Nations.* New York: Viking Press, 2006.

Books for Students

Stark, Sam. *Diderot: French Philosopher and Father of the Encyclopedia.* New York: Rosen Publishing Group, 2006.

Whitelaw, Nancy. *Catherine the Great and the Enlightenment in Russia.* Greensboro, North Carolina: Morgan Reynolds Publishing, 2005.

CD-ROM/Software

World History: the French Revolution. Planet CDROM (MAC/XP/Vista), multimedia and interactive.

World History: the Industrial Revolution. Planet CDROM (MAC/XP/Vista), multimedia and interactive.

Videos

Inspired by Bach. (50 minutes) Sony Classical, 2000. (Yo-Yo Ma performing Bach's Cello Suite No.1)

Industrial Revolution. (44 minutes) Educational Video Network, 2004. (describes how the Industrial Revolution transformed society, beginning in England)

The French Revolution. (1 hour) The History Channel, 2005. (describes the causes and events of the French Revolution)

Web Sites

www.agsglobewh.com/page458a (interactive site on the life of Napoleon Bonaparte)

www.agsglobewh.com/page458b (provides a summary of economic factors leading to the early 19th century Industrial Revolution)

Unit 4

Enlightenment and Revolution

I n this unit, you will meet thinkers who wanted to use reason to improve society. These enlightened people include rulers, writers, and composers. You will march with revolutionaries in search of freedom. You will learn about factories and how the industrial revolution changed the lives of workers. And you will read about revolutions that changed the face of Europe and Latin America.

459

Introducing the Unit

Tell students that Unit 4 introduces a time when military and industrial revolutions changed societies in many regions of the world. Write the word *revolution* on the board. Ask students what impact they think a revolution has on a society in terms of social, political, and economic change. List their ideas on the board under the word *revolution*.

Then read the quote from Marie Curie on page 458 and the title of Unit 4 on page 459. Ask students to define the term *enlightenment* and note their ideas on the board. Then, as a unit overview, have students read through the list of chapter titles appearing in Unit 4. Point out that revolution in one region of the world had a direct impact on political and economical events in other regions. Together, page through the unit, pausing to discuss the photographs and drawings that capture students' interest.

Ask:

- In what way do you think revolutions change society?
(Answers will vary. Governments change; land is taken or divided; cultures are influenced or altered.)

Read aloud the quote on page 458 again, but this time pause after each phrase to allow students to explain their understanding of Marie Curie's words. Ask students to write a sentence that summarizes the quote and have volunteers share their sentences with the class.

Presenting the Unit Activity

Assign Unit 4, Activity 1 to help students gain an understanding of the variety of inventions during the 18th and 19th centuries. If possible, create categories of inventions, such as inventions in the areas of textile manufacturing, communications, industry, and transportation. Assign students to a particular category for study. Have student share their information.

Use Unit 4, Activity 2 to help students recognize that inventions can have both positive and negative effects. At the conclusion of the activity, write the names of several inventions on the board. Ask students to share their findings on the positive and negative effects of this sampling of inventions.

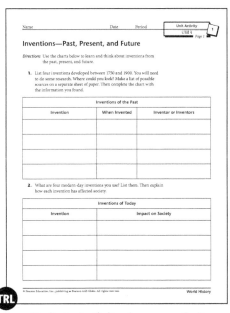

Unit 4, Activity 1, pages 1–2   Unit 4, Activity 2

Enlightenment and Revolution Unit 4 **459**

Introducing the Chapter

The Age of Reason in Europe was an
exciting time. People found new ways of
looking at the world and its place in the
solar system. They also looked differently
at government and its relationship
to its people. European scholars and
enlightened rulers contributed their
views and implemented changes.

The Age of Reason

In 1687, Isaac Newton published an important scientific
book. It changed the way people thought about the universe
and about society. His scientific reasoning led to the Age of
Reason. In this chapter, you will learn about people like Locke
and Voltaire who had theories about people and government.
You will spend time with enlightened rulers like Maria Theresa
of Austria. You will experience the wonder of the music of
Mozart—a musical genius. They will all help you understand
the belief that order and balance rule the universe.

Goals for Learning

- To explain how Isaac Newton's work influenced the
  Age of Reason and why historians call this historical
  period the Age of Reason
- To explain the views of three important philosophers
  of this time
- To describe the period called the Enlightenment
- To name enlightened thinkers, rulers, musicians,
  and writers

1651 Hobbes publishes book on absolute power

1690 Locke publishes book on human rights

1748 Montesquieu publishes book on three types of government

1774 Empress Maria Theresa establishes school for children

1650 — 1700 — 1750 — 1800

Newton publishes book about the Universal Law of Gravitation

1726 Swift publishes *Gulliver's Travels*

1762 Rousseau publishes book on the general will

Ask:

- Which years does this timeline
  cover? Which centuries? (1650–
  1800; 17th and 18th centuries)

- How many events on this timeline
  relate to the publication of a
  book? (six)

- Which book's title is mentioned?
  Who was its author? (*Gulliver's
  Travels*; Swift)

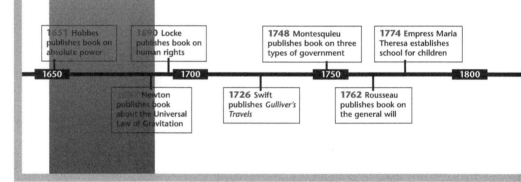

Chapter 19 Self-Study Guide, pages 1–2

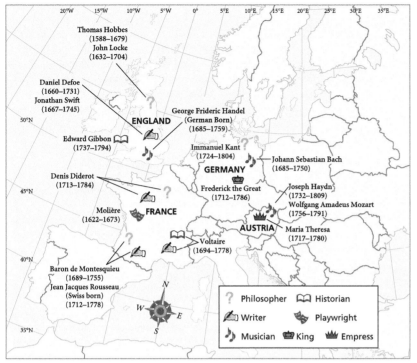

During the Age of Reason—from about 1687 to 1789—many famous people tried to think reasonably about government, the arts, and society. They made important contributions to history, philosophy, and culture. We remember some of them for their novels and plays. We remember others for the music they wrote. We remember many of them for the way they changed people's ways of thinking.

Study the map, then answer the following questions:

1. In what country did Bach write his music?

2. In what year did the philosopher John Locke die?

3. In what year was Maria Theresa of Austria born?

4. For what is Molière famous?

5. In what country did the historian Edward Gibbon live?

1687 – 1789

Remind students of the title of the chapter. Then ask a volunteer to read the map title, "Notable People (1687–1789)." Ask students why they think the people on the map are notable.

Ask:

- During which years did the events on this map take place? (1687–1789)

- Which countries are represented by notable people? (Germany, England, Austria, and France)

- What kind of contributions did these notable people make? (Answers will vary; students may mention that they wrote books or music)

Have students read the paragraph below the map, and then read and answer the questions.

Map Skills Answers

1. Germany
2. 1704
3. 1717
4. He was a playwright.
5. England

Chapter Project

Organize the class into three groups, and assign each group to one of the following topics: Enlightenment Thinkers, Enlightenment Rulers, or Music and Literature of the Enlightenment. Students will use Internet and library resources to research their assigned topic for a class display on the Enlightenment. Tell students that they will also need to gather visual images to illustrate their section of the display. Remind students that all members in their group should be included in researching and producing the final product.

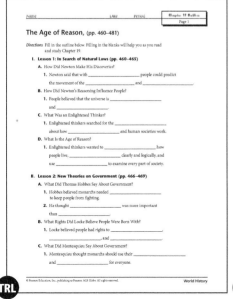

Chapter 19 Outline, pages 1–3

Visualizing

Emphasize that visualizing helps individuals remember what they have read. Explain that some concepts, such as the ideas of the Enlightenment, can be difficult to grasp. Visualizing, or making pictures of the words in your mind, helps. For example, the concept of liberty may be difficult to understand. However, by visualizing people moving freely from place to place, the word *liberty* gains meaning.

Ask:

- What do you visualize when you think of the word *prejudice*? (Answers will vary; students may use an example of prejudice in their community or in the media.)

- What do you visualize when you think of the word *symphony*? (Answers will vary; I visualize several people playing different instruments in a grand concert hall.)

- What do you visualize when you think of the word *classical*? (Answers will vary; I think of people wearing wigs and playing violins.)

Key Vocabulary Words

Point out that these chapter words are presented in the order they appear in each lesson. They are also found in the Glossary. Explain that students should use visualizing when reading to help them understand and remember what they read.

Ask:

- Which key vocabulary words are the easiest to visualize? (Answers will vary; *salon, symphony*)

- Which key vocabulary words are the most difficult to visualize? (Answers will vary; *Enlightenment, ban*)

- How is visualizing a helpful reading strategy? (Answers will vary; Visualizing helps me remember words because I make pictures of them in my mind.)

Reading Strategy:
Visualizing

Visualizing is like creating a movie in your mind. It is also a strategy to help you understand what you are reading. These are some ways you can visualize a text:

◆ As you read this chapter, notice the images of people from this time in history. How does this help you visualize the events described in the chapter?

◆ Think about experiences in your own life that may add to the images. For example, does a salon sound like an early online "chat room"?

Key Vocabulary Words

Lesson 1
Enlightened Having a belief in reasoning; moving away from ignorance

Lesson 2
Contract A legal agreement

Lesson 3
Enlightenment A time in European history when thinkers and writers tried to solve the problems of society by using reason

Salon A meeting of artists, writers, and thinkers in a Paris home during the Enlightenment

Prejudice An unfair and unreasonable opinion

Ban To get rid of; to make something not legal

Lesson 4
Classical A type of music from the 1700s and early 1800s that is orderly and balanced; in the style of ancient Greece or Rome

Symphony A long musical work played by a group of musicians using many different instruments

OBJECTIVES

◆ To explain how Isaac Newton influenced other people

◆ To list the three goals of the Age of Reason

In Chapter 16, you learned about Isaac Newton and his Universal Law of Gravitation. In 1687, he published his law in a book. In it, he showed how this law applied to the universe. He also showed how to use mathematics to describe the law.

How Did Newton Make His Discoveries?

Newton discovered these things using reason, or thinking in a logical way. He did not experiment. Instead, by reason alone, he discovered a mathematical law that controls the movement of planets and other objects in space.

Reading Strategy:
Visualizing

Visualize the clock mentioned in this paragraph. How does this image help you understand the way people began to view the universe?

How Did Newton's Reasoning Influence People?

After reading Newton's book, people began to think of the universe as a kind of huge clock. A clock ticks off the minutes of the day in a predictable, orderly way. They believed that the universe works this way too. It is predictable. That is, people can discover what will happen in the universe.

Newton influenced many scientists. They decided to use careful, scientific reasoning to find the truth about how nature worked. He influenced nonscientists too. They now knew that nature followed natural laws. Perhaps other natural laws controlled the actions of human beings. If so, then scientific reasoning was a tool. They could use this tool to solve the problems of society.

Enlightened

Having a belief in reasoning; moving away from ignorance

What Was an Enlightened Thinker?

People who believed in scientific reasoning called themselves **enlightened** thinkers. They had found the light! No longer did they walk in the darkness of ignorance, or lack of knowledge. Enlightened thinkers asked difficult questions. They searched for the truth about how nature and human societies really work.

1687 – 1789

The Age of Reason Chapter 19 **463**

Overview This lesson explains the profound impact of Isaac Newton's process of reasoning.

Objectives

■ To explain how Isaac Newton influenced other people

■ To list the three goals of the Age of Reason

Student Pages pages 463–464

Teacher's Resource Library TRL

Workbook Activity 87

Activity 87

Modified Activity 87

Vocabulary

enlightened

Have students share what they visualize when they think of the word *light*. Explain that being enlightened means to bring light to an idea through reason and knowledge. Have students generate sentences using the word *enlightened*.

1 Warm-Up Activity

Present students with the following problem: If you put a small coin into an empty bottle and replace the cork, how would you get the coin out of the bottle without taking out the cork or breaking the bottle? (Push the cork into the bottle and shake out the coin.) Have students use reasoning to address the problem and to generate possible answers until a reasonable solution is reached. This brain teaser and others can be found at www. agsglobewh.com/page463.

2 Teaching the Lesson

Have students look back through the pages of Chapter 16 to recall what they learned about the work of Isaac Newton. Students should share recollections. Then have them read pages 463–464 to find out the effect Newton's writing had on other people's way of looking at the world.

Ask:

- What kind of laws did Newton think controlled the universe? (natural laws)
- What did people who believed in scientific reasoning say about themselves? (Answers will vary; students will probably say that they saw themselves as being enlightened.)

Reading Strategy: Visualizing

Have students share their mental images of what the clock looks like. Ask a volunteer who enjoys drawing to create the image on the board as students offer their descriptions. Then have students answer the Reading Strategy question. (Answers will vary; Visualizing helps me better understand how Newton and others thought about the workings of the universe.)

Ask:

- What did enlightened thinking replace? (ignorance)
- What age was inspired by the enlightened views of Newton? (Age of Reason)

Reading Strategy: Visualizing

(Student pictures should depict the ability to learn about improving people's lives, thinking clearly and without feelings, and using reasoning to understand education, government, and so on.)

Have students read to find out how even people who thought themselves to be enlightened could be fooled. When students finish, ask them to share any commercials they have heard or seen that might make one suspect quackery. You can prompt discussion by asking if they have ever heard a claim that seems too good to be true.

Fake Science and Miracle Cures

Even in the Age of Reason, people could be fooled. They bought "miracle cures" from "quacks." Quacks were individuals who offered fake cures for illnesses. The name *quack* came from their loud sales talk. Quacks often used scientific-sounding explanations and names for their cures.

One quack treated patients with tools called "Metallic Tractors." He said the tractor could draw a sickness out of someone. This idea fooled even great thinkers such as Benjamin Franklin.

The German Franz Mesmer used a mysterious force called "animal magnetism."

In this treatment, patients sat around a tub of water and held hands. Animal magnetism was then supposed to flow through them. Mesmer also used a kind of hypnotism, which put people into a trancelike state. Later, doctors used this technique.

In England, many people were convinced that a woman named Mary Tofts could give birth to rabbits! She became so popular, the king of England was willing to support her. However, it was found out that she was a fake. She was secretly buying rabbits at a local market. She and many others had fooled everyone during a time when science and careful thinking were popular.

Reading Strategy: Visualizing

Draw a picture to help you remember the three goals of enlightened thinkers.

What do you think

Are there natural laws that can help us predict how people will act? Explain your answer.

What Is the Age of Reason?

Newton's ideas helped begin the Age of Reason. During this age, many enlightened thinkers had three goals:

1. They wanted to improve how people live.

2. They wanted to think clearly and logically, without letting their feelings guide them.

3. They wanted to use scientific reasoning to examine every part of society—education, religion, economics, law, and government.

Lesson 1 Review On a sheet of paper, write the answer to each question. Use complete sentences.

1. How did Newton discover natural laws?

2. In what way are Newton's ideas of the universe like a clock?

3. Why did people who believed in scientific reasoning think of themselves as enlightened?

4. How did enlightened thinkers search for the truth?

5. During the Age of Reason, enlightened thinkers had three goals. What were they?

---

3 Reinforce and Extend

ELL/ESL STRATEGY

Language Objective: *To describe the contributions of enlightened thinkers*

ELL students may have difficulty linking the people in this chapter with their contributions. Pair them with English-proficient students; have them listen to the recording of the chapter together. Have students write down the name, nation, and contribution of each person as they listen. Then have students tell their partners what they learned about each person.

Lesson 1 Review Answers

1. He discovered these by using reason. **2.** Just as a clock ticks off minutes, the universe also works in a predictable pattern. **3.** They had gained knowledge and could now ask difficult questions. **4.** They searched for truth by asking difficult questions. **5.** The goals were to improve people's lives, to think clearly and logically, and to use reasoning to understand society.

Answers will vary. Students should respond that there are some simple human behaviors that can be predicted. However, for complex situations and circumstances, people are often very difficult to predict.

Objectives

- To compare the views of Thomas Hobbes and John Locke
- To understand Baron de Montesquieu's idea of balance of powers
- To explain Jean Rousseau's views concerning the general will

Contract

A legal agreement

The enlightened thinkers of the Age of Reason asked questions about government. What was the best form of government? Are there natural laws that people should follow in setting up a government? These thinkers used logic and reason to find answers.

What Did Thomas Hobbes Say About Government?

In 1651, English philosopher Thomas Hobbes published a book on government. According to Hobbes, at one time people lived without any government. Their lives were short and unhappy. At some point, people agreed to give up their freedom to a ruler to gain order and safety.

Hobbes thought that an agreement existed between the ruler and the ruled. Under this agreement, people agreed to obey the rulers even if they ruled poorly. Hobbes said that monarchs needed absolute power to keep people from fighting among themselves. For Hobbes, order was more important than freedom.

What Rights Did Locke Believe People Were Born With?

In 1690, Englishman John Locke published another book on government. Like Hobbes, Locke thought that government should keep order in a society. He also thought that government was a **contract**, or legal agreement, between the ruler and those who are ruled. But the two men had different ideas too. For example, Locke believed that people were reasonable. Given the chance, they would act in an orderly manner.

John Locke said every person has the right to life, property, and liberty. He thought government should protect these rights.

1687 – 1789

The Age of Reason   Chapter 19   465

Chapter 19: Lesson 2

Overview With enlightened thinking came an array of ideas about the purpose of government and the obligations of the governed. This lesson explains the contributions of Hobbes, Locke, Montesquieu, and Rousseau to the intellectual discussion.

Objectives

- To compare the views of Thomas Hobbes and John Locke
- To understand Baron de Montesquieu's idea of balance of powers
- To explain Jean Rousseau's views concerning the general will

Student Pages pages 465–468

Teacher's Resource Library

Workbook Activity 88

Activity 88

Modified Activity 88

Vocabulary

contract

Discuss the difference between a written and oral contract. Discuss the importance of contracts and where they would be necessary, such as in buying a house or car. Have the class create and sign a contract for the completion of work in Lesson 2. Write and retain the contract, complete with signatures, on the board.

1 Warm-Up Activity

Have students refer to a copy of the *United States Declaration of Independence.* Together, read through the second paragraph of the document. Have students identify the reasons behind the writing of the *Declaration.* Write these reasons on the board as students identify them. Refer to these reasons as students complete Lesson 2. Help students recognize the influence of John Locke and other enlightened thinkers on the framers of America's government.

Teaching the Lesson

Have students recall the name of the age in which the enlightened thinkers lived. Then ask them to read pages 465–468 to find out what enlightened thinkers reasoned about government and the people who are ruled by a government.

Ask:

- Which writer thought the king or queen should have absolute power? (Hobbes)

- When did Locke think that people acquired rights? (when they were born)

- What rights did Locke think the people had? (life, property, and liberty, or freedom)

- What did Montesquieu call goodness? (virtue)

- Who thought that government should be separated into three branches? What were the branches? (Montesquieu; Parliament, the king, the courts)

Reading Strategy: **Visualizing**

(Parliament made the laws—legislative branch, the king enforced the laws—executive branch, and the courts interpreted the laws—judicial branch. Separation of powers between three branches created a system of checks and balances.)

ONLINE CONNECTION

The Web Site www. agsglobewh.com/page466 provides a complete biography of John Locke. Students can also link to his other writings.

Unlike Hobbes, Locke believed that people had rights. He believed that they were born with three rights: the right to life; property; and liberty. The job of government was to protect these rights. Locke said that people kept these rights even when they agreed to be governed. He believed that people had a right to rebel when the ruler or government did not protect their rights.

In France, Baron de Montesquieu believed that the government must have separate branches to divide the power.

What Did Montesquieu Say About Government?

Across the English Channel in France, two enlightened thinkers also published books about government. One of them was Baron de Montesquieu. He studied the government of ancient Rome and governments in his own time. Then, in 1748, he published a book about his studies.

Montesquieu thought that the best monarchs used their wealth and power for the good of everyone. Virtue, or goodness to one another, held a republic together. Montesquieu said that people in a republic needed to elect people who would serve the good of the community.

What Are Separate Powers?

Montesquieu admired the English government of the 1700s. It divided power into three branches.

1. Parliament made the laws.

2. The king enforced the laws.

3. The courts interpreted the laws.

Reading Strategy: **Visualizing**

Make a chart showing the three branches of the English government of the 1700s. How did this division keep any one branch from becoming too powerful?

CAREER CONNECTION

Today, discovering the general will of the people is an important business. What kind of cars will people buy? What kind of books will they read? Market researchers try to answer these questions for makers of cars, books, and countless other products. Market researchers check the pulse of the marketplace by asking a sample of people their views. Students interested in these fields should check reference sources in the library or on the Internet.

Montesquieu said that separating these powers kept each of the three branches from becoming too powerful. Each branch checked and balanced the powers of the two other branches.

How Did Rousseau Differ from Hobbes?

The other French thinker and writer of this time was Jean Jacques Rousseau. Rousseau said that people had once done only good things. They began to do bad things when civilizations developed.

This was just the opposite of what Hobbes had said. The English philosopher believed that people were born greedy and selfish. Civilization made them responsible and orderly.

Rousseau turned Hobbes's idea upside down. He said that people were born good and that civilization made them do bad things. "Man is born free," he wrote, "but everywhere he is in chains."

Rousseau strongly believed that peasants were just as good as kings and nobles. He said that no one was better than anyone else, so no one should have any special privileges, or rights. All were equal.

Reading Strategy:
Visualizing

Create a graphic organizer that shows how the views of Montesquieu and Rousseau are alike and different.

What Did Rousseau Mean by "General Will"?

In 1762, Rousseau published his book on government. In it, he disagreed with Hobbes and Locke and their idea of a contract between the ruler and the ruled. Rousseau said that in order to get along, people made a contract with each other, not with a ruler. He thought that shared customs, traditions, and values held together a community of people.

Rousseau called these shared customs, traditions, and values the "general will." According to Rousseau, a community expressed what it wanted through its general will. Because of this, Rousseau favored rule by the majority.

Ask:
- Who said that people were born free? (Rousseau)
- What did Rousseau mean when he talked about the "general will" of the people? (the shared customs, traditions, and values of a people)
- What kind of rule did Rousseau favor? (majority)
- Who did Rousseau think were better, peasants or kings and queens? (neither—he thought all people were equal)

Reading Strategy:
Visualizing

Have students brainstorm about the views of Montesquieu and Rousseau. List their ideas on the board. Then have students create a Venn diagram or similar graphic organizer to show the similarities and differences between the two philosophers. (Montesquieu: Monarchs use their wealth and power for the good of everyone, virtue holds a republic together, and people should elect leaders. Rousseau: People are born good, man is born free, civilization makes people do bad things, all people are of equal status, and no groups should have special status over another group.)

STUDY SKILLS

Invite students to create a chart to organize the views that the people named in this section had about government. They can title the chart *About Governments and People.* Have students set up two columns—*Person* and *Views.* Encourage students to enter information on the chart as they read this lesson.

Have students read "An Enlightened Government" to find out more about Montesquieu's ideas and where they were put into practice.

 3 Reinforce and Extend

Lesson 2 Review Answers

1. Hobbes thought that monarchs with absolute power should rule.
2. John Locke believed that we are born with three basic rights: the right to life, liberty, and property. **3.** Montesquieu thought that powers should be separated so that no branch of government would get too powerful. **4.** Rousseau thought that people were born good and that civilization spoiled them. Hobbes believed people were born uncivilized and that government brought them order. **5.** According to Rousseau, a community expressed what it wanted through its shared customs, traditions, and values, or its general will.

Answers will vary. Locke's theory still appeals to people today because the rights of life, property, and liberty are still important.

An Enlightened Government

Montesquieu thought that a government should have three parts. If political power were split, no one group would have too much power. Each branch would balance the other. This idea has become a driving force for many governments today.

These ideas were put to practice in England first; then they spread to America. Americans such as Thomas Jefferson and James Madison had studied Locke and Montesquieu. In 1787, Americans who believed in these ideas designed a government based on "separation of powers." It had three branches. The legislative branch made laws, the executive branch carried them out, and the judicial branch decided what the laws mean. The United States government and other governments still use this system.

Lesson 2 Review On a sheet of paper, write the answer to each question. Use complete sentences.

1. According to Thomas Hobbes, who should rule a government?

2. With what rights did John Locke believe people were born?

3. Why did Montesquieu believe that powers should be separated into several branches of government?

4. What did Rousseau say about people that was different from what Hobbes said?

5. What does Rousseau's term "general will" mean?

 What do you think

Why might Locke's theory of rights appeal to people today?

- To explain how the Paris salons helped advance the Enlightenment
- To describe the importance of Diderot's encyclopedia

Enlightenment

A time in European history when thinkers and writers tried to solve the problems of society by using reason

Salon

A meeting of artists, writers, and thinkers in a Paris home during the Enlightenment

Reading Strategy:
Visualizing

Study the image on this page. Does this help you visualize how a gathering might have looked?

Enlightened thinkers wanted to improve government. They also wanted to change or reform unreasonable customs and traditions. They asked society to allow people to have political, economic, and religious freedom. In fact, they thought that more liberty could improve the lives of everyone.

What Is the Enlightenment?

During the middle 1700s, many French writers and artists criticized their society. They wanted to use reason to solve society's problems. Their writings began a movement that historians call the **Enlightenment.** Enlightened thinkers lived all over Europe, but Paris became the center of the Enlightenment.

What Was a Salon?

Enlightened people met to talk about new ideas. In Paris, wealthy women invited writers, artists, and educated nobles to gather in their homes. They called these meetings **salons.** During the evening, a guest might read a poem aloud. Another guest might play some music. The guests talked about new books, plays, and the latest scientific ideas. They loved to talk and share their opinions.

People used salons during the Enlightenment to share new ideas, poetry, and music.

1687 – 1789

Chapter 19: Lesson 3

Overview This lesson covers the beginning of the Enlightenment and the effect that the notion of freedom had on the distribution of knowledge and on education.

Objectives

- To explain how the Paris salons helped advance the Enlightenment
- To describe the importance of Diderot's encyclopedia

Student Pages pages 469–473

Teacher's Resource Library **TRL**

Workbook Activity 89

Activity 89

Modified Activity 89

········

Vocabulary

ban	prejudice
Enlightenment	salon

Invite students to offer definitions for the vocabulary words without looking in their textbook. If they have trouble defining a word, encourage them to find the word in the dictionary and read the entire definition aloud. Then have them read the words and their definitions in the textbook.

········

1 **Warm-Up Activity**

Move desks aside and arrange chairs in a circle to resemble a salon setting. Discuss a recent school event, current political event, favorite movie, or other topic of interest to the students. Encourage the free flow of ideas. Explain that during the Enlightenment, wealthy Parisians routinely gathered in homes to talk about music, literature, or scientific ideas. Discuss the value of the salon during the 18th century.

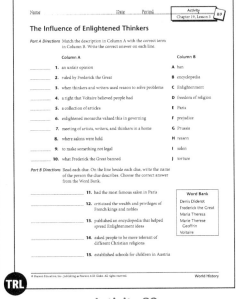

Workbook Activity 89

Activity 89

2 Teaching the Lesson

Have students recall how enlightened thinkers influenced the way people thought about themselves, their government, and the world. Then have students read pages 469–473 to find out more about how people's ideas were changing.

Ask:

- Which city was the center of the Enlightenment? (Paris)

- What did enlightened thinkers do in salons? (Answers will vary; students may say they discussed new ideas.)

Reading Strategy: Visualizing

Have students point out different aspects of the painting, such as the inclusion of women, the number of people, how they are dressed, the details of the room, and so forth. Then have students answer the question. (Answers will vary; The painting gives me an idea of the importance of the salon.)

- Why did the king of France put Voltaire in jail? (for criticizing the wealth and privileges of French kings and nobles)

- What specific freedoms did Voltaire think people had? (speech, press, and religion)

- Which enlightened thinker decided to publish a set of books to share knowledge? (Diderot)

- What was the effect of Diderot's encyclopedia? (It helped spread the ideas of the Enlightenment.)

IN THE COMMUNITY

Ask students to list places in their community where people exercise freedom of speech, press, and religion. Give students an opportunity to share and compare lists. (Answers will vary; students may say school or neighborhood meetings, printed advertisements or newspapers, church services, and so on.)

What Rights Did Voltaire Think People Had?

Free speech, free press, and religious freedom are important human rights, according to Voltaire.

Voltaire was an enlightened French thinker who influenced many people. He wrote histories, poetry, and over 50 plays. In these, he criticized the wealth and privileges of French kings and nobles. Twice, King Louis XV put Voltaire in jail to keep him from criticizing the French monarchy.

Voltaire defended a person's right to think and to say anything. He is reported to have said, "I do not agree with a word you say, but I will defend to the death your right to say it." Voltaire also supported freedom of religion. Free speech, free press, and religious freedom seemed to him to be rights that belonged to every person. According to Voltaire, governments had to respect these rights.

Why Did Diderot Publish an Encyclopedia?

During the Age of Reason, scientists and other people discovered many new things. Frenchman Denis Diderot decided to publish a set of books containing all this new knowledge. He wanted to put together all this knowledge so that everyone could learn it.

LEARNING STYLES

 Body/Kinesthetic
Have students work in small groups to prepare a skit set in a Paris salon during the Enlightenment. Each student should play the role of a famous enlightened person. When they present the skit for their classmates, students should not tell which role they are playing. Rather, classmates should try to identify each character by what the character says.

How Long Did Diderot Work on His Encyclopedia?

Beginning in the 1740s, Diderot spent 30 years working on his encyclopedia. More than 200 important thinkers—such as Rousseau and Voltaire—wrote articles for the encyclopedia. Madame Geoffrin, famous for her salon, helped finance Diderot's work.

Diderot's encyclopedia was a collection of articles that explored new learning. It also questioned people in authority in every field of learning. Diderot published the first volume of his encyclopedia in 1751. For 21 years, he worked to complete his encyclopedia. Finally, in 1772, he published the final book. Publishers sold thousands of this 28-volume set in France and other countries in Europe. The work of Diderot helped spread the ideas of the Enlightenment.

What Enlightened Things Did Frederick the Great Do?

The Enlightenment influenced several monarchs in Europe. These enlightened monarchs accepted reason as important in governing. Two of these monarchs were Frederick the Great of Prussia and Empress Maria Theresa of Austria.

Frederick the Great rejected the divine right of a king to rule. He thought that the idea was unreasonable. The Prussian ruler said that he was king because he was the person most able to lead. Frederick wanted to fight the ignorance and the **prejudices** in Prussia. A prejudice is an unfair and unreasonable opinion. People who are prejudiced form an opinion without having all the facts.

Frederick the Great wanted to enlighten his people and reform his country. He made the court system more fair. During this time, governments often used torture to get people to confess to a crime. Frederick **banned,** or got rid of, torture, except for the crimes of murder and treason.

Reading Strategy:
Visualizing

Make one or two stacks using 28 of something—textbooks, for example. Does this help you visualize the amount of "knowledge" that Diderot's encyclopedia contained?

Writing About History

Compare a modern encyclopedia with Diderot's. Why were they written? What kinds of articles do they contain? How large are they? Write your findings in your notebook.

Ask:

- How many people contributed to Diderot's encyclopedia? (more than 200)

Reading Strategy:
Visualizing

After students finish making their "stacks," have them answer the question. (Answers will vary; It makes me realize how much information Diderot gathered.)

- Which two rulers' actions demonstrated that they were enlightened? (Frederick the Great and Empress Maria Theresa)
- What is one way in which Frederick the Great showed that he was an enlightened ruler? (Answers will vary; students may say that he did not believe in the divine right of kings.)

 ### Writing About History

Have students read the Writing About History feature. Before they work on this assignment, discuss with them places where they can find encyclopedias to compare with Diderot's.

ELL/ESL Strategy

Language Objective:
To locate terms in an encyclopedia

As a class, identify different ideas, people, and places in Lesson 3. Write these on the board as students identify them. Pair ELL students with English-speaking students. Have each group choose three ideas, people, or places to research using an encyclopedia from the classroom or school library. Have each pair of students report on three interesting facts they discovered by reading the encyclopedia.

Ask:

- What things did Frederick the Great do to help the people of Prussia? (He made the court system more fair, banned torture, encouraged greater tolerance of different religions, and improved the lives of farmers.)

- What did Empress Maria Theresa do to improve the lives of Austrian children? (She set up schools for them.)

Biography

When Holy Roman Emperor Charles V's only son died, he put forth what was called the Pragmatic Sanction. This royal act made it possible for a daughter to succeed to the throne. After the emperor died, despite the Pragmatic Sanction, Maria Theresa was not allowed to succeed to the throne. When Francis Stephen of Lorraine married Maria Theresa, he became Holy Roman Emperor instead. He had to exchange his ancestral lands in France to become ruler of the Hapsburg land. Because of their strong relationship, Maria Theresa was able to exert her enlightened influence, improving the lives of many people.

 3 Reinforce and Extend

Frederick asked people to be more tolerant of different Christian religions. He improved the lives of German farmers by giving them seed and rebuilding homes and barns. Frederick so impressed Voltaire that the French thinker called him "Frederick the Great." Voltaire was the first person to give the Prussian ruler that name.

What Enlightened Thing Did Empress Maria Theresa Do?

The Enlightenment also influenced other European rulers. Many of them tried to change old customs and traditions. They tried to improve the lives of their people. In 1774, Empress Maria Theresa of Austria used government money for an enlightened cause. She established schools for all children between the ages of 6 and 13.

 Biography

Maria Theresa: 1717–1780

Empress Maria Theresa had to fight for her throne because she was a woman. Her father was the Holy Roman Emperor. When he died, other rulers denied her right to become empress. In the war that followed, she lost one province to Frederick the Great. Her husband, Francis Stephen, became Holy Roman Emperor. They had 16 children. Her daughter, Marie Antoinette, became queen of France.

Maria Theresa was a wise ruler who followed Enlightenment ideas. She established public education in Austria. Its goal was a better-educated workforce. Maria Theresa also made the lives of Hungarian serfs better.

WORLD CULTURES

 The Enlightenment belief in the importance of spreading knowledge eventually came to America. In 1886, a wealthy American named Andrew Carnegie donated a library to the town of Allegheny, PA. By the time of his death, Carnegie had donated about 1,700 free public libraries to New York City and small towns throughout the United States. Historians remember Carnegie as an industrialist who made a fortune in the steel industry. But generations of Americans knew his name from the *Free Carnegie Library* he donated to their town.

Word Bank
Diderot
Frederick
Geoffrin
Paris
Voltaire

Lesson 3 Review On a sheet of paper, use the words from the Word Bank to complete each sentence correctly.

1. The center of the Enlightenment was the city of _____.

2. Madame _____ held famous parties, or salons, for enlightened thinkers.

3. _____ was an enlightened thinker who favored free speech, free press, and religious freedom.

4. The encyclopedia by _____ spread the learning of the Enlightenment.

5. The enlightened ruler _____ the Great urged his people to be more tolerant of different Christian religions.

Are free speech, free press, and religious freedom important? Explain your answer.

STUDY SKILLS

Create the following graphic organizer on the board. Have students copy and complete it.

Person or Practice	Place	Accomplishment
the salon	(France)	(sharing of ideas)
Voltaire	(France)	(supported freedom of religion, free speech, and free press)
Diderot	(France)	(first encyclopedia)
Frederick the Great	(Prussia)	(enlightened his people and reformed his country)
Maria Theresa	(Austria)	(established public education)

Lesson 3 Review Answers

1. Paris 2. Geoffrin
3. Voltaire 4. Diderot 5. Frederick

Answers will vary. All three are important because they enable a people to express themselves and their deepest wishes and dreams. Today, many people from all over the world who did not have these rights have rebelled against their governments to get them.

Chapter 19: Lesson 4

Overview This lesson explains how the Enlightenment brought about changes in music and literature.

Objectives

- To explain how music was influenced by enlightened thinking
- To describe the kinds of books that were written during the Age of Reason

Student Pages pages 474–476

Teacher's Resource Library TRL

Workbook Activity 90

Activity 90

Modified Activity 90

Vocabulary

classical   **symphony**

Encourage students to work in pairs. Instruct one student to read a definition from this and previous lessons. Ask the other student to supply the word that matches the definition. Then have the student restate in his or her own words the meaning of the word.

 Warm-Up Activity

Invite a music teacher to your classroom to share different works of baroque composers, including Bach, Handel, and Vivaldi. Students should also listen to examples of classical works from Mozart and Haydn. Have students discuss which pieces they enjoyed the most.

 Teaching the Lesson

Ask students to talk about the types of music and reading they enjoy. Then have them read pages 474–476 to discover the new trends in music and in writing that emerged as a result of the Enlightenment.

Objectives

- To explain how music was influenced by enlightened thinking
- To describe the kinds of books that were written during the Age of Reason

Reading Strategy: Visualizing

Examine the details in this drawing of people dancing a minuet. Does this help you visualize the slow and careful way people danced during this period?

Enlightenment ideas influenced scientists, philosophers, reformers, and rulers. But the idea of an orderly universe governed by natural laws also influenced musicians, writers, and painters.

What Is Baroque Music?

The Age of Reason produced important new musical forms. At the end of the 1600s and during the early 1700s, baroque music became popular. (The French word *baroque* means "strange.") Renaissance music had sounded simple; baroque music sounded more complex.

During this time, composers—people who make up music for musicians to play—wrote fugues. In a fugue, the composer uses different musical instruments to repeat a melody. Perhaps the composer has the flute play the melody first. Then the composer changes the melody a little and repeats it on a trumpet. Sometimes, the composer uses two or three melodies in one fugue. Johann Sebastian Bach and George Friderick Handel were great baroque composers.

What Is Classical Music?

By the mid-1700s, another type of music appeared. Following the ideas of the Enlightenment, this new music was orderly and balanced. Musicians called it **classical** music. Historians used the word classical to describe the order and balance of ancient Greek art. The musicians of the Age of Reason used the same word to describe their music.

Dancing during the Age of Reason followed a precise pattern of movement. The minuet was a popular dance. It involved slow movements, bowing, and toe pointing.

474   Unit 4   *Enlightenment and Revolution*

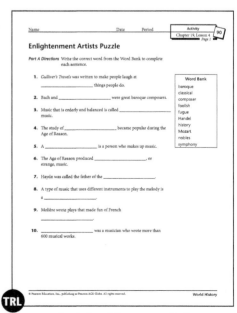

Classical

A type of music from the 1700s and early 1800s that is orderly and balanced; in the style of ancient Greece or Rome

Symphony

A long musical work played by a group of musicians using many different instruments

The classical period of European music lasted from 1750 to 1820. Classical musicians developed forms of music that are still popular today. One of the most important of these new forms was the **symphony**. It is a long musical work played by a group of musicians using many different instruments.

Why Is Haydn the "Father of the Symphony"?

Joseph Haydn and Wolfgang Amadeus Mozart were two of the most important classical composers. Historians call Haydn the "father of the symphony." He was the first European to compose a complete symphony using string and woodwind musical instruments. A woodwind instrument is one that a musician plays by blowing into it. During this time, artisans made these instruments out of wood.

One of the most famous composers of classical music was Wolfgang Amadeus Mozart of Austria. As a young boy, he shocked people with his musical talent. He died young and poor, but he left behind some of the world's most beautiful music.

How Did Mozart Show He Was a Musical Genius?

Wolfgang Amadeus Mozart was a musical genius. Haydn's student, Mozart began to compose music at age 5 and played the piano for European nobles at age 8. By age 13, he had written his first opera. He wrote more than 600 musical works before he died at age 35. However, he died a poor man. Today, his music is more popular than when he was alive. Singers and musicians perform his operas *The Magic Flute* and *The Marriage of Figaro* around the world.

Which Writers Examined Human Nature?

During the Age of Reason, writers carefully observed what was going on around them. They often wrote books about the foolish actions they had seen. In 1726, Englishman Jonathan Swift published *Gulliver's Travels*. In this book, Swift made his readers laugh at the foolish things people do. Writers observed foolish actions in France too. It was there that Molière wrote plays. His plays made fun of the behavior of French nobles and middle-class people.

Ask:

- What was the first complex form of music to become popular at the end of the 1600s? (baroque)

Reading Strategy:
Visualizing

Have students discuss the details shown in the painting, including the postures and clothing of the dancers, and the evidence of wealth. Then have students answer the question. (Answers will vary; It appears that the dance partners are moving gracefully.)

- What did Enlightenment musicians mean when they described their music as classical? (Answers will vary; students may say that classical describes order and balance in the way ancient Greek art was balanced.)

- What musical form was developed during the classical period of European music? (the symphony)

- Who was the father of the symphony? Who was his greatest pupil? (Haydn; Mozart)

LEARNING STYLES

Auditory/Verbal

Have students listen to a portion of baroque music, particularly by Handel or Bach. Then, as students become familiar with the form, change to symphonic music, either by Mozart or Haydn, in order to compare the two musical forms. Encourage students to write down their comparisons as they listen. Students may note differences such as melody, complexity, number and kinds of instruments used, and so on.

ELL/ESL STRATEGY

Language Objective:
To read and write musical terms

Have music students in your class share musical terms, such as note, staff, chord, harmony, and so on. Write the terms and their meanings on the board. If possible, have a music student create a musical staff with several notes on the board. Pair ELL students with English-speaking students. Have ELL students use as many musical terms as possible in sentences, such as "Musical sounds are shown by notes on a staff."

STUDY SKILLS

Have students look at the images on pages 474 and 475. Explain that musical gatherings were an important part of 18th-century life, and that children of wealth were expected to learn to play an instrument and sing. Have students discuss what they can learn about 18th-century life from these paintings.

- Who were some of the important writers during the Age of Reason? (Students may mention Jonathan Swift, Daniel Defoe, Molière, or Edward Gibbon.)

- Who was the author of *Gulliver's Travels*? of *Robinson Crusoe*? of *The Decline and Fall of the Roman Empire*? (Jonathan Swift; Daniel Defoe; Edward Gibbon)

 3 Reinforce and Extend

LEARNING STYLES

 Logical/Mathematical
Have students make a timeline that shows the works of three writers—the English author Jonathan Swift, the French playwright Molière, and the American author Washington Irving. Research the works of each writer to find the common element in all of their work. Write a paragraph that explains what the three writers had in common.

AT HOME

Invite students to discuss with family members Robinson Crusoe's dilemma—being stranded on a deserted island. Poll family members to find out what three things they would take with them if they knew they would be stranded on a deserted island. Give students the opportunity to share and compare their findings.

Lesson 4 Review Answers

1. C **2.** B **3.** A **4.** D **5.** C

Answers will vary. Painters might have begun to work more on composition in their paintings. They might have tried to balance one part of the painting with another part. Also, they might have chosen for their subject matter the enlightened people of their day or the scientific instruments of the time.

Other books were written based on real events. In the novel *Robinson Crusoe*, English author Daniel Defoe told the story of a shipwrecked man named Robinson Crusoe. Living on a deserted island, Crusoe had to find a way to continue his life without civilization.

What Kind of History Did People Study?

The study of history also became popular during the Age of Reason. Historians studied the civilization of ancient Greece and Rome. Edward Gibbon wrote an important book called *The Decline and Fall of the Roman Empire*.

Lesson 4 Review On a sheet of paper, write the letter of the answer that correctly completes each sentence.

1. During the Enlightenment, baroque musicians developed the _____, a new form of music.

   A classical   **C** fugue
   B symphony   **D** melody

2. Classical musicians developed the _____, a new form of music.

   A opera   **C** baroque
   B symphony   **D** flute

3. _____ was a great baroque musician.

   A Bach   **B** Mozart   **C** Haydn   **D** Defoe

4. _____ was a great classical musician.

   A Bach   **B** Defoe   **C** Molière   **D** Mozart

5. _____ wrote plays during the Enlightenment.

   A Mozart   **B** Haydn   **C** Molière   **D** Bach

 What do you think

How might the Enlightenment have influenced painters? Hint: Think about order and balance!

Chapter Project Follow-up

Have students who enjoy making displays create a large wall mural of three large interlocking circles. Have them create the title, *The Enlightenment*, across the top of the display. Have each project group (Enlightenment Thinkers, Enlightenment Rulers, and Music and Literature of the Enlightenment) add information to one circle. Remind students that each section should be visually interesting. When the display is completed, encourage students to view the entire display. Then lead a discussion on how the beliefs and actions of all three areas interacted.

What Is the Enlightenment?

Immanuel Kant

Immanuel Kant was a German philosopher (1724–1804). He believed in using reason to solve human problems. People who did so were called "enlightened." This excerpt is from an essay Kant wrote in 1784. In it, he explains the term "enlightenment."

Enlightenment is man's leaving his self-caused immaturity. Immaturity is the incapacity to use one's intelligence without the guidance of another. Such immaturity is self-caused if it is not caused by lack of intelligence, but by lack of determination and courage to use one's own intelligence without being guided by another. . . . Have the courage to use your own intelligence! is therefore the motto of the enlightenment.

Through laziness and cowardice a large part of mankind . . . gladly remain immature. It is because of laziness and cowardice that it is so easy for others to usurp the role of guardians. It is so comfortable to be a minor! If I have a book which provides meaning for me, a pastor who has conscience for me, a doctor who will judge my diet for me and so on, then I do not need to exert myself. I do not have any need to think; if I can pay, others will take over the tedious job for me. The guardians who have kindly undertaken the supervision will see to it that by far the largest part of mankind, including the entire "beautiful sex," should consider the step into maturity, not only as difficult but as very dangerous. . . .

But it is more nearly possible for a public to enlighten itself: this is even inescapable if only the public is given its freedom. . . .

All that is required for this enlightenment is *freedom;* and particularly the least harmful of all that may be called freedom, namely, the freedom for man to make *public use* of his reason in all matters. . . .

The question may now be put: Do we live at present in an enlightened age? The answer is: No, but in an age of enlightenment. Much still prevents men from being placed in a position . . . to use their own minds securely and well in matters of religion. But we do have very definite indications that this field of endeavor is being opened up for men to work freely and reduce gradually the hindrances preventing a general enlightenment and an escape from self-caused immaturity. In this sense, this age is the age of enlightenment. . . .

Document-Based Questions

1. How does Kant define immaturity?

2. For Kant, what is the motto of the enlightenment?

3. According to Kant, how do people avoid becoming mature?

4. What does the public need to become enlightened?

5. Did Kant think that he lived in an enlightened age? Why or why not?

1687 – 1789

The Age of Reason   Chapter 19   **477**

Read the title, "What Is the Enlightenment?" and the introductory paragraph to students. Then have students read this selection with a partner, jotting down words or phrases that are unfamiliar to both of them. When students finish reading, have them share which words or phrases were unfamiliar. Write their words and phrases on the board and explain what they mean. (possible words or phrases: usurp—take over; tedious—tiresome, dull) Have students silently reread the selection. Students should then write answers to the Document-Based questions.

Answers to Document-Based Questions:

1. He says that it is the incapacity to use one's mind without the guidance of another.

2. It is "Have the courage to use your own intelligence!"

3. They let something or someone else (books, pastor, doctor) do their thinking for them; they pay someone to do it for them.

4. People need the freedom to make public use of their reason in all matters.

5. He believed that he did not live in an enlightened age because people were not allowed to use their reason with regard to religion.

In Defense of Women's Rights

Before students begin reading, ask them to compare the rights of men and women in today's society. Do students believe any inequalities exist? If so, have them say what the inequalities are. After students silently read "In Defense of Women's Rights," let volunteers read the selection aloud. Explain that Wollstonecraft chose to spread her message about women's rights by writing books, the dominant medium of her time. Ask students what medium Wollstonecraft might use to spread her message if she were alive today. (Answers will vary; students may say she would have her own Web site.) Students should read and answer the Wrap-Up questions.

Answers to Spotlight Story Wrap-Up:

1. They could own property, keep their pay, and divorce a wife and take the children.

2. It was A *Vindication of the Rights of Women.*

3. She thought men and women should be educated equally and that women should be encouraged to develop their minds.

4. He was a political writer whom Mary Wollstonecraft married.

5. She was Mary Shelley, the author of *Frankenstein.*

Enlightenment thinkers often wrote about the rights of men. Nearly all ignored the rights of women. Mary Wollstonecraft tried to change that attitude. In the 1700s, women had few rights. They could not own property. If they worked, their pay went to their fathers or husbands. A husband could divorce his wife and take the children. A woman could not do the same.

Mary Wollstonecraft was born in London in 1759. As was typical, her brother Edward was sent away to a good school. Mary went to a day school where she learned French and composition. Years later, she and her sisters started a school for small children. From this experience, she wrote her first book. It was called *Thoughts on the Education of Daughters.* It contained ideas that she would develop in the future.

Finally, her luck changed. She began working for a publisher. In 1792, she went to France where the French Revolution was under way. There she wrote two more books. One was a collection of original stories for children. The other book defended the ideals of the French Revolution.

French political ideas led to Mary's most important book. Published in 1792, it was called *A Vindication of the Rights of Women.* Vindication means "defense." She wrote, "I wish to see women as neither heroines nor brutes; but reasonable creatures." Women, she argued, should have the same rights as men. They should be entitled to a good education to develop their minds. Her book is still important in the history of women's rights.

Mary Wollstonecraft

Her book became popular. Mary became famous throughout Europe. She met other people who held similar ideas. One was William Godwin, a free-thinking political writer, whom she married. In August 1797, their daughter was born. Mary died a few days later at the age of 38.

Her daughter, Mary Godwin, also became a writer. She married the poet Percy Bysshe Shelley. In 1818, Mary Wollstonecraft Shelley wrote a book that is still famous. It tells about a scientist who created a monster. The scientist's name is the title of the book: *Frankenstein!*

Wrap-Up

1. In the 1700s, men had many rights that women did not. What were some of them?

2. What was Mary Wollstonecraft's most important book?

3. What were her views about education?

4. Who was William Godwin?

5. Why is Mary Wollstonecraft's daughter famous today?

- The Age of Reason changed the way people thought about the universe. Ideas of order and balance influenced ideas about government.

- Newton's scientific discoveries introduced the ideas of natural, universal laws that could predict natural events. People began to look for natural laws in human behavior and society. Believers in reason were enlightened thinkers. They wanted to use reason to improve people's lives and all parts of society. This movement is called the Enlightenment.

- Thomas Hobbes, an English philosopher, believed strong rulers were needed to keep peace in society. John Locke thought that people and their government made a contract, or agreement. He wrote that people had rights to life, liberty, and property. Government was to protect those rights.

- Montesquieu and Rousseau were enlightened French thinkers. Montesquieu thought that government powers should be divided among separate branches. Rousseau believed that people were naturally good, but that civilization made them evil. He wrote that people made a contract with each other. Their shared values, the general will, created a community.

- During the Enlightenment, people met to discuss ideas. In Paris, these meetings were known as salons.

- Voltaire was a French philosopher and writer. He defended people's right to free speech, a free press, and religious freedom.

- Denis Diderot in France wrote a many-volume encyclopedia including the knowledge of the Age of Reason.

- Some European monarchs adopted Enlightenment ideas. Frederick the Great of Prussia rejected the idea of the "divine right" of kings. He believed in religious tolerance and made the court system more just. Maria Theresa of Austria set up schools for children.

- Enlightenment ideas influenced artists as well as scientists and rulers. In baroque music, composers such as Bach and Handel wrote complex pieces such as fugues.

- Classical music was balanced and orderly. Joseph Haydn developed the symphony form. Wolfgang Amadeus Mozart, his student, wrote hundreds of works in his short lifetime.

- Enlightenment writers used reason to examine society and history. These writers included Swift, Defoe, and Gibbon in England, and Molière in France.

1687 – 1789

Using the Chapter Summary

Have students read the Chapter Summary on page 479 to review the main ideas presented in Chapter 19.

Ask:

- What ideas influenced government during the Age of Reason? (order and balance)

- What kind of laws did Newton's scientific discoveries introduce? (natural, universal laws)

- What did Hobbes, Locke, Montesquieu, and Rousseau all write about? (government)

- Which enlightened philosopher thought individuals had the right to life, liberty, and property? (Locke)

- Which enlightened philosopher thought that there should be three separate branches of government? (Montesquieu)

- Which freedoms did Voltaire think people had? (speech, press, religion)

- Which source of knowledge did Diderot publish? (an encyclopedia)

- Which European monarch rejected the idea of the "divine right"? (Frederick the Great)

- What form of classical music first written by Haydn was also written by Mozart? (the symphony)

- What did the writers during the Age of Reason examine? (society and history)

TEACHER'S RESOURCE

The AGS Globe Teaching Strategies in Social Studies Transparencies may be used with this chapter. The transparencies add an interactive dimension to expand and enhance the *World History* program content.

Chapter 19 Review

Use the Chapter Review to prepare students for tests and to reteach content from the chapter.

Chapter 19 Mastery Test

The Teacher's Resource Library includes two forms of the Chapter 19 Mastery Test. Each test addresses the chapter Goals for Learning. An optional third page of additional critical-thinking items is included for each test. The difficulty level of the two forms is equivalent.

Chapter 19 Review Answers

1. Newton
2. Hobbes
3. Locke
4. Montesquieu
5. Rousseau
6. Frederick the Great
7. Voltaire
8. Diderot
9. Maria Theresa
10. Handel
11. B
12. A
13. C
14. D
15. A
16. During these years, many thinkers thought that they could solve the problems of society and government by using reason.

Word Bank

Handel
Diderot
Frederick the Great
Hobbes
Locke
Maria Theresa
Montesquieu
Newton
Rousseau
Voltaire

On a sheet of paper, use the words from the Word Bank to complete each sentence correctly.

1. _____ discovered a law that made Europeans begin to use scientific reasoning.

2. _____ believed that rulers should have absolute power.

3. _____ believed that people had the right to life, liberty, and property.

4. _____ believed in separation of powers in government.

5. _____ said that all people were born good.

6. _____ rejected the divine right of a king to rule.

7. _____ criticized the French government and the king put him in jail.

8. _____ published the first encyclopedia.

9. Empress _____ of Austria was an enlightened ruler.

10. _____ was a famous baroque composer.

On a sheet of paper, write the letter of the answer that correctly completes each sentence.

11. Enlightened thinkers believed that _____ could lead them to truth.

   A feeling   **C** traditions
   B reason   **D** government

12. According to Montesquieu, _____ held a republic together.

   A virtue   **B** fear   **C** honor   **D** rebellion

13. Hobbes thought that order was more important than _____ in a society.

   A government   **B** writing   **C** freedom   **D** virtue

---

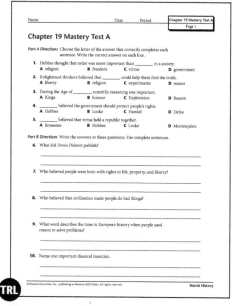

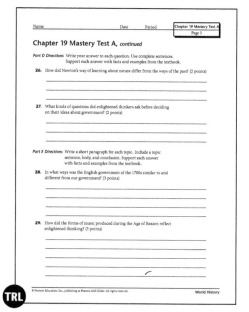

14. _____ composed music during the Age of Reason.

  A Handel   **C** Bach
  B Mozart   **D** all of the above

15. Many enlightened thinkers thought that reason could solve the problems of _____.

  A society   **B** fugue   **C** woodwind   **D** privilege

On a sheet of paper, write the answer to each question. Use complete sentences.

16. Why do historians call the years 1687 to 1789 the Age of Reason?

17. Why do historians also call these years the Enlightenment?

18. What did Hobbes and Locke agree and disagree about with regard to government?

Critical Thinking On a sheet of paper, write your response to each question. Use complete sentences.

19. The enlightened thinkers during the Age of Reason believed that they could make societies and people better by using reason. Do you agree with this belief?

20. According to Rousseau, people are born good. Society creates people who do bad things. What do you think of this theory? If possible, give examples to explain your answer.

If you do not know a word in a question, read the question again but leave out the word. Then see if you can figure out the word from its use in the sentence.

17. People who believed in scientific reasoning called themselves "enlightened" thinkers. They no longer walked in the darkness of ignorance.

18. Like Hobbes, Locke thought that government should keep order in a society. He also thought that government was a contract between the ruler and those ruled. Unlike Hobbes, Locke believed that people were reasonable. Given the chance, they would act in an orderly manner. Locke also believed that people had rights to life, property, and liberty. The job of government was to protect these rights. Hobbes thought that people gave up any rights they had so as to obtain order in their world.

Critical Thinking

19. Answers will vary. Sample answer: Thinking logically about problems can bring solutions. We see this as neighborhood watch groups and city councils meet and debate.

20. Answers will vary. Sometimes we hear about a person who even as a child did hurtful things. Then we wonder if all people are born good. Often we hear about people who abuse others because they were abused when they were children. Then we say for certain that society creates people who do bad things.

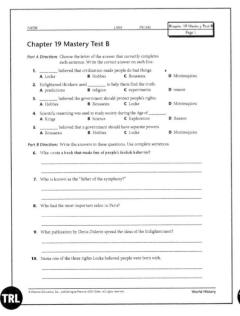

Chapter 19 Mastery Test B, pages 1–3

The Age of Reason   Chapter 19   **481**

Introducing the Chapter

In the last quarter of the 18th century, revolutions brought dramatic changes in France and North America. After winning independence from England, the United States became a nation. In France, revolution was followed by a Reign of Terror. Napoleon emerged first as a military dictator and then as emperor of France. Then, almost as suddenly as he

Revolutions and Napoleon

Economic and political revolutions bring change. In this chapter, you will become part of the American Revolution. This change brought about a new nation—the United States. Across the ocean, the French watched this revolution and learned from it. You will see how they too revolted. Then you will meet Napoleon, a military leader. With him, you will march into a Russian winter and end up on a rocky island in the Atlantic. This chapter will help you understand how revolution changed Europe and America.

Goals for Learning

◆ To list the causes of the American Revolution

◆ To explain how the American Revolution changed the world

◆ To describe the causes of the French Revolution

◆ To describe the Reign of Terror in France

◆ To list the accomplishments and failures of Napoleon

1775 Battle of Lexington and Concord is fought

1781 American Revolutionary War ends

1793 French execute Louis XVI

1815 Wellington defeats Napoleon at Waterloo

1750   1775   1800   1825

1776 Declaration of Independence signed

1789 French Revolution begins

1804 Napoleon becomes emperor of France

burst into prominence, Napoleon was banished.

Ask:

• Where did revolution begin first, in America or in France? (America)

• When was the battle of Lexington and Concord fought? (1775)

• When did the French execute their king? (1793)

• When and where did Napoleon meet defeat? (1815; Waterloo)

Name _____ Date ____ Period ____   *SELF-STUDY GUIDE*

Chapter 20: Revolutions and Napoleon

Goal 20.1 To list the causes of the American Revolution

Date	Assignment	Completed
_____	**1.** Read pages 482–487.	_____
_____	**2.** Complete the Lesson 1 Review on page 487.	_____
_____	**3.** Complete Workbook Activity 91.	_____

Comments:

Goal 20.2 To explain how the American Revolution changed the world

Date	Assignment	Completed
_____	**4.** Read pages 488–492.	_____
_____	**5.** Complete the Lesson 2 Review on page 492.	_____
_____	**6.** Complete Workbook Activity 92.	_____

Comments:

Goal 20.3 To describe the causes of the French Revolution

Date	Assignment	Completed
_____	**7.** Read pages 493–495.	_____
_____	**8.** Complete the Lesson 3 Review on page 495.	_____
_____	**9.** Complete Workbook Activity 93.	_____

Comments:

Chapter 20 Self-Study Guide, pages 1–2

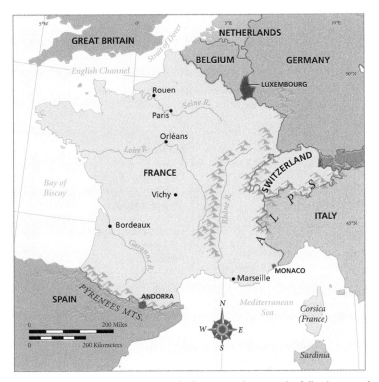

GREAT BRITAIN · NETHERLANDS · BELGIUM · GERMANY · LUXEMBOURG · Rouen · Paris · Seine R. · Orléans · Loire R. · FRANCE · SWITZERLAND · ALPS · Vichy · Rhône R. · ITALY · Bordeaux · Garonne R. · Bay of Biscay · MONACO · Marseille · English Channel · Strait of Dover · SPAIN · PYRENEES MTS. · ANDORRA · Mediterranean Sea · Corsica (France) · Sardinia

During this time, revolution started in America, then spread to France. Great changes took place in this European country. The common people revolted and took power away from the nobles and the king. Their cry was "Liberty, equality, and fraternity!" They wanted everyone to be part of a brotherhood in which all were free and equal.

Study the map and answer the following questions:

1. What city in France is near the Mediterranean?

2. What island in the Mediterranean did France hold?

3. What are the names of four rivers in France?

4. What mountains separate France from Spain?

5. What mountains form the boundary between Italy and France?

1775 – 1815

Revolutions and Napoleon   Chapter 20   483

Ask students to read the title of the map, "France." Encourage students to study the map.

Ask:

• Which bodies of water touch the shores of France? (English Channel, Bay of Biscay, Mediterranean Sea)

• Which lands border France? (Spain, Andorra, Italy, Switzerland, Germany, Luxembourg, and Belgium)

Have students read the paragraph below the map with a partner and then read and answer the questions.

Map Skills Answers

1. Marseille

2. Corsica

3. the Garonne River, the Loire River, the Seine River, and the Rhone River

4. the Pyrenees Mountains

5. the Alps

Chapter Project

Divide the class into two groups. Assign one group to research the French Revolution and the other group to research the American Revolution. Then have the students in each group arrange themselves into smaller subgroups of two to three students to research in detail a specific topic related to their assigned revolution. You may want to list specific topics for students to study. At the end of Chapter 20, all students in each group should be prepared to be part of a panel discussion or presentation.

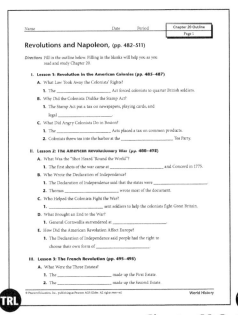

Chapter 20 Outline, pages 1–3

Revolutions and Napoleon   Chapter 20   483

Inferencing

Introduce the reading strategy of *inferencing*. Draw students' attention to the definition. Explain that when they make an inference, they will combine what they already know with what they read. Tell students that active readers watch for clues within a text that will help them make inferences and understand what is happening. Read aloud the first paragraph on page 485.

Ask:

- Land was cheap and people could work and earn money. Can you infer that this made people satisfied or angry? (satisfied)

- What knowledge do you have that helps you make this inference? (People with money are able to buy cheap land.)

- What inference can you make about life in England between 1607 and 1733? (Land in England must have been expensive and people must have been poor, since it was the opposite situation in the 13 American colonies.)

Point out the bulleted list on page 484. Encourage students to use these ideas as they read the lessons in Chapter 20.

Key Vocabulary Words

Explain that the list of words here is a glossary of the Key Vocabulary that students will read in Chapter 20. Call on volunteers to read aloud the words and their definitions.

Ask:

- What is the Declaration of Independence? (a document declaring the colonists' freedom from Great Britain)

- What does *repeal* mean? ("to get rid of a law")

- What was the Estates-General? (the French governmental body made up of representatives from the three estates)

- What is the difference between a *moderate* and a *radical*? (A moderate wants to change things little by little; a radical wants to change things all at once.)

Reading Strategy:
Inferencing

Sometimes the meaning of a text is not directly stated. You have to "read between the lines" to understand what is really being said.

- ◆ What You Know + What You Read = Inference

- ◆ As you read, look for clues that help you understand what is happening.

Key Vocabulary Words

Lesson 1
Quarter To provide soldiers with a place to live

Violate To go against

Repeal To do away with a law

Lesson 2
Boycott To refuse to buy something

Minutemen Colonial soldiers in the Revolutionary War who were ready to fight at any time

Declaration of Independence A document the American colonists signed declaring their freedom from Great Britain

Complaint A statement about something that that tells why a person is unhappy

American Revolution The American struggle against Great Britain for independence

Lesson 3
Estate A class of people in France

Estates-General The French governmental body made up of representatives from the three estates

Bastille A prison in Paris

French Revolution The war that the common people of France fought to achieve freedom

Lesson 4
Equality The same rights for everyone

Enforce To make sure that people follow the laws and rules

Convention A group of people who meet to get something done

Émigré A French noble who fled France during the French Revolution

Moderate One who wants to change things little by little

Radical One who wants to change things all at once

Jacobin A radical leader during the French Revolution

Reign of Terror The one-year period in French history when radical leaders put many people to death

Guillotine A machine used to execute people by chopping off their head

Legislature The lawmaking body of government

Executive The branch of government that enforces laws

Lesson 5
Tactic A plan that helps someone win a game or a battle

Neutral Not choosing either side in a war

Exile To send someone away from his or her own country

Code of Napoleon A code of law Napoleon passed that made all men equal in France

484　Unit 4　Enlightenment and Revolution

Between 1607 and 1733, England established 13 colonies in North America. For the people living in America, the colonists, life was different from life in England. Land was cheap. People could earn money and not be poor anymore. For more than 150 years, England pretty much left the colonists alone. Then, in 1763, England changed the way it treated the colonies.

What Law Took Away the Colonists' Rights?

From 1754 to 1763, the English and the French fought to control North America. The war cost a lot of money. After it ended, England left British soldiers in the colonies to protect the colonists. But Great Britain needed money to pay these soldiers and to pay off the bills from the war.

To raise money, the British government tried for the first time to make the colonists obey the Navigation Acts. These laws said that the colonists had to ship their trading goods on British ships. The money England got from the colonists would pay for the cost of protecting them. The colonists said that they did not need British protection.

Then, in 1765, the British government passed the Quartering Act. This law said that the colonists had to let British soldiers **quarter** in their homes. That is, colonists had to provide the soldiers with a place to live. The colonists also had to feed these soldiers. The colonists said that this law **violated,** or went against, their rights.

Why Did the Colonists Dislike the Stamp Act?

In 1765, the English Parliament also passed the Stamp Act to raise money. This law put a tax on colonial newspapers, playing cards, and legal documents. In England, this type of tax was common.

Before the Stamp Act, the price of everything included a British tax. But most colonists did not know this, so they thought that the Stamp Act was new. They thought that it was the first direct tax England had placed on them.

Objectives

◆ To identify the Stamp Act and the Townshend Acts

◆ To identify the cause of the Boston Massacre

◆ To explain what happened at the Boston Tea Party

Quarter

To provide soldiers with a place to live

Violate

To go against

Geography Note

Beginning in the late 1700s, many American settlers moved westward on the Wilderness Road. Daniel Boone, on behalf of the Transylvania Company, had blazed a trail through the wilderness. The road began in Virginia and spanned the Appalachian Mountains.

Chapter 20: Lesson 1

Overview This lesson explains the events that began in 1763 that brought England and the 13 English colonies in North America to the brink of war.

Objectives

■ To identify the Stamp Act and the Townshend Acts

■ To identify the cause of the Boston Massacre

■ To explain what happened at the Boston Tea Party

Student Pages pages 485–487

Teacher's Resource Library

Workbook Activity 91

Activity 91

Modified Activity 91

....

Vocabulary

quarter   violate
repeal

Write each vocabulary word in a vertical list on the board. Then write the definition for each word in another vertical list next to the words, but write the definitions out of order. Have student volunteers draw lines to match each word to its correct definition. Then have students write each definition in their own words.

....

1 Warm-Up Activity

Explain to students that during the American Revolution, there was a law in place that stated that colonists had to allow British soldiers to stay in their homes. The colonists had to provide food for the soldiers as well. Have students discuss the benefits and the downside of this law for both the colonists and the soldiers.

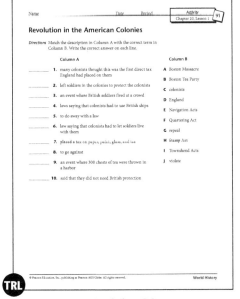

Workbook Activity 91   **Activity 91**   *Revolutions and Napoleon*   *Chapter 20*   **485**

2   Teaching the Lesson

Students may not be aware that the colonists were taxed by England without any representation in the British government. Explain that this "taxation without representation" is what colonists found most unfair.

Ask:

• What act did England pass to force colonists to house soldiers? (Quartering Act)

• What is one thing the Stamp Act taxed? (answers will vary; students may say newspapers, playing cards, and legal documents)

Geography Note

Have students look at a current map of the United States and point out Virginia where the Wilderness Road began, the Appalachian Mountains, and the Ohio River. Discuss with students the difficulties settlers may have faced while traveling westward on this route.

Ask:

• What did colonists insist that they must do before they could be taxed? (agree to be taxed)

Reading Strategy: Inferencing

(Students may say that they know the colonists dressed up as Indians and threw tea into Boston Harbor so it could not be sold in the colonies. They may also know that this was an act of rebellion.)

• What do historians call Great Britain's attack on colonists in Boston in 1770? the colonists' raid of an English ship in 1773? (Boston Massacre; Boston Tea Party)

Repeal
To do away with a law

Reading Strategy: Inferencing

What do you already know about the Boston Tea Party?

The colonists did not like the Quartering Act. They also did not like the Stamp Act, even though it was a small tax. They said that Great Britain had not asked them if they wanted this tax. The colonists believed that England had no right to tax them unless they agreed to taxation. They refused to pay the tax, and in 1766, the British Parliament **repealed**, or did away with it.

What Did Angry Colonists Do in Boston?

In 1767, the British Parliament passed a new group of laws called the Townshend Acts. These laws placed a tax on common products, such as paper, paint, glass, and tea. Once again, the colonists said that England could not tax them without their consent.

The bad feelings between Great Britain and the colonists got worse. Then, in 1770, British soldiers in Boston fired into a crowd that had tossed sticks and snowballs at them. Historians call this event the Boston Massacre.

In 1773, some colonists in Boston dressed up as American Indians. Then they climbed on board a British merchant ship that was carrying tea. The colonists threw the tea into the harbor. Historians call this event the Boston Tea Party.

The Boston Tea Party was a protest against Britain's unfair control of the tea trade. Colonists dumped over 300 chests of tea into Boston Harbor.

ELL/ESL STRATEGY

Language Objective:
To prepare and give a group presentation

Ask students to name the actions that the colonists took to show their displeasure with the British government's policies. Write them on the board. Then divide the class into groups of five or six, including ELL students in each group; have each group choose one of the actions. Have them research the action, when and where it occurred, who was involved, and the result of the action. All group members should prepare and participate in a skit to present their information.

3   Reinforce and Extend

STUDY SKILLS

Invite students to make a chart of the steps in this lesson and the next that led to the American Revolution. Have them title the chart *Steps Leading to the American Revolution.* They should make one column for *Actions* and one for *Results.*

How does what you already know about the Boston Tea Party add to what you have just read?

Word Bank

Boston Tea Party
Navigation Acts
Quartering Act
Stamp Act
Townshend Acts

Why did the colonists do this? Before this, British companies had sold tea to merchants in the colonies. Then these merchants had sold tea to the colonists. In that way, the colonial merchants ran a business and made money. But Parliament had now given a British company the right to sell tea directly to colonists. This cut out colonial merchants. Clearly, the colonists and the British were not getting along.

Lesson 1 Review On a sheet of paper, use the words from the Word Bank to complete each sentence correctly.

1. The _____ made colonists ship goods on British ships.

2. The _____ put a tax on items such as paper and glass.

3. The _____ required colonists to let British soldiers live in the colonists' homes.

4. The _____ put a tax on colonial newspapers, playing cards, and legal documents.

5. The _____ was some colonists' response to the Townshend Acts.

Do you think that England had the right to tax the colonists to pay for the soldiers' protection? Explain your answer.

 Biography

Abigail Adams: 1774–1818

Abigail Smith Adams was the wife of one American president (John Adams) and the mother of another (John Quincy Adams). She was very active in her husband's career. Abigail was also one of the most influential women of her day. She supported equal education for women. She often spoke out against slavery.

We know a great deal about Abigail from her letters. She wrote to her husband while he was attending Congress during the American Revolution. There are also letters from when he was a diplomat in Europe. Still more letters present a clear picture of Washington, D.C., up to 1800.

1775 – 1815

Revolutions and Napoleon Chapter 20 **487**

(Students may say that they used the new information and the details they knew to infer how angry and displeased the colonists were and to better understand the motivation behind their action.)

 IN THE COMMUNITY

Ask students to check with merchants in their community to find out what taxes customers pay when they buy items such as newspapers and tea at a store. Have students report and compare their findings. If you live in a state with no sales tax, find out how the state government collects tax dollars.

Lesson 1 Review Answers

1. Navigation Acts 2. Townshend Acts
3. Quartering Act 4. Stamp Act
5. Boston Tea Party

Answers will vary. The British needed to get money from somewhere to pay the soldiers and to provide lodging, food, and supplies for them. These soldiers were protecting the colonists, so it seems reasonable that the colonists should pay taxes that would pay for the protection. However, some colonists did not really object to the taxes. What they wanted was representation in the British Parliament. Then they could be part of passing any law that affected the colonies.

Biography

Abigail Adams is well-known as the wife of President John Adams, but she is equally well-known for the letters she wrote. Her letters to her husband and friends were such a compelling record of her time that they were published in a book in 1840. Explain to students that what made her letters so interesting was how they featured somewhat trivial events, like her lunch that day or her trip to the market, alongside events of vast historical significance, like the Revolutionary War and the Continental Congress.

Chapter 20: Lesson 2

Overview This lesson explains why the colonies decided to separate from England and fight for independence.

Objectives

- To identify the minutemen
- To identify the writer of the Declaration of Independence
- To describe how the Revolutionary War ended

Student Pages pages 488–492

Teacher's Resource Library **TRL**

Workbook Activity 92

Activity 92

Modified Activity 92

Vocabulary

American Revolution
boycott
complaint
Declaration of Independence
minutemen

Have students make three columns with these headings: *Causes, Events,* and *People.* After they study the vocabulary definitions, have students write each vocabulary word under the appropriate heading. Then have students write two or three sentences using the words in each category. Have students meet in small groups to share what they wrote and correct others' use of vocabulary as needed.

1 Warm-Up Activity

Read aloud the sentence of the Declaration of Independence that begins "We hold these truths to be self-evident, . . ." Write the words *Life, Liberty,* and *the pursuit of Happiness* on the board. Discuss why the colonists may have felt that life (or safety), liberty (or freedom), and the pursuit of happiness were important to the colonists. Explain that the Declaration of Independence was the final act of the colonists that led to a full war between the colonies and Great Britain.

Objectives

- To identify the minutemen
- To identify the writer of the Declaration of Independence
- To describe how the Revolutionary War ended

Boycott
To refuse to buy something; to refuse to deal with a person, business, or country

Minutemen
Colonial soldiers in the Revolutionary War who were ready to fight at any time

Because of the Boston Tea Party, Parliament closed the port of Boston. It also forced the colony of Massachusetts to accept military rule. This upset the colonists. In 1774, representatives from 12 colonies met in Philadelphia. They agreed to **boycott**—or refuse to buy—any British goods; to send a protest to King George III in England; and to meet again.

What Was the "Shot Heard 'Round the World"?

Before the representatives could meet again, something happened. In April 1775, British soldiers marched to Concord, Massachusetts, to seize colonial weapons. At Lexington, some colonial soldiers called **minutemen** met the British soldiers. (These soldiers were ready to fight at any time.) Someone fired a gun. This started a small battle. An American poet later wrote that this was the "shot heard 'round the world."

The British soldiers began to march back toward Boston. But their bright red uniforms were easy to see. As they retreated, the minutemen fired on them from behind trees and rocks. By the time the British "redcoats" reached Boston, the colonists had killed a third of them.

The first shots of the American Revolutionary War were fired at Lexington and Concord in 1775.

Name _____ **Date** _____ **Period** _____ Workbook Activity 92 Chapter 20, Lesson 2

Do You Remember?

Directions Write the answers to these questions. Use complete sentences.

1. When and where did the first fighting of the American Revolutionary War happen?

2. What are three things that the Declaration of Independence said?

3. What troubles did George Washington's soldiers face?

4. Who was General Cornwallis?

5. What did the French fleet do near Yorktown, Virginia?

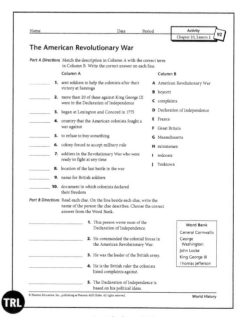

Name _____ **Date** _____ **Period** _____ Activity 92 Chapter 20, Lesson 2

The American Revolutionary War

Part A Directions Match the description in Column A with the correct term in Column B. Write the correct answer on each line.

Column A	Column B
1. sent soldiers to help the colonists after their victory at Saratoga	A American Revolutionary War
2. more than 20 of these against King George III were in the Declaration of Independence	B boycott
3. began at Lexington and Concord in 1775	C complaints
4. country that the American colonists fought a war against	D Declaration of Independence
5. to refuse to buy something	E France
6. colony forced to accept military rule	F Great Britain
7. soldiers in the Revolutionary War who were ready to fight at any time	G Massachusetts
8. location of the last battle in the war	H minutemen
9. name for British soldiers	I redcoats
10. document in which colonists declared their freedom	J Yorktown

Part B Directions Read each clue. On the line beside each clue, write the name of the person the clue describes. Choose the correct answer from the Word Bank.

1. This person wrote most of the Declaration of Independence.

2. He commanded the colonial forces in the American Revolutionary War.

3. He was the leader of the British army.

4. He is the British ruler the colonists listed complaints against.

5. The Declaration of Independence is based on his political ideas.

Word Bank
General Cornwallis
George Washington
John Locke
King George III
Thomas Jefferson

Declaration of
Independence

A document the
American colonists
signed in which
they declared their
freedom from Great
Britain

Complaint

A statement about
something that
tells why a person
is unhappy

American
Revolution

The American
struggle against
Great Britain for
independence

Who Wrote the Declaration of Independence?

In May 1775, the colonial representatives met again. They agreed to pay for an army that George Washington would command. On July 4, 1776, they signed the **Declaration of Independence.** In this document, they declared that the colonies were free states. They were no longer part of the British Empire. The Declaration of Independence also listed more than 20 **complaints** against King George III. That is, it told why the colonists were unhappy.

Thomas Jefferson wrote most of the document. He accepted the political ideas of John Locke. Jefferson wrote that people could change their government if that government no longer protected their rights of life and liberty. Jefferson also said that people had the right to try to find happiness.

Who Helped the Colonists Fight the War?

The struggle against Great Britain—the **American Revolution**—lasted from 1776 to 1781. The battles fought during this war did not go well for the colonists at first. George Washington's soldiers had little training and lacked supplies, but they managed to win some battles.

George Washington commanded the colonial forces in the Revolutionary War.

As students read, have them make a list of the events that led up to the Revolutionary War. Have students write a sentence about each one that they can use to study for the chapter test.

AT HOME

Have students discuss with their families the colonists' tactic of boycotting British goods. Ask if anyone in their family has ever been part of a boycott or knows about any other local, national, or international boycotts. (Possible boycotts: United States boycott of the Olympic Games in Moscow in 1980 to protest the USSR's invasion of Afghanistan; consumer boycotts to protest labor practices) Have students report the results of their discussions to the class.

Ask:

- How did 12 of the colonies fight back against England for closing the port of Boston and imposing military rule? (They boycotted, or refused to buy, British goods.)

- Which document listed colonial complaints against King George III? (Declaration of Independence)

- What was George Washington's role in the Revolutionary War? (He commanded the colonial forces.)

- What challenges did the colonists face in fighting battles? (lack of training and supplies)

LEARNING STYLES

 Auditory/Verbal
Have students find a copy of the poem "Paul Revere's Ride" by Henry Wadsworth Longfellow. It should be relatively easy to find in the school library or on the Internet. Have students practice reading the poem more than once. Encourage students to recite the poem aloud, either as a class or by dividing the poem in sections and reciting in groups.

Ask a volunteer to read the title: "Major Battles of the Revolutionary War." Have other volunteers point to and name the 13 colonies that became the United States of America. Then have students read the caption under the map and answer the questions. (Four battles the Americans won include Cowpens, Yorktown, Trenton, and Saratoga. Two battles the British won include Bunker Hill and Camden. The final battle was Yorktown in October 1781; the colonists won.)

Ask:

• Which European countries helped the United States win independence from England? (France, Spain, the Netherlands)

• How did the French help the Americans win the Battle of Yorktown? (Their ships kept the British ships from rescuing General Cornwallis.)

LEARNING STYLES

Visual/Spatial

Have students trace a map of Western Europe, filling in the borders of Spain, France, and the Netherlands. Have students research the contributions each country made to the American Revolution. Students should title their maps "European Countries Help Colonists." Have students write a few sentences or create a map key with symbols that explain what each country did to help the Americans and place that information on the map.

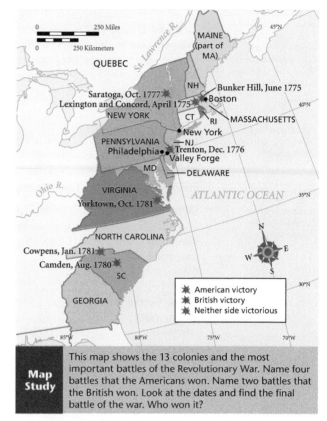

Map Study This map shows the 13 colonies and the most important battles of the Revolutionary War. Name four battles that the Americans won. Name two battles that the British won. Look at the dates and find the final battle of the war. Who won it?

In 1777, the colonists won an important victory at Saratoga. Because of this, France sent soldiers to help the colonists defeat Great Britain. In 1779, Spain declared war on Great Britain. In 1780, the Netherlands joined the American fight. Great Britain was now at war with the colonies and with France, Spain, and the Netherlands.

What Brought an End to the War?

Finally, in 1781, the colonial army rushed southward to Yorktown, Virginia. Here, the British army, led by General Cornwallis, was trapped. In front, it faced the colonial army. At its back was the sea and the French fleet.

Reading Strategy:
Inferencing

What can you infer about the ability of the colonial army?

Because of these French ships, the British navy could not rescue Cornwallis and his soldiers. Cornwallis surrendered. Some political leaders in Great Britain began to oppose the war. Two years later, the colonists and England signed a peace treaty in Paris, France. Great Britain accepted the independence of the 13 American colonies. The American Revolution had ended.

How Did the American Revolution Affect Europe?

The British soldiers marched out of Yorktown in 1781. As they did so, their band played the song "The World Turned Upside Down." And the world had turned upside down. The American Revolution brought change for Americans and for Europeans.

The Declaration of Independence said that "all men are created equal." The declaration also said that people had a right to choose their own form of government. In 1789, the people of France followed the lead of the Americans. The French also turned their world upside down.

1775 – 1815

Ask:

- What did the colonists and England do two years after the Revolutionary War ended? (signed a peace treaty in Paris, France)

- Who followed the lead of the Americans in 1789 and started their own Revolutionary War? (the people of France)

Reading Strategy:
Inferencing

(Some students may say that they can infer that the colonial army was skilled at gathering the help of other countries and at plans of attack.)

ELL/ESL Strategy

Language Objective:
To identify verbs and their effect on sentences

After students read the text on pages 490–491, have pairs of students work together to find all the verbs they can on these two pages. Have students make a list of the verbs. Then bring the class together again. Make a list on the board of the verbs the students found. Encourage students to discuss how the specific verbs used make the text more understandable. Discuss why the author may have chosen specific verbs over other verbs that would have also fit the sentence. For example, discuss why the author used "rushed" instead of "went" in the first sentence on page 491. ("Rushed" tells the reader that the army moved quickly, while "went" doesn't give enough detail.)

3 Reinforce and Extend

ONLINE CONNECTION

A facsimile and the text of the Declaration of Independence can be viewed at www.agsglobewh.com/page492a. Specific information on the battles of the American Revolution can be found at www.agsglobewh.com/page492b.

Lesson 2 Review Answers

1. The minutemen were colonists who were ready to fight at a minute's notice. **2.** The American Revolutionary War began in Lexington and Concord, Massachusetts. **3.** They signed it on July 4, 1776. **4.** France, Spain, and the Netherlands helped the colonists win the war. **5.** The war ended at Yorktown, Virginia, in 1781.

Answers will vary. The United States would very likely still be under rule of Great Britain today if the revolution had not been a success. Or perhaps another revolution years later would have been a success. Either way, it would have changed American history significantly.

After students read "Independence Day," ask them to share how they celebrate their Independence Day. Also encourage students to find out how countries besides the United States celebrate independence.

Lesson 2 Review On a sheet of paper, write the answer to each question. Use complete sentences.

1. Who were the minutemen?

2. In what place did the American Revolutionary War begin?

3. When did the colonial representatives sign the Declaration of Independence?

4. What European countries helped the colonists win the war?

5. Where and when did the fighting in the American Revolution end?

What do you think

What do you think life would be like in America today if the American Revolution had been a failure?

Independence Day

The Fourth of July is the anniversary of American independence. It celebrates the signing of the Declaration of Independence. This national holiday first took place in Philadelphia on July 8, 1776. The Declaration was read aloud, city bells rang, and bands played. Independence is now celebrated with parades, picnics, and fireworks. In 1976, the United States was 200 years old. During the whole year, cities and towns held special events to remember independence.

Other countries also have independence days. Mexico marks its independence from Spain on September 16. Ghana celebrates independence from Great Britain on March 6.

♦ To identify the three estates

♦ To explain the importance of the Bastille

Estate

A class of people in France

In the early 1770s, France probably had more money than any other nation in Europe. Throughout Europe, most educated people spoke French. Many of the most important ideas of the Enlightenment came from French thinkers. However, France had two big problems. First, French society was still like the feudal societies of the Middle Ages. Second, the king—an absolute monarch—was a weak ruler.

What Were the Three Estates?

French society was divided into three **estates,** or classes. The clergy—1 percent of the population—made up the First Estate. These religious leaders owned 10 percent of the land. The nobles—5 percent of the population—made up the Second Estate. They held all the important jobs in the government. They also controlled most of the money and property in their country. The Third Estate included three different groups of common people. At the top were doctors, teachers, bankers, business people, and lawyers. In the middle were city workers. At the bottom were farmers, who made up more than 80 percent of the population.

Who Paid Taxes in France?

The clergy and the nobility paid no taxes to the government. But the three groups of the Third Estate had to pay taxes on the money they made and on their land. They also had to pay taxes when they bought salt, tobacco, and soap.

The farmers paid about half of their money in taxes. They also had to work once a year on government projects without pay. The members of the Third Estate paid a lot of taxes, but they had little or no political power.

Chapter 20: Lesson 3

Overview This lesson describes how the discontent most of the people in France felt over taxes and representation in government brought about the French Revolution.

Objectives

■ To identify the three estates

■ To explain the importance of the Bastille

Student Pages pages 493–495

Teacher's Resource Library **TRL**

Workbook Activity 93

Activity 93

Modified Activity 93

Vocabulary

Bastille	**Estates-General**
estate	**French Revolution**

Have students write the definition of each vocabulary word on one side of an index card. Then have them draw a simple picture or icon to represent the word on the other side. Have students pair up and use the index cards as flash cards. One partner shows the picture, while the other partner names it and gives the definition. The partner holding the card can check the definition on the back of the card. Let students pair up with other students until they feel they know all of the definitions.

1 **Warm-Up Activity**

Have students review what they have learned about the causes of the American Revolution. Make a two-column chart on chart paper or on the board. In the left column, write the heading "Causes of the American Revolution." List the causes that students suggest. In the right column, write the heading "Causes of the French Revolution." As the class reads Lesson 3, add the causes of the French Revolution to the chart.

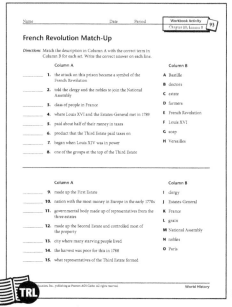

Workbook Activity 93

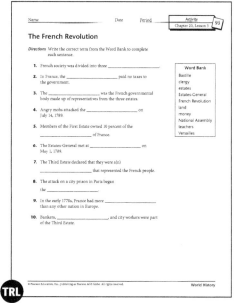

Activity 93

2 ▶ Teaching the Lesson

To help students understand the percentages of people in the three French estates or classes, write the number of students in the class on the board. Assign 1 percent of the class to the First Estate (most likely one student sitting on the floor to represent a very small amount), 5 percent (most likely one or two students) to the nobles, and the rest of the class to represent the common people.

Ask:

- Which group made the important decisions in government? (the nobles or Second Estate)

- People in which estate in France were not happy about the tax situation? (Third Estate)

- Why did the French government need money? (because it had spent money helping the Americans)

- How many votes did the 610 representatives of the Third Estate have in the Estates-General? (one)

- When the Third Estate could get only one vote for its 610 representatives in the Estates-General, what did it do? (declared it was a National Assembly representing the people of France)

- Who called for an end to the monarchy in 1789? (the Third Estate)

Estates-General
The French governmental body made up of representatives from the three estates

Why Did the French Government Need Money in 1789?

In 1789, the French treasury was empty. France had spent a lot of money helping the American colonies revolt against Great Britain. To raise money, the government decided to find a way to tax the nobles. They did not like this and demanded that the king call a meeting of the **Estates-General.** This was a government body made up of the representatives from the three estates. The last time the Estates-General had met was in 1614.

Louis XVI agreed. The Estates-General met at Versailles on May 5, 1789. At this meeting, the representatives would decide if the nobles had to pay taxes. But each of the three estates had only one vote. So, the First and Second Estates—the clergy and the nobles—could defeat the Third Estate, which was already paying all the taxes.

What Did the Third Estate Do in 1789?

The 610 representatives of the Third Estate wanted everyone at the meeting to have a vote. They could then outvote the 591 representatives of the other two estates. But the king said that the meeting would follow the old rule of three votes.

The representatives of the Third Estate declared that they were a National Assembly that represented the French people. The king locked them out of the meeting hall. But they simply marched outside and decided to write a constitution. They called for an end to absolute monarchy. Under pressure, Louis XVI ended the meeting of the Estates-General. He told the clergy and the nobles to join the National Assembly.

The storming of the Bastille, a prison in France, became a symbol of the French Revolution.

3 ▶ Reinforce and Extend

CAREER CONNECTION

One of the ways we know about what happened in Paris on July 14, 1789, is the press. On-site reporting by a free press is an important factor in an effective democracy. Discuss with students why they think the Fourth Estate is a term commonly used for the press. Students interested in becoming reporters should know that most employers today require applicants to have a Bachelor's degree in journalism as a minimum requirement. Previous experience, even on school papers, is also helpful. Students should check with their guidance counselor to find out what courses to take to prepare for entering a college journalism program.

Bastille

A prison in Paris

French Revolution

The war that the common people of France fought against the king, nobles, and one another to achieve freedom

Reading Strategy:
Inferencing

Based on their actions, what can you infer about the poor people in Paris?

Why do you think the French people attacked the Bastille?

What Did Mobs Do in Paris in 1789?

In the 1780s, many poor people lived in Paris. Mostly, they ate bread. If the price of bread increased, they starved. Sometimes, mobs—large groups of people—seized carts of grain and bread because of their hunger.

In 1788, the grain harvest in France was poor, so bread doubled in price. In the spring of 1789, the starving people in Paris got mad. Angry mobs rioted in the streets. On July 14, 1789, these mobs attacked a city prison called the **Bastille.** The government kept a few political prisoners there as well as gunpowder. When the French soldiers joined the mob, the Bastille fell!

A noble woke Louis XVI from his sleep and told him what had happened. The angry king said, "Why, this is a revolt!" "No," the noble said. "It is a revolution." It was the beginning of the **French Revolution.** The common people of France fought against the king, nobles, and one another to achieve freedom.

Lesson 3 Review On a sheet of paper, write the letter of the answer that correctly completes each sentence.

1. In the early 1770s, France probably had more _____ than any other nation in Europe.

   A bread   **B** grain   **C** money   **D** population

2. The Third Estate was made up of _____.

   A clergy   **C** nobles
   B kings   **D** common people

3. Members of the Third Estate wanted to end France's _____.

   A clergy   **C** grain harvest
   B absolute monarchy   **D** Bastille

4. The Bastille in Paris is a _____.

   A prison   **B** palace   **C** castle   **D** navy yard

5. The French Revolution began in _____.

   A 1775   **B** 1780   **C** 1789   **D** 1791

Revolutions and Napoleon   Chapter 20   **495**

Reading Strategy:
Inferencing

(Students may say that the poor people of Paris were out of options and had no choice but to get angry and take decisive action.)

ELL/ESL Strategy

Language Objective:
To speak in front of a group

In this lesson, students have learned about the roles of the people in each of the three estates in France. Assign each student to a different estate. For those students assigned to the third estate, give them each a specific role, such as doctor, banker, worker, or farmer. Have students reread the text on their role. Then have students prepare a brief presentation for the class about their role. Have students give the presentations, acting as if they are the person they have studied. Each student should tell what his or her life is like in the class system. Have students do additional research as needed.

Lesson 3 Review Answers

1. C **2.** D **3.** B **4.** A **5.** C

Answers will vary. They probably wanted to get the gunpowder that was there. Also, they wanted to release any prisoners and give them freedom. For many years, many common people had been sent to prison for life, so the Bastille was a natural place for revolt.

LEARNING STYLES

Logical/Mathematical

Have students draw pyramids to illustrate the following:

1. The number of people in France's three estates, with the Third Estate at the bottom and the First Estate on top. (Students should make the space within the pyramid proportionate to the number of people.) 2. The proportion of taxes paid by people in the Third Estate 3. The representation of each estate in the Estates-General.

Chapter 20: Lesson 4

Overview This lesson describes the French Revolution, its terrifying conclusion, and the subsequent government takeover by three military leaders.

Objectives

■ To identify the government formed by the National Assembly

■ To describe what the Jacobins wanted

■ To identify the Directory

Student Pages pages 496–499

Teacher's Resource Library

Workbook Activity 94

Activity 94

Modified Activity 94

Vocabulary

convention	Jacobin
Émigré	legislature
enforce	moderate
equality	radical
executive	Reign of Terror
guillotine	

Read a definition to students and have a volunteer write the defined word on the board. Continue until all of the words are on the board. Have volunteers select a word and use it in a sentence. Ask other students to say whether the word usage is correct or, if not, suggest changes in the sentence. Cross out the words as they are used in sentences. Continue until all of the words have been crossed out.

1 Warm-Up Activity

Have students think about the different forms of government that they are familiar with, such as a democracy, a monarchy, and a socialist government. On the board, write facts about each type of government that students generate. Explain that after the National Assembly took over the French government, there were many changes in the type of government that ran France.

Objectives

◆ To identify the government formed by the National Assembly

◆ To describe what the Jacobins wanted

◆ To identify the Directory

Equality
The same rights for everyone

Enforce
To make sure that people follow the laws and rules

The National Assembly quickly started to reform French government. On August 4, 1789, it ended the feudal privileges of the clergy and the nobles. It also adopted a document that gave citizens three rights—free speech, freedom of religion, and **equality** under the law. Equality means that everyone shares the same rights.

Why Did the King Leave Versailles?

In October 1789, thousands of women rioted over the cost of bread. They marched on Versailles, which was ten miles from Paris. When they got to Versailles, the women broke into the palace and killed several guards. Then they demanded that the king and queen move to Paris. Frightened, the rulers agreed to do so. In June 1790, Louis XVI and his family tried to escape from France. But someone recognized the king. He and his family had to return to Paris.

What Type of Government Did the Assembly Form?

The National Assembly continued to make changes. By 1791, it had created a new form of government. Members of the assembly wrote a constitution that limited the king's power. This new government was a constitutional monarchy.

According to the constitution, the new Legislative Assembly had the power to make laws. The king had the power to **enforce** the laws, or make sure people follow them. The new constitution said that all men were equal before the law. However, only property owners—less than 1 percent of the population—could be elected to the government.

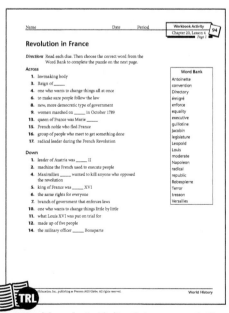

Workbook Activity 94, pages 1–2

Activity 94

Reading Strategy:
Inferencing

After reading about the unstable governments, what can you infer about life in France at this time?

What Was the Next Government of France?

The new constitutional government lasted only 11 months. In September 1792, the French abolished it. Then they elected a National Constitutional **Convention.** A convention is a group of people who meet to get something done. The Constitutional Convention met to form a new, more democratic government for France—a republic.

The new government took away all of Louis XVI's power. It gave all French men the right to vote and to hold political office. The government also decided to fight to bring freedom to all the common people in Europe.

Which Nations Tried to Stop the French Revolution?

Many French nobles, called **émigrés,** had fled France. They asked Leopold II of Austria to overthrow the new French government. In August 1791, Leopold and the king of Prussia said that all kings had the duty to "restore order to France." The armies of Great Britain, Austria, Prussia, and Spain joined together to try and defeat the French and end the French Revolution.

What Happened to Louis XVI?

The French no longer thought of Louis XVI as king. He was just a common citizen. In June 1790, he had written a letter condemning the revolution. In December 1792, the government put him on trial for treason. On January 21, 1793, it executed him. That same year, France raised a citizen army of 300,000 men. Many French women went to war with the men.

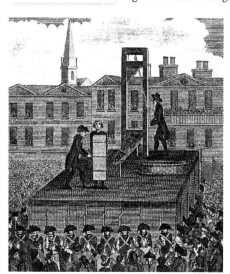

The French created a horrible way to put people to death: the guillotine. This picture shows Louis XVI before his execution by the guillotine.

1775 – 1815

Revolutions and Napoleon Chapter 20   **497**

PRONUNCIATION GUIDE

Use this list to help students pronounce difficult words in this lesson.

Robespierre   (rōbz´ pyer)

 Teaching the Lesson

Ask students to recall the American colonists' complaints against England. Then have them read pages 496–499 to find out what happened after the National Assembly took control of France.

Ask:

- **What did the National Assembly do about the privileges of clergy and nobles?** (It ended the privileges.)
- **Why did thousands of women riot in 1789?** (They were protesting the cost of bread.)
- **How long did the new constitution last?** (11 months)
- **How did the French decide what kind of government to have next?** (There was a National Constitutional Convention to form a new government.)
- **What power did the new government give the king?** (none)
- **Which countries sent armies to France to try to end the French Revolution?** (Great Britain, Austria, Prussia, and Spain)
- **For what crime was Louis XVI tried?** (treason)

Reading Strategy:
Inferencing

(Students may say that life in France was chaotic and unpredictable. The government was constantly changing.)

ELL/ESL STRATEGY

 Language Objective:
To read for meaning

Divide the class into pairs. Have partners reread pages 496–497 together and ask them to focus on what life was like for the king during the time period of 1789 through 1793. Have partners work together to make a poster about what it was like to be the

king of France during this time. Have students make illustrations to visually represent the challenges the king faced and who caused those challenges. The posters should also include the decisions the king made and why. Encourage partners to share their posters with the class in a brief presentation.

Queen of France Marie Antoinette was one of the first to be sent to the guillotine in France.

Moderate

One who wants to change things little by little

Radical

One who wants to change things all at once

Jacobin

A radical leader during the French Revolution

Who Were the Jacobins?

After the king was executed, the French peasants rebelled. Then, **moderate** and **radical** leaders in the government began to fight one another for power. Moderates wanted to bring about reform little by little. Radicals wanted to change everything at once.

In Paris, a mob rushed into the Convention and arrested all the moderate leaders. Then the radicals—called **Jacobins**—controlled the government. The Convention formed a Committee of Public Safety. Maximilien Robespierre led the committee. He wanted to kill anyone who opposed the revolution.

Reign of Terror

The one-year period in French history when radical leaders put many people to death

Guillotine

The machine used to execute people by chopping off their head

Legislature

The lawmaking body of government

Executive

The branch of government that enforces laws

Word Bank

Leopold
Louis XVI
Marie Antoinette
Robespierre
Versailles

What Was the Reign of Terror?

Between July 1793 and July 1794, the Jacobins executed thousands of people by chopping off their heads. Historians call this the **Reign of Terror.** One of the first people to lose her head was the woman who had been queen—Marie Antoinette. The radicals executed many nobles, but mostly they put common people to death.

For one year, Robespierre was a dictator. But the Reign of Terror ended on July 28, 1794, when the radicals sent Robespierre himself to the **guillotine.** (This was the machine the French used to execute someone by chopping off their head.)

What Was the Directory?

During the next five years, the National Convention drew up another new constitution. (This was the third one since 1789.) They divided the **legislature,** or lawmaking body, into two houses. They established an **executive** branch—the Directory—made up of five people. (The executive branch enforced the laws.)

For a time, the Directory brought order to France. Then, in November 1799, it also fell from power. Three men took control of the government. One of them was a 30-year-old military officer named Napoleon Bonaparte.

Lesson 4 Review On a sheet of paper, use the words from the Word Bank to complete each sentence correctly.

1. In 1789, women marched on _____ and demanded that their rulers return to Paris.

2. The king of France at this time was _____.

3. The queen of France was _____.

4. _____ led the Reign of Terror for a year.

5. _____ of Austria called all kings to bring order to France.

Why do you think the kings of other nations opposed the French Revolution?

WORLD CULTURES

The revolution put an end to royalty and nobility in France, but the French were left with two magnificent royal palaces. What did they do with these structures and the spacious grounds surrounding them? After Louis XVI was sent to the guillotine, the palace of Versailles was abandoned. Since then, it has been restored. It is occasionally used for government purposes and was the place where the treaty ending World War I was written. About 3,000,000 tourists visit the Palace of Versailles every year. The Louvre in Paris is an art museum. It was last used as a royal residence in 1682. It houses exquisite paintings—its collection of Impressionist paintings is considered by many to be the most famous in the world. The Louvre, like Versailles, is a major tourist attraction.

Lesson 4 Review Answers

1. Versailles **2.** Louis XVI **3.** Marie Antoinette **4.** Robespierre **5.** Leopold

Answers will vary. The French were fighting to get rid of the absolute monarch and to give freedom and equality to all people in France. The kings in other nations probably feared that these feelings would spread and that their people would revolt too.

Chapter 20: Lesson 5

Overview This lesson covers Napoleon's rise to power, his military exploits, his exile and return to power, and his ultimate defeat at Waterloo.

Objectives

- To explain why soldiers supported Napoleon
- To describe how Napoleon was crowned emperor
- To explain what happened when Napoleon invaded Russia
- To identify ways that Napoleon affected history

Student Pages pages 500–506

Teacher's Resource Library TRL

Workbook Activity 95

Activity 95

Modified Activity 95

Vocabulary

Code of Napoleon   neutral
exile   tactic

Write the vocabulary words on the board and discuss the meaning of each with students. Ask a volunteer to choose a word and make up a sentence that is a clue to one of the words. Classmates should try to guess the word from the clue. Continue until all the words have been guessed.

1 Warm-Up Activity

Have students work with a partner to make a list of what it takes to be a good leader. Have students add the personality traits that make world leaders appealing to large groups of people. Ask students to share their lists with the class and write list items on the board. Explain that in this lesson, students will read about Napoleon, a prominent leader in France.

Lesson 5 | Napoleon and the French Empire

Objectives

- To explain why soldiers supported Napoleon
- To describe how Napoleon was crowned emperor
- To explain what happened when Napoleon invaded Russia
- To identify ways that Napoleon affected history

Tactic

A plan that helps someone win a game or a battle

Reading Strategy: Inferencing

After reading this section, what can you infer about the kind of person Napoleon was?

Napoleon Bonaparte was born in 1769 on the small island of Corsica. As a boy, he went to a military school in France. When he was 16, he joined the king's army. The French Revolution began in 1789. At that time, Napoleon was a little-known, low-level military officer. But he developed a new military **tactic,** or plan that would help him win. He moved his soldiers quickly, then put most of them at the weakest point of the enemy line.

Soldiers liked to fight for Napoleon. He was a natural leader and helped them win battles against stronger armies. Within four years, he became a general. (He was only 24.) Six years later, Napoleon took control of the disorganized government of France. Later, he said, "I found the crown of France lying on the ground, and I picked it up with a sword."

For the next 15 years, Napoleon ruled France as a military dictator. As time passed, he conquered most of Europe. His actions dominated European history from 1800 to 1815. Historians call those years the Age of Napoleon.

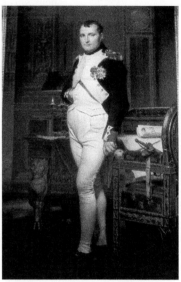

Napoleon Bonaparte saw himself as a conqueror like Alexander the Great. He became emperor of France in 1804.

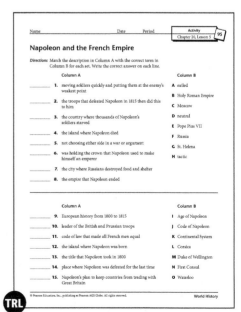

Workbook Activity 95   **Activity 95**

When Did Napoleon Become First Consul?

Napoleon dreamed of making France into a mighty empire like that of ancient Rome. He saw himself as a modern-day Alexander the Great. When Napoleon first came to power, he acted as if he was the elected leader of a democratic republic. Then, in 1800, he asked the people of France to approve a new constitution. It gave him the title of First Consul. (Consuls led the ancient Roman republic.) As First Consul, Napoleon had more power than any other French official.

Who Crowned Napoleon As the Emperor?

In 1802, the French people elected Napoleon their First Consul for life. More than 3 million people voted, and only 9,000 of them voted against Napoleon. Then, on December 2, 1804, Pope Pius VII came to Paris. He waited at the Cathedral of Notre Dame to crown Napoleon emperor of France. Napoleon, dressed in purple, entered the cathedral. He walked up to the pope, took the crown from him, and placed it on his own head! Through his own military skill, he had risen to power. Now, by his own hand, he made himself Emperor Napoleon I.

A Song for the Revolution

In 1792, more than 500 soldiers marched from Marseilles to Paris. They were all volunteers, caught up in the spirit of the Revolution. On the way, they sang "The War Song of the Rhine Army." This emotional song of liberty had captured the feeling of hope and revolutionary change. It was written by Claude-Joseph Rouget de L'isle, a young French army captain.

The song was renamed "The Marseillaise." In 1795, it became the national anthem of France. When France became an empire,

Napoleon banned "The Marseillaise." He feared it would continue to rouse the French to revolution. However, in 1875 France, once again, adopted "The Marseillaise" as its national anthem.

> Arise, ye sons of France!
> Your day of glory has arrived!
> Oh army of citizens!
> Form your battalions.
> March on, march on!
> All hearts dedicated
> to liberty or death!

Explain that at different times throughout history, world leaders have outlawed creative works. With the help of students, make a list on the board of the arguments a leader or government might use to restrict access to a book, movie, or song. When the list is complete, discuss with students the validity of each argument. Then have students read "A Song for the Revolution" to find out about a song that is very important to the French people and why one of their leaders once banned it.

2 Teaching the Lesson

As students read the lesson, have them make a chart listing the achievements and the failures of Napoleon during his time as emperor of France. Encourage students to use this chart to study for the test at the end of the chapter.

Reading Strategy:
Inferencing

(Students may say that Napoleon was an ambitious leader who took advantage of the opportunities that he saw.)

Ask:

- Why do historians call 1800–1815 the Age of Napoleon? (Napoleon was a dominant force in European history during that time.)

- What title did the people of France give Napoleon in 1800? (First Consul)

- What happened when the pope came to crown Napoleon emperor? (Napoleon crowned himself.)

ELL/ESL STRATEGY

Language Objective:
To learn specific content vocabulary

Have students read the definition for *tactic* given on page 500. On a sheet of paper, have each student write one or two sentences telling how they used a tactic to play a game. Students might use an example from an organized sport, a casual sport they play with friends, a board game, or a card game. Encourage students to use the word *tactic* correctly in their sentences. Have students read their sentences to a partner. Have partners work together to make sure they used the vocabulary word correctly. Repeat the activity with other content vocabulary in Lesson 5.

Ask:

- Which countries were allied against France in 1805? (Britain, Austria, Russia)

- Which empire did Napoleon end? (the Holy Roman Empire)

- What was the Confederation of the Rhine? (a loose alliance of German states)

- What was the Continental System? (a plan to ruin the British economy by ordering other European nations to stop trading with Great Britain)

- Did Napoleon's plan to ruin the British economy work? Why or why not? (The tactic failed because Great Britain retaliated by preventing any ships from entering French and other European ports; European nations suffered and some turned against Napoleon.)

- Why did Napoleon invade Russia? (to punish Russia for trading with Britain)

Neutral
Not choosing either side in a war or argument

What Was the Confederation of the Rhine?

In 1805, Britain, Austria, and Russia formed a military alliance against France. Napoleon quickly defeated the armies of Austria and Russia. From 1806 to 1812, his power increased in Europe. He took control of Italy and made himself king there. Then he ended the Holy Roman Empire. (This empire had lasted for many centuries.) In its place, he created a loose alliance of German states. He called this alliance the Confederation of the Rhine.

Napoleon let his brothers rule some of this conquered land. Louis Bonaparte became king of Holland. Jerome Bonaparte ruled over the Kingdom of Westphalia in Germany. Joseph Bonaparte ruled over the Kingdom of Naples and Sicily and later became the king of Spain.

What Mistakes Did Napoleon Make?

Only Great Britain stood against the spreading French power. In 1805, England destroyed the French fleet off the coast of Spain. In 1806, Napoleon decided to ruin the British economy by ordering other European countries to stop trading with Great Britain. He called his plan the Continental System.

But Napoleon misjudged the power of the British navy. It prevented trading ships from entering French and other European ports. The successful actions of the British navy hurt the economy of France and these other countries.

Because of their lost trade, the **neutral** European nations quickly turned against France. (A neutral country is one that does not choose either side in a war.) Napoleon's mistake had weakened French power. In 1812, he made a second mistake—a bigger one. He invaded Russia.

Why Did Napoleon Invade Russia?

In 1807, Czar Alexander I of Russia had agreed to support the Continental System. But lack of trade hurt the Russian economy. In 1812, Alexander began to trade with Britain once again. His decision made Napoleon angry.

Napoleon was a natural military leader. This painting shows him at the Battle of Eylau in 1807. Perhaps his greatest mistake was invading Russia in 1812.

Ask:

• What tactic did the Russians use against Napoleon? (Students may say the Russians destroyed anything that could help Napoleon's army before retreating from it.)

• When did Napoleon's invasion of Russia begin and end? (began in May 1812; ended in October 1812)

To punish Russia, Napoleon organized the largest army in history up to that time. His Grand Army of 500,000 was made up of soldiers from all parts of the French Empire. In May 1812, this army set out to invade Russia.

How Did the Russian Army Fight?

Napoleon thought that he could defeat Russia in a few months. But the Russian army did not want to fight one big battle. Instead, it kept retreating. As the French army followed, the Russian soldiers retreated eastward, deeper and deeper into Russia. As they pulled back, the soldiers destroyed anything that could help Napoleon's invading army. The Russians left behind only burned fields and houses.

Near Moscow, the French and Russian armies finally met. The French won the battle. But when the soldiers entered the capital, they found only a burned-out and deserted city. Once again the Russians had destroyed food and shelter that Napoleon's army needed.

Have a volunteer read the title, "The Napoleonic Empire." Have other volunteers mention which lands were included in Napoleon's empire.

Ask:

• **Which areas did not belong to Napoleon's empire?** (Portugal, United Kingdom, Sweden, Russia, Sardinia, Sicily, and the Ottoman Empire)

Have students write answers to the questions in the caption. (The Austrian Empire had an alliance with France. The Battle of Moscow was fought in Russia.)

Reading Strategy:
Inferencing

(Students may say that fighting a war in Russia in the winter would be difficult because of the cold weather.)

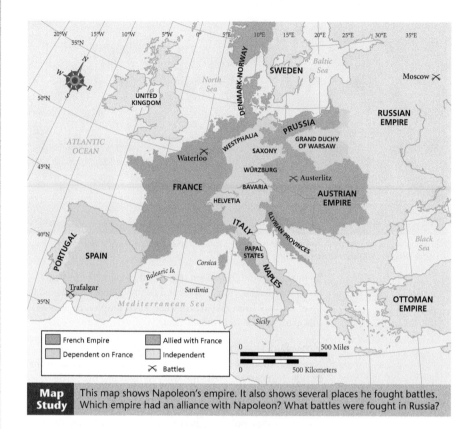

French Empire	Allied with France
Dependent on France	Independent
✕ Battles	

Map Study This map shows Napoleon's empire. It also shows several places he fought battles. Which empire had an alliance with Napoleon? What battles were fought in Russia?

Reading Strategy:
Inferencing

What can you infer about fighting a war in Russia during the winter?

What Happened When Napoleon Left Russia?

Napoleon sent several messages of peace. However, he heard nothing from the Russians. In October 1812—after five weeks of waiting—Napoleon ordered his army to return to France. The Grand Army had already lost thousands of soldiers. Many had died of disease. Now the soldiers faced a cold Russian winter without food and warm clothing.

The Russian winter was a hard enemy. As the French army moved slowly westward, thousands of soldiers died of starvation. Many froze to death. Over 500,000 soldiers had marched boldly into Russia. Only 40,000—tired and beaten—returned to France. And only 10,000 of them were still able to fight. Napoleon's retreat from Russia was a military disaster.

Who Defeated Napoleon the First Time?

Seeing the weakened French army, Napoleon's enemies attacked. In March 1814, the British, Russian, Prussian, and Austrian armies captured Paris. The leaders removed Napoleon from power and sent him to Elba, an island off the coast of Italy. Then they restored the monarchy to France. (The brother of the executed Louis XVI became king.)

In February 1815, Napoleon escaped from Elba and returned to France. First, he declared himself emperor. Then he began to raise an army. The French king quickly sent his soldiers to stop Napoleon. When Napoleon met the king's soldiers, he asked if any one of them wished "to kill his emperor." They all cried, "Long live the emperor!"

Who Defeated Napoleon the Second Time?

For the next three months, Napoleon was once again the hero of France. During that time, he organized an army of 125,000 men. On June 18, 1815, his new army met the combined armies of Britain and Prussia at Waterloo in present-day Belgium.

The Duke of Wellington led the British and Prussian troops. On the battlefield at Waterloo, these troops finally defeated Napoleon. Once again, he was **exiled,** or sent away, to a lonely island, this time in the South Atlantic. He was ordered not to come back to France.

In 1821, six years after the Battle of Waterloo, Napoleon Bonaparte died at the age of 52 on the rocky island of St. Helena. For a few years, his dream of a French empire came true. No one could stop his army. Then he met a Russian winter and Waterloo.

Writing About History

In your notebook, write an epitaph, or writing on a tombstone, for Napoleon. What were his dreams? his accomplishments? Why did he capture the French imagination? Why did Napoleon fall from power?

Ask:

- **How did the climate affect the war in Russia?** (Answers will vary; students will probably say that the French were not prepared to fight through the harsh Russian winter.)

- **When the armies of Britain, Russia, Prussia, and Austria captured Paris, what did they do to Napoleon?** (sent him to the island of Elba)

- **Which military leader is credited with leading the army that defeated Napoleon?** (the Duke of Wellington)

 Writing About History

Explain to students that tombstones, especially those of famous people, sometimes have a phrase inscribed on them that summarizes what the person is remembered for. These phrases are called epitaphs. Because they are written on stone, they are usually brief. Have students read the Writing About History feature and write an epitaph for Napoleon.

 Reinforce and Extend

BACKGROUND INFORMATION

 Waterloo, the site of Napoleon's final defeat, was a small town near Brussels. When word that Napoleon had escaped from exile and returned to France reached the British, Dutch, Belgians, and Germans, they were alarmed. Weary of decades of Napoleon's wars, these countries quickly combined forces and assembled in Belgium under the command of England's Duke of Wellington. Napoleon heard about this and marched his army north to meet the challenge. Historians disagree about why Napoleon met defeat at Waterloo. It might have been that he delayed his attack, or it might have been the additional pressure from the Prussian army. But at day's end, the French army was in retreat. Napoleon's defeat and reversal of fate have given rise to an expression: a person suffering a similar defeat is said to be meeting her or his Waterloo.

Ask:

- What did Napoleon's Code say about the rights of people? (All men were equal before the law.)

Lesson 5 Review Answers

1. The Age of Napoleon is from 1800 to 1815. **2.** Napoleon was a soldier. **3.** He became emperor of France on December 2, 1804. **4.** His invasion of Russia was a disaster for France and for Napoleon. **5.** Napoleon met his final defeat at Waterloo.

Answers will vary. The Russians probably wanted to keep him in Moscow for as long as possible. They knew winter was coming and that his soldiers would have to march hundreds of miles through snow and sleet to France.

Chapter Project Follow-up

Give each of the two groups, the French Revolution group and the American Revolution group, time to meet and discuss the information group members found. Tell each smaller subgroup to explain the information they found to their larger group, and have the larger group decide the order of the presentations. Explain to students that for each panel discussion or presentation, they will act as the experts on their topic and you will ask them questions about it. Assess students on their ability to state accurate facts about their topic in a clear, understandable way.

Code of Napoleon
A code of law Napoleon passed that made all men equal in France

How Did Napoleon Affect History?

Napoleon's leadership had many important effects. In France, he achieved one important goal of the French Revolution—he made every man equal before the law. He did this with a new code of laws called the **Code of Napoleon.**

Napoleon's success as a military conqueror changed the political boundaries of Europe. The leaders of the French Revolution had wanted liberty and equality. Napoleon's success spread these ideas throughout Europe.

These ideas changed people. Napoleon had conquered many people. Many of them now wanted their own nation. This rising spirit of nationalism helped to shape European history throughout the 19th century.

Lesson 5 Review On a sheet of paper, write the answer to each question. Use complete sentences.

1. What years in French history do historians call the Age of Napoleon?

2. What did Napoleon do before he came to power in France?

3. When did Napoleon become the emperor of France?

4. How successful was Napoleon's invasion of Russia?

5. At which battle did Napoleon meet his final defeat?

What do you think

Why do you think the Russians did not answer Napoleon's messages of peace near Moscow?

Declaration of the Rights of Man and of the Citizen

The National Assembly of France approved this document in 1789. It was based on two other important documents: the English Bill of Rights and the American Declaration of Independence. The basic principles of the French declaration, such as freedom and equality of all male citizens, helped start the revolution. The declaration also presumed that women were inferior. In response to this, a woman named Olympe de Gouges wrote the Declaration of the Rights of Women in 1791. It began, "Woman is born free and lives equal to man in her rights…" For writing that document, de Gouges was executed by guillotine!

Here are some excerpts from the 1789 document.

1. Men are born and remain free and equal in rights. Social distinctions may be founded only upon the general good.

4. Liberty consists in the freedom to do everything which injures no one else. . . .

5. Law can only prohibit such actions as are hurtful to society. Nothing may be prevented which is not forbidden by law, and no one may be forced to do anything not provided for by law.

6. Law is the expression of the general will. Every citizen has a right to participate personally, or through his representative, in its foundation. . . .

11. The free communication of ideas and opinions is one of the most precious of the rights of man. Every citizen may, accordingly, speak, write, and print with freedom, but shall be responsible for such abuses of this freedom as shall be defined by law.

16. A society in which the observance of the law is not assured, nor the separation of powers defined, has no constitution at all.

Document-Based Questions

1. Why do you think the Declaration of the Rights of Man did not include any reference to the rights of women?

2. Would you describe liberty the same way that it is described in number 4 above?

3. Number 6 says that every citizen has the right to participate in making laws. Do you think that every citizen did this?

4. What rights are listed in number 11?

5. According to number 16, what is important for a society to have?

Read aloud

Read aloud the title "Declaration of the Rights of Man and of the Citizen." Point out that at the time this document was written, it was common to not include women in documents such as these, as women were not seen as equals to men. Then read aloud the introductory paragraph. Explain that because women were not considered equals under the law, Olympe de Gouges did not have the right to compose a document such as the "Declaration of the Rights of Women" in 1791. Under the laws of the day, the French government could execute her for speaking out. Finally, ask volunteers to take turns reading the excerpts from the document from 1789.

Answers to Document-Based Questions:

1. Women were viewed as inferior to men, so women had no rights under the law.

2. Answers will vary. Some students may say that liberty is more restricted than that because restrictions help to prevent chaos.

3. Answers will vary. Students may say that every person eligible to be a citizen probably did not participate in making laws, because not everyone gets involved all the time.

4. Number 11 lists the rights to speak, write, and print with freedom; or the right of free speech or free communication.

5. It is important for a society to have laws that are observed by all, and the separation of powers.

Find a recording of Beethoven's "Ode to Joy" from his Ninth Symphony to play for students. Explain that the composition was first performed in 1824, in the hopes of uplifting people's spirits after years of war and revolution in Europe. Play "Ode to Joy," and then have students silently read "Another Kind of Hero." Have students write answers to the Wrap–Up questions.

Answers to Spotlight Story Wrap-Up:

1. Beethoven was born in Bonn, Germany.

2. His music was based on his feelings.

3. Beethoven lost his hearing.

4. He said that life's struggles could end in peace and joy.

5. Answers will vary. Not letting his handicap defeat him and his musical genius make him a hero.

LEARNING STYLES

Body/Kinesthetic

Obtain a CD of Beethoven's work from your school or local public library. Give students some drawing paper and colored pencils. As students listen to the music, encourage them to draw pictures that show how each piece of music makes them feel. Have students share their drawings with the class and talk about why they "drew the music" the way they did.

Another Kind of Hero

During the French Revolution and the Age of Napoleon, many people were heroes. However, not all heroes are political or military leaders. There is another kind of hero. In spite of great problems, this person reaches for worthy goals. One such hero was a musician named Ludwig van Beethoven.

He was born in Bonn, Germany, in 1770. He was trained in classical music. When he was 12, he became the assistant organist to the royal court in Bonn. Then at age 22, Beethoven went to Vienna to study with Joseph Haydn. Haydn was Europe's greatest classical composer.

Near the end of the 1700s, Beethoven began to compose a new style of music. It was based on his own feelings.

Then a terrible thing happened to him. He started losing his hearing. In 1802, Beethoven wrote, "I was soon compelled to withdraw myself, to live life alone. If at times I try to forget all this . . . I am flung back by the doubly sad experience of my bad hearing. Yet, it is impossible for me to say to people, 'Speak louder, shout, for I am deaf.'" Fate had played a horrible trick on him. He was a great composer. But he was less and less able to hear the beautiful sounds that he created.

Beethoven did not give up. In 1808, he wrote his *Fifth Symphony*. It opens with Fate knocking on the door: *Dah-Dah-Dah Daaaaaaah!* In the end, Music wins the battle with Fate.

Beethoven was going deaf, but his deafness did not stop him from creating music.

In 1824, Beethoven conducted his *Ninth Symphony,* his last work for a large orchestra. In the last movement, a chorus sings the "Ode to Joy." It calls for brotherhood among people throughout the world. It also states that the human struggle against Fate can end in peace and joy. When the *Ninth Symphony* ended, Beethoven stood staring at the orchestra. He could not hear the audience's thunderous applause! A musician made Beethoven turn around and face them. Then he saw what he could not hear.

Ludwig van Beethoven

Beethoven died on March 26, 1827. More than 20,000 people attended his funeral in Vienna. What did Beethoven think about his talent as a composer? In a letter years before, Beethoven had written a possible answer to that question. "There will always be thousands of princes, but there is only one Beethoven." And so there was.

Wrap-Up

1. Where was Beethoven born?

2. How was Beethoven's music different from composers before him?

3. What terrible thing happened to Beethoven?

4. What feeling did Beethoven try to express in his *Ninth Symphony?*

5. Do you think that Beethoven was a hero? Explain your answer.

Chapter 20   SUMMARY

■ After 1763, Britain wanted its North American colonies to pay for the war against France. Britain used the Navigation Acts, the Quartering Act, the Stamp Act, and the Townshend Acts to raise money. The colonists protested. The Boston Massacre and the Boston Tea Party followed. Representatives of the 12 colonies met in Philadelphia in 1775. They agreed to boycott British goods. Then minutemen fought British soldiers at Lexington and Concord.

■ Jefferson wrote most of the Declaration of Independence. It stated people could change their government if it did not protect their rights. Colonial representatives signed it on July 4, 1776.

■ The American victory at Saratoga earned French help. The Revolutionary War ended in 1781. An American army and French ships forced the British under Cornwallis to surrender.

■ France in the 1770s consisted of three estates—the clergy, the nobles, and the common people. The Third Estate paid all the taxes. This group wanted each representative in the Estates-General to have a vote. The other estates and Louis XVI refused. The Third Estate established a constitutional monarchy. It gave everyone freedom of speech and religion and equality under the law. Mobs stormed the Bastille, and the French Revolution began.

■ During the Revolution, there were several governments. In 1792, the National Constitutional Convention created a republic. It wanted to spread the revolution to other countries. Other European countries united to stop France.

■ After an attempted escape, the king was executed and peasants rebelled. Moderates and radicals fought to control the government. The Jacobins under Robespierre came to power and began the Reign of Terror. Then came the Directory and the Consulate. Napoleon became First Consul and then First Consul for life. In 1804 he crowned himself emperor.

■ Napoleon's victories increased French power, but he made two mistakes. The Continental System turned countries against France instead of ruining the British economy. His Russian invasion destroyed his army. Britain, Prussia, Russia, and Austria defeated Napoleon in 1814 and exiled him. He returned and was defeated at Waterloo.

■ In France, the Code of Napoleon made every man equal under the law. Napoleon's conquests spread the ideas of the French Revolution.

1775 – 1815

TEACHER'S RESOURCE

The AGS Globe Teaching Strategies in Social Studies Transparencies may be used with this chapter. The transparencies add an interactive dimension to expand and enhance the *World History* program content.

Using the Chapter Summary

Have students read the Chapter Summary on page 509 to review the main ideas presented in Chapter 20.

Ask:

- **What made the American colonists angry with the British king?** (Answers will vary; students may mention taxes, having to house troops in their homes, and military rule.)

- **What two events in Boston increased hostile feelings between England and the colonies?** (the Boston Massacre and the Boston Tea Party)

- **What document explained why the Americans believed they should be independent?** (the Declaration of Independence)

- **Who led the American forces to victory over the British?** (George Washington)

- **Which European country helped defeat the British in the final battle of the American Revolution?** (France)

- **In France, which people held power and which paid taxes?** (Students may say the poor people in the Third Estate paid taxes and the king and nobility had the power.)

- **What action by French mobs in Paris was the beginning of the French Revolution?** (the storming of the Bastille)

- **What do historians call the year during which radical Jacobins ran the French government?** (the Reign of Terror)

- **Following the Reign of Terror, what military leader became emperor of France?** (Napoleon)

- **Which country was Napoleon unable to conquer in 1812? Why?** (Russia; students may say because of the harsh Russian winter or because the Russians burned everything in a town before they retreated.)

- **Which military leader led the British and Prussian troops against Napoleon at Waterloo?** (the Duke of Wellington)

Chapter 20 Review

Use the Chapter Review to prepare students for tests and to reteach content from the chapter.

Chapter 20 Mastery Test

The Teacher's Resource Library includes two forms of the Chapter 20 Mastery Test. Each test addresses the chapter Goals for Learning. An optional third page of additional critical–thinking items is included for each test. The difficulty level of the two forms is equivalent.

Chapter 20 Review Answers

1. George III
2. Jefferson
3. Locke
4. Washington
5. Cornwallis
6. Louis XVI
7. Antoinette
8. Bonaparte
9. Alexander I
10. Wellington
11. C
12. D
13. A
14. C
15. B
16. The colonists did not want to pay the taxes the British demanded. Also they wanted representation in the British Parliament.

Word Bank

Alexander I
Antoinette
Bonaparte
Cornwallis
George III
Jefferson
Locke
Louis XVI
Washington
Wellington

On a sheet of paper, use the words from the Word Bank to complete each sentence correctly.

1. _____ was the British king when the colonists rebelled.

2. Thomas _____ was the main writer of the Declaration of Independence.

3. The Declaration of Independence is based on many of the ideas of John _____.

4. George _____ commanded the colonial army.

5. General _____ surrendered the British army at Yorktown.

6. During the reign of _____, the French Revolution began.

7. The French executed Marie _____, the queen of France.

8. Napoleon _____ became the emperor of France.

9. Czar _____ of Russia decided to trade with England, so Napoleon invaded Russia.

10. The Duke of _____ defeated Napoleon at Waterloo.

On a sheet of paper, write the letter of the answer that correctly completes each sentence.

11. England enforced the _____ that said that colonists had to ship their trading goods on British ships.

   A Stamp Act   **C** Navigation Acts
   B Townshend Acts   **D** Quartering Act

12. _____ helped the colonists win the Revolutionary War.

   A France   **C** The Netherlands
   B Spain   **D** all of the above

13. At this time, French society was divided into _____ classes, or estates.

   A 3   **B** 6   **C** 9   **D** 19

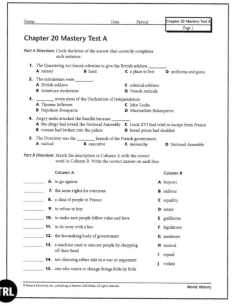

14. The French wanted liberty and _____ for all people.

   A constitutions   **C** equality
   B consuls   **D** boycotts

15. The leader of the French Reign of Terror was _____.

   A Antoinette   **C** Cornwallis
   B Robespierre   **D** Wellington

On a sheet of paper, write the answer to each question. Use complete sentences.

16. What were the colonists rebelling against during the American Revolution?

17. What were the French rebelling against during the French Revolution?

18. What is one way in which the American Revolution changed Europe and one way in which the French Revolution changed Europe?

Critical Thinking On a sheet of paper, write your response to each question. Use complete sentences.

19. Which revolution—the American or the French—would you like to have been part of and why?

20. Pretend that Napoleon's army is marching across Russia and that you are advising the czar. What would you tell him to do?

17. The French did not like to be ruled by an absolute monarch. The common people did not want to be the only ones paying taxes. The people wanted liberty, equality, and fraternity.

18. Answers will vary. The American Revolution gave people in some European countries—France in particular—the courage to rebel. The French Revolution ultimately brought Napoleon to power. His thinking about equality changed the face of Europe.

Critical Thinking

19. Answers will vary. Students should give examples from the text in their response.

20. Answers will vary. The Russians knew that as Napoleon's armies got farther and farther away from France, food and supplies would become more scarce. The czar's advisor probably said, "Keep them here until they face winter. A Russian winter will defeat them!"

Read test questions carefully to identify those that require more than one answer.

1775 – 1815

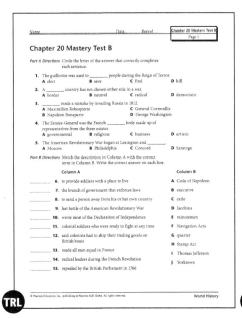

Introducing the Chapter

In the middle of the 18th century, the power of machines began to replace the human hand in the production of goods. Factories replaced home workshops and people left their farms for jobs in the city. New inventions allowed these changes to take place.

The Industrial Revolution Begins

Beginning in the 1750s, workers left farms and moved to cities. There, they labored in factories instead of at home. In this chapter, you will learn more about these factories. You will meet inventors who changed the way people worked and lived. You will discover inventions such as the flying shuttle, the steam locomotive, the light bulb, and the telephone. These inventions and other great changes were all part of the Industrial Revolution.

Goals for Learning

◆ To name the economic conditions needed for industrialization to take place

◆ To explain what was revolutionary about the economic changes that took place in England during the Industrial Revolution

◆ To identify improvements in transportation that helped industrialization

◆ To describe the benefits and problems of industrialization

1793 Whitney invents cotton gin

1823 Lowell builds model factory town in Massachusetts

1856 Bessemer makes steel from iron

1879 Edison invents light bulb

| 1750 | 1800 | 1850 | 1900 |

1814 Stephenson builds steam locomotive

1844 Morse sends first telegraph message

1876 Bell invents telephone

This period of rapid change from farming to industry—from about 1750 to 1850—is known as the Industrial Revolution.

Ask:

• Who invented the cotton gin? (Whitney)

• Which was invented first, the steam locomotive or the telephone? (steam locomotive)

• Name two inventors who improved communication. (Morse and Bell)

Name   Date   Period   *SELF-STUDY GUIDE*

Chapter 21: The Industrial Revolution Begins

Goal 21.1 To name the economic conditions needed for industrialization to take place

Date	Assignment	Completed
	1. Read pages 512–518.	
	2. Complete the Lesson 1 Review on page 518.	
	3. Complete Workbook Activity 96.	

Comments:

Goal 21.2 To explain what was revolutionary about the economic changes that took place in England during the Industrial Revolution

Date	Assignment	Completed
	4. Read pages 519–523.	
	5. Complete the Lesson 2 Review on page 523.	
	6. Complete Workbook Activity 97.	

Comments:

TRL

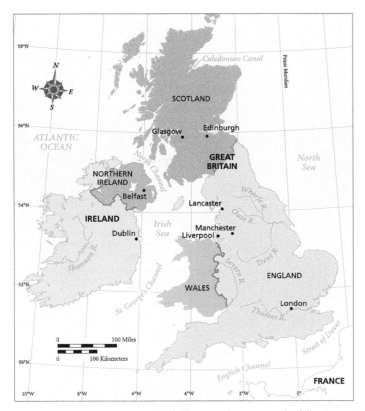

58°N

Caledonian Canal

SCOTLAND

Glasgow ● ● Edinburgh

GREAT BRITAIN

56°N

ATLANTIC OCEAN

North Sea

North Channel

NORTHERN IRELAND

● Belfast

54°N

IRELAND

Irish Sea

Lancaster ●

Wharfe R.

Dublin ●

Manchester ●
Liverpool ●

Ouse R.

Shannon R.

Trent R.

52°N

WALES

ENGLAND

Severn R.

St. George's Channel

London ●

Thames R.

0   100 Miles

0   100 Kilometers

50°N

English Channel

Strait of Dover

FRANCE

10°W   8°W   6°W   4°W   2°W   0°

The British Isles consists of two large islands and many smaller ones. Scotland, Wales, and England are on the larger island that we call Great Britain. Between 1750 and 1850, Great Britain became the center of the Industrial Revolution. Industry changed the way people worked and where they lived.

Study the map, then answer the following questions:

1. What channels separate Ireland from Great Britain?

2. What are the names of three cities in England?

3. What is the major river of Ireland?

4. In what area of Great Britain is the Caledonian Canal located?

5. What sea is to the east of Great Britain?

1750 – 1885   *The Industrial Revolution Begins*   Chapter 21   513

Have students study the map of the British Isles on page 513. Ask them to list the different types of bodies of water that are shown on this map. (ocean, sea, channel, strait, canal, river) Have students point out the cities that are located near some of these bodies of water. (London, Liverpool, Lancaster, Edinburgh, Belfast, Dublin)

Ask:

• What body of water is west of the British Isles? (the Atlantic Ocean)

• What river passes through London? (the Thames River)

• What bodies of water separate England from France? (the English Channel and the Strait of Dover)

Have students read the paragraph about the map and write answers to the questions.

Map Skills Answers

1. St. George's Channel and the North Channel

2. Cities in England include London, Manchester, Lancaster, and Liverpool.

3. the Shannon River

4. northern Scotland

5. the North Sea

Chapter Project

Have students each work with a partner to choose an invention from the era of the Industrial Revolution. The invention might be other than those mentioned in this chapter. Have students use the Internet and library resources to research date, description, inventor, and impact of their invention. Each pair of students should prepare a computer presentation, and if possible a visual model, of the invention for a presentation to the class.

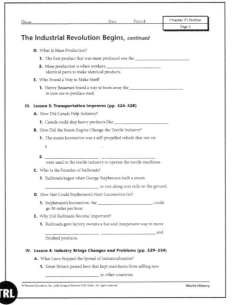

Chapter 21 Outline, pages 1–3

Industrial Rev. Begins Chapter 21   **513**

Metacognition

Introduce the reading strategy *metacognition*. Draw students' attention to the definition. Explain that active readers are aware of the way they learn in order to choose the best way to read the text.

Read aloud the bulleted list on page 514.

Ask:

- **What is a good strategy to use before you read?** (Previewing the text by looking at the headings, pictures, maps, and graphs.)

- **What is a good strategy to use when you read something that you do not understand?** (go back and reread that part)

- **Why is summarizing a good strategy?** (Summarizing helps you remember important facts and make inferences about the text.)

Point out to students that when they think about how they learn as they read, they are using metacognition.

Key Vocabulary Words

Point out that these Key Vocabulary Words are presented in the order that they appear in each lesson. They are also found in the Glossary. Call on volunteers to read aloud the words and their definitions.

Ask:

- **What is *capital*?** (money used to start a business)

- **Which word describes the process of getting machines to do work?** (industrialization)

- **What is a vehicle that runs on rails?** (a locomotive)

- **What is an organized group of workers called?** (labor union)

Reading Strategy:
Metacognition

Metacognition means being aware of the way you learn. It will help you become a better reader.

- ◆ Preview the text, noting the main idea, details, and any questions you have.

- ◆ If you don't understand something, go back and read it again.

- ◆ Summarize what you have read. Make inferences about the meaning.

Key Vocabulary Words

Lesson 1 ───────────────
Industrial Revolution An important change in the way people work

Natural resources Things—such as coal, ore, and water—that come from nature and help humans

Capital Money used to start a business

Industrialization The process of getting machines to do work

Economist A person who studies money

Lesson 2 ───────────────
Manufacturer A person who hires people to work with machines to make something to sell

Mass production A way of making large amounts of the same thing in a factory

Lesson 3 ───────────────
Transportation The movement of people and things from one place to another

Locomotive A self-propelled vehicle that runs on rails

Efficient Working well with little loss of time or energy

Raw materials The materials that are used to make things

Lesson 4 ───────────────
Labor union An organized group of workers who try to improve their working conditions

Internal combustion engine An engine that burns gasoline to produce power

Beginning in the 1750s, quick economic change came to England. Before then, workers made things by hand in their homes. Now they began to work in factories and use machines to produce goods. Before this time, people had used their own strength or the strength of animals to provide power. Now they used the steam engine.

What Is an Industrial Revolution?

We call all these changes the **Industrial Revolution.** What does this term mean? *Industrial* means related to work or labor. *Revolution* means an important change in the way something is done. So the term *Industrial Revolution* means an important change in the way people work. During the Industrial Revolution, people stopped making goods by hand. They began to use machines to produce goods.

In the mid-1700s, England had three things that helped it industrialize: **natural resources,** plenty of workers, and **capital** to build factories and machines. (Natural resources are things that come from nature and help humans. Capital is money used to start a business.)

What Are Natural Resources?

Factory owners need power to run machines. In the 1750s, England could industrialize because it had a source of power. In fact, it had three: coal, iron ore—a rock that contains metal—and rivers. The heat from burning coal turned water into steam power. The iron ore in rocks was made into iron tools and machines. Fast-moving rivers provided power for machines. Nature supplied the coal, the ore, and the rivers. We call these things natural resources. They come from nature, so they are natural. They help us, so they are resources.

Objectives (margin)

- To list three things that helped England industrialize
- To explain how the Industrial Revolution spread beyond England
- To explain the difference between industrialized nations and developing nations

Reading Strategy:
Metacognition

Before you read this section, think about what you can do that will help you understand the text.

Industrial Revolution

An important change in the way people work

Natural resources

Things—such as coal, ore, and water—that come from nature and help humans

Capital

Money used to start a business

1750 – 1885

The Industrial Revolution Begins Chapter 21 515

Chapter 21: Lesson 1

Overview This lesson describes the beginning of the Industrial Revolution in England and includes how it spread to other parts of the world.

Objectives

- To list three things that helped England industrialize
- To explain how the Industrial Revolution spread beyond England
- To explain the difference between industrialized nations and developing nations

Student Pages pages 515–518

Teacher's Resource Library TRL

Workbook Activity 96

Activity 96

Modified Activity 96

Vocabulary

capital	industrialization
economist	natural resources
Industrial Revolution	

Write the headings *People, Things,* and *Events* in a three-column chart on the board. Read aloud each vocabulary word with students and discuss its definition. Have students classify each word under the correct heading. Once all words have been classified, invite students to use each word in a sentence. Write each sentence on the chart.

1 Warm-Up Activity

Divide the class into groups of three or four students. Read the definition of *natural resources* on page 515 and have students work in their groups to list all the natural resources they can. Then have students use the Internet to find products for which those natural resources are used. Have groups share their information with the class. If time permits, have students discuss which natural resources are renewable and which are nonrenewable.

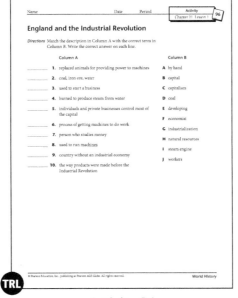

Workbook Activity 96   Activity 96

Industrial Rev. Begins Chapter 21 **515**

Teaching the Lesson

As students read the lesson, it may be challenging for them to understand what life was like prior to the Industrial Revolution. Explain that before the Industrial Revolution, most people made a living by farming, or by doing jobs related to farming. People who made things made them using hand tools. The Industrial Revolution was a time when a lot of machinery was invented that could help people with their jobs.

Reading Strategy:
Metacognition

(Some students may say that they can write questions about the text before and as they read and answer those questions after reading each lesson.)

Ask:

• What three things did England have that helped it industrialize? (natural resources, workers, and capital)

• What new food source caused England's population to increase by 50 percent? (the potato)

Reading Strategy:
Metacognition

(Students may predict that England had so many workers because the country had plenty of food so people were healthier and living longer than they used to.)

Have a volunteer read the title of the map on page 516: "The Industrial Revolution in Great Britain." Have students study the map and the map key.

Ask:

• What do you notice about the location of industrial areas in relation to iron ore deposits and coal fields? (They are generally near one another.)

• Why do you think industrial areas usually developed near natural resources? (Answers will vary; students may say that factories needed natural resources to produce goods, and transportation costs would be lower if factories were located near natural resources.)

Have students read and write answers to the questions in the caption. (There are 14 coal fields. Liverpool was a large coal and industrial area. The Thames River passes through London. Cardiff, Birmingham, and Glasgow had coal and iron ore nearby.)

Map Study

This map shows the sources of industrial power in Great Britain. How many coal fields do you see? Which city in the western part of Great Britain was a large coal and industrial area? What river passes through the industrial city of London? Which industrial cities had both coal and iron ore nearby?

Reading Strategy:
Metacognition

Make a prediction about why England had so many workers in the 1850s. Check your prediction as you continue reading and revise if needed.

Why Did England Have So Many Workers?

Factory owners need workers to run their machines. In the 1850s, England had a large group of workers. Between 1750 and 1800, the population of England increased by 50 percent because there was a new food source from the Americas—the potato.

516   Unit 4   Enlightenment and Revolution

LEARNING STYLES

Auditory/Verbal
To help auditory learners process the information in this lesson, have students listen to the recording for Lesson 1. Encourage them to follow along in their book and to write down key facts as they listen. Invite students to listen to sections of the lesson as many times as necessary to gain understanding of the concepts.

516   Unit 4   *Enlightenment and Revolution*

Biography

Adam Smith: 1723–1790

In 1776, Adam Smith published one of the most important books on economics. It was called *An Inquiry into the Nature and Causes of the Wealth of Nations.* Smith thought that people should be free to produce and sell products at a profit. Government should not interfere in this process. Competition would produce the best goods at the lowest prices.

Smith's ideas are called "capitalism." Capital is money that is used to produce more money. In a capitalist system, individuals and private businesses own and control most of the capital. Today, the United States is the most powerful capitalist nation in the world.

Industrialization

The process of getting machines to do work

At the same time, the English government forced farmworkers off the land. How did they do this? The government passed a law that allowed rich landowners to fence in open fields. For hundreds of years, poor families had farmed these unfenced lands. Now they had no land to farm. So factory owners now had two work sources—an increased population and farmers who had no land to farm.

What Is Capital Used For?

Factory owners need power to run machines and people to work these machines. But where do the machines and the factories come from? The factory owners must buy and build them. Owners do this with capital to start a business and to make more money.

Did the Industrial Revolution Spread Beyond England?

This change in the way people worked began in England, but it soon spread to other countries. By 1860, Germany was industrialized. By the 1870s, the United States became a powerful industrial nation. Today, the process of **industrialization,** or getting machines to do work, is still going on.

Smith's book, An Inquiry Into the Nature of the Wealth of Nations, begins with a famous story about a pin factory. In this factory there are 10 workers, each responsible for one task in the pin-making process. Smith argued that this system—called division of labor—could produce 48,000 pins a day. Working alone, according to Smith, each worker could only produce a few pins a day. Ask students why they think division of labor, as with an assembly line, is more efficient than one person making something from start to finish. (Students may say that by specializing in just one task, a worker would become good at it and be able to work quickly.)

Ask:

• How did the English government force farmworkers off their land? What effect did this have on industrialization? (They passed a law that allowed rich landowners to fence in open fields, leaving farmers with no land to farm; the farmers found work in factories.)

• Why do factory owners need capital? (to buy and build machines and factories)

ELL/ESL Strategy

Language Objective:
To practice using correct punctuation

Give students practice with using proper punctuation. Photocopy the paragraph under the heading "What Is Capital Used For?" and use white-out to delete all of the punctuation from the heading and the paragraph. Make a photocopy of this new page for each student. Have students read the selection independently and fill in the punctuation that they think best suits each sentence. When all students are finished, use choral reading to read the text again, with students saying the type of punctuation they used at the end of each sentence. Discuss with students what makes a complete sentence. Discuss why a period is appropriate for some sentences, while a question mark is appropriate for others.

Ask:

● What do economists call nations that do not yet have an industrial economy? *(developing nations)*

3 Reinforce and Extend

Lesson 1 Review Answers

1. England **2.** Germany **3.** the United States **4.** industrialized nations **5.** developing nations

Answers will vary. Today, factory owners use electricity and oil. Some government factories use atomic or nuclear energy.

After reading this feature, encourage students to find information about other suspension bridges such as the Golden Gate Bridge in California, the Humber Bridge in England, or the Akashi Kaikyo Bridge in Japan.

ONLINE CONNECTION

Descriptions and animated diagrams tell and show students about the steam engine, an integral component of the Industrial Revolution, at this Web site: www.agsglobewh.com/page518.

Economist

A person who studies money

Word Bank

developing nations
England
Germany
industrialized nations
United States

Economists, or people who study money, often divide the people of the world into two groups. One group lives in industrialized nations that have factories to produce goods. The second group lives in developing nations that do not have an industrial economy. Nations need these things to industrialize: capital to buy machines and start up factories, a source of power to make machines work, and workers to run the machines.

Lesson 1 Review On a sheet of paper, use the words from the Word Bank to complete each sentence correctly.

1. Important economic changes beginning in the 1750s took place mainly in _____.

2. By 1860, _____ was industrialized.

3. By the 1870s, the _____ became an industrial nation.

4. Nations that have factories to produce goods are called _____.

5. Nations that do not have an industrial economy are called _____.

What do you think

What are some new sources of power that factory owners use today as they industrialize?

 Marc Seguin and the Bridge

French engineer Marc Seguin built the first wire-cable suspension bridge in 1825. The bridge spanned the Rhone River near Lyons, in eastern France. A suspension bridge uses bearing cables attached to towers at either end. Suspender cables, connected to the bridge platform, are attached vertically to those bearing cables. Suspension bridges had been around since ancient times. However, the cables of those bridges were most often made of hemp rope. The rope could not support all that much weight and it did wear out.

Marc Seguin initiated or supervised the construction of 186 bridges throughout France.

Objectives

- To list the inventions that helped the textile industry
- To explain the advantages of mass production
- To describe how iron is made into steel

Reading Strategy:
Metacognition

Before you read this lesson, think about what you can do that will help you understand how industries began.

For industry, people had to invent new machines and discover new sources of power. In the 1700s, English inventors made several new machines for the textile industry. A textile is a cloth that workers weave from cotton, silk, or wool.

What Inventions Helped the Textile Industry?

In 1733, an English weaver named John Kay invented a "flying shuttle." A shuttle is the part of a weaving machine that carries the thread from one side to the other. The flying shuttle did this more quickly than the human hand could. Because of the flying shuttle, workers could weave twice as much cloth.

To weave more cloth, workers needed more yarn. At that time, people working at home used a spinning wheel to spin yarn. Each spinning wheel had only one spindle. (A spindle twists thread into yarn.) But all the spinning wheels in England could not produce all the yarn the weavers needed.

Then, in 1764, James Hargreaves invented a machine to spin wool or cotton yarn. He called his machine the "spinning jenny." It was a spinning wheel with eight spindles instead of one. In the same year, Richard Arkwright invented a large machine that produced tighter cotton yarn than the spinning jenny.

Manufacturers built large textile mills like this one in Lancashire, England. These mills could produce large amounts of textiles quickly.

1750 – 1885   *The Industrial Revolution Begins*   Chapter 21   **519**

Chapter 21: Lesson 2

Overview This lesson describes inventions that helped the textile industry, mass production, and the development of steel.

Objectives

- To list the inventions that helped the textile industry
- To explain the advantages of mass production
- To describe how iron is made into steel

Student Pages pages 519–523

Teacher's Resource Library

  Workbook Activity 97

  Activity 97

  Modified Activity 97

Vocabulary

manufacturer   **mass production**

Have students look up definitions for *manufacturer* and *mass production*. Have students read and write the definition for each. Then ask students to think of an example of a mass-produced product that they use. Assign students to write a paragraph about the production of that product using the vocabulary words.

PRONUNCIATION GUIDE

Use this list to help students pronounce difficult words in this lesson.

Hargreaves   (här´ grēvz´)

1 Warm-Up Activity

As a class, make a list of everything in the classroom that students think is mass produced. Then discuss whether or not those products existed prior to the Industrial Revolution. For example, a calculator did not exist. If the item did exist prior to the Industrial Revolution, discuss how it was produced. For example, before the sewing machine, clothing was sewn by hand.

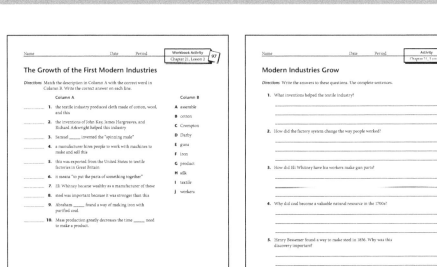

2 Teaching the Lesson

Reading Strategy: Metacognition

(Students may say that they will read and think about the questions in the subheads and look at the illustrations and read the captions.)

Ask:

- Name five inventions that helped the textile industry. (flying shuttle, spinning jenny, Arkwright's machine, spinning mule, and the cotton gin)

- How did the factory system change the way people worked? (The manufacturer determined the location, hours, and amount of work to be done.)

STUDY SKILLS

 To help students identify and summarize the main ideas in this lesson, have them write answers to each of the heading questions. Challenge students to answer each question in a single sentence. Then invite volunteers to write their sentences on the board. Encourage students to answer the heading questions for the entire chapter—their answers will be a helpful study guide.

Manufacturer
A person who hires people to work with machines to make something to sell

In 1778, Samuel Crompton combined the spinning jenny and Arkwright's invention into the "spinning mule." This machine could spin a thread 150 miles long from a single pound of cotton!

Why Did Manufacturers Build Factories?

Before this time, people spun yarn at home and wove it into cloth. Textile **manufacturers** brought wool, cotton, and silk to the workers' homes. (A manufacturer hires people to work with machines to make something to sell.) But hand work at home was slow and costly, and manufacturers wanted to save time and money. They built factories, and workers then left their homes and came to the factory to work. The factory system brought workers, machines, and a source of power together to produce a product.

This system changed the way people worked. The worker now had to work when and where the manufacturer said. The worker had to work the hours the manufacturer wanted. And the worker had to do the amount of work the manufacturer demanded.

The cotton gin allowed workers to separate seeds from cotton faster than doing it by hand. It made cotton, which is used to make cloth, a much more valuable material.

What Problem Did Cotton Growers Have?

Textile workers in factories now needed more cotton to spin into yarn and to weave into cloth. Getting cotton from the field to the factory was hard work. Natural cotton contains sticky, tightly-held seeds. In the 1700s, people had to remove these seeds by hand. This took a lot of time.

Then, in 1793, Eli Whitney invented a machine that solved the problem. While fixing other machines in Georgia, Whitney invented the cotton gin. His invention was a wooden box with a wire brush and grille, or screen. Workers placed cotton on one side of the grille. Then the revolving brush grabbed the cotton and pushed it through the grille. The seeds were too large to pass through the screen, so the machine separated the seeds from the cotton thread.

With the cotton gin, workers could clean cotton 50 times faster than by hand. Within 20 years, cotton became the most important export from the southern United States. Cotton farmers exported most of this cotton to the textile factories in Great Britain.

Reading Strategy:
Metacognition

Note the main idea and important details of this paragraph. Summarize what you have read to make sure you understand the importance of mass production.

What Is Mass Production?

Whitney made little money from his invention of the cotton gin. But he became wealthy as a gun manufacturer. Before Whitney, workers made guns one at a time. Each part of a gun was a little different from the same part on another gun. Whitney had workers make gun parts that were identical, or exactly alike.

Then the workers assembled, or put together, these identical parts to make identical guns. The guns were alike in every way. If a part from one gun needed to be replaced, that same part from another gun of the same kind could be used. We call this **mass production.** It is a way of making large amounts of the same thing in a factory. It greatly cuts the time workers need to make something, so they can produce more.

Ask:

- Why was it a problem to make things with iron? (It had impurities that caused it to break easily.)

- What did Bessemer create by burning the impurities out of melted iron? (steel)

- How did Bessemer make iron into steel? (He forced air into melted iron to burn away the impurities.)

LEARNING STYLES

Interpersonal/ Group Learning

Have students work in groups of three or four to research the importance of steel to the Industrial Revolution and to our lives today. Suggest concentrating on the following issues: how the Bessemer process works, the advantages of steel over iron, what engineers can build from steel (possibilities include skyscrapers, bridges, and better railroad tracks), and what it's like to work in a steel mill today. Encourage groups to use visual aids. Have them present their reports to the class.

Henry Bessemer developed a low-cost way to make steel. Steel became an important building material after it was invented. This picture shows a steel mill.

Who Found a Way to Make Steel?

Manufacturers built their new industrial machines from iron. In 1709, Englishman Abraham Darby found a way of making iron with coke, or purified coal. However, making iron was still a problem because iron ore had impurities, or materials in it that made it not pure and made iron products break easily. In the late 1700s, it was discovered that stirring hot iron helped burn off the impurities.

In 1856, Englishman Henry Bessemer found a way to get rid of more impurities in iron. He discovered that air forced into melted iron burned away these impurities. His process produced a new product—steel. It was stronger than iron and did not break as easily. Soon, steel manufacturing became an important industry in many industrial countries. Those countries that had large amounts of coal and iron ore built steel mills.

The English built their steel mills in the north. In Germany, the Ruhr Valley became a great steel center. In the United States, Pittsburgh, Pennsylvania, became an important steel-producing city.

Lesson 2 Review On a sheet of paper, write the letter of the answer that correctly completes each sentence.

1. The _____ industry became more profitable with the invention of the flying shuttle, spinning jenny, and spinning mule.

   A steel   **C** cotton
   B iron   **D** textile

2. The factory system brought together _____ to produce a product.

   A workers   **C** a source of power
   B machines   **D** all of the above

3. _____ invented the cotton gin.

   A Whitney   **C** Hargreaves
   B Kay   **D** Bessemer

4. The term _____ means producing identical products in great number.

   A spinning jenny   **C** textile
   B mass production   **D** industry

5. _____ discovered a way to make steel from iron.

   A Whitney   **C** Bessemer
   B Kay   **D** Hargreaves

What is good and what is bad about the factory system?

Lesson 2 Review Answers

1. D 2. D 3. A 4. B 5. C

Answers will vary. The workers had to give up some personal freedom to work in factories. Working at home, people could work when they wanted. They had no boss watching them work. Also, to work in factories, a person had to live in a city, not on the farm. However, factories could produce more, so workers might have made more money.

Chapter 21: Lesson 3

Overview This lesson describes improvements in roads and canals and the development of railroads and their effects on industry.

Objectives

- To explain how improvements in the construction of roads and canals helped industrialization
- To describe how the steam engine led to the development of railroads

Student Pages pages 524–528

Teacher's Resource Library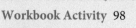

Workbook Activity 98

Activity 98

Modified Activity 98

Vocabulary

efficient   raw materials
locomotive   transportation

On the board, write original sentences that contain the vocabulary words. Based on your sentences, have students guess the definition of each word. Then have students write their own sentences using the words.

Warm-Up Activity

Divide the class into pairs of students. Have partners make a list of all of the transportation methods they can think of for transporting manufactured goods. Have students share their lists with the class. Then discuss how each transportation method would be affected if the roads, canals, and railroad tracks were not well maintained.

Teaching the Lesson

Ask students to think about transportation routes including railroads and waterways that are in or near your community. Discuss the advantages of having these routes nearby.

Objectives

- To explain how improvements in the construction of roads and canals helped industrialization
- To describe how the steam engine led to the development of railroads

Transportation

The movement of people and things from one place to another

Reading Strategy:
Metacognition

Notice the structure of this chapter. Look at the titles, headings, and boldfaced words.

Improved **transportation** also helped industrialization. Transportation is the movement of people and things from one place to another. Industry needs good transportation.

The problem with transportation in the early 1700s was that people had to travel on dirt roads. When rain fell, the dirt turned into thick mud into which horses and carriages sunk. In 1770, two Scotsmen—Thomas Telford and John McAdam—developed better road-building methods. Telford built roads in two layers, so water quickly ran off. McAdam built roads of crushed stone.

How Did Canals Help Industry?

For many years, manufacturers used roads to move products that were not so heavy. Then, in the 1760s, workers dug the first modern canal in England. (The United States built its first canal in 1825.) The seven-mile-long canal stretched from Manchester to a coal mining area nearby. Now, manufacturers could easily move large amounts of coal from mines to cities, so coal became cheaper.

On a canal, manufacturers could ship heavy products like coal. Canals cost a lot of money to dig, and they needed a source of water. Good roads were a faster means of transportation for moving light products from place to place. But no one could travel fast on them in rainy weather.

English manufacturers had a problem. They needed to quickly move large amounts of products—light or heavy—to different places in any type of weather. But roads got muddy and canals needed water. What could these manufacturers do?

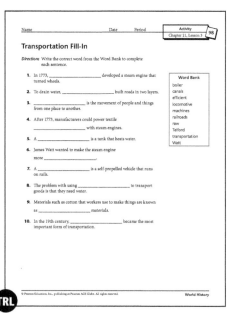

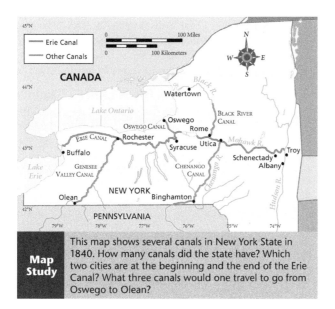

Map Study

This map shows several canals in New York State in 1840. How many canals did the state have? Which two cities are at the beginning and the end of the Erie Canal? What three canals would one travel to go from Oswego to Olean?

Locomotive

A self-propelled vehicle that runs on rails

Efficient

Working well with little loss of time or energy

How Did the Steam Engine Change the Textile Industry?

The answer to the manufacturers' transportation problem was a steam **locomotive.** This is a self-propelled vehicle that runs on rails. But before learning about that, you need to know about steam engines. In 1705, the simple steam engine was invented. Workers used it to pump water out of coal mines.

In 1763, James Watt began to look for a way to improve the steam engine and make it more **efficient,** or work better with little time or energy wasted. In 1773, Watt developed a steam engine that turned wheels. Textile machines had wheels, so this new engine could operate those machines.

1750 – 1885   *The Industrial Revolution Begins*   *Chapter 21*   525

Reading Strategy:
Metacognition

(Students may notice that each lesson has a title that gives them clues about the main idea of the lesson. Each heading is a question that students should be able to answer after reading the section of text.)

Ask:

• How did Telford and McAdam fix the problem of muddy roads in rainy weather? (Telford built roads in two layers that allowed water to run off; McAdam built roads of crushed stone.)

• What products were easier to ship via water than via road? (heavy products, such as coal)

• What did James Watt invent in 1773? (a steam engine that could turn wheels)

Have a volunteer read the title of the map on page 525: "Canals in New York, 1840." Have students study the map carefully.

Ask:

• In which direction does the Erie Canal run? (east and west)

• In which direction do the other canals run? (north and south)

• What river joins the Erie Canal at its eastern end? (the Hudson River)

Have students write answers to the questions in the caption. (New York had five canals. Schenectedy and Buffalo are at the beginning and end of the Erie Canal. The three canals people used to travel from Oswego to Olean would be the Oswego Canal, the Erie Canal, and the Genesee Valley Canal.)

LEARNING STYLES

Visual/Spatial

Have students locate a photograph or illustration of a steam engine in a magazine or on the Internet. Ask them to bring the picture to class and explain how the steam engine works. Students who enjoy drawing might wish to draw a diagram of a steam engine on construction paper or poster board. Students should clearly label its parts.

Ask:

- Before the development of the steam engine, where did manufacturers have to build textile factories? Why? (next to streams; the swiftly falling water provided the power to run textile machines)

- When did George Stephenson build the first steam locomotive? (1814)

- How fast could *Blucher* pull 30 tons of coal? (four miles per hour)

BACKGROUND INFORMATION

The construction of the transcontinental railroad in the United States had two starting points. The Union Pacific Railroad started laying tracks at Omaha, Nebraska, and headed westward. The Central Pacific Railroad started in Sacramento, California, and headed eastward. Conditions for the European and Chinese immigrants who laid the track were brutal: many lost their lives due to accidents, illness, and disputes with American Indians. Workers had to construct tunnels through mountains—sometimes making only a few feet of progress after a full day of work. Finally, after several years of grueling labor, the two railroad lines were joined at Promontory Point, Utah. This occasion was marked by a ceremony in which a golden spike was driven into the last link of track.

Up to that time, swiftly falling water produced the power to run textile machines. Manufacturers had to build textile factories next to fast-moving streams. Now manufacturers could power their textile machines with steam engines. They could build their factories anywhere. By 1800, more than 500 steam engines were powering machinery in British factories.

Who Is the Founder of Railroads?

Early in the 1800s, workers used a little steam engine on wheels to pull small carts of coal out of mines. This steam engine did the work of one or two horses. Then, in 1814, George Stephenson—a mining engineer—built a steam locomotive. It moved along iron rails, or bars, on the ground. These rails went on and on and became a kind of road, so the locomotive traveled on a road of rails, or a railroad.

Stephenson called his locomotive *Blucher*. He had discovered a way to increase the heat in the boiler. (A boiler is the tank that heats water.) By increasing the heat, Stephenson produced steam under higher pressure. *Blucher* could pull almost 30 tons of coal at a speed of four miles per hour.

George Stephenson's Rocket could reach a top speed of 30 miles per hour.

How Fast Could Stephenson's Next Locomotive Go?

In 1829, Stephenson built the *Rocket*—a faster locomotive. At that time, some businessmen wanted to build a railroad between Liverpool and Manchester. They had a contest to find a locomotive to quickly go this distance. Stephenson entered the contest and won.

Stephenson's *Rocket* pulled a train of cars for more than 30 miles. It reached a speed of 30 miles per hour. This meant that the *Rocket* was more powerful than 80 horses pulling together. Stephenson went on to design railroad bridges, tunnels, and the roadbed for the Liverpool and Manchester Railway. Today, historians call him the "founder of the railways."

Why Did Railroads Become Important?

Railroads became the most important form of transportation in the 19th century. During the 1840s and 1850s, they went back and forth across England. They greatly helped factory owners. How? By providing them with a fast and inexpensive way to move **raw materials** and finished products. (Raw materials are the materials such as cotton, wood, iron, and oil that workers use to make things.)

Railroads needed metal rails, cars, and locomotives. The iron and steel industry grew quickly. Railroad owners hired thousands of workers to clear land and lay railroad tracks. Other European countries also built railroad lines. In 1869, the United States completed the transcontinental railroad. It ran from one side of the continent to the other and linked the Atlantic and Pacific coasts together.

Ask:

- **How did railroads help factory owners?** (They were a fast and inexpensive way to transport raw materials and finished products.)

- **Why was George Stephenson called "the founder of the railways?"** (He designed locomotives, railroad bridges, tunnels, and roadbeds.)

- **What industry grew as a result of railroads?** (the iron and steel industry)

ELL/ESL STRATEGY

Language Objective: *To prepare and give a group presentation*

Divide the class into groups of 4 or 5 students. Have students reread the sections about early railroads on pages 526 and 527 with their group. Then have each group choose and research an early locomotive. Have students work together and use the Internet, books, and encyclopedias to find important and interesting facts about their locomotive. Have students record their facts and sources on index cards. Ask each group to compile all of their facts into an interesting presentation for the class. Encourage students to make the presentations as entertaining as possible. Students may choose to use the facts in song lyrics, or create a skit that includes their facts.

Have students read the Then and Now feature, "Railroads," silently. Then have a volunteer read it aloud.

Ask:

- What are the three types of locomotives? Which type is the fastest? (steam, diesel, electric; electric)

- How fast can high-speed trains in Japan and France travel? (more than 200 miles per hour)

- What is the world's longest railroad line? How long is it? (the Trans-Siberian Railroad; 5,700 miles)

- What percentage of city passenger transportation in the United States is by rail? (less than one percent)

 3 Reinforce and Extend

Lesson 3 Review Answers

1. Manufacturers need a way to get raw materials and products to different places, so they need good roads, canals, and railroads. **2.** One big problem with transportation was that roads got muddy and carriages and people got stuck in them. **3.** Canals were expensive to dig, and they had to be near a source of water. **4.** James Watt found a way to make the steam engine more efficient. **5.** Historians credit George Stephenson with being the founder of the railroad. He built steam locomotives, railway bridges and tunnels, and railway roadbeds.

Answers will vary. When natural resources cost less money, the manufacturer has less cost and can make more profit on goods. As manufacturers make more profit, they may build more factories in other places, so industry spreads. Also, when manufacturers have fewer costs and make more profit, they sometimes pay more to workers. Then workers have more to spend and want more goods to buy. This means that manufacturers produce more goods and the cycle continues.

Railroads

Stephenson's invention of the steam locomotive started a race. Who could develop the fastest, most efficient transportation for people and goods? After the steam locomotive came the diesel, and then the even faster electric locomotive. The first trains traveled about four miles per hour. Today, Japan and France have high-speed trains that travel more than 200 miles per hour.

Countries also began to build miles and miles of tracks. The world's longest railroad line is the Trans-Siberian Railroad. It runs 5,700 miles—from Moscow to Vladivostock, Russia.

The United States has over 140,000 miles of rail in use today. About 40 percent of goods are still shipped by rail. But less than 1 percent of city passenger transportation is by rail.

Lesson 3 Review On a sheet of paper, write the answer to each question. Use complete sentences.

1. Why is good transportation needed for the growth of industry?

2. What was one big problem with transportation in the 1770s?

3. Why were canals not the best type of transportation for industry?

4. Who found a way of making the steam engine more efficient?

5. Why is George Stephenson important in the history of transportation?

How would cheap coal help industry grow?

Lesson 4 — Industry Brings Changes and Problems

Objectives

- To explain why cities grew during the Industrial Revolution
- To describe the problems factory workers faced
- To identify two new sources of power

Reading Strategy:
Metacognition

Look at the photographs and illustrations, and note the descriptive words. This will help you visualize the inventors and inventions named in this lesson.

Before the 1750s, most people worked as farmers in small villages. Each family grew its own food and made its own clothing. Many people never traveled more than 10 miles from where they were born.

Industrialization changed all this. People in Great Britain were the first to experience these changes. In the 1800s, industrialization also changed Europe and the United States. However, British textile factories still made more than half of the world's cotton cloth. In fact, British factories produced so many goods that people called Great Britain the "workshop of the world."

What Laws Stopped the Spread of Industrialization?

For many years, Great Britain tried to keep other countries from learning the lessons of industrialization. In fact, Britain passed laws so that merchants could not sell new machines to other countries. Up until the 1840s, Britain also refused to let skilled workers leave the country. People feared that these workers could design or make tools and machinery that would help other countries industrialize.

How Did A British Worker Help the United States?

In 1789, Samuel Slater—a British factory worker—memorized plans for building a spinning machine. Then he dressed himself as a simple farmer and got on a ship sailing to the United States. (British officials would have stopped him if they had known he could build a spinning machine.) Once in the United States, Slater met Moses Brown—a Rhode Island businessman. In 1793, Brown built the first thread-making factory in the United States. He used spinning machines that Slater built.

Chapter 21: Lesson 4

Overview This lesson describes the changes and problems brought about by industrialization.

Objectives

- To explain why cities grew during the Industrial Revolution
- To describe the problems factory workers faced
- To identify two new sources of power

Student Pages pages 529–534

Teacher's Resource Library

Workbook Activity 99

Activity 99

Modified Activity 99

Vocabulary

internal combustion engine
labor union

Discuss with students the definitions of the vocabulary words. Then have them write two short paragraphs explaining how each word relates to industrialization. Encourage volunteers to read their paragraphs aloud.

1 Warm-Up Activity

Tell students that once the Industrial Revolution began, many people gave up the farming lifestyle and moved to cities to work in factories. Divide the class into pairs. Have one partner role-play the part of a farm worker and the other role-play a factory worker at the time of the Industrial Revolution. Have each student describe their job to their partner. Encourage students to add to or correct their descriptions as they read Lesson 4.

2 Teaching the Lesson

As students read the lesson, have them think about the benefits and drawbacks of an industrialized society. You may wish to have students include the information in a two-column chart that can be used to study for the chapter test.

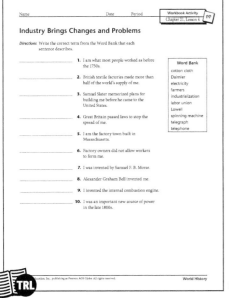

Workbook Activity 99   **Activity 99**   *Industrial Rev. Begins* Chapter 21   **529**

(Students might work with a partner to scan the lesson and look at the photos and write down descriptive words.)

Ask:

• Where did most people live before the Industrial Revolution? Where did they live after? (farms; cities)

• How did Great Britain try to prevent other countries from learning the lessons of industrialization? (Great Britain passed laws to prevent British merchants from selling new machines to other countries and refused to allow skilled workers to leave the country)

• Who were the workers in Francis Lowell's textile factory? (young farm women)

Have students study the graph, "The Population Growth of Five British Cities." Have students work in teams to find the answers to the questions. (Bristol had the largest population in 1685. Liverpool had the largest population in 1881. It had 555,425 people.)

Have students work in small groups to create a list of laws to protect children from unfair or dangerous working conditions. Ask them to consider the following questions: What should be the minimum age for employment? When should young people be allowed to work? What type of work should young people be prohibited from doing? Have groups share their laws with the class. Then have students read "Child Labor Laws" to find out about the dangers of child labor and the laws that exist to protect children.

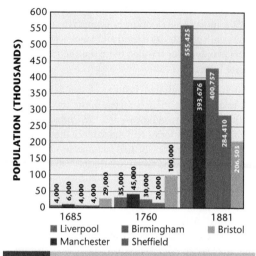

Population (Thousands) by city and year

1685 — Liverpool 4,000; Manchester 6,000; Birmingham 4,000; Sheffield 4,000; Bristol 29,000

1760 — Liverpool 35,000; Manchester 45,000; Birmingham 30,000; Sheffield 20,000; Bristol 100,000

1881 — Liverpool 555,425; Manchester 393,676; Birmingham 400,757; Sheffield 284,410; Bristol 206,503

■ Liverpool   ■ Birmingham   ■ Bristol
■ Manchester ■ Sheffield

Graph Study Which city had the largest population in 1685? Which city had the largest population in 1881? How many people did it have?

Child Labor Laws

As industry increased, factory owners began to hire children. They could pay them much lower wages than men. Children might work as many as 14 hours a day. Their working conditions were often dangerous as well. Some British orphans were treated almost like slaves.

Reformers began to force governments to stop the evils of the factory system. Reformers wanted to protect children and give them a chance to go to school. Early laws failed to correct these evils. Later laws carried more power. Today, Europe, North America, Australia, Japan, and New Zealand enforce child labor laws. In the United States, the minimum age for employment is 14. The work must be done outside of school hours, and it cannot be in manufacturing.

In less developed countries, however, millions of children still work. Some as young as seven years old work in quarries, mines, and factories.

What Did Lowell Do for His Factory Workers?

In 1823, Francis Lowell built a factory town in Massachusetts and named it after himself. He hired young farm women to work in his factory. First, he taught them how to work the textile machines. Then he set up a school to teach them how to read and write. Finally, he gave them a clean place to live. Soon, textile mills spread throughout the New England states. However, few factory owners followed Lowell's ideas.

530   Unit 4   Enlightenment and Revolution

IN THE COMMUNITY

Have students research the influence of industrialization on the growth of their own town or city. Ask them to consider the following questions: What industries developed in your town or city? What happened to the population when those industries grew? Has the population increased or decreased over time? What industries are located in your town or city today? Students might call the local library or historical society to find this information. Have them summarize their findings in a brief report.

Industry greatly changed many cities. This picture shows the crowded living conditions and soot-filled air of Manchester, England, in 1876.

What Did Industrialization Do to Cities?

Industrialization changed the way people worked. It also changed where they lived. Before the Industrial Revolution, most people lived on farms, not in cities. Then manufacturers began to build factories near cities. People from the country then moved to the cities to get work.

Industrialization caused city populations to grow quickly. For example, in 1750, the English town of Manchester had less than 16,000 people. By 1850, it had become a major textile center with a population of more than 300,000. From 1800 to 1850, the number of European cities with a population of more than 100,000 doubled to nearly 50.

But bigger cities created problems. People lived in unhealthy conditions. Garbage filled the streets. Bad water and sanitation caused disease. Still, people moved to the cities to find jobs. In fact, by 1900, almost 75 percent of the people of Great Britain lived in cities.

What Problems Did Factory Workers Have?

As you know, during the Industrial Revolution, unskilled workers came to cities for work. Whole families labored in factories. Children as young as six years old worked 8 to 14 hours a day. They worked among dangerous machines. But factory owners refused to pay for doctors to help workers hurt by these machines. Also, owners refused to pay workers if they were hurt or sick and could not work for a while.

Ask:

- List the problems that arose as cities grew bigger. (Answers will vary; garbage filled the streets and bad water and sanitation caused disease.)

- Who worked in factories? (entire families, including young children)

 Writing About History

Have students consult a variety of resources—books, encyclopedias, the Internet—as they perform their research. Suggest to students that they select the most interesting facts from a number of reputable resources instead of relying on just one. When they write their paragraphs, have students note the sources they used.

WORLD CULTURES

Manchester, England, is widely regarded as the first major urban center of the Industrial Revolution. While surrounding towns continue to depend on manufacturing today, the city itself has been turning away from its industrial past and turning toward a service economy. Banks and financial services have taken the place of factories. Almost half of the manufacturing jobs once available in the city are gone, resulting in high unemployment rates for unskilled workers.

Ask a volunteer to read "Telegraph Provides Instant Communication" to the class. Discuss with students how the invention of the telegraph revolutionized communication in the 19th century. Some observers say we are currently experiencing a new communication revolution. Ask students what communication tools are part of this revolution. (Students may say e-mail, the Internet, cellular telephones, instant messaging, text messaging, and so on.) Then have students speculate what new tools might revolutionize communication in the future.

Ask:

- Why couldn't the workers change the law to make factories safer? (They had no political power because they were not allowed to vote.)
- What new sources of power were being used by the late 19th century? (electricity and oil)
- How did the telegraph work? (It sent messages long distances over wires by making and breaking an electrical current.)

Reading Strategy:
Metacognition

Students might ask themselves questions such as: "What was the telegraph used for?" (sending messages over long distances)

AT HOME

Some students may have family members who belong to labor unions. Have students interview them to find out why they choose to be a member. What benefits do they receive? Some students do not have family members in labor unions. Have those students interview a family member about the safety precautions that are taken so they can do their jobs safely. Have students summarize their interviews in a brief report and share their findings with the class.

Telegraph Provides Instant Communication

Samuel F. B. Morse, an artist and inventor, invented the telegraph in the United States in the 1830s. Two British men, Charles Wheatstone and William Cooke, also made a telegraph machine.

The telegraph freed communication from the problems of long distance transportation. In the United States, the Pony Express service was the fastest way to communicate. However, it was discontinued in 1861 because the telegraph was much faster.

The telegraph also solved a traffic control problem for railroads. Using the telegraph, railroad workers could keep track of trains. This helped them avoid accidents. Railroads also used the telegraph to check on schedules, passengers, and freight shipments.

Labor union

An organized group of workers who try to improve their working conditions

Workers wanted safer factories, more pay, and shorter hours. They could not get what they wanted because the law did not let them form **labor unions.** A labor union is an organized group of workers who try to improve their working conditions.

The workers could not change the law because they had no political power. In England, only people who owned property could vote. But most factory workers owned no property, so they could not vote. Without a vote, they could not change the laws that kept them from forming unions.

What Two New Sources of Power Changed the World?

As you know, coal and steam provided power for the Industrial Revolution. But in the late 19th century, inventors discovered two new sources of power—electricity and oil.

Reading Strategy:
Metacognition

Remember to ask yourself questions as you read. This will help you make sure that you understand what you are reading.

The use of electricity began in the 1840s when Samuel F. B. Morse invented the telegraph. With this machine, he could send messages over long distances by making and breaking an electric current. In 1844, Morse sent his first message from Washington, D.C., to Baltimore, Maryland. For the message, he used a code he had created. In this code, a different pattern of long or short electrical signals represented each letter of the alphabet. This was called Morse code.

Alexander Graham Bell demonstrates how to use his telephone, which he invented in 1876.

In 1866, workers laid a cable on the floor of the Atlantic Ocean to carry electrical messages between the United States and Europe. Before this, messages took days to deliver; now they took minutes.

In 1876, Alexander Graham Bell invented the telephone. For the first time, a human being could hear another person's voice over an electrical wire. In 1879, Thomas Edison invented the light bulb. It provided safe light to homes, businesses, and factories.

Why Was the Discovery of Gasoline Important?

Internal combustion engine

An engine that burns gasoline to produce power

Oil was another important new source of power. Before the 1860s, people mostly used oil to grease wheels. Now, they began to use it to provide heat and to power machinery.

People learned that they could make gasoline from oil. Gasoline ran the **internal combustion engine** that Gottlieb Daimler invented in 1885. The internal combustion engine burned gasoline to produce power. It made the automobile possible.

Thomas Edison poses with perhaps his greatest invention, the light bulb. He invented it in 1879.

The Industrial Revolution Begins   Chapter 21   533

Lesson 4 Review Answers

1. Slater **2.** Lowell **3.** Morse
4. Bell **5.** Daimler

Answers will vary. Some manufacturers are so interested in profits that they do not care a great deal about workers. So labor unions can help workers get better working conditions, better pay, fewer hours, and greater benefits. However, other owners are more sensitive to the needs of workers. In their factories, unions might not be necessary.

Chapter Project Follow-up

Give student pairs time to finish the preparation of their computer presentations on their chosen invention. Have students give their presentations to the class and turn in a bibliography of reliable sources to you. Evaluate students on the accuracy of their research, the creativity of their presentation, and their ability to interest other students in their chosen invention.

In 1903, Wilbur and Orville Wright—two American men who liked to work with machines—were the first to fly an airplane successfully. They used a gasoline engine.

The Wright brothers were the first people to fly an airplane successfully.

Lesson 4 Review On a sheet of paper, use the words from the Word Bank to complete each sentence correctly.

Word Bank
Bell
Daimler
Lowell
Morse
Slater

1. In 1789, Samuel _____ left England and came to the United States to build spinning machines.

2. In 1823, Francis _____ built a model factory town in Massachusetts.

3. In 1844, Samuel F. B. _____ sent the first telegraph message.

4. In 1876, Alexander _____ invented the telephone.

5. In 1885, Gottlieb _____ built the internal combustion engine.

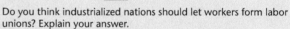

What do you think

Do you think industrialized nations should let workers form labor unions? Explain your answer.

A Manchester Housewife's Weekly Budget in 1833

Living and working conditions were terrible in manufacturing areas during the early 1800s in England. As a result, Parliament formed committees in the 1830s to see if workers earned enough to feed, clothe, and house themselves. This report discusses the weekly budget of a housewife in Manchester, a manufacturing city.

A word about English money: the "s" after a number stands for shilling. A "d" means pence. One shilling contains 12 pence. At this time, 20 shillings were equal to $5.

Mrs. B., Manchester. This witness was accidentally met with, 13th May, 1833. She was waiting for Dr. Hawkins, to consult him about her niece's health. I took her into a room, and examined her about the customs and comforts of operative families. . . .

Her husband is a fine spinner, at Mr. M's, where he has been from 1816, has five children. Her eldest daughter, now going on 14, has been her father's helper for three years. At present her husband's earnings and her daughter's together amount to about 25s a week.

Breakfast is generally porridge, bread, and milk, lined with flour or oatmeal. On Sunday, a cup of tea and bread and butter. Dinner, on weekdays, potatoes and bacon, and bread, which is generally white. On a Sunday, a little fresh meat, no butter, egg, or pudding. Tea time every day, tea, and bread and butter; nothing extra on Sunday at tea. Supper, oatmeal porridge and milk; sometimes potatoes and milk. Sunday, sometimes a little bread and cheese for supper; never have this on a weekday. Now and then buys eggs when they are as low as a halfpenny apiece, and fries them with bacon.

They never taste any other vegetable than potatoes; never use any beer or spirits; now and then may take a gill of beer when ill, which costs a penny. . . .

The house consists of four rooms, two on each floor; the furniture consists of two beds in the same room, one for themselves and the other for the children; have four chairs, one table in the house, boxes to put clothes in, no chest of drawers, two pans and a tea kettle for boiling, a gridiron and frying pan, half a dozen large and small plates, four pair of knives and forks, several pewter spoons.

Document-Based Questions

1. What kind of work does the husband in this family do?

2. How much money does the family make in a week?

3. How many people are in this family?

4. Do you think this family's diet is a healthy one? Why or why not?

5. Do you think that the family's housing is adequate? Why or why not?

Read aloud the introduction to "A Manchester Housewife's Weekly Budget in 1833." Then have volunteers take turns reading paragraphs aloud. Ask students to calculate the husband's earnings of 25 shillings a week into dollars. (at the time, 20 shillings were equal to 5 dollars; therefore, 25 shillings were equal to 6 dollars and 25 cents) Have students write their answers to the Document–Based questions.

Answers to Document-Based Questions:

1. He was a spinner.

2. The family earns 25 shillings a week.

3. There are seven people in the family— a father, a mother, and five children.

4. Answers will vary. Their diet is not healthy because it does not include fruits and vegetables and contains very little protein. Bacon was fried and would include lots of fat.

5. Answers will vary. While seven people would be crowded in four rooms, it probably was not unusual for that time. More furnishings would make the house more comfortable. They probably had to sleep in the same room because they did not have enough money to buy coal to heat separate rooms.

Spotlight Story

Hard Times and Charles Dickens

"Now what I want is, Facts. Teach these boys and girls nothing but Facts. Facts alone are wanted in life. Plant nothing else, and root out everything else. . . . This is the principle on which I bring up my own children, and this is the principle on which I bring up these children. Stick to the Facts, Sir!"

So wrote Charles Dickens in *Hard Times,* one of his many novels. *Hard Times* is a story about the difficult lives of textile workers. Through Dickens's novels, a reader can relive the world of 19th-century England. He was the greatest observer of his times. And, like the schoolmaster in *Hard Times,* Dickens gathered the facts of his world. He used actual people, places, and social groups in England in his writings. But unlike the schoolmaster, Dickens's mind took "a fanciful photograph" of a person or place. He turned facts into unforgettable stories. The schoolroom and master in *Hard Times* are only examples of this ability. Dickens had a gift for describing places and creating memorable characters. As a result, he is called "the greatest master of English character since Shakespeare."

Dickens's novels captured the sights and sounds of a world that no longer exists. Today, there are no debtors' prisons. But Dickens helps the reader picture these terrible places. There are no more stagecoaches, but he makes you feel their bumpy ride. There are no more workhouses for poor orphaned children. But Dickens shows you the children. You see the poverty, hopelessness, and hard work that ages them beyond their years.

When he was a young man in the 1830s, Dickens found work as a journalist. In 1836, he published his first novel *The Pickwick Papers.*

Then he wrote *Oliver Twist.* Oliver is a boy caught in a world of crime and workhouses for the poor. The novel appeared in parts in a monthly magazine. *A Christmas Carol* came later. It is the story of Ebenezer Scrooge, a greedy man with a heart of stone. In the end, Scrooge comes to a new understanding about life. He learns that joy can come from kindness to others.

Charles Dickens

Dickens's stories are a time machine to the past. Through them, we travel through time and experience a different world.

Wrap-Up

1. Who was Charles Dickens?

2. Dickens said that he would take a "fanciful photograph" of a person or place. What did he mean?

3. What kind of work did Dickens do when he was young?

4. How did readers first experience the story of Oliver Twist?

5. Why are Dickens's novels valuable for historical purposes?

Chapter 21   S U M M A R Y

■ The Industrial Revolution began in England in the 1750s. England could industrialize because it had coal, iron ore, and rivers as natural resources. A growing population and farmers looking for work increased the workforce. There was capital to build factories and buy machinery.

■ By 1860, Germany was industrialized. By the 1870s, so was the United States. The world became divided into industrialized and developing nations.

■ The English invented new machines, making textile manufacturing possible. Kay invented the flying shuttle to make weaving faster. Hargreaves developed the spinning jenny to spin yarn faster. Crompton invented the spinning mule to spin thread faster.

■ The factory system brought workers, machines, and power together to make a product. Manufacturers built factories to save time and money.

■ Whitney's cotton gin removed cotton seeds from the fiber faster. He also developed mass production to speed up the assembly of goods.

■ Darby developed an improved way of making iron with coke. In 1856, Bessemer discovered how to make steel.

■ Manufacturers could use roads for light-weight loads, but not when they were muddy. In the 1760s, manufacturers started using canals for heavy loads, but canals needed water.

■ Watt improved the steam engine, so it could power factories. Stephenson built the first steam locomotive. Railroads were the most important means of transportation in the nineteenth century. They were a fast and cheap way to move raw materials and finished goods.

■ England kept information about industrialization secret. However, in 1789, Slater built the first spinning machine in the United States.

■ Industrialization caused the growth of cities. Workers moved to cities for jobs in factories.

■ Workers wanted better working conditions and wages. Laws kept them from forming unions. Most workers could not vote because they did not own land.

■ In the late 19th century, electricity and oil were new sources of power. Morse invented the telegraph. Bell developed the telephone. Edison invented the electric light. Daimler invented the internal combustion engine. The Wright Brothers made the first successful airplane flight.

1750 – 1885

Using the Chapter Summary

Have students read the Chapter Summary on page 537 to review the main ideas presented in Chapter 21.

Ask:

- **Name the three things England had that helped it industrialize.** (natural resources, workers, and capital to build factories and machines)

- **Why did manufacturers build factories?** (handwork was slow and expensive; factories saved time and money)

- **What invention made cleaning cotton faster?** (the cotton gin)

- **Who developed mass production?** (Eli Whitney)

- **Why were roads and canals a problem?** (Manufacturers needed to be able to transport all sorts of products in any type of weather; but roads got muddy, and canals needed water, which was not always available.)

- **Who invented the steam locomotive?** (George Stephenson)

- **What effect did industrialization have on the populations of cities?** (It caused populations to grow quickly.)

- **Why were factory workers unable to get safer factories, more pay, and shorter hours?** (The law did not let them form labor unions.)

- **What two new sources of power did inventors discover in the late 19th century?** (electricity and oil)

TEACHER'S RESOURCE

The AGS Globe Teaching Strategies in Social Studies Transparencies may be used with this chapter. The transparencies add an interactive dimension to expand and enhance the *World History* program content.

Chapter 21 Review

Use the Chapter Review to prepare students for tests and to reteach content from the chapter.

Chapter 21 Mastery Test

The Teacher's Resource Library includes two forms of the Chapter 21 Mastery Test. Each test addresses the chapter Goals for Learning. An optional third page of additional critical-thinking items is included for each test. The difficulty level of the two forms is equivalent.

Chapter 21 Review Answers

1. Kay
2. Hargreaves
3. McAdam
4. Watt
5. Whitney
6. Stephenson
7. Slater
8. Morse
9. Bessemer
10. Daimler
11. D
12. B
13. A
14. C
15. A

Word Bank

Bessemer
Daimler
Hargreaves
Kay
McAdam
Morse
Slater
Stephenson
Watt
Whitney

On a sheet of paper, use the words from the Word Bank to complete each sentence correctly.

1. In 1733, the English weaver John _____ invented the flying shuttle.

2. In 1764, James _____ invented a machine that increased the amount of yarn that one person could spin.

3. In 1770, John _____ built roads of crushed rock and improved transportation.

4. In 1773, James _____ developed a way to make the steam engine turn wheels.

5. In 1793, Eli _____ invented a simple machine that separated the seeds from cotton.

6. In 1814, George _____ built a steam locomotive called Blucher.

7. In 1789, Samuel _____ brought plans for a spinning machine to the United States.

8. In 1844, Samuel F. B. _____ sent the first telegraph message.

9. In 1856, Henry _____ invented a way to remove impurities from iron to make steel.

10. In 1885, Gottlieb _____ invented the internal combustion engine.

On a sheet of paper, write the letter of the answer that correctly completes each sentence.

11. Something from nature that people use is called a(n) _____.

   A mass production   **C** capital
   B industrial revolution   **D** natural resource

12. New machinery first helped the _____ industry.

   A steel   **B** textile   **C** gasoline   **D** electric

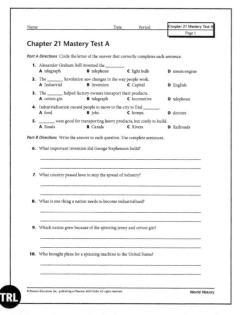

13. The automobile was made possible by the _____ engine.

   A internal combustion   **C** iron

   B steel   **D** steam

14. A(n) _____ is a person who hires people to work with machines to make something to sell.

   A economist   **C** manufacturer

   B capital   **D** labor union

15. _____ is a way of making large amounts of the same, or identical, thing in a factory.

   A Mass production   **C** Natural resource

   B Raw material   **D** Capital

On a sheet of paper, write the answer to each question. Use complete sentences.

16. Why do historians use the word *revolution* to describe the industrial changes that took place in England during the 1700s?

17. What three conditions are necessary for an industrial revolution to take place in a country?

18. Why is a good transportation system needed for the growth of industry?

Critical Thinking On a sheet of paper, write your response to each question. Use complete sentences.

19. Which invention from the Industrial Revolution was the most important and why?

20. During this period, would you have moved from the farm to the city to work in a factory? Explain your answer.

Make flash cards to study vocabulary. Write the word on the front of the card. Write the definition on the back. Use the flash cards in a game to test your vocabulary skills.

1750 – 1885

The Industrial Revolution Begins   *Chapter 21*   **539**

16. The changes brought about by industrialization revolutionized, or greatly changed, how people worked and where they lived.

17. Industry needs natural resources to run machines, workers to work the machines, and capital to build or buy the machines and to build factories.

18. Manufacturers need a way to get both light and heavy raw materials and products to different places as quickly as possible.

Critical Thinking

19. Answers will vary. Students should give details to support why they think each invention was most important.

20. Answers will vary. Students should list in their response the pros and cons of living in a city or on a farm.

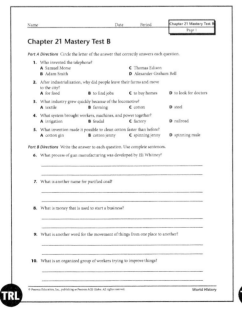

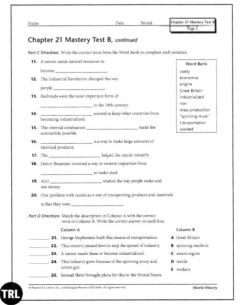

Chapter 21 Mastery Test B, pages 1–3

Industrial Rev. Begins   *Chapter 21*   **539**

Introducing the Chapter

After the violent French Revolution and Reign of Terror, the leaders of Austria, Great Britain, Prussia, and Russia met in Vienna. In 1815, they redrew the map of Europe to try to put an end to nationalism. However, in the years to

Revolutions in Europe and Latin America

The French Revolution changed Europe. The leaders of Austria, Britain, Prussia, and Russia did not like change. They feared nationalism, so they met in Vienna to stop it. In this chapter, you will see how they divided the map of Europe. Then you will find out how people rebelled—first in Greece, then in the Spanish colonies of Latin America. You will see how Simón Bolívar and José San Martín liberated South America. You will sail to Europe and learn about Metternich and Marx. Finally, you will witness 1848, when nearly 50 rebellions broke out in Europe.

Goals for Learning

◆ To state the purpose and outcome of the Congress of Vienna

◆ To explain the idea of nationalism

◆ To describe the wars of national liberation in Latin America

◆ To explain the difference between radicals, conservatives, and liberals

◆ To explain the ideas of the socialists

1804 Haiti wins independence

1821 Mexico wins independence

1822 Brazil wins independence

1800 — 1810 — 1820 — 1830 — 1840 — 1850

6 Argentina gains independence

1821 Santo Domingo wins independence

1829 Greece wins independence

1848 Revolutions break out in Europe

follow, new countries in Greece and in Latin America were born of rebellion. The height of revolutionary enthusiasm came in 1848, when rebellions broke out all over Europe.

Ask:

• When did the island nation of Haiti win independence from Spain? (1804)

• What are some of the countries in Latin America that fought for independence? (Argentina, Santo Domingo, Mexico, and Brazil)

• When did Greece win its independence? (1829)

| Name | Date | Period | SELF-STUDY GUIDE |

Chapter 22: Revolutions in Europe and Latin America

Goal 22.1 To state the purpose and outcome of the Congress of Vienna

Date	Assignment	Completed
	1. Read pages 540–545.	
	2. Complete the Lesson 1 Review on page 545.	
	3. Complete Workbook Activity 100.	

Comments:

Goal 22.2 To explain the idea of nationalism

Date	Assignment	Completed
	4. Read pages 546–547.	
	5. Complete the Lesson 2 Review on page 547.	
	6. Complete Workbook Activity 101.	

Comments:

Goal 22.3 To describe the wars of national liberation in Latin America

Date	Assignment	Completed
	7. Read pages 548–552.	
	8. Complete the Lesson 3 Review on page 552.	
	9. Complete Workbook Activity 102.	

Comments:

(TRL)

© Pearson Education, Inc., publishing as Pearson AGS Globe. All rights reserved.

World History

CENTRAL AMERICA

Caribbean Sea

SOUTH AMERICA

Lima•

Brasilia•

Rio de Janeiro•

PACIFIC OCEAN

Santiago•

ATLANTIC OCEAN

Falkland Islands (U.K.)

Strait of Magellan

0   1000 Miles
0   1000 Kilometers

This is a map of modern South America. Portugal and Spain once controlled all this land of high mountains, dry deserts, and steamy tropical rain forests. The largest river system in the world flows through South America.

Study the map, then answer the following questions:

1. What are the names of four cities in South America?

2. What are the names of five rivers in South America?

3. On which coast of South America do the Andes Mountains stand?

4. What sea is on the north coast of South America?

5. What two oceans touch the shores of South America?

Ask a volunteer to read aloud the title of the map, "South America," and the introductory paragraph.

Ask:

• **Which bodies of water surround South America?** (the Pacific Ocean, the Caribbean Sea, the Atlantic Ocean)

Have students trace the route of the Amazon River from its mouth back to its source and many tributaries. Then have them trace from the tributaries and source to its mouth. Finally, have students read and answer the questions.

Map Skills Answers

1. Lima, Santiago, Rio de Janeiro, and Brasilia

2. Rivers include Negro, Uruguay, Paraguay, Paraná, São Francisco, Tocantins, Xingu, Tapajós, Amazon, and Orinoco

3. the west coast

4. the Caribbean Sea

5. the Pacific and Atlantic oceans

ELL/ESL STRATEGY

Language Objective:
To make a map and describe its features to the class

For ELL students or students who need help visualizing the Western Hemisphere, have them work with partners to trace a map of North America, Central America, and South America. Have students label the continents, Mexico, and the surrounding bodies of water. Then have students "read" their maps to classmates, pointing out where certain places on their maps are in relation to South America. For example, North America is north and west of South America, Central America connects North America and South America, and so on.

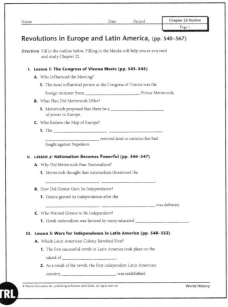

Name   Date   Period   Chapter 22 Outline
                                                  Page 1

Revolutions in Europe and Latin America, (pp. 540–567)

Directions Fill in the outline below. Filling in the blanks will help you as you read and study Chapter 22.

I. **Lesson 1: The Congress of Vienna Meets (pp. 543–545)**
   A. Who Influenced the Meeting?
      1. The most influential person at the Congress of Vienna was the foreign minister from _____, Prince Metternich.
   B. What Plan Did Metternich Offer?
      1. Metternich proposed that there be a _____ of power in Europe.
   C. Who Redrew the Map of Europe?
      1. The _____ _____ _____ restored land to nations that had fought against Napoleon.

II. **Lesson 2: Nationalism Becomes Powerful (pp. 546–547)**
   A. Why Did Metternich Fear Nationalism?
      1. Metternich thought that nationalism threatened the _____
   B. How Did Greece Gain Its Independence?
      1. Greece gained its independence after the _____ _____ was defeated.
   C. Who Wanted Greece to Be Independent?
      1. Greek nationalism was favored by many educated _____

III. **Lesson 3: Wars for Independence in Latin America (pp. 548–552)**
   A. Which Latin American Colony Revolted First?
      1. The first successful revolt in Latin America took place on the island of _____
      2. As a result of the revolt, the first independent Latin American country, _____, was established.

© Pearson Education, Inc., publishing as Pearson AGS Globe. All rights reserved.   World History

Chapter Project

Arrange students into groups of three or four students. Assign each group a country whose revolution is discussed in Chapter 22 and make a poster to graphically describe the country's struggle for independence. Posters might include a timeline to place the revolution within a historical context, photographs of important figures of the revolution, and drawings and captions that help explain the how, when, and why behind the revolution.

TRL

Summarizing

Introduce the reading skill *summarizing*. Draw students' attention to the process of summarizing. Then ask volunteers to read the three bullet point questions on page 542.

Explain that as they read nonfiction material they should look for important ideas and put those ideas into their own words. Tell students that key or important ideas will help them identify and remember the main idea of what they read. After students read Lesson 1, discuss the key ideas and phrases.

Guide the class to use the key ideas to help them write a summarizing statement of the main idea of Lesson 1. (The Congress of Vienna was formed to restructure Europe and the balance of power after Napoleon was defeated.)

Key Vocabulary Words

Have students create a crossword puzzle using the Key Vocabulary Words. They can use the definitions in the textbook or write their own as clues. When puzzles have been completed, students should exchange and solve them.

Reading Strategy:
Summarizing

When readers summarize, they look for key ideas and phrases. Then they rewrite them in their own words, using as few words as possible. A summary of key points will help you remember the important ideas you have read. As you read the text, ask yourself these questions:

◆ What are some important ideas or phrases in the text?

◆ How can I write these ideas or phrases in just a few words?

◆ How will this remind me of the main idea in the section or the lesson?

Key Vocabulary Words

Lesson 1
Congress of Vienna An important meeting in 1814 and 1815 in which leaders restructured Europe

Influential Having the power to change things or to affect what happens

Foreign minister A person who handles one country's dealings with other nations

Balance of power The condition that exists when all countries or all sections of government have equal strength

Confederation A union, or group, of states or nations

Lesson 2
Nationality A group of people who share the same language, culture, and history

Lesson 3
Peninsular A person who came to South America from Spain and held an important office in the colonial government

Creole A wealthy landowner who had been born in a Spanish colony in the Americas but whose ancestors came from Spain

Lesson 4
Conservative A person who likes the old political order and is against revolution or change

Liberal A person who wants change; a person who wants to limit the absolute power of kings and nobles and give power to the middle class

Ordinance A law set forth by someone in government

Lesson 5
Socialist A person who wants to end private ownership of land and factories

Utopia A type of society in which everyone works peacefully together for the good of all

Proletariat The working class, according to Marx

Objectives

◆ To describe the plan that Prince Metternich of Austria brought to the meeting

◆ To identify the ideas Congress had about nationalism

Reading Strategy:
Summarizing

What is the main idea of this paragraph?

Congress of Vienna

An important meeting in 1814 and 1815 in which leaders restructured Europe

Influential

Having the power to change things or to affect what happens

Foreign Minister

A person who handles one country's dealings with other nations

The French Revolution, which began in 1789, changed France. Ten years later, Napoleon Bonaparte seized power. The wars he fought changed Europe because he conquered other countries and gathered them into his empire.

In 1814 and 1815, four European countries—Austria, Prussia, Great Britain, and Russia—defeated Napoleon and sent him into exile. Then the leaders of these countries met in Vienna, Austria. Historians call this meeting the **Congress of Vienna.** Leaders restructured Europe during this meeting.

Who Influenced the Meeting?

Many powerful leaders attended the meeting. Two were kings— William III of Prussia and Czar Alexander of Russia. The Duke of Wellington and Lord Castlereagh represented Great Britain. Charles Talleyrand came for France. But Prince Metternich of Austria was the most **influential.** He had the power to affect what happened.

Prince Metternich was Austria's **foreign minister.** That is, he handled his country's dealings with other nations. He hated the democratic goals of the French Revolution. In fact, he thought that they had made Europe weak. The Congress of Vienna had to cure Europe of this disease called revolution.

Overview This lesson explains why the Congress of Vienna met and the results of the meeting.

Objectives

■ To describe the plan that Prince Metternich of Austria brought to the meeting

■ To identify the ideas Congress had about nationalism

Student Pages pages 543–545

Teacher's Resource Library (TRL)

Workbook Activity 100

Activity 100

Modified Activity 100

Vocabulary

balance of power	foreign minister
confederation	influential
Congress of Vienna	

Challenge students to study the definitions and spellings of the vocabulary words. Write the words on the board for students' reference. Then have students number a sheet of paper from one to five. As you read the definitions, have students write the word that matches the definition on their papers. Then ask volunteers to state the definitions for each word on their list, starting with the first word. Class members should concur with the definitions or provide corrections.

1 Warm-Up Activity

Ask students to imagine that they are members of a powerful ruling royal family in a European country. Tell students that in neighboring countries, ruling families are being overthrown and democratic goals are being achieved. As a ruling family, would they feel threatened or safe? Would they flee the country, stay and fight the revolutionaries, or help reorganize the government to the will of the revolutionaries?

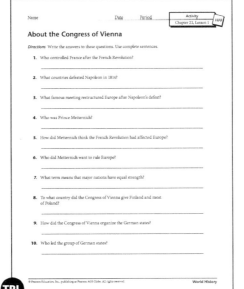

Workbook Activity 100   **Activity 100**   *Rev. Europe/Latin Am.   Chapter 22*   **543**

PRONUNCIATION GUIDE

Use this list to help students pronounce difficult words in this lesson.

| Castlereagh | (kas´ əl rā) |
| Tallyrand | (ta´ lē rand) |

2 Teaching the Lesson

Ask students how they think the rulers of other nations in Europe felt about what happened during the French Revolution. Then have students read pages 543–545 to find out about a meeting to put an end to the violence.

Ask:

• What meeting of European leaders was held after Napoleon was defeated and exiled? (the Congress of Vienna)

• Which four countries were represented at the meeting? (Great Britain, Austria, Russia, and Prussia)

• Who dominated the discussions? (Prince Metternich of Austria)

Reading Strategy: Summarizing

(Prince Metternich thought the democratic goals of the French Revolution made Europe weak and he wanted to stop the revolutionary process.)

• What were the three parts of Metternich's plan? (to make sure France could not threaten other nations again, to have a balance of power, to return royal families to power)

Ask for a volunteer to read the title, "Europe in 1815." Have students locate countries that played an important role at the Congress of Vienna—Great Britain, Russia, Prussia, and Austria. Ask which of these countries borders on France. (none)

Balance of power

The condition that exists when all countries or all sections of government have equal strength

What Plan Did Metternich Offer?

Metternich had a plan to make Europe what it had been before the French Revolution. His plan had three main parts. First, Metternich wanted to make sure that France could not threaten other nations again. Second, he wanted a **balance of power** in Europe. That is, he wanted the major nations to have equal strength so as to keep peace. Third, Metternich wanted to return royal families to power.

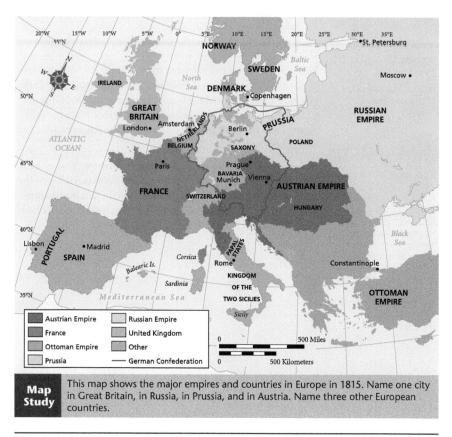

Map Study This map shows the major empires and countries in Europe in 1815. Name one city in Great Britain, in Russia, in Prussia, and in Austria. Name three other European countries.

Then have students read the paragraph under the map and answer the questions. (Great Britain: London; Russia: Moscow and St. Petersburg; Prussia: Berlin; Austria: Vienna and Prague; Other European countries include Portugal, Spain, France, Switzerland, Hungary, Poland, Belgium, the Netherlands, Denmark, Sweden, Norway, and Ireland)

ELL/ESL STRATEGY

Language Objective: *To explain an abstract idea*

Show students a two-pan laboratory balance scale. Explain that if equal weights are placed in both pans, the pans will be level and will no longer swing up and down. Ask ELL students to explain how a balance of power of European countries is like a lab balance. Have students draw simple pictures of an unequal balance of power between France and Austria, and another picture of Metternich's plan for an equal balance of power.

Confederation
A union, or group, of states or nations

Writing About History

The Congress of Vienna redrew the map of Europe. How did redrawing the map accomplish Metternich's goals? In your notebook, write an essay explaining your opinion. Include facts to support your beliefs.

Reading Strategy:
Summarizing

How did Europe change during Napoleon's reign?

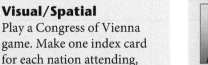

Why would a balance of power among the major nations help to keep peace?

The Congress decided to restore all the kings whom Napoleon had driven from power. But what if some of them had died? Then relatives, or family members, would take their place on the throne. The Congress placed kings on the thrones of France, Spain, Portugal, and Sardinia in Italy.

Who Redrew the Map of Europe?

During Napoleon's reign, several nations had lost land to France. (This land became part of his empire.) The Congress gave land to the nations that had lost land to France and that had fought against Napoleon.

The Congress gave Finland and most of Poland to Russia. It gave part of northern Italy to Austria. Great Britain got the island of Ceylon, some of South Africa, and Malta in the Mediterranean Sea. Sweden gained control of Norway. Then the Congress organized the many German states into a German **Confederation.** A confederation is a union, or group, of states or countries. Austria would lead this group.

What about the people in Finland, Ceylon, South Africa, and other places? What they wanted did not matter to the leaders of the Congress of Vienna. The Congress felt that this nationalism was part of the "disease" of the French Revolution.

Lesson 1 Review On a sheet of paper, write the answer to each question. Use complete sentences.

1. Which four large nations were against the goals of the French Revolution?

2. What was the name of the meeting that these four nations held after the defeat of Napoleon?

3. Who was the most influential leader at the Congress of Vienna?

4. What were the three major parts of Metternich's plan to cure Europe of the disease of nationalism?

5. What is one way that the Congress of Vienna changed the map of Europe?

1814 – 1850   *Revolutions in Europe and Latin America*   Chapter 22   **545**

• Which people did the Congress of Vienna decide to restore to power? (the kings that Napoleon had driven from power)

Reading Strategy:
Summarizing

(During Napoleon's reign, several countries lost land to France and many kings were driven from power.)

Writing About History

Ask students to think about what it must have felt like to live in a country such as Norway, which was given to another country as the result of the Congress of Vienna. (Responses will vary; students may say that they would have resented it if their country had been put under the control of another country.) Then have students read this feature and write responses in their notebooks.

3 **Reinforce and Extend**

Lesson 1 Review Answers

1. Austria, Prussia, Great Britain, and Russia were against the goals of the French Revolution. 2. The four nations met at the Congress of Vienna. 3. The most influential leader there was Prince Metternich of Austria. 4. First, Metternich wanted to make sure that France could not threaten other nations again. Second, he wanted a balance of power in Europe. Third, he wanted to return royal families to power. 5. The Congress gave Finland and most of Poland to Russia. It gave part of northern Italy to Austria. Great Britain got the island of Ceylon, some of South Africa, and Malta. Sweden gained control of Norway. The many German states were organized into a German Confederation.

Answers will vary. If all the nations had the same strength, no one would declare war on anyone else because no one could hope to win.

LEARNING STYLES

Visual/Spatial
Play a Congress of Vienna game. Make one index card for each nation attending, Metternich's three points, nations that had royalty restored, nations that were given territory, and nations or territories given to other countries. Have students select a partner, then put the cards face down. Have each student, in turn, draw two cards. If the two cards relate in some way, students can keep them. When no cards or only one card remains, the player having the most cards wins.

CAREER CONNECTION

Some students may be interested in joining the diplomatic corps and representing their country at international conferences, such as the Congress of Vienna. The United States State Department has an exam for individuals who are interested in positions in the United States or in other countries. Successful candidates usually have a college degree and are proficient in English, world geography, and history. Invite students to find out which courses are needed to prepare for a career in foreign service.

Chapter 22: Lesson 2

Overview This lesson explains why some people in Europe feared nationalism, how Greece succeeded in becoming independent, and the role of literary romanticism during this period of history.

Objectives

- To explain how nationalism remained a strong movement in Europe
- To describe how nationalism affected Greece's independence

Student Pages pages 546–547

Teacher's Resource Library **TRL**

Workbook Activity 101

Activity 101

Modified Activity 101

Vocabulary

nationality

Have students study the definition and then write a sentence that uses the word in correct context. Have students trade papers and examine each other's sentences, saying whether the use of the word is correct, and offering suggestions if it is not. Volunteers can read their sentence to the class for feedback.

PRONUNCIATION GUIDE

Use this list to help students pronounce difficult words in this lesson.

Dumas   (dü mä´)

1   **Warm-Up Activity**

Have students set up a page in their notebook for each revolution that is mentioned in this chapter, starting with the revolution in Greece that is discussed in this lesson. For each revolution, students should note where it occurred, who led it, who helped, and what the result was. Students can use this information to prepare for the Chapter 22 Review.

Objectives

- To explain how nationalism remained a strong movement in Europe
- To describe how nationalism affected Greece's independence

Nationality

A group of people who share the same language, culture, and history

Reading Strategy: **Summarizing**

What event is described in this section?

Through all of history, people have organized themselves into groups. In the 19th century, nationalism became an important way to organize. (Nationalism is loyalty to one's country.) People who shared the same history, traditions, customs, and language wanted to unite under one government. They wanted to become a nation. They would then be loyal to this huge family.

Why Did Metternich Fear Nationalism?

The French Revolution and the Age of Napoleon helped nationalism develop. Before the French Revolution, European armies fought for money or for kings. But the army of revolutionary France fought for the nation of France. This citizen army was loyal to, and willing to die for, their homeland.

Metternich feared nationalism. He believed that it would lead to war. He also thought that nationalism threatened the Austrian Empire. People of different **nationalities** made up the empire. (A nationality is a group of people who share the same language, culture, and history.)

Allowing each nationality to have its own nation would end the Austrian Empire. The leaders of the Congress of Vienna tried to stop nationalism. But nationalists continued to meet in secret. They published books and planned revolutions to set up national governments.

How Did Greece Gain Its Independence?

The first successful national revolution in Europe began in Greece in 1821. For several centuries, Greece had been part of the Ottoman Empire. Now the Greeks wanted independence. They fought long and hard for it. But Greek nationalists needed help to break away from the Ottoman Empire. They got that help in 1827 when France, Britain, and Russia entered the war. These three nations sent a fleet of ships to defeat the Ottoman

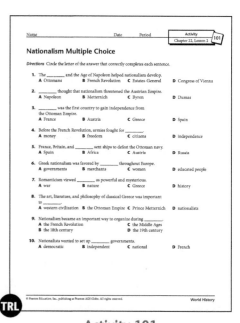

navy. Finally, after eight years of fighting, Greece became an independent nation.

Who Wanted Greece to Be Independent?

Even though some leaders feared nationalism, many educated people throughout Europe favored Greek nationalism. They respected the Greeks for their ancient civilization. In fact, the art, literature, and philosophy of classical Greece had become an important part of Western civilization.

Lesson 2 Review On a sheet of paper, write the answer to each question. Use complete sentences.

1. Describe nationalism in your own words.
2. Why did Metternich fear nationalism?
3. Why did Metternich think nationalism threatened the Austrian Empire?
4. How did Greece gain its independence?
5. Why was Greek independence important to the rest of Europe?

Why would people of different nationalities want to form different countries?

Romanticism

Romanticism became important during the first half of the 19th century. It affected all the arts—literature, art, and music. Romanticism contained four basic ideas. First, feeling was as important as thinking. Second, it stressed the importance of the individual. It was especially interested in heroes. Third, it viewed nature as powerful and mysterious. Fourth, it focused on the past.

Romanticists wrote many novels and poems that people still read today. *The Three Musketeers* by Alexander Dumas is about 17th-century France. Victor Hugo wrote *The Hunchback of Notre Dame.* Sir Walter Scott's *Ivanhoe* tells about the adventures of a knight during the Middle Ages.

WORLD CULTURES

Victor Hugo continues to stir the hearts of millions of people through the arts of live theater and film. The hit musical *Les Miserables*, which is based on Hugo's novel by the same name, opened in London in 1985 and has toured in more than 120 cities on five continents. Hugo's timeless story takes place in Paris around the time of the French Revolution and is a reminder that liberty is the birthright of every person.

BACKGROUND INFORMATION

Vienna, the site of the Congress of Vienna, is Austria's capital and largest city. In the 1200s, the city was named the capital of the Holy Roman Empire. During the 1500s and 1600s, Vienna successfully repelled attacks from the Turks. Vienna became the capital of the Republic of Austria after World War I. Nazi Germany occupied the city from 1938 until 1945. It was heavily damaged by Allied bombs during World War II, but most damaged areas have since been restored.

Chapter 22: Lesson 3

Overview This lesson describes how Spanish colonies in Latin America gained independence.

Objectives

- To describe the liberation of South America and Mexico
- To identify key figures in Latin America's fight for independence

Student Pages pages 548–552

Teacher's Resource Library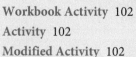

Workbook Activity 102

Activity 102

Modified Activity 102

....

Vocabulary

creole   peninsular

Have students study the definitions and then complete the following two sentences: A peninsular thinks.... A creole thinks.... Have students read their sentences to a partner. Both partners should check the other student's use of the vocabulary words and work with that person to correct the word usage if necessary.

....

 Warm-Up Activity

Ask volunteers to participate in a skit about obtaining independence. Some students should play the role of colonized people who want to become an independent nation. They should tell why they want to be independent. Other students can represent the rulers of the mother country. They should tell why they do not want the colony to become independent. Both sides should meet to try to work out a compromise. If compromise does not work, the nationals might plan a revolt.

Objectives

- To describe the liberation of South America and Mexico
- To identify key figures in Latin America's fight for independence

Reading Strategy:
Summarizing

What character is being introduced in this section?

Nationalism became a force in Latin America. This geographic region includes Mexico, Central America, the islands of the Caribbean Sea, and the continent of South America. In the early 19th century, Spain, France, and Portugal ruled most of this large area.

Which Latin American Colony Revolted First?

The first successful revolt in Latin America took place on the island of Hispaniola in the Caribbean Sea. France controlled the western half of the island. Spain controlled the eastern half. African slaves worked the island's sugar plantations. In 1794, a former slave named Toussaint L'Ouverture led a revolt of free blacks and slaves. They forced the French to leave the island. L'Ouverture became the first governor of the western half of the island.

However, in 1802, the French put L'Ouverture in prison, where he died. Then Napoleon tried to retake the island, but he failed. In 1804, black rebels established the independent country of Haiti

Toussaint L'Ouverture led a revolt of free blacks and slaves against the French in Hispaniola in 1794.

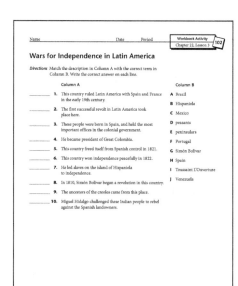

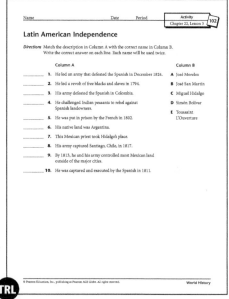

Peninsular

A person who came to South America from Spain and held an important office in the colonial government

Creole

A wealthy landowner who had been born in a Spanish colony in the Americas but whose ancestors came from Spain

on the western half of the island. It was the first independent country in Latin America. Santo Domingo—the eastern half of the island—gained its independence from Spain in 1821.

Who Rejected Spanish Rule in South America?

Napoleon conquered Spain in 1808. To keep control of Spain, Napoleon made his brother king. That meant a Frenchman ruled Spain and the Spanish colonies. Some people in the colonies did not want a French ruler.

Two groups of people dominated the Spanish colonies in South America. The most important group was the **peninsulars.** They had been born in Spain, and they held the most important offices in the colonial government. The second group was the **creoles.** These wealthy landowners had been born in South America, but their ancestors had come from Spain. When Napoleon's French brother became king of Spain, many peninsulars became loyal to him. But many creoles did not.

Two creole leaders rejected Spanish rule. One was Simón Bolívar in New Granada, the northern area of South America. The other was José San Martín in the southern area. Together they freed much of South America from Spanish rule.

When Did Bolívar Free New Granada?

Simón Bolívar was born into a wealthy family in Venezuela. In 1810, he led a revolution to free this colony from Spanish control. At first, he had little success. Then in 1819, his army defeated the Spanish in Colombia.

Simón Bolívar came from a wealthy creole family. His army defeated the Spanish in Colombia in 1819.

Use this list to help students pronounce difficult words in this lesson.

Simón Bolívar
        (sē mōn´ bō lē´ vär)

Miguel Hidalgo y Costilla
        (mē gel´ ē thäl´ gō ē käs tē´ yä)

Toussaint L'Ouverture
        (tü´ san lü ver te´)

José San Martín
        (hō zā´ sän mär tēn´)

Jose Morelos
        (hō zā´mō re´ lōs)

2 Teaching the Lesson

Ask students to recall how Greece was able to win its independence. Have them read pages 548–552 to find out how Spanish colonies won their independence.

Reading Strategy:
Summarizing

(former slave, Toussaint L'Ouverture, who led the first successful revolt in Latin America)

Ask:

• Which was the first Spanish colony to win independence? (Haiti)

• Who did Napoleon put on the throne of Spain? (his brother)

• Who were the important South Americans who were born in Spain and held office in the colonial government? (peninsulars)

• Who were the wealthy South Americans who were born in South America but whose descendants were born in Spain? (creoles)

• Which two creole leaders rejected Spanish rule? (Simón Bolívar and José San Martín)

• Who was the leader of the revolution that resulted in Spain losing its South American colonies? (Simón Bolívar)

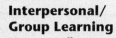

Interpersonal/ Group Learning

Have a small group of students develop a skit to help the class distinguish between the creoles and the peninsulars. Two students can begin role-playing—one as a creole and one as a peninsular. Role-playing alternates should sit behind the two, following the dialogue carefully. Ask an alternate to interrupt the dialogue by standing and tapping the role-player on the shoulder. With the tap, both role-players should freeze and allow the alternate to take over the dialogue. The skit should continue until all members of the group have had an opportunity to participate in the dialogue.

As a young priest, Father Miguel Hidalgo y Costilla tried to help his parishioners improve economically by introducing new methods of farming. Spanish officials were somewhat suspicious of his activities. But when Napoleon defeated Spain and named his brother to the throne, the attention of the authorities turned elsewhere. Secret societies formed. Some supported the deposed King Ferdinand, and others supported independence. Father Hidalgo favored independence. A spy reported the existence of Father Hidalgo's group. Some members were arrested, but Father Hidalgo fled. On September 6, 1810, Father Hidalgo rang the church bell in the village of Dolores, calling together his parishioners. He told them it was time to begin a revolt against Spain. That bell tolled the beginning of the Mexican war for independence.

Ask:

- What was Bolívar's dream for the new nation of Great Colombia? (He hoped that all of Spain's South American colonies would become one country.)

- Who did San Martín meet with in an effort to increase the size of his army? (Bolívar)

- What happened after that meeting? (Bolívar took charge of both armies and San Martín left South America.)

Father Miguel Hidalgo y Costilla: 1753–1811

As a priest, Father Hidalgo worked to improve the lives of his people. He taught them farming. He helped them operate small industries such as brick making. Father Hidalgo believed that Mexicans would be better off without Spanish control. On September 16, 1810, he led a revolt against the Spanish. Thousands joined him.

Father Hidalgo was defeated, but many Mexicans consider him a saint for the revolution he started. The Mexican state of Hidalgo is named for him. His parish, Dolores, was renamed Dolores Hidalgo. In his honor, Mexicans celebrate September 16 as Independence Day.

Bolívar became president of the new nation of Great Colombia. He dreamed of uniting all the colonies of South America into one great nation. But his dream did not come true. Great Colombia became the nations of Colombia, Ecuador, and Venezuela.

What Colonies Did San Martín Free?

José San Martín's native land was Argentina. Argentina had gained its independence in 1816, and San Martín wanted it to remain free.

But San Martín feared that Argentina would lose its freedom. Spain still controlled Chile and Peru, Argentina's neighbors, in the southern part of South America. San Martín organized an army. It crossed the Andes Mountains and captured Santiago, Chile, in 1817.

In 1821, San Martín moved his army by sea to Lima, Peru. The Spanish forces retreated into the mountains. San Martín now needed a larger army to force the Spanish out of the mountains, so he met with Simón Bolívar.

No one knows what the two men said to each other during their historic meeting. After the meeting, Bolívar took command of San Martín's army. San Martín left South America and sailed to Europe. He never returned, and died there in 1850.

LEARNING STYLES

Logical/Mathematical

To help students understand how South America colonies gained their freedom from Spain, have them make a graphic organizer that illustrates and outlines the events of the lesson. For example, students may want to write Simón Bolívar and José San Martín on opposite sides of a page and list the important events and dates of each. Students then may want to show how both men worked together by drawing arrows to the center of the page and listing the remaining events. Encourage students to be creative with their graphic organizers.

ELL/ESL STRATEGY

Language Objective:
To use a map to describe geographic locations

Display a map of the Caribbean that shows the island of Hispaniola. Have an ELL student indicate that Hispaniola is the entire island. Then ask the student to point out the countries of Haiti and Santo Domingo. Ask the student to describe where Hispaniola, Haiti, and Santo Domingo are each located. (Hispaniola is an island in the Caribbean Sea; Haiti is the western half of the island. Santo Domingo is the eastern half.) Guide students to use direction words to tell where Haiti and Santo Domingo are in relation to other Caribbean countries. (for example, Haiti is east of Cuba. Santo Domingo is west of Puerto Rico.) Ask other students to tell who controlled each half of the island of Hispaniola prior to their gaining independence from Europe. (France controlled Haiti, the western half; Spain controlled Santo Domingo, the eastern half.)

Reading Strategy:
Summarizing

What are some important details that help you understand this section?

Bolívar led his army and San Martín's up into the Andes Mountains. In December 1824, they defeated the Spanish army. The last of the Spanish colonies in South America were now free.

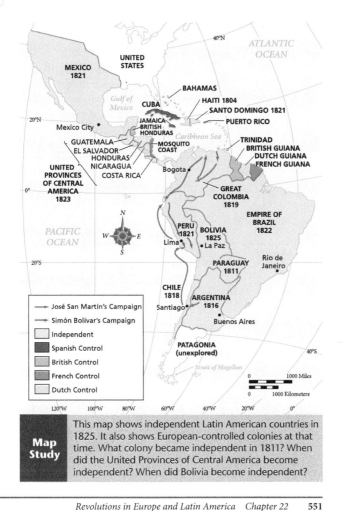

- José San Martín's Campaign
- Simón Bolívar's Campaign
- Independent
- Spanish Control
- British Control
- French Control
- Dutch Control

Map Study

This map shows independent Latin American countries in 1825. It also shows European-controlled colonies at that time. What colony became independent in 1811? When did the United Provinces of Central America become independent? When did Bolivia become independent?

Reading Strategy:
Summarizing

(Answers will vary. Students may say that knowing where each revolutionary came from, when he lived, and where each colony is located in South America helps them understand the section.)

Ask a volunteer to read the title of the map, "Independence in Latin America (1825)." Be sure that students can interpret the key information.

Ask:

- How many independent countries are there in 1825? (15 independent countries)

- How many colonies remain? (10 colonies remain)

Have students read the caption and answer the questions. (Paraguay became independent in 1811. The United Provinces of Central America became independent in 1823. Bolivia became independent in 1825.)

Ask:

- What happened to Hidalgo after the Spanish captured him? (He was executed.)

- What did the Mexican creoles fear might happen if Mexico became independent? (They feared that a new government would take away their land and give it to the peasants)

- In what year did Mexico's fight for independence end? (1821)

3 Reinforce and Extend

LEARNING STYLES

Body/Kinesthetic

Have students make a South American map in the form of a puzzle by cutting out each country into a separate puzzle piece. Ask them to color the Spanish colonies and Portugal's Brazil in contrasting color and to make a key to indicate the colonies of Spain and Portugal. Students should put the names of the countries and the dates of independence on the puzzle pieces. Students can use the map to explain events in the revolutions in South America. For example, students may display a puzzle piece and explain what happened to make that country independent.

ONLINE CONNECTION

The Web site www. agsglobewh.com/page552 from the Office of Latin American Programs and Mexico Center of Texas A&M University offers a brief history of Mexico in both English and Spanish.

Lesson 3 Review Answers

1. L'Ouverture 2. Bolívar
3. San Martín 4. Hidalgo 5. Morelos

Who Led Mexico to Independence?

In 1821, Mexico freed itself from Spanish control after an 11-year struggle. The Indians played an important role in the revolution. It began when Miguel Hidalgo, a poor Mexican priest, challenged the Indian peasants to rebel against their Spanish landowners. Quickly, they formed an army and began a 200-mile march to Mexico City. By the time it got there, the army had 60,000 men. When they met the Spanish army, the Spanish captured and executed Hidalgo.

José Morelos, another priest, took Hidalgo's place. Morelos and his army of peasant rebels were successful. By 1813, they controlled most Mexican land outside of the major cities. Representatives of the peasants met and declared Mexico an independent republic.

What Did Mexican Creoles Fear?

The Indians in Mexico wanted independence from Spain. Wealthy Mexican creoles wanted it, too. However, they feared that a new government would give their land to the landless peasants. In 1815, creole soldiers captured and executed Morelos. Six years later, in 1821, creole leaders successfully revolted against Spain and achieved independence.

Brazil, the largest colony in South America, won its independence from Portugal peacefully in 1822.

Lesson 3 Review On a sheet of paper, use the words from the Word Bank to complete each sentence correctly.

Word Bank
Bolívar
Hidalgo
Morelos
L'Ouverture
San Martín

What do you think

What might San Martín and Bolívar have said to one another at their famous meeting?

1. Toussaint _____ led slaves on the island of Hispaniola to independence.

2. Simón _____ led the people of New Granada, in the northern part of South America, to independence.

3. The armies of José _____ freed Chile and Peru.

4. Miguel _____, a priest, began a revolution in Mexico.

5. José _____, another priest, also led the Mexican peasants in their revolt.

Answers will vary. Perhaps they realized that they could not work together because both wanted to lead. So perhaps San Martín agreed to let Bolívar lead. Maybe he loved freedom for his country so much that he willingly sacrificed his own ambitions. Or perhaps San Martín thought that Bolívar was the better military leader and was more likely to defeat the Spanish.

Objectives

◆ To understand the political views that divided Europeans

◆ To explain France's struggle with various leaders and governments after Napoleon's defeat

The French Revolution promoted the ideas of nationalism, liberty, and equality. These ideas and the events of the French Revolution brought into being three political groups—conservatives, liberals, and radicals.

What Is a Conservative?

Conservatives were mainly rich landowners and nobles. They formed the upper class of most societies. As a group, they liked the old political order. In fact, conservatives thought that revolution was dangerous. They thought that it brought only disorder and pain. Because of this, they supported the absolute power of kings.

What Is a Liberal?

Usually, **liberals** were wealthy businessmen and merchants. As such, they belonged to the upper middle class. But many people in the middle class had no political power. The liberals wanted to limit the absolute power of kings and nobles and give power to the middle class. How did they plan on doing this? They would write a constitution and elect a parliament.

Most liberals wanted only some people to have the right to vote. They feared democracy because they did not trust that the uneducated working class and the poor would vote reasonably.

What Is a Radical?

The word *radical* means "root." Radicals wanted to change society down to its very roots. They wanted monarchies to become democracies in which every man had the right to vote.

Many radicals were willing to use violence, or great physical force, to bring about change in society. The French Reign of Terror had frightened conservatives and liberals. It did not frighten radicals. They saw it as necessary to make France into a true democracy.

Conservative
A person who likes the old political order and is against revolution or change

Liberal
A person who wants change; a person who wants to limit the absolute power of kings and nobles and give power to the middle class

Reading Strategy:
Summarizing

What is the main idea of this paragraph? What key words help you identify it?

Chapter 22: Lesson 4

Overview This lesson defines three political groups and describes how France and other European countries fought for freedom and reform.

Objectives

■ To understand the political views that divided Europeans

■ To explain France's struggle with various leaders and governments after Napoleon's defeat

Student Pages pages 553–556

Teacher's Resource Library **TRL**
Workbook Activity 103
Activity 103
Modified Activity 103

Vocabulary

conservative   ordinance
liberal

Review the definitions of these vocabulary words with students. Then have them write sentences that use each word correctly. Invite student volunteers to write their sentences on the board.

PRONUNCIATION GUIDE

Use this list to help students pronounce difficult words in this lesson.

Louis Philippe   (lü′ ē fi lēp′)

Joseph Niepce   (jō′sef nyeps)

1 **Warm-Up Activity**

Ask students if they have heard the words *conserve* and *conservative* used in a non-political way. Ask them what the words mean. (Students have probably used *conserve* in an ecological sense to mean saving resources.) Ask students to write a sentence using the word *liberal* in a non-political sense. (Example: He poured a liberal amount of salt on his food.) Finally have them write a sentence using the word *radical* or *radically*. (Example: She dressed in a radical fashion.)

Workbook Activity 103   **Activity 103**   *Rev. Europe/Latin Am. Chapter 22* **553**

2 Teaching the Lesson

Have students imagine how they might have felt if they had lived through the Reign of Terror. Tell them to read pages 553–556 to find out about the political views of three groups after the French Revolution.

Ask:

• Which political group did most of the rich landowners and nobles support? (the conservatives)

• Which political group did most of the wealthy businessmen and merchants support? (the liberals)

• What did the radicals want? (Radicals wanted to change society down to its roots.)

Reading Strategy: Summarizing

(The main idea is to tell what a radical is and what he or she believes in. Key words are *violence, change, democracy*.)

• Which of the three political groups participated in the French Reign of Terror? (the radicals)

• Which king ruled France after Napoleon was defeated? What did he try to do? (Louis XVIII; he tried to please both the conservatives and the liberals.)

Reading Strategy: Summarizing

(Louis XVIII wanted to please both conservatives and liberals to broaden his appeal. Since the philosophies of the two groups were different, he could not please either group.)

• Which king tried to return France to an absolute monarchy? (Charles X)

The condition of the poor in Paris in 1831 was a reminder why radicals were calling for reforms.

Who Ruled France From 1814 to 1824?

In 1793, the French had executed Louis XVI for treason. The monarchy ended. Then, after Napoleon's defeat in 1814, the monarchy was restored to France. The king's brother became King Louis XVIII. He ruled from 1814 to 1824.

Louis XVIII tried to please both the conservatives and the liberals. Conservatives wanted him to support the right of nobles to rule. Liberals wanted him to give more people in the middle class the right to vote. The king could not please both groups, so neither group was happy with him.

What Kind of Power Did Charles X Want?

When Louis XVIII died in 1824, his brother became King Charles X. He wanted to be an absolute monarch. He asked the French legislature to pass laws that limited the rights of many people. When the legislature refused to do this, Charles X closed it down.

Next, Charles X called for an election to get representatives for a new legislature. He thought it would be a conservative one. However, the election results surprised him. The French people voted for liberals.

Reading Strategy: **Summarizing**

Summarize the conflict that Louis XVIII faced in this section.

---

554   Unit 4   *Enlightenment and Revolution*

How Did Charles X Bring About a Rebellion?

Ordinance

A law set forth by someone in government

Charles wanted to end the power of this new liberal legislature. In July 1830, he issued new laws. These laws abolished the legislature, limited voting rights, and ended freedom of the press. Historians call these laws the July **Ordinances.** An ordinance is a law set forth by someone in government. French newspapers encouraged their readers to ignore the king's laws.

On July 28, 1830, middle-class liberals, workers, and students took to the streets of Paris in protest. They built barriers in the streets. The king then sent his soldiers to break up the riots. But many soldiers refused to shoot the rioters. In fact, some troops joined the protest movement. When Charles X saw this, he fled to England. Once again, the French had forced a king from his throne.

Who Became the "Citizen King"?

Many of the working-class rebels thought that the July Revolution, as it was called, would make France a republic. They wanted this to happen because in a republic, every man could vote. Middle-class leaders wanted a constitutional monarchy instead of a republican form of government.

With middle-class support, Louis Philippe (the cousin of Charles X) became king. Historians call him the "citizen king" because he dressed like a middle-class businessman. He often walked through Paris and spoke to the people he met there.

Louis Philippe was known as the "citizen king" because he sided with the middle class.

Ask:

- How did the French newspapers react to Charles X's July Ordinances? (They encouraged people to disobey the laws.)

- Why did people take to the streets of Paris in 1830? (Students may say to protest Charles X's July Ordinances.)

- Who became king after Charles X fled from France? (Louis Philippe)

- How was the "citizen king" different from previous kings? (He dressed like a businessman and he walked through Paris and talked to the people.)

ELL/ESL STRATEGY

Language objective:
To organize and summarize information

Have ELL students skim through the material on pages 554–555 and make a list of the kings that ruled France from 1814 to 1831. Then guide students in making a timeline for this period of time and, using their list, have them mark the timeline with the reign of each king. Ask students to display their timelines and describe in two or three sentences what each king did and what groups of French people (conservatives, liberals, or radicals) were happy with the king and his rule.

LEARNING STYLES

Auditory/Verbal

Have students make three columns on a sheet of paper with the headings *Conservatives*, *Liberals*, and *Radicals*. Then ask students to listen to the audio recording from the beginning of Lesson 4 that explains each of these groups. Have them write down who belongs to each group, what the groups believe, and what they do. Students can listen to the recording a second time to check their notes, filling in any information they initially missed.

Ask:

- Where else in Europe were there rebellions between 1830 and 1848? (Answers will vary; students may mention Belgium, Poland, and Italy.)

- Which European country won its independence as a result of France's influence? (Belgium)

- In which European countries did rebellions fail between 1830 and 1848? (Poland, Italy, and Germany)

3 Reinforce and Extend

Lesson 4 Review Answers

1. The conservatives, the liberals, and the radicals came out of the French Revolution. **2.** Charles X followed Louis XVIII as the king of France. **3.** The July Revolution took place in 1830. **4.** Louis Philippe, the cousin of Charles X, was the "citizen king." **5.** Belgium freed itself from the Netherlands in 1830.

Answers will vary. Charles X believed in an absolute monarchy, in which the king held power over the people. The conservatives believed in that type of government too.

Ask students to think when they last had their picture taken. Explain that some of the earliest work with photography was done by French people. Then have students read "Photography" to find out who made the first photograph and how widely cameras are used today. Ask students if photographs still "tell the truth." (Answers will vary. Students may know that digital technology allows a person to alter the "truth" in a photograph.)

What Other European Nationalists Rebelled?

Between 1830 and 1848, France influenced rebels in other countries. People in Belgium rebelled against the Netherlands in 1830 and won their independence. Polish people also tried to rebel and win their independence from Russia. But the Russian army defeated them. Nationalists in Italy and Germany also rebelled. Austrian troops put down the revolt in Italy. The Confederation of German States used force to end the rebellion in Germany.

Lesson 4 Review On a sheet of paper, write the answer to each question. Use complete sentences.

1. What three political groups came out of the French Revolution?

2. Who followed Louis XVIII as king of France?

3. In what year did the July Revolution in France take place?

4. Who was known as the "citizen king"?

5. When did Belgium free itself from rule by the Netherlands?

Why would Charles X want a conservative legislature?

Photography

Did you know that you probably see more than 1,000 camera images a day? Yet the photograph was unknown before 1827!

French inventor Joseph Niepce made the first photograph from nature that year. It showed the courtyard of his house. In 1844, the first book of photographs was published in Paris. It contained photos of the Egyptian countryside.

Photographs have become popular for several reasons. They tell the truth. Photographs of the United States Civil War first showed what war is really like. Scientists use photos to record information about whatever they are studying—humans, animals, space. People have used them to win support for causes, such as helping the poor. Photographs also record important personal events. Museums even consider photography an art form.

AT HOME

Have students ask members of their family if they had ever attended a speech or rally in support of a political figure. Then have them ask if they had ever met or spoken with a political figure. Suggest that students think about how personal perceptions can change as distances are shortened.

Objectives

♦ To describe how socialism changed Europe
♦ To explain what the utopian socialists thought
♦ To describe the kind of society that Karl Marx wanted

In 1848, revolutions swept through Europe. Once again, the French rebelled against their government. This time, French radicals demanded that workers be given the right to vote. Louis Philippe, the citizen king, said, "There will be no reform. I do not wish it."

In February 1848, the people of Paris took to the streets in a protest against their government. The king sent troops to restore order. Then a mob marched on the king's palace. After he fled to England, revolutionary leaders set up a Second French Republic to govern the nation. (The French established the First Republic during the French Revolution of 1789.)

What Did Socialists Want?

The new republican government had trouble because the radical leaders were divided into two groups. One group wanted to reform only the French political system. The second group wanted both political and economic reform.

Revolutions swept through Europe in 1848.

Chapter 22: Lesson 5

Overview This lesson describes the revolutions that swept through Europe in 1848 and how they changed forever the way people viewed government.

Objectives

■ To describe how socialism changed Europe
■ To explain what the utopian socialists thought
■ To describe the kind of society that Karl Marx wanted

Student Pages pages 557–562

Teacher's Resource Library (TRL)

Workbook Activity 104

Activity 104

Modified Activity 104

Vocabulary

proletariat   **utopia**
socialist

Have students study the vocabulary definitions and select one to think about further. Put students who select the same word together in a group. Give each group a card with a task and an example of how to respond to the task. For example, the task might be to list five things that members of the proletariat (or the socialists or the utopians) would probably want. (Examples of the response might be: proletariat—good wages; socialists to have the government run the airlines and other services; utopians—to close down the police department and other services that keep order and protect). Have a spokesperson report each group's findings.

1 Warm-Up Activity

Have students recall France and other countries they read about in Lesson 4 that fought for independence. Then tell students that in Lesson 5 they will learn about European countries' continued struggles for freedom.

2 ▸ Teaching the Lesson

Have students recall the goals of the conservatives, liberals, and radicals. Then have students read pages 557–562 to find new groups who wanted reform.

Ask:

- What happened when Louis Philippe refused to let the workers of France have the right to vote? (Answers will vary; students may say the workers took to the streets to protest.)

- Why did the socialists want to end private ownership? (Only a few people had enough money to own land or start factories.)

- Who feared the socialists? Why did they fear them? (The middle class feared the socialists because they demanded an end to the middle-class way of life.)

BACKGROUND INFORMATION

Louis Blanc lived in poverty as he studied law in Paris. He wrote many essays in newspapers and journals about his views. Blanc blamed the pressure of competition for everything that was wrong with society. For example, if several people applied for the same job, the person who asked for the lowest wage would get the work. The others might starve. Blanc advocated the equalization of wages as a cure for this problem. He set up social workshops, similar to trade unions or cooperatives, where workers could bring together their efforts for the common benefit of all.

Socialist

A person who wants to end private ownership of land and factories

---

Louis Blanc—a **socialist**—led the second group. Socialists wanted to end the private ownership of land and factories. In Chapter 21, you read about the Industrial Revolution. In that chapter, you learned that a nation needs three things to industrialize—natural resources, plenty of workers, and capital. In France, as in most countries, only a few people owned land and had the capital to build factories and machines.

How Did Socialists Frighten the Middle Class?

The socialists believed that private ownership caused the poor economic conditions of the working class. They wanted the state to control the land and the factories. This radical idea frightened the middle class.

Blanc demanded that the government establish workshops to give jobs to people who had none. For a time, the government did this, but then it closed the workshops. This angered the workers, so they rioted.

Before the riots ended, government soldiers had killed thousands of workers. This violence upset the French people. They blamed the radical socialists for these riots and disorder. The French then wrote a new constitution. It called for the election of a parliament and a powerful president.

Louis Blanc, a French socialist, set up workshops to give jobs to people who had none.

ELL/ESL STRATEGY

Language Objective:
To describe events in historical images

Ask students to examine the historical illustrations on pages 557 and 558. Have ELL students describe what is happening in each picture. Ask questions about the pictures, such as what is the mob at the palace doing on page 557, and what are the men being trained to do in the workshop on page 558. (The mob is throwing the king's furniture and other belongings out of the windows of the palace. The men in the workshop are being trained to work with their hands.) Have students write two or three descriptive sentences of their own about each illustration.

Who Brought Peace to France?

In December 1848, the French voters elected Louis Napoleon Bonaparte (Napoleon III) as their new president. (Napoleon Bonaparte was his uncle.) Louis Napoleon brought order to France. Soon after his election, he set aside the republican form of government.

In 1851, Louis Napoleon declared that he was the only ruler of France. Many French people liked this change. In an election, more than 90 percent of the voters supported Napoleon III as a single powerful leader. France achieved peace, but lost democracy. Napoleon III ruled France for nearly 20 years.

What Did Utopian Socialists Think?

Not all socialists agreed on the best way to improve the lives of the working class. One group—the **utopian** socialists— thought that they could reform society peacefully. The word *utopian* comes from a book Thomas More, an Englishman, wrote in 1516. It was about a future society where everyone worked together peacefully for the good of all. Utopia was a perfect society. No one was poor, no one committed any crimes, and no one fought. Utopian socialists believed that people could live and work together peacefully if they had the chance to do so.

What Did Marx Think About Factory Owners?

A German named Karl Marx thought that the utopian socialists were dreamers. Marx said that all societies were made up of the "haves" and the "have-nots." The "haves" have power and wealth. The "have-nots" have nothing. They have no money and no power.

Marx said that powerful leaders would never willingly give up their power. He thought workers would always fight with factory and landowners. Marx believed that all of history was a class struggle between the rich (the "haves") and the poor (the "have-nots"). He thought that factory owners grew rich from the labor of the workers. Factory owners paid workers low wages and kept the profit from the business for themselves.

1814 – 1850   *Revolutions in Europe and Latin America*   Chapter 22   **559**

Ask:

• How did Louis Napoleon surprise the people of France? (He ended the republican government, and he ruled like an absolute ruler.)

• Which group thought they could make changes in the lives of working people peacefully? (the utopian socialists)

Reading Strategy:
Summarizing

(Responses will vary. Students may say that in a utopian society, everyone works together peacefully for the good of all.)

• What did Karl Marx have to say about the utopian socialists? (He thought they were dreamers.)

• According to Marx, society was made up of which two groups? ("haves" and "have-nots")

• What did Marx think about factory owners? (Answers will vary; students may suggest that Marx thought factory owners used the workers or that they paid low wages.)

STUDY SKILLS

Have students work in groups to find out about former utopian societies in the United States. Examples include Oneida, NY, and New Harmony, IN. Students will use the information that they find to fill in a graphic organizer that you have drawn on the board. Possible categories for the organizer could include *When Began, Years Lasted,* and *Important Details.* When all groups have completed their research, invite them to add their data to the graphic organizer.

Ask:

- How did Marx think workers should make changes? (by violent revolution)

- Which book by Marx set forth his views? (*The Communist Manifesto*)

Proletariat

The working class according to Marx

What Kind of Society Did Marx See in the Future?

Marx believed that workers could improve their lives and gain power only by violent revolution. In a pamphlet called *The Communist Manifesto*, written by Marx and Friedrich Engels, we read, "Workers of the world, unite!" Marx believed that workers had ". . . nothing to lose . . . but their chains." Marx called these industrial workers the **proletariat.**

In the future, Marx saw a society that had no need for government. Each member of this society would be equal. There would be no rich or poor. The ideas of Karl Marx influenced history from the last years of the 19th century to the present.

Karl Marx believed that only violent revolution could improve workers' lives.

Ask:

- By 1848, what was the most important force for organizing societies in Europe? (nationalism)

What Ended the Old Ways of Government?

Throughout 1848, violent revolutions occurred in the Italian states, in Prussia, and in the Austrian Empire. Nearly 50 rebellions broke out in different areas of Europe. Some revolutionaries wanted national independence. Others wanted more say in who governed them. Some rebellions combined both goals. In the end, all these revolutions failed.

However, the rebellions ended the system that the Congress of Vienna established in 1814. When a revolt broke out in Austria, Prince Metternich fled to England. The old ruling order was finished. Nationalism had become the most important organizing force for societies.

As time passed, noble families lost their power and privilege. Like all members of the royal class, Czar Nicholas of Russia was nervous. He said, "What remains standing in Europe?"

Reading Strategy:
Summarizing

Look for important details in this section. Why did these revolutions fail?

Reading Strategy:
Text Structure

(Answers will vary. Students may suggest that the revolutions failed because the revolutionaries were divided. They did not focus on a single goal.)

Communication in History

Ask students what they know about Braille. Then have them read "Reading with Fingertips" to find out where the idea for Braille came from and how Braille is printed. When students finish, have them share where they have seen Braille. (Students may mention that they have seen Braille in elevators or on signs.)

Communication in History

Reading with Fingertips

The Frenchman Louis Braille was a blind teacher of blind children and teenagers. In 1824, he invented a reading system that enables blind people to read. He based it on Charles Barbier's night reading principle. Barbier developed it so that the military could read messages at night. His system was made up of dots pressed into paper.

Braille's system uses six raised dots arranged in cells, or letter spaces. Each cell contains three rows and two columns. Each letter, number, and punctuation mark has its own layout of larger and smaller dots. Braille taught people how to read these dots with their fingertips.

Braille was first printed by hand. A sharp, pointed tool raised small dots on heavy paper. In 1892, the stereotyping machine made it possible to transfer dots to printing plates. For today's books, computer programs translate print into Braille. The blind can also write Braille. They use a Braillewriter, which resembles a typewriter.

---

3 Reinforce and Extend

IN THE COMMUNITY

Explain to students that in the United States, neither the government nor private citizens own everything. Have them find out about their local government services, such as the recycling program or the fire department. Have students list services that the government provides and services that private companies provide. Give students an opportunity to share their findings.

Lesson 5 Review Answers

1. D **2.** B **3.** A **4.** C **5.** D

Answers will vary. The radicals thought that privately owned land and factories were responsible for the poor economic conditions of the working class. The owners could pay the workers a low wage and reap profits. The radicals believed that the state would be more evenhanded and fairer to the worker. All would be equal.

Chapter Project Follow-up

Student posters for their chapter project should contain historically accurate information. They should show a timeline for historical context, captioned illustrations, and some of the most important events of the revolution. Poster information should also include the year or time period of the revolution, the ruling country before the revolt, and important events following the revolution. Posters might be displayed in the classroom and groups might make oral presentations to the class as study aids for students' review of Chapter 22.

Lesson 5 Review On a sheet of paper, write the letter of the answer that correctly completes each sentence.

1. The "Year of Revolutions" is _____.

  A 1776   **C** 1815
  B 1789   **D** 1848

2. Louis Blanc, a(n) _____, wanted to end the private ownership of land and factories.

  A absolute monarch   **C** conservative
  B socialist   **D** liberal

3. The _____ socialists believed that they could peacefully bring about a perfect society.

  A utopian   **C** conservative
  B communist   **D** radical

4. _____ called industrial workers the "proletariat."

  A Louis Philippe
  B Louis Napoleon Bonaparte
  C Karl Marx
  D Prince Metternich

5. The authors of *The Communist Manifesto* said that society is made up of _____.

  A the "haves"   **C** class struggle
  B the "have-nots"   **D** all of the above

What do you think

Why did the radicals want the state to control land and factories?

The Communist Manifesto

Karl Marx and Friedrich Engels were the leaders of a new social movement. They believed that a workers' revolution would take place in England. They were wrong, however. Then in 1848, the two men published a pamphlet. This Communist Manifesto stated their beliefs. Marx and Engels argued that workers (proletariat) would overthrow the owners of business (bourgeoisie). Marx and Engels called themselves Communists. Their revolutionary ideas would become an important force in the 20th century.

Karl Marx and Friedrich Engels

In the earlier times of history, we find almost everywhere a complicated arrangement of society into various orders of social rank. In ancient Rome, we have patricians, knights, plebeians, slaves; in the Middle Ages, feudal lords, vassals, guild-masters, journeymen, apprentices, serfs.

The modern bourgeois society [middle class factory owners] that has sprouted from the ruins of feudal society . . . has but established new classes, new conditions of oppression, new forms of struggle in place of the old ones. . . .

The modern labourer . . . instead of rising with the progress of industry, sinks deeper and deeper below the conditions of existence of his own class. He becomes a pauper [poor person]. . . . And here it becomes evident that the bourgeoisie is unfit any longer to be the ruling class in society. What the bourgeoisie therefore produces, above all, are its own grave diggers. Its fall and the victory of the proletariat are equally inevitable. . . .

The Communists turn their attention chiefly to Germany, because that country is on the eve of a bourgeois revolution that . . . will be but the prelude to an immediately following proletarian revolution. . . .

The Communists openly declare that their ends can be attained only by the forcible overthrow of all existing social conditions. Let the ruling classes tremble at a Communist revolution. The proletarians have nothing to lose but their chains. They have a world to win.

Working men of all countries, unite!

Document-Based Questions

1. According to this writing, what two classes made up society in his day?

2. Who were the bourgeoisie?

3. The authors said that workers were sinking "deeper and deeper below the conditions of existence." What did they mean?

4. Why might non-Communists fear the Communists?

5. Why did the authors believe that workers should rebel?

Ask students if they can think of any Communist countries. (Students may mention Cuba and China.) Explain to students that Communism, as defined by Karl Marx and Frederick Engels, has never been fully realized by any country. Throughout history, many countries have claimed to embody Marx and Engels's vision of Communism, yet they actually operated under a different political system or set of ideologies, such as Socialism, Maoism, or Stalinism. Have a volunteer read the title of the Document-Based Reading. Read the introductory paragraph to students. Then have students read *The Communist Manifesto* to find out what Marx and Engels wanted the workers of the world to do. Students should read and answer the Document-Based questions.

Answers to Document-Based Questions:

1. They were the proletariat and the bourgeoisie.

2. They were the middle-class factory owners.

3. The workers were finding it more and more difficult to provide themselves and their families with food, clothing, and shelter.

4. Answers will vary. The Communists said that they would use force to change the existing social conditions. The Communists would take everything for themselves.

5. The proletariat had the whole world to win and nothing to lose but their chains.

Before students begin reading, ask them what kinds of clothes they like to wear. If initial responses are vague ("Because it looks cool.") or evasive ("I don't follow fashion."), challenge students to explain themselves further ("What do you mean when you say 'cool'?" "What is 'following fashion'?"). Explain that the importance of clothing and fashion has come into play throughout the course of world history. Have students read "Dressing for Success" and then read and answer the Wrap-Up questions.

Answers to Spotlight Story Wrap-Up:

1. The style of a person's clothes often shows his or her success, social status, and wealth.

2. Buttons made tighter-fitting clothing possible. Men began wearing tighter-fitting jackets.

3. He wore the simple clothes of the "natural man" to the French court.

4. It ended the role of the nobility as fashion setters. The clothing of the middle class became the acceptable style of dress. Men began dressing in dark-colored jackets and trousers.

5. Answers will vary. Students may suggest that fashion trends are set by Paris designers and by people in the entertainment fields—musicians, athletes, and movie stars.

Dressing for Success

Throughout history, clothes have been a symbol of success, social status, and wealth. Fashions change for many reasons. For example, during the Middle Ages in Europe, both men and women wore long gowns. They only had buckles to hold their clothing together. Clothing, therefore, had to be large enough to pull over the head. Then in the 1200s, the crusaders returned from the Middle East, bringing back buttons. Buttons could make clothes fit closer to the body.

People wore fancy, elaborate clothing in Europe during the 1700s.

In the 1400s, women still dressed mostly in floor-length gowns. Men began to wear tight-fitting jackets though. They also wore hose to show off the shape of their legs. Over the years, the dress of upper class men became more fancy and colorful. This trend continued for the next three centuries.

Benjamin Franklin's arrival at the French court in 1779 showed how men's clothing would change. Franklin decided not to wear the fancy, colorful clothes in style at the time. He wore a simple black coat and matching knee breeches. Franklin's dress caused a new fashion trend. His clothes were thought to be the perfect symbol of the "natural man" of the middle class.

In 1789, the French-Estates General met. Members of the Third Estate, or common people, could not wear colors or decorated ornaments. After the French Revolution swept the upper class from power, their fashion-setting days ended. Instead, the clothing of the middle class became the acceptable style of dress. Men dressed in dark-colored jackets and trousers. Men's fashion kept this same basic suit well into the 20th century.

Here is an interesting fact from the history of clothing styles. The upper classes often passed clothing styles down to the working class. In the 1700s, the upper class wore powdered wigs, colorful jackets, and knee breeches. In the 1800s, household servants dressed this way. To get dressed up, gentlemen of the 19th century wore a tuxedo. In the 20th century, waiters in fancy restaurants sported tuxedos.

Wrap-Up

1. Besides modesty and warmth, why do people dress as they do?

2. How did the button change men's clothing in Europe?

3. Why was Benjamin Franklin's clothing the talk of the French court?

4. What impact did the French Revolution have on clothing styles?

5. In your opinion, how are fashion styles set today?

Chapter 22   S U M M A R Y

- Britain, Prussia, Austria, and Russia defeated and exiled Napoleon in 1814. They met at the Congress of Vienna to decide France's fate.

- Metternich had three goals. France should never threaten other nations again. Major European nations should have equal strength. This balance of power would keep the peace. Royal families should return to power and end nationalism.

- The Congress of Vienna divided the French empire among European countries and established a German Confederation. It also put royal families back on their thrones.

- The ancient Greeks contributed much to Western civilization. Many Europeans supported Greek independence for this reason.

- Nationalism spread to Latin America. Led by L'Ouverture, Haiti gained its independence from France. Later Santo Domingo won independence from Spain.

- In northern South America, Bolívar freed Colombia, Ecuador, and Venezuela. San Martín freed Chile and Peru. Later Brazil got its freedom from Portugal peacefully.

- Fathers Hidalgo and Morelos led Mexican peasants successfully against the Spanish. But Mexican creoles wanted power for themselves. This struggle delayed Mexican independence until 1821.

- In France, conservatives were mainly rich landowners and nobles. They supported absolute royal power. Liberals were usually wealthy businessmen and merchants. They wanted a say in the government. Radicals wanted to change monarchies to democracies and were willing to use force.

- A series of kings ruled France. Charles X's desire to be an absolute ruler caused the Revolution of 1830. Between 1830 and 1848 other people revolted: Belgians, Poles, Italians, and Germans.

- Europe was torn by revolutions in 1848, but they all failed. In France, revolution founded a republic. The revolutionaries, however, were divided. Liberals wanted to reform the political system. Socialists wanted to end the private ownership of land and factories. Louis Napoleon was elected president and declared himself Napoleon III.

- Karl Marx and Friedrich Engels wrote *The Communist Manifesto*. They believed only violent revolution could improve workers' lives.

TEACHER'S RESOURCE

The AGS Globe Teaching Strategies in Social Studies Transparencies may be used with this chapter. The transparencies add an interactive dimension to expand and enhance the *World History* program content.

- Why did the French Revolution of 1848 fail? (Answers will vary; students may say that the revolutionaries were divided and were not focused on one set of goals.)

- Who was Karl Marx? (He wrote *The Communist Manifesto* and believed in violent revolution.)

Using the Chapter Summary

Have students read the Chapter Summary on page 565 to review the main ideas presented in Chapter 22.

Ask:

- Where did the leaders of European nations meet after Napoleon was sent into exile? What did they do? (Vienna; students may say they redrew the map of Europe or they put dethroned kings back in power.)

- Who had the most influence at the Congress of Vienna? What were his goals? (Metternich; he wanted France to never threaten other nations again, for major European countries to have balanced power, and for nationalism to end.)

- What did the Congress of Vienna accomplish? (It divided up the French empire, established a German Confederation, and put royal families back on their thrones.)

- Where did the first successful revolution that created a new independent European country take place? (Greece)

- Where did the first successful revolt in Latin America take place? (Haiti)

- What did Simón Bolívar and José San Martín do? (Answers will vary; students may say they liberated much of South America from European rule.)

- Why did Mexican creoles cause a delay of independence from Spain? (They wanted power for themselves.)

- What were the political groups that developed in Europe after the French Revolution? (the conservatives, the liberals, and the radicals)

- Why did the people of France revolt against King Charles X? (Answers will vary; students may say he wanted to take power away from the people.)

Chapter 22 Review

Use the Chapter Review to prepare students for tests and to reteach content from the chapter.

Chapter 22 Mastery Test

The Teacher's Resource Library includes two forms of the Chapter 22 Mastery Test. Each test addresses the chapter Goals for Learning. An optional third page of additional critical-thinking items is included for each test. The difficulty level of the two forms is equivalent.

Chapter 22 Review Answers

1. Metternich
2. Alexander
3. Ottoman
4. L'Ouverture
5. Bolívar
6. San Martín
7. Hidalgo
8. Philippe
9. Blanc
10. Marx
11. D
12. D
13. A
14. C
15. B
16. Nationalism is the belief that people who share the same history, customs, traditions, and language should be united under and loyal to one government.

Word Bank
Alexander
Blanc
Bolívar
Hidalgo
L'Ouverture
Marx
Metternich
Ottoman
Philippe
San Martín

On a sheet of paper, use the words from the Word Bank to complete each sentence correctly.

1. Prince _____ of Austria was the most influential leader at the Congress of Vienna.

2. Czar _____ of Russia represented his nation at the Congress of Vienna.

3. Before it won its independence, Greece was part of the _____ Empire.

4. Toussaint _____ led the slave revolt against the French in Haiti.

5. Simón _____ liberated New Granada from Spain.

6. José _____ led an army into Chile to free it from Spanish control.

7. The Mexican priest Miguel _____ challenged the Indian peasants to rebel against the Spanish.

8. Louis _____ became the "citizen king" of France in 1830.

9. Louis _____ led one group of French socialists.

10. Karl _____ and Friedrich Engels wrote *The Communist Manifesto*.

On a sheet of paper, write the letter of the answer that correctly completes each sentence.

11. The French Revolution promoted the idea(s) of _____.

   A nationalism **C** equality
   B liberty **D** all of the above

12. _____ led revolts against the Spanish in Latin America.

   A Byron **C** Metternich
   B Blanc **D** San Martín

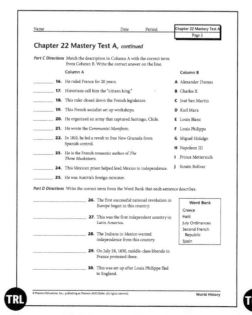

13. At the Congress of Vienna, _____ said that nationalism was a disease and that he had the cure for it.

A Metternich   **C** Louis Philippe

B Marx   **D** Byron

14. A _____ is a person who likes the old order of things.

A liberal   **B** radical   **C** conservative   **D** socialist

15. A _____ is a person who wants to end the private ownership of land and factories.

A conservative   **C** monarch

B socialist   **D** peninsular

On a sheet of paper, write the answer to each question. Use complete sentences.

16. What is nationalism?

17. Why did the leaders at the Congress of Vienna fear nationalism?

18. How did events in France in the 19th century influence other European and colonial revolutionaries?

Critical Thinking On a sheet of paper, write your response to each question. Use complete sentences.

19. Prince Metternich believed nationalism was like a disease. He said, "When France sneezes, Europe catches cold." What did Metternich mean? If possible, use an example of a "sneeze" and a "cold" in your answer.

20. The political group called the conservatives thought that revolution was a danger to society. Do you agree with them? Why or why not?

When taking a matching test, first match the items you know belong together. Cross these items out. Then try to match the items that are left.

1814 – 1850   *Revolutions in Europe and Latin America*   **Chapter 22**   **567**

---

17. The leaders at the Congress of Vienna feared nationalism because they would lose land and power if groups of nationalists broke away from the four major nations and empires.

18. The French Revolution and the Age of Napoleon taught people in Europe and in the Latin American colonies that they could revolt.

Critical Thinking

19. Answers will vary. A sneeze is a sign that someone has a cold or a disease. When France did something revolutionary (sneezed), people in other countries did it too. The sneeze became a cold, and the disease spread. We can see this in the July Revolution of 1830. France sneezed and took a king off his throne. In that same year, Belgium caught the "cold" and won independence from the Netherlands.

20. Answers will vary. Revolution usually brings change, and change can be good. Change can sometimes lead to great violence as in the Reign of Terror in France. The conservatives wanted to protect the rights of the upper class and the nobles. They did not like change. In this century, we have seen violent change and peaceful change throughout the world.

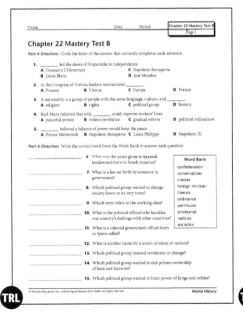

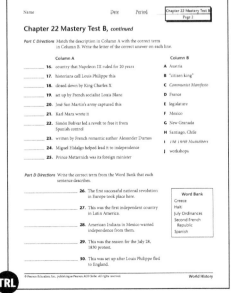

Chapter 22 Mastery Test B, pages 1–3

Rev. Europe/Latin Am.   **Chapter 22**   **567**

To introduce the Skill Builder Lesson on page 568, display as many different reference materials as possible. Show examples of an almanac, atlas, a volume of an encyclopedia, gazetter, newspaper, periodical index, and an informational Web Site page. Turn to a table of contents or index, or show a few sample pages to review what each reference source contains and how it is organized. Ask volunteers to read the definitions of the reference material examples on page 568.

Ask:

- **Where would you find current maps?** (an atlas, gazetteer; Internet)

- **Where would you find facts about Napoleon?** (encyclopedia, almanac, Internet)

- **Where would you find information on current events?** (newspaper, Internet)

Have students read and answer Skill Builder questions 1–10. Then assign one question to each of 10 groups and have each group find the information in the appropriate reference source. If possible, combine the lesson with a trip to the school media center and a talk with a media specialist.

Unit 4 Skill Builder Answers

1. encyclopedia
2. almanac, encyclopedia
3. periodical index
4. atlas, gazetteer
5. gazetteer, atlas, encyclopedia, almanac
6. encyclopedia
7. newspaper
8. encyclopedia
9. atlas, gazetteer, encyclopedia
10. almanac, encyclopedia

Unit 4
Skill Builder

Using Reference Materials

Reference materials are sources for finding different kinds of information. Here are some examples of reference materials and the kinds of information you can find in them.

General information almanac — Book of recent and historical facts and figures about many subjects

Atlas — Book of maps of countries, states, and some cities

Encyclopedia — One book or a set of books with summaries and histories of many different subjects

Gazetteer — Dictionary of geographic place names and information

Newspaper — Daily or weekly publication with national, local, sports, and business news and regular features

Periodical index — Listing of magazine articles by subject and the publication in which they appear

Internet — Worldwide computer network with information on a variety of subjects; includes on-line encyclopedias, newspapers, and periodicals

Here is a list of research questions. You could probably find the answers to all of them somewhere on the Internet. Name at least one other listed source that you could use to answer each question.

1. Where could you find a short biography of Queen Isabella of Spain?

2. What kind of government does Austria have today?

3. You remember seeing a magazine article about foods and dishes brought from Africa by slaves. Where can you find the date and name of the publication in which it appeared?

4. Where could you find a map of Spain with an inset of Madrid?

5. Where could you find information about the Andes Mountains?

6. Where could you find information about instruments used for navigation in modern submarines?

7. Where could you look for results of a vote taken in Congress yesterday?

8. What are the names of some compositions by Joseph Haydn?

9. In what part of England is Plymouth located?

10. Who is the present king of Spain?

Unit Skills Activity

Distribute the Unit 4 Skills Activity. List the names of the six revolutions noted on the Skills Activity on the board under the title *Revolutions*. Title a second column *In Common* and a third column *In Contrast*. As students discuss their information, connect lines from each pair of revolutions to the *In Common* and *In Contrast* columns. Write one idea in each column. At the conclusion, have students note what is common to all revolutions.

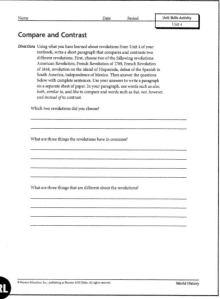

Unit Skills Activity

Unit 4   S U M M A R Y

- Newton's discovery of natural, universal laws introduced the Age of Reason.

- Enlightenment thinkers wanted to use reason to improve society. Hobbes, Locke, Montesquieu, Rousseau, and Voltaire wrote about government. Locke said people had natural rights to life, liberty, and property.

- Handel and Bach were baroque composers. Haydn and Mozart were classical composers. The Age of Reason influenced writers such as Swift and Molière.

- After 1763, Britain wanted its North American colonies to pay for the war against France. The colonists protested. Then colonial representatives signed the Declaration of Independence. The French helped Americans win a revolution against Britain.

- France in the 1770s consisted of three estates—the clergy, the nobles, and the common people. The Third Estate paid all the taxes. This group established a constitutional monarchy in 1789. In 1792, the National Constitutional Convention created a republic. The Jacobins under Robespierre began the Reign of Terror. Then came the Directory and the Consulate. In 1804, Napoleon crowned himself emperor.

- Napoleon's victories increased French power, but he made two mistakes. The Continental System turned countries against France. His Russian invasion destroyed his army. The allies defeated Napoleon in 1814 and again at Waterloo. In France, the Code of Napoleon made every man equal under the law. Napoleon's conquests spread the ideas of the French Revolution.

- The Industrial Revolution began in England in the 1750s. England could industrialize because it had natural resources, workers, and capital.

- The English invented new machinery. The factory system brought workers, machines, and power together.

- Under Metternich's lead, the Congress of Vienna reorganized Europe. It promoted the balance of powers.

- Nationalism was a major force. Bolívar and San Martín freed South American countries from Spain. Father Hidalgo began the Mexican fight for independence.

- Conservatives supported absolute royal power. Liberals favored a constitutional monarchy. Radicals wanted to change monarchies to democracies. In 1848, there were revolutions throughout Europe. None succeeded. In France, Napoleon III became emperor. Marx believed only violent revolution could improve workers' lives.

1687 – 1850   *Enlightenment and Revolution   Unit 4*   **569**

Using the Unit Summary

Read and discuss the Unit 4 Summary statements on page 569 with students.

Ask:

- Which scientist introduced the Age of Reason? (Isaac Newton)
- Which country helped Americans with a revolution against Britain? (France)
- What were the three estates of the France during the 1770s? (the clergy, the nobles, and the common people)
- What was the Code of Napoleon? (every man was equal under the law)
- Why was England able to industrialize in the 1750s? (It had natural resources, workers, and capital.)
- What did the Congress of Vienna promote? (balance of powers between nations)
- Which two revolutionary leaders helped South America gain independence from Spain? (San Martín and Bolívar)
- What was Marx's belief about revolution? (only violent revolution could improve workers' lives)

Unit 4 Mastery Test

The Teacher's Resource Library includes a two-page Unit Mastery Test. An optional third page of additional critical thinking items is included for each test. The Unit 4 Mastery Test is pictured on page 862 of this Teacher's Edition.

Unit Activity Follow-Up

Discuss with students some of the ideas they had for future inventions. Discuss how each invention would affect the lives of individuals.

To evaluate student performance, consider the following questions:

- Did students complete Unit 4 Activity 1 and Unit 4 Activity 2?
- Did students identify a way to improve their chosen inventions?
- Did the students write paragraphs comparing and contrasting two revolutions?

Enlightenment and Revolution   Unit 4   **569**

Planning Guide
A New Global Age

		Student Text Lesson				
		Student Pages	Vocabulary	Lesson Review	Critical-Thinking Questions	Chapter Summary	Chapter Review
Chapter 23	Nationalism	572–589	✔		✔	587	588
Lesson 1	Nationalism	575–576	✔	576	✔		
Lesson 2	Growing Nationalism in Italy	577–579	✔	579	✔		
Lesson 3	The Unification of Germany	580–584	✔	584	✔		
Chapter 24	Imperialism	590–607	✔		✔	605	606
Lesson 1	Imperialism	593–595	✔	595	✔		
Lesson 2	The Effect of Imperialism on Asia	596–599	✔	599	✔		
Lesson 3	The Effect of Imperialism on Africa	600–602	✔	602	✔		

Unit Activities

Student Text
Unit 5 Summary
Unit 5 Skill Builder

Teacher's Resource Library
Unit 5 Activities 1–2
Unit 5 Skills Activity

Assessment Options

Teacher's Resource Library
Chapter 23 Mastery Tests A and B
Chapter 24 Mastery Tests A and B
Unit 5 Mastery Test

Reading Strategy	Map Study/Map Skills	Writing About History	Geography Note	Biography	History in Your Life	Communication in History	Technology Connection	Then and Now	Spotlight Story	Document-Based Reading	Background Information	Applications (Home, Career, Community)	World Cultures	Study Skills	Online Connection	ELL/ESL Strategy	Auditory/Verbal	Visual/Spatial	Body/Kinesthetic	Interpersonal/Group Learning	Logical/Mathematical	Activities/Modified Activities	Workbook Activities	Self-Study Guide	Chapter Outline
574	573								586	585														✔	✔
✔			576													576		576				105	105		
✔		578				578	579						579		579	578	579					106	106		
✔	583		584								581	582, 584	582			581			582	583	581	107	107		
592	591								604	603										603				✔	✔
✔						595						595	595			594			594			108	108		
✔	597										598	599				598	599	599			597	109	109		
✔		601		602								602		602	602	602						110	110		

Student Text Features | Teaching Strategies | Learning Styles | Teacher's Resource Library

Other Resources

Books for Teachers

Anderson, Benedict. *Imagined Communities: Reflections on the Origin and Spread of Nationalism*, Revised Ed. New York: Verso, 2006. (elaborates on nationalism and addresses questions of why people live, die, and kill in the name of nations)

Greenfeld, Liah. *Nationalism: Five Roads to Modernity*, Reprint Ed. Cambridge MA: Harvard University Press, 2007. (traces the rise of nationalism in England, France, Germany, Russia, and the United States)

Hobson, J. A. *Imperialism: A Study*. New York: Cosimo Classics, 2006. (explores the principals and hidden motives of imperialist policy)

Books for Students

Lace, William W. *The British Empire: The End of Colonialism (History's Great Defeats)* Lucent Books, 2000. (describes the factors that lead to the gradual decline of the British Empire, and the changes in world views about colonies)

Nardo, Don. *The Age of Colonialism*. Lucent, 2006. (documents the rise and fall of the great colonial empires in North and South America, Africa, the Far East, and the Pacific region)

CD-ROM/Software

European Imperialism: 1800–1914 Culver City, CA: Social Studies School Service (1-800-421-4246), 2007. (PowerPoint presentation of European imperialism in Africa and Asia)

Videos

South Africa: Free at Last (50 minutes). The History Channel. (explores the problems South Africa has faced in the past 50 years, first under colonial rule, and then under independence)

Web Sites

www.agsglobewh.com/page570a
(Includes a description, including maps, of nationalism in India, leading to its partition and independence in 1947; it also includes a timeline: 1600–1971)

www.agsglobewh.com/page570b
(contains statistics on the extent of European colonial holdings)

www.agsglobewh.com/page570c
(contains links to aspects of colonialism in Africa, including timelines, BBC Web Sites, maps, and biographical information)

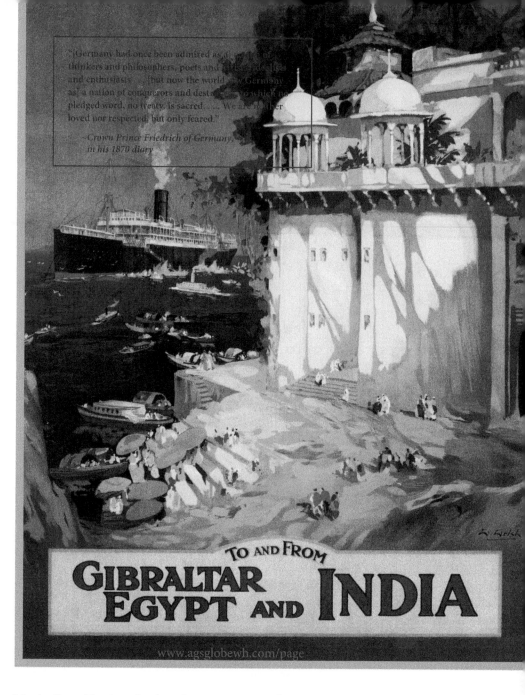

"[Germany had once been admired as a . . . . . . of
thinkers and philosophers, poets and . . . . . . idealists
and enthusiasts . . . . but now the world . . . Germany
as a nation of conquerors and dest . . . . . . which n . . .
pledged word, no treaty, is sacred. . . . . . . We are n . . .
loved nor respected, but only feared."

—*Crown Prince Friedrich of Germany,
in his 1870 diary*

**TO AND FROM
GIBRALTAR
EGYPT AND INDIA**

www.agsglobewh.com/page

Unit 5

A New Global Age

European leaders fought to create strong nations, and nationalism spread. In Italy, revolts exploded between 1820 and 1848. Germany was brought together as one nation by the Franco-Prussian War.

Imperialism also swept across the world during the 19th century. European nations established colonies in Africa and Asia.

In this unit, you will meet nationalism and imperialism face to face. First you will read about the ways nationalism can bring people together. You will learn why Europeans thought that imperialism helped the colonized nations. You will also learn why the people in those colonized nations did not think that imperialism was a good thing.

Chapters in Unit 5

571

Introducing the Unit

Read aloud the quotation from Crown Prince Friedrich of Germany. Have students look at the picture on page 570. Explain that in this unit, students will learn about nationalism and imperialism, the creation of strong European nations and their desire to take over weaker nations to establish colonies. Have volunteers read aloud the introductory material on page 571.

Ask:

- **What mood might Prince Friedrich have been in when he wrote the diary entry in 1870?** (He was sad that Germany's image in the world had changed so much. Instead of being admired and respected for their learning, Germany was now feared for their destruction and deceit.)

- **Where did European countries establish colonies in the 19th century?** (Africa and Asia)

- **What happens when a country becomes a colony?** (The native people in the country lose control of their government and their lives.)

Presenting the Unit Activity

Distribute copies of Unit 5, Activity 1. Discuss nationalism and what it means to students. Ask whether it is possible for a person to have nationalistic feelings for more than one country. (Many immigrants have feelings for both their native country and their adopted country.) Be sure students understand the instructions on the activity.

In Unit 5, Activity 2, students will play a game to simulate spheres of power. Students can draw rough outlines of the United States or Canada to use in the game. They need not be detailed. Alternatively, you may wish to prepare outline maps of the country. If students are not familiar with geography and the location of states or provinces, use a map that has them outlined. Have index cards available. Each student team will need 12 cards.

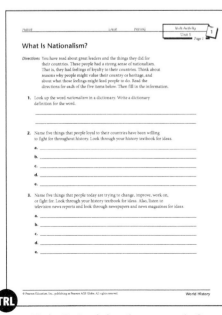

Unit 5, Activity 1, pages 1–2

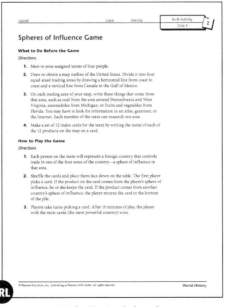

Unit 5, Activity 2

 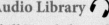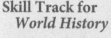
Introducing the Chapter

Nationalism swept across Europe in the
late 19th and early 20th centuries. Many
changes occurred throughout the world
as nationalism brought unification to
Italy and Germany.

23 Nationalism

As you have read, nationalism is the loyalty people have for their country. This became a powerful force for change in the world during the 1800s. In this chapter, you will meet Giuseppe Mazzini, who led a rebellion in 1848. You will meet Camillo di Cavour, who united most of Italy. You will also meet Giuseppe Garibaldi, known for his military ability. Then you will see how Germany was brought together as one nation.

Goals for Learning
◆ To explain nationalism
◆ To identify the leaders of Italian unification
◆ To explain how Germany became a unified nation

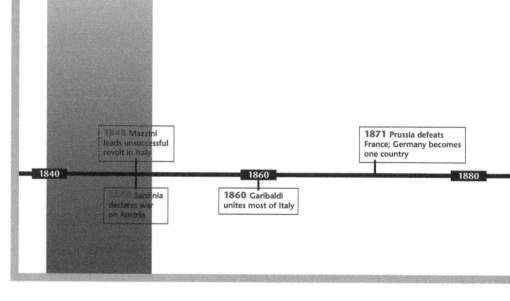

1848 Mazzini leads unsuccessful revolt in Italy

1871 Prussia defeats France; Germany becomes one country

1840

1860

1880

1848 Sardinia declares war on Austria

1860 Garibaldi unites most of Italy

Ask:

- What is nationalism? (loyalty to one's country)

- How many years after Mazzini's revolt was Italy largely unified? (12 years later)

- In what year was Germany fully unified? (1871)

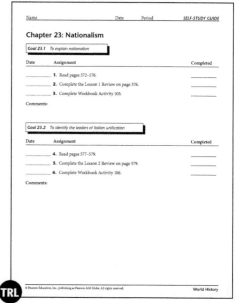

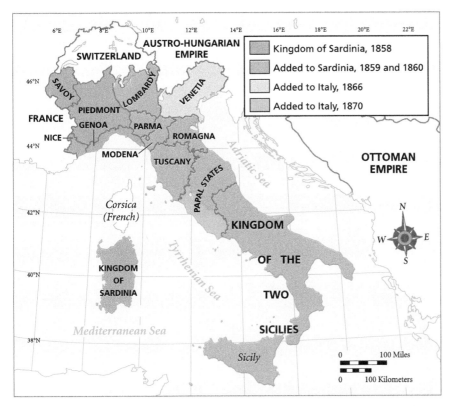

This map shows how Italy became unified as one country by adding territory between 1858 and 1870. In 1870, the last independent state became part of Italy. Rome became the capital of Italy.

Study the map, then answer the following questions:

1. What states became part of the Kingdom of Sardinia in 1859 and 1860?

2. What state was added to Italy in 1866?

3. When did the last independent state become part of Italy?

4. What sea separates Italy from the Ottoman Empire?

5. Which sea lies to the west of Italy?

Ask a volunteer to read the map title, "Unification of Italy (1858–1870)." Have students explain what unification means. Draw attention to the territories and dates shown on the map key.

Ask:

• **What is shown in the map key?** (the territories added to Italy and their dates)

• **What two other seas surround Italy?** (the Tyrrhenian and Mediterranean seas)

• **What do you notice about Italy?** (Answers will vary; It is made up of several territories; It is shaped like a boot.)

Have students read the paragraph below the map, and then read and answer the questions.

Map Skills Answers

1. Kingdom of the Two Sicilies, the Papal States, Tuscany, Romagna, Modena, Parma, and Lombardy became part of Sardinia.

2. Venetia was added in 1866.

3. The last independent state became part of Italy in 1870.

4. The Adriadic Sea separates Italy from the Ottoman Empire.

5. The Tyrrhenian Sea lies to the west of Italy.

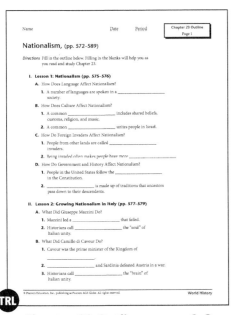

Chapter Project

Divide the class into two large groups. One group will study the unification of Italy. The other group will examine the unification of Germany. Explain that each group will create two puzzle boards that highlight the geography of unification and two games that highlight the events leading to unification. Encourage groups to subdivide tasks among themselves based on group members' interests. Have students use library resources and the Internet to gather information.

Questioning

Have students page through the chapter and note that the text in each lesson is divided by headings written in the form of questions. Explain that these questions provide a reason for reading the text. The question in each heading should be answered after reading the section that follows it. Tell students that a good study technique is to write down the question in a notebook, read the section, and then write down the answer. Point out that the same technique also can be used with new vocabulary words.

Ask:

- How would answering the first heading on page 575 help you understand the material? (It will give me an understanding of the importance of language in each country.)

- What question could you ask after reading the first heading on page 577? (Who was Giuseppe Mazzini?)

- What question could you ask before reading the "Then and Now" information on page 579? (Answers will vary; Where is the Vatican City? What is the Vatican City? What importance did the Vatican City have in the unification of Italy?)

Key Vocabulary Words

Point out that these chapter words are presented in the order they appear in each lesson. They are also found in the Glossary. Remind students that they should use questioning when reading to help them understand and remember what they read.

Reading Strategy:
Questioning

As you read this chapter, ask yourself questions. You will understand and remember more information if you ask yourself questions as you read. As you read, ask yourself:

◆ What is my reason for reading this text?

◆ What connections can I make between this text and my own life, or something I have read before?

Key Vocabulary Words

Lesson 1 —————
Multilingual A society in which a number of languages are spoken

Heritage The traditions ancestors have passed down

Lesson 2 —————
Prime minister The leader in some democratic government systems

Lesson 3 —————
Militarism A nation's warlike policy or practice

Policy A plan that helps a person or a country make a decision

Ambassador A person sent to represent his or her government in another country

Siege The act of surrounding a city or fort with an army and cutting off its supplies

Negotiate To talk together, make bargains, and agree on something

Kaiser The emperor of Germany

Reich The German word for empire

Ask:

- What question can you make using the word *heritage*? (What is heritage?)

- Where will you find the answer to your question? (Lesson 1; the dictionary)

- What question can you ask about the word *siege*? (Answers will vary. Did a siege take place in Italy?)

- What questions can you ask about the kaiser? (Answers will vary; What does the word *kaiser* mean? Who was the kaiser of Germany? When did he come to power? How did he come to power?)

Objectives

♦ To identify how language and culture affect nationalism

♦ To explain how foreign invaders, government, and history affect nationalism

Multilingual

A society in which a number of languages are spoken

Reading Strategy: Questioning

What do you think you will learn about by reading this lesson?

Nationalism swept across Europe in the 1800s and early 1900s. As you have already learned, nationalism is loyalty to one's country. But there are many other things that make up nationalism.

How Does Language Affect Nationalism?

A common language is an important part of nationalism. Usually the people of one country speak the same language. This unites them. In some countries, however, people speak more than one language. This kind of society is **multilingual.** However, they are still loyal to their country.

How Does Culture Affect Nationalism?

A common culture is another part of nationalism. The people of a nation often share the same beliefs, customs, religion, music, and way of life. A belief in freedom, democracy, and equality unites Americans. A common religion unites people in nations such as Israel or Iran. Both Japan and China have a culture that is different from other countries. In any country, the citizens may be different from one another. But they all love their country and feel loyal to it.

How Do Foreign Invaders Affect Nationalism?

Sometimes people lose their land. Foreign invaders (people from other countries) might take it over. For example, powerful neighbors have taken over Poland over the years. Also, for many years, non-Chinese leaders ruled China.

But nationalism can remain even if people lose their land or government. In fact, being invaded often makes people have more nationalism. For example, today many Palestinians are scattered throughout the Middle East. They are now fighting for a land of their own.

1840 – 1914

Nationalism Chapter 23 575

Chapter 23: Lesson 1

Overview This lesson describes the various factors that can affect nationalism as it develops in a country.

Objectives

■ To identify how language and culture affect nationalism

■ To explain how foreign invaders, government, and history affect nationalism

Student Pages pages 575–576

Teacher's Resource Library

Workbook Activity 105

Activity 105

Modified Activity 105

Vocabulary

heritage   **multilingual**

Ask students to write each vocabulary word on a separate index card. As you read the definition for a vocabulary word, have students hold up the card on which the defined word is written. Repeat the definitions in a random order to be certain students understand the words. Then ask for volunteers to provide definitions in their own words. ESL students may have particularly interesting definitions.

1 Warm-Up Activity

Explain that every country has certain symbols that unify the country. Hold up a picture or point to an American flag. Ask students what the flag symbolizes. Hold up a picture of a baseball game, apple pie, hot dog stand, football game, and/or a bald eagle. Discuss how each item in some way symbolizes the American way of life and creates a feeling of national pride. Have students suggest other symbols that convey a strong feeling of national identity or unity. Create a list of such symbols on the board.

Name_____ Date_____ Period_____

Workbook Activity 105
Chapter 23, Lesson 1

The Rise of Nationalism

Directions Write the answers to these questions. Use complete sentences.

1. What is a multilingual society?

2. What are two beliefs that unite Americans?

3. How can an invasion affect nationalism?

4. What document contains laws that unite all Americans?

5. What is heritage?

Name_____ Date_____ Period_____

Activity 105
Chapter 23, Lesson 1
Page 1

Nationalism

Part A Directions Write the correct word from the Word Bank to complete each sentence.

1. Customs, religion, music, and beliefs make up a country's _____.

2. _____ invaders come from outside of one's own country.

3. Usually, the people of one country speak the same _____.

4. A belief in freedom, _____, and equality unites Americans.

5. _____ is made up of what our ancestors have passed down to us.

6. Nationalism is a feeling of _____ to one's country.

7. Students study their country's _____ so they will understand the past.

8. The main _____ of the United States is based in Washington, D.C.

9. In a(n) _____ society, a number of languages are spoken.

10. _____ have passed down things to their descendents.

Word Bank
ancestors
culture
democracy
foreign
government
heritage
history
language
loyalty
multilingual

2 Teaching the Lesson

Ask students what makes people feel loyal to their country. Have them read pages 575–576 to find out what nationalism is and how it is affected.

Ask:

- How does an outside threat, like an invasion, affect nationalism? (It increases it.)

- Why does studying your country's history help instill nationalism? (it helps citizens value their common heritage.)

- Do people have to practice the same religion to share a common culture? Why or why not? (No; religion is only one element of culture.)

Reading Strategy:
Questioning

(The effect of language, culture, foreign invasion, and history on nationalism.)

3 Reinforce and Extend

Heritage
The traditions ancestors have passed down to their descendants

 Geography Note

Not all people in European countries felt a sense of nationalism. Many traveled to the United States to find a better life. Ellis Island, in New York Bay, was the first stop for most. It was the main U.S. immigration station beginning in 1892. By the time it closed in 1954, more than 20 million people had passed through its gates.

How Do Government and History Affect Nationalism?

Having only one government is another part of nationalism. For example, people who live in the 50 states of the United States follow the laws in the Constitution. They also follow the laws made by the government in Washington, D.C.

A common history is another part of nationalism. In American schools, students study the history of the United States. They feel pride in their shared history. The flag, the symbol of Uncle Sam, and the "Star-Spangled Banner" mean something special to all Americans.

Students in other countries also study their history so they will love their country, be loyal to it, and value their **heritage.** Heritage is made up of all the traditions our ancestors have passed down to us.

Lesson 1 Review On a sheet of paper, write the answer to each question. Use complete sentences.

1. Why is a common language an important part of nationalism?

2. What three things do the people of a nation often share?

3. How can nationalism remain even when people lose their land?

4. How does having one government unite people in different parts of a country?

5. Why do students in other countries study the history of their country?

What do you think

What do you think is the most important symbol of your country? Why?

Lesson 1 Review Answers

1. A common language unites people.
2. People of a nation often share a common language, culture, and religion.
3. If people lose their land, they often join together to fight for it. **4.** One government unites people because they follow the same laws. **5.** Students study their history to learn about their heritage.

Answers will vary.

Geography Note

Ask a volunteer to read the Geography Note on this page. Point out that most immigrants who passed through Ellis Island came from Europe. Other immigrants came from Asian nations, Mexico, South America, Australia, New Zealand and a few from Africa. Ask students if they have moved to the U.S. or Canada from a different country (or state). Discuss the things that excited students about the move. (moving to a new house, making new friends) What things did students fear about the move? (attending a new school or eating unfamiliar foods) Ask if they think early immigrants had the same concerns.

Objectives

- To identify three important leaders in Italy and what they did
- To identify the first king of Italy

Prime minister

The leader in some democratic government systems

Reading Strategy:
Questioning

What details are important to understanding nationalism in Italy?

The Napoleonic Wars gave birth to nationalism in Italy. In Chapter 21, you read about the Congress of Vienna, which met in 1814 after Napoleon's defeat. The leaders of this meeting divided Italy into about 30 states and provinces. Austria, France, and Spain controlled these provinces.

What Did Giuseppe Mazzini Do?

Many people in Italy had strong nationalist feelings. In 1848, revolts broke out in many states. Giuseppe Mazzini led the rebellion. Historians call him the "soul" of Italian unity because he stood for its spirit of freedom. But Mazzini's rebellion failed. Thousands of soldiers from Austria and France marched into Italy and put down the revolt. For the next 20 years, French troops controlled Rome.

What Did Camillo di Cavour Do?

Count Camillo di Cavour then stepped forward to lead the fight for unity. He was the **prime minister** of the Kingdom of Sardinia. A prime minister is the leader in some democratic government systems.

Sardinia was the only Italian state that an Italian king ruled. (Remember that France, Austria, and Spain ruled all the other Italian states.)

Cavour was a skilled politician, and he figured out a way to free the Italian states from outside rule. First, he made a secret agreement with France. Together, they declared war against Austria in 1859. The combined French-Sardinian army defeated Austria. This action won the respect of people in all the states of Italy.

Next, nationalist revolts broke out in the northern provinces that Austria controlled. By 1860, all these provinces had become part of the Kingdom of Sardinia. Cavour planned how to get two major powers to fight one another and leave Italy alone. Historians call him the "brain" of Italian unity.

1840 – 1914

Nationalism *Chapter 23* 577

Chapter 23: Lesson 2

Overview This lesson introduces the key players in the unification of Italy and describes the contributions made by each.

Objectives

- To identify three important leaders in Italy and what they did
- To identify the first king of Italy

Student Pages pages 577–579

Teacher's Resource Library

Workbook Activity 106

Activity 106

Modified Activity 106

Vocabulary

prime minister

Ask students to research five countries that have prime ministers. Have them find out the names of the people who hold that office. Then ask them to briefly explain the difference between the duties of a president or king and a prime minister. (A prime minister is head of the government; a king or president is in charge of all other affairs of a country.)

1 Warm-Up Activity

Have students gather around a chess set. Using the pieces of the chess set, spread out the kings and queens on the board. Use the rest of the chess pieces to create groups around each king and queen. Place one knight in the center of the chess board. Explain that the knight's goal is to unite the groups living under the kings and queens, and that the kings and queens are very protective of their respective lands. Have students suggest why and how unification could be accomplished. Point out that in this lesson, students will learn how one man united Italy.

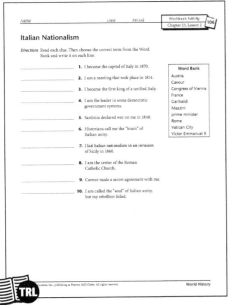

Workbook Activity 106 **Activity 106, pages 1–2**

PRONUNCIATION GUIDE

Use this list to help students pronounce difficult words in this lesson.

Giuseppe Mazzini
(jü zep´ pe mät tse´ ne)

Camillo di Cavour
(kä mel´ lo de kä vür´)

2 Teaching the Lesson

Ask students to recall the definition of nationalism they learned in Lesson 1. Then have students read from pages 577–579 to learn about the "soul," the "brain," and the "sword" of Italy during the time of nationalism and unification.

Ask:

- Why did Mazzini's rebellion fail? (Thousands of soldiers from Austria and France marched into Italy.)

- What was the name of the only Italian state not under foreign rule? (Sardinia)

Reading Strategy: Questioning

(Answers should include the language, culture, and heritage of Italy.)

- With which country did Cavour join forces to defeat Austria? (France)

- What island did Garibaldi's troops invade in 1860? (Sicily)

- Who were the "Red Shirts?" (Garibaldi's army)

- Who chose King Victor Emmanuel II of Sardinia to be the ruler of Italy? (the Italian parliament)

- What land did the parliament set aside for the pope? (part of Rome, called Vatican City)

Communication in History

Ask students to read the feature to themselves. Then have them do library or Internet research and draw a rough timeline of the inventions of Marconi, Fessenden, Alexanderson, and de Forest. Point out that scientists and inventors often build on the work of others to develop new inventions.

Writing About History

What is your opinion of nationalism? Use examples to explain your opinion. Are there events in the current news that influence what you think? How about the recent past? Write your opinion in your notebook.

What Did Giuseppe Garibaldi Do?

Cavour united the northern states of Italy, while secretly helping nationalists in the southern states. In May 1860, a small army of Italian nationalists invaded the island of Sicily. Giuseppe Garibaldi led them.

Garibaldi always wore a red shirt in battle. His supporters imitated him, and the red shirt became their uniform. The "Red Shirts" swept

Giuseppe Garibaldi, the "sword" of Italian unity, united most of Italy.

through Sicily and marched northward toward Rome. There, Garibaldi's army met up with Sardinian troops. Together, they had united almost all of Italy. Because of his great military feats, historians call Garibaldi the "sword" of the revolution.

Who Became Italy's First King?

In March 1861, a parliament representing most of the Italian states chose a ruler. King Victor Emmanuel II of Sardinia became the first king of a unified Italy. In 1870, the last independent state became part of Italy. Rome became the capital. The parliament set aside part of Rome for the pope's use. Vatican City is still the home of the pope and the center of the Roman Catholic Church.

Communication in History

The Wireless Telegraph
The Italian engineer Guglielmo Marconi invented the wireless telegraph in 1895. He performed his first experiment near his home in Bologna, Italy. There he transmitted signals on radio waves across a mile of countryside. In 1901, he sent messages by telegraph a much longer distance, across the Atlantic

Ocean from England to Newfoundland. Marconi went on to build communication products for ships at sea. A few years later, Canadian Reginald Fessenden and American Ernst Alexanderson learned how to send speech and music on the same radio waves. Another American, Lee de Forest, created a device to make these radio messages louder.

Writing About History

Have students read the feature independently and ask a volunteer to read it aloud. Discuss both positive and negative aspects of nationalism. (examples: positive—it can bring people together during difficult times; negative—can cause civil war over which brand of nationalism should dominate) Then have students write personal responses to the questions in their journals. Remind students that opinions are personal feelings and answers cannot be considered right or wrong.

ELL/ESL STRATEGY

Language Objective:
To use description
Write "red shirts" on the board. Ask an ELL student to write words that have the same meaning in his or her native language on the board. Then have the student read both sets of words. Next, break the class into small groups. Provide a colorful picture from a magazine to each group. Have students share a list of descriptive terms in both English and the ELL student's native language.

Vatican City

From 756 to 1870, the pope ruled much of central Italy. However, with the unification of Italy, the pope's rule was reduced to one city-state, Vatican City. Established in 1929, Vatican City is the world's smallest independent country. Located in northwestern Rome, it has an area of 110 acres.

Medieval and Renaissance walls surround the city. The most important building is Saint Peter's Church. The Vatican, the pope's palace, is also within these walls. The Sistine Chapel is part of this palace. Michelangelo painted its ceiling. The government offices of the Roman Catholic Church are also found here.

Vatican City has its own currency, postal system, and telephone and telegraph services. It also has a railroad station and a radio station. Its population is less than 1,000.

Lesson 2 Review On a sheet of paper, write the letter of the answer that correctly completes each sentence.

1. After 1814, _____ controlled most of the 30 states in Italy.

    A Austria   **C** Spain

    B France   **D** all of the above

2. The "soul" of Italian unity was _____.

    A Mazzini   **C** Cavour

    B Garibaldi   **D** Victor Emmanuel II

3. The "brain" of Italian unity was _____.

    A Mazzini   **C** Cavour

    B Garibaldi   **D** Victor Emmanuel II

4. The "sword" of Italian unity was _____.

    A Mazzini   **C** Cavour

    B Garibaldi   **D** Victor Emmanuel II

5. The first king of Italy was _____.

    A Mazzini   **C** Cavour

    B Garibaldi   **D** Victor Emmanuel II

Red is an easy color to shoot at. Why would Garibaldi wear red in battle?

Have students read "Vatican City" on page 579. Explain that the Sistine Chapel is a prominent cultural attraction and that it is decorated with important works of art. Invite students to work in pairs or small groups to find examples of this artwork and the names of the artists who created them. Have students bring in photocopies or, if possible, books with reproductions to share with the class.

3 Reinforce and Extend

LEARNING STYLES

Auditory/Verbal

Have students turn Lesson 2 into an oral story. Have one student begin the story by relating the first set of information from the lesson. Have the next student provide a sentence with the next set of information from the lesson. Continue with a third student providing the next set of information, and so on. Students should try to avoid reading from the text, but instead use the information in the paragraph to construct their own informational sentences.

STUDY SKILLS

To help students organize this material, ask them to create a chart with three columns and three rows. They can title the chart "Italian Nationalists." Have students write *Soul*, *Brain*, and *Sword* in separate rows in the first column. In the second column, students should provide the names of the three Italian nationalists, placing them in the proper rows. The third column should contain explanations as to why each term was associated with each nationalist.

ONLINE CONNECTION

Students can gain additional information by accessing the following Web sites:

www.agsglobewh.com/page579a
(Students will read the speech given by Giuseppe Garibaldi to the "Red Shirts.")

www.agsglobewh.com/page579b
(Students will read a section of Otto von Bismarck's memoirs.)

www.agsglobewh.com/page579c
(Students will read the reasons Marie Curie was awarded the Nobel Peace Prize in 1903.)

Lesson 2 Review Answers

1. D **2.** A **3.** C **4.** B **5.** D

Answers will vary. Garibaldi might have wanted to show his followers how brave he was. He might have wanted to show his enemies how little he feared them. He might have thought that his bravery would inspire his followers. Perhaps he thought the aggressive color red would inspire his followers.

Nationalism Chapter 23 **579**

Chapter 23: Lesson 3

Overview This lesson describes the series of wars through which Germany became unified.

Objectives

- To explain how the failed German Revolution of 1848 affected Germany
- To identify the role Otto von Bismarck played in German unification
- To identify the first ruler of Germany

Student Pages pages 580–584

Teacher's Resource Library TRL

Workbook Activity 107

Activity 107

Modified Activity 107

Vocabulary

ambassador	policy
kaiser	reich
militarism	siege
negotiate	

Have students study the definitions of the vocabulary words. Then ask them to rewrite the definitions in their own words, each one containing one of the other vocabulary words. Invite volunteers to read their definitions to the class.

1 Warm-Up Activity

Draw a three-column chart on the board, and label the columns as *Resources, Nationalism,* and *Strategy,* respectively. Have students brainstorm factors that enable a country to become a military power. Examples of such factors might include availability of industry, natural resources, financial backing, soldiers, common heritage and history, leadership, and a strategy that will lead to victory over adversaries. Write their ideas under the proper columns. Have students copy the information and refer to it as they read through the lesson.

Objectives

- To explain how the failed German Revolution of 1848 affected Germany
- To identify the role Otto von Bismarck played in German unification
- To identify the first ruler of Germany

Reading Strategy: Summarizing

What do you think you will learn by reading about the 1848 German Revolution?

The Napoleonic Wars also gave birth to nationalism in Germany. Germany had many independent states. From 1814 to 1815, the Congress of Vienna organized the German Confederation. It included 38 German states and their rulers. But the confederation was weak.

Soon, the idea of unifying Germany became popular. The people in all the German states spoke German. They also had the same culture and shared the same land.

Why Did the 1848 German Revolution Fail?

The revolts that swept over Europe in 1848 affected Germany. In April 1849, representatives of the German states met in a parliament and issued a constitution. The parliament asked the Prussian king, Frederick Wilhelm IV, to become king of all the German states. (Prussia was the largest German state.)

The king refused the offer because the people of Germany, and not the princes of all the states, had offered him the crown. He wanted the nobles, not the common people, to choose him.

Soon, fighting broke out between the liberals and the conservatives. The liberals wanted gradual change and a democratic government; the conservatives wanted none of this. Then King Wilhelm sent his Prussian army to break up the parliament. When the liberal leaders fled, the conservatives once again controlled the German states.

How Did Bismarck Plan to Unite the German States?

After the 1848 revolution failed, most German nationalists thought that only Prussia could unite Germany. Prussia was the strongest German state and had the best army. In 1862, Otto von Bismarck became prime minister of Prussia. Bismarck, a member of the rich landlord class, was loyal to the Prussian king. He wanted to unite all the German states under Prussia's leadership.

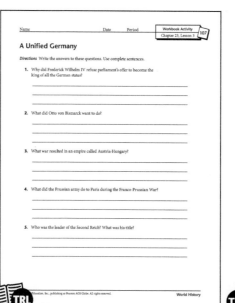

Workbook Activity 107

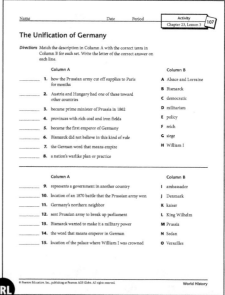

Activity 107

Militarism

A nation's warlike policy or practice

Policy

A plan that helps a person or a country make a decision

Reading Strategy:
Questioning

As you read, notice the details in the text. What questions can you ask yourself about these details?

Bismarck, who was a conservative, did not believe in democratic rule. In his first speech as prime minister, he told the Prussian parliament that the only way to solve problems was "by blood and iron." For him, "blood" meant war and "iron" meant a king with absolute power.

What Is Militarism?

Bismarck wanted to make Prussia into a great military power. He forced the Prussian parliament to give him money to build a strong army. He believed that war would unite the German states. Historians have a name for this belief: **militarism.** For such a country, nothing is more important than the military.

Who Won the Austro-Prussian War?

In 1864, Bismarck's army defeated Germany's northern neighbor, Denmark. Then, in 1866, his army defeated Austria in just seven weeks. To do this, Bismarck used Prussia's new railroads and better weapons. After Austria's defeat, Bismarck forced its neighbor to give up some of its German land.

Austria gave Hungary more independence. Austria and Hungary each had its own parliament and officials. However, the Austrian emperor was still the king of Hungary. Also, the two countries had one **policy,** or plan, toward other countries. They also shared one army. Historians call this new empire Austria-Hungary.

Have students turn to the timeline on page 572. Ask them to find the year in which Germany became unified. (1871) Have students read pages 580–584 to learn about the steps that led up to German unification.

Ask:

- What was the name of the Prussian king who refused the German parliament's offer to make him king in 1849? (Frederick Wilhelm IV)
- Who became the prime minister of Prussia in 1862? (Otto von Bismarck)
- What political belief led Bismarck to lead his armies into war? (militarism)
- Which countries did Bismarck's armies defeat? (Denmark, Austria, and France)

Reading Strategy:
Questioning

(Answers will vary; factors that lead to revolution, leaders of the revolution, results of the revolution)

- What is the name of the empire that formed after the Austro-Prussian War? (Austria-Hungary)

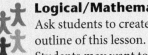
LEARNING STYLES

Logical/Mathematical
Ask students to create an outline of this lesson. Students may want to list prominent figures as main points and their accomplishments as subpoints. Alternatively, students could create a chronology of revolts and wars as main points and list the importance of each as subpoints.

BACKGROUND INFORMATION

The Austro-Prussian War, also called the Seven Weeks' War, took place between June and August of 1866. Otto von Bismarck used this war to make Prussia the most powerful state in the German Confederation and to force Austria out of the Confederation. The Prussians' skillful use of new inventions such as the railroad and telegraph led them to victory.

ELL/ESL STRATEGY

Language Objective:
To explain a sequence of events

Divide the class into small groups. Include an ELL student in each group, if possible. Using the information in Lesson 3, have each group create a flow chart showing how one event lead to another in Germany. Ask each ELL student to explain the flow of events using transition words, such as *first, second, next, then, after,* and so forth.

Ask:

- What was the cause of the Franco-Prussian War? (Bismarck lied, which forced each country to defend its national honor)
- What French ruler was captured by the Prussian army at the Battle of Sedan? (Napoleon III)
- Which war brought all of the German states together? (Franco-Prussian War)
- What action of the Prussian army caused Paris to surrender? (a four-month siege)
- What is the name of the treaty that Bismarck forced the French to sign? (the Treaty of Frankfurt)
- Which two territories did France have to surrender to Germany? (Alsace and Lorraine)

WORLD CULTURES

Throughout the second half of the 19th century, German immigrants represented the largest group of immigrants in America. Before the turn of the century more than five million Germans arrived in the United States. Many settled in Ohio and in Wisconsin, where farmland was plentiful, bringing their German heritage, foods, and traditions with them. The German word "burg," meaning castle, is attached to the names of numerous small cities and villages in Wisconsin, such as Reedsburg, Harrisburg, and Johnsburg. One large subgroup of these German immigrants were the Amish. Today, Amish communities in Ohio, Wisconsin, and other states maintain their German heritage through their language and traditions.

Ambassador
A person sent to represent his or her government in another country

Siege
The act of surrounding a city or fort with an army and cutting off its supplies

Negotiate
To talk together, make bargains, and agree on something

How Did Bismarck Start the Franco-Prussian War?

Next, Bismarck and Prussia went to war with France. It started when the French **ambassador,** a representative of the French government, came to Prussia. He wanted to talk to the king about who should become the next king of Spain.

Bismarck then lied to the newspapers about what the two men said to one another. His lie made the French think that the Prussian king had said something rude to their ambassador. It made the Germans think that the French ambassador had threatened them. Nationalists in both countries felt that they had to go to war. Only then could they defend their national honor.

Who Won the Franco-Prussian War?

The well-trained Prussian army moved quickly. In 1870, German soldiers poured into northern France. At the Battle of Sedan, the Prussian army defeated the French and captured about 100,000 French soldiers. Included among them was the French ruler, Napoleon III.

The Prussian army surrounded Paris and cut off its supplies. After this four-month **siege,** Paris surrendered. Bismarck forced the French to sign a treaty called the Treaty of Frankfurt. According to the treaty, France had to pay Prussia a huge sum of money. It also had to give up two important territories, Alsace and Lorraine. These provinces, which lay on the border with Germany, contained France's richest coal and iron fields.

What Was the Second Reich?

The Franco-Prussian War brought all the German states together. After the Austro-Prussian War, Prussia took control of northern Germany. Then it formed the North German Confederation. After the Franco-Prussian War, the people in the four southern states joined the rest of Germany.

AT HOME

Have students discuss their heritage with family. Have students collect photos of family members, learn from which country or countries their family originated, and to where and when their family members migrated. Have students write a paragraph and create posters of what they learned about their family's heritage.

LEARNING STYLES

Body/Kinesthetic
Invite students to take part in dramatically interpreting the lesson text. Ask for two volunteers to interpret each paragraph: one student to read with dramatic expression and another to pantomime what is read. Ask the class to refrain from applause until all paragraphs are read.

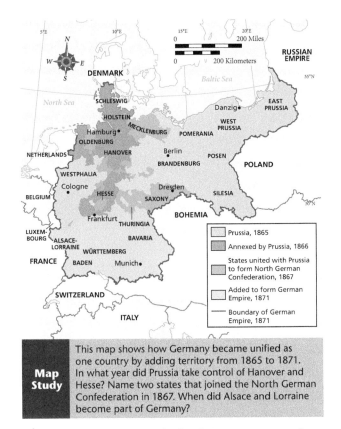

Prussia, 1865

Annexed by Prussia, 1866

States united with Prussia to form North German Confederation, 1867

Added to form German Empire, 1871

Boundary of German Empire, 1871

Map Study This map shows how Germany became unified as one country by adding territory from 1865 to 1871. In what year did Prussia take control of Hanover and Hesse? Name two states that joined the North German Confederation in 1867. When did Alsace and Lorraine become part of Germany?

Kaiser

The emperor of Germany

Reich

The German word for empire

Wilhelm I agreed to become the first **kaiser,** or emperor, of Germany. He was crowned in January 1871 at the French palace of Versailles. Historians call this new German empire the Second **Reich.** The German word *reich* means empire or nation. The Holy Roman Empire was the First Reich in that part of Europe.

Ask for a volunteer to read the title of the map, "Unification of Germany, 1865–1871." Ask students to locate West and East Prussia. Then have students read the caption and answer the questions. (Prussia took over Hanover in 1866 and Hesse in 1867. States that joined the North German Confederation in 1867 include Saxony, Oldenburg, Hesse, and Mecklenburg. Alsace and Lorraine became part of Germany in 1871.)

Ask:

• Where was Wilhelm I crowned Kaiser of Germany in 1871? (the French palace of Versailles)

3 Reinforce and Extend

LEARNING STYLES

Interpersonal/ Group Learning

Divide the class into small groups. Explain that the sovereignty of Alsace and Lorraine remained in dispute between Germany and France during the 20th century. Assign each group a characteristic of Alsace and Lorraine to research, such as natural resources, geography, agriculture, trade, language, traditions, and the like. Have each group share what it learned. Discuss the importance of the region's attributes.

Lesson 3 Review Answers

1. Prussia **2.** Wilhelm IV
3. Bismarck **4.** Sedan **5.** Wilhelm I

Answers will vary. France must have already felt ashamed because its soldiers had allowed Prussia to capture Napoleon III, the French ruler. Then France had to give away two provinces that provided it with coal and iron. These two natural resources would then help Prussia become even more powerful.

Biography

Provide students with this background information: Marie Curie was born in Warsaw, Poland. She met Pierre Curie in Paris, where she was studying mathematics, physics, and chemistry. After their marriage, the Curies worked together to research the source of radioactivity. Their success led to the 1903 Nobel Prize in physics for the Curies and a physicist who worked with them, Antoine Henri Becquerel. Marie went on to isolate the element radium, which earned her the 1911 Nobel Prize in Chemistry.

After students read the biography, encourage them to share personal experiences of being X-rayed.

CAREER CONNECTION

The work of Marie Curie has paved the way for a number of careers in the field of medicine. Nuclear Medicine Technologists, for example, work with radioactive materials and X-rays to diagnose and treat such diseases as cancer, heart disease, and Alzheimer's disease. A person interested in this career should get good grades in science and math in high school, then go on to a one-to four-year professional program. Ask students to research this career further and write a brief summary of their findings.

Word Bank
Bismarck
Prussia
Sedan
Wilhelm I
Wilhelm IV

Lesson 3 Review On a sheet of paper, use the words from the Word Bank to complete each sentence correctly.

1. Germans looked to _____ for leadership in unifying Germany.

2. _____ refused the offer to become king of all the German states.

3. In 1862, _____ became prime minister of Prussia.

4. In the Battle of _____, the Prussian army defeated the French army.

5. _____ became the first kaiser of Germany.

What do you think

Why do you think the Treaty of Frankfurt probably made the French feel ashamed?

Biography

Marie Curie: 1867–1934

Marie Curie was a Polish-born French chemist. She and her husband, Pierre, studied radioactivity, which is the energy in atoms. Marie received the Nobel Prize in physics in 1903 and in chemistry in 1911.

The Curies wanted everyone to benefit from their studies. During World War I, Marie helped equip ambulances with X-ray equipment to help wounded soldiers. She even drove ambulances to the front lines. She also taught others how to use the equipment.

Her work meant that she was often near radioactive materials. Its dangers were not known at the time. Radiation gave her cancer. In a twist of fate, today we use controlled radiation to treat cancer.

Chapter Project Follow-up

Provide time for students to share and explain their puzzle boards and games based on the unification of Italy or Germany. Then allow groups to play each others' games and puzzles.

A Lady's Glimpse of the Late War in Bohemia

Little is known about Lizzie Selina Eden, who wrote this account in 1867. She was traveling in Europe when the Austro-Prussian War broke out in 1866. The Prussian army defeated Austria in seven weeks.

"Love oft since this strange world began,

Walking his path of awe and wonder,

Has brought a better age to man

In blood, and fire, and battle thunder.

Angels, that with the evening star

Looked down upon the field of doom,

Wept – but serenely, for they saw

Beyond the veil the good to come."

We went over to Tetschen in the evening, but a gloomy distrust seemed on every face – a dim foreshadowing of the dismal tidings that burst on us next morning, when the sad fact could no longer be withheld, and we learnt the melancholy truth that Austria had been beaten – utterly and completely beaten. . . .

It was piteous this evening, and on many succeeding days, to see . . . raftsmen and wood-cutters out of employ, and many other sturdy-looking Bohemians who had nothing to do, for there was no work to be had – standing the whole day on the banks of the Elbe, watching for the first sight of the victorious Prussian army.

The weather even seemed now to share in the general depression, and changed from the intense heat of the previous week to cold, chilly days. A melancholy little robin, too, used to come and perch itself close to my window, and sing its dreary song all day, so that I felt in my room as melancholy as if I were in a churchyard. I quite longed to be told some day with a grin by our cheery-looking little waiter . . . that there were robins for dinner, among which this one might be included, so that henceforth we should be rid of its doleful song.

Scarcely anyone in England will ever know the extent of the misery and beggary which that fatal six weeks has brought on Bohemia. Many who were rich and prosperous are now fearfully reduced, and thousands are literally beggars. All, however, bear their hard doom with wonderful resignation, and make the best of their sad fate.

Document-Based Questions

1. What event is Eden describing?

2. Why is there such sadness around her?

3. Why does Eden mention the weather?

4. Why does she want the robin to go away?

5. Why are the rich people now beggars?

Source: A Lady's Glimpse of the Late War in Bohemia, by Lizzie Selina Eden, 1867.

Have students recall the details of the Austro-Prussian War. Read the document title, "A Lady's Glimpse of the Late War in Bohemia," and the introductory paragraph to the class. Have a student who enjoys poetry read the opening poem. Briefly discuss its meaning with the class. Then have students finish reading the selection independently. Discuss phrases that indicate despair. Write the phrases on the board and explain how they bring emotion and a sense of doom to the selection. (possible phrases: dismal tidings, melancholy truth, completely beaten, general depression, literally beggars) Have students silently reread the selection. Then have students write answers to the Document-Based Questions. Discuss students' answers as a group.

Answers to Document-Based Questions:

1. Eden is describing the despair she finds in Austria following the Austro-Prussian War.

2. People realize their way of life is about to dramatically change.

3. Answers will vary. The cold and rainy weather is used to help describe the general feeling of gloom in Austria.

4. Answers will vary. The robin represents the feeling of despair felt by the people.

5. Answers will vary. Austria has been defeated.

Spotlight Story

Read the Spotlight Story title to the students. Then have the students read the story to find out what the *Kulturkampf* was. Point out that Bismarck's attempt to make Catholics put loyalty to the state above loyalty to the Catholic Church backfired. About a third of the German population was Catholic, and they rallied behind the church. Even though Bismarck realized that he had made a mistake by establishing the *Kulturkampf* and ended it, he never regained the widespread support he had enjoyed.

Answers to Spotlight Story Wrap-Up:

1. The *Kulturkampf* was a program that Bismarck started to limit the power of the Catholic Church.

2. Laws included forcing the Jesuits to leave Germany, making other clergy obey rules about what they could teach, and banning Catholics from government jobs.

3. The Catholics helped Bismarck by supporting his trade and economic policies.

4. He ended the *Kulturkampf* to gain political support from Catholics.

5. The *Kulturkampf* lasted from 1871–1887.

Bismarck's *Kulturkampf*

For centuries the Roman Catholic pope has exercised power over European land owned by the church. Many of those properties were in Germany. Otto von Bismarck wanted to reduce the power of the Roman Catholic Church in his empire.

Bismarck was a devoted Protestant. He was afraid that the Catholics in Germany would not be loyal to his empire. He believed that their only real loyalty was to Rome. In 1871 he began a program called *Kulturkampf,* or "struggle for the minds controlling civilization."

Bismarck led the German parliament to pass laws limiting the power of the church. The Jesuits, an important order of teaching priests, had to leave Germany. Other clergy members had to obey strict rules about what they could teach. Those who did not agree to these rules were imprisoned. Catholics were banned from all jobs connected to government. In 1872 Germany ended all ties with the Vatican.

Bismarck's government had a very hard time enforcing these rules. In many cases, the government authorities were secretly working for the Catholic Church. Reaction to the *Kulturkampf* brought new support for the Roman Catholic Center Party. Even many non-Catholics who opposed the chancellor's actions joined the new party. A growing contempt for the *Kulturkampf* had become widespread within a very short time. One angry Catholic even tried to assassinate Bismarck!

Bismarck had encouraged free trade with other countries. This was weakening the Germany economy, as the country became flooded with foreign goods. People throughout the empire began to blame Bismarck for their money problems.

The groups that had previously supported Bismarck also favored free trade. He needed to find backing from more conservative voters. Many of those voters were the very Catholics he was trying to control. The Catholic political party members agreed to support Bismarck if he agreed to end his *Kulturkampf.*

Bismarck began to repeal the laws against Catholics. He reestablished ties with the Vatican. By 1887 he had completely ended the *Kulturkampf.* Otto von Bismarck knew he had made a mistake and he worked to correct it. However, he never regained the support of many people in the growing German middle class.

Wrap-Up

1. What was the *Kulturkampf*?

2. What laws were enacted under the *Kulturkampf*?

3. How could the Catholics help Bismarck?

4. Why did Bismarck end the *Kulturkampf*?

5. For how long did the *Kulturkampf* last?

- Nationalism grows stronger when a group of people have one language, one culture, one government, and a common history. They share the same customs, music, way of life, and religion. Nationalism can remain even if people lose their land or their government.

- Giuseppe Mazzini was called the soul of Italian independence because he stood for its spirit of freedom. He led a failed revolt in 1848.

- Count Camillo di Cavour was known as the brain of Italian unity. He got French support for Sardinia's war against Austria. The war won independence for several Italian provinces.

- Giuseppe Garibaldi was called the sword of Italian independence because of his military accomplishments. He and his Red Shirts freed Sicily. They joined Sardinian troops near Rome and united Italy.

- Victor Emmanuel II became Italy's first king. The parliament set aside part of Rome for the pope. It became Vatican City.

- The German Revolution of 1848 failed. The Prussian ruler refused to become king of all the German states. German nationalists believed only Prussia, the strongest German state, could unite Germany.

- In 1862, Otto von Bismarck became Prussia's prime minister. Prussia was the largest German state. Bismarck did not believe in democratic rule.

- Bismarck used militarism to conquer the German states. He defeated Austria in just seven weeks. A new empire, Austria-Hungary, was formed.

- In the Franco-Prussian War of 1870, Prussia defeated France and won French territory. The remaining independent German states joined Prussia to become a united Germany. Wilhelm I became its first kaiser in 1871.

1840 – 1914

Using the Chapter Summary

Have students read the Chapter Summary on page 587 to review the main ideas presented in Chapter 23.

Ask:

- What is the word for the devotion people have for their country? (nationalism)
- Why was Giuseppe Mazzini called the soul of Italian independence? (He stood for its spirit of freedom.)
- Which country did Cavour enlist to support Sardinia's war against Austria? (France)
- Why was Giuseppe Garibaldi called the sword of Italian independence? (because of his military accomplishments)
- Which three nationalists helped bring about Italian unification? (Mazzini, Cavour, and Garibaldi)
- Who was Italy's first king? (Victor Emmanuel II)
- Where did German nationalists look for help in uniting Germany? (to Prussia)
- Who became prime minister of Prussia in 1862? (Otto von Bismarck)
- What strategy did Bismarck use to defeat Austria? (militarism)
- Which country was defeated in the Franco-Prussian War of 1870? (France)
- When was Germany unified? (1871)

TEACHER'S RESOURCE

The AGS Globe Teaching Strategies in Social Studies Transparencies may be used with this chapter. The transparencies add an interactive dimension to expand and enhance the *World History* program content.

Chapter 23 Review

Use the Chapter Review to prepare students for tests and to reteach content from the chapter.

Chapter 23 Mastery Test

The Teacher's Resource Library includes two forms of the Chapter 23 Mastery Test. Each test addresses the chapter Goals for Learning. An optional third page of additional critical-thinking items is included for each test. The difficulty level of the two forms is equivalent.

Chapter 23 Review Answers

1. Napoleonic Wars
2. Red Shirts
3. Victor Emmanuel II
4. Mazzini
5. Cavour
6. Garibaldi
7. Bismarck
8. Prussia
9. Napoleon III
10. Wilhelm I
11. A
12. C
13. C

Word Bank
Bismarck
Cavour
Garibaldi
Mazzini
Napoleon III
Napoleonic Wars
Prussia
Red Shirts
Victor Emmanuel II
Wilhelm I

On a sheet of paper, use the words from the Word Bank to complete each sentence correctly.

1. The _____ started nationalism in Italy.

2. The _____ were supporters of Giuseppe Garibaldi.

3. Italy's first king, chosen in 1861, was _____.

4. _____ was an Italian nationalist and the "soul" of Italian unity.

5. _____ was a skilled politician and the "brain" of Italian unity.

6. _____ was a fine soldier and the "sword" of Italian unity.

7. _____ was the Prussian prime minister who wanted to unite all the German states under Prussia's leadership.

8. The strongest German state was _____.

9. In the Battle of Sedan, Prussian soldiers captured _____ and 100,000 other prisoners.

10. The first kaiser of a united Germany was _____.

On a sheet of paper, write the letter of the answer that correctly completes each sentence.

11. The love people have for their country is _____.

   A nationalism   C colonialism
   B militarism   D protectorate

12. Another name for a German emperor is _____.

   A conservative   C kaiser
   B liberal   D protectorate

13. Bismarck believed in _____ for Germany.

   A imperialism   C militarism
   B nationalism   D all of the above

Chapter 23 Mastery Test A

Part A Directions Circle the letter of the answer that correctly completes each sentence.

1. American _____ includes a belief in freedom and democracy.
   A monarchy   B culture   C religion   D property

2. Studying the history of the United States helps students value their _____.
   A heritage   B policy   C province   D kingdom

3. _____ planned how to get France and Austria to fight one another to help unite Italy.
   A Giuseppe Mazzini   B Otto von Bismarck   C Giuseppe Garibaldi   D Camillo di Cavour

4. The German _____ was weak, and it included 38 states and their rulers.
   A Alliance   B Unity   C Independence   D Confederation

5. France had to give up the territories of _____ and Lorraine.
   A Paris   B Hungary   C Alsace   D Hesse

Part B Directions Match the definition in Column A with the correct term in Column B. Write the letter of the correct answer on each line.

Column A	Column B
_____ 6. a society in which a number of languages are spoken	A ambassador
_____ 7. a nation's warlike policy or practice	B foreign
_____ 8. a person sent to represent his or her government in another country	C heritage
_____ 9. the emperor of Germany	D kaiser
_____ 10. traditions that ancestors pass down to their descendants	E militarism
_____ 11. the German word for empire	F multilingual
_____ 12. the act of surrounding a city or fort and cutting off its supplies	G policy
_____ 13. from outside of one's country	H prime minister
_____ 14. a plan that helps a person or a country make a decision	I reich
_____ 15. the leader in some democratic government systems	J siege

World History

Chapter 23 Mastery Test A, *continued*

Part C Directions Write the answers to these questions. Use complete sentences.

16. Why is Giuseppe Garibaldi called the "sword"?

17. What is Vatican City?

18. Which countries controlled the Italian provinces after 1814?

19. What action did Sardinia take in 1848?

20. What did Otto von Bismarck believe in?

Part D Directions Write the correct word from the Word Bank to complete each sentence.

21. After the Franco-Prussian War, _____ gave up provinces that were near Germany.

22. Historians call the German empire the _____ Reich.

23. Nationalism is a feeling of loyalty to one's _____.

24. Garibaldi's army and _____ troops teamed up to unify most of Italy.

25. The _____ Wars gave birth to nationalism in Italy and in Germany.

Word Bank
country
France
Napoleonic
Sardinian
Second

World History

Chapter 23 Mastery Test A, *continued*

Part E Directions Write your answer to each question. Use complete sentences. Support each answer with facts and examples from the textbook.

26. Giuseppe Mazzini led a rebellion that failed. Why is he important to the history of Italy? Explain. (2 points)

27. What did Otto von Bismarck lie about? What was the result of his lie? (2 points)

Part F Directions Write a short paragraph for each topic. Include a topic sentence, body, and conclusion. Support each answer with facts and examples from the textbook.

28. Explain nationalism, and describe the things that affect it. (3 points)

29. Explain how militarism was important to the unification of Germany. (3 points)

World History

14. After the Franco-Prussian War, Bismarck forced the French to sign the Treaty of _____.

    A France   **C** Frankfurt
    B Prussia   **D** Lorraine

15. Prussian King Frederick Wilhelm IV refused to become king because he wanted the _____ to choose him.

    A nobles   **C** Germans
    B common people **D** liberals

On a sheet of paper, write the answer to each question. Use complete sentences.

16. Why did the 1848 German Revolution fail?

17. How can an invasion of their land make people have more nationalism?

18. Why is a common language an important part of nationalism?

Critical Thinking On a sheet of paper, write your response to each question. Use complete sentences.

19. Do you agree or disagree with Bismarck that leaders must decide problems with "blood and iron"? Explain your answer.

20. Do you think that nationalism is always a good thing? Explain your answer.

Read multiple-choice questions completely before reading the answer choices.

1840 – 1914

Nationalism Chapter 23   **589**

14. C

15. A

16. The Prussian king, Frederick Wilhelm IV, refused to become king of all German states unless the nobles offered him the crown.

17. Answers will vary. An invasion of a country can draw people together to rise up against the invaders to protect their heritage and culture.

18. Answers will vary. A common language creates a sense of pride in a shared heritage and culture, and the preservation of national unity.

Critical Thinking

19. Answers will vary. Some students may believe that military conquest is required when there are disputes between countries that seem irresolvable. Others may feel that compromise and diplomacy can solve any dispute.

20. Answers will vary. Some students may feel that nationalism binds a country and gives it a focus and purpose. Others may feel that a sense of nationalism creates an arrogance that harm foreign relations.

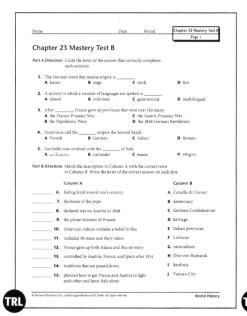

Chapter 23 Mastery Test B, pages 1–3

Nationalism Chapter 23   **589**

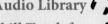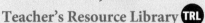
Introducing the Chapter

The wave of nationalism that swept
through Europe in the late 19th century
was followed by a period of imperialism.
European powers began to look outside
their borders to enlarge their respective
empires. Their chief targets were Asia
and Africa. The countries on these
continents provided much-needed raw
materials and natural resources for
European industry. The people in these
countries provided cheap labor to harvest
and mine these resources. They also
provided a market for European goods.

Imperialism

In this chapter you will learn about imperialism, when
European powers took control of Asia and Africa. There
were several reasons for this. Manufacturers in Europe needed
new natural resources. Some missionaries and doctors were
concerned for the well being of people in these countries.
Another reason was that many Europeans thought they were
superior to everyone else. They thought it was up to them to
"improve" life for the people in these countries. The results
were often violent.

Goals for Learning

◆ To explain imperialism
◆ To describe the effects of imperialism on Asia
◆ To describe the effects of imperialism on Africa

1842 Europeans divide China into spheres of influence

1859 Workers begin to build the Suez Canal

1904 Japan defeats Russia and gains Korea

| 1840 | 1860 | 1880 | 1900 | 1920 |

British government begins to rule India

1867 Japanese revolution returns power to Emperor Meiji

1909 South Africa becomes a British colony

1912 Italy controls Tripoli

Ask:

- When did Europeans divide China
  into spheres of influence? (1842)

- When did South Africa become a
  British colony? (1909)

- Which Asian country took over
  another Asian country? Which
  country was taken over? (Japan
  took over Korea.)

- How many years after the British
  colonized India did they take over
  South Africa? (51 years)

Name   Date   Period   *SELF-STUDY GUIDE*

Chapter 24: Imperialism

Goal 24.1 *To explain imperialism*

Date	Assignment	Completed
	1. Read pages 590–595.	
	2. Complete the Lesson 1 Review on page 595.	
	3. Complete Workbook Activity 108.	

Comments:

Goal 24.2 *To describe the effects of imperialism on Asia*

Date	Assignment	Completed
	4. Read pages 596–599.	
	5. Complete the Lesson 2 Review on page 599.	
	6. Complete Workbook Activity 109.	

Comments:

TRL

Chapter 24 Self-Study Guide, pages 1–2

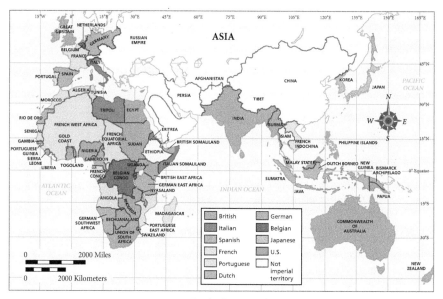

Between 1850 and 1900, the world went through great change. By 1900, a few powerful nations dominated the map. Many countries in Europe had huge empires in Africa and Asia. The European powers divided nearly all of Africa among themselves. Outsiders also controlled much of Asia. This map shows European and American imperialism in Africa, Europe, and Asia.

Study the map, then answer the following questions:

1. Which European power controlled the largest empire?

2. What country controlled the island of Madagascar, off the east African coast?

3. What are the names of three African colonies that Portugal controlled?

4. What were the major Dutch colonies in Asia?

5. What country controlled Australia?

Ask a volunteer to read the title of the map on page 591: "Imperialism." Call attention to its key. Make sure students understand the symbols.

Ask:

- Which three continents are not shown on this map? (North America, South America, Antarctica)
- Australia is in which direction from Africa? (east)
- What was the southernmost country controlled by a European power? (New Zealand)
- Which two African countries were not under European control? (Liberia, Ethiopia)

Have students read the paragraph under the map and answer the questions.

Map Skills Answers

1. the British

2. France

3. Portuguese Guinea, Angola, and Portuguese East Africa

4. Sumatra, Java, Dutch Borneo, Bismarck Archipelago, and New Guinea

5. Great Britain

Chapter Project

Organize students into several small groups. Have each group research and write a report about the Suez Canal. Reports should focus on how the canal influenced the spread of imperialism into Asia and Africa, and also how these continents were changed by the canal. Suggest that each member of a group should focus on a different area of the story, such as the digging of the canal, the fight to control the canal, the changes in Africa and Asia during and after the canal was finished, and how all of this, in turn, affected Europe. Encourage students to illustrate their written reports with photographs, drawings, and other visual elements.

Name _____ Date _____ Period _____ | Chapter 24 Outline Page 1

Imperialism, (pp. 590–607)

Directions: Fill in the outline below. Filling in the blanks will help you as you read and study Chapter 24.

I. **Lesson 1: Imperialism (pp. 593–595)**
  A. How Did Industrialism Help Imperialism?
    1. The Industrial Revolution helped spread _____ or colonialism.
    2. A _____ is a place to sell goods.
    3. The nation that controls a colony is the _____ country.
  B. How Did Nationalism Help Imperialism?
    1. Nations thought _____ would make them as powerful as England and France.
  C. How Did Militarism Help Imperialism?
    1. Nations used sea power to control _____ routes.
    2. Mother countries used colonies as _____ bases.
  D. What Attitudes Helped Promote Imperialism?
    1. People in Europe and the United States thought they were _____ than Africans.
    2. Westerners wanted to bring _____ civilization to other countries.

II. **Lesson 2: The Effect of Imperialism on Asia (pp. 596–599)**
  A. Why Was India Important to Britain?
    1. _____ and Britain fought for control of India.
    2. In 1858, the British _____ took over direct rule of India.
    3. India provided raw _____ for British industry.
  B. Why Was Southeast Asia Important to Europe?
    1. French colonies were called French _____
    2. Britain took over _____, now called Myanmar.

Name _____ Date _____ Period _____ | Chapter 24 Outline Page 2

Imperialism, continued

  C. When Did Europe Insist on More Trade With China?
    1. European countries forced China to give them special _____ rights.
    2. A trading area is called a _____ of influence.
    3. _____ rulers had no say in the European-controlled trade.
  D. What Happened in Japan in 1867?
    1. A _____ in 1867 ended the rule of the shogun.
    2. Emperor _____ gained political power.
    3. Japan _____ feudalism.
  E. How Did Japan Become Imperialistic?
    1. All young men had to serve in the _____
    2. Japan defeated _____ in a war that ended in 1895.
    3. In 1904, Japan went to war against _____

III. **Lesson 3: The Effect of Imperialism on Africa (pp. 600–602)**
  A. What Colonies Did Britain Control in Africa?
    1. Britain controlled what are now Sudan, Nigeria, Ghana, Kenya, and _____
    2. The _____ Canal connected the Mediterranean Sea and the Red Sea.
    3. A major power controls the foreign policy of a _____
  B. How Big Was the French Empire in Africa?
    1. France's holdings were large but not _____
    2. Countries respected France for having such a large _____
  C. How Big Was the German Empire in Africa?
    1. Germany asked other countries to come to Berlin to talk about _____ boundaries.

© Pearson Education, Inc., publishing as Pearson AGS Globe. All rights reserved. | World History

Chapter 24 Outline, pages 1–3

Imperialism Chapter 24 **591**

Predicting

Introduce the reading skill *predicting*. Ask for volunteers to read the three bullet-point questions on page 592. Then have students read the two introductory paragraphs on page 593. Ask students to think about the question in the last line of paragraph two, and then look at the heading questions in the lesson (without reading the lesson). Tell students to write a short paragraph that predicts how imperialism happened. When students finish their paragraphs, have them read Lesson 1.

Ask:

- Were your predictions correct? (Answers will vary; Yes, my predictions were correct.)

- If so, what helped you predict correctly? (Answers will vary; I paid close attention to details in the text.)

- If your predictions were incorrect, how could you make a stronger prediction? (Answers will vary; I could pay closer attention to details in the text.)

Key Vocabulary Words

Have students write a fill-in-the-blank sentence for each of the six vocabulary words. Then ask students to exchange papers and complete the sentences by writing the correct words or phrases. Students who complete the sentences should assess them for correct usage of the vocabulary words.

Reading Strategy:
Predicting

Previewing a text helps prepare readers to look for new information—to predict what will come next. A prediction is your best guess about what might happen next:

- ◆ As you read the text, notice details that could help you make predictions.

- ◆ While you read, check your predictions.

- ◆ You may have to change your predictions as you learn more information.

Key Vocabulary Words

Lesson 1

Imperialism Control or influence a powerful nation has over a weaker nation

Colonialism The controlling of colonies; another name for imperialism

Market A place to sell goods

Mother country A nation that controls a colony

Lesson 2

Sphere of influence An area in which only one foreign country can trade

Lesson 3

Protectorate An independent country whose foreign policy is controlled by a major power

Objectives

♦ To explain how industrialization and nationalism helped spread imperialism

♦ To describe how people's attitudes and the quest for military power helped imperialism

Reading Strategy:
Predicting

Preview the lesson title. Predict what you will learn in this lesson.

Imperialism
Control or influence a powerful nation has over a weaker nation

Colonialism
The controlling of colonies; another name for imperialism

Market
A place to sell goods

Mother country
A nation that controls a colony

Imperialism occurs when a powerful nation controls a weaker nation. During the 1500s, many European countries set up colonies in the Americas. Spain controlled most of Latin America and England controlled most of North America. **Colonialism**, or the controlling of colonies, is another name for imperialism.

By the beginning of the 1800s, however, wars like the American Revolutionary War had changed Europe's opinion about colonialism. Colonies seemed to cause more trouble than they were worth. However, by 1900, the industrialized countries of Europe, Japan, and the United States controlled nearly the whole world. How did this happen? There are many reasons.

How Did Industrialism Help Imperialism?

The Industrial Revolution was one reason why imperialism spread. Factory owners in industrialized nations needed the natural resources and raw materials of other countries. To keep their factories running, they needed coal, iron ore, gold, silver, tin, and copper. They could get these from colonies.

These same nations needed places to sell their manufactured goods. That is, they needed markets. By taking over colonies, they could control **markets.** Each major nation let its colonies buy only those goods manufactured in the **mother country**—the nation that controls a colony.

How Did Nationalism Help Imperialism?

Some countries thought that an empire would make them look important in the eyes of the world. Italy, Germany, Japan, and the United States thought colonies would make them as powerful as England and France. Many countries agreed with the statement that "there has never been a great power without great colonies."

1840 – 1914

Chapter 24: Lesson 1

Overview This lesson explains what imperialism is and how it is driven by industrialism, nationalism, militarism, and by people's attitudes toward one another.

Objectives

■ To explain how industrialization and nationalism helped spread imperialism

■ To describe how people's attitudes and the quest for military power helped imperialism

Student Pages pages 593–595

Teacher's Resource Library **TRL**

Workbook Activity 108

Activity 108

Modified Activity 108

Vocabulary

| colonialism | market |
| imperialism | mother country |

Ask students to create fill-in-the-blank sentences that use these vocabulary words. Have students exchange papers with a neighbor and complete each other's sentences.

1 Warm-Up Activity

Discuss the definition of imperialism, and compare imperialism with nationalism. Have students suggest some differences between the two. Ask if nationalism must always come before imperialism. (Usually a country has to solidify the support of its people before it can conquer other countries.) Tell students to make a chart with two columns, labeled *Nationalism* and *Imperialism*. Then have students write down some distinguishing features of each.

2 Teaching the Lesson

Encourage students to share what they know about imperialism. Then have them read pages 593–595 to learn more about how and why imperialism spread.

Ask:

- In what way was the Industrial Revolution a cause of imperialism? (Factory owners needed more natural resources, raw materials, and markets for their goods, which they could get from colonies.)

Reading Strategy: Predicting

(Students will probably predict that they will learn about imperialism, although they will not yet know exactly what imperialism is.)

- Why was sea power important to imperialism? (Sea power helped countries control trade routes.)

- How did having large numbers of colonies give a country more military power? (Colonies could be used as military bases and as shipping ports for stocking up on supplies. Having many colonies allowed a country to control trade routes.)

Reading Strategy: Predicting

(Answers will vary. Students may have to change at least part of their predictions based on information they read in the lesson.)

- What was the attitude of Westerners toward the people of Africa and Asia? (They thought they were better than Africans and Asians, who they believed to be ignorant and uncivilized.)

- What role did religion play in imperialism? (Europeans thought they should bring Christianity to colonized countries.)

Queen Victoria of England rides on top of an elephant in Delhi, India, in this picture.

Reading Strategy: Predicting

Think about what you predicted earlier. Was your prediction correct, or do you need to change your prediction?

How Did Militarism Help Imperialism?

In the late 1800s, many countries built up their military power. Sea power was especially important, because it helped nations control trade routes. Mother countries could use their colonies as military bases. Ships from these mother countries could stop at colonial ports to get supplies for the military.

What Attitudes Helped Promote Imperialism?

Many people in Europe and the United States thought that they were better than people from the East. They thought that these people—especially Africans and Asians—were ignorant and uncivilized. Westerners believed that they should bring Christianity and western civilization to these countries.

LEARNING STYLES

Body/Kinesthetic

Have students present a skit in which they are merchants on a ship that has just docked at a colonial port. Their job is to get supplies for the mother country. Have the merchants negotiate with the colonist traders for natural resources and other supplies. The two sides must agree on a price and terms of a sale.

ELL/ESL STRATEGY

Language Objective:
To change the meaning of words by adding the suffix -ism

Have ELL students go through the lesson and make a list of words that end in -ism. Ask what the words have in common. Elicit the response that they are all processes or theories. Have students explore how adding the suffix -ism changes the meaning of the word. For example, *imperial* is an adjective that relates to a ruler or an empire. *Imperialism* is a noun that refers to the process by which a powerful country colonizes a weaker country.

Lesson 1 Review On a sheet of paper, write the answer to each question. Use complete sentences.

1. What is imperialism?

2. Why did many countries lose interest in imperialism at the beginning of the 1800s?

3. What is the connection between the Industrial Revolution and imperialism?

4. What is the connection between nationalism and imperialism?

5. Why do you think Europeans and Americans thought of themselves as better than people from Africa and Asia?

Was imperialism a good thing? Explain your answer.

The Color Khaki

During the American Revolution, British soldiers wore white pants, a shiny black hat, and a bright red coat. Because of these bright coats, people called them "redcoats" or "lobster backs." Their uniforms looked great in a parade, but an enemy could easily see these red coats.

Years later, while fighting in India, the British soldiers decided to make the enemy's job harder. They covered their uniforms with brown dirt in the dry season and with mud in the wet season. In time, the British adopted the dull yellowish-brown color of Indian dirt for their battle uniforms. Today, we call this "khaki." It comes from the Indian word for dust.

Lesson 1 Review Answers

1. Imperialism is the control or influence a powerful nation has over a weaker country. **2.** After the American Revolution, many European nations thought that having colonies caused more trouble than they were worth. **3.** An increase in industry meant that factory owners needed more raw materials and natural resources. Europeans discovered that African and Asian countries were rich in resources, so they took control of these countries to get the materials. Also, colonies gave Europeans an expanded market where they could sell their manufactured goods. **4.** Some countries thought that an empire would make them look important in the eyes of the world. Some nationalists thought that "there has never been a great power without great colonies." **5.** Many people in Europe and the United States thought that Africans and Asians were ignorant and uncivilized. Westerners thought that they should bring Christianity and Western civilization to these countries.

Answers will vary. Students may suggest that imperialism was good for the mother country but bad for people in the colonies.

Ask students to raise their hands if they own a pair of khaki pants. Ask them if they know the source of this fashion term. Then read Then and Now, "The Color Khaki" together to find out about the camouflage British soldiers used while fighting in India. Ask students if they know any other fashion terms that are derived from Indian words. (*Dungaree* is also an Indian word.)

WORLD CULTURES

Negative effects of imperialism still linger today. In South Africa, descendants of European colonists formed a white supremacist government and set up a system legally separating blacks from whites. This system was called *apartheid*. South Africa did not have an all-race parliamentary election until 1994. Efforts have been made in recent years to correct abuses of human rights. On March 28, 1998, President Clinton became the first United States president to visit South Africa. Previous leaders had stayed away as an expression of their disapproval of apartheid.

CAREER CONNECTION

The spread of imperialism resulted in increased trade between colonies and mother countries. Today, most countries have a global economy, which is based on trade with many countries. Some students may be interested in careers in international trade, sales, marketing, or banking. To be successful in any of these fields, a person should have a degree in business or public administration, international business, or a related field. Fluency in a foreign language and familiarity with multi-ethnic issues also are important. Invite students to find out which courses are needed to prepare for a career in international business.

Chapter 24: Lesson 2

Overview This lesson describes the steps taken by Great Britain to secure its interests in India, how Europeans forced China to trade with them, and how Japan became an industrialized and imperialistic country.

Objectives

- To explain why India was important to Britain
- To explain why Southeast Asia was important to Europe
- To describe how Japan became imperialistic

Student Pages pages 596–599

Teacher's Resource Library

Workbook Activity 109

Activity 109

Modified Activity 109

Vocabulary

sphere of influence

Have students name products they have bought in America that were made in other countries. (Students might mention clothing, bicycles, cars, or food items.) Read the definition of *sphere of influence* aloud to the class. Ask students to think about how their lives would change if the United States was allowed to trade with only one other country. Have them write a sentence or two describing this change, using the term *sphere of influence*. Ask for volunteers to share what they have written.

1 Warm-Up Activity

Have students make a set of index cards, with the name of a powerful Western country written on each. Use a world map to point to a country in Africa or Asia. Ask students to hold up the card that shows the name of that country's mother country during the age of imperialism. Encourage students to play this game in groups when reviewing the chapter content.

Objectives

- To explain why India was important to Britain
- To explain why Southeast Asia was important to Europe
- To describe how Japan became imperialistic

By the 1600s, Britain was the greatest sea power in the world. It was also the most industrialized country and the country that did the most trading. Because of all this, Britain wanted colonies in Asia. Soon, the British would brag that "the sun never sets on the British empire."

Why Was India Important to Britain?

The Mogul Empire ruled most of India in the 1500s and 1600s, but it collapsed in 1707. India was then divided into many weak, independent states. By the mid-1700s, France and Britain were fighting each other for control of India. Britain won. At first, the British ruled India through a privately owned company—the British East India Company. However, in 1858, the British government took over direct rule of India.

India won its independence in 1947. But for nearly 100 years, India was very important to Britain. It provided Britain with natural resources and raw materials for industry. Its large population also provided an important market for British goods.

Because India was important to Britain, the British did everything they could to protect India from other imperialistic countries. In the late 1800s, Russia threatened India on its northwest boundaries. To protect India, Britain took over neighboring Afghanistan.

This picture shows the Prince of Wales being welcomed to India.

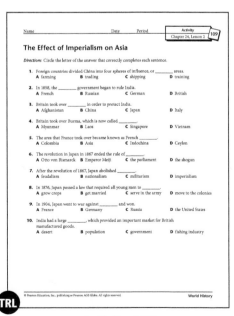

Workbook Activity 109

Imperialism in Asia

Directions Write the answers to these questions. Use complete sentences.

1. What is a sphere of influence?

2. How long did the British government control India?

3. What countries today were parts of French Indochina?

4. Who ruled Japan after the revolution of 1867?

5. How was Japan imperialistic?

Activity 109

The Effect of Imperialism on Asia

Directions Circle the letter of the answer that correctly completes each sentence.

1. Foreign countries divided China into four spheres of influence, or _____ areas.
   A farming   B trading   C shipping   D training

2. In 1858, the _____ government began to rule India.
   A French   B Russian   C German   D British

3. Britain took over _____ in order to protect India.
   A Afghanistan   B China   C Japan   D Italy

4. Britain took over Burma, which is now called _____.
   A Myanmar   B Laos   C Singapore   D Vietnam

5. The area that France took over became known as French _____.
   A Colombia   B Asia   C Indochina   D Ceylon

6. The revolution in Japan in 1867 ended the rule of _____.
   A Otto von Bismarck   B Emperor Meiji   C the parliament   D the shogun

7. After the revolution of 1867, Japan abolished _____.
   A feudalism   B nationalism   C militarism   D imperialism

8. In 1876, Japan passed a law that required all young men to _____.
   A grow crops   B get married   C serve in the army   D move to the colonies

9. In 1904, Japan went to war against _____ and won.
   A France   B Germany   C Russia   D the United States

10. India had a large _____, which provided an important market for British manufactured goods.
    A desert   B population   C government   D fishing industry

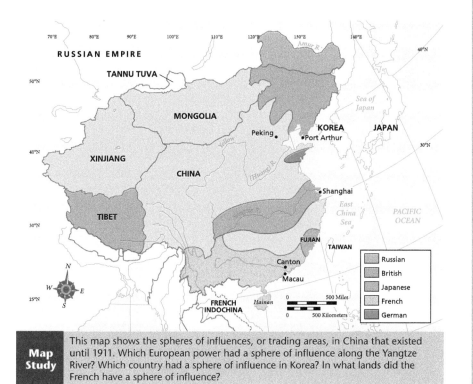

Map Study
This map shows the spheres of influences, or trading areas, in China that existed until 1911. Which European power had a sphere of influence along the Yangtze River? Which country had a sphere of influence in Korea? In what lands did the French have a sphere of influence?

Legend:
- Russian
- British
- Japanese
- French
- German

Reading Strategy:
Predicting

Based on what you have just read, predict what will happen to Southeast Asia as imperialism spreads.

Why Was Southeast Asia Important to Europe?

France also threatened British interests in India. France took over much of Southeast Asia, an area that became known as French Indochina. (Today, this area includes the countries of Vietnam, Laos, and Cambodia.) The British took over Burma to keep the French from expanding westward. (India lies to the west of Burma, now called Myanmar.) Soon Ceylon, Malaya, and Singapore also fell under British control.

1840 – 1914

Use this list to help students pronounce difficult words in this lesson.

Laos	(lous)
Mogul	(mug´ əl)
Myanmar	(myän mär´)

2 Teaching the Lesson

Ask students to list products they own that were made in China or Japan. Have them read pages 596–599 to find out how the United States began trading with these countries.

Ask:

- **What was the name of the British company that ruled India?** (the British East India Company)
- **Which five countries did Great Britain take over to protect its interests in India?** (Afghanistan, Burma, Ceylon, Malaya, and Singapore)
- **What are the modern names of the three countries of French Indochina?** (Vietnam, Laos, and Cambodia)
- **Why did the British take over Burma?** (to keep the French from expanding westward from Indochina)

Reading Strategy:
Predicting

(Answers will vary. Students may predict, incorrectly, that all of Southeast Asia was colonized by Britain. Point out that Britain took control of Burma, Ceylon, Malaya, and Singapore, but not Indochina.)

Ask a student to read the title of the map on page 597: "Spheres of Influence in China to 1911." Point out that China's long coast and major rivers made the country an important trading partner. Have students read and answer the questions in the caption. (The British had a sphere of influence along the Yangtze River. The Japanese controlled Korea. The French had a sphere of influence in southern China and French Indochina.)

LEARNING STYLES

Logical/Mathematical

Remind students that maps usually have symbols to represent different information. Ask students to look at the map on this page and list the symbols used, explaining what information each symbol imparts. Have students suggest other symbols that might make the map more useful to them. (Answers will vary; students may suggest adding arrows to show the movement of imperialism in the region or adding the dates when each country fell.)

Ask:

- Which four countries took over Chinese land and sea ports to control trade there? (Great Britain, France, Germany, and Russia)

- Who became the ruler of Japan after the revolution of 1867? (Emperor Meiji)

- What did Japan use as a model for its constitution? (the German system developed by Bismarck)

- Which two countries did Japan go to war with in order to become an imperialistic power? (China and Russia)

- How did Japan build up an army and a navy? (It passed a law requiring all young men to serve.)

- How did Japan acquire Korea in 1904? (It defeated Russia.)

3 Reinforce and Extend

ELL/ESL STRATEGY

Language Objective:
To explain the meaning of the phrase sphere of influence

Ask ELL students to explain to the class what is meant by the phrase *sphere of influence*. Have students dissect the phrase. Ask what the word *sphere* means and why it is part of the phrase. (*Sphere* is used to indicate an encompassing area, the area in which the mother country controls the trade.) Ask what the word *influence* means. (*Influence* means to have an effect on something.) Have the class question the presenting students about their definitions and the meaning of the phrase.

Sphere of influence
An area in which only one foreign country can trade

When Did Europe Insist on More Trade with China?

China lies east of India. For years Chinese rulers had allowed only limited trade with other countries. By the late 1800s, however, this limited trade no longer satisfied the Europeans. They forced China to give them special trade rights. After 1842, Great Britain, France, Germany, and Russia took over Chinese land and important sea ports. These nations divided China up into four different trading areas. Each European power controlled the trade in one of these areas. Historians call this a **sphere of influence.** The Europeans said that China was still an independent country. However, its rulers had no say in the European-controlled trade.

What Happened in Japan in 1867?

For a while, people thought that Japan, too, might fall to Europe's imperialism. However, a revolution in 1867 ended the rule of the shogun and returned political power to Emperor Meiji. This revolution brought great change to Japan.

After 1867, new leaders governed Japan in the emperor's name. They introduced many reforms, and Japan set out to become a modern, industrialized nation. It adopted western ideas in transportation and education. It abolished feudalism. Then the Japanese leaders wrote a constitution based on the German system Bismarck had developed.

How Did Japan Become Imperialistic?

Next, Japan began to develop a western-style army. In 1876, its leaders passed a law that ordered all young men to serve in the army. Soon Japan had a modern army and navy. Japan used its new military power to become imperialistic. From 1894 to 1895, it went to war with China. China lost and had to give Japan some of its territory.

In 1904, Japan went to war with Russia and won again. It took over Korea and gained important trading rights in Russian-controlled lands in China. Like many European countries, Japan was now an imperialistic world power.

---

598   *Unit 5   A New Global Age*

BACKGROUND INFORMATION

On the last day of 1600, a group of London businessmen became incorporated as the East India Company. They were given exclusive privileges by the British Crown to trade in spices with the East Indies. Company ships arrived in India in 1608, but they soon faced competition and hostility from Dutch and Portuguese traders. After a brief naval battle in which the company defeated the Portuguese traders in India, British trade began increasing. Many trading posts were established on the east and west coasts of India. Large

British communities grew up in Bombay, Calcutta, and Madras. As the East India Company became more influential, it was transformed into a ruling enterprise with its own army and the right to collect taxes. Over the next 50 years, the company expanded its territory by engaging in a series of wars. However, poor management and a severe famine left the region destitute, and in 1857–1858, the people rebelled. The company was dissolved, and the British government took over rule of India, ending the strange situation of a private company ruling a nation.

598   *Unit 5   A New Global Age*

Word Bank

Afghanistan
France
Great Britain
Japan
Russia

Lesson 2 Review On a sheet of paper, use the words from the Word Bank to complete each sentence correctly.

1. In 1858, _____ took over direct rule of India.

2. In the late 1800s, Great Britain took over _____.

3. In the late 1800s, _____ took over much of Southeast Asia.

4. _____ became a military power after its revolution in 1867.

5. Japan became a world power after it defeated China in 1895 and _____ in 1904.

China was once the most powerful and richest country in the world. But in the 1800s, Europeans began to control its trade. Why did that happen?

Lesson 2 Review Answers

1. Great Britain **2.** Afghanistan
3. France **4.** Japan **5.** Russia

Answers will vary. In Chapter 13, students read that China began a period of isolationism in the 1500s. That chapter told them that China changed from one of the most advanced civilizations to one that was backward. Students may suggest that this explains the ease with which Europe took control of China's trade.

Chapter 24: Lesson 3

Overview This lesson lists the European countries that colonized Africa and describes the effect imperialism had on the African people.

Objectives

- To identify colonies that Britain controlled in Africa
- To identify other countries that controlled colonies in Africa
- To describe how Europeans treated native people

Student Pages pages 600–602

Teacher's Resource Library TRL

Workbook Activity 110

Activity 110

Modified Activity 110

Vocabulary

protectorate

Have a volunteer read the vocabulary word and its definition to the class. Ask students who they think some of the major powers mentioned in the definition might be. (Answers will vary; students may mention Great Britain, Germany, France, or the United States.) Then have them write a paragraph explaining whether they would rather live in a protectorate or in a major power, and why. (Answers will vary; in a major power, their government would be in control and have more freedom of trade.) Encourage students to share what they have written with the class.

 Warm-Up Activity

Have a student volunteer explain what a bully is and how a bully behaves. Ask students to give an example of how a bully might act in the classroom. Have a class discussion in which students compare imperialism with bullying. Ask if powerful nations act like bullies when they take over weaker countries.

Objectives

- To identify colonies that Britain controlled in Africa
- To identify other countries that controlled colonies in Africa
- To describe how Europeans treated native people

Reading Strategy: Predicting

Based on the first two lessons in this chapter, how do you think the Africans will be treated by other countries?

Protectorate

An independent country whose foreign policy is controlled by a major power

As you know, Europeans wanted colonies in Asia. They wanted them in Africa, too. In the 1870s, Europeans raced one another for colonies there.

What Colonies Did Britain Control in Africa?

By the end of the 1800s, Great Britain controlled what are now the nations of Sudan, Nigeria, Ghana, Kenya, and Uganda. In 1900, it took over Nigeria. South Africa became a British colony in 1909.

In 1859, workers began to build the Suez Canal. When it was finished over 10 years later, it connected the Mediterranean and Red Seas. The canal made the trip from Europe to India and the Far East much shorter. In 1875, Britain took control of the canal.

The Suez Canal was finished in 1869. It links the Mediterranean Sea and the Red Sea. This image shows the opening ceremony of this important waterway.

A few years later, Egypt became a British **protectorate.** As a protectorate, Egypt stayed independent, but Britain controlled its foreign policy. In return, Britain protected Egypt from attacks by other countries.

How Big Was the French Empire in Africa?

By 1847, France had gained control of Algeria. Soon, France established the largest European empire in Africa. This empire stretched 2,500 miles from the Atlantic Ocean eastward to Sudan. France's holdings in Africa were large, but not rich. Still, other countries respected France for having such a large empire.

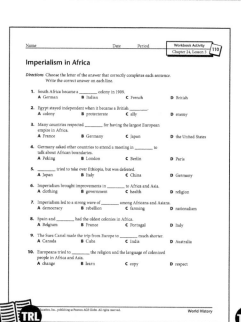

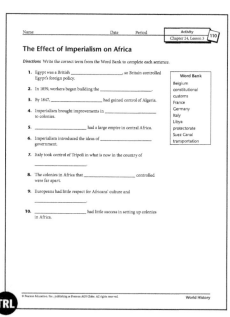

How Big Was the German Empire in Africa?

Germany united as a nation in 1871. It entered the race for African colonies late. Even so, by 1900, only France and Britain had larger empires in Africa. Germany's colonies were far apart and not rich. However, its military strength worried other European countries. When Germany asked these countries to come to a meeting in Berlin, they came. There they talked about African boundaries. However, no one asked any Africans to come to the meeting.

What Other European Countries Controlled Africa?

Many other nations had colonies in Africa. Spain and Portugal had the oldest colonies. Belgium had a large empire in central Africa. Italy, which came late to Africa, had little success there. It tried to take over Ethiopia, but was defeated. In 1912, Italy did take control of Tripoli in what is now the nation of Libya. Tripoli was large, but poor.

Many European nations scrambled for empires, but some nations got little or nothing of value. They felt angry at those who got wealth from their colonies. This led to fighting.

Reading Strategy:
Predicting

Think about your prediction. Was it accurate? Why or why not?

Was Imperialism Good or Bad?

Europeans said that imperialism was good. It brought great improvements in health, transportation, and education to Africa and Asia. It introduced the ideas of constitutional government. It also brought jobs and industry to the colonies.

However, many of the colonial people thought that imperialism was bad. They felt that Europeans got more out of imperialism than they did. Factories in Africa and Asia supplied cheap goods to Europe. But these factories—owned by Europeans—destroyed native industry and many people lost their jobs.

Also, the colonial people had no control over their government or their country's natural resources. Europeans took the best land and the richest sources of gold, iron, silver, copper, or other valuable natural resources found in the ground.

1840 – 1914   *Imperialism   Chapter 24*   **601**

 Teaching the Lesson

Have students name as many African countries as they can without consulting a map. Write the names of these countries on the board. Have students read pages 600–602 to learn what effect imperialism had on these countries.

Ask:

• How many African countries did Great Britain control by 1909? (seven—Sudan, Nigeria, Ghana, Kenya, Uganda, South Africa, Egypt)

• Which two bodies of water are connected by the Suez Canal? (Mediterranean Sea and Red Sea)

Reading Strategy:
Predicting

(Answers will vary. Students may predict that the Africans would not be respected, would lose their homes, and would be poorly treated.)

• Which country established the largest European empire in Africa? (France)

• Which European country arranged a meeting to discuss African boundaries? (Germany)

• Which country failed in its attempt to take over Ethiopia? (Italy)

• How did the Europeans think Africa and Asia benefited from imperialism? (They got improvements in health, transportation, and education, and more jobs and industry.)

• What did Europeans take from the colonies? (Answers will vary; students may say that the Europeans took the best land and richest sources of gold, iron, silver, copper, and other natural resources.)

Point out to the students that Germany, France, and Britain gathered in Berlin to make important decisions that would affect Africa, without hearing from any Africans. In their short speech, the students should say how they felt being left out of these discussions, how they felt about being colonized by other countries, and what the impact on their country might be (e.g., loss of jobs, customs, and culture, bad treatment by people from other countries).

Reading Strategy:
Predicting

(Answers will vary. Students should use details from the reading to tell why their predictions were accurate or not.)

• What were some of the effects of imperialism? (Answers will vary; students may suggest that imperialism brought social improvements but caused loss of jobs and political power.)

- **How did Europeans show a lack of respect for the native people?** (Answers will vary; students may say they tried to change their religion, language, culture, and customs.)

ELL/ESL STRATEGY

Language Objective:
To research a topic and write a summary
Pair ELL students with English-proficient classmates. Ask each pair to choose a country in Africa and find out how it was affected by imperialism. If the country is now independent, students should also find out when and how independence was achieved. Have each pair of students work together to write a one-page summary of their information.

3 Reinforce and Extend

ONLINE CONNECTION

Students can gain additional information from this Web site from the Nobel Prize organization: www.agsglobewh.com/page602. It gives an account of Albert Schweitzer's life and work as a medical missionary in Africa and includes an extensive list of books that describe his life as a doctor, a theologian, and a musician.

IN THE COMMUNITY

Explain that although most African nations are no longer colonies, their standard of living is much lower than that in Western countries. Many social and religious organizations send volunteers to these countries to help improve the lives of people there. Have students find out if any churches or social organizations in their community have programs in Africa. Give them an opportunity to share their findings.

How Did Europeans Treat Native People?

Europeans thought they were better than the native people of Africa and Asia. They tried to change the religion, the language, and the way of life of these colonized people. This showed that they had little respect for native culture and customs. In time, this led to a wave of nationalism among the people of Africa and Asia.

Lesson 3 Review On a sheet of paper, write the letter of the answer that correctly completes each sentence.

1. The Suez Canal connected and Mediterranean Sea and the _____ Sea.

   A Algerian   **B** Asian   **C** Black   **D** Red

2. By 1847, France had gained control of _____.

   A Algeria   **B** Sudan   **C** Germany   **D** Britain

3. In 1875, _____ took control of the Suez Canal.

   A Britain   **B** Germany   **C** Italy   **D** Nigeria

4. Italy tried to take over _____, but was defeated.

   A Belgium   **B** Britain   **C** Ethiopia   **D** Spain

5. By 1900, only France and Britain had African empires larger than _____.

   A Belgium   **B** Germany   **C** Spain   **D** Egypt

What do you think?

Why would Europeans want Africans to give up their language, religion, and customs?

Biography

Leopold II of Belgium: 1835–1909

Leopold II was born in the Belgian capital of Brussels. At age 20, he entered the Belgian senate. As a senator, he urged the Belgian government to acquire colonies in Africa. When the government did not cooperate, Leopold used his own money to pay for an expedition to central Africa. In 1865, Leopold became king of Belgium, and in 1885, he founded the Congo Free State. Leopold used a private army to force Africans in the area to work. They helped Leopold gather a huge personal fortune. About a year before his death, Leopold turned over the Congo Free State to the Belgian government. It was renamed the Belgian Congo.

602   *Unit 5   A New Global Age*

Lesson 3 Review Answers

1. D **2.** A **3.** A **4.** C **5.** B

Answers will vary. When people take away the language, religion, and customs of another people, they take away their identity. Without identity, native people may lose their self-esteem and their power to resist the more powerful country.

Biography

Have a volunteer read the biography. Leopold was a strong advocate of imperialism, in both his private life and as king of Belgium. This also explains why the country is named the Belgian Congo.

STUDY SKILLS

To help students organize the material in this lesson, ask them to create a four-column chart. Have students label the columns from left to right as *Colony*, *Controlled By*, *When Colonized*, and *Today*. In each row, students should list the information about a colonized country discussed in the lesson. Students may also use information from Lesson 2 to make a similar chart for the countries in Asia.

"That Was No Brother"

The first meeting between white explorers and Africans must have been terrifying to both groups. The Africans had never seen white-skinned people before. The whites were far from home and few in number compared to the Africans. Misunderstandings were likely to occur. This excerpt describes such a meeting from an African's viewpoint.

When we heard that the man with the white flesh was journeying down the [river] we were open-mouthed with astonishment. We stood still. All night long the drums announced the strange news—a man with white flesh! That man, we said to ourselves, has a white skin. He will be one of our brothers who were drowned in the river. All life comes from the water, and in the water he has found life. Now he is coming . . . home. . . .

We will prepare a feast, I ordered. We will go to meet our brother and escort him into the village with rejoicing! We donned our ceremonial garb. We assembled the great canoes. We listened for the gong which would announce our brother's presence . . . Presently the cry was heard: He is approaching. . . . Now he enters the river! Halloh! We swept forward, my canoe leading, . . . to meet the first white man our eyes had beheld, and to do him honor.

But as we drew near his canoes there were loud reports, bang! bang! and fire staves spat bits of iron at us. We were paralyzed with fright; our mouths hung wide open and we could not shut them. Things such as we had never seen, never heard of, never dreamed of— they were the work of evil spirits! Several of my men plunged into the water. . . . Some screamed dreadfully, others . . . were dead, and blood flowed from little holes in their bodies. "War! That is war!" I yelled. "Go back!" The canoes sped back to our village with all the strength our spirits could impart to our arms.

That was no brother! That was the worst enemy our country had ever seen. . . .

Now tell me: has the white man dealt fairly by us? Oh, do not speak to me of him! You call us wicked men, but you white men are much more wicked! You think because you have guns you can take away our land and our possessions. You have sickness in your heads, for that is not justice.

Document-Based Questions

1. Who did the Africans think the white man was?

2. How did the Africans prepare to greet the white man?

3. How did the white man greet the Africans?

4. Why does the writer call white men wicked?

5. After reading the excerpt, what is your opinion of what the white man did?

Source: From The Quest for Africa. *© 1957 by Dr. Heinrich Schiffers, G. P. Putnam's Sons, New York.*

Call attention to the title of this feature, "That Was No Brother." Read the introductory paragraph to students and explain that the writing style of this feature is different from that of the rest of the chapter. Ask students to read page 603 to find out how an African leader might have responded to the arrival of white explorers. Ask how the writing style is different. (The feature is written in the first person and is conversational in tone. The writing is very emotional, happy at first and then very angry.) Then have students answer the Document-Based Questions.

Answers to Document-Based Questions:

1. They thought he was a fellow tribesman who had drowned in the river and come back to life.

2. They prepared a feast, put on ceremonial garb, and assembled the great canoes.

3. He shot at them, killing some and wounding others.

4. Answers will vary. Because they have guns (superior force), white men thought that they could take the Africans' land and possessions; the white man's attack was unprovoked.

5. Answers will vary. The white man was wrong, because the Africans were not attacking him; we do not know how the Africans appeared to the white man. Maybe he thought they were coming to attack him.

Chapter Project Follow-up

Student reports should contain historically accurate information. They should accurately describe the history of the Suez Canal project, some of the canal's specifications, which country dug it, which countries fought over it, and which country controlled it after it was completed. You may wish to have each group make an oral presentation to the class as a chapter review.

LEARNING STYLES

Interpersonal/ Group Learning

Have students form into small groups to discuss how trying to see things from another perspective makes it easier to understand the reactions of others. Ask students to rewrite a paragraph of the Document-Based Reading from the white man's perspective, showing what might have made the white man act as he did. (Answers will vary; students may say he was afraid, outnumbered, or he misunderstood the intent of the Africans.)

Have a volunteer read the title, "Dr. Livingstone, I Presume?" Ask students if they have ever heard this expression. Then have students read the story to find out the source of this expression as well as finding out who Dr. Livingstone was and the role he played in the exploration of Africa.

Have students examine the picture in the feature. Ask them to guess which man is Henry Stanley, and why they think this. (The man raising his hat on the left is Stanley. A man in his group is holding an American flag.)

Answers to Spotlight Story Wrap-Up:

1. Africa's desert and the waterfalls and rapids on its rivers made exploration difficult.

2. They wanted to spread Christianity and educate Africans.

3. Livingstone explored the Zambezi River and Victoria Falls.

4. Stanley was a newspaper reporter for the *New York Herald*. He looked for and found David Livingstone. He also sent back daily reports about what he was seeing in Africa.

5. Their writings and speeches made people more interested in Africa.

"Dr. Livingstone, I Presume?"

For many years, Africa was called the unexplored continent. The African desert made it hard to travel there by land. Africa's rivers had many waterfalls and rapids that made travel difficult.

In the 19th century, religious explorers set out for Africa. They wanted to bring Christianity and education to the Africans. One of the most famous was David Livingstone. Livingstone went to Africa to spread Christianity. He also hated slavery and wanted to end the slave trade. In time, he became well known and was loved by many Africans.

Between 1841 and 1873, Livingstone made three long trips to Africa. In 1849, he crossed the vast Kalahari Desert. On this trip he explored the Zambezi River. Six years later, he followed that river eastward to the coast. On that trip, he explored a giant waterfall. He named it Victoria Falls after the English queen, Queen Victoria.

In 1865, he set out to find the source of the Nile River. He began at Cape Town on the southern tip of Africa and went north. For many years nothing was heard from him. Many people thought he had died or become lost.

An American newspaper, the *New York Herald*, sent a reporter to find Livingstone. The reporter, Henry Stanley, traveled for 126 days in search of Livingstone. He sent back daily accounts of what he was seeing and learning in Africa. Some African guides took him to Ujiji on Lake Tanganyika. In his newspaper account, Stanley described what happened next. "The expedition at last comes to a halt. . . . I alone have a few more steps to make. . . . As I come nearer I see the white face of an old man. . . .

Henry Stanley met up with David Livingstone near Lake Tanganyika in Africa.

We raise our hats and I say, "Dr. Livingstone, I presume?"

The two men became friends and explored together. By the end of the trip, Africa fascinated Stanley. In 1873, Dr. Livingstone died. Stanley continued to explore.

Explorers like Livingstone and Stanley were very important in the scramble for African territory. Their writings and speeches made people more interested in Africa. They also convinced some people that slavery was evil and should be stopped.

Wrap-Up

1. Why did African geography discourage its exploration?

2. Why did the missionary explorers go to Africa?

3. What river and waterfall did Livingstone explore on his expeditions?

4. On his first trip to Africa, for whom did Henry Stanley work? What did he do?

5. How did Livingstone and Stanley contribute to the scramble for Africa?

Chapter 24 SUMMARY

- In imperialism or colonialism, a stronger nation controls weaker ones for its own benefit. The Industrial Revolution contributed to this policy. Factory owners needed raw materials from colonies and used them as markets for their goods.

- Countries believed that having colonies made them important world powers. Since sea power was especially important, colonies were used as naval bases.

- In Asia, Britain took control of India, Burma, Ceylon, Malaya, and Singapore. France took Indochina.

- The Industrial Revolution made colonies into sources of raw materials and markets. Imperialism made large parts of Asia and Africa into European colonies.

- After 1842, Britain, France, Germany, and Russia divided China into trading areas. They were called spheres of influence.

- After 1867, Japan modernized and went to war against China and then Russia. It took over Korea and won trading rights in China.

- European powers divided Africa into colonies. Britain controlled Egypt and the Suez Canal, South Africa, and several other colonies. French colonies were mainly in West Africa. Germany, Portugal, Spain, and Belgium also had colonies.

TEACHER'S RESOURCE

The AGS Globe Teaching Strategies in Social Studies Transparencies may be used with this chapter. The transparencies add an interactive dimension to expand and enhance the *World History* program content.

Using the Chapter Summary

Have students read the Chapter Summary on page 605 to review the main ideas presented in Chapter 24.

Ask:

- How did the Industrial Revolution contribute to the spread of imperialism? (As industry increased, factory owners needed raw materials to manufacture goods. These materials were plentiful in Asia and Africa, so by controlling these countries, imperial powers could get resources, and also use the countries as a market for the goods.)

- Why were colonies used as military bases? (Colonies were used as military bases so the mother country could control the trade routes. Having colonies with military bases also made countries seem important and more powerful.)

- What Asian countries did Great Britain take control of? (Great Britain took control of India, Burma, Ceylon, Malaya, and Singapore.)

- What happened to Asian and African countries under imperialism? (They became European colonies.)

- What happened to China after 1842? (China was divided into four trading areas, called spheres of influence, which were controlled by Britain, France, Germany, and Russia.)

- What happened to Japan after 1867? (Japan modernized, developed an army, and went to war against China and then Russia. It won Korea and trading rights in China.)

- What African countries were controlled by Britain? By France? (Britain controlled Egypt and the Suez Canal, South Africa, and several other countries. France controlled several West African countries.)

Chapter 24 Review

Use the Chapter Review to prepare students for tests and to reteach content from the chapter.

Chapter 24 Mastery Test

The Teacher's Resource Library includes two forms of the Chapter 24 Mastery Test. Each test addresses the chapter Goals for Learning. An optional third page of additional critical-thinking items is included for each test. The difficulty level of the two forms is equivalent.

Chapter 24 Review Answers

1. India
2. China
3. Meiji
4. Mogul Empire
5. Japan
6. Suez Canal
7. Bismarck
8. British East India Company
9. Great Britain
10. Algeria
11. D
12. B
13. D
14. C
15. A
16. B

Word Bank

Algeria
Bismarck
British East India Company
China
Great Britain
India
Japan
Meiji
Mogul Empire
Suez Canal

On a sheet of paper, use the words from the Word Bank to complete each sentence correctly.

1. _____ won its independence in 1947.

2. After 1842, Great Britain, France, Germany, and Russia divided _____ up into four different trading areas.

3. Emperor _____ began to make Japan a modern and powerful nation.

4. _____ ruled most of India in the 1500s and 1600s.

5. _____ defeated Russia in 1904 and won control of Korea.

6. The _____ connected the Mediterranean and Red Seas.

7. After 1867, new leaders in Japan wrote a constitution based on the German system _____ had developed.

8. The British ruled India through their _____.

9. By the end of the 1800s, _____ controlled what are now the nations of Sudan, Nigeria, Ghana, Kenya, and Uganda.

10. By 1847, France had gained control of _____.

On a sheet of paper, write the letter of the answer that correctly completes each sentence.

11. A nation's warlike policy or practice is called _____.

    A imperialism   **C** nationalism
    B colonialism   **D** militarism

12. The control by a powerful nation of a weaker one is _____.

    A militarism   **C** nationalism
    B imperialism   **D** Kaiser

13. Europeans said that imperialism brought _____ to Africa and Asia.

    A improvements in health   **C** better education
    B jobs and industry   **D** all of the above

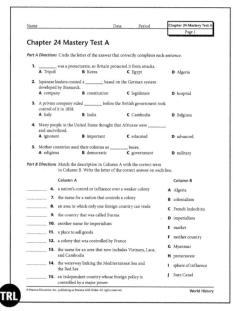

Chapter 24 Mastery Test A, pages 1–3

14. By the 1600s, _____ was the greatest sea power in the world.

   A Korea   **B** India   **C** Britain   **D** China

15. In 1904, Japan went to war with _____ and won.

   A Russia   **B** China   **C** Germany   **D** France

16. By 1900, only Great Britain had a larger empire in Africa than _____.

   A France   **B** Germany   **C** China   **D** Russia

On a sheet of paper, write the answer to each question. Use complete sentences.

17. What is imperialism?

18. Which countries became imperial powers during the 19th century?

Critical Thinking On a sheet of paper, write your response to each question. Use complete sentences.

19. Do you believe imperialism was more a force for good or a force for evil? Explain your answer.

20. Why do you think Europeans gained control over Africa so easily?

17. Imperialism is the control that large, powerful countries have over weaker countries. The large, powerful countries take control of weaker countries and turn them into colonies.

18. Great Britain, France, Germany, Russia, Japan, and the United States became major imperial powers. But Italy, Spain, Portugal, Belgium, and the Netherlands also became imperial powers.

Critical Thinking

19. Answers will vary. Some students will say that imperialism was good because it brought improvements in health, education, and transportation to the colonies. Other students may suggest that imperialism was bad because it led to many devastating and bloody wars. It destroyed native industry and jobs, depleted natural resources, and was resented by natives.

20. Answers will vary. Students may suggest that African countries were easily defeated because they had weaker militaries and governments and had far less money than the European countries.

Restate the test directions in your own words. Tell yourself what you are expected to do.

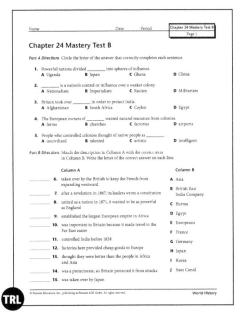

Write these sentences on the board:

Mazzini, Cavour, and Garibaldi were all Italian nationalists.

However, Mazzini was known as the "soul" of the revolution, Cavour was known as the "brain" of the revolution, and Garibaldi was known as the "sword" of the revolution.

Ask:

- What three people are mentioned in the first sentence? (Mazzini, Cavour, and Garibaldi)
- What is being said about these three people? (They were all Italian nationalists.)
- What three people are mentioned in the second sentence? (Mazzini, Cavour, and Garibaldi)
- What is being said about these three people? (They were known as being the "soul," the "brain," and the "sword" of the revolution.)

Point out that the first sentence tells how the three people are alike, whereas the second sentence tells how the same three people are different. Then have students read the first column of the Skill Builder on page 608. Ask them which word or words in the sentences on the board signal comparison and contrast. Circle the word. (however) Have students complete items 1–10. For item 10, encourage them to write both a sentence that compares and a sentence that contrasts.

Unit 5 Skill Builder Answers

1. contrasts
2. contrasts
3. compares
4. compares
5. contrasts
6. Answers will vary. Both France and Britain wanted to control India.
7. Answers will vary. France took over much of Southeast Asia, but Britain gained control of Burma.
8. Answers will vary. China seemed like an independent country; however, European countries controlled its important seaports and some of its land.

608 Unit 5 *A New Global Age*

Unit 5
Skill Builder

Compare and Contrast

Comparing and contrasting reveals how things are alike and how they are different. People, ideas, and events are sometimes compared and contrasted in writing. Look for words that signal comparing and contrasting when you read.

> To compare, ask: "How are these things alike?"
>
> To contrast, ask: "How are these things different?"

- To decide if things are being compared, look for words, such as:

also	both	like	similar

Cavour, like Garibaldi, was a leader in the unification of Italy.

- To decide if things are being contrasted, look for words, such as:

but	however	instead
not	only	while

Cavour was called the "brain" of the revolution while Garibaldi was called the "sword."

Decide whether each of these sentences compares or contrasts.

1. Mazzini's revolt was unsuccessful; however, Cavour's gained Sardinia's freedom.

2. Cavour worked to unite the northern Italian states while Garibaldi fought in the south.

3. Both Cavour and Garibaldi were Italian heroes.

4. Germany, like Italy, had many independent states.

5. Ironically, it was not a German, but Napoleon, who began German unification.

Compare and contrast the effects of imperialism. Focus on what happened between imperialistic European nations and the named areas. In your notebook, write one sentence about each item. Be sure to use words that compare and contrast.

6. India
7. Southeast Asia
8. China
9. Japan
10. Egypt

608   Unit 5   *A New Global Age*

---

9. Answers will vary. Instead of becoming a European colony, Japan remained independent because it took steps to become a modern industrialized nation.

10. Answers will vary. Britain wanted control of Egypt because of the Suez Canal, which was an important route to India and Asia, not because Egypt had valuable resources.

Unit Skills Activity

Have volunteers read aloud their sentences. Ask their classmates to identify each sentence as comparing or contrasting and to explain how they knew. Then distribute the Unit 5 Skills Activity. Have them write their paragraphs independently.

Name	Date	Period	**Unit Skills Activity**
			Unit 5

Compare and Contrast

Directions Using what you have learned about the revolutions and rebellions that led first to nationalism and then to imperialism, you will compare and contrast these two movements. First, answer the questions below with complete sentences. Then, use your answers to write a paragraph on a separate sheet of paper. In your paragraph, use words such as *also, both, similar to,* and *like* to compare nationalism and imperialism. Use words such as *but, not, however,* and *instead of* to contrast the two movements.

What are some things the two movements have in common?

What are some things that are different about the movements?

How are the outcomes of the two movements alike and different?

Which movement is more likely to produce military heroes?

© Pearson Education, Inc., publishing as Pearson AGS Globe. All rights reserved.   **World History**

Unit Skills Activity

Unit 5   SUMMARY

- Nationalism means that a group of people have one language, one culture, one government, and a common history.

- Giuseppe Mazzini was called the soul of Italian independence because he stood for its spirit of freedom.

- Count Camillo di Cavour was known as the brain of Italian unity. He got French support for Sardinia's war against Austria.

- Giuseppe Garibaldi was called the sword of Italian independence because of his military accomplishments. He and his Red Shirts freed Sicily.

- The German Revolution of 1848 failed. The Prussian ruler refused to become king of all the German states. German nationalists believed only Prussia could unite Germany.

- Prussia was the largest German state. In 1862, Otto von Bismarck became Prussia's prime minister. Bismarck did not believe in democratic rule.

- Bismarck used militarism to conquer the German states. He defeated Austria in seven weeks. A new empire, Austria-Hungary, was formed.

- In the Franco-Prussian War of 1870, Prussia defeated France and won French territory. The remaining independent German states joined Prussia to become Germany.

- In imperialism, a stronger nation controls weaker ones. The Industrial Revolution contributed to this because Europeans needed the raw materials and markets in Asia and Africa.

- Countries believed that having colonies made them important world powers. Since sea power was important, colonies were used as naval bases.

- In Asia, Britain took control of India, Burma, Ceylon, Malaya, and Singapore. France took Indochina.

- Many Europeans thought that imperialism was good because it improved health, transportation, and education. Also, it brought jobs and industry to the colonies.

- Many of the colonial people thought imperialism was bad. European factories in Africa and Asia destroyed native industry. The colonial people had no control over their government or natural resources.

- After 1842, Britain, France, Germany, and Russia divided China into trading areas, or spheres of influence.

- After 1867, Japan modernized and went to war against China and then Russia. It won Korea and trading rights in China.

1840 – 1914

Using the Unit Summary

Read and discuss the Unit Summary statements on page 609 with students.

Ask:

- **What is shared by a group of people experiencing nationalism?** (They share language, culture, government, common history, customs, music, way of life, and religion.)

- **What were Mazzini, Cavour, and Garibaldi known for?** (Italian independence and Italian unity)

- **What did German nationalists believe?** (They believed that only Prussia could unite Germany.)

- **What did Otto von Bismarck accomplish?** (He conquered the German states and defeated Austria, which resulted in the formation of Austria-Hungary.)

- **How did the Industrial Revolution contribute to imperialism?** (Europeans needed raw materials and markets in Asia and Africa to make and sell increased numbers of goods.)

- **Why were colonies used as important military bases?** (Sea power was important and having colonies allowed a country to have more ships covering a greater area.)

- **What colonies did Britain control in Asia?** (India, Burma, Ceylon, Malaya, and Singapore.)

- **What was good and what was bad about imperialism?** (Europeans thought it was good because it improved health, education, and transportation in Africa and Asia and provided jobs and industry. Many colonial people thought it was bad because they lost native industry and the best land and had no control over their government or natural resources.)

Unit 5 Mastery Test

The Teacher's Resource Library includes a two-page Unit Mastery Test. An optional third page of additional critical-thinking items is included for each test. The Unit 5 Mastery Test is pictured on page 863 of this Teacher's Edition.

Unit Activity Follow-Up

Follow up on Unit 5, Activity 1 by asking students to read their definitions of nationalism. Ask students for their views on what it means to be an American. Be sure to include any ELL students in your class. Follow up on Unit 5, Activity 2 by asking students to explain what a sphere of influence is. Ask them why the player with the most cards at the end of the game represents the most powerful country. (That player, or country, controls the most trade.)

Planning Guide
World Wars and Revolutions

Unit Activities

Student Text
Unit 6 Summary
Unit 6 Skill Builder

Teacher's Resource Library
Unit 6 Activities 1–2
Unit 6 Skills Activity

Assessment Options

Teacher's Resource Library
Chapter 25 Mastery Tests A and B
Chapter 26 Mastery Tests A and B
Chapter 27 Mastery Tests A and B
Unit 6 Mastery Test

	Student Text Features											Teaching Strategies						Learning Styles					Teacher's Resource Library			
Reading Strategy	Map Study/Map Skills	Writing About History	Geography Note	Biography	History in Your Life	Communication in History	Technology Connection	Then and Now	Spotlight Story	Document-Based Reading	Background Information	Applications (Home, Career, Community)	World Cultures	Study Skills	Online Connection	ELL/ESL Strategy	Auditory/Verbal	Visual/Spatial	Body/Kinesthetic	Interpersonal/Group Learning	Logical/Mathematical	Activities/Modified Activities	Workbook Activities	Self-Study Guide	Chapter Outline
614	613								636	635							635							✔	✔
✔															616							111	111		
✔		619					620	621			620				618	619, 621			620		619	112	112		
✔	626												624			625		624		625		113	113		
✔													628									114	114		
				631							631	630				631						115	115		
					633											633						116	116		
642	641								662	661														✔	✔
✔		645		646							644		645	644		646						117	117		
✔	649							650				648			649	650				648		118	118		
✔		652									652					652			653			119	119		
✔																	655					120	120		
✔												658				657					657	121	121		
✔												660						660				122	122		
668	667								696	695														✔	✔
✔	670														671	670				671		123	123		
✔		674										674				673						124	124		
✔	677		676								676		679			677	678	679		678	676	125	125		
✔	682						684				684					681			683			126	126		
✔				685	687						687			686						687		127	127		
✔	689										691	691				690					690	128	128		
✔		694													694	693						129	129		

TRL Activities

The Teacher's Resource Library (TRL) contains a set of lower-level worksheets called Modified Activities. These worksheets cover the same content as the standard Activities but are written at a lower reading level.

Skill Track

Use Skill Track for *World History* to monitor student progress and meet the demands of Adequate Yearly Progress (AYP). Make informed instructional decisions with individual student and class reports of lesson and chapter assessments. With immediate and ongoing feedback, students will also see what they have learned and where they need more reinforcement and practice.

Other Resources

Books for Teachers

Lewis, Jon E. (editor) *The Mammoth Book of Eyewitness World War I: Over 280 First-Hand Accounts of the "War to End All Wars,"* New York: Carroll & Graf, 2003. (contains extracts of speeches, letters, memoirs, diaries, and articles about World War I)

Wiesel, Elie. *After the Darkness: Reflections on the Holocaust.* New York: Schocken, 2002. (Wiesel sums up the most important aspects of Hitler's years in power and includes testimonies from Holocaust survivors.)

Books for Students

Boyd, Bentley. *World War 2 Tales.* Williamsburg, VA: Chester Comix, 2005. (Graphic novel format tells the story of World War 2, including the Battle of Britain, Pearl Harbor, and the Pacific island campaign.)

Fridell, Ron. *Dictatorship (Political Systems of the World).* NY: Marshall Cavendish Benchmark, 2007. (examples of dictatorships throughout history with emphasis on Hitler, Stalin, and Mao)

CD-ROM/Software

World War I and the Jazz Age. Culver City, CA: Social Studies School Service (1-800-421-4246). (CD-ROM presentation that includes timelines, maps, photographs, and essays)

Videos

America Goes to War: World War II (5 hours). Culver City, CA: Social Studies School Service (1-800-421-4246). (10-part collection of primary sources)

Web Sites

www.agsglobewh.com/page610a (Web Site offers World War II material, including a year-by-year holocaust timeline from 1933 to 1945, a slide show of Pearl Harbor photographs, battle photos, and the rise, triumph, and defeat of Hitler)

www.agsglobewh.com/page610b (contains primary source material that describes different aspects of the Czarist state, Russian Revolution, Bolshevik rule, and Stalinism)

"Human beings come in all sizes and shapes and in a variety of colors. This rich diversity is match by an equal diversity in regard to religion beliefs and political ideologies. We are thrown together on this planet. . . . That is why the Charter imposes the imperative on all human beings to . . . live together in peace with one another as good neighbors."

~U Thant, Secretary-General of the United Nations (1962–1971), speaking in 1964

Unit 6

World Wars and Revolutions

Wars unlike history had ever seen before filled the first half of the 20th century. World War I and World War II were large and devastating. Millions of people were killed or injured.

You will learn how World War I began in 1914 and lasted four long years. During this time, a revolution started in Russia. You will see how and why it started. After World War I, you will see how World War II started in 1939. After World War II, you will see how the United Nations formed. You will also learn how this organization got involved in a war in Korea in 1950 to try to prevent the spread of Communism.

Chapters in Unit 6

611

Introducing the Unit

Read aloud the quotation on page 610. Ask students to study the picture on page 610. Explain that in this unit, students will learn about a time of great unrest in Europe and Asia. Then have volunteers read aloud the unit introduction.

Ask:

• What does the quotation tell you about U Thant as a leader of the United Nations? (He recognizes the diversity among people, but insists that all peoples must learn to live together in peace. This implies that he will do everything in his power to uphold world peace.)

• What five kinds of diversity does U Thant recognize in people? (size, shape, color, religious belief, and political ideology)

• Which of the five kinds of diversity do you think causes the most world conflict? (Answers will vary. Students will probably say either religious belief or political ideology.)

Presenting the Unit Activity

World War I, World War II, and the Russian Revolution all played major roles in world history. Students have an opportunity to study one of these three topics in greater detail. Provide each student with a copy of Unit 6 Activity 1. Read through the instructions with them and answer any questions they might have. Point out that there are many events that could be listed. Ask students to select the five they think are the most important. Allow time for students to do research. Also, periodically monitor their progress in the unit activity during the course of the unit. Unit 6 Activity 2 can be used by students who chose the same topic to compare and discuss their results.

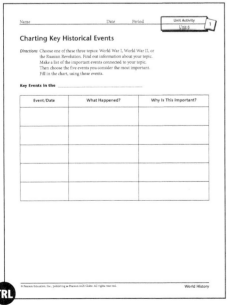

Unit 6, Activity 1

Unit 6, Activity 2

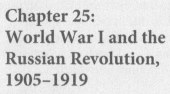

Introducing the Chapter

This chapter explains how the buildup of nationalism, imperialism, and militarism was set off by a single event—an assassination in Sarajevo—to start a

25 World War I and the Russian Revolution

You learned about imperialism, nationalism, and militarism in earlier chapters. Now you will see how these caused World War I. This war was unlike any before it. It featured modern weapons, terrible fighting conditions, and great loss of life. In this chapter, you will learn how it started, how it was fought, how it ended, and what it meant for those involved. You will also learn how powerful groups started a revolution in Russia.

Goals for Learning
◆ To explain how imperialism, nationalism, and militarism caused war
◆ To identify the countries that fought in the war
◆ To describe the different goals the Big Four powers had at the peace conference
◆ To describe the social, economic, and political effects of World War I
◆ To describe life in czarist Russia
◆ To list the causes and effects of the Revolution of 1905

1914 Archduke Ferdinand is assassinated

1917 United States enters World War I

1918 World War I ends

1910   1915   1920

1914 World War I begins

1917 Revolution breaks out in Russia

1919 Treaty of Versailles is signed

chain of declarations of war that became World War I. When the war was over, people were appalled at the devastation wrought by terrifying new weapons. The tally of human casualties went into the millions. Winners licked their wounds and determined to make the losing nations pay.

In 1894 the czar of Russia declared war on Japan to distract the impoverished serfs and workers from their troubles. The beginning of the new century brought a bloody confrontation between the czar and workers, and participation in a world war and a revolution.

Ask:
• How many alliances were in place in Europe in 1914? (two)

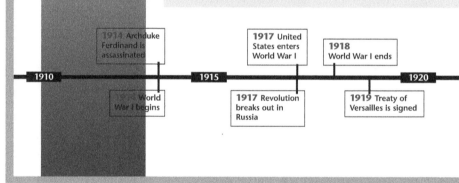

Chapter 25 Self-Study Guide, pages 1–3

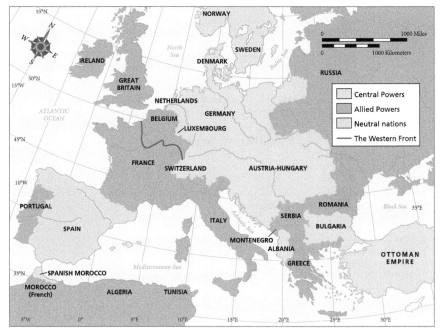

During World War I, Europe was divided into two alliances. Germany and Austria-Hungary were the major Central Powers. France, Russia, and Great Britain were the main Allied Powers. Some countries were neutral. That is, they took neither side. This map shows the central, allied, and neutral powers in Europe during World War I. It also shows the western front.

Study the map and answer the following questions:

1. To what alliance did Italy belong?

2. To what alliance did Bulgaria belong?

3. Where was the western front?

4. What are the names of three neutral countries shown on this map?

5. German U-boats were an important weapon against British naval power. In what sea would they have been most effective?

• When did World War I begin? (1914)

• In what year did the United States enter the war? (1917)

• The signing of which treaty officially brought World War I to an end? (Treaty of Versailles)

• Why do you think the assassination of Archduke Ferdinand is on this timeline? (answers will vary; students may conclude correctly that this was the incident that caused World War I to begin)

Ask a volunteer to read aloud the title of the map, "Europe During World War I," and have students read the paragraph under the map silently to find out which nations were at war.

Ask:

• Which were the major nations in the Central Powers? In the Allied Powers? (Germany, Austria-Hungary, Turkey [Ottoman Empire], and Bulgaria; Great Britain, France, Italy, and Russia)

• What does it mean to be neutral during a war? (not to take sides)

Have students read and answer the questions independently.

Map Skills Answers

1. Allied Powers

2. Central Powers

3. France and Belgium

4. Neutral countries included: Norway, Sweden, Denmark, the Netherlands, Belgium, Luxembourg, Switzerland, Spain, Spanish Morocco, and Albania.

5. U-boats would have been most effective in the North Sea.

Chapter 25 Outline, pages 1–3

Chapter Project

Adapt sections of the book *All Quiet on the Western Front* into a Reader's Theater script. Divide the class into small groups; give each copies of one section. Discuss the time and political context of the book. Have each group organize its script into character- and narrative-reading parts; decide who will read which parts. Groups will present their sections of the book in chronological order. (See http://bms.westport.k12.ct.us/mccormick/rt/RTHOME.htm.)

Text Structure

Teaching students to recognize common text structures found in expository text can help students monitor their comprehension. Draw the following structures on the board:

(1) a blank "TV Guide" matrix, with channels and times listed down the side and across the top; and

(2) a blank store-receipt structure, with blanks for items, prices, and totals.

Ask:

• What information would be contained in each of these text structures? (program listings, itemized list of purchases).

• How did you know? (the structure of the text gives a suggestion of the contents).

• How is the subhead text in the lessons in this book structured? (in question and answer format)

Key Vocabulary Words

Point out that these chapter words are presented in the order that they appear in each lesson. They are also found in the Glossary. Have students ask adults in their families what the saying "in the trenches" means in their line of work. Discuss the responses in class and relate them to World War I.

Reading Strategy:
Text Structure

Readers can look at the organization of the text to help them identify the most important information.

◆ Before you begin reading this chapter, look at the chapter title, the names of the lessons and the sections, the boldfaced words, and photographs.

◆ You will notice that the section titles are in the form of questions. The answer to each question is provided in the paragraph(s) in that section. In this way, the text is structured in a question and answer format.

Key Vocabulary Words

Lesson 1
Rival One who tries to outdo another country or person

Lesson 2
Central Powers The allied nations of Germany, Austria-Hungary, Turkey, and Bulgaria

Allied Powers The allied nations of Great Britain, France, Russia, Italy, and eventually, the United States and Japan

Trench A long narrow ditch

Barbed wire Wire that has sharp metal spikes on it

Unrestricted warfare War that is not limited to a certain area or boundary

Armistice An agreement to stop fighting

Lesson 3
Reparation Payment for war damage

Treaty of Versailles The treaty that ended World War I

League of Nations A group of leaders from many nations who met to solve problems between countries

Lesson 5
Autocracy A government in which one person rules with unlimited power

Standard of living A way to judge how well a person or a family is living

Democratic Having to do with a government in which all people have equal rights

Duma The Russian parliament

Lesson 6
Abdicate To give up power as a ruler

Socialism An economic and political theory in which the government owns and controls the major means of production

Objectives

♦ To explain how mistrust of one another led powerful nations to build bigger militaries

♦ To identify the event that directly started the war

Reading Strategy:
Text Structure

Preview this lesson. Notice the headings, features, and boldfaced words.

Rival

One who tries to outdo another country or person

In Chapter 24, you read about the powerful imperialistic nations of France, Great Britain, Germany, Austria-Hungary, Italy, and Russia. These imperialistic powers did not have equal shares of land and riches, so they became rivals. That is, they tried to outdo one another. At first, this led to jealousy. Then it led to mistrust. Finally, it led to war.

Why Did Imperial Nations Become Militarized?

As they became more mistrustful of one another, these imperial nations built bigger armies and navies. For example, Wilhelm II, Germany's kaiser, wanted his navy to be equal to Britain's. Britain then had to build an even larger navy. All these industrialized nations also built bigger, more deadly weapons. Countries were becoming more militarized.

What Was the Alliance System?

At first, the countries of Europe tried to prevent war. They formed alliances and agreed to aid one another if attacked. After all, one country would surely not attack another if that meant fighting with several countries instead of one. By 1914, two **rival** alliances were in place. Germany, Austria-Hungary, and Italy made up the Triple Alliance. Great Britain, France, and Russia made up the Triple Entente.

The assassination of Archduke Franz Ferdinand and his wife, Sophie, was the spark that caused World War I. This photo shows Ferdinand and Sophie just before they were killed.

Chapter 25: Lesson 1

Overview This lesson describes the military buildup of the imperialistic nations in Europe, Europe's system of alliances, and the incident that led to World War I.

Objectives

■ To explain how mistrust of one another led powerful nations to build bigger militaries

■ To identify the event that directly started the war

Student Pages pages 615–616

Teacher's Resource Library

  Workbook Activity 111

  Activity 111

  Modified Activity 111

....

Vocabulary

rival

Discuss situations where rivalry often exists (e.g., between siblings or sports teams). Ask volunteers to write sentences on the board in which the word *rival* is used in various contexts. Classmates should confirm correct word usage.

....

① **Warm-Up Activity**

Write these statements on the board:

• Due to food rationing during WWI, the diet of German civilians was reduced to bread and turnips.

• Germany spent 83 percent of the public budget on military items; 2 percent was spent on civilians.

• 25,000 German civilians died from starvation during the war.

• In his 1913 book *Germany in Arms*, Crown Prince Wilhelm wrote enthusiastically about war as an essential factor for preserving Germany and the German way of life.

Read sections of the document (www.firstworldwar.com/source/crownprincewilhelm1913.htm) to the class. Discuss the prince's argument in the context of the effects of war on humans.

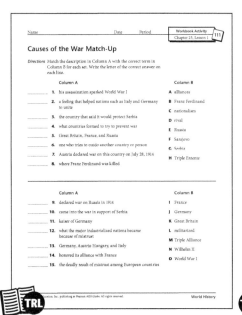

Workbook Activity 111

Activity 111

PRONUNCIATION GUIDE

Use this list to help students pronounce difficult words in this lesson.

Sarajevo   (sär´ ə yä´ vō)

2 Teaching the Lesson

Ask students to recall which nations combined their strength to defeat Napoleon. Have them read pages 615–616 to find out how and why European countries formed alliances.

Ask:

- Because of mistrust among powerful nations in Europe, what did nations invest in? (Answers will vary; students may say bigger armies and navies.)

- Which nations were in the Triple Alliance? the Triple Entente? (Germany, Austria-Hungary, Italy; Britain, France, Russia)

- Why did Archduke Ferdinand's assassination lead to World War I? (answers will vary: students may say Austria-Hungary was in one of the alliances or blamed Serbia for Archduke Ferdinand's death; Russia, a member of the other alliance, said it would protect Serbia)

- Which nation came into the war on the side of Austria-Hungary? (Germany)

- Which nations came into the war on the side of Serbia? (Russia, France, and Great Britain)

STUDY SKILLS

On an index card, have students write in separate columns the names of the nations who were the Allies and those who were the Central Powers. Students can use this card as a bookmark as they read the rest of this chapter. They can refer to it if they have any questions about which nations were the Allies and which nations were the Central Powers.

What Event Started World War I?

Nationalism had helped nations like Italy and Germany to unite. But by the 1900s, the spirit of nationalism had become a problem for some nations.

Serbs living in Austria-Hungary wanted to be part of Serbia, a neighboring country. Many Serbs lived in Sarajevo, which was a city in Austria-Hungary. To try to improve relations with the Serbs, the Austrian emperor sent his nephew Franz Ferdinand to Sarajevo. On Sunday, June 28, 1914, Ferdinand and Sophie, his wife, were killed as they rode through the streets of Sarajevo.

Austria-Hungary blamed the Serbians. On July 28, 1914, Austria declared war on Serbia. Next, Russia said it would protect Serbia. A few days later, Germany declared war on Russia. France then came into the war in support of Serbia. Next, Great Britain honored its alliance with France. What started out as a small revolt exploded into a big war.

Lesson 1 Review On a sheet of paper, write the answer to each question. Use complete sentences.

1. How did imperialism cause World War I?
2. How did militarism cause World War I?
3. How did the alliance system cause World War I?
4. How did nationalism cause World War I?
5. What event in Sarajevo led to World War I?

What do you think

What could have kept World War I from happening?

Reading Strategy: Text Structure

(Guide students through identifying the headings, features, and boldfaced words in Lesson 1. Point out how these elements create structure.)

3 Reinforce and Extend

Lesson 1 Review Answers

1. During the 19th century, nations began to take over other countries. These powers did not have equal shares of land, so they became rivals. This ultimately led to war. **2.** Imperial nations began a military buildup, making them even more aggressive rivals. **3.** When nations formed alliances, individual countries agreed to protect their allies. **4.** Serbs living in Austria-Hungary wanted to be part of Serbia, a neighboring country. This nationalism led to war. **5.** The assassination of Archduke Ferdinand and his wife was the immediate spark of the war.

Answers will vary. If leaders around the world had moved away from imperialism, militarism, nationalism, and alliances, World War I may not have happened.

Reading Strategy:
Text Structure

As you read the next paragraphs, use a graphic organizer to record the countries of the Central Powers and the Allied Powers.

Objectives

- To identify the Central Powers and the Allied Powers
- To describe trench warfare and new weapons used in World War I
- To explain why the United States entered the war
- To describe how the war ended

Central Powers

The allied nations of Germany, Austria-Hungary, Ottoman Empire, and Bulgaria

Allied Powers

The allied nations of Great Britain, France, Russia, Italy, and eventually, the U.S. and Japan

When fighting started in August 1914, millions of soldiers marched eagerly to battle. They thought they would be home by Christmas. But Christmas came and went and still they fought. In fact, they fought for four long years.

On one side of the war were Austria-Hungary, Germany, Bulgaria, and the Ottoman Empire. Historians call them the **Central Powers** because they were countries in central Europe.

Historians call the other side the **Allied Powers,** or the Allies. The Allies included France, Russia, Great Britain, Italy, and several smaller countries. Italy, originally allied with Germany, had now switched sides. Later, Japan and the United States joined the Allies.

Where Was the Western Front of the War?

The Central Powers and the Allies fought World War I all over the world. During the earliest months of the war, most fighting took place in Belgium and northern France. This was known as the western front. Germany wanted a quick victory over France. It could then turn east and defeat Russia on the eastern front. When the Allies stopped the Germans at the Marne River, Germany's hope for a quick victory over France ended.

Soldiers spent much of World War I fighting in trenches. Many new weapons made World War I the first modern war.

1905 – 1919

World War I and the Russian Revolution   Chapter 25   **617**

Chapter 25: Lesson 2

Overview This lesson describes action along the eastern and western fronts, Russia's treaty with Germany, the new weapons of war, and the United States' entry into World War I.

Objectives

- To identify the Central Powers and the Allied Powers
- To describe trench warfare and new weapons used in World War I
- To explain why the United States entered the war
- To describe how the war ended

Student Pages pages 617–622

Teacher's Resource Library TRL

Workbook Activity 112

Activity 112

Modified Activity 112

Vocabulary

Allied Powers	trench
armistice	unrestricted
barbed wire	warfare
Central Powers	

Have students work in pairs, with one student reading the definitions and the other supplying the correct word and an example sentence. Students should switch roles and continue to quiz each other until they feel comfortable with the vocabulary.

1 Warm-Up Activity

Play a recording of George M. Cohan's "Over There," the song that American soldiers sang when they sailed across the ocean to fight in WWI. Distribute copies of a shortened version of Woodrow Wilson's April 2, 1917, message to Congress and ask a volunteer to read it aloud. Then tell the class that after Wilson finished speaking, the congressmen cheered and cheered. When Wilson went back to his office, he said to his aide, "Isn't it strange that men should cheer for war." He put his head on his desk and wept.

Reading Strategy:
Text Structure

ONLINE CONNECTION

Students can gain additional information by accessing the following Web sites:

www.agsglobewh.com/page618a
(This site houses the World War I Document Archive, featuring an extensive collection of official papers, diaries, personal reminiscences, collections of photographs, and links to other sites .)

www.agsglobewh.com/page618b
(This Web site offers links organized by significant events, and containing photos, illustrations, and articles from war-time publications.)

www.agsglobewh.com/page618c
(This music-based site has copies of sheet music from the WWI years.)

www.agsglobewh.com/page618d
(Students can visit this site for information on the Russian Revolutions.)

Reading Strategy:
Text Structure

(Work with students and guide them through finding the answer for one section.)

Many submarines, or "U-boats," were used to sink enemy ships in World War I.

Trench
A long narrow ditch
Barbed wire
Wire that has sharp metal spikes on it

Reading Strategy:
Text Structure

Notice that the section headings are written as questions. After you read each section, try to answer the question asked in the heading.

What Was Trench Warfare?

For the next two years, both sides fought a bitter war on the western front. Soldiers dug **trenches,** or long, narrow ditches, where they ate, slept, and watched the enemy. **Barbed wire** protected these trenches. This type of wire has sharp metal spikes on it. Between the two series of trenches was an area the soldiers called "no man's land."

Many soldiers died fighting in the trenches, but neither side won much territory. For example, in the Battle of Verdun in 1916, each side lost more than 300,000 men. However, the German army advanced only four miles.

What Weapons Were Used in World War I?

During World War I, nations fought in the air for the first time. However, the use of airplanes in World War I was limited. But both sides used submarines on a large scale. Germany called its submarines U-boats. They sank many Allied and neutral ships carrying food and supplies.

 2 **Teaching the Lesson**

Remind students about how the Spanish soldiers had amazed the natives in South America with their weapons. (They read about this in Chapter 17.) Then have students read pages 617–622 to find out about the weapons and methods of warfare that were new to the world during World War I.

Ask:

• What type of warfare was carried out along the western front? (trench warfare)

• What military vehicles were introduced in World War I? What kind of weapons were used? (airplanes, tanks, and submarines or U-boats; machine guns and poison gas)

• Why did Russia pull out of the war? Why did the United States enter? (answers will vary—students may say the Russians went home because of the heavy losses they were taking and because they were angry with the czar; because German U-boats were sinking U.S. ships)

• Which type of German ship sank both Allied and neutral ships? (the U-boat)

This cartoon shows the Allies fighting the Central Powers, represented here as a dragon.

Writing About History

In World War I, most American soldiers had never traveled far from home before. Imagine that you are an 18-year-old soldier in France. Write a letter home. What is happening? How does it feel?

Both sides also developed new weapons. The machine gun changed war forever. This type of gun fires bullets rapidly without reloading. It fired so fast that the only way an army could protect itself was to take cover in trenches.

Early in 1915, the Germans introduced poison gas. The Allies quickly followed the German example. This deadly gas settled in the trenches and blinded and choked the soldiers there. But gas was risky. If the wind suddenly shifted, the gas could drift back to the troops using the gas.

The tank was another new weapon. The British introduced it in 1916 to smash through the barbed wire that protected the trenches. By the end of the war, both sides were using tanks.

Who Fought on the Eastern Front?

Russians and Serbs fought Austrians, Germans, and Ottoman Turks along the eastern front. Allied soldiers were poorly prepared and sometimes went to battle without weapons. The Central Powers forced the Russians to retreat. But the Russian army kept thousands of German troops fighting for over three years.

In 1916, a million Russian soldiers died in an attack on Austria. Short on food, guns, and supplies, the Russians grew tired of war. They blamed their problems on the czar.

1905 – 1919

World War I and the Russian Revolution   Chapter 25   **619**

 ## Writing About History

Have students brainstorm the different sights and sounds that they might experience when visiting a foreign country for the first time. Then have them read the Writing About History feature and write their letters home.

Ask:

- **What protection did soldiers have against the machine gun?** (the trenches)

- **Why was it risky to use poison gas?** (the wind might shift, causing the gas to kill your own soldiers)

- **Who did the Russian soldiers blame for the shortage of food and weapons?** (the czar)

LEARNING STYLES

Logical/Mathematical
To help students gain a reference for the economic cost of war, ask them to find out the current cost of barbed wire. They can call a feed store or search on the Internet. Have students use the information to calculate the cost to protect trenches along one mile of the western front at today's prices. Students should remember that soldiers on both sides needed protection. They should take into account that several parallel strands of wire would have been needed to protect each side. Have students report their findings to the class.

ELL/ESL STRATEGY

Language Objective: *To recognize that listening is an active process*

Point out to students that listening allows people to gather information, follow directions, participate in a discussion, form an opinion, and analyze information received. Pair ESL students with English-speaking students. Have them listen to the recording for each lesson in this chapter, following along in their text as they do. Challenge them to agree on the answer to each subhead question. Students can listen to the recording again to make sure that their answers are correct. They should produce a list of questions and answers for each section and study the lists as they prepare for the Chapter Review.

Body/Kinesthetic

Have students research the type of ships that carried cargo from the United States to Britain and France during World War I and the naval ships that escorted them in convoys. Students should use this information to create a diorama of a convoy crossing the Atlantic in World War I. Ask them to include a German U-boat in the diorama. Have students write a few sentences about each type of vessel on index cards. Have them use the cards as they explain their dioramas to classmates.

BACKGROUND INFORMATION

Millions of people were killed in World War I. Millions were also wounded. Many more lives might have been lost were it not for the efforts of an organization called the Red Cross. Founded in 1863 by Jean Henri Dunant, a Swiss philanthropist, the organization gives medical care to the wounded, regardless of their race or nationality. Similarly, under the terms of the Geneva Conventions, no nation is allowed to fire upon a Red Cross worker while assisting someone in need—even if the someone is an enemy soldier. The Red Cross is part of the International Committee of the Red Cross, which also includes the Red Crescent society (in Muslim countries).

Ask:

• When did Germany begin unrestricted warfare at sea? Where did this happen? What did it mean?
(1917; around the British Isles; Germany would sink any ship in those waters)

Unrestricted warfare

War that is not limited to a certain area or boundary

In 1918, after a revolution in Russia, Russia and Germany signed the Treaty of Brest Litovsk. It ended the war for Russia. Because of the treaty, Russia had to give Finland, Estonia, Latvia, Lithuania, the Ukraine, and part of Poland to Germany.

Where Else Did Fighting Take Place?

As the war expanded, fighting broke out in many places besides the western and eastern fronts. There was fighting in Italy and Asia. Japan moved to take over areas of China that were under German influence. Australia and New Zealand forces took over some islands Germany held in the Pacific. Some of the heaviest battles were fought in Turkey, part of the Ottoman Empire. The war even extended into Africa, where British and French troops took over former German colonies.

When Did the United States Enter the War?

In 1917, Germany announced that it would begin **unrestricted warfare** in waters around Britain. That is, German U-boats would sink any ship—even ones from neutral countries—that sailed into the waters surrounding the British Isles.

German U-boats

Germans launched their first U-boat (for the German word *Unterseeboot,* meaning "undersea boat") in 1906. During World War I, Germany used U-boats in many successful attacks on British ships. Germany built more than 400 new, larger, and more powerful U-boats that sank more than 4,000 ships.

The Germans put hundreds of U-boats into use in World War II. During three days in October 1940, eight of these vessels destroyed 38 British ships. Not one of those U-boats was damaged. However, Germany was eventually overcome by the Allied forces. By the end of World War II, Germany had lost 821 U-boats. Its largest remaining boat, the U-234, was forced to surrender by an American destroyer in the North Atlantic as the war ended.

The most celebrated action in Germany's unrestricted warfare campaign was the sinking of the British ocean liner *Lusitania* on May 7, 1915, off the coast of Ireland. A German U-boat sent a torpedo into the side of the *Lusitania* without warning. Two massive explosions followed, and the ship sank in 18 minutes. Of the 1,200 or so people who perished, 128 were Americans. Posters circulated in the United States urged men to "Remember the *Lusitania*" and enlist in the army. The United States' reaction was so hostile that Germany ceased U-boat attacks for a time. Their resumption in 1917 caused the United States to declare war against Germany.

Armistice
An agreement to stop fighting

Germany knew that this plan would lead to war with the United States, which had been a neutral country. Its leaders thought that they could force Britain to surrender before American troops and supplies arrived in Europe. On April 6, 1917, the U.S. Congress declared war on Germany. Soon more than a million American soldiers landed in Europe.

When Did World War I End?

By 1918, after four long years of war, both the Central Powers and the Allies were tired. Germany no longer had trained troops to replace those killed in battle. The fresh American troops tipped the balance in favor of the Allies. On November 11, 1918, Germany agreed to an **armistice,** or an end to fighting. On the 11th day at the 11th hour of the 11th month, the great war ended.

The World War I "Doughboy"

In the early 1900s, most men became soldiers just for the length of a war. Then they returned to civilian life. World War I soldiers were called "doughboys." This may be because the buttons on soldiers' uniforms looked like doughboys—what we now call doughnuts. When America entered the war, the army was very small. A draft law was passed in 1917, calling up all men between 21 and 30. The ages later became 18 to 45. Draftees received combat training. They learned how to be part of a bayonet charge, use a gas mask, and fire a rifle.

Today, the United States has a professional volunteer army. Volunteers sign up for a set number of years. They can then choose whether or not to re-enlist. Besides combat training, the army trains people in medicine, languages, computers, and other fields. It has changed in other ways, too. The military was segregated in World War I. African Americans served in separate army units. In 1918, there were no black marines and few women in the military. Today, these groups make up almost 25 percent of the army.

Ask:

- When did World War I end? How long did it last? (November 11, 1918; four years)

- What did they call the agreement that ended the fighting? (an armistice)

Ask students how the United States navy, army, air force, and marines recruit men and women into the service. Have a volunteer read the title of the Then and Now feature, "The World War I 'Doughboy'." Have students read the feature to find out how the United States recruited troops for World War I.

 Reinforce and Extend

ELL/ESL STRATEGY

Language Objective:
To read with a specific purpose in mind

Point out that reading with a specific purpose helps with other reading strategies, such as summarizing main ideas. Keeping a purpose in mind as you read helps you to clarify and extend your thinking. It also helps you to gather information more efficiently and to organize ideas when you are preparing to make an oral presentation.

Have students work in small groups to

- use multiple sources to collect background information about the draft and all-volunteer systems for enrollment in military service;

- create graphic organizers comparing the advantages and disadvantages of each system;

- organize a debate about which is the better system for our country.

Lesson 2 Review Answers

1. D **2.** C **3.** B **4.** D **5.** B

Answers will vary. The United States had been neutral. However, it had been sending supplies to the Allies. The Germans knew that United States ships would be in the waters around Britain. They knew, too, that if they attacked these ships, the United States would retaliate and enter the war.

Lesson 2 Review On a sheet of paper, write the letter of the answer that correctly completes each sentence.

1. _____ fought on the Allied side in World War I.

   A Turkey   **C** Austria

   B Bulgaria   **D** Great Britain

2. On the western front, soldiers lived in _____ and faced one another across a "no man's land."

   A tanks   **C** trenches

   B airplanes   **D** U-boats

3. World War I lasted for _____ years.

   A two   **C** six

   B four   **D** seven

4. The United States entered the war in _____.

   A 1914   **C** 1916

   B 1915   **D** 1917

5. World War I ended in _____.

   A 1917   **C** 1919

   B 1918   **D** 1920

What do you think

Germany decided to attack any ship in the waters around Britain. Why did this lead to war with the United States?

- ◆ To identify Woodrow Wilson's Fourteen Points
- ◆ To describe what other countries wanted after the war
- ◆ To describe the League of Nations

Reparation

Payment for war damage

Reading Strategy:
Text Structure

As you read, look for words like *first, then, next,* and *finally.* These words will help you understand the order of the text

World War I ended in November 1918, and the Allies won. The next year, the Allied leaders met at Versailles in France to create a peace treaty. The "Big Four"—Britain, France, Italy, and the United States—made most of the big decisions. Each of them wanted something different from the peace meeting.

What Did the United States Want?

President Woodrow Wilson represented the United States at the peace meeting. He had written a peace plan called the Fourteen Points. Part of his plan was to end secret treaties between nations. He also wanted to reduce the size of armies and navies in each nation. Most of all, Wilson wanted to organize a league of nations to keep the peace.

What Did Other Countries Want?

The leaders from France, Great Britain, and Italy had plans that were different from Wilson's Fourteen Points. France had suffered greatly during the war. Premier Clemenceau, who represented France, wanted Germany to make **reparations** for the war. That is, he wanted Germany to pay for the cost of the war. He also wanted Germany to return land to France.

Prime Minister Lloyd George of Great Britain also wanted Germany to pay for the war. In addition, Britain wanted Germany's African colonies. However, they did not want the French to become too powerful. Prime Minister Vittorio Orlando represented Italy at the meeting. He wanted the Allies to honor a treaty that had been signed in 1915. The Allies had promised to give Italy more land if it entered the war on the Allied side.

Chapter 25: Lesson 3

Overview This lesson explains what the U.S., France, Britain, and Italy wanted to add to the Treaty of Versailles and what the leaders of those countries agreed on.

Objectives

- ■ To identify Woodrow Wilson's Fourteen Points
- ■ To describe what other countries wanted after the war
- ■ To describe the League of Nations

Student Pages pages 623–625

Teacher's Resource Library 🅣🅡🅛

    Workbook Activity 113

    Activity 113

    Modified Activity 113

Vocabulary

| League of Nations | Treaty of |
| Reparation | Versailles |

Discuss what the terms mean with students. Encourage them to make a connection between the terms and similar terms or events they know about. Examples may include *League of Nations/ the United Nations; Treaty of Versailles/ treaty between American Indians and the United States.*

① Warm-Up Activity

Ask students if anyone knows why Veterans of Foreign Wars (VFW) volunteers give you a paper poppy after you give them a donation. (As early as the Napoleonic wars, red poppies grew on the graves of dead soldiers in the fields of northern Europe. In 1915, they covered the graves of WWI soldiers.) Distribute copies of the poem "In Flanders Field," by John McCrae. Read the poem aloud. Discuss the location of Flanders Field, the change of mood between stanzas two and three, and whether students view this as a pro-war or antiwar poem.

PRONUNCIATION GUIDE

Use this list to help students pronounce difficult words in this lesson.

Clemenceau   (kle mä sō´)

2 Teaching the Lesson

Ask students to remember the decisions made at the Congress of Vienna, which gave certain countries control over others. Then have students read pages 623–625 to find out what happened at the end of World War I.

Ask:

• Which of the Allies had suffered most during World War I? (France)

• Which of the Allies wanted to punish Germany by making it pay reparations? (France)

• What concern did the British have about the French? (they did not want them to become too powerful)

• Why was Italy given more land? (because Italy had secretly entered the war on the side of the Allies)

• According to the Treaty of Versailles, which country was given complete blame for causing World War I? (Germany)

• According to the Treaty of Versailles, which areas did Germany have to return to France? On which continent did Germany have to give up its colonies? (Alsace and Lorraine; Africa)

• What were the four countries carved out of what had once been in the western part of the Russian Empire? (Finland, Estonia, Latvia, and Lithuania)

• What made the League of Nations weak? (answers will vary; students may say it could not force countries to obey its rulings)

Reading Strategy:
Text Structure

(Guide students in finding one of these words in the first paragraph. Ask a volunteer to explain how the word gives structure to the text.)

The four Allied leaders at the peace conference were (from left): Vittorio Orlando (Italy), Lloyd George (Great Britain), George Clemenceau (France), and Woodrow Wilson (United States).

Treaty of Versailles
The treaty that ended World War I

League of Nations
A group of leaders from many nations who met to solve problems between countries

What Happened to Germany?

The leaders at Versailles finally agreed to a treaty. The **Treaty of Versailles** forced Germany to accept responsibility for causing the war. Germany also had to pay for the cost of the war. In addition, Germany gave the land of Alsace and Lorraine to France. It divided its African colonies between France and Great Britain. It also gave its colonies in the Pacific to Japan.

Even though the German leaders thought the Allies had treated them unfairly, they signed the treaty in 1919.

What Happened to the Austro-Hungarian Empire?

The Treaty of Versailles broke up the Austro-Hungarian Empire. Austria and Hungary became two countries. The treaty also created two new countries—Yugoslavia and Czechoslovakia. Some Austro-Hungarian land went to Poland, Latvia, and Romania. The treaty carved Finland, Estonia, Latvia, and Lithuania out of the western part of the old Russian Empire.

What Was the League of Nations?

The Treaty of Versailles created the **League of Nations** to try to keep peace. This was a group of leaders from many nations who met to solve problems between countries. These leaders met in Geneva, Switzerland, to talk over their problems. However, the League was weak because some countries did not join. Also, the League could not force countries to obey its rulings.

LEARNING STYLES

Visual/Spatial

Have students make a poster that shows what each of the Big Four nations—England, France, Italy, and the United States—wanted in the Treaty of Versailles. Students could list each country's points along with an illustration of its flag. Students could title the poster, "The Making of the Treaty of Versailles." Have students use this poster to study for the Chapter Review.

AT HOME

Have students find a video to watch with their families about World War I. A number of documentaries have been made on this subject, as well as feature-length movies, such as *All Quiet on the Western Front.* Students should share with family members their knowledge of the weapons used for the first time during World War I. Ask them to discuss with their families whether the film presents an accurate picture of warfare. Have students share the reactions of their families in class.

Lesson 3 Review On a sheet of paper, write the answer to each question. Use complete sentences.

1. What countries were represented at the peace meeting in France?

2. What were the Fourteen Points?

3. Why did Germany think the Treaty of Versailles treated it unfairly?

4. What two new countries were created by the Treaty of Versailles?

5. Why was the League of Nations weak?

The Treaty of Versailles treated Germany and the other Central Powers poorly. What were the problems this caused for those countries?

LEARNING STYLES

Interpersonal/ Group Learning

The League of Nations created new countries, and some existing countries had their borders changed. Some groups found themselves living in new or different countries after the war. Have a group of students research and report on ethnic groups in the Balkans. They can begin by finding the area known as the

Balkans on a map and researching five or six groups who live there. Each student should select a different ethnic group on which to write a report. Students should write down events in their group's history on index cards. Make available a map of the Balkans for the group to display when they report to the class. Students can use their index cards when they report orally about the ethnic group they researched.

- Which countries were carved out of the Austro Hungarian Empire? Which countries received land as a result of the treaty? (Austria, Hungary, Yugoslavia, Czechoslovakia; Poland, Italy, Romania)

- Where did the League of Nations meet? What was its purpose? (Geneva; to keep peace among nations)

 Reinforce and Extend

ELL/ESL STRATEGY

Language Objective: *To make connections to prior knowledge*

Divide students into groups of three or four, making sure to group ELL/ESL students with fluent English speakers. Have students look over the list of countries that Russia gave to Germany, and then assign one of those countries to each group. Explain that each group will use an encyclopedia or other reference book to learn what has happened to their country since 1918. They will then use their findings to give a brief presentation to the class about that country. Each member of the group should deliver a portion of the presentation.

Lesson 3 Review Answers

1. Britain, France, Italy, and the U.S. were represented. **2.** The Fourteen Points was Wilson's peace plan to end secret treaties and reduce the size of military organizations. **3.** Germany thought it was being treated unfairly because it had to pay reparations. **4.** The Treaty of Versailles created Yugoslavia and Czechoslovakia. **5.** It was weak because it could not force countries to obey its rulings.

Answers will vary. Germans could become angry, ready to fight again. The defeated nations could also go into deeper and deeper debt and suffer from lack of food and other supplies. This, too, would lead to bitterness and frustration.

Ask a volunteer to read the map titles: "Europe Before World War I" and "Europe After World War I." Encourage students to suggest what the biggest change was. (answers will vary; students may mention Russia is smaller or there are more countries) Then have students read the caption and answer the questions in it. (There were more countries after the war. Austria-Hungary was divided into Austria and Hungary. Two new countries, Yugoslavia and Czechoslovakia, were also formed with former Austro-Hungarian land.)

Map Study

The top map shows what Europe looked like just before World War I. The bottom map shows Europe after the war. Were there more countries in Europe before or after the war? What happened to Austria-Hungary after the war?

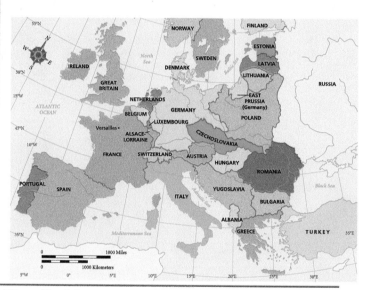

Objectives

◆ To explain the loss of life and financial cost of the war

◆ To identify the problems caused by the Treaty of Versailles

Reading Strategy:
Text Structure

As you read this lesson, use a graphic organizer to list the social, economic, and political effects of World War I

What Were the Social and Economic Effects of the War?

World War I was the first total war. Cities, farms, factories, and people living at home all become part of a total war. Because of this, there were many social effects of the war. The years between the wars were difficult for people everywhere. Russia, Germany, Austria-Hungary, and France lost a whole generation. A generation is all the people born around the same time. In fact, France lost one out of every five men between the ages of 20 and 44.

World War I also had economic effects. Historians do not know what the war cost. One guess is about $350 billion. Many governments raised taxes and borrowed large sums of money to pay for the war. However, by the end of the war, every major European country was bankrupt. They could not pay off their debts because they had no money. Cities and farms lay in ruins. Many people had no jobs. Because of the war, Europe lost much of its power and wealth. Countries like the United States and Japan took over the European markets.

Many soldiers were wounded in the war.

What Were the Political Effects of the War?

Democracy spread because of the war. In Germany, Austria-Hungary, and Russia, governments elected by the people replaced monarchies. However, in Russia, a dictatorship soon replaced the new democratic government.

Chapter 25: Lesson 4

Overview This lesson explains the enormous social and financial cost of WWI and how the war's outcome reduced chances for a lasting peace.

Objectives

■ To explain the loss of life and financial cost of the war

■ To identify the problems caused by the Treaty of Versailles

Student Pages pages 627–628

Teacher's Resource Library TRL

  Workbook Activity 114

  Activity 114

  Modified Activity 114

Vocabulary

The concept of "total war" is difficult to grasp. Almost everyone in the countries fighting World War I was affected by the war. The loss of a generation, the monetary cost, and the ruin of cities and farms were suffered by countries in Europe, but not the United States. Discuss how this fact might affect the attitudes of European and U.S. citizens toward wars.

1   Warm-Up Activity

Distribute copies of the following passages:

• From *All Quiet on the Western Front*:

  "This book . . . will try simply to tell of a generation of men who, even though they may have escaped shells, were destroyed by the war."

• From the *New York Times*, November 11, 1918:

  ARMISTICE SIGNED, END OF THE WAR!

  BERLIN SEIZED BY REVOLUTIONISTS;

  NEW CHANCELLOR BEGS FOR ORDER;

  OUSTED KAISER FLEES TO HOLLAND

Discuss how you think the future of the world would be affected by the happenings described here.

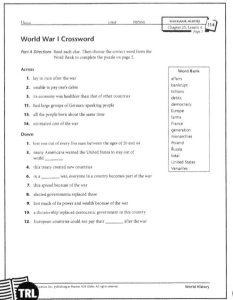

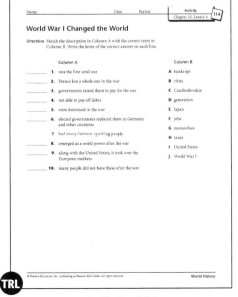

Workbook Activity 114, pages 1–2   **Activity 114**   *WWI/Russian Revolution*   Chapter 25   **627**

Reading Strategy:
Text Structure

(Demonstrate the structure of a
graphic organizer suited for this
strategy, such as a table. Show
students how to get started with it.)

 Teaching the Lesson

Have students discuss what they think
the German leaders thought about the
Treaty of Versailles. Have students read
pages 627–628 to learn the cost of WWI
and the problems that emerged shortly
after it ended.

Ask:

- **What was the financial situation in
  Europe after World War I?**
  (countries were bankrupt)

- **Which nations took over the
  markets of European countries?**
  (the United States and Japan)

- **What advantage did the United
  States have over other countries at
  the end of World War I?** (it had a
  healthy economy)

 Reinforce and Extend

WORLD CULTURES

Ernest Rutherford, who
was born in New
Zealand and worked in
Great Britain, made
three discoveries that played a large
part in the beginning of the nuclear
age: he found out that the structure
of elements can change; developed
the nuclear model of the atom; and
in 1919, changed the world by
splitting the atom. During WWI,
Rutherford said he hoped that an
efficient way of extracting the energy
of the atom would not be found until
men were at peace again.

The Treaty of Versailles created new countries. But some of
these had large numbers of foreign people. For example, Poland
and Czechoslovakia had large groups of German-speaking
people. This caused problems in the future.

As a result of World War I, the United States emerged as a
world power. Its economy was healthier than that of other
countries. However, many Americans wanted the United States
to stay out of world affairs.

Lesson 4 Review On a sheet of paper, write the answer to each
question. Use complete sentences.

1. What is a "total war"?
2. How did World War I affect the economy of Europe?
3. What happened to the new democratic government
   of Russia?
4. What was one problem that the Treaty of Versailles caused?
5. What were three effects of World War I?

 What do you think

How do you think the deaths of so many people in World War I
made soldiers feel about the war?

Lesson 4 Review Answers

1. In a total war, a country uses all its
resources; citizens are involved. **2.** After
WWI, every major European country
was bankrupt. **3.** A dictatorship replaced
the Russian democracy. **4.** The Treaty
of Versailles created new countries that
combined different ethnic groups.
5. After WWI, the U.S. was a world
power; Europe lost much of its power
and wealth; democracy spread.

Answers will vary. Both the victors and
the defeated in WWI may have felt bitter.

Chapter Project Follow-up

Schedule the Reader's Theater
performances to begin after
Lesson 4. Have the groups
present the script in the same
order as in the novel. See the
Web site on page 613 for
assessment.

Objectives

♦ To explain what an autocracy is

♦ To identify changes that Alexander II and III made

♦ To describe what happened under the rule of Czar Nicholas II

♦ To explain what happened on Bloody Sunday

Autocracy

A government in which one person rules with unlimited power

Standard of living

A way to judge how well a person or a family is living

Reading Strategy:
Text Structure

Choose an event in this section. Use a graphic organizer to illustrate cause and effect for that event.

One important result of World War I was the Russian Revolution of 1917. In less than a week, rebels overthrew the czar. But people before them had planted the seeds of the revolution.

What Was the Autocracy of Russia?

In the 1800s, Russia was an **autocracy**—a government in which one person rules with unlimited power. In Russia, that person was the czar. He controlled the lives of his people and expected them to obey without question.

In 1855, Alexander II became czar. He ended serfdom and introduced the jury system. He gave Russians more rights, and allowed more people to attend school. Around the same time, the Industrial Revolution reached Russia. When this happened, many farmers left their land to go to the cities to work. Russian cities of St. Petersburg, Moscow, and Baku became centers of industry. The Russian **standard of living**—a way to judge how well a person or family is living—also improved.

People in Russia were experiencing their first taste of freedom. But they wanted more. When the czar refused to give them more rights, the Russian people revolted. During one of these revolts, a young revolutionary killed Czar Alexander.

Czar Alexander II freed the serfs and their families in 1861, ending serfdom in Russia.

Chapter 25: Lesson 5

Overview This lesson explains how poverty and the czar's refusal to listen to the people's demands brought Russia closer to revolution.

Objectives

■ To explain what an autocracy is

■ To identify changes that Alexander II and III made

■ To describe what happened under the rule of Czar Nicholas II

■ To explain what happened on Bloody Sunday

Student Pages pages 629–631

Teacher's Resource Library

Workbook Activity 115

Activity 115

Modified Activity 115

....

Vocabulary

autocracy	**Duma**
democratic	**standard of living**

Have students read the vocabulary words and study their definitions. Ask volunteers to explain the differences between an autocracy and a democracy. Then ask which kind of government would likely have a Duma. Next, have students suggest things that they think contribute to a high standard of living. Write students' suggestions on the board.

....

1 **Warm-Up Activity**

Distribute copies of this statement:

"It is better to abolish serfdom from above than to wait for it to abolish itself from below."

-Alexander II, czar of Russia

On January 22, 1905, Nicholas II of Russia ordered his soldiers to open fire upon a crowd of workers peacefully parading to ask him for help. They were carrying large pictures of the czar as a sign of their respect and loyalty. The massacre of demonstrators came to be known as Bloody Sunday. Discuss with students what they can infer about the natures of the two czars from this information.

---

2 Teaching the Lesson

Ask students to recall what caused the French and American revolutions. Then have them read pages 629–631 to find out what life was like in Russia under the czars.

Ask:

- In what ways did Czar Alexander II improve the lives of Russian people? (answers will vary; students may say he freed the serfs and sold them land, introduced a jury system, gave them more rights, and let more people go to school)

- Why did Russians remain unhappy with the czar? (he refused to give them more rights)

- Why did Nicholas II declare war on Japan? (to distract people from thinking about change)

- How did Nicholas II respond to the people who marched to his palace, requesting better working conditions? (he had his troops fire on them)

- Why did Czar Nicholas dismiss the Duma after only three months? (he believed that he alone had the right to govern Russia)

3 Reinforce and Extend

IN THE COMMUNITY

Have students interview people in businesses in their community to find out what types of communications systems they rely on. Have students report the results of their interviews. Classmates should decide in which ways these systems are alike and different from those in 19th-century Russia.

Democratic

Having to do with a government in which all people have equal rights

Duma

The Russian parliament

In 1894, Nicholas II became czar. He faced many problems. Educated Russians wanted a more **democratic** government in which all people had equal rights. Instead of listening to his people, Czar Nicholas II tried to get them to think about something else. Nicholas II declared war on Japan in 1904. This was called the Russo-Japanese War. When Russia lost the war, people demanded more change.

In 1905, another revolt took place. Russians call this day Bloody Sunday. Workers had marched in peace to the czar's palace in St. Petersburg. They wanted better working conditions, more freedom, and an elected national assembly. The czar's soldiers fired on the crowd and killed hundreds of workers.

After Bloody Sunday, Russian workers refused to work. Riots broke out. Peasants attacked the nobles and burned their estates. The czar promised to give the people more freedom if they would stop the violence. He even agreed to the election of a Russian parliament, or **Duma.** However, Czar Nicholas dismissed the Duma after three months. He believed that he alone had the right to govern.

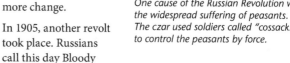

One cause of the Russian Revolution was the widespread suffering of peasants. The czar used soldiers called "cossacks" to control the peasants by force.

AT HOME

Encourage students to invite family members to watch a videotape of David Lean's 1965 film *Doctor Zhivago*, based on the novel by Boris Pasternak. This is the story of a doctor in Russia and his experiences during World War I, the Russian Revolution, and the Civil War. Students will recognize Bloody Sunday and the Trans-Siberian Railroad from their reading. Have students discuss the film with their families and bring to class some observations of Russia prior to the revolution to share with other students.

Lesson 5 Review On a sheet of paper, use the words from the Word Bank to complete each sentence correctly.

1. In the late 1800s, the nobles completely controlled the _____.

2. In 1855, _____ ended serfdom.

3. During the Industrial Revolution, the Russian cities of St. Petersburg, Moscow, and _____ became centers of industry.

4. In 1904 Czar Nicholas II declared war on _____.

5. Russian soldiers killed hundreds of workers on January 22, 1905; Russians call this day Bloody _____.

Why would both Russian serfs and Russian nobles want reform?

Biography

Grigori Rasputin: c. 1872–1916

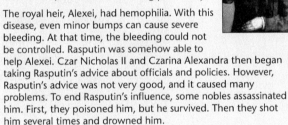

Rasputin was a Siberian peasant who became a monk and healer. Later, he moved to St. Petersburg. Although Rasputin lived an immoral life, he had an interesting personality.

The royal heir, Alexei, had hemophilia. With this disease, even minor bumps can cause severe bleeding. At that time, the bleeding could not be controlled. Rasputin was somehow able to help Alexei. Czar Nicholas II and Czarina Alexandra then began taking Rasputin's advice about officials and policies. However, Rasputin's advice was not very good, and it caused many problems. To end Rasputin's influence, some nobles assassinated him. First, they poisoned him, but he survived. Then they shot him several times and drowned him.

BACKGROUND INFORMATION

Alexei was the only son of Czar Nicholas and Alexandra, their youngest of six children. Hemophilia was usually fatal before adulthood because the blood failed to clot and internal bleeding could not be stopped. When blood transfusions became possible, hemophilia was less often fatal. Sadly, in the late 20th century, hemophiliacs became vulnerable to another disease: AIDS. Before a test was invented to screen the blood that was the lifeline for victims of hemophilia, the blood supply became contaminated by the virus that causes AIDS. Since blood is now screened for the AIDS virus, hemophiliacs can again safely receive transfusions.

Biography

Grigory Yefimovich Rasputin was a well-known holy man and faith healer in St. Petersburg. However, many people believed he was a sorcerer. The czarina called upon him to cure her son because none of the medical doctors had been successful. She believed Rasputin's methods could save her son's life. Some people thought that Rasputin gained influence with the royal family by hypnotizing Prince Alexei and Czarina Alexandra. A few nobles who feared him and his influence on the czarina decided to kill him. The assassination took several attempts, however, and legends still persist about the sorcerer priest who could not be killed.

Lesson 5 Review Answers

1. serfs 2. Alexander II 3. Baku
4. Japan 5. Sunday

Answers will vary. The czar controlled the lives of both Russian serfs and nobles. Both wanted more freedom.

ELL/ESL Strategy

Language Objective:
To plan for writing and speaking

Have students work in a small group and use multiple resources to get information about actions taken by czars Nicholas I, Alexander II, Alexander III, and Nicholas II of Russia. Students should use a graphic organizer to list the names, dates, and actions of the four czars. Then use that information to create an illustrated mindmap on mural paper. Point out that students should begin at the far left of paper and progress in time toward the right. Remind students to give the mindmap a title. Hang the mindmap on the wall for the class presentation.

Chapter 25: Lesson 6

Overview This lesson explains the growing spirit of rebellion in Russia, the disagreement among people about how to change the government, Russia's experience with World War I, and the abdication of the czar.

Objectives

■ To describe socialism

■ To explain why Nicholas II gave up his power

Student Pages pages 632–634

Teacher's Resource Library

Workbook Activity 116

Activity 116

Modified Activity 116

....

Vocabulary

abdicate   **socialism**

Have students work in pairs to study the definitions and then use the words correctly in three sentences.

....

1 Warm-Up Activity

Copy and display or distribute images of two posters from the Russian Revolution:

• Imperial Russia's social structure derided in an anonymous cartoon made in 1900

• The Tsar, the Priest, and the Rich Man on the shoulders of the Labouring People, 1918.

These images can be found on the Internet at www.agsglobewh.com/page632. Lead a class analysis and discussion of the messages sent by these posters.

Reading Strategy: Text Structure

(Guide students in answering the question asked by the heading in the first section.)

Lesson 6 — Russia Moves Toward Revolution

Objectives

◆ To describe socialism

◆ To explain why Nicholas II gave up his power

Reading Strategy: Text Structure

The section headings are written as questions. After you read each section, try to answer the question asked in the heading

After the Revolution of 1905, the spirit of rebellion continued to grow in Russia. But the revolutionaries could not agree on how change should happen. Some wanted to limit the czar's power and create a constitutional monarchy like Great Britain's. Others thought a completely new form of government was needed.

How Did World War I Affect Russia?

World War I was probably the single most important cause of the Russian Revolution of 1917. Millions of Russians were killed, wounded, or taken prisoner. The people had to live with little food, fuel, and other needed supplies. They became very angry at Czar Nicholas.

Women marched on St. Petersburg in 1917 demanding bread. This forced Czar Nicholas II to step down as ruler of Russia.

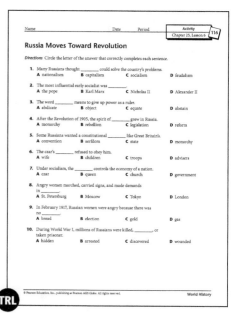

The Russian Orthodox Church

Byzantine missionaries took Christianity to Russia in the 900s. By the 1400s, the Russian Orthodox Church was self-governing. The patriarch, the head of the church, lived in Moscow. For centuries, Orthodox priests and monks had great influence. The church was central in the lives of many ordinary Russians. They kept icons in their homes. Some czars used the church to support their absolute rule.

The Russian Revolution was a disaster for the church. It lost power and property. Still, millions of people remained faithful. After the Soviet Union collapsed in 1991, Russia had a great religious revival. Some Russians have joined other churches. The Russian Orthodox Church, however, remains the most important.

Abdicate

To give up power as a ruler

Socialism

An economic and political theory in which the government owns and controls the major means of production

Why Did Czar Nicholas II Abdicate?

On the morning of February 24, 1917, news came that stores in St. Petersburg had no bread. Women became angry. "We want bread! We want bread!" they shouted. Soon a crowd formed. They carried banners, shouted, and sang. Some of their signs said "End the War" and "Down with the Czar."

His troops even refused to obey him. He had to **abdicate** as ruler. That is, he gave up his power. After the czar abdicated, no one was sure who would govern Russia. Many Russians thought **socialism** would solve the country's problems. Socialism is an economic and political theory in which the government owns and controls the major means of production

What Do Socialists Want?

Under socialism, the government controls the economy of a nation. Representing the people, the government owns all the land, industries, and transportation. The most influential of all the early socialists was a German named Karl Marx.

Have students discuss what prevents the United States from having an official religion. (students should mention that religion is separate from government) Then have students read the Then and Now feature to find out the connection between the Russian Orthodox Church and some of the czars.

 Teaching the Lesson

Ask students to explain why Russian people marched on the palace of the czar on Bloody Sunday. Then have them read pages 632–634 to find out how Russians were able to overthrow the czar.

Ask:

- What made the Russian people angry during World War I? (answers will vary; students may say that many were killed and injured and that soldiers didn't have the right equipment to fight)

- Why were people in St. Petersburg upset on February 24, 1917? (there was no bread in the stores)

- What action caused the czar to resign? (his troops would not obey him)

 Reinforce and Extend

ELL/ESL STRATEGY

Language Objective: *To summarize major ideas*

Have students work in small groups to get information about demonstrations in the years leading up to the Russian Revolution. One example is the women's march for bread. Each group should create three banners or placards containing protest signs for a chosen demonstration. The group should then identify a protest movement in American history or current events and create three protest banners or placards that could be used in a demonstration for that movement. Have a class discussion about the similarities and differences between the signs for the two movements chosen by each group.

Lesson 6 Review Answers

1. C **2.** B **3.** A **4.** D **5.** A

Answers will vary. Perhaps the soldiers had families that had suffered under the czar. Or perhaps the soldiers balked at fighting the Russian people.

Lesson 6 Review On a sheet of paper, write the letter of the answer that correctly completes each sentence.

1. Under _____, a government owns all the land, the industries, and the means of transportation.

  A democracy   **C** socialism

  B monarchy   **D** constitutional monarchy

2. _____ was a German who influenced the Russian Revolution.

  A Czar Nicholas II   **C** Alexander II

  B Karl Marx   **D** Rasputin

3. Probably the single most important cause of the Russian Revolution was _____.

  A World War I   **C** a provisional government

  B Bloody Sunday   **D** the Duma

4. During World War I, conditions in Russia got worse because _____.

  A factories could not produce bullets and guns

  B food was scarce

  C millions of soldiers died or were wounded

  D all of the above

5. In 1917, the Russians forced _____ to abdicate.

  A Czar Nicholas II   **C** Alexander II

  B Karl Marx   **D** Rasputin

What do you think

Why do you think the czar's soldiers joined the workers who were rebelling on February 25, 1917?

The Next War

This picture, titled "Shadows," shows the bleakness of World War I.

In August 1914, European nations plunged into the Great War. World War I ended four years later. It had destroyed millions of lives. Many soldiers had gone to war with grand ideas of honor and glory. The reality was different. War was wet trenches, poison gas, and artillery fire. Soldiers saw lives being wasted. Their views quickly changed. This change is clear in the poetry written during the war. Early poems are often about heroism. Later poems show shock and anger.

Britain had many fine soldier-poets. One was Siegfried Sassoon. He wrote bitterly, "when it was all said and done, the war was mainly a matter of holes and ditches." The poem that follows is by Wilfred Owen, a young British officer. He was killed a week before the war ended.

War's a joke for me and you,

While we know such dreams are true. Out there, we've walked quite friendly up to Death;

Sat down and eaten with him, cool and bland,
Pardoned his spilling mess-tins in our hand.
We've sniffed the green thick odour of his breath,
Our eyes wept, but our courage didn't writhe.
He's spat at us with bullets and he's coughed
Shrapnel. We chorused when he sang aloft;
We whistled while he shaved us with his scythe.
Oh, Death was never enemy of ours!
We laughed at him, we leagued with him, old chum.
No soldier's paid to kick against his powers.
We laughed, knowing that better men would come,
And greater wars; when each proud fighter brags
He wars on Death for lives; not men for flags.

Document-Based Reading Questions

1. How have the soldiers in this poem become friendly with Death?

2. What weapons has Death used against the soldiers?

3. Death is often pictured with a scythe, a long blade used for cutting grass. How does Owen use that image?

4. Many soldiers could not talk about the war. Would civilians think of death like Owen did in this poem?

5. Owen says that a proud fighter, "Wars on Death for lives; not men for flags." What does he mean?

Read the title, "The Next War," and the two introductory paragraphs to students. Then have them read the poem and jot down any words or phrases that they do not understand. When students finish, clarify meanings of words and phrases.

Ask:

• Did the poet really think that war was a joke? How do you know? (no; answers will vary—students may say the poet said that death was always close)

Have students reread the poem and answer the questions below.

Answers to Document-Based Questions:

1. They have walked up to and eaten with Death.

2. Death has used poison gas ("green thick odour"), bullets, and shrapnel.

3. Answers will vary. Death came so close that it was like getting a shave as in the expression, "That was a close shave."

4. Answers will vary. Civilians would probably be very frightened of Death.

5. He means that a proud fighter doesn't fight to capture flags (which are symbols of victory), but to preserve lives from Death.

LEARNING STYLES

Auditory/Verbal
Explain to students that poetry is often read aloud to groups of people. Have students listen to the recording of the poem. Give them an opportunity to record and listen to their own reading of the poem.

Spotlight
Story

Explain to students that they are about to read an account of the assassination that started World War I. Tell students that the political alliances were already in place, and the assassinations were enough to set countries against each other in war. Then have students silently read "Death at Sarajevo." When students are finished, ask volunteers to recite the chain of events in the reading that led to World War I. Give classmates the opportunity to disagree with the order of events and explain their reasons. Write the links in the chain of events on the board as volunteers name them. Then have students read and answer the Wrap-Up questions.

Answers to Spotlight Story Wrap-Up:

1. He was the archduke of Austria, heir to the throne of the Austro-Hungarian Empire.

2. They were Slavs. Bosnia had become independent, but the Austro-Hungarian Empire took it over. Some Bosnians wanted unity with Serbia.

3. It was a Serbian secret society.

4. A Bosnian Serb nationalist named Gavrilo Princip killed them. He was sentenced to 20 years in prison.

5. The Austrians and then the Serbians called on their allies for help, and both sides got ready for war. It triggered World War I.

Spotlight
Story

Death at Sarajevo

June 28, 1914, was a hot Sunday in Sarajevo. Despite the heat, crowds of people filled the streets. They were waiting for Archduke Franz Ferdinand and his wife, Sophie. People were curious to see the archduke. He would be the next emperor of Austria-Hungary. His visit was supposed to improve Austria's image.

Sarajevo was the capital of Bosnia, a small Balkan state. Bosnia's people were Slavs. They had become independent of the Ottoman Empire less than 40 years earlier. Then the Austro-Hungarian Empire had taken control of the area. Many Bosnians hated Austrian rule. They wanted to be part of nearby Serbia, a Slav state. Some joined a secret society known as the Black Hand. Its slogan was "Union or Death."

That June morning, the archduke and duchess rode to the town hall in an open car. With them was the military governor of Bosnia. No one realized that several Black Hand members were waiting along the route. Suddenly a man stepped forward and threw a bomb. It exploded in the street and wounded officers in the next car. The official party went on with the scheduled program. At its end, the archduke decided to visit a wounded officer in the hospital. The duke had his driver stop while he gave him new directions.

Standing only a few feet away was 19-year-old Gavrilo Princip. He was one of the Black Hand members in the plot. Princip pulled out a small gun and fired twice. The first shot struck the Duchess Sophie. She died instantly. The second bullet struck Franz Ferdinand near the heart. He uttered a few last words, then his head fell back. He died a few minutes later.

Police seized Princip, kicking and beating him. They took him to jail. Next, the Austrians arrested every known revolutionary in Sarajevo. Because he was young, Princip was sentenced to only 20 years in jail. That was the maximum sentence.

The sudden, brutal murders shocked the world. Austrian officials blamed Serbia. They were determined to punish Serbia. Austria called on its ally, Germany, for help. Then Austria declared war on Serbia. Serbia asked its ally, Russia, to come to its aid. Within a few days, Russia and Germany had declared war. Soon most of Europe was involved. Members of both European alliances immediately got ready for war. The shots in Sarajevo triggered World War I.

Wrap-Up

1. Who was Franz Ferdinand?

2. Why did many people in Sarajevo dislike Austrian rule?

3. What was the Black Hand?

4. Who killed the archduke and duchess? How was he punished?

5. What were the effects of the shootings at Sarajevo?

Chapter 25 SUMMARY

- In the late 1800s, powerful European nations competed for both land and military power. They formed alliances to aid each other in case of war. Germany, Austria-Hungary, and Italy made up the Triple Alliance. Great Britain, France, and Russia were the Triple Entente.

- A Serbian nationalist killed Austrian Archduke Franz Ferdinand and his wife in June 1914. This act triggered World War I. The alliance system brought the major European nations into the war.

- The nations in World War I divided into the Central Powers (Austria-Hungary, Germany, Bulgaria, and Turkey) and the Allied Powers (France, Russia, Britain, Italy, and smaller nations). Japan and the United States later joined the Allies.

- World War I relied on trench warfare. New weapons were also used: airplanes, submarines, machine guns, poison gas, and tanks.

- The United States was neutral until April 1917, when Germany declared unrestricted war on shipping. The United States joined the Allies. In November 1918, Germany agreed to an armistice.

- The "Big Four"—Britain, France, Italy, and the United States—shaped the peace treaty. Each nation had different goals.

- The Treaty of Versailles gave Germany's colonies to France, Britain, and Japan. Germany had to give land back to France and pay the costs of war. The treaty broke up the Austro-Hungarian Empire.

- In the 1800s, Russia was an autocracy. The czar was an absolute ruler. More than 80 percent of Russians were serfs.

- In the mid-1800s, Czar Alexander II freed the serfs, reformed education, and gave people more rights. Revolutionaries killed him. His son Nicholas II ignored calls for reform.

- The Industrial Revolution reached Russia in the late 1800s. The standard of living for factory workers improved, but most people remained poor.

- In 1894, Nicholas II became czar. He declared war on Japan in 1904. Russia lost.

- In 1905, workers held a peaceful march in St. Petersburg. Soldiers killed hundreds on that "Bloody Sunday."

- Many Russians wanted socialism, a system in which the government runs a nation's economy.

- World War I made things worse for the Russians. In 1917, a revolution forced Nicholas II to resign. Leaders of the Duma formed a government.

1905 – 1919 *World War I and the Russian Revolution* Chapter 25 **637**

Using the Chapter Summary

Have students read the Chapter Summary on page 637 to review the main ideas presented in Chapter 25.

Ask:

- How many great alliances was Europe divided into during World War I? (two)

- What were the alliances originally designed to do? (prevent wars)

- What kind of fighting took place along the western front? (trench warfare)

- Which army on the eastern front retreated? (the Russian army)

- What new weapons were used during World War I? (airplanes, submarines, automatic machine guns, poison gas, and tanks)

- Who entered the war in 1917 on the side of the Allies? (the United States)

- What did the Treaty of Versailles force Germany to do? (accept full responsibility for causing the war; pay reparations; give up its colonies in Africa; give other territories in Europe to other European countries)

TEACHER'S RESOURCE

The AGS Globe Teaching Strategies in Social Studies Transparencies may be used with this chapter. The transparencies add an interactive dimension to expand and enhance the *World History* program content.

Chapter 25 Review

Use the Chapter Review to prepare students for tests and to reteach content from the chapter.

Chapter 25 Mastery Test **TRL**

The Teacher's Resource Library includes two forms of the Chapter 25 Mastery Test. Each test addresses the chapter Goals for Learning. An optional third page of additional critical-thinking items is included for each test. The difficulty level of the two forms is equivalent.

Chapter 25 Review Answers

1. alliance
2. neutral
3. Russia
4. U-boat
5. armistice
6. Italy
7. bankrupt
8. reparations
9. Alexander II
10. Nicholas II
11. D
12. D
13. A
14. B
15. C
16. Nationalism, imperialism, militarism, and the alliances in Europe caused World War I. The assassination of the Austrian emperor's nephew, Ferdinand, and his wife sparked the war.
17. The Treaty of Versailles forced Germany to do the following:
   • Return Alsace and Lorraine to France.
   • Divide its African colonies between France and Great Britain.
   • Give its colonies in the Pacific to Japan.
   • Accept full responsibility for causing the war.
   • Repay the Allies for most of the cost of the war.

Chapter 25 R E V I E W

Word Bank

Alexander II
alliance
armistice
bankrupt
Italy
neutral
Nicholas II
reparations
Russia
U-boat

On a sheet of paper, use the words from the Word Bank to complete each sentence correctly.

1. Before the war, many countries made a(n) _____ with one another and agreed to help one another.

2. Belgium was a(n) _____ country during the war because it chose neither side.

3. The Treaty of Brest Litovsk ended the war for _____.

4. The Germans used the _____, a type of submarine, to destroy Allied ships.

5. On November 11, 1918, Germany agreed to a(n) _____, or an end to the fighting.

6. After World War I ended, the "Big Four" nations—Britain, France, _____, and the United States—met to create a peace treaty.

7. As a result of the war, all the major European countries were _____ and had no money to pay their debts.

8. At Versailles, France demanded that Germany make _____, or payments for war debts.

9. Czar _____ introduced change into Russia and gave his people some freedom.

10. "Bloody Sunday" took place during the rule of Czar _____.

On a sheet of paper, write the letter of the answer that correctly completes each sentence.

11. _____ fought as part of the Central Powers in World War I.

  A Japan   **C** the United States
  B France   **D** Germany

12. During World War I, the industrial nations developed _____.

  A tanks   **C** machine guns
  B poison gas   **D** all of the above

Chapter 25 Mastery Test A, pages 1–3

13. _____ represented France at the Versailles peace meeting.

A Clemenceau   **C** George

B Wilson   **D** Ferdinand

14. _____ represented Britain at the peace meeting.

A Orlando   **C** Wilson

B George   **D** Clemenceau

15. Under the czars, Russia was a(n) _____.

A democracy   **C** autocracy

B constitutional monarchy   **D** duma

On a sheet of paper, write the answer to each question.
Use complete sentences.

16. What were the causes of World War I?

17. What were three terms of the Treaty of Versailles?

18. Why did the Russians revolt against Czar Nicholas II?

Critical Thinking On a sheet of paper, write your response to
each question. Use complete sentences.

19. If you had been a German in 1919, how would you have
felt about the Treaty of Versailles?

20. Do you think having a large and powerful military causes
or prevents war? Explain your answer.

> For multiple-choice or word bank questions, cross off answers
> you know are wrong. Then choose the correct answer from the
> remaining choices.

It also broke up the Austro-Hungarian Empire. Austria and Hungary became two countries. The treaty created two new countries, Yugoslavia and Czechoslovakia. Some Austro-Hungarian land went to Poland, Italy, and Romania. The treaty carved Finland, Estonia, Latvia, and Lithuania out of the western part of the old Russian Empire. Finally, the treaty created the League of Nations.

18. The Russians revolted against Czar Nicholas II because they had little food, fuel, or other supplies.

Critical Thinking

19. Answers will vary. Most Germans probably hated the treaty. They had been at war and known deprivation. Now they had no money to start new businesses or buy food or have any of the niceties of life. Their standard of living was going to plunge downward.

20. Answers will vary. Some people say that weapons deter war. Others say that having weapons makes the military want to use them. Also, having weapons can make a nation feel tough. This might lead to an unwillingness to negotiate.

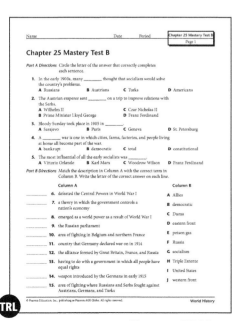

Chapter 25 Mastery Test B, pages 1–3

26 Nationalism, Revolution, and Totalitarianism Around the World

In this chapter, you will learn about the results of the Russian Revolution. You will witness the creation of Communism and the Soviet Union. You will also learn how nationalism and hard economic times led to the rise of dictators, including the Nazis in Germany. You will see how these changes affected Europe and Asia and set the stage for World War II.

Goals for Learning

◆ To explain how Russia became the Soviet Union

◆ To describe life in the Soviet Union under Stalin

◆ To explain why dictators came to power in Italy

◆ To explain how the Nazis gained power in Germany

◆ To describe how the Chinese began to build a modern nation after the overthrow of the government in 1911

◆ To explain how military leaders took over the government of Japan

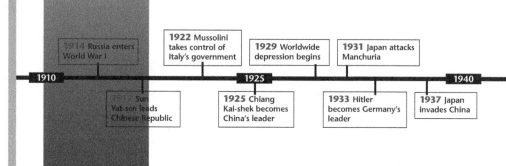

1914 Russia enters World War I

1922 Mussolini takes control of Italy's government

1929 Worldwide depression begins

1931 Japan attacks Manchuria

1910

1925

1940

1911 Sun Yat-sen leads Chinese Republic

1925 Chiang Kai-shek becomes China's leader

1933 Hitler becomes Germany's leader

1937 Japan invades China

Introducing the Chapter

During the first part of the 20th century, governments in many countries went through dramatic changes. Communist, fascist, and nationalist movements gained power. Leaders such as Stalin, Mussolini, Hitler, and Chiang Kai-shek rose to power as despairing people turned to them for relief from economic difficulties.

Ask:

• Who was the leader of the Chinese Republic in 1917? (Sun Yat-sen)

• Who took control of Italy's government in 1922? (Mussolini)

• Who became China's leader in 1925? (Chiang Kai-shek)

• When did the Great Depression begin? (1929)

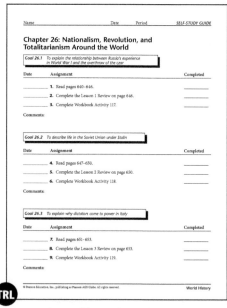

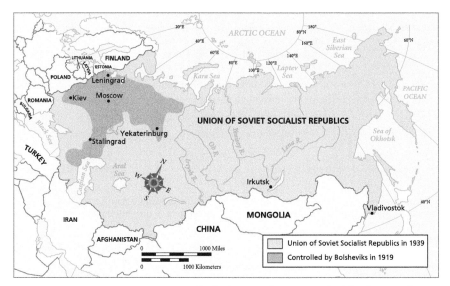

This chapter is about revolution and change in Russia. A group called the Bolsheviks led the revolution. This map shows the area that the Bolsheviks controlled in 1919. The map also shows the border of the Soviet Union in 1939. This was the new nation that formed as a result of this revolution.

Study the map, then answer the following questions:

1. What cities did the Bolsheviks control in 1919?

2. What seas are shown on this map?

3. What rivers are shown on this map?

4. What countries bordered the Soviet Union to the south?

5. What does this map tell you about the size of the Soviet Union in 1939?

Have a student read the title of the map, "The Development of the Soviet Union." Ask students to study the map and note which areas of land were part of the Soviet Union in 1939. Have students read the Map Skills paragraph independently.

Map Skills Answers

1. Moscow, Leningrad, Kiev, Stalingrad, Yekaterinburg

2. Black Sea, Kara Sea, Laptev Sea, East Siberian Sea, Sea of Okhotsk, Caspian Sea

3. Volga, Irtysh, Ob, Yenisey, Lena

4. Iran, Afghanistan, China, Mongolia

5. The map tells me that the Soviet Union in 1939 was much larger than the surrounding countries.

Chapter Project

In this chapter, students are introduced to several dictators who were leaders during the first part of the 20th century. Divide the class into groups of four to five students. Assign each group a historical leader, such as Lenin, Trotsky, Stalin, Mussolini, Hitler, or Chiang Kai-shek. Have groups use library resources and reliable Internet resources to learn about the lives of these men beyond what is in the text. Have each group prepare their research information for a five-minute lesson for the class. Encourage students to make their lessons engaging as well as informative.

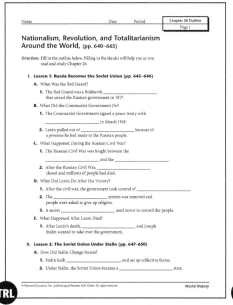

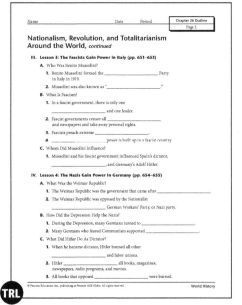

Visualizing

Introduce the reading strategy *visualizing*. Draw students' attention to the explanation of visualizing. Tell students that good readers use visualization, or creating a picture in their mind as they read, to help them understand what they are reading.

Explain that visualizing can also help them predict what might happen next in a text, and that as they visualize, they should also combine their own experiences with the information they are reading.

Ask students to read the first two paragraphs on page 643 and try to visualize what they read.

Ask:

• What did you see as you read the first paragraph? (Answers will vary. Students may say that they saw a group of people making plans against another person.)

• What did you visualize as you read the second paragraph? (Answers will vary. Students may say that they saw a man as a leader and spokesman for the group.)

Encourage students to pause in their reading and ask themselves, "What do I see?" as they read Chapter 26.

Key Vocabulary Words

Explain that the list of words here is a glossary of the Key Vocabulary they will read in Chapter 26. Call on volunteers to read aloud the words and their definitions.

Reading Strategy: Visualizing

When readers create pictures in their head about what they are reading, they are using visualization. This is another strategy that helps readers understand what they are reading. Use the following ways to visualize a text:

◆ Notice the order in which things are happening and what you think might happen next.

◆ Look at the photographs, illustrations, and descriptive words.

◆ Think about experiences in your own life that may add to the images.

Key Vocabulary Words

Lesson 1 —————
Bolshevik A revolutionary socialist group in Russia

Militia A group of people who can be called to military service when something dangerous happens suddenly

Communism An economic system in which there is little private property and the government produces goods

Minority A small group of like people within a larger group

Successor One who follows another in a position

Lesson 2 —————
Heavy industry The manufacturing of products, such as machines and raw materials, for use in other industries

Consumer goods Products that people buy

Collective farm A large farm owned by the government and worked by many peasants

Totalitarian state A government in which a small group totally controls the lives of its country's citizens

Purge To remove from office; to clean by getting rid of unwanted things

Lesson 3 —————
Veteran A person who has served in the military, especially during a war

Fascism A form of government in which a dictator and the dictator's party totally control a government

Lesson 4 —————
Inflation A quick increase in prices

Swastika The Nazi symbol of a cross with its arms bent

Depression A time of economic collapse when businesses lose money and many people become poor

Reichstag The national assembly of the Weimar Republic

Fuehrer The name given to Adolf Hitler meaning "leader"

Gestapo Hitler's secret police force

Lesson 6 —————
Great Depression The worldwide depression that began in the United States in 1929

Ask:

• What is Communism? (an economic system in which the government owns all property)

• What is a totalitarian state? (a government that has a small group of people who control everyone)

• Which word describes a person who has served in the military? (veteran)

• What name given to Adolf Hitler means "leader"? (Fuehrer)

• In what country did the Great Depression begin? (The United States)

OBJECTIVES

◆ To identify Lenin and the changes the Bolsheviks brought to Russia
◆ To describe the Russian Civil War
◆ To describe how Joseph Stalin came to power

Bolshevik

A revolutionary socialist group in Russia

Militia

A group of people who can be called to military service when something dangerous happens suddenly

Communism

An economic system in which there is little private property and the government produces goods

The **Bolsheviks** were a revolutionary socialist group. For many years, they plotted against the czar. Their party was small, but it was well organized.

A man who called himself Lenin led the Bolsheviks. He became a revolutionary when the czar's soldiers killed his brother. Many Russians liked his promise of "Peace, Land, and Bread." The Russian government arrested him and then exiled him. Lenin stayed away from Russia for 17 years.

What Was the Red Guard?

In the fall of 1917, the Bolsheviks took over the Russian government. They formed a **militia**—a group of people who can be called to military service very quickly when needed. This militia, called the Red Guard, seized the government by force on November 6 and 7. The Red Guard then arrested the leaders of the provisional government.

This change in government was almost bloodless. The Bolsheviks moved quickly to establish control. They gave their party a new name— the Communist Party. Lenin became its leader. This party believed in **Communism.** Communism is an economic system in which there is little private property and the government produces goods.

The Communist Party gave Russia a new name. It became the Union of Soviet Socialist Republics (U.S.S.R.), or the Soviet Union.

Lenin was the leader of the Communist Party, which took over the Russian government in 1917.

1911 – 1939   *Nationalism, Revolution, and Totalitarianism Around the World*   Chapter 26   **643**

Chapter 26: Lesson 1

Overview This lesson covers the Bolshevik takeover of the Russian government, the civil war that followed, and the changes Lenin made.

Objectives

■ To identify Vladimir Lenin and the changes the Bolsheviks brought to Russian government

■ To describe the Russian Civil War

■ To describe how Joseph Stalin came to power

Student Pages pages 643–646

Teacher's Resource Library

Workbook Activity 117

Activity 117

Modified Activity 117

Vocabulary

Bolshevik   minority
Communism   successor
militia

Have students study the words and write sentences including those words. Students should then work with a partner and read each other's papers to confirm word usage or suggest changes to make the usage correct. Give volunteers an opportunity to write sentences on the board for classmates' approval or correction.

1 **Warm-Up Activity**

Have students share what they have learned or heard about the Communist form of government. Make a list of their ideas on the board. Make corrections to students' ideas as necessary. Explain that in this lesson, students will be reading about how Communism started in Russia.

Ask:

● When did the Bolsheviks take over the government? (fall of 1917)

● What did the Bolsheviks name their new party? (the Communist Party)

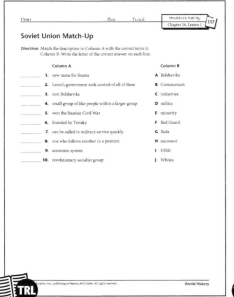

Workbook Activity 117

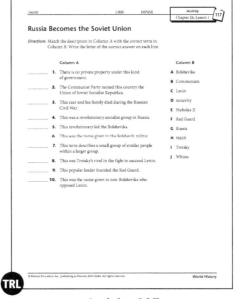

Activity 117

② Teaching the Lesson

As students read the lesson, have them make a list of reasons why the Russian people might have liked Lenin as a leader. This may help students understand why Lenin was able to gain so much control.

BACKGROUND INFORMATION

From 1917 to 1998, no one knew for sure what had become of Czar Nicholas II and his family. Rumors that one or more of his children had survived persisted for many years. Throughout the years, various individuals have claimed to be a surviving child of Nicholas II. Then, in 1998 the remains of what was thought to be the czar and his family were positively identified. Two living relatives of the deceased royal family gave DNA samples which positively identified the skeletal remains discovered in a shallow grave near the city of Yekaterinburg in 1991 as those of the Czar and his family. A formal reburial of the royal family took place on July 18, 1998 on what is believed to have been the 80th anniversary of their murder. The remains were interred in St. Petersburg's Saint Catherine Cathedral, where members of the Romanov dynasty have been interred since the time of Peter the Great.

Reading Strategy:
Visualizing

(Students may say that they visualize a map of the world with the "White" countries shown in white and the "Red" countries shown in red.)

Ask:

• Which groups made up the "White" army? (minorities)

• Who led the "Red" army to victory? (Lenin)

• How did the Russian government control people after the Civil War? (It created a dictatorship to control industry, society, government, and the economy, and used a secret police force to control the people.)

Minority
A small group of like people within a larger group

Reading Strategy:
Visualizing

How can visualizing help you remember which countries were "Whites" and which were "Reds"?

What Did the Communist Government Do?

Many Russians did not support the Communists. In the first free elections to choose an assembly, they received only one-third of the vote. The Communists simply closed the assembly after only one day. Lenin then kept his promise to the Russian people and pulled Russia out of World War I. The Communists signed a peace treaty with Germany in March 1918. Russia had to give up about a third of its European territory.

Some Russians opposed Lenin and the Communists. These non-Bolsheviks formed a "White" army. A number of national **minorities** in Russia supported the Whites. (A minority is a small group of like people within a larger group.) Countries like Great Britain, France, Japan, and the United States sent troops to fight the "Reds"—the Bolshevik army.

What Happened During the Russian Civil War?

The Whites and the Reds fought a civil war that lasted until 1920. Among those who died was Czar Nicholas II and his family. The Bolsheviks shot them because they did not want the White army to rescue the royal family.

The Reds finally defeated the Whites, but the civil war left Russia with many problems. Factories had closed and there was nothing to trade. Some of the millions who had died included the brightest and most skilled people in Russia.

What Did Lenin Do After His Victory?

After the Reds won the Russian Civil War, Lenin and the Communists changed Russia. The government took control of industry. They also divided land among the peasants. The government taxed extra grain. However, it allowed the peasants to sell their goods to make extra money. The Communists also removed Russia's class system and asked people to give up religion. They created a powerful dictatorship that controlled the government and the economy. Finally, they established a secret police that used terror to control the Russian people.

644 Unit 6 World Wars and Revolutions

• What promise did Lenin keep? (to take Russia out of the war)

• What happened to the czar and his family? (they were shot)

• Which side did the United States support during the Russian civil war? the peasants and workers? (the "Whites"; the "Reds")

• What change did the Communist government make in the ownership of factories? the ownership of land? (the Communists took over; the land was divided among the peasants)

STUDY SKILLS

Have students work with a partner to research and list visual resources available in the library or on the Internet about Russia or one of the other countries that were republics in the former USSR. They should write a brief description about each resource listed. Challenge students to make the description inviting. Their goal should be to entice others to check out the resource. Students should duplicate the lists and make them available to other students.

Writing About History

Choose one person from this chapter who was important in Russian history or culture. Research his or her life. Then write a short biography of that person in your notebook.

Many people starved during the Russian civil war. This picture shows barefoot and starving children during the war.

Successor

One who follows another in a position

What Happened After Lenin Died?

In 1922, Lenin became sick. Two Communist leaders began fighting to become his **successor**—the one who would take over the government.

Most people expected Leon Trotsky to become the new party leader. He had founded the Red Guard and had beaten the Whites in the civil war. He was a well-known, popular leader. He was also an excellent writer and speaker.

Trotsky's rival was Joseph Stalin. He was a quiet man and not well known, but he had a high-ranking position in the Communist Party. Stalin had used his power to appoint his followers to key positions in the government.

 3 Reinforce and Extend

Writing About History

Have students brainstorm a list of individuals mentioned in this chapter and why that person was included. (for example, Lenin, because he changed the form of government in Russia)

Ask:

• Which two men fought to lead the Communists after Lenin's death? Who won? (Trotsky and Stalin; Stalin)

WORLD CULTURES

The Cossacks were a group of men who organized themselves as a militia, or a military group for hire, beginning in the fourteenth century. The word *Cossack* is from the Turkish word that means "vagabond." Most of the Cossacks were escaped serfs who needed a means of support. The Cossacks were fiercely against the Red cause and were crushed by the Stalinist forces. Many were deported. As many as three million still live in Russia. Large numbers of Cossacks also live in other parts of Europe and in North America.

Ask students to imagine a country that is almost twice as large as the United States. Tell them that was the size of the Soviet Union. Explain that like the United States, the Soviet Union had many different geographical features. Ask students to read the History in Your Life feature "The World's Largest Country," listing as they do the different geographical features, such as mountains and rivers, in the Soviet Union. When students finish, have them share and compare their lists.

Lesson 1 Review Answers

1. Lenin **2.** Reds **3.** Whites
4. Trotsky **5.** Stalin

Answers will vary. The peasants were fighting World War I, so they wanted peace. The nobles owned most of the land, so the peasants wanted their own land. Things were so bad that food was scarce. Lenin's slogan named the needs of the Russian peasants.

ELL/ESL STRATEGY

Language Objective:
To summarize reading
Work with students on writing a summary of the text in Lesson 1. Using an overhead or a computer projection system, model how to summarize the introductory paragraph on page 643 in your own words. Use a think aloud to help students understand why you are writing specific facts. Point out the most important information from the section and model how to include it in the summary. Give examples of text that should not be included in the summary because they are not the most important text. Repeat this process with each section of Lesson 1. Have students copy the summary you make onto their own paper. As you work through the process, encourage students to help you decide which facts should be included in the summary.

The World's Largest Country

Russia is the largest country in the world. It sprawls across northern Europe and Asia. Russia has about 6,600,000 square miles of land. It is almost twice as large as China or the United States. The Volga is the longest river in Europe. It flows near Moscow into the Caspian Sea.

Steppes, or grasslands, cover much of western and central Russia. They run from Ukraine across Russia into Kazakhstan.

Summers are short and hot. Winters are long and snowy. A low mountain range, the Urals, separates the steppes from Siberia.

Siberia is the Asian part of Russia. It stretches east to the Pacific Ocean. Northern Siberia has a subarctic climate—the ground is partly frozen all year. Huge, thick forests cover other areas. Siberia has about three-quarters of Russia's mineral wealth.

Word Bank
Lenin
Reds
Stalin
Trotsky
Whites

Lesson 1 Review On a sheet of paper, use the words from the Word Bank to complete each sentence correctly.

1. The formerly exiled leader of the Bolsheviks was _____.

2. The Bolsheviks came to be called the _____.

3. The people who opposed the Bolsheviks became known as the _____.

4. The founder of the Red Guard was _____.

5. _____ became leader of the Soviet Union after Lenin's death.

What do you think ❓

Why was Lenin smart to promise "Peace, Land, and Bread" to the Russian people?

Objectives

◆ To describe the ways Joseph Stalin changed Russia

◆ To describe a totalitarian state

When Lenin died in 1924, two leaders—Leon Trotsky and Joseph Stalin—fought to become Lenin's successor. They both wanted to be the one who would follow Lenin and take over the government.

How Did Stalin Change Russia?

Finally, in 1927, Joseph Stalin won the support of party members. Stalin wanted to industrialize Russia. He set up a series of Five-Year Plans. Stalin built **heavy industry**—factories that make basic products like steel or machines for use in other industries. The government gave a lot of money to heavy industry, but there was little money to produce **consumer goods.** These goods that people buy, like clothing and shoes, became scarce in Russia.

Heavy industry

The manufacturing of products, such as machines and raw materials, for use in other industries

Consumer goods

Products that people buy

Collective farm

A large farm owned by the government and worked by many peasants

Stalin also set up **collective farms.** He believed that fewer workers could produce more food on these large farms. Each farm was owned by the government and worked by many peasants. The peasants had to sell their crops at fixed prices. The government paid the workers according to the amount of

Reading Strategy:
Visualizing

What words in this paragraph help you visualize what you are reading?

work they had done. Most peasants hated these collective farms. Some burned grain and killed farm animals. Stalin sent these people to Siberia. He ordered the death of thousands of farmers and their families. Historians believe that between 5 and 10 million peasants died.

Joseph Stalin ruled the Soviet Union harshly. He turned his country into an industrialized nation, but he used cruel methods to do it.

Overview This lesson explains what life was like for the people of Russia under Stalin's rule.

Objectives

■ To describe the ways Joseph Stalin changed Russia

■ To describe a totalitarian state

Student Pages pages 647–650

Teacher's Resource Library 🆃🆁🅻

Workbook Activity 118

Activity 118

Modified Activity 118

Vocabulary

collective farm   purge
consumer goods   totalitarian state
heavy industry

Have students work with a partner to study the definitions. Then have them make a three-column chart with words in the first column, definitions in the second, and clues to the words in the third. Have partners form a team and try to stump another two-person team. One team will put their paper face down and wait for the other team to give them a clue. If they can identify the word and define it, they get a point. Teams should alternate. The first pair to identify and define all the words correctly wins.

1 Warm-Up Activity

Pose this problem to students: Suddenly the materials to make new clothing have become scarce. As a result, clothing racks in stores are empty. People still need clothes. What can people do to solve this problem? Have students work in small groups to come up with realistic solutions to the problem. Have each group share their solutions with the class.

Reading Strategy:
Visualizing

(Students may say that the words *peasants, large farms, burned grain, killed farm animals, thousands of farmers,* help them visualize the text.)

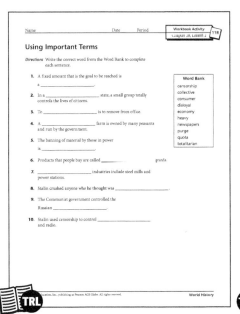

Workbook Activity 118   **Activity 118**

2 Teaching the Lesson

As students read the section of text on collective farms, have them create a word web using the term *collective farms* in a circle in the center of the web. Have students write facts about collective farms on lines that radiate from the center circle.

Ask:

- What did the Russian factories produce instead of shoes and clothes? (answers may vary; students may say steel or products factories used)

- Who decided how much peasants working on collective farms were paid? (the government)

- How many peasants did Stalin execute? (5 to 10 million)

- What did Stalin encourage children to do? (report their parents if they were disloyal to the government)

- What services did people get during the Stalin era? (answers will vary; students may mention health care or education)

CAREER CONNECTION

Every government, whether a totalitarian state or a democracy, has a need for correctional institutions—places to incarcerate some people who violate the law. In the United States, corrections officers are needed for prisons at the federal, state, and local level. Students who might be interested in corrections work can search the Internet or contact their state's civil service department to find out what a person needs to do to become a corrections officer.

Totalitarian state

A government in which a small group totally controls the lives of its country's citizens

Purge

To remove from office; to clean by getting rid of unwanted things

Stalin's "Great Purge" caused great suffering among the Russian people. Historians believe millions died from Stalin's plan to rid his enemies.

Stalin made the Soviet Union a **totalitarian state.** A totalitarian state is a government in which a small group controls the lives of its country's citizens. That is, people have no rights. Under Stalin, everyone in the Soviet Union lived in fear. People who spoke out against the government were sometimes never seen again. Stalin encouraged children to report their parents if they did or said anything disloyal. His secret police watched everyone. Stalin even **purged,** or removed from office, thousands of members of the Communist Party.

Stalin died in 1953. As a ruler, he had changed the Soviet Union—some for the good, but mostly for the bad. Millions of Russians suffered and died. Living conditions remained poor. The government completely controlled the lives of the people

But the Soviet Union became a powerful industrialized nation with improved health care and education.

LEARNING STYLES

Interpersonal/ Group Learning

On slips of paper, print the warning, "You are being watched. Be careful!" Give these to all but four students. Slips of paper for the remaining four students will read "You are a spy. Turn in anyone who criticizes Russia." Fold slips so that no one can see what is on them. At the beginning of a class period, remind students that

people living in Russia during Stalin's rule were always afraid that they were being spied upon. Tell students that today they are going be spied upon, or be spies. Distribute the folded slips of paper. Then continue with class as usual. Allow time before class ends for spies to report and for students to discuss how they felt not knowing who might be spying on them.

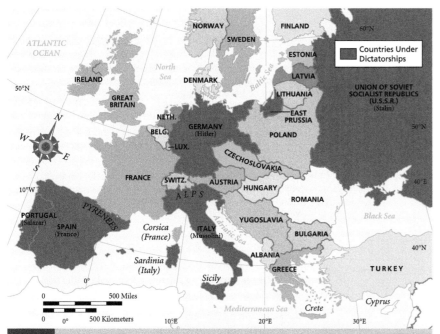

Map Study

This map shows what Europe looked like at the end of 1938. It also shows the countries under the control of a dictator. What were the names of five European dictators? Which dictator controlled the most land? In case of war, why would Britain be more difficult to conquer than France?

Countries Under Dictatorships

Have a volunteer read the title of the map and have students study the map with a partner. Then have students read the caption and answer the questions. (Salazar in Portugal, Franco in Spain, Mussolini in Italy, Stalin in the Soviet Union, Hitler in Germany) (Stalin in the USSR) (Great Britain is more isolated because it is surrounded by water.)

Ask:

- Which country was most vulnerable to attack from a country with a dictator? (France)
- Which country with a dictator shared a border with Romania? (Soviet Union)

3 **Reinforce and Extend**

ONLINE CONNECTION

After World War I ended in 1918, many events occurred in Europe that led to the beginning of World War II in 1939. View a timeline of events that led to the war and read about the people who influenced the war at www.agsglobewh.com/page649a.

Find out more about the historical facts, figures, and people of the year 1938, by following the links at www.agsglobewh.com/page649b.

Have a volunteer read the title of this feature: "Dictators."

Ask:

- What is it like to live under the rule of a dictator? (answers will vary; students may say that you could not criticize the government or that you might be afraid of the secret police)

Have students read "Dictators" independently to find out where some dictators have ruled and where some dictators have been overthrown by the people.

Lesson 2 Review Answers

1. heavy industry 2. collective farms
3. totalitarian 4. rights 5. Siberia

Answers will vary. They probably felt betrayed by Stalin. They wanted consumer goods to make their lives easier, but Stalin used heavy industry to produce things that other factories could use to produce equipment, weapons, and other big items. The people wanted bread, food, clothes, and homes. These things would make them feel as if their standard of living was higher.

Dictators

Throughout history, powerful leaders have taken power by force. They have absolute power and do not allow opposition. Their word is law. In the early 1800s, Napoleon Bonaparte conquered much of Europe. Napoleon began as an enemy of monarchy, but then he became a dictator. Also in the 1800s, most of Latin America won its independence from Spain. Since then, dictators called "caudillos" have often ruled these countries.

In the 1930s, Franco won the civil war in Spain and became its dictator. Two other dictators—Mussolini in Italy and Hitler in Germany—took the world to war.

In recent years, people have overthrown dictators in the Philippines and Indonesia. Yet dictators keep coming to power. Unfortunately, dictators still rule smaller nations around the world today.

Word Bank
collective farms
heavy industry
rights
Siberia
totalitarian

Lesson 2 Review On a sheet of paper, use the words from the Word Bank to complete each sentence correctly.

1. Stalin stressed _____, factories that make industrial products such as machines.

2. Stalin forced farmers to work on _____ owned by the government.

3. Under Stalin, the Soviet Union became a _____ state.

4. Under totalitarianism, people had no _____.

5. Peasants who disagreed with Stalin were sent to _____.

What do you think

How might the Russian people have felt when their factories produced only a few consumer goods?

ELL/ESL STRATEGY

Language Objective: *To learn content-area vocabulary*

Have students create a word wall using the vocabulary words for this lesson. On a wall or bulletin board, display the vocabulary words and Word Bank words for Lesson 2 (*collective farm, consumer goods, heavy industry, purge, totalitarian state, rights, Siberia*). Provide pictures that represent each word. Pictures might be taken from magazines, copied from books, or printed from the Internet. Choose one word and read it aloud. Give a definition for it in your own words and write the definition on an index card. Think aloud about which picture best shows the word. Find the picture and pin or tape the picture and the definition next to the word on the word wall. Have volunteers repeat the activity with the other words. Display the words, pictures, and students' definitions on the word wall.

- To identify Benito Mussolini
- To describe fascism and its influence on others

Veteran

A person who has served in the military, especially during a war

Reading Strategy: Visualizing

Create a graphic organizer to help you remember some things about fascism.

During World War I, Italy fought on the side of the Allies. The Italians wanted to win territory from Germany and Austria-Hungary. After the war, the Treaty of Versailles disappointed them. They wanted more land than the treaty gave them.

World War I also brought economic and political problems to Italy. The war left the country in debt. Many people lost their jobs. Many political parties arose, and the government was weak.

Who Was Benito Mussolini?

Many Italians blamed the democratic government for all of their nation's problems. Some feared a Communist revolution in Italy like the one in Russia. Benito Mussolini used this deep fear of Communism and revolution to win power. Most of his followers were **veterans.** That is, they had fought for Italy in World War I. They became known as "Black Shirts." In 1919, Mussolini formed the Fascist Party. It opposed both Communism and democracy. Mussolini promised to make Italy as great as the ancient Roman Empire. In 1922, he became the dictator of Italy. His followers called him "Il Duce," or "the leader."

Mussolini became dictator of Italy in 1922. He was known as "Il Duce," which means "the leader."

Chapter 26: Lesson 3

Overview This lesson tells how Mussolini became the fascist dictator of Italy and about the conditions that made it possible for him to come to power.

Objectives

- To identify Benito Mussolini
- To describe fascism and its influence on others

Student Pages pages 651–653

Teacher's Resource Library TRL

Workbook Activity 119

Activity 119

Modified Activity 119

Vocabulary

fascism **veteran**

Have students work with a partner to write definitions in their own words for each vocabulary word. Each definition should appear on its own index card. Have partners exchange cards with another pair of students and then write the vocabulary word that matches each definition on the reverse side of the card.

1 Warm-Up Activity

As a class, have students name political leaders of today. Write this list on the board. Then in small groups, have students talk about and make a list of some of the promises politicians commonly make today to gain the support of the people. Have each group share its list with the class.

Ask:

- Why were Italians disappointed with the Treaty of Versailles? (they wanted more land)
- What did Mussolini's fascists oppose? (democracy and Communism)

---

2 ▶ Teaching the Lesson

As students read the lesson, have them make a list of the things Mussolini promised to the people of Italy. Tell students that they should keep their lists to use when studying for the chapter test.

Reading Strategy:
Visualizing

(Students might create a chart with rows and columns for listing facts about fascism, or they might create a web with *fascism* in the middle and facts around the center.)

BACKGROUND INFORMATION

 Remind students that nationalism is a force that unites the people of a nation, especially when the nation is threatened, such as in times of war. Tell students that Hitler's brand of nationalism excluded groups of people, including Jews and gypsies, who were citizens of Germany. Explain that these groups were among those later sent to concentration camps.

Writing About History

Invite students to find sample newspaper articles to study before writing their own article.

Ask:

- How many political parties are allowed by fascist governments? (one)
- Which dictators followed in Mussolini's footsteps? (Franco of Spain and Hitler of Germany)
- How did Mussolini limit people's freedom? (answers will vary; students might say the people could not read what they wanted because books were censored)

Fascism

A form of government in which a dictator and the dictator's party totally control a government

Writing About History

Imagine that you are a foreign correspondent in the 1930s. In your journal, write a news story about one event mentioned in this chapter. Include details that tell who, what, where, when, why, and how.

What Is Fascism?

Fascism developed during the 20th century. This government system is a little different in each country, but they share the following:

1. They have only one party and one leader. All other political parties are banned.

2. All fascist governments demand obedience to the state and to its leader.

3. They take away individual rights and freedom. That is, the state takes away freedoms that belong to each person. The government censors all books and newspapers.

4. They preach extreme nationalism. They believe their country is the best and should be the strongest.

5. They build up military power. Fascists believe that military force wins land for their country and makes it great.

Whom Did Mussolini Influence?

Fascists from other countries admired Italy's fascist dictatorship and borrowed ideas from it. In Spain, a fascist named Francisco Franco set himself up as dictator. In Germany, Adolf Hitler carefully watched Mussolini. In a few years, Hitler would become the most feared fascist leader in the world.

---

3 ▶ Reinforce and Extend

ELL/ESL STRATEGY

Language Objective:
To discuss an assigned topic as a small group

After students have read about fascism, briefly review what it is and what it means to be a fascist. Review what life was like under the fascist government in Italy. Then divide the class into groups of 4 or 5 students. Ask students to discuss the benefits and drawbacks of this form of government. Encourage students to support their opinions with their own background knowledge. Tell students that each person in their group must have an opportunity to voice their opinions, and any disagreements should be expressed respectfully and calmly. As students talk, circulate among the groups and observe students' communication skills.

The League of Nations Fails

When World War I ended, world leaders met to discuss peace. U.S. President Woodrow Wilson wanted to create an organization to which every nation belonged. He thought this organization could prevent war. That is, it could keep wars from happening.

The Treaty of Versailles formed this organization—the League of Nations. The nations of the league promised to defend the territory and independence of all its members.

A test of the league's strength came in October 1935 when Italy attacked Ethiopia. Ethiopian Emperor Haile Selassie asked the league for help. It voted to force Italy to withdraw through economic means. That is, member nations refused to buy goods from Italy or to sell it war materials.

However, Great Britain and France did not want to upset Italy. They wanted Italy's support against Germany. Great Britain continued to allow Italy to send troops and supplies through the Suez Canal. Italy was then able to defeat Ethiopia.

In 1935, the league failed to stop Italy. It tried to make everyone happy. Instead, it made everyone mad. Ethiopia lost its independence and the league lost its best chance of preventing war through nations working together.

Lesson 3 Review On a sheet of paper, write the answer to each question. Use complete sentences.

1. What problems led to the rise of Mussolini in Italy?

2. Who supported the Fascist Party in Italy?

3. Who were the "Black Shirts"?

4. What are five ways in which most fascist governments are alike?

5. What are the names of two fascist leaders influenced by Mussolini?

Dictators often do terrible things. Why do you think people allow dictators to rule them?

The League of Nations Fails

Explain that the League of Nations was intended to keep peace in the world after World War I, just as the United Nations does in the world today. But the league had a weakness. Have students read this feature on page 653 to find out what caused the League of Nations to fail.

Ask:

- Where did the League of Nations fail to stop Mussolini? (in Ethiopia)

Lesson 3 Review Answers

1. Italy's problems were that it was in debt, many people had no jobs, and the government was weak. **2.** Industrialists, the members of the aristocracy, and the middle class supported the fascist party in Italy. **3.** The "Black Shirts" were veterans who were followers of Mussolini. **4.** Fascist governments are alike in the following five ways: 1. They have only one party and one leader; 2. They demand total obedience to the state and to its leader; 3. They take away individual rights and freedom; 4. They preach extreme nationalism; 5. They build up military power. **5.** Franco was the dictator in Spain. Hitler was Germany's dictator.

Answers will vary. People may feel desperate and think that a dictator is the only option. They may also fear to say or do anything against such a cruel leader. They may also have no power to change the system because a dictator has complete control. Some people may even like being ruled by a cruel dictator.

LEARNING STYLES

Body/Kinesthetic
Have students work in small groups to make a model that illustrates the fascist system of government. The chief item on the model should be the title "Fascism." Following this would be the five common characteristics of a fascist government, as described on page 651. Students may wish to make a mobile, a train, or some other representative piece. Ask students to explain their models to the class.

Chapter 26: Lesson 4

Overview This lesson tells about the Nazi Party's rise to power in Germany and the nation they created.

Objectives

- To describe the conditions that allowed the Nazis to gain control
- To describe Hitler's rise to power

Student Pages pages 654–655

Teacher's Resource Library TRL

Workbook Activity 120

Activity 120

Modified Activity 120

Vocabulary

depression	Nazi
Fuehrer	Reichstag
Gestapo	swastika
inflation	

The vocabulary terms in this lesson all have more than one syllable. Write each syllable of each word on a card. Mix the cards and display them randomly on a board ledge or bulletin board. Read a definition of one of the vocabulary terms and challenge a volunteer to piece the word defined together by placing the cards with its syllables in the proper order.

 Warm-Up Activity

Divide the class into pairs of students. Write the word *dictator* on the board. Have partners work together to make a list of what they agree a dictator does. Have students share their lists with the class. Discuss the common idea threads that run through the lists. Encourage students to add to or revise their lists as they read Lesson 4.

 Teaching the Lesson

As students read the lesson, have them create a timeline of Hitler's rise to power. Encourage students to use their timelines when studying for the chapter test.

Objectives

- To describe the conditions that allowed the Nazis to gain control
- To describe Hitler's rise to power

Inflation
A quick increase in prices

Swastika
The Nazi symbol of a cross with its arms bent

Depression
A time of economic collapse when businesses lose money and many people become poor

Reading Strategy: Visualizing

Look for clues in this lesson that help you visualize how Hitler came to power.

When German soldiers returned home after World War I, they found little work. Because the war had destroyed many factories, people had few goods to sell at home or to foreign markets. Prices went up quickly. This is called **inflation.**

What Was the Weimar Republic?

At the end of the war, the Allies forced Kaiser William II of Germany to step down. Then the German people set up a democratic government and wrote a constitution. They called their new government the Weimar Republic. However, the new government had problems. Some Germans blamed it for accepting the terms of the Treaty of Versailles.

One party that opposed the new government was the Nationalist Socialist German Workers' Party. It was called *Nazi* for short. The Nazis adopted a red flag with a black **swastika** as its symbol. A swastika is a cross with its arms bent. Adolf Hitler became the Nazi leader.

In 1923, Hitler tried to take control of the German government by force, but he failed. Then the leaders of the Weimar Republic arrested and jailed him. During his jail term, he wrote *Mein Kampf,* which means "My Struggle."

In his book, Hitler said that the German people were better than other people. He also said that everyone else was less important than the German people. Hitler came up with a plan to make Germany a powerful nation once again.

How Did the Depression Help the Nazis?

In 1929, a long drop in business activity—a **depression**—took place all over the world. By 1932, nearly 40 percent of the factory workers in Germany had no jobs. Many turned to Communism. But the middle class and the wealthy were tired of inflation; they feared the Communists. Many of them turned to Hitler because he opposed Communism. Soon the Nazis became the largest political party in Germany.

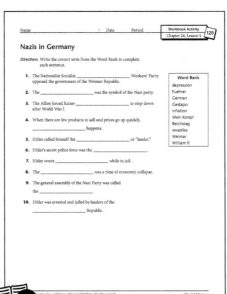

Workbook Activity 120

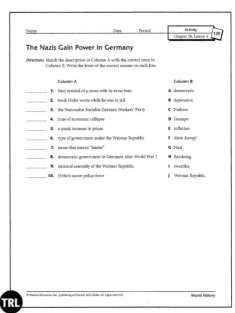

Activity 120

What Did Hitler Do As Dictator?

In 1933, Hitler became head of the German government. Then he called for an election. (The Nazi Party still did not have a majority in the German assembly, or **Reichstag.** Hitler needed a majority to become really powerful.)

Just before the election, someone set the Reichstag building on fire. No one knows who started the fire, but Hitler blamed the Communists. In the election, many German people, fearing revolution, voted for the Nazis. The Nazis did not win the election, but Hitler later took control of the Reichstag.

Next, Hitler made himself dictator. He called himself the **Fuehrer,** which means "leader." As dictator, Hitler did the following:

1. Banned all other political parties and all labor unions.

2. Made all army officers promise to obey his orders.

3. Censored all books, magazines, newspapers, radio programs, and movies.

4. Burned all books that contained ideas opposed to Nazism.

5. Established a secret police force called the **Gestapo.** It made sure that no one said anything against Hitler or the Nazis.

6. Rebuilt the German army into a powerful war machine.

Lesson 4 Review On a sheet of paper, write the answer to each question. Use complete sentences.

1. Why did the government of the Weimar Republic have problems?

2. What is the symbol of the Nationalist Socialist German Worker's (Nazi) Party?

3. What economic conditions caused the people of Germany to turn to Hitler?

4. What did Hitler censor as soon as he became dictator?

5. What was the secret police force that Hitler established? What did it do?

Reichstag

The national assembly of the Weimar Republic

Fuehrer

The name given to Adolf Hitler meaning "leader"

Gestapo

Hitler's secret police force

Hitler forced Jews to wear yellow stars. Why do you think he did so?

Ask:

- **What was the symbol for the Nazi Party?** (the swastika)
- **Why was Hitler jailed in 1923?** (he tried to take over the government)
- **Which people did Hitler say were superior?** (the German people)
- **What happened during the Depression?** (students may say that many people lost their jobs)
- **Which party became the largest political party in Germany?** (Nazis)
- **What did Hitler blame on the Communists? How did this help him?** (the burning of the Reichstag; it turned the public against the Communists)
- **What is the name of the secret police that Hitler established?** (the Gestapo)

Reading Strategy:
Visualizing

(Student responses will vary. Students may say that they visualize soldiers returning home and not being able to find jobs or the flag of the Nazi Party.)

3 Reinforce and Extend

LEARNING STYLES

Auditory/Verbal

Tell students that Hitler was an excellent public speaker—that some say he had a hypnotic effect on crowds. Explain that even listeners who do not know German can appreciate the roar of the crowds as they listen to Hitler. Encourage students to locate and listen to audio recordings of Hitler's speeches and report back to the class about what they heard. Many clips of Hitler's speeches can be heard on various sites on the Internet.

Lesson 4 Review Answers

1. The government of the Weimar Republic had problems mainly because some Germans blamed it for accepting the Treaty of Versailles. **2.** The symbol of the Nazi Party is a swastika. **3.** They turned to Hitler because they were in an economic depression. Also, Hitler opposed Communism, which the people feared. **4.** Hitler censored all other political parties and labor unions, as well as books, magazines, newspapers, radio programs, and movies. **5.** Hitler's secret police force was the Gestapo, which made sure no one said anything agianst Hitler or the Nazis.

Probably because he wanted to have them identified publicly as Jews.

Chapter 26: Lesson 5

Overview This lesson explains how the Chinese freed themselves from imperialism and overcame civil war.

Objectives

- To describe what Sun Yat-sen did as leader of the Chinese nationalists
- To explain why the peasants support Mao Zedong

Student Pages pages 656–658

Teacher's Resource Library

Workbook Activity 121

Activity 121

Modified Activity 121

1 Warm-Up Activity

Ask students what they already know about China. Have students share their ideas with the class. List their ideas on the board and ask students to look for categories of ideas, for example, geography, history, and government. Rearrange students' ideas into the categories. As students read Lesson 5, have them add to and correct the information on the board.

2 Teaching the Lesson

As students read, have them write an answer for each heading question. Have students share their answers with the class.

Reading Strategy: Visualizing

(Answers will vary. Students might draw a picture of people living in nice homes to show something that Sun Yat-sen wanted for the people of China.)

Ask:

- Who wrote the book *Three Principles of the People?*
  (Sun Yat-sen)

Objectives

- To describe what Sun Yat-sen did as leader of the Chinese nationalists
- To explain why the peasants support Mao Zedong

Reading Strategy: Visualizing

Draw a picture to help you visualize what Sun Yat-sen wanted for China. How does this image help you remember?

During the Age of Imperialism, Europe and Japan carved out spheres of influence in China. European powers controlled Chinese mines, railroads, and some factories. But Chinese nationalists hated imperialism. They wanted to free China from foreign influence.

What Did Sun Yat-sen Want for China?

Sun Yat-sen led the Chinese nationalists. He wrote a book called *Three Principles of the People*, which greatly influenced his country. In his book, he wrote that he wanted three things for China:

1. A strong national government free of foreign control.

2. A democratic government that the Chinese people controlled.

3. Better living conditions for all the Chinese people.

Why Did the Soviet Union Help Sun Yat-sen?

In 1911, Sun Yat-sen and the Chinese revolutionaries overthrew the government and formed a republic. However, for the next five years, civil war tore China apart. In 1917, Sun Yat-sen became leader of the republic. But military leaders who wanted power for themselves still controlled much of China.

Sun Yat-sen was the leader of the Chinese nationalists. He wanted to free China from foreign influence.

Sun Yat-sen asked the European nations for help. They would not help, because Sun Yat-sen had criticized them for being imperialists. Sun Yat-sen then turned to the Soviet Union. Lenin, the Russian leader at the time, agreed to send money and military supplies to China. He thought that his country and China faced the same enemies. Lenin also wanted to introduce Communism to China.

What Started a Civil War in China?

Reading Strategy:
Visualizing

How could this paragraph be written differently to create a stronger picture in your mind?

In 1925, Sun Yat-sen died. Then Chiang Kai-shek, an army general, became China's leader. Chiang did not trust the Soviet Union or the Communists. Soon after taking power, he ordered the Soviet advisers out of China and nearly wiped out the Chinese Communist Party. Only a few Communists managed to escape.

Mao Zedong was one of the Communists who fled to the Chinese countryside. With his supporters, he fought a long civil war against Chiang. Several times during this war, Chiang almost destroyed the Communists.

What United the Chinese People?

In this war, bankers and business people in the cities along China's coast supported Chiang. The peasants supported Mao Zedong because the Communists took land from the rich and divided it among the landless peasants.

China's civil war stopped for a while in 1937 when Japan invaded China. The Japanese killed many Chinese people and destroyed cities, farms, and factories. Then all the Chinese people united to fight their common enemy.

LEARNING STYLES

Logical/Mathematical

Have students make timelines for each of the following countries: the Soviet Union, Germany, Italy, Japan, and China. Each timeline should include significant events between 1911 and 1938.

Ask:

- Why wouldn't European nations help Sun Yat-sen? (he had criticized them)
- Which Communist leader fled to the Chinese countryside? (Mao Zedong)
- What event served to unify the people of China? (In 1937, the Chinese people united to fight their common enemy of Japan.)

Reading Strategy:
Visualizing

Answers will vary. Students may say that a description of how the Chinese Communist Party was nearly wiped out would create a stronger picture.

 Reinforce and Extend

ELL/ESL STRATEGY

Language Objective:
To use comparing and contrasting to understand text

Draw a three-column chart on the board. Write the names Sun Yat-sen, Chiang Kai-shek, and Mao Zedong for the three column headings. Have students read the names with you as you point to each one. Write one fact about Sun Yat-sen from the lesson in the column under his name. Read this fact aloud. Have students generate more facts about Sun Yat-sen from the lesson and write and read aloud these facts as well. Repeat the activity for Chiang Kai-shek and Mao Zedong. Then have students use the information in the three-column chart to answer the following questions.

- How was Chiang Kai-shek different from Sun Yat-sen?
- How were Chiang Kai-shek and Mao Zedong alike?
- How were Chiang Kai-shek and Sun Yat-sen alike?

Encourage students to point to the fact or facts in the chart that support their responses.

Lesson 5 Review Answers

1. B **2.** D **3.** A **4.** C **5.** A

Answers will vary. Some Chinese people, especially nationalists, probably hated imperialism because it benefited only the mother country. These people probably felt used, and they wanted their country back.

At Home

Sun Yat-sen wanted the people of China to have good lives, and he wanted the government to run smoothly and for the benefit of the people. Have students talk to their household and/or extended family members about the things that family members do to improve the quality of life for the whole family. Students might want to make a list of some of the things the family discussed. Ask volunteers to share their lists with the class.

Lesson 5 Review On a sheet of paper, write the letter of the answer that correctly completes each sentence.

1. Chinese _____ hated foreign influence in China.

  A industrialists   **C** imperialists

  B nationalists   **D** Communists

2. Sun Yat-sen wanted _____ for the Chinese people.

  A a strong national government

  B a democratic government

  C better living conditions

  D all of the above

3. After Sun Yat-sen died, _____ led China.

  A Chiang Kai-shek   **C** Hitler

  B Lenin   **D** Mao Zedong

4. The leader of the Chinese Communists was _____.

  A Chiang Kai-shek   **C** Mao Zedong

  B Sun Yat-sen   **D** Lenin

5. In 1937, _____ invaded China and the Chinese people stopped their civil war.

  A Japan   **C** Italy

  B Germany   **D** Russia

What do you think

Why do you think some Chinese people hated imperialism?

Objectives

◆ To describe how the Great Depression in the United States affected Japan

◆ To explain how Japan's government was like the fascist governments of Germany and Italy

◆ To explain why Japan attacked Manchuria

Great Depression

The worldwide depression that began in the United States in 1929

Reading Strategy: Visualizing

What words in this paragraph help you visualize what you are reading?

The **Great Depression** started in the United States in 1929 and spread all over the world. It was hard on Japan, because people no longer had money to buy Japanese silk. Some Japanese companies that had exported goods to other countries went out of business. Many workers had no jobs. The Japanese people blamed its government for their problems.

Who Became the Real Leaders of Japan?

In the 1920s, the Japanese government had become more democratic. Before then, it had not allowed many people to vote. Now they had this right. When the depression hit in the 1930s, some people blamed democracy. Military officers did so because they wanted more power.

In the fascist countries of Italy and Germany, one military man ruled all the people. This was not true in Japan. In the 1930s, a small group of military men gained power in the government. They said that the emperor ruled. But in fact, the military ruled in his name. General Hideki Tojo—the minister of war—was the chief speaker for the military.

However, Japan's government had at least four things in common with the fascist governments of Germany and Italy.

1. It arrested anyone who spoke out against it.

2. It controlled the press and censored newspapers and radio.

3. It ordered schools to teach children that they must always obey.

4. Its secret police made people afraid to say or do anything against the government.

General Hideki Tojo led a group of military leaders in Japan. He would lead a government takeover in 1941.

Overview This lesson explains how military officers took control of Japan's government and ruled in the name of the emperor.

Objectives

■ To describe how the Great Depression in the United States affected Japan

■ To explain how Japan's government was like the fascist governments of Germany and Italy

■ To explain why Japan attacked Manchuria

Student Pages pages 659–660

Teacher's Resource Library TRL

Workbook Activity 122

Activity 122

Modified Activity 122

Vocabulary

Great Depression

Draw a triangle on the board. At each corner write one of the following sentences:

1. people do not have money to buy goods;

2. factories that make goods shut down;

3. people lose their jobs.

Use this diagram to show the downward spiral of an economic depression. Explain that in 1929, the Great Depression that began in the United States spread worldwide, people who did not have work felt helpless, and countries that had many unemployed people were vulnerable to takeover by dictators.

1 Warm-Up Activity

Have students find Japan on a world map. Ask students to think about geographic reasons why it might have been easy for the Japanese government to control its people in the 1930s. (Japan is an island, and people in the 1930s probably didn't have an easy way to leave the island.)

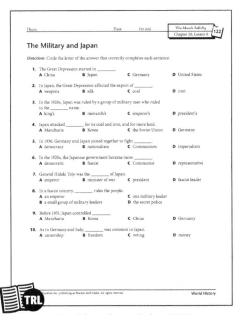

Workbook Activity 122   **Activity 122**   *National./Rev./Total.* Chapter 26   **659**

PRONUNCIATION GUIDE

Use this list to help students pronounce difficult words in this lesson.

Tojo   (tō´ jō)

2 Teaching the Lesson

After students read page 659, work with them to write a summary explaining how the Great Depression affected the people of Japan.

Reading Strategy: Visualizing

(Answers will vary. Students might say *arrested, controlled, newspapers, radio, ordered, schools, obey, secret, police*.)

Ask:

- Which group took control over Japan? (the military)
- Who made people afraid to criticize the government? (the secret police)
- What name did the Japanese give Manchuria? (Manchukuo)
- Which three countries agreed to work together to fight the spread of Communism? (Germany, Japan, and Italy)
- During which decade did the leaders of Germany, Japan, and Italy agree to fight the spread of Communism? (1930s)

3 Reinforce and Extend

IN THE COMMUNITY

Ask students to look for current news stories about countries that are experiencing political change. Have students search in newspapers, magazines, Internet news sites, or on television. Then have them write a report for each country that they investigated and have them note where they found each story, whether they portrayed the leader in a positive way, and whether the story was an editorial or a news report.

Why Did Japan Attack Manchuria?

In September 1931, Japan attacked Manchuria. (This Chinese province bordered on Japanese-controlled Korea.) Japan quickly overran Manchuria. The Japanese said that they had freed the province from China. But Japan completely controlled this new state, which it renamed Manchukuo. Why had Japan attacked Manchuria? For two reasons. First, Japan's military leaders wanted Manchuria's coal and iron for industry. Second, Japan had too many people. But Manchuria had few people. The Japanese leaders wanted people from Japan to move to Manchuria and settle there.

What Alliance Developed?

During the 1930s, Germany and Italy had developed close ties. In 1936, Germany and Japan agreed to join together to fight the spread of Communism. In 1937, Italy agreed to this, too. The three nations would later agree to help each other if one of them went to war. That war—World War II—was coming closer and closer.

Word Bank

Germany
Great Depression
Italy
Manchuria
Tojo

Lesson 6 Review On a sheet of paper, use the words from the Word Bank to complete each sentence correctly.

1. Because of the _____, many Japanese companies went out of business after 1929.

2. In the 1930s, General _____ ruled Japan

3. Japan attacked _____ in 1931.

4. In 1936, _____ and Japan formed an alliance to fight the spread of Communism.

5. Japan, Germany, and _____ formed an alliance.

What do you think

In Chapter 13, you read about Japanese feudalism and the samurai. How might this tradition have prepared the Japanese people for military leadership?

LEARNING STYLES

Visual/Spatial

To help students understand the relationship between the aggressive nations in World War II and more peaceful, neighboring nations, show students a large map of Europe. Ask volunteers to point to Germany, Italy, and Japan on the map. Explain to students how an alliance of these three countries threatens many parts of the world. Have students come to the map and show Germany's proximity to eastern and western Europe, Italy's with Mediterranean countries, and Japan's with Asian countries.

Lesson 6 Review Answers

1. Great Depression **2.** Tojo
3. Manchuria **4.** Germany **5.** Italy

Answers will vary. The samurai, who were the Japanese nobles for hundreds of years, were warriors, so the Japanese were used to being led by soldiers or warriors.

The Importance of the Peasant Problem

Mao Zedong

Mao Zedong was leader of the People's Republic of China and first secretary of the Chinese Communist Party beginning in 1943. He died in 1976. Mao wrote this speech in 1927 after spending 32 days in Hunan Province investigating the concerns of peasants and their potential as revolutionaries. Mao went on to lead the Communists in the struggle to control China.

During my recent visit to Hunan I made a first-hand investigation of conditions in the five counties of Hsiantan, Hsianghsiang, Henshan, Liling and Changsha. In the thirty-two days from January 4 to February 5, I called together fact-finding conferences in villages and county towns, which were attended by experienced peasants and by comrades working in the peasant movement, and I listened attentively to their reports and collected a great deal of material. Many of the hows and whys of the peasant movement were the exact opposite of what the gentry [people of high social position] in Hankow and Changsha are saying. I saw and heard of many strange things of which I had hitherto been unaware. I believe the same is true of any other places, too. All talk directed against the peasant movement must be speedily set right. All the wrong measures taken by the revolutionary authorities concerning the peasant movement must be speedily changed.

Only thus can the future of the revolution be benefited. For the present upsurge of the peasant movement is a colossal event. In a very short time, in China's central, southern and northern provinces, several hundred million peasants will rise like a mighty storm, like a hurricane, a force so swift and violent that no power, however great, will be able to hold it back. They will smash all the trammels [things that limit movement] that bind them and rush forward along the road to liberation. They will sweep all the imperialists, warlords, corrupt officials, local tyrants and evil gentry into their graves. Every revolutionary party and every revolutionary comrade will be put to the test, to be accepted or rejected as they decide. There are three alternatives. To march at their head and lead them. To trail behind them, gesticulating [gesturing] and criticizing. Or to stand in their way and oppose them. Every Chinese is free to choose, but events will force you to make the choice quickly.

Document-Based Reading Questions

1. Why did Mao Zedong visit counties in the Hunan Province?

2. How did he respond to what he learned?

3. What was Mao Zedong's biggest concern?

4. What did he think might happen to the warlords?

5. What action did he decide to take?

Source: "Report on the Investigation of the Peasant Movement in Hunan," Mao Zedong, March 1927.

In China, the oppressed poor were the peasants rather than industrial workers. Mao Zedong was himself a Hunanese peasant who became a founding member of the Chinese Communist Party and an active rural organizer. As an influential leader in China, Mao was very popular among the peasant population. He realized that since the majority of the population was peasants, it was going to be important to the revolution to have the peasants on the side of the Communists.

Read aloud the title "The Importance of the Peasant Problem By Mao Zedong." Then read aloud the introductory paragraph about Mao. With students, draw a timeline on the board to organize the facts in this paragraph. Next read aloud the remainder of the selection to students, pausing at and rereading Mao's figurative use of similes, such as "rise like a mighty storm, like a hurricane," and his use of strong verbs, such as *smash, bind, rush, sweep.* Guide students to put the three alternatives at the end of the document into their own words. (to march and lead, to trail behind, to stand in the way) Then have students answer the questions independently.

Answers to Document-Based Questions:

1. He went to investigate their potential as fighters in the revolution.

2. He reported on his experience in this 1927 speech.

3. His biggest concern was that the leaders were unaware of what was really going on with the peasants.

4. Mao thought the warlords would be killed or eliminated.

5. He decided to present this information to the other leaders.

Chapter Project Follow-up

Give students time to put the finishing touches on their presentations on early 20th-century dictators. Make sure students include visuals in their lessons, using computer presentation software if possible. Then have each group give their five-minute lesson to the class. Assess students' ability to communicate effectively and present accurate and interesting information about the leader they were assigned.

Call on volunteers to read the title "Hitler's Rise to Power" aloud. Have students read the selection independently to find out more about how Hitler took control in Germany. Once the reading is completed, ask students to state the advancements and setbacks during Hitler's rise to power. As students recall the events, make a timeline of Hitler's rise on the board, labeling each event. Ask students to keep these events in mind as they answer the Wrap-Up questions.

Answers to Spotlight Story Wrap-Up:

1. The Treaty of Versailles set the stage for nationalism because many Germans thought it was unfair. It took away their military strength, they resented paying war debts, the economy was bad, and the Weimar government was weak.

2. He blamed the Versailles Treaty, the Weimar government, capitalists, and Jews.

3. Hitler and his followers tried to take over the Bavarian government, but they failed. Hitler and other Nazi leaders were sent to prison.

4. It was the book in which Hitler outlined his ideas and plans.

5. Workers who were unemployed because of the Depression supported the Nazis, as did people who preferred Nazism to Communism, and the Nazis became the single largest German party. When there was a government crisis in 1933, Hitler agreed to support the government and was named chancellor.

Hitler's Rise to Power

In 1919, Germany was defeated and in ruins. The Treaty of Versailles took away its military strength. The treaty also ordered Germany to pay $33 billion in war damages to the Allies. Germans were angry and bitter. Things got worse in the next few years. Inflation soared. By late 1923, German money was worth almost nothing. Many people were out of work and hungry. The Weimar government was too weak to do anything. The times were ripe for revolution.

Playing on these feelings, many nationalist groups formed. One was the Nazi Party. Adolf Hitler became its leader. In fiery speeches, Hitler blamed Germany's troubles on the Versailles Treaty. He attacked the Weimar government. He denounced capitalists and the Jews. Hitler organized a private army of 15,000 "brown shirts."

In 1923, the Nazis staged a *putsch*—an attempt to overthrow the state government of Bavaria. About 3,000 people, including government leaders, were holding a rally at a Munich beer hall. Hitler's "brown shirts" surrounded the hall. They set up a machine gun in the entrance. Hitler jumped up on a table and fired his gun into the air. He shouted, "The national revolution has begun!" He then led his men toward the center of the city, but police stopped them. They arrested Hitler and most of the top Nazi leaders.

Hitler and other top Nazi leaders were sent to prison for treason. It was there that he wrote *Mein Kampf* (My Struggle). The book stressed nationalism and racism. It also made Hitler famous in Germany.

From 1924 to 1929, the German economy began to recover. Many Nazis lost interest and drifted away. Then the worldwide depression hit Germany. Slowly, Hitler began to rebuild the Nazi Party.

By late 1932, the Nazi Party was the strongest in Germany. Hitler was getting valuable help from people who preferred Nazism to Communism. In 1933, another government crisis occurred. Hitler promised to support the government if he were made leader. On January 30, 1933, he took office as chancellor. Six months later, he was dictator of Germany.

The dictator in Germany was Adolf Hitler. He took control of the German government in 1933.

Wrap-Up

1. What conditions set the stage for the rise of nationalism in Germany?

2. Who did Hitler blame for Germany's hard times?

3. What happened at the Beer Hall rally?

4. What was *Mein Kampf*?

5. How did Hitler eventually become leader of Germany?

Chapter 26 SUMMARY

- The Bolsheviks were revolutionary socialists led by Lenin. They took over the Russian government in 1917 and became the Communist Party. They called Russia "the Soviet Union." It then dropped out of World War I.

- Non-Bolsheviks formed a "White" army to fight the Bolshevik "Red" army. Civil war continued until 1920.

- With the support of peasants and workers, the Red army won. Lenin took over industry, gave land to peasants, and set up a dictatorship.

- After Lenin died, Joseph Stalin defeated his rival, Leon Trotsky, and became the new leader of Russia.

- Russia became a totalitarian state. In the 1930s, Stalin held purges. Millions were arrested. Russia became a powerful industrialized nation, but its people had few freedoms.

- Italians felt that the Allies had cheated them in the Treaty of Versailles.

- In 1919, Mussolini formed the Fascist Party. It opposed both democracy and Communism. Italy's dictator, Mussolini, became known as "Il Duce."

- Fascism demands total obedience to one party and leader. The state censors books and newspapers and denies free speech. Fascists believe in nationalism and military power.

- In Germany, the Weimar Republic was the democratic government after World War I. Many small political groups opposed it.

- Adolf Hitler led a fascist party known as the Nazis. In 1923, Nazi leaders were jailed for trying to take over the government. While in jail, Hitler wrote *Mein Kampf*. It described Hitler's plan to make Germany strong again.

- An economic depression and fear of Communism helped Hitler gain power. By 1933, he was head of the government.

- In China, Sun Yat-sen led a nationalist movement. A revolution in 1911 overthrew the monarchy but led to civil war. Only the Soviet Union sent Sun Yat-sen help.

- After Sun Yat-sen died, Chiang Kai-shek led the Nationalists. He conducted a long civil war against Mao Zedong's Chinese Communists.

- Japan's government became more democratic after World War I. However, the depression hurt the economy. Military leaders used this as an excuse to gain power.

- In 1931, Japan invaded Manchuria, a Chinese province rich in iron and coal. Later Japan became allies with Germany and Italy against Communism.

Using the Chapter Summary

Have students read the Chapter Summary on page 663 to review the main ideas presented in Chapter 26.

Ask:

- When the Bolsheviks came to power, what party was in control? Who was its leader? (the Communist Party; Lenin)

- Which army won the Russian civil war? (the Red army)

- Who came to power after Lenin died? (Stalin)

- Why were the Italians disappointed with the Treaty of Versailles? (they wanted more land than the treaty gave them)

- What was the name of the German government immediately after World War I? (the Weimar Republic)

- Why did many Germans turn to Nazism? (because they feared the spread of Communism)

- How did the Soviet Union become involved in the Chinese civil war? (it gave money and military supplies to Chinese nationalists)

- Who ruled Japan after World War I? (military leaders)

- Why did Japan invade Manchuria? (to control Manchuria's coal and iron and to obtain new territory to settle)

TEACHER'S RESOURCE

The AGS Globe Teaching Strategies in Social Studies Transparencies may be used with this chapter. The transparencies add an interactive dimension to expand and enhance the *World History* program content.

Chapter 26 Review

Use the Chapter Review to prepare students for tests and to reteach content from the chapter.

Chapter 26 Mastery Test

The Teacher's Resource Library includes two forms of the Chapter 26 Mastery Test. Each test addresses the chapter Goals for Learning. An optional third page of additional critical-thinking items is included for each test. The difficulty level of the two forms is equivalent.

Chapter 26 Review Answers

1. Japan
2. Lenin
3. Bolshevik
4. Stalin
5. Totalitarian
6. Mussolini
7. Il Duce
8. Hitler
9. Nazi
10. Fuehrer
11. D
12. B
13. A
14. C
15. B

Chapter 26   R E V I E W

Word Bank
Fuehrer
Hitler
Il Duce
Japan
Lenin
Mussolini
Totalitarian
Bolshevik
Stalin
Nazi

On a sheet of paper, use the words from the Word Bank to complete each sentence correctly.

1. When Russia lost its war with _____, people began to demand more change.

2. The leader of the Bolsheviks was _____.

3. In the Russian civil war, several foreign countries sent troops to fight the _____ army.

4. _____ had a plan to industrialize Russia.

5. _____ states are governments in which a small group totally controls the lives of all the citizens.

6. Benito _____ became Italy's dictator.

7. Italians called their dictator _____, which means "leader."

8. Adolf _____ led the Nationalist Socialist German Workers' Party.

9. _____ is another name for the Nationalist Socialist German Workers' Party.

10. Germans called their dictator _____, which also means "leader."

On a sheet of paper, write the letter of the answer that correctly completes each sentence.

11. After Lenin and his followers came to power, he _____.

   A took control of all industry

   B gave land to the peasants

   C swept away the class system

   D all of the above

12. Stalin conducted a _____ in which the government killed millions of workers that he thought were disloyal.

   A minority   B purge   C militia   D study

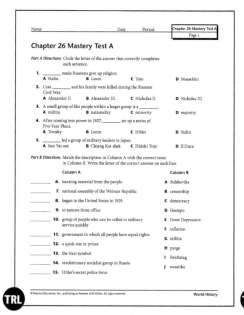

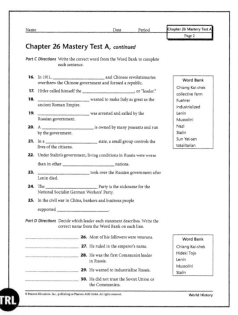

Chapter 26 Mastery Test A, pages 1–3

13. A person who has served in the military, especially during a war, is a _____.

   A veteran   **C** extremist
   B Gestapo   **D** swastika

14. The Nazi Party chose a cross with its arms bent, the _____, as a symbol.

   A Reichstag   **C** swastika
   B Gestapo   **D** Nazi

15. The name of Germany's government after World War I was the _____.

   A Fascist Party   **C** Nationalist Party
   B Weimar Republic **D** Communist Party

On a sheet of paper, write the answer to each question. Use complete sentences.

16. Why did Italy and Germany choose fascism and dictators after World War I?

17. What are six things Hitler did when he became dictator?

18. What are four things that Japan had in common with Nazi Germany and fascist Italy during the 1930s?

Critical Thinking On a sheet of paper, write your response to each question. Use complete sentences.

19. Stalin wanted to change Russia into a modern industrial power. What was it about the way he did it that prevented him from being successful?

20. Mussolini wrote that fascism "was born of the need for action." What do you think he meant?

> Cross off items on matching tests as you use them. Be sure you use each item only once.

1911 – 1939   *Nationalism, Revolution, and Totalitarianism Around the World*   **Chapter 26**   **665**

16. Both Italy and Germany disliked the Treaty of Versailles. Also, both countries had economic problems that the people blamed on the new democratic governments established immediately after the war.

17. Hitler banned all other political parties and all labor unions; made all army officers promise to obey his orders; censored all books, magazines, newspapers, radio programs, and movies; burnt all books that contained ideas opposed to Nazism; established a secret police force to ensure that no one would speak out against Hitler or the Nazis; and rebuilt the German army into a powerful war machine.

18. Japan's government arrested anyone who spoke out against it; controlled the press and censored newspapers and radio; ordered schools to teach children that they must always obey; and created a secret police force that made people afraid to say or do anything against the government.

Critical Thinking

19. Answers will vary. In general, a people's standard of living goes up with industrialization. However, most people need consumer goods to feel that their standard of living is improving. Stalin paid little attention to that. Sending people to Siberia was also extremely cruel.

20. Answers will vary. After the war, Italy faced many economic problems with a weak government that seemed unable to do anything. According to Mussolini, someone had to do something and take action. He did.

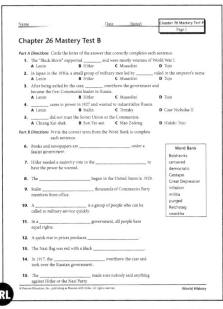

Introducing the Chapter

In the late 1930s, Germany invaded
neighboring countries. Great Britain and

27 World War II and Its Aftermath

More than 50 countries fought in World War II. The war
was fought in Europe, Asia, and North Africa. Millions
of troops and civilians died. In this chapter, you will watch as
Hitler ignores the Treaty of Versailles. You will read about the
Battle of Britain, a German army facing a cold winter in the
Soviet Union, and the destruction at Pearl Harbor. You will see
what ended World War II and the result of that war. Then you
will learn how Europe was rebuilt after the war.

Goals for Learning

◆ To explain the major causes of World War II

◆ To list the countries that fascist dictators and nations
  invaded and explain why appeasement failed

◆ To list the successes of the Axis Powers and the Allies

◆ To explain what brought an end to World War II

◆ To explain what the Holocaust was and why it
  happened

◆ To describe the social, economic, and political results
  of World War II

◆ To describe the makeup of the United Nations

1939 World War II begins	
1941 Japan attacks Pearl Harbor	
1944 Allies invade Europe on D-Day	
1945 United States drops atomic bombs on Japan	

1935   1940   1945

1941 Hitler invades Soviet Union

1945 World War II ends

1945 World representatives write United Nations Charter

France tried to stop Germany without
fighting but in 1939, they declared war.
WWII spread throughout Europe and
parts of Africa and the Pacific Islands.
After the war ended, the world's two new
superpowers, the U.S. and the Soviet
Union, grew apart. Germany was divided.
The UN was created to establish security
and peace.

Ask:

● How long did World War II
  last? (six years)

● When was Japan's first battle in the
  war? What did Japan do? (1941;
  Japan attacked Pearl Harbor.)

● What happened on D-Day? (The
  Allies invaded Europe.)

Name   Date   Period   *SELF-STUDY GUIDE*

Chapter 27: World War II and Its Aftermath

Goal 27.1   *To explain the major causes of World War II*

Date	Assignment	Completed
	1. Read pages 666–671.	
	2. Complete the Lesson 1 Review on page 671.	
	3. Complete Workbook Activity 123.	

Comments:

Goal 27.2   *To list the countries that fascist dictators and nations invaded and explain why appeasement failed*

Date	Assignment	Completed
	4. Read pages 672–674.	
	5. Complete the Lesson 2 Review on page 674.	
	6. Complete Workbook Activity 124.	

Comments:

Goal 27.3   *To list the successes of the Axis Powers and the Allies*

Date	Assignment	Completed
	7. Read pages 675–679.	
	8. Complete the Lesson 3 Review on page 679.	
	9. Complete Workbook Activity 125.	

Comments:

© Pearson Education, Inc., publishing as Pearson AGS Globe. All rights reserved.   World History

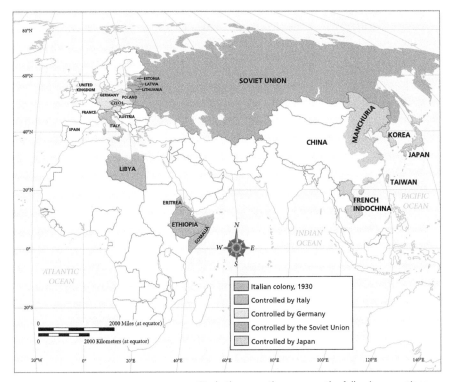

80°N
60°N
UNITED
KINGDOM
GERMANY POLAND
CZECH
FRANCE AUSTRIA
ITALY
SPAIN
ESTONIA
LATVIA
LITHUANIA
SOVIET UNION
40°N
20°N
LIBYA
ERITREA
ETHIOPIA
SOMALIA
0°
ATLANTIC
OCEAN
20°S
MANCHURIA
KOREA
CHINA
JAPAN
TAIWAN
FRENCH
INDOCHINA
PACIFIC
OCEAN
INDIAN
OCEAN
N
W   E
S

0   2000 Miles (at equator)
0   2000 Kilometers (at equator)

Italian colony, 1930
Controlled by Italy
Controlled by Germany
Controlled by the Soviet Union
Controlled by Japan

20°W   0°   20°E   40°E   60°E   80°E   100°E   120°E   140°E

In the 1930s, Japan, Germany, Italy, and the Soviet Union took over the land and resources of neighboring countries. Because they were strong, they believed they had the right to rule other nations. This map shows aggression in Europe and Asia from 1930 to 1940.

Study the map, then answer the following questions:

1. What area of China did the Japanese conquer?

2. What French territory in Asia did the Japanese capture?

3. What countries did Germany conquer?

4. What African colonies did Italy control?

5. Which country—Germany, Italy, Japan, or the Soviet Union—controlled the most land?

1939 – 1945

World War II and Its Aftermath   Chapter 27   **667**

Have a volunteer read aloud the title of the map, "Aggression in Europe and Asia (1930–1940)," and the paragraph underneath the map.

Ask:

- What country controls land on the northern border of China? On the eastern border? (Soviet Union; Japan)

- What country controls much of the land between the Atlantic Ocean and the Soviet Union? (Germany)

Have students read and write answers to the questions.

Map Skills Answers

1. Manchuria
2. French Indochina
3. Austria, Czechoslovakia, and Poland
4. Libya, Ethiopia, Eritrea, and Somalia
5. the Soviet Union

Chapter Project

Divide the class into small groups. Have the groups prepare reports on activities that the United Nations and its various councils and organizations are engaged in today. Students should search current newspapers, magazines, television newscasts, and the Internet for stories about the United Nations, write brief summaries of the articles or newscasts, and then compile the summaries into a report. Refer students to the Web site in the Online Connection on page 694. You might suggest that students start by looking into the activities of UNICEF, although they should research other parts of the UN as well. Each student in a group should be responsible for at least one item in the report.

Inferencing

Introduce the reading skill *inferencing.* Draw students attention to the explanation. Ask volunteers to read the two bullet points on page 668. Then have students read the paragraph headed "Why Did Nationalism Lead to War?" on page 669.

Write the equation on the board:

What you know + What you read = Inference.

Ask:

• **What do you already know about the topic in the paragraph?** (Nationalists want to bring their people together and make them strong. Germany went to war earlier. Hitler was gaining power in Germany.)

• **What new information is in the paragraph?** (Italy, Germany, and Japan thought they were superior and had the right to rule others.)

Discuss what inferences students can make from what they knew about nationalism and what they learned in the paragraph. (Students might infer that Italy, Germany, and/or Japan invaded other countries; that the three countries fought each other.)

Key Vocabulary Words

Have students use the vocabulary and definitions to make a matching test using the vocabulary words. On a blank piece of paper, have students draw two columns. Column 1 will show the vocabulary words. Column 2 will contain the definitions of the words, written in random order. Have students exchange papers and draw lines to match each word to its definition.

Reading Strategy:
Inferencing

Sometimes the meaning of a text is not directly stated. You have to make an inference to figure out what the text means.

◆ What You Know + What You Read = Inference

◆ To make inferences, you have to think "beyond the text." Predicting what will happen next and explaining cause and effect are helpful strategies for making inferences.

Key Vocabulary Words

Lesson 1
Axis A make-believe line
Axis Powers The alliance of Germany, Italy, and Japan during World War II

Lesson 2
Appeasement Making others content
Front The place where armies fight

Lesson 3
Blitzkrieg The quick and forceful method of attack that Germany used in World War II
Arsenal A place where weapons are kept
Destroyer A small, fast warship that uses guns to protect ships from submarines
Lend-Lease program Franklin Roosevelt's program that allowed Britain to borrow war supplies from the U.S. during World War II

Lesson 4
Occupy To take over and stay in a place
Resistance Groups of people who used hit and-run tactics to fight the Nazis
Guerilla warfare A kind of fighting that involves small attacks against an enemy
D-Day The Allied invasion of France in 1944
Kamikaze A Japanese pilot who crashed his plane into an enemy ship
V-E Day The day the allies completed their victory in Europe: May 8, 1945

Atomic bomb A nuclear bomb
Nuclear Having to do with atoms
V-J Day The day the Allies completed their victory in Japan: September 2, 1945

Lesson 5
Holocaust Hitler's killing of many of the Jews in Europe
Ghetto The parts of cities where Jewish people had to live during World War II
Genocide The mass murder of a group of people
Concentration camp A prison death camp

Lesson 6
Refugee A person who is forced to flee from his or her country
Superpower A nation that has more power and money than other countries
Satellite A nation that is tightly controlled by another nation

Lesson 7
United Nations (UN) The international organization that works to settle disagreements
Charter A constitution; a set of statements that explains a group's purpose
Trust territory A territory that the Allies took from the countries that lost World War I and World War II

668 *Unit 6 World Wars and Revolutions*

Objectives

♦ To describe how nationalism and imperialism led to war

♦ To explain how the formation of the Axis Powers led to war

♦ To identify four other causes of the war

The 1930s brought danger to the whole world. Once again, the countries of Europe stood ready to fight. In Chapter 25, you learned that nationalism, imperialism, and militarism caused World War I. They also led to World War II.

Why Did Nationalism Lead to War?

Italy's Mussolini and Germany's Hitler were nationalists. So were the military leaders of Japan. Mussolini promised to make Italy as great as the Roman Empire. Hitler called the German people the "master race." He preached that all other people were inferior. Italy, Germany, and Japan thought that they were superior. They believed that they had the right to rule all the other people in the world.

Why Did Imperialism Lead to War?

Axis

A make-believe line that goes through the middle of an object that spins around it

Axis Powers

The alliance of Germany, Italy, and Japan during World War II

These three countries were also imperialistic. They wanted to take over the land and resources of other countries. Japan tried to create a new empire. Italy expanded into Africa and tried to make the Mediterranean Sea into an "Italian lake." Germany annexed Austria and Czechoslovakia.

Why Did Militarism Lead to War?

Italy, Germany, and Japan tried to form a military **axis** around which the world would turn. An axis is a make-believe line that goes through the middle of an object. The object spins on the axis. For this reason, historians called the three nations the **Axis Powers.**

Reading Strategy:
Inferencing

What do you already know about the start of World War II?

The three Axis nations spent great sums of money on the military. They developed new weapons and built large armies. They welcomed war. They said that dying for their country was the highest honor a person could ever have.

1939 – 1945

Chapter 27: Lesson 1

Overview This lesson explains the major causes of World War II.

Objectives

■ To describe how nationalism and imperialism led to war

■ To explain how the formation of the Axis Powers led to war

■ To identify four other causes of the war

Student Pages pages 669–671

Teacher's Resource Library

Workbook Activity 123

Activity 123

Modified Activity 123

....

Vocabulary

axis   **Axis Powers**

Have students read the definition of the word *axis.* Ask them to use the word in a way that is not political or historical. (Earth spins on its axis; a top pivots on its axis; a line of reference such as an x-axis) Have students write three sentences, each using the word with one of the meanings.

....

1 Warm-Up Activity

Discuss the ways conditions in Germany and Austria were different just before World War I and just before World War II. Ask students how living conditions might have been different for the average person. (Before World War II, the economies of Germany and Austria were shattered. People were out of work, and money was almost worthless. People were willing to follow a leader who promised a better way of life.)

Reading Strategy:
Inferencing

(Answers will vary. Most students will know that Hitler was gaining power and that European countries were bankrupt. Germany felt that they had been treated unfairly after World War I.)

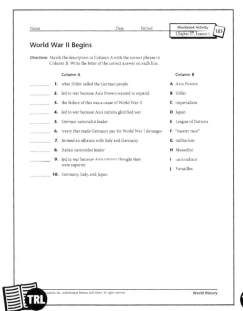

Workbook Activity 123

Activity 123

2 Teaching the Lesson

Ask students to recall the causes of World War I. Then have them read pages 669–671 to find out in what ways the causes of both wars were similar and in what ways they were different.

Ask:

- **Which three causes of World War I were also causes of World War II?** (nationalism, imperialism, and militarism)

- **Why were Germany, Italy, and Japan together called the Axis Powers?** (An axis is an imaginary line on which an object turns. These three countries wanted to act as the world's axis, that is, to be at the center or controlling point.)

- **What two factors caused Germany's economy to disintegrate after World War I?** (The Treaty of Versailles forced Germany to pay large amounts of money for World War I damages. The worldwide depression after 1929 caused Germany's economy to suffer further.)

- **Why didn't the League of Nations make the Axis countries obey the rules of the Treaty of Versailles?** (The League of Nations was weak because its most powerful nations refused to cooperate.)

Writing About History

Before students begin writing, discuss with them the concepts of nationalism, imperialism, and militarism. Ask them to give examples of these traits from other chapters they have studied. Then have students write their ten items. Remind students that some or all of their items may provide steps toward preventing wars, although each one may not necessarily be a solution.

Reading Strategy:
Inferencing

(Answers will vary. Students may suggest that knowing how bad the economy was in Germany helped them to understand why the German people followed Hitler.)

Writing About History

Pretend that you represent a world organization that tries to prevent wars around the world. In your notebook, write 10 things that your organization would do to try to prevent a world war.

Reading Strategy:
Inferencing

How does what you already know about World War II add to what you have just read?

What Are Four Other Causes of World War II?

Nationalism, imperialism, and militarism led to World War II. But four other things did, too.

First, the Treaty of Versailles, which ended World War I, punished Germany severely. Hitler and the German people wanted to make the Allies pay for what Germany had suffered.

Second, the breakdown of the world economy after 1929 helped nations turn to war. During the Great Depression, many businesses failed. World trade almost stopped. The money of some countries became almost worthless. The Treaty of Versailles made Germany and Austria pay for World War I damages. This destroyed the economies of these two countries. These hard times encouraged the rise of dictators. People were willing to follow leaders who promised a better way of life.

Third, the three Axis countries were totalitarian dictatorships. They did not believe in personal freedom or in free elections. They did not believe in freedom of speech or equality. They wanted to destroy democracy.

Fourth, the failure of the League of Nations was a cause of World War II. The league had little power to use against countries that broke its rules. The United States never joined the league. Germany and Japan dropped out in 1933; Italy left it in 1937. The league expelled Russia in 1939.

All of these set the stage for World War II. It would be even more destructive than World War I.

The Great Depression ruined the world economy. In the United States, people had to wait in line for food and jobs.

ELL/ESL Strategy

Language Objective:
To make a graphic organizer

Have ELL students make a graphic organizer that shows the seven causes of World War II, as described in the lesson. Encourage students to chose a graphic organizer that fits this kind of information. Many students will make a simple chart. However, students might benefit from the suggestion and modeling of a web diagram. Show them how to write the main idea in the center. Then draw seven spokes, or radiating lines, around the center on which to write seven causes for World War II. After students complete their graphic organizers, ask them to present their organizer to the class as a summary of the lesson.

Lesson 1 Review On a sheet of paper, write the letter of the answer that correctly completes each sentence.

1. _____ was one cause of World War II.

   A Communism   **C** Revolution
   B Monarchy   **D** Nationalism

2. Germany, Japan, and Italy formed the _____ Powers.

   A Allied   **C** European
   B Axis   **D** democratic

3. All three countries felt _____ to other people.

   A superior   **C** weaker
   B inferior   **D** less powerful

4. The _____ was a cause of World War II.

   A failure of the League of Nations
   B Great Depression
   C Treaty of Versailles
   D all of the above

5. _____ never joined the League of Nations.

   A Russia   **C** The United States
   B Germany   **D** Italy

What do you think was the most important cause of World War II?

 3 **Reinforce and Extend**

STUDY SKILLS

 Reproduce a large version of the timeline from page 666 on the bulletin board. Leave plenty of space between the dates. As students study the chapter, ask volunteers to fill in the timeline with additional dates and events as they are discussed. Students may also wish to create icons to signify Allied and Axis powers.

LEARNING STYLES

Interpersonal/ Group Learning

Arrange students into small groups of three to four students. Ask them to research the causes of the Great Depression in the United States and write a short report. Ask students to discuss both the causes and the details of the Great Depression. They should describe how the depression affected the average American family.

Lesson 1 Review Answers

1. D   **2.** B   **3.** A   **4.** D   **5.** C

Answers will vary. Lesson 1 gave the students seven causes: nationalism, imperialism, militarism, the harsh Treaty of Versailles, the Great Depression, the Axis dislike of democracy, and a weak League of Nations. However, some students may think of something else as the most important cause—such as arrogance, greed, hatred, or revenge.

Chapter 27: Lesson 2

Overview This lesson explains Hitler's steps toward world dominance, the policy of appeasement, and the invasion of Poland, which sparked the beginning of World War II.

Objectives

- To identify countries that Hitler invaded
- To explain the policy of appeasement and why it failed
- To identify the countries that fought in World War II

Student Pages 672–674

Teacher's Resource Library

   Workbook Activity 124

   Activity 124

   Modified Activity 124

Vocabulary

appeasement **front**
conference **Munich Pact**

Have students read and pronounce the vocabulary words and study the definitions. Then have them work in pairs to write four sentences of dialogue, with each sentence using one of the vocabulary words. Invite students to read their dialogues to the class.

1 Warm-Up Activity

Tell students that they will learn in this lesson that before the outbreak of World War II, Adolf Hitler said, "Today, Germany; tomorrow, the world." Discuss with students what this slogan might mean. Write their ideas on the board and have them revisit their ideas after reading Lesson 2 to revise, correct, or confirm them.

Reading Strategy: Inferencing

(Answers will vary. Students will probably suggest that Hitler will invade Czechoslovakia.)

Objectives

- To identify countries that Hitler invaded
- To explain the policy of appeasement and why it failed
- To identify the countries that fought in World War II

Conference
A meeting to discuss ideas and plans

Reading Strategy: Inferencing

After reading this section, what inference can you make about Hitler's plans?

The Treaty of Versailles limited the size of Germany's army and the number of weapons it could have. Hitler ignored the treaty. He ordered all young German men to serve in the army. He ordered Germany's factories to produce guns, tanks, airplanes, and other weapons. Hitler said, "Today, Germany; tomorrow, the world!"

How Did Hitler Break the Treaty of Versailles?

The Treaty of Versailles barred German troops from the Rhineland, an area of Germany that bordered France. In March 1936, Hitler sent troops there. Great Britain and France protested, but did nothing because they feared war.

The Treaty of Versailles also said that Germany and Austria—who were allies in World War I—could not unite again. In 1938, Hitler said that all German-speaking people should be one. He ignored the treaty again by invading and annexing Austria. Once again, Britain and France took no military action.

Why Did Hitler Want the Sudetenland?

Hitler had invaded the Rhineland and Austria and no one did anything. He then demanded control over Czechoslovakia. (It was one of the new countries that the Treaty of Versailles created after World War I.) About three million Germans lived in the area of northwestern Czechoslovakia that bordered Germany. (People called this area the Sudetenland.)

What Did the Munich Pact Give Hitler?

The British and the French had promised to protect Czechoslovakia against its enemies. On September 29, 1938, British Prime Minister Neville Chamberlain met with Hitler in Munich, Germany. Chamberlain invited French and Italian leaders to participate in the **conference,** or meeting. However, he did not invite leaders from the Soviet Union or from Czechoslovakia.

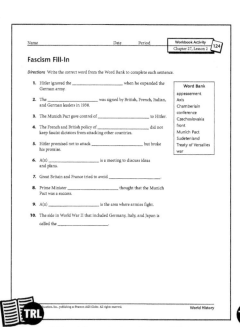

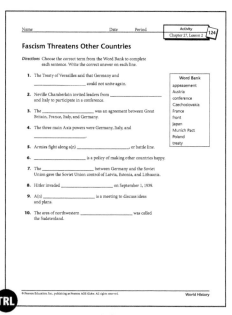

Munich Pact

A 1938 agreement between Great Britain and Germany to appease Hitler

Appeasement

A policy of making others happy or content

Front

The place where armies fight

At the conference, the leaders signed the **Munich Pact.** It gave Hitler control of the Sudetenland. In return, he promised not to attack the rest of Czechoslovakia. When Chamberlain returned to England, cheering crowds greeted him. He said that now they would have "peace in our time." However, six months later, Hitler took over the rest of Czechoslovakia.

Why Did Appeasement Fail?

Neither Great Britain nor France helped Austria or Czechoslovakia. They hoped to avoid war. They followed a policy of **appeasement.** That is, they gave in to the fascist dictators. Britain and France hoped that the dictators would be happy with what they had and would not attack other countries. This policy failed.

Why Did Germany and Russia Sign a Treaty?

Soon, Germany and Russia signed a treaty. They agreed not to make war against each other. No one could understand why Hitler and Stalin signed this treaty. After all, Hitler hated Communism, and Stalin hated Fascism.

Both countries gained something from their treaty. The Soviets got two things. First, the treaty allowed them to avoid war—for the time being. It gave them time to strengthen their military forces. Second, the treaty gave them control of Latvia, Estonia, and Lithuania.

Germany also gained two things from the treaty. First, it protected Germany against fighting a two-**front** war. (A front is the place where armies are fighting.) Second, the treaty left Germany free to invade Poland.

Hitler (right) met with European leaders in Munich, Germany, in 1938. There they signed the Munich Pact, which gave Hitler control of the Sudetenland. Pictured to the left is Britain's Prime Minister Neville Chamberlain.

1939 – 1945

World War II and Its Aftermath   Chapter 27   **673**

 2   Teaching the Lesson

Explain to students that when nations choose to not get involved in the conflicts and problems of other nations, they are said to have a policy of isolationism. Ask students to think of reasons why many nations chose not to come to the aid of Hitler's earliest victims. Have students read pages 672–674 to find out how Great Britain and France responded to Hitler's increasing aggression.

Ask:

• **What limitations did the Treaty of Versailles set against Germany?** (German troops were not allowed in the Rhineland, and Germany and Austria were not allowed to reunite.)

• **Why did Hitler want the Sudetenland?** (The area had been part of Germany until the Treaty of Versailles, and many Germans still lived there.)

• **Which countries were represented at the Munich Pact conference?** (Germany, Great Britain, France, and Italy)

• **What did British Prime Minister Chamberlain think had been gained by the signing of the Munich Pact?** (He felt the Munich Pact ensured "peace in our time.")

• **What did Germany gain from its treaty with Russia? What did the Soviets gain from its treaty with Germany?** (The Germans avoided fighting a two-front war and could concentrate forces to invade Poland. The Russians avoided war, had time to strengthen their military forces, and took control of Latvia, Estonia, and Lithuania.)

Ask:

- Who were the major Axis powers? (Germany, Italy, and Japan)
- Who were the major Allied countries? (Great Britain, France, and later the Soviet Union, the United States, Canada, and 47 other nations)

Geography Note

Display a map of Europe. Have students find and point to The Netherlands, Luxembourg, and Belgium. Tell students that the Netherlands declared themselves neutral in 1939 at the onset of World War II, just as they had done during World War I. However they were invaded by Germany on May 10, 1940. Five days later, on May 15, the Dutch surrendered after the city of Rotterdam was heavily bombed. The invasion resulted in thousands of dead, missing, or wounded Dutch soldiers and the deaths of almost 1,000 civilians.

 3 **Reinforce and Extend**

IN THE COMMUNITY

 Arrange for students to go on a field trip to the local historical museum to view World War II artifacts and exhibits. If this is not an option, take a virtual field trip with students on the Internet or invite a veteran of World War II to speak to the class. Follow up with a class discussion on how World War II affected all American communities.

Lesson 2 Review Answers

1. Italy and Germany invaded the Rhineland, Austria, Czechoslovakia, Ethiopia, and Poland **2.** The treaty limited the size of Germany's army and its number of weapons. However, Hitler ordered all young German men to serve in the army and all factories to produce guns, tanks, airplanes, and other weapons. The treaty also barred German troops from the Rhineland and from uniting with Austria. However, Hitler invaded both. **3.** France and Great Britain did not want to go to war. **4.** The Soviets got two things from the treaty. First, it allowed them to avoid war—for

Geography Note

During the 1800s, the Low Countries of Europe became the Netherlands, Luxembourg, and Belgium. The Netherlands remained neutral in World War II, while Germans occupied the other two countries.

What Sparked World War II?

In September 1939, Hitler, believing that Great Britain and France would do nothing, invaded Poland from the west. At the same time, the Soviet Union attacked from the east.

Now the British and French leaders gave up their policy of appeasement. They had proof that the policy did not work. On September 3, 1939, Britain and France declared war on Germany. World War II had begun.

Who Fought World War II?

Historians call the two sides in the war the Axis and the Allies. The three major Axis powers were Germany, Italy, and Japan. A few other nations supported them. When war broke out, the Allies included only France and Britain. Later, the Soviet Union, the United States, Canada, and 47 other nations joined the Allies.

Lesson 2 Review On a sheet of paper, write the answer to each question. Use complete sentences.

1. What countries did Italy and Germany invade during the 1930s?
2. How did Germany ignore the Treaty of Versailles?
3. Why did France and Great Britain do nothing to stop Hitler's annexation of Austria and Czechoslovakia?
4. What did the Soviet Union get from its treaty with Germany?
5. What happened in September 1939 that sparked the beginning of World War II?

 What do you think

What does the saying from the Nazi Party, "Today, Germany; tomorrow, the world!" mean?

the time being. It gave them time to strengthen their military forces. Second, it gave them control of Latvia, Estonia, and Lithuania. **5.** Hitler invaded Poland.

Answers will vary. He probably meant that the superior Germans would be first today, making Germany into a great power. Then, tomorrow, the "master race" would control the world.

Objective

◆ To identify the terms Maginot line and total war

◆ To describe the Battle of Britain

◆ To describe Hitler's invasion of the Soviet Union

Blitzkrieg

The quick and forceful method of attack that Germany used in World War II; "lightning war"

Maginot line

A line of concrete forts built by France along its border with Germany

---

Reading Strategy:
Inferencing

What can you infer about the damage and hardship resulting from a total war?

World War II began on September 3, 1939. But for seven months, no fighting took place. Then, in April 1940, German troops began to attack. Within days they conquered Denmark, Norway, the Netherlands, Luxembourg, and Belgium.

To do this, Germany invented a quick and forceful method of attack called the **blitzkrieg,** or "lightning war." Using the fastest new machines, the Germans rushed deep into enemy territory. They defeated an enemy country before it could defend itself.

What Was the Maginot Line?

After World War I, the French built a line of concrete forts along its border with Germany. France's defense was called the **Maginot line.** Hitler got around the Maginot line by conquering Belgium. On June 16, 1940, German troops marched into Paris. Six days later, the French surrendered to Germany. Hitler now controlled almost all of Western Europe.

How Was World War II a Total War?

Now Great Britain stood alone. It prepared for a German invasion. The new British Prime Minister Winston Churchill said, "We shall defend our island, whatever the cost may be. . . . We shall never surrender."

The Axis tried to force England's surrender by waging "total war." In a total war, both soldiers and civilians suffer from bombing, sickness, and lack of food. A country uses all its resources to destroy all the resources of another country.

Where Did the Battle of Britain Take Place?

The battle between Hitler's air force and the British air force began in August 1940 and lasted for over a year. Day and night, German planes bombed London, Britain's capital. To escape the bombs, thousands of Londoners slept in underground railroad stations.

1939 – 1945   *World War II and Its Aftermath*   *Chapter 27*   **675**

Chapter 27: Lesson 3

Overview This lesson describes the first years of the war and some of its major battles. It also describes how the United States helped the Allies while remaining neutral—until Japan bombed Pearl Harbor.

Objectives

■ To identify the terms *Maginot line* and *total war*

■ To describe the Battle of Britain

■ To describe Hitler's invasion of the Soviet Union

Student Pages pages 675–679

Teacher's Resource Library 🆃🆁🅻

Workbook Activity 125

Activity 125

Modified Activity 125

....

Vocabulary

arsenal   Lend-Lease program
blitzkrieg   Maginot line
destroyer

Explain to students that the Maginot line was named after France's minister of war André Maginot, who oversaw its construction from 1929 until he died in 1933. It was completed in 1938. After students read the definitions for the vocabulary words, have them write sentences about WWII using the words.

....

1   Warm-Up Activity

Explain to students that the Allies probably would not have won the war if they had not helped and cooperated with each other. Have students brainstorm ways in which a country can help another country in time of war without actually sending in troops to fight. (A country could donate money and equipment, help develop strategies, or accept refugees.)

Reading Strategy:
Inferencing

(Students will probably infer that damage and hardship from a total war are extremely severe.)

---

2 Teaching the Lesson

Have students read pages 675–679 to find out how World War II began and progressed from 1939 to 1941.

Ask:

- What was the date of the beginning of World War II? (September 3, 1939)
- When did the fighting actually begin? (April, 1940)
- How long did it take Hitler to conquer France? (six days)
- What is a "total war"? (when a country uses all its resources to destroy all the resources of another country, including its people)
- What did Germany do after it stopped the air war with Britain in 1941? (It attempted to starve the English into surrendering.)
- What position did the United States take when war broke out? (The United States declared itself neutral.)

Communication in History

Have students read the Communication in History feature, "Breaking the Enemy's Code." Discuss with students how breaking these codes made a significant difference in the outcome of the war. You may want to extend the discussion to include a kind of code that has been the topic of many television and news reports and programs: encryption codes. These are codes that keep private information on the Internet from being accessed by unauthorized people. Invite students to discuss why encryption codes are important, especially as retail business on the Internet increases.

LEARNING STYLES

LOGICAL/MATHEMATICAL
Have students form into groups to develop a code language and write ten questions about the chapter written in the code they develop. The code could employ symbols, pictures, gestures, or words they make up. Then have groups exchange questions. Students should try to crack the code and answer the questions.

Arsenal
A place where someone stores or makes weapons

Destroyer
A small, fast warship that uses guns and other weapons to protect ships from submarines

Lend-Lease program
A program developed by Franklin Roosevelt that allowed Britain to borrow war supplies from the United States during World War II

In the Battle of Britain, as it was called, Germany lost 2,300 planes, while England lost only 900. In October 1941, Hitler stopped the air war. This was his first defeat. Now he decided to starve the English into surrendering. German submarines began sinking merchant ships headed for Britain. As British supplies got low, Churchill asked the United States for help.

How Did the United States Help Britain?

When war broke out in Europe, the United States declared itself neutral. However, President Roosevelt asked the United States to become an "**arsenal** of democracy." (An arsenal is a place where someone stores or makes weapons.)

Roosevelt sent 50 old **destroyers** to Britain. These small, fast warships used guns and other weapons to protect merchant ships from submarines. In return, the United States received the use of eight British naval bases along the Atlantic Coast. Roosevelt also developed the **Lend-Lease program.** Through this program, Britain borrowed supplies from the United States.

Why Did Hitler Invade the Soviet Union?

After the failure of the Battle of Britain, Hitler decided to attack his ally—the Soviet Union. He ignored their treaty because he wanted the Soviet oil fields, grain, and other resources.

Communication in History

Breaking the Enemy's Code

Even in peacetime, governments send messages in code. In wartime, breaking codes can help win the war. During World War II, the Allies broke several top-secret German and Japanese codes. Much of the information about these codes is still secret, however.

In 1939, Polish spies got a German coding machine. It was called "Enigma." British mathematicians and code-breakers worked for months to solve Enigma's system. When they did, it was called the "Ultra secret."

Ultra let the British decode messages between Hitler and his generals. Sometimes the British knew battle plans before the German generals did.

By August 1939, American code-breakers had cracked Japan's diplomatic code. The Japanese used it in messages between Tokyo and its embassies. The code-breakers named it "Magic." They then faced two problems until war broke out in 1941. First, they were a small team, but they received a huge volume of messages. Second, the decoded messages were in Japanese. Few Americans could read it.

BACKGROUND INFORMATION

Hitler's willingness to wage a total war was one reason many countries in Europe surrendered without battle. These countries recognized what he would do and what their limitations were. Great Britain chose to go to war. Many people in British cities sent their children to stay with relatives in the countryside, because the cities—especially London—were being bombed day and night. Many who didn't have relatives in the country sent their children to live with strangers who volunteered. Some children spent the war years in the United States and other countries.

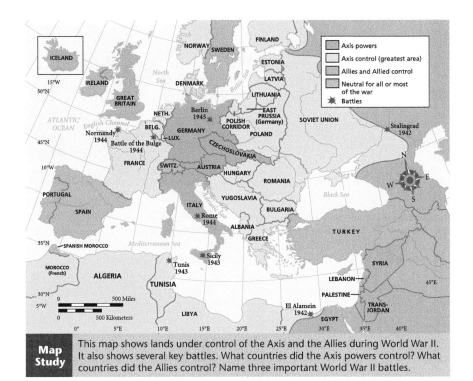

- Why do you think the Germans made the same mistake in 1941 that Napoleon made in 1812 when they were caught unprepared in the Battle of Stalingrad? (Answers will vary. Students may suggest that the Germans may have felt they could not be defeated.)

- When did the Soviets defeat Hitler at Stalingrad? (by February, 1943)

Have students read the title "World War II in Europe." After they have examined the map, ask students which neutral country was surrounded by Axis conquests and Axis countries. (Switzerland)

Ask students to read the caption under the map and answer the questions. (The Axis powers controlled Morocco, Algeria, Tunisia, Libya, Greece, Albania, Bulgaria, Yugoslavia, Romania, Hungary, Austria, Czechoslovakia, France, Poland, Denmark, Norway, Finland, Estonia, Latvia, Lithuania, East Prussia, Germany, Italy, Luxembourg, the Netherlands, Belgium, and part of the Soviet Union. The Allies controlled Great Britain, Iceland, Syria, Lebanon, Palestine, Egypt, Trans-Jordan, and part of the Soviet Union. Battles include: Normandy, the Battle of the Bulge, Berlin, Rome, Sicily, Tunis, Stalingrad, and El Alamein.)

Map Study This map shows lands under control of the Axis and the Allies during World War II. It also shows several key battles. What countries did the Axis powers control? What countries did the Allies control? Name three important World War II battles.

At first, the Germans won one battle after another. But soon a terribly cold winter caught the Germans unprepared. Many soldiers in both armies died. Historians call the six-month Battle of Stalingrad a turning point in the war. Before Stalingrad, the Soviets retreated. After Stalingrad, the Germans did.

Hitler did not expect such a cold winter. The Russian army had destroyed anything that might help Hitler. They burned crops and blew up houses, dams, and bridges. By February 1943, they had defeated Hitler.

1939 – 1945

World War II and Its Aftermath   Chapter 27   **677**

ELL/ESL STRATEGY

Language Objective:
To demonstrate how Germany avoided the Maginot line

Invite pairs of students to come in front of the class to "show and tell" how Germany avoided the Maginot line and conquered France. Have pairs of students locate France and Germany on a class map and indicate France's border with Germany, where the Maginot line was built. Ask partners to show the class how Hitler avoided the Maginot line by taking over Belgium. Then have them locate Paris and show how conquering Belgium put the Germans closer to Paris than crossing the Maginot line would have done. Encourage students who speak a second language to share equally in the verbal portion of the presentation.

Tanks were very important weapons in World War II.

Where Else Did the Axis Fight?

In 1940 and 1941, the Axis invaded Greece and Yugoslavia. Then they attacked British possessions in North Africa. Next, they threatened the Suez Canal, which was the British lifeline to India. But in May 1943, the Axis forces in North Africa surrendered. Historians consider the Battle of El Alamein in Egypt another turning point in the war. As Churchill said: "Up to Alamein we survived; after Alamein we conquered."

Why Did Japan Attack Pearl Harbor?

Between 1939 and 1941, Japan tried to gain more power. It depended on the United States for gasoline and old iron to help it wage war. Then the United States stopped selling the Japanese these materials. Japan prepared for war with the United States. Japanese leaders decided to cripple the U.S. Pacific Fleet, which was stationed in Pearl Harbor, Hawaii.

On Sunday, December 7, 1941, Japanese planes attacked Pearl Harbor. In this surprise raid, the Japanese killed over 2,500 Americans; sank or badly damaged 18 American ships; and destroyed 188 American planes. The next day, the United States declared war on Japan and its Axis partners.

Within months, Japan conquered northern and central China. It took over the Philippines, most of Southeast Asia, the Dutch East Indies, and French Indochina. Japan also helped to capture the island of New Guinea and then prepared to invade Australia.

Word Bank
Blitzkrieg
Britain
El Alamein
Pearl Harbor
Stalingrad

Lesson 3 Review On a sheet of paper, use the words from the Word Bank to complete each sentence correctly.

1. _____ war was different from fighting during World War I because it was a quick attack.

2. During the Battle of _____, Germany fought an air and bombing war and lost.

3. During the Battle of _____, Germany fought a bitter winter and lost.

4. The Allies won a major victory at _____ in Egypt.

5. On December 7, 1941, the Japanese attacked _____, killed many Americans, and destroyed many ships and planes.

Americans were faced with a difficult problem when the Japanese bombed Pearl Harbor. What would have been your reaction to the problem?

Lesson 3 Review Answers

1. Blitzkrieg 2. Britain
3. Stalingrad 4. El Alamein
5. Pearl Harbor

Answers will vary.

LEARNING STYLES

Visual/Spatial

On April 26, 1937, the tiny village of Guernica in the Basque section of Spain was bombed by 43 German planes. The Spanish Civil War was raging, and the Germans used it as an excuse for their war machine to practice new methods of bombing. In addition, Germany wanted to make Spain a Fascist state. The bombs destroyed more than half the town and killed 1,600 of Guernica's 7,000 residents. Spanish painter Pablo Picasso's masterpiece, *Guernica*, was completed a month later. It is 25 feet by 11 feet and painted in shades of black and white. The painting is a powerful example of Picasso's use of symbols to represent feelings. The painting hung in New York's Museum of Modern Art for many years and then was returned to Spain. Have students look at a print or a poster of this painting, and invite them to talk about the feelings it evokes in them.

WORLD CULTURES

On February 19, 1942, ten weeks after Japan bombed Pearl Harbor, President Roosevelt authorized the military to identify citizens and aliens of Japanese heritage from specially designated areas for security reasons. The army proceeded to remove all Japanese-Americans living on the West Coast of the United States and place them in camps. About 110,000 Japanese-Americans were detained. Ironically, while they were interned, 23,000 Japanese-American men fought in Italy. In 1998 Congress and the president signed a document stating that the Japanese-Americans were confined "without adequate security reason and without any acts of espionage or sabotage." Their heirs and the remaining survivors received $1.25 billion in reparations for the wrongs done to them.

Chapter 27: Lesson 4

Overview This lesson details the last several years of the war. It also describes the lives of civilians and their contributions to the war effort.

Objectives

- To describe the Allies' victories in the Pacific and Europe
- To identify D-Day
- To describe the effects of the atomic bomb on Hiroshima

Student Pages 680–684

Teacher's Resource Library

Workbook Activity 126

Activity 126

Modified Activity 126

....

Vocabulary

atomic bomb	**nuclear**
D-Day	**occupy**
defensive	**resistance**
guerilla warfare	**V-E Day**
kamikaze	**V-J Day**

After students read the vocabulary words and their definitions, ask them to name the words that were created during World War II. (D-Day, atomic bomb, kamikaze, nuclear, V-E Day, V-J Day) Then have students write a paragraph about World War II, using the vocabulary words.

....

1 Warm-Up Activity

Have students review what they have learned so far about World War II by playing 20 Questions. One student should think of something related to the war—such as a battle, a country, or a place. The other students should ask questions that can be answered by *yes* or *no*. Students will try to identify the word in 20 or fewer questions.

PRONUNCIATION GUIDE

Use this list to help students pronounce difficult words in this lesson.

Hiroshima (hir ō shē´ mə)

Objectives

- To describe the Allies' victories in the Pacific and Europe
- To identify D-Day
- To describe the effects of the atomic bomb on Hiroshima
- To identify the resistance

Defensive
Protecting oneself rather than attacking others

Occupy
To take over and stay in a place

Resistance
Those who opposed the Germans occupying their country

Guerilla warfare
A kind of fighting that involves small attacks against an enemy or the things it needs and uses

From September 1939 to the summer of 1942, the Axis Powers had things pretty much their own way. Then the tide turned; the Allies began to win in the Pacific and in Europe.

In June 1942, the Allies won a great naval victory at Midway Island. Historians call this battle a turning point in the Pacific. The Allies forced Japan to go on the **defensive,** or to defend oneself rather than attack others. When the Allies captured Guadalcanal in 1943, Japan went into full retreat.

In 1943, the Soviets defeated Hitler at Stalingrad. At about the same time, Allied troops swept enemy troops out of North Africa.

What Was the Resistance?

During the war, Germany **occupied,** or took over, many European countries. In these occupied countries, even in Germany itself, civilians secretly fought against the Nazis. People with great courage secretly organized and fought for their freedom. They were members of "the **Resistance**." That is, they resisted, or opposed, the Germans occupying their country. They used **guerilla warfare** to get at the enemy. In this kind of fighting, Resistance fighters blew up bridges, railroads, and factories. Hitler sent thousands of troops into these occupied countries to guard important transportation and supply centers.

How Long Did the Allies Fight in Italy?

On July 10, 1943, the Allies invaded Italy and opened up a new front. They quickly overran the island of Sicily. This forced Mussolini to resign and a new government was formed.

This new government signed an armistice with the Allies. However, thousands of German troops remained in Italy. It was not until June 1944 that Allied troops freed Rome from German control. However, parts of Italy stayed under German control until the spring of 1945.

Based on the title of the next section, what can you infer about the text in the section?

D-Day

The Allied invasion of France in 1944

Kamikaze

A Japanese pilot who crashed his plane into an enemy ship and destroyed it and himself

V-E Day

The day the allies completed their victory in Europe: May 8, 1945; stands for "Victory in Europe Day"

What Was D-Day?

In the early morning hours of June 6, 1944, a large Allied army invaded France. Historians call this **D-Day.** By the end of August, Paris was free for the first time since 1940. The Allies had driven the Germans out of Paris. Now they prepared to attack Germany.

D-Day brought an Allied attack from the west. At the same time, Soviet forces attacked Germany from the east. During 1944, the Soviets successfully pushed the Germans back. By October 1944, almost all of eastern and central Europe was under Soviet control.

What Was the Allied Battle Plan in the Pacific?

In the Pacific, the Allies used a plan called "island hopping." They fought their way north to Japan by leapfrogging from one island to another. They attacked some Japanese-controlled islands but ignored, or leapfrogged, others. The Allies then cut off supplies to the islands they ignored.

Things were going badly for Japan. It called on its young pilots to die for their country with honor. These pilots were called **kamikazes.** They crashed their planes, loaded with bombs, into Allied ships.

What Ended World War II in Europe?

In March 1945, the Allies crossed the Rhine River on Germany's western border. Soviet forces marched toward Berlin from the east. In April, the Allied forces met at the Elbe River and Russian troops captured Berlin. On April 30, 1945, Hitler killed himself. On May 7, Germany surrendered. Historians call the next day, May 8, **V-E Day**—Victory in Europe Day.

What Ended World War II in the Pacific?

Now the Allies turned their full attention to Japan. Day and night, American planes bombed Japanese cities. President Harry Truman, who took office after President Roosevelt died in 1945, did not want to invade Japan. He knew that many American soldiers would be killed.

(Answers will vary. Students may suggest that they will read about the Allies' battle plan to win the war in the Pacific.)

 2 Teaching the Lesson

Have a volunteer read the lesson title. Discuss with students what is meant by the phrase "the tide turns." Then ask students to listen to the recording of pages 680–684 to find out how the Allies were able to defeat the Axis.

Ask:

- **What was the war's turning point in the Pacific?** (Allies forced Japan to retreat and go on the defensive.)
- **What was the Resistance?** (secret organizations of civilians in occupied countries that used guerrilla warfare to fight the Nazis)
- **What was D-Day?** (D-Day was the day the Allies invaded France, June 6, 1944)
- **What was "island hopping"?** (The Allies attacked some Japanese-held islands and cut off supplies of others.)
- **What event led to the end of the war in Europe?** (The Allies captured Berlin. Hitler saw the end in sight and killed himself.)
- **What happened May 7, 1945? What do we call the following day?** (Germany surrendered; V-E Day)

ELL/ESL STRATEGY

Language Objective:
To make a Venn diagram
Show ELL students how to make a two-circle Venn diagram to compare and contrast two important historic days of World War II: V-E Day and V-J Day. Draw the two intersecting circles of a Venn diagram on the board. Label one circle V-E Day and the other V-J Day. Ask students to list some things that the two days have in common, such as "Allied victories," in the section where the two circles overlap. Then have students list things that are different, each in the appropriate section where the circles do not overlap. For example, students might write "commemorates victory in Asia" in the section that is singular to V-J Day.

Ask:

- On what Japanese cities did the Allies drop atomic bombs? (Hiroshima and Nagasaki)

- When did Japan surrender? What do historians call this day? (September 2, 1945; V-J Day)

- What island in the Pacific was partially controlled by the Japanese? (the island divided between New Guinea and Papua New Guinea)

- What Allied battle plan does this map illustrate? (island hopping)

Have students study the map, titled "World War II in the Pacific (1941–1945)," on page 682. Then have students read the caption and answer the questions. (Major battles in the Pacific were fought at Midway, Iwo Jima, Okinawa, Leyte Gulf, and Guadalcanal.) (Areas under Japanese control include Manchuria, Korea, Burma, Thailand, French Indochina, Malaya, Sumatra, Borneo, Celebes, New Guinea, Papua New Guinea, and the Philippines.)

Atomic bomb

A bomb that uses nuclear energy and has much destructive power

Nuclear

Having to do with atoms or energy from atoms

V-J Day

The day the Allies completed their victory in Japan: September 2, 1945; stands for "Victory in Japan Day"

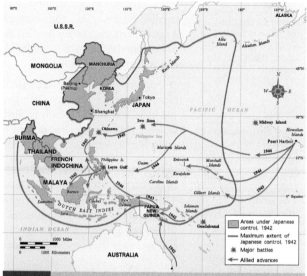

Map Study This map shows major battles in the Pacific, Japanese-controlled lands and waters, and Allied advances during World War II. Name three major battles in the Pacific. Name four areas in Asia that Japan controlled in 1942.

General Dwight D. Eisenhower was the Allied commander in Europe. He became president of the United States in 1953.

On August 6, 1945, Truman approved the use of the world's first **atomic bomb.** This type of bomb was **nuclear.** This meant it used energy from atoms, which gave it much destructive power. The United States dropped it on the Japanese city of Hiroshima. Japan did not surrender. Three days later, the United States dropped a second atomic bomb on the city of Nagasaki. On August 14, 1945, Japan agreed to end the war. On September 2, Japan officially surrendered. Historians call this **V-J Day**—Victory in Japan Day. World War II was over.

"A Blinding Flash Cut Sharply Across the Sky"

In May 1941, President Roosevelt set up a secret program—the Manhattan Project—to build a special bomb. On August 6, 1945, three American planes flew over Hiroshima, Japan. At exactly 8:15 a.m., a B-29 bomber called the *Enola Gay* dropped this ten-foot atomic bomb.

The bomb weighed about 8,000 pounds. It carried about two pounds of uranium, which gave it enormous energy. In fact, the bomb had the explosive power of 20,000 tons—or 40 million pounds—of TNT.

A Japanese man who was about three miles from the blast center described the scene. He said, "A blinding flash cut sharply across the sky. . . . At the same moment as the flash, the skin over my body felt a burning heat . . . and then a . . . huge 'boom.'" He saw a large mushroom-shaped cloud rise nearly 27,000 feet over Hiroshima.

The temperature at the center of the blast was at least about 10,800° Fahrenheit. Fires broke out everywhere. Then rain began to fall. It was made up of large, black drops. This black rain was radioactive. It caused blood cancer, loss of hair, high fever, and death.

No one knows how many people died in the attack on Hiroshima. Perhaps as many as 140,000 to 150,000 persons died immediately from burns. However, during the months that followed, more than 200,000 people died from the aftermath of the bomb.

In a park in downtown Hiroshima, the Japanese have built a monument to those who died. On it, they wrote "Let all the souls here rest in peace; For we shall not repeat the evil." Let us hope the world never does.

The atomic bomb that was dropped on Hiroshima destroyed almost everything it touched. Hundreds of thousands of Japanese people were killed.

"A Blinding Flash Cut Sharply Across the Sky"

Have students read this feature silently at first, and then ask for volunteers to read each paragraph aloud. When the reading is finished, ask students whether or not they feel the bombing was justified. Allow students to speak freely without leading the discussion.

LEARNING STYLES

Body/Kinesthetic

Have students work in two large groups to create memorial plaques or models commemorating V-E Day and V-J Day. Have students include facts from the text and other information they find through research. Members of each group should decide who will plan the design, who will find the added research, and who will build the memorials.

Have students read "The Nuclear Age." Tell them that the use of nuclear power can pose unforeseeable dangers. On April 26, 1986, a nuclear reactor at the Soviet Union's Chernobyl power plant exploded. This was the world's worst nuclear accident. Nuclear contamination was carried for thousands of miles across the Northern Hemisphere. The area is still contaminated, and parts are off-limits for humans.

 Reinforce and Extend

The Nuclear Age

The Nuclear Age began in August 1945. Atomic fireballs burned Hiroshima and Nagasaki to the ground. Many people were grateful that the war had ended, but they were also horrified. They feared this immense new energy source. Soon several other countries developed this bomb. For years, nations competed in a nuclear arms race. Finally, many countries agreed to limit nuclear tests and weapons. Some have refused to follow these rules, however.

Nuclear energy has peaceful uses too. Some people believe it is a clean, safe source of energy. France, the Soviet Union, and other countries depend on nuclear power plants. But many people in the United States doubt its safety. Nuclear medicine is another peaceful use. Tiny amounts of radioactive materials find and treat disease.

Word Bank
Allies
D-Day
Midway
Resistance
Truman

Lesson 4 Review On a sheet of paper, use the words from the Word Bank to complete each sentence correctly.

1. Historians consider the Battle of _____ a turning point in the war in the Pacific.

2. Many European civilians fought the war as members of the _____.

3. The _____ invaded Italy in 1943.

4. _____ is the name for the Allied invasion of France on June 6, 1944.

5. President _____ gave the command to drop an atomic bomb on Japan to end the war.

What do you think

Do you think the United States did the right thing by dropping atomic bombs on Japan? Explain your answer.

Lesson 4 Review Answers

1. Midway **2.** Resistance **3.** Allies **4.** D-Day **5.** Truman

Answers will vary.

Objectives

◆ To explain why Germans thought the Jews were responsible for Germany's problems

◆ To describe how the Germans treated the Jews

Holocaust
Hitler's killing of many of the Jews in Europe

Ghetto
The special parts of cities where the Jewish people were forced to live during World War II

Reading Strategy:
Inferencing

What do you already know about the Holocaust?

At the end of the war, Allied forces discovered that the Nazis were guilty of horrible crimes against humanity. Hitler and the Nazis thought there were two groups of people. They thought the German people were a "master race." They said that everyone else was below them, or inferior. Nazi leaders told the German people that the Jews were responsible for Germany's problems. They discussed a plan to murder all the Jews of Europe. Nazi officials called this plan the "Final Solution." Historians call Hitler's carrying out his plan to kill Jews the **Holocaust.**

What Were the First Steps the Nazis Took?

The Nazis began to treat the Jews badly almost as soon as Hitler took power. All Jews working in the German government lost their jobs. Hitler also ordered all Jews to wear a yellow star on their clothes. Finally, Jews were forced to move to **ghettos,** which were special parts of the cities.

Biography

Anne Frank: 1929–1945
Anne Frank's diary has made her a symbol of Nazi cruelty. In July 1942, Nazi troops began rounding up Jews in Amsterdam. With her parents and sister, Anne went into hiding. She had just turned 13. The family and others lived in a secret attic above her father's former business. Anne also began a diary, writing about her hopes and dreams. For two years, non-Jewish friends brought them food. Then in August 1944, the Gestapo found and sent them to concentration camps. Only her father survived. Anne died at Bergen-Belsen. After the war, her father found the diary and published it.

Overview This lesson describes some of the atrocities that the Nazis committed against the Jewish people and how some Jews fought back.

Objectives

■ To explain why Germans thought the Jews wee responsible for Germany's problems

■ To describe how the Germans treated the Jews

Student Pages pages 685–687

Teacher's Resource Library **TRL**

Workbook Activity 127

Activity 127

Modified Activity 127

Vocabulary

concentration camp   **ghetto**
genocide   **Holocaust**

Have students read the vocabulary words and discuss the definitions. Ask students to write sentences in which they use a vocabulary word in each. Have them circle the word. Students should then exchange papers with a partner, who should rewrite the sentence, substituting the definition for the circled word.

1 Warm-Up Activity

Tell students that the following list of items can be found in a museum: a yellow six-pointed star sewn on a jacket, the diary of Anne Frank, a map showing the locations of Auschwitz and Dachau, a Nazi SS officer's uniform. Ask students what they think the subject of the museum is. Write their ideas on the board. Then after reading Lesson 5, have students revisit their ideas for revision or confirmation.

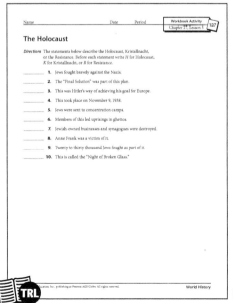

Workbook Activity 127

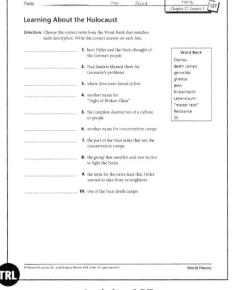

Activity 127

PRONUNCIATION GUIDE

Use this list to help students pronounce difficult words in this lesson.

Auschwitz	(oush´ vits)
Dachau	(dä´ kou)
Kristallnacht	(kris´ təl näkt)
Lebensraum	(lā´ bəns roum)

2 Teaching the Lesson

Ask students to recall how Hitler took away personal freedoms of the German people, such as censoring and burning books, and banning political parties that opposed him. Then have them read pages 685–687 to find out Hitler's plan to kill the Jewish people.

Ask:

- **Why did Hitler hate the Jews?** (He blamed them for all of Germany's problems.)

- **What is a ghetto?** (a special section of a city where certain people are forced to live)

- **How many Jews did the Nazis kill during World War II?** (about 6 million)

- **Where were many Jews killed?** (They were taken to concentration camps, where most of those in the camps were killed.)

- **What was Kristallnacht?** (the events of November 9, 1938, when Germans broke into many Jewish businesses and synagogues)

- **What happened in concentration camps?** (Strong, healthy prisoners were forced to work. The others were killed.)

Reading Strategy:
Inferencing

(Answers will vary. Students should know that Hitler believed the Germans were superior to other groups of people. They may have heard about Anne Frank and may have read her diary.)

Genocide

The mass murder of a group of people

Concentration camp

A large prison death camp

What Was Kristallnacht?

Soon Hitler took his hatred of Jews one step further. On November 9, 1938, non-Jewish Germans broke into and destroyed many Jewish owned businesses and many synagogues, where the Jews worshipped. Historians call this Kristallnacht, or "Night of Broken Glass."

What Happened in the Holocaust?

Starting in June 1941, the German government began an organized program of **genocide.** Genocide is the complete destruction of a culture or people. Hitler ordered millions of Jews arrested. The Nazis rounded up Jews from Germany and from all the countries the Nazis had conquered. Individuals and entire families were crowded into cattle cars and brought to large prison death camps called **concentration camps.**

A special Nazi army unit called the SS ran the concentration camps. Six of the camps, including Auschwitz and Dachau, were death camps. When the prisoners arrived, those who seemed strong and healthy were forced to work. Everyone else was put to death right away. This group included babies, young children, sick people, and elderly people.

Before the war, there were about 11 million Jews living in Europe. By the end of the war, the Nazis had murdered nearly six million Jews. Every Jewish community in Europe that the Nazis had taken over suffered losses. Experts guess that another five million non-Jews were killed.

Did the Jews Fight Back?

It was difficult and dangerous to resist the Nazis, but many Jews fought back. If a prisoner escaped or attacked a Nazi, the army would round up and kill a large number of Jews. The Jews were isolated and had no weapons. Nevertheless, during the war, some 20,000 to 30,000 Jews fought bravely against the Nazis. The fighters were completely outnumbered by the Nazis and had few weapons. Still, they led uprisings in many ghettos. Even though they knew they had little hope of success, fighters led uprisings in several camps.

STUDY SKILLS

 The United States Holocaust Memorial Museum has a Web site on the Internet. Have students develop their computer and research skills by doing a search for the site and writing a report on what the site has to offer. Some students may wish to follow some of the links on the site and report on a particular aspect of the Holocaust itself. Caution students that they may find many of the images on the site disturbing. Monitor students who could be particularly uneasy with what they see.

Biography

The Diary of Anne Frank has been made into a play and a movie. The diary has been translated into 55 languages and read by millions since it was discovered by Anne's father in the family's hiding place after the war. Suggest that interested students find out more about a firsthand account of a teenager hiding from the Nazis in Holland during World War II.

Hitler and *Lebensraum*

Hitler wanted to rebuild Germany into a great power. To do this, Hitler said that Germany needed more living space, or *Lebensraum*. This idea was a basic part of his policy. In theory, Hitler meant empty lands where Germans could settle. But in reality, any land that Germany would take already belonged to other people. Germany was no more crowded than most of Europe.

Many historians think that *Lebensraum* was just an excuse. It justified Hitler's

plans to conquer his neighbors. He found other reasons to claim their land, too. For example, many ethnic Germans lived in Czechoslovakia. Nearby Austria was another German-speaking country. Also, the Treaty of Versailles, which ended World War I, had deeply wounded German pride. France had gotten land from Germany. So had Poland. Beyond Poland were the rich farmlands of Ukraine in the Soviet Union. Taking more land would bring Hitler more power.

Hitler almost succeeded in destroying the Jewish culture and people. It is important to remember what happened during the Holocaust so that we can prevent it from ever happening again.

Lesson 5 Review On a sheet of paper, write the answer to each question. Use complete sentences.

1. Why did the German people think that Jews were inferior to them?

2. What was Kristallnacht?

3. About how many Jews were killed in concentration camps?

4. How did Jews fight back?

5. Why is it important to remember what happened in the Holocaust?

What are some ways that reminders of the Holocaust have been kept alive through the years?

---

 3 **Reinforce and Extend**

Lesson 5 Review Answers

1. Hitler told them that they were a "master race" and everyone else was inferior. Also, Hitler believed that the Jews were responsible for all of Germany's problems. **2.** Kristallnacht was a night when Nazis broke into and destroyed Jewish businesses and synagogues. **3.** Nearly six million Jews were killed. **4.** Many Jews led uprisings against Nazis. **5.** The Holocaust must be remembered so that it never happens again.

Answers will vary. Holocaust museums, memorials, special exhibits, books, television programs, movies, and books help to keep reminders of the Holocaust alive through the years.

BACKGROUND INFORMATION

 The Nazis had created more than 100 concentration camps throughout Europe. By 1942, most of Europe's Jews had been shipped to one of them or murdered elsewhere. Other victims were members of the religious sect Jehovah's Witnesses, who opposed Hitler, and people with disabilities. The Nazis also performed medical experiments on their victims, especially women and twins. Many of the Nazis' crimes were revealed immediately after the war. The Nazis apparently never thought that they might lose the war so, without fear or shame, they kept very detailed records of their terrible actions.

LEARNING STYLES

 Interpersonal/ Group Learning

The Anne Frank House in Amsterdam is open for people to visit. However, it's not really a house, just two rooms tucked away in an attic where the four members of the Frank family and four other people lived for two years. Have a group of students research the size of the annex where these eight people lived. The Anne

Frank House has a Web site, and some editions of Anne's diary have the specifications. Have students map the area on the floor of their classroom and ask eight volunteers to "reside" inside the outline. Invite the volunteers to discuss their feelings about what it would be like to live in such a small area for two years. Ask students what adjustments to daily life they would have to make.

Chapter 27: Lesson 6

Overview This lesson details the aftermath of World War II.

Objectives

- To identify ways that the war destroyed the economies of some countries
- To explain why refugees fled their countries
- To identify changes in Italy, Germany, Eastern Europe, and Japan

Student Pages pages 688–691

Teacher's Resource Library

Workbook Activity 128

Activity 128

Modified Activity 128

Vocabulary

Iron Curtain	**satellite**
refugee	**superpower**

Have students study the definitions of the vocabulary words. Ask them to use the definitions as clues to a word search puzzle. When their puzzles are complete, have students exchange puzzles with a partner and work their partner's puzzle.

1 Warm-Up Activity

Tell students that Lesson 6 is about change. With students, brainstorm a list of things that they think will change at the end of a huge war. Then after reading Lesson 6, return to the list so students can revise and add to the list on the board.

2 Teaching the Lesson

Have students read pages 688–690 to find out what happened after the war ended.

Ask:

- What happened to the economies of most European countries?
  (Most economies were wrecked.)

World War II ended in 1945. Millions of people had been killed or injured. The economies of many countries were destroyed, and the political power of the world shifted. We still live with the social, economic, and political results of the war.

Before the war, Europe had led the world's economy. Large empires had made Britain and France rich and powerful. Now they no longer controlled many of their colonies. Their economies had fallen apart.

Some historians have guessed that the war may have cost four trillion dollars. It wrecked the economy of most countries—except the United States. Most countries had borrowed money to pay for weapons. If they had goods to export after the war, they could pay back this money. But they had nothing to sell because the war had destroyed their factories.

Objectives

- To identify ways that the war destroyed the economies of some countries
- To explain why refugees fled their countries
- To identify changes in Italy, Germany, Eastern Europe, and Japan

Those in concentration camps suffered through terrible treatment, including cramped living conditions. This photo shows prisoners at Dachau in Germany.

688 *Unit 6 World Wars and Revolutions*

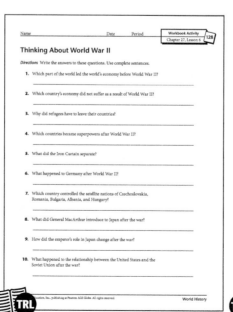

Thinking About World War II

Directions Write the answers to these questions. Use complete sentences.

1. Which part of the world led the world's economy before World War II?

2. Which country's economy did not suffer as a result of World War II?

3. Why did refugees have to leave their countries?

4. Which countries became superpowers after World War II?

5. What did the Iron Curtain separate?

6. What happened to Germany after World War II?

7. Which country controlled the satellite nations of Czechoslovakia, Romania, Bulgaria, Albania, and Hungary?

8. What did General MacArthur introduce to Japan after the war?

9. How did the emperor's role in Japan change after the war?

10. What happened to the relationship between the United States and the Soviet Union after the war?

The Results of World War II

Directions Each statement describes a social result, a political result, or an economic result of World War II. Write *S* for social, *E* for economic, or *P* for political on each line.

____ 1. Some historians say that the war may have cost four trillion dollars.

____ 2. The Nazis carried out a program of genocide against the Jews.

____ 3. Britain and France no longer controlled many of their colonies.

____ 4. The Soviet Union and the United States became superpowers.

____ 5. Most countries could not pay back the money they borrowed for weapons.

____ 6. As many as 60 million people may have died in the war.

____ 7. The Communists took control of Eastern Europe.

____ 8. Germany was divided into four zones.

____ 9. The Allies discovered German concentration camps.

____ 10. The United States placed Japan under the control of General Douglas MacArthur.

____ 11. Countries had nothing to sell because the war had destroyed their factories.

____ 12. The Iron Curtain separated democratic Western Europe from Communist controlled Eastern Europe.

____ 13. Many civilians died in this total war.

____ 14. The Japanese gave up militarism.

____ 15. Countries in Eastern Europe became satellites of the Soviet Union.

Workbook Activity 128

Activity 128

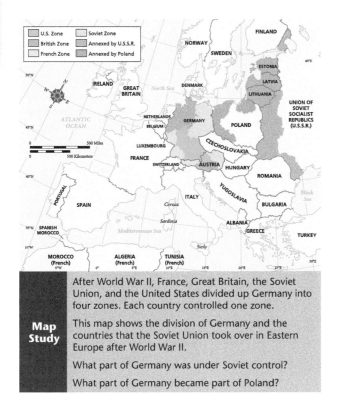

U.S. Zone	Soviet Zone
British Zone	Annexed by U.S.S.R.
French Zone	Annexed by Poland

Map Study

After World War II, France, Great Britain, the Soviet Union, and the United States divided up Germany into four zones. Each country controlled one zone.

This map shows the division of Germany and the countries that the Soviet Union took over in Eastern Europe after World War II.

What part of Germany was under Soviet control?

What part of Germany became part of Poland?

How Did the World Change?

The war also destroyed homes, farms, highways, bridges, and railroads. People had no food. Because of this, millions of **refugees** were forced to flee their countries. Their cities lay in ruins. The war damaged the capitals of Germany, Poland, Austria, the Netherlands, and Hungary. Many people went to other countries to find a new and better life.

Ask:

- What countries became the superpowers after the war? (the United States and the Soviet Union)

- What was the Iron Curtain? (an invisible boundary between democratic and Communist countries)

- What type of government did Italy vote for after the war? (Italy became a republic.)

- Which Allied countries controlled the four zones of divided Germany after the war? (Britain, France, the Soviet Union, and the United States)

 3 Reinforce and Extend

Superpower

A nation that has more power and money than other countries

Iron Curtain

The invisible boundary between Western Europe and Eastern Europe after World War II

Satellite

A nation that is tightly controlled by another nation

Because of the war, the political power of the world shifted. The United States and the Soviet Union became much more powerful than any other country. For this reason, historians called them **superpowers.**

The United States and the Soviet Union had been allies in World War II. But after the war, they grew apart. Before long, an invisible boundary separated democratic Western Europe from Communist-controlled Eastern Europe. Winston Churchill called this invisible boundary the **Iron Curtain.**

What Changes Took Place in Italy and Germany?

After the war, the Italians voted to set up a republic. The Allies divided Germany into four zones. Britain, France, the Soviet Union, and the United States each controlled one zone. In 1949, the western zones united under a new democratic government called the Federal Republic of Germany, or West Germany. The Soviets set up a Communist government in their zone called the German Democratic Republic, or East Germany.

What Changes Took Place in Eastern Europe?

The Communists took control of Eastern Europe. Poland, Yugoslavia, Czechoslovakia, Romania, Bulgaria, Albania, and Hungary set up Communist governments. They became **satellites** of the Soviet Union. A satellite nation is tightly controlled by another nation.

What Changes Took Place in Japan?

After the war ended, the United States placed Japan under the control of General Douglas MacArthur. (He had been a leader in the war in the Pacific.) He introduced the Japanese to democracy. The Japanese wrote a new constitution that protected individual rights. The Allies told the Japanese they could have only a small military force for self-defense. The emperor remained as head of state, but the people no longer viewed him as a god.

Lesson 6 Review On a sheet of paper, write the letter of the answer that correctly completes each sentence.

1. Many countries in Eastern Europe became _____ of the Soviet Union.

A refugees   **C** superpowers
B satellites   **D** colonies

2. Bombs and troops destroyed _____ and left Europe in ruins.

A factories   **C** homes
B railroads   **D** all of the above

3. The Soviets set up a _____ government in East Germany after the war.

A Communist   **C** Slavic
B democratic   **D** military

4. After the war, the Allies divided Germany into _____ zones.

A two   **C** four
B three   **D** five

5. The invisible boundary separating democratic Western Europe from Communist-controlled Eastern Europe was known as the _____.

A Iron Curtain   **C** superpowers
B satellite   **D** Italian zone

Why do you think refugees wanted to leave their countries and go to other European countries after the war?

WWII and Its Aftermath   *Chapter 27*   **691**

IN THE COMMUNITY

 Communities of all sizes often have memorials to the people who served in the military in World War II. Plan a field trip to a memorial in your area. Have students find answers to the following questions: Who is represented in the memorial? What is the tribute to them? Who maintains the memorial?

BACKGROUND INFORMATION

 "Rosie the Riveter" was an American heroine of a World War II song. When Rosie's boyfriend was drafted, she went to work in a defense plant. Rosie became the symbol for female war workers. They made bombs and tanks and welded battleships. Until the war, most women had worked in more traditional fields such as teaching or nursing. The war opened up new kinds of work to women.

When the war ended, returning soldiers wanted their jobs back. Women were encouraged to quit their jobs and stay home with their families. American women never left the workforce, however. According to the U.S. Census, 60 percent of the American workforce today is composed of women over the age of 16.

Lesson 6 Review Answers

1. B 2. D 3. A 4. C 5. A

Answers will vary. These European refugees hoped that something better waited for them elsewhere. They felt they had lost their old way of life and had nothing to lose by leaving the old, which was useless and wrecked. They set out to find a new way of life, which they hoped would be better.

Chapter 27: Lesson 7

Overview This lesson describes the founding and the purpose of the United Nations and explains the makeup and function of each of the six UN councils.

Objectives

- To identify the six parts of the United Nations and the job of each
- To explain some successes and failures of the United Nations

Student Pages pages 692–694

Teacher's Resource Library

Workbook Activity 129

Activity 129

Modified Activity 129

Vocabulary

agency   trust territory
charter   United Nations
organization   (UN)

Read the definitions randomly from the list. Have students volunteer to identify the correct word for each definition and write it on the board. Then have students work in pairs to write sentences using each word.

 Warm-Up Activity

Discuss with students the reasons why world leaders might want to start an organization that would establish safety in the world. Suggest that World War II devastated the world so much that world leaders felt it must never happen again.

2 Teaching the Lesson

Have students discuss ways that different countries might start an international organization. Then have students read pages 692–694.

Ask:

- What does the General Assembly do? (It debates world problems and votes on whether the UN should take action.)

Objectives

- To identify the six parts of the United Nations and the job of each
- To explain some successes and failures of the United Nations

Organization

A group of people joined together for a common purpose

United Nations (UN)

The international organization that works to settle disagreements, improve the way people live, and keep peace around the world

Charter

A constitution; a set of statements that explains a group's purpose

In August 1941, President Roosevelt and Prime Minister Churchill began to work together to establish safety in the world. In April 1945, representatives of many nations met in San Francisco, California. They met to establish an **organization,** or group, to replace the League of Nations. It was called the **United Nations** (UN). This is an international organization that works to settle disagreements, improve the way people live, and keep peace around the world. Its representatives wrote a **charter,** or constitution, for this new organization. It has six major parts. Each has a special job.

The first branch is the General Assembly. All member nations belong to it. Each nation—no matter how large or how small—has one vote. The assembly debates world problems. If it votes for UN action on an issue, the matter goes to the Security Council.

The Security Council tries to settle arguments between nations peacefully. It has 15 members. Britain, China, France, the United States, and the Soviet Union became the permanent members of the council. Ten other nations are elected to it. They serve two-year terms. The five permanent members of the council have veto power. Any one of them can stop the council from taking any action. The council members have used this power many times.

The Secretariat handles the day-to-day work of the UN. The Secretary-General of the UN heads the Secretariat. People from many countries help. They work in the UN building in New York.

The International Court of Justice handles questions of law that arise between member nations. It listens to arguments between countries and decides what can be done. However, it has no power to carry out the actions of its rulings.

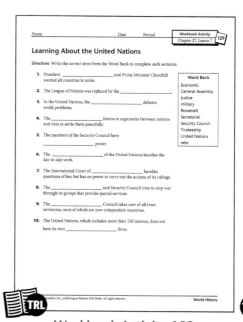

Workbook Activity 129

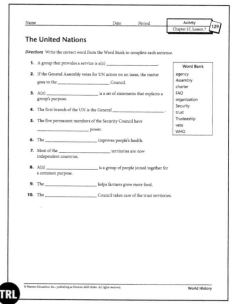

Activity 129

What Does the Economic and Social Council Do?

The Economic and Social Council tries to stop wars by improving the way people live. It does this through five groups.

- The United Nations Educational, Scientific, and Cultural Organization (UNESCO) gives advice to needy countries in Africa, Asia, and Latin America.

- The United Nations International Children's Emergency Fund (UNICEF) cares for sick, starving, and homeless children in dozens of countries.

- The Food and Agricultural Organization (FAO) helps farmers grow more food.

- The World Health Organization (WHO) improves people's health.

- The International Labor Organization (ILO) improves working conditions and living standards around the world.

Reading Strategy:
Inferencing

What does this section tell you about the importance of the United Nations?

The Trusteeship Council takes care of all **trust territories.** These are territories that the Allies took from countries that lost World War I and World War II. The council prepares these territories to rule themselves. Most of them are now independent countries.

How Successful Has the UN Been?

The UN can be proud of what it has done since 1945. Over 150 nations are now members. It provides a place where nations can present their views to the world. It has helped colonial people gain independence. It has helped keep peace in many places in the world. It has protected millions of people from diseases.

However, the UN has failed to stop some wars. It has not been able to get nations to give up their weapons. It still does not have its own military force. Instead, it depends on its members to volunteer soldiers. Some nations refuse to obey UN orders or pay their share of the UN's costs.

Ask:

- Who is the head of the UN Secretariat? (the Secretary-General)

- Name some ways that agencies of the Economic and Social Council try to improve the way people live. (They give advice to needy countries; care for sick and homeless children; help farmers; and work to improve people's health and working conditions.)

- Why do you think the United Nations set up an emergency fund (UNICEF) only for children? (Answers will vary. Students may say that children are dependent and cannot care for themselves.)

- What does the Trusteeship Council do? (It takes care of all trust territories and prepares them for self-rule.)

- How many countries are members of the United Nations? (more than 150)

- Does the UN have its own military force? How does it keep the peace? (No, it depends on its members to volunteer soldiers for peacekeeping missions.)

Reading Strategy:
Inferencing

(Answers will vary. Students may infer that the United Nations is very important to keeping peace in the world, helping colonial people gain independence, and protect people from diseases. However, students may point out that the UN has failed to stop some wars and has not been able to get all nations to give up their weapons.)

3 Reinforce and Extend

ELL/ESL STRATEGY

Language Objective:
To make a flow diagram

Draw a simple flow diagram of your school or school system. Show, name and connect the position of principal or superintendent at the top, teachers on the next level, support staff next, and students on the lower level. Then using the information on pages 692–693, guide ELL students in making a poster of a flow diagram to show the structure of the United Nations. Have them present their diagrams to the class. Ask class members to describe fictitious problems and have the presenting student name the UN agencies that would handle the issues. For example, students may say that a certain area of a country is having trouble raising enough crops to feed the people. The presenting student should refer to the Food and Agricultural Organization (FAO).

Writing About History

Before students begin writing, have them discuss some of the problems that people in other parts of the world face daily. (Students might mention war, disease, political oppression, poverty, and famine.) Then divide the class into small groups and have them brainstorm some goals that would be appropriate for an international organization. Encourage students to think in broad terms. For example, "stopping the conflict between Israel and Palestinians" is an important goal but it is limited. "Promoting world peace" or "working to ensure safety and security to all people" are broad goals that can be applied to many situations. Have students work individually to list what they consider to be the three or four most important goals. Make sure students give reasons for each goal. After they have completed their list, you may wish to refer them to the excerpt from the United Nations Charter on page 695.

ONLINE CONNECTION

The UN Web site www. agsglobewh.com/page694 includes an extensive list of links, including an organization chart, symbolism of its flag, history, and the activities of its many agencies. Students will find this Web site useful when researching the chapter project.

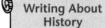

Writing About History

The founders of the United Nations listed its goals. In your opinion, what should be the goals of such an international organization? List your choices in your notebook. Include supporting reasons.

Lesson 7 Review On a sheet of paper, write the answer to each question. Use complete sentences.

1. What are the six major branches of the United Nations?

2. Which five countries became the permanent members of the Security Council?

3. What are three agencies of the Economic and Social Council?

4. Why is the Trusteeship Council almost out of business?

5. What is one success and one failure of the UN?

What do you think

Why did the representatives who wrote the UN charter give five powerful nations on the Security Council veto power?

Lesson 7 Review Answers

1. The six major branches of the UN are the General Assembly, the Security Council, the Secretariat, the International Court of Justice, the Economic and Social Council, and the Trusteeship Council. **2.** Great Britain, China, France, the United States, and the Soviet Union became the permanent members of the Security Council. **3.** Among the agencies of the Economic and Social Council are UNESCO, UNICEF, FAO, WHO, and ILO. **4.** The Trusteeship Council is almost out of business because so many of the places it held in trust are now independent countries.

5. The UN provides a place where nations can present their views to the world. It has helped colonial peoples gain independence, kept peace in many places in the world, wiped out smallpox, and protected millions of people from other diseases. However, it has failed to stop war, has been unable to get nations to give up their weapons, and has no military force but depends on its members to volunteer soldiers. Also, some nations refuse to obey UN orders or to pay their share of the UN's costs, so it is short on money.

Answers will vary. Students may suggest that veto power allows countries to differ and to stop actions that might hurt them.

The United Nations Charter

The United Nations Charter was signed in 1945.

One important result of World War II was the creation of the United Nations (UN). It replaced the League of Nations. The United States had refused to join the League, which weakened it. The League could not keep the peace.

During World War II, Allied leaders had met often to plan strategy and future cooperation. In January 1942, 26 Allied nations held a meeting. They first used the name "United Nations" to describe their group. In April 1945, before the war ended, representatives of about 50 nations drew up a charter, or constitution, for the new organization. The UN Charter begins:

We the people of the United Nations are determined to save future generations from the scourge of war, which twice in our lifetime has brought untold sorrow to mankind. We are determined to reaffirm our faith in fundamental human rights, in the dignity and worth of the human person, and in the equal rights of men and women and of nations large and small. We are determined to establish conditions under which justice and respect for the duties arising from treaties and other parts of international law can be maintained. We are determined to promote social progress and better standards of life in greater freedom. To achieve these goals, we will practice tolerance and will live together in peace with one another as good neighbors. We are also determined to unite our strength to maintain international peace and security, and to insure that armed force shall not be used except in the interests of all. And, finally, we are determined to use international means to promote the economic and social advancement of all peoples. To accomplish these aims we have resolved to combine our efforts. And so our Governments have agreed to present this Charter of the United Nations. And they do hereby establish an international organization to be known as the United Nations.

Document-Based Questions

1. What two wars is the Charter referring to in its opening sentence?

2. What rights does the Charter reaffirm?

3. What are two other goals of the United Nations according to the Charter?

4. How will member nations achieve those goals?

5. Does the Charter expect possible threats to international peace in the future? If yes, how will the United Nations deal with them?

Source: The United Nations Charter, 1945.

1939 – 1945   *World War II and Its Aftermath   Chapter 27*   **695**

Call attention to the title of the Document-Based Reading, "The United Nations Charter." Read aloud the introduction to students. Remind them that the United Nations charter was written at the close of World War II. The people writing the charter had lived through World War I, which almost completely destroyed an entire generation of young European men. They were coming to the end of World War II, which involved almost every nation on Earth directly or indirectly and in which as many as 60 million people had died.

Have a student read the charter aloud. Discuss the events of the first half of the 20th century that might have led to some of the goals mentioned in the charter. For example, when the framers of the charter wrote about "the dignity and worth of the human person," they might have been thinking about the Nazi concentration camps and slave labor camps. Then as a class, read and answer the Document-Based Questions. Ask students what issues they think the UN should focus on today. Answers may include illness, racism, poverty, hunger, and war.

Answers to Document-Based Questions:

1. It is referring to World Wars I and II.

2. It mentions fundamental human rights, the dignity and worth of each person, the equal rights of men and women, and the equal rights of large and small nations.

3. Answers will vary. Other goals include establishing conditions under which international justice and treaty obligations can be met, maintaining international law, promoting social progress, improving standards of living, and promoting the economic and social advancement for all peoples.

4. Nations will practice tolerance, live in peace as good neighbors, and work together.

5. Yes, the Charter mentions the need to maintain international peace and security and to ensure that armed force is not used except in the interests of all. The members of the United Nations promise to use their united strength to maintain peace and security and to prevent the use of armed force.

Chapter Project Follow-up

Student reports should contain accurate and current information about the activities of the United Nations and its councils. They should be factual, but students also may wish to add their own opinions about whether the activities are accomplishing their goals or are successful. Have students display their reports or present them to the class.

Have a volunteer read the title, "The Dachau Concentration Camp." Some students may find this story disturbing. Read the story aloud in class, allowing time for students to express their feelings and opinions. You may wish to guide the discussion with the following three points:

- People deported to the death camps were told they were going to "relocation centers" or work camps. Although they heard rumors of gas chambers, few people believed such a thing could happen.

- The Nazis were able to carry out their "final solution" in part because they were so well-organized. Their railroads could efficiently move thousands of people from one place to another.

- Few people resisted the Nazis, partly because they didn't believe they were going to death camps. Also, the Nazis systematically "dehumanized" their victims by stripping them of all their belongings, beating them, separating them from their families, forcing them to stand for hours in all kinds of weather, and starving them. All of these actions took away the people's will to resist.

Close the discussion by pointing out that there are many memorials around the world commemorating those who died in the death camps, including the United States Holocaust Memorial Museum in Washington, D.C. You may also wish to have students view the web site for Dachau.

After reading and discussion, have the class work together to complete the Wrap-Up questions.

The Dachau Concentration Camp

Dachau was the first Nazi concentration camp in Germany. It became a model for camps built later. Dachau opened in March 1933. It was on the grounds of a former ammunition factory near Munich. Prisoners included political opponents, Jews, and people who were not considered normal. Some were religious leaders who spoke out against the Nazis.

It is hard to know how many people were held at Dachau. The camp originally held 5,000 persons. It was expanded in 1937. Between 1938 and 1945, the camp registered more than 200,000 people. Thousands more passed through on their way to other camps. Others died before their names were recorded.

The prisoners lived in 32 "blocks," or barracks. Each block was built for 180 persons. Later, more than 800 people lived in that same space. To prevent escapes, the camp was fenced with electric barbed wire and a wall. On one side was a water-filled ditch. Guards with machine guns kept watch. If one prisoner escaped, all the others were punished.

The camp crematorium and gas chamber stood outside the walls. A crematorium is where bodies of the dead are burned. New arrivals at Dachau were told to undress and shower. But the "showers" contained poison gas, not water. Thousands of people were gassed and then burned. The smell of burning bodies often filled the air. Perhaps 70,000 people died at Dachau.

Over the camp gate hung the sign reading *Arbeit Macht Frei*. That means, "Work makes you free." This was a lie. Prisoners worked in the gravel pits. They worked from sunrise to sunset. If workers stopped, Nazi guards kicked or hit them with rifles.

A prisoner of Dachau shows an American soldier the crematorium.

Prisoners never had enough food. On April 29, 1945, American troops freed Dachau. The camp had nearly 30,000 prisoners. Many looked like walking skeletons. Some were so ill and weak that they soon died. The soldiers were horrified by what they found. General Dwight D. Eisenhower wrote, ". . . I have never at any other time experienced an equal sense of shock."

Some years later, the acting mayor of Berlin said, "Every German . . . must feel responsible . . . for the sins committed . . . in the name of Germany." Today there are chapels and a museum at Dachau.

Wrap-Up

1. What and where was Dachau?

2. Who was sent to Dachau?

3. How did the Nazis try to prevent prisoners from escaping?

4. What happened in the "showers"?

5. What did American soldiers find when they freed Dachau?

Answers to Spotlight Story Wrap-Up:

1. Dachau was the first Nazi concentration camp. It was near Munich, Germany.

2. Prisoners included political opponents, Jews, those who were not considered normal, and religious leaders who opposed the Nazis.

3. There was an electric barbed-wire fence, a wall, a water-filled ditch, and watch towers with armed guards. When someone escaped, the other prisoners were punished.

4. People were killed with poison gas in the showers. Their bodies were burned in the crematorium.

5. They found 30,000 starved and ill prisoners.

Chapter 27 SUMMARY

- Italy, Germany, and Japan—the Axis Powers—were strongly nationalistic and imperialistic in the 1930s. They built strong military forces.

- German anger at the Treaty of Versailles and worldwide economic problems caused World War II. Other causes were the Axis dictatorships and the failure of the League of Nations.

- Hitler broke many provisions of the Treaty of Versailles. He invaded the Rhineland and Austria. In 1938, he demanded the Sudetenland section of Czechoslovakia.

- To avoid war, France and Britain followed a policy of appeasement. They did not act against Italy or Germany. The Munich Pact gave Hitler the Sudetenland.

- Germany and the Soviet Union signed a treaty not to attack one another. In September 1939, the two countries invaded Poland. Then Britain and France declared war on them.

- In 1940, Germany launched the "blitzkrieg" and quickly conquered most of Western Europe. The Maginot line of defense failed, and France surrendered.

- The Axis waged total war against Great Britain. German planes bombed England in the Battle of Britain. The United States aided Britain through the Lend-Lease program.

- Germany invaded the Soviet Union for its oil and grain. The Russian winter stopped the Germans, and after the battle of Stalingrad the Germans retreated.

- In December 1941, Japanese forces attacked the American fleet at Pearl Harbor, Hawaii. The United States declared war on the Axis Powers.

- To avoid invading Japan, President Harry Truman decided to drop atomic bombs on Hiroshima and Nagasaki in August 1945. Japan surrendered.

- World War II killed about 60 million soldiers and civilians. Millions of Jews and others were killed in Nazi concentration camps. This killing of innocent people is called the Holocaust.

- World War II hurt the economies of most nations except the United States. Major nations lost their colonial empires. Refugees moved to other countries.

- An invisible "Iron Curtain" separated Soviet-dominated Eastern Europe from democratic Western Europe. Germany was divided into democratic West Germany and Communist East Germany.

- The United Nations (UN) was formed in 1945 to prevent future wars. It has both succeeded and failed. Soldiers from member nations serve as peacekeepers.

1939 – 1945

World War II and Its Aftermath   Chapter 27   697

- What were some aftermaths of World War II? (The economies of most countries were badly hurt, millions of people were killed, major countries lost their colonies, refugees moved to other countries, and an invisible Iron Curtain divided democratic Western Europe from Communist Eastern Europe.)

- Why was the United Nations formed? (The UN was formed to prevent future wars.)

Using the Chapter Summary

Have students read the Chapter Summary on page 697 to review the main ideas presented in Chapter 27.

Ask:

- What caused World War II? (Germany's anger at the Treaty of Versailles, worldwide economic problems, Axis dictatorships, and the failure of the League of Nations all helped to cause World War II.)

- What were some of the things Hitler did to provoke France and Britain? (He broke many provisions of the Treaty of Versailles, invaded the Rhineland and Austria, and demanded the Sudetenland region of Czechoslovakia.)

- What caused France and Britain to declare war on Germany and the Soviet Union? (Germany and the Soviet Union invaded Poland.)

- How did Germany conquer most of Europe so quickly? (Blitzkrieg tactics and total war, in which the German army rushed quickly and deeply into Allied territory, allowed them to capture a lot of territory quickly.)

- What were the outcomes of Germany's invasions of Great Britain and the Soviet Union? (Germany's total war against Britain killed many soldiers and civilians. The invasion of the Soviet Union failed and Germany retreated.)

- What caused the United States to enter the war (Japan attacked the American fleet at Pearl Harbor, Hawaii.)

- Why did Japan surrender? (The United States dropped atomic bombs on Japan to force them to surrender.)

- What was the Holocaust? (The killing of 6 million Jews and others in concentration camps is called the Holocaust.)

Chapter 27 Review

Use the Chapter Review to prepare students for tests and to reteach content from the chapter.

Chapter 27 Mastery Test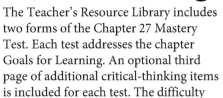

The Teacher's Resource Library includes two forms of the Chapter 27 Mastery Test. Each test addresses the chapter Goals for Learning. An optional third page of additional critical-thinking items is included for each test. The difficulty level of the two forms is equivalent.

Chapter 27 Review Answers

1. League of Nations
2. Roosevelt
3. Rhineland
4. Munich Pact
5. Maginot Line
6. Hiroshima
7. Japan
8. General Assembly
9. Security Council
10. Secretariat
11. B
12. A
13. D
14. C
15. D
16. Japan attacked Pearl Harbor on December 7, 1941.

Word Bank
General Assembly
Hiroshima
Japan
League of Nations
Maginot Line
Munich Pact
Rhineland
Roosevelt
Secretariat
Security Council

On a sheet of paper, use the words from the Word Bank to complete each sentence correctly.

1. The _____ could not prevent World War II, because it was weak and its most powerful members would not cooperate.

2. When war broke out, President _____ asked the United States to become an "arsenal of democracy."

3. Hitler ignored the Treaty of Versailles when he sent German troops into the _____.

4. The _____ gave Hitler control of the Sudetenland.

5. France's line of concrete forts along its border with Germany was called the _____.

6. The United States dropped an atomic bomb on _____ on August 6, 1945.

7. World War II ended when _____ agreed to end the fighting on August 14, 1945.

8. Every member nation in the United Nations is represented in the _____.

9. Britain, China, France, the United States, and the Soviet Union became the five permanent members of the UN _____.

10. The _____ handles the day-to-day operations of the UN.

On a sheet of paper, write the letter of the answer that correctly completes each sentence.

11. Japan, Germany, and Italy were the three _____ Powers in World War II.

    A Allied   **B** Axis   **C** Pacific   **D** Western

12. Great Britain, France, the United States, the Soviet Union, Canada, and 47 other nations were the _____ in World War II.

    A Allies   **C** League of Nations
    B Axis   **D** Eastern Powers

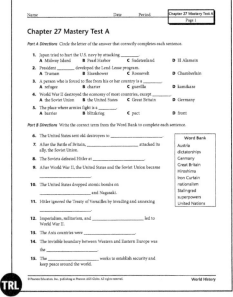

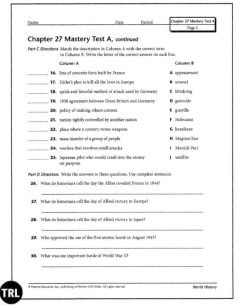

Chapter 27 Mastery Test A, pages 1–3

13. The _____ was a turning point in World War II.

A Battle of Stalingrad   **C** Battle of Midway

B Battle of El Alamein   **D** all of the above

14. Japan tried to cripple the U.S. Navy with a surprise attack on _____.

A Midway   **C** Pearl Harbor

B Guadalcanal   **D** San Francisco

15. A special Nazi unit called the _____ ran the concentration camps.

A Kamikaze   **C** Maginot line

B Blitzkrieg   **D** SS

On a sheet of paper, write the answer to each question. Use complete sentences.

16. What caused the United States to stop being neutral and to enter World War II?

17. What is one social, one economic, and one political outcome of World War II?

18. After the Battle of Britain, Hitler attacked the Soviet Union. Why?

Critical Thinking On a sheet of paper, write your response to each question. Use complete sentences.

19. Why do you suppose appeasement was popular at first? What happened in World War I that might explain appeasement? Why did it fail?

20. Could Germany have won World War II if it had not attacked the Soviet Union? Explain your answer.

> Spend most of your time on essay tests answering the question. Don't write long introductions or conclusions.

1939 – 1945

World War II and Its Aftermath   Chapter 27   **699**

17. The social results of WWII are that as many as 60 million people may have died in the war and many homeless and starving people became refugees. The economic results of the war are that European economies fell apart; the war may have cost four trillion dollars; the war destroyed factories, homes, farms, highways, bridges, and railroads. The political results of the war are that the U.S. and the Soviet Union became superpowers and began a cold war; Italy set up a republic; the Allies divided Germany into four zones; the Communists took control of Eastern Europe; Poland, Yugoslavia, Czechoslovakia, Romania, Bulgaria, Albania, and Hungary set up Communist governments; and Japan become more democratic.

18. Hitler attacked the Soviet Union because he wanted the Soviet oil fields, grain and other resources.

Critical Thinking

19. Appeasement was popular because Britain and France wanted to avoid war. They had lost so many soldiers in WWI, and the war had gone on so long, that they did not want to fight again. Appeasement failed because Hitler kept taking over countries.

20. Answers will vary. Fighting on two fronts is always difficult because the generals have to divide up their armies. Many German soldiers died in the battle against the Soviets, and German morale suffered. However, without the atomic bomb–which Germany did not have–Germany could probably not have won the war.

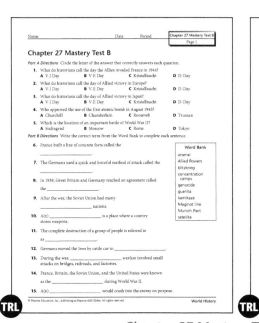

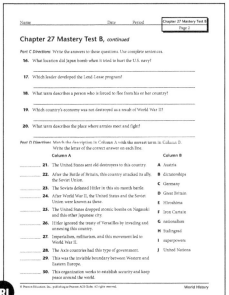

Chapter 27 Mastery Test B, pages 1–3

To introduce the Skill Builder on page 700, have students examine the details of the cartoon. Point out that although political cartoons can be amusing, they usually have a serious message. Read the Skill Builder together as a class, and have students complete the questions. Then have volunteers explain in their own words what point the cartoonist is trying to make. (Possible response: Even though we think we are using the atomic bomb to bring peace and security to our nation, the bomb can bring world destruction.)

Unit 6 Skill Builder Answers

1. The house and family stand for people in general.

2. Answers will vary. Students may suggest that it is necessary to have the bomb to control what happens in the world, but that the bomb could also cause world destruction.

3. It shows that people were worried and frightened about the possibility of a nuclear war.

4. Answers will vary. The caption points out the strange and ironic situation in which people find themselves: the very thing that they need to protect themselves (the atomic bomb) may also be what destroys everything.

5. Answers will vary. Explanations should show that students understand the cartoon.

Unit Skills Activity

Distribute copies of the Unit 6 Skills Activity. Have students read the directions. Before students begin the activity, you may want to brainstorm a list of issues faced by your community and discuss with students why these issues are important and how they impact students' lives. Encourage students to share their political cartoons with their classmates.

Unit 6
Skill Builder

Political Cartoons

Political cartoons are drawings about political events. Some are intended to make people laugh. They may poke fun at a political figure. However, the main point of a political cartoon is to encourage people to think about current issues. Political cartoons express a viewpoint about a political issue or topic. Cartoonists reveal various opinions in a drawing. They can persuade others to support their opinion through the cartoon.

Cartoons often use symbols, or objects that stand for something else. In the cartoon on this page, the bomb-shaped object stands not just for the atomic bomb but also for the climate of fear around it. Notice that a house and family are perched on the bomb. What do you think they stand for?

Cartoonists use labels or captions to help readers interpret their drawing. This cartoon has three labels. One is "atomic bomb." The others are "world control" and "world destruction." The bomb is balanced on the cliff labeled "world control." It is teetering over a deep canyon called "world destruction." The cartoonist, Ruben Goldberg, has added a caption, too: "Peace Today." The cartoon was published in 1948, only three years after the first atomic bombs were dropped on Japan.

Peace Today

Study the cartoon. Then answer these questions.

1 What do the house and family stand for?

2 Why is the bomb balanced between "world control" and "world destruction"?

3 What does the cartoon show about people's feelings in 1948?

4 What does the caption "Peace Today" add to the cartoon?

5 Find a current political cartoon in your newspaper. Write what you think it means.

| Name | Date | Period | **Unit Skills Activity** |
| | | | Unit 6 |

Interpreting Political Cartoons

Directions Political cartoons get people thinking about current issues.
Look through current magazines and newspapers and find a political cartoon that expresses an opinion on an issue or event in today's society. Read and study the cartoon, and then answer the following questions to try to understand what the cartoon is trying to say.

1. What issue or event is the cartoon commenting on or making fun of?

2. Political cartoons often use symbols to help make a point. What drawings are used in the cartoon you chose? What do you think they symbolize, or stand for?

3. Some political cartoons include labels or captions. Does your cartoon have labels, captions, or other words that help explain the cartoon? If so, how do they help the reader interpret what the cartoon is trying to say?

4. What do you think is the main point of your cartoon?

5. Think about your reaction to the cartoon you chose. Is the cartoonist revealing his or her opinion about an issue? Is the cartoonist trying to persuade the reader to feel a certain way?

© Pearson Education, Inc., publishing as Pearson AGS Globe. All rights reserved.

TRL   World History

Unit Skills Activity

Unit 6 SUMMARY

- Military alliances and nationalism led to World War I (1914–1918). The Allies were France, Russia, Britain, Italy, Japan, and the United States. They defeated the Central Powers (Austria-Hungary, Germany, Bulgaria, and the Ottoman Empire).

- World War I was a total war. Armies used trench warfare and many new weapons.

- The Treaty of Versailles blamed Germany for the war and broke up the Austro-Hungarian Empire. It created new democratic nations.

- Russia had begun to industrialize in the 1800s, but most people were poor. In 1905, workers rebelled and Nicholas II briefly gave in to some demands. A revolution in 1917 overthrew him.

- Lenin's Bolsheviks (later called Communists), took over the Russian government. Russia became the Soviet Union.

- Stalin made the Soviet Union a totalitarian state. The government developed heavy industry and collective farms. Stalin had opponents killed or sent to Siberia.

- Fascism opposed both democracy and communism. It demanded total obedience to the state. Mussolini gained power in Italy. Adolf Hitler led the Nazis in Germany.

- In China, Sun Yat-sen led a nationalist revolution in 1911. Later Chiang Kai-shek led a civil war against Mao Zedong's Chinese Communists. Military leaders took power in Japan in the 1930s.

- The Axis Powers (Italy, Germany, and Japan) were nationalistic. They seized territory in the 1930s, but France and Britain did not stop them. In 1939, Germany and the Soviet Union invaded Poland. France and Britain then declared war.

- Hitler conquered Western Europe. Japan conquered Southeast Asia and much of China. The United States entered the war in 1941.

- The battles of Stalingrad (Russia), El Alamein (North Africa), and Midway (Pacific) were turning points in the war. Allied forces invaded France in June 1944. Germany surrendered in May 1945. The United States used atomic bombs against Japan, which surrendered in August 1945.

1905 – 1945

World Wars and Revolutions   Unit 6   **701**

Using the Unit Summary

Read and discuss the Unit Summary Statements on page 701 with students.

Ask:

- What countries made up the Allies during World War I? the Central Powers? (Allies—France, Russia, Britain, Italy, Japan, and the United States; Central Powers—Austria-Hungary, Germany, Bulgaria, and Turkey)

- What changes were made in Europe as a result of the Treaty of Versailles? (The Austro-Hungarian Empire was broken up and new democratic nations were formed.)

- What changes were brought to Russia after the Communists took over? (Russia became a totalitarian state, it developed heavy industry and collective farming, and Stalin's opponents were exiled or killed.)

- What was fascism and what did it demand of the people? (Fascism was a system of government that opposed both democracy and Communism. It demanded total obedience to the state.)

- Who led a Chinese nationalist revolution in 1911? (Sun Yat-sen)

- Who led a civil war against Mao Zedong's Chinese Communists? (Chiang Kai-shek)

- What event caused France and Britain to declare war on Germany and the Soviet Union? When did this happen? (In 1939, Germany and the Soviet Union invaded Poland.)

- What major events happened after the United States entered the war in 1941? (Allied forces invaded and liberated France in 1944, Germany surrendered in May 1945, and the United States used atomic bombs in Japan to force its surrender in August 1945.)

Unit 6 Mastery Test

The Teacher's Resource Library includes a two-page Unit Mastery Test. An optional third page of additional critical-thinking items is included for each test. The Unit 6 Mastery Test is pictured on page 863 of this Teacher's Edition.

Unit Activity Follow-Up

As a wrap-up for the Unit Activity, encourage students to create the combined list suggested on Unit 6 Activity 2. Provide a place where these lists can be displayed.

For further evaluation, the following questions may prove helpful:

- Did students list key events and give accurate dates for the events?

- Did students accurately assess the importance of each event listed?

World Wars and Revolutions   Unit 6   **701**

Planning Guide
The World Since 1945

	Student Pages	Vocabulary	Lesson Review	Critical-Thinking Questions	Chapter Summary	Chapter Review
Chapter 28 **The Cold War**	704–727	✔		✔	725	726
Lesson 1 The Cold War Begins	707–708	✔	708	✔		
Lesson 2 Conflicts Between Superpowers	709–712	✔	712	✔		
Lesson 3 Reforming the Soviet Union	713–716	✔	716	✔		
Lesson 4 Europe Experiences Great Change	717–722	✔	722	✔		
Chapter 29 **New Nations Emerge**	728–755	✔		✔	753	754
Lesson 1 Many African Colonies Become Nations	731–736	✔	736	✔		
Lesson 2 Israel Becomes a Nation	737–741	✔	741	✔		
Lesson 3 India Gains Its Independence	742–744	✔	744	✔		
Lesson 4 The Struggle to Control China	745–747	✔	747	✔		
Lesson 5 Vietnamese Wars for Independence	748–750	✔	750	✔		
Chapter 30 **The Developing World**	756–781	✔			779	780
Lesson 1 African Nations Face Many Challenges	759–761	✔	761	✔		
Lesson 2 The Middle East Remains in Conflict	762–767	✔	767	✔		
Lesson 3 The Booming Asian Economies	768–771	✔	771	✔		
Lesson 4 Latin America Struggles to Overcome Problems	772–776	✔	776	✔		
Chapter 31 **The World Today**	782–813	✔			811	812
Lesson 1 Energy and Technology Create a Global Village	785–792	✔	792	✔		
Lesson 2 Global Trade and Economic Development	793–796	✔	796	✔		
Lesson 3 Social and Environmental Challenges	797–802	✔	802	✔		
Lesson 4 The Threat of Global Terrorism	803–805	✔	805	✔		
Lesson 5 Looking to the Future	806–808		808	✔		

Unit Activities

Student Text
Unit 7 Summary
Unit 7 Skill Builder

Teacher's Resource Library
Unit 7 Activities 1–2
Unit 7 Skills Activity

Assessment Options

Teacher's Resource Library
Chapter 28 Mastery Tests A and B
Chapter 29 Mastery Tests A and B
Chapter 30 Mastery Tests A and B
Chapter 31 Mastery Tests A and B
Unit 7 Mastery Test

Reading Strategy	Map Study/Map Skills	Writing About History	Geography Note	Biography	History in Your Life	Communication in History	Technology Connection	Then and Now	Spotlight Story	Document-Based Reading	Background Information	Applications (Home, Career, Community)	World Cultures	Study Skills	Online Connection	ELL/ESL Strategy	Auditory/Verbal	Visual/Spatial	Body/Kinesthetic	Interpersonal/Group Learning	Logical/Mathematical	Activities/Modified Activities	Workbook Activities	Self-Study Guide	Chapter Outline
706	705								724	723				705										✔	✔
✔																708						130	130		
✔	711						709					710, 711			710	711		711	712			131	131		
✔			716									715	715			714				715	716	132	132		
✔	721	720		722							718			721		720			719			133	133		
730	729								752	751				751										✔	✔
✔	732		734									736			733	733			736			134	134		
✔	739						741					740	739			740						135	135		
✔												744				743		744		744		136	136		
✔				746												746	746				747	137	137		
✔	750	748									750					749					750	138	138		
758	757								778	777														✔	✔
✔	760											761				760					760	139	139		
✔											763, 765		764, 766	763	763	764			766			140	140		
✔			770									769, 771				770				769		141	141		
✔				776			774					773		775		774	774			773		142	142		
784	783								810	809														✔	✔
✔			792	786	788						789	791	791			786	792		789	787	788	143	143		
✔	795			796								795				794		796				144	144		
✔											799	802		798		800		801				145	145		
✔															805	804					804	146	146		
✔	807										807	808				807					808	147	147		

TRL Activities

The Teacher's Resource Library (TRL) contains a set of lower-level worksheets called Modified Activities. These worksheets cover the same content as the standard Activities but are written at a lower reading level.

Skill Track

Use Skill Track for *World History* to monitor student progress and meet the demands of Adequate Yearly Progress (AYP). Make informed instructional decisions with individual student and class reports of lesson and chapter assessments. With immediate and ongoing feedback, students will also see what they have learned and where they need more reinforcement and practice.

Other Resources

Books for Teachers

Aiyobe, Leo E. *Nation Insane! The Plight
of African Children: A Personal and
Political Journey.* Victoria, B.C. Canada:
Trafford Publishing, 2006. (personal
account of a Nigerian who left his
homeland because of the uncertainty of
life in Nigeria)

Westad, Odd Arne. *The Global Cold
War: Third World Interventions and
the Making of Our Times.* New York:
Cambridge University Press, 2007.
(scholarly account of how the newly-
emerging nations of Africa, Asia, and
Latin America became involved in the
Cold War)

Books for Students

Diagram Group. *African Nations and
Leaders (History of Africa).* Facts on
File, 2003. (each of the 53 independent
countries is highlighted on a two-page
spread)

DK Publishing. *Vietnam War (DK
Eyewitness Books).* New York: DK
Children, 2005. (photos, diagrams,
timeline, and text identify the major
political and military figures of the
conflict)

CD-ROM/Software

Escalation. Culver City, CA: Social
Studies School Service (1-800-421-4246),
2001. (Web-based interactive simulation
about the Vietnam War)

Videos

Gandhi (200 minutes). Burbank,
CA: RCA/Columbia Pictures, 1983.
(Ben Kingsley's Academy Award-
winning portrayal, directed by Richard
Attenborough)

Web Sites

www.agsglobewh.com/page702a
(contains the text of Israel's 1948
declaration of independence)

www.agsglobewh.com/page702b
(describes some of the actions the United
Nations is taking to combat world
terrorism)

Unit 7

The World Since 1945

The contemporary world is the world in which you are living today. This world is an interdependent one. That is, you depend on people around the world. You eat food that farmers grew in Asia and Africa. You listen to Latin American music. Your family may drive a car made in Europe. These products, mass communication, and technology link you to people around the globe.

With this unit, you end your study of world history. What an adventure it has been! You have visited the past. Now you will look at the present. You will see new nations develop. You will also see how your global village changes. You will learn the lessons that prepare you to greet the future. Where will the 21st century take you? Changes lie ahead. Be ready to meet it and to grow into a good citizen of this global village we call the earth.

Chapters in Unit 7

703

Introducing the Unit

Have students study the picture on page 702. Ask what it shows. (a wind energy farm) Explain that in this unit, students will learn about some of the threats to the environment as increasing amounts of energy are needed by an increasing world population. Students will also learn about changes that have occurred throughout the world in the post–cold war era. Then have volunteers read aloud the unit introduction.

Ask:

- In what way are we currently living in an interdependent world? (People all over the world are dependent on each other for goods and information.)

- Why is today's world sometimes referred to as a "global village"? (Students may suggest that people seem to be living close to each other, as in a village, because of sharing and dependency across the globe.)

- What are some of the advantages and disadvantages of living in a global village? (Students' answers will vary. Advantages may include broader access to diverse cultural influences, such as food and art, and a greater appreciation for world history. Disadvantages may include shorter attention spans as a result of having too much information from which to choose.)

Presenting the Unit Activity

Students will soon be completing their textbook and their study of world history. Unit 7, Activity 1 will help students focus in depth on the history and interesting places of a nation of their choice. They will research information about the nation and create a travel brochure about it. Distribute copies of Unit 7, Activity 1. Allow time for students to research their nations. During the course of the unit, check on the progress that students have made.

Unit 7, Activity 2 encourages students to focus on a key event in world history and to give reasons why they think that event is important. Remind students to review their textbook for ideas.

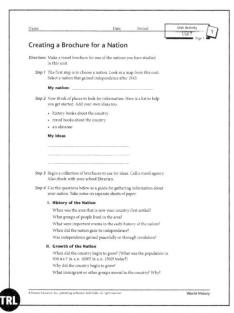

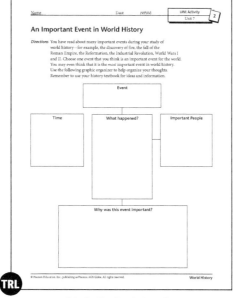

Unit 7, Activity 1, pages 1–2

Unit 7, Activity 2

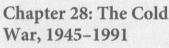

Chapter 28: The Cold War, 1945–1991

pages 704–727

Introducing the Chapter

After World War II, the world's two new superpowers, the United States and the Soviet Union, grew apart. Germany was divided. The Truman Doctrine was put into place in an effort to stop the spread of Communism, and the Marshall Plan was established to help Europe rebuild. One of its first tasks was to monitor a war between the two new republics of Korea.

The Cold War

Both the United States and the Soviet Union came out of World War II as superpowers. The United States lost 300,000 men and women in battle, but Germany and Japan had losses of several million people. More than 18 million Soviets lost their lives. The Soviet Union fought much of the war on its own soil.

Between the end of World War II and the collapse of the Soviet Union in 1991, the United States and the Soviet Union were engaged in a "cold" war. This was a war of ideas, not bombs.

Goals for Learning

◆ To explain how the cold war began

◆ To describe U.S. conflicts with the Soviets and explain the Korean War

◆ To explain why Communism failed in the Soviet Union and Eastern Europe

◆ To describe the changes in European countries

1949 NATO formed by 12 European countries

1953 Korean War ends with a truce

1991 Soviet Union breaks up and Cold War ends

1945 World War II ends

1950 Korean War begins

1959 Fidel Castro leads Communist revolution in Cuba

1989 Berlin Wall falls

| 1945 | 1955 | 1965 | 1975 | 1985 | 1995 |

1947 U.S. begins Marshall Plan to rebuild Europe

1955 Soviet Union and its allies form Warsaw Pact

1961 Berlin Wall is built

1989 Communist rulers overthrown in Eastern Europe

Reforms in the Soviet Union eventually led to the collapse of the Soviet Union and the establishment of independent countries.

Ask:

• How long after the end of World War II did the Korean War begin? (five years)

• What event took place in 1948? (U.S. begins Marshall Plan to rebuild Europe.)

• In what year was the Warsaw Pact formed? What superpower was part of the Warsaw Pact? (1955; the Soviet Union)

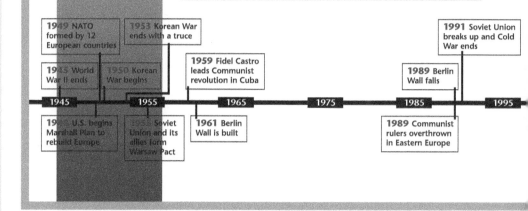

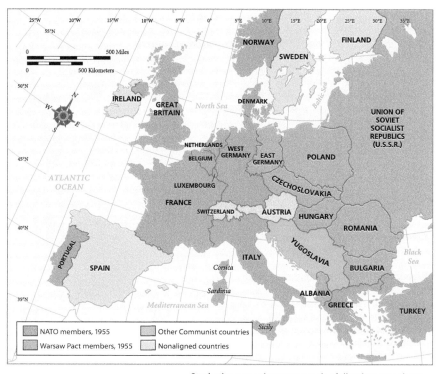

This map shows how Europe was divided by two alliances—NATO and the Warsaw Pact. The map legend tells you what countries were NATO members in 1955, Warsaw Pact members in 1955, other Communist countries, and nonaligned countries, or countries that are not in any of these groups.

Study the map, then answer the following questions:

1. Which countries were NATO members in 1955?

2. Which countries were members of the Warsaw Pact?

3. Which alliance did most countries of Western Europe join?

4. Which country in the Warsaw Pact was probably the most powerful?

5. Which countries did not belong to either NATO or the Warsaw Pact?

Ask a volunteer to read the title of the map, "Europe Divided." Inform students that the boundaries of many countries had shifted following World War II, causing these countries to change governments.

Ask:

- In general, where were countries belonging to NATO located? (Western Europe)
- Where were countries belonging to the Warsaw Pact located? (Eastern Europe)

Have students read the paragraph under the map silently and then read and answer the questions.

Map Skills Answers

1. Great Britain, France, Denmark, Iceland, Italy, Norway, Portugal, Belgium, Netherlands, Luxembourg, Greece, Turkey, West Germany

2. Soviet Union, Albania, Bulgaria, Czechoslovakia, Hungary, East Germany, Poland, Romania

3. NATO

4. Soviet Union

5. Spain, Ireland, Sweden, Finland, Austria, Switzerland, Yugoslavia

STUDY SKILLS

Have students look at the timeline and write three observations about events occurring between 1949 and 1991. Then have students write and answer three questions based on the information in the timeline. Require students to list another source other than the textbook that they can use to find answers to their questions.

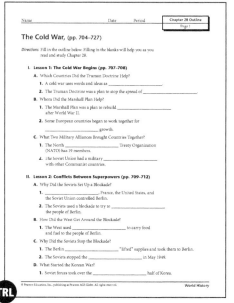

Chapter 28 Outline, pages 1–3

Chapter Project

Divided the class into five groups. Assign each group a 10-year period from 1945 through 1995. Explain that many world events occurred that were related to the Cold War. Have each group use library sources and the Internet to research its assigned time period. Explain that information from each group's research will be compiled into a larger class timeline.

Metacognition

Draw students' attention to the explanation of *metacognition*. Tell students that being aware of how they think and learn will help them understand and remember the information they read.

Have students page through the chapter noting the chapter headings, photos, and maps. Have students create four columns horizontally on a sheet of paper and write the heading of each chapter as a column heading. Then have them use each heading to write a question in each column. Next have students write down what they know to answer each question. Tell students to add to each column as they read through the chapter.

Ask:

- How does writing questions about each heading help you organize information? (It makes me think about what I might be learning.)

- How do photos and maps help you visualize the information on each page? (Answers will vary; the photos help to me understand how and under what circumstances people lived.)

....

Key Vocabulary Words

Point out that these chapter words are presented in the order they appear in each lesson. They are also found in the Glossary.

....

Metacognition means "thinking about your thinking." Use metacognition to become a better reader:

- ◆ Write the main idea, details, and any questions you have as you read the text.

- ◆ Make predictions and ask yourself what you already know about the topic.

- ◆ Summarize what you have read and make inferences about the meaning.

- ◆ Visualize what is happening in the text. If something doesn't make sense, go back and read it again.

Key Vocabulary Words

Lesson 1 ─────────────────
Cold war The war of ideas between the United States and the Soviet Union after World War II

Propaganda One-sided information meant to change people's thinking

Truman Doctrine President Truman's plan to stop the spread of Communism

Marshall Plan The American plan to rebuild Europe after World War II

Lesson 2 ─────────────────
Truce An agreement to stop a war for a time

Lesson 3 ─────────────────
Glasnost A Russian word that means openness; under Gorbachev it meant openness in government

Perestroika An economic policy used by Gorbachev to encourage factories to produce the goods people wanted

Coup A takeover of the government

Lesson 4 ─────────────────
Strike The act of refusing to work until certain demands are met

Solidarity The name of the Polish shipbuilder's union that went out on strike in 1980

Berlin Wall The wall that divided the people of East and West Berlin

Ethnic cleansing The act of getting rid of a group of people because their religion or race is different from the majority group

Tariff A tax that countries put on goods they import or export

Currency The form of money a country uses

706 Unit 7 *The World Since 1945*

Ask:

- What questions can you ask about the *Cold War*? (What was it? When was it? Who was involved?)

- What predictions can you make after reading the definition of the *Marshall Plan*? (Europe will benefit economically from the Marshall Plan.)

- What inference can you make when you read the definition of *perestroika*? (People in Russia wanted to participate in a free market system.)

- What do you visualize when you read the definition of the word *coup*? (chaos, the military, armed conflict)

Soon after World War II, the United States and the Soviet Union began a **cold war.** That is, they became rivals who used words and ideas as weapons instead of bullets. They fought the cold war with **propaganda,** or one-sided information. They used this propaganda to change people's way of thinking.

Which Countries Did the Truman Doctrine Help?

At the end of the war, the Communists threatened to take control of Greece and Turkey. But American President Harry Truman wanted to prevent the spread of Communism.

In 1947, Truman announced the **Truman Doctrine.** This plan gave economic and military help to nations threatened by an outside power. The Truman Doctrine helped Greece and Turkey defeat the Communists. But it also showed the world that the United States would do everything short of war to stop the spread of Communism.

The Marshall Plan helped European nations rebuild after World War II.

◆ To explain what the cold war was

◆ To identify the Truman Doctrine and the Marshall Plan

◆ To explain why NATO was formed

Reading Strategy:
Metacognition

Before you read this lesson, think about what you can do that will help you understand all the reasons for the cold war.

Cold war

The war of ideas between the United States and the Soviet Union after World War II

Propaganda

One-sided information meant to change people's thinking

Truman Doctrine

President Truman's plan to stop the spread of Communism

Chapter 28: Lesson 1

Overview The Soviet Union and the United States came out of World War II as the most powerful nations in the world and as enemies. They developed alliances with other nations against each other.

Objectives

■ To explain what the cold war was

■ To identify the Truman Doctrine and the Marshall Plan

■ To explain why NATO was formed

Student Pages pages 707–708

Teacher's Resource Library

Workbook Activity 130

Activity 130

Modified Activity 130

....

Vocabulary

cold war	**propaganda**
Marshall Plan	**Truman Doctrine**

Have students work in pairs, taking turns to give the definitions and identify the correct words. Then have them work individually to write definitions using their own words.

....

1 **Warm-Up Activity**

Write the word *IDEAS* on the board. Ask students for ideas on how government should run a country. Write students' ideas on the board. Then have them offer suggestions on how a government could convince the people in the country that its rule is best. Discuss the pros and cons of allowing a government to control the flow of ideas in a country.

Reading Strategy:
Metacognition

(Review with students the following steps in a reading strategy that uses metacognition: question, make predictions, summarize, and visualize.)

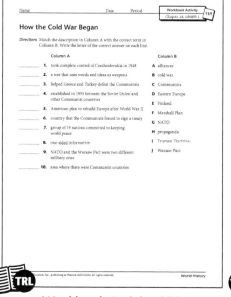

2 Teaching the Lesson

Ask students what they know about the cold war. When did it start? Who were the opponents? What nations were allies of each opponent? Then have students read pages 707–708 to learn more about the cold war and how the U.S. helped rebuild Europe after World War II.

Ask:

- What did the Soviets use to change peoples' thinking? (propaganda)
- How did the Truman Doctrine help prevent the spread of Communism? (by giving military and economic aid to nations threatened by an outside power)
- How did the Marshall Plan help Europe recover from the war? (The U.S. donated food, fuel, machines, and other goods to needy countries.)
- How did the Marshall Plan affect some European nations? (It helped them begin to produce more goods and to work together for economic growth.)
- Why was NATO formed? (Democratic nations wanted protection against Communist countries.)

Reading Strategy: Metacognition

(As a group, have students brainstorm and answer five questions about the material in Lesson 1. Ask how visualizing helps them answer the questions.)

3 Reinforce and Extend

Lesson 1 Review Answers

1. Communism 2. propaganda
3. Marshall Plan
4. Truman Doctrine 5. NATO

Alliances can always lead to war because if one country in the alliance is threatened, they all respond. However, perhaps the nations of the world felt having an alliance system was worth the risk.

Marshall Plan

The American plan to rebuild Europe after World War II

Reading Strategy: Metacognition

Remember to ask yourself questions as you read. This will help you understand what you are reading.

Word Bank

Communism
Marshall Plan
NATO
propaganda
Truman Doctrine

What do you think?

In Chapter 25, you learned that alliances led to World War I. Why do you think nations once again formed alliances?

Whom Did the Marshall Plan Help?

Both Communism and economic collapse threatened Europe. In 1948, the U.S. Congress approved the **Marshall Plan,** or European Recovery Program. It helped European nations get back on their feet after the war.

The Marshall Plan was a big success. By 1950, countries were producing more goods than they had before the war. Instead of being rivals, some European countries began to work together for economic growth.

What Two Military Alliances Brought Countries Together?

In 1948, the Communists took complete control of Czechoslovakia. They forced Finland to sign a treaty with them and tried to take over Berlin. The West was afraid that the cold war might suddenly become hot.

Several nations formed the North Atlantic Treaty Organization (NATO). They said that an attack on any one of them would be an attack on all of them. Today, NATO has 19 members. It has taken part in many missions to keep world peace.

In 1955, the Soviet Union established the Warsaw Pact. This treaty set up a military alliance between the Soviet Union and other Communist countries in Eastern Europe.

Lesson 1 Review On a sheet of paper, use the words from the Word Bank to complete each sentence correctly.

1. President Truman wanted to contain _____.
2. The cold war used _____ to try to change people's way of thinking.
3. The _____ helped rebuild Europe after World War II.
4. The _____ helped Greece and Turkey defeat the Communists.
5. _____ is an alliance among 19 countries of Western Europe.

ELL/ESL STRATEGY

Language Objective: To understand acronyms Explain that NATO is an acronym, or word formed from the first letters of other words. Write NATO vertically on the board and complete each word using the initial letter: North Atlantic Treaty Organization. Tell students that we use acronyms because they are easier to use than the longer titles for which they stand. Divide the class into small groups. Ask each group to think of five acronyms and write the words they stand for, such as UN (United Nations), USSR (United Soviet Socialist Republic), FEMA (Federal Emergency Management Agency), AIDS (Acquired Immune Deficiency Syndrome), WHO (World Health Organization), ZIP Code (Zone Improvement Plan Code). Have each group share their acronyms and explain their meanings. ELL students might use these acronyms to begin a word bank of acronyms.

Objectives

◆ To describe the blockade of Berlin and the Berlin Airlift

◆ To explain how the Korean War began and ended

In 1948, the cold war threatened to become a real war in Berlin. After World War II, Germany was divided into four sections. The United States, Britain, France, and the Soviet Union each controlled one zone. Its capital, Berlin, was located completely within the Soviet zone. The four countries agreed that each would control a part of Berlin.

Why Did the Soviets Set Up a Blockade?

In June 1948, the Soviets tried to take over all of Berlin by starving the people living there. To do this, they used a blockade. That is, they "blocked" all roads, waterways, and railroads into the city. The people of Berlin had no food, fuel, or other necessary supplies.

How Did the West Get Around the Blockade?

President Truman said, "The United States is going to stay. Period." Almost immediately the West began to use planes to fly in supplies. For more than a year, American and British planes brought tons of food and fuel to the people of Berlin. Planes took off and landed around the clock at the rate of one every three minutes. During the blockade, the pilots flew over 277,000 flights. They delivered more than two million tons of supplies.

The Mariinsky Theatre

The Mariinsky Theatre was named for Maria, wife of Tsar Alexander II. It was built in 1860 in St. Petersburg, Russia. It became a thriving center for the ballet. After the Russian Revolution, the Bolsheviks renamed it the Academic Theater. When government support ended, many performers had to leave. During the Cold War era, three famous dancers—Rudolf Nureyev, Natalia Makarova, and Mikhail Baryshnikov—defected to

Western nations from their ballet home at the Mariinsky (then called the Kirov). This caused strife between the theater management and Soviet authorities.

Today, the renamed Mariinsky Theater is a renowned performance center, featuring its own opera and ballet companies. Every year in June, it hosts the St. Petersburg White Nights Festival. Performers and tourists, once afraid of the Soviet Union, now visit St. Petersburg and the Mariinsky Theatre.

1945 – 1991

Chapter 28: Lesson 2

Overview This lesson describes the Soviet blockade of Berlin, the Berlin Airlift, the Korean War, China's involvement in it, and the truce that ended it.

Objectives

■ To describe the blockade of Berlin and the Berlin Airlift

■ To explain how the Korean War began and ended

Student Pages pages 709–712

Teacher's Resource Library

Workbook Activity 131

Activity 131

Modified Activity 131

Vocabulary

truce

Read the definition of *truce*. Tell students that the concept of a truce is important to this lesson. Discuss the word and its relationship to compromise and mediation.

1 Warm-Up Activity

Place two different color pieces of paper of unequal size on either side of a divider, such as a ruler or pencil. Explain that the smaller paper represents a city that needs food and supplies and the other paper represents several countries that have food and supplies. Pose the problem that the two sides are hostile toward each other and the barrier cannot be crossed. Discuss with students the problems of and solutions for getting supplies to the city in need.

2 Teaching the Lesson

The blockade of Berlin and the Korean War were two major conflicts in which the U.S. played an important role. Remind students of the Truman Doctrine and ask them to recall President Truman's main goal. (to stop Communism) Tell them that the Berlin Airlift and the Korean War were part of that commitment. Then have students read pages 709–712.

3 Reinforce and Extend

Explain that the Russian ballet dancers Rudolf Nureyev, Natalia Makarova, and Mikhail Baryshnikov had outstanding performance careers as ballet dancers in the United States. Have students read "The Mariinsky Theatre."

Ask:

- **What is a blockade?** (blocking by force roads, waterways, and railways to prevent people and goods from getting through)

- **Why did the Soviet Union blockade Berlin?** (They wanted to force the Western nations to give up their claim on the city.)

- **How long did the blockade of Berlin last?** (more than a year)

- **Why was Korea divided into North and South Korea?** (The superpowers divided Korea after World War II; the Soviet Union took over the north and American forces occupied the south.)

- **What was the border between the two Korean republics?** (the 38th parallel)

- **On what date did Communist troops cross this border into South Korea?** (June 25, 1950)

ONLINE CONNECTION

 Students can gain additional information by accessing the following Web sites:

www.agsglobewh.com/page710a (interactive learning site about the cold war)

www.agsglobewh.com/page710b (interactive government site that provides audio and visual information about the Marshall Plan)

www.agsglobewh.com/page710c (Web site dedicated to Russian leader Mikhail Gorbachev and the events surrounding his presidency)

Why Did the Soviets Stop the Blockade?

Historians call this the Berlin Airlift because the West "lifted" supplies into the air and took them to Berlin. With this airlift, the Western powers showed one big thing—they would not let the Communists control any more European land. The West was not going to allow Communism to spread.

All this made the Soviets mad, but they did not shoot down any Western planes. They did not want to start a war. In May 1949, the Soviets stopped blockading Berlin.

What Started the Korean War?

Korea lies between China and Japan. In 1910, Japan made Korea part of its empire. When World War II ended, Soviet forces took over the northern half of Korea. American forces occupied the south. The 38th parallel of latitude became the border that divided the two republics. On June 25, 1950, Communist troops crossed this border into South Korea.

How Did the UN Help South Korea?

South Korea asked the United Nations to stop the North Koreans. The UN Security Council voted to send aid to South Korea. (The Soviet Union was not attending the UN meetings at that time. If it had been, the Soviets probably would have vetoed any UN action.) The United Nations sent soldiers to help South Korea. The Chinese and Soviet Union helped North Korea.

More than 54,260 American soldiers were killed in battle during the Korean War, which was fought 1950–1953.

CAREER CONNECTION

 One of the effects of the cold war was the Space Race—the competition between the United States and the Soviet Union to be the first in space and to make the greatest advances in space technology. Today the National Aeronautics and Space Administration (NASA) continues to develop space technology. NASA employs many different specialists in science and engineering in its programs. Have students research NASA to find out what types of workers it employs. Then have them choose one specialty and find out more about that field and its educational requirements. They might use reference books, the Internet, or check a university catalog. Have students write brief summaries of their findings and share with the class.

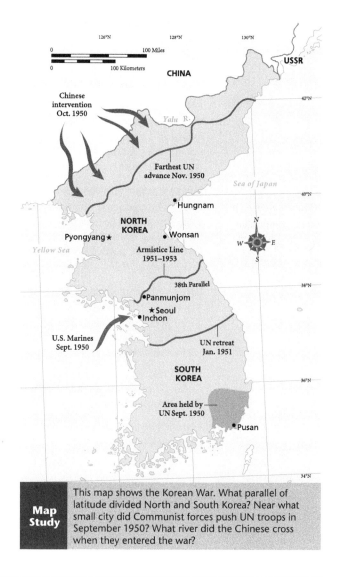

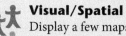

Map Study This map shows the Korean War. What parallel of latitude divided North and South Korea? Near what small city did Communist forces push UN troops in September 1950? What river did the Chinese cross when they entered the war?

Have students examine the map on page 711. Call attention to its title: "Korean War (1950–1953)." Ask a volunteer to read in chronological order the labels for the advance line, retreat line, and armistice line as the rest of the class points to the areas on their maps. Then have students read the caption and answer the questions. (The 38th parallel divided North and South Korea. Communist forces pushed the UN near Pusan, South Korea. The Chinese crossed the Yalu River.)

LEARNING STYLES

Visual/Spatial
Display a few maps that you have cut from current newspapers or magazines. Discuss with students the ways in which the maps illustrate the intended information. Then have them work in small groups to choose a current event that could be illustrated on a map. For example, students may want to map areas of conflict in Iraq or the route of the Boston Marathon. Then have the groups create maps that illustrate their topics of interest. Have the groups display their maps in class.

AT HOME

Encourage students to talk to their parents and grandparents about their experiences in the cold war. Students can ask about family members' experiences in school with air raid drills and bomb shelters. Students should ask how children of the time felt about the cold war threat. Did they think the threat was serious? Were they afraid? Ask volunteers to share their findings with the class.

ELL/ESL STRATEGY

Language Objective:
To explain information using a timeline
Divide the class into small groups of three to four students. Include ELL students in as many groups as possible. Ask students to identify the dated information on the Korean War map on page 711, such as Chinese intervention Oct. 1950. Have the groups make a list of the dates and events. Show students how to draw a timeline for the years 1950 to 1953. Then have students make their own timeline and place the events in their list along the timeline. Have students in the group quiz each other on the information in both their timeline and on the map, for example, When was the city of Pusan held by the UN? (September 1950)

Ask:

- How successful were the UN troops at first in holding back the Communist forces? (They pushed the Communist forces back to the border of China.)

- How did Chinese troops affect the war? (Chinese troops pushed UN troops back to nearly the 38th parallel.)

- What was the result of the Korean War? (Korea remained divided much as it was before the war.)

3 Reinforce and Extend

Reading Strategy:
Metacognition

Ask students to identify the important details and write the details on the board. Then have students use the details to write a short paragraph about the cold war. (Paragraphs should include the idea of two superpowers and the desire of the West to contain Communism.)

LEARNING STYLES

Body/Kinesthetic
Have students work in small groups to create a papier-mâché model of North and South Korea, using the map on page 711 and topographical maps located in atlases as guides. Make sure they indicate the 38th parallel and the Yalu River on their model. Then ask students: What difficulties might UN soldiers encounter in pushing North Korean forces back? (rough, mountainous terrain) What reasons might China have for coming to North Korea's aid? (If UN troops took over North Korea, they would be sitting right on China's border.)

Truce
An agreement to stop a war for a time

Reading Strategy:
Metacognition

Note the important details in this lesson. Summarize what you have read about the cold war.

What do you think?

Since neither the Communists nor the UN troops won the Korean War, was it worth fighting?

How Did the UN Troops Push Back the Communists?

By September 1950, the Communists controlled most of Korea. However, the UN forces got behind the North Korean lines. Then they made a surprise attack that cut the Communist forces in two and forced them to retreat.

By November, UN forces had pushed the Communists back to the Yalu River, the border between China and North Korea. It looked as if the war was over. The UN hoped that Korea would become one country again. But then China sent in thousands of troops to help the North Koreans. The fighting continued.

What Ended the Korean War?

In July 1951, **truce** talks began. A truce is an agreement to stop a war for a time. The talks dragged on for two years. Finally, the two sides signed an armistice. It left Korea divided. The border between the two Koreas was almost what it had been before the war.

Why Was the Korean War Important?

The Korean War showed that the UN could stop an attack on a member nation. It showed that China could hold its own in a war that did not use atomic weapons. It also showed that the cold war between the two superpowers would continue.

Since 1953, the United States has continued to support South Korea. It has become an industrial powerhouse in Asia. North Korea remains Communist.

Lesson 2 Review On a sheet of paper, write the answer to each question. Use complete sentences.

1. Why did the Soviets blockade Berlin in June 1948?
2. What caused the Soviets to stop the blockade?
3. What event started the Korean War?
4. How did the United Nations help South Korea?
5. What were the effects of the war on Korea?

Lesson 2 Review Answers

1. The Soviets tried to starve the people living there. **2.** They did not want to start a war. **3.** Communists from North Korea crossed the 38th Parallel into South Korea. **4.** The United Nations provided soldiers to fight the Communists. **5.** The countries remained much as they did before the war, but the United Nations showed it could stop an attack on a member nation.

Answers will vary. Historians differ as to the "value" of the Korean War. It taught the North Korean and Chinese Communists that the United States would fight to contain Communism. It also taught the United States that Communist troops would fight to the bitter end and knew how to defend their own terrain.

Objectives

- ◆ To describe the reform efforts of Khrushchev and Gorbachev
- ◆ To explain why the Soviet Union collapsed
- ◆ To describe Russia under Putin

Reading Strategy:
Metacognition

Note the main idea and important details of this paragraph. Summarize what you have read to make sure you understand this important event.

Throughout its history the Soviet Union has had serious economic problems. Soviet dictator Joseph Stalin tried to industrialize the Soviet Union. By the late 1930s, the Soviet Union had become a major industrial nation. Still, the standard of living in the Soviet Union remained very low.

Why Did Khrushchev's Reform Efforts Fail?

Stalin died in 1953. Nikita Khrushchev became the leader of the Soviet Union. He wanted to reform the weak Soviet economy and to end the government's cruel treatment of the Soviet people. To raise the people's standard of living, factories produced more consumer goods. Artists and writers were allowed some freedom to create what they wanted for the first time.

In 1964, all this changed. Leonid Brezhnev replaced Khrushchev. He opposed reform. Brezhnev punished anyone who spoke out against the government.

What Role Did Gorbachev Play in Reforming the Soviet Union?

In 1985, Mikhail Gorbachev became the new Soviet leader. Gorbachev was a younger man with new ideas. He faced big problems. The Soviet economy was falling apart. Almost one-third of the Soviet population lived in a state of poverty. People spent hours a day standing in lines to buy food and clothing. Prices were high and wages low. (A pair of winter boots cost the average citizen a month's wages!)

In the 1980s and 1990s, Russian citizens had to wait in long lines to buy things they needed because goods were scarce. Prices were very high and wages were low.

1945 – 1991

The Cold War Chapter 28 **713**

Chapter 28: Lesson 3

Overview This lesson describes the breakup of the Soviet Union and the creation of the Commonwealth of Independent States.

Objectives

- ■ To describe the reform efforts of Khrushchev and Gorbachev
- ■ To explain why the Soviet Union collapsed
- ■ To describe Russia under Putin

Student Pages pages 713–716

Teacher's Resource Library

Workbook Activity 132

Activity 132

Modified Activity 132

....

Vocabulary

coup   **glasnost**   **perestroika**

Challenge students to write a statement using each vocabulary word. For example, they might imagine themselves the newly elected leader of a country, addressing the population for the first time. Invite volunteers to share their statements.

....

1 Warm-Up Activity

Have students brainstorm a list of factors that would cause the government of a country to dissolve. Write each idea on the board, grouping the ideas into economic, political, and social factors. Ask students if one factor alone could cause collapse, or if the interaction of all factors is required. Tell students they will learn about the collapse of the USSR in this lesson.

Reading Strategy:
Metacognition

Have students reread the first section. Then have them write the question and each reason, and then a short summary paragraph. (Brezhnev replaced Krushchev; he opposed reform and punished anyone who opposed the government.)

Workbook Activity 132   **Activity 132**   *The Cold War Chapter 28* **713**

PRONUNCIATION GUIDE

Use this list to help students pronounce difficult words in this lesson.

Nikita Khrushchev
(ni kē´ tə krüsh´ chef)

Mikhail Gorbachev
(mi kīl´ gôr´ bə chôf´)

Leonid Brezhnev
(lā´ ə nid brezh´ nef)

2 Teaching the Lesson

Recall what life was like for people in the Soviet Union under Stalin. Then have students read pages 713–716 about how the Soviet Union came to an end and what replaced it.

Ask:

- How did life change for artists and writers under the leadership of Khrushchev? How did this change under Brezhnev? (They gained some creative freedom; he took their freedom away.)

- What happened under Gorbachev's policy of glasnost? (Answers will vary; students may say that the press became freer or that people could criticize the government.)

- Between 1988 and 1990 how many republics of the Soviet Union demanded independence? (seven)

- When was the Soviet flag lowered for the last time, signaling the end of the Soviet Union? (December 25, 1991)

- How has life in Russia changed under Putin? (loss of some freedoms but an improved economy and standard of living)

- What was the result of Gorbachev's perestroika? (Factories could produce all the goods people wanted.)

- What did the Russian people do for the first time in May of 1989? (elected a parliament)

- How many different languages were spoken in the Soviet Union? (112)

Soviet leader Mikhail Gorbachev (right) meets with U.S. President Ronald Reagan (left).

Glasnost

A Russian word that means "openness"; under Gorbachev it meant openness in government

Perestroika

An economic policy used by Gorbachev to encourage factories to produce the goods people wanted

Coup

A takeover of the government

Gorbachev introduced a policy of **glasnost** or openness, in government. For the first time, people could speak out against the government. He allowed more freedom of the press. To help rebuild the economy, he introduced **perestroika**. That is, he let factories produce the goods people wanted. Gorbachev called for the beginning of a market economy with less government interference.

Then, Gorbachev moved his country toward a more democratic government by creating a new Soviet parliament. The Russian people elected representatives to this parliament. Other political parties besides the Communists were allowed to run candidates. In May 1989, the Soviet parliament met for the first time. The elected representatives were allowed to speak freely. The entire meeting was carried live on Soviet television. Glasnost was being put into practice.

Gorbachev struggled with the problems that resulted from his reforms. He began to back away from them. The army and the KGB, the secret police, were worried. They knew that a breakup of the Soviet Union would mean a loss of power and influence for them. They tried to arrest Gorbachev. The attempted **coup**, or overthrow of the government, failed. A new leader named Boris Yeltsin led thousands of Russians against the army and police. Yeltsin became a national hero.

What Caused the Collapse of the Soviet Union?

The Soviet Union continued to have economic and social problems. Part of the problem was that the Soviet Union was a country made up of more than 100 different ethnic groups. It had 92 nationalities and its people spoke 112 different languages. The new policy of glasnost encouraged some groups to demand an independent country of their own. Between 1988 and 1990, people in Soviet Georgia, Latvia, Estonia, Moldavia, Uzbekistan, Azerbaijan and Lithuania demanded independence.

714   Unit 7   The World Since 1945

ELL/ESL STRATEGY

Language Objective:
To use a photograph to compare and contrast
Divide the class into small groups. Have students in their groups discuss the photo and caption on page 713, comparing and contrasting the purchase of goods in Russia in the 1980s and 1990s with shopping in local grocery stores in the United States today. Bring the class together to make a two-column chart on the board. Head one column Russia 1980s and 1990s and the other column U.S. Today. Write students' ideas about buying goods in the appropriate column. Then have students use the chart information to make statements comparing and contrasting the purchasing of goods. Ask ELL students to describe food stores in his or her native country or neighborhood. As a follow up, have students write a paragraph comparing food shopping in a familiar grocery store with food shopping in a Russian meat market.

Reading Strategy:
Metacognition

Make a prediction about what you think will happen next in the Soviet Union. As you continue reading, check to see if your prediction was right and revise it if necessary.

On December 1, 1991, the Ukraine voted for independence from the Soviet Union. Within days other Soviet republics declared their independence. Gorbachev tried to stop the breakup, but he could not. He resigned. On December 25, 1991, the Soviet flag was lowered from the Kremlin for the last time. The Soviet Union no longer existed.

Yeltsin was elected president of the new Russian republic. It had the most people and was the largest republic of the old USSR. He tried to maintain some unity among the newly independent republics by forming the Commonwealth of Independent States (CIS). Yeltsin had great difficulties governing. At the end of 1999, he resigned and was replaced by Vladimir Putin.

Boris Yeltsin (waving) became the president of Russia after the collapse of the Soviet Union. Though many Russians disagreed with how he ran the country, he was re-elected in 1996.

What Is Russia Like Under Putin?

One of the problems Yeltsin faced was an unpopular war in Chechnya. Chechnya is a largely Muslim area in southwestern Russia. Fighting continued for almost ten years. Putin took strong action to put down the rebellion. This helped him win election as president in 2000.

1945 – 1991

The Cold War   Chapter 28   **715**

WORLD CULTURES

Satellite nations of the Soviet Union often were made up of several ethnic groups. Soviet influence kept peace among these various groups. Following the breakup of the Soviet Union, some of these nations struggled violently for their own identity. The former Czechoslovakia separated peacefully into two nations—the Czech Republic and Slovakia. On the other hand, the former nation of Yugoslavia has had a stormy recent history. In the early 1990s, Croatia, Macedonia, Bosnia and Herzegovina, and Slovenia, all part of Yugoslavia, declared independence from the Yugoslavian government dominated by the Serbs. Since then the former Yugoslavia has been plagued by ethnic and territorial wars, especially among Croatians, Muslims, and Serbs.

Ask:

- What are some of the problems that have developed within the reformed nation of Russia? (Answers will vary; students may say the government cannot collect taxes or that they cannot take care of the elderly and the poor.)

- Why have people been willing to support Putin? (Life has improved for many people in Russia.)

Geography Note

Explain that Georgia sits on the east coast of the Black Sea and is bordered by Russia to the north, Turkey to the south, and Azerbaijan to the east. The Caucasus Mountains cross Georgia. Its landscape ranges from snowy alpine regions to marshland to temperate rainforests. Its diverse landscape creates an equally diverse climate.

Lesson 3 Review Answers

1. government 2. Gorbachev
3. Yeltsin 4. 1991 5. dictatorship

Answers will vary. Students may recognize that some Russians are willing to give up personal freedoms for a better economy. Others may state that the Russians have little choice in the matter and are making the best of a bad situation.

Geography Note

Georgia is a republic in southeastern Europe made up of Abkhazia, Ajaria, and South Ossetia. It was part of the former USSR. It declared its independence in 1991.

Since then, Putin has become more and more powerful. These moves are supported by most Russians. He has brought peace and stability back, but at a high price. The Russian people have lost some of their freedom. Newspapers that have criticized the president have been shut down. The government had taken over national television. The power of the country's governors has been greatly reduced. The Russian parliament has been turned into a rubber stamp. Many former members of the KGB, the secret police, hold positions of power.

The Russian people have been willing to support Putin because for many of them the quality of life has improved. His move to seize control over the nation's rich natural resources was popular. Russian oil, natural gas, and coal are in great demand and are its chief exports. The economy is booming. Russians, in particular those living in cities, are enjoying higher living standards. The Russian government is spending millions of dollars it earns on its vast natural resources to build roads, schools, shopping centers, and hotels.

Lesson 3 Review On a sheet of paper, write the word or name in parenthesis that best completes each sentence.

1. Under Communism, all major economic decisions are made by (government, consumers, investors).

2. The Soviet leader who introduced openness in government was (Khruschev, Gorbachev, Yeltsin).

3. The man who became a hero for putting down an attempt by the KGB and the army to overthrow the Soviet government was (Khruschev, Gorbachev, Yeltsin).

4. The Soviet Union broke up in (1981, 1991, 2001).

5. Under its President Vladimir Putin, Russia has become more of a (dictatorship, democracy, monarchy).

What do you think

Why do you think Russian President Putin is popular with many Russian people ?

- ◆ To describe how Eastern Europe forced their Communist leaders out
- ◆ To describe the reunification of Germany and the fall of the Berlin Wall
- ◆ To explain the ethnic cleansing in Kosovo

Reading Strategy:
Metacognition

Remember to look at the photographs and maps as you read this lesson. Note the descriptive words. This will help you visualize what you are reading.

Eastern Europe revolted against Communist rule many times. The people of Hungary revolted in 1956. Their revolt was crushed by 2,500 tanks and 200,000 soldiers of the Soviet Union. Soviet tanks also put an end to a brief period of freedom in Czechoslovakia in the spring of 1968. Poland rebelled against the dictatorship of their Communist leaders in 1956, 1979, and in 1981. All these rebellions failed. Then, in 1989, the people of Eastern Europe finally were able to force their Communist leaders out.

How Did Hungary Cut a Hole in the Iron Curtain?

Since Gorbachev had encouraged a policy of glasnost, the Hungarian government began to allow its citizens more freedom of speech and assembly. Then, on May 2, 1989, Hungarian soldiers were ordered to begin cutting down the barbed-wire fence between Austria and Hungary.

The 150-mile fence and its minefield had been built in 1969. On one side of the fence was the Communist nation of Hungary. On the other was the democratic nation of Austria. The barbed-wire fence was part of the Iron Curtain. Cutting the fence that separated the two countries was historic. Hungary was the first country in Eastern Europe to allow people to freely travel to a Western nation. Word quickly spread that there was an opening in the Iron Curtain. Soon thousands of people from East Germany, Poland, and Czechoslovakia moved through Hungary to freedom in the West. For the first time in decades, people were being allowed to "vote with their feet" about whether they wished to live in a Communist country. In October of 1989, the Communist party in Hungary ceased to exist. Hungarian leaders set about trying to create a new democratic constitutional state.

Chapter 28: Lesson 4

Overview This lesson covers the opening of the Iron Curtain and the fall of the Berlin Wall. It also explains the breakup of Yugoslavia and the formation of the European Union.

Objectives

- ■ To describe how Eastern Europe forced their Communist leaders out
- ■ To describe the reunification of Germany and the fall of the Berlin Wall
- ■ To explain the ethnic cleansing in Kosovo

Student Pages pages 717–722

Teacher's Resource Library

Workbook Activity 133

Activity 133

Modified Activity 133

Vocabulary

Berlin Wall	**solidarity**
currency	**strike**
ethnic cleansing	**tariff**

Discuss the vocabulary words and their meanings. Ask a volunteer to choose a word and make up a sentence that is a clue to the word. Classmates should try to guess the word from the clue. Continue until all the words have been guessed.

1 Warm-Up Activity

Direct students to the photo on page 718. Have students suggest words to describe the emotions felt by the people of East and West Berlin as the Berlin Wall crumbled. Discuss problems societies may have when there is a dramatic change in government.

Reading Strategy:
Metacognition

Have students write other captions for the photos on pages 718 and 719. (Answers will vary, but should capture the emotions shown.)

---

2 Teaching the Lesson

Ask students what they know about the Iron Curtain and the Berlin Wall. Have them read pages 719–724 to find out how these symbols of Communist repression were taken down and of the great changes that followed in Europe.

Ask:

- Where was the first "hole" cut in the Iron Curtain? (between Hungary and Austria)

- What did the workers in the Gdansk shipyard call their union? (Solidarity)

- What did the Berlin Wall separate? (Answers will vary; students may say the eastern part of the city from the western part of the city.)

Reading Strategy:
Metacognition

Have students list the events so far. Then have students answer the Reading Strategy question. (Answers will vary; there will be chaos in the country until a new government is formed.)

Strike

The act of refusing to work until certain demands are met

Solidarity

The name of the Polish shipbuilders' union that went out on strike in 1980

Reading Strategy:
Metacognition

Predict what will happen next in the collapse of Communist rule in Europe.

How Did Communists in Poland Give Up Power?

In 1980, a group of workers in a shipyard in the city of Gdansk, Poland went on **strike**. That is, they refused to work until their working conditions improved. (Striking was not legal in Poland.) The workers wanted Poland's Communist government to recognize their union as legal. They called their union "**Solidarity**," or unity.

For eight years, Solidarity struggled to bring about reform. In the past, protests against the government would have led to a Soviet crackdown. But in 1989, things were different. The Soviet Union stayed out of the dispute. The Communist Polish government agreed to share power. In free elections held in June of 1989, the citizens of Poland elected representatives. Solidarity won a huge victory.

How Was Germany Able to Reunite?

In Chapter 27, you learned that after World War II, Germany was divided. Since 1949, there had been two Germanys. West Germany was a democracy; East Germany was Communist. In 1989, East Germans took to the streets demanding reform. In November 1989, the entire East German government gave up their positions. The new government now said its people were free to travel where they wanted, even to West Germany.

German citizens hammered down the Berlin Wall in 1989.

BACKGROUND INFORMATION

In 1945 Germany was divided into four sectors that were occupied by four separate armies. The entire city of Berlin was within the Soviet sector of Germany, which later became known as East Germany. A year later, Berlin held free elections, but the Soviets did not want that, so they cut off East Berlin from West Berlin, hoping to make Berliners accept communism instead. The Allies came to the aid of West Berlin. In 1961, the Soviets began building the Berlin Wall to keep East Berliners who did not want to live under communism from fleeing to West Berlin. Thus, West Berlin became an island of democracy within Communist East Germany.

Berlin Wall

The wall that divided the people of East and West Berlin

Ethnic cleansing

The act of getting rid of a group of people because their religion or race is different from the majority group

Thousands of Germans rushed to the **Berlin Wall.** (Since 1961 the wall had divided the people of East and West Berlin.) They climbed up on the wall and with hammers began to break down the wall. People danced and cried, and cheered. In February 1990, representatives of the East German and West German governments agreed to reunite.

What Caused the Breakup of Yugoslavia?

Like the Soviet Union, Yugoslavia was made up of many different ethnic groups. In 1990, the Yugoslav republics of Croatia, Bosnia-Herzegovina, Slovenia, and Macedonia began a push for independence. Slobodan Milosevic, who became the leader of the Serbian republic, rejected the idea. He made war against the other republics. His forces, helped by the Serbian minority in Croatia, captured one-third of Croatia's territory. In early 1992, Bosnia-Herzegovina declared its independence. Bosnia's large Muslim population favored independence, but the Christian Serbs living there did not. By mid-1993 over 70 percent of the republic was controlled by Serb forces. They began a policy of **"ethnic cleansing."** Bosnian Muslims were forced out of their homes and property. Over two million were left homeless and nearly 250,000 Bosnians were killed. Finally, a treaty was signed that divided Bosnia into two parts.

Secretary of State Madeleine Albright visits American troops in Kosovo in 1999.

Milosevic next began a war in Kosovo, a small province of Serbia. About 90 percent of its people are ethnic Albanians. They are related more to the people of Albania than they are to the Serbs. Just as he had in Bosnia, Milosevic tried to force the non-Serbs out. Thousands of refugees fled. Many of their villages were burned and many people were killed.

Ask:

- What occurred in Yugoslavia following a push for independence? (Milosevic carried out a policy of ethnic cleansing, resulting in the deaths of thousands of non-Serbs.)
- Which government began the policy of ethnic cleansing in Eastern Europe? (the Serbian government)
- Which ethnic group was in the majority in Kosovo when Serbian troops invaded? (Albanians)

LEARNING STYLES

Body/Kinesthetic

Have students work in groups to make blocks with the names of the nations that belong to NATO. Then have students decide what type of structure to build with their blocks: a castle, bridge, or other shape. Have students work together to build their model. Students may want to top their model with a NATO flag.

Ask:

- How did NATO force Serbia to let Kosovo govern itself? (with air strikes)

- Besides going to a single currency, what have some European nations agreed to do to cooperate? (reduce trade barriers)

- What formed in 1970 as a way to reduce trade barriers in Europe? (the European Economic Community or Common Market, later called the European Union)

Writing About History

Discuss with students how opinions are taken for granted in a democracy, but that expressing an opinion under some Communist governments could get a person arrested and sent to jail. Explain to students that editorials are a writer's opinion about a particular topic, such as what should be done to protect the environment. Then have students read the Writing About History feature and write their editorials.

Tariff

A tax that countries put on goods they import or export

Writing About History

In recent decades, many nations have struggled to establish democratic governments. In your notebook, write an editorial for your local paper. Explain what you think democracy is. Tell how you feel about it

---

On March 24, 1999 NATO began air strikes against Serbia. NATO hoped that bombing would force Milosevic to stop his attacks in Kosovo. After two months of air strikes, Serbian leaders finally took their forces out of Kosovo.

The region still has many problems, but the fighting has stopped. Milosevic was put on trial for war crimes, but died during the trial. Yugoslavia no longer exists. All its former parts—Slovenia, Croatia, Bosnia and Herzegovina, Serbia, Montenegro, Kosovo, and Macedonia—are now all independent countries.

What Steps Has Europe Taken Toward Union?

After World War II a number of European countries sought closer ties. Many wanted to get rid of trade barriers and **tariffs**. A tariff is a tax that countries put on exports or imports. In 1952, six European nations agreed to create a tariff-free market for European coal and steel products. This was so successful that the same countries decided to reduce trade barriers even more. In 1970, they created the European Economic Community, also known as the Common Market.

During the 1980s and 1990s the European Community grew. In 1992, the name was changed to the European Union. In 2007, the EU had 27 members with nearly 500 million people.

Currency

The form of money a country uses

Just as people in all 50 states of the United States use the same **currency**, members of the European Union use the same euro. The EU has a parliament that makes rules and regulations about almost every aspect of economic and social life. It is working toward a common defense and foreign policy for all the members.

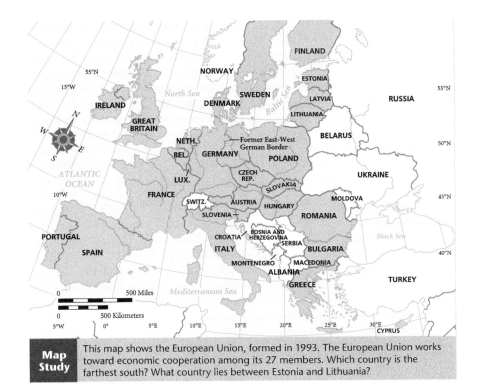

This map shows the European Union, formed in 1993. The European Union works toward economic cooperation among its 27 members. Which country is the farthest south? What country lies between Estonia and Lithuania?

Ask:

• What form of government does the European Union have? (a parliament)

• How many countries were members of the EU in 2007? (27)

• What is the name of the currency used by most nations in Western Europe? (the euro)

• What is one goal of the EU? (Answers will vary; common defense and foreign policy for all members)

Ask a volunteer to read the title of the map, The European Union, and other volunteers to identify the member nations of the European Union. Explain that Croatia, Macedonia, and Turkey are candidates for the EU. Then have students read the caption and answer the questions. (Cyprus; Latvia)

3 Reinforce and Extend

STUDY SKILLS

Have students research the names of each of the countries that use the euro. Next to the country name, have them write the name of the currency that the euro replaced.

Have students read the feature, titled "The Jet Age." Inform students that jets are still important in warfare, and they have become much more sophisticated. Have students research one of the jet fighters such as the F-15 and prepare a report that tells what it is used for, how fast it can fly, and other special features. Have students share their reports with the class.

Chapter Project Follow-up

Provide a length of banner paper to each group. Have students create a timeline of events occurring during their assigned time period. Have each group add visuals to its timeline. Connect the timelines to create a timeline mural. Discuss the events within each period and how the events of earlier years affected later events. Have students decide on a title for the timeline.

Lesson 4 Review Answers

1. Because the Hungarian border was now open, people in other countries controlled by the Soviet Union were able to flee to the West. **2.** Solidarity was the non-Communist union in Poland that fought for recognition in a one-party country. **3.** The tearing down of the Berlin Wall led, ultimately, to the unification of East and West Germany. **4.** Yugoslavia was made up of many different ethnic groups who each wanted independence. **5.** A number of European countries are now using only one currency—the euro, some countries have joined together to get rid of trade barriers and tariffs, members of the EU work to create one foreign policy and a common defense.

Answers will vary. Some students may state having a united Europe will help to insure its defense and economic health. Others may state that uniting so many cultures under one government will create many problems and ultimately result in a clash of cultures and world conflict.

The Jet Age

New technology often comes out of war. In 1939, Germany made the first successful flight of a plane powered by jet engines. By 1944, German Messerschmitt fighters were flying combat missions. They flew at nearly 550 miles an hour. The first American jet was built in 1942. After the war, the United States and the Soviet Union worked to build faster warplanes. By the Korean War in the 1950s, they had succeeded. The Americans had the F-86 Sabre jet. The Soviets had the MiG-15.

Jet planes soon changed passenger travel. Trips were faster, and there were fewer stops to refuel. Britain built the first large passenger jet in 1952. American companies soon followed. In 1958, a Boeing 707 carried passengers across the Atlantic. The first "jumbo jet" was the Boeing 747 in 1970. It could carry more than 400 people. Now, millions of people travel by jet every day.

Lesson 4 Review On a sheet of paper, write the answers to these questions. Use complete sentences.

1. Why was cutting the barbed-wire fence in Hungary important to the people behind the Iron Curtain?

2. What was Solidarity in Poland?

3. Why was the tearing down of the Berlin Wall important?

4. What caused the breakup of Yugoslavia?

5. What are some ways in which European countries are uniting?

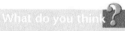

What do you think

Would a United States of Europe be good or bad for the world? Why?

The Fall of the Berlin Wall

On November 11, 1989, the Berlin Wall, which had separated East Berlin from West Berlin since 1961, fell. This is an excerpt from a personal account of that event by Andreas Ramos. Ramos, an author and computer technology expert, was in Denmark when the wall fell.

From the East German side we could hear the sound of heavy machines. With a giant drill, they were punching holes in the wall. Every time a drill poked through, everyone cheered . . . People shot off fireworks and emergency flares and rescue rockets. Many were using hammers to chip away at the wall. There were countless holes. At one place, a crowd of East German soldiers looked through a narrow hole. We reached through and shook hands. . . .

Everything was out of control. Police on horses watched. There was nothing they could do. The crowd had swollen. People were blowing long alpine horns which made a huge noise. There were fireworks, kites, flags and flags and flags, dogs, children. The wall was finally breaking. The cranes lifted slabs aside. East and West German police had traded caps. . . . The final slab was moved away. A stream of East Germans began to pour through. People applauded and slapped their backs . . . Packed in with thousands, I stood at the break in the wall. Above me, a German stood atop the wall, at the end, balanced, waving his arms and shouting reports to the crowd. With all of the East Germans coming into West Berlin, we thought it was only fair that we should go to East Berlin. A counterflow started. Looking around, I saw an indescribable joy in people's faces. It was the end of the government telling people what not to do, it was the end of the Wall, the war, the East, the West. If East Germans were going west, then we should go east, so we poured into East Berlin. Around me, people spoke German, French, Polish, Russian, every language. A woman handed her camera to someone who was standing atop rubble so that he could take her picture. . . . On top of every building were thousands of people. Berlin was out of control. There was no more government, neither in East nor in West. The police and the army were helpless. The soldiers themselves were overwhelmed by the event. They were part of the crowd. Their uniforms meant nothing. The Wall was down.

Document-Based Questions

1. How do you know this is an important event?

2. What did the Berlin Wall represent?

3. Why might someone want their picture taken atop the rubble of the wall?

4. Why do you think people were helping each other to climb on and through the wall?

5. People traveled from many surrounding countries to witness this event. Why do you think they did this?

Have students revisit and discuss the photo on page 718. Read the title of the Document-Based Reading, "The Fall of the Berlin Wall," and the introductory paragraph aloud to students. Have the class read the article silently. Discuss the series of events. Then ask four or five students who enjoy reading orally to read the excerpt to the class. Give these students a moment to meet to divide the excerpt into sections. The students should position themselves in several parts of the room for the oral reading. Allow students to be as theatrical as possible. Have students explain why they chose to portray their oral reading section as they did. Students should then write answers to the Document-Based Questions. Discuss students' answers as a group.

Answers to Document-Based Questions:

1. Answers will vary. People are cheering and taking photos, fireworks and rockets are being shot into the air.

2. Answers will vary. The division between Communism and democracy; the power and control imposed by the Communists.

3. Answers will vary. To record an important and unique moment in history. Being on top of the wall is a sign of triumph.

4. Answers will vary. They were very happy to be free to move independently from East to West and West to East.

5. Answers will vary. The fall of the wall represented the fall of Communism and the hope for an independent Europe.

Ask students to recall empires they have learned about in this book. In general, how did these empires grow? (by conquering other nations) What made them fall? (The empire grew too large to manage; people grew restless for their own governments.) Then write these questions on the board.

Ask:

- When did Gorbachev take over? (1985)
- What happened in 1989? (the Berlin Wall came down)
- Who was elected as the first president of Russia? (Boris Yeltsin)
- What was the name of the alliance that Russia, Ukraine, and Belarus formed in 1991? (Commonwealth of Independent States)

Have students skim "Fall of an Empire" to find the answers to the questions on the board. When all of the questions have been answered, have students read the selection silently. Then have students write answers to the Wrap-Up questions.

Answers to Spotlight Story Wrap-Up:

1. Originally, it was made up of 13 republics; later, Latvia, Lithuania, and Estonia were added.

2. The Russians made up the largest and most powerful group in the USSR.

3. The republics in Europe gained more freedom.

4. Some hard-line Communists plotted to get rid of Gorbachev.

5. Russians elected him president.

Fall of an Empire

Some historians call the Soviet Union the world's last empire. In 1917, the Russian Revolution ended the empire of the czars. The Soviet Union, though, took over its territory. Officially, the country's name was the Union of Soviet Socialist Republics. It had 13 republics, based somewhat on ethnic groupings. The Russians made up the largest and most powerful group.

In 1985, Mikhail Gorbachev became the Soviet leader. Gorbachev's reforms changed Eastern Europe first. He gave the republics more independence. Events were quick and dramatic. In 1989, the Berlin Wall between East and West Berlin fell. Then Germany was reunited in late 1990. Later, other Iron Curtain countries formed democratic governments.

Inside the Soviet Union, events also moved quickly. In 1990, reform parties were formed in Russia. A reformer named Boris Yeltsin quit the Communist Party. In 1991, the Russian Republic held its first free election. The people elected Yeltsin president.

In August 1991, some hard-line Communists plotted to get rid of Gorbachev. He and his family were on vacation near the Black Sea. Armed men surrounded his country house. In Moscow, security troops tried to take control. Tanks blocked the streets. They surrounded the parliament building. But thousands of Russians who wanted democracy protested. Yeltsin climbed on a tank and encouraged them. The crisis soon ended, but the Soviet Union was crumbling. In late August, the Soviet legislature took away the Communist Party's power. Then even more republics broke away from the Soviet Union.

A Russian family shares a meal.

In December 1991, Russia, Ukraine, and Belarus formed a new alliance. It was called the Commonwealth of Independent States (CIS). Russia took over running most of the Soviet central government. Then on December 25, Gorbachev resigned. The huge red Soviet flag over the Kremlin came down. The Soviet Union, formed in 1922, was over.

Spotlight Story Wrap-Up

1. What was the structure of the former Soviet Union?

2. Who made up the largest and most powerful group in the USSR?

3. How did Gorbachev's reforms affect Eastern Europe?

4. Who plotted to get rid of Gorbachev in August 1991?

5. How did Boris Yeltsin become president of Russia?

Chapter 28   SUMMARY

- Rivalry between the United States and the Soviet Union became the Cold War. Under the Truman Doctrine, the United States helped Greece and Turkey resist Communist takeovers. The Marshall Plan helped Western Europe rebuild.

- In 1948, the United States and its European allies formed the North Atlantic Treaty Organization (NATO), a military alliance. In 1955, the Soviet Union set up the Warsaw Pact with its satellite countries.

- There were many conflicts between the superpowers, including the Berlin Airlift in Germany and the Korean War.

- Mikhail Gorbachev became the Soviet leader in 1985. He allowed more freedom (glasnost), reformed the economy (perestroika), and moved toward democracy.

- In 1991, the Soviet Union broke into independent republics. Boris Yeltsin was elected president of Russia. He tried to continue economic reforms, but crime and poverty hurt many Russians.

- Changes in the Soviet Union affected Eastern Europe. In 1989, people in Hungary, Poland, and East Germany overthrew Communist governments. The Berlin Wall came down, and Germany was reunited.

- The breakup of Yugoslavia brought conflicts. Serbian leader Slobodan Milosevic went to war against other ethnic groups in Bosnia and Kosovo.

- Western European nations worked toward economic unity. In 1992 they became the European Union. They adopted a new currency, the euro. In 2007, the European Union had 27 members, with nearly 500 million people.

Using the Chapter Summary

Have students read the Chapter Summary on page 725 to review the main ideas presented in Chapter 28.

Ask:

- **What was the purpose behind the Truman Doctrine? The Marshall Plan?** (assist Turkey and Greece to resist Communism; to help Western Europe rebuild)

- **When was NATO established?** (1948)

- **What were two conflicts between the superpowers?** (Berlin Airlift, Korean War)

- **What were three reforms accomplished by Mikhail Gorbachev?** (allowed more freedom, reformed the economy, moved toward democracy)

- **Why did Boris Yeltsin find it difficult to continue the reforms of Mikhail Gorbachev?** (Crime and poverty hurt many Russians.)

- **What happened as a result of the fall of the Berlin Wall?** (Berlin and Germany were reunited.)

- **What occurred following the breakup of Yugoslavia?** (Serbian leader Slobodan Milosevic went to war against other ethnic groups.)

- **How many people are included in the European Union?** (nearly 500 million people)

Chapter 28 Review

Use the Chapter Review to prepare students for the tests and to reteach content from the chapter.

Chapter 28 Mastery Test

The Teacher's Resource Library includes two forms of the Chapter 28 Mastery Test. Each test addresses the chapter Goals for Learning. An optional third page of additional critical-thinking items is included for each test. The difficulty level of the two forms is equivalent

Chapter 28 Review Answers

1. Marshall Plan
2. Berlin
3. South Korea
4. truce
5. Truman Doctrine
6. China
7. glasnost
8. perestroika
9. Warsaw Pact
10. currency
11. B
12. D

Chapter 28   R E V I E W

Word Bank
Berlin
China
currency
glasnost
Marshall Plan
perestroika
South Korea
truce
Truman Doctrine
Warsaw Pact

On a sheet of paper, use the words from the Word Bank to complete each sentence correctly.

1. The _____ helped Europe recover from World War II.

2. In 1948, the Soviets tried to blockade _____.

3. In June 1950, the Communists tried to expand into _____.

4. A _____ is an agreement to stop a war for a time.

5. The _____ was an attempt to stop the spread of Communism.

6. Communist soldiers from _____ crossed into North Korea to join the fighting there.

7. Gorbachev introduced _____, or openness, to the Soviet Union.

8. Gorbachev also introduced _____, which was a looser economic policy.

9. The _____ set up a military alliance between the Soviet Union and its satellite nations.

10. Several European countries have also agreed to use one _____, or form of money.

On a sheet of paper, write the letter of the answer that correctly completes each sentence.

11. In 1985, _____ became the Soviet leader.

  A Joseph Stalin   **C** Nikita Khrushchev
  B Mikhail Gorbachev   **D** Boris Yeltsin

12. The Soviet Union came to an end in _____.

  A 1980   **B** 1986   **C** 1990   **D** 1991

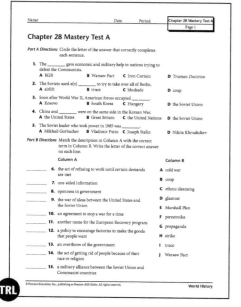

13. When Boris Yeltsin resigned at the end of 1999, he was replaced by _____.

  A Mikhail Gorbachev   **C** Vladimir Putin

  B Nikita Khrushchev   **D** Slobodan Milosevic

14. Workers in Poland called their union _____.

  A Gdansk   **C** Solidarity

  B Iron Curtain   **D** Glasnost

15. All the countries of the European Union use the same _____.

  A currency   **C** office building

  B flag   **D** language

On a sheet of paper, write the answer to each question. Use complete sentences.

16. How did the Marshall Plan help Europe?

17. What was the purpose of NATO?

18. Why was the Korean War important?

Critical Thinking On a sheet of paper, write your response to each question. Use complete sentences.

19. The United States and Great Britain used an airlift to help the people in Berlin during the Soviet blockade. If they had not done this, what might have happened?

20. In Chapter 25, you read about the Russian Revolution of 1917. Which is more important—that revolution or the Russian Revolution of 1991? Explain your answer.

Be sure you understand what a test question is asking. Reread the questions if you have to.

1945 – 1991

The Cold War   Chapter 28   **727**

---

13. C

14. C

15. A

16. By providing needed funds, the Marshall Plan allowed Europeans to rebuild.

17. The original nations that formed NATO wanted to create a mutual defense against Communist aggression.

18. Answers will vary. It showed that the United Nations could stop an aggressive attack against a member nation.

Critical Thinking

19. Answers will vary. Most likely all of Berlin would have come under Soviet control.

20. Answers will vary. Some students may say that the Russian Revolution in 1917 was more important because it signaled a rise of Communism in Russia. Others may say the Russian Revolution in 1991 was more important because it signaled the fall of Communism in Russia.

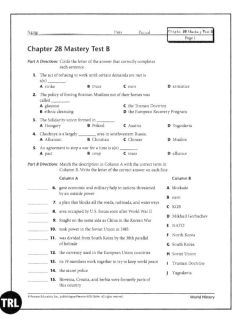

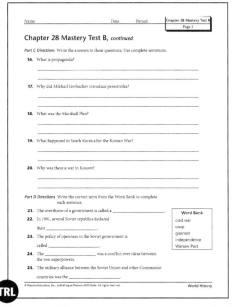

Chapter 28 Mastery Test B, pages 1–3

The Cold War   Chapter 28   **727**

Introducing the Chapter

After World War II, colonies in Africa, Asia, and the Middle East sought independence from foreign rule. Mandela worked to free the people of South

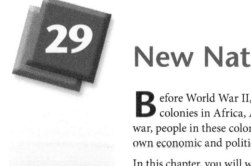

29 New Nations Emerge

Before World War II, European nations controlled many colonies in Africa, Asia, and the Middle East. After the war, people in these colonies wanted to be free to make their own economic and political decisions.

In this chapter, you will watch colonies in Africa become independent and learn about apartheid. You will journey to the Middle East, where Israelis and Palestinians have been fighting for many years. You will read about Gandhi in India, and you will travel to China and Vietnam, where fierce wars were fought.

Goals for Learning

◆ To explain how the countries of Africa gained their independence, and to describe apartheid

◆ To explain the problems that exist between the Israelis and the Palestinians

◆ To explain the two problems that faced Gandhi in unifying India

◆ To describe the two groups that fought for control of China and to detail the outcome of this struggle

◆ To detail the events of the Vietnam War

1947 British India is divided into the free nations of India and Pakistan

1957 Vietnam War begins

1976 North and South Vietnam unite

1994 Nelson Mandela is elected president of South Africa

1945   1970   1995

1949 Nationalists and Communists begin to fight a civil war in China

1948 Israel becomes a nation; fighting begins with Arabs

1975 North Vietnamese take control of Saigon

1995 Israeli Prime Minister Yitzhak Rabin is assassinated

Africa from the policy of apartheid, and Gandhi brought independence to India. Meanwhile, wars broke out in the Middle East, China, and Vietnam.

Ask:

• When did Israel become a nation? (1948)

• In what year did the unification of North and South Vietnam occur? (1976)

• Which political leader was assassinated in 1995? (Yitzhak Rabin)

Name   Date   Period   *SELF-STUDY GUIDE*

Chapter 29: New Nations Emerge

Goal 29.1 To explain how the countries of Africa gained their independence, and to describe apartheid

Date	Assignment	Completed
	1. Read pages 728–736.	
	2. Complete the Lesson 1 Review on page 736.	
	3. Complete Workbook Activity 134.	

Comments:

Goal 29.2 To explain the problems that exist between the Israelis and the Palestinians

Date	Assignment	Completed
	4. Read pages 737–741.	
	5. Complete the Lesson 2 Review on page 741.	
	6. Complete Workbook Activity 135.	

Comments:

Goal 29.3 To explain the two problems that faced Gandhi in unifying India

Date	Assignment	Completed
	7. Read pages 742–744.	
	8. Complete the Lesson 3 Review on page 744.	
	9. Complete Workbook Activity 136.	

Comments:

© Pearson Education, Inc., publishing as Pearson AGS Globe. All rights reserved.   World History

TRL

Chapter 29 Self-Study Guide, pages 1–2

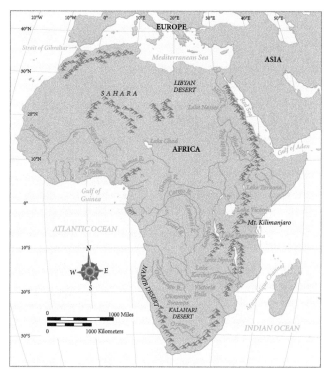

This is a topographic map of current-day Africa. That is, it shows Africa's mountains, deserts, lakes, swamps, and rivers.

Study the map, then answer the following questions:

1. Which African coast—the east or the west—has the most mountains?

2. What are the names of three deserts in Africa?

3. What are the names of three lakes in Africa?

4. What are the names of three rivers in Africa?

5. What ocean lies to the east of Africa?

Ask a volunteer to read the title of the map, "Africa." Then have students read the paragraph under the map.

Ask:

- What is the name of the lake located at approximately 30° east longitude and 20° north latitude? (Nasser)
- Which lake is located on the equator (0° latitude)? (Victoria)
- Which lake is located on the prime meridian (0° longitude)? (Volta)

Have students read and write answers to the questions.

Map Skills Answers

1. Most are on the east coast.

2. Deserts in Africa include: Sahara, Libyan Desert, Namib Desert, and the Kalahari Desert

3. Lakes in Africa include: Lake Nasser, Lake Chad, Lake Volta, Lake Turkana, Lake Victoria, Lake Tanganyika, Lake Nyasa, and Lake Kariba.

4. Rivers in Africa include: Senegal River, Niger River, Benue River, Nile River, Blue Nile, White Nile, Ubangi River, Congo River, Lomami River, Lualabu River, Kasai River, Okavango River, Zambezi River, and the Orange River.

5. Indian Ocean

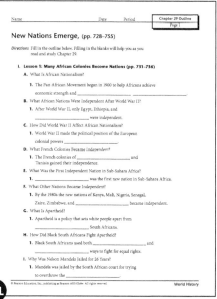

Chapter Project

Divide the class into five groups. Explain that each group will create an illustrated timeline of events that took place between 1946 and 1999 in relation to one of the following topics: India and Independence; Israel: The Struggle for a Homeland; The Many Faces of Africa; Changes in China; Vietnam: War and Peace. Students should consult multiple sources to gather information for the timeline, which should include text, illustrations, and artifacts associated with the events that transpired and the philosophies behind these. Encourage students to cover positive events and outcomes as well as conflicts and wars. Timelines should be constructed on mural paper and displayed in the classroom.

Summarizing

Prepare a template listing the words *who, what, when, where, why,* and *how,* with a blank space next to each word for the corresponding information. Leave space at the bottom for a written summary. Distribute copies of the template, along with a high-interest newspaper article. Working in small groups, have students read the sample article and then fill in the template together. Ask students to write their summaries while you write your own. Ask volunteers to share their summaries, and then share yours. Guide students in applying this strategy to content reading in the textbook.

Key Vocabulary Words

Point out that these chapter words are presented in the order that they appear in each lesson. They also are found in the Glossary. Ask students to write a description of a political demonstration that they have seen, or that they have heard or read about.

Reading Strategy:
Summarizing

When readers summarize, they ask questions about what they are reading. As you read the text in this chapter, ask yourself the following questions:

◆ Who or what is this about?

◆ What is the main thing being said about this topic?

◆ What details are important to the main idea or event?

Key Vocabulary Words

Lesson 1 ——————————
African Nationalism The struggle by native African people to gain their economic and political freedom from European colonial rulers

Pan-African Movement A group that planned ways in which Africans could achieve economic strength and political peace

British Commonwealth of Nations A group of nations that is loyal to the British monarch

Apartheid The official policy of the Union of South Africa that refused to give black and other nonwhite people any political, economic, or social rights

African National Congress (ANC) A black nationalist group in South Africa

Demonstrate To join together with other people to protest and march against something

Legalize To make lawful

Multiracial Having to do with all people and all races

Lesson 2 ——————————
Displace To move people from their home or land; to force people to leave their home or land

Palestinian Liberation Organization (PLO) The group of Palestinians dedicated to regaining from Israel their homeland in Palestine

Terrorist A person who uses violence to frighten people and to get them to obey

Lesson 3 ——————————
Passive resistance A nonviolent way of protesting for political and social change

Lesson 5 ——————————
Election An act by which people choose someone or something by voting

Vietnamization The U.S. plan to turn the fighting of the Vietnam War over to the South Vietnamese army

◆ To explain how African nations gained their independence

◆ To describe apartheid

African Nationalism

The struggle by native African people to gain their economic and political freedom from European colonial rulers

Pan-African Movement

A group that planned ways in which Africans could achieve economic strength and political peace

Between 1945 and 1990, more than 50 African countries became independent nations. The number is large because Africa is large. It has many different cultures.

Africa has three different geographic areas. The first is North Africa. It is the land between the Mediterranean Sea and the Sahara. Muslim Arabs and Muslim Berbers live there. But they have different cultural and religious roots.

The second geographic area in Africa is the sub-Sahara. It lies below the Sahara. People from many different cultures live on the land south of the Sahara. The third geographic area in Africa is its southern tip.

What Is African Nationalism?

For many years, native Africans struggled to gain economic and political freedom from their European colonial rulers. We call their struggle **African Nationalism.** Beginning in 1900, the Pan-African Movement met several times to plan for the political independence of Africa.

The **Pan-African Movement** wanted Africans to achieve economic strength and political peace. To do this, they had to work with what they had in common. The movement helped native Africans and their descendants in every part of the world. The group trained people who became political leaders of several new African nations.

What African Nations Were Independent After World War II?

When World War II ended, North Africa had only three independent nations—Egypt and Ethiopia, and Liberia. At the southern tip of the continent lay South Africa, which also had self-rule. Between North Africa and South Africa lay all the other land of this huge continent. Britain, France, Belgium, and Portugal controlled most of this in-between land.

1946 – 1999

Chapter 29: Lesson 1

Overview Students will learn how more than 50 African countries gained their independence between 1945 and 1990. They will also learn about the policy of apartheid in South Africa and how it was abolished.

Objectives

■ To explain how African nations gained their independence

■ To describe apartheid

Student Pages pages 731–736

Teacher's Resource Library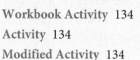

   Workbook Activity 134

   Activity 134

   Modified Activity 134

Vocabulary

African National Congress
African Nationalism
apartheid
British Commonwealth of Nations
demonstrate
legalize
multiracial
Pan-African Movement

Encourage students to write sentences combining multiple vocabulary words in the correct context. Have them write as many sentences as necessary to use every term on the list at least once. Have students exchange papers with a partner. If students notice that word usage needs to be changed in their partners' sentences, have them make suggestions.

1 Warm-Up Activity

Have each student write a one-paragraph description of his or her idea of everyday life in Africa. Ask for volunteers to read their paragraphs aloud to the class. To illustrate the contrast between the positive and the problematic characteristics of modern African life, show two or more cultural artifacts that express these extremes. For example, have the class watch a DVD performance of the Soweto Gospel Choir, and then

---

pass around a news magazine story featuring photographs from a famine-stricken or war-torn African country. Engage students in a discussion on this mix of positive and challenging aspects of everyday life in Africa today.

PRONUNCIATION GUIDE

Use this list to help students pronounce difficult words in this lesson.

apartheid   (ə pärt´ hāt)

Kwame Nkrumah

                   (kwä´ mē ən krü´ mə)

 Teaching the Lesson

Have students look at the map of Africa on page 729. Tell students that in addition to differences in physical landscape, each African nation also has a unique government and culture. Have students read pages 731–736 to learn more about the differences among African cultures.

Ask:

- Which two Muslim groups live in North Africa? (Muslim Arabs and Muslim Berbers)

- What is sub-Sahara Africa? (the portion of Africa south of the Sahara)

- When was the first meeting of the Pan-African Movement? (1900)

- Which European countries controlled most of Africa after World War II? (Britain, France, Belgium, and Portugal)

- How many Africans fought on the side of their European rulers in World War II? (200,000)

Have a student read the title of the map, "Independence in Africa." Explain that the dates on the map reflect the year each nation became independent.

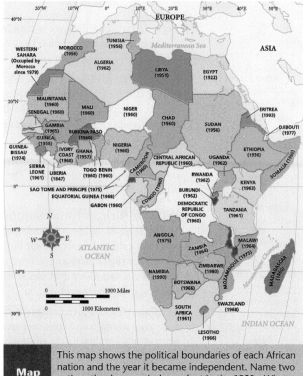

Map Study This map shows the political boundaries of each African nation and the year it became independent. Name two nations that became independent in the 1950s. What was the last country in Africa to become independent? How long has South Africa been an independent nation?

How Did World War II Affect African Nationalism?

World War II weakened the political position of all the European colonial powers. During World War II, more than 200,000 Africans fought on the side of their British and French colonial rulers. After the war, these people felt they had earned the right to rule themselves.

Ask:

- When did Egypt become independent? (1922)

- When did Eritrea become independent? (1993)

- When did South Africa become independent? (1961)

Then have students read the caption and answer the questions.

(These nations became independent in the 1950s: Morocco [1956], Libya [1951], Tunisia [1956], Sudan [1956], Guinea [1958], and Ghana [1957]. Niger became independent in 1960. The last country in Africa to become independent was Eritrea [1993]. South Africa has been independent since 1961.)

Kwame Nkrumah (center) became the leader of Ghana after it gained its independence in 1957.

British Commonwealth of Nations

A group of nations that is loyal to the British monarch

Reading Strategy:
Summarizing

Stop often as you read. Try to sum up the events using your own words.

What French Colonies Became Independent?

The European colonial powers denied self-rule and independence. France in particular did not want to lose its colonies in North Africa. However, Morocco and Tunisia—both French colonies—gained their independence.

France wanted to hold on to the colony of Algeria. The French went to war with the Arab and Berber people living there. This war lasted from 1954 to 1961. But in 1962, Algeria, the last French colony in North Africa, finally won its independence.

What Was the First Independent Nation in Sub-Sahara Africa?

African Nationalism also spread to the European colonies in sub-Sahara Africa. The first new nation in this area was Ghana. Its people gained their independence in 1957.

Great Britain had ruled this area—called the Gold Coast—for 83 years. The people living there named their new nation after an ancient African empire. Kwame Nkrumah was the new African leader of Ghana. He said, "There is a new Africa in the world."

What Other Nations Became Independent?

Over the next 20 years, the "new Africa" continued to grow. In 1960 alone, 17 African nations gained their independence. Because of this, historians call 1960 "the year of Africa."

By the 1980s, more than 50 African countries had become independent nations. These new nations included Kenya, Mali, Nigeria, Senegal, Zaire, and Zimbabwe. Eritrea—the last area to gain its independence—became a nation in 1993.

What Is Apartheid?

Until the 1960s, the Union of South Africa was the only self-governing nation in the southern part of the continent. It belonged to the **British Commonwealth of Nations**—a group of nations that is loyal to the British monarch.

1946 – 1999

New Nations Emerge   Chapter 29   **733**

ONLINE CONNECTION

Students can gain additional information by accessing the following Web sites:

www.agsglobewh.com/page733a (This global network enables teachers and students to collaborate with their peers around the world on service-learning projects that enhance both classroom knowledge and intercultural communication on a worldwide scale.)

www.agsglobewh.com/page733b (This site offers a comprehensive collection of primary and secondary resources, slides, photographs, sounds, and texts on Africa.)

www.agsglobewh.com/page733c (The events of 1947 and the road to India's independence, as reported in the pages of the New York Times, are available in this online archive.)

Biography

Ask students whether the name they are called is their birth name or a nickname. Encourage volunteers to share whether they chose their nicknames themselves or, if not, who did. Then have students read the biography to find out how a man named Johnstone Kamau came to be known as Jomo Kenyatta. After reading the feature together as a class, discuss with students the appropriateness of Jomo as a new name for this freedom fighter.

Ask:

- **Which three kinds of rights were denied nonwhites under apartheid?** (political, economic, and social rights)

- **What group claimed responsibility for the 1983 car bombing near a South African military base?** (African National Congress)

- **Who won the Nobel Peace Prize in 1984 for his nonviolent protests in South Africa?** (Bishop Desmond Tutu)

Apartheid
The official policy of the Union of South Africa that refused to give black and other nonwhite people any political, economic, or social rights

African National Congress (ANC)
A black nationalist group in South Africa

South Africa was different from the rest of Africa because whites living there controlled it. In 1948, the white-controlled government in South Africa made **apartheid** its official policy. This policy set blacks and other nonwhite South Africans apart from whites. White South Africans refused to give black and other nonwhite people any political, economic, or social rights. Whites also decided where nonwhites could live.

Great Britain and other nations protested this apartheid policy. South Africa then withdrew from the British Commonwealth. In 1961, South Africa became a republic.

How Did Black South Africans Fight Apartheid?

In 1976, a protest against apartheid turned into a riot. More than 500 people—mostly blacks—were killed. In 1983, a car bomb near a military base killed or injured more than 100 people. The **African National Congress (ANC),** a black nationalist group, said it had done the bombing.

As black South Africans struggled for equal rights, some used violence. Others did not. Bishop Desmond Tutu led nonviolent protests against apartheid. For his efforts to free South Africa from apartheid, Tutu was awarded the Nobel Peace Prize in 1984.

Biography

Jomo Kenyatta: c. 1890–1978

Jomo Kenyatta spent his life working for black rule in Kenya. As a boy, he attended a Scottish mission school. There he was called Johnstone Kamau.

As an adult, Kenyatta joined a political group. It was trying to change British colonial rule. Local government officials would not listen, however. In 1931, Kenyatta went to England to work there for the changes he desired. In England, he took the name *Jomo,* or "burning spear."

Kenyatta returned to Kenya in 1946 and worked for independence. Then he was jailed for his beliefs and actions. After Kenya gained independence in 1963, he became its first president.

Nelson Mandela (center) was sent to prison for 26 years for his actions against the white minority government in South Africa. However, when he was released from prison, he helped end apartheid and became the president of South Africa.

In 1986, the South African government said that blacks could no longer **demonstrate** against apartheid. That is, they could not join together with other blacks to protest and march against apartheid. But blacks continued to protest. The South African government put many black political leaders in jail.

Reading Strategy:
Summarizing

What important person is introduced in this section?

Demonstrate

To join together with other people to protest and march against something

Legalize

To make lawful

Why Was Nelson Mandela Jailed for 26 Years?

On the first day that young Rolihlahla Mandela went to school in South Africa, his teacher gave him an English name—Nelson. In his native language, *Rolihlahla* means "he who pulls the branch of a tree." The English translate this word as "trouble maker." As an adult, Nelson Mandela did make trouble for those who wanted apartheid. He changed the history of his country.

In June 1964, a South African court sentenced Mandela to life in prison. The court said that Mandela had tried to overthrow the white minority government. The government wanted to silence Mandela because he worked to gain political, economic, and social rights for black South Africans. For 26 years, he remained in prison.

Who Released Mandela from Prison?

The South African government locked Mandela behind prison walls. But he was still a hero for black South Africans. In 1989, F. W. de Klerk became president of the Republic of South Africa. By this time, the black protest to end apartheid was growing stronger. President de Klerk **legalized** the African National Congress. (That is, he said that people could join it without breaking the law.) In 1990, de Klerk released Mandela from prison.

Reading Strategy:
Summarizing

(Have students complete the following: _____ is introduced in this section.)

Ask:

- In what year did the South African government outlaw demonstrations against apartheid? (1986)

- What was Nelson Mandela's birth name? What does this name mean in English? (Rolihlahla; "troublemaker")

- How many years was Mandela imprisoned? (26 years)

- Which South African president legalized the African National Congress and freed Mandela from prison? (F. W. de Klerk)

Ask:

- Which two leaders arranged South Africa's first multiracial election? (Mandela and de Klerk)
- What prize was awarded to de Klerk and Mandela for their joint efforts against apartheid? (1993 Nobel Peace Prize)
- Who was elected president of South Africa in 1994? (Nelson Mandela)

 3 Reinforce and Extend

LEARNING STYLES

 Body/Kinesthetic
Ask for volunteers to stage a silent drama. Have one volunteer play the role of Bishop Desmond Tutu leading others in a peace march and receiving the Nobel Peace Prize. Have other volunteers play the parts of fellow marchers, prize committee members who vote on and present the award, and other supporting roles.

IN THE COMMUNITY

 Most human rights groups are international in scope. Students can get a flavor of human rights advocacy in their own community through researching social service organizations. Ask each student to contact a social service group in which they have particular interest. Examples include organizations that help disabled or homeless citizens, the Salvation Army, or senior persons services. Encourage students to visit the organization and interview a member or gather information through available literature. Have students write a summary of the community service and report their findings to the class.

Multiracial
Having to do with all people and all races

How Did Mandela Help South Africans?

The ANC made Mandela its leader. Right away, Mandela called for an end to white privileges. For four years, Mandela and de Klerk negotiated over black political, economic, and social rights.

Finally, the two leaders agreed to a plan. It provided for South Africa's first **multiracial** election. *Multiracial* means all the people and all races. A multiracial election means people of all races can vote. Because of their work together, de Klerk and Mandela were awarded the 1993 Nobel Peace Prize.

In 1994, the people of South Africa elected Mandela to be their president. He served one term. Then, in 1999, at the age of 80, he retired from public office. People around the world honored him. He had broken down apartheid and united a divided nation.

Lesson 1 Review On a sheet of paper, write the answer to each question. Use complete sentences.

1. Into how many geographic areas is Africa divided?
2. What is African Nationalism?
3. What is the name of the first nation created south of the Sahara?
4. How was the nation of South Africa different from other African nations?
5. Why do many South Africans and other people think that Nelson Mandela is a hero?

 What do you think
Why do you think the small white minority in South Africa adopted a policy of apartheid?

Lesson 1 Review Answers

1. Africa is divided into three geographic areas. **2.** African Nationalism is the struggle of Africans to win freedom from their European colonial rulers. **3.** Ghana is the first nation created south of the Sahara. **4.** Unlike other African nations, South Africa had a policy of apartheid, or separateness, for its nonwhites. **5.** Nelson Mandela spent 26 years in prison because he fought against apartheid. After being released from prison, he negotiated the end of apartheid. Then he became the first black president of South Africa in modern times.

Answers will vary. The small white minority probably feared that if blacks had the right to vote they would vote the whites out of office and live wherever they pleased.

Objectives

◆ To explain the problems that exist between the Israelis and the Palestinians
◆ To describe the Arab-Israeli War and its outcome

More than 3,000 years ago, Palestine was the home of the Jewish people. But because of wars and troubles, many Jews moved to countries in Europe. However, in these places, some people persecuted them. That is, people were mean and unfair to the Jews because of their beliefs. For centuries, they dreamed of a Jewish homeland. There they would be safe; they could follow their own traditions.

What Homeland Did the Jewish People Choose?

In the 19th century, Jewish leaders began to discuss the idea of creating a Jewish nation in Palestine. By 1900, Jews were moving into the dry, desert land of Palestine. However, for many generations, Palestine had been the home of Palestinian Arabs.

How Did World War II Affect the Jewish People?

When World War I ended, Britain gained control of Palestine. In the 1930s, many Jews moved there to escape the Nazis in Germany. As you know, during World War II, the Nazis murdered over six million Jews. After the war, Jewish people wanted a homeland more than ever. They believed that only there would they be safe.

How Did Israel Become a Nation?

After World War II, thousands of Jews left Europe to create their own nation in Palestine. The British could not stop them from settling there. Finally, Britain decided to leave Palestine. The United Nations was left to control it.

In 1947, the United Nations voted to divide Palestine into Jewish and Arab states. In May 1948, the new nation of Israel was declared by Jewish leader David Ben-Gurion. The neighboring Arab nations opposed the creation of a Jewish nation.

Reading Strategy:
Summarizing

What are some important details that help you understand why Israel was created?

Chapter 29: Lesson 2

Overview This lesson describes the history of the problems that developed in the Middle East as Jewish people moved into Palestine seeking a homeland.

Objectives

■ To explain the problems that exist between the Israelis and the Palestinians
■ To describe the Arab-Israeli War and its outcome

Student Pages pages 737–741

Teacher's Resource Library TRL

Workbook Activity 135

Activity 135

Modified Activity 135

Vocabulary

displace
Palestinian Liberation Organization (PLO)
terrorist

Have students read aloud definitions for the vocabulary words. As each is read, ask a volunteer to name the word, define it in his or her own words, and write it on the board. Have classmates listen to the definitions and, if they are not accurate, explain how to change them.

1 Warm-Up Activity

Write the following questions on the board or distribute to students:

1. Where is your homeland?
2. Why do you think of that place as your homeland?

Ask students to write out their answers. Then have students discuss them with the class. On chart paper, list the students' definitions of "homeland" and analyze them.

Reading Strategy:
Summarizing

(Answers will vary but may include that Jews left Europe, and that Palestine was divided into Israel and Arab states.)

Workbook Activity 135

Activity 135

2 Teaching the Lesson

Ask students to think about what it would be like to have to give up something of great importance to them. Explain that they will be reading about two groups of people that felt strongly about the same territory. Have students read pages 737–741 to find out about these two groups.

Ask:

- Which five Arab countries attacked Israel in 1948? (Egypt, Iraq, Jordan, Lebanon, and Syria)

- Where did Palestinian Arabs relocate when they fled Israel? (Lebanon, Jordan, and Syria)

- How many more wars have been fought between Israel and the Arab nations since the 1948 war? (four more)

- Where were displaced Palestinian Arabs forced to live? (in refugee camps)

Dr. Chaim Weizmann took the oath as the first president of Israel in 1948.

Displace
To move people from their home or land; to force people to leave their home or land

What Was the Outcome of the 1948 Arab-Israeli War?

These Arab countries—Egypt, Iraq, Jordan, Lebanon, and Syria—attacked Israel. Nearly 400,000 Arabs in Palestine fled the area because of the fighting. These Palestinian refugees settled mostly in Lebanon, Jordan, and Syria.

The Israeli army quickly defeated the invading Arab armies. As a result, Israel gained most of the land in Palestine. Egypt and Jordan took the remaining land.

In the next 30 years, Israel fought four more wars against the Arab nations that surrounded it. Each time, Israel defeated their armies. However, the defeated Arab nations still refused to admit that Israel was a nation. Arab leaders even refused to meet with Israeli officials to discuss peace.

What Did the PLO Want?

These wars **displaced** many Palestinian Arabs. These people were forced to leave their homes. They ended up in refugee camps. They had no land of their own to live on. These displaced people demanded that they be given their own nation within Palestine.

Some Palestinian Arabs formed the **Palestinian Liberation Organization (PLO).** By the 1970s, many members of the PLO had become **terrorists**. They used violence to frighten Israeli citizens and to force them to leave Palestine. The PLO staged raids on Israel from neighboring Arab nations, such as Lebanon. In the early 1980s, Israel invaded Lebanon to rid it of the PLO.

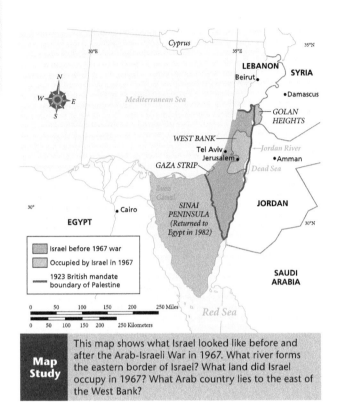

Map Study This map shows what Israel looked like before and after the Arab-Israeli War in 1967. What river forms the eastern border of Israel? What land did Israel occupy in 1967? What Arab country lies to the east of the West Bank?

Ask:

• What is the name of the group that tried to force Israelis to leave Palestine? (the Palestinian Liberation Organization)

• Which country did Israel attack in an effort to eliminate the PLO? (Lebanon)

Have a volunteer read the title of the map, "Israel in 1967." Ask students to examine the map and its key. Have students identify the city on the border of Israel and its occupied land on the West Bank. (Jerusalem) Have students read the caption and answer the questions. (Beirut is in Lebanon. The Jordan River is the eastern border of Israel. Israel occupied the Sinai Peninsula, the Gaza Strip, the Golan Heights, and the West Bank in 1967. Syria lies to the east of the Golan Heights. Jordan lies to the east of the West Bank.)

STUDY SKILLS

 Israel is a land of turmoil due to conflicting claims laid upon it by Jews and Palestinian Arabs. Ask students to make two lists. One list should give reasons supporting Israeli claims to the land. The other list should give reasons supporting Palestinian claims to the land. Discuss these lists as a class. Encourage students to keep these lists to help them study for the Chapter Review.

Reading Strategy:
Summarizing

(Have students answer the question
in the who-what-when format.)

Ask:

- Who attacked Israeli soldiers in the
West Bank and the Golan Heights
in 1987? (Palestinian women and
children)

- Israel allowed Palestinians to control
parts of which two areas? (the
Gaza Strip and the West Bank)

- What do the Palestinians want from
Israel? (answers will vary; students
may say the Palestinians want more
land to create their own nation)

 Reinforce and Extend

ELL/ESL STRATEGY

Language Objective:
To write descriptively
Provide students in
small groups with copies
of a newspaper or newsmagazine
street-scene photograph of the
Israeli-Palestinian conflict. Tell
students that they will write a
description of the sights, and the
imagined sounds and smells, that
surround the scene. Ask students to
use evidence from the photograph,
as well as their knowledge of the
conflict, in their descriptions.
Have students examine the image
to find clues about the economics,
commerce, and/or living conditions
of the area. Encourage groups to
share their written descriptions with
the class.

When Did Children Get Involved in the Fight?

In 1987, violence spread to areas that lay south of Lebanon
called the West Bank and the Golan Heights. Young Palestinian
children and women put up barriers in the streets. Then they
threw rocks at Israeli soldiers. They killed a few soldiers and
injured others. But the soldiers also killed and injured some
Arab women and children.

After this, the Israeli soldiers arrested hundreds of Palestinians.
Israel believed that controlling the West Bank was necessary
for its security. In fact, hundreds of Israeli families had already
built homes in the West Bank.

Reading Strategy:
Summarizing

What is the main idea
of this paragraph?

How Did the Israelis and the Palestinians Work Together?

During the 1990s, the Palestinian Arabs began to work with
the Israelis to obtain Palestinian self-rule. In 1994, the Israelis
allowed the Palestinians to take control of much of the Gaza
Strip and the West Bank. (A few hundred thousand Jewish
settlers and more than two million Palestinians live in the West
Bank and the Gaza Strip.)

Why Do the Israelis Not Want to Give Up Land?

In 1998, Israel celebrated because it had been a nation for 50
years. The Israelis had fought again and again to keep their
homeland. However, the Palestinians did not celebrate.

Instead, the Palestinians called, once again, for the creation
of their own nation. They began to argue and fight with the
Israelis over land. The Palestinians wanted Israel to give up
land in return for peace. The government of Israel thought that
giving up land would weaken its security.

World leaders want the Israelis and Palestinians to negotiate
again and to create peace in the Middle East. Both sides
continue to search for the right solution.

AT HOME

 Some students may have
vague perceptions of the
Middle East and Israel. You
might suggest that these
students invite their family members
to rent a travel or documentary video
that highlights Israel. Ask students to
write a report that describes Israel's
culture, history, and topography, and
also its modern cities and high-tech
features. For students who have
traveled to Israel or the Middle East,
or who are natives of the ME, ask
them to spend time with their
families and select artifacts to bring
to class. Students could feature their
artifacts in their reports.

Jerusalem

Jerusalem is one of the world's oldest cities. People have lived there for about 4,000 years. It was the center of ancient Jewish culture. Jewish kings ruled from there. King Solomon built the Temple on the Temple Mount. One of its walls still stands. It is called the Western Wall. Jews go there to pray.

Today the city is the capital of modern Israel. That country took control of East Jerusalem in the 1967 war. Palestinians also claim Jerusalem as their capital.

Jerusalem is holy to Christians and Muslims, too. Jesus taught in Jerusalem. The Last Supper and the Crucifixion both took place there. For Muslims, the Dome of the Rock is a holy shrine. They believe Muhammad rose to heaven from there.

Lesson 2 Review On a sheet of paper, use the words from the Word Bank to complete each sentence correctly.

Word Bank
Arabs
Ben-Gurion
Israel
Lebanon
PLO

1. _____ occupied Palestine when some Jewish people returned to it in 1900.

2. _____ became a nation in 1948.

3. Israel was declared a nation by Jewish leader David _____.

4. The _____ is an organization that wants the Arab Palestinians to have their own nation.

5. In the early 1980s, Israel invaded _____ to rid it of the PLO.

Do you think the Arab Palestinians should have their own nation? Explain your answer.

Ask students to read the feature titled "Jerusalem." Have students brainstorm in small groups about compromises that could be made between Israelis and Palestinians regarding the city of Jerusalem. Then ask a spokesperson from each group to share the group's ideas with the rest of the class.

Lesson 2 Review Answers

1. Arabs **2.** Israel **3.** Ben-Gurion
4. PLO **5.** Lebanon

Answers will vary. Today, people throughout the world continue to fight to create a nation that will represent their language and common background. Most people have this, so the Arab Palestinians want it, too. One of the problems, however, is that Palestine is small and the Israelis have settled on much of it. The Israelis do not want to leave their homes and the land they worked to make productive. But the Palestinians deserve someplace that is their own. They feel as if the Israelis drove them off their land.

Chapter 29: Lesson 3

Overview In this lesson, students will read about Mohandas Gandhi and the struggle for Indian independence.

Objectives

- To explain the two problems Gandhi faced in unifying India
- To define passive resistance

Student Pages pages 742–744

Teacher's Resource Library

Workbook Activity 136

Activity 136

Modified Activity 136

Vocabulary

passive resistance

Have students write brief scenarios in which they could use passive resistance to accomplish a political goal. Ask for volunteers to share their scenarios.

1 Warm-Up Activity

Use the Rudyard Kipling poem "Gunga Din" to illustrate India's colonial past. The poem tells of the courage and loyalty of an Indian man who carries water to British troops. Distribute copies of the poem and ask for 13 volunteer readers. The teacher should read the first verse aloud; verses 2–14 should each be read aloud by one of the 13 volunteers.

Ask:

- Who is telling the story? (a British soldier)
- Who was Gunga Din? (an Indian water-carrier)

Discuss the author's attitude toward Gunga Din, and whether the British soldiers are prejudiced.

Reading Strategy: Summarizing

(Call on volunteers to identify the topic, the main point, and important details about the text under each subheading on this page.)

Objectives

- To explain the two problems Gandhi faced in unifying India
- To define passive resistance

Passive resistance
A nonviolent way of protesting for political and social change

Reading Strategy: Summarizing

As you read, notice the topic, the main thing being said about the topic, and important details.

India is located on the huge continent of Asia. For much of its history, many different people speaking many different languages have lived in India. This happened partly because many different groups of people have invaded India.

What European Countries Took Control of India?

Since the 1500s, Europeans have traded with India. By the 1700s, France controlled much of southern India. In addition, the British East Indian Trading Company sold Indian silks and other products throughout the world.

In 1763, Great Britain took control of large areas of India. As time passed, Britain drove the French from their trading posts in India. In 1858, Britain made all of India into a colony.

Why Did Indians Want Self-Rule?

Many Indians did not want their country to be a British colony. They wanted independence. They felt that the British treated them as second-class citizens in their own country. New industries and transportation served British needs, not the needs of the Indian people. The best jobs in India went to the British.

How Did Gandhi Bring Independence to India?

In 1885, a group of Indian leaders founded the Indian National Congress. Soon, it developed into the Congress Party. Its purpose was to gain political power for Indians.

In 1920, India's most important nationalist leader began to help India achieve independence. Mohandas Gandhi and his followers used **passive resistance** to fight British rule. This is a nonviolent way of protesting to get political and social change. For nearly 30 years, Gandhi led boycotts, protests, and work stoppages against the British. Finally, in 1947, Britain gave India its independence.

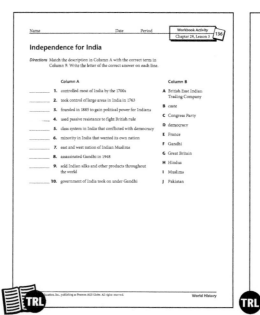

Workbook Activity 136

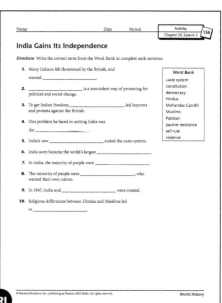

Activity 136

Gandhi wanted to make India a united nation. But he faced two major problems. The first problem was the caste system. The second problem was religious differences.

Why Was the Caste System a Problem for India?

There are four main castes, or classes, of people in India. These castes are divided according to work, money, skin color, and religious beliefs.

The members of each caste remained in the caste for life and followed its rules. For example, a person could marry only within the same caste. Another rule was that all the people in a caste did the same kind of work.

Gandhi knew that India could never be a true democracy as long as the caste system existed, so India's new constitution ended it. This constitution gave every Indian the right to vote. It opened schools that would educate all Indian children. It taught all these students Hindi, the national language. In time, India became the world's largest democracy.

Why Were Religious Differences a Problem for India?

The second problem that stood in the way of uniting India was religious differences. The majority of people in India were Hindus. They followed the Hindu religion. However, millions of Indians were Muslims. This Muslim minority wanted its own nation.

In August 1947, two new nations were created: India and Pakistan. Muslim Pakistan was further divided into East and West Pakistan. These two areas were more than 1,000 miles apart.

Reading Strategy:
Summarizing

What important details will help you remember how India and Pakistan were created?

2 Teaching the Lesson

Ask students to share what they know about Mohandas Gandhi. Ask them to read pages 742–744 to learn more about this dynamic individual and the role he played in unifying India.

Ask:

- Which European country ruled India from 1858 to 1947? (Britain)
- What two major problems did Gandhi face in the unification of India? (the caste system and religious differences)
- How many major castes were there in India before it became a democracy? (four castes)
- What brought an end to the caste system in India? (India's new constitution)
- What was the national language of India after the new constitution? (Hindi)
- Which two religious groups dominated India? (Hindus and Muslims)
- Which two nations were created in 1947? (India and Pakistan)

Reading Strategy:
Summarizing

(Tell students to look for details about why the two new nations were created as they were.)

ELL/ESL Strategy

Language Objective:
To interpret text

Do a search online for quotes by Mohandas Gandhi. Distribute copies of about 12 Gandhi quotes, as well as this quote by Dr. Martin Luther King, Jr.: "If humanity is to progress, Gandhi is inescapable. He lived, thought, and acted, inspired by the vision of humanity evolving toward a world of peace and harmony. We may ignore Gandhi at our own risk." Have students study the quotes and consider what they mean. Then, working in small groups, have students create a 3-column graphic organizer, and label the columns "Nonviolence," "Justice," and "Character Education." Have groups classify each quote according to its message and write it in the appropriate column. Have a class discussion about the results.

- How did Gandhi protest the violence between Hindus and Muslims? (he fasted)
- Who assassinated Gandhi? Why? (a Hindu; he believed that Gandhi no longer supported the Hindus)

 3 Reinforce and Extend

Lesson 3 Review Answers

1. Great Britain **2.** Gandhi
3. Hindus **4.** Muslims **5.** Pakistan

Answers will vary. In a democracy, all people are equal. They have equal rights under the law. But the caste system made some people better than others.

Religious differences between Hindus and Muslims led to violence. More than 500,000 people died in this struggle. Gandhi wanted to stop the violence. As a protest, he did not eat food for many days. But on January 30, 1948, a Hindu assassinated him. This man believed that Gandhi no longer supported the Hindus.

Lesson 3 Review On a sheet of paper, use the words from the Word Bank to complete each sentence correctly.

Word Bank
Gandhi
Great Britain
Hindus
Muslims
Pakistan

1. In 1858, _____ took control of India and made it a colony.
2. In 1920, _____ began to lead the Indian people in passive resistance.
3. The majority of people in India were _____.
4. The minority of people in India were _____.
5. In 1947, part of India became the nation of _____.

 What do you think

Why would the caste system have kept India from becoming a true democracy?

European nations had colonies both in Africa and in Asia. China was not a colony. But Europe still had economic control over it. After World War II, China wanted to be independent from European nations.

What Two Groups Fought to Control China?

In Chapter 26, you read about the struggle between the Communists and the non-Communists for control of China. This struggle began in 1927. Mao Zedong led the Communist forces. Chiang Kai-shek led the Nationalists. For ten years their two armies fought each other. This civil war left China weak and divided.

What Happened When Japan Invaded China?

In 1937, Japan invaded China. Chiang Kai-shek and Mao Zedong stopped fighting each other; they united to fight the Japanese. But neither side trusted the other.

Each side fought the Japanese in a different way. The Communists used guerilla warfare against the Japanese. In this kind of warfare, bands of fighters made surprise attacks against the Japanese and their supplies. The Communists worked closely with the Chinese peasants. The Nationalists, however, did not use guerilla warfare. They stayed mostly in the cities of southwest China.

How Did the Two Groups Differ After World War II?

When World War II ended in 1945, the fighting between the Communists and the Nationalists started again. Their civil war lasted from 1946 to 1949.

Chiang Kai-shek's Nationalists had a large army. The United States sent them billions of dollars for weapons and training. But Chiang's government was both greedy and inefficient. His military officers argued with each other.

Objectives

◆ To describe the two groups that fought for control of China and the outcome of this struggle

◆ To explain the role the United States played in China's conflicts

Chapter 29: Lesson 4

Overview This lesson describes the struggle between the Communist and Nationalist forces for control of China, and the involvement of the United States in the conflicts.

Objectives

■ To describe the two groups that fought for control of China and the outcome of this struggle

■ To explain the role the United States played in China's conflicts

Student Pages pages 745–747

Teacher's Resource Library

Workbook Activity 137

Activity 137

Modified Activity 137

1 Warm-Up Activity

Display pictures of Chinese propaganda posters from the Mao era. Have students form small groups, and have each group analyze one of the posters. Monitor groups and guide them to ask questions about the content of the posters and how the message is delivered. For example, a message can be delivered through the appearance of its subjects, or through the uses of symbolism, color, mood, or language. Lead a class discussion about each group's analysis.

2 Teaching the Lesson

Ask students to recall what they have learned about Communism (discussed in Chapter 26). Then have them read pages 745–747 to learn how China came under Communist rule.

Ask:

• Who was the leader of the Chinese Communist forces? (Mao Zedong)

• Who was the leader of the Chinese Nationalist forces? (Chiang Kai-shek)

• Which group did the United States support during the civil war in China after World War II? (the Nationalists)

Workbook Activity 137   **Activity 137**   *New Nations Emerge Chapter 29* **745**

(Answers may vary. The main idea
is that the Communists won central
control of China by defeating Chiang
Kai-shek's government in 1949.)

Ask:

- Which country supported
  Communist forces during the
  Chinese civil war? (the Soviet
  Union)

- What Chinese leader was forced
  to flee to Taiwan after the civil
  war? (Chiang Kai-shek)

- What did the Communists call their
  new government? (the People's
  Republic of China)

- Why didn't the United States
  government trust Mao Zedong?
  (the United States thought that the
  Chinese Communists threatened
  freedom in Asia)

3 Reinforce and Extend

After students have read "Made in Asia,"
ask them to work in groups to research
industries in Asian countries, such as
Japan, China, Korea, Taiwan, Singapore,
Hong Kong, and Indonesia. Have each
group identify the current exports of one
of these countries and report their
findings to the class.

LEARNING STYLES

Auditory/Verbal
Have the class step back in
time to China's civil war
during the 1940s. Stage a
debate over whether the United
States should support the Chinese
Nationalists. Have one group of
volunteers support United States
involvement while another group of
volunteers protests it. Give students
time to prepare their arguments.
Then have a volunteer from each
group give a one-minute summary
of the group's argument. Have the
class decide which side of the debate
is more persuasive.

However, Mao Zedong's Communist forces were united in
their cause. Many of the Chinese people supported them.
The Soviet Union—the first Communist nation—sent them
weapons and supplies.

Which Group Won Control of China?

By 1948, the Communists had the upper hand in China. One
city after another fell to them. As this happened, thousands of
soldiers deserted Chiang's army and joined Mao's forces. By
the fall of 1949, Chiang Kai-shek and his government had lost
control of China.

Chiang and his followers fled the mainland of China and
crossed over to the small island of Taiwan. After 22 years of
struggle, the Communists set up a new government in China.
They called it the People's Republic of China.

Why Did Mao Zedong and the United States Not Trust One Another?

Mao Zedong did not trust the United States for two reasons.
First, the United States had helped Chiang Kai-shek. Second,
the United States had supported imperialism around the world.

The United States did not trust Mao either. The U.S.
government thought that the Chinese Communists threatened

"Made in Asia"

Where were your shoes made? Your CD
player? Many products like these come from
Japan, China, or Korea. Since 1945, Asian
economies have grown quickly. Postwar
Japan had the fastest-growing economy
in the world. Other countries like South
Korea, Taiwan, Singapore, and Hong Kong
also grew. China, India, and Indonesia have
developed more recently.

Asian nations differ greatly. Still, they share
some attitudes. People will work hard for
long hours. They want to learn new things.

For example, the Japanese studied other
countries' methods. They became efficient at
making quality products. In addition, most
governments help industries develop.

At first, Asian countries depended on selling
their goods to Europe and America. Things
have changed in Asian societies, however. A
middle class has grown up in these nations.
People can buy cars, color TVs, and washing
machines. They travel and use credit cards.
Asian consumers have become the fastest-
growing market for Asian goods.

ELL/ESL STRATEGY

Language Objective:
*To organize ideas
appropriately*
Discuss the fact that,
in our country today, television
commercials and "photo-ops" have
largely replaced propaganda posters
in political advertising. As examples
of this methodology, show students a
television commercial for a political
candidate, and then display an example

of a photo-op (such as President Bush's
"Mission Accomplished" appearance
on an aircraft carrier). Have each small
group of students create three pieces of
propaganda supporting Mao, but using
modern methodology (for example, a
television announcement supporting
Mao). For each piece, students should
create an illustration and a short written
description. Encourage students to
share their work with the class.

freedom in Asia. The United States refused to recognize the Communist government as the legal government of China. Instead, the United States supported the Nationalist government on the island of Taiwan.

But in 1972, the United States changed its policy toward the People's Republic of China. For the first time, the United States recognized it as the legal government of the Chinese people.

Lesson 4 Review On a sheet of paper, write the letter of the answer that correctly completes each sentence.

1. The leader of the Chinese Nationalists was _____.

   A Mao Zedong   **C** Lenin

   B Chiang Kai-shek   **D** Gandhi

2. The leader of the Chinese Communists was _____.

   A Mao Zedong   **C** Tojo

   B Chiang Kai-shek   **D** Mandela

3. The Chinese Nationalists and Communists united to fight against the _____ in World War II.

   A Americans **B** British **C** Japanese **D** French

4. After the war, the two groups fought one another again and the _____ won.

   A Nationalists   **C** Nazis

   B Republicans   **D** Communists

5. In 1972, the United States recognized that the legal government of China was the _____.

   A People's Republic of China **C** Nationalists

   B Nazis   **D** Chiang Kai-shek Party

Why did Mao Zedong and his followers win the civil war in China?

Ask:

• In what year did the United States officially recognize the People's Republic of China as the legal government of China? (1972)

LEARNING STYLES

Logical/Mathematical
Have students outline the details of United States involvement in China's civil war. Ask students to speculate on why the United States became involved and what its involvement was during the war. After studying the Vietnam War in Lesson 5, students may refer to this outline to compare and contrast how the United States was involved in the two wars.

Lesson 4 Review Answers

1. B **2.** A **3.** C **4.** D **5.** A

Answers will vary. Mao Zedong had the support of the peasants. Also, his followers were united and had one goal. Chiang's followers fought among themselves and were corrupt.

Chapter 29: Lesson 5

Overview This lesson describes the Vietnamese struggle for independence, the formation of the Socialist Republic of Vietnam, and the reasons behind the United States' involvement in the Vietnam War.

Objectives

■ To show the development of the Socialist Republic of Vietnam

■ To explain the role of the United States in the Vietnam War

Student Pages pages 748–750

Teacher's Resource Library **TRL**

Workbook Activity 138

Activity 138

Modified Activity 138

Vocabulary

election   **Vietnamization**

Write these two words on the board, and help students break these words into smaller parts by circling each part. Ask volunteers to look up the definitions of these parts: *elect; -ion; Vietnam; -ize;* and *-ation.* Discuss how studying a word's parts can help students understand its meaning.

1 Warm-Up Activity

Display or distribute copies of newspaper articles or pictures of fliers protesting the Vietnam war. If possible, you may wish to distribute copies of the poster "Vietnam, An Eastern Theatre Production" (available on the Internet). Have students analyze the text and/or graphics of the artifacts. Discuss the nature of the protest materials. Display the photograph "Remembering Vietnam," or other photos of veterans standing at the Vietnam War Memorial. Ask students to interview older relatives or friends about their recollections of protests in the period 1964–1975, and then share them with the class.

Objectives

◆ To show the development of the Socialist Republic of Vietnam

◆ To explain the role of the United States in the Vietnam War

Election

An act by which people choose someone or something by voting

Writing About History

Choose a nation from this chapter that gained its independence. Research key events in its fight for independence. In your notebook, write the words for an imaginary national anthem.

After World War II, nationalist independence movements spread across Southeast Asia. In 1946, the United States gave the Philippine Islands their independence. South of the Philippines, the Netherlands gave freedom to Indonesia. However, France refused to free its colonial lands in Indochina.

What Did Ho Chi Minh Want for Vietnam?

Japan had conquered Indochina during World War II. The Vietnamese, under the leadership of Ho Chi Minh, fought against the Japanese. After the war, Ho Chi Minh wanted Vietnam to be an independent nation, not a French colony.

Between 1946 and 1954, Ho Chi Minh and his Communist followers fought a fierce guerrilla war against the French. The United States sent aid to the French. The United States did not want another Communist government in Asia. However, in 1954, the Vietnamese Communist forces captured a French fort. Because of this, the French government decided that it could not win the war.

What Happened After the Communists Defeated France?

Ho Chi Minh and the French agreed to divide Vietnam into two areas. The Communist area became known as North Vietnam. The non-Communist area became South Vietnam. Two other areas in Indochina became independent: Cambodia and Laos.

The division of Vietnam was not meant to be permanent. The government of South Vietnam was supposed to hold an **election**. In an election, people choose someone or something by voting. In this election, the Vietnamese people would choose how to unite their country.

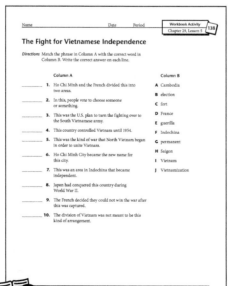

Workbook Activity 138

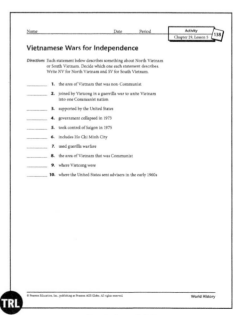

Activity 138

Despite sending 500,000 American troops to fight in Vietnam, the United States could not win the war.

Vietnamization

The U.S. plan to turn the fighting of the Vietnam War over to the South Vietnamese army

Reading Strategy:
Summarizing

What important details help you understand the events of the Vietnam War?

But this election never took place. North Vietnam began a guerrilla war to unite Vietnam into one Communist nation. Communists in South Vietnam, called the Vietcong, joined this struggle.

What Did the United States Do About the Guerrilla War?

In the early 1960s, the United States began to send military advisers to South Vietnam. Their job was simply to help the South Vietnamese government. But by 1968, nearly 500,000 American troops were fighting a war in South Vietnam. However, many Americans protested this war.

The Vietnam War lasted from 1960 to 1975. In 1969, the United States government started to gradually withdraw its forces from South Vietnam. The American plan was to turn the fighting of the war entirely over to the South Vietnamese army. The United States called this plan **Vietnamization.**

What United North and South Vietnam?

After the United States pulled all its soldiers out of Vietnam in 1975, the South Vietnamese government collapsed. The North Vietnamese took control of South Vietnam's capital city, Saigon.

The next year, North and South Vietnam united into one Communist country, the Socialist Republic of Vietnam. The government gave a new name to Saigon, the former capital of South Vietnam. It became Ho Chi Minh City.

After many years of struggle, the United States and the Socialist Republic of Vietnam found ways to work together. Trade between the countries increased, and the United States investment in Vietnam grew. There was more travel and tourism in the country. There was also a renewed effort to locate American soldiers that had been missing in Vietnam since the war.

2 Teaching the Lesson

Ask students if they know someone who fought in the Vietnam War. Invite students to share what they know about the war and how the American people feel about it. Then ask students to read pages 748–750 to learn more about the conflict in Vietnam.

Ask:

• Who was the Communist leader who led Vietnam in the fight against France? (Ho Chi Minh)

• Why did the United States support French forces? (the United States didn't want another Communist government in Asia)

• Which part of the divided Vietnam was the Communist area? (North Vietnam)

• How many American troops were in Vietnam by 1968? (nearly 500,000)

Writing About History

Give students a copy of the first verse of the "Star-Spangled Banner," and of another country's national anthem. Read the words together and talk about the images they bring to mind; what things do both anthems have in common? Then have students read the feature on page 748. Students may work in groups to compile research, but should write their anthems independently.

Reading Strategy:
Summarizing

Use the "who, what, when, where, why, and how" template to list the details.

Ask:

• What name did Vietnam adopt after its unification? (Socialist Republic of Vietnam)

• What new name did the Communist government give Saigon? (Ho Chi Minh City)

ELL/ESL Strategy

Language Objective:
To observe and describe details in a photograph

Download or have students access Vietnam war photographs at www.agsglobewh.com/page749. Tell each group to select three photos to analyze, using the following framework:

• Describe your overall impression of the photo and then describe the individual items.

• Divide the photo into quadrants and study each section. List the people, objects, and activities that you observe.

• Based on your observations, list three things you might infer from this photograph.

• What questions does this photo raise in your mind?

• Where could you find answers to these questions?

Encourage groups to share their impressions with the class.

3 Reinforce and Extend

BACKGROUND INFORMATION

Many Americans disapproved of the United States' involvement in the Vietnam War. Some Americans staged antiwar demonstrations, while others left the country to avoid serving in the military. Many Americans who disapproved of the Vietnam War transferred this resentment to returning soldiers. When veterans of the Vietnam War came home, they did not receive the welcome given to veterans of other wars. As a group, Vietnam veterans were either ignored or criticized. This made them feel that the sacrifices they had made were unappreciated. The Vietnam Veterans Memorial in Washington, D.C., was created to help rectify this mistreatment. It was dedicated in 1982.

Have a student read the title of the map, "Southeast Asia." Ask students to study the map, then help them locate Vietnam and Ho Chi Minh City. Have students read the caption and answer the questions. (China borders Vietnam to the north. Ho Chi Minh City (Saigon) is in the southern part of Vietnam. Laos is to the northeast of Thailand. Cambodia is to the southeast of Thailand.)

Lesson 5 Review Answers

1. France controlled Vietnam in 1954. **2.** Ho Chi Minh led the Communists. **3.** The Communist area was North Vietnam; the non-Communist area was South Vietnam. **4.** The U.S. supported the S. Vietnamese army. **5.** After the U.S. Army pulled out, the S. Vietnamese government collapsed, and N. and S. Vietnam united into one Communist country.

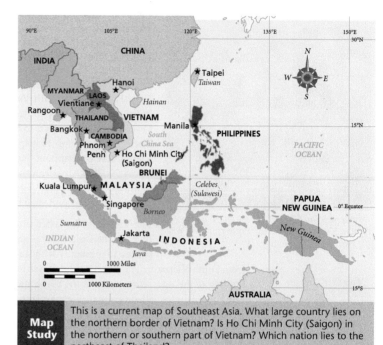

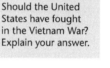

Map Study This is a current map of Southeast Asia. What large country lies on the northern border of Vietnam? Is Ho Chi Minh City (Saigon) in the northern or southern part of Vietnam? Which nation lies to the northeast of Thailand?

Lesson 5 Review On a sheet of paper, write the answer to each question. Use complete sentences.

1. Who controlled Vietnam until 1954?

2. Who led the Communists in their fight for an independent Vietnam?

3. What was the Communist area of Vietnam called? the non-Communist area?

4. Which army did the United States support in the Vietnam War?

5. What happened after the United States Army pulled out of Vietnam in 1975?

What do you think? Should the United States have fought in the Vietnam War? Explain your answer.

Answers will vary. At that time, the United States believed in the domino theory. That is, the U.S. government thought that if one country in Asia fell to Communism other countries would follow, just as one domino knocks down the next. However, the United States was fighting guerrillas on foreign soil, so it was impossible to win.

LEARNING STYLES

Logical/Mathematical
After students read pages 748–750, ask them to outline the details regarding the United States' involvement in the civil war in Vietnam. Ask students to speculate about the reasons why the United States became involved and how their involvement affected the war. Then have students refer to the outlines they completed for the civil war in China. Ask students to identify details that appear on both outlines.

Statement of Nelson Mandela

This is an excerpt from the statement of the president of the African National Congress, Nelson Rolihlahla Mandela, at his inauguration as president of the Democratic Republic of South Africa. He spoke in Pretoria, South Africa, on May 10, 1994.

Today, all of us do, by our presence here, and by our celebrations in other parts of our country and the world, confer glory and hope to newborn liberty.

Out of the experience of an extraordinary human disaster that lasted too long, must be born a society of which all humanity will be proud.

Our daily deeds as ordinary South Africans must produce an actual South African reality that will reinforce humanity's belief in justice, strengthen its confidence in the nobility of the human soul and sustain all our hopes for a glorious life for all . . . each one of us is as intimately attached to the soil of this beautiful country as are the famous jacaranda trees of Pretoria and the mimosa trees of the bushveld.

Each time one of us touches the soil of this land, we feel a sense of personal renewal. The national mood changes as the seasons change.

That spiritual and physical oneness we all share with this common homeland explains the depth of the pain we all carried in our hearts as we saw our country tear itself apart in a terrible conflict . . .

We understand it still that there is no easy road to freedom

We know it well that none of us acting alone can achieve success.

We must therefore act together as a united people, for national reconciliation, for nation building, for the birth of a new world.

Let there be justice for all.

Let there be peace for all.

Let there be work, bread, water and salt for all.

Never, never and never again shall it be that this beautiful land will again experience the oppression of one by another and suffer the indignity of being the skunk of the world.

Let freedom reign.

The sun shall never set on so glorious a human achievement!

God bless Africa!

Document-Based Questions

1. What is the disaster Mandela refers to?

2. What does Mandela say happens when each South African touches the soil?

3. How does Mandela say is the way to achieve success?

4. To what animal does Mandela compare South Africa?

5. What does work, bread, water, and salt represent?

1946 – 1999

New Nations Emerge   Chapter 29   **751**

Nelson Mandela, who led the struggle to replace the apartheid regime of South Africa with a multiracial democracy, remains one of the world's most revered statesmen. Despite many years in jail, he emerged to become South Africa's first black president, and to play a leading role in the drive for peace in other conflict-ridden areas. He won the Nobel peace prize in 1993. Since stepping down as president in 1999, Mr. Mandela has become South Africa's highest-profile ambassador, campaigning against HIV/AIDS, and securing his country's right to host the 2010 World Cup. He has also been actively involved in peace negotiations in numerous African countries and in other areas of the world as well.

Answers to Document-Based Questions:

1. The disaster that Mandela refers to is the existence of apartheid.

2. When each South African touches the soil, he/she feels a sense of personal renewal.

3. To achieve success, Africans must act together as a united people.

4. Mandela compares South Africa to "the skunk of the world."

5. Work, bread, water, and salt represent economic security.

Chapter Project Follow-up

Hang the mural sections on the walls around the room for group presentations to the class. An assessment rubric, distributed to students at the start of the project, should include content and presentation objectives, such as the presence of illustrations, breadth of resources consulted, creativity in displaying, and so forth.

WORLD CULTURES

During the Vietnam War, many citizens of Laos, called Hmong, aided American troops. After the Communist victory, many Hmong soldiers and their families relocated to the United States. Usually the Hmong settle in the agricultural centers, such as California's Central Valley, so that they can take advantage of their skills as farmers, which they learned in the mountainous regions of China, Vietnam, Laos, and Thailand. Hmong have faced the challenge of learning new trades and a new language while also maintaining their culture. Hmong parents teach their children Hmong values and history to help them maintain their identity and ethnic pride.

Ask students to look up the word *mahatma* in the dictionary. Discuss why this is an appropriate title for Ghandi. Have a volunteer read the title of the Spotlight Story, "The Spinning Wheel and Salt—Weapons of the Indian Revolution." Then have students read the feature to learn how the spinning wheel and salt became weapons in the Indian fight for independence.

Ask students to answer the Spotlight Story Wrap-Up questions.

Answers to Spotlight Story Wrap-Up:

1. Passive resistance is a nonviolent protest.

2. A crowd had gathered for a political meeting. British soldiers fired on the crowd, killing or injuring hundreds.

3. He led the Congress Party (Indian National Congress).

4. Gandhi urged people to spin and weave their own cloth instead of buying British textiles so that Britain would think that India was less valuable as a colony.

5. It was a peaceful protest against a law that prevented people from making salt from seawater. British law made people buy salt that was expensive.

The Spinning Wheel and Salt—Weapons of the Indian Revolution

Mahatma Gandhi was the father of Indian independence. He was a man of ideas, trained as a lawyer. Gandhi believed in nonviolence. He thought that passive resistance was his people's best weapon. This is a form of nonviolent protest. It is used against laws seen as unfair. Gandhi believed that the force of truth could defeat British military force. Violence would not work.

In 1919, British colonial laws changed. Some Indian leaders organized strikes and riots against the laws. That led to a tragedy in the town of Amritsar, when British soldiers fired on a gathering of unarmed people. Hundreds were killed.

Gandhi decided to work for independence. In 1920, he became head of the Indian National Congress. The Congress Party became India's largest political party.

Indian leaders wanted both political and economic freedom. Great Britain sold India a lot of cotton cloth. That made the colony a valuable market for British industry. Gandhi urged Indians not to buy British cotton goods but to spin cotton thread and weave their own cloth. He hoped that this would make India less valuable to Britain. The simple spinning wheel became a powerful symbol. Gandhi himself wore only homespun cloth. He was often seen beside a spinning wheel.

Gandhi told his followers to disobey unfair British laws. One of those laws was the Salt Act. The law made it a crime to make salt from sea water. Indians had to buy expensive salt from the government. In 1930, Gandhi started a "salt march" to the sea in protest. He began the 200-mile march with 78 followers. Every day more and more people joined the march.

Gandhi (center) used passive resistance to gain India's independence.

The march lasted 24 days. When it reached the sea, there were hundreds of people. They began to make salt the traditional way. They boiled sea water to get the salt out of it. More Indians joined Gandhi and his followers. Thousands of people—including Gandhi— were arrested.

Under constant pressure, the British changed many laws. In 1935, India won some self-government. Full independence finally came in 1947. When the country was divided, violence did occur. Still, India had won independence with two simple weapons—salt and the spinning wheel.

Wrap-Up

1. What is passive resistance?

2. Describe what happened in Amritsar in 1919.

3. What political party did Gandhi lead?

4. Why did the spinning wheel become a symbol of Indian independence?

5. What was the salt march?

Chapter 29   SUMMARY

- In 1900, European nations controlled most of Africa. The Pan-African Movement led the struggle for African independence.

- African nationalism grew after World War II. Ghana, a British colony, became the first independent nation in sub-Saharan Africa in 1957.

- A minority of white settlers controlled South Africa. The policy of apartheid strictly separated nonwhite and white South Africans.

- The African National Congress was one nationalist group. Its leader Nelson Mandela spent 26 years in prison for protesting apartheid. In 1994, he was elected president in South Africa's first multiracial election.

- After World War II, many Jews moved to Palestine, but Arabs already lived there. In 1947, the United Nations divided Palestine into Jewish and Arab states. Jewish leaders declared the new nation of Israel.

- Israel won several wars against neighboring Arab countries. Because of these wars, many Palestinians became refugees. Some formed the Palestinian Liberation Organization (PLO), which led terrorist attacks on Israel. In the 1990s, some Arab and Israeli leaders worked toward peace and Palestinian self-rule.

- India was a British colony. Many Indians wanted independence. The Congress Party under Mohandas Gandhi fought the British, using passive resistance.

- India became an independent democracy in 1947. People in every caste had political rights. Religious differences led to the creation of Pakistan as a Muslim state.

- Beginning in 1927, Chinese Nationalists and Communists fought a civil war. They united to fight the Japanese in World War II.

- The Chinese civil war began again after World War II. The Communists won in 1949. Mao Zedong set up a Communist government—the People's Republic of China. In 1972, the United States accepted the People's Republic as a legal government.

- Southeast Asia was a French colony, Indochina. Ho Chi Minh, a Communist, led the Vietnamese fight for independence. After a French defeat, Indochina was divided into North and South Vietnam, Cambodia, and Laos.

- North Vietnam began a guerrilla war to unite Vietnam under Communist rule. The United States helped South Vietnam. After the United States left in 1975, all Vietnam became one Communist nation.

1946 – 1999

Using the Chapter Summary

Have students read the Chapter Summary to review the main ideas presented in Chapter 29.

Ask:

- What colony became an independent nation in 1957? (Ghana)

- What was the policy that separated nonwhite and white South Africans? (Apartheid)

- Which two groups were fighting over land in the Middle East? (Israelis and Palestinians)

- Who was the leader of India's independence movement? (Mohandas Gandhi)

- In what year did Britain grant India its independence? (1947)

- What four countries was Indochina divided into? (North and South Vietnam, Cambodia, and Laos)

- What country did the United States help during the Vietnam War? (South Vietnam)

TEACHER'S RESOURCE

The AGS Globe Teaching Strategies in Social Studies Transparencies may be used with this chapter. The transparencies add an interactive dimension to expand and enhance the *World History* program content.

Chapter 29 Review

Use the Chapter Review to prepare students for tests and to reteach content from the chapter.

Chapter 29 Mastery Test

The Teacher's Resource Library includes two forms of the Chapter 29 Mastery Test. Each test addresses the chapter Goals for Learning. An optional third page of additional critical-thinking items is included for each test. The difficulty level of the two forms is equivalent.

Chapter 29 Review Answers

1. Ethiopia
2. Tutu
3. Mandela
4. Ben-Gurion
5. Great Britain
6. Gandhi
7. Chiang
8. Mao
9. Vietnam
10. France
11. C
12. A

Chapter 29   R E V I E W

Word Bank

Ben-Gurion
Chiang
Ethiopia
France
Gandhi
Great Britain
Mao
Mandela
Tutu
Vietnam

On a sheet of paper, use the words from the Word Bank to complete each sentence correctly.

1. After World War II, _____ was one of the independent nations in Africa.

2. Bishop Desmond _____, who worked to get rid of apartheid, was awarded the Nobel Peace Prize in 1984.

3. The white minority in South Africa put Nelson _____ in jail for 26 years.

4. In 1948, David _____ announced a new nation: Israel.

5. _____ controlled India from 1858 to 1947.

6. Mohandas _____ used passive resistance to gain freedom for India.

7. The nationalist leader in China in 1927 was _____ Kai-shek.

8. The Communist leader in China in 1927 was _____ Zedong.

9. The Communist leader in _____ in 1946 was Ho Chi Minh.

10. _____ had colonies in Indochina after World War II.

On a sheet of paper, write the letter of the answer that correctly completes each sentence.

11. The South African policy of not letting blacks vote or choose where to live is _____.

   A Vietnamization   C apartheid
   B African Nationalism   D Pan-African Movement

12. In _____ soldiers hide, make surprise attacks, and set traps for the enemy.

   A guerilla warfare   C persecution
   B multiracial   D apartheid

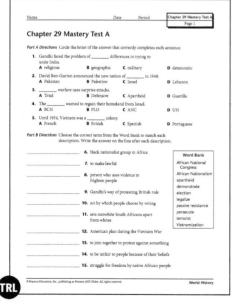

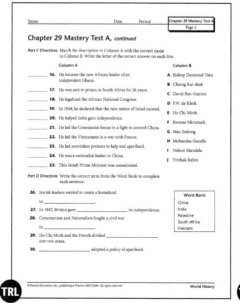

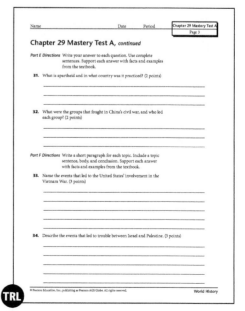

13. _____ have fought the Israelis for land to set up a nation.

A Arab Palestinians   **C** Chinese Communists
B Vietnamese Communists   **D** Japanese

14. The United States used a plan called _____ to get out of a war in Southeast Asia.

A African Nationalism   **C** Pan-African Movement
B Vietnamization   **D** British Commonwealth

15. _____, the president of the Republic of South Africa, and ANC leader Nelson Mandela, were awarded the Nobel Peace Prize in 1993.

A F. W. de Klerk   **C** Ho Chi Minh
B Desmond Tutu   **D** Yitzhak Rabin

On a sheet of paper, write the answer to each question. Use complete sentences.

16. Why did India divide into two countries?

17. What two Chinese groups fought over control of China? Which side won? Why?

18. Why did the United States fight a war in Vietnam?

Critical Thinking On a sheet of paper, write your response to each question. Use complete sentences.

19. How would you solve the problems in the Middle East between the Palestinians and the Israelis?

20. Do you think Gandhi's passive resistance would have worked to end apartheid in South Africa? Explain your answer.

> Learn from your mistakes. Review corrected homework and quizzes. Correct any errors you may have made.

1946 – 1999

13. A
14. B
15. A
16. India divided into two nations because its majority was Hindu, but it had a large minority of Muslims.
17. The Nationalists and the Communists fought for control of China. The Communists won because they were united and had the support of the peasants.
18. The United States wanted to contain Communism and not have it spread to South Vietnam.

Critical Thinking

19. Answers will vary. The problem is how to make the Israelis give up land and still feel secure in the midst of Arab nations. But the problem is also the tendency both sides—the Israelis and the Palestinians—have of always reacting violently to events and often overreacting. Solving the problem of distribution of land, displacement, and security is difficult. It demands an ability to see possibilities and adopt a long-range view.

20. Answers will vary. Passive resistance is often effective in creating change.

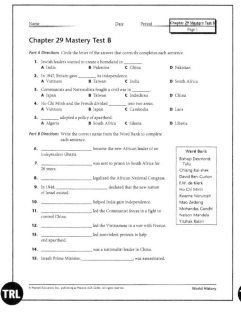

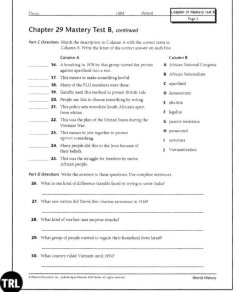

Chapter 29 Mastery Test B, pages 1–3

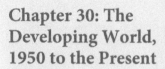

Introducing the Chapter

In the last decades of the 20th century
and into the 21st century, dramatic
political change reshaped the world.
Populations of African nations migrated
in increasing numbers to urban areas;
historic conflicts in the Middle East
continued; Asian economies had a global
impact; and Latin America echoed with
campesinos' cries for land reform.

756 *Unit 7 World Since 1945*

30 The Developing World

In this chapter, you will learn about the many changes in
world history that have taken place since the end of World
War II. Japan and China became economic powers. Still, many
challenges remain, especially in Africa and Latin America. The
Middle East continues to be a troubled region. Many Africans
face the problems of poverty, hunger and disease. Latin
Americans are pushing for change.

Goals for Learning

- ◆ To explain the problems facing Africa today
- ◆ To describe why conflict still exists in the Middle East
- ◆ To explain the changes in Asian countries
- ◆ To list the problems Latin America faces

1959 Fidel Castro overthrows the pro-American leader of Cuba

1978 Israeli and Egyptian leaders sign Camp David Accords in United States

1989 Chinese students protest in Tiananmen Square

1991 Persian Gulf War begins and ends

2002 United States and allies begin Iraq War

1960 — 1980 — 2000

1978 Deng Xiaoping begins economic reforms in China

1990 Iraq invades Kuwait

1997 Economic crisis in Asia

Ask:

- What are Africa's biggest problems? (poverty, hunger, and disease)
- Which leaders signed the Camp David Accords in 1978? (Israeli and Egyptian)
- What caused the Persian Gulf War? (the invasion of Kuwait by Iraqi forces)

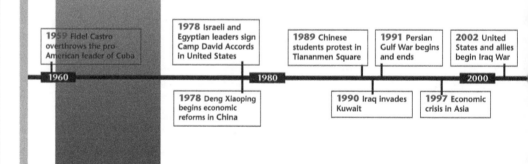

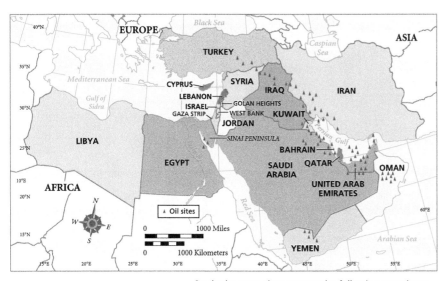

This map of the Middle East shows the oil sites in several countries. This area has oil resources that are important to many other countries. The countries with the largest oil reserves are Saudi Arabia, Iran, Iraq, Kuwait, and the United Arab Emirates. All of these nations belong to the Organization of Petroleum Exporting Countries (OPEC).

Study the map, then answer the following questions:

1. Which country is larger—Iraq or Iran?

2. In what direction does Kuwait lie from Iraq?

3. Where in the Middle East is the most oil?

4. What body of water lies between Iran and United Arab Emirates?

5. What body of water lies between Egypt and Saudi Arabia?

Ask a volunteer to read the map title, "The Middle East." Inform them that Saudi Arabia is a peninsula and ask them to point to and name the bodies of water that surround it on three sides. (Red Sea, Arabian Sea, and Persian Gulf) Then have them read the caption and answer the questions.

Ask:

• What sea lies north of Iran? (the Caspian Sea)

• What body of water is south of Yemen and Oman? (the Arabian Sea)

• What body of water separates Europe from Africa? (the Mediterranean Sea)

• What body of water separates Saudi Arabia from Iran? (the Persian Gulf)

Have students read the paragraph below the map, and then read and answer the questions.

Map Skills Answers

1. Iran is bigger than Iraq.

2. Kuwait is southeast of Iraq.

3. Oil is mostly along the east coast of Saudi Arabia, in the Persian Gulf, and along the border of Iran and Iraq.

4. The Persian Gulf is between Iran and the United Arab Emirates.

5. The Red Sea lies between Egypt and Saudi Arabia.

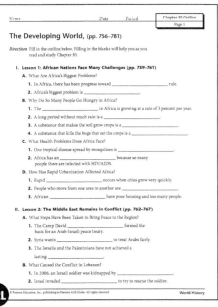

Chapter Project

Divide the class into four groups, and assign each to one of the following regions: Africa, the Middle East, Asia, or Latin America. Tell groups to use newspapers, magazines, and Internet sources to research current events occurring in its assigned region. Ask each group to decide the most efficient way to conduct research to learn about current events affecting the region. Tell students that at the end of their research, each group will create a collage of images that will visually explain the problems and accomplishments experienced by its assigned region.

Questioning

Have students page through the chapter and note that the text in each lesson is divided by subheadings composed as questions. Remind students that these questions provide a reason for reading the text, and that the questions should be answered after reading each section. Remind students that a good study technique is to write down the question in a notebook, read the section, and then write down the answer. Explain that the same technique can be used with new vocabulary words.

Ask:

• How would answering the first question on page 759 help you understand problems experienced by Africa? (It will allow me to list current problems, which will help me to understand them.)

• What questions could you ask after reading the first question on page 763? (Answers will vary; Where is Lebanon? Did Lebanon have a problem with another country in the Middle East?)

• What question could you ask before reading the "Biography" information on page 770? (Answers will vary; Who is Aung San Suu Kyi? What were her accomplishments?)

Key Vocabulary Words

Point out that these chapter words are presented in the order they appear in each lesson. They are also found in the Glossary. Remind students that they should use questioning when reading to help them understand and remember what they read.

Ask:

• What question can you make using the key vocabulary word *drought*? (What is a drought?)

• Where will you find the answer to your question? (Lesson 1; the dictionary)

Reading Strategy:
Questioning

Questioning what you are reading helps you understand and remember more information. It also makes you a more active reader. When reading this chapter, ask yourself:

◆ Why am I reading this text?

◆ What key points can I draw from the facts and details in this text?

◆ How can I connect this text to experiences in my own life?

Key Vocabulary Words

Lesson 1 ————————————
Investment Money given to a company to use to make more money

Drought A long period of time without much rain

Fertilizer A substance that helps the soil grow crops

Pesticide A substance that kills the bugs that eat the crops

Conflict Fighting; not being able to agree on something

Urbanization Becoming more like a city

Migrant A person who has left one place and moved to another

Slum An area of a city with too many people, poor housing, and low-income families

Lesson 2 ————————————
Accords Agreements

Shah An Iranian ruler

Ayatollah A Muslim religious leader

Hostage Someone held against his or her will until certain demands are met

Lesson 3 ————————————
Human rights Political and civil liberties, including the right to life, liberty and the pursuit of happiness

Lesson 4 ————————————
Campesino A peasant who works the land but does not own it

Western Hemisphere The half of the earth that includes North and South America

Embargo An act that stops all trade

• What question can you ask about the key vocabulary word *human rights*? (Answers will vary; What human rights issues were there in Asia? Are human rights an issue in other regions of the world?)

• What questions can you ask about the key vocabulary word *embargo*? (Answers will vary; What is an embargo? Which countries have experienced an embargo? How effective is an embargo?)

◆ To explain the problems that African nations face today

◆ To list some reasons why African people suffer from a lack of food

Investment

Money given to a company to use to make more money

Reading Strategy: Questioning

What do you think you will learn about by reading this lesson?

Africa is a continent in change. It has experienced many changes in a relatively short time. It has changed from being a colonial possession to a continent of independent nations.

Today, some African economies are growing at an average rate of over 5 percent. There has been real progress toward democratic rule. Trade and **investment** are growing, and Africa is reconnecting with the world economy.

What Are Africa's Biggest Problems?

Africa is also in crisis. Economic growth is uneven. The countries with natural resources, especially oil, have the fastest growing economies. Despite the progress, much of Africa still faces many problems.

Poverty is Africa's biggest problem. Between one quarter and one half of the population of Africa lives on less than two dollars a day. The average American makes more than 63 times what the average person in the Democratic Republic of Congo makes. One third of the people do not get enough food to eat. One out of every six children dies before the age of five.

Lack of food and water causes many problems in a number of African countries.

1950 to the Present

Chapter 30: Lesson 1

Overview This lesson explains several problems that challenge African nations: conflict among its peoples, swelling populations in many cities, and famine.

Objectives

■ To explain the problems that African nations face today

■ To list some reasons why African people suffer from a lack of food

Student Pages pages 759–761

Teacher's Resource Library

Workbook Activity 139

Activity 139

Modified Activity 139

Vocabulary

conflict	migrant
drought	pesticide
fertilizer	slum
investment	urbanization

After reading each word and discussing its meaning, ask volunteers to name one of the words. Have them call on another student who provides a sentence using the word or supplies a definition for the word.

1 **Warm-Up Activity**

Write the following phrases on the board: severe drought, rapid urbanization, AIDS epidemic. Have students brainstorm the consequences of each situation. Write their ideas on the board as students generate them. Students should recognize the devastating results of all three situations. Explain that currently, Africa is dealing with the consequences of severe drought, rapid urbanization, and the AIDS epidemic occurring at the same time.

2 **Teaching the Lesson**

Ask students to name some of the nations that gained independence in Africa. Then have them read pages 759–761 to find out about some challenges facing African nations in the new century.

Ask:

- What type of growth indicates that Africa is reconnecting with the world economy? (growing trade)
- How fast is the population of Africa growing? (3 percent per year)
- What do farmers in Africa need to produce more food? (fertilizer, pesticides, and fuel)
- What are three medical problems faced by the people of Africa? (malaria, HIV/AIDS, poor medical care)

 Writing About History

Before students start this assignment, brainstorm a list of situations that students know cause suffering, from either the lesson or the media. Each student should choose one, state a goal, and list at least three steps he or she would take to "fix" the problem.

 3   Reinforce and Extend

LEARNING STYLES

 Logical/Mathematical
Have students prepare a bar graph that illustrates the population of the capital cities of African nations north of the Sahara. Students should give their graphs a title and place the cities along one axis and the population along the other axis. Display students' graphs on the bulletin board. Give students an opportunity to explain how they gathered their information.

Drought
A long period of time without much rain

Fertilizer
A substance that helps the soil grow crops

Pesticide
A substance that kills the bugs that eat the crops

Conflict
Fighting; not being able to agree on something

 Writing About History
This lesson describes things that are happening right now. Think of one way you could help stop the suffering of so many people.
In your notebook, state your goal, and then write the steps you would take to reach it.

Why Do So Many People Go Hungry in Africa?

Famine is a big problem in Africa. Since the 1970s, many people have starved to death. There are five main causes of famine in Africa.

1. The population in Africa is growing at a rate of 3 percent per year, which is faster than any other region of the world. This means that the population will double in less than 24 years!

2. Since the 1970s, Africa has experienced several **droughts.** A drought is a long period without much rain.

3. Africa is growing less food, because its farmers have little **fertilizer, pesticides,** and fuel that are necessary for agriculture. Fertilizer helps the soil produce more crops; pesticides kill the bugs that eat the crops.

4. Many African countries pay more attention to industry than to agriculture.

5. In many parts of Africa, civil wars and armed **conflicts** have greatly damaged agriculture.

What Health Problems Does Africa Face?

Africa's people face many health problems. Many people become ill from malaria, a tropical disease spread by mosquitoes. About one million people in Africa die each year from malaria.

A big problem in Africa is AIDS. Africa accounts for 70 percent of the world's population infected with HIV/AIDS. The AIDS epidemic has a big effect on the economy. The death of so many farmers has cut food production. The number of orphans and old people that need care has grown. Some children cannot attend school because they have to take care of sick family members. Because most African countries are poor, they are unable to provide much medical care for people who are sick.

ELL/ESL STRATEGY

 Language Objective:
To explain cause and effect
Divide the class into groups of five. Tell each group to discuss several problems experienced by the people of Africa. Have each group create a two-column chart on a sheet of paper, and label the left column "Cause," and the right column "Effect." Ask students to determine the cause and effect of five problems noted in Lesson 1. Then have each student explain one cause and one effect to the other students in his or her group.

Reading Strategy:
Questioning

Think beyond the text. Consider your own thoughts and experiences as you read about Africa.

Urbanization

Becoming more like a city

Migrant

A person who has left one place and moved to another

Slum

An area of a city with too many people, poor housing, and low-income families

How Has Rapid Urbanization Affected Africa?

One of the biggest problems in Africa is rapid **urbanization.** This means that African cities are growing at a very fast rate. Many people are leaving the countryside in hopes of escaping poverty and finding a better life in the cities. Often they are disappointed. Many of the newcomers have few skills and little education. There are few jobs available to them.

This large number of **migrants**—people who move from one area to another—puts a strain on city services. Housing is poor. Many people are forced to live in **slums** with no electricity, running water, or sewers. A slum is an area of a city with too many people, poor housing, and unhealthy living conditions.

Lesson 1 Review On a sheet of paper, write the word in parentheses that makes each statement true.

1. Malaria is a tropical disease spread by (fertilizer, mosquitoes, pesticides).

2. Because many African countries pay more attention to (democracy, malaria, industry) than to agriculture, there is not enough food in Africa.

3. Africa's greatest problem is probably (poverty, low birth rate, high prices).

4. (AIDS, Anorexia, Measles) is a big problem in many African countries.

5. Many rural people who migrate to Africa's cities live in (factories, slums, apartments).

How would a civil war damage farming?

Ask:

- What is urbanization? (the growth of cities)

- What is one consequence of rapid urbanization? (Answers will vary; poverty, lack of housing, lack of jobs, limited city services)

- Why is it difficult for many people to find work in cities? (Jobs are limited; They lack skills or education.)

Reading Strategy:
Questioning

(Answers will vary; My community needs to improve job and housing opportunities for people moving into the city.)

AT HOME

Ask students to discuss the problems of Africa with their families. Then have students and their families make a list of all of the different industries they depend on to live, such as the food industry, the clothing industry, the housing industry, etc. Each student should make a chart that notes each industry identified and how his or her family would manage if the ability to depend on that industry were removed. For example, what if the food industry was no longer accessible? Students can share their charts with the class.

Lesson 1 Review Answers

1. mosquitoes 2. industry
3. poverty 4. AIDS 5. slums

A civil war would damage the crops themselves, as well as disrupt planting and harvesting.

Chapter 30: Lesson 2

Overview This lesson describes the Middle East peace process, revolution in Iran, war between Iran and Iraq, the Persian Gulf War, war in Iraq, and the influence of Islamic fundamentalists.

Objectives

- To describe why conflict still exists in the Middle East
- To explain the causes of the Persian Gulf War

Student Pages pages 762–767

Teacher's Resource Library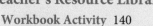

Workbook Activity 140

Activity 140

Modified Activity 140

Vocabulary

accords   shah

Ayatollah   terrorist

hostage

Have students demonstrate their knowledge of the vocabulary words by using them in a paragraph that describes the conflict between the United States and Iran during the late 1970s.

Warm-Up Activity

Have students return to the map of the Middle East on page 757. Discuss the geographic location of each country in the Middle East. Have students note the size and proximity of one country to another. Explain that oil has brought great wealth to some people of the Middle East while others live in extreme poverty. Have students speculate on the strategic importance of the Persian Gulf.

Reading Strategy:
Questioning

(Answers should include an understanding of the historical significance of religion, cultural clashes, changes in political borders, and economic rivalries.)

Objectives

- To describe why conflict still exists in the Middle East
- To explain the causes of the Persian Gulf War

Accords

Agreements

Reading Strategy:
Questioning

What details are important for understanding the history of the Middle East?

The major countries in the Middle East continue not to trust in one another. The Middle East has been an area of conflict and violence for the last 100 years or so. One problem is that the Palestinians and the Israelis both claim Palestine as their own. You read about that in Chapter 29.

What Steps Have Been Taken to Bring Peace to the Region?

The United States has tried to encourage Israel and its neighbors to settle their differences. In 1978, U.S. President Jimmy Carter brought Egypt's President Sadat together with Israel's Prime Minister Begin at Camp David, Maryland. The Camp David **Accords,** or agreements, formed the basis for an Egyptian-Israeli peace treaty.

Israeli Prime Minister Yitzhak Rabin agreed to the idea of trading some of the land Israel had taken in the 1967 war for a guarantee of peace.

In November 1995 Rabin was killed by an Israeli who was against the peace process. The leaders who followed Rabin have made little progress in securing peace. Some Arabs opposed to the peace support terrorist groups like Hamas. Hamas uses violence like suicide bombings to try to prevent peace. On the other side, some Israelis fear that a self-ruling Palestine would be a threat to the security of their country.

Israel also reached out to its other Arab neighbors: Jordan and Syria. In 1994, Jordan signed a peace treaty with Israel. Talks were also held between Syria and Israel. The two sides distrust each other. Israel believes the Syrians must recognize the state of Israel as the homeland of the world's Jewish people. It also believes that Syria must control the Hezbollah. This is an organization close to Iran and Syria that Israel believes sponsors terrorism. Syria wants Israel to return the Golan Heights. This is an area overlooking the northeast corner of Israel that was taken

---

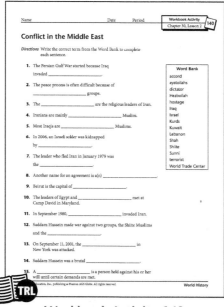

Workbook Activity 140

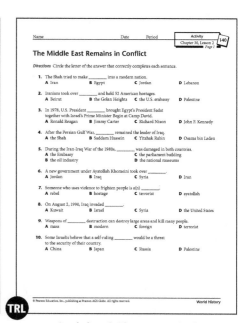

Activity 140, pages 1–2

Shah
An Iranian ruler

Ayatollah
A Muslim religious leader

over by Israel in the 1967 war. It also wants Israel to stop what it considers the racist attitude toward and treatment of Arabs.

In October 1998, leaders of the Middle East met with U.S. President Bill Clinton for nine days. Israel agreed to withdraw from more Palestinian land. The Palestinians agreed to get rid of terrorism. The United States agreed to guarantee security. Unfortunately, the agreement was broken and a lasting peace has not been achieved.

What Caused the Conflict in Lebanon?

In 2006, an Israeli soldier was kidnapped by Hezbollah. Even before the kidnapping, Hezbollah had fired many rockets at Israeli settlements. Israel invaded Lebanon to try to rescue their soldier. They also bombed Beirut, Lebanon's capital, killing many civilians and destroying many buildings. Thousands of people on both sides were forced to flee their homes. The UN arranged for the fighting to stop and Israel withdrew its soldiers.

What Are the Roots of U.S. Problems with Iran?

Until 1979, Iran was ruled by a **Shah.** The Shah tried to make Iran into a modern nation. He began new industry. He built schools, highways, and factories. He gave women more freedom.

But many Iranians opposed the Shah. Many peasants were still without land of their own. Unemployment was high. The **ayatollahs,** the Muslim religious leaders of Iran, thought that the Shah was destroying traditional values. The Shah used his secret police to arrest and torture anyone who opposed him. He became a cruel dictator.

In the late 1970s, many people began to support Ayatollah Khomeini. Khomeini had long opposed the Shah. He wanted Iran to become an Islamic republic ruled by religious leaders. In January 1979 the Shah was forced to flee Iran. A new government under the Ayatollah took over Iran.

Ayatollah Khomeini took control of Iran in 1979.

1950 to the Present

The Developing World Chapter 30 **763**

2 **Teaching the Lesson**

Ask students to name some nations that are in the Middle East. Then have them read pages 762–766 to find out about some conflicts that have led to violence in the Middle East.

Ask:

- Which United States president brought the Arab and Israeli leaders to Camp David for peace talks? (Jimmy Carter)
- Which Iranian leader did the United States support in the 1970s? (the Shah)
- What did Iran do to display its hatred for the United States? (took Americans hostage)
- How long did the Iran-Iraq war last? (eight years)
- Why did the United States attack Iraq? (The United States believed Saddam Hussein had weapons of mass destruction.)
- What does Syria want Israel to do? (return the Golan Heights)
- Which religious leader gained support of the Iranian people during the 1970s? (Ayatollah Khomeini)

ONLINE CONNECTION

Students can gain additional information by accessing the following Web sites:

www.agsglobewh.com/page763a (Students will read about the great difficulties experienced by the people of Darfur.)

www.agsglobewh.com/page763b (This interactive site provides information on the events and results of the Gulf War, including an oral history.)

www.agsglobewh.com/page763c (Students will read about Beijing— the Imperial City and the site of the Tiananmen Square Massacre and the 2008 Summer Olympics.)

STUDY SKILLS

To help students understand the flow of events in the Middle East, have them work as a group to create a timeline. First, have students identify the time and place of events highlighted in Lesson 2. List the events on the board as they are identified. Create a timeline on the board for students to copy. Discuss the sequence of events and the involvement of several countries in the Middle East in conflict.

BACKGROUND INFORMATION

The historic peace treaty signed in 1979 between Egypt and Israel is known as the Camp David Accords. Camp David is in Maryland, about 60 miles from Washington, D.C., in a scenic, wooded area. It is off-limits for everyone except the president of the United States, family members, and invited guests. The first president to use the camp was Franklin Roosevelt. President Eisenhower named the camp after his grandson.

Ask:

- On which nation did Khomeini focus his anger? (the United States)
- What does the United States believe about Iran? (Iran is developing nuclear weapons.)
- When did the Iran-Iraq war begin? (1980)
- Which industry was damaged in both Iran and Iraq during the war? (oil)

WORLD CULTURES

Literature is important in Iran. Iranians especially enjoy poetry, and, even in this modern era, many Iranians can recite from memory long passages of epic poetry in Persian, their native tongue. The poetry of Omar Khayyam is revered throughout the world. His most famous work, "The Rubaiyat of Omar Khayyam," has been translated into many languages and includes the famous verse that begins "The Moving Finger writes; and having writ,/Moves on..."

3 **Reinforce and Extend**

ELL/ESL STRATEGY

Language Objective:
To use a list of facts to write a summary
Divide the class into six groups. Assign a section of the lesson to each group. Each group should turn the question that leads its assigned section into a statement. One member of the group should read the assigned section aloud. Facts supporting the statement should be listed under the statement. Each group should write a short paragraph summarizing the facts. Then each group should use its list of facts and summary paragraph to generate three questions that could be answered by further research. Have groups share their paragraphs and questions with the class.

Hostage
Someone held against his or her will until certain demands are met

Reading Strategy:
Questioning

Ask yourself: "Did I understand what I just read about the United States and Iran?" If not, read the material again.

Much of the anger against the Shah was directed towards the United States. It was accused of being the "Great Satan," the protector of Israel, and the enemy of all Muslims. In November 1979, some Iranians took over the U.S. embassy. They captured 52 Americans and made them **hostages** for almost 15 months. Eventually, the hostages were released.

Since then, relations between the United States and Iran have been strained. The United States believes Iran is developing nuclear weapons. It accuses Iran of interfering in neighboring Iraq. It claims Iran is supplying Iraq with weapons used to kill American soldiers. Iran is accused of supporting terrorist groups like Hezbollah in Lebanon. Iran says it is not building nuclear weapons, but that it has the right to develop nuclear power. It also denies giving help to Iraqis fighting the United States.

Why Did Iraq and Iran Go to War?

Iran and Iraq are neighbors. Iranians are mainly Shiite Muslim; most Iraqis are Sunni Muslims. Iranians are Persians; most Iraqis are Arabs. Because of differences in language, culture, and religion, the two neighbors have a long history of conflict.

After its revolution in 1979, Iran tried to influence the large Shiite community in Iraq. This caused alarm among the Sunni Muslims who led the Iraqi government. In September 1980, Iraqi troops invaded Iran. The war between the two countries lasted eight years. More than one million people were killed. The oil industries in both countries were heavily damaged.

The Iraqis had better weapons, and they used poison gas. The Iranians, however, had the larger army and better airplanes. Both sides attacked international shipping. Because of this, the United States sent ships to the area. They protected the shipping lanes through which ships transported much of the world's oil. In 1988, the United States helped to end the war.

Reading Strategy:
Questioning

(Answers should either provide a reason why the material was understood or why there is a need to reread the material.)

The Persian Gulf War in 1991 lasted only about 100 hours. UN forces defeated the Iraqis and freed Kuwait.

What Caused the Persian Gulf War?

The war with Iran left Iraq with a weakened economy and big debts. Iraq owed money to its neighbor, Kuwait. On August 2, 1990, Iraqi troops invaded Kuwait. They wanted to take over its rich oil fields. Saudi Arabia feared that Iraq might attack it too. If Iraq took over both Kuwait and Saudi Arabia, it would control nearly 40 percent of the world's oil. This would give it great power in the world.

The UN Security Council ordered Iraq to withdraw from Kuwait, but Iraq refused. In January 1991, an international force began an air war against Iraq. Iraq responded by firing missiles on Saudi Arabia and Israel. Iraqi soldiers did terrible things to the people of Kuwait. Gold and cash worth $1.6 billion was stolen from Kuwait's central bank and taken to Iraq.

Iraq would not leave Kuwait willingly. An international force of soldiers from 34 countries led by the United States invaded Iraq. After about 100 hours of fighting, the allies defeated Iraq. Kuwait was freed. Historians call this conflict the Persian Gulf War.

Ask:

• What country invaded Kuwait in 1990? (Iraq)

• Why did Saudi Arabia fear that Iraq would invade it also? (because Iraq would then control nearly 40 percent of the world's oil)

• During the UN air war against Iraq, what nations did Iraq attack? What weapons did it use? (Saudi Arabia and Israel; missiles)

BACKGROUND INFORMATION

Long ago, the term *Arab* referred to any of the Arabic-speaking people on the Arabian peninsula. However, after the rise of Islam in the seventh century, most Arabs converted and became Muslims. As Islam spread beyond its Arabian borders into central Asia and across the southern coast of the Mediterranean Sea into Spain, the Arabic language and culture traveled with it. As a result, many people who are Arabs belong to widely diverse cultures, some with Spanish, African, or Turkish traditions, among others. What links most Arabs together, however, are their religion and common language.

- What did President George W. Bush believe about Hussein? (He had supported and cooperated with al Qaeda.)

- How did the attitude of the Iraqis toward foreign troops change? (At first many Iraqis supported foreign troops, but eventually many Iraqis opposed them.)

WORLD CULTURES

Storytelling has deep roots in Iraqi culture, and Iraqi stories are well appreciated in many parts of the world. Children love the classic tale of Sinbad the sailor's perilous adventures on the sea. His seven journeys all began and ended in his hometown of Baghdad in Iraq. Americans also love to retell the Iraqi tale "The One Thousand and One Nights." This story pits the clever Scheherazade against the ruthless Sultan Shahryar. Within the tale itself are numerous other tales, which Scheherazade must make up on the spot to keep the sultan happy. One of the best-loved stories from this collection is "Ali Baba and the Forty Thieves."

LEARNING STYLES

Visual/Spatial

Have students study the photo on page 765. Have them brainstorm about the difficulties of fighting a war in the desert. List the problems they identify. Divide the class into small groups. Have each group determine the best plan for mobilizing soldiers and machines for desert conflict. Have groups share their strategies. Then have the class speculate on why the Persian Gulf War only lasted 100 hours.

After the war, Iraq's leader, Saddam Hussein, remained in power. Two groups in Iraq—the Shiite Muslims and the Kurds—had not supported him in the war. Hussein made war against them. Hundreds of thousands were killed. Many people were forced out of their homes.

Why Did the United States Attack Iraq in 2002?

On September 11, 2001, the World Trade Center in New York was attacked. The United States suspected that Iraq was behind the attack. In December 2002, the United States and its allies attacked Iraq. There were several reasons given for the attack.

1. President George W. Bush believed that Hussein supported and cooperated with al Qaeda, a terrorist group led by Osama bin Laden. Bush called Iraq an evil country that supported terrorism.

2. The United States and others believed that Iraq's leader, Saddam Hussein, had weapons of mass destruction. These are weapons that can destroy large areas and kill many people.

3. The United States accused Hussein of taking away the basic rights of the Iraqi people.

4. President Bush believed the world was right to attack Iraq in self-defense; he believed that Iraq was a threat to the world.

At first, many other countries agreed with the United States. Hussein was quickly overthrown. At the beginning, most Iraqi people were happy to be free of their brutal dictator. Soon, however, some people began to view the foreign troops as invaders and occupiers, not as people bringing them freedom. Thousands of Iraqi people have been killed in what many people now call a civil war.

Lesson 2 Review Choose the letter of the answer that correctly completes each sentence. Write your answer on a sheet of paper.

1. The prime minister of Israel in the 1990s was _____.

   A Hamas   **B** Rabin   **C** Clinton   **D** Hussein

2. In 1979, Ayatollah _____ took over the Iranian government.

   A Shah   **B** Hussein   **C** Khomeini   **D** Hamas

3. In 1980, _____ invaded Iran.

   A Iraq   **C** Kuwait
   B Saudi Arabia   **D** the United States

4. In 1990, Iraq invaded _____.

   A Iran   **B** Libya   **C** Kuwait   **D** Israel

5. _____ fought Shiite Muslims and Kurds in his own country.

   A Rabin   **C** Hussein
   B Khomeini   **D** Shah

Why is oil such an important resource for the Middle East?

Chapter 30: Lesson 3

Overview This lesson describes political developments and economic trends in China, Japan, and other Asian nations.

Objectives

- To explain political changes in Asian countries
- To describe economic changes that have occurred in Asian countries

Student Pages pages 768–771

Teacher's Resource Library (TRL)

Workbook Activity 141

Activity 141

Modified Activity 141

Vocabulary

human rights

Have students study the definition and discuss the context in which they have heard this word used. Ask for volunteers to use the word in sentences.

 Warm-Up Activity

Ask students to list all the things they purchase that come from China, Japan, Korea, or another Asian country. List the items on the board as they are identified. Have students create categories of items, such as clothing, hardware, electronics, etc. Discuss how the economies of the United States and Asian countries closely interact.

 Teaching the Lesson

Ask students to name some Asian countries that they have studied in previous chapters. Then have them read pages 768-771 to find out about recent political and economic developments in Asia.

PRONUNCIATION GUIDE

Use this list to help students pronounce difficult words in this lesson.

Deng Xiaoping   (dung′ shou′ ping′)

Objectives

- To explain political changes in Asian countries
- To describe economic changes that have occurred in Asian countries

---

After Mao Zedong died in 1976, China began to change. China's new leader, Deng Xiaoping, proposed major economic reforms. His economic plan was called the Four Modernizations. The plan called for reform and change in agriculture, industry, science, and defense. There were many changes. One was that privately owned businesses and private property were again permitted. Another was that investment from foreign countries including the United States was welcomed. Although major industries were still controlled by the government, factory managers were given new powers to make them more efficient and profitable.

The new economic reforms resulted in a big increase in the standard of living for many people. Many Chinese families were able to buy such things as televisions, refrigerators, fans, and even cars. Until recently, these items were considered luxuries that most people could not afford. But the reforms had a bad side, too. A big gap developed between those people who had become successful and rich and those who had not. Crime and corruption increased. Food prices went up. Many people lost their jobs as some factories were closed.

China's capital city is Beijing. Many people ride bicycles rather than motorized vehicles.

China's economy is one of the fastest growing economies in the world today. Many foreign companies are investing in China. They are taking advantage of the low cost of labor in China compared to most developed countries. They also see China's huge population as a market for their products. One of China's biggest customers is the United States.

Name _____ Date _____ Period _____ Workbook Activity 141 | Chapter 30, Lesson 3

Economic Challenges in Asia

Directions Write the answers to these questions. Use complete sentences.

1. How did the economic reforms of Deng Xiaoping help the Chinese people? How did they hurt the Chinese people?

2. Why did students go on a hunger strike in Tiananmen Square?

3. What does the phrase "human rights" mean?

4. What are three important reasons for Japan's economic success?

5. What five Asian countries besides China and Japan have experienced economic growth?

Name _____ Date _____ Period _____ Activity 141 | Chapter 30, Lesson 3

Asian Countries Face Economic Challenges

Directions Write the correct term from the Word Bank to complete each sentence.

1. A person's human rights include _____ and _____ civil liberties.

2. Tiananmen Square is in _____, China's capital city.

3. The country with the largest economy in the world is _____.

4. Many workers in Japan are well _____ and highly skilled.

5. The "little tigers" are South Korea, Taiwan, _____, Hong Kong, and Thailand.

6. The Bank of _____ is owned by the Japanese government.

7. Deng Xiaoping proposed major _____ reforms.

8. In June 1997, the money supply of _____ collapsed.

9. Asian businesses had borrowed too much money from _____ in the 1980s.

10. The country with the third-largest economy is _____.

11. The West has called for more _____ in China.

12. The economic crisis in Thailand spread to Indonesia, _____, the Philippines, and South Korea.

13. The _____ was an economic plan to change agriculture, industry, science, and defense.

14. China has a low cost of _____ compared to most developed countries.

15. During an economic crisis, foreign investors pulled their money out of some _____ countries.

Word Bank

Asian
banks
Beijing
China
economic
educated
Four Modernizations
human rights
Japan
labor
Malaysia
political
Singapore
Thailand
the United States

Workbook Activity 141   **Activity 141**

Reading Strategy: Questioning

What do you already know about what went on in Tiananmen Square in 1989?

What Happened at Tiananmen Square?

In May 1989, more than 3,000 students went on a hunger strike in Tiananmen Square in Beijing, China's capital city. They wanted a democratic, not a communist, government. Soon, more than a million people went out on the streets and called for a change.

Through television, the whole world learned about the protest. But on June 4, 1989, soldiers marched into Tiananmen Square and killed hundreds of protestors. The government put many of the student leaders in jail and tortured or killed them.

Since the Tiananmen Square massacre, China's relations with the West have been strained. The West led by the United States has called for more **human rights** in China. Human rights refer to political and civil liberties, including the right to life, liberty, and the pursuit of happiness. They also include economic, social, and cultural rights.

Why Has Japan Become an Economic Power?

Japan is among the world's top producers of goods and services. It is the second largest economy in the world. (Only the economy of the United States is bigger.) People who study economics give three reasons for its success.

1. The government works with large companies to plan and promote industrial growth.

2. These companies get money from banks. Since Japanese people have one of the highest savings rates in the world, the banks have a lot of money to loan out. The Bank of Japan (owned by the Japanese government) guarantees the loans.

3. The Japanese people are group oriented. It is natural and easy for them to work with one another. They are generally hard workers who produce many products quickly and at low cost. Workers are well educated and highly skilled.

Ask:

- Why did students go on a hunger strike in Tiananmen Square in 1989? (They wanted a democratic government.)

- What role does the government play in business in Japan? (It helps plan industrial growth.)

- Which countries are known as the "Little Tigers"? (South Korea, Taiwan, Singapore, Hong Kong, and Thailand)

- Which nation's money supply collapsed in 1997? (Thailand)

- Which woman has led her nation's fight for democracy? What is her country? (Aung San Suu Kyi; Myanmar)

- Which Asian country has one of the fastest growing economies in the world? (China)

- How many people called for a change in China in 1989? (a million)

- Which country has the second largest economy in the world? (Japan)

Reading Strategy: **Questioning**

(Answers will vary; People in China wanted a democratic government, went on a hunger strike, had a mass protest, and so on.)

Learning Styles

Body/Kinesthetic

Direct student attention to the photo on page 768. Discuss the image. Clear an area in your classroom. Have students volunteer to create a street in Beijing. Have student take on different roles in portraying what it might be like to navigate a Beijing street. Some students should pantomime riding a bike, some crossing the street, some walking among others, etc. Discuss the difference between navigating a street in Beijing and a street in the students' community.

Career Connection

People would not be able to buy manufactured goods if there were not wholesale and retail buyers. These buyers anticipate what the customer will want and find and buy it at the lowest possible price. Wholesale buyers purchase goods directly from the manufacturer; retail buyers purchase goods from wholesale buyers. Training for buyers can be done on the job.

Colleges and trade associations also offer courses. A buyer's work is very competitive, and often entails working overtime. Buyers often must travel across the country and even around the world. Students can find out whether they might enjoy being a buyer by working part-time in retail. They can check with their counselor to find out what courses to take to prepare for a career as a buyer.

Ask:

- Why are several Asian countries called "Little Tigers"? (They have experienced strong economic growth in recent years.)

- Why did many Asian banks and businesses go bankrupt? (They borrowed too much money; foreign investors pulled their money out of some Asian countries.)

Reading Strategy:
Questioning

(Answers should provide a reason why the material was understood or why there is a need to reread the material.)

3 ◆ **Reinforce and Extend**

ELL/ESL STRATEGY

Language Objective:
To understand and use banking terms

Write the word "bank" on the board. Under "bank" write several banking terms including currency, coins, deposit, withdrawal, checking, savings, interest, borrow, and loan. Explain the meaning of each term. ELL students should add these words to their word banks. If possible, invite a local banker to talk to your class about establishing checking accounts, debit cards, credit cards, and similar topics.

Biography

As a child, Aung San Suu Kyi was inspired by the teachings of Mohandas Gandhi, one of India's greatest spiritual and political leaders. Suu Kyi's mother held important government posts in Burma when the country was independent. The family moved when Suu Kyi was 15 years old and her mother began serving as ambassador to India. Suu Kyi attended college in England and then went to New York City, where she worked at the United Nations. Shortly after, she was married and spent 16 happy years before returning to Myanmar in 1988 to visit her dying mother. That was when Suu Kyi became

Reading Strategy:
Questioning

Ask yourself: "Did I understand what I just read?" If not, read the material again.

Biography

Aung San Suu Kyi: 1945–

Since 1988, Aung San Suu Kyi has led the fight for democracy in Myanmar (Burma). Leadership is a family trait. Her father, Aung San, is called the father of independent Burma.

In 1988, Myanmans protested against military rule. As a result, troops shot or arrested thousands. Aung San spoke out for human rights. She helped the National League for Democracy win 80 percent of the seats in parliament. The military rulers ignored this and kept her under house arrest for six years. In 1991, she won the Nobel Peace Prize. She was free for a short time; in 2003, she was returned to house arrest.

Who Are the "Little Tigers"?

Several other Asian nations have experienced economic growth in recent years. Known as the "little tigers," they are South Korea, Taiwan, Singapore, Hong Kong, and Thailand. South Korea builds ships and automobiles. Taiwan produces everything from toys to electronics. Singapore and Hong Kong are manufacturing and banking centers. Much of Thailand's economic growth is the result of huge foreign investment and loans. Investors were hoping to make money and take advantage of Thailand's lower cost of labor.

What Caused the Economic Crisis in Asia in 1997?

In June 1997, the money supply of Thailand collapsed. Soon, the crisis spread to Indonesia, Malaysia, the Philippines, and South Korea. Many Asian banks and businesses went bankrupt. This happened for two reasons.

First, many Asian businesses had borrowed too much money from banks in the 1980s. Then, factories began to produce more than they could sell and prices went down. The businesses could not pay back what they had borrowed. Soon, both the banks and the businesses had no money.

involved in Myanmar politics. At that point, her passion for nonviolent protest connected with political reality, and Aung San Suu Kyi took up the cause of peace and democracy for her people.

Second, foreign investors got worried. They pulled their money out of some Asian countries. Without this money, many Asian businesses could no longer stay in business.

Lesson 3 Review On a sheet of paper, write the answers to these questions. Use complete sentences.

1. How did Deng's Four Modernizations program change China?

2. Which group led the protest movement in China in 1989?

3. List at least two reasons why Japan became the most important economy of Asia.

4. Who are the "Little Tigers"?

5. What two problems led to the economic crisis in Asia?

If you had to choose one human right that was most important to you, what would it be? Why?

Lesson 3 Review Answers

1. Deng permitted private ownership of businesses and property and allowed foreign investment. This led to a big increase in the standard of living. **2.** Students led the protest movement in China. **3.** Answers will vary, but should include two of the following ideas: a unique relationship between government and business, a high rate of savings that provides banks with a lot of money to loan out, a culture that promotes a group spirit and values hard work and education. **4.** South Korea, Taiwan, Singapore, Hong Kong, Thailand **5.** The economic crisis in Asia came about because of the weakness of the banking and finance system and the outflow of foreign investment.

Answers will vary. Students should explain that human rights refer to political and civil liberties, including the right to life, liberty, happiness, in addition to economic, social, and cultural rights. Students should provide an reason to support the human right they believe is most important to them.

Chapter 30: Lesson 4

Overview This lesson explains the problems of land ownership and the trade agreements that affect Latin America.

Objectives

- To explain why campesinos demanded land reform
- To describe ways the United States has caused changes in Latin America

Student Pages pages 772–776

Teacher's Resource Library

Workbook Activity 142

Activity 142

Modified Activity 142

Vocabulary

campesino
Western Hemisphere
embargo

Ask students to write sentences that use a simple definition of each vocabulary word. Have them exchange papers. Classmates can underline the definition used and write, in a different color above the definition, the vocabulary word being defined.

1 Warm-Up Activity

Have students turn to the map of South America on page 821 of the Atlas in the back of the textbook. Have students locate Panama. Ask students to speculate as to the economic value of the Panama Canal. Explain that the canal continues to be used for both military and merchant vessels, and cuts about 12,875 kilometers (8,000 miles) from the lengthy crossing from the Atlantic to the Pacific Ocean.

2 Teaching the Lesson

Remind students that nations in the Americas from Mexico to the south are considered part of Latin America. Then have students read pages 772–776 to find out about major problems that confront Latin America.

Objectives

- To explain why campesinos demanded land reform
- To describe ways the United States has caused changes in Latin America

Campesino

A peasant who works the land but does not own it

One of the biggest problems facing Latin America is an extreme of wealth and poverty. Most Latin American countries have agricultural economies. The majority of people are poor people. They are peasants, landless farm workers, and factory workers. Poverty is widespread. It affects all groups but affects native peoples, minorities, women, and children the most. A small but rich elite controls much of the wealth. This group includes the landowners, factory owners, and military leaders.

Why Do Campesinos Want Land Reform?

A big problem is that a small group of people own so much of the land. For example, in Paraguay, a few big landowners control 80 percent of the land that can be farmed! This is true in most of the rest of Latin America. Many poor people, called **campesinos**, live and work on the land, but do not own it.

In many countries, campesinos are demanding land reform. They want the government to break up the large farms and divide the land among the poor. Land reform has been most successful in Mexico, Cuba, Peru, and Nicaragua.

Women buying and selling food in Guatemala, Central America.

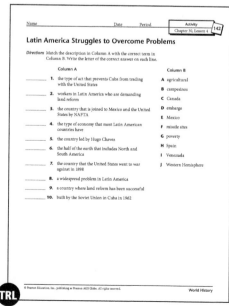

Name _____ Date _____ Period _____ **Workbook Activity**
Chapter 30, Lesson 4 **142**

Struggles in Latin America

Directions Write the answers to these questions. Use complete sentences.

1. What are three natural resources that Latin America exports?

2. Who are the campesinos? What do they want from the government?

3. Why did the United States encourage the people of Panama to revolt?

4. What happened in Cuba in 1959? What happened there in 1962?

5. What does the name NAFTA stand for? What does it do?

Workbook Activity 142

Name _____ Date _____ Period _____ **Activity**
Chapter 30, Lesson 4 **142**

Latin America Struggles to Overcome Problems

Directions Match the description in Column A with the correct term in Column B. Write the letter of the correct answer on each line.

Column A	Column B
1. the type of act that prevents Cuba from trading with the United States	A agricultural
2. workers in Latin America who are demanding land reform	B campesinos
3. the country that is joined to Mexico and the United States by NAFTA	C Canada
4. the type of economy that most Latin American countries have	D embargo
5. the country led by Hugo Chavez	E Mexico
6. the half of the earth that includes North and South America	F missile sites
7. the country that the United States went to war against in 1898	G poverty
8. a widespread problem in Latin America	H Spain
9. a country where land reform has been successful	I Venezuela
10. built by the Soviet Union in Cuba in 1962	J Western Hemisphere

Activity 142

Western
Hemisphere

The half of the earth
that includes North
and South America

Population growth is another big challenge. In 1940 Latin America had about 126 million people. In 2007 there are nearly 600 million! Families are typically large. Improved health care also means that fewer people die.

Economic development is another problem. The leaders of Latin America believe that industrialization is the way to solve many of the region's problems. In the 1980s and 90s, Latin America made great progress. The region has large deposits of oil, tin, copper, iron ore, and bauxite, the main ingredient in aluminum. Export sale of these natural resources provides much of the foreign income needed to finance development. But relying on one product can be very bad. When the price drops, governments are forced to borrow money to make up the difference. Many Latin American countries got into trouble when they began borrowing too much money.

How Do Latin America and the United States Get Along?

Reading Strategy:
Questioning

What details are
important to
understanding the
relationship between
Latin America and the
United States?

In Chapter 22, you read about the struggle for freedom in Latin America. During this time, the United States encouraged the wars of independence. In 1823, President James Monroe warned European nations to stay out of the **Western Hemisphere.** That is the half of the earth that includes North and South America.

Conflict developed when Americans settled in territories of northern Mexico in the 1830s and 1840s. In 1846, Mexico and the United States went to war. At the end of the war, Mexico had to give up California and all the land between Texas and California.

In 1898, the United States went to war against Spain in the Spanish-American War. Cuba, a Spanish colony, was given its independence but U.S. forces stayed in Cuba for four more years. The United States took control of Puerto Rico, another Spanish colony. By now, the United States was becoming a major world power.

1950 to the Present

The Developing World   Chapter 30   **773**

Ask:

- **What are campesinos in some Latin American countries demanding?** (land reform)
- **What land did the United States get from Mexico after a war in the mid-19th century?** (California, Texas, and all the land in between)
- **When did the United States acquire Puerto Rico?** (1898)
- **What are two major challenges faced by Latin America?** (population growth and economic development)
- **What was the result of the Spanish American War?** (Cuba became independent.)

Reading Strategy:
Questioning

(economic and social problems facing Latin America, importance of the region's natural resources, history of the region)

LEARNING STYLES

Interpersonal/ Group Learning
Explain that the class is going to research the building of the Panama Canal. Ask students what different topics could be researched to learn more about the canal. (geography, climate, political events of the early 20th century, actually construction, reasons for building the canal, etc.) Have students divide into groups according to student interests. Provide time for each group to make use of library resources and the Internet to complete its research. Have each group present what it learned to the class in a visually interesting report.

AT HOME

Pass out outline maps of Latin America to students and ask them to play a game with their families. Each family member takes a turn placing a label with the name of a Latin American country on the correct spot on the map. Ask students to share their families' game experiences with classmates. You may want students to work in groups to complete or correct family game maps.

Ask:

- When did NAFTA take effect? (January 1, 1994)
- What is the purpose of NAFTA? (to promote free trade)
- Which nations' economies are linked by the North American Free Trade Agreement? (Canada, Mexico, and the United States)

Have students read "The 'Tourist Capital of Peru.'" Explain that Cuzco is a World Heritage site identified by the United Nations Educational, Scientific and Cultural Organization (UNESCO), established in 1972. A World Heritage site is considered of great natural and cultural value to people of the world.

3 ◆ **Reinforce and Extend**

LEARNING STYLES

Auditory/Verbal

Ask students to research sports that are popular in Latin America today or that have a long history in Latin America. Have students organize their research into a two-to-three minute speech.

ELL/ESL STRATEGY

Language Objective: *To describe foods of Latin America*
Today, many Spanish food terms have become commonplace, such as tacos, burritos, and gazpacho. Divide the class into small groups. Have each group research the food of an assigned Latin American country. Have each group describe favorite foods, how they are produced, prepared, and served. If possible, have a food day where students can share dishes from Latin America. Provide time for each ELL student to describe a favorite food from his or her native country.

The "Tourist Capital of Peru"

Cuzco is a city in southern Peru. It is believed to be one of the oldest cities in the world, dating back to 2000 B.C. Cuzco was the capital of the Incan civilization beginning in A.D. 1200. When Spain conquered the empire in 1533, they moved the capital to Lima.

Colorful reminders of Inca art and architecture are still found in Cuzco. Much of the Incan Temple of the Sun still stands, as do pieces of wall that once surrounded the city. The same is true of the Renaissance cathedral built by Spaniards, as well as explorer Francisco Pizzaro's palace. A major earthquake destroyed much of Cuzco in 1950. The historical buildings have been restored since that time. Cuzco, now a major center for archaeological research, is often called the "tourist capital of Peru."

The navy needed a fast way to move its warships from the Atlantic to the Pacific Ocean. It was decided to build a canal through Central America. The shortest route for a canal was through Panama, but Panama was a part of Colombia. The United States encouraged the people of Panama to revolt. U.S. President Theodore Roosevelt bragged, "I took Panama." The canal was built and opened to shipping in 1914.

The United States and Latin America have taken steps to reduce tariffs and trade barriers. They have joined together in regional trade agreements such as the North American Free Trade Agreement, or NAFTA. It took effect on January 1, 1994. It links together the economies of the United States, Mexico, and Canada. The United States has tried to promote free trade, that is, trade between countries that is free of taxes and other barriers.

What Major Problems Exist Between the United States and Latin America Today?

Several countries in Latin America have elected leaders who are critical of the United States government. In 1959, Fidel Castro overthrew the pro-American leader of Cuba. He became a dictator who would not allow free elections or a free press. He took over U.S.-owned businesses. The United States put an **embargo** on all trade with Cuba, which still exists. An embargo stops all trade. In 1961, a U.S.-trained group invaded Cuba and tried to overthrow Castro. The landing at the Bay of Pigs had little popular support. In July, 1962, the Soviet Union began to build missile sites in Cuba. The United States demanded their removal. It looked as if the United States and the USSR would go to war. Fortunately, the missile crisis ended peacefully. The Soviets agreed to remove the missiles, and the United States promised not to invade Cuba.

Venezuela's leader is Hugo Chavez. Like Castro, he is anti-American and wants to reduce America's influence in the region. His government has taken over several major oil businesses owned by foreign corporations. In Bolivia, Evo Morales, a critic of free market economics, is president.

Reading Strategy:
Questioning

Think about the purpose of this lesson. Ask yourself what you hope to learn by reading it.

Ask:

- In what year did Fidel Castro become the dictator of Cuba? (1959)
- What did a U.S.-trained group try to do in 1961? (overthrow Castro)

Reading Strategy:
Questioning

(Answers will vary; I hope to learn more about the history of U.S.-Cuban relations.)

STUDY SKILLS

Encourage students who are interested in learning more about the Bay of Pigs or the Cuban Missile Crisis to research their topic of interest on the Internet. Many photos and other primary source documents are readily available. Students may also be interesting in researching the difficulties faced by Cuban refugees.

Ask students to brainstorm the names of players on United States baseball teams that are from other countries. Then have them read the History in Your Life feature to find out about the popularity of the game all over the world.

Lesson 4 Review Answers

1. Answers will vary; The landowners also hold political power in Latin America. **2.** They also would like to own land so they could live independently. **3.** People are forced to work for large landholders; they have poor health care and living conditions. **4.** The purpose of NAFTA is to promote free trade between the United States, Canada, and Mexico. **5.** The Unites States hoped to establish a democratic government in Cuba.

Answers will vary. The United States could provide assistance that would allow the Latin American countries to improve health, transportation, sanitation, housing, education, and economic development. The U.S. government could support land reform and also could demand that U.S. businesses practice human rights in Latin America and give up their support of dictatorships.

Chapter Project Follow-up

Provide each group with poster board. Have students use the images collected from the Internet to create a collage depicting current events in Africa, the Middle East, Asia, or Latin America. Have each group display and explain its collage. Ask a student who enjoys creating displays to use the posters to develop a current events display for the classroom.

Baseball Around the World

Do you love béisbol? Do you play besoboru? These are the words for baseball in Spanish and Japanese. Baseball has been popular in countries around the world for more than a hundred years. Players from countries such as Cuba and Japan now play for American major league teams.

How did baseball spread outside the United States? American missionaries took it to Japan in the 1870s. During the Spanish-American War (1898), American soldiers brought the game to the Philippines.

The Japanese saw baseball as a new kind of martial art. By the early 1900s, it was the country's most popular sport. American major league players toured Japan in the 1920s and 1930s. Baseball then spread to Korea and Taiwan.

Baseball is played in Mexico, the Caribbean, and Central America, too. Tours and spring training also helped introduce it there. Each year, national teams from these areas play in the Caribbean Series.

Lesson 4 Review On a sheet of paper, write the answer to each question. Use complete sentences.

1. Why do you think that a few landowners, factory owners, and military leaders control most of Latin America's wealth?

2. Why did campesinos demand land reform?

3. How does poverty affect the people of Latin America?

4. What is the purpose of NAFTA?

5. Why did the United States try to overthrow Cuba's leader, Fidel Castro, in the Bay of Pigs invasion?

What do you think

What should the United States do to improve the life of poor people in Latin America?

Poverty Is a Threat to Peace

Muhammad Yunus received the Nobel Peace Prize in 2006 for starting Grameen Bank. This bank provides small loans—the average is $200— to poor people so they can invest in business and change their lives. Today the bank has 3.5 million borrowers. Most of them are women. Here is an excerpt from his acceptance speech.

Ladies and Gentlemen:
By giving us this prize, the Norwegian Nobel Committee has given important support to the proposition that peace is inextricably linked to poverty. Poverty is a threat to peace. . . .

Poverty is the denial of all human rights. Peace should be understood in a human way, in a broad social, political and economic way. Peace is threatened by unjust economic, social and political order, absence of democracy, environmental degradation and absence of human rights.

Poverty is the absence of all human rights. The frustrations, hostility and anger generated by abject poverty cannot sustain peace in any society. For building stable peace we must find ways to provide opportunities for people to live decent lives.

The creation of opportunities for the majority of people—the poor—is at the heart of the work that we have dedicated ourselves to during the past 30 years. . . .

We create what we want. We get what we want, or what we don't refuse. We accept the fact that we will always have poor people around us, and that poverty is part of human destiny. This is precisely why we continue to have poor people around us. If we firmly believe that poverty is unacceptable to us, and that it should not belong to a civilized society, we would have built appropriate institutions and policies to create a poverty-free world.

We wanted to go to the moon, so we went there. We achieve what we want to achieve. If we are not achieving something, it is because we have not put our minds to it. We create what we want.

I believe that this honor that you give us will inspire many more bold [projects] around the world to make a historical breakthrough in ending global poverty.

Document-Based Questions

1. How does Yunus define poverty?

2. How is poverty connected to peace?

3. What are the emotions that people experience from living in poverty?

4. According to Yunus, what do we achieve?

5. What does Yunus hope that his receiving the Nobel Peace Prize will inspire in others?

Source: Nobel lecture by Muhammad Yunus, December 20, 2006.

1950 to the Present

The Developing World   Chapter 30   **777**

Read the title, "Poverty Is a Threat to Peace," by Muhammad Yunus and the introductory paragraph to students. Talk about the difference between $200 in the United States and $200 in poverty-stricken countries. In 2006, for example, the average salary was $10 per month. Have students read the selection silently. Then write the opening sentence of each paragraph on the board. Have students list supporting details from each paragraph. Discuss the general idea of the selection. Focus on the second to last paragraph. Have students discuss this paragraph in particular. Have interested students research the Grameen Bank (www.agsglobewh.com/ page777) and share what they learned with the class. Have students silently reread the selection. Students should then write answers to the Document-Based questions.

Answers to Document-Based Questions:

1. Poverty is the absence of all of human rights.

2. Peace is threatened by the absence of human rights and is directly linked to poverty.

3. People living in poverty experience hostility and anger.

4. We achieve what we want to achieve.

5. Yunus hopes others will be inspired to start projects that address global poverty.

Ask students to think back over recent world events. Encourage them to compare these events to historical events they have studied. Ask volunteers to make connections between recent wars, economic crises, and natural disasters and similar events from the past. Write their responses on the board. Then have students silently read "Themes in History" and write answers to the Wrap-Up questions.

Answers to Spotlight Story Wrap-Up:

1. Some ancient empires were those of Babylon, Egypt, Persia, Alexander the Great, and Rome.

2. Empires fall because of the death of a strong leader, gradual decline and then invasion, and new technology with better weapons.

3. They have rebelled against their own monarchs and ruling colonial powers.

4. Answers will vary. Students may mention things besides those in the Spotlight Story.

5. Answers will vary.

Themes in History

An old saying goes, "History repeats itself." Look back over the thousands of years you have studied. Probably you can see many continuing themes. Certain types of events seem to happen again and again.

One theme in history is the rise and fall of empires. In every time and place, leaders have wanted power. They have conquered and ruled other lands and people. The earliest empires began in Mesopotamia more than 4,000 years ago. Ancient history, in fact, sometimes looks like the history of empires. Babylon, Egypt, and Persia each ruled huge territories. Alexander the Great and Genghis Khan built the largest empires of all.

Empires fall for different reasons. Some, like Alexander's, depended on one strong leader. After the leader's death, the empire fell apart. Other empires grew weak before they were defeated. The Roman Empire declined for centuries. Finally, Germanic invaders brought it to an end. Sometimes empires were defeated by new technology. North Africans with guns defeated Songhai. Spaniards with guns and horses conquered the Incas.

The search for freedom is another major theme. Throughout history, individuals have rebelled against power. In the 1790s, the people of France began a bloody revolution. It ended the monarchy. In the 1800s, Latin American colonies won independence from Spain. After World War II, colonies around the world struggled to become independent. Some went to war. In India, Gandhi used a new way to win independence from Britain. He urged nonviolent methods like strikes.

Today there is a new emphasis on human rights. This issue combines justice with freedom. Human rights supporters want fair treatment for all people. They work particularly on behalf of people without power. Human rights is not a new issue. Gandhi wanted fair treatment for India's "untouchables." Today, activists work for the rights of children, the poor, and others.

Technology is another theme in human history. The earliest men and women made tools. Technology helped build civilizations. It has also changed history. Iron tools changed warfare and farming. The Chinese learned to make silk and porcelain. That encouraged trade ties between Asia and Europe. With better ships and navigation, explorers could make long sea voyages. Printing helped spread learning. Today, cell phones and the Internet link the whole world.

Wrap-Up

1. Name some empires from ancient times.

2. What are some causes for the fall of empires?

3. How have people shown their desire for freedom?

4. Name one advance in technology that changed history. What did it change?

5. Identify a theme in history that you have noticed. Include an example.

Chapter 30 SUMMARY

- Africa continues to face the challenges of poverty, famine, and disease.

- The United States has tried to bring peace to the Middle East. Israel made peace with Egypt (1978) and Jordan (1994). Conflicts continue in the Middle East.

- The Shah of Iran tried to modernize the country but used harsh methods. A religious leader, Ayatollah Khomeini, led a revolution against him in 1979.

- Iranians and Iraqis follow different branches of Islam and belong to different ethnic groups. Iraq invaded Iran in 1980, starting an eight-year war. The war threatened world oil supplies.

- In 1990, Iraqi leader Saddam Hussein invaded Kuwait to take control of its oil fields. In the Persian Gulf War, an international military force defeated Iraq.

- The United States and its allies invaded Iraq in 2002 because they suspected that Iraq was behind the attack on the World Trade Center on 9/11.

- After Mao Zedong's death, Chinese leader Deng Xiaoping made economic changes. He encouraged private business and foreign investment. Now, China has one of the fastest growing economies in the world.

- In 1989 in Tiananmen Square, soldiers attacked students. They were marching for democracy and human rights.

- Japan has the world's second largest economy. The economies of other Asian nations have also grown.

- An economic crisis hit Asian nations in 1997. Many banks and businesses failed.

- Land reform is an issue in many Latin American nations. Most people are poor.

- Mexico, Canada, and the United States signed the North American Free Trade Agreement (NAFTA) to encourage trade.

- Several countries in Latin America have elected leaders who do not like the United States government. Cuba's leader, Fidel Castro, came to power in 1959. The United States tried to overthrow him in 1961.

1950 to the Present

Using the Chapter Summary

Have students read the Chapter Summary to review the main ideas presented in Chapter 30.

Ask:

- What are three challenges faced by the people of Africa? (poverty, famine, disease)

- What are two causes of famine in Africa? (Answers will vary; students may mention a growing population, droughts, lack of fertilizer and pesticides, or war.)

- Which two countries in the Middle East were at war for years during the 1980s? (Iraq and Iran)

- Which leader sent troops into Kuwait, hoping to capture oil fields? (Saddam Hussein)

- Which nation killed hundreds of pro-democracy protesters in Tiananmen Square in 1989? (China)

- The United States' economy is the largest in the world; whose economy is second? Whose is third? (Japan; China)

- What economic crisis occurred in many Asian nations in 1997? (Many banks and businesses failed.)

- What is the trade agreement that links Canada, Mexico, and the United States? (North American Free Trade Agreement, or NAFTA)

- What is the current political situation between leaders of Latin America and the United States? (Some leaders work with the United States, while others do not like the United States government.)

Chapter 30 Review

Use the Chapter Review to prepare students for tests and to reteach content from the chapter.

Chapter 30 Mastery Test

The Teacher's Resource Library includes two forms of the Chapter 30 Mastery Test. Each test addresses the chapter Goals for Learning. An optional third page of additional critical-thinking items is included for each test. The difficulty level of the two forms is equivalent.

Chapter 30 Review Answers

1. urbanization
2. ayatollah
3. malaria
4. Accords
5. shah
6. Kuwait
7. Modernizations
8. Japanese
9. Thailand
10. campesinos
11. B
12. A

Word Bank

Accords
ayatollah
campesinos
Japanese
Kuwait
malaria
Modernizations
Shah
Thailand
urbanization

On a sheet of paper, use the words from the Word Bank to complete each sentence correctly.

1. Because many people are flocking to the cities, Africa faces rapid _____.

2. The name for a religious leader in Iran is _____.

3. Millions of people in Africa suffer from AIDS or _____, which is spread by mosquitos.

4. The Camp David _____ formed the basis for an Arab-Israeli peace treaty.

5. Until 1979, Iran was ruled by a(n) _____.

6. In August 1990, Iraqi troops invaded _____.

7. Deng Xiaoping's economic plan was called the Four _____.

8. _____ people have one of the highest rates of saving money in the world.

9. In June 1997, the money supply of _____ collapsed.

10. The _____ in Latin America are demanding land reform.

On a separate sheet of paper, write the letter of the answer that correctly completes each sentence.

11. In 1979, _____ took 52 Americans hostage.

   A Iraq   **B** Iran   **C** Cuba   **D** Israel

12. The Persian Gulf War started after Iraq invaded _____.

   A Kuwait   **C** Iran
   B Saudi Arabia   **D** Israel

13. Pro-democracy protests in Tiananmen Square were led by _____.

   A peasants   **C** merchants
   B students   **D** government leaders

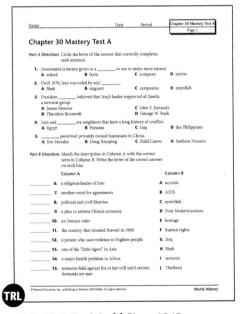

Chapter 30 Mastery Test A, pages 1–3

14. China's economy is the _____ largest economy in the world.

    A second   **B** third   **C** fourth   **D** fifth

15. In 1978, U.S. President _____ brought Egypt's Sadat and Israel's Begin together at Camp David, Maryland.

    A Nixon   **B** Reagan   **C** Carter   **D** Clinton

On a sheet of paper, write the answers to the following questions. Use complete sentences.

16. What is one problem that Africans face today?

17. What is one problem that people in the Middle East face today?

18. What is one problem that people in Latin America face today?

Critical Thinking On a sheet of paper, write your response to each question. Use complete sentences.

19. The conflict in the Middle East has gone on for many years. If you could talk to leaders in the Middle East, what advice would you give them about ending the conflict?

20. There are many countries in the world that suffer from extreme poverty. If you could choose one country to help, where would you go and what would you do?

> Make sure you have the same number of answers on your paper as there are items on the test.

1950 to the Present

The Developing World   *Chapter 30*   **781**

---

13. B

14. B

15. C

16. Africans face rapid urbanization, health problems, famine, and drought.

17. People in the Middle East face war because of the Palestinian situation and because of the presence of Saddam Hussein, the Iraqi dictator. Also, the gap between the rich and the poor seems to be growing and families are breaking down.

18. People in Latin America face a division between the few who have extreme wealth and the many who live in extreme poverty.

Critical Thinking

19. Answers will vary. Students may suggest strategies such as telling the leaders that they are destroying their countries and their people by continuing to fight.

20. Answers will vary. Students should choose an appropriate country and suggest some steps to help ease poverty there.

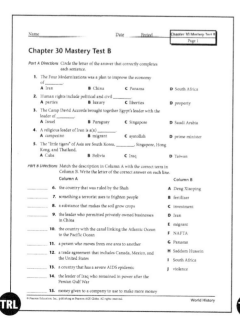

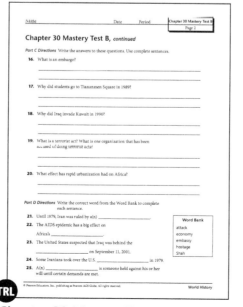

Chapter 30 Mastery Test B, pages 1–3

The Developing World   *Chapter 30*   **781**

Introducing the Chapter

Tell students that at the beginning of the 1900s, people found it difficult to contact the more remote places on Earth. The Internet and other communication systems made it possible for people to connect with areas around the world almost instantly. Other advances in

---

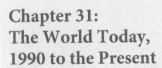

The World Today

This is the last chapter of your world history book. In this text, you have traveled through time from ancient India, China, and Sumeria to modern nations. Now, in this final chapter, you will discover the global village that is Earth. You will see how the Internet and mass communication link the nations of our global village. Then you will learn how modern technology can be harmful. You will also learn about the joining together of the world economies. Finally, you will see what farming and industry have done to the environment. This chapter shows you what life is like today.

Goals for Learning

◆ To explain how technology and energy help build a global village

◆ To describe the economic interdependence of modern industrial nations and developing countries

◆ To identify some health concerns and environmental problems the world faces

◆ To describe how the threat of terrorism has changed the world

◆ To consider what the future may hold

1990s Internet expands the use of computers

1997 Recession begins in Thailand and spreads worldwide

2001 September 11 attacks; U.S. Department of Homeland Security created

| 1990 | 1995 | 2000 |

International leaders meet to discuss environmental problems

1997 International leaders meet once again to discuss environmental problems

---

technology improved methods of farming, medicine, and manufacturing. But rapid technological growth has had drawbacks as well. Modern farming methods and industrial development are taking a toll on the world's ecosystem. New communication systems have brought fears about invasion of privacy.

Ask:

• What decade is featured on this timeline? (1990s)

• This decade was the last in which century? Which millennium? (20th; second)

• What information system made the world seem smaller? (the Internet)

Name _____ Date _____ Period _____   *SELF-STUDY GUIDE*

Chapter 31: The World Today

Goal 31.1 *To explain how technology and energy help build a global village*

Date	Assignment	Completed
	1. Read pages 782–792.	
	2. Complete the Lesson 1 Review on page 792.	
	3. Complete Workbook Activity 143.	

Comments:

Goal 31.2 *To describe the economic interdependence of modern industrial nations and developing countries*

Date	Assignment	Completed
	4. Read pages 793–796.	
	5. Complete the Lesson 2 Review on page 796.	
	6. Complete Workbook Activity 144.	

Comments:

Goal 31.3 *To identify some health concerns and environmental problems the world faces*

Date	Assignment	Completed
	7. Read pages 797–802.	
	8. Complete the Lesson 3 Review on page 802.	
	9. Complete Workbook Activity 145.	

Comments:

© Pearson Education, Inc., publishing as Pearson AGS Globe. All rights reserved.   **World History**

Chapter 31 Self-Study Guide, pages 1–2

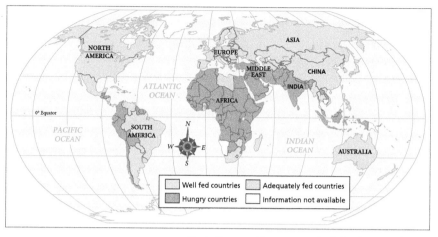

Many countries of the world have enough food to feed their people. But some countries do not. The climate is much hotter and drier near the equator than it is farther away, so that is where growing food is difficult. Many of these hungry nations have deserts in their land. This world map shows world hunger.

Study the map, then answer the following questions:

1. Which continent has the most serious problem with hunger?

2. What are three places where people are well fed?

3. On which coast of South America is there a hunger problem?

4. Do people in China have more or less food than people in Australia?

5. Do people in India have more or less food than people in North America?

Ask students to read the title of the map, "World Hunger." Then have a volunteer read the caption below the map. Ask how the different categories in the key might have been determined. (Answers will vary. Students may suggest that the data is based on the amount of food produced in the country or the number of people that go to sleep hungry every night.)

Ask:

• On which continents is hunger a problem? (parts of Asia and South America, and most of Africa)

• How would you define the United States with respect to hunger? (well-fed)

Map Skills Answers

1. Africa

2. North America, parts of Asia, Europe, Australia, southern America, and S. Africa are well fed.

3. the west coast

4. The Chinese have less food than the Australians.

5. The people in India have less food than those in North America.

Chapter Project

List the following alternative, or renewable, energy sources on the board: hydroelectricity, solar power, wind power, geothermal power, ocean thermal energy and wave power, and bioenergy. Divide the class into groups and assign an energy source to each group. Have groups research and prepare reports on their energy source. Students might make a "How It Works" poster or a model to show how the energy source produces electricity or heats homes and offices. Have students find out if their energy source is used in their community. And, if possible, have them present data comparing their energy source to fossil fuels in terms of cost, pollution, and availability.

Chapter 31 Outline, pages 1–3

Predicting

Introduce the reading skill *predicting*. Tell students that predicting as they read will help them be active readers and help them better understand the information they are reading.

Ask a volunteer to read the three bullet points on page 784. Then have students read the title of Lesson 1. Explain that the title "Energy and Technology Create a Global Village" leads you to predict that this lesson is about how people in the world know more about each other and how we depend upon each other, like people in a small village do.

Read aloud the Objectives in the left-hand column on page 785.

Ask:

- What do you know about the meanings of the words *global* and *village*? (Answers will vary. Most students will identify *global* as meaning "the whole world" and *village* as a small town or a place where people live.)

- What do you think a "global village" might be? (Answers will vary.)

- How has mass communication changed our world? (Answers will vary. Students may suggest that mass communication has made it easier, and faster, to connect with people all over the world.)

Remind students to revise their predictions as new information is presented in the lesson.

....

Key Vocabulary Words

Have students work with a partner. Ask one student of each pair to read a definition of a vocabulary word. Have the other student give the word that matches the definition and restate the definition in his or her own words. Partners should take turns supplying the words and the definitions.

....

Reading Strategy:
Predicting

In order to predict what will come next, it is helpful to first preview a text. Previewing helps readers think about what they already know about a subject. When making predictions, consider the following:

- Consider what you already know about the topic. Make your best guess as to what might happen next.

- Be sure to include details that support your prediction.

- As you read, you may learn new information that changes your prediction. Check your predictions as you read.

Key Vocabulary Words

Lesson 1 —————————————
Technology The use of science to do practical things

Global village The term used to describe the sharing of ideas, cultures, and traditions throughout the world

Mass communication Messages directed at many people

Internet An international computer network

International Around the world; involving different nations

World Wide Web A network of information on the Internet open to businesses and individuals

Renewable Energy that will never run out

Photoelectric cell An invention that can produce electricity from light

Laser A tool that produces high-energy beams of light

Lesson 2 —————————————
Interdependent Depending on one another

Free-market economy An economy in which manufacturers try to satisfy consumers' wants and needs

Northern Hemisphere The half of the earth north of the equator

Developing country A nation that is slowly developing its industry and economy

Southern Hemisphere The half of the earth south of the equator

Subsistence farming A type of farming in which people grow crops mostly for their own use, not to sell

Recession An economic slowdown

Lesson 3 —————————————
Deforestation The destruction of forests

Fossil fuel Fuel made from coal, oil, or natural gas

Global warming The worldwide heating up of Earth, caused in part by human activity

Lesson 4 —————————————
Regime The form of government

Tyranny Harsh, absolute power

Objectives

- To define global village
- To identify ways mass communication has changed our world
- To identify the cost of energy to the environment

Technology
The use of science to do practical things

Global village
The term used to describe the sharing of ideas, cultures, and traditions throughout the world

Reading Strategy:
Predicting

Preview the lesson title. Predict what you will learn in this lesson.

Today, the earth seems smaller than it used to be. Its physical size is the same as it was for the ancient Romans. The distance between Spain and Cuba is the same as it was for Christopher Columbus. The miles from France to Russia are still the same as they were for Napoleon. So what has changed?

What Has Made the World into a Global Village?

Today, people around the world share ideas, art, music, and different ways of living. This has happened because of advances in **technology.** Technology is the use of science to do practical things. Because of this technology, the world is changing into a **global village.**

What is a global village? The word *global* comes from the word *globe*, which means "the earth." As you know, a village is a place where a few hundred people live and work together. People who live in a village know most, if not all, their neighbors. Villagers share ideas and traditions. They share their lives. A global village, then, is a term used to describe the sharing of ideas, cultures, and traditions around the world.

Today, for the first time in history, modern technology—motion pictures, computers, video cameras, CD players, television—allows people from around the world to share their lives. Technology also enables businesses to employ workers all over the world.

Technology links the whole world together. Technology makes the globe we live on into one village—a global village. We have begun to share our cultures around the globe.

We all live in Earth's global village. This picture shows Tokyo, Japan.

Overview This lesson explains how the World Wide Web and other forms of mass communication have transformed Earth into a global village, the energy needed to make technological advancements possible, and the drawbacks of energy and technology use.

Objectives

- To define global village
- To identify ways mass communication has changed our world
- To identify the cost of energy to the environment

Student Pages pages 785–792

Teacher's Resource Library

Workbook Activity 143

Activity 143

Modified Activity 143

....

Vocabulary

global village	photoelectric cell
international	renewable
Internet	technology
laser	World Wide Web
mass communication	

Have students work with a partner to make a crossword puzzle that uses all the vocabulary words, with no space between terms that have more than one word. Students can write fill-in-the-blank sentences as clues. Have students exchange with another pair of students and solve each other's puzzles.

....

1 Warm-Up Activity

Remind students that they have learned about many emerging nations. Have them imagine that they are leaders who have just led a fight for independence. A new country has been formed, and the leaders are preparing to set up a government. Have students brainstorm a list of bold, new ideas for this country, including environmental, social, health, economic, and governmental issues.

Workbook Activity 143

Name _____ Date _____ Period _____ Workbook Activity 143
Chapter 31, Lesson 1

Creating a Global Village

Directions Write the correct term from the Word Bank to match each description.

1. I describe the sharing of ideas, cultures, and traditions throughout the world.
2. I am the use of science to do practical things.
3. I am produced when air, water, or land become unclean and unhealthy.
4. I made the Internet easier to use.
5. I was the source of energy in the 19th century.
6. I am messages directed at many people.
7. People use me to announce or sell things.
8. I am an international computer network.
9. I started a technological revolution as important as the Industrial Revolution.
10. I produce energy from light.

Word Bank
advertising
coal
computer
global village
Internet
mass communication
photoelectric cell
pollution
technology
World Wide Web

Activity 143

Name _____ Date _____ Period _____ Activity 143
Chapter 31, Lesson 1

Energy and Technology Create a Global Village

Directions Match the description in Column A with the correct term in Column B for each set. Write the letter of the correct answer on each line.

Column A	Column B
1. the first space satellite	A advertising
2. network of information on the Internet	B Columbia
3. the selling or the announcing of something	C computer
4. the name of the space shuttle	D Internet
5. started a technological revolution	E oil
6. an international computer network	F Sputnik
7. major source of energy in the 21st century	G technology
8. the use of science to do practical things	H World Wide Web

Column A	Column B
9. involving different nations	I culture
10. landed on Mars and took photos	J electronic
11. lets us write messages to people almost instantly	K E-mail
12. world-wide sharing of ideas, cultures, and traditions	L global village
13. messages directed at many people	M international
14. powered by electricity	N mass communication
15. what technology allows us to share around the globe	O Pathfinder

Have students recall the projects they have done in school that required information about countries other than the United States. Then have students read pages 785–792 to find out how technology has made it easy to access that information quickly.

Ask:

- What has made it possible for people all over the world to share ideas, cultures, and traditions? (Answers will vary. Students may suggest technology or mass communication.)

- What is one way that global culture has influenced your life? (Answers will vary. Students may suggest that music, technology, and food from other cultures have become part of their lives.)

- How is the International Space Station an example of global cooperation? (Many different countries worked together to build it, and astronauts and scientists from various countries work there.)

Reading Strategy:
Predicting

(Answers will vary. Students might make the same predictions as in the Reading Strategy activity, or they might revise or expand on those ideas.)

Ask:

- What are some examples of mass communication? (Answers will vary. Students may mention advertising, television, radio, or movies.)

- What language is spoken by many businesspeople and government officials around the world? (English)

Reading Strategy:
Predicting

As you read, think about what might come next. Do you think that mass communication has played an important role in creating the global village?

Mass communication

Messages directed at many people

Reading Strategy:
Predicting

(Answers will vary. Students may suggest that the world could not have become a global village if mass communication didn't spread messages to all parts of the world.)

Communication in History

Ask students to read "Your Phone Is Ringing" to find out about the changes cell phones have made in our lives. When they finish reading, ask students where the low-power transmission towers are in their community. If no one knows, ask volunteers to find out and report back to the class.

How Has Mass Communication Created Our Global Village?

Mass communication is one of the major reasons that the world is becoming a global village. Mass communication is messages directed at many people. Businesses and private or governmental groups prepare these messages.

Newspaper and magazine advertising provides mass communication in print. Advertising is the selling or the announcing of something. Motion pictures, television, radio, and musical recordings provide mass communication electronically.

Today, electronic communications connect people everywhere. Since the end of World War II, American television, movies, music, fast food, and clothing styles have helped to shape this new global culture. Around the world, many business people and government officials speak English.

But the global culture has also changed the United States. Music from Asia, Africa, and Latin America influences American popular music. Americans eat foods from around the world.

Communication in History

Your Phone Is Ringing

You hear them ringing everywhere. Cell phones ring in pockets and purses. People talk on the street and in their cars. Regular telephone messages move through wires and cables. Cell phones, however, send messages through the air. They travel much like radio waves. A World War II invention inspired the cell phone. It was the "walkie-talkie" used by soldiers in combat. After the war, inventors worked to adapt this technology. The first commercial cell phone clicked on in 1983.

Cellular phone technology spread quickly. Wireless networks put a low-power transmission tower in each area, or "cell." As the phone user travels, the call moves from cell to cell. Over longer distances, global networks use satellites to relay messages.

Cell phones are more than a convenience. People in a dangerous situation can call for help. In some places around the world, telephone wires did not reach distant towns. Cell phones have brought phone service there.

 ELL/ESL Strategy

Language Objective:
To compare and contrast

Have ELL students make a list of different kinds of mass communication. (e.g., newspapers, magazines, motion pictures, TV, radio) Ask how they are alike and how they are different. (They all send messages directed at many people at once. Newspapers and magazines are printed. The others are electronic.) Ask if a cell phone is used for mass communication. (No, a cell phone transmits messages from one person to another.)

How Has the Internet Linked Our World?

The computer started a technological revolution as important as the Industrial Revolution. People use computers in businesses, schools, and homes. They are used to store information, figure math problems, and write things.

In the 1990s, the **Internet** expanded the use of computers. The Internet is an **international** computer network. (That is, the information on it goes around the world. It involves different nations.) This computer network connects millions of computer users all over the world. However, for some time, only universities and governmental agencies used the Internet.

All this changed with the development of the **World Wide Web.** It made the Internet easier to use and opened it to businesses and individuals. Because of the Internet, the whole world is linked electronically for the first time in history. E-mail lets us send messages to people anywhere in the world almost instantly.

How Does Space Exploration Create Our Global Village?

In October 1957, the Soviet Union placed *Sputnik,* the first space satellite, into orbit around the earth. Today, dozens of communication satellites send and receive radio, television, and telephone signals. Because of this, people around the globe can see television shows produced thousands of miles away. They can talk on the telephone to friends who live halfway around the globe.

On July 20, 1969, nearly a billion people watched on television as Neil Armstrong stepped from his spaceship. An American was the first person to land on the moon, but Americans do not own it. The nations of the world have agreed that the moon and all of outer space are international areas.

Internet

An international computer network

International

Around the world; involving different nations

World Wide Web

A network of information on the Internet open to businesses and individuals

Ask:

- What system made it possible for businesses and individuals to use the Internet? (the World Wide Web)

- Which nation was the first to put a satellite into orbit? In what year did this happen? (The Soviet Union put *Sputnik* into orbit in 1957.)

- In what year did Neil Armstrong walk on the moon? (1969)

LEARNING STYLES

Interpersonal/ Group Learning

Ask students to imagine a conversation between Christopher Columbus and a contemporary astronaut. Then ask for volunteers to prepare and act out a conversation between a person from the 1400s and a person today. The conversation should involve a contrast between technology then and now. You might want to set up the skit in a talk-show format, with a host and two guests. The rest of the class can participate as the "studio audience," asking questions of the two guests. As the audience listens to the skit, have them evaluate it by writing down the things that could only have happened in the past or that could only happen in the present.

Ask:

- How have Russia and the
  United States worked together
  in space? (U.S. space shuttles
  delivered supplies and astronauts
  to the Russian space station, *Mir.*
  Both countries have sent people
  to live and work together on the
  International Space Station.)

- What energy source was used in
  the 19th century? (coal)

- What does oil provide energy for
  in the 21st century? (heating,
  powering cars and other vehicles,
  and running factories)

LEARNING STYLES

Logical/Mathematical

Have students create a
timeline to chart technological
progress during the period
from 1990 to the present. Ask them,
as a group, to create a title to display
above the timeline. Mark off part of
the line for each year. Then students
can add information related to
improvements in technology as they
discover them in the chapter or in
their daily lives.

Tell students that at one time, lands west
of the Mississippi River were considered
the American frontier. Then have students
read "Space: The Final Frontier . . ." to
find out if they agree with the idea that
space is the last frontier. If they disagree,
ask what they think the final frontier is.

"Space: the Final Frontier . . ."

In the 1500s, explorers needed courage and imagination. They
sailed to new parts of the world. They had few maps to guide
them. New technology helped, however. Better instruments
measured speed and location. Shipbuilders designed sturdy
ocean-going ships.

Nearly 500 years later, explorers traveled to new worlds in outer
space. Courage and technology were still important. In April
1961, a Soviet cosmonaut became the first person in space. The
first American space flight came a month later. From there, space
exploration has reached greater and greater successes with many
new types of spacecraft. Several unmanned ships have been sent
deep into outer space. In 1996, *Pathfinder* landed on Mars and
took many amazing photos of its surface. Some day, people may
even live on the moon or on other planets.

Russia and the United States are now working together. U.S.
space shuttles regularly delivered supplies and people to the
Russian space station *Mir.* In 1998, work began on building the
International Space Station. It is an orbiting science laboratory
that goes around the earth more than 15 times a day. The
station is serviced mostly by the United States and Russia.
However, crew members have come from many countries.
Fifteen governments are involved in the Space Station project.
When the International Space Station is complete, it will have
a mass of almost 1 million pounds and be larger than a five-
bedroom house and measure 361 feet end-to-end. People have
been living on it permanently since 2000.

What Have Coal and Oil Done to Our Global Village?

Coal was a source of energy in the 19th century. It produced
energy for factories, homes, and steam locomotives. Oil has
continued to be the major source of energy into the 21st
century. It runs our factories, heats our homes, and powers
our cars, trucks, trains, and planes.

But the burning of coal and oil has also created serious problems for our world. Air and water pollution creates health problems for humans. Pollution occurs when air, water, or land becomes unclean and unhealthy. Pollution threatens the life of many plants and animals. It threatens our environment—the land, sea, and air of our world.

What Is Wrong with Using Nuclear Energy?

Scientists have been looking for a clean source of energy that will not hurt our environment. They once thought that nuclear power was a clean source of energy. But it produces deadly waste products.

Also, people have died from accidents at nuclear power plants in the United States, Russia, and India. Even so, nuclear power plants produce about 20 percent of the electricity in the United States, Japan, and Great Britain. In France, 70 percent of the nation's electricity comes from nuclear power.

Some scientists look to wind, water in oceans and rivers, and the sun as clean sources of energy. These are **renewable** sources of energy. That means they'll never run out. Technology can use all of them to produce electricity. The **photoelectric cell** is an invention that can produce electricity from light. Today, many businesses and homes use photoelectric cells to create electricity. Engineers have designed cars that run on electricity produced by photoelectric cells.

Is nuclear energy the answer to the world's energy needs? Although it is used in many countries, it can be dangerous. This photo shows a destroyed nuclear power plant in Chernobyl, Ukraine. It exploded in 1986, killing 31 people.

1990 to the Present

Ask:

- What new technology do doctors use to cut and seal wounds? (lasers)

- What do you think is the most amazing thing that doctors are now able to do for people? (Answers will vary. Students may mention transplanting organs or removing and fixing the human heart.)

- How is it possible to talk on the computer to someone who does not speak the same language? (Software programs are available that translate what an individual types from one language to another.)

Reading Strategy: Predicting

(Answers will vary. Students might revise their prediction to include deaths due to accidents in Chernobyl, the United States, and India.)

Read the title of the graph, "The World's Major Consumers of Energy." Ask students to study the graph and then read the caption and the questions that follow. (The United States uses the most energy. Answers will vary; students may suggest that the United States uses the most energy because it has the most wealth to spend on modern conveniences that use energy.) Ask students if they thought population was the most important factor in ranking the countries on the graph. If so, explain that some countries with large populations, such as India, do not necessarily have the widespread technology that other countries with smaller populations, such as Canada, do.

Laser

A tool that produces high-energy beams of light

Reading Strategy: Predicting

Think about your prediction. What details can you now add to make your prediction more specific?

How Has Technology Changed Medicine?

Doctors now remove a person's heart and fix it. They replace livers and hips. They sew fingers, arms, and legs onto a person who has lost them in an accident. Technology makes all this possible.

Engineers have invented new machines to help doctors figure out what diseases people have. One machine helps doctors see the inside of the body. Doctors use lasers to cut and seal wounds. A **laser** is a tool that produces high-energy beams of light.

What Is the Electronic Superhighway?

The electronic superhighway sends information from telephones, television, and computers. This information is now reaching many areas of the world. As this happens, cultures around the world influence one another. Today, some electronic programs translate one language into another. People can communicate even though they do not speak or write the same language. This "electronic culture" is going to change our global village.

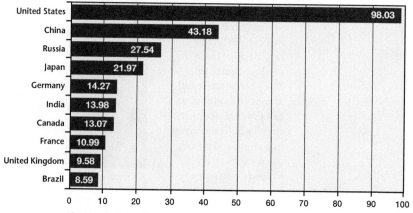

The World's Major Consumers of Energy
Numbers indicate quadrillion British thermal units (Btu).

Country	Btu
United States	98.03
China	43.18
Russia	27.54
Japan	21.97
Germany	14.27
India	13.98
Canada	13.07
France	10.99
United Kingdom	9.58
Brazil	8.59

This graph shows the countries that use the most energy and how much they use (estimated). Which country uses the most energy? Why do you think this is true?

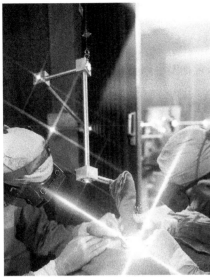

Doctors now use lasers and other technology to treat people. Medicine is one area that technology has influenced greatly.

Can New Technology Harm Our Global Village?

In the early part of the 20th century, people predicted that technology would solve many of the world's problems. Electricity would provide the energy for many labor-saving machines. People would work only a few hours a week. Everyone would have an automobile. Airplanes would fill the sky.

At the time, people did not see how the military would use technology to fight World War I and II. They did not see what technology would do to our environment.

Today, some people think that we are losing our freedom. People can find out too much information about us. Every time we use a credit card, a computer files the information away. Computers also contain information about medicines we take. The government collects information about us and stores it on computers.

But who will decide how to use all this information? How can we control what people know about us? Does having this information give some people control over us? If technology can cause harm, should we limit its development? Who will decide what that limit is? These important questions have no easy answers.

AT HOME

Have students discuss with their families the ways in which technology affects their lives. As an at-home assignment, students should create a list of the ten most important technologies their family relies on. Give students an opportunity to share and compare their lists in class.

Ask:

• Why can the use of computers threaten people's privacy?
(Answers will vary. Students may say that computers store large amounts of personal information, including medical records, which was once considered private. This information can be stolen or the government can use it inappropriately.)

 Reinforce and Extend

WORLD CULTURES

Carrying a cell phone means you can be interrupted at any time. Watching videos at home can substitute for going to the movies. By shopping on the computer, you may never have to enter a store. Some people suspect that technology is robbing us of the opportunities to interact with other people—with people in a theater, with people in stores, even with our own families. One group of people that don't take part in these concerns is the Amish. Amish communities have existed for more than 300 years. During that time, their way of life has changed very little. The Amish believe that to be obedient to God, they must live simply, without worldly distractions. Their entire culture, from the clothes they wear to the way they work and spend their free time, is governed by this premise. They avoid popular culture, including television, modern farming equipment, and clothing styles. Amish communities have struggled with the dramatic changes that the technological revolution has brought to the world around them. But to the Amish people, community and the family are of primary importance.

Biography

In 1978, Stephen Hawking published a book to explain the incredible advances in the field of astrophysics. The book was written in terms nonscientists could easily understand, thus providing an extraordinary service to the millions of people puzzled by the dramatic new knowledge. Some students may have seen the TV documentary series that drew its script from Hawking's book *A Brief History of Time*. Ask students who have watched some of these programs to comment on the series. Then have students read the Biography feature to find out more about Stephen Hawking's work. After they have read the feature, ask them to discuss the various ways in which Stephen Hawking is dependent upon technology.

LEARNING STYLES

Auditory/Verbal

Students may enjoy listening to some of the audiotapes of *A Brief History of Time*. Tell students not to be overwhelmed by the information on the tapes, but to listen to capture the wonder of the discoveries scientists are making about our universe. Give students an opportunity to discuss their listening experiences in class.

Lesson 1 Review Answers

1. Mass communication has made it possible for people to communicate and do business with others throughout the world, thus causing the world to become a global village. **2.** Scientists believe that wind and water, as well as the photoelectric cell, can be clean sources of energy. **3.** Doctors now remove a person's heart and fix it. They replace livers and hips. They reattach fingers, arms, and legs onto a person who has lost them in an accident. They also have new machines that help them diagnose disease and see inside the body. With lasers, they cut and seal wounds. **4.** The Internet makes it possible for people to store and retrieve large amounts of information, and communicate it to people around the world. However, misuse of the Internet can mean a loss of our privacy.

Biography

Stephen Hawking: 1942–

If you've ever heard of a black hole, you know something about Stephen Hawking. This physicist has made major discoveries about the universe. A black hole, for instance, is a region in space with intense gravity. The collapse of a huge star would have caused it. Not even light can escape a black hole. Hawking's main field is quantum physics, the study of units that make up the atom.

Hawking is a professor of mathematics at Cambridge University in England. Because of a disease of the nervous system, he uses a wheelchair. He speaks with the help of a computer.

Lesson 1 Review On a sheet of paper, write the answers to these questions. Use complete sentences.

1. How has mass communication changed our world?
2. What is one example of a clean source of energy?
3. What is one improvement that technology has brought to medicine?
4. What are one good thing and one bad thing about the Internet?
5. Why do some people consider nuclear energy very dangerous?

What do you think

What is your favorite form of mass communication and why?

5. Nuclear energy produces dangerous waste products. People can die from accidents at nuclear power plants.

Answers will vary. Students' answers should reflect their understanding of what mass communication is.

Objectives

- To describe economies in developing nations
- To identify economic and other problems that developing countries have

Interdependent

Depending on one another

Free-market economy

An economy in which manufacturers try to satisfy consumers' wants and needs

Northern Hemisphere

The half of Earth north of the equator

Developing country

A nation that is slowly developing its industry and economy

Subsistence farming

A type of farming in which people grow crops mostly for their own use, not to sell

Southern Hemisphere

The half of Earth south of the equator

The global village is **interdependent.** What happens in one nation affects every other nation. For example, when the price of oil from the Middle East goes up, manufacturers in the United States have to spend more to produce goods. Consumers then pay more when they buy these goods.

What Is a Free-Market Economy?

Most rich countries have a **free-market economy.** In such an economy, manufacturers satisfy the wants and needs of consumers. The government lets factories produce what they like.

The **Northern Hemisphere**—the half of Earth north of the equator—contains most of the successful free-market countries. Among these are the United States, Canada, Germany, France, and Great Britain. Asia's strongest economy is in Japan. These countries have well-organized farming and industrial systems and make use of technology.

What Problems Do Developing Countries Have?

Developing countries are countries that are slowly developing their industries and economies. In these poor nations, most people do **subsistence farming.** This means that they grow crops mostly for their own use. They do not sell what they grow. Most of these nations are in the **Southern Hemisphere**—the half of Earth south of the equator.

These developing nations face many problems. First, they are overpopulated. More than half of the people in the world live in developing countries. This leads to hunger, pollution, and political unrest. It has also led to the destruction of the Amazon rain forest and the overuse of croplands in Asia. Second, in many developing countries, students attend school for only two or three years. Only about half the people in these countries can read and write. Third, industrialization requires money.

Chapter 31: Lesson 2

Overview This lesson describes the economic connections among members of the new global village and how the actions of one nation can have an impact on many others.

Objectives

- To describe economies in developing nations
- To identify economic and other problems that developing countries have

Student Pages pages 795–798

Teacher's Resource Library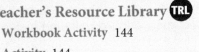

  Workbook Activity 144

  Activity 144

  Modified Activity 144

Vocabulary

developing country
free-market economy
interdependent
Northern Hemisphere
recession
Southern Hemisphere
subsistence farming

Ask students to write each vocabulary word on the front of an index card and the definition on the back of the card. Have students pair up and use these materials as flash cards. One partner should show the word; the other should give the definition. The partner holding the card can check the definition on the back. Students should take turns until they feel they know all the definitions.

1 Warm-Up Activity

To demonstrate the concept of economic interdependence, have each student think of a manufactured product, such as a bicycle, a frozen pizza, or a tank of gasoline. Name a raw material such as crude oil, wheat, or iron ore. Ask students to raise their hand if this raw material is important in the making of their product. Ask students how an increase or decrease in price, or a shortage in the raw material, will affect the price of their manufactured product.

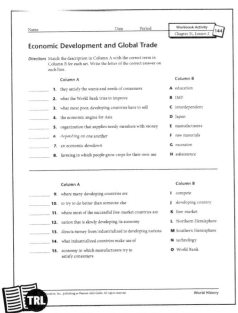

Workbook Activity 144

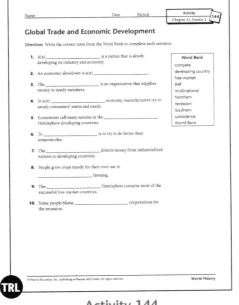

Activity 144

2 Teaching the Lesson

Have students think about times when their own actions affected other people. Tell them that in a global economy, the actions of one country can have a strong impact on other countries. Then have students read pages 793–796 to find out just how interdependent the nations of our world have become.

Ask:

- What part of the world has the strongest free-market economy? (Northern Hemisphere)

- What is the primary problem in developing nations? (overpopulation)

- In what part of the world are most of the world's developing nations located? (Southern Hemisphere)

- What type of products do most developing countries have for sale? (raw materials)

- In what year did the money supply of Thailand collapse? (1997)

- Which nation is most important to the Asian economy? (Japan)

- How did the Asian recession affect the United States? (American companies lost money and laid off workers because Asians had no money to buy American goods. However, the price of oil dropped because bankrupted Asian companies no longer needed oil to run their factories.)

- What is a multinational company? (a company that manufactures and sells goods in many countries)

- Why is it difficult for independent businesses to compete against multinational corporations? (Multinationals can sell the same products more cheaply.)

Reading Strategy: Predicting

(Students might suggest that Asian countries had no money to buy goods. U.S. companies were also affected because Asians could not afford to buy American goods.)

Recession

An economic slowdown

Reading Strategy: Predicting

Predict what effect the recession will have on Asian countries and the United States.

Most developing countries have only raw materials to sell. (The industrialized countries set the cost for these raw materials.) They have no consumer goods to trade to other countries. But poor countries want consumer goods, so they buy more than they sell. Money flows out of these countries.

What Is a Recession?

After the money supply of Thailand collapsed in 1997, the crisis spread to South Korea, Indonesia, Malaysia, and Russia. Soon, banks and businesses went bankrupt. People lost their jobs and had no money to buy things. Because no one was buying consumer goods, even more businesses closed down. Economists call this a **recession**, or an economic slowdown.

How Did the Recession Affect Japan and the United States?

Many people in Japan lost their jobs because of the recession. This is important because Japan is the economic engine for Asia. It keeps things moving there.

The recession also affected the United States. People in other countries had no money to buy goods from the United States. U.S. companies lost money, and some workers lost jobs. However, the bankrupted Asian companies no longer had a need for oil to supply energy to their factories. The Middle East lowered its oil price. This meant that the United States had to pay less for oil, so gasoline prices in the United States went down.

Who Is to Blame for the Recession?

Some people blame multinational corporations, which manufacture and sell goods in many countries. They compete with businesses in developing countries. These businesses cannot win when they are up against huge foreign corporations. For example, a small business might make the same product that a multinational makes. But the multinationals can sell their products cheaper. They can move their factories from one developing country to another to get the lowest cost for labor and materials.

ELL/ESL STRATEGY

Language Objective:
To locate nations on a world map

Trace a world map such as the map on page 795. Do not label the countries. Make copies of the map for ELL students. Then have them work as a group to label their maps with the names of countries from this lesson. Have volunteers find the countries on a globe and then identify their placement on their maps. Have volunteers come up to a large world map to point out for the class the most industrialized nations and the poorest developing nations.

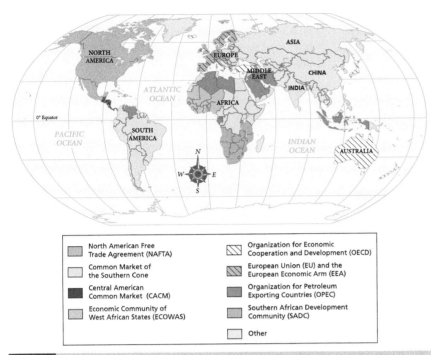

North American Free Trade Agreement (NAFTA)	Organization for Economic Cooperation and Development (OECD)
Common Market of the Southern Cone	European Union (EU) and the European Economic Arm (EEA)
Central American Common Market (CACM)	Organization for Petroleum Exporting Countries (OPEC)
Economic Community of West African States (ECOWAS)	Southern African Development Community (SADC)
	Other

Map Study

This map shows eight major economic groups in today's world. The North American Free Trade Agreement (NAFTA) relates to countries on which continent? In what areas of the world are the Organization for Petroleum Exporting Countries (OPEC) located?

Reading Strategy:
Predicting

Think about your prediction. What details can you now add to make your prediction more specific?

Who Helps Nations That Have Economic Problems?

For 50 years, industrialized nations have given money, food, medicine, tools, and machinery to developing nations. Each year, the 21 most industrialized nations provide billions of dollars to roughly 182 nations. In one third of these countries, people live on less than two dollars a day.

Reading Strategy:
Predicting

(Students can add details about the effect of the Asian recession on American companies, the lowering of oil prices, and the dominance of multinational companies in a global economy.)

Have students study the map titled "Major World Economic Groups." Then have them read and answer the questions in the caption. (The North American Free Trade Agreement relates to those countries in North America. The Organization for Petroleum Exporting Countries are located in the Middle East, southeast Asia, northern Africa, and a small area of northern South America.)

CAREER CONNECTION

Many people are trying to find ways to increase the amount of food countries, especially developing countries, are able to grow and to make sure that the food is safe. One of the people who help safeguard the food supply is an agricultural lab technician. Independent and government laboratories, county farm cooperatives, and dairy processing plants all need laboratory technicians. To do this type of work a person must have math skills, curiosity about science, and decision-making abilities. Tell students that in this type of work, advancement comes with experience and training. Interested students can check with their counselor about high school, junior college, or technical school courses that will give them the background needed for this career.

Ask:

- **What does the World Bank do?**
  (It directs money from industrialized nations to developing nations. It helps build roads, dams, mines, and bridges. It helps improve education, health, and the environment.)

- **What do the initials IMF stand for? What does the organization do?**
  (The International Monetary Fund helps 182 developing countries in times of economic crisis.)

Ask students to read "What Will a Dollar Buy?" silently. Tell them that the eleven members of the European Union (EU) that adopted the euro as their national currency are Austria, Belgium, Finland, France, Germany, Ireland, Italy, Luxembourg, The Netherlands, Portugal, and Spain. The four remaining members of the EU that are holding out, at least for the time being, are Denmark, Greece, Sweden, and Great Britain.

3 Reinforce and Extend

LEARNING STYLES

Visual/Spatial
Encourage students to make a chart that shows the current rate of exchange of Italian and Australian currency with the U.S. dollar. Tell them that they can make the chart as simple or elaborate as they like, but the information (.75 euros = $1 American, or 1 euro = $1.33 American; $1.50 Australian = $1 American) should be the same in each case.

The industrialized nations send their money through two international organizations: the World Bank and the International Monetary Fund (IMF). The World Bank directs money from industrialized nations to developing ones. It helps build dams, mines, roads, and bridges. It also helps to improve education, health, and the environment. The IMF is an organization of 182 nations. It has a supply of money to help its members in times of economic crisis.

Lesson 2 Review On a sheet of paper, write the word from the Word Bank that best completes each sentence.

Word Bank
free-market
interdependent
overpopulation
recession
subsistence

Would the earth be in better shape if countries did not depend on one another? Explain your answer.

1. The world's richest countries generally have a _____ economy.
2. People of less developed countries are often _____ farmers.
3. Economists call an economic slowdown a _____.
4. Nations of the world are _____, because what happens in one affects all the others.
5. Many developing countries face the problem of _____, which has led to hunger and pollution.

What Will a Dollar Buy?

Do you have a dollar? If you were in Capri, Italy, you could buy a small pizza. In Sydney, Australia, you could buy a toy koala bear. First, though, you would have to exchange your dollar for the local money. In Italy, you would get about .75 euros for a dollar. In Sydney, you would get about $1.50 in Australian dollars.

In some countries, people like to be paid in U.S. dollars. This happens because the United States' economy is strong. That makes the U.S. dollar strong. The British pound is another strong currency.

In 1999, some members of the European Union agreed to gradually give up their national currencies. They now use a new currency called the "euro." A euro has the same value in every country that joins this agreement. This makes trade among these countries easier.

Lesson 2 Review Answers

1. free-market 2. subsistence
3. recession 4. interdependent
5. overpopulation

Answers will vary. Many of the things we enjoy in the United States come from other countries. Also, our standard of living is high partly because U.S. companies sell their products to other countries. If companies did not have foreign markets, they would not sell as much and that would lead to a loss of jobs and wages in the United States. A global village is interdependent. The problem is that the corporations of some countries have the power to hurt the economies of others.

Objectives

◆ To identify important problems in our environment

Millions of people around the world die every day from illnesses related to unsanitary living conditions. Some do not have clean water to drink. Others simply do not have enough of the right foods to remain healthy. At the same time, air pollution and global warming are affecting every part of our world, from human beings to oceans, animals, and plants. These are serious concerns that need to be addressed.

What Diseases Are Threatening Our World?

AIDS continues to infect people all over the world. In 2006, nearly 40 million people worldwide were living with the HIV virus. New medications are helping more people with HIV live longer and avoid developing AIDS.

There is a growing crisis in developing countries, where many children have lost one or both parents to AIDS. One report says that by 2005, there were more than 15 million "AIDS orphans" worldwide. About 95 percent of the people who have HIV live in developing countries.

Several new diseases prompted concern in the 1990s and 2000s. A disease called SARS (Severe Acute Respiratory Syndrome) is believed to have been carried by Chinese horseshoe bats. More than 8,000 people in 26 countries have become infected with SARS. Lyme disease, spread by deer ticks, infected 25,000 people in the United States alone during 2002. The West Nile virus is most often spread to people and animals through mosquitoes. Scientists are working to learn more about how to control all of these diseases.

1990 to the Present

The World Today   Chapter 31   **797**

Chapter 31: Lesson 3

Overview This lesson describes the world's current social and environmental problems and explains some of the steps that are being taken to solve them.

Objectives

■ To identify important problems in our environment

Student Pages pages 797–802

Teacher's Resource Library

   Workbook Activity 145

   Activity 145

   Modified Activity 145

Vocabulary

deforestation   **global warming**
fossil fuel

Read the definitions for the vocabulary words to students and have a volunteer write the defined words on the board. Have volunteers select one of the words and use it in a sentence. Ask the class to decide whether the word usage is correct or, if not, suggest changes in the sentence.

1 Warm-Up Activity

On the board, list the social and environmental problems discussed in this lesson: disease, unsafe or not enough water, lack of food, air pollution, and global warming. Ask a volunteer to act out an action that illustrates one of these problems. The student who correctly identifies the problem and describes it in his or her own words will choose the next student to act out another problem.

Challenges to Society and the Environment

Directions Write the answers to these questions. Use complete sentences.

1. Where is the problem of water pollution from fertilizers and pesticides the most serious?

2. Why do many people fear global warming?

3. What kinds of pollution do cities in Asia have major problems with?

4. What is an "AIDS orphan"?

5. Where do most of the people who have HIV live?

Workbook Activity 145

Social and Environmental Challenges

Directions Write the correct term from the Word Bank to complete each sentence.

1. Fertilizers and _____ can cause people who eat animals like fish to get sick.

2. Most air pollution is caused by the burning of fossil fuels such as _____.

3. Cars and factories give off high levels of _____.

4. _____ is the heating up of Earth caused in part by human activity.

5. Trees release _____ into the air for us to breathe.

6. Many cities in America suffer from _____ air pollution.

7. The _____ of the polar ice caps will raise the sea levels and flood some cities.

8. The term "_____" refers to the move toward cleaner power and technology.

9. Reducing, reusing, and _____ things can help the environment.

10. The destruction of forests, or _____, is taking place all over the globe.

Word Bank
carbon monoxide
coal
deforestation
global warming
greening
industrial
melting
oxygen
pesticides
recycling

Activity 145

The World Today   Chapter 31   **797**

PRONUNCIATION GUIDE

Use this list to help students pronounce difficult words in this lesson.

monoxide   (mon ok´ sīd)

2 Teaching the Lesson

Ask students to think about what they already know about pollution and problems such as acid rain and global warming. Then have students read pages 797–802 to find out how the world is being affected by pollution and what is being done to solve the problem.

Ask:

- **What are three diseases that threaten developing countries?** (AIDS, SARS, malaria)

- **What are two causes of water pollution?** (fertilizers and pesticides used in farming)

- **Where is the water pollution problem most serious?** (developing countries)

- **What harmful gas is released through the burning of wood, coal, oil, and natural gas?** (carbon monoxide)

- **What is happening to the world's forests and jungles?** (They are being cut down to make farmland, towns, and firewood for human use.)

- **What is the difference between HIV and AIDS?** (HIV is the name of the virus that causes the disease AIDS.)

- **Where do most people who are infected with HIV live?** (in developing countries)

- **What three diseases have emerged in the last 15 years?** (SARS, Lyme disease, and West Nile disease)

- **What are two problems that result from deforestation?** (Less oxygen is produced, and animals lose their habitats.)

- **What causes most air pollution?** (burning of fossil fuels)

Deforestation
The destruction of forests

Fossil fuel
Fuel made from coal, oil, or natural gas

What Is the Growing Population Doing to Our Environment?

As the numbers of people increase all around the world, so do problems of damage to the environment. More people are driving cars. More factories are using more energy to make products. More space is needed to house and grow food.

Vehicles, factories, and energy-generating plants produce gases from burning fuels such as oil or coal. These gases pollute the air. They may contribute to breathing illnesses in people. They produce acid rain, which damages plants and harms animals that eat those plants. Dangerous global warming occurs when gases surrounding the earth trap the heat from sunlight. Factories, careless farming practices, and poor sewage disposal are affecting water quality in many countries of the world.

Lands that were once wilderness are becoming farms or towns. **Deforestation**, or the destruction of forests, is taking place all over the globe. When there are fewer trees and plants, the valuable oxygen they contribute to the earth's air also declines. Animals are losing the wild areas where they live. Many of those animals and the plants that once surrounded them are facing extinction. Some scientists estimate that around the world, up to 100 species become extinct every day!

What Pollutes Our Air and Water?

Air pollution affects our health, and it may change our climate. The burning of coal, oil, and natural gas causes most air pollution. These kinds of fuels are called **fossil fuels.** We also have water pollution. Farming and industry have poisoned lakes and rivers.

Farmers around the world now use fertilizers to help crops grow and pesticides to kill bugs. Rain makes these chemicals run off into rivers, lakes, and oceans. Then they end up in the bodies of fish and other animals. People who eat these animals or drink the water get sick. The problem is most serious in developing countries, where many people cannot get clean water.

Reading Strategy:
Predicting

What do you think the text will identify as the biggest sources of pollution?

Reading Strategy:
Predicting

(Students might predict the burning of fossil fuels in vehicles, factories, and energy-generating plants as the biggest sources of air pollution, and farming and industry as the biggest sources of water pollution.)

STUDY SKILLS

Encourage students to research and report about deforestation of the Amazon rain forest, worldwide pollution, or worldwide hunger. Remind them that when they take notes from published source material, they can summarize the information by creating bulleted or numbered lists. Explain that summarizing does not mean writing down information word for word; they should write down only the most important points of their research and they need not write in complete sentences.

What Is Global Warming?

Since the 1980s, scientists have warned us about **global warming.** Global warming is the worldwide heating up of Earth, caused in part by human activity. Scientists believe that gases from cars and factories are heating up the earth. Burning wood, coal, oil, or natural gas releases carbon dioxide. Trees remove this gas from the air and release oxygen into the air for us to breathe. But overpopulated countries are now cutting down forests and jungles to provide farmland and firewood.

Many people fear that this will increase the carbon dioxide in the air and raise the earth's temperature. This might change rainfall patterns around the world. Too much rain would cause floods; too little rain would cause droughts and famine. Scientists also believe that the polar ice caps are melting. This will raise the sea levels and flood cities like New York, which are on the coast. If this happens, two billion people around the world would have to move inland.

What Nations Have Environmental Problems?

Many American cities suffer from industrial air pollution. Russia and Eastern Europe suffer from it, too. When the Communists controlled them, they kept producing goods, no matter what happened to the environment.

Many developing African countries made the same mistake. They wanted to develop their economies quickly, but they ignored the environment. Now many Africans are starving to death. Farmers have killed their animals for food. Some ate the seeds they needed for next year's crop.

Asia depends on coal and oil for fuel. Its cars and factories are giving off high levels of carbon monoxide. The worst problems are in the cities. Most big cities have major problems with air and water pollution.

Global warming

The worldwide heating up of the earth, caused in part by human activity

Ask:

- What will happen to the world's coastal cities if the polar ice caps continue to melt? (Two billion people around the world will have to move inland.)
- What has been the result of Africa's economies developing too quickly and ignoring the environment? (Many Africans are starving to death.)
- What continent contains 8 of the world's 15 largest cities? (Asia)

BACKGROUND INFORMATION

People first began to keep weather records in 1880. Between then and 1950, the world's air temperature rose an average of 1 degree Fahrenheit. Thirty years later, the average air temperature had climbed another degree. As a comparison, tell students that during the last Ice Age, it took 18,000 years for the world's air temperature to rise by 9 degrees. Yet the temperature rose 2 degrees within one hundred years— from 1880 to 1980. In 1996, the scientific debate on how to stop the threat of global warming took a new turn. According to some experts, there was more to global warming than just a rise in air temperatures. Some experts are now claiming that the increasingly common severe-weather events, such as hurricanes, earthquakes, floods, and droughts, are being made worse by global warming. Encourage students to talk about weather systems they have experienced, read about, or seen on television over the last year.

Ask:

- What did 178 nations decide to do when they met in 1992? (They agreed to reduce air pollution and to save forests.)

- Why is it difficult to solve environmental problems in a global village? (What may be good for one country may cause problems in another country.)

- What natural resources are people using up that cannot be replaced? (clean water, forests, topsoil, and fish)

3 Reinforce and Extend

ELL/ESL Strategy

Language Objective:
To describe ways to clean up polluted areas
Invite ELL students to examine the photograph on page 800. Have the students make a list of possible pollution in the photo. Then have students list actions they could take to clean up the areas in the photo. Have students write the tools they would need, such as a rake or wheelbarrow, to do the job. Ask students to list separately any pollution that would have to be cleaned up by government or private environmental agencies. Encourage students to share their lists with the class in an oral presentation. Suggest that classmates help expand the lists by adding their own ideas.

Reading Strategy:
Prediction

Think about your prediction. Were you right, or do you need to change your prediction?

The developing countries of Latin America have problems, too. Just breathing the air in Mexico City is equal to smoking two packs of cigarettes a day. The city's pollution may cause 100,000 deaths a year.

How Are Nations Attacking Environmental Problems?

People all over the world care about the environment. In 1992, representatives from 178 countries met to talk about it. They agreed to reduce air pollution and to save forests.

In June 1997, world leaders met again. But many thought that the nations of the world had not made much progress since 1992. What is good for one nation may be bad for another. For example, many developing countries depend on the production and export of wood, coal, and oil. But what happens if the industrial countries cut back on the use of these fuels? The environment may improve, but the economies of the developing countries go downhill.

Farming, industry, and carelessness cause water pollution.

The truth is that the global environment is less healthy than it once was. Air pollution is growing. Also, people are using up resources like water, forests, topsoil, and fish faster than they can be replaced.

How Can We Help Save the Environment?

We can do at least three things to help the environment. We can reduce the kinds of packages manufacturers sell things in. We can reuse things. We can recycle things that we no longer use. All of us depend on the same earth to supply us with our needs. Laws are being passed to preserve places where animals live and to protect endangered animals.

In fact, something happened as we entered the new century. The "greening" of countries around the world became more important as we learned about the costs of a polluted environment. *Greening* refers to the move toward cleaner power and technology. Although most people in developed nations were aware of the problem of global warming, industries were slow to change. Many companies are now using greener sources of energy. Green architecture is becoming more popular. New buildings are more energy-efficient and are built using recycled materials. People are making more environmentally sound choices in transportation, clothing, and food. However, there is still a long way to go.

The clear-cutting of trees, by loggers and others, damages the environment.

Ask:

• What are some positive things that are being done to help the environment? (Laws are being passed to preserve animal habitats and protect endangered animals, many companies are using greener energy sources, new buildings are more energy-efficient, and people are making more environmentally-sound choices in transportation, clothing, and food.)

• What are three things people can do to help the environment? (reduce the amount of packaging manufacturers use, reuse things, and recycle)

LEARNING STYLES

Visual/Spatial
Have students make illustrated posters encouraging all the students in the school to practice the three "*R*s"—reduce, reuse, and recycle. Posters should explain and show people actively doing each practice. Hang the posters in the classroom or throughout the school to encourage students to help protect the environment.

Lesson 3 Review Answers

1. Habitats are being destroyed through deforestation as more areas are developed for human use. **2.** Due to an increasing world population, more people are driving cars, more factories are using more energy to make products, and more space is needed to build houses and grow food. **3.** The trees in forests remove carbon dioxide from the air and produce the oxygen we need to breathe. Forests also are important to the habitats of animals and other plants. **4.** Global warming is the worldwide heating up of Earth, caused partly by human activity. **5.** The people of developing nations are starving because they cannot grow enough food. Their air and water are polluted because factories and cars put pollutants into the air and water.

Answers will vary, but should reflect information in the lesson.

Lesson 3 Review On a sheet of paper, write your answers to the following questions. Use complete sentences.

1. What are the reasons that so many species are becoming extinct every day?
2. What are three things that cause damage to our environment?
3. Why is it important that forests are not destroyed?
4. What is global warming?
5. What are some environmental problems that developing nations have?

What do you think

What do you think is the single most important problem in the world today? Why?

Objective

- To identify ways the world has changed since the attacks of 2001
- To describe the reasons for the war in Iraq that began in 2002
- To describe things that can be done to help prevent terrorist attacks

Regime

A form of government

Tyranny

Harsh, absolute power

After the September 11, 2001, terrorist attacks on the United States, all planes were grounded for two days. When they started flying again, airport security screening for all passengers was much more strict. Security was also increased near public places where large groups of people gather, such as sports arenas. Lawmakers in the United States began developing the new Department of Homeland Security. This department organizes all security and emergency agencies into one department.

How Has the Threat of Terrorism Changed the World?

The Taliban **regime,** or form of government, in Afghanistan was known to allow training camps for members of al Qaeda. The United States government had asked the Taliban to turn over Osama bin Laden, who had admitted leading the 9/11 terror attacks on America. The Taliban refused. The United States attacked Taliban sites in Afghanistan in October 2001. Taliban and al Qaeda members fled the country, as did bin Laden. American and NATO troops have remained in Afghanistan to help rebuild the country under a new government.

In 2002, a report by the American Central Intelligence Agency (CIA) warned that Iraq was hiding weapons of mass destruction. Iraq refused to cooperate with United Nations weapons inspectors. President George Bush insisted that Saddam Hussein's government was aiding terrorist groups. He said that the people of Iraq had to be freed of Hussein's **tyranny,** or harsh, absolute power. On March 19, 2003, troops from the United States, Britain, and many smaller nations invaded Baghdad, the capital of Iraq. Operation Iraqi Freedom had begun. Saddam Hussein went into hiding. Within 43 days

Overview This lesson identifies how the world has changed because of the threat of terrorism and describes what can be done to prevent future attacks.

Objectives

- To identify ways the world has changed since the attacks of 2001
- To describe the reasons for the war in Iraq that began in 2003
- To describe things that can be done to help prevent terrorist attacks

Student Pages pages 803–805

Teacher's Resource Library

Workbook Activity 146

Activity 146

Modified Activity 146

Vocabulary

regime   tyranny

Have student volunteers come to the board and write a plausible sentence that uses both vocabulary words. An example might be "The war in Afghanistan brought an end to the Taliban regime's tyranny."

1 Warm-Up Activity

Review with students what they know about the events of September 11, 2001, al Qaeda, Osama bin Laden, and the attack on the World Trade Center in New York City, the Pentagon in Washington, DC, and the airplane crash in Shanksville, Pennsylvania. Provide students with enough background information to understand the events discussed in the lesson.

Workbook Activity 146   Activity 146   *The World Today* Chapter 31   **803**

PRONUNCIATION GUIDE

Use this list to help students pronounce difficult words in this lesson.

al Qaeda   (äl kā′ də)

Osama bin Laden
             (ō säm′ ə bin lah′ dən)

Saddam Hussein   (sä däm′ hü sān′)

2 Teaching the Lesson

Have a volunteer read the lesson title. Discuss with students what is meant by the term terrorism. Ask whether *terrorism* differs from war and, if so, how. Then have students read pages 803–805 to find out about some terrorist attacks of the past and what can be done to prevent future attacks.

Ask:

- **What is the goal of the Department of Homeland Security?** (to monitor the activities of terrorist groups and prevent future terrorist attacks in the United States)

- **Who was Saddam Hussein and what was his fate?** (Saddam Hussein was the ruler of Iraq. He was captured, found guilty of crimes against humanity, and executed.)

- **What is the United States' goal in Iraq?** (to help establish a democratic government in Iraq)

- **What terrorist attack occurred in London in 2005?** (Bombs planted on a subway and buses killed 52 people.)

- **What can be done to prevent future attacks?** (People must be aware of dangers, especially when they travel and are in crowds. Government agencies can work together to monitor activities of terrorist groups.)

---

the troops had taken over the country. In July 2003, Saddam Hussein's two sons were killed in a raid. Hussein was captured in December of the same year. An Iraqi court found him guilty of crimes against humanity, and he was executed in December 2006. The American and British troops found no weapons of mass destruction.

Americans wanted to help establish a democratic government in Iraq. Aided by other governments, the Iraqis began forming a representative government. They wrote a constitution and held their first free elections in 2005. Unfortunately, since that time, fighting between groups for control of the country has increased. As of early 2007, tens of thousands of Iraqi civilians had been killed. More than 3,000 American soldiers have been killed and about 20,000 injured.

Have There Been Other Terrorist Attacks?

According to the U. S. State Department, there were 9,474 terrorist attacks worldwide between 1982 and 2003. In the five-year period between 1998 and 2003, there were 1,865. Regular acts of terror continue in both Iraq and Afghanistan.

In many countries of the world, increased security has reduced the number of terrorist attacks. However, some have occurred. For instance, bombs planted on a subway and buses in London killed 52 people in 2005.

What Can Be Done to Prevent Further Attacks?

Further attacks can be prevented by increasing awareness of dangers. This is especially important with travel and in situations involving large groups of people.

Passengers on a flight from Paris to New York in December 2001 noticed another passenger acting suspiciously. They were able to subdue him before he could light explosives in his shoes.

---

3 Reinforce and Extend

ELL/ESL STRATEGY

 Language Objective: *To describe orally the meaning of "weapon of mass destruction"*

Remind the class that mass communication is directing messages to many people at one time. Ask ELL students if they can explain what a weapon of mass destruction is. (a weapon that kills or harms many people at one time) Ask students if they can name a weapon of mass destruction. (Bombs and poison gas are two examples.)

LEARNING STYLES

 Logical/Mathematical
Have students calculate the average number of terrorist attacks per year between 1982 and 2003 and also between 1998 and 2003. Ask if the number of terrorist attacks per year is increasing or decreasing. (There were 451 attacks per year between 1982 and 2003 and 373 per year between 1998 and 2003. The number of attacks is decreasing.) Students can also calculate the average number of attacks per year between 1982 and 1998 from the data given in the text. (There were 476 attacks per year between 1982 and 1998.)

In August 2006, British officials uncovered a plot to blow up 9 or 10 planes leaving London for the United States. The 24 men arrested were going to use liquid explosives in carry-on bags to destroy the planes mid-air. As a result, the airlines placed limits on the amount of liquid that travelers could carry on future flights.

The U.S. State Department has identified dozens of terrorist groups training members in different countries. One important task for the Department of Homeland Security is monitoring the activities of such groups. Agents and offices in foreign countries help them do this. A law called the Patriot Act allows the U.S. government more power to check the background of people in the country.

Lesson 4 Review On a sheet of paper, write the answers to the following questions. Use complete sentences.

1. How has security changed since the attacks of September 11?
2. What did Osama bin Laden admit to doing?
3. What information did the CIA report in 2002 contain?
4. Why have troops stayed in Afghanistan?
5. What is the purpose of the Patriot Act?

Do you think it is OK for people to lose some of their freedoms in exchange for greater security?

Chapter 31: Lesson 5

Overview This lesson describes some of the problems that face the world today as well as lessons from the past that might guide us in the future.

Objectives

- To identify some good things and some bad things that could happen
- To suggest ways the world might change in the future

Student Pages pages 806–808

Teacher's Resource Library

Workbook Activity 147

Activity 147

Modified Activity 147

....

Vocabulary

The concept of *billion* is so large that many students will not truly understand how large it is. Write the words *billions, millions, thousands, hundreds,* and *tens* on the board. Ask students which word estimates the number of students in an average class (tens), the number of students in an average high school (hundreds), the number of people in a full sports stadium (thousands), the number of people in a large city such as New York (millions), and the number of people in the world (billions).

....

1 Warm-Up Activity

Have students make a list of the five most important inventions of the 20th century. Now have them make a list of the five biggest problems of the 21st century. Ask students if the same or related items are on both lists, for example, invention of the automobile and air pollution. Tell them that new technology often introduces problems that are unexpected or unintended.

Objectives

- To identify some good things and some bad things that could happen
- To suggest ways the world might change in the future

Spaceships to the moon, automobiles that speed people to their destinations, airplanes, television, telephone. At one time, all of these things existed only in the imaginations of inventors and dreamers.

Looking to the future, we can see promises and problems. Promises of new treatments for diseases; new technologies we cannot even guess at; new ways to feed the starving people of the world; promises of human rights and an improved standard of living for everyone, everywhere.

However, there are also problems--big problems that will require big solutions. Global problems such as extreme poverty and epidemics of diseases. Natural disasters that destroy the lives of people who have no way to rebuild and recover. Around the world, wars and the fear of terrorism continue. And problems that result from a growing world population, such as pollution and global warming.

What Is the Population Explosion?

At the time of the Roman Empire, the population of the world was 200 million. Since then, this is how it has grown:

- 1800: 1 billion
- 1920: 2 billion
- 1960: 3 billion
- 1975: 4 billion
- 1988: 5 billion
- 1999: 6 billion

Do you notice how the population is growing faster? The time between 1 billion and 2 billion was 120 years. The time between 5 billion and 6 billion was only 11 years. Scientists have calculated that by 2025, the population of the world will be 9 billion. By the year 2200, if we keep growing at the same rate, it will be 138 billion!

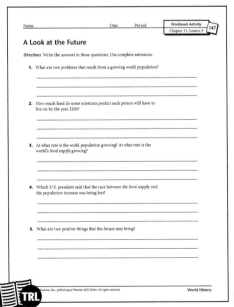

Workbook Activity 147

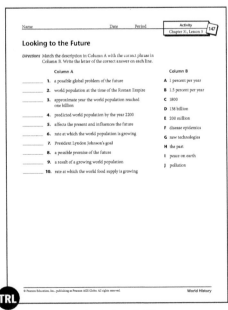

Activity 147

In the past, increases in the food supply and control of disease allowed people to live longer. Today, however, the food supply is not growing as fast as the population is. The world's food supply is increasing at about 1 percent a year. The world's population, however, has been increasing at the rate of 1.5 percent a year.

In 1965, President Lyndon Johnson said that the most important thing we had to do was to work for peace on earth. But the next most important challenge to the human family was the "race between the food supply and the population increase." President Johnson said that the race was being lost. As time moves on, our growing population will continue to be a major problem for the governments of the world.

What Are Some Lessons of History?

Human history has been going on for thousands of years. What does it teach us? One thing we learn is that people from many different cultures faced hard problems in the past. We know the following about these people and their problems:

• Some met challenges with courage, good sense, and goodwill. They improved our world, and we owe them our thanks. We can learn from them.

• Others acted badly. They created terrible problems and caused many people to suffer. But even their terrible actions can teach us something—what not to do!

• Some ignored the past. We can do this, too, but then we will make the same mistakes others have made. The past shapes the present. It influences the future.

• No one has ever been able to predict for sure what the future will bring. But we can say one sure thing—the future belongs to all of us.

1990 to the Present

The World Today   Chapter 31   **807**

Ask students to brainstorm a list of problems that result from overpopulation. Tell them that psychologists have found that people and other animals act more aggressively when they are crowded together. Ask if overpopulation can cause wars. Then have students read pages 806–808 to find out how the world population is growing.

Ask:

• What does the statement "The earth will not support such a huge population" mean? (People will not be able to grow enough crops or raise enough animals to feed themselves because of a lack of space.)

• Why is the race between food supply and population increase being lost? (We are running out of space to grow crops. We are also running out of space and feed for the animals we use for food.)

 Writing About History

When the *Pioneer* and *Voyager* spacecrafts of the 1970s and 1980s left on their space missions to the vast regions beyond our solar system, they each carried a special kind of cargo: a time capsule. In each time capsule was a disk that featured audio recordings and pictures showing life on Earth. The sounds included selections of popular and classical music, sounds from nature, and greetings spoken in 55 different languages. The time capsules were created as a way of communicating with other life-forms, if in fact any exist. Encourage students to think about the various sounds and images they would put into a time capsule. Have them use a tape recorder to record sounds they think might be useful as an indication of life on Earth. Encourage students who speak languages other than English to record greetings.

3 Reinforce and Extend

Lesson 5 Review Answers

1. Answers will vary. Students suggest inventions in this time period and provide reasons for their choices.

2. Answers will vary. Students should state whether increased food production will solve all the world's problems and give reasons for their opinions.

3. Answers will vary, but students should choose a real problem in the world.

4. Answers will vary, but generallly students should understand that ignoring past mistakes will make it likely that those mistakes will be repeated.

5. Answers will vary. Students should give reasons for their choices.

Answers will vary. Possible answers could involve new technology, or changes in the way people eat or live.

Lesson 5 Review On a sheet of paper, write the answers to the following questions. Use complete sentences.

1. What do you think is the most amazing invention of the last 50 years? Why?

2. Do you think that increased production of food will solve all the world's problems? Why or why not?

3. If you could fix one problem in the world today, what would you choose?

4. How can ignoring mistakes and problems of the past lead to problems in the future?

5. Name one person you admire and tell how he or she made a difference in the world.

What do you think?

What do you think the biggest change in the world could be 50 years from now?

Al Gore on Global Warming

Former Vice President Al Gore has been very concerned about the environment for many years. In 1993, he wrote the book Earth in the Balance: Ecology and the Human Spirit. *In 2006, his book and documentary film* An Inconvenient Truth *brought attention to the urgent issues surrounding global warming. On September 9, 2005, Al spoke to the Sierra Club about the need to change the direction the world—the United States in particular—is heading. Here are some excerpts from that speech.*

Ladies and gentlemen, the warnings about global warming have been extremely clear for a long time. We are facing a global climate crisis. It is deepening. We are entering a period of consequences. . . .

Abraham Lincoln said, "The occasion is piled high with difficulty and we must rise with the occasion. As our case is new, we must think anew and act anew. We must disenthrall [free] ourselves and then we shall save our country."

My friends, the truth is that our circumstances are not only new; they are completely different than they have ever been in all of human history. The relationship between humankind and the earth had been utterly transformed in the last hundred years. We have quadrupled the population of our planet. The population in many ways is a success story . . . but the reality of our new relationship with the planet brings with it a moral responsibility to accept our new circumstances and to deal with the consequences of the relationship we have with this planet

Document-Based Questions

1. What is Al Gore's greatest concern?

2. What is the purpose of the quote from Abraham Lincoln?

3. What does it mean to "rise with the occasion," as Lincoln said? What do people need to do to rise with (or to) the occasion?

4. Why has the relationship between humankind and the earth changed in the last hundred years?

5. What does Gore say we have to move beyond in order to change the situation?

Source: Excerpt from Al Gore's speech at the Sierra Summit, September 9, 2005.

Call attention to the title of the Document-Based Reading, "Al Gore on Global Warming." Read aloud the introduction to students. Remind them that Al Gore was the 45th vice president under President Bill Clinton from 1993 to 2001. He also represented the state of Tennessee in the U.S. House of Representatives from 1977 to 1985 and in the United States Senate from 1985 to 1993. Senator Gore was the Democratic nominee for president in the 2000 presidential election.

Explain that the Sierra Club Web site tells us that it is an environmental organization that "works to promote solutions to global warming using current and cutting-edge technology that will reduce our use of fossil fuels."

Have a student read the speech excerpts aloud. Ask them how serious Gore thinks the global warming problem is. Ask if they think the bulleted points about lessons of history on page 807 are relevant to the problems of global warming. Then as a class, read and answer the Document-Based Questions.

If possible, purchase a videotape or DVD of *An Inconvenient Truth* or borrow one from the public library. Play it for students and have a class discussion afterwards.

Answers to Document-Based Questions:

1. His greatest concern is the global climate crisis.

2. Answers will vary. Abraham Lincoln said that people must think of new solutions to new and difficult problems. Global warming is also a new and difficult problem that will need new solutions.

3. Answers will vary. The phrase means that we must be willing to tackle solutions to difficult problems, no matter how difficult the solutions are.

4. The human population in the world has quadrupled.

5. Answers will vary. We must move beyond old solutions and "think outside the box" to come up with new solutions.

Spotlight Story

Have a volunteer read the title, "The Search for New Sources of Energy." Read the article aloud in class. Ask students if they or their families use one of the new energy sources described. If they do not think their family does, have them think about appliances and electronic devices. Hand-held calculators are often powered by solar energy. Most gasoline sold today contains a small amount of ethanol. Tell students that simply heating a room of a house with the warmth of sunlight is a form of passive solar energy.

Show students a photo of a wind farm, in which hundreds of wind turbines rotate to supply energy. Show students a photo of an old-fashioned windmill, which also captures wind energy.

Show students a picture of Niagara Falls in New York and Canada. Tell them that huge amounts of electricity are generated by the falling water.

Close the discussion by pointing out that alternative energy sources are used throughout the world, but other sources must be found to generate power.

After reading and discussion, have the class work together to complete the Wrap-Up questions.

Spotlight Story

The Search for New Sources of Energy

Today's high prices for energy have caused many countries to look for other ways to generate power. Cars and trucks are some of the biggest users of gasoline. Americans use about 382 million gallons of gasoline every day. Almost 65 percent of the oil used in the United States is imported from other countries.

Some countries have turned to ethanol as a substitute for gasoline. Ethanol is a fuel made from the sugar in plants. The United States and Brazil are the world's leaders in ethanol production. Brazil makes ethanol from the large amounts of sugar cane it grows. In the United States, most ethanol is made from corn.

Many countries have started using solar energy. Solar energy is energy from the sun that is converted into electrical energy. It is already used to heat homes and swimming pools. It is used to operate such things as lighthouses and road traffic warning signals. It could also be used to run cars and power plants.

Wind power is another energy source that does not harm the environment. Wind power uses wind turbines (similar to aircraft propeller blades) to generate electricity. They turn in the moving air and power an electric generator that supplies an electric current. Electricity from these turbines is fed into the local utility and then distributed to customers. However, the turbines are both noisy and dangerous to birds.

Other sources of energy are used in some countries. These sources include geothermal power, tidal energy, and hydroelectric power from falling water.

Wrap-Up

1. Why are many countries looking for new ways to generate energy?

2. What is ethanol and who are the world's biggest producers?

3. What are some of the uses of solar energy today?

4. How is wind used to generate electricity?

5. What are three other sources of energy besides solar energy and wind power?

Answers to Spotlight Story Wrap-Up:

1. Answers will vary. Most energy sources have drawbacks. None is perfect for all uses. More than one energy source is needed to supply the amount of power the modern world needs.

2. Ethanol is a fuel made from the sugar in plants. The United States and Brazil are the world's biggest producers of ethanol.

3. Solar energy is used to heat homes and swimming pools, and to operate lighthouses and road traffic warning signals. It could also be used to run cars and power plants.

4. Wind turns the blades of a turbine, which powers an electric generator that supplies an electric current.

5. Other sources include geothermal power, tidal energy, and hydroelectric power.

Chapter 31 S U M M A R Y

- Modern technology has made the world a "global village." People around the world share ideas and cultures. Technology helps businesses become multinational corporations that have workers in many countries.

- Mass communication includes advertising and electronic communication. American culture influences other parts of the world.

- Computers have many uses. The Internet is an international computer network. The World Wide Web links people through electronics. These media are part of the "electronic superhighway."

- The United States and the Soviet Union competed in space for many years. Now, the two countries are among the 15 that are working on the International Space Station.

- Modern technology depends on energy from various sources. However, burning coal and oil pollutes the environment. Nuclear power plants produce deadly waste; accidents are a danger.

- Modern technology has also changed medicine with new equipment, such as lasers.

- Most rich countries have a free-market economy and well-developed industries and technology. Most of these nations are in the Northern Hemisphere.

- Developing nations are building their industries and economies. Many people in these nations live by subsistence farming. Overpopulation and education are problems. Developing nations also lack money. Most industrialized nations supply aid to poorer countries. Aid comes through the World Bank and International Monetary Fund.

- A recession in 1997 hurt the economies of Asian nations. This crisis affected the entire world economy. Some people blamed it on multinational corporations.

- Land, air, and water pollution is a global problem.

- Developing nations have pollution problems because of fast, uncontrolled growth.

- The threat of global terrorism has changed the world. There is more concern about security since the attacks of 9/11. There is a concern that this greater security results in the loss of privacy.

- More terrorist attacks are possible. It is important for everyone to be aware of their surroundings.

- In the future, a growing world population will strain the world's supplies of food and water.

1990 to the Present

TEACHER'S RESOURCE

The AGS Globe Teaching Strategies in Social Studies Transparencies may be used with this chapter. The transparencies add an interactive dimension to expand and enhance the *World History* program content.

Using the Chapter Summary

Have students read the Chapter Summary to review the main ideas presented in Chapter 31.

Ask:

- Why is the world sometimes called a global village? (People around the world share ideas and cultures. Many businesses are multinational and have workers in many countries.)

- What is mass communication? (Advertising and electronic communication reach all parts of the world, especially through the use of computers and the Internet.)

- How are the United States and Russia working together in space? (They are among five nations working on the International Space Station.)

- What energy problems are caused by modern technology? (Large amounts of energy are needed, but burning fossil fuels cause pollution and nuclear power can be dangerous.)

- What new equipment has changed modern medicine? (Lasers are an example.)

- What kind of economy do most nations in the Northern Hemisphere have? (They have a free-market economy and well-developed industry and technology.)

- What are some economic problems in developing nations? (Many people live by subsistence farming, industry is still being built, and overpopulation, education, and lack of money are problems.)

- What was a result of the recession of 1997? (The economies of Asian nations were hurt, and the entire world economy was affected.)

- What global problems are caused by a growing world population? (Land, water, and air pollution and an insufficient supply of food and water are global problems.)

- How has global terrorism changed the world? (There is more security and a growing concern that this security results in loss of privacy.)

Chapter 31 Review

Use the Chapter Review to prepare students for tests and to reteach content from the chapter.

Chapter 31 Mastery Test

The Teacher's Resource Library includes two forms of the Chapter 31 Mastery Test. Each test addresses the chapter Goals for Learning. An optional third page of additional critical-thinking items is included for each test. The difficulty level of the two forms is equivalent.

Chapter 31 Review Answers

1. international
2. mass communication
3. technology
4. energy
5. photoelectric cell
6. environment
7. developing
8. interdependent
9. free-market
10. global warming
11. A
12. D
13. C
14. A
15. Mass communication connects people everywhere. Since the end of World War II, American television, movies, music, fast food, and clothing styles have helped to shape this new global culture.
16. Answers will vary. Students may suggest wind, hydroelectric, geothermal, or solar energy.
17. Answers will vary. Developing nations face overpopulation. This leads to hunger, pollution, and political unrest. Also, students in developing nations attend school for only two or three years. Only about half the people in these countries can read and write. Finally, industrialization requires money. Most developing countries have only raw materials to sell. They have no consumer goods to trade to other countries. But poor countries want consumer goods, so they buy more than they sell. Money flows out of the country.

Chapter 31   R E V I E W

Word Bank
developing
energy
environment
free-market
global warming
interdependent
international
mass communication
photoelectric cell
technology

On a sheet of paper, use the words from the Word Bank to complete each sentence.

1. The Internet is a(n) _____ computer network that goes around the world and among many nations.

2. Television, advertising, and movies are examples of _____, which is messages directed at many people.

3. The global village is partly the result of advances in _____, which is the use of science to do practical things.

4. Progress in technology depends on _____, which makes machines work and produces heat.

5. The _____ can produce electricity from light from the sun.

6. The burning of coal and oil threatens our _____, which is the land, sea, and air of Earth.

7. The Southern Hemisphere has many _____ countries, which are just beginning to grow their economies.

8. The nations of the world have become _____. They depend on one another.

9. Most industrial countries have a(n) _____ economy in which manufacturers meet the needs of consumers.

10. Many scientists are worried about _____, which could change the earth's temperature.

On a sheet of paper, write the letter of the answer that correctly completes each sentence.

11. A _____ is a tool that produces high-energy beams of light.

   A laser   C recession
   B technology   D subsistence

12. The _____ directs money from industrialized nations to developing countries.

   A IMF   C World Wide Web
   B Internet   D World Bank

Chapter 31 Mastery Test A, pages 1–3

13. The _____ has 182 members whom it helps in times of economic crisis.

   A World Bank

   B World Wide Web

   C International Monetary Fund

   D Internet

14. A _____ corporation does business around the world.

   A multinational   **C** advertising

   B electronic   **D** mass communication

On a sheet of paper, write the answers to the following questions. Use complete sentences.

15. What is one way that mass communication has helped create a global village?

16. What is one source of energy that may be safe and may not pollute our environment?

17. What is one problem that developing countries have?

18. What is the biggest problem facing the world today?

Read each question, then write your opinion on a sheet of paper. Use complete sentences.

19. Should the countries with the greatest wealth do more to help the less developed countries? Explain your answer.

20. What is one way you can reduce, reuse, or recycle to help the environment?

> Read all test directions carefully. Do not assume that you know what you are supposed to do.

18. Answers will vary. Students may say overpopulation or global warming.

Critical Thinking

19. Answers will vary. Students may believe that the richer countries have an obligation to their own people and are already doing enough to help less developed countries. Others may believe that the rich countries are getting richer while the poor countries are getting poorer, so it is only fair that the rich should give more.

20. Answers will vary. Students may suggest using products with less wrapping, not using paper plates, or reusing plastic containers. Student answers should reflect an understanding of reducing, reusing, and recycling.

Chapter Project Follow-up

Student reports on alternative, or renewable, energy sources should contain accurate and current information. Posters should show how the alternative energy source can be converted into electrical energy. Data will probably show that alternative energy sources are more expensive but less polluting that fossil fuels. Some, such as solar energy, are readily available in many regions, and others, such as geothermal or hydroelectric, are available only in certain regions. Have students display their reports or present them to the class.

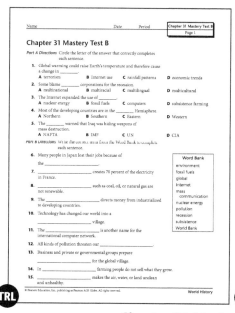

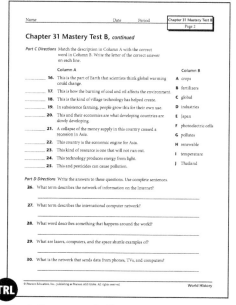

Chapter 31 Mastery Test B, pages 1–3

Have students read the Skill Builder and answer the questions that follow. Explain to students that even though they may be too young to vote now, each of them can still make a strong statement through action. Discuss with students how they can express their views and make an impact by getting involved with organizations such as the World Wildlife Fund, the National Humane Society, or through local fundraising or volunteerism. Another way students can make their opinions known is by sending a letter to an elected official stating a problem and proposing a solution. You may want to help students draft such a letter or help them gather addresses of organizations whose views they wish to support.

Unit 7 Skill Builder Answers

1–8. Answers will vary according to local requirements.

9. Answers will vary. You can determine whether candidates support programs and ideas that you think are important. You can find out by following what the media—radio, television, newspapers, news magazines, Internet Web sites and bloggers—report and what the political parties say about the candidate. You can hear candidates speak in person and check their voting records against these statements.

10. Answers will vary. What happens in government depends on who is elected. You can influence the government's actions by voting for candidates who stand for issues that are important to you; if you don't vote, you let other people control how government affects your life.

Unit Skills Activity

Ask students for their advice about how to fill out forms. (read the whole form through first, be sure of directions, fill out a practice copy of the form first, ask questions when confused or unsure, write carefully and neatly) Then distribute copies of the Unit 7 Skills Activity to students. You may wish to review the form as a group before students fill out the form.

Unit 7
Skill Builder

Voting

As American citizens, we vote to elect leaders and decide certain issues. As voters, we can do many things to find out about different candidates and issues. We can read newspapers. We can listen to political debates on radio and TV. Or we can attend political rallies and hear candidates speak in person. We can read articles about candidates in news magazines. We can get information from the political party of our choice. We can study the voting record of a candidate already in office.

Many people around the world vote for their political leaders. Each country has its own voting process. Here is how it works in the United States. To vote, qualified persons 18 and older must first register at a city or county clerk's office. In some places, they can register by mail or at the polls on election day. Polling places are usually open from 7 a.m. to 8 p.m. Each voter must vote at the assigned polling place in his or her district. Local newspapers usually list polling places and hours. Voters also can get this information from local government offices. Voters who will be out of town on election day may request an absentee ballot in person or by mail. They may then mark and send in the absentee ballot ahead of the election.

At the polls, voters fill out a ballot. If necessary, election judges can show voters how to mark a ballot. Different districts use various machines and methods. Voters may have to pull a lever on a machine or punch holes. On paper, they may mark Xs with a pen. To ensure privacy, voters make their choices in a private booth.

After the polls close, election judges at each polling place count the votes. They deliver the count to the city or county clerk's office. When all the votes are counted, a winner is declared. Television, radio, and newspapers then give election results.

Find out the answers to these questions. Then you'll be ready to vote when the time comes.

1. How long must you live in your state and district before you can vote?

2. Where do you register to vote?

3. How do you register to vote?

4. Where do you vote?

5. How can you get an absentee ballot?

6. How do you fill out the ballot?

7. How are the votes counted?

8. In what day, month, and year can you vote in a national election for the first time?

As a future voter, explain how you would answer these questions.

9. How can you decide which candidates to vote for?

10. Why do you think it is important to vote in elections?

Unit Skills Activity

Unit 7 SUMMARY

- The U.S. and the Soviet Union fought a "cold war" of words after WWII.

- In 1945, European nations controlled most of Africa. By the 1980s, there were 50 new African countries. African economies are growing quickly, but famine and overcrowded cities are problems.

- Apartheid hurt the black majority in South Africa. Nationalist leader Nelson Mandela helped end apartheid and became its president in 1994.

- The Jewish state of Israel fought several wars with Arab countries. Some displaced Palestinians became terrorists. By the 1990s, Arab and Israeli leaders were working toward peace. Palestinian self-rule is a major issue.

- Indian nationalists used passive resistance to gain independence from Britain in 1947. Pakistan was established as a separate Muslim state.

- In China, a Communist victory in the civil war established the People's Republic in 1949.

- The French colony of Indochina was divided into North and South Vietnam, Cambodia, and Laos. When Communist North Vietnam waged war against South Vietnam, the United States helped South Vietnam. Many Americans opposed the war. A Communist government united Vietnam in 1975.

- Oil and religion continued to cause conflict in the Persian Gulf region. A religious revolution in Iran overthrew the Shah. Iraq and Iran fought a long war. Iraqi leader Saddam Hussein invaded Kuwait but was stopped by an international force.

- The Chinese Communist government violently stopped pro-democracy demonstrators at Tiananmen Square in 1989.

- People in Eastern Europe overthrew Communist governments in 1989. Ethnic wars broke out in the former Yugoslavia. Western European nations moved toward economic union, with a common currency, the euro.

- Land reform is a major problem in Latin America.

- Modern technology made the world a "global village." Mass communication lets people share ideas and culture.

- Russia and the United States cooperate with other nations on space projects.

- Technology depends on energy. Many energy sources cause pollution or other hazards. World leaders try to balance the needs of rich and poor nations while protecting the environment.

- The threat of global terrorism has caused increased security since the attacks of 9/11. More terrorist attacks are possible.

1990 to the Present

Unit Activity Follow-Up

After students have presented their brochures, display them for the class to see. Use these questions to evaluate each student brochure for Activity 1:

- Did the student create a brochure that is clear and easy to follow?

- Did the students include any visual aids?

- Did the student show good research skills for the brochure's content?

For Unit 7, Activity 2, have students meet in small groups to share their choices of important events in world history. For further evaluation, use this question:

- Did the student give good reasons for why the event he or she chose was important?

Using the Unit Summary

Read and discuss the Unit Summary statements on page 815 with students.

Ask:

- What was the "cold war?" (The cold war was a war of ideas between the United States and the Soviet Union that lasted from World War II until 1991.)

- What are some of the problems facing the 50 new countries in Africa? (famine, disease, and overpopulation)

- What kind of resistance did Indian nationalists use to gain its independence from Britain? (passive resistance)

- Which Asian countries established Communist governments in 1949 and in 1975? (China in 1949 and the combined North and South Vietnam in 1975)

- What are two causes of conflict in the Middle East? (religion and oil)

- Which two Asian countries are most successful economically? (China and Japan)

- How are international space projects examples of the world as a global village? (Many countries cooperate and work together closely to build space labs.)

- What are the most serious environmental problems of the future? (pollution, global warming, dwindling energy supplies, not enough food and water for a growing world population)

Unit 7 Mastery Test

The Teacher's Resource Library includes a two-page Unit Mastery Test. An optional third page of additional critical-thinking items is included for each test. The Unit 7 Mastery Test is pictured on page 864 of this Teacher's Edition.

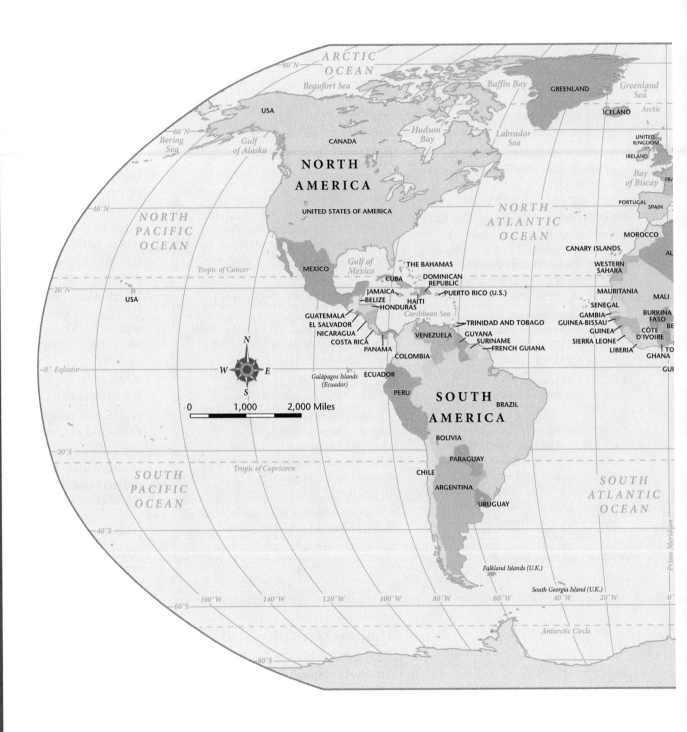

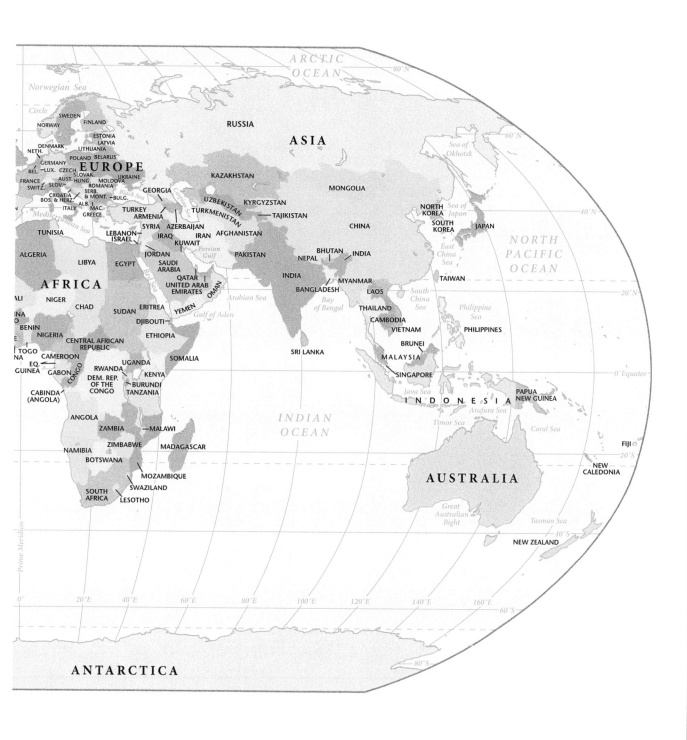

ARCTIC OCEAN

Norwegian Sea

80°N

Circle

SWEDEN
NORWAY   FINLAND

RUSSIA

ASIA

60°N

Sea of Okhotsk

DENMARK
NETH.   ESTONIA
            LITHUANIA   LATVIA
GERMANY
BEL. LUX. CZECH   POLAND BELARUS
FRANCE   AUST. HUNG.   MOLDOVA
SWITZ. SLOV.   UKRAINE
      ROMANIA
CROATIA   SERB.
BOS. & HERZ. & MONT. BULG.
      ITALY   ALB.   MAC.
            GREECE

EUROPE

KAZAKHSTAN

MONGOLIA

NORTH
KOREA   Sea of
         Japan

40°N

SOUTH
KOREA   JAPAN

Black Sea

GEORGIA

Caspian Sea

UZBEKISTAN   KYRGYZSTAN

TURKEY
ARMENIA

TURKMENISTAN   TAJIKISTAN

CHINA

NORTH
PACIFIC
OCEAN

TUNISIA

Mediterranean Sea

LEBANON
ISRAEL

SYRIA
IRAQ

AZERBAIJAN
KUWAIT

AFGHANISTAN

East
China
Sea

TAIWAN

20°N

ALGERIA

LIBYA

JORDAN

EGYPT

Persian
Gulf

SAUDI
ARABIA

QATAR

UNITED ARAB
EMIRATES

PAKISTAN

NEPAL

BHUTAN

INDIA

MYANMAR

South
China
Sea

Philippine
Sea

AFRICA

Red Sea

OMAN

Arabian Sea

INDIA

BANGLADESH

LAOS

THAILAND

PHILIPPINES

NIGER

CHAD

SUDAN

ERITREA

YEMEN

Gulf of Aden

Bay
of Bengal

CAMBODIA

VIETNAM

BENIN

DJIBOUTI

BRUNEI

NIGERIA

CENTRAL AFRICAN
REPUBLIC

ETHIOPIA

SRI LANKA

MALAYSIA

TOGO

CAMEROON

EQ.
GUINEA   GABON

UGANDA

CONGO

RWANDA
DEM. REP.
OF THE
CONGO

SOMALIA

KENYA

BURUNDI
TANZANIA

SINGAPORE

Java Sea

INDONESIA

PAPUA
NEW GUINEA

0° Equator

CABINDA
(ANGOLA)

Arafura Sea

Timor Sea

Coral Sea

ANGOLA

ZAMBIA   MALAWI

INDIAN
OCEAN

FIJI

20°S

ZIMBABWE

MADAGASCAR

NAMIBIA
BOTSWANA

NEW
CALEDONIA

MOZAMBIQUE

AUSTRALIA

SOUTH
AFRICA   SWAZILAND
          LESOTHO

Great
Australian
Bight

Tasman Sea

40°S

NEW ZEALAND

0°   20°E   40°E   60°E   80°E   100°E   120°E   140°E   160°E   60°S

80°S

ANTARCTICA

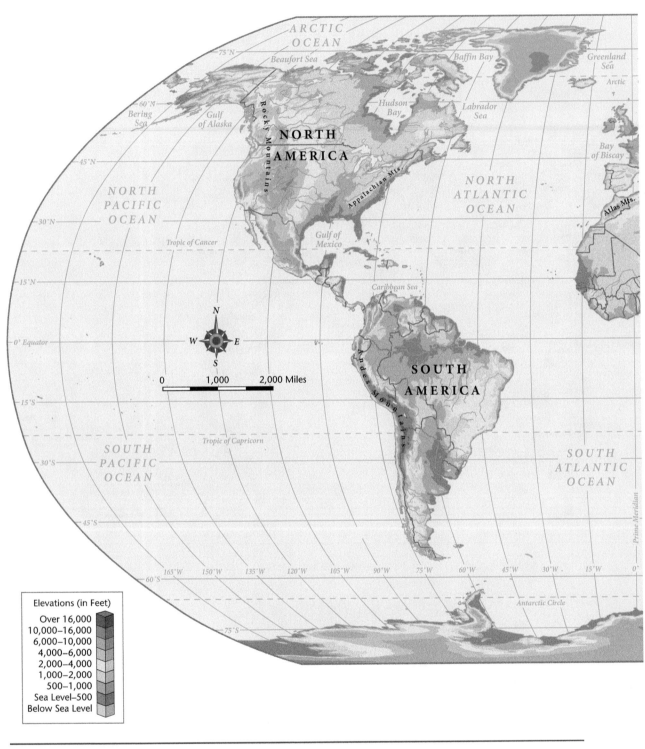

ARCTIC
OCEAN

Beaufort Sea

Baffin Bay

Greenland
Sea

Arctic

60°N

Bering
Sea

Gulf
of Alaska

Hudson
Bay

Labrador
Sea

Bay
of Biscay

**NORTH
AMERICA**

75°N

Rocky Mountains

45°N

NORTH
ATLANTIC
OCEAN

Appalachian Mts.

Atlas Mts.

NORTH
PACIFIC
OCEAN

30°N

Tropic of Cancer

Gulf of
Mexico

15°N

Caribbean Sea

N

0° Equator

W   E

S

SOUTH
AMERICA

Andes Mountains

0   1,000   2,000 Miles

15°S

Tropic of Capricorn

SOUTH
PACIFIC
OCEAN

30°S

SOUTH
ATLANTIC
OCEAN

45°S

Prime Meridian

165°W   150°W   135°W   120°W   105°W   90°W   75°W   60°W   45°W   30°W   15°W   0°

60°S

Antarctic Circle

75°S

Elevations (in Feet)

Over 16,000
10,000–16,000
6,000–10,000
4,000–6,000
2,000–4,000
1,000–2,000
500–1,000
Sea Level–500
Below Sea Level

ARCTIC
OCEAN

Norwegian Sea

Circle

Ural Mts.

S i b e r i a
ASIA

Sea of
Okhotsk

60°N

75°N

45°N

EUROPE

Alps

Black Sea

Caucasus

Caspian Sea

Gobi Desert

Sea of
Japan

Mediterranean Sea

Mts.

AFRICA

S a h a r a
D e s e r t

Persian
Gulf

Plateau of Tibet

H i m a l a y a

East
China
Sea

NORTH
PACIFIC
OCEAN

30°N

Red Sea

Arabian Sea

Gulf of Aden

*Bay
of Bengal*

South
China
Sea

Philippine
Sea

15°N

0° Equator

Java Sea

INDIAN
OCEAN

Arafura Sea

Timor Sea

Coral Sea

15°S

Kalahari
Desert

AUSTRALIA
Victoria Desert

30°S

Great
Australian
Bight

Tasman Sea

45°S

Prime Meridian

0°   15°E   30°E   45°E   60°E   75°E   90°E   105°E   120°E   135°E   150°E   165°E

60°S

75°S

ANTARCTICA

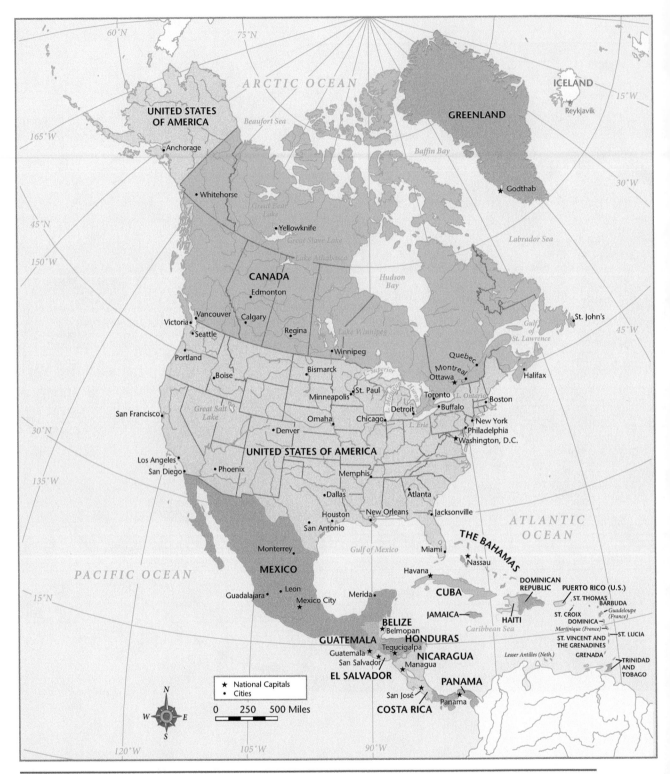

Caribbean Sea

Managua ★

San José ★

Panama

Barranquilla

Caracas

TRINIDAD AND TOBAGO

Valencia

VENEZUELA

Cúcuta

Medellín

Georgetown ★

Paramaribo

GUYANA

Cayenne ★

Bogotá ★

SURINAME

FRENCH GUIANA

COLOMBIA

Mitú

Quito ★

ECUADOR

Guayaquil

Galápagos Islands (Ecuador)

Manaus

Belém

Fortaleza

Talara

PERU

Trujillo

Recife

Huánuco

Pôrto Velho

BRAZIL

Lima ★

Ica

Cuzco

BOLIVIA

La Paz ★

Salvador

Santa Cruz

★ Brásilia

Goiânia

Sucre ★

Iquique

20°S

PACIFIC OCEAN

Antofagasta

PARAGUAY

Rio de Janeiro

São Paulo

Asunción ★

CHILE

Córdoba

Rosario

Santiago ★

URUGUAY

Buenos Aires ★

Montevideo

Concepción

ARGENTINA

ATLANTIC OCEAN

Valdivia

Puerto Montt

N

W   E

S

Comodoro Rivadavia

★ National Capitals
• Cities

0   250   500 Miles

Falkland Islands (U.K.)

South Georgia Island (U.K.)

90°W   80°W   70°W   60°W   50°W   40°W

10°N

Equator 0°

10°S

30°S

40°S

50°S

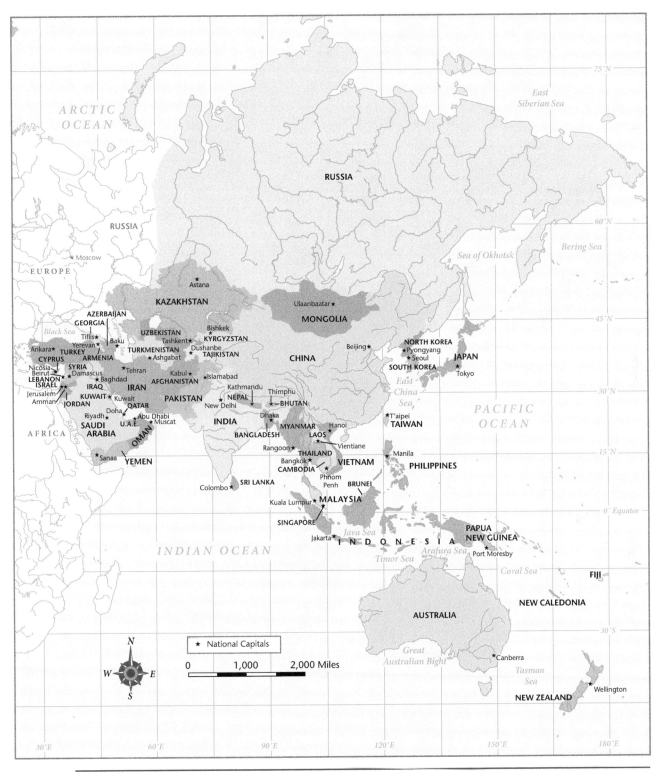

ARCTIC OCEAN

East Siberian Sea

RUSSIA

75°N

RUSSIA

60°N

Moscow

EUROPE

Sea of Okhotsk

Bering Sea

Astana

KAZAKHSTAN

Ulaanbaatar

MONGOLIA

45°N

AZERBAIJAN
GEORGIA

Black Sea

Bishkek

UZBEKISTAN

Tashkent

KYRGYZSTAN

Tiflis

Baku

Ankara

TURKEY

Yerevan

TURKMENISTAN

Dushanbe

TAJIKISTAN

Beijing

NORTH KOREA

Pyongyang

JAPAN

CYPRUS

ARMENIA

Ashgabat

CHINA

Seoul

SOUTH KOREA

Nicosia

SYRIA

Tehran

Kabul

Islamabad

Tokyo

Beirut

Damascus

AFGHANISTAN

East China Sea

LEBANON

Baghdad

IRAN

Kathmandu

Thimphu

PACIFIC OCEAN

ISRAEL

IRAQ

KUWAIT

PAKISTAN

NEPAL

BHUTAN

30°N

Jerusalem

Amman

Kuwait

JORDAN

Riyadh

Doha

QATAR

Abu Dhabi

New Delhi

Dhaka

SAUDI

U.A.E.

Muscat

INDIA

MYANMAR

Hanoi

T'aipei

ARABIA

OMAN

BANGLADESH

LAOS

TAIWAN

AFRICA

Red Sea

Rangoon

THAILAND

Vientiane

15°N

Sanaa

YEMEN

Bangkok

VIETNAM

Manila

CAMBODIA

PHILIPPINES

Colombo

SRI LANKA

Phnom Penh

BRUNEI

Kuala Lumpur

MALAYSIA

SINGAPORE

Java Sea

0° Equator

Jakarta

INDONESIA

PAPUA NEW GUINEA

INDIAN OCEAN

Timor Sea

Arafura Sea

Port Moresby

FIJI

Coral Sea

NEW CALEDONIA

N
W E
S

★ National Capitals

0   1,000   2,000 Miles

AUSTRALIA

30°S

Great Australian Bight

Canberra

Tasman Sea

Wellington

NEW ZEALAND

30°E   60°E   90°E   120°E   150°E   180°E

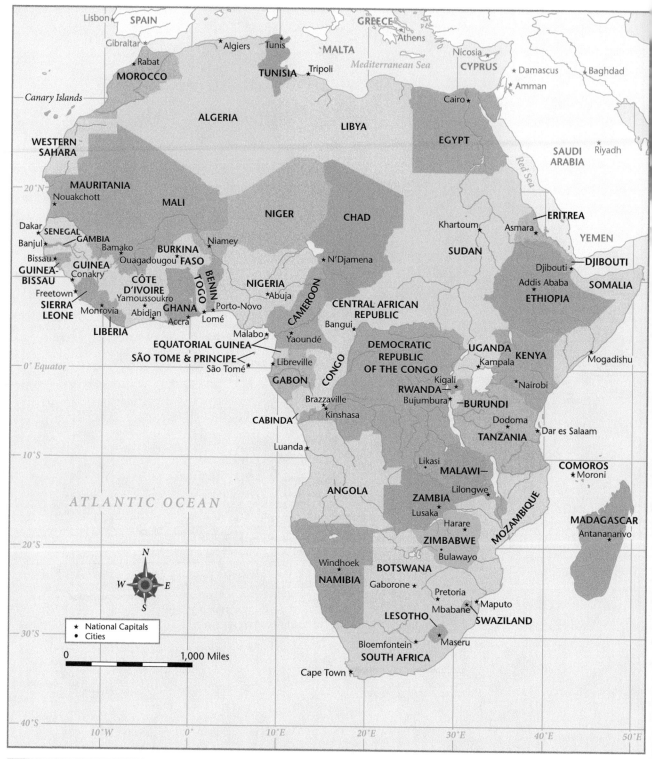

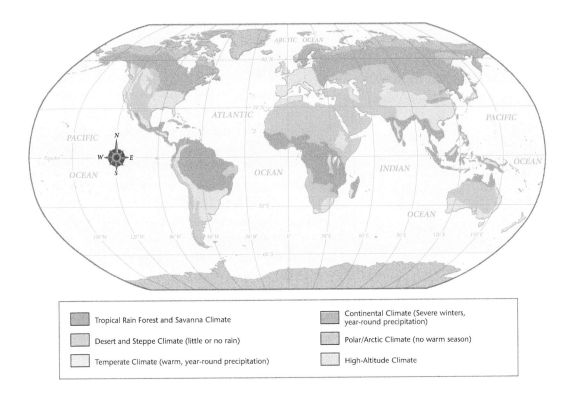

Tropical Rain Forest and Savanna Climate		Continental Climate (Severe winters, year-round precipitation)
Desert and Steppe Climate (little or no rain)		Polar/Arctic Climate (no warm season)
Temperate Climate (warm, year-round precipitation)		High-Altitude Climate

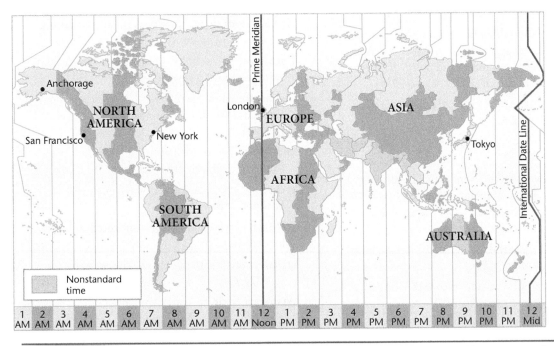

A

Abacus (ab´ ə kəs) A tool that helps people add and do other things with numbers (p. 303)

Abdicate (ab´ də kāt) To give up power as a ruler (p. 633)

Abolish (ə bol´ ish) To get rid of something (p. 414)

Absolute monarch (ab´ sə lüt mon´ ərk) A king or queen who had complete and unlimited power over his or her people (p. 430)

Abundant (ə bun´ dənt) More than enough (p. 71)

Accords (ə kords´) Agreements (p. 762)

Acropolis (ə krop´ ə lis) A hill on which the people in a Greek city built their main temple (p. 122)

Advanced (ad vanst´) Beyond the beginning stage (p. 149)

Advisor (ad vī´ zər) A person who gives advice (p. 444)

African National Congress (ANC) (af´ rə kən nash´ ə nəl kong´ gris) A black nationalist group in South Africa (p. 734)

African Nationalism (af´ rə kən nash´ ə nə liz əm) The struggle by native African people to gain their economic and political freedom from European colonial rulers (p. 731)

Agency (ā´ jən sē) A group that provides a service (p. 693)

Alliance (ə lī´ əns) An agreement to help one another (p. 50)

Allied Powers (al´ īd pou´ ərs) The allied nations of Great Britain, France, Russia, Italy, and eventually, the United States and Japan (p. 617)

Ally (al´ ī) A friend; a country or person who helps another (p. 156)

Alms (ämz) The money or care that one gives to the poor and needy (p. 275)

Ambassador (am bas´ ə dər) A person sent to represent his or her government in another country (p. 582)

Amber (am´ bər) The hard, yellowish remains of a liquid that comes out of trees (p. 388)

American Revolution (ə mar´ ə kən rev ə lü´ shən) The American struggle against Great Britain for independence (p. 489)

Anatomy (ə nat´ ə mē) The structure of a human or animal body (p. 387)

Anglican Church (ang´ glə ken chėrch) The Church of England (p. 361)

Annex (ə neks´) To take over; to add a piece of land to one's country (p. 76)

Annul (ə nul´) To announce that a marriage never existed between two people (p. 360)

Anthropologist (an thrə pol´ ə jist) A scientist who studies the beginnings and the behavior of people (p. 9)

Apartheid (ə pärt´ hīt) The official policy of the Union of South Africa that refused to give black and other nonwhite people any political, economic, or social rights (p. 734)

Appeasement (ə pēz´ mənt) A policy of making others happy or content (p. 673)

Aqueduct (ak´ wə dukt) A structure that carries water from far away (p. 171)

Archaeologist (är kē ol´ ə jist) A scientist who finds and studies the things people left behind (p. 9)

Archbishop (ärch´ bish əp) The top religious leader in a church province (p. 361)

Archer (är´ chər) A soldier who fights with a bow and arrows (p. 47)

Architect (är´ kə tekt) A person who draws plans for buildings (p. 335)

Architecture (är´ kə tek chər) The art of building (p. 127)

Aristocrat (ə ris´ tə krat) A member of the powerful ruling class (p. 122)

Armada (är mä′ də) A large fleet of warships (p. 435)

Armistice (är′ mə stis) An agreement to stop fighting (p. 621)

Armor (är′ mər) A strong metal covering that protects the body in battle (p. 74)

Arsenal (är′ sə nəl) A place where someone stores or makes weapons (p. 676)

Artifact (är′ tə fakt) An object made by a person for a practical purpose (p. 9)

Artisan (är′ tə zən) A person who works with his or her hands to create something (p. 47)

Assassinate (ə sas′ n āt) To kill someone important (p. 160)

Assembly (ə sem′ blē) A meeting (p. 124)

Astronomer (ə stron′ ə mər) A person who keeps track of the sun, the planets, and the stars (p. 53)

Astronomy (ə stron′ ə mē) The study of the stars (p. 135)

Atomic bomb (ə tom′ ik bom) A bomb that uses nuclear energy and has much destructive power (p. 682)

Attract (ə trakt′) To pull something toward oneself (p. 385)

Authority (ə thôr′ ə tē) Power (p. 353)

Autocracy (ȯ tok′ rə sē) A government in which one person rules with unlimited power (p. 629)

Axis (ak′ is) A make-believe line that goes through the middle of an object that spins around it (p. 669)

Axis Powers (ak′ is pou′ ərs) The alliance of Germany, Italy, and Japan during World War II (p. 669)

Ayatollah (ä yä tō′ lə) A Muslim religious leader (p. 763)

B

Balance of power (bal′ əns ov pou′ ər) The condition that exists when all countries or all sections of government have equal strength (p. 544)

Ban (ban) To get rid of; to make something not legal (p. 471)

Baptism (bap′ tiz əm) A ritual by which a person becomes a Christian (p. 358)

Barbarian (bär bâr′ ē ən) An uncivilized person (p. 306)

Barbaric (bär bar′ ik) Not civilized (p. 252)

Barbed wire (bärbd wīr) Wire that has sharp metal spikes on it (p. 618)

Bastille (ba stēl′) A prison in Paris (p. 495)

Berlin Wall (bər lin′ wȯl) The wall that divided the people of East and West Berlin (p. 719)

Betray (bi trā′) To stop being loyal to someone (p. 178)

Bible (bī′ bəl) The Hebrew and Christian book that is thought to be holy (p. 36)

Biology (bī ol′ ə jē) The study of living things (p. 135)

Bishop (bish′ əp) A priest who is in charge of other priests and a number of churches (p. 239)

Blacksmith (blak′ smith) A person who works with iron and makes tools and weapons (p. 235)

Blitzkrieg (blits′ krēg) The quick and forceful method of attack that Germany used in World War II; "lightning war" (p. 675)

Bolshevik (bōl′ shə vik) A revolutionary socialist group in Russia (p. 643)

Boundary (boun′ dər ē) Dividing line (p. 429)

Boyar (bō yär′) A Russian noble who owned land (p. 257)

a	hat	e	let	ī	ice	ȯ	order	u̇	put	sh	she		a	in about
ā	age	ē	equal	o	hot	oi	oil	ü	rule	th	thin	ə {	e	in taken
ä	far	ér	term	ō	open	ou	out	ch	child	ᴛʜ	then		i	in pencil
â	care	i	it	ȯ	saw	u	cup	ng	long	zh	measure		o	in lemon
													u	in circus

Boycott (boi´ kot) To refuse to buy something; to refuse to deal with a person, business, or country (p. 488)

British Commonwealth of Nations (brit´ ish kom´ ən welth ov nā´ shəns) A group of nations that is loyal to the British monarch (p. 733)

Buddha (bü´ də) A name meaning the "Enlightened One"; the name given to Siddhartha Gautama, the founder of Buddhism (p. 100)

Bushido (bü´ shē dō) The Samurai code of honor in Japan (p. 311)

C

Calligraphy (kə lig´ rə fē) The art of beautiful handwriting (p. 311)

Calvinism (kal´ və niz əm) The religious movement founded by John Calvin (p. 363)

Campesino (käm pā sē´ nō) A peasant who works the land but does not own it (p. 772)

Canal (kə nal´) A waterway made by humans (p. 104)

Capital (kap´ ə təl) The city from which a ruler, or emperor, rules (p. 48); money used to start a business (p. 515)

Caravan (kar´ ə van) A group of traders traveling together, often through deserts (p. 69)

Cardinal (kärd´ n əl) A high official of the Roman Catholic Church (p. 444)

Caste (kast) A class of people in India (p. 98)

Catholic Reformation (kath´ ə lik ref ər mā´ shən) The Catholic Church's reforms that attempted to fight Protestant beliefs; also known as the Counter-Reformation (p. 366)

Cavalier (kav ə lir´) A person who fought for the king in the English Civil War (p. 440)

Cavalry (kav´ əl rē) Soldiers on horseback (p. 47)

Censor (sen´ sər) To prevent someone from reading or viewing something (p. 366)

Central Powers (sen´ trəl pou´ ərs) The allied nations of Germany, Austria-Hungary, Turkey, and Bulgaria (p. 617)

Chapel (chap´ əl) A small church (p. 343)

Chariot (char´ ē ət) A two-wheeled, horse-drawn carriage (p. 47)

Charter (chär´ tər) A constitution; a set of statements that explains a group's purpose (p. 692)

Christianity (kris chē an´ ə tē) The religion based on the teachings of Jesus Christ (p. 177)

City-state (sit´ ē - stāt) A city surrounded by smaller villages (p. 27)

Civilian (sə vil´ yən) A person who is not in the military (p. 300)

Civilization (siv ə lə zā´ shən) A large group of people who have cities and government, and a high level of development as a group (p. 17)

Civilized (siv´ ə līzd) Having good government and the things that make life easier (p. 172)

Civil service (siv´ əl sėr´ vis) A system of government run by civilians (p. 300)

Civil war (siv´ əl wôr) Fighting between people within their own country (p. 72)

Classical (klas´ ə kəl) A type of music from the 1700s and 1800s that is orderly and balanced; in the style of ancient Greece or Rome (p. 475)

Clergy (klėr´ jē) Leaders of religious groups (p. 329)

Co-emperor (kō - em´ pər ər) A person who rules part of an empire while another person rules the other part (p. 181)

Code of Napoleon (kōd ov nə pō´ lē ən) A code of law Napoleon passed that made all men equal in France (p. 506)

Cold war (kōld wôr) The war of ideas between the United States and the Soviet Union after World War II (p. 707)

Collective farm (kə lek´ tiv färm) A large farm owned by the government and worked by many peasants (p. 647)

Colonialism (kə lō´ nē ə liz əm) The controlling of colonies; another name for imperialism (p. 593)

Colonist (kol´ ə nist) A person who settles in a new place (p. 416)

Column (kol´ əm) A tall post used to support a building (p. 132)

Commandment (kə mand´ mənt) A rule, or a way to act (p. 37)

Communion (kə myü´ nyən) A ritual by which Christians grow in their faith (p. 358)

Communism (kom´ yə niz əm) An economic system in which there is no private property and the government produces goods (p. 643)

Community (kə myü´ nə tē) A group of people with something in common (p. 387)

Complaint (kəm plānt´) A statement about something that tells why a person is unhappy (p. 489)

Compromise (kom´ prə mīz) An agreement in which both sides give up something to stop an argument (p. 362)

Concentration camp (kon sən trā´ shən kamp) A large prison death camp (p. 686)

Conclude (kən klüd´) To decide by using facts (p. 380)

Conclusion (kən klü´ zhən) An answer; a decision reached through step-by-step thinking (p. 377)

Confederation (kən fed ə rā´ shən) A union, or group, of states or nations (p. 545)

Conference (kon´ fər əns) A meeting to discuss ideas and plans (p. 672)

Conflict (kon´ flikt) Fighting; not being able to agree on something (p. 760)

Congress of Vienna (kong´ gris ov vē en´ ə) An important meeting in 1814 and 1815 in which leaders restructured Europe (p. 543)

Conquistador (kon kē´ stə dôr) A Spanish conqueror (p. 406)

Conservative (kən sėr´ və tiv) A person who likes the old political order and is against revolution or change (p. 553)

Constitution (kon stə tü´ shən) A body of laws that states the rights of the people and the power of the government (p. 449)

Constitutional monarchy (kon stə tü´ shə nəl mon´ ər kē) A form of government in which a king and queen rule, but there are laws of a democracy to protect the people (p. 443)

Consul (kon´ səl) A Roman leader who served a one-year term in the government (p. 151)

Consumer goods (kən sü´ mər gůds) Products that people buy (p. 647)

Contract (kon´ trakt) A legal agreement (p. 465)

Convention (kən ven´ shən) A group of people who meet to get something done (p. 497)

Core (kôr) The center of something (p. 388)

Coup (kü) A takeover of the government (p. 715)

Courtyard (kôrt´ yärd) A large open area inside the castle walls (p. 237)

Covenant (kuv´ ə nənt) An agreement (p. 38)

Creole (krē´ ōl) A wealthy landowner who had been born in a Spanish colony in the Americas but whose ancestors came from Spain (p. 549)

Cro-Magnon (krō - mag´ nən) The hominid *Homo sapiens*, a direct ancestor of modern humans (p. 14)

Crucify (krü´ sə fī) To hang someone on a cross to die (p. 178)

Crusade (krü sād´) Any of the military journeys taken by Christians to win the Holy Land from the Muslims (p. 229)

a	hat	e	let	ī	ice	ô	order	ů	put	sh	she		a	in about
ā	age	ē	equal	o	hot	oi	oil	ü	rule	th	thin	ə {	e	in taken
ä	far	ėr	term	ō	open	ou	out	ch	child	ŦH	then		i	in pencil
â	care	i	it	ȯ	saw	u	cup	ng	long	zh	measure		o	in lemon
													u	in circus

World History Glossary **829**

Cubit (kyü´ bit) A measurement that is the length of an arm from the end of the middle finger to the elbow (p. 80)

Culture (kul´ chər) The values, attitudes, and customs of a group (p. 5)

Cuneiform (kyü nē´ ə fôrm) The writing invented by Sumerians (p. 29)

Currency (kėr´ ən sē) The form of money a country uses (p. 721)

Cycle (sī´ kəl) The events that keep happening, one after another (p. 97)

Cyrillic alphabet (si ril´ ik al´ fə bet) The alphabet invented by Cyril and Methodius and used to translate the Bible into Slavic languages (p. 255)

Czar (zär) The ruler of Russia; a Russian title that means "caesar" (p. 258)

D

Daimyos (dī´ myos) The highest nobles next to the shogun (p. 311)

D-Day (dē - dā) The Allied invasion of France in 1944 (p. 681)

Declaration of Independence (dek lə rā´ shən ov in di pen´ dəns) A document the American colonists signed in which they declared their freedom from Great Britain (p. 489)

Decline (di klīn´) To lose power (p. 175)

Defensive (di fen´ siv) Protecting oneself rather than attacking others (p. 680)

Deforestation (dē fôr´ ist ā shən) The destruction of forests (p. 798)

Delta (del´ tə) An area of fertile land at the mouth of a river (p. 67)

Democracy (di mok´ rə sē) Rule by the people (p. 123)

Democratic (dem ə krat´ ik) Having to do with a government in which all people have equal rights (p. 630)

Demonstrate (dem´ ən strāt) To join together with other people to protest and march against something (p. 735)

Depression (di presh´ ən) A time of economic collapse when businesses lose money and many people become poor (p. 654)

Desire (di zīr´) To wish for something (p. 101)

Destroyer (di stroi´ ər) A small, fast warship that uses guns and other weapons to protect ships from submarines (p. 676)

Developing country (di vel´ ə ping kun´ trē) A nation that is slowly developing its industry and economy (p. 793)

Dictator (dik´ tā tər) A leader who has full control of laws and rules with force (p. 151)

Direct democracy (də rekt´ di mok´ rə sē) A type of government in which each citizen votes on everything (p. 124)

Disciple (də sī´ pəl) A follower of someone (p. 178)

Displace (dis plas´) To move people from their home or land; to force people to leave their home or land (p. 738)

Divine right (də vīn´ rīt) The belief that God chooses the ruler of a nation (p. 437)

Dominate (dom´ ə nāt) To control (p. 47)

Drama (drä´ mə) A story that is acted out on stage (p. 338)

Drawbridge (drô´ brij) A bridge that can be raised or lowered over a moat (p. 236)

Drought (drout) A long period of time without much rain (p. 760)

Duma (dü´ mə) The Russian parliament (p. 630)

Dynasty (dī´ nə stē) A family that rules a country over a long period of time (p. 106)

E

Economist (i kon´ ə mist) A person who studies money (p. 518)

Economy (i kon´ ə mē) The system of making and trading things (p. 72)

Efficient (ə fish´ ənt) Working well with little loss of time or energy (p. 525)

Elder (el´ dər) An experienced, older person (p. 363)

Elect (i lekt´) A Calvinist term for those whom God has chosen to save (p. 363)

Election (i lek´ shən) An act by which people choose someone or something by voting (p. 748)

Ellipse (i lips´) The shape of an egg (p. 380)

Embargo (em bär´ gō) An act that stops all trade (p. 775)

Émigré (em´ ə grā) A French noble who fled France during the French Revolution (p. 497)

Emperor (em´ pər ər) A person who is ruler of an empire (p. 161)

Empire (em´ pīr) A large area of land ruled by one person (p. 47)

Encomienda (en kōmē´ endə) The Spanish system of forced physical labor (p. 410)

Enforce (en fôrs´) To make sure that people follow the laws and rules (p. 496)

Enlightened (en līt´ nd) The state of knowing the truth (p. 100); having a belief in reasoning; moving away from ignorance (p. 463)

Enlightenment (en līt´ n mənt) A time in European history when thinkers and writers tried to solve the problems of society by using reason (p. 469)

Enslave (en slāv´) To force people to become slaves (p. 126)

Equality (i kwol´ ə tē) The same rights for everyone (p. 496)

Estate (e stāt´) A large piece of land with a house on it (p. 311); a class of people in France (p. 493)

Estates-General (e stāts´ - jen´ ər el) The French governmental body made up of representatives from the three estates (p. 494)

Eternal (i tėr´ nl) Lasting forever (p. 171)

Ethics (eth´ iks) The study of what is right and wrong (p. 135)

Ethnic cleansing (eth´ nik klenz´ ing) The act of getting rid of a group of people because their religion or race is different from the majority group (p. 719)

Excommunicate (ek skə myü´ nə kāt) To say that someone can no longer be a member of a church (p. 358)

Executive (eg zek´ yə tiv) The branch of government that enforces laws (p. 499)

Exile (eg´ zīl) To send someone away from his or her own country and to order this person not to come back (p. 505)

Experimental science (ek sper ə men´ tl sī´ əns) The science that begins with and depends on careful experiments and measurements (p. 383)

Exploration (ek splə rā´ shən) The act of looking around some unknown place (p. 402)

Extinct (ek stingkt´) No longer existing; died out (p. 13)

F

Famine (fam´ ən) A time when crops do not grow and there is no food (p. 37)

Fascism (fash´ iz əm) A form of government in which a dictator and the dictator's party totally control a government (p. 652)

Fast (fast) To give up eating food for a while (p. 273)

Fertile Crescent (fėr´ tl kres´ nt) The area in the Middle East shaped like a quarter moon (crescent) where one of the earliest civilizations developed (p. 35)

Fertilizer (fėr´ tl ī zər) A substance that makes the soil grow crops (p. 760)

Feudalism (fyü´ dl iz əm) A political and military system based on the holding of land (p. 232)

Fief (fēf) The land and peasants who farmed it, which a lord gave to a vassal (p. 232)

a	hat	e	let	ī	ice	ȯ	order	u̇	put	sh	she		ə {	a	in about
ā	age	ē	equal	o	hot	oi	oil	ü	rule	th	thin			e	in taken
ä	far	ėr	term	ō	open	ou	out	ch	child	ᵺ	then			i	in pencil
â	care	i	it	ȯ	saw	u	cup	ng	long	zh	measure			o	in lemon
														u	in circus

Fleet (flēt) A group of ships (p. 128)

Foreign minister (fôr´ ən min´ ə stər) A person who handles one country's dealings with other nations (p. 543)

Formation (fôr mā´ shən) A shape or pattern (p. 436)

Fossil fuel (fos´ əl fyü´ əl) Fuel made from coal, oil, or natural gas (p. 798)

Founded (found´ əd) To have begun a country or city (p. 149)

Free-market economy (frē - mär´ kit i kon´ ə mē) An economy in which manufacturers try to satisfy consumers' wants and needs (p. 793)

French Revolution (french rev ə lü´ shən) The war that the common people of France fought against the king, nobles, and one another to achieve freedom (p. 495)

Fresco (fres´ kō) A painting done in wet plaster on a wall (p. 342)

Front (frunt) The place where armies fight (p. 673)

Fuehrer (fyür´ ər) The name given to Adolf Hitler meaning "leader" (p. 655)

G

Genocide (jen´ ə sīd) The mass murder of a group of people (p. 686)

Gentile (jen´ tīl) A non-Jew (p. 178)

Geometric (jē ə met´ rik) Simple designs made up of straight lines and circles (p. 199)

Geometry (jē om´ ə trē) The study of the measurement of flat and round things (p. 139)

Gestapo (gə stä´ pō) Hitler's secret police (p. 655)

Geography (jē og´ rə fē) The science that deals with land, weather, bodies of water, and plant and animal life (p. 91)

Ghetto (get´ ō) The special parts of cities where the Jewish people were forced to live during World War II (p. 685)

Glacier (glā´ shər) A thick sheet of ice (p. 195)

Glasnost (glas´ nost) A Russian word that means "openness"; under Gorbachev it meant openness in government (p. 714)

Global village (glō´ bəl vil´ ij) The term used to describe the sharing of ideas, cultures, and traditions throughout the world (p. 785)

Global warming (glō´ bəl wôrm ing) The worldwide heating up of Earth, caused in part by human activity (p. 799)

Glorious Revolution (glôr´ ē əs rev ə lü´ shən) The overthrow of James II and the crowning of William and Mary as monarchs of England (p. 442)

Goddess (god´ is) A female god (p. 132)

Gospel (gos´ pəl) One of four books of the New Testament part of the Bible; a word that means "good news" (p. 177)

Gothic (goth´ ik) A style of architecture with thin walls, pointed arches, many windows, and flying buttresses (p. 240)

Govern (guv´ ərn) To rule (p. 50)

Great Depression (grāt di presh´ ən) The worldwide depression that began in the United States in 1929 (p. 659)

Guerilla warfare (gə ril´ ə wôr´ fâr) A kind of fighting that involves small attacks against an enemy or the things it needs and uses (p. 680)

Guillotine (gil´ ə tēn) The machine used to execute people by chopping off their head (p. 499)

H

Habeas Corpus (hā´ bē as kôr´ pəs) A law that says that the government has to charge someone with a crime before putting the person in prison (p. 442)

Hajj (haj) The pilgrimage to Mecca that is a religious duty of all Muslims (p. 275)

Hari-kari (har´ ē - kar´ ē) To kill oneself with a knife (p. 311)

Heavy industry (hev´ ē in´ də strē) The manufacturing of products, such as machines and raw materials, for use in other industries (p. 647)

Hegira (hi jī′ rə) Muhammad's journey from Mecca to Medina; his flight from danger (p. 273)

Hellenism (hel′ ə niz əm) The blend of Western and Eastern cultures made possible by Alexander the Great (p. 138)

Hellenistic Age (hel ə nis′ tik āj) The time between 323 B.C. and 31 B.C., when Greek culture influenced the world (p. 139)

Helot (hel′ ət) A slave in Sparta (p. 126)

Heretic (her′ ə tik) A person who holds a belief that a religious authority thinks is false (p. 354)

Heritage (her′ ə tij) The traditions ancestors have passed down to their descendants (p. 576)

Heroic (hi rō′ ik) Being brave and bold (p. 119)

Hieroglyphics (hī ər ə glif′ iks) A kind of picture writing in Egypt (p. 77)

Hinduism (hin′ dü iz əm) The main religion of India that stresses the belief in the Vedas (p. 97)

Historian (hi stôr′ ē ən) One who is an expert in history (p. 5)

History (his′ tər ē) The record of past events (p. 5)

Holocaust (hol′ ə kȯst) Hitler's killing of many Jews in Europe (p. 685)

Holy Land (hō′ lē land) Palestine; the area where Jesus of Nazareth lived (p. 228)

Homeland (hōm′ land) The land that belongs to a people (p. 177)

Hominids (hom′ ə nids) A group that includes humans and their closest relatives (p. 13)

Hostage (hos′ tij) Someone held against his or her will until certain demands are met (p. 764)

Huguenot (hyü′ gə not) A French Calvinist (p. 364)

Humanism (hyü′ mə niz əm) A belief that human actions, ideas, and works are important (p. 331)

Human rights (hyü′ mən rīts) Political and civil liberties, including the right to life, liberty and pursuit of happiness (p. 769)

Hypothesis (hī poth′ ə sis) An educated guess based on what a scientist already knows (p. 377)

I

Ice Age (īs āj) A period of time when much of Earth and Earth's water was frozen (p. 13)

Icon (ī′ kon) A small picture of a saint or Jesus (p. 253)

Idol (ī′ dl) A statue of a god that people worship (p. 274)

Ikebana (i kā bä′ nə) One Japanese art of arranging flowers (p. 316)

Imperfection (im pər fek′ shən) Something that makes an object or person less than perfect (p. 184)

Imperialism (im pir′ ē ə liz əm) Control or influence a powerful nation has over a weaker nation (p. 593)

Independence (in di pen′ dəns) Being free; being able to govern one's self (p. 130)

Indulgence (in dul′ jəns) A church paper that says that a person will not be punished after death for their sins (p. 355)

Industrialization (in dus′ trē līz ā shən) The process of getting machines to do work (p. 517)

Industrial Revolution (in dus′ trē əl rev ə lü′ shən) An important change in the way people work (p. 515)

Infidel (in′ fə dəl) One who does not believe in the religion of another person (p. 283)

Inflation (in flā′ shən) A quick increase in prices (p. 654)

a	hat	e	let	ī	ice	ȯ	order	u̇ put
ā	age	ē	equal	o	hot	oi	oil	ü rule
ä	far	ér	term	ō	open	ou	out	ch child
â	care	i	it	ȯ	saw	u	cup	ng long

sh	she		a	in about
th	thin	ə	e	in taken
∓ң	then		i	in pencil
zh	measure		o	in lemon
			u	in circus

Influential (in flü en′ shəl) Having the power to change things or to affect what happens (p. 543)

Inherit (in her′ it) To receive money, land, or a title from someone who has died (p. 433)

Inspector (in spek′ tər) A person who looks at how things are being done (p. 55)

Interdependent (in tər di pen′ dənt) Depending on one another (p. 793)

Internal combustion engine (in tėr′ nl kəm bus′ chən en′ jən) An engine that burns gasoline to produce power (p. 533)

International (in tər nash′ ə nəl) Around the world; involving different nations (p. 787)

Internet (in′ tər net) An international computer network (p. 787)

Invade (in vād′) To attack or march into another country (p. 104)

Investment (in vest′ mənt) Money given to a company to use to make more money (p. 759)

Iron Curtain (ī′ ərn kėrt′ n) The invisible boundary between Western Europe and Eastern Europe after World War II (p. 690)

Irrigate (ir′ ə gāt) To bring water to crops (p. 94)

Isolate (ī′ sə lāt) To keep apart or away from others (p. 103)

J

Jacobin (jak′ ə bən) A radical leader during the French Revolution (p. 498)

Jesuit (jesh′ ü it) A member of the Catholic religious order known as the Society of Jesus (p. 367)

Jihad (ji häd′) A holy war fought by Muslims to spread Muhammad's teachings (p. 278)

Joust (joust) A contest between two knights carrying lances and riding horses (p. 237)

Judaism (jü′ dē iz əm) The religion of the Hebrews that Jews practice today (p. 37)

Jury (jür′ ē) A group who listens to court cases and decides the outcome (p. 125)

K

Kabuki (kä bü′ kē) A Japanese play with exaggerated actions (p. 316)

Kaiser (kī′ zər) The emperor of Germany (p. 584)

Kami (ka′ mi) The spirits of the Shinto religion (p. 308)

Kamikaze (kä mi kä′ zē) A Japanese pilot who crashed his plane into an enemy ship and destroyed it and himself (p. 681)

Kiva (kē′ və) A small underground building used for ceremonies (p. 199)

Knighted (nīt′ əd) To be made a knight (p. 234)

Kremlin (krem′ lən) The center of the Russian church and the Russian government (p. 258)

L

Labor union (lā′ bər yü′ nyən) An organized group of workers who try to improve their working conditions (p. 532)

Laborer (lā′ bər ər) A person who does hard work with his or her hands (p. 152)

Laser (lā′ zər) A tool that produces high-energy beams of light (p. 790)

League of Nations (lēg ov nā′ shəns) A group of leaders from many nations who met to solve problems between countries (p. 624)

Legalize (lē′ gə līz) To make lawful (p. 735)

Legislature (lej′ ə slā chər) The lawmaking body of government (p. 499)

Lend-Lease program (lend - lēs prō′ gram) A program developed by Franklin Roosevelt that allowed Britain to borrow war supplies from the United States during World War II (p. 676)

Liberal (lib′ ər əl) A person who wants change; a person who wants to limit the absolute power of kings and nobles and give power to the middle class (p. 553)

Literature (lit′ ər ə chùr) The written works that have lasting influence (p. 260)

Locomotive (lō kə mō′ tiv) A self-propelled vehicle that runs on rails (p. 525)

Logic (loj′ ik) The science of thinking (p. 135)

Lord (lôrd) A king or a noble who gave land to someone (p. 232)

Lottery (lot´ ər ē) A system of picking names from a container so that each person has an equal chance of being chosen (p. 124)

Lutheran Church (lü´ thər ən chèrch) The church established by Martin Luther (p. 358)

M

Maginot line (mazh´ ə nō līn) A line of concrete forts built by France along its border with Germany (p. 675)

Majority (mə jôr´ ə tē) More than half of a group of people or group of things (p. 416)

Maneuver (mə nü´ vər) To move around easily (p. 130)

Manor (man´ ər) The part of a fief that peasants farm to support the lord's family (p. 235)

Manufacturer (man yə fak´ chər ər) A person who hires people to work with machines to make something to sell (p. 520)

Market (mär´ kit) A place to sell goods (p. 593)

Marshall Plan (mär´ shəl plan) The American plan to rebuild Europe after World War II (p. 708)

Massacre (mas´ ə kər) The act of killing many people who are often defenseless (p. 364)

Mass communication (mas kə myü nə kā´ shən) Messages directed at many people (p. 786)

Mass production (mas prə duk´ shən) A way of making large amounts of the same thing in a factory (p. 521)

Masterpiece (mas´ tər pēs) A piece of art that seems almost perfect (p. 303)

Mayflower Compact (mā´ flou ər kom´ pakt) The agreement made by the Pilgrims that set up a form of government for their new colony (p. 417)

Messiah (mə sī´ ə) A king sent by God to save people (p. 177)

Migrant (mī´ grənt) A person who has left one place and moved to another (p. 761)

Militarism (mil´ ə tə riz əm) A nation's warlike policy or practice (p. 581)

Military (mil´ ə ter ē) Having to do with the army (p. 27)

Military state (mil´ ə ter ē stāt) A place in which a leader rules through the military (p. 449)

Militia (mə lish´ ə) A group of people who can be called to military service when something dangerous happens suddenly (p. 643)

Minister (min´ ə stər) A person who can lead a religious ceremony in a Lutheran church (p. 358)

Minority (mə nôr´ ə tē) A small group of like people within a larger group (p. 644)

Minutemen (min´ it men) Colonial soldiers in the Revolutionary War who were ready to fight at any time (p. 488)

Moat (mōt) A dug-out area filled with water that circles a castle (p. 236)

Moderate (mod´ ər it) One who wants to change things little by little (p. 498)

Monarch (mon´ ərk) A king or a queen (p. 429)

Monk (mungk) A member of a religious order (p. 255)

Monsoon (mon sün´) A seasonal wind (p. 92)

Monument (mon´ yə mənt) An object or building honoring a person or event, usually made of stone (p. 16)

Mosque (mosk) A Muslim place of worship (p. 279)

Mother country (muᴛʜ´ ər kun´ trē) A nation that controls a colony (p. 593)

a	hat	e	let	ī	ice	ô	order	u̇	put	sh	she		ə	a	in about
ā	age	ē	equal	o	hot	oi	oil	ü	rule	th	thin			e	in taken
ä	far	ėr	term	ō	open	ou	out	ch	child	ᴛʜ	then			i	in pencil
â	care	i	it	ȯ	saw	u	cup	ng	long	zh	measure			o	in lemon
														u	in circus

Multilingual (mul ti ling′ gwəl) A society in which a number of languages are spoken (p. 575)

Multiracial (mul ti rā′ shəl) Having to do with all people and all races (p. 736)

Mummify (mum′ ə fī) To wrap a dead body in strips of cloth to keep the body from decaying (p. 74)

Munich Pact (myü′ nik pakt) A 1938 agreement between Great Britain and Germany to appease Hitler (p. 673)

Muslim (muz′ ləm) A follower of the religion that Muhammad founded in Arabia in the 7th century (p. 228)

N

Nationalism (nash′ ə nə liz əm) Loyalty to one's country or nation (p. 429)

Nationality (nash ə nal′ ə tē) A group of people who share the same language, culture, and history (p. 546)

Natural resources (nach′ ər əl ri sôrs′ əs) Things—such as coal, ore, and water—that come from nature and help humans (p. 515)

Navigation (nav ə gā′ shən) The science of planning and directing a ship's journey (p. 399)

Negotiate (ni gō′ shē āt) To talk together, make bargains, and agree on something (p. 582)

Neolithic Age (nē ə lith′ ik āj) The age when people made polished stone tools; also called the New Stone Age (p. 15)

Neutral (nü′ trəl) Not choosing either side in a war or argument (p. 502)

Nirvana (nir vä′ nə) A condition of complete emptiness in which a person's soul finds perfect peace (p. 101)

Noble (nō′ bəl) A person of high birth (p. 106)

Noh drama (nō drä′ mə) A Japanese play with only two actors (p. 316)

Nomad (nō′ mad) A person who moves from place to place (p. 15)

Northern Hemisphere (nôr′ ᵺərn hem′ ə sfir) The half of the earth north of the equator (p. 793)

Nuclear (nü′ klē ər) Having to do with atoms or energy from atoms (p. 682)

O

Obelisk (ob′ ə lisk) A tall, pointed stone pillar (p. 77)

Occupy (ok′ yə pī) To take over and stay in a place (p. 680)

Ordinance (ôrd′ n əns) A law set forth by someone in government (p. 555)

Organization (ôr gə nə zā′ shən) A group of people joined together for a common purpose (p. 692)

P

Page (pāj) A young noble who learned to become a knight (p. 232)

Paleolithic Age (pā lē ə lith′ ik āj) The earliest period of human history; called the Old Stone Age (p. 14)

Palestinian Liberation Organization (PLO) (pal ə stin′ ē ən lib′ ə rā shən ôr gə nə zā′ shən) The group of Palestinians dedicated to regaining from Israel their homeland in Palestine (p. 739)

Palisade (pal′ ə sād) A wooden fence (p. 204)

Pan-African Movement (pan - af′ rə kən müv′ mənt) A group that planned ways in which Africans could achieve economic strength and political peace (p. 731)

Papyrus (pə pī′ rəs) A reed from the Nile River used to make paper (p. 80)

Parliament (pär′ lə mənt) The English council or lawmaking assembly (p. 241)

Passive resistance (pas′ iv ri zis′ təns) A nonviolent way of protesting for political and social change (p. 742)

Patriarch (pā′ trē ärk) A leader of the church (p. 253)

Patrician (pə trish′ ən) A Roman who owned land and helped a ruler govern (p. 149)

Patriotic (pā trē ot´ ik) Being loyal toward one's country (p. 127)

Patron (pā´ trən) A person who supports an artist with money (p. 342)

Pax Romana (paks rō mä´ nə) The Roman peace that began during the reign of Augustus Caesar (p. 172)

Peninsula (pə nin´ sə lə) A piece of land surrounded on three sides by water (p. 91)

Peninsular (pə nin´ sə lər) A person who came to South America from Spain and held an important office in the colonial government (p. 549)

Perestroika (per ə stoi´ kə) An economic policy used by Gorbachev to encourage factories to produce the goods people wanted (p. 714)

Pesticide (pes´ tə sīd) A substance that kills the bugs that eat the crops (p. 760)

Petition of Right (pə tish´ ən ov rīt) An English document that brought about more democracy (p. 437)

Pharaoh (fâr´ ō) An Egyptian ruler (p. 70)

Philosopher (fə los´ ə fər) A person who tries to understand the basic nature of knowledge and reality (p. 133)

Photoelectric cell (fō tō i lek´ trik sel) An invention that can produce electricity from light (p. 789)

Physics (fiz´ iks) The science of matter and energy (p. 135)

Pictogram (pik´ tə gram) A figure that tells a story (p. 95)

Pilgrim (pil´ grəm) A person who travels to visit a holy place (p. 228)

Plague (plāg) A disease that spreads from person to person and kills many people (p. 175)

Plantation (plan tā´ shən) A large area of farmland (p. 410)

Plateau (pla tō´) A flat area that rises above the land close by (p. 103)

Plebeian (pli bē´ ən) A common person in Rome who was not wealthy (p. 152)

Policy (pol´ ə sē) A plan that helps a person or a country make a decision (p. 581)

Polis (pō´ ləs) The Greek name for a city-state (p. 122)

Political (pə lit´ ə kəl) Having to do with governing (p. 153)

Politician (pol ə tish´ ən) A government leader (p. 159)

Politics (pol´ ə tiks) The work of government (p. 135)

Pope (pōp) The head of the Roman Catholic Church (p. 261)

Portrait (pôr´ trāt) A drawing of a person (p. 341)

Prehistory (prē his´ tər ē) The time before humans left written records (p. 13)

Prejudice (prej´ ə dis) An unfair and unreasonable opinion (p. 471)

Priest (prēst) A religious leader (p. 28)

Primary source (prī´ mer ē sôrs) A first-hand account of a historical event (p. 5)

Prime minister (prīm min´ ə stər) The leader in some democratic government systems (p. 577)

Prism (priz´ əm) A three-sided object that can be seen through (p. 385)

Proletariat (prō lə târ´ ē ət) The working class according to Marx (p. 560)

Propaganda (prop ə gan´ də) One-sided information meant to change people's thinking (p. 707)

Prophet (prof´ it) A person who speaks for God (p. 177)

Protectorate (prə tek´ tər it) An independent country whose foreign policy is controlled by a major power (p. 600)

a	hat	e	let	ī	ice	ô	order	ù	put	sh	she		ə {	a	in about
ā	age	ē	equal	o	hot	oi	oil	ü	rule	th	thin			e	in taken
ä	far	ėr	term	ō	open	ou	out	ch	child	₮H	then			i	in pencil
â	care	i	it	ȯ	saw	u	cup	ng	long	zh	measure			o	in lemon
														u	in circus

Protestant (prot′ ə stənt) A reformer who protested against the Catholic Church (p. 359)

Province (prov′ əns) An area, such as a state, that is part of a larger country (p. 50)

Purgatory (pėr′ gə tôr ē) A place of suffering after death (p. 356)

Purge (pėrj) To remove from office; to clean by getting rid of unwanted things (p. 648)

Purify (pyür′ ə fī) To make clean (p. 362)

Puritan (pyür′ ə tən) An English Protestant who wanted to purify the Anglican Church (p. 362)

Q

Quarter (kwör′ tər) To provide soldiers with a place to live (p. 485)

Qur'an (kô rän′) The holy book of the Muslims that contains the teachings of Islam; also spelled *Koran* (p. 274)

R

Radical (rad′ ə kəl) One who wants to change things all at once (p. 498)

Radiocarbon dating (rā dē ō kär′ bən dāt′ ing) A way of measuring the radioactivity of historic artifacts to determine how old they are (p. 10)

Raw materials (rȯ mə tir′ ē əls) The materials that are used to make things (p. 527)

Rebel (ri bel′) To disobey or fight against (p. 50)

Rebellion (ri bel′ yən) A fight by people against a government; a struggle for change (p. 330)

Recession (ri sesh′ ən) An economic slowdown (p. 794)

Reform (ri fôrm′) To make something better through change (p. 158)

Reformation (ref ər mā′ shən) A movement that challenged and changed the Catholic religion in Europe (p. 355)

Reformer (ri fôr′ mər) A person who tries to change something (p. 353)

Refugee (ref yə jē′) A person who is forced to flee from his or her country (p. 689)

Regime (ri zhēm′) A form of government (p. 803)

Reich (rīk) The German word for empire (p. 584)

Reichstag (rīk′ stag) The national assembly of the Weimar Republic (p. 655)

Reign (rān) To rule; the period of time a king or queen rules (p. 33)

Reign of Terror (rān ov ter′ ər) The one-year period in French history when radical leaders put many people to death (p. 499)

Reincarnation (rē in kär nā′ shən) The rebirth of the soul into a new body (p. 97)

Relic (rel′ ik) A holy object from the past (p. 251)

Renaissance (ren′ ə säns) Rebirth; a period in European history that focused on being an individual and expanding on creative thoughts and ideas (p. 330)

Renewable (ri nü′ ə bl) Will not run out; will last forever (p. 789)

Reparation (rep ə rā′ shən) Payment for war damage (p. 623)

Repeal (ri pēl′) To do away with a law (p. 486)

Representative (rep ri zen′ tə tiv) A person who speaks and governs for others (p. 151)

Republic (ri pub′ lik) A type of government with no king in which a few people represent, or speak for, everyone (p. 151)

Resistance (ri zis′ təns) Those who opposed the Germans occupying their country (p. 680)

Resolution (rez ə lü′ shən) A formal statement that a governmental body writes (p. 438)

Restoration (res tə rā′ shən) The period that saw monarchy return to England in 1660 (p. 441)

Retire (ri tīr′) To give up one's job (p. 161)

Revolve (ri volv′) To move around something (p. 379)

Ritual (rich′ ü əl) A ceremony (p. 358)

Rival (rī′ vəl) One who tries to outdo another country or person (p. 615)

Romanesque (rō mə nesk´) A style of building that was like what the Romans built with thick walls and arches (p. 240)

Roman Inquisition (rō´ mən in kwə zish´ ən) A Catholic court that inquired into people's religious beliefs (p. 366)

Roundhead (round´ hed) A Puritan who fought for Parliament in the English Civil War (p. 441)

S

Saint (sānt) A person who follows God's ways (p. 251)

Salon (sə lon´) A meeting of artists, writers, and thinkers in a Paris home during the Enlightenment (p. 469)

Salvation (sal vā´ shən) Eternal happiness for one's soul (p. 355)

Samurai (sam´ ů rī) A Japanese warrior who received land from a daimyo and fought for him (p. 311)

Sanitation (san ə tā´ shən) The act of keeping something clean and free from disease (p. 185)

Satellite (sat´ l īt) A nation that is tightly controlled by another nation (p. 690)

Schism (skiz´ əm) A permanent separation (p. 229)

Scientific law (sī ən tif´ ik lȯ) A pattern in nature that someone can predict (p. 386)

Scientific method (sī ən tif´ ik meth´ əd) A set of steps scientists follow for study (p. 377)

Scribe (skrīb) A person from ancient times who could read and write (p. 107)

Scroll (skrōl) A roll of papyrus (p. 80)

Sculptor (skulp´ tər) A person who carves statues (p. 335)

Secondary source (sek´ ən der ē sȯrs) A second-hand account of a historical event; an account written by a person who was not there (p. 5)

Senate (sen´ it) A governing body (p. 149)

Senator (sen´ ə tər) A member of a senate, a governing body (p. 157)

Serf (sėrf) A peasant who was bound to the land and whose life was controlled by the lord of the manor (p. 235)

Shah (shä) An Iranian ruler (p. 763)

Shinto (shin´ tō) The Japanese religion that involves a love of nature and worship of spirits (p. 307)

Shogun (shō´ gun) A Japanese word that means "great general"; a military dictator (p. 310)

Siege (sēj) The act of surrounding a city or fort with an army and cutting off its supplies (p. 582)

Silt (silt) A rich layer of soil left behind after a flood (p. 67)

Slavery (slā´ vər ē) The owning of human beings as property (p. 413)

Slum (slum) An area of a city with too many people, poor housing, and low-income families (p. 761)

Socialism (sō´ shə liz əm) An economic and political theory in which the government owns and controls the major means of production (p. 633)

Socialist (sō´ shə list) A person who wants to end the private ownership of land and factories (p. 558)

Society (sə sī´ ə tē) A group of people whose members live together for the good of all (p. 107)

Solidarity (sol ə dar´ ə tē) The name of the Polish shipbuilder's union that went out on strike in 1980 (p. 718)

Sonnet (son´ it) A 14-line poem about one idea (p. 338)

Soul (sōl) A person's spirit (p. 101)

a	hat	e	let	ī	ice	ȯ	order	ů	put	sh	she		a	in about
ā	age	ē	equal	o	hot	oi	oil	ü	rule	th	thin	ə	e	in taken
ä	far	ér	term	ō	open	ou	out	ch	child	ᵺ	then		i	in pencil
â	care	i	it	ȯ	saw	u	cup	ng	long	zh	measure		o	in lemon
													u	in circus

Southern Hemisphere (suŦH´ ərn hem´ ə sfir) The half of the earth south of the equator (p. 793)

Sphere of influence (sfir ov in´ flü əns) An area in which only one foreign country can trade (p. 598)

Squire (skwīr) A 15-year-old page who learned how to ride a horse and use weapons to become a knight (p. 232)

Standard of living (stan´ dərd ov liv´ ing) A way to judge how well a person or a family is living (p. 629)

Static electricity (stat´ ik i lek tris´ ə tē) The electricity that builds up in something and is produced when one object rubs up against another (p. 388)

Strait (strāt) A narrow strip of water that connects two bigger bodies of water (p. 404)

Strike (strīk) The act of refusing to work until certain demands are met (p. 718)

Stupa (stü´ pə) A large building in which a monk is buried (p. 297)

Subcontinent (sub kon´ tə nənt) A large landmass that is somewhat smaller than a continent (p. 91)

Subsistence farming (səb sis´ təns fär´ ming) A type of farming in which people grow crops mostly for their own use, not to sell (p. 793)

Successor (sək ses´ ər) One who follows another in a position (p. 645)

Superpower (sü´ pər pou ər) A nation that has more power and money than other countries (p. 690)

Swastika (swäs´ tə kə) The Nazi symbol of a cross with its arms bent (p. 654)

Symbol (sim´ bəl) Something that stands for something else (p. 106)

Symphony (sim´ fə nē) A long musical work played by a group of musicians using many different instruments (p. 475)

T

Tactic (tak´ tik) A plan that helps someone win a game or a battle (p. 500)

Tariff (tar´ if) A tax that countries put on goods they import or export (p. 720)

Technology (tek nol´ ə jē) The use of science to do practical things (p. 785)

Temple (tem´ pəl) A place in which to honor gods (p. 28)

Terraced (ter´ ist) Going upward like steps (p. 52)

Terrorist (ter´ ər ist) A person who uses violence to frighten people and to get them to obey (p. 739)

Theory (thir´ ē) A statement that explains why or how something happens (p. 379)

Thesis (thē´ sis) A statement that people argue about or try to prove (p. 356)

Tory (tôr´ ē) A person who supported a strong monarchy in England (p. 442)

Totalitarian state (tō tal ə ter´ ē ən stāt) A government in which a small group totally controls the lives of its country's citizens (p. 648)

Tradition (trə dish´ ən) A custom, idea, or belief handed down from one person to the next (p. 429)

Translate (tran slāt´) To change the words of one language into those of another (p. 31)

Transportation (tran spər tā´ shən) The movement of people and things from one place to another (p. 524)

Treason (trē´ zn) The act of turning against the laws and people of your own country (p. 438)

Treaty of Versailles (trē´ tē ov ver sī´) The treaty that ended World War I (p. 624)

Trench (trench) A long narrow ditch (p. 618)

Tribune (trib´ yün) A representative who protected the rights of the plebeian class (p. 152)

Tribute (trib´ yüt) A payment given to a stronger ruler or nation (p. 48)

Triumvirate (trī um´ vər it) Rule by three people (p. 159)

Truce (trüs) An agreement to stop a war for a time (p. 712)

Truman Doctrine (trü´ mən dok´ trən) President Truman's plan to stop the spread of Communism (p. 707)

Trust territory (trust ter´ ə tôr ē) A territory that the Allies took from the countries that lost World War I and World War II (p. 693)

Tutor (tü´ tər) A teacher who teaches one person at a time (p. 332)

Tyranny (tir´ ə nē) Harsh, absolute power (p. 803)

Tyrant (tī´ rənt) A leader who rules by force and not by law (p. 122)

U

Unify (yü´ nə fī) To bring together as one (p. 55)

Unite (yü nīt´) To bring together as one (p. 69)

United Nations (UN) (yü nī´ tid nā´ shəns) The international organization that works to settle disagreements, improve the way people live, and keep peace around the world (p. 692)

Universe (yü´ nə vėrs) All the planets and stars that exist in space (p. 379)

Unrestricted warfare (un ri strik´ tid wôr´ fâr) War that is not limited to a certain area or boundary (p. 620)

Urbanization (ėr bə nə zā´ shən) Becoming more like a city (p. 761)

Utopia (yü tō´ pē ə) A type of society in which everyone works peacefully together for the good of all (p. 559)

V

Vassal (vas´ əl) A person who received land from a king or noble (p. 232)

Vatican (vat´ ə kən) The home of the pope (p. 343)

Vaulted (vȯl´ təd) A ceiling that is high, arched, and covers a large space (p. 183)

V-E Day (vē´ - ē´ dā) The day the Allies completed their victory in Europe: May 8, 1945; stands for "Victory in Europe Day" (p. 681)

V-J Day (vē´ - jā´ dā) The day the Allies completed their victory in Japan: September 2, 1945; stands for "Victory in Japan Day" (p. 682)

Veche (ve´ chuh) The Russian assembly that represented all free, adult male citizens (p. 257)

Veteran (vet´ ər ən) A person who has served in the military, especially during a war (p. 651)

Veto (vē´ tō) To say no to a decision (p. 151)

Viceroy (vīs´ roi) An official who governs land for the king or queen (p. 410)

Vietnamization (vē et nə miz ā´ shən) The U.S. plan to turn the fighting of the Vietnam War over to the South Vietnamese army (p. 749)

Violate (vī´ ə lāt) To go against (p. 485)

Vision (vizh´ ən) A visit from God's angel (p. 273)

W

Western Hemisphere (wes´ tərn hem´ ə sfir) The half of the earth that includes North and South America (p. 773)

Whig (wig) A person who supported the English Parliament (p. 442)

World Wide Web (wėrld wīd web) A network of information on the Internet open to businesses and individuals (p. 787)

Worldly (wėrld´ lē) Having nothing to do with religion (p. 336)

Worship (wėr´ ship) To honor and praise a god (p. 28)

a	hat	e	let	ī	ice	ȯ	order	u̇	put	sh	she	ə {	a in about
ā	age	ē	equal	o	hot	oi	oil	ü	rule	th	thin		e in taken
ä	far	ėr	term	ō	open	ou	out	ch	child	ŦH	then		i in pencil
â	care	i	it	ȯ	saw	u	cup	ng	long	zh	measure		o in lemon
													u in circus

Index

European, 232–34, 245, 312–13, 323
Japanese, 310–14, 319, 323
vs. nationalism, 429
Fief, defined, 232
Fire, discovery of, 15, 221
Florence, Italy, 334–37, 347
Folsom Point, 196, 217
Formation, defined, 436
Fossil fuels, 811
defined, 798
Founded, defined, 149
Fourteen Points Plan, 623
France
absolute monarchy in, 444–47, 453, 457
African colonies, 733
as American allies, 490, 509, 569
Canada, colonization of, 417, 423, 457
constitutional monarchy in, 496, 509, 569
government, pre-Revolution, 493, 509, 569
imperialism by, 598, 605, 609, 742
maps, 483
Napoleon, 500–506, 509, 545, 548–49, 569
Protestantism in, 365
revolution in, 493–99, 509, 554–59, 565, 569
taxation, 493–94, 569
timelines, 426, 482
women's rights, 507
in WWI, 623, 624, 627, 637
in WWII, 672–74, 681, 697, 701
Franco-Prussian War, 581–82, 587, 609
Franklin, Benjamin, 388, 393, 564
Franks, 261, 267, 323, 432
Frederick II (the Great), 449, 453, 471–72, 479
Frederick Wilhelm IV, 580
Frederick William I, 449
Free-market economy, defined, 793

Fresco, defined, 342
Front, defined, 673
Fuehrer, defined, 655
Fugues, 474, 479

G

Galen, 185, 387
Galilei, Galileo, 382–84, 393, 457
Gandhi, Mohandas, 742–44, 752, 753
Ganges River, 91, 113
Garibaldi, Giuseppe, 578, 587, 609
Gasoline, 533, 534
Gautama, Siddhartha, 100, 113, 221
Genghis Khan, 305, 323
Genocide, defined, 686
Gentile, defined, 178
Geography, defined, 91
Geography Note
Atacama Desert, 407
Ellis Island, 576
Fertile Crescent, 35
Georgia, 716
Wilderness Road, 485
WWII, 674
Geometric, defined, 199
Geometry, defined, 139
George, Lloyd, 623, 624
George III, 488, 489
Germanic tribes, 263, 265, 267
Germany
in Africa, 601
Lutheran church in, 359, 363, 370, 371
maps, 583
Nazis, 654–55, 662, 663, 685–87, 697, 701
reunification of, 718–19, 725
the Second Reich, 582–83
taxation, 370
unification of, 580–84, 587, 609
in WWI, 616, 617, 619–21, 623, 624, 627, 637
in WWII, 669, 670, 672–79, 690, 697, 701
Gestapo, defined, 655

Ghana, 282–83, 291, 323, 733, 753
Ghetto, defined, 685
Gilbert, William, 388, 393
Glacier ,defined, 195
Glasnost, defined, 725
defined, 714
Global village
defined, 785
disease issues, 797
economic development in, 793–96, 811
environmental issues, 798–802, 815
factors affecting, 785–91, 815
global warming, 799, 809
history, lessons from, 807
pollution issues, 798, 811
population issues, 806–7, 811
terrorism, 803–5, 811, 815
timeline, 782
Global warming, 809
defined, 799
Glorious Revolution, 453
defined, 442
Goddess, defined, 132
Gorbachev, Mikhail, 713–15, 724, 725
Gore, Al, 809
Gospel, defined, 177
Gothic, defined, 240
Gothic architecture, 245, 323
Govern, defined, 50
Grand Canal of China, 104
Graph Study, 411, 530
Gravity, 385
Great Britain. *See* England
Great Depression, 670
defined, 659
Great Plains Indians, 205–6, 217
Great Wall of China, 104, 113
Greece
Alexander the Great, 137–39, 143
architecture in, 132
arithmetic in, 139
Athens, 124–25, 134–35, 141, 143
Europe, influence on, 330, 331
government, 122–23, 143

Europe, WWII, 677, 689

European Colonies in the Americas, 419

European Union, 721

Europe, 544

German unification, 583

Hapsburg Land, 434

Independence in Latin America, 552

India, 96

Industrial Revolution in Great Britain, 516

Islam, spread of, 277

Israel, 739

Japan, 309

Korean War, 711

Major World Economic Groups, 795

Mogul Empire, 299

Napoleonic Empire, 504

Phoenicia/Hebrew Kingdoms, 36

Revolutionary War, 490

Rome, 150, 158, 176

Russia, 256

Southeast Asia, 750

Spheres of Influence in China, 597

Trade Routes From Asia to Italy, 336

Vikings, 262

wind currents, Egypt, 68

WWII in the Pacific, 682

Marathon, Battle of, 128, 143

Marcus Aurelius, 175, 189

Maria Theresa, 449, 453, 471, 472, 479

Market, defined, 593

Marshall Plan, 725

defined, 708

Marx, Karl, 559–60, 563, 565, 569, 633

Mary (Queen), 361, 371, 442

Massacre, defined, 364

Mass communication, 786, 811, 815

Mass production, defined, 521

Masterpiece, defined, 303

Mayans, 193, 209–10, 214, 217, 221

Mayflower Compact, 416–17, 423

defined, 417

Mazarin (Cardinal), 444, 447

Mazzini, Giuseppe, 577, 587, 609

Measles, 408, 422

Medes, 50

Medici, Lorenzo de, 335–37, 342, 347

Medicine, 790, 791, 811

Medieval, 227

Menes, King, 69, 85

Mesoamerica

Aztecs, 193, 210–11, 217, 221, 406–7, 423

Incas, 193, 212–13, 215, 217, 221, 407–9, 423

map of, 193

Mayans, 193, 209–10, 214, 217, 221

Olmecs, 193, 208, 217, 221

overview, 208–14, 217, 221

Toltecs, 210, 217

Mesopotamia

Akkadians, 31, 41

Assyrians, 47–50, 61, 221

Babylonians, 32–34, 50–54

Chaldeans, 50–54, 61

map of, 34

overview, 24–25, 41, 221

Persians, 54, 57, 59, 61, 79, 85, 128–30, 143

Phoenicians, 35–36, 40, 41

Sumerians, 27–30, 41, 221

Messiah, defined, 177

Metal coins, 55

Metternich, Prince of Austria, 543–44, 546, 561, 565

Mexico, 457, 552, 565, 569, 773, 779

Michelangelo, 342–44, 347, 457

Microscopes, 389, 393, 457

Middle Ages

architecture, 240, 245

armor, 233, 234

art, 239

castles, 236–37, 245

Crusades, 225, 229–31, 243, 245, 323

Dark Ages, 260, 267

education in, 236, 239–42, 245, 260 (See also Roman Catholic Church)

farming, 236, 245, 323

feudalism, 232–34, 245

legal reforms, 241, 245

literature, 240–41, 245, 260

manors, 235–37, 245

population growth during, 236, 245

timeline, 224

women's rights, 235

Middle East. See also specific countries

conflicts in, 762–67, 779

maps, 45, 757

timelines, 24, 44, 756

Midway, Battle of, 680, 701

Migrant, defined, 761

Militarism, 587, 594, 609, 669

defined, 581

Military, defined, 27

Military state, defined, 449

Militia, defined, 643

Milosevic, Slobodan, 719, 725

Ming dynasty, 306

Minh, Ho Chi, 748, 753

Minister defined, 358

Minoans, 119, 143

Minority, defined, 644

Minutemen defined, 488

Mir, 788

Moat, defined, 236

Moderate, defined, 498

Mogollons, 198, 199, 217

Mogul Empire, 299–300, 319, 323, 596

Mohenjo-Daro, 94, 113

Molière, 475, 479, 569

Monarch, defined, 429

Mongols, 257, 267, 298, 305–6, 319, 323

Monks, 227, 245, 255, 297

Monotheism, 37, 38, 78

Monroe, James, 773

Monsoon, defined, 113

defined, 92

Montesquieu, Baron de, 466–67, 479

Montezuma, 406–7, 421

Pesticide, defined, 760
Peter the Great, 448, 453
Petition of Right, 437–38, 453
Pharaoh, defined, 70
Philip II, 130, 435–36, 453
Philip III, 430
Philip IV, 353
Philosopher, defined, 133
Phoenicians, 35–36, 40–41
Photoelectric cell, defined, 789
Photography, 556
Physics, defined, 135
Pictogram, defined, 95
Pilgrim, defined, 228
Pius VII, 501
Pizarro, Francisco, 407–8, 423, 457
Plague, defined, 175
Plantation, defined, 410
Plateau, defined, 103
Plato, 135, 221
Plebeian, defined, 152
Plymouth colony, 417, 423, 457
Poison gas, 619
Poland, 624, 628, 673, 674, 697, 717, 718
Policy, defined, 581
Polis, defined, 122
Political, defined, 153
Politician, defined, 159
Politics, defined, 135
Pompey the Great, 159, 160
Pope, defined, 261. *See also specific Popes*
Porcelain, 304, 323
Portrait, defined, 341
Portugal, 399–400, 402–3, 413, 414
Pottery, 15, 21, 199, 204
Poverty Point culture, 203
Prehistory, 13–17, 21, 221
Prejudice, defined, 471
Priest, defined, 28
Primary source, 6, 21
    defined, 5
Prime minister, defined, 577
Printing, invention of, 301, 323, 339
Prism, defined, 385
Proletariat, defined, 560

Propaganda, defined, 707
Prophet, defined, 177
Protectorate, defined, 600
Protestant, defined, 359
Province, defined, 50
Prussia, 426, 448–50, 453, 505, 580, 587, 609
Ptolemy, 379, 393
Public education, establishment of, 472, 479
Puerto Rico, 773
Purgatory, defined, 356
Purge, defined, 648
Purify, defined, 362
Puritans, 369, 439–41, 453, 457
    defined, 362
Putin, Vladimir, 715–16
Pyramids, 28
    building instructions, 71
    Egyptian, 70–72, 80, 85, 221
Pythagoras, 140

Q

Quarter, defined, 485
Quartering Act, 486
Qur'an, 274–75, 284, 289, 291, 323
    defined, 274

R

Rabin, Yitzhak, 740, 762
Radical, defined, 498, 553, 565, 569
Radiocarbon dating, 21
    defined, 10
Railroads, 526–28, 537
Raleigh, Sir Walter, 416
Ramps, invention of, 30
Ramses III, 78
Raphael, 344, 347, 457
Raw materials, defined, 527
Reading Strategy
    inferencing, 118, 296, 484, 668
    metacognition, 148, 328, 514, 706
    predicting, 46, 226, 398, 592, 784
    questioning, 26, 194, 376, 574, 758

summarizing, 4, 170, 352, 542, 730
text structure, 66, 250, 428, 614
visualizing, 90, 272, 462, 642
Rebel, defined, 50
Rebellion, defined, 330
Recession, defined, 811
    defined, 794
Red Guard, 643
Reformation, 353–57, 457
    defined, 355
Reformer, defined, 353
Refugee, defined, 689
Regime, defined, 803
Reich, defined, 584
    defined, 583
Reichstag, defined, 655
Reign, defined, 33
Reign of Terror, 499, 509, 553, 569
Reincarnation, defined, 97, 113
Relic, defined, 251
Renaissance
    artists, 341–44, 347, 457
    defined, 330
    Elizabethan Age, 338
    Italy, 334–37, 347
    literature, 338–40
    overview, 330, 347, 457
    reforms, 331–33
    timeline, 326
    women's rights, 332
    writers, 338–40, 457
Renewable, defined, 789
Reparation, defined, 623
Repeal, defined, 486
Representative, defined, 151
Republic, defined, 151
Resistance, defined, 680
Resolution, defined, 438
Restoration, defined, 441
Retire, defined, 161
Revolutionary War, 485–92, 509
Revolve, defined, 379
Richelieu, Armand (Cardinal), 444, 447
Ritual, defined, 358
Rival, defined, 615

Cover Image100/Punchstock; Cover © Robert Glusic/ Corbis; Cover © Reed Kaestner/Corbis; Cover © Steve Estvanik/Corbis; Cover Big Stock Photo; Cover © Blend Images/Superstock; page iii Digital Juice; page iv Digital Juice; page v Digital Juice; page vi Digital Juice; page vii Digital Juice; page viii Digital Juice; page ix Courtesy of Daren Hastings; page x Digital Juice; page xxiv Andres Rodriquez/Shutterstock; page xxvi © Steve Estvanik/ Corbis; page 7 Courtesy of Charmaine Whitman; page 9 Rechitansorin/Big Stock Photo; page 10 Kenneth V. Pilon/Shutterstock; page 11 © Bettmann/CORBIS; page 16 Photodisc/Getty Images; page 19 Photos.com/Jupiter Images; page 20 Vladislav Gurfinkel/Shutterstock; page 28 Dean Conger/National Geographic Image Collection; page 32 Marcel Lewinski; page 37 The Granger Collection, New York; page 39 © Bettmann/ CORBIS; page 40 The Granger Collection, New York; page 49 © Gianni Dagli Orti/CORBIS; page 52 Marcel Lewinski; page 57 The Granger Collection, New York; page 59 The Granger Collection, New York; page 60 Marcel Lewinski; page 70 Steve Vidler/ImageState/ Jupiter Images; page 72 Frederic Neema/Workbook Stock/Jupiter Images; page 73 Vladimir Korostyshevskiy /Shutterstock; page 76 Vova Pomortzeff/Shutterstock; page 77 Marcel Lewinski; page 81a CJ Photography/ Shutterstock; page 81b © SuperStock, Inc./SuperStock; page 83 © Kurt Scholz/SuperStock; page 84 The Granger Collection, New York; page 93 Tony Waltham/ Robert Harding/Jupiter Images; page 95 Kim Winship; page 97 Hitesh Brahmbhatt/Shutterstock; page 98 © SuperStock, Inc./SuperStock; page 100 The Granger Collection, New York; page 103 James Stanfield/ National Geographic Image Collection; page 106 Giraudon/Art Resource, NY; page 109 The Granger Collection, New York; page 111 Scala/Art Resource, NY; page 112 © Stephanie Maze/Woodfin Camp; page 120 © William Hubbell/Woodfin Camp; page 122 Albert Barr/Shutterstock; page 124 © Spiros Tselentis/ SuperStock; page 130 Vanni/Art Resource, NY; page 131 Scala/Art Resource, NY; page 132 Library of Congress; page 134 © SuperStock, Inc./SuperStock; page 135 The Granger Collection, New York; page 137 TAOLMOR/Shutterstock; page 141 Library of Congress; page 142 Scala/Art Resource, NY; page 151 © Bettman/ Corbis; page 154 © SuperStock, Inc./SuperStock; page 157 Library of Congress; page 160 Scala/Art Resource, NY; page 161 The Granger Collection, New York; page 164 Library of Congress; page 171a Pippa West/ Shutterstock; page 171b Richard Nowitz/National Geographic Image Collection; page 172 The Granger Collection, New York; page 175 Danilo Ascione/

Shutterstock; page 181 The Granger Collection, New York; page 184 Photos.com/Jupiter Images; page 187 wikipedia.org; page 188 The Granger Collection, New York; page 196 © Warren Morgan/CORBIS; page 200 IRC/Shutterstock; page 204 The Granger Collection, New York; page 209 Ales Liska/Shutterstock; page 211 Tomasz Otap/Shutterstock; page 212 © John Van Hasselt/CORBIS SYGMA; page 213 Photodisc/Getty Images; page 215 © Bettmann/CORBIS; page 216 SGM/ Stock Connection/Jupiter Images; page 222 © Atlantide Phototravel/Corbis; page 227 Marcel Lewinski; page 230 The Granger Collection, New York; page 231 © SuperStock, Inc./SuperStock; page 233 © Blue Lantern Studio/Corbis; page 235 © Musee Dobree, Nantes, France/Giraudon/The Bridgeman Art Library; page 237 © Castello del Buonconsiglio, Trent, Italy/ Alinari/The Bridgeman Art Library; page 239 © Bettman/Corbis; page 240 © Ray Manley/SuperStock; page 243 The Granger Collection, New York; page 244 The Granger Collection, New York; page 252 © SuperStock, Inc./SuperStock; page 255 © Bettman/ Corbis; page 257 Judy King; page 259 Andrey Armyagov/Shutterstock; page 261 © Bettman/Corbis; page 265 ©Musee Saint-Remi, Reims, France/Giraudon/ The Bridgeman Art Library; page 266 Scala/Art Resource, NY; page 274 © Murat Ayranci/SuperStock; page 280 The Granger Collection, New York; page 283 The Granger Collection, New York; page 285 The Granger Collection, New York; page 289 © Earl & Nazima Kowall/CORBIS; page 290 © SuperStock, Inc./ SuperStock; page 297 © Hubertus Kanus/SuperStock; page 302 The Granger Collection, New York; page 303 © Burstein Collection/CORBIS; page 305 The Granger Collection, New York; page 308 Victoria & Albert Museum, London/Art Resource, NY; page 311 The Granger Collection, New York; page 315 Manfred/ Shutterstock; page 317 © SuperStock, Inc./SuperStock; page 318 Photodisc/Getty Images; page 324 The Granger Collection, New York; page 329 The Granger Collection, New York; page 332 Erich Lessing/Art Resource, NY; page 333 The Granger Collection, New York; page 334 Scala/Art Resource, NY; page 335 The Granger Collection, New York; page 339 © Culver Pictures, Inc./SuperStock; page 340 Erich Lessing/Art Resource, NY; page 341 © SuperStock, Inc./SuperStock; page 342a © Bettman/Corbis; page 342b Scala/Art Resource, NY; page 343 The Granger Collection, New York; page 344 © Bettman/Corbis; page 345 The Granger Collection, New York; page 346 The Granger Collection, New York; page 353 The Granger Collection, New York; page 356 © Bettmann/CORBIS; page 360

The Granger Collection, New York; page 364 The Granger Collection, New York; page 367 The Granger Collection, New York; page 370 © SuperStock, Inc./ SuperStock; page 379 © Bettman/Corbis; page 380 © Bettman/Corbis; page 383 © SuperStock, Inc./ SuperStock; page 385 The Granger Collection, New York; page 389 The Granger Collection, New York; page 390 Judy King; page 391 © National Portrait Gallery/ SuperStock; page 392 The Granger Collection, New York; page 399 © Bettmann/CORBIS; page 401 The Granger Collection, New York; page 408 The Granger Collection, New York; page 411 The Granger Collection, New York; page 414 The Granger Collection, New York; page 416 The Granger Collection, New York; page 417 © SuperStock, Inc./SuperStock; page 418 © SuperStock, Inc./SuperStock; page 421 Michel Zabe/Art Resource, NY; page 422 © Newberry Library/SuperStock; page 430 © Peter Willi/SuperStock; page 433 The Granger Collection, New York; page 435 The Granger Collection, New York; page 438 The Granger Collection, New York; page 439 The Granger Collection, New York; page 441 © National Portrait Gallery/SuperStock; page 444 The Granger Collection, New York; page 445 © Peter Willi/ SuperStock; page 447 © National Gallery Collection; By kind permission of the Trustees of the National Gallery, London/CORBIS; page 449 The Granger Collection, New York; page 451 The Granger Collection, New York; page 452 © Christie's Images/SuperStock; page 458 © Christie's Images/CORBIS; page 465 The Granger Collection, New York; page 466 The Granger Collection, New York; page 469 The Granger Collection, New York; page 470 Bridgeman-Giraudon/Art Resource, NY; page 472 © Christie's Images/SuperStock; page 474 The Granger Collection, New York; page 475 The Granger Collection, New York; page 477 The Granger Collection, New York; page 478 Tate Gallery, London/Art Resource, NY; page 486 © Bettmann/CORBIS; page 487 The Granger Collection, New York; page 488 The Granger Collection, New York; page 489 The Granger Collection, New York; page 494 © SuperStock, Inc./SuperStock; page 497 The Granger Collection, New York; page 498 © SuperStock, Inc./SuperStock; page 500 © Bettmann/ CORBIS; page 503 Photo Credit: Scala/Art Resource, NY; page 507 ©Musee de la Ville de Paris, Musee Carnavalet, Paris, France/Giraudon/The Bridgeman Art Library; page 508 Photo Credit: Erich Lessing/Art Resource, NY; page 517 The Granger Collection, New York; page 519 The Granger Collection, New York; page 520 © Bettman/Corbis; page 522 The Art Archive/JFB; page 526 The Granger Collection, New York; page 531 The Granger Collection, New York; page 533a © Culver Pictures, Inc./SuperStock; page 533b © SuperStock, Inc./SuperStock; page 534 © Culver Pictures, Inc./ SuperStock; page 535 The Granger Collection, New York; page 536 © National Portrait Gallery/SuperStock;

page 548 The Granger Collection, New York; page 549 © Bettmann/CORBIS; page 550 The Granger Collection, New York; page 554 The Art Archive/Saint Sulpice Seminary Paris/Dagli Orti; page 555 Giraudon/ Art Resource, NY; page 557 The Granger Collection, New York; page 558 The Art Archive/Musée National de la voiture et du tourisme Compiègne/Dagli Orti; page 560 Library of Congress; page 563 The Granger Collection, New York; page 564 The Granger Collection, New York; page 570 © Swim Ink 2, LLC/CORBIS; page 578 The Granger Collection, New York; page 584 The Granger Collection, New York; page 585 The Granger Collection, New York; page 586 Erich Lessing/Art Resource, NY; page 594 The Granger Collection, New York; page 596 The Granger Collection, New York; page 600 The Granger Collection, New York; page 602 © Stapleton Collection/Corbis; page 603 © SuperStock, Inc./SuperStock; page 604 The Granger Collection, New York; page 610 © Swim Ink 2, LLC/CORBIS; page 615 The Granger Collection, New York; page 617 © Bettmann/CORBIS; page 618 © Bettmann/CORBIS; page 619 The Granger Collection, New York; page 624 © Woodfin Camp; page 627 © Bettmann/CORBIS; page 629 The Granger Collection, New York; page 630 © Jaime Abecasis/SuperStock; page 631 © Culver Pictures, Inc./SuperStock; page 632 © Bettmann/ CORBIS; page 635 © Hulton-Deutsch Collection/ CORBIS; page 636 © SuperStock, Inc./SuperStock; page 643 Library of Congress; page 645 Library of Congress; page 647 The Granger Collection, New York; page 648 © Bettman/Corbis; page 651 Library of Congress; page 656 Library of Congress; page 659 The Granger Collection, New York; page 661 TAOMOR/Shutterstock; page 662 Library of Congress; page 670 © Bettmann/ CORBIS; page 673 © Bettmann/CORBIS; page 678 The Granger Collection, New York; page 682 Library of Congress; page 683 © Woodfin Camp; page 685 © Reuters/Corbis; page 688 AP Images; page 695 © Bettman/Corbis; page 696 © Bettman/Corbis; page 700 The Granger Collection, New York; page 702 Volker Kreinacke/Shutterstock; page 707 © Bettmann/ CORBIS; page 710 © Bettmann/CORBIS; page 713 © Dean Conger/CORBIS; page 714 © Larry Downing/ Woodfin Camp; page 715 © Reuters/CORBIS; page 718 © Alexandra Avakian/Woodfin Camp; page 719 © Reuters/CORBIS; page 723 Carsten Medom Madsen/ Shutterstock; page 724 © Gideon Mendel/CORBIS; page 733 © Bettmann/CORBIS; page 734 © Jason Laure/ Woodfin Camp; page 735 © David Modell/Katz/ Woodfin Camp; page 738 © SuperStock, Inc./ SuperStock; page 749 © William Strode/Woodfin Camp; page 751 © Peter Turnley/CORBIS; page 752 Library of Congress; page 759 © Mike Goldwater/ Alamy; page 763 © Bettmann/CORBIS; page 765 © John Ficora/Woodfin Camp; page 768 Kwan, Heungman/

Index Stock Imagery/Jupiter Images; page 770 © Reuters/CORBIS; page 772 © SuperStock, Inc./SuperStock; page 777 Martial Trezzini/AP Images; page 778 http://visibleearth.nasa.gov/; page 785 © George Hunter/SuperStock; page 789 © Chuck Nacke/Woodfin Camp; page 791 © Tony Linck/SuperStock; page 792 © Mike Yamashita/Woodfin Camp; page 796 Nikolai Okhitin/iStock Photo; page 800 © SuperStock, Inc./SuperStock; page 801 David Hyde/Shutterstock; page 807 Juergen Sack/iStock Photo; page 809 © Jeff Morgan Hay on Wye/Alamy; page 810 Jiri Castka/ Shutterstock

Staff Credits

Rosalyn Arcilla, Mel Benzinger, Karen Blonigen, Carol Bowling, Laura Chadwick, Nancy Condon, Barb Drewlo, Marti Erding, Daren Hastings, Brian Holl, Patrick Keithahn, Mary Kaye Kuzma, Daniel Milowski, Stephanie Morstad, Carol Nelson, Carrie O'Connor, Julie Theisen, LeAnn Velde, Mike Vineski, Amber Wegwerth, Susan Weinlick

Acknowledgments

Grateful acknowledgment is made to the following for copyrighted material:

Andreas Ramos
"A Personal Account of the Fall of the Berlin Wall: The 11th and 12th of November 1989" by Andreas Ramos from www.andreas.com/berlin.html. Used by permission of Andreas Ramos.

Estate of Moses Hadas
"How to Get Elected in Rome" by Moses Hadas from *A History of Rome.* Courtesy of the Estate of Moses Hadas.

Liveright Publishing Corporation
"The Travels of Marco Polo" by Manuel Komroff from *The Travels of Marco Polo.* Copyright © 1926 by Boni & Liveright, Inc., renewed 1953 by Manuel Komroff. Copyright © 1930 by Horace Liveright, Inc., renewed © 1958 by Manuel Komroff. Used by permission of Liveright Publishing Corporation.

New Directions Publishing Corporation
"The Next War" by Wilfred Owen from *The Collected Poems of Wilfred Owen,* copyright © 1963 by Chatto & Windus, Ltd. Reprinted by permission of New Directions Publishing Corp.

Norwegian Nobel Institute
"Nobel Lecture given by The Nobel Peace Prize Laureate 2006, Muhammad Yunus (Oslo, December 10, 2006)" from Nobelpeaceprize.Org/Eng_Lect_2006b. Copyright © Nobel Foundation. Reprinted with permission from the Norwegian Nobel Institute.

Pearson Prentice Hall, Inc.
"A Manchester Housewife's Weekly Budget in 1833" by Bernard from *Reading In European History.* Copyright © 1958. Used by permission of Pearson Education College Division.

Penguin Group U.K.
60 line (approximately 217 words) (pp. 62-63) from *The Bhagavad Gita,* translated by Juan Mascaro (Penguin Classics, 1962) Copyright © Juan Mascaro, 1962. "Pericles' Funeral Oration" (approximately 3,355 words) by Thucydides from *The History of The Peloponnesian War,* translated by Rex Warner, with an introduction and notes by M.I. Finley (Penguin Classics 1954, Revised edition 1972.) Translation copyright © Rex Warner, 1954. Introduction and Appendices copyright © M.I. Finley, 1972. Used by permission of Penguin Group U.K.

Random House, Inc.
"What is Enlightenment" by Immanuel Kant from *The Philosophy of Kant,* translated by Carl Friedrich, copyright © 1949 by Random House, Inc. Used by permission of Random House, Inc.

Roman Ghirshman, Vladimir Minorsky and Ramesh Sanghvi
"It's Hard to be Humble" by Roman Ghirshman, Vladimir Minorsky and Ramesh Sanghvi from Persia, *The Immortal Kingdom.*

University of Texas Press
"Royal Commentaries of the Incas and General History of Peru" by Garcilaso de la Vega from *Royal Commentaries of The Incas And General History of Peru,* translated by Harold V. Livermore, Copyright © 1966. Used by permission of The University of Texas Press.

University of Utah Press
"The Capture and Death of Moctezuma" translated by Arthur J.O. Anderson and Charles E. Dibble from *The War of Conquest: How It Was Waged Here In Mexico.*

Westminster John Knox Press
"John Calvin's Strict Code of Conduct" translated by Ford Lewis Battles, edited by John T. McNeill from *Institutes of The Christian Religion,* Vol. Xx. Used by permission of Westminster John Knox Press.

Note: Every effort has been made to locate the copyright owner of material reproduced in this component. Omissions brought to our attention will be corrected in subsequent editions.

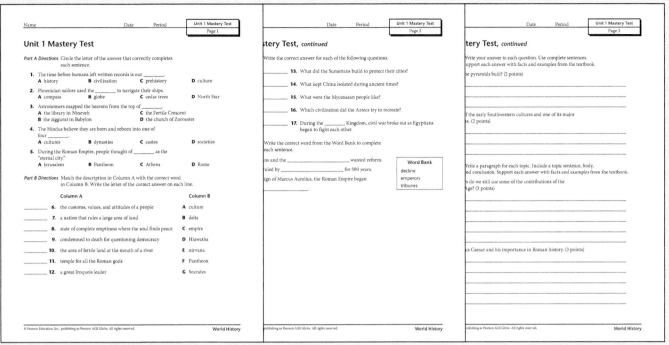

Unit 1 Mastery Test Page 1

Name _____ Date _____ Period _____ **Unit 1 Mastery Test** Page 1

Unit 1 Mastery Test

Part A Directions Circle the letter of the answer that correctly completes each sentence.

1. The time before humans left written records is our _____.
   A history   B civilization   C prehistory   D culture

2. Phoenician sailors used the _____ to navigate their ships.
   A compass   B globe   C cedar trees   D North Star

3. Astronomers mapped the heavens from the top of _____.
   A the library in Nineveh   C the Fertile Crescent
   B the ziggurat in Babylon   D the church of Zoroaster

4. The Hindus believe they are born and reborn into one of four _____.
   A cultures   B dynasties   C castes   D societies

5. During the Roman Empire, people thought of _____ as the "eternal city."
   A Jerusalem   B Pantheon   C Athens   D Rome

Part B Directions Match the description in Column A with the correct word in Column B. Write the letter of the correct answer on each line.

Column A   Column B

_____ 6. the customs, values, and attitudes of a people   A culture

_____ 7. a nation that rules a large area of land   B delta

_____ 8. state of complete emptiness where the soul finds peace   C empire

_____ 9. condemned to death for questioning democracy   D Hiawatha

_____ 10. the area of fertile land at the mouth of a river   E nirvana

_____ 11. temple for all the Roman gods   F Pantheon

_____ 12. a great Iroquois leader   G Socrates

© Pearson Education, Inc., publishing as Pearson AGS Globe. All rights reserved.   World History

Unit 1 Mastery Test Page 2

... Date _____ Period _____ **Unit 1 Mastery Test** Page 2

...stery Test, *continued*

Write the correct answer for each of the following questions.

_____ 13. What did the Sumerians build to protect their cities?

_____ 14. What kept China isolated during ancient times?

_____ 15. What were the Mycenaean people like?

_____ 16. Which civilization did the Aztecs try to recreate?

_____ 17. During the _____ Kingdom, civil war broke out as Egyptians began to fight each other.

Write the correct word from the Word Bank to complete each sentence.

...ans and the _____ wanted reform.

...ruled by _____ for 500 years.

...ign of Marcus Aurelius, the Roman Empire began

Word Bank
decline
emperors
tribunes

...ublishing as Pearson AGS Globe. All rights reserved.   World History

Unit 1 Mastery Test Page 3

... Date _____ Period _____ **Unit 1 Mastery Test** Page 3

...tery Test, *continued*

Write your answer to each question. Use complete sentences. ...upport each answer with facts and examples from the textbook.

...he pyramids built? (2 points)

...f the early Southwestern cultures and one of its major ...s. (2 points)

Write a paragraph for each topic. Include a topic sentence, body, ...nd conclusion. Support each answer with facts and examples from the textbook.

...s do we still use some of the contributions of the ...ge? (3 points)

...us Caesar and his importance in Roman history. (3 points)

...ublishing as Pearson AGS Globe. All rights reserved.   World History

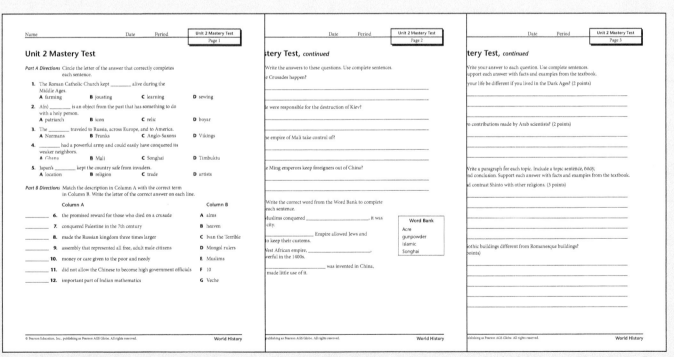

Unit 2 Mastery Test Page 1

Name _____ Date _____ Period _____ **Unit 2 Mastery Test** Page 1

Unit 2 Mastery Test

Part A Directions Circle the letter of the answer that correctly completes each sentence.

1. The Roman Catholic Church kept _____ alive during the Middle Ages.
   A farming   B jousting   C learning   D sewing

2. A(n) _____ is an object from the past that has something to do with a holy person.
   A patriarch   B icon   C relic   D boyar

3. The _____ traveled to Russia, across Europe, and to America.
   A Normans   B Franks   C Anglo-Saxons   D Vikings

4. _____ had a powerful army and could easily have conquered its weaker neighbors.
   A Ghana   B Mali   C Songhai   D Timbuktu

5. Japan's _____ kept the country safe from invaders.
   A location   B religion   C trade   D artists

Part B Directions Match the description in Column A with the correct term in Column B. Write the letter of the correct answer on each line.

Column A   Column B

_____ 6. the promised reward for those who died on a crusade   A alms

_____ 7. conquered Palestine in the 7th century   B heaven

_____ 8. made the Russian kingdom three times larger   C Ivan the Terrible

_____ 9. assembly that represented all free, adult male citizens   D Mongol rulers

_____ 10. money or care given to the poor and needy   E Muslims

_____ 11. did not allow the Chinese to become high government officials   F 10

_____ 12. important part of Indian mathematics   G Veche

© Pearson Education, Inc., publishing as Pearson AGS Globe. All rights reserved.   World History

Unit 2 Mastery Test Page 2

... Date _____ Period _____ **Unit 2 Mastery Test** Page 2

...stery Test, *continued*

Write the answers to these questions. Use complete sentences.

...e Crusades happen?

...e were responsible for the destruction of Kiev?

...he empire of Mali take control of?

...e Ming emperors keep foreigners out of China?

Write the correct word from the Word Bank to complete each sentence.

...Muslims conquered _____, it was ...city.

..._____ Empire allowed Jews and ...to keep their customs.

...West African empire, _____, ...werful in the 1400s.

..._____ was invented in China, ...made little use of it.

Word Bank
Acre
gunpowder
Islamic
Songhai

...ublishing as Pearson AGS Globe. All rights reserved.   World History

Unit 2 Mastery Test Page 3

... Date _____ Period _____ **Unit 2 Mastery Test** Page 3

...tery Test, *continued*

Write your answer to each question. Use complete sentences. ...upport each answer with facts and examples from the textbook.

...your life be different if you lived in the Dark Ages? (2 points)

...o contributions made by Arab scientists? (2 points)

Write a paragraph for each topic. Include a topic sentence, body, ...nd conclusion. Support each answer with facts and examples from the textbook.

...d contrast Shinto with other religions. (3 points)

...othic buildings different from Romanesque buildings? ...points)

...ublishing as Pearson AGS Globe. All rights reserved.   World History

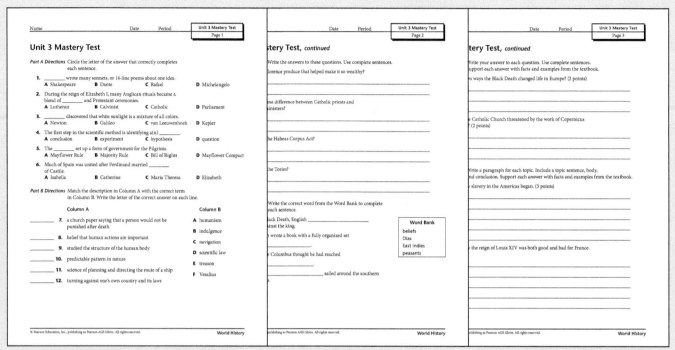

Unit 3 Mastery Test Page 1 Unit 3 Mastery Test Page 2 Unit 3 Mastery Test Page 3

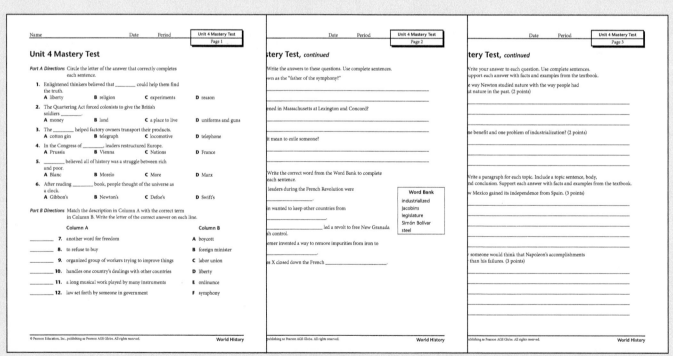

Unit 4 Mastery Test Page 1 Unit 4 Mastery Test Page 2 Unit 4 Mastery Test Page 3

Unit 5 Mastery Test

Part A Directions Circle the letter of the answer that correctly completes each sentence.

1. The German _____ was weak, and it included 38 states and their rulers.
   A Alliance   B Unity   C Independence   D Confederation

2. Garibaldi was involved with the _____ of Italy.
   A unification   B surrender   C music   D religion

3. A private company ruled _____ before the British government took control of it in 1858.
   A Italy   B India   C Cambodia   D Belgium

4. Mother countries used their colonies as _____ bases.
   A religious   B democratic   C government   D military

5. Japanese leaders created a _____ based on the German system developed by Bismarck.
   A company   B constitution   C legislature   D hospital

Part B Directions Match the description in Column A with the correct term in Column B. Write the letter of the correct answer on each line.

Column A

_____ 6. planned how to get France and Austria to fight each other and leave Italy alone

_____ 7. was important to Britain because it made travel to the Far East easier

_____ 8. controlled by Austria, France, and Spain after 1814

_____ 9. the home of the pope

_____ 10. an area in which only one foreign country can trade

_____ 11. taken over by the British to keep the French from expanding westward

Column B

A Burma
B Camillo di Cavour
C Italian provinces
D sphere of influence
E Suez Canal
F Vatican City

World History

Unit 5 Mastery Test Page 1

...stery Test, *continued*

Write the answers to these questions. Use complete sentences.

...itage?

...militarism important to the unification of Germany?

...des did Europeans have toward African people and Asian people?

...owerful nations divide China into spheres of influence?

...n did Sardinia take in 1848?

Write the correct word from the Word Bank to complete each sentence.

...Franco-Prussian War, _____ gave ... that were near Germany.

...n is a feeling of loyalty to one's _____.

...blished the largest European empire

...factories in Africa and Asia supplied cheap goods to _____

Word Bank
Africa
country
Europe
France

World History

Unit 5 Mastery Test Page 2

...tery Test, *continued*

Write your answer to each question. Use complete sentences. ...upport each answer with facts and examples from the textbook.

...to von Bismarck lie about? What was the result of his lie? (2 points)

...tatue of Giuseppe Garibaldi in New York City. What did ... that made people want to honor him with a statue? (2 points)

Write a paragraph for each topic. Include a topic sentence, body, and conclusion. Support each answer with facts and examples from the textbook.

...erialism? What is the connection between industrialism ...lism? Explain. (3 points)

...meaning of this expression: "The sun never sets on the ...re." (3 points)

World History

Unit 5 Mastery Test Page 3

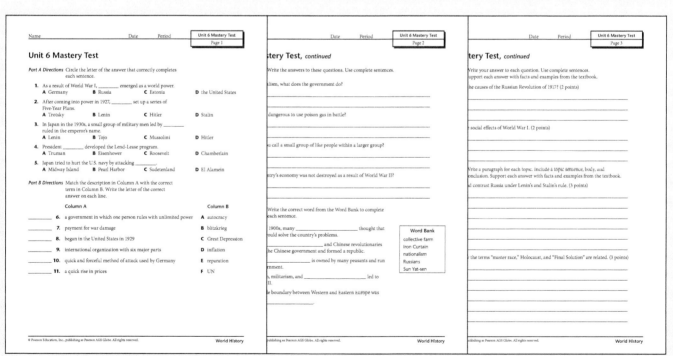

Unit 6 Mastery Test

Part A Directions Circle the letter of the answer that correctly completes each sentence.

1. As a result of World War I, _____ emerged as a world power.
   A Germany   B Russia   C Estonia   D the United States

2. After coming into power in 1927, _____ set up a series of Five-Year Plans.
   A Trotsky   B Lenin   C Hitler   D Stalin

3. In Japan in the 1930s, a small group of military men led by _____ ruled in the emperor's name.
   A Lenin   B Tojo   C Mussolini   D Hitler

4. President _____ developed the Lend-Lease program.
   A Truman   B Eisenhower   C Roosevelt   D Chamberlain

5. Japan tried to hurt the U.S. navy by attacking _____.
   A Midway Island   B Pearl Harbor   C Sudetenland   D El Alamein

Part B Directions Match the description in Column A with the correct term in Column B. Write the letter of the correct answer on each line.

Column A

_____ 6. a government in which one person rules with unlimited power

_____ 7. payment for war damage

_____ 8. began in the United States in 1929

_____ 9. international organization with six major parts

_____ 10. quick and forceful method of attack used by Germany

_____ 11. a quick rise in prices

Column B

A autocracy
B blitzkrieg
C Great Depression
D inflation
E reparation
F UN

World History

Unit 6 Mastery Test Page 1

...stery Test, *continued*

Write the answers to these questions. Use complete sentences.

...lism, what does the government do?

...dangerous to use poison gas in battle?

...u call a small group of like people within a larger group?

...ntry's economy was not destroyed as a result of World War II?

Write the correct word from the Word Bank to complete each sentence.

...1900s, many _____ thought that ...ould solve the country's problems.

...and Chinese revolutionaries ...he Chinese government and formed a republic.

...is owned by many peasants and run ...rnment.

...n, militarism, and _____ led to ...II.

...e boundary between Western and Eastern Europe was

Word Bank
collective farm
iron Curtain
nationalism
Russians
Sun Yat-sen

World History

Unit 6 Mastery Test Page 2

...tery Test, *continued*

Write your answer to each question. Use complete sentences. ...upport each answer with facts and examples from the textbook.

...he causes of the Russian Revolution of 1917? (2 points)

...e social effects of World War I. (2 points)

Write a paragraph for each topic. Include a topic sentence, body, and conclusion. Support each answer with facts and examples from the textbook.

...d contrast Russia under Lenin's and Stalin's rule. (3 points)

...the terms "master race," Holocaust, and "Final Solution" are related. (3 points)

World History

Unit 6 Mastery Test Page 3

Unit 7 Mastery Test Page 1

Name _____ Date _____ Period _____

Unit 7 Mastery Test — Page 1

Unit 7 Mastery Test

Part A Directions Circle the letter of the answer that correctly completes each sentence.

1. Soon after World War II, American forces occupied _____.
   A Kosovo   B South Korea   C Hungary   D the Soviet Union

2. The Soviet leader who took power in 1985 was _____.
   A Mikhail Gorbachev   B Vladimir Putin   C Joseph Stalin   D Nikita Khrushchev

3. _____ warfare uses surprise attacks.
   A Total   B Defensive   C Apartheid   D Guerilla

4. _____ permitted privately owned businesses in China.
   A Evo Morales   B Deng Xiaoping   C Fidel Castro   D Saddam Hussein

5. The _____ is an organization that gives money to needy members.
   A NAFTA   B IMF   C UN   D CIA

6. Something that involves different nations is _____.
   A photoelectric   B developing   C subsistence   D international

Part B Directions Match the description in Column A with the correct term in Column B. Write the letter of the correct answer on each line.

Column A	Column B
_____ 7. an agreement to stop a war for a time	A African National Congress
_____ 8. A bombing in 1976 by this group turned the protest against apartheid into a riot.	B Iraq
	C Mao Zedong
_____ 9. He led the Communist forces in a fight to control China.	D pollution
_____ 10. the country that invaded Kuwait in 1990	E truce
_____ 11. makes the air, water, or land unclean and unhealthy	

World History

Unit 7 Mastery Test Page 2

Date _____ Period _____ Unit 7 Mastery Test — Page 2

...stery Test, *continued*

...Write the answers to these questions. Use complete sentences.

...ems helped cause the collapse of the Soviet Union?

_____

...o of people wanted to regain their homeland from Israel?

_____

...apan's government help the country's economy?

_____

...many people in Africa starved?

_____

...Write the correct word from the Word Bank to complete each sentence.

..._____ is a largely Muslim area in ...rn Russia.

...th and the French divided _____ ...nas.

...s of _____ happens when an area ...ore like a city.

...hink global warming could change the _____.

...ce farming, people grow _____ ...m use.

Word Bank
Chechnya
crops
temperature
urbanization
Vietnam

World History

Unit 7 Mastery Test Page 3

Date _____ Period _____ Unit 7 Mastery Test — Page 3

...tery Test, *continued*

...Write your answer to each question. Use complete sentences. ...upport each answer with facts and examples from the textbook.

... Chinese civil war end? (2 points)

_____

...e no trade between Cuba and the United States? (2 points)

_____

...Write a paragraph for each topic. Include a topic sentence, body, ...nd conclusion. Support each answer with facts and examples from the textbook.

...r terrorism has changed the world. (3 points)

_____

...meaning of this statement: "Hungary cut a hole in the ...h." (3 points)

_____

World History

Midterm Mastery Test

Part A Directions Circle the letter of the answer that correctly completes
each sentence or answers each question.

1. The earliest period of human history is the _____.
   A Bronze Age   **B** Paleolithic Age   **C** Neolithic Age   **D** Cro-Magnon Age

2. Phoenicians were known as successful _____.
   A farmers   **B** lawmakers   **C** pottery-makers   **D** sea traders

3. The Egyptian civilization developed in the valley of the _____ River.
   A Indus   **B** Cairo   **C** Nile   **D** Tiber

4. The _____ was built to protect China from invaders.
   A Great Wall   **B** Huang He   **C** Grand Canal   **D** Khyber Pass

5. Which group assassinated Julius Caesar?
   A Etruscans   **B** tribunes   **C** plebeians   **D** senators

6. What kind of evidence did the "bone pit" bones provide?
   A how long American Indians had lived in North America
   B how the first Americans set up their communities
   C how American Indians farmed their land
   D how the first Americans reached North America

7. _____ made the Russian kingdom three times larger.
   A William the Conqueror   **C** Ivan the Terrible
   B Ivan the Great   **D** Justinian

8. The monk _____ preached against the Renaissance.
   A Miguel de Cervantes **B** Michelangelo   **C** Shakespeare   **D** Savonarola

9. Copernicus believed that the planets revolved around the _____.
   A moon   **B** sun   **C** universe   **D** earth

10. Hernando Cortés conquered the _____.
   A Aztecs   **B** Incas   **C** Portuguese   **D** French

World History

Midterm Mastery Test Page 1

Midterm Mastery Test, *continued*

Part B Directions Write the correct term from the Word Bank to complete each sentence.

11. Scientists use radiocarbon dating to figure out the age
   of _____.

12. Assyrians developed an empire in _____.

13. The Greek city-state, _____,
   created democracy.

14. _____ ruled during the "Golden Age
   of Rome."

15. _____ conquered Palestine in the
   7th century.

16. William, the Duke of Normandy, became king of England after the
   _____.

17. Ghana became powerful because it controlled the
   _____ trade.

18. The *Pietà* is a famous sculpture created by _____.

19. The Edict of Nantes gave Protestant _____
   more political and religious rights.

20. A _____ was a person who supported the
   English Parliament.

Word Bank
artifacts
Athens
Augustus Caesar
Battle of Hastings
gold
Huguenots
Mesopotamia
Michelangelo
Muslims
Whig

Part C Directions Write the answer to these questions. Use complete sentences.

21. What are two facts about life in Sumer?

22. Why were the changes that happened during the Shang Dynasty important to later dynasties?

23. How did aqueducts and sewers improve the lives of Romans?

24. What is the fifth pillar of Islam, the Hajj?

25. How did Frederick the Great expand Prussia's territory?

World History

Midterm Mastery Test Page 2

Midterm Mastery Test, *continued*

Part D Directions Match the description in Column A with the correct term in
Column B for each set. Write the letter of the correct answer on each line.

Column A	Column B
26. This calendar has dates that contain the letters B.C. or A.D.	**A** Anasazi
27. These people conquered the Assyrians.	**B** caravans
28. These groups of traders traveled together across the desert.	**C** Chaldeans
29. This was the Minoan city discovered by Arthur Evans.	**D** Christian
30. Marc Antony formed an alliance with this Egyptian leader.	**E** Cleopatra
31. He was the first Christian emperor of Rome.	**F** Constantine
32. This North American civilization built a "wagon wheel" community.	**G** crusade
33. Pope Urban II called for this against the Muslims.	**H** Knossos

Column A	Column B
34. This leader was known as the "Emperor of the Romans."	**I** Calvin
35. This kind of person had the most political power in Japanese feudalism.	**J** Charlemagne
36. This leader ruled England when Shakespeare lived.	**K** eastern
37. This religious leader taught that people are full of sin when they are born.	**L** Elizabeth I
38. This scientist disproved Aristotle and Ptolemy.	**M** Kepler
39. The French settled in this part of Canada.	**N** Restoration
40. This describes the period when Charles II ruled.	**O** shogun

World History

Midterm Mastery Test Page 3

Midterm Mastery Test, *continued*

Part E Directions Write your answer to each question. Use complete sentences.
Support each answer with facts and examples from the textbook.

41. How do you think the Assyrian rebels felt when the empire fell?
   Why? (2 points)

42. Do you agree with Plato that the rulers of a country should be philosophers?
   Why or why not? (2 points)

Part F Directions Write a paragraph for each topic. Include a topic
sentence, body, and conclusion. Support each answer
with facts and examples from the textbook.

43. Explain how Henry VIII became the head of the Anglican Church. (3 points)

44. Explain how slavery began in the Americas. (3 points)

World History

Midterm Mastery Test Page 4

Final Mastery Test

Final Mastery Test

Part A Directions Write the correct term from the Word Bank to complete each sentence.

1. Scientists called _____ study the beginnings and the behavior of people.

2. The Chinese teacher, _____, taught that a ruler should govern by good example.

3. An early Southwestern culture known as the _____ built canals to provide water for crops and for drinking.

4. In the T'ang dynasty, China had a ruling class made up of _____.

5. Catherine the Great improved education and allowed more _____ freedom.

6. In 1774, representatives from 12 colonies agreed to _____ British goods.

7. Henry Bessemer invented a way to remove impurities from _____ to make steel.

8. Mexican priest _____ helped lead Mexico to independence.

9. During the _____ of Paris, the city was surrounded and its supplies were cut off.

10. Japan defeated _____ in a war that ended in 1895.

11. After being exiled by the czar, _____ overthrew the government and became the first Communist leader in Russia.

12. The Treaty of _____ made Germany pay for World War I damages.

13. German citizens broke down the _____ in 1989.

14. _____ was sent to prison in South Africa for 26 years.

15. The _____ is a trade agreement that includes Canada, Mexico, and the United States.

Word Bank
anthropologists
Berlin Wall
boycott
China
Confucius
Hohokam
iron
Lenin
Miguel Hidalgo
NAFTA
Nelson Mandela
religious
scholars
siege
Versailles

World History

Final Mastery Test, *continued*

Part B Directions Circle the letter of the answer that correctly completes each sentence.

16. _____ led the Hebrews out of slavery in Egypt.
    A Sargon I   **B** Moses   **C** Hammurabi   **D** Abraham

17. The ancient Greek philosopher _____ wrote *The Republic*.
    A Aristotle   **B** Aristophanes   **C** Socrates   **D** Plato

18. The years from 1050 to about 1500 are the late Middle Ages, or _____ times.
    A ancient   **B** medieval   **C** modern   **D** Renaissance

19. Johan Gutenberg is known because he _____.
    A was a famous sculptor   **C** printed the first book in Europe
    B was a famous painter   **D** brought back many goods from China

20. Much of Spain was united after Ferdinand married _____ of Castile.
    A Isabella   **B** Catherine   **C** Maria Theresa   **D** Elizabeth

21. _____ believed the government should protect people's rights.
    A Hobbes   **B** Rousseau   **C** Locke   **D** Montesquieu

22. The _____ helped factory owners transport their products.
    A cotton gin   **B** telegraph   **C** locomotive   **D** telephone

23. _____ and his army captured Santiago, Chile, in 1817, and Lima, Peru, in 1821.
    A José San Martín   **B** Miguel Hidalgo   **C** José Morelos   **D** Simón Bolívar

24. After the _____, France gave up provinces that were near Germany.
    A Franco-Prussian War   **C** Austro-Prussian War
    B Napoleonic Wars   **D** 1848 German Revolution

25. A private company ruled _____ before the British took control in 1858.
    A Italy   **B** India   **C** Cambodia   **D** Belgium

26. Bloody Sunday took place in 1905 in _____.
    A Sarajevo   **B** Paris   **C** Geneva   **D** St. Petersburg

27. After World War II, the _____ separated the United States and the Soviet Union.
    A Great Wall   **B** Iron Curtain   **C** Grand Canal   **D** Maginot Line

28. The _____ gave economic and military help to nations trying to defeat the Communists.
    A KGB   **B** Warsaw Pact   **C** Iron Curtain   **D** Truman Doctrine

29. Ho Chi Minh and _____ agreed to divide Vietnam.
    A France   **B** the United States   **C** China   **D** the Soviet Union

30. Until 1979, Iran was ruled by a(n) _____.
    A Shah   **B** migrant   **C** campesino   **D** ayatollah

World History

Final Mastery Test, *continued*

Part C Directions Match the description in Column A with the correct term in Column B for each set. Write the letter of the correct answer on each line.

Column A

_____ 31. This religious leader preached to Persians.

_____ 32. This soldier led the Carthaginians in the Second Punic War.

_____ 33. The Kremlin was rebuilt by this Russian leader.

_____ 34. This Catholic ruler married the queen of England.

_____ 35. The name taken by Siddartha Gautama.

_____ 36. This composer is called the "Father of the Symphony."

_____ 37. The Declaration of Independence listed more than 20 complaints against this king.

_____ 38. This was the last battle of the American Revolutionary War.

Column B

A Buddha
B Hannibal
C Haydn
D George III
E Ivan the Great
F Philip II
G Yorktown
H Zoroaster

Column A

_____ 39. Karl Marx believed that workers could improve their situation only by this kind of revolution.

_____ 40. This area now includes Vietnam, Laos, and Cambodia.

_____ 41. Under this type of government, the government controls the economy of a nation.

_____ 42. This is the nickname for the National Socialist German Workers' Party.

_____ 43. After the collapse of the Soviet Union, this man was elected president of the new Russian republic.

_____ 44. This plan was designed to reform China's economy.

_____ 45. In this type of economy, the government lets manufacturers produce what they want.

Column B

I Bortis Yeltsin
J Four Modernizations
K free-market
L French Indochina
M Nazi
N socialism
O violent

World History

Final Mastery Test, *continued*

Part D Directions Write the answer to these questions. Use complete sentences.

46. How was Roman art different from Greek art?

47. What were the three West African empires that became powerful between A.D. 400 and A.D. 1586?

48. What did the discoveries of the Arab scholar Jabir lead to?

49. What is the origin and meaning of the word *science*?

50. What did the conquistadors do to the Incas?

51. Name two things a nation needs to become industrialized.

52. Who fought in the Russian Civil War?

53. What are two things that the United Nations tries to prevent?

54. What is the term used to describe the international computer network?

55. What happened to North and South Vietnam after the United States pulled its troops out?

World History

Final Mastery Test, *continued*

Part E Directions Write the correct term from the Word Bank to complete each sentence.

56. A group's _____ includes its attitudes, values, and customs.

57. The _____ is the region between the Tigris and the Euphrates rivers.

58. Scientific reasoning was used to study society during the Age of _____.

59. Napoleon I was crowned and named by _____.

60. In 1810, _____ led a revolt to free New Granada from Spanish control.

61. _____ was once a British colony called Burma.

62. The Austrian emperor sent Franz Ferdinand on a trip to improve relations with the _____.

63. Benito Mussolini formed the _____ in Italy in 1919.

64. The _____ is another name for the European Recovery Program.

65. In 1997, the economy of _____ collapsed.

Word Bank
culture
fascist party
Fertile Crescent
Marshall Plan
Myanmar
Napoleon
Reason
Serbs
Simón Bolívar
Thailand

World History

Final Mastery Test, *continued*

Part F Directions Write your answer to each question. Use complete sentences. Support each answer with facts and examples from the textbook.

66. How were Lower and Upper Egypt united? (2 points)

_____

_____

67. In what two locations did the French set up settlements in North America? (2 points)

_____

_____

Part G Directions Write a paragraph for each topic. Include a topic sentence, body, and conclusion. Support each answer with facts and examples from the textbook.

68. Explain how militarism was important to the unification of Germany. (3 points)

_____

_____

_____

_____

69. Describe the recession and how it affected the world economy. (3 points)

_____

_____

_____

_____

_____

World History

The lists below show how items from the Midterm and Final correlate to the chapters in the student edition.

Midterm Mastery Test
Chapter 1: 1, 11, 26
Chapter 2: 2, 12, 21
Chapter 3: 27
Chapter 4: 3, 28
Chapter 5: 4
Chapter 6: 13, 29
Chapter 7: 5, 30
Chapter 8: 14, 23, 31
Chapter 9: 6, 32
Chapter 10: 15, 33
Chapter 11: 7, 16, 34
Chapter 12: 17, 24
Chapter 13: 35
Chapter 14: 8, 18, 36
Chapter 15: 19, 22, 37
Chapter 16: 9, 38
Chapter 17: 10, 39
Chapter 18: 20, 25, 40

Critical-Thinking Items
41. Chapter 3
42. Chapter 6
43. Chapter 15
44. Chapter 17

Final Mastery Test
Chapter 1: 56
Chapter 2: 16, 57
Chapter 3: 31
Chapter 4:
Chapter 5: 2, 35
Chapter 6: 17
Chapter 7: 32
Chapter 8: 46
Chapter 9: 3
Chapter 10: 18

Chapter 11: 33
Chapter 12: 47, 48
Chapter 13: 4
Chapter 14: 19
Chapter 15:
Chapter 16: 49
Chapter 17: 50
Chapter 18: 5, 20, 34
Chapter 19: 21, 36, 58
Chapter 20: 6, 37, 59
Chapter 21: 7, 22, 38, 51
Chapter 22: 8, 23, 39, 60
Chapter 23: 9, 24
Chapter 24: 10, 25, 40, 61
Chapter 25: 12, 26, 41, 62
Chapter 26: 11, 42, 52, 63
Chapter 27: 27, 53
Chapter 28: 13, 28, 43, 64
Chapter 29: 14, 29, 55
Chapter 30: 15, 30, 44
Chapter 31: 45, 54, 65

Critical-Thinking Items
66. Chapter 4
67. Chapter 17
68. Chapter 23
69. Chapter 31

Activities

Activity 1—Studying History
1. history 2. diary 3. eyewitness 4. culture 5. historian
6. humanity 7. interpret 8. primary 9. secondary 10. combined

Activity 2—Connecting with the Past
Sample Answers 1. What happened when my ancestors left their home country? 2. When did they make the move? 3. Where did they originally come from? 4. Who decided to make the move?
5. Why did they decide to leave their country?

Activity 3—Prehistory Puzzle
1. archaeologist 2. artifacts 3. jigsaw 4. calculate
5. anthropologist 6. carbon 7. Latin 8. dating 9. calendars
10. bones
Mystery Word
historians

Activity 4—Descriptions and Discoveries in Prehistory
Java Man—C, D
Neanderthals—A, E, G
Cro-Magnons—B, F, H
Paleolithic—K, N
Neolithic—I, L, M
Bronze—J, O

Activity 5—Sumerians Puzzle
1. temples 2. legal 3. arches 4. Euphrates 5. ziggurats
6. cuneiform 7. priests 8. city-states 9. dike 10. stylus
Mystery Word
sacrifices

Activity 6—Akkadian and Babylonian Choices
1. B 2. C 3. C 4. D 5. A 6. B 7. A 8. B 9. C 10. D 11. A 12. B
13. C 14. A 15. D

Activity 7—Identifying Terms and People
Part A
1. F 2. H 3. I 4. C 5. J 6. A 7. B 8. E 9. G 10. D
Part B
11. Fertile Crescent 12. Abraham 13. Egyptians 14. North Star
15. Palestine

Activity 8—Important Terms
1. capital 2. dominated 3. archers 4. chariot 5. smelt 6. tribute
7. province 8. cavalry 9. alliances 10. governor 11. rebel
12. Artisans 13. batter 14. library 15. govern

Activity 9—Who Were the Chaldeans?
1. The Chaldeans' ancestors were the people Hammurabi ruled hundreds of years before. 2. Nebuchadnezzar defeated many armies, which helped to expand his empire. He also made the city of Babylon beautiful. 3. Nebuchadnezzar's palace was brightly colored and had beautiful, terraced gardens. 4. Chaldean priests learned to map the stars and planets, and they saw constellations that they believed could tell the future. 5. The Chaldean Empire collapsed because war broke out after Nebuchadnezzar died, and Babylon fell under the control of the Persian Empire.

Activity 10—Persians Puzzle
1. coins 2. unify 3. stretchers 4. Egypt 5. relay 6. Cyrus 7. cheat
8. Zoroaster 9. barter 10. Christianity
Mystery Word
inspectors

Activity 11—The Nile River
1. Possible answers: It is the longest river in the world; it begins in the mounts of central Africa; it flows northward to the Mediterranean Sea; it is 4,000 miles long; it forms a large delta just before it reaches the Mediterranean Sea. 2. It spreads out into a delta, or area of fertile land. 3. The Egyptians used the floodwater of the Nile River to irrigate their fields. 4. They used the fertile banks of the Nile River for planting their crops. 5. The Nile River made a water highway for traders, government workers, and rulers. The Nile River was traveled in both directions, north and south.

Activity 12—The Old Kingdom
1. Old Kingdom 2. Menes 3. priests 4. afterlife 5. pyramids
6. civil war 7. economy 8. Egypt 9. Ra 10. Giza

Activity 13—The Middle Kingdom
1. B 2. D 3. C 4. B 5. D 6. D 7. A 8. C 9. B; 10. B

Activity 14—The New Kingdom
1. J 2. G 3. A 4. F 5. B 6. D 7. H 8. C 9. E 10. I

Activity 15—Gifts from the Egyptians
1. Egyptians used papyrus to make paper. It was easier to write on paper than on stone. Because they needed to write with something, Egyptians also invented ink. 2. The scrolls described how to set broken bones, how to check for a heartbeat, and how to treat fevers and accidents. 3. The temples are in ruins today. 4. The cubit was used to measure length. This helped in measuring and surveying land. 5. Egyptian artists had to make sure important people were the largest figures in a piece of art. Also, figures in paintings and sculpture had to face forward.

Activity 16—Identifying Places and Terms
1. C 2. G 3. F 4. D 5. A 6. B 7. E 8. H
9. N 10. I 11. K 12. O 13. L 14. J 15. M

Activity 17—Ancient India Boxes
1. The Indus River Valley has both water and fertile soil to grow crops. The soil, or silt, is left behind when flood waters from melting snow retreat. 2. The people raised grain and vegetables, irrigated their fields, and had plenty of food for everyone. They had time to make pottery, cloth, jewelry and metal tools and traded with other civilizations. 3. Some homes were two stories high and had a patio open to the sky and stairs that led to the roof. They had windows that the light could shine through, and indoor plumbing and toilets. The cities were surrounded by walls with towers to watch for enemies. The center of the city had a walled fort, a place to store food, and a large bath. 4. Clay tablets were covered with pictograms, figures that tell a story. No one can read the Harappan language. 5. A change in the coastline may have made trading harder. Disease, an earthquake, or a flood might have struck. Farmers may not have been able to grow enough food, or armies from central Asia might have invaded.

Activity 18—Hinduism Puzzle

Across

3. Brahmin 4. Vedas 7. slaves 9. reincarnation 10. cows
11. outcast 12. Sanskrit

Down

1. Brahma 2. cycle 3. Brahman 5. warrior 6. Hinduism
7. Shiva 8. Vishna 10. caste

Activity 19—Complete the Story

1. India 2. Hindu 3. Four Noble Truths 4. Buddha 5. Enlightened
One 6. Buddhism 7. food 8. shelter 9. selfish 10. suffering
11. Eightfold Path 12. desire 13.nirvana 14. emptiness 15. soul
16. monks 17. monasteries 18. countries 19. China/Japan
20. Japan/China

Activity 20—Ancient China Geography Match

1. A 2. A 3. B 4. F 5. D 6. B 7. E 8. C 9. A 10. B 11. F 12. A
13. E 14. E 15. F

Activity 21—Chinese History Puzzle

1. China 2. Han 3. dynasty 4. scribes 5. paper 6. society 7. tomb
8. nobles 9. Ancestor 10. symbols

Mystery Word

characters

Activity 22—Early Civilizations of the Aegean Sea

Across

6. Mediterranean 7. Crete 8. Iliad 9. peninsula

Down

1. warlike 2. heroic 3. horse 4. Helen 5. Knossos
6. Mycenae

Activity 23—The Greek City-States

1. polis 2. mountains 3. Athenians 4. acropolis 5. kings
6. aristocrats 7. tyrants 8. Solon 9. democracy 10. temple

Activity 24—Athens

1. lottery 2. jury 3. citizens 4. vote 5. direct democracy
6. assembly 7. defend 8. bribe 9. seaport 10. loyal

Activity 25—Sparta

1. Spartans did not build protective walls around their city because
they thought that their military skills would protect them. 2. When
a boy was seven, he left his parents. At age 20, he became a citizen.
He married at 30, but could not return home until he was 60.
3. Spartan women were independent and patriotic to their city-state.
4. The Spartans sent people to spy on the helots and they killed any
helot who made trouble. 5. The Spartans did not trade with others,
they feared new ideas, and they were not interested in art and
architecture.

Activity 26—War Tests the Greeks

First Persian Invasion: B, K; Marathon: C, F;
Thermopylae: A, D, G; Salamis: H, L;
Peloponnesian War: E, I, J, O; Greece is conquered: M, N

Activity 27—Greek Culture Puzzle

1. philosophers 2. Athena 3. goddess 4. ethics 5. acropolis
6. chorus 7. comedy 8. tragedy 9. column 10. Plato

Mystery Word

instrument

Activity 28—Alexander the Great Spreads Greek Culture

1. M 2. K 3. C 4. O 5. A 6. N 7. B 8. L 9. D 10. J 11. E 12. H 13. F
14. I 15. G

Activity 29—Early Rome

1. The legend says that twin babies, Romulus and Remus, were left
on the banks of the Tiber River. A she-wolf found them and cared
for them. Then a shepherd killed the wolf and raised the twins as his
own. As adults, the twins built a city and fought over who should
rule. Romulus killed Remus, became king, and named the city
Rome. 2. The Latins lived on a plain called Latium in small villages
near the Tiber River. Rome grew from these small villages. 3. The
Etruscans were a tribe that lived north of the Tiber River. They had
written language and made pottery and fine clothing. They were
also expert sailors. They conquered Rome by 600 B.C.
4. The Etruscans were more advanced than the Latins. The
Etruscans had written language. 5. The Etruscan king appointed a
senate. The senate helped the king make decisions. The senate also
controlled large amounts of land.

Activity 30—Plebeians and Patricians

1. Plebeians 2. Plebeians 3. Patricians 4. Patricians 5. Patricians
6. Plebeians 7. Plebeians 8. Patricians 9. Plebeians 10. Plebeians

Activity 31—Important Terms and People

1. F 2. E 3. D 4. B 5. C 6. A 7. G 8. H 9. N 10. O 11. L 12. K
13. J 14. M 15. I

Activity 32—Choose the Correct Answer

1. reform 2. Lucius Sulla 3. army 4. triumvirate 5. plebeians
6. riot 7. tribune 8. Crassus 9. soldiers 10. senators 11. territory
12. politician 13. challenge 14. taxes 15. Marius

Activity 33—The End of the Republic

1. B 2. D 3. D 4. A 5. C

Activity 34—The Age of Augustus

1. B 2. C 3. D 4. A 5. B 6. D 7. D 8. A 9. B 10. C

Activity 35—Roman Empire Sentences

1. simple 2. declined 3. life 4. Nero 5. emperors 6. Trajan
7. plague 8. lyre 9. peace 10. Caligula

Activity 36—The Rise of Christianity

1. hang 2. Augustus Caesar 3. homeland 4. disciples 5. divine
6. Greek 7. prophet 8. emperor 9. gentiles 10. Rome 11. king
12. loyal 13. New Testament 14. Paul 15. miracle

Activity 37—The Fall of Rome

1. Adrianople 2. Constantine 3. Visigoths 4. Odoacer 5. Attila
6. co-emperor 7. Byzantium 8. survive 9. Vandals 10. Huns

Mystery Word

Diocletian

Activity 38—Roman Culture

1. fair 2. art 3. influence 4. medicine 5. vaulted 6. sanitation
7. Pantheon 8. respected 9. bridges 10. entertainment

Activity 39—The First Americans

1. The first Americans walked from Asia over the Bering Strait and into North and South America. **2.** The land grew warmer, and American Indians settled in communities all over North America and South America. **3.** George McJunkin was an African American cowboy who found a "bone pit" of large animal bones. **4.** The "bone pit" was important because it showed that American Indians had been living in North America for at least 9,000 years. **5.** Scientists think the Clovis people came to the Americas about 13,000 years ago.

Activity 40—Early Southwestern Cultures

1. Hohokam **2.** growing **3.** kivas **4.** pottery **5.** Anasazi
6. Chaco Canyon **7.** canals **8.** Snaketown **9.** Mogollon
10. Golden Age

Activity 41—Early Regional Cultures

1. A **2.** B **3.** J **4.** I **5.** F **6.** G **7.** C **8.** E **9.** H **10.** D

Activity 42—Civilizations of Mesoamerica

1. A **2.** D **3.** C **4.** D **5.** B

Activity 43—The Church During the Middle Ages

1. religious **2.** Benedict **3.** Palestine **4.** crusaders **5.** Crusades
6. spices **7.** Muslims **8.** pilgrims **9.** convents **10.** heaven

Activity 44—Feudalism Puzzle

1. church **2.** feudalism **3.** armor **4.** fief **5.** money **6.** sword
7. weapons **8.** squires **9.** brave **10.** jousting
Mystery Word
ceremonies

Activity 45—The Manor

1. Serfs did farm work, cut wood, built fences, cooked, made clothing, and cared for the house. **2.** A manor was self-sufficient because the people who lived on it could grow, raise, or make nearly everything they needed. **3.** The three-field system allowed the soil to rest. The soil produced more food when crops were planted a year later. **4.** Courtyards had many small buildings and sheds, such as a blacksmith's shop, a bakery, a kitchen, a stable for horses, and storage areas for weapons and extra food. **5.** Better farming enabled people to grow more food than they needed. People then had more time to do activities other than farming. People used their extra time to study and learn new things.

Activity 46—Culture in the Middle Ages

1. buttresses **2.** warrior **3.** bishop **4.** Latin **5.** cathedral
6. Parliament **7.** Romanesque **8.** faith **9.** Gothic **10.** jury

Activity 47—The Byzantine Empire Crossword

Across
3. Justinian **5.** relic **11.** goods **13.** Constantine **14.** code **15.** Rome
Down
1. plague **2.** saint **4.** Turks **6.** icons **7.** patriarch **8.** Greek
9. Istanbul **10.** barbaric **12.** Orthodox

Activity 48—The Russians Match-Up

1. F **2.** B **3.** N **4.** J **5.** D **6.** G **7.** E **8.** I **9.** C **10.** A **11.** N **12.** K
13. O **14.** M **15.** L **16.** Q **17.** S **18.** R **19.** T **20.** P

Activity 49—Europe During the Middle Ages

1. C **2.** A **3.** B **4.** D **5.** C **6.** B **7.** A **8.** C **9.** D **10.** A **11.** C **12.** B
13. D **14.** B **15.** A

Activity 50—The Rise of Islam

1. Mecca **2.** Hegira **3.** vision **4.** Kaaba **5.** idols **6.** Muslims
7. Qur'an **8.** Gabriel **9.** pillars **10.** alms **11.** Hajj **12.** Ramadan
13. Christianity **14.** fast **15.** Islam

Activity 51—Islamic Civilization

1. Europe **2.** jihads **3.** respect **4.** trade **5.** Jabir

Activity 52—African Kingdoms

1. G **2.** M **3.** M **4.** M **5.** S **6.** G **7.** M **8.** S **9.** G **10.** G

Activity 53—India

1. A **2.** C **3.** A **4.** D **5.** C **6.** B **7.** A **8.** D **9.** B **10.** D

Activity 54—China

1. D **2.** B **3.** F **4.** E **5.** H **6.** G **7.** A **8.** C **9.** L **10.** I **11.** N **12.** M
13. J **14.** K **15.** O

Activity 55—The Mongols Conquer China

Part A
1. B **2.** A **3.** E **4.** D **5.** C
Part B
6. Genghis Khan **7.** Kublai Khan **8.** Ming **9.** foreigners
10. Chinese

Activity 56—History and Culture of Japan

1. Chinese **2.** Shinto **3.** Nippon **4.** missionaries **5.** Jimmu
6. nobles **7.** Buddhists **8.** invaders **9.** books **10.** spirits

Activity 57—Japan Develops Its Own Culture

1. daimyo **2.** samurai **3.** estates **4.** bushido **5.** haiku
6. self-discipline **7.** calligraphy **8.** hari-kari **9.** tanka **10.** shogun
Mystery Phrase
martial arts

Activity 58—A Unified Japan

1. Japanese shoguns isolated Japan because they thought Western influence would take away their power. **2.** Japan developed ikebana, the art of arranging flowers; Noh dramas, plays with only two actors; kabuki, plays with exaggerated actions; and beautiful paintings and gardens. **3.** People in Japan were not allowed to be Christians. The shogun ordered all foreign missionaries to leave, and many Christian Japanese were killed. **4.** Japanese paintings usually show the beauty of Japan. Some paintings show war. **5.** The shogun forced the daimyos to move to Edo so that he could keep an eye on them.

Activity 59—The Troubled 14th Century

1. Fleas spread the Black Death from one person to the next.
2. Governments had less money because there were fewer people to pay taxes. **3.** The serfs and peasants were fighting for their rights. **4.** When the Renaissance began, the Middle Ages ended.
5. During the Middle Ages, the nobles and clergy were at the top of society.

Activity 60—The Spirit of the Renaissance

1. B **2.** I **3.** G **4.** J **5.** D **6.** E **7.** F **8.** A **9.** H **10.** C

Activity 61—The Renaissance Begins in Italy

1. wool **2.** Lorenzo **3.** worldly **4.** republican **5.** criticize
6. Florence **7.** architect **8.** Savonarola **9.** city-states **10.** Venice

Activity 62—Renaissance Literature
1. A 2. E 3. F 4. H 5. G 6. I 7. B 8. C. 9. J 10. D

Activity 63—Great Renaissance Artists
1. L 2. L 3. R 4. L 5. M 6. R 7. M 8. L 9. M 10. R

Activity 64—The Reformers Multiple Choice
1. C 2. B 3. B 4. A 5. C 6. D 7. D 8. A 9. C 10. B

Activity 65—The Reformation Puzzle
1. faith 2. lightning 3. deed 4. purgatory 5. salvation
6. Germany 7. Reformation 8. monk 9. church 10. printed
Mystery Word
indulgence

Activity 66—Lutheran Match-Up
1. D 2. B 3. C 4. H 5. A 6. G 7. J 8. F 9. E 10. I

Activity 67—Protestant Ideas Multiple Choice
1. A 2. B 3. D 4. D 5. A 6. C 7. B 8. A 9. D 10. C

Activity 68—John Calvin Organizes a New Religion
1. G 2. H 3. F 4. E 5. C 6. D 7. B 8. I 9. A 10. J

Activity 69—All About the Catholic Reformation
1. Paul 2. Trent 3. Catholic 4. salvation 5. censor 6. Jesuits
7. counter 8. Ignatius 9. missionaries 10. Inquisition
Mystery Word
Protestant

Activity 70—Modern Science Develops
1. Scholars decided what was true or false by reading the Bible and studying the works of Greek and Roman writers. 2. There are five steps in the scientific method. The last step is the scientist drawing a conclusion from the notes of the experiment. 3. A hypothesis is an educated guess about an answer to a problem. Making a hypothesis is the second step of the scientific method. 4. Scientists discover the truth in an experiment by carefully controlling a test. The test helps them find the truth for themselves, so they do not to depend on others to tell them with is true or false. 5. In the fourth step of the scientific method, a scientist observes what is happening during the experiment and makes notes.

Activity 71—Recognizing People and Ideas
1. C 2. A 3. B 4. D 5. A 6. C 7. D 8. B 9. B 10. A 11. C 12. B
13. A 14. C 15. D

Activity 72—Questions About Galileo
1. Galileo used a telescope to observe the night sky. 2. He observed the rough surface of the moon, dark spots on the sun, and the four moons of Jupiter. 3. He concluded that the sun, rather than the earth, was the center of the universe. 4. The Catholic Church said Galileo's book was an attack on Catholic teaching, so they put him on trial and imprisoned him. 5. Galileo concluded that gravity makes all objects on Earth fall at the same speed.

Activity 73—Newton's Discoveries
1. light 2. absorbs 3. scientific law 4. gravity 5. Galileo 6. prism
7. Copernicus 8. universe 9. planets 10. reflects

Activity 74—Identifying Important People
1. B 2. C 3. H 4. D 5. F 6. G 7. E 8. A 9. O 10. J 11. I 12. N
13. K 14. L 15. M

Activity 75—Europeans Search for New Trade Routes
1. East 2. Portugal 3. Navigation 4. gold 5. Africa 6. India
7. Cape of Storms 8. Cape of Good Hope 9. Gold Coast
10. Arab merchants

Activity 76—Exploring New Lands
1. Magellan 2. exploration 3. Spain 4. native 5. Vasco da Gama
6. profit 7. strait 8. Columbus 9. *Santa Maria* 10. the pope

Activity 77—Spanish Empires in America
1. Many of the American Indians who helped Cortés hated their Aztec rulers. 2. The Incas carried no weapons, so the Spanish were able to kill many of them and capture their emperor. 3. Atahualpa offered Pizarro a room filled with gold in exchange for his release. 4. After Atahualpa kept his promise, Pizarro put Atahualpa on trial and executed him. 5. Indians had never seen horses before. They thought that a horse and its rider was a two-headed god.

Activity 78—Spain Establishes Colonies in America
1. F 2. G 3. I 4. B 5. A 6. J 7. H 8. C 9. D 10. E

Activity 79—The Growth of the Slave Trade
1. B 2. A 3. B 4. D 5. A 6. B 7. D 8. D 9. A 10. C

Activity 80—The Results of Exploring and Establishing Colonies
1. G 2. I 3. D 4. H 5. E 6. J 7. C 8. B 9. A 10. F

Activity 81—The Rise of Nations
1. C 2. A 3. B 4. C 5. D 6. B 7. D 8. A 9. B 10. D

Activity 82—The Rise and Fall of Spain
1. C 2. B 3. A 4. B 5. A 6. D 7. C 8. D 9. C 10. A

Activity 83—English Monarchs Struggle for Power
Part A
1. F 2. I 3. D 4. J 5. G 6. H 7. C 8. E 9. Av10. B
Part B
1. James I 2. Elizabeth I 3. citizens 4. Charles I 5. Parliament

Activity 84—England Rejects Absolute Monarchy
1. Restoration 2. Habeas Corpus 3. Cavaliers 4. Tory 5. William
6. Roundheads 7. constitutional 8. Whig 9. Catholic 10. England
Mystery Word
Revolution

Activity 85—Absolute Monarchy in France
1. C 2. G 3. D 4. J 5. B 6. I 7. F 8. H 9. E 10. A

Activity 86—Russia and Prussia Produce Strong Monarchs
1. C 2. D 3. B 4. D 5. D 6. A 7. B 8. A 9. C 10. B

Activity 87—In Search of Natural Laws
1. D 2. B 3. C 4. A 5. C 6. B 7. D 8. A 9. C 10. B

Activity 88—Who Said It?
1. L 2. M 3. R 4. M 5. H 6. L 7. L 8. R 9. H 10. M 11. M
12. R 13. R 14. L 15. H

Activity 89—The Influence of Enlightened Thinkers
Part A
1. F 2. G 3. C 4. D 5. B 6. H 7. I 8. E 9. A 10. J
Part B
11. Marie Therese Geoffrin 12. Voltaire 13. Denis Diderot
14. Frederick the Great 15. Maria Theresa

Activity 90—Enlightenment Artists Puzzle
1. foolish 2. Handel 3. classical 4. history 5. composer
6. baroque 7. symphony 8. fugue 9. nobles 10. Mozart
Mystery Word
instrument

Activity 91—Revolution in the American Colonies
1. H 2. D 3. A 4. E 5. G 6. F 7. I 8. J 9. B 10. C

Activity 92—The American Revolutionary War
Part A
1. E 2. C 3. A 4. F 5. B 6. G 7. H 8. J 9. I 10. D
Part B
1. Thomas Jefferson 2. George Washington 3. General Cornwallis
4. King George III 5. John Locke

Activity 93—The French Revolution
1. estates 2. clergy 3. Estates-General 4. Bastille 5. land
6. Versailles 7. National Assembly 8. French Revolution 9. money
10. teachers

Activity 94—Reforms and Terror in France
1. A 2. C 3. D 4. B 5. D 6. B 7. B 8. A 9. A 10. C 11. D
12. D 13. C 14. A 15. C

Activity 95—Napoleon and the French Empire
1. H 2. A 3. F 4. G 5. D 6. E 7. C 8. B 9. I 10. M 11. J 12. L
13. N 14. O 15. K

Activity 96—England and the Industrial Revolution
1. I 2. H 3. B 4. D 5. C 6. G 7. F 8. J 9. E 10. A

Activity 97—Modern Industries Grow
1. The "spinning jenny," Arkwright's machine that produced tighter
yarn, and the "spinning mule" are inventions that helped the textile
industry. 2. The factory system made workers work a certain
number of hours and at a certain time. 3. Eli Whitney had workers
make identical gun parts, and then the workers put together the
identical parts to make identical guns. 4. Coal became a valuable
natural resource in the 1700s for powering steam engines. Later it
became valuable because of its importance in producing steel.
5. Steel production was important because steel was stronger than
iron and did not break as easily. As a result, machines and other steel
products lasted longer.

Activity 98—Transportation Fill-In
1. Watt 2. Telford 3. Transportation 4. machines 5. boiler
6. efficient 7. locomotive 8. canals 9. raw 10. railroads

Activity 99—Problems with Industry
1. C 2. B 3. C 4. A 5. D 6. B 7. B 8. B 9. C 10. D

Activity 100—About the Congress of Vienna
1. Napoleon Bonaparte controlled France after the French
Revolution. 2. Austria, Prussia, Great Britain, and Russia defeated
Napoleon. 3. The Congress of Vienna restructured Europe.
4. Prince Metternich was Austria's foreign minister. 5. He thought
the French Revolution had made Europe weak. 6. Metternich
wanted royal families to rule Europe. 7. Balance of power means
major nations have equal strength. 8. Russia gained Finland and
most of Poland through the Congress of Vienna. 9. The German
states were organized into a confederation. 10. Austria led the
German states.

Activity 101—Nationalism Multiple Choice
1. B 2. B 3. C 4. A 5. D 6. D 7. B 8. A 9. D 10. C

Activity 102—Latin American Independence
1. D 2. E 3. D 4. C 5. E 6. B 7. A 8. B 9. A 10. C

Activity 103—Conservatives, Liberals, and Radicals
1. R 2. L 3. C 4. C 5. L 6. C 7. R 8. C 9. L 10. L

Activity 104—Revolutions in 1848
1. The first group wanted political reform only, and the second
group—the socialists—wanted political and economic reform.
2. State control of the land and of factories frightened the middle
class. 3. A utopian society is a perfect society with no war, no
poverty, and no crime. 4. Marx saw a society with no need for
government. 5. These rebellions accomplished nothing; all of the
rebellions failed.

Activity 105—Nationalism
1. culture 2. Foreign 3. language 4. democracy 5. Heritage
6. loyalty 7. history 8. government 9. multilingual 10. Ancestors
Mystery Word
traditions

Activity 106—Growing Nationalism in Italy Puzzle
1. prime minister 2. Cavour 3. Italy 4. Mazzini 5. Austria
6. Garibaldi 7. Sicily 8. Sardinia 9. Emmanuel 10. France
Mystery Word
politician

Activity 107—The Unification of Germany Match-Up
1. G 2. E 3. B 4. A 5. H 6. C 7. F 8. D 9. I 10. N 11. J 12. L
13. M 14. K 15. O

Activity 108—Imperialism
1. mother 2. imperialism 3. colonialism 4. supplies 5. tin
6. Christianity 7. market 8. Industrial 9. sea 10. materials
Mystery Word
militarism

Activity 109—The Effect of Imperialism on Asia
1. B 2. D 3. A 4. A 5. C 6. D 7. A 8. C 9. C 10. B

Activity 110—The Effect of Imperialism on Africa
1. protectorate 2. Suez Canal 3. France 4. transportation
5. Belgium 6. constitutional 7. Libya 8. Germany 9. customs
10. Italy

Activity 111—The Causes of the War
1. C 2. B 3. C 4. D 5. D 6. A 7. B 8. A 9. C 10. D

Activity 112—The War Years: 1914–1918
Part A
1. I 2. B 3. G 4. J 5. F 6. D 7. E 8. A 9. C 10. H
Part B
11. machine gun 12. Brest Litovsk 13. the United States
14. November 11, 1918 15. Verdun

Activity 113—Making Peace
1. Woodrow Wilson wanted to end secret treaties between nations, reduce the size of armies and navies in each nation, and organize a league of nations that would keep the peace. 2. Premier Georges Clemenceau represented France at Versailles. Prime Minister Lloyd George represented Great Britain, and Prime Minister Vittorio Orlando represented Italy. 3. The Treaty of Versailles forced Germany to accept responsibility for causing the war, pay for the cost of the war, give the land of Alsace and Lorraine to France, divide its African colonies between France and Great Britain, and give its colonies in the Pacific to Japan. 4. The treaty created Yugoslavia and Czechoslovakia. 5. The League of Nations was a group of leaders from the nations of the world. It wanted to keep the peace.

Activity 114—World War I Changed the World
1. J 2. D 3. H 4. A 5. B 6. G 7. C 8. I 9. E 10. F

Activity 115—Life in Czarist Russia
1. czar 2. autocracy 3. Alexander II 4. freedom 5. nobles
6. standard of living 7. Nicholas II 8. democratic 9. Bloody Sunday 10. Duma

Activity 116—Russia Moves Toward Revolution
1. C 2. B 3. A 4. B 5. D 6. C 7. D 8. A 9. A 10. D

Activity 117—Russia Becomes the Soviet Union
1. B 2. G 3. E 4. A 5. C 6. F 7. D 8. H 9. I 10. J

Activity 118—The Soviet Union Under Stalin
1. Setting up heavy industry factories hurt Russia because they produced only steel or machines. As a result, consumer goods became scarce. 2. Farmers who protested the collective farm system were sent to Siberia where many were killed. 3. In a totalitarian state, a small group controls the lives of its country's citizens. 4. Under Stalin's rule, the Soviet Union became a powerful industrialized nation and improved its health care and education systems. 5. Historians believe that between 5 and 10 million peasants died under Stalin's rule.

Activity 119—The Fascists Gain Power in Italy
1. Il Duce 2. obedience 3. Extreme 4. Mussolini 5. Black Shirts
6. military 7. fascist 8. Hitler 9. Communism 10. fascism

Activity 120—The Nazis Gain Power in Germany
1. I 2. F 3. G 4. B 5. E 6. A 7. C 8. J 9. H 10. D

Activity 121—The Chinese Begin to Build a Modern Nation
1. B 2. D 3. B 4. B 5. A 6. D 7. D 8. C 9. C 10. A

Activity 122—Military Leaders Take Over in Japan
1. Hideko Tojo 2. fascist 3. newspapers 4. Italy 5. Manchuria
6. silk 7. democracy 8. coal 9. Germany 10. secret police

Activity 123—The Causes of World War II
1. C 2. D 3. B 4. B 5. A 6. D 7. C 8. B 9. A 10. D

Activity 124—Fascism Threatens Other Countries
1. Austria 2. France 3. Munich Pact 4. Japan 5. front
6. Appeasement 7. treaty 8. Poland 9. conference
10. Czechoslovakia

Activity 125—Axis Successes in Europe and Asia
1. German 2. blitzkrieg 3. French 4. Maginot 5. England
6. Britain 7. arsenal 8. Lend-Lease 9. Soviet Union 10. Stalingrad
11. destroyer 12. Hitler 13. Axis 14. Japan 15. United States

Activity 126—The Tide Turns in Favor of the Allies
1. Members of the Resistance used guerilla warfare to fight the Germans. They worked in secret and blew up bridges, railroads, and factories. 2. D-Day is the day the allied army invaded France. It took place on June 6, 1944. 3. "Island hopping" was the plan the Allies used to fight or ignore islands in the Pacific Ocean. Allied forces attached Japanese-controlled islands but ignored, or leapfrogged, others. This is how Allied forces made their way north to Japan. 4. The war in the Pacific ended after the second atomic bomb was dropped. 5. V-E Day, May 8, 1945, was Victory in Europe Day. V-J Day, September 2, 1945, was Victory in Japan Day. It marked the end of World War II.

Activity 127—Learning About the Holocaust
1. "master race" 2. Jews 3. ghettos 4. Kristallnacht 5. genocide
6. death camps 7. SS 8. Resistance 9. Lebensraum 10. Dachau

Activity 128—The Results of World War II
1. E 2. S 3. P 4. P 5. E 6. S 7. P 8. P 9. S 10. P 11. E 12. P
13. S 14. P 15. P

Activity 129—The United Nations
1. agency 2. Security 3. charter 4. Assembly 5. veto 6. WHO
7. trust 8. organization 9. FAO 10. Trusteeship

Activity 130—The Cold War Begins
1. Marshall Plan 2. Truman Doctrine 3. cold war 4. Warsaw Pact
5. NATO 6. Greece 7. European 8. Communism 9. Finland
10. alliance
Mystery Word
propaganda

Activity 131— Conflicts Between Superpowers
1. D 2. A 3. D 4. C 5. B 6. B 7. C 8. A 9. C 10. B 11. B 12. C
13. D 14. B 15. A

Activity 132—Reforming the Soviet Union
1. Chechnya 2. perestroika 3. glasnostv 4. Nikita Khrushchev
5. KGB 6. poverty 7. Ukraine 8. Boris Yeltsin 9. coup
10. Vladimir Putin

Activity 133— Europe Experiences Great Change
1. Hungary 2. Communist 3. glasnost 4. Poland 5. cleansing
6. Albanians 7. Solidarity 8. Kosovo 9. strike 10. tariff
Mystery Word
Yugoslavia

Activity 134—Many African Colonies Become Nations
1. A 2. C 3. D 4. A 5. B 6. C 7. Dv8. A 9. Dv10. B 11. D
12. A 13. B 14. C 15. B

Activity 135—Israel Becomes a Nation
1. D 2. C 3. F 4. G 5. H 6. E 7. A 8. B 9. I 10. O 11. J 12. N 13. M 14. L 15. K

Activity 136—India Gains Its Independence
1. self-rule 2. Passive resistance 3. Mohandas Gandhi 4. caste system 5. constitution 6. democracy 7. Hindus 8. Muslims 9. Pakistan 10. violence

Activity 137—The Struggle to Control China
1. Mao Zedong led the Communists and Chiang Kai-shek led the Nationalists during the fighting in China. 2. Japan invaded China in 1937. 3. The Nationalists fought with the Communists against the Japanese. 4. Guerilla warfare is a kind of warfare in which small bands of fighters make surprise attacks against the enemy. 5. The Nationalists and the Communists restarted their fighting when World War II ended. 6. The Soviet Union supported the Communists and the United States supported the Nationalists during their conflict. 7. The Communists were more organized during the conflict between the Nationalists and the Communists. 8. The Communists finally won control of China. 9. Chiang Kai-shek and the Nationalists fled to the island of Taiwan. 10. The United States recognized the People's Republic of China as the legal government in China in 1972.

Activity 138—Vietnamese Wars for Independence
1. SV 2. NV 3. SV 4. SV 5. NV 6. SV 7. NV 8. NV 9. SV 10. SV

Activity 139—African Nations Face Many Challenges
1. conflicts 2. pesticides 3. drought 4. investment 5. epidemic 6. slum 7. independent 8. urbanization 9. poverty 10. migrants
Mystery Word
fertilizer

Activity 140—The Middle East Remains in Conflict
1. A 2. C 3. B 4. B 5. B 6. D 7. C 8. A 9. A 10. D 11. C 12. B 13. B 14. B 15. D

Activity 141—Asian Countries Face Economic Challenges
1. political 2. Beijing 3. the United States 4. educated 5. Singapore 6. Japan 7. economic 8. Thailand 9. banks 10. China 11. human rights 12. Malaysia 13. Four Modernizations 14. labor 15. Asian

Activity 142—Latin America Struggles to Overcome Problems
1. D 2. B 3. C 4. A 5. I 6. J 7. H 8. G 9. E 10. F

Activity 143—Energy and Technology Create a Global Village
1. F 2. H 3. A 4. B 5. C 6. D 7. E 8. G 9. M 10. O 11. K 12. L 13. N 14. J 15. I

Activity 144—Global Trade and Economic Development
1. developing country 2. recession 3. IMF 4. free-market 5. Southern 6. compete 7. World Bank 8. subsistence 9. Northern 10. multinational

Activity 145—Social and Environmental Challenges
1. pesticides 2. coal 3. carbon monoxide 4. global warming 5. oxygen 6. industrial 7. melting 8. greening 9. recycling 10. deforestation

Activity 146—The Threat of Global Terrorism
1. D 2. A 3. B 4. D 5. C

Activity 147—Looking to the Future
1. F 2. E 3. C 4. D 5. H 6. B 7. I 8. G 9. J 10. A

Modified Activities

Modified Activity 1—Studying History
1. history 2. historian 3. primary 4. culture 5. questions
6. interpret 7. secondary 8. combined

Modified Activity 2—Connecting with the Past
Sample Answers 1. What choice did my ancestors make? 2. When did they make the choice? 3. Who was involved in the choice?
4. Why did they make the choice?

Modified Activity 3—Prehistory Puzzle
1. archaeologist 2. artifacts 3. jigsaw 4. calculate
5. anthropologist 6. carbon 7. Latin 8. dating 9. calendars
Mystery Word
historians

Modified Activity 4—Descriptions and Discoveries in Prehistory
Java Man—C
Neanderthals—A, E
Cro-Magnons—B, D, F
Paleolithic—K
Neolithic—G, I, J
Bronze—H, L

Modified Activity 5—Sumerians Puzzle
1. temples 2. legal 3. arches 4. Euphrates 5. ziggurats
6. cuneiform 7. priests 8. city-states 9. dike
Mystery Word
sacrifice

Modified Activity 6—Akkadian and Babylonian Choices
1. D 2. B 3. B 4. C 5. C 6. A 7. A 8. C 9. D 10. A 11. B 12. A

Modified Activity 7—Identifying Terms and People
Part A
1. E 2. G 3. H 4. C 5. A 6. B 7. D 8. F
Part B
1. Fertile Crescent 2. Abraham 3. North Star 4. Palestine

Modified Activity 8—Important Terms
1. capital 2. archers 3. chariot 4. tribute 5. province 6. cavalry
7. governor 8. rebel 9. artisans 10. batter 11. library 12. govern

Modified Activity 9—Who Were the Chaldeans?
1. Nebuchadnezzar expanded his empire by defeating armies from other countries. He also made the city of Babylon beautiful.
2. The Hanging Gardens had terraced gardens that rose up like a mountain. There were many flowers and bushes. Water was pumped up to the terraces to water the plants. 3. Chaldean priests learned to map the stars and planets. They saw constellations that they believed could tell the future. 4. The Chaldean Empire collapsed because war broke out after Nebuchadnezzar died. The Persians killed King Belshazzar and the Chaldean Empire became part of the Persian Empire

Modified Activity 10—Persians Puzzle
1. Egypt 2. cheat 3. relay 4. Zoroaster 5. coins 6. barter 7. unify
8. Cyrus
Mystery Word
Persians

Modified Activity 11—The Nile River
1. Possible answers: It is 4,000 miles long. It is the longest river in the world. It starts in the mountains of Africa. It ends at the Mediterranean Sea. 2. Possible answers: They used the river to water their fields. They planted crops on the banks of the river.
3. Traders and important people traveled up and down the river.
4. It spreads out into a delta, or area of fertile land.

Modified Activity 12—The Old Kingdom
1. Old Kingdom 2. Menes 3. afterlife 4. pyramids 5. civil war
6. Ra

Modified Activity 13—The Middle Kingdom
1. B 2. D 3. D 4. D 5. A 6. C 7. B 8. B

Modified Activity 14—The New Kingdom
1. F 2. D 3. A 4. C 5. B 6. E 7. H 8. G

Modified Activity 15—Gifts from the Egyptians
1. They used papyrus for writing. 2. The scrolls described how to set broken bones. 3. They used the cubit to measure how long something was.

Modified Activity 16—Identifying Places and Terms
1. C 2. F 3. E 4. D 5. A 6. B 7. K 8. G 9. H 10. L 11. I 12. J

Modified Activity 17—Ancient India Boxes
1. The Indus River Valley has both water and fertile soil to grow crops. The soil, or silt, is left behind when flood waters from melting snow retreats. 2. The people raised grain and vegetables, irrigated their fields, and had plenty of food for everyone. They had time to make pottery, cloth, jewelry and metal tools and traded with other civilizations. 3. Some homes were two stories high and had a patio open to the sky and stairs that led to the roof. They had windows that the light could shine through, and indoor plumbing and toilets. The cities were surrounded by walls with towers to watch for enemies. The center of the city had a walled fort, a place to store food, and a large bath. 4. Clay tablets were covered with pictograms, figures that tell a story. No one can read the Harappan language.

Modified Activity 18—Hinduism Puzzle
Across 2. reincarnation 4. Brahman 5. Vedas 6. cows 8. warrior
9. Sanskrit
Down 1. Shiva 3. caste 4. Brahma 5. Vishna 6. cycle
7. Hinduism

Modified Activity 19—Complete the Story
1. India 2. Four Noble Truths 3. Buddha 4. Enlightened One
5. Buddhism 6. selfish 7. suffering 8. Eightfold Path 9. desire
10. nirvana 11. soul 12. monks 13. monasteries 14. countries
15. China/Japan 16. Japan/China

Modified Activity 20—Ancient China Geography Match
1. A 2. E 3. B 4. A 5. C 6. B 7. D 8. A 9. B 10. E 11. D 12. E

Modified Activity 21—Chinese History Puzzle
1. China 2. Han 3. dynasty 4. scribes 5. paper 6. society 7. tomb
8. nobles 9. ancestor
Mystery Word
character

Modified Activity 22—Early Civilizations of the Aegean Sea

Across
3. Aegean 4. peninsula 7. Knossos 8. heroic
Down
1. Crete 2. warlike 5. Troy 6. horse

Modified Activity 23—The Greek City-States
1. acropolis 2. tyrants 3. independent 4. polis 5. aristocrats 6. mountains 7. Solon 8. temple

Modified Activity 24—Athens
1. citizens 2. bribe 3. lottery 4. direct democracy 5. assembly 6. defend 7. jury 8. seaport

Modified Activity 25—Sparta
1. Spartans planned to protect themselves with military skills—a wall of men instead of a wall of bricks. 2. Spartan women were independent and patriotic to their city-state. 3. When a boy was seven, he left his parents. At age 20, he became a citizen. He married at 30, but could not return home until he was 60. 4. The Spartans did not trade with others, they feared new ideas, and they were not interested in art and architecture.

Modified Activity 26—War Tests the Greeks
First Persian invasion: F, J; Marathon: C, E; Thermopylae: B, D; Salamis: G; Peloponnesian War: A, H, I; Greece is conquered: K, L

Modified Activity 27—Cultural Contributions
1. chorus 2. column 3. comedy 4. acropolis 5. Plato 6. Athena 7. goddess 8. ethics
Mystery Word
Socrates

Modified Activity 28—Alexander the Great Spreads Greek Culture
1. G 2. D 3. L 4. A 5. K 6. B 7. J 8. C 9. F 10. H 11. I 12. E

Modified Activity 29—Early Rome
1. The two brothers were Romulus and Remus. 2. The first settlements were in the hills near the Tiber River. 3. The Etruscans ruled Rome in 600 B.C. 4. Senators helped the king rule Rome. They also controlled large amounts of land.

Modified Activity 30—Plebeians and Patricians
1. Plebeians 2. Plebeians 3. Patricians 4. Patricians 5. Patricians 6. Plebeians 7. Plebeians 8. Plebeians

Modified Activity 31—Important Terms and People
1. E 2. C 3. D 4. B 5. G 6. H 7. F 8. A

Modified Activity 32—Choose the Correct Answer
1. reform 2. army 3. triumvirate 4. plebeians 5. riot 6. politician 7. challenge 8. taxes

Modified Activity 33—The End of the Republic
1. D 2. D 3. A 4. C

Modified Activity 34—The Age of Augustus
1. B 2. D 3. A 4. B 5. D 6. D 7. A 8. C

Modified Activity 35—Roman Empire Sentences
1. life 2. Nero 3. emperors 4. Trajan 5. plague 6. lyre 7. peace 8. Caligula

Modified Activity 36—The Rise of Christianity
1. disciples 2. divine 3. Greek 4. prophet 5. emperor 6. gentiles 7. Rome 8. king 9. loyal 10. New Testament 11. Paul 12. miracle

Modified Activity 37—The Fall of Rome
1. Adrianople 2. Constantine 3. Visigoths 4. Odoacer 5. Attila 6. co-emperor 7. Byzantium 8. survive 9. Vandals 10. Huns
Mystery Word
Diocletian

Modified Activity 38—Roman Culture
1. C 2. D 3. H 4. G 5. E 6. F 7. A 8. B

Modified Activity 39—The First Americans
1. George McJunkin was an African American cowboy who found a "bone pit" of large animal bones. 2. The first Americans walked from Asia over the Bering Strait and into North and South America. 3. The land grew warmer, and American Indians settled in communities all over North America and South America. 4. The "bone pit" was important because it showed that American Indians had been living in North America for at least 9,000 years.

Modified Activity 40—Early Southwestern Cultures
1. Hohokam 2. growing 3. kivas 4. Anasazi 5. Chaco Canyon 6. Snaketown 7. Mogollon 8. Golden Age

Modified Activity 41—Early Regional Cultures
1. A 2. H 3. E 4. F 5. B 6. D 7. G 8. C

Modified Activity 42—Civilizations of Mesoamerica
1. C 2. D 3. B 4. A

Modified Activity 43—The Church During the Middle Ages
1. monks 2. Benedictines 3. Holy 4. pilgrims 5. Muslim 6. crusaders 7. convents 8. Pope Urban II

Modified Activity 44—Feudalism Puzzle
1. church 2. feudal 3. armor 4. fief 5. money 6. sword 7. weapons 8. squires 9. brave 10. jousting
Mystery Word
ceremonies

Modified Activity 45—The Manor
1. A serf was a peasant who was bound to the land and whose life was controlled by the lord of the manor. 2. Answers will vary. Possible answer The people who lived on the manor could grow or raise all the food they ate. 3. The three-field system, the horseshoe, a better plow, the waterwheel, and the windmill all improved farming. 4. Courtyards had many small buildings and sheds, such as a blacksmith's shop, a bakery, a kitchen, a stable for horses, and storage areas for weapons and extra food.

Modified Activity 46—Middle Ages Culture
1. buttress 2. *Beowulf* 3. bishop 4. Latin 5. cathedral 6. jury 7. Romanesque 8. Thomas Aquinas

Modified Activity 47—Byzantine Empire Crossword
Across
1. patriarch 6. Constantine 11. relic 12. Justinian
Down
2. Turks 3. Greek 4. Rome 5. barbaric 7. Istanbul 8. code 9. saint 10. Orthodox

Modified Activity 48—The Russians Match-Up
1. C 2. B 3. F 4. H 5. D 6. G 7. E 8. A 9. K 10. L 11. J 12. I
13. N 14. O 15. M

Modified Activity 49—Europe During the Middle Ages
1. C 2. C 3. D 4. C 5. B 6. A 7. A 8. C 9. B 10. D 11. B 12. A

Modified Activity 50—The Rise of Islam
1. Muhammad 2. Hegira 3. idols 4. Qur'an 5. Gabriel 6. pillars
7. alms 8. Hajj 9. Christianity 10. Islam

Modified Activity 51—Islamic Civilization
1. Baghdad 2. jihads 3. trade 4. Jabir

Modified Activity 52—African Kingdoms
1. G 2. M 3. M 4. S 5. M 6. S 7. G 8. G

Modified Activity 53—India
1. A 2. A 3. D 4. C 5. B 6. A 7. D 8. B

Modified Activity 54—China
1. E 2. B 3. F 4. A 5. D 6. C 7. G 8. L 9. J 10. H 11. I 12. K

Modified Activity 55—The Mongols Conquer China
Part A
1. B 2. A 3. C 4. E 5. D
Part B
6. Genghis Khan 7. Ming 8. foreigners

Modified Activity 56—History and Culture of Japan
1. religion 2. Nipon 3. missionaries 4. Jimmu 5. nobles
6. Buddhists 7. invaders 8. spirits

Modified Activity 57—Japan Develops Its Own Culture
1. daimyo 2. samurai 3. estates 4. bushido 5. self-discipline
6. calligraphy 7. hari-kari 8. shogun
Mystery Phrase
martial arts

Modified Activity 58—A Unified Japan
1. The daimyos were the highest nobles next to the shogun.
2. Ikebana is the art of arranging flowers. 3. People in Japan
were not allowed to be Christians. The shogun ordered all foreign
missionaries to leave, and many Christian Japanese were killed.
4. Japanese paintings usually show the beauty of Japan. Some
paintings show war.

Modified Activity 59—The Troubled 14th Century
1. The Black Death was a disease that affected many during the
Middle Ages. 2. The Black Death caused the population, food, and
money to decrease. 3. The peasants and serfs were fighting for their
rights during the rebellion. 4. The Middle Ages ended with the
Renaissance began.

Modified Activity 60—The Spirit of the Renaissance
1. B 2. E 3. D 4. F 5. A 6. C 7. H 8. G

Modified Activity 61—The Renaissance Begins in Italy
1. Lorenzo 2. worldly 3. republican 4. Medici 5. architect
6. city-states 7. Savonarola 8. Venice

Modified Activity 62—Renaissance Literature
1. E 2. D 3. F 4. G 5. A 6. B 7. H 8. C

Modified Activity 63—Great Renaissance Artists
1. L 2. L 3. R 4. L 5. M 6. R 7. M 8. L

Modified Activity 64—The Reformers Multiple Choice
1. A 2. D 3. B 4. C 5. D 6. B 7. A 8. D

Modified Activity 65—The Reformation Puzzle
1. faith 2. lightning 3. deed 4. purgatory 5. salvation
6. Germany 7. Reformation 8. monk 9. church 10. printed
Mystery Word
indulgence

Modified Activity 66—Lutheran Match-Up
1. B 2. G 3. A 4. E 5. D 6. H 7. C 8. F

Modified Activity 67—Protestant Ideas Multiple Choice
1. B 2. B 3. D 4. D 5. A 6. C 7. D 8. C

**Modified Activity 68—John Calvin Organizes
a New Religion**
1. F 2. G 3. E 4. D 5. C 6. B 7. H 8. A

Modified Activity 69—Counter-Reformation Puzzle
1. Paul 2. Trent 3. Catholic 4. salvation 5. censor 6. Jesuits
7. counter 8. Ignatius 9. missionaries 10. Inquisition
Mystery Word
Protestant

Modified Activity 70—Modern Science Develops
1. One way that scholars decided what was true or false was by
reading the Bible. (Students may also answer that scholars studied
the works of Greek and Roman writers.) 2. Francis Bacon worked
out the five steps of the scientific method in the 1620s. 3. A
hypothesis is an educated guess about an answer to a problem.
Making a hypothesis is the second step of the scientific method.
4. Scientists discover the truth in an experiment by carefully
controlling a test. The test helps them find the truth for themselves,
so they do not to depend on others to tell them with is true or false.

Modified Activity 71—Recognizing People and Ideas
1. C 2. A 3. B 4. D 5. A 6. C 7. D 8. B 9. B 10. A 11. C 12. B

Modified Activity 72—Questions about Galileo
1. He observed the rough surface of the moon, dark spots on the
sun, and the four moons of Jupiter. 2. He concluded that the sun,
rather than the earth, was the center of the universe.
3. The Catholic Church said Galileo's book was an attack on
Catholic teaching, so they put him on trial and imprisoned him.
4. Galileo concluded that gravity makes all objects on Earth fall at
the same speed.

Modified Activity 73—Newton's Discoveries
1. gravity 2. prism 3. scientific law 4. light 5. planets 6. absorbs
7. Copernicus 8. universe

Modified Activity 74—Identifying Important People
1. A 2. B 3. F 4. C 5. E 6. D 7. G 8. H 9. L 10. I 11. J 12. K

**Modified Activity 75—Europeans Search for
New Trade Routes**
1. East 2. Portugal 3. gold 4. India 5. Cape of Storms
6. Cape of Good Hope 7. navigation 8. Arab merchants

Modified Activity 76—Exploring New Lands
1. Magellan 2. Spain 3. Vasco da Gama 4. profit 5. strait
6. Columbus 7. exploration 8. native

Modified Activity 77—Spanish Empires in America
1. Hernando Cortes of Spain conquered the Aztec empire.
2. Francisco Pizarro of Spain conquered the Inca Empire. 3. The Inca emperor offered Pizarro a room full of gold. 4. Pizarro put the Inca emperor on trial and executed him.

Modified Activity 78—Spain Establishes Colonies in America
1. E 2. F 3. H 4. B 5. A 6. G 7. C 8. D

Modified Activity 79—The Growth of the Slave Trade
1. B 2. A 3. B 4. D 5. B 6. D 7. D 8. A

Modified Activity 80—The Results of Exploring and Establishing Colonies
1. B 2. D 3. C 4. F 5. E 6. G 7. A

Modified Activity 81—The Rise of Nations
1. C 2. A 3. B 4. C 5. D 6. A 7. B 8. D

Modified Activity 82—The Rise and Fall of Spain
1. C 2. B 3. A 4. B 5. A 6. D 7. C 8. A

Modified Activity 83—English Monarchs Struggle for Power
Part A
1. E 2. G 3. C 4. F 5. B 6. D 7. A
Part B
8. James I 9. Elizabeth I 10. Charles I

Modified Activity 84—England Rejects Absolute Monarchy
1. Restoration 2. Habeas Corpus 3. Cavaliers 4. Tory 5. William
6. Roundheads 7. constitutional 8. Whig 9. Catholic 10. England
Mystery Word
Revolution

Modified Activity 85—Absolute Monarchy in France
1. C 2. G 3. D 4. H 5. B 6. F 7. E 8. A

Modified Activity 86—Russia and Prussia Produce Strong Monarchs
1. C 2. D 3. D 4. A 5. B 6. A 7. C 8. B

Modified Activity 87—In Search of Natural Laws
1. C 2. D 3. A 4. C 5. B 6. A 7. D 8. B

Modified Activity 88—Who Said It?
1. L 2. H 3. R 4. M 5. H 6. L 7. L 8. M 9. M 10. R 11. R
12. H

Modified Activity 89—The Influence of Enlightened Thinkers
Part A
1. F 2. B 3. F 4. D 5. E 6. G 7. A 8. H
Part B
9. Marie Therese Geoffrin 10. Voltaire 11. Denis Diderot
12. Maria Theresa

Modified Activity 90—Enlightenment Artists Puzzle
1. classical 2. history 3. Mozart 4. composer 5. Handel
6. baroque 7. nobles 8. melody
Mystery Word
symphony

Modified Activity 91—Revolution in the American Colonies
1. G 2. C 3. A 4. D 5. F 6. E 7. H 8. B

Modified Activity 92—The American Revolutionary War
Part A
1. C 2. A 3. B 4. E 5. F 6. H 7. G 8. D
Part B
1. Thomas Jefferson 2. George Washington 3. King George III

Modified Activity 93—The French Revolution
1. estate 2. clergy 3. Estates-General 4. Bastille 5. land
6. Versailles 7. National Assembly 8. French Revolution

Modified Activity 94—Reforms and Terror in France
1. A 2. C 3. B 4. D 5. B 6. B 7. A 8. C 9. D 10. D 11. C 12. A

Modified Activity 95—Napoleon and the French Empire
1. F 2. A 3. E 4. D 5. C 6. B 7. G 8. J 9. H 10. K 11. L 12. I

Modified Activity 96—England and the Industrial Revolution
1. E 2. G 3. B 4. C 5. F 6. D 7. H 8. A

Modified Activity 97—Modern Industries Grow
1. The "spinning jenny" helped the textile industry. 2. The factory system made people work at certain times. 3. Eli Whitney used mass production to make identical guns. 4. Steel was better than iron because it is stronger and doesn't break as easily.

Modified Activity 98—Transportation Fill-In
1. Watt 2. Transportation 3. machines 4. boiler 5. efficient
6. locomotive 7. canals 8. raw

Modified Activity 99—Problems with Industry
1. C 2. A 3. A 4. D 5. B 6. B 7. B 8. C

Modified Activity 100—About the Congress of Vienna
1. Napoleon Bonaparte controlled France after the French Revolution. 2. The Congress of Vienna restructured Europe.
3. Prince Metternich was Austria's foreign minister. 4. He thought the French Revolution had made Europe weak. 5. Metternich wanted royal families to rule Europe. 6. Balance of power means major nations have equal strength. 7. Russia gained Finland and most of Poland through the Congress of Vienna. 8. The German states were organized into a confederation.

Modified Activity 101—Nationalism Multiple Choice
1. C 2. B 3. C 4. D 5. D 6. B 7. D 8. C

Modified Activity 102—Latin American Independence
1. E 2. D 3. C 4. B 5. A 6. B 7. A 8. C

Modified Activity 103—Conservatives, Liberals, and Radicals
1. C 2. R 3. C 4. C 5. R 6. C 7. L 8. L

Modified Activity 104—Revolutions in 1848
1. Both groups wanted political reform. **2.** Socialists wanted the state to control factories and land. **3.** A utopian society is perfect. **4.** Marx thought society could do without government.

Modified Activity 105—Growing Nationalism Puzzle
1. culture **2.** Foreign **3.** language **4.** democracy **5.** Heritage **6.** loyalty **7.** history **8.** government **9.** multilingual **10.** Ancestors
Mystery Word
traditions

Modified Activity 106—Growing Nationalism in Italy Puzzle
1. prime minister **2.** Cavour **3.** Italy **4.** Mazzini **5.** Austria **6.** Garibaldi **7.** Sicily **8.** Sardinia **9.** Emmanuel **10.** France
Mystery Word
politician

Modified Activity 107—The Unification of Germany Match-Up
1. E **2.** C **3.** A **4.** F **5.** D **6.** B **7.** H **8.** K **9.** I **10.** L **11.** G **12.** J

Modified Activity 108—Imperialism Puzzle
1. mother **2.** imperialism **3.** colonialism **4.** supplies **5.** tin **6.** Christianity **7.** market **8.** Industrial **9.** sea **10.** materials
Mystery Word
militarism

Modified Activity 109—The Effect of Imperialism on Asia Multiple Choice
1. B **2.** D **3.** A **4.** C **5.** D **6.** C **7.** C **8.** B

Modified Activity 110—The Effect of Imperialism on Africa
1. protectorate **2.** Suez Canal **3.** France **4.** transportation **5.** Belgium **6.** Germany **7.** customs **8.** Italy

Modified Activity 111—The Causes of the War
1. C **2.** B **3.** C **4.** D **5.** A **6.** B **7.** C **8.** D

Modified Activity 112— The War Years: 1914–1918
Part A
1. H **2.** B **3.** F **4.** I **5.** D **6.** E **7.** A **8.** C **9.** G
Part B
10. machine gun **11.** the United States **12.** Battle of Verdun

Modified Activity 113—Making Peace
1. The Allied leaders met at Versailles to create a peace treaty.
2. The "Big Four" at Versailles were Britain, France, Italy, and the United States. **3.** The treaty created Yugoslavia and Czechoslovakia.
4. The League of Nations was a group of leaders from the nations of the world. It wanted to keep the peace.

Modified Activity 114—World War I Changed the World
1. G **2.** D **3.** F **4.** A **5.** B **6.** C **7.** H **8.** E

Modified Activity 115—Life in Czarist Russia
1. czar **2.** autocracy **3.** Alexander II **4.** freedom **5.** Nicholas II **6.** democratic **7.** Bloody Sunday **8.** Duma

Modified Activity 116—Russia Moves Toward Revolution
1. C **2.** B **3.** A **4.** B **5.** D **6.** C **7.** D **8.** A

Modified Activity 117—Russia Becomes the Soviet Union
1. F **2.** D **3.** A **4.** B **5.** H **6.** G **7.** C **8.** E

Modified Activity 118—The Soviet Union Under Stalin
1. Joseph Stalin became the leader after Lenin died. **2.** Heavy industry factories hurt Russia because money was used for them instead of producing consumer goods. **3.** In a totalitarian state, a small group controls the lives of the citizens. **4.** Under Stalin, the Soviet Union became a powerful industrialized nation.

Modified Activity 119—The Fascists Gain Power in Italy
1. Italy **2.** Mussolini **3.** Il Duce **4.** obedience **5.** Black Shirts **6.** military **7.** Hitler **8.** fascist

Modified Activity 120—The Nazis Gain Power in Germany
1. F **2.** H **3.** G **4.** B **5.** E **6.** A **7.** C **8.** D

Modified Activity 121—The Chinese Begin to Build a Modern Nation
1. B **2.** D **3.** B **4.** B **5.** B **6.** A **7.** C **8.** A

Modified Activity 122—Military Leaders Take Over in Japan
1. Hideko Tojo **2.** fascist **3.** newspapers **4.** Italy **5.** Manchuria **6.** silk **7.** democracy **8.** Germany

Modified Activity 123—The Causes of World War II
1. B **2.** C **3.** C **4.** D **5.** B **6.** A **7.** C **8.** A

Modified Activity 124—Fascism Threatens Other Countries
1. Versailles **2.** Neville Chamberlain **3.** Munich Pact **4.** Japan **5.** front **6.** Appeasement **7.** Poland **8.** conference

Modified Activity 125—Axis Successes in Europe and Asia
1. German **2.** blitzkrieg **3.** French **4.** Maginot **5.** England **6.** Britain **7.** arsenal **8.** Soviet Union **9.** Stalingrad **10.** destroyer **11.** Japan **12.** United States

Modified Activity 126—The Tide Turns in Favor of the Allies
1. The Battle at Midway Island is considered the turning point in the war in the Pacific. **2.** D-Day is the day the Allied army invaded France. **3.** World War II ended in the Pacific when Japan surrendered on august 14, 1945. **4.** V-E Day was Victory in Europe Day. V-J Day is Victory in Japan Day.

Modified Activity 127—Learning About the Holocaust
1. Final Solution **2.** Holocaust **3.** Kristallnacht **4.** genocide **5.** death camps **6.** SS **7.** Resistance **8.** Dachau

Modified Activity 128—The Results of World War II
1. E **2.** S **3.** P **4.** P **5.** S **6.** P **7.** P **8.** S **9.** E **10.** S **11.** P **12.** P

Modified Activity 129—The United Nations
1. Roosevelt **2.** Security **3.** charter **4.** veto **5.** WHO **6.** organization **7.** FAO **8.** Trusteeship

Modified Activity 130—The Cold War Begins
1. Marshall Plan **2.** Truman Doctrine **3.** cold war **4.** Warsaw Pact **5.** NATO **6.** Greece **7.** European **8.** Communism **9.** Finland **10.** alliance
Mystery Word
propaganda

Modified Activity 131— Conflicts Between Superpowers
1. D 2. A 3. D 4. C 5. B 6. C 7. A 8. B 9. B 10. C 11. B 12. A

Modified Activity 132—Reforming the Soviet Union
1. Chechnya 2. perestroika 3. glasnost 4. Nikita Khrushchev
5. KGB 6. Ukraine 7. coup 8. Vladimir Putin

Modified Activity 133— Europe Experiences Great Change
1. Hungary 2. Communist 3. glasnost 4. Poland 5. cleansing
6. Albanians 7. Solidarity 8. Kosovo 9. strike 10. tariff
Mystery Word
Yugoslavia

Modified Activity 134—Many African Colonies Become Nations
1. A 2. A 3. C 4. C 5. D 6. A 7. D 8. D 9. A 10. B 11. C
12. B

Modified Activity 135—Israel Becomes a Nation
1. D 2. F 3. A 4. C 5. E 6. B 7. K 8. H 9. I 10. L 11. G 12. J

Modified Activity 136—India Gains Its Independence
1. India 2. British 3. self-rule 4. Mohandas Gandhi
5. constitution 6. democracy 7. Hindus 8. Pakistan

Modified Activity 137—The Struggle to Control China
1. The Communists and the Nationalists fought during the Chinese
civil war. 2. Mao Zedong led the Communists. Chiang Kai-shek led
the Nationalists. 3. Guerilla warfare uses bands of fights that make
surprise attacks. 4. The United States supported the Nationalists.
5. The Communists were more organized. 6. The Communists
finally won control of China. 7. Chiang Kai-shek and the
Nationalists fled to Taiwan. 8. The United States recognized the
People's Republic of China in 1972.

Modified Activity 138—Vietnamese Wars for Independence
1. NV 2. NV 3. SV 4. SV 5. SV 6. SV 7. NV 8. NV

Modified Activity 139—African Nations Face Many Challenges
1. conflict 2. pesticide 3. drought 4. investment 5. epidemic
6. slum 7. independent 8. urbanization 9. poverty 10. migrants
Mystery Word
fertilizer

Modified Activity 140—The Middle East Remains in Conflict
1. A 2. C 3. B 4. B 5. D 6. C 7. A 8. A 9. D 10. C 11. B 12. D

Modified Activity 141—Asian Countries Face Economic Challenges
1. human rights 2. Beijing 3. the United States 4. educated
5. Singapore 6. Japan 7. economic 8. Thailand 9. banks
10. China 11. Four Modernizations 12. Asian

Modified Activity 142—Latin America Struggles to Overcome Problems
1. C 2. B 3. A 4. G 5. H 6. F 7. E 8. D

Modified Activity 143—Energy and Technology Create a Global Village
1. B 2. C 3. A 4. F 5. D 6. E 7. K 8. H 9. J 10. L 11. I 12. G

Modified Activity 144—Global Trade and Economic Development
1. E 2. B 3. F 4. D 5. C 6. A 7. H 8. G

Modified Activity 145—Social and Environmental Challenges
1. Global warming 2. melting 3. coal 4. carbon monoxide
5. industrial 6. pesticides 7. oxygen 8. recycling

Modified Activity 146—The Threat of Global Terrorism
1. D 2. A 3. B 4. D

Modified Activity 147—Looking to the Future
1. H 2. E 3. C 4. B 5. F 6. D 7. G 8. A

Workbook Activities

Workbook Activity 1—Do You Remember?

1. We have learned about what happened to people in the past from the work of archaeologists and anthropologists. 2. A primary source is a first-hand account of an event, and a secondary source is a second-hand account. Primary source examples may include eyewitness accounts, newspapers, diaries, or letters. Secondary source examples may include textbooks, or accounts heard from someone else. 3. Historians ask *What?*, *When?*, *Where?*, *Who?*, and *Why?*. 4. One person's account of an event may be different from someone else's because people interpret events differently. 5. A group's culture is made up of its customs, and values.

Workbook Activity 2—The Importance of History

1. past 2. the present 3. the future 4. cause 5. question 6. history 7. connects 8. roots 9. global 10. humanity

Workbook Activity 3—Exploring the Past

1. pottery 2. anthropologists 3. when 4. artifacts 5. archaeologists 6. Calendars 7. Jewish 8. radiocarbon dating 9. artifacts 10. Christian 11. bones and teeth 12. garbage 13. putting together a jigsaw puzzle 14. Muslim 15. material

Workbook Activity 4—Prehistory Match-Up

1. F 2. C 3. A 4. B 5. E 6. G 7. D 8. O 9. L 10. H 11. K 12. I 13. N 14. K 15. M

Workbook Activity 5—Do You Remember?

1. The Tigris and the Euphrates Rivers were important to the people of Mesopotamia because they made the land fertile, helping the people raise crops and animals. 2. Sumerians owned their own houses or farms. Sumerian women and slaves had legal rights. 3. Sumerians built ziggurats, kept statues of the gods, and sacrificed animals to keep their gods happy. 4. Writing is the most important Sumerian invention because the Sumerians were the first people to write down history. They left the first written record of what their life was like. 5. Sample Answers: They were the first to use a plow and sailboat, and to put wheels on carts. They created arches and ramps. We use their number system to measure time.

Workbook Activity 6—Chart for Akkadians and Babylonians

Akkadians

kingdom arose around 2340 B.C.; ruled by Sargon I; used Sumerian cuneiform to make written records; leader repaired dikes and made irrigation systems longer; army used bronze weapons

Babylonians

kingdom arose around 1800 B.C.; ruled by Hammurabi; leader improved roads and helped develop trade; leader created the first system of laws; leader built a wall around the city

Workbook Activity 7—Phoenicians and Hebrews

1. D 2. F 3. B 4. C 5. G 6. E 7. H 8. A 9. K 10. N 11. O 12. L 13. I 14. M 15. J

Workbook Activity 8—Assyrian Crossword

Across

2. Nineveh 3. artisan 4. dominate 5. cavalry 7. tribute 8. iron 9. provinces 13. laws 14. Medes

Down

1. chariot 3. archers 6. library 10. Empire 12. governor ~~rebels~~ *(handwritten: rebels / 11.)*

Workbook Activity 9—Complete the Description

1. empire 2. Nineveh 3. Nebuchadnezzar 4. Egypt 5. Hebrew 6. Nebuchadnezzar 7. Babylon 8. Ischtar 9. glaze 10. sculptures 11. Hanging Gardens 12. queen 13. astronomers 14. ziggurat 15. constellations 16. future 17. 562 B.C. 18. Persian 19. Cyrus 20. Babylon

Workbook Activity 10—Important People and Terms

1. D 2. A 3. C 4. G 5. E 6. F 7. H 8. B 9. K 10. I 11. J 12. L 13. N 14. M 15. O

Workbook Activity 11—Nile River Facts

1. B 2. D 3. B 4. B 5. C 6. A 7. D 8. C 9. B 10. A

Workbook Activity 12—What Am I?

1. Lower Egypt 2. pharaohs 3. pyramids 4. afterlife 5. unite 6. caravan 7. Upper Egypt 8. Memphis 9. Old Kingdom 10. civil war

Workbook Activity 13—About the Middle Kingdom

1. The Middle Kingdom began in 2040 B.C. with a new dynasty. 2. Egyptians of the Middle Kingdom dug a canal to join the Nile River with business centers near the Red Sea. 3. The natural basin contained water drained from the swamps. It was used by farmers the water for irrigation. 4. Any one of the following. Egyptians in the Old Kingdom thought their pharaohs had complete power. Pharaohs of the Middle Kingdom had to share their power. Or, Egyptians in the Old Kingdom thought only the pharaoh lived forever. In the Middle Kingdom, Egyptians thought all people lived forever. Or, Egyptians in the Old Kingdom buried their pharaohs in pyramids. Egyptians of the Middle Kingdom buried their pharaohs in tombs cut into cliffs near Thebes. 5. The Hyksos were nomads who invaded Egypt around 1630 The Hyksos knew about war and ruled Egypt until 1570 B.C.

Workbook Activity 14—The New Kingdom Fill-In

1. Queen Cleopatra 2. Hatshepsut 3. Ikhnaton 4. Ikhanton 5. Ramses III 6. Queen Cleopatra 7. Thutmose III 8. Hatshepsut 9. Thutmose III 10. Thurmose III 11. Ikhnaton 12. Queen Cleopatra 13. Thutmose III 14. Ikhaton 15. Hatshepsut

Workbook Activity 15—Egyptian Gifts

1. B 2. A 3. D 4. C 5. A 6. B 7. D 8. C 9. A 10. D

Workbook Activity 16—India Crossword Puzzle

Across

2. Indus 5. summer 7. fertile 8. Ganges 10. peninsula

Down

1. winter 3. subcontinent 4. Khyber 6. geography 9. monsoon

Workbook Activity 17—What Am I?

1. irrigate 2. Indus River 3. cotton 4. tablet 5. flood 6. 1500 B.C. 7. alabaster 8. silt 9. Harappa 10. wall 11. patio 12. tower 13. pictogram 14. clay 15. grain

Workbook Activity 18—Identifying People, Places, and Things
1. H 2. E 3. A 4. G 5. B 6. F 7. C 8. D 9. M 10. K 11. I 12. L
13. J 14. N 15. O

Workbook Activity 19—Buddhism
1. Siddartha Gautama met several suffering people. After that, he walked the countryside and studied the Hindu holy books for several years. One day he discovered four noble truths about life. People called him Buddha, meaning "Enlightened One." The religion based on his truths is called Buddhism. 2. The four holy truths are: life is full of suffering; our own selfish wishes cause this suffering; we stop suffering when we stop being jealous, greedy, and selfish; and we can stop wishing for, or desiring, more. 3. They could enter a spiritual place called nirvana where their soul will find perfect peace. 4. They are alike because they both believe in reincarnation and that life is sad and evil. Both religions refuse to kill animals or eat meat. They are different because Buddhists treat all people the same and believe that people can reach nirvana in their own lifetime by following the Eightfold Path. 5. After seeing more than 100,000 people die, he realized the evil of war and became shoka, or powerful. He accepted Buddhism and was called "without sorrow," or ashoka.

Workbook Activity 20—Ancient China Facts
1. B 2. A 3. C 4. C 5. D 6. B 7. A 8. D 9. C 10. A

Workbook Activity 21—Chinese Dynasty Fill-In
1. dynasty 2. paper 3. wood 4. symbols 5. Qin 6. scribes
7. society 8. Shang 9. nobles 10. ancestor 11. Han 12. clay
13. iron 14. Silk Road 15. Confucius

Workbook Activity 22—Do You Remember?
1. The Minoan civilization began on the island of Crete. 2. The Greek civilization developed when the people from the north moved south into the peninsula of Greece and built cities there.
3. The Mycenaeans were warlike people. They raided other cities around the Aegean Sea. 4. We know about the Trojan War from the poems the Iliad and the Odyssey. 5. The Mycenaean warriors hid inside the wooden horse they had pretended to leave as a gift to the Trojans. The hidden warriors were able to let the Mycenaean army into the city.

Workbook Activity 23—The Greek City-State Facts
1. B 2. C 3. A 4. C 5. D 6. B 7. D 8. A 9. C 10. D

Workbook Activity 24—The Athenians
1. people 2. citizens 3. vote 4. men 5. loyal 6. government
7. defend 8. direct democracy 9. assembly 10. council 11. lottery
12. juries 13. bribing 14. seaport 15. artists

Workbook Activity 25—Sparta Puzzle
1. city-state 2. architecture 3. peninsula 4. patriotic 5. helots
6. soldiers 7. victor 8. military 9. enslaved 10. steal
Mystery Word
supportive

Workbook Activity 26—Greeks Wars Crossword
Across
2. Philip 7. Thermopylae 9. independence 11. Salamis
12. Ionians 13. Marathon
Down
1. Macedon 2. Peloponnesian 3. Athenian 4. alliance 5. Xerxes
6. fleet 8. Darius 10. maneuver 14. Nike

Workbook Activity 27—Greek Culture
1. Athena 2. goddess 3. acropolis 4. columns 5. beauty 6. chorus
7. comedies 8. philosophers 9. Socrates 10. ethics 11. Plato
12. Aristotle 13. politics 14. brains 15. logic

Workbook Activity 28—Alexander the Great
1. F 2. A 3. B 4. C 5. D 6. G 7. H 8. E 9. K 10. M 11. O 12. L
13. J 14. I 15. N

Workbook Activity 29—What Am I?
1. Latium 2. Remus 3. Etruscans 4. founded 5. patriciam
6. senate 7. Italy 8. advanced 9. Tiber 10. Latins

Workbook Activity 30—Learning About the Roman Republic
1. patricians 2. republic 3. representatives 4. consuls 5. veto
6. senate 7. democracy 8. patricians 9. plebeians 10. power
11. slavery 12. political 13. tribunes 14. senate 15. tablets
16. laws 17. patricians 18. plebeians 19. senate 20. centuries

Workbook Activity 31—Rome Expands Its Boundaries
1. The Punic Wars began when Rome and Carthage both tried to control the island of Sicily. 2. In the First Punic War, Romans used planks to board the Carthage ships. This made it possible for the Romans army to defeat the Carthaginian navy. 3. The Second Punic War ended when the Roman general Scipio defeated Hannibal's at Zama. 4. Carthaginians starved during the Third Punic War because Romans cut off their food supplies. 5. After the Punic Wars, Romans burned Carthage to the ground and sold its people into slavery. A legend says that after the Punic Wars, Romans covered the farmlands in Carthage with salt. This kept anything from growing.

Workbook Activity 32—The Republic Faces Problems
1. C 2. D 3. H 4. G 5. A 6. J 7. F 8. B 9. E 10. I

Workbook Activity 33—The End of the Republic
1. C 2. B 3. A 4. D 5. B

Workbook Activity 34—Age of Augustus Crossword
Across
1. Golden 2. Rhine 3. Egypt 5. eternal 6. ~~promises~~ 6 provinces 9. empire
10. civilized 11. Augustus 12. peace 13. taxes
Down
1. government 3. Euphrates 4. Octavian 7. Roman 8. aqueduct

Workbook Activity 35—Roman Emperors
Claudius: 4, 12, 18
Tiberius: 3, 7, 15
Nero: 8, 13, 16
Trajan: 5, 14
Caligula: 2, 6, 19
Hadrian: 9, 11, 17
Marcus Aurelius: 1, 10, 20

Workbook Activity 36—Christianity Match-Up
1. A 2. B 3. F 4. C 5. G 6. D 7. H 8. E 9. O 10. L 11. K 12. M
13. J 14. N 15. I

Workbook Activity 37—Do You Remember?
1. Diocletian thought that the Roman Empire was too large for one person to govern, so he divided it into two parts. Diocletian ruled the eastern part, and another person, called a co-emperor, ruled the western part. 2. Constantine became emperor in A.D. 306, and he decided to move to capital to Byzantium. He named the new capital after himself, calling it Constantinople. 3. The Huns were a non-Germanic tribe from central Asia. Their leader was Attila the Hun. The Huns were expert horsemen and fierce warriors. The Visigoths feared the Huns. 4. The Vandals were a German tribe that attacked Rome in A.D. 455. They destroyed much of Rome's beauty. This is why we use the modern word vandal to describe someone who destroys property. 5. In A.D. 378, at the Battle of Adrianople, the Visigoths defeated the Romans. This was an important historical event because for the first time in hundreds of years, Rome could not defend itself.

Workbook Activity 38—Rome's Contributions
1. A 2. H 3. C 4. B 5. E 6. G 7. D 8. F 9. O 10. I 11. M 12. J
13. K 14. N 15. L

Workbook Activity 39—First Americans Fill-In
1. nomads 2. artifacts 3. bone pit 4. glaciers 5. Folsom Point
6. Clovis Point 7. Ice Age 8. American Indians
9. George McJunkin 10. Bering Strait

Workbook Activity 40—Southwestern Culture Facts
1. M 2. H 3. H 4. Av5. A 6. M 7. H 8. H 9. M 10. A

Workbook Activity 41—All About Early Regional Cultures
1. A 2. B 3. C 4. C 5. B 6. A 7. C 8. B 9. D 10. A

Workbook Activity 42—Mesoamerican Match-Up
1. E 2. F 3. D 4. A 5. I 6. H 7. C 8. B 9. G 10. J

Workbook Activity 43—Middle Ages Religion Crossword

Workbook Activity 44—Feudalism Match-Up
Part A
1. H 2. A 3. B 4. F 5. G 6. C 7. E 8. D
Part B
9. L 10. I 11. O 12. N 13. K 14. J 15. M

Workbook Activity 45—Manor Life
1. A 2. D 3. D 4. B 5. C 6. C 7. A 8. D 9. A 10. B

Workbook Activity 46—Culture in the Middle Ages Match-Up
Part A
1. B 2. D 3. E 4. H 5. F 6. C 7. G 8. A
Part B
9. K 10. I 11. M 12. L 13. J 14. O 15. N

Workbook Activity 47—What Am I?: The Byzantine Empire
1. code 2. Constantinople 3. icon 4. patriarch 5. relics
6. Justinian 7. Eastern Orthodox Church 8. Hippodrome 9. saint
10. Constantine 11. churches 12. goods 13. plague 14. Istanbul
15. barbaric

Workbook Activity 48—The Russians
1. The Slavs learned about Christianity and could read the Bible because the monks invented the Cyrillic alphabet, and used it to translate the Bible and write about Christian ceremonies.
2. The Russian king Vladimir married the sister of the Byzantine emperor. The Byzantine Empire traded with Russia. Russians built their churches in the style of Byzantine churches. 3. Kiev was important because it was located at the center of three trading routes. 4. Ivan the Great freed Russia from foreign rule, set up a strong government, and rebuilt the Kremlin. 5. Ivan IV is known as Ivan the Terrible because he was cruel. He ordered his government officials to kill many Russians and enemy soldiers.

Workbook Activity 49—The Story of Europe During the Middle Ages
1. Rome 2. soldiers 3. Germanic 4. kingdoms 5. towns 6. villages
7. interest 8. literature 9. knowledge 10. Dark Ages 11. Franks
12. Clovis 13. Paris 14. Roman Catholic 15. Charlemagne
16. religion 17. pope 18. Vikings 19. Leif Eriksson
20. Newfoundland 21. Canute 22. Romans
23. Edward the Confessor 24. William 25. Norman

Workbook Activity 50—Understanding the Rise of Islam
1. Muhammad and his followers fled Mecca because it was too dangerous to stay. The people of Mecca worshipped hundreds of gods. Muhammad and his followers worshipped only one god.
2. When Muhammad returned to Mecca, he destroyed the statues of the gods, and took control of the city. 3. The five pillars are: statement of faith, prayer, giving of alms; fasting; and a pilgrimage to Mecca. 4. The Arabic language spread as Islam spread around the world. 5. Muslims recognize the teachings of Judaism and Christianity.

Workbook Activity 51—Understanding the Islamic Civilization
Part A
1. B 2. A 3. A 4. B 5. C
Part B
6. culture 7. medicine 8. light 9. Arabic numbers
10. decimal system

Workbook Activity 52—African Kingdoms Match-Up
1. E 2. G 3. C 4. A 5. F 6. I 7. B 8. H 9. D 10. J

Workbook Activity 53—Learning About India

1. Golden Age 2. Gupta 3. Hindus 4. religion 5. stupas 6. unique 7. scientists 8. moon 9. gravity 10. mathematicians 11. surgery 12. inoculate 13. decline 14. Huns 15. Mongols 16. Timur the Lame 17. Babur 18. provinces 19. civilians 20. Muslim 21. religious 22. Taj Mahal 23. tomb 24. Red Fort 25. gold

Workbook Activity 54—China Multiple Choice

1. B 2. C 3. D 4. C 5. A 6. A 7. D 8. A 9. C 10. B

Workbook Activity 55—The Mongols and Trade Between China and Europe

From the Chinese: porcelain, printing, gunpowder
From the Europeans: glass, clothes, cotton, silver, carpets, honey

Workbook Activity 56—Japan

1. The waters that surround Japan have kept out invaders, and have brought ideas to Japan from Korea and China. 2. The Japanese adopted the Chinese writing system, Chinese art and literature, Chinese clothing, the Chinese calendar, and the Chinese civil service. 3. Shinto is different from Christianity, Islam, and Buddhism because it has no holy books like the Bible, the Qur'an, or the Vedas. Shinto followers worship thousands of gods and spirits. 4. The Japanese call their country *Nippon,* which means "source of the sun." The royal family of Japan traces its ancestors back to Jimmu. They believe Jimmu was related to the sun goddess. 5. Young Japanese men became Buddhists when they went to China to study. They brought the religion with them when they returned. Buddhist missionaries came to Japan to spread Buddhism.

Workbook Activity 57—Japanese Culture Match-Up

1. H 2. D 3. C 4. B 5. F 6. E 7. G 8. A 9. N 10. J 11. O 12. L 13. K 14. I 15. M

Workbook Activity 58—The Tokugawa Unify Japan

1. merchants 2. Christian 3. Dutch 4. Edo 5. Sesshu 6. beauty 7. Noh 8. missionaries 9. ikebana 10. Tokyo 11. Kabuki 12. Tokugawa 13. rocks 14. painted 15. Nagasaki

Workbook Activity 59—14th Century Problems

1. C 2. B 3. A 4. A 5. B 6. D 7. C 8. B 9. C 10. D

Workbook Activity 60—Renaissance Ideas

1. tutor 2. Isabella d'Este 3. humanist 4. Renaissance 5. Greece 6. ignorant 7. Latin 8. Humanism 9. learning 10. Middle Ages

Workbook Activity 61—Italian Renaissance Match-Up

1. F 2. I 3. E 4. G 5. B 6. H 7. A 8. J 9. C 10. D

Workbook Activity 62—Literature of the Renaissance

1. Queen Elizabeth I 2. Geoffrey Chaucer 3. William Shakespeare 4. Miguel de Cervantes 5. William Shakespeare 6. Johann Gutenberg 7. Miguel de Cervantes 8. Johann Gutenberg 9. Queen Elizabeth I 10. Miguel de Cervantes

Workbook Activity 63—About Renaissance Artists

1. Michelangelo was born near Florence 2. Lorenzo de Medici helped Michelangelo. 3. Michelangelo painting the celing of the Sistine Chapel. 4. Rafael Santi was born in 1483. 5. The Vatican is the hope of the pope. 6. Michelangelo carved the Pietà. 7. Leonardo da Vinci painted the Last Supper using the fresco painting method. 8. Rafael's painting, the School of Athens, shows the Greek philosophers Plato and Aristotle. 9. A genius was an artist who was born with special skills and was different from ordinary people. 10. Patrons were people who supported artists by giving them money.

Workbook Activity 64—People Challenge the Church's Authority

1. E 2. D 3. J 4. A 5. I 6. B 7. G 8. C 9. H 10. F

Workbook Activity 65—Martin Luther Leads the Reformation

1. Germany 2. Reformation 3. Catholic 4. salvation 5. faith 6. promise 7. indulgences 8. Tetzel 9. purgatory 10. Rome 11. theses 12. argue 13. officials 14. printed 15. influence

Workbook Activity 66—Luther Starts His Own Church

1. B 2. D 3. C 4. C 5. A 6. A 7. D 8. C 9. B 10. D

Workbook Activity 67—Protestant Ideas Spread to England

1. Henry VIII had not always agreed with Luther. In 1521, Henry VIII attacked Luther's ideas, and Pope Leo X called Henry the "Defender of the Faith." 2. The Reformation in England began when King Henry VIII wanted to divorce Catherine of Aragon, but the Catholic Church would not allow it. In 1534, Parliament made the king the head of the Church of England, or Anglican Church. 3. Henry wanted a divorce. He appointed a new archbishop, who said that the king's marriage to Catherine was not legal. 4. Anglican rituals became a blend of Catholic and Protestant ceremonies after Elizabeth I tried to join together the Protestants and Catholics into the Anglican Church. 5. The Puritans were a group of people who wanted to make the Anglican Church clean. They did not like Elizabeth I's compromise. They wanted to rid the Anglican Church of Catholic rituals. Many Puritans left England and settled in North America.

Workbook Activity 68—What Am I?

1. Huguenot 2. Paris 3. Calvinist 4. elder 5. dancing 6. Geneva 7. Martin Luther 8. John Calvin 9. massacre 10. elect

Workbook Activity 69—The Catholic Reformation

1. D 2. C 3. A 4. B 5. C 6. C 7. A 8. D 9. B 10. D

Workbook Activity 70—The Development of Modern Science

1. method 2. certainty 3. experiment 4. observe 5. question 6. truth 7. Bible 8. conclusion 9. five 10. Aristotle
Mystery Word
hypothesis

Workbook Activity 71—Copernicus

1. B 2. C 3. A 4. D 5. B 6. D 7. B 8. A 9. C 10. A

Workbook Activity 72—Galileo

1. Copernicus' 2. mathematics 3. telescope 4. moon 5. sun
6. Jupiter 7. sun 8. earth 9. universe 10. scholars 11. Bible
12. censored 13. experimented 14. gravity 15. father

Workbook Activity 73—Isaac Newton

1. E 2. I 3. J 4. F 5. H 6. C 7. D 8. B 9. A 10. G

Workbook Activity 74—Other Early Scientists

Workbook Activity 75—New Trade Routes

1. J 2. G 3. I 4. C 5. H 6. A 7. F 8. B 9. D 10. E

Workbook Activity 76—Countries Gain New Lands

1. Spain 2. Portugal 3. India 4. China 5. Portugal 6. Spain
7. Portugal 8. China 9. India 10. Spain

Workbook Activity 77—The Spanish Conquest Match-Up

1. A 2. G 3. B 4. D 5. C 6. F 7. H 8. E 9. M 10. K 11. I 12. J
13. N 14. L 15. O

Workbook Activity 78—Spanish Colonies Multiple Choice

1. C 2. A 3. C 4. C 5. B 6. D 7. B 8. A 9. B 10. A

Workbook Activity 79—Questions About the Slave Trade

1. In the ancient world, a person could become a slave if they had not paid a debt, or if they were captured in a war. 2. Slavery had existed in Africa for many centuries. 3. Spain allowed Portugal to bring African slaves to the Americas. 4. The slave trade grew because European settlements grew. 5. Slavery lasted for almost 400 years in the Americas.

Workbook Activity 80—Exploring and Establishing the New Colonies

1. Netherlands 2. money 3. medicine 4. potatoes 5. Asia
6. majority 7. Roanoke Island 8. Samuel de Champlain 9. cacao
10. "New World"

Workbook Activity 81—Nations Fill-In

1. nobles 2. nationalism 3. country 4. boundaries 5. language
6. traditions 7. government 8. Hobbes 9. monarch 10. unify
11. power 12. absolute 13. Age of Kings 14. Spain 15. disobey

Workbook Activity 82—Do You Remember?

1. The Moors built their civilization in southern Spain around 732. Their civilization lasted almost 800 years. 2. Isabella went to war against Granada and then said everyone in Spain had to be a Catholic. If Moors or Jews refused, Isabella said they had to leave Spain. 3. Charles V inherited lands in France from his father, and Austria from his grandfather. He also controlled land in Italy, the Netherlands, Germany, Belgium, and the Americas. 4. Philip II (who was a Roman Catholic) invaded England because Elizabeth I had made England a strong Protestant nation. He wanted to stop the spread of Protestantism. 5. The English defeated the Spanish Armada by sending burning ships into the Spanish fleet and scattering them, and because they had smaller and faster ships than the Spanish Armada.

Workbook Activity 83— English Monarchs Multiple Choice

1. A 2. D 3. B 4. B 5. C 6. A 7. C 8. D 9. D 10. A

Workbook Activity 84—What Am I?

1. Cavalier 2. monarchy 3. Mary 4. constitutional monarchy
5. Tory 6. Roundhead 7. English Bill of Rights 8. habeas corpus
9. Whig 10. Glorious Revolution 11. William 12. Oliver Cromwell
13. Charles I 14. Restoration 15. tolerant

Workbook Activity 85—France's Monarchy

1. A cardinal is a high official of the Roman Catholic Church.
2. Cardinal Mazarin ruled because Louis XIV was too young to make decisions. 3. Louis XIV centralized the government because he wanted to rule France alone. To do this, he had to lessen the nobles' power, appoint officials to collect taxes, and expand and reorganize the French army. 4. Louis XIV built a grand palace at Versailles. It took 30 years to build and cost millions of dollars.
5. People called Louis XIV the "Sun King" because all of France seemed to revolve around him like planets around the sun. His reign was an absolute monarchy.

Workbook Activity 86—Russia and Prussia Match-Up

1. F 2. B 3. A 4. J 5. H 6. G 7. D 8. E 9. I 10. C

Workbook Activity 87—Do You Remember?

1. Newton's Law showed that, with good information, people can correctly predict the movement of falling objects on Earth. They can also predict the movement of the moon and planets. 2. Newton discovered things by using reason rather than experimenting.
3. People began to think of the universe as a clock, whose movements are predictable and orderly. They believed the universe was predictable and that people can predict what will happen.
4. An enlightened thinker was a person who believed in scientific reasoning and asked difficult questions. They searched for truth about how nature and human societies work. 5. Enlightened thinkers wanted to improve how people live. They wanted to think clearly and logically, without letting their feelings guide them. They wanted to use scientific reasoning to examine every part of society.

Workbook Activity 88—New Government Crossword

Across

5. Hobbes 6. Locke 7. life 8. contract 11. Montesquieu
12. Rousseau 13. reasonable 14. Parliament

Down

1. balance 2. property 3. liberty 4. absolute 9. order 10. virtue
11. majority

Workbook Activity 89—Enlightened Thinkers
1. C 2. B 3. D 4. A 5. B 6. B 7. C 8. C 9. A 10. D

Workbook Activity 90—Enlightenment Artists Match-Up
1. H 2. B 3. G 4. E 5. D 6. C 7. A 8. F 9. K 10. J 11. N 12. M
13. I 14. L 15. O

Workbook Activity 91—American Colonies Multiple Choice
1. B 2. D 3. C 4. A 5. C 6. D 7. B 8. A 9. C 10. A

Workbook Activity 92—Do You Remember?
1. The first fighting of the American Revolution took place in 1775 at Lexington and Concord in Massachusetts. 2. The Declaration of Independence said that the colonies were free states; that the colonies were no longer a part of the British Empire; that people could change or choose their government if that government did not protect their rights of life and liberty; that people had the right to try to find happiness. 3. George Washington's soldiers faced defeats in the early part of the war. The soldiers had little training and lacked supplies. 4. General Cornwallis led the British troops at Yorktown, where he surrendered after a battle that took place in 1781. 5. The French fleet helped the colonial soldiers defeat the British at Yorktown in 1781. The French fleet prevented the British navy from rescuing General Cornwallis and his soldiers.

Workbook Activity 93—French Revolution Match-Up
1. A 2. F 3. C 4. H 5. D 6. G 7. E 8. B 9. I 10. K 11. J 12. N
13. O 14. L 15. M

Workbook Activity 94—Napoleon and the French Empire
Across
1. legislature 3. terror 4. radical 6. enforce 8. republic
9. Versailles 13. Antoinette 15. émigré 16. convention 17. Jacobin
Down
1. Leopold 2. guillotine 4. Robepierre 5. Louis 6. equality
7. executive 10. moderate 11. treason 12. Directory 14. Napoleon

Workbook Activity 95—Do You Remember?
1. Napoleon moved his soldiers quickly, and then put most of them at the weakest point of the enemy line. 2. Napoleon replaced the Holy Roman Empire with the Confederation of the Rhine, a loose alliance of German states. 3. The Continental System hurt France's economy and caused neutral European nations to turn against France. 4. Napoleon's retreat from Russia was a military disaster because thousands of soldiers starved or froze to death, and very few of the surviving soldiers were able to fight when they returned to France. 5. In 1814, the British, Russian, Prussian, and Austrian armies captured Paris. They sent Napoleon to Elba. In 1815, the armies of Britain and Prussia defeated Napoleon at Waterloo (in present-day Belgium).

Workbook Activity 96—The Industrial Revolution Begins
1. machines 2. natural resources 3. coal 4. population
5. economists 6. potato 7. capital 8. industrialized 9. developing
10. power

Workbook Activity 97—The Growth of the First Modern Industries
1. H 2. I 3. C 4. G 5. B 6. A 7. E 8. F 9. D 10. J

Workbook Activity 98—Transportation Improves
1. Industry needs good transportation to move people and things from one place to another. 2. Canals helped industry by making it easier to move products. 3. James Watt's steam engine helped textile manufacturers because the engine was used to operate textile machines. This made it possible to build factories anywhere. 4. George Stephenson is called the "founder of the railways" because he built a steam locomotive that went on rails on the ground. He also designed railroad bridges and tunnels. 5. The most important form of transportation in the 19th century was the railroad.

Workbook Activity 99—Industry Brings Changes and Problems
1. farmers 2. cotton cloth 3. spinning machine 4. industrialization
5. Lowell 6. labor unions 7. telegraph 8. telephone 9. Daimler
10. electricity

Workbook Activity 100—The Congress of Vienna Meets
1. Congress of Vienna 2. Napoleon 3. foreign minister
4. revolution 5. Metternich 6. nationalism 7. land
8. confederation 9. kings 10. Austria

Workbook Activity 101—Nationalism Becomes Powerful
1. Nationality describes people with the same culture, language, and history. 2. Metternich thought nationalism would lead to war. 3. The Congress of Vienna wanted to stop nationalism. 4. Greece was part of the Ottoman Empire. 5. France, Britain, and Russia helped Greece gain independence. 6. Alexander Dumas wrote *The Three Musketeers*. 7. Greece's fight for independence lasted eight years. 8. The army fought for the nation of France. 9. The French Revolution and Napoleon helped developed nationalism. 10. The first successful revolution began in Greece in 1821.

Workbook Activity 102—Wars for Independence in Latin America
1. F 2. B 3. E 4. G 5. C 6. A 7. I 8. J 9. H 10. D

Workbook Activity 103—New Revolution and Reform in Europe
1. political 2. revolution 3. constitution 4. Liberals 5. radicals
6. violence 7. monarchy 8. Charles X 9. July Ordinances
10. republic 11. Louis XVIII 12. Netherlands 13. Russia
14. nationalists 15. root

Workbook Activity 104—The Year of Revolutions—1848
1. H 2. E 3. B 4. A 5. C 6. D 7. F 8. G 9. N 10. J 11. I 12. K
13. O 14. M 15. L

Workbook Activity 105—The Rise of Nationalism
1. A multilingual society is one in which multiple languages are spoken. 2. Americans are united by their beliefs in freedom, democracy, equality, fairness, freedom of speech, freedom of religion, and electing leaders through the voting process. 3. Nationalism can remain even after a foreign invasion. Sometimes an invasion can result in an increase in nationalism because people feel more loyal to their country. 4. People who live in the United States follow the laws in the Constitution, and this unites all Americans. 5. Heritage is made up of all the traditions that ancestors pass down to their descendents.

Workbook Activity 106—Italian Nationalism

1. Rome **2.** Congress of Vienna **3.** Victor Emmanuel II
4. prime minister **5.** Austria **6.** Cavour **7.** Garibaldi
8. Vatican City **9.** France **10.** Mazzini

Workbook Activity 107—A Unified Germany

1. Frederick Wilhelm IV refused the offer because he did not want
to be chosen by the common people. **2.** Otto von Bismarck wanted
to unite all the German states under Prussia's leadership.
3. Austria-Hungary was formed after the Austro-Prussian War.
4. The Prussian army surrounded Paris and cut off its supplies in a
four-month siege. **5.** William I was the leader of the Second Reich.
He was a kaiser.

Workbook Activity 108—The Rise of Imperialism

1. A mother country is a nation that controls a colony. **2.** An
example of colonialism, or imperialism, is the way that England
controlled colonies in North America, or the way that Spain
controlled colonies in Latin America. **3.** Each major nation let
its colonies buy only those goods that were manufactured in the
mother country. **4.** Militarism was an important part of imperialism
because mother countries used sea power to control trade routes;
mother countries used colonies as military bases; and mother
countries stopped in colonial ports to get supplies for the military.
5. In 1900, many people in Europe thought of themselves as superior
to Africans because they thought that Africans were ignorant,
uncivilized, and in need of Christian teaching and other aspects of
western civilization.

Workbook Activity 109—Imperialism in Asia

1. A sphere of influence is an area in which only one foreign country
can trade. **2.** The British government took over direct rule of India
in 1858, but India won its independence in 1947. Britain ruled
India for 89 years. **3.** Today, this area includes Vietnam, Laos, and
Cambodia. **4.** In 1867, political power returned to Emperor Meiji.
New leaders were appointed to rule in the emperor's name. **5.** After
1867, Japan developed a western-style army. It also developed a
modern navy, and its leaders passed a law in 1876 requiring men
to serve in the army. Japan defeated China in 1895, and it gained
territory in China. It went to war with Russia in 1904 and won.
Japan took over Korea and it gained important trading rights in
Russian-controlled lands in China.

Workbook Activity 110—Imperialism in Africa

1. D **2.** B **3.** A **4.** C **5.** B **6.** C **7.** D **8.** C **9.** C **10.** A

Workbook Activity 111—Causes of the War Match-Up

1. B **2.** C **3.** E **4.** A **5.** H **6.** D **7.** G **8.** F **9.** J **10.** I **11.** N **12.** L
13. M **14.** K **15.** O

Workbook Activity 112—The Allied and Central Powers

Allied Powers
B, F, G, I, K, L, O
Central Powers
A, C, D, E, H, J, M, N

Workbook Activity 113—Peace Fill-In

1. Clemenceau **2.** reparation **3.** Japan **4.** Italy **5.** Yugoslavia
6. League of Nations **7.** Great Britain **8.** Lorraine **9.** Switzerland
10. the United States

Workbook Activity 114—World War I Crossword

Across
1. farms **2.** bankrupt **5.** United States **11.** Poland **13.** generation
14. billions
Down
1. France **3.** affairs **4.** Versailles **6.** total **7.** democracy
8. monarchies **9.** Europe **10.** Russia **12.** debts

Workbook Activity 115—Czarist Russia

1. standard of living **2.** Alexander **3.** Duma **4.** Moscow **5.** czar
6. jury **7.** Japan **8.** cities **9.** parliament **10.** elected
Mystery Word
democratic

Workbook Activity 116—Toward Revolution

1. Socialism is an economic and political theory. Under socialism,
the government controls the economy of a nation. **2.** Karl Marx
was the most influential of all the early socialists. **3.** Czar Nicholas
II was forced to give up his power because citizens were rebelling,
people were angry because there was little food, and the czar's troops
refused to obey him. **4.** World War I was the most important cause
of the revolution. **5.** Living conditions in Russia got worse. Millions
of Russians were killed, wounded, or taken prisoner. People lived
with little food, fuel, and other needed supplies.

Workbook Activity 117—Soviet Union Match Up

1. I **2.** C **3.** J **4.** E **5.** G **6.** F **7.** D **8.** H **9.** B **10.** A

Workbook Activity 118—Using Important Terms

1. quota **2.** totalitarian **3.** purge **4.** collective **5.** censorship
6. consumer **7.** Heavy **8.** disloyal **9.** economy **10.** newspapers

Workbook Activity 119—Italy and the Fascists

1. B **2.** D **3.** C **4.** D **5.** B **6.** A **7.** A **8.** D **9.** B **10.** C

Workbook Activity 120—Nazis in Germany

1. German **2.** swastika **3.** William II **4.** inflation **5.** Fuehrer
6. Gestapo **7.** *Mein Kampf* **8.** depression **9.** Reichstag **10.** Weimar

Workbook Activity 121—A Modern China

1. Sun Yat-sen wanted a democratic government for China.
2. Chiang Kai-shek became China's leader after Sun Yat-sen died.
3. The peasants supported Mao Zedong. **4.** Chinese nationalists
wanted to free China from foreign influence.
5. The Soviet Union sent money and military supplies to China. **6.**
Sun Yat-sen formed an alliance with the Soviet Union. **7.** When
Japan invaded China in 1937, the civil war stopped. **8.** Lenin
wanted to introduce communism to China. **9.** Sun Yat-sen wrote
the book *Three Principles of the People*. **10.** Chiang Kai-shek
ordered the Soviet advisers out of China.

Workbook Activity 122—The Military and Japan

1. D **2.** B **3.** C **4.** A **5.** C **6.** A **7.** B **8.** C **9.** A **10.** A

Workbook Activity 123—World War II Begins

1. F **2.** C **3.** E **4.** G **5.** B **6.** J **7.** D **8.** H **9.** I **10.** A

Workbook Activity 124—Fascism Fill-In

1. Treaty of Versailles **2.** Munich Pact **3.** Sudetenland
4. appeasement **5.** Czechoslovakia **6.** conference **7.** war
8. Chamberlain **9.** front **10.** Axis

Workbook Activity 125—Success for the Axis Powers

1. B 2. D 3. C 4. B 5. A 6. C 7. A 8. A 9. D 10. B

Workbook Activity 126—Allied Victories

1. guerilla 2. Defensive 3. Nazis 4. occupied 5. D-Day
6. Pacific 7. kamikaze 8. Europe 9. V-J Day 10. Nagasaki 11. atomic 12. Berlin 13. Soviet 14. Germany
15. Truman

Workbook Activity 127—The Holocaust

1. R 2. H 3. H 4. K 5. H 6. R 7. K 8. H 9. R 10. K

Workbook Activity 128—Thinking About World War II

1. Europe led the world's economy before World War II.
2. The economy of the United States did not suffer as a result of World War II. 3. Refugees had to leave their countries because their homes, farms, highways, bridges, and railroads, and factories were destroyed. 4. The Untied States and the Soviet Union became superpowers after World War II. 5. The Iron Curtain separated Western and Eastern Europe. 6. After World War II, Germany was divided into four zones. 7. The Soviet Union controlled Czechoslovakia, Romania, Bulgaria, Albania, and Hungary. 8. General MacArthur introduced democracy to Japan.
9. After the war, the emperor in Japan was no longer viewed as a god. 10. After the war, the United States and the Soviet Union grew apart and were no longer allies.

Workbook Activity 129—Learning About the United Nations

1. Roosevelt 2. United Nations 3. General Assembly
4. Security Council 5. veto 6. Secretariat 7. Justice
8. Economic 9. Trusteeship 10. military

Workbook Activity 130—How the Cold War Began

1. C 2. B 3. I 4. J 5. F 6. E 7. G 8. H 9. A 10. D

Workbook Activity 131—The Superpowers in Conflict

1. The Soviets tried to take over all of Berlin by setting up a blockade. They blocked all the roads, waterways, and railroads into the city so the people living there could not get food and supplies. 2. The West began to use planes to fly in supplies. In the Berlin Airlift, the West lifted supplies into the air and took them to Berlin. The planes delivered more than two million tons of supplies. 3. After World War II ended, Soviet forces occupied North Korea, and American forces occupied South Korea. 4. The 38th parallel of latitude became the border that separated North Korea from South Korea. When the Korean War ended, the border was almost what it had been before the war. 5. The Korean War was important because it showed that the UN could stop an attack on a member nation, it showed that China could hold its own in a war that did not use atomic weapons, and it showed that the cold war between the two superpowers would continue.

Workbook Activity 132—Changes in the Soviet Union

1. Nikita Khrushchev wanted to reform the economy and the government. Khrushchev gave artists and writers more freedom. In contrast, Leonid Brezhnev opposed reform. Brezhnev punished anyone who spoke out against the government. 2. Mikhail Gorbachev introduced glasnost, a policy of openness in the Soviet government. Glasnost involved more freedom for the press, and eventually, a more democratic government in which elected representatives were allowed to speak freely. 3. Perestroika was an economic policy used by Mikhail Gorbachev to encourage factories to produce the goods people wanted. 4. On December 1, 1991, the Ukraine voted for independence from the Soviet Union. Other Soviet republics declared their independence, and the Soviet Union broke up.
5. Under Vladimir Putin, the economy improved. The Russian government took control over the nation's rich natural resources, such as oil, natural gas, and coal. The government made millions of dollars by selling these resources, and the money was used to build roads, schools, shopping centers, and hotels.

Workbook Activity 133—Changes in Europe

1. D 2. C 3. C 4. A 5. D 6. B 7. C 8. B 9. A 10. D

Workbook Activity 134—Forming African Nations

1. geographic 2. Europeans 3. Pan-African 4. Egypt
5. Ghana 6. Apartheid 7. Desmond Tutu 8. de Klerk
9. Nelson Mandela 10. African National

Workbook Activity 135—The New Nation of Israel

1. Palestinian Arabs lived in Palestine when Jewish leaders discussed making it a Jewish nation. 2. Great Britain controlled Palestine at the end of World War I. 3. Jews moved to Palestine during and after World War II to escape the Nazis. 4. In 1947, the United Nations voted to divide Palestine into Jewish and Arab states. 5. Egypt, Iraq, Jordan, Lebanon, and Syria fought Israel during the Arab-Israeli War. 6. Israel won the Arab-Israeli War and the four wars that followed it. 7. The PLO wanted to regain their homeland from Israel. 8. In 1994, the Israelis let the Palestinian Arabs take control of most of the Gaza Strip and the West Bank. 9. An Israeli citizen who opposed the Israeli peace policy assassinated Yitzhak Rabin, the prime minister of Israel. 10. Israelis and Palestinians are still trying to reach a peaceful solution to their conflict.

Workbook Activity 136—Independence for India

1. E 2. G 3. C 4. F 5. B 6. I 7. J 8. H 9. A 10. D

Workbook Activity 137—Control Over China

1. D 2. B 3. B 4. A 5. C 6. C 7. D 8. C 9. A 10. B

Workbook Activity 138—The Fight for Vietnamese Independence

1. I 2. B 3. J 4. D 5. E 6. H 7. A 8. F 9. C 10. G

Workbook Activity 139—Challenges in Africa

1. F 2. B 3. I 4. G 5. A 6. H 7. J 8. D 9. E 10. C

Workbook Activity 140—Conflict in the Middle East

1. Kuwait 2. terrorist 3. ayatollahs 4. Shiite 5. Sunni
6. Hezbollah 7. Shah 8. accord 9. Lebanon 10. Israel 11. Iraq 12. Kurds 13. World Trade Center 14. dictator
15. hostage

Workbook Activity 141—Economic Challenges in Asia

1. The economic reforms raised the standard of living in China, so people could buy televisions, refrigerators, and cars. The reforms also created a gap between the rich and the poor. In this environment, there was an increase in crime, corruption, and food prices. Inefficient factories closed, causing many people to lose their jobs. **2.** Students went on a hunger strike because they wanted a democratic, not a Communist, government. **3.** Human rights involves political and civil liberties, including the right to life, liberty, and the pursuit of happiness. **4.** Japan's economy is successful because the government works with large companies to plan industrial growth, because the banks have a lot of money to loan to companies, and because many Japanese workers are skilled and educated. **5.** South Korea, Taiwan, Singapore, Hong Kong, and Thailand have experienced economic growth.

Workbook Activity 142—Struggles in Latin America

1. Latin America exports oil, tin, copper, iron ore, and bauxite. **2.** The campesinos are poor peasants who work on the land, but do not own it. They want the government to divide large farms among the poor. **3.** The United States encouraged the people of Panama to revolt because it wanted to build a canal there so it could sail its ships from the Atlantic Ocean to the Pacific Ocean. **4.** In 1959, Fidel Castro overthrew the leader of Cuba. Castro took over and became a dictator. In 1962, the Soviet Union began to build missile sites in Cuba. This almost led to war between the United States and the Soviet Union. **5.** NAFTA stands for the North American Free Trade Agreement. It links together the economies of Canada, Mexico, and the United States.

Workbook Activity 143—Creating a Global Village

1. global village **2.** technology **3.** pollution
4. World Wide Web **5.** coal **6.** mass communication
7. advertising **8.** Internet **9.** computer
10. photoelectric cell

Workbook Activity 144—Economic Development and Global Trade

1. E **2.** A **3.** F **4.** D **5.** B **6.** C **7.** G **8.** H **9.** M **10.** I **11.** L **12.** J **13.** O **14.** N **15.** K

Workbook Activity 145—Challenges to Society and the Environment

1. The problem of water pollution from fertilizers and pesticides is most serious in developing countries.
2. People fear global warming because it could cause flooding in some areas, and drought in other areas.
3. Cities in Asia have major problems with air and water pollution. **4.** An "AIDS orphan" is a child who has lost both parents to AIDS. **5.** Most of the people who have HIV live in developing countries.

Workbook Activity 146—Terrorism in a Global Age

1. B **2.** D **3.** C **4.** A **5.** B

Workbook Activity 147—A Look at the Future

1. Two problems that result from a growing world population are pollution and global warming. **2.** Scientists predict that each human being will have one square foot of land to live on by the year 2200. **3.** The world's population is growing at a rate of 1.5 percent a year. The world's food supply is increasing at a rate of about 1 percent a year.
4. President Lyndon Johnson said that the race between the food supply and the population increase was being lost.
5. The future may bring new treatments for diseases, new ways to feed people all over the world, and improvements in the standard of living for all people.

Chapter Outlines

Chapter 1 Outline

I.   A.   1. values, attitudes, customs
     B.   1. primary sources
          2. secondary sources
     C.   1. newspapers, diaries, letters
          2. a textbook
     D.   1. explanations
          2. differ

II.   A.   1. discover
          2. their problems
     B.   1. global community

III.   A.   1. artifacts, archaeologists
          2. beginnings, anthropologists
     B.   1. measure time
     C.   1. Jewish
          2. Muslim
     D.   1. radioactivity
     E.   1. material

IV.   A.   1. Africa, Asia, and Europe
     B.   1. Ice Age
          2. animal bones and stones
     C.   1. cave
          2. ancestors
     D.   1. Paleolithic Age
          2. weapons, tools
     E.   1. stay warm, cook
     F.   1. plant seed
          2. animals, food
     G.   1. insects, mice, dampness
     H.   1. animals, cave wall
     I.   1. monument, Salisbury in England
     J.   1. copper, tin
          2. sharper edge
     K.   1. new tools
     L.   1. nomads, hunted, gathered
          2. farm, or grow crops
          3. small groups

Chapter 2 Outline

I.   A.   1. Mesopotamia
          2. city-states
          3. military leaders
     B.   1. citizens
          2. women, slaves
     C.   1. clay bricks
     D.   1. temple, pyramid
          2. priests, a part of each farmer's crop
     E.   1. rivers flood , crops fail
          2. sacrificed
     F.   1. cuneiform (or writing)
          2. symbol for each sound or word
          3. clay tablet, stylus
          4. first people
     G.   1. plow, sailboat
          2. wheels
          3. arches and ramps
          4. measure time

II.   A.   1. Sumerian
          2. Akkad
          3. translated
          4. dikes, irrigation system
     B.   1. 1800
          2. Hammurabi, Babylon
          3. India, China
     C.   1. system of laws
          2. Golden Age of Babylon

III.   A.   1. Fertile Crescent
          2. Canaan
          3. sea traders
          4. Tyre, Sidon
     B.   1. England, Africa
          2. sea routes, the North Star
     C.   1. alphabet
          2. culture and products
     D.   1. Bible, Hebrews, Christians
     E.   1. Abraham, Mesopotamia
          2. Egypt, famine
          3. slaves
     F.   1. Moses
          2. 10 commandments
     G.   1. commandments, worship
          2. Canaan, Judah, Israel
          3. Palestine, Israel

Chapter 3 Outline

I. A. 1. Mesopotamia
    2. smelt, Hittites
    3. chariots, cavalry, archers
  B. 1. shoulder to shoulder
    2. battered down, tunneled, climbed
  C.1. slaves, forced
  D. 1. tribute
    2. Assurbanipal, Nineveh
  E. 1. library
    2. Sumer, Akkad
  F. 1. provinces
    2. governor, collected taxes
    3. roads
  G. 1. govern
II. A. 1. expanded, Syria, Canaan
    2. Egypt
    3. Jews
  B. 1. blue glaze, animal sculptures
    2. red brick, message
  C. 1. Terraced
  D. 1. astronomers
    2. constellations
  E. 1. war broke out
    2. conquered
    3. Cyrus the Great, Babylon
III. A. 1. Darius I, 20 provinces
    2. inspectors
    3. weights and measures
  B. 1. coins, Lydians
  C. 1. fairly
    2. keep their own language, religion, and laws
    3. pay taxes
  D. 1. art
  E. 1. preach, 570 B.C.
    2. affected

Chapter 4 Outline

I. A. 1. 4,000
    2. delta
  B. 1. irrigation
  C. 1. highway
II. A. 1. Menes
  B. 1. business
    2. farmers
  C. 1. pharaohs
    2. gods
  D. 1. pyramids
  E. 1. afterlife
    2. buried
  F. 1. stones
  G. 1. civil war broke out
III. A. 1. complete power
    2. live forever
    3. cliffs
  B. 1. Hyksos
  C. 1. 1570
IV. A. 1. Hatshepsut
  B. 1. Thutmose III
  C. 1. slaves
    2. hieroglyphics
  D. 1. temples
  E. 1. Aton
  F. 1. Ikhnaton
    2. Ramses III
  G. 1. Persians
V. A. 1. check heartbeat
  B. 1. survey
  C. 1. statues
    2. artwork or drawings

Chapter 5 Outline

I. A. 1. Khyber Pass
    2. culture
  B. 1. Ganges; Indus; Brahma Putra
  C. 1. Indian Ocean; rain
    2. crops fail

II. A. 1. irrigate
    2. cotton cloth; traded
  B. 1. clay bricks; alabaster
    2. plumbing; toilets
  C. 1. protected; enemy
  D. 1. pictographs; Harappan

III. A. 1. Vedas
    2. Brahman
  B. 1. souls; reincarnation
  C. 1. castes; work; money; skin color; religious beliefs
  D. 1. caste; thrown out
  E. 1. Sanskrit

IV. A. 1. Hindu; noble truths
    2. Buddha; ìEnlightened Oneî
    3. Buddhism
  B. 1. Eightfold Path
    2. desire; nirvana
  C. 1. reincarnation
    2. Buddhists

V. A. 1. Gobi Desert; Tibetan mountain plateau; Himalayas; seas
  B. 1. deep; runs swiftly
  C. 1. shallow; cities; farms
    2. ìChinaís Sorrowî
  D. 1. Huang He; Yangtze
  E. 1. invaders
  F. 1. 1400

VI. A. 1. palace; temple; nobles
  B. 1. pictograms; symbols
  C. 1. read and write
  D. 1. ancestors; religion
  E. 1. invaders; declined
  F. 1. unite
    2. writing; laws
  G. 1. Silk Road
    2. Confucius

Chapter 6 Outline

I. A. 1. Crete; Minos
  B. 1. Achaeans; warlike
  C. 1. Iliad; Odyssey
  D. 1. Helen; Paris
  E. 1. wooden horse

II. 1. isolated
    2. acropolis; temple
  A. 1. self-governing
    2. aristocrats
  B. 1. Solon; democracy

III. A. 1. council; assembly
  B. 1. juries
  C. 1. seaport
    2. artists, writers, teachers

IV. A. 1. protective walls
  B. 1. boys; steal food
  C. 1. patriotic
    2. victors
  D. 1. art; architecture

V. A. 1. Ionian Greeks
    2. ships; Darius
  B. 1. Athenians
  C. 1. mountain pass; Greek army
  D. 1. the Persians; maneuver
  E. 1. Athens, Sparta
    2. independence; Philip II

VI. A. 1. Parthenon; columns
  B. 1. tragedy; hero
    2. comedy; important people or ideas
  C. 1. truth
  D. 1. Socrates
  E. 1. society
  F. 1. government

VII. A. 1. Asia Minor
    2. Egypt; Alexandria
  B. 1. Indus River
    2. Babylon; 32
  C. 1. Macedon; Egypt; Syria; culture
    2. Hellenism
  D. 1. lighted; paved
    2. lighthouse; library
  E. 1. geometry
    2. levers; pulleys
    3. Hippocrates; medicine
    4. shaped; Mediterranean

Chapter 7 Outline

I. A. 1. south
   2. north
   3. Latin

II. A. 1. consuls; senate
   B. 1. patrician
   C. 1. laborers
   D. 1. tribunes
   2. veto
   E. 1. twelve bronze tablets
   F. 1. 280 B.C.

III. A. 1. Sicily
   B. 1. planks
   C. 1. Pyrenees; Alps
   D. 1. destroyed/defeated

IV. A. 1. taxes
   2. votes
   B. 1. Tiberius Gracchus
   2. reform
   C. 1. Marius
   D. 1. Crassus, Pompey, Julius Caesar
   2. 10

V. A. 1. the poor
   2. calendar
   B. 1. senators
   C. 1. Mark Antony, Octavian
   D. 1. Mark Antony, Cleopatra

Chapter 8 Outline

I. A. 1. Augustus Caesar
   B. 1. Italy
   2. senate
   C. 1. peace

II. A. 1. guards
   2. orderly
   3. worst
   4. Trajan
   5. Hadrian
   6. Marcus Aurelius
   B. 1. emperor
   2. wars
   3. plague

III. A. 1. homeland
   B. 1. equally
   2. love
   C. 1. rebel
   2. crucified
   D. 1. disciples
   E. 1. dead
   F. 1. Christian
   2. Theodosius I

IV. A. 1. Constantinople
   B. 1. warriors
   2. weapons
   C. 1. Visigoths
   2. Vandals
   3. Odoacer

V. A. 1. property
   2. punished
   B. 1. road
   C. 1. temple
   D. 1. imperfections
   2. sanitation
   3. medicine

Chapter 9 Outline

I. A. 1. ice
   B. 1. 9,000
      2. Folsom
   C. 1. 4,000
II. A. 1. Hohokam, Mogollan, Anasazi
   B. 1. water
   C. 1. rock art
   D. 1. wagon wheel
   E. 1. religious
III. A. 1. east
      2. dead
   B. 1. quarter
   C. 1. Mississippi River
   D. 1. rivers
   E. 1. agricultural
   F. 1. Europeans
   G. 1. Sioux
   H. 1. fishermen
      2. longhouses
   I. 1. Eskimo
      2. igloos
IV. A. 1. writing
   B. 1. pyramid
   C. 1. written
      2. astronomers
      3. cities
   D. 1. warriors
   E. 1. Tenoch
   F. 1. food
   G. 1. Andes
      2. "Land of the Four Quarters"

Chapter 10 Outline

I. A. 1. Monks
      2. Nuns
      3. Benedictines
      4. books
   B. 1. Holy Land
      2. pilgrimage
      3. Muslims
   C. 1. Roman Catholic Church
      2. Greek Orthodox Church
      3. Schism
   D. 1. Crusade
      2. control
      3. Acre
   E. 1. Middle East
      2. fought
II. A. 1. Feudalism
      2. land
   B. 1. lords
      2. loyalty
      3. fief
   C. 1. page
      2. squire
      3. knighted
      4. strong
III. A. 1. clothing
      2. blacksmith
      3. manor
   B. 1. plow
      2. power
      3. learning
   C. 1. drawbridge
      2. courtyard
      3. joust
IV. A. 1. schools
      2. Latin
      3. Christianity
   B. 1. Romanesque
      2. buttresses
   C. 1. common
      2. story
   D. 1. Henry II
      2. truth
      3. lawmaking

Chapter 11 Outline

I. A. 1. Byzantine Empire
2. Constantinople
3. new Rome
4. Greek
5. churches; relics; pray
B. 1. Justinian
2. Roman
3. laws
4. Constantinople
C. 1. emperor
2. icons
3. Roman Catholic Church; Eastern Orthodox Church
D. 1. civil war
2. Turks
II. A. 1. monks; Cyrillic
2. Orthodox; Roman Catholic
3. traded
B. 1. Dnieper; north-south
2. boyars; Veches
3. Constantinople
4. Mongol
C. 1. powerful
2. Great; freed; government;
3. Kremlin
4. czar
III. A. 1. Roman; kingdoms
2. art; architecture; literature
3. Dark Ages
B. 1. Clovis; Roman Catholic
2. Charlemagne; religion; Pope Leo III
C. 1. Russia; Europe; America
2. Iceland; Greenland
3. Vinland
D. 1. Britain
2. Canute; England
3. William; Hastings; Normans

Chapter 12 Outline

I. A. 1. angel
2. Allah
B. 1. Mecca, Medina
2. Hegira
C. 1. army
2. Mecca
D. 1. Islam
E. 1. duties
2. Hajj
II. A. 1. jihad
B. 1. Baghdad
2. four
C. 1. traders
2. religions
D. 1. doctors
E. 1. earth
2. light
3. Jabir
F. 1. India
2. Hindus
G. 1. animals
III. A. 1. gold
B. 1. tribute
2. army
C. 1. Arabs
2. Kumbi
3. Almoravids
D. 1. Ghana
E. 1. Mansa Musa
F. 1. 60,000
G. 1. salt

Chapter 13 Outline

I. A. 1. stupas
    2. unique
    3. moon
    4. inoculate
  B. 1. Huns
  C. 1. Mongols
    2. Timur
  D. 1. Babur
    2. Akbar
    3. Civilians
    4. Taj Mahal
II. A. 1. traders
    2. ideas/knowledge
  B. 1. nature
    2. black
  C. 1. printing
    2. knowledge
  D. 1. Hangzhou
    2. gunpowder
    3. abacus
    4. masterpieces
    5. scrolls
III. A. 1. Kublai Khan
    2. Beijing
  B. 1. protected
  C. 1. plays
    2. sing
  D. 1. barbarians
IV. A. 1. invaders
    2. writing
  B. 1. Shinto
    2. spirits
  C. 1. China
    2. Buddhists
V. A. 1. loyalty
    2. Shogun
  B. 1. daimyos
    2. estate
    3. Samurai
  C. 1. bushido
    2. hari-kari
  D. 1. morality
    2. son
    3. calligraphy
VI. A. 1. isolate
    2. killed
  B. 1. beauty
    2. ikebana
    3. kabuki

Chapter 14 Outline

I. A. 1. pay taxes
    2. less
    3. dropped, farmers
  B. 1. rebellion
  C. 1. philosophy
II. A. 1. human actions
    2. Greeks, Romans
  B. 1. writings
  C. 1. educated
    2. Isabella d'Este
III. A. 1. trade
  B. 1. republican
    2. ruling
  C. 1. artists, scholars
  D. 1. Savonarola
  E. 1. French
  F. 1. pope
    2. executed
IV. A. 1. William Shakespeare
  B. 1. Miguel de Cervantes
  C. 1. Bible
V. A. 1. inventor
    2. Mona Lisa
  B. 1. Pietà
  C. 1. Sistine Chapel
  D. 1. Madonna

Chapter 15 Outline

I. A. 1. tax
    2. France
  B. 1. change
    2. Bible
  C. 1. qworldly
    2. heretic
II. A. 1. Reformation
    2. faith
  B. 1. Indulgences
    2. purgatory
  C. 1. statements
    2. printed
III. A. 1. excommunicated
    2. Edict of Worms
  B. 1. Jesus Christ
    2. truth
  C. 1. Lutheran
    2. Ministers
  D. 1. Protestants
    2. Charles V
IV. A. 1. annul
    2. Anne Boleyn
  B. 1. Anglican
  C. 1. Protestant
  D. 1. Mary
    2. Catholic
  E. 1. join
    2. Puritans
V. A. 1. born
    2. elect
  B. 1. religious
    2. Elders
  C. 1. Huguenots
    2. killed
VI. A. 1. counter
    2. court
  B. 1. sale
    2. translation
  C. 1. St. Ignatius or Ignatius of Loyola
    2. Jesuit
  D. 1. Protestant
    2. Catholic

Chapter 16 Outline

I. 1. the Bible; Greek and Roman writers
    2. science
  A. 1. steps; studying the natural world
    2. Francis Bacon
    3. experiments
  B. 1. problem (or question); hypothesis; experiment; observation; conclusion
II. A. 1. Ptolemy; earth
    2. 1400
    3. Copernicus; the sun
  B. 1. Copernicus; Mars
    2. ellipse
III. A. 1. the moon; the sun
    2. Jupiter; four; Copernicus
  B. 1. challenged the Bible
    2. experimented; gravity; at the same speed
    3. experimental science
IV. A. 1. all colors
    2. reflect
    3. prism
  B. 1. force gravity; attract
    2. greater attractive force
    3. Gravitation; law
V. 1. community
  A. 1. Andreas Vesalius; anatomy
  B. 1. blood vessels; pump
  C. 1. points north; amber; electric
  D. 1. static electricity
  E. 1. symbols; multiplication; division; equality
    2. mathematics
    3. René Descartes
    4. Isaac Newton; Gottfried Leibniz
  F. 1. Anton van Leeuwenhoek
    2. clock
    3. Fahrenheit; Celsius

Chapter 17 Outline

I. A. 1. navigation
    B. 1. India
II. A. 1. East Indies
    B. 1. Spain
    C. 1. south
    D. 1. Dutch
    E. 1. Ferdinand Magellan
    F. 1. Pacific Ocean
III. A. 1. Quetzalcoatl
    B. 1. gods
    C. 1. Aztec Empire
    D. 1. Atahualpa
    E. 1. Incan Empire
    F. 1. a. time; weapons
           b. Tribes
           c. horses; diseases
IV. A. 1. Spain
    B. 1. landowners
    C. 1. African
V. A. 1. Portuguese
    B. 1. chains
    C. 1. colonies
    D. 1. 400
VI. A. 1. Roanoke
    B. 1. American Indians
    C. 1. Great Lakes
    D. 1. corn, potatoes
    E. 1. Europe

Chapter 18 Outline

I. A. 1. country
        2. traditions
    B. 1. monarch
    C. 1. absolute
II. A. 1. Islam
        2. Spain
    B. 1. learning
    C. 1. Isabella
        2. nobles
    D. 1. Catholic
    E. 1. emperor
    F. 1. Italy
    G. 1. Ferdinand I
    H. 1. Protestantism
    I. 1. formation
        2. English
III. A. 1. God
    B. 1. soldiers
    C. 1. Parliament
IV. A. 1. Parliament
    B. 1. Cavaliers
        2. Roundheads
    C. 1. beheaded
        2. dictator
    D. 1. monarchy
        2. Restoration
    E. 1. body
        2. rights
    F. 1. Tories
        2. Whigs
    G. 1. constitutional
V. A. 1. Cardinal
        2. Louis XIV
    B. 1. nobles
    C. 1. taxes
        2. army
    D. 1. Versailles
VI. A. 1. capital
    B. 1. religious
    C. 1. state
    D. 1. Frederick

Chapter 19 Outline

I.   A.   **1.** reason; planets; other objects in space
     B.   **1.** orderly; predictable
     C.   **1.** truth; nature
     D.   **1.** improve; think; scientific reasoning
II.   A.   **1.** absolute power
         2. order; freedom
     B.   **1.** life; property; liberty
     C.   **1.** wealth; power
         2. virtue
     D.   **1.** Parliament; the king; the courts
     E.   **1.** good; civilization
     F.   **1.** majority
III.   A.   **1.** writers; artists; society
         2. Paris
     B.   **1.** salons; wealthy women
         2. scientific ideas
     C.   **1.** speech; press; religious
     D.   **1.** books; knowledge
     E.   **1.** 21 years
     F.   **1.** torture; Voltaire
     G.   **1.** government; schools
IV.   A.   **1.** fugues
         2. Bach; Handel
     B.   **1.** orderly; balanced
         2. symphony
     C.   **1.** symphony; string; woodwind
     D.   **1.** 5; 13
     E.   **1.** Molière
         2. Daniel Defoe
     F.   **1.** Greece; Rome

Chapter 20 Outline

I.   A.   **1.** Quartering
         2. violated
     B.   **1.** documents
     C.   **1.** Townshend
         2. Boston
II.   A.   **1.** Lexington
     B.   **1.** free
         2. Jefferson
     C.   **1.** France
     D.   **1.** Yorktown
     E.1. government
III.   A.   **1.** clergy
         2. nobles
         3. farmers
     B.   **1.** Third
     C.   **1.** nobles
         2. representatives
     D.   **1.** Assembly
         2. constitution
     E.   **1.** Bastille
IV.   A.   **1.** Versailles
     B.   **1.** constitutional
     C.   **1.** republic
     D.   **1.** Austria
     E.   **1.** treason
     F.   **1.** moderates
         2. Jacobins
     G.   **1.** queen
         2. guillotine
     H.   **1.** executive
V.   A.   **1.** Rome
         2. Pius VII
     B.   **1.** Russia
     C.   **1.** Alexander
     D.   **1.** destroyed
     E.   **1.** starvation
     F.   **1.** Prussian
     G.   **1.** Waterloo
     H.   **1.** equality

Chapter 21 Outline

I. A. 1. work
   B. 1. coal, iron, water
   C. 1. potato
   D. 1. business
   E. 1. Germany
II. A. 1. flying shuttle
      2. spinning jenny
   B. 1. factories
   C. 1. seeds
   D. 1. gun
      2. assemble
   E. 1. impurities
III. A. 1. coal
   B. 1. track or rail
      2. steam engines
   C. 1. locomotive
   D. 1. Rocket
   E. 1. raw materials
IV. A. 1. machines
      2. skilled workers
   B. 1. spinning machines
   C. 1. Francis Lowell
   D. 1. city
      2. jobs
   E. 1. dangerous
      2. shorter
      3. labor unions
   F. 1. electricity
   G. 1. power
      2. oil
      3. airplane

Chapter 22 Outline

I. A. 1. Austria
   B. 1. balance
   C. 1. Congress of Vienna
II. A. 1. Austrian Empire
   B. 1. Ottoman Empire
   C. 1. Europeans
III. A. 1. Hispaniola
      2. Haiti
   B. 1. creole
   C. 1. 1819
   D. 1. Chile, Peru
   E. 1. Miguel Hidalgo
   F. 1. land
IV. A. 1. kings
   B. 1. middle
   C. 1. democracy
   D. 1. Louis XVIII
   E. 1. absolute
   F. 1. voting rights, press
   G. 1. businessman
   H. 1. Poland
      2. Germany
V. A. 1. factories
   B. 1. state
   C. 1. democracy
   D. 1. reformed
   E. 1. labor
   F. 1. violent
   G. 1. Prince Metternich

Chapter 23 Outline

I. A. 1. multilingual
   B. 1. culture
      2. religion
   C. 1. foreign
      2. nationalism
   D. 1. laws
      2. Heritage
II. A. 1. rebellion
      2. Mazzini
   B. 1. Sardinia
      2. France
      3. Cavour
   C. 1. Sicily
      2. red
      3. Garibaldi
   D. 1. Emmanuel
      2. Vatican
III. A. 1. king
      2. conservatives
      3. parliament
   B. 1. Prussia
      2. minister
      3. democratic
   C. 1. militarism
   D. 1. Denmark
      2. Austria
      3. Hungary
   E. 1. ambassador
      2. war
   F. 1. Sedan
      2. Paris
      3. Frankfurt
   G. 1. kaiser
      2. Reich

Chapter 24 Outline

I. A. 1. imperialism
      2. market
      3. mother
   B. 1. colonies
   C. 1. trade
      2. military
   D. 1. better
      2. western
II. A. 1. France
      2. government
      3. materials
   B. 1. Indochina
      2. Burma
   C. 1. trade
      2. sphere
      3. Chinese
   D. 1. revolution
      2. Meiji
      3. abolished
   E. 1. army
      2. China
      3. Russia
III. A. 1. Uganda
      2. Suez
      3. protectorate
   B. 1. rich
      2. empire
   C. 1. African
   D. 1. Portugal
      2. Belgium
      3. Tripoli
   E. 1. education
      2. factories
      3. natural
   F. 1. religion
      2. culture
      3. nationalism

Chapter 25 Outline

I. A. 1. militarized
   B. 1. Alliance
      2. Entente
   C. 1. Ferdinand
      2. Serbia
II. A. 1. Central
      2. Allied
      3. France
   B. 1. trenches
      2. barbed
   C. 1. submarines
      2. machine
      3. poison
   D. 1. Serbs
      2. Russia
   E. 1. China
      2. Africa
   F. 1. Germany
   G. 1. armistice
III. A. 1. Wilson
      2. Fourteen
      3. peace
   B. 1. reparations
      2. colonies
      3. treaty
   C. 1. Versailles
   D. 1. Hungary
      2. Yugoslavia
      3. Latvia
   E. 1. leaders
IV. A. 1. generation
      2. debts
   B. 1. monarchies
      2. dictatorship
      3. economy
V. A. 1. unlimited
      2. democratic
      3. parliament
VI. A. 1. rebellion
      2. constitutional
      3. Revolution
   B. 1. power
   C. 1. government

Chapter 26 Outline

I. A. 1. militia
   B. 1. Germany
      2. World War I
   C. 1. Reds, Whites
      2. factories
   D. 1. industry
      2. class
      3. police
   E. 1. Leon Trotsky
II. A. 1. factories
      2. totalitarian
III. A. 1. Fascist
      2. Il Duce
   B. 1. party
      2. books
      3. nationalism
      4. military
   C. 1. Francisco Franco
IV. A. 1. World War I
      2. Socialist
   B. 1. Communism
      2. Hitler
   C. 1. political parties
      2. censored
      3. Nazism
      4. Gestapo
V. A. 1. foreigners
      2. living conditions
   B. 1. Communism
   C. 1. Communists
      2. Chiang Kai-shek
   D. 1. Japan
VI. A. 1. military
   B. 1. coal, iron
   C. 1. Italy

Chapter 27 Outline

I.   A. 1. superior
     B. 1. land, resources
     C. 1. Axis powers
     D. 1. Germany
        2. Austria
II. A. 1. Rhineland and Austria
     B. 1. Germans
     C. 1. Hitler
     D. 1. fascist dictators
     E. 1. war
        2. Germany
     F. 1. Poland
        2. France, Britain
     G. 1. Allies
III. A. 1. France
     B. 1. destroy
     C. 1. Hitler
     D. 1. warships/destroyers
     E. 1. oil fields
     F. 1. Suez Canal
     G. 1. gasoline
IV. A. 1. Resistance
     B. 1. 1945
     C. 1. Allied
     D. 1. island hopping
     E. 1. Berlin
     F. 1. nuclear/atomic bomb
V.   A. 1. Jews
     B. 1. Night of Broken Glass
     C. 1. concentration camps
     D. 1. organized
VI. A. 1. Iron Curtain
     B. 1. republic
        2. West, East
     C. 1. satellites
     D. 1. democracy
VII. A. 1. wars
     B. 1. military force

Chapter 28 Outline

I.   A. 1. weapons
        2. Communism
     B. 1. Europe
        2. economic
     C. 1. Atlantic
        2. alliance
II. A. 1. Britain
        2. starve
     B. 1. planes
     C. 1. Airlift
        2. blockade
     D. 1. northern
        2. southern
        3. latitude
     E. 1. soldiers
        2. North
     F. 1. surprise
     G. 1. truce
        2. armistice
     H. 1. attack
        2. superpowers
III. A. 1. reform
        2. freedom
        3. Brezhnev
     B. 1. Gorbachev
        2. glasnost
        3. perestroika
     C. 1. independence
        2. Soviet
        3. Yeltsin
     D. 1. Chechnya
        2. oil
IV. A. 1. Hungarian
        2. Austria
        3. Communist
     B. 1. strike
        2. elections
     C. 1. democracy
        2. East
        3. Berlin
     D. 1. Milosevic
        2. cleansing
        3. Muslims
     E. 1. tariff
        2. parliament

Chapter 29 Outline

I.   A. 1. political peace
    B. 1. Liberia
    C. 1. weaker
    D. 1. Morocco
    E. 1. Ghana
    F. 1. Eritrea
    G. 1. nonwhite
    H. 1. violent, nonviolent
    I. 1. government
    J. 1. de Klerk
    K. 1. social

II.   A. 1. Palestine
    B. 1. Nazis
    C. 1. Arab
    D. 1. defeated
    E. 1. Palestine
    F. 1. 1987
    G. 1. self-rule
    H. 1. security

III.   A. 1. Great Britain
    B. 1. second-class
    C. 1. passive resistance
    D. 1. equal
    E. 1. Hindus

IV.   A. 1. Nationalists
    B. 1. Mao Zedong
    C. 1. united
    D. 1. Taiwan
    E. 1. imperialism

V.   A. 1. independent
    B. 1. non-Communist
    C. 1. military advisers
    D. 1. United States

Chapter 30 Outline

I.   A. 1. democratic
      2. poverty
    B. 1. population
      2. drought
      3. fertilizer
      4. pesticide
    C. 1. malaria
      2. epidemic
    D. 1. urbanization
      2. migrants
      3. slums

II.   A. 1. Accords
      2. Israel
      3. peace
    B. 1. Hezbollah
      2. Lebanon
    C. 1. ayatollahs
      2. Khomeini
      3. hostages
    D. 1. Shiite
      2. Sunni
      3. Iraq
    E. 1. Kuwait
      2. international
      3. Gulf
    F. 1. New York
      2. terrorist

III.   A. 1. economic
      2. Beijing
      3. democratic
    B. 1. government
      2. banks
      3. skilled
    C. 1. South Korea
      2. Hong Kong
    D. 1. Thailand
      2. Indonesia
      3. investors

IV.   A. 1. campesinos
      2. industrialization
      3. oil
    B. 1. Texas
      2. canal
      3. Mexico
    C. 1. Cuba
      2. embargo
      3. Venezuela

Chapter 31 Outline Answers

I.   A.   **1.** technology
      B.   **1.** television
      C.   **1.** world wide web
      D.   **1.** satellites
      E.   **1.** pollution
      F.   **1.** deadly
      G.   **1.** Lasers
      H.   **1.** electronic
      I.   **1.** information

II.   A.   **1.** Great Britain
      B.   **1.** overpopulated
           2. consumer goods
      C.   **1.** slowdown
      D.   **1.** goods
      E.   **1.** multinational
      F.   **1.** industrialized

III.   A.   **1.** HIV
           2. SARS
      B.   **1.** pollution
           2. deforestation
      C.   **1.** fossil fuels
      D.   **1.** warming
      E.   **1.** industrial
      F.   **1.** resources
      G.   **1.** Greening

IV.   A.   **1.** Iraq
      B.   **1.** security
      C.   **1.** Homeland

V.   A.   **1.** 200 million
           2. 9 billion
      B.   **1.** past

Unit Activities

Unit 1 Activity 1— Early Civilizations Chart

Ancient Middle East Civilzation:
Time Period: 5000 B.C. to 600 B.C.
Where: along the Tigris and Euphrates Rivers in what is called the Fertile Crescent
Beliefs: believed in one or many gods that both protected and punished
Characteristics: Answers will vary; invented cuneiform, Hammurabi's Code, strong armies; trade with neighboring civilizations

Egyptian Civilization:
Time Period: 3100 B.C. to 30 B.C.
Where: along the Nile River
Beliefs: believed in an afterlife, the forces of nature, and in many gods; most important gods were Ra, the sun-god and Hapi, the river god
Characteristics: built pyramids, highly organized society, traded with other civilizations; made great use of technology

Ancient China:
Time Period: about 8000 years ago
Where: along the Yellow River Valley
Beliefs: the gods controlled all things like sickness and flooding, the spirits of nature gave the rulers power, ancestor worship
Characteristics: built the Great Canal and the Great Wall; built cities, farmed with stone tools, developed a system of writing based on characters

The Roman Republic:
Time Period: 753 B.C. to 27 B.C.
Where: boot shaped peninsula of Italy and much of the northern Mediterranean coast, parts of Asia Minor, and small area on the African coastline
Beliefs: believed in many gods; Roman rulers believed they had godlike powers
Characteristics: established a republic and a written set of laws, society based on class system, often at war

Unit 1 Activity 2—Early Civilizations Report

1. Answers will vary but should note that early civilizations began along a water source.
2. Answers will vary but note that most civilizations believed in many gods that exercised great control.
3. Answers will vary; established social system, worship of gods, development of villages and cities along water routes, war and conquest, established order based on rule or written laws.
4. Answers will vary but should note that though each of the civilizations were alike, within those similarities were many differences, such as the worship of different gods, different systems of rule and order, and different writing systems.
Student paragraphs should include at least three similarities among the civilizations.

Unit 2 Activity 1— Powerful Leaders Game

Each student in each group should choose two leaders and complete the needed information, using the textbook and other sources of information to find the answers. Students should then use their information to play the game.

Unit 2 Activity 2—Powerful Leaders Information

Student choices will vary. Most information about the leaders can be found in Chapters 10–13 (pp. 222–323) of the student text.

Unit 3 Activity 1—Understanding Shakespeare's Writing: Romeo and Juliet

1. Two equal families
2. in Verona, where the play takes place
3. face new problems that come from an old disagreement
4. where political struggles make people do bad things
5. from the troubled pasts of these fighting families
6. two fated lovers kill themselves
7. their actions are misunderstood
8. their deaths overshadow the old disagreement between their families
9. how they kill themselves for love
10. and how their parents' feud
11. which would not end until their children had died
12. is what this play is about
13. pay attention to the play
14. and what you don't hear or understand, we hope to explain

Unit 3 Activity 2—Expressing Opinions

1. Answers will vary. Students may say that the prologue tells the audience what to expect.
2. Answers will vary. Most students will say the language is difficult to understand and pronounce. Students may say that actors practice repeating the lines until they are comfortable with the language.
3. Answers will vary. Students may say Shakespeare created tension because he wanted the audience to be interested in the play.
4. Answers will vary.
5. Answers will vary. Make sure students support their opinions with three reasons.

Unit 4 Activity 1—Inventions—Past, Present, and Future

1. Answers will vary. Possible answers include the following: spinning jenny, 1769, James Hargreaves; cotton gin, 1793, Eli Whitney; telephone, 1876, Alexander Graham Bell; light bulb, 1879, Thomas Edison.
2. Answers will vary. Possible answers include the following: microwave oven, 1947, Percy Spencer; polio vaccine, 1953, Jonas Salk; compact disk, 1972, RCA.
3. Answers will vary.
Students' answers should show some creativity, and the inventions they name should have a realistic purpose.

Unit 4 Activity 2—The Positives and Negatives of an Invention

Choice of inventions will vary. Under "Ways the Invention Helps People," students may indicate that it helps people save time, does something more effectively and efficiently than people can, or does something a person could not do. Under "Problems the Invention Causes," students might indicate that the invention causes pollution, uses up valuable natural resources, or can be dangerous to use if operated improperly.

Unit 5 Activity 1—What Is Nationalism?

1. loyalty to a nation

2. Answers will vary. Students might include these ideas: freedom or independence, a different form of government, religious rights, and better working conditions.

3. Answers will vary. Students might include these ideas: helping the poor and hungry, equal rights for everyone, regulating the use of nuclear weapons, keeping our environment clean and healthy, and religious freedom.

4. Answers will vary. Students might include these ideas: our many rights, our desire to help others, our willingness to fight for what we believe in, our ability to work together when it really matters, and our right to disagree and to argue for our point of view.

5. Answers will vary. Students may combine the dictionary definition with some of the ideas they listed in the various exercises.

Unit 5 Activity 2—Spheres of Influence Game

Each student in each group should research products that come from one of the four areas of the country using an atlas, a gazetteer, or the Internet. Students should then use their information to play the game. The player holding the most cards after 10 minutes of play represents the most powerful sphere of influence and wins the game.

Unit 6 Activity 1—Charting Key Historical Events

Choice of topics will vary. Possible answers for each topic are given. World War I: Alliance System, 1914; the Triple Alliance and the Triple Entente formed; this set up a rivalry between the two alliances. Assassination of Archduke Ferdinand, June 28, 1914; the archduke and his wife were killed as they rode through the streets of Sarajevo; Austria-Hungary blamed the Serbians and declared war on them, causing Russia, Germany, France, and Great Britain to honor their alliances and enter the war. Germany begins unrestricted warfare, 1917; German U-boats sank any ship that sailed into the waters surrounding the British Isles; this caused the United States to enter the war. Germany agreed to armistice, November 11, 1918; Germany agreed to stop fighting; World War I ended. World War II: Invasion of Poland, 1939; Hitler invaded Poland from the west and the Soviet Union attacked from the east, Britain and France declared war on Germany. Attack on Pearl Harbor, December 7, 1941; the Japanese damaged the American navy in a surprise raid; the United States declared war on Japan. D-Day, June 6, 1944; the Allies invaded France; by October 1944, almost all of eastern and central Europe was under Soviet control. V-E Day, May 8, 1945; the allies completed victory in Europe; Germany surrendered. U.S. drops atomic bomb on Japan, August 6, 1945; the United States bombed Hiroshima and later Nagasaki; Japan agreed to end the war. V-J Day, September 2, 1945; Japan surrendered; World War II ended. The Russian Revolution: In the second half of the 19th century, Alexander II became czar; the Russian standard of living improved, but the people wanted even more freedom. Alexander refused. 1894; the people revolted and killed the czar. 1904; the next czar, Nicholas II, tried to get the peoples' minds off democracy by declaring war on Japan. Russia lost this war, and the people demanded more changes. 1905; Bloody Sunday revolt; people refused to work and nobles were attacked. Although the spirit of rebellion grew, the revolutionaries could not agree on how change should happen. 1917; World War I caused great suffering in Russia and was a major cause of the 1917 Russian Revolution; Czar Nicholas II abdicates.

Unit 6 Activity 2—Comparing Results

1. Answers will vary and will depend on the events chosen by the group.

2. Answers will vary, but at least one specific reason should be given.

3. Answers will vary. The total number of different events will vary depending on what events where chosen by each group member.

4. Answer will vary but should include an event and at least one specific reason.

5. Lists will vary. For each person, a specific reason for including him or her should be given. Displays will vary but should include the information in a clear and interesting way.

Unit 7 Activity 1—Creating a Brochure for a Nation

Brochure descriptions will vary. Students should describe their plans for how the brochure will look and what information it will contain. The historical information should be accurate. Brochures should contain descriptions of interesting places to visit and may include pictures. The completed brochures should be interesting; visually appealing; and correctly written in terms of grammar, spelling, and punctuation.

Unit 7 Activity 2—An Important Event in World History

Answers will vary. Students should correctly complete each section of the chart and should give at least one reason why they consider the event important.

Unit Skills Activities

Unit 1 Skills Activity—Time of Your Life
Student timelines will vary but should indicate a clear sequence of important events, such as the student's birth, starting school, getting a pet, an important game, meeting a new friend, etc.

Unit 2 Skills Activity—In My Opinion, As a Matter of Fact
Part A:
1. Fact; the statement can be proven true or false.
2. Fact; the statement can be proven true or false.
3. Opinion; the statement gives someone's belief.
4. Opinion; the statement gives someone's belief.
Part B:
1. Letters will vary but should include a clear statement as to the reason for the letter, the writer's opinion, and facts in support of the opinion.

Unit 3 Skills Activity—Cause and Effect
1. Nearly 10 percent of Western Europeans died from starvation.
2. The Bubonic Plague hit Western Europe in 1348.
3. Farmers left the country to find work elsewhere.
4. English peasants did not like their place in society.
5. People began to study the ideas of ancient Greece and Rome.

Unit 4—Compare and Contrast
Answers will vary. Students' paragraphs should include similarities and differences between two of the revolutions.

Unit 5 Skills Activity—Compare and Contrast
Answers will vary. Students' paragraphs should include similarities and differences between nationalism and imperialism.

Unit 6 Skills Activity—Interpreting Political Cartoons
Answers will vary depending on the cartoon each student chooses. Students should show an understanding of the cartoon's topic and message.

Unit 7 Skills Activity—Getting Voter Power
Part A:
1. personal information that identifies the voter
2. to prove who you are, to establish legal identity nationwide
3. Yes or no. Yes, if the person was not born in this country. No, if the person was born in this country.
4. those who are unable to write due to illiteracy or disability (A friend or a clerk may need to fill out this part for the voter.)
5. to formally swear or affirm before a witness that the information on the application is accurate
Part B:
Answers will vary. Students should correctly complete the form.

Chapter Mastery Tests

See page 953 for the Scoring Rubric for Short-Response and Essay Items on the last page of the Mastery Tests.

Chapter 1 Mastery Test A

Part A

1. B 2. D 3. C 4. A 5. D

Part B

6. G 7. F 8. D 9. H 10. A 11. C 12. E 13. B 14. J 15. I

Part C

16. People interpret, or explain, artifacts in different ways. 17. Secondary sources are things written by people who weren't actually at the event. 18. We study history to learn about ideas that people had in the past and understand their problems and how they solved them. 19. The global community is the whole world back to the beginning of humanity. 20. Different groups of people start their calendars with different events in history.

Part D

21. Cro-Magnons 22. artifacts 23. humanity 24. fire 25. Neolithic

Part E

Answers will vary. Students should support their answers with at least some of these facts: 26. Scientists could use radiocarbon dating to tell whether the animals were the same age. 27. We wouldn't know about what people did in the past and how they solved their problems, so every time there was a problem, we'd have to figure out how to solve it. We'd also have to come up with the same ideas over and over.

Part F

Answers will vary. Students' paragraphs should include at least some of these ideas: 28. The earliest hominids were nomads. They had to move around to hunt and gather food, so they didn't stay in villages. 29. The Cro-Magnons were most like modern humans because they had a spoken language, understood the phases of the moon, kept a calendar, wore jewelry, and were creative artists.

Chapter 1 Mastery Test B

Part A

1. B 2. A 3. D 4. C 5. A

Part B

6. J 7. F 8. A 9. B 10. D 11. C 12. I 13. H 14. G 15. E

Part C

16. History connects us to the past and the "roots" of our family tree. 17. History helps us understand how people lived, what ideas they had, and how they solved their problems. 18. Different groups of people start their calendars with different events in history, so year 1 starts at different times. 19. People explain artifacts and other things they find in different ways, just as people see the same event today in different ways. 20. A primary source is written by an eyewitness. A secondary source comes from someone who wasn't at the event.

Part D

21. Cro-Magnons 22. pottery 23. nomads 24. artifacts
25. Neolithic

Part E

Answers will vary. Students should support their answers with at least some of these facts: 26. We wouldn't know about what people did in the past and how they solved their problems, so every time there was a problem, we'd have to figure out how to solve it. We'd also have to come up with the same ideas over and over. 27. Scientists could use radiocarbon dating to tell whether the animals were the same age.

Part F

Answers will vary. Students' paragraphs should include at least some of these ideas: 28. The Cro-Magnons were most like modern humans because they had a spoken language, understood the phases of the moon, kept a calendar, wore jewelry, and were creative artists. 29. Remains of villages from Neanderthals might be found because Neanderthals appeared almost 2 million years after Java Man. Neanderthals made tools and buried their dead, so there might be tools and bones that could be found.

Chapter 2 Mastery Test A

Part A

1. B 2. D 3. C 4. D 5. D

Part B

6. city-state 7. Fertile Crescent 8. Phoenicians 9. cuneiform
10. Bible

Part C

11. H 12. B 13. C 14. E 15. D 16. G 17. F 18. A 19. L 20. N
21. O 22. K 23. M 24. J 25. I

Part D

Answers will vary. Students should support their answers with
at least some of these facts: **26.** Writing was the most important
because there wouldn't be written laws, books, or records of history
without it. **27.** You would never know if what you were doing was
wrong. Leaders could change the laws any time they wanted.

Part E

Answers will vary. Students' paragraphs should include at least some
of these ideas: **28.** The people in the Middle East wouldn't have
known about other parts of the world. They would only have the
things they made locally. Culture wouldn't have been shared until
later. **29.** The Sumerians sacrificed animals to their gods to keep
them from getting angry. They thought the gods would punish them
if they did the wrong thing. The Hebrew god gave them a set of rules
to follow. The Hebrews agreed to follow them and, in return, their
god protected them.

Chapter 2 Mastery Test B

Part A

1. D 2. B 3. D 4. B 5. B

Part B

6. arches and ramps 7. Mesopotamia 8. Bible 9. city-state
10. Phoenicians

Part C

11. G 12. J 13. C 14. E 15. D 16. H 17. F 18. A 19. L 20. I
21. O 22. K 23. M 24. J 25. N

Part D

Answers will vary. Students should support their answers with at
least some of these facts: **26.** Without writing, the history of the
Sumerians would have been lost. The Akkadians wouldn't have had
a written language, and Hammurabi wouldn't have written laws. The
Hebrews couldn't have written their stories and the Bible. **27.** You
would never know if what you were doing was wrong. Leaders could
change the laws any time they wanted.

Part E

Answers will vary. Students' paragraphs should include at least some
of these ideas: **28.** The people in the Middle East learned about
other parts of the world. They got to trade for things that weren't
made locally. Culture spread between countries a lot faster.
29. The Sumerians thought the gods would punish them if they did
the wrong thing. They sacrificed animals to their gods to keep them
from getting angry. The Hebrew god gave the people a set of rules to
follow. The Hebrews agreed to follow them and, in return, their god
protected them.

Chapter 3 Mastery Test A

Part A

1. D 2. A 3. A 4. C 5. C

Part B

6. Darius I 7. cavalry 8. bartering 9. Persians 10. Belshazzar

Part C

11. C 12. H 13. E 14. B 15. G 16. F 17. A 18. D 19. K
20. O 21. L 22. J 23. I 24. N 25. M

Part D

Answers will vary. Students should support their answers with at
least some of these facts: **26.** The Assyrian rebels were already
disobeying so they were probably happy when the empire fell. The
Assyrians treated captured people very badly. **27.** Students may say
that they would like to live in the Chaldean Empire because Babylon
was so beautiful and people were studying the stars. Some may
prefer the Persian Empire because they treated people more kindly.

Part E

Answers will vary. Students' paragraphs should include at least some
of these ideas: **28.** If a country had enough money, paying tribute
could save lives and keep the cities from being destroyed. **29.** It took
a long time to travel great distances, even with roads. If an empire
was too large, things might happen far from the capital and it would
be months before anyone knew about it. It would also take a long
time to solve problems.

Chapter 3 Mastery Test B

Part A

1. B 2. A 3. B 4. A 5. D

Part B

6. Assyrians 7. archers 8. Babylon 9. Assyrians 10. Cyrus the Great

Part C

11. D 12. C 13. E 14. B 15. A 16. G 17. H 18. F 19. J
20. N 21. K 22. I 23. O 24. M 25. L

Part D

Answers will vary. Students should support their answers with at least some of these facts: **26.** Students may say that they would like to live in the Chaldean Empire because Babylon was so beautiful and people were studying the stars. Some may prefer the Persian Empire because they treated people more kindly. **27.** Students may answer if they had been one of the Assyrian rebels who were already disobeying, they would probably be happy when the empire fell, since the Assyrians treated captured people very badly.

Part E

Answers will vary. Students' paragraphs should include at least some of these ideas: **28.** The people knew they could be killed if the Assyrian army attacked. If they had enough money, paying tribute could save lives and keep the cities from being destroyed. **29.** It took a long time to travel great distances, even with roads. If an empire was too large, things might happen far from the capital and it would be months before anyone knew about it. It would also take a long time to solve problems.

Chapter 4 Mastery Test A

Part A

1. C 2. B 3. D 4. A 5. B

Part B

6. G 7. A 8. B 9. J 10. I 11. C 12. D 13. F 14. E 15. H

Part C

16. Egypt 17. sails 18. irrigation 19. afterlife 20. Old
21. Hyksos 22. tributes 23. obelisks 24. paper 25. civil

Part D

Answers will vary. Students should support their answers with at least some of these facts: **26.** During the Old Kingdom, Upper and Lower Egypt were united; Egyptian cities became centers of business; and the pyramids were built. **27.** The pyramids were built by slaves, who carried blocks of stone weighing 5,000 pounds each, for about 20 years.

Part E

Answers will vary. Students' paragraphs should include at least some of these ideas: **28.** During the New Kingdom, strong pharaohs ruled Egypt; Egypt's influence spread into Africa; and Egyptian army bases were set up in other conquered lands. Egyptians rulers and nobles became rich. These rulers and nobles used some of their money to build temples, palaces, and statues. Schools and religious centers were set up as well. Toward the end of the New Kingdom disagreements about religion caused the pharaoh and priests to fight. The fighting within Egypt prevented the pharaoh from paying attention to the empire, and the empire became weak. **29.** Egyptians artists created statues, wooden, bronze, and copper figures, drawings, paintings, jewelry, pottery, and furniture. Egyptian paintings and sculpture show figures facing forward, with arms and legs turned to the side so they can be seen more easily. Also, important people were always shown to be the largest figures in a piece of art.

Chapter 4 Mastery Test B
Part A
1. B 2. C 3. A 4. B 5. D
Part B
6. D 7. I 8. E 9. B 10. A 11. C 12. J 13. F 14. H 15. G
Part C
16. afterlife 17. money 18. economy 19. Old
20. hieroglyphics 21. unified 22. stone 23. south 24. longest
25. war
Part D
Answers will vary. Students should support their answers with at least some of the following facts: **26.** We do not know how Upper and Lower Egypt were united; one story is that Menes, the god-king, conquered Lower Egypt and built his capital where Upper Egypt and Lower Egypt meet. **27.** The pyramids were built as tombs for Egypt's dead ruler; Egyptians believed that their rulers continued to rule after death, so they wanted to provide a place for their bodies.
Part E
Answers will vary. Students' paragraphs should include at least some of these ideas: **28.** In the Old Kingdom people believed the pharaoh lived forever; in the Middle Kingdom they believed that all people, not just the pharaoh, lived forever. In the Old Kingdom, pharaohs were buried in pyramids; in the Middle Kingdom, pharaohs were buried in tombs cut into cliffs near Thebes, the capital. In both kingdoms, people thought the pharaoh was a god. In the Old Kingdom, people thought the pharaohs had complete power; in the Middle Kingdom, the people thought that the pharaoh had to share power with other officials. **29.** The Egyptian civilization developed the use of irrigation, the process of mummification, the base ten counting system, the use of geometry to survey land, the art of hieroglyphics, the process of making paper out of papyrus, medical knowledge such as how to set bones, how to check for a heartbeat, how to deal with fevers and accidents; beautiful artwork, sculpture, paintings, furniture, and jewelry.

Chapter 5 Mastery Test A
Part A
1. B 2. C 3. A 4. D 5. B
Part B
6. geography 7. reincarnation 8. monsoons 9. Confucius
10. Ganges
Part C
11. B 12. A 13. F 14. C 15. E 16. H 17. G 18. D 19. N 20. K
21. O 22. I 23. M 24. L 25. J
Part D
Answers will vary. Students should support their answers with at least some of these facts: **26.** Answers will vary: They could grow a lot of crops in the Indus River Valley because the soil was very fertile. Because there was plenty of food for everyone, people didn't have to spend all their time growing food, so they had time to do other things like making art. **27.** The Shang Dynasty developed Chinese writing and put all of China under a single ruler. That made it easier for later dynasties to rule and gave them time to do and invent other things.
Part E
Answers will vary. Students' paragraphs should include at least some of these ideas: **28.** Answers will vary: The geography of both India and China cut them off from the rest of the world for a long time and let them develop their own culture before it was affected by the outside. The rivers in both countries made most of the people depend on farming for their work. **29.** Answers will vary: If symbols or characters such as those in Sanskrit are used in other languages, you can understand them, but if not, you can't be sure what they mean. Some characters, such as Chinese symbols are still being used, so we know what they mean. We don't know what the Harappan pictographs mean because no one uses them and there aren't any books that use both them and another familiar language.

Chapter 5 Mastery Test B

Part A

1. B 2. A 3. A 4. B 5. A

Part B

6. noble 7. reincarnation 8. Han 9. Confucius
10. Harappa or Mohenjo-Dara

Part C

11. B 12. A 13. F 14. C 15. E 16. H 17. G 18. D 19. N
20. K 21. O 22. I 23. M 24. L 25. J

Part D

Answers will vary. Students should support their answers with at least some of these facts: **26.** Answers will vary: The Shang Dynasty developed Chinese writing and put all of China under a single ruler. That made it easier for the Qin and Han dynasties to rule and gave them time to do and invent other things. **27.** Answers will vary: The geography of both India and China cut them off from the rest of the world for a long time and let them develop their own culture before it was affected by the outside. The rivers in both countries made most of the people depend on farming for their work.

Part E

Answers will vary. Students' paragraphs should include at least some of these ideas: **28.** Answers will vary: Other languages were based on Sanskrit, so you can understand them. Harappan symbols weren't used by later people and there aren't any dictionaries, so we don't know what the Harappan pictographs mean or how they were used. **29.** Answers will vary: They could grow a lot of crops in the Indus River Valley because the soil was very fertile. Because there was plenty of food for everyone, people didn't have to spend all their time growing food, so they had time to do other things. Earlier people had to spend all their time growing food and had no time for art.

Chapter 6 Mastery Test A

Part A:

1. A 2. D 3. A 4. C 5. D

Part B

6. The Mycenaean people were very warlike. **7.** People know about the Trojan War because Homer wrote about it in the *Iliad* and the *Odyssey*. **8.** The Persians won the battle at Thermopylae. '
9. The name of the hill around which a Greek polis was built is an acropolis. **10.** Athens created democracy.

Part C

11. A 12. B 13. E 14. H 15. F 16. D 17. C 18. G 19. K
20. J 21. O 22. L 23. M 24. I 25. N

Part D

Answers will vary. Students should support their answers with at least some of these facts: **26.** In a direct democracy, every citizen must vote on every issue. If all the laws that are passed required everyone to vote on them, it would take too long to get anything done. **27.** Sample answer: Philosophers might spend too much time thinking about things and never get anything done. Leaders should be thinkers, but they should also be doers.

Part E

Answers will vary. Students' paragraphs should include at least some of these ideas: **28.** I would rather live in Sparta because they had a very strong army and military things interest me. I am more interested in protecting land and in military battles than in beautiful art and architecture. **29.** We base our science on the physics, biology, astronomy, and medicine that started during the Hellenistic Age.

Chapter 6 Mastery Test B

Part A

1. B 2. A 3. D 4. C 5. D

Part B

6. The Minoans were the first Greek civilization. 7. The *Iliad* and the *Odyssey* describes the Trojan War. 8. The councils replaced the Greek assembly. 9. The Parthenon was built on the acropolis. 10. The Parthenon was built for the goddess Athena.

Part C

11. G 12. F 13. C 14. A 15. E 16. B 17. D 18. H 19. O 20. K 21. J 22. N 23. L 24. I 25. M

Part D

Answers will vary. Students should support their answers with at least some of these facts: 26. In a direct democracy, every citizen must vote on every issue. The United States has lawmakers who represent the people. These lawmakers vote on issues and the American people follow the decisions of the lawmakers. 27. Leaders should be thinkers, but they should also be doers. Philosophers might spend too much time thinking about things and never get anything done.

Part E

Answers will vary. Students' paragraphs should include at least some of these ideas: 28. Sample answer: Athens had a better way of life because people didn't have a choice about what they did in Sparta. All the men had to be soldiers and women would never see their husbands. Athens also had beautiful buildings and art, which Sparta didn't care about. 29. Today's society still uses geometry, pulleys, and levers. We also use information about astronomy and medicine from the Hellenistic Age.

Chapter 7 Mastery Test A

Part A

1. A 2. D 3. D 4. A 5. B

Part B

6. B 7. E 8. I 9. D 10. J 11. H 12. F 13. A 14. C 15. G

Part C

16. Rome won the first Punic War. 17. Citizens vote to elect representatives in a republic. 18. A common person in Rome is called a plebeian. 19. Carthage was destroyed in the Third Punic War. 20. A triumvirate is rule by three people.

Part D

21. citizen-soldiers 22. Rome 23. plebeians 24. Carthage 25. emperors

Part E

Answers will vary. Students should support their answers with at least some of the following facts: 26. Rome and Carthage both wanted control of the island of Sicily. 27. Citizens voted to elect representatives. There were two consuls, and members of each served a one-year term. The senate was made up of 300 patricians who passed the laws.

Part F

Answers will vary. Students' paragraphs should include at least some of these ideas: 28. The earliest Romans were the Latins who lived on the plain of Latium south of the Tiber River. The city of Rome grew from the Latin settlements. The Etruscans lived north of the Tiber River. The Etruscans were more advanced than the Latins. By 600 B.C., the Etruscans had conquered the plain of Latium, where the Latins lived. Etruscan kings ruled the Romans for more than a century. 29. Julius Caesar was part of the First Triumvirate. Caesar challenged the power of the Roman senate, and eventually Caesar gained more power than the Roman senate. Caesar passed laws against crime, forgave old enemies and made them government officials, and made the Roman calendar more accurate. The senate made Caesar dictator for life, but some senators were afraid that Caesar wanted to be king, which would end the republic. The fearful senators assassinated Caesar to "save the republic."

Chapter 7 Mastery Test B

Part A

1. B 2. A 3. B 4. C 5. A

Part B

6. Hannibal led the Carthaginians in the Second Punic War.
7. Gaius Gracchus helped the poor with Tiberius. 8. Hannibal's army was defeated at Zama to end the Second Punic War. 9. A consul replaced the Etruscan king. 10. The Etruscans lived north of the Tiber River.

Part C

11. Sicily 12. representatives 13. laborers 14. Third 15. Julius Caesar

Part D

16. I 17. J 18. C 19. G 20. H 21. B 22. F 23. A 24. D 25. E

Part E

Answers will vary. Students should support their answers with at least some of the following facts: 26. The First Punic War lasted 23 years. At the end of the First Punic war, Rome took control of Sicily. 27. There were two consuls in the Roman republic. One consul could veto a decision by the other consul. Each consul served a one year term, which kept the consuls from becoming too powerful.

Part F

Answers will vary. Students' paragraphs should include at least some of these ideas: 28. The Etruscan government had a king as a leader. The Etruscan king appointed a senate to help him make decisions. In the republic, citizens elected representatives. Instead of one king, there were two consuls that served only one year.

29. Octavian was Caesar's 19-year-old son and part of the Second Triumvirate. Octavian; Octavian ruled the West and was afraid that Mark Antony and Cleopatra were going to form their own empire. Octavian defeated the Egyptians in 31 B.C., and in 27 B.C., the Roman Republic ended and the senate made Octavian Rome's first emperor, or king.

Chapter 8 Mastery Test A

Part A

1. D 2. B 3. D 4. C 5. A

Part B

6. A 7. C 8. B 9. H 10. G 11. J 12. F 13. I 14. D 15. E

Part C

16. Romans built sewers, which are underground pipes used to carry away dirty water and human waste. Sewers reduce the spread of disease because dirty water can contain germs that cause people to get sick. Aqueducts transported water to places where it was needed. 17. Augustus Caesar's reign began the *Pax Romana,* a time of peace and prosperity in Rome. Augustus built new temples, theaters, public buildings, roads, and a large aqueduct. Provinces traded with other provinces. People led civilized lives. Two government officials took care of the business of each province, and this made government officials more honest. 18. Roman law said that everyone must honor the emperor as a god, but Christians refused to obey this law. Romans killed many Christians because of this strong difference in beliefs. 19. Jesus's disciples carried on his teachings. Paul traveled to many places (such as Greece and Italy) telling people about the teachings of Jesus. 20. Roman art contained imperfections. Statues, for example, had wrinkles and broken noses. This differed from Greek art, which celebrated perfection and idealized beauty.

Part D

21. Jews 22. god 23. decline 24. plague 25. Augustus Caesar

Part E

Answers will vary. Students should support their answer with at least some of these facts: 26. The Roman Empire declined because the government never found a simple way to choose a new emperor, civil war often broke out after the death of an emperor, wars were a financial strain on the government, and a plague killed many Romans. 27. Modern society has been influenced by the accomplishments of the Romans. We still believe, as the Romans did, that laws should be fair, just, and reasonable. The Romans built roads, used concrete, developed vaulted ceilings, made realistic art, studied medicine, had a health-care system, and used sewers and aqueducts.

Part F

Answers will vary. Students' paragraphs should include at least some of these ideas: 28. The difference between a good leader and a bad leader is that a good leader listens to the needs of the people. A bad leader is only concerned about himself or herself. For example, in Rome, Trajan was a good leader. He allowed poor farmers to borrow money at a very low cost. Nero, however, was a bad leader. He didn't listen to anyone and is also thought to have started a fire that damaged Rome. 29. Although it was civilized for its time, Roman society lacked many of the modern conveniences we enjoy today, such as electricity, televisions, computers, digital clocks, telephones, easily obtained medicine, and products for good hygiene.

Chapter 8 Mastery Test B

Part A

1. B 2. C 3. A 4. A 5. D

Part B

6. J 7. A 8. B 9. D 10. C 11. I 12. G 13. E 14. F 15. H

Part C

16. The Pantheon was built by Hadrian, and it still stands today. It is a temple for all the Roman gods, and it has a vaulted ceiling. 17. Romans built sewers, which are underground pipes used to carry away dirty water and human waste. Sewers reduce the spread of disease because dirty water can contain germs that cause people to get sick. 18. Augustus Caesar's reign began the *Pax Romana,* a time of peace and prosperity in Rome. Augustus built new temples, theaters, public buildings, roads, and a large aqueduct. Provinces traded with other provinces. People led civilized lives. Two government officials took care of the business of each province, and this made government officials more honest. 19. Roman law said that everyone must honor the emperor as a god, but Christians refused to obey this law. Romans killed many Christians because of this strong difference in beliefs. 20. Roman art contained imperfections. Statues, for example, had wrinkles and broken noses. This differed from Greek art, which celebrated perfection and idealized beauty. Romans built structures that were both functional and beautiful, such as aqueducts and the Colosseum.

Part D

21. disciples 22. divine 23. Roman Empire 24. disease 25. common

Part E

Answers will vary. Students should support their answer with at least some of these facts: 26. The empire might have lasted longer if the Romans had used elections or a systematic way to choose an emperor. Better ways of collecting and managing money might also have helped the empire to survive longer. 27. Modern life owes much to things that were developed in ancient Rome. We still believe, as the Romans did, that laws should be fair, just, and reasonable. The Romans built roads, used concrete, developed vaulted ceilings, made realistic art, studied medicine, and had a health-care system.

Part F

Answers will vary. Students' paragraphs should include at least some of these ideas: 28. Some of the bad Roman emperors were Caligula (who was mentally ill) and Nero (who may have started a fire that damaged Rome.) Some of the good emperors were Augustus Caesar (who oversaw the "Golden Age of Rome"), Trajan (who let farmers borrow money at low cost), Hadrian (who lowered taxes and passed progressive laws), and Marcus Aurelius (who was a soldier but was also a leader who worked for peace.) 29. Life in the Roman Empire was civilized. During the *Pax Romana,* there was peace and prosperity. Romans enjoyed the benefits of living in a society with fair laws, excellent architecture, realistic artwork, underground sewers, fine bridges and aqueducts, and a health-care system.

Chapter 9 Mastery Test A

Part A

1. B 2. A 3. D 4. A 5. D

Part B

6. D 7. C 8. H 9. A 10. B 11. E 12. G 13. I 14. J 15. F

Part C

16. McJunkin's major discovery was the Folsom Point. 17. The Hohokam built canals to bring water to their land. 18. The Iroquois descended from the Mississippian people. 19. The Aztecs tried to recreate the Toltec civilization. 20. The Inca Empire included parts of Ecuador, Peru, Chile, Argentina, and Bolivia.

Part D

21. Hohokam 22. Chaco Canyon 23. mound 24. Mississippian 25. Mandan

Part E

Answers will vary. Students should support their answers with at least some of these facts: 26. The first Americans were nomads who were probably following herds of animals. They came from Asia across a land bridge that connected Asia to North America. 27. The Hohokam, Mogollon, and Anasazi are the early southwestern cultures. The Hohokam built canals and Snaketown. The Mogollon created rock art and built kivas to hold religious ceremonies. The Anasazi were master builders who created cliff dwellings, pueblos, and Chaco Canyon. They also made mirrors out of obsidian.

Part F

Answers will vary. Students' paragraphs should include at least some of these ideas: 28. The Anasazi built a massive complex of ceremonial buildings and roads. At the center of their complex was Chaco Canyon, which contained cliff dwellings. Roads were built from the hub of the wheel like spokes, and each road led to a village as far as 10 miles away. Leaders communicated from the central great houses using signal fires. 29. The Olmecs and the Mayas were both good mathematicians and astronomers. The Olmecs and the Mayas developed special calendars and were led by priests and religious leaders. The Toltecs were led by powerful warriors and valued their military strength. The Toltecs conquered other groups with their military force.

Chapter 9 Mastery Test B

Part A

1. C 2. B 3. A 4. D 5. C

Part B

6. Anasazi roads had a wagon wheel design. All of the roads started from the same central location. 7. The Mississippian people built Cahokia. 8. The Iroquois tribe formed a democracy. The United States government is based on the Iroquois democracy. 9. The Mayas created a calendar based on 13 cycles of 400 years each. 10. The Incas called their empire the "Land of the Four Quarters."

Part C

11. New Mexico 12. Snaketown 13. Southeastern 14. Aztec 15. Tenochtitlán

Part D

16. C 17. B 18. E 19. J 20. D 21. A 22. F 23. I 24. H 25. G

Part E

Answers will vary. Students should support their answers with at least some of these facts: 26. The Folsom Point first showed that Indians had been in North America for at 9,000 years. The discovery of the Clovis Point showed that Indians had been in North American for at least 13,000 years. 27. The Mogollon Indians carved thousand of mysterious images into rock surfaces. The rock art images include those of insects, fish, reptiles, birds, mammals, human faces, and masks.

Part F

Answers will vary. Students' paragraphs should include at least some of these ideas: 28. The Hohokam civilization began about A.D. 300. The Hohokam people built hundreds of miles of canals from A.D. 800–1000, and by A.D. 1450, most people had abandoned the area. The reason for the end of the Hohokam civilization is thought to be a lack of water and a failed irrigation system. 29. The Incas divided their empire into four geographic areas. The leader of each conquered tribe was asked to be a partner in the Inca Empire. The tribal leaders had to follow certain rules but could still make decisions for their own tribe.

Chapter 10 Mastery Test A

Part A

1. B 2. C 3. D 4. A 5. B

Part B

6. A 7. H 8. D 9. I 10. C 11. F 12. B 13. J 14. E 15. G

Part C

16. Romanesque churches had rounded arches, think walls, and narrow openings for windows, so they were dark and gloomy. Around 1200, the Gothic style started, with its narrow ribs of stone to support the roof, flying buttresses to hold up the walls, and pointed arches, which drew the eyes upward. 17. The Crusades were fought over control of Palestine, or the Holy Land. For 400 years, Muslims had allowed Christian pilgrims to visit the Holy Land, but then another group of Muslims took control of Palestine. Pope Urban II called for a crusade against the Muslims. Crusaders believed that they were following God's orders in these battles. 18. Lords gave land and peasants to vassals in exchange for their loyalty. The vassal would serve the lord and help him in battle. The vassal had a fief and needed his own soldiers. The vassal could offer smaller pieces of land to other people in exchange for their loyalty. 19. A manor was that part of the fief that peasants farmed to support a lord's family. A manor was self-sufficient because people who lived on it grew, raised, or made nearly everything that they needed without help. 20. The jury helped a judge decide whether a person (who had been accused of doing something wrong) was innocent or guilty. The jury asked questions to discover the truth. A jury examined information and facts.

Part D

21. marry 22. patriarch 23. power 24. Christian 25. weapons

Part E

Answers will vary. Students should support their answer with at least some of these facts: 26. The crusaders were Christians who fought against Muslims over control of the Holy Land. Christians and Muslims both wanted control of the same area, and their differences in religious beliefs added to the tension. Pope Urban II called for a war against Muslims, and he said that Christians who died for this cause would go to heaven. Crusaders' religious beliefs caused them to fight. They wanted to obey the pope, they believed they would go to heaven, they believed they were following God's orders, and they believed that Christians should control the area where Jesus of Nazareth had lived. 27. Feudalism was based on the exchange of land for loyalty. When a lord gave a vassal land and peasants, the vassal promised the lord his loyalty. The vassal promised he would help in battle, so he was making a promise that he was willing to die for his lord. Today, workers feel a much smaller degree of loyalty to their employers. Workers make a promise not to violate any laws or break the company's rules, but they do not make a promise that they would give their lives for the good of the company. A modern worker's loyalty to his or her employer is not nearly as important as a vassal's loyalty to his lord was.

Part F

Answers will vary. Students' paragraphs should include at least some of these ideas: **28.** The manor was self-sufficient because people used tools and resources to grow, raise, or make everything they needed. The dwellers of a manor did not need to venture outside of it for any necessities because they had forests, which supplied wood for buildings and tools; they grew crops to feed everyone; they had sources for water, including a moat; a blacksmith living on the manor made their tools; and they raised sheep for wool to make clothing. If a manor or castle fell under attack, the people inside would not have to risk their lives by going to the outside world. **29.** A jury was similar to Parliament because both were groups that discussed and debated issues to try to come up with the best resolution or idea. A judge did not have to rely only on his own thoughts and opinions because he could seek advice from the members of a jury. Getting multiple people involved in a decision-making process usually results in a good final decision. Parliament was a group of people who discussed and made laws. Members of a jury offered differing points of view while working toward the resolution of a court case. Similarly, members of Parliament offered differing points of view while working on the development of laws. In this way, a jury and Parliament both bring to mind the old expression "Two heads are better than one."

Chapter 10 Mastery Test B

Part A

1. B **2.** A **3.** C **4.** D **5.** B

Part B

6. A **7.** F **8.** I **9.** C **10.** J **11.** B **12.** H **13.** G **14.** E **15.** D

Part C

16. Students at cathedral schools studied religion, Latin, rhetoric, arithmetic, geometry, astronomy, logic, and music. **17.** A knight wore armor and was trained to fight using a lance, a two-edged sword, a dagger, and a battle ax. **18.** Benedict wrote a rule saying that monks and nuns should promise not to marry, own property, or disobey the head of the monastery or convent. **19.** These killings caused a lasting split between the Roman Catholic Church and the Eastern Orthodox Church. **20.** Europe began to trade with the Middle East, so Europeans bought sugar, lemons, spices, and other things. The crusaders learned about Arab art, architecture, medicine, and mathematics. Europeans gained an increased sense of adventure and a greater willingness to explore other parts of the world, such as Africa and Asia.

Part D

21. loyalty **22.** Greek Orthodox Church **23.** Acre **24.** noble **25.** squire

Part E

Answers will vary. Students should support their answer with at least some of these facts: **26.** A manor was the part of a fief that peasants would farm to support the lord's family. Serfs lived on a manor. Serfs were peasants bound to the land; their lives were controlled by the lord of the manor. Serfs made clothing from the wool of sheep they raised. Serfs cut down wood for building fences. Serfs grew crops and raised animals so that they and the lord's family would have food to eat. A blacksmith on the manor made tools and weapons. Male serfs did agricultural work. Female serfs worked in the fields, cooked, made clothing, and cared for the house. About 60 percent of what each serf raised went to the lord of the manor and to the church. **27.** Until about 1100, most churches looked like Roman buildings. These Romanesque churches had rounded arches, think walls, and narrow openings for windows, so they were dark and gloomy. Around 1200, the Gothic style started, with its narrow ribs of stone to support the roof, flying buttresses to hold up the walls, and pointed arches, which drew the eyes upward. Two examples of Gothic architecture in France are the cathedral of Notre Dame and the Rheims Cathedral.

Part F

Answers will vary. Students' paragraphs should include at least some of these ideas: **28.** Religious differences were a chief cause of the Crusades, which were fought over control of Palestine. For nearly 400 years, Muslims had allowed Christian pilgrims to visit the Holy Land, but then another group of Muslims took control of Palestine. According to some reports, this group was not as tolerant toward Christians. Pope Urban II called for a crusade against the Muslims. Thousands of people joined the Crusades. Many people believed that they were following God's orders in these battles. Some people fought in the Crusades because they wanted adventure. Some went because they wanted to escape hard work at home. Kings and nobles joined the Crusades to get more power. The pope encouraged them to do this by forgiving their debts and letting them pay fewer taxes. **29.** A lord was a king or a noble who gave land to someone. A vassal was a noble who received land. Lords gave land and peasants to vassals in exchange for their loyalty. The vassal would serve the lord and help him in battle. This meant that a vassal might die in a battle because of his loyalty to his lord. The land and peasants given to a vassal was called a fief. The vassal could offer smaller pieces of this land to other people in exchange for their loyalty.

Chapter 11 Mastery Test A

Part A

1. B **2.** C **3.** D **4.** A **5.** D **6.** B **7.** C **8.** A **9.** D **10.** B

Part B

11. Western Europe **12.** the Mongols **13.** Eastern Orthodox **14.** Leif Eriksson **15.** the Turks

Part C

16. C **17.** E **18.** D **19.** A **20.** F **21.** B **22.** G **23.** H **24.** O **25.** M **26.** K **27.** J **28.** N **29.** I **30.** L

Part D

Answers will vary. Students should support their answers with at least some of these facts: **31.** With a spoken language, you can only talk to small groups of people at a time. A written language lets you write books and pass ideas around faster to more people.

32. If religions and government are run by the same people, everyone would have to have the same religion. The leaders would have too much power over people's lives.

Part E

Answers will vary. Students' paragraphs should include at least some of these ideas:

33. The Eastern Orthodox Christians used the building, language, and customs of the Byzantine Empire. They didn't know about inventions and discoveries made in Europe, which was Roman Catholic. **34.** I wouldn't go to school or know anything about history or art or where buildings came from. I wouldn't be able to read or write. It would be dangerous to travel.

Chapter 11 Mastery Test B

Part A
1. F 2. G 3. D 4. A 5. C 6. B 7. E 8. H 9. O 10. L 11. J 12. K 13. N 14. I 15. M

Part B
16. C 17. B 18. D 19. B 20. A 21. C 22. A 23. D 24. C 25. B

Part C
11. Leif Ericksson founded a colony in Vinland. 12. Justinian wrote a code of laws. 13. Western Europe accepted Roman Catholicism. 14. The Kremlin is the center of the Russian church and government. 15. Constantine built the Hippodrome to look like Rome's Colosseum.

Part D
Answers will vary. Students should support their answers with at least some of these facts: **31.** With a spoken language, you can only talk to small groups of people at a time. However, people can more easily convey emotion when talking face-to-face. A written language is spread faster and to more people. This is because with written language allows you to write books, etc. **32.** Some Christians did not want an emperor the government and religion to be run by the same people because it would give the leaders too much power over people's lives. Also, if religion and government are run by the same people, everyone would have the same religion.

Part E
Answers will vary. Students' paragraphs should include at least some of these ideas:

33. The split of the Christian Church separated Europe. The Eastern Orthodox Christians did not know about inventions and discoveries made in Europe, which was Roman Catholic. Also, the Eastern Orthodox Christians used the building, language, and customs of the Byzantine Empire. **34.** If I lived in the Dark Ages, I wouldn't be able to read or write because I wouldn't go to school. It would be dangerous to travel because of the frequent wars. I would stay in my kingdom and have no contact with anyone outside of it. The towns and villages around me would be in a state of ruin. I would only live for my day-to-day needs.

Chapter 12 Mastery Test A

Part A:
1. E 2. D 3. H 4. C 5. B 6. G 7. F 8. A

Part B
9. Muhammad 10. vision 11. Muslims 12. pillars 13. Islamic 14. Ghana 15. Songhai

Part C
16. B 17. A 18. C 19. D 20. A 21. D 22. B

Part D
23. prayer 24. respect for others 25. Mali 26. Arab astronomers 27. infidel 28. Mansa Musa 29. civil war 30. Abbasid

Part E
Answers will vary. Students should support their answers with at least some of the following facts: **31.** Muhammad founded Islam. Muhammad went to a desert to pray and to fast. One year, Muhammad had a vision in which an angel told him he was the messenger of Allah. Muhammad began preaching about a religion that had only one god. **32.** Muslim doctors studied medicine carefully. Arab astronomers figured out that the earth is round and that it is about 25,000 miles around.

Part F
Answers will vary. Students' paragraphs should include at least some of these ideas: **33.** Ghana was founded about 400 A. D. and quickly became a center of trade. Ghana controlled the important trade routes from the Sudan to North Africa. Ghana collected taxes from trade caravans and built a large army with its extra money. Almoravids from North Africa invaded Ghana in 1076 and destroyed Kumbi. The war with the Almoravids weakened Ghana. Mali replaced Ghana as the strongest empire. **34.** Songhai became powerful in the 1400s by controlling the gold and salt trade. Other countries wanted the riches that Songhai had. At first, Songhai easily defeated its invaders. Finally, an army from North Africa defeated Songhai by using a new weapon—the gun.

Chapter 12 Mastery Test B

Part A

1. jihad 2. Allah 3. Gabriel 4. fast 5. Mali 6. Ghana 7. alms
8. mosque

Part B

9. C 10. B 11. A 12. D 13. C 14. A 15. C

Part C

16. The Hajj is a pilgrimage to Mecca. 17. Mali took control of important trade routes. 18. Historians call Muhammad's journey from Mecca to Medina Hegira. 19. Muslims had a surplus of food because they improved farming. 20. Jabir's discoveries led to chemistry. 21. There are more Sunnis today. About 90 percent of Muslims are Sunnis. 22. Ghana's government became rich by taxing trade caravans.

Part D

23. infidel 24. respect for others 25. civil war 26. Mali 27. Mansa Musa 28. Abbasid 29. Arab astronomers 30. prayer

Part E

Answers will vary. Students should support their answers with at least some of the following facts: 31. The Qur'an is the holy book of the Muslims. The Qur'an contains the teachings of Islam with the words God spoke to Muhammad through the angel Gabriel. 32. Jabir was the greatest Muslim scholar. His discoveries formed the foundation of chemistry.

Part F

Answers will vary. Students' paragraphs should include at least some of these ideas: 33. Mali formed a new empire when Ghana lost its power. Mali's leader, Sandiata Keita, helped Mali rise to greatness. Keita took control of the gold fields. As Keita's armies moved across Africa, divided the Mali empire into provinces and put a general in charge of each one. Mansa Musa was a powerful Mali king. Musa made Mali safe and peaceful. When Musa died, civil war broke out, and within 150 years, the Mali empire fell. 34. Both the Ghana and Mali empires became strong because they controlled trade routes. Both were involved in the trading of gold and had a strong army. Unlike Mali, Ghana didn't use its army to conquer other lands. Ghana did not have a Muslim king, like Mali did.

Chapter 13 Mastery Test A

Part A

1. C 2. D 3. A 4. B 5. D

Part B

6. H 7. I 8. G 9. A 10. E 11. J 12. D 13. B 14. F 15. C

Part C

16. The emperors thought that the people who lived in other countries were barbarians. They wanted to keep China free from the influences of uncivilized people. 17. The shogun was the ruler with the most power. The emperor held the highest rank in society, but he had no political power. The shogun was a military dictator who controlled officials, judges, and armies. 18. A Noh drama is a Japanese play with only two actors. It involves a storyteller, musicians, and two actors who act out the story. The actors wear masks. 19. Akbar did these things to keep peace. Akbar ruled the Mogul Empire from 1556 to 1605. Like all the Mogul rulers, Akbar was a Muslim. He tried to give people religious freedom and to treat them all fairly. 20. Educated people in T'ang China were literate and they wrote poetry. The poems were about nature and the problems of ordinary people.

Part D

21. India 22. scholars 23. printing 24. gunpowder 25. Japan

Part E

Answers will vary. Students should support their answer with at least some of these facts: 26. Inventions that came out of Sung China include gunpowder, the compass, the abacus, the clock, and a machine to detect earthquakes. Chinese rulers had little use for gunpowder, but the compass allowed Chinese ships to travel far, and the abacus led to advancements in mathematics. Sung China was so advanced that Hangzhou had streetlights and a fire department. 27. The shoguns kept foreigners, missionaries, and Christians out of Japan because they thought that the influence of outsiders was a potential threat to the shoguns' power. This sense of isolation allowed Japan to develop unique art forms, such as ikebana, Noh dramas, and kabuki plays.

Part F

Answers will vary. Students' paragraphs should include at least some of these ideas: 28. The Mongol rulers were the opposite of isolationists. They encouraged trade by building great highways and protecting merchants and travelers. The exchange of goods led to an exchange of ideas as Europeans and Arabs learned from the Chinese. Europeans got paper, porcclain, printing, gunpowder, and other inventions. The Chinese got glass, clothes, cotton, silver, carpets, honey, and slaves. This exchange of goods and ideas had an impact on the entire world, not just China. 29. European and Japanese feudalism were similar in that they both involved the exchange of land for loyalty and military service. They were different, however, in that in Europe, the relationship between a lord and a vassal was a legal one, whereas in Japan the connection was based on morality. When a vassal died in Europe, the property was divided among his sons, but in Japan, a man chose (or adopted) a son to care for the land. Unlike their European counterparts, Japanese warriors expected women to be tough and self-disciplined. Unlike their European counterparts, Japanese warriors valued education and literary and artistic expression (such as poetry and calligraphy).

Chapter 13 Mastery Test B

Part A

1. D 2. C 3. A 4. B 5. C

Part B

6. B 7. G 8. D 9. E 10. F 11. J 12. H 13. A 14. I 15. C

Part C:

16. Indian mathematicians used a number system based on 10; we still use their symbols for 1 to 9 today; they used the number zero, and they used the decimal. 17. A masterpiece is a work of art that seems nearly perfect. Paintings from Sung China are considered masterpieces today because of their beauty and the skills that the artists had. 18. A samurai obeyed because he believed his daimyo had the right to rule. In Europe, the relationship between a lord and a vassal was a legal one, but in Japan the connection was based on morality. 19. China did little trading for 250 years because the Ming emperors thought that outsiders were barbarians. During this time, China fell behind other civilizations because it was not being exposed to the advancements of other cultures. 20. An opera is a play in which people sing all the words. In ancient China, opera performers were men who acted, sang, and danced while musicians played.

Part D

21. civilian 22. ruling 23. compass 24. shoguns 25. house

Part E

Answers will vary. Students should support their answer with at least some of these facts: 26. The Chinese invented printing around 1040 by using carved blocks of wood, ink, and paper. The Chinese began printing books about 400 years before the Europeans. This development meant that people no longer had to copy a book by hand. Since books could be made much more quickly, knowledge and education spread throughout the world. 27. Sung artisans made beautiful bowls and vases out of porcelain. European artisans traveled to China to learn how to make porcelain. While in China, Europeans would have been exposed to new ideas. They brought European ideas and products with them to China. Under the Mongol rulers, porcelain became an important item that the Chinese traded with Arabs and Europeans in exchange for things like glass, clothes, cotton, silver, carpets, honey, and slaves. The exchange of goods like porcelain led to an exchange of ideas.

Part F

Answers will vary. Students' paragraphs should include at least some of these ideas: 28. Like Christianity, Judaism, and Islam, Shinto is a religion based on a set of beliefs. Unlike those religions, however, Shinto has no holy books. In Christianity, Judaism, and Islam, followers worship one all-powerful God. Shinto followers, however, worship thousands of gods and spirits. The goddess of the sun is the most important Shinto entity. Shinto followers believe that kami, or spirits, control the forces of nature. 29. A civilization can be isolated because of geography or politics. Japan, for example, has been isolated from other countries because the waters surrounding the Japanese islands kept invaders out. Another kind of isolation is political and cultural isolation. In the 1600s, the shoguns kept foreigners, missionaries, and Christians out of Japan because they thought that the influence of outsiders was a potential threat to the shoguns' power. This sense of isolation allowed Japan to develop unique art forms, such as ikebana, Noh dramas, and kabuki plays. In the 1500s, China also experienced isolation because the Ming emperors thought that foreigners were barbarians. They kept foreigners out, and they kept the Chinese in the country. The lack of travel and trade kept China from being exposed to exciting new ideas happening elsewhere. As a result, Chinese civilization fell behind other civilizations.

Chapter 14 Mastery Test A

Part A

1. B 2. C 3. D 4. C 5. B

Part B

6. D 7. F 8. B 9. H 10. G 11. E 12. A 13. I 14. J 15. C

Part C

16. humanist 17. learning 18. Bible 19. Rafael Santi
20. peasants 21. Renaissance 22. Mantua 23. city-states
24. Florence 25. Latin

Part D

26. Elizabeth I 27. rebellion 28. humanism 29. Gutenberg
30. Sistine Chapel

Part E

Answers will vary. Students should support their answers with at least some of the following facts: 31. Humanism is the belief that human actions, ideas, and works are important. Humanists believe that people should be happy while they are alive. 32. Michelangelo was an Italian sculptor and painter. Michelangelo is best know for his sculpture of David, the Pietà, and the fresco painting on the ceiling of the Sistine Chapel in Rome.

Part F

Answers will vary. Students' paragraphs should include at least some of these ideas: 33. Lorenzo de Medici used his family's wealth to help artists and scholars. Lorenzo de Medici, or Lorenzo the Magnificent, ruled Florence in the 1400s. The ancient Athenians came together frequently to discuss ideas, drink, and eat. Lorenzo de Medici brought scholars together in Florence to discuss ideas, eat, and drink. 34. During the Middle Ages, millions of people died. People of the Middle Ages believed that life after death was their only reason for living. During the Middle Ages the arts, literature, and science were not important. By the end of the Middle Ages, people needed a change. The Renaissance was a rebirth of learning. The Middle Ages are also called the "Dark Ages."

Chapter 14 Mastery Test B

Part A

1. A 2. C 3. B 4. A 5. D

Part B

6. C 7. E 8. A 9. G 10. I 11. H 12. F 13. J 14. B 15. D

Part C

16. patron 17. Shakespeare 18. humanism 19. rebellion
20. Renaissance 21. Michelangelo 22. fresco 23. Savonarola
24. Black Death 25. sonnets

Part D

26. wool 27. Savonarola 28. geniuses 29. Italy 30. Greece.

Part E

Answers will vary. Students should support their answers with at least some of the following facts: **31.** As a result of the Black Death, the population decreased; with fewer people, fewer taxes could be paid; less food was needed so the price of food dropped; farmers made less money; many people left the cities and fled to the country. **32.** William Shakespeare wrote sonnets and dramas, Chaucer wrote stories, Cervantes wrote Don Quixote.

Part F

Answers will vary. Students' paragraphs should include at least some of these ideas: **33.** The Renaissance began in 1350 in a few city-states in northern Italy. People rebelled against the Middle Ages and wanted to use their imaginations to make things. People began to look back and to study ancient Greece and Rome. People started to study art, literature, science, and philosophy. People focused on being individuals and expanding creative thought and ideas. **34.** A man of the Middle Ages focused on getting ready for life after death. A man of the Middle Ages believed that happiness came only after death. A man of the Renaissance believed that we should be happy while alive. A man of the Middle Ages did not spend time learning about the arts, sciences, or philosophy. A man of the Renaissance was well educated, read about ancient Greece and Rome, learned about science and art, had good manners and a sense of humor, and also could play music, dance, write

Chapter 15 Mastery Test A

Part A

1. C 2. A 3. B 4. C 5. D

Part B

6. C 7. F 8. D 9. G 10. E 11. H 12. I 13. A 14. B 15. J

Part C

Answers will vary. Students should support their answer with at least some of these facts: **16.** To excommunicate someone is to say that the person can no longer be a member of a church. Pope Leo X said that Martin Luther's beliefs were wrong, and the pope excommunicated him. **17.** Catholic priests were not allowed to marry, but Lutheran ministers could. Also, Lutheran ministers did not perform the same rituals as priests because the Lutheran Church got rid of most of the ceremonies of the Catholic Church.
18. These women were all wives of King Henry VIII. The king married Catherine of Aragon, and after he tried to get the marriage annulled, he secretly wed Anne Boleyn. Henry said that Anne Boleyn was unfaithful, so he executed her and then married Jane Seymour, who gave birth to Edward. **19.** The Reformation was a movement that challenged and changed the Catholic religion in Europe. Martin Luther was the key figure of the Reformation. In his 95 theses, Luther criticized the practice of selling indulgences and other practices of the Catholic Church. Luther's ideas caused people to question the religious authority of the Catholic Church.
20. The Counter-Reformation was the Catholic Church's process of reforming itself. The Catholic Church made reforms to counter, or fight against, Protestant beliefs.

Part D

21. Catholic 22. beliefs 23. church 24. Jesuits 25. Protestant

Part E

Answers will vary. Students should support their answer with at least some of these facts: **26.** Martin Luther was the key figure of the Reformation. In his 95 theses, Luther criticized the selling of indulgences and other practices of the Catholic Church. Luther said that people could not buy forgiveness for their sins. Luther believed that people could win salvation by faith alone. Luther's ideas caused people to question the religious authority of the Catholic Church. Luther formed the Lutheran Church. Luther's religious reform movement quickly spread beyond Germany. By 1534, it had reached England. **27.** John Calvin taught that people are full of sin when they are born. Calvin believed that few people would be saved from sin, and that God had already chosen those who would be saved. These special people were called the "elect." Calvin believed that the elect of God had a political mission. They were called upon to rule Christian society. In Geneva, Switzerland, Calvin set up a religious community, which was overseen by a council of 12 elders. Calvin gave these elders the power to make laws saying what was right and what was wrong. These elders said that the following things were sinful: playing cards, gambling, drinking alcohol, singing, and dancing. The council could imprison people who did not live the Calvinist way.

Part F

Answers will vary. Students' paragraphs should include at least some of these ideas: **28.** King Henry VIII wanted to end his marriage to Catherine, but the Catholic Church did not allow divorce. Henry asked Pope Clement VII to annul the marriage. Catherine was opposed to this, so she asked her nephew, Charles V, to influence the pope's decision. The pope refused to annul the marriage. Henry secretly wed Anne Boleyn anyway. Henry appointed a new archbishop of Canterbury, who said that the marriage to Catherine was not legal. In 1534, Parliament made Henry the head of the Church of England, or Anglican Church. Henry took control of all lands the Catholic Church owned in England. **29.** In Geneva, Switzerland, John Calvin set up a religious community, which was overseen by a council of 12 elders. These elders were older, experienced men. Calvin gave these elders the power to make laws saying what was right and what was wrong. These elders said that the following things were sinful: playing cards, gambling, drinking alcohol, singing, and dancing. The council could imprison people who did not live the Calvinist way. The members of the council could visit people in their homes to make sure they were leading good lives. The council could force people to leave the city. One big difference between this council and the Roman Inquisition was that Calvinists were Protestants, but the members of the Roman Inquisition were Catholics. During the Counter-Reformation, Pope Paul III set up the Roman Inquisition, which was a special court that inquired into people's religious beliefs. The court could execute heretics.

Chapter 15 Mastery Test B

Part A

1. A **2.** D **3.** B **4.** D **5.** C

Part B

6. I **7.** C **8.** F **9.** H **10.** J **11.** E **12.** G **13.** B **14.** A **15.** D

Part C

16. John Calvin wrote this book, which contained what he thought each person should believe about religious questions. The book gave the Protestant movement a fully organized set of beliefs. Calvin taught that people are full of sin when they are born. Calvin believed that few people would be saved from sin, and that God had already chosen those who would be saved. These special people were called the "elect." Calvin believed that the elect of God had a political mission. They were called upon to rule Christian society. **17.** The Catholic Church formed the Council of Trent in 1545. The council wrote down the most important beliefs of the Catholic Church; stopped the sale of indulgences; said that people only found salvation through the Catholic Church; said people had to go to church and do good deeds; declared that the pope was the only leader of the Christian Church; said that Catholics had to agree with the Church's interpretation of the Bible; and ordered its own new translation of the Bible. **18.** Ignatius of Loyola founded a new Catholic religious order called the Society of Jesus. Members of this order were called Jesuits. They wanted to help Catholics stay in the Catholic Church, and they wanted to help Protestants return to it. **19.** The Edict of Worms said that anyone could kill Martin Luther without being punished. Several German princes protected Luther from this. Many German princes liked Luther's ideas. They began to protest the ways of the Catholic Church, and that is why they were called Protestants. **20.** John Tetzel was a monk who sold indulgences near Martin Luther's university. Tetzel said that a person who bought an indulgence could be sure of salvation. Luther said this was wrong because he believed that people could not buy their forgiveness. Tetzel criticized Luther for this statement.

Part D

21. indulgences **22.** Baptism **23.** Huguenots **24.** authority **25.** Puritans

Part E

Answers will vary. Students should support their answer with at least some of these facts: **26.** In his 95 theses, Martin Luther criticized the selling of indulgences and other practices of the Catholic Church. Luther said that people could not buy forgiveness for their sins. He called for three reforms. First, Luther believed that people achieved salvation only through faith in Jesus Christ. Second, Luther taught that religious truth came from the Bible. Third, Luther said that people should read the Bible and decide for themselves what it means, rather than relying on clergy to tell them how to think about the Bible. Luther translated the Bible into German so that more people could read it. Luther's ideas caused people to question the religious authority of the Catholic Church. Luther formed the Lutheran Church. **27.** The Counter-Reformation happened because religious leaders did not want more people to leave the Catholic Church. The Counter-Reformation was the Catholic Church's process of reforming itself. The Catholic Church made reforms to counter, or fight against, Protestant beliefs. The Roman Inquisition and the Council of Trent were key features of the Counter-Reformation.

Part F

Answers will vary. Students' paragraphs should include at least some of these ideas: **28.** King Henry VIII wanted to end his marriage to Catherine, but the Catholic Church did not allow divorce. Henry asked Pope Clement VII to annul the marriage. Catherine was opposed to this, so she asked her nephew, Charles V, to influence the pope's decision. The pope refused to annul the marriage. Henry secretly wed Anne Boleyn anyway. Henry appointed a new archbishop of Canterbury, who said that the marriage to Catherine was not legal. In 1534, Parliament made Henry the head of the Church of England, or Anglican Church. Henry took control of all lands the Catholic Church owned in England. **29.** In Geneva, Switzerland, John Calvin set up a religious community, which was overseen by a council of 12 elders. These elders were older, experienced men. Calvin gave these elders the power to make laws saying what was right and what was wrong. These elders said that the following things were sinful: playing cards, gambling, drinking alcohol, singing, and dancing. The council could imprison people who did not live the Calvinist way. The members of the council could visit people in their homes to make sure they were leading good lives. The council could force people to leave the city.

Chapter 16 Mastery Test A

Part A

1. B **2.** D **3.** A **4.** C **5.** D **6.** B **7.** C **8.** A **9.** D **10.** B

Part B

11. magnifying lens **12.** thermometer **13.** static electricity **14.** calculus **15.** new clock

Part C

16. H **17.** B **18.** I **19.** J **20.** F **21.** E **22.** C **23.** D **24.** G **25.** A

Part D

26. Aristotle believed everything in the heavens moved in circles. **27.** Kepler proved Copernicus' theory. **28.** Gilbert explained why a compass needle points north. **29.** The word *science* means to know. **30.** Experimental science begins with and depends on careful experiments and measures.

Part E

Answers will vary: **31.** The Bible had been the source of truth for scholars before the Middle Ages. The new ideas based on personal observation or experiments threatened the authority of the church. **32.** Answers will vary: Using the scientific method means that everyone will study nature in the same way, so they can compare their answers.

Part F

Answers will vary: **33.** Fancy writing would be big words or making descriptions too flowery. Bacon wanted everyone to say things in a simple way that everyone could understand.

34. Aristotle was a philosopher so he just thought about the way things acted and made up explanations. Galileo actually did experiments and made observations. They studied at different times, which meant that Galileo had more scientific information.

Chapter 16 Mastery Test B

Part A
1. C 2. A 3. B 4. D 5. A 6. C 7. B 8. C 9. D 10. A

Part B
11. blood circulates 12. static electricity 13. analytic geometry
14. thermometer 15. Universal Gravitation

Part C
16. B 17. C 18. E 19. J 20. I 21. G 22. H 23. A 24. D 25. F

Part D
26. Experimental science depends on careful experiments and measures. 27. Gilbert worked with amber and used the word "electric." 28. Science is a word that means to know. 29. The Catholic Church imprisoned Galileo for his scientific theories.
30. Aristotle believed everything in the heavens moved in circles.

Part E
Answers will vary: 31. The Bible had been the source of truth for scholars before the Middle Ages. The new ideas based on personal observation or experiments threatened the authority of the church. 32. Using the scientific method means that everyone will study nature in the same way, so they can compare their answers.

Part F
Answers will vary: 33. No, because they didn't have the tools or mathematics they needed to figure things out. During the Roman and Byzantine Empires, people were supposed to accept what the Bible or Greek and Roman writers said and not question or experiment on things themselves. 34. Galileo actually did experiments and made observations. He studied centuries after Aristotle when there was more scientific information available. Aristotle was a philosopher so he just thought about the way things acted and made up explanations.

Chapter 17 Mastery Test A

Part A
1. A 2. D 3. B 4. B 5. D

Part B
6. Prince Henry 7. Dias 8. Magellan 9. Pizarro 10. de las Casas 11. Columbus 12. Raleigh 13. de Champlain 14. de Soto 15. Quetzalcoatl

Part C
16. J 17. F 18. C 19. I 20. G 21. D 22. B 23. A 24. H 25. E

Part D
26. conquistador 27. encomienda 28. East Indies 29. Spanish
30. pilgrims

Part E
Answers will vary. Students should support their answers with at least some of the following facts: 31. King John II of Portugal wanted his country to be wealthy and powerful. A water route to India and China would bring in goods that Portugal could sell for a profit. 32. The priest, de las Casas wanted to stop the cruel treatment of American Indian slaves. De las Casas suggested to Spain that African workers be used instead.

Part F
Answers will vary. Students' paragraphs should include at least some of these ideas: 33. The Spaniards killed the Aztec emperor, Montezuma. The Spaniards broke their promise to the Inca emperor and executed him. Pizarro, who killed the Inca emperor, was killed by his own men because of an argument over gold. Millions of Indians died or were killed because of diseases introduced by the Spaniards, or by Spanish guns and cannons. 34. The first English colony in North America was Roanoke Island, set up by Sir Walter Raleigh in 1585. This colony did not last. The first permanent English colony was Jamestown, set up in 1607. The first French colony in North America was Quebec, set up by Samuel de Champlain in 1608. The French also founded settlements along the Great Lakes and the Mississippi River.

Chapter 17 Mastery Test B

Part A

1. A 2. D 3. C 4. B 5. A

Part B

6. viceroy 7. native 8. economic 9. strait 10. Navigation
11. exploration 12. descendant 13. colonist 14. settlement
15. import

Part C

16. Another name for conquistador is conqueror. 17. The Encomienda caused thousands of American Indians to suffer and die. 18. Columbus thought he had landed on the East Indies.
19. The Spanish used canons, guns, and horses to defeat the Aztecs.
20. The Pilgrims came to North American for religious freedom.

Part D

21. G 22. A 23. D 24. E 25. B 26. C 27. J 28. I 29. F 30. H

Part E

Answers will vary. Students should support their answers with at least some of the following facts: 31. Bartholomeu Dias, of Portugal, was the first explorer to sail around the southern tip of Africa. This means that it was possible to sail south and then eastward from Portugal to India and China. 32. Bartolomé de las Casas wanted to do something about the suffering and cruel treatment of the American Indian slaves.

Part F

Answers will vary. Students' paragraphs should include at least some of these ideas: 33. The Aztecs thought a legend was coming true when Cortés arrived. The Incas were in the middle of a civil war when Pizarro arrived. Tribes that didn't like the Incas or Aztecs joined the Spanish. The Spanish had horses, which had never been seen by the Aztecs or Incas. The Spanish had guns and cannons. The Spanish brought smallpox and measles. The Indians had no natural protection against these diseases. As a result, the diseases killed many American Indians. 34. After the Spanish conquered the Aztec and Inca Empires, Spanish conquistadores controlled large areas of land. To make money off the land, the landowners needed farmworkers and miners to work on their land. The Spanish forced American Indians to do the work for them. Within 100 years, the Indian population went from 20 million to 4 million. After the efforts of Bartolomé de las Casas, Spain started to import Africans to the Americas. This was the beginning of African slavery in the Americas.

Chapter 18 Mastery Test A

Part A

1. C 2. A 3. A 4. D 5. B

Part B

6. B 7. A 8. H 9. F 10. J 11. C 12. G 13. D 14. I 15. E

Part C

16. The Habeas Corpus Act said that the government has to charge someone with a crime before putting the person in prison.
17. The Glorious Revolution is the period in England that involved the overthrow of James II and the crowning of William and Mary.
18. An adviser is a person who gives advice. 19. Frederick the Great expanded Prussia's territory by invading Silesia and taking it away from Austria. 20. The Petition of Right said that no one, not even the king, can force citizens to house soldiers unless those citizens want to.

Part D

21. nobility 22. Puritans 23. Whig 24. government 25. resolution

Part E

Answers will vary. Students should support their answer with at least some of these facts: 26. The Spanish fleet was defeated by the English fleet because the Spanish ships broke out of their protective formation, and because the English ships were smaller and faster. The lessons to be learned include: always stay in formation, know your enemy's strengths, and use speedy forms of transportation in battle. 27. Nationalism began in Europe in the 11th century when England became a nation. People started to feel loyal to their nations. People in the new nations shared the same language, history, and traditions. People today still feel a great deal of pride about their countries. This pride can lead to positive things (such as competition in the Olympics) or negative things (such as wars or border disputes).

Part F

Answers will vary. Students' paragraphs should include at least some of these ideas: 28. The reign of Louis XIV was good for France because he reorganized and expanded the army. The nobility was weakened, beautiful churches and palaces were built, and art and music spread. Louis XIV's reign was bad for France because the taxpayers had to pay for his love of beautiful things, such as the grand palace at Versailles. It was also bad because he fought too many wars, which were paid for by taxpayers, and which drained the French treasury. At the end of his life, Louis XIV urged his grandson to keep peace, saying, "I have been too fond of war."

29. In an absolute monarchy, the king or queen has complete and unlimited power over his or her people. Everyone must do whatever the monarch says. Philip III of Spain and Louis XIV of France both had absolute power. In a constitutional monarchy, the monarchy's powers are limited because there are the laws of a democracy to protect the people. England under the rule of William and Mary was a constitutional monarchy. Between 1628 and 1689, Parliament passed the Petition of Rights, the Habeas Corpus Act, and the English Bill of Rights. These documents showed that England did not want an absolute monarch. In an absolute monarchy, a ruler like Louis XIV could spend taxpayers' money on whatever luxury or war he wanted. In a constitutional monarchy, as in England, the king would have to ask Parliament for money to pay for a war, and Parliament could refuse.

Chapter 18 Mastery Test B

Part A

1. D 2. B 3. D 4. C 5. A

Part B

6. E 7. D 8. I 9. B 10. G 11. F 12. A 13. H 14. C 15. J

Part C

16. The Tories were people who supported a strong monarchy in England. 17. To inherit is to receive money, land, or a title from someone who has died. (Today, a person's inheritance is usually described in the deceased person's will.) 18. A resolution is a formal statement written by a governmental body. 19. The Restoration is the period that saw monarchy return to England in 1660 with the crowning of Charles II. Historians call his 25-year reign the Restoration. 20. Nationalism began in Europe in the 11th century when England became a nation. France soon followed. Nationalism began when people started to feel loyal to their country because they shared boundaries, traditions, a history, and a language.

Part D

21. Spain 22. England 23. tradition 24. treason 25. loyalty

Part E

Answers will vary. Students should support their answer with at least some of these facts: 26. Louis XIV was a bad leader because he was selfish. He cared more about himself than about serving the French people. Louis XIV's reign was bad for France because the taxpayers had to pay for his love of beautiful things, such as the grand palace at Versailles. It was also bad because he fought too many wars, which were paid for by taxpayers, and which drained the French treasury. At the end of his life, Louis XIV urged his grandson to keep peace, saying, "I have been too fond of war." 27. Peter the Great and Catherine the Great accomplished many things. Peter the Great improved Russia's culture by inviting scholars and artists to his country. He increased trade with nations in Western Europe. He gained control of ports to the Baltic Sea and the Black Sea. He also built a new, modern capital called St. Petersburg. Catherine the Great was a strong Russian ruler who improved education. She allowed more religious freedom. She also tried to get a constitution written for her country. For a time, Catherine favored freedom for serfs.

Part F

Answers will vary. Students' paragraphs should include at least some of these ideas: 28. Spain's rise to power began with the Moors, who settled in southern Spain. In 1469, the marriage of Ferdinand and Isabella united much of Spain under two strong rulers. After Ferdinand's death, Charles became king of Spain and then emperor of the vast Holy Roman Empire. Gold and silver found by explorers in the Americas made Charles V's empire rich. When Charles V retired, Philip II became the king of Spain, and he wanted to defeat England and make Europe Catholic again. In 1588, the English navy defeated the Spanish Armada, and a sudden storm sank many of the Spanish ships. This defeat led to Spain's decline. In the next two centuries, England and France replaced Spain as the most powerful nations in Europe. 29. In an absolute monarchy, the king or queen has complete and unlimited power over his or her people. Everyone must do whatever the monarch says. James I of England and Scotland refused to share power with Parliament because he said that he ruled by divine right. He thought that God had chosen him to rule, and that no one had the right to question him or his decisions. An absolute monarch's sense of power and authority was often increased by the idea that God had chosen that person to rule. An absolute monarch would think, "I have God on my side, so no one can disobey me."

Chapter 19 Mastery Test A

Part A

1. B 2. D 3. D 4. B 5. D

Part B

6. Denis Diderot published an encyclopedia. 7. Locke believed that people were born with these rights. 8. Rousseau believed that civilization made people do bad things. 9. Enlightenment was the time when people used reason to solve problems. 10. Mozart and Haydn were important classical musicians.

Part C

11. D 12. H 13. A 14. G 15. B 16. F 17. C 18. E 19. J
20. L 21. I 22. O 23. K 24. N 25. M

Part D

Answers will vary. Students should support their answers with at least some of these facts: 26. In the past, people had learned about nature from the Bible or Aristotle. Galileo had done experiments. Newton used mathematics and reason to figure out how nature works. 27. What are people really like? What is a government for? Do people have any natural rights? If so, what are they? How will government work best?

Part E

Answers will vary. Students' paragraphs should include at least some of these ideas: 28. We have three branches of government like the English government. Both systems have a court that interprets the laws. In our government, Congress makes laws instead of Parliament. The President enforces the laws instead of the king. 29. In the Age of Reason, people thought about things in more complex ways. They also believed in order. Baroque music was more complex than the simpler music of the Renaissance. Classical music, such as fugues, showed order in playing the same melody but on different instruments.

Chapter 19 Mastery Test B

Part A

1. C 2. D 3. C 4. D 5. D

Part B

6. Swift wrote a book about people's foolish behavior. 7. Haydn is the father of the symphony. 8. Madame Geoffrin had the most important salon in Paris. 9. Diderot published an encyclopedia. 10. Locke believed in the rights of life, property, and liberty.

Part C

11. C 12. H 13. E 14. A 15. B 16. G 17. D 18. F 19. M 20. L 21. I 22. N 23. J 24. O 25. K

Part D

Answers will vary. Students should support their answers with at least some of these facts: 26. We have three branches of government like the English government. Both systems have a court that interprets the laws. In our government, Congress makes laws instead of Parliament. The President enforces the laws instead of the king. 27. People had a lot of different ideas about government, society, art, music, and writing. Each person gave the best information about the thing he or she knew most about.

Part E

Answers will vary. Students' paragraphs should include at least some of these ideas: 28. In the past, people had learned about nature from the Bible or Aristotle. Galileo had done experiments. Newton used mathematics and reason to figure out how nature works.

29. In the Age of Reason, people thought about things in more complex ways. They also believed in order. Baroque music was more complex than the simpler music of the Renaissance. Classical music, such as fugues, showed order in playing the same melody but on different instruments.

Chapter 20 Mastery Test A

Part A

1. C 2. C 3. A 4. D 5. B

Part B

6. J 7. C 8. D 9. A 10. B 11. I 12. F 13. E 14. H 15. G

Part C

16. In 1781, General Cornwallis surrendered at Yorktown, Virginia. The British troops were trapped by colonial soldiers in front of them and by French ships in the sea behind them. 17. The Stamp Act placed a tax on colonial newspapers, playing cards, and legal documents. 18. To exile means to send someone away from his or her home country and to order this person not to come back. 19. Some causes of the French Revolution were that people wanted to do away with the feudal aspects of French society (such as the fact that nobility and clergy did not have to pay taxes); that people wanted a more democratic form of government instead of an absolute monarchy; that people wanted equality under the law; and that the French people were influenced by the actions of the colonists in the American Revolution. 20. In April 1775, the first shots of the American Revolutionary War were fired at Lexington after British troops had marched to Concord to seize colonial weapons. The minutemen killed one third of the "redcoats" as they marched back to Boston.

Part D

21. National Assembly 22. Russia 23. Napoleon 24. Jacobins 25. Estates-General

Part E

Answers will vary. Students should support their answer with at least some of these facts: 26. The American Revolutionary War was fought because the monarch in Great Britain did not respect the colonists' rights. The colonists wanted to break free from the British Empire because England started interfering with colonists' lives. If England had treated the colonists with respect and not passed so many tax laws, the colonists would have had little reason to revolt. 27. The Reign of Terror lasted between July 1793 and July 1794. The Jacobins, led by Maximilien Robespierre, wanted to kill anyone who disagreed with them. They killed thousands of people with the guillotine. Ironically, Robespierre himself was sent to the guillotine. His death showed that the French people were not going to stand for a dictator while they were fighting for democracy.

Part F

Answers will vary. Students' paragraphs should include at least some of these ideas: **28.** The American Revolution changed the world because people in other countries adopted the ideas that the colonists promoted. The Declaration of Independence said that "all men are created equal." This idea, and the actions of the colonists, inspired people in France to start the French Revolution, which, in turn, inspired people in other countries to fight for equality and liberty. The American Revolution had a ripple effect that promoted the idea of democracy around the world. **29.** Napoleon's failures were the invasion and retreat from Russia, his defeat in 1814, and his defeat at Waterloo. These were important events, but they were not as great as Napoleon's accomplishments. Napoleon was a a smart military leader whose soldiers liked fighting for him. He conquered most of Europe and ended the Holy Roman Empire. After his defeat in March 1814, he escaped from exile on Elba and returned to France to become a hero again. His Code of Napoleon made every man in France equal before the law; and he helped spread the ideas of liberty and equality throughout Europe.

Chapter 20 Mastery Test B

Part A

1. D 2. B 3. B 4. A 5. C

Part B

6. G 7. B 8. C 9. J 10. I 11. E 12. F 13. A 14. D 15. H

Part C

16. In 1789, starving French people became angry when the price of bread doubled. Angry mobs rioted and attacked the Bastille, which contained political prisoners and gunpowder. **17.** Equality means that everyone shares the same rights. **18.** The clergy made up the First Estate; the nobles made up the Second Estate; and the Third Estate was made up of groups such as doctors, teachers, bankers, business people, lawyers, city workers, and farmers. **19.** The legislature is the lawmaking body of government. **20.** In 1789, the representatives of the Third Estate (who believed it was unfair that they were paying all the taxes) declared that they were a National Assembly that represented the French people. They called for an end to absolute monarchy. Under pressure, Louis XVI ended the meeting of the Estates-General, and he told the clergy and nobles to join the National Assembly.

Part D

21. violated 22. French 23. moderates 24. enforces 25. boycott

Part E

Answers will vary. Students should support their answer with at least some of these facts: **26.** The Navigation Acts forced colonists to use British ships; the Quartering Act forced colonists to house British soldiers; the Stamp Act put a tax on newspapers, playing cards, and legal documents; the Townshend Acts put a tax on common goods, such as paint. These acts angered the colonists and increased the calls for freedom from the British Empire because people believed that these laws were unfair. **27.** Historians use this term because it describes a period when terror itself seemed to rule over the people of France during the French Revolution. The Reign of Terror lasted between July 1793 and July 1794, and the Jacobins killed thousands of people with the guillotine.

Part F

Answers will vary. Students' paragraphs should include at least some of these ideas: **28.** The American Revolution changed the world because people in other countries adopted the ideas that the colonists promoted. The Declaration of Independence said that "all men are created equal." This idea, and the actions of the colonists, inspired people in France to start the French Revolution, which, in turn, inspired people in other countries to fight for equality and liberty. The American Revolution had a direct effect on Great Britain, which lost its valuable colonies and gained a dangerous enemy in the form of General Washington's troops. **29.** Napoleon could have prevented his military disaster in one of two ways. First of all, he could have decided not to invade Russia in the first place. He wanted to punish Russia because Czar Alexander I stopped supporting the Continental System. Secondly, after invading Russia, Napoleon should have retreated much sooner. After moving deep into Russia, the troops found it very difficult to get out because they faced disease, freezing temperatures, and starvation. The retreating Russian army destroyed shelter and food so that the invaders would not have the things they needed. Over 500,000 soldiers had marched into Russia, but only 40,000 returned to France.

Chapter 21 Mastery Test A

Part A

1. B 2. A 3. C 4. B 5. B

Part B

6. George Stephenson built the steam locomotive. **7.** Great Britain passed laws to stop the spread of industry. **8.** Nations need natural resources and workers to become industrialized. **9.** The textile industry grew because of the spinning jenny and the cotton gin. **10.** Samuel Slater brought the spinning machine plans to the United States.

Part C

11. natural resources 12. Revolution 13. Railroads
14. industrialized 15. automobile 16. identical 17. textile
18. steel 19. money 20. Canals

Part D

21. B 22. C 23. A 24. E 25. D

Part E

Answers will vary. Students should support their answers with at least some of the following facts: **26.** Benefits—produced many goods for many people, city populations grew; Problems—conditions for workers were bad at first, bigger cities had more garbage, bad water, and bad sanitation. **27.** Before the steam locomotive people used canals, dirt roads, two layer roads, and gravel roads to transport products and materials.

Part F

Answers will vary. Students' paragraphs should include at least some of these ideas: **28.** During the Industrial Revolution, the population of cities in Great Britain grew very quickly. Great Britain became the "workshop of the world" because it produced so many goods in its factories. A people moved to cities, fewer people lived on farms. With more people living there, sanitary conditions in the cities got worse. **29.** In 1773, James Watt developed a steam engine with wheels. The steam engine could be used to turn the wheels of textile machines so that workers didn't have to do it. Steam engines made it possible to build factories anywhere since moving water was no longer necessary to power the textile machines.

Chapter 21 Mastery Test B

Part A

1. D 2. B 3. D 4. C 5. A

Part B

6. Eli Whitney developed the process of mass production.
7. Another name for purified coal is coke. 8. Money used to start a business is called capital. 9. Transportation is the movement of things from place to place. 10. A labor union is an organized group of workers trying to improve things.

Part C

11. industrialized 12. work 13. transportation 14. Great Britain 15. engine 16. Mass production 17. spinning mule 18. iron 19. economist 20. costly

Part D

21. C 22. A 23. E 24. D 25. B

Part E

Answers will vary. Students should support their answers with at least some of the following facts: 26. Labor unions gave workers more political power. They also helped make factories safer, gave workers more pay, and allowed them to work shorter hours. 27. The locomotive gave factory owners a fast and inexpensive way to move raw materials and finished products from one place to another.

Part F

Answers will vary. Students' paragraphs should include at least some of these ideas: 28. The Industrial Revolution happened because machines were used to make products instead of making them by hand. Using machines instead of hand labor meant that many more products could be produced in less time. Factories made it possible to produced goods in even less time because workers came together for certain hours on certain days to work. 29. Electricity replaced steam as a source of power and made it possible to send messages by cable across long distances, even across oceans. Electricity and electrical wiring made the telephone and the invention of the light bulb possible. Electricity provided safe light to homes, businesses, and factories. Oil was used to power machinery in factories. Gasoline was made from oil and was used to run the internal combustion engine, which led to the invention of the gasoline engine.

Chapter 22 Mastery Test A

Part A

1. B 2. B 3. C 4. D 5. C

Part B

6. C 7. F 8. I 9. H 10. D 11. G 12. A 13. B 14. J 15. E

Part C

16. H 17. F 18. B 19. E 20. C 21. D 22. J 23. A 24. G 25. I

Part D

26. Greece 27. Haiti 28. Spain 29. July Ordinances
30. Second French Republic

Part E

Answers will vary. Students should support their answers with at least some of the following facts: 31. Socialists were one of two political groups during the Second French Republic. Socialists wanted political and economic reform and also wanted the state to control land and factories. 32. A nationalist believes that people who share the same history, traditions, customs, and language should be organized in separate nations. Nationalists do not believe that an empire should rule over many different people.

Part F

Answers will vary. Students' paragraphs should include at least some of these ideas: 33. As a result of the Congress of Vienna, monarchies that had lost their power to Napoleon Bonaparte were restored. Kings were put into power in France, Spain, Portugal, and Sardinia. The Congress gave Finland and most of Poland to Russia; gave part of northern Italy to Austria; gave Ceylon, some of south Africa, and Malta to Great Britain; and gave Norway to Sweden. The Congress organized the German states into a German Confederation. 34. Before 1794, the western half of Hispaniola was controlled by France, and Spain controlled the eastern half. Toussaint L'Ouverture was a former African salve who led the revolt of free blacks and slaves and forced the French to leave the western half of Hispaniola. In 1804, the western half of Hispaniola became the independent country of Haiti. In 1821, the eastern half of Hispaniola became Santo Domingo.

Chapter 22 Mastery Test B

Part A

1. A 2. C 3. D 4. B 5. A

Part B

6. creoles 7. ordinance 8. radicals 9. proletariat 10. foreign minister 11. peninsular 12. confederation 13. conservatives 14. socialists 15. liberals

Part C

16. D 17. B 18. E 19. J 20. H 21. C 22. G 23. I 24. F 25. A

Part D

26. Greece 27. Haiti 28. Spanish 29. July Ordinances 30. Second French Republic

Part E

Answers will vary. Students should support their answers with at least some of the following facts: **31.** The Congress of Vienna met after Napoleon Bonaparte was defeated and sent into exile. Leaders from Austria, Prussia, Great Britain, and Russia met in 1814 to restructure Europe. **32.** Simón Bolívar was a Creole leader who was born in Venezuela. He led a revolution to free Venezuela from Spanish control in 1810. In 1819, he freed Columbia from Spanish rule and then became president of the new nation of Great Colombia.

Part F

Answers will vary. Students' paragraphs should include at least some of these ideas: **33.** The three political groups came into existence after the French Revolution were the conservatives, liberals, and radicals. The conservatives were made up mostly of rich landowners and nobles and formed the upper class of most societies. They thought revolution was dangerous and supported the absolute power of kings. The liberals were made up mostly of wealthy businessmen and merchants and belonged to the upper middle class. Liberals wanted to limit the absolute power of kings and give more power to the middle class. Radicals believed every man should have the right to vote and believed that violence was sometimes necessary to bring change in society. **34.** It took 11 years for Mexico to become independent. In 1811, Father Hidalgo organized the Indians into an army that rebelled against the Spanish landowners. After Hidalgo was executed by the Spanish, Father Morelos continued Father Hidalgo's fight. By 1813, Indians controlled most of the land outside the major cities of Mexico. In 1815, Creole soldiers captured and executed Morelos because they didn't want Mexico to be ruled by peasants. In 1821, Creole leaders revolted against Spain and made Mexico independent.

Chapter 23 Mastery Test A

Part A

1. B 2. A 3. D 4. D 5. C

Part B

6. F 7. E 8. A 9. D 10. C 11. I 12. J 13. B 14. G 15. H

Part C

16. Giuseppe Garibaldi is called the "sword" because of his great military feats. **17.** Vatican City is the home of the pope and the center of the Roman Catholic Church. **18.** Austria, France, and Spain controlled the Italian provinces. **19.** In 1848, Sardinia declared war on Austria. **20.** Otto von Bismarck was a conservative who believed in militarism, absolute power, and the unification of the German states. He did not believe in democratic rule.

Part D

21. France 22. Second 23. country 24. Sardinian 25. Napoleonic

Part E

Answers will vary. Students should support their answer with at least some of these facts: **26.** Giuseppe Mazzini is called the "soul" of Italian unity because he stood for its spirit of freedom. Although the rebellion he led failed, his actions promoted nationalist feelings in Italy. **27.** Otto von Bismarck lied to the newspapers about a meeting he had with a French ambassador. His comment caused such a strong reaction that it helped start the Franco-Prussian War. Prussia won this war in 1871, and France had to give up Alsace and Lorraine. These territories contained France's richest coal and iron fields.

Part F

Answers will vary. Students' paragraphs should include at least some of these ideas: **28.** Nationalism is a feeling of loyalty toward one's country. Nationalism can be affected by language, culture, foreign invasions, government, history, and heritage. Speaking the same language, sharing a culture, feeling united against invaders, believing in a form of government, having a shared history, and valuing a country's heritage all contribute to nationalism. **29.** Militarism is a nation's warlike policy or practice. Otto von Bismarck, the prime minister of Prussia, believed that war was a means for solving problems. He forced the Prussian parliament to give him money to built a strong army. Prussia defeated Denmark in 1864, Austria in 1866, and France in 1871. France had to give up Alsace and Lorraine. All these military victories contributed to the movement for a unified Germany. William I became the first kaiser of Germany. This German empire is called the Second Reich.

Chapter 23 Mastery Test B

Part A

1. C **2.** D **3.** A **4.** B **5.** A

Part B

6. G **7.** J **8.** I **9.** H **10.** B **11.** C **12.** F **13.** E **14.** D **15.** A

Part C

16. A policy is a plan that helps a person or a country make a decision. **17.** Heritage is made up of the traditions that are passed down from ancestors to their descendents. **18.** Prussia's military victories over Denmark in 1864, Austria in 1866, and France in 1871 contributed to the movement for a unified Germany. **19.** The Napoleonic Wars gave birth to nationalism in Italy and in Germany. **20.** Nationalism is a feeling of loyalty toward one's country. Nationalism can be affected by language, culture, foreign invasions, government, history, and heritage.

Part D

21. militarism **22.** foreign **23.** democratic **24.** government **25.** siege

Part E

Answers will vary. Students should support their answer with at least some of these facts: **26.** Giuseppe Mazzini is called the "soul" of Italian unity because he stood for its spirit of freedom. The rebellion he led in Italy in 1848 failed. Thousands of soldiers from Austria and France marched into Italy and put down the revolt. Although the rebellion failed, Mazzini's actions promoted nationalist feelings in Italy. **27.** Historians call Giuseppe Garibaldi the "sword" because of his great military feats. He led an army of Italian nationalists on an invasion of Sicily in May 1860. Garibaldi and his "Red Shirts" swept through Sicily and marched northward toward Rome. His troops and Sardinian troops teamed up to unite almost all of Italy.

Part F

Answers will vary. Students' paragraphs should include at least some of these ideas: **28.** People in the United States feel very loyal to their country. They have a democratic government, and they have a shared history, culture, and heritage. No matter what language people speak or religion they practice, all people in this country feel loyal toward the United States. This loyalty is stronger than most disagreements or differences that people have with other people within the country. **29.** Otto von Bismarck lied to the newspapers about a meeting he had with the French ambassador. His lie made the French think that the Prussian king had said something rude to their ambassador. It made the Germans think that the French ambassador had threatened them. This controversy helped cause the Franco-Prussian War. Prussia won this war, and France had to give up Alsace and Lorraine. These territories contained France's richest coal and iron fields.

Chapter 24 Mastery Test A

Part A

1. C **2.** B **3.** B **4.** A **5.** D

Part B

6. D **7.** F **8.** I **9.** G **10.** B **11.** E **12.** A **13.** C **14.** J **15.** H

Part C

16. To protect India, Britain took over neighboring Afghanistan. **17.** European nations forced China to give them special trade rights. China was divided into spheres of influence so that a nation like Great Britain could benefit without competing with a nation like France, which had its own sphere of influence. Chinese rulers had no say in this European-controlled trade. **18.** After the revolution of 1867, Japan ended the rule of the shogun. It returned political power to Emperor Meiji and introduced reforms. It adopted western ideas in transportation and education. It abolished feudalism and wrote a constitution. It developed a modern army and navy and passed a law requiring all young men to serve in the army. It defeated China and Russia in wars and took over Korea. It gained important trading rights in Russian-controlled lands in China. **19.** Factory owners wanted natural resources and raw materials from colonies. These raw materials included coal, iron ore, gold, silver, tin, and copper. Owners also wanted workers for their factories, and they wanted markets to sell their manufactured goods. **20.** Attitudes that helped imperialism included the idea that Europeans and people in the United States were superior to Africans and Asians. Another idea was that native people were ignorant and uncivilized. The idea that westerners should bring Christianity and western civilization to the East helped imperialism, as did the idea that imperialism was good because it improved the native population's health, transportation, and education. The idea that outsiders could bring jobs and industry to colonies helped imperialism. Also, the idea that Europeans had a right to take gold and other valuable natural resources from the ground in colonies helped. There was also an idea that native people would be better off if they adopted western ways.

Part D

21. Africa **22.** Burma **23.** Korea **24.** Europe **25.** Germany

Part E

Answers will vary. Students should support their answer with at least some of these facts: **26.** Imperialism occurs when a powerful nation controls a weaker colony. Industrialization helped spread imperialism. Factory owners wanted natural resources and raw materials from colonies. Manufacturers also wanted markets for their goods. Each major nation let its colonies buy only those goods manufactured in the mother country. **27.** Imperialism was bad because Europeans benefited much more from it than the native people did. Imperialism destroyed native industry, which caused people to lose their jobs. Colonial people had no control over their government or their country's natural resources. Europeans did not respect the culture, religion, language, and customs of native people, and Europeans tried to force them to change their way of life. One could argue that imperialism was good because it brought great improvements in health, transportation, and education. It was also good because it introduced the ideas of constitutional government and because it brought jobs and industry to the colonies.

Part F

Answers will vary. Students' paragraphs should include at least some of these ideas: **28.** This expression means that British colonies were so spread out around the world that it was always daylight somewhere in Britain's empire. Britain took control of India, Afghanistan, South Africa, Burma (now Myanmar), Ceylon, Malaya, and Singapore, as well as areas that are now Sudan, Nigeria, Ghana, Kenya, and Uganda. Britain took control of the Suez Canal, and Egypt became a protectorate. **29.** The Suez Canal connected the Mediterranean Sea and the Red Sea, which made the journey from Britain to India (and other British colonies) much shorter. The British government controlled India from 1858 to 1947. The Suez Canal made it much easier for British military ships and cargo boats to go to the Far East, where they could establish military bases or pick up raw materials. Britain took control of the Suez Canal in 1875, and a few years later, Britain made Egypt a protectorate.

Chapter 24 Mastery Test B

Part A

1. D 2. B 3. A 4. C 5. A

Part B

6. C 7. H 8. G 9. F 10. J 11. B 12. A 13. E 14. D 15. I

Part C

16. A sphere of influence is an area in which only one foreign country can trade. **17.** A mother country is a nation that controls a colony. **18.** French Indochina included what is now Vietnam, Laos, and Cambodia. **19.** Europeans did not respect the culture, religion, language, and customs of native people in Africa and Asia. Europeans tried to force them to change their way of life. Europeans viewed them as uncivilized, ignorant, and in need of help. **20.** A protectorate is an independent country whose foreign policy is controlled by a major power.

Part D

21. market **22.** military **23.** Myanmar **24.** colonialism **25.** Algeria

Part E

Answers will vary. Students should support their answer with at least some of these facts: **26.** Colonialism, or imperialism, is the control or influence that a powerful nation has over a weaker colony. Mother countries wanted colonies that they could use as military bases. Ships from these mother countries could stop at colonial ports to get supplies for the military. Powerful nations competed with other nations to gather colonies, and they used sea power to control trade routes. **27.** Imperialism was good because it brought great improvements in health, transportation, and education. It was also good because it introduced the ideas of constitutional government and brought jobs and industry to the colonies. Imperialism was bad, however, because Europeans benefited much more from it than the native people did. It was also bad because colonial people had no control over their government or their country's natural resources. Another negative effect was that Europeans did not show respect for the culture, religion, language, and customs of native people.

Part F

Answers will vary. Students' paragraphs should include at least some of these ideas: **28.** This meaning of this expression is that powerful nations felt that they could not achieve greatness without establishing colonies around the world. Nationalism contributed to imperialism. Italy, Germany, Japan, and the United States thought colonies would make them as powerful as England and France. Powerful nations relied on colonies for natural resources and raw materials, such as coal, iron ore, gold, silver, tin, and copper. Colonies also provided markets. Major nations forced their colonies to buy only those goods manufactured in the mother country.
29. After the revolution of 1867, Japan ended the rule of the shogun. It returned political power to Emperor Meiji and introduced reforms. It also adopted western ideas in transportation and education. Japan abolished feudalism and wrote a constitution. It developed a modern army and navy and passed a law requiring all young men to serve in the army. It defeated China and Russia in wars and took over Korea. It also gained important trading rights in Russian-controlled lands in China.

Chapter 25 Mastery Test A

Part A

1. C 2. D 3. B 4. D 5. A

Part B

6. H 7. G 8. J 9. D 10. B 11. E 12. F 13. A 14. C 15. I

Part C

16. Poison gas was risky because the wind could shift and blow the deadly gas back to the troops who were using it. 17. A democratic government is one in which all people have equal rights.

18. Under socialism, the government owns all the land, industries, and transportation. Under this political and economic theory, the government controls the economy of a nation. 19. A total war is one in which cities, farms, factories, and people living at home all become part of the war. 20. Bloody Sunday is the name of a 1905 revolt in Russia in which the czar's soldiers killed hundreds of workers. The workers wanted better working conditions, more freedom, and an elected national assembly.

Part D

21. socialists 22. Allies 23. Austrians 24. Russians 25. Serbs

Part E

Answers will vary. Students should support their answer with at least some of these facts: 26. Imperialistic powers became rivals. They became jealous and mistrustful of each other. Industrialized nations began building bigger armies and navies with more deadly weapons. Countries formed alliances, which meant that the nations agreed to aid one another if attacked. Germany, Austria-Hungary, and Italy made up the Triple Alliance. Great Britain, France, and Russia made up the Triple Entente. The assassination of Franz Ferdinand in Sarajevo led to World War I. On July 28, 1914, Austria declared war on Serbia. Russia said it would protect Serbia; Germany declared war on Russia; France came into the war to support Serbia; and then Great Britain honored its alliance with France. What started as a small revolt became a big war. 27. World War I was the most important cause of the Russian Revolution of 1917. Millions of Russians were killed, wounded, or taken prisoner. Russians had to live with very little food, fuel, and other necessary supplies. Russians became very angry with Czar Nicholas II, and they wanted a more democratic form of government. Things were going very poorly for the people of Russia, and many people thought that socialism would solve the country's problems.

Part F

Answers will vary. Students' paragraphs should include at least some of these ideas: 28. President Woodrow Wilson came to the peace conference with a plan called the Fourteen Points. Wilson wanted to end secret treaties between nations; he wanted to reduce the size of armies and navies in each nation; and he wanted to organize a league of nations to keep the peace. 29. The cost of World War I was in the hundreds of billions of dollars. Governments raised taxes and borrowed large sums of money to pay for the war. By the end of the war, every major European nation was bankrupt. Millions of people had been killed, cities and farms lay in ruins, and many people were unemployed. Europe lost much of its power and wealth, and as a result of the war, the United States and Japan took over the European markets. The United States emerged as a world power because its economy was much healthier than that of other countries.

Chapter 25 Mastery Test B

Part A

1. A 2. D 3. D 4. C 5. B

Part B

6. A 7. G 8. I 9. C 10. J 11. F 12. H 13. B 14. E 15. D

Part C

16. Germany used U-boats, or submarines, to sink Allied and neutral ships carrying food and supplies. Germany used U-boats for unrestricted warfare in the waters around Britain.

17. An autocracy is a government in which one person rules with unlimited power. 18. Unrestricted warfare is war that is not limited to a certain area or boundary. In 1917, Germany announced that it would begin unrestricted warfare in the waters around Britain. Germany said it would sink any ship that sailed into those waters. 19. An armistice is an agreement to stop fighting. 20. This treaty required Germany to accept responsibility for causing the war. Germany had to pay for the cost of the war; it gave Alsace and Lorraine to France; it divided its African colonies between France and Great Britain; and it gave its colonies in the Pacific to Japan.

Part D

21. trenches 22. rival 23. Germany 24. reparations 25. France

Part E

Answers will vary. Students should support their answer with at least some of these facts: 26. Prior to the war, nations were becoming more mistrustful of each other. Industrialized nations began building bigger armies and navies with more deadly weapons. Nationalism made Serbs living in Austria-Hungary want to be a part of Serbia, which was a neighboring country. The Austrian emperor sent his nephew, Franz Ferdinand, on a trip to try to improve relations with the Serbs. Ferdinand was assassinated in Sarajevo, and this led to World War I. On July 28, 1914, Austria declared war on Serbia. Russia said it would protect Serbia; Germany declared war on Russia; France came into the war to support Serbia; and then Great Britain honored its alliance with France. What started out as a small revolt became a big war. 27. Educated Russians wanted a more democratic government. When Russia lost the Russo-Japanese War, people demanded change. In 1905, on Bloody Sunday, Russian workers marched to the czar's palace in St. Petersburg. They wanted better working conditions, more freedom, and an elected national assembly. The czar's soldiers killed hundreds of workers. Then Russian workers refused to work. Riots broke out. Peasants burned nobles' estates. The czar promised to give the people more freedom if they would stop the violence. The czar agreed to the election of a Russian parliament. However, Czar Nicholas II dismissed the Duma after only three months because he believed that he alone had the right to rule.

Answers will vary. Students' paragraphs should include at least some of these ideas: **28.** At the peace conference, France wanted Germany to make reparations for the war. France wanted Germany to return land to France. Great Britain also wanted Germany to pay for the war, and the British wanted Germany's African colonies. Britain, however, did not want France to become too powerful. Italy wanted the Allies to honor a treaty from 1915, which said that if Italy entered the war on the Allied side, it would be rewarded with land. **29.** The social effects of World War I were widespread because it was a total war that affected cities, farms, factories, and civilians. A generation was lost in the war. France lost one out of every five men between the ages of 20 and 44. Many soldiers who had fought in the war came home wounded. Cities and farms lay in ruins, and many people were unemployed.

Chapter 26 Mastery Test A

Part A

1. B **2.** C **3.** C **4.** D **5.** C

Part B

6. B **7.** I **8.** E **9.** H **10.** G **11.** C **12.** F **13.** J **14.** A **15.** D

Part C

16. Sun Yat-sen **17.** Fuehrer **18.** Mussolini **19.** Lenin **20.** collective farm **21.** totalitarian **22.** industrialized **23.** Stalin **24.** Nazi **25.** Chiang Kai-shek

Part D

26. Mussolini **27.** Hideki Tojo **28.** Lenin **29.** Stalin **30.** Chiang Kai-shek

Part E

Answers will vary. Students should support their answers with at least some of the following facts: **31.** The Reds were the Bolsheviks, or Communists. The Whites were the non-Bolsheviks who opposed Lenin and the Communists. **32.** Sun Yat-sen's three principles were to have a strong national government free of foreign control, a democratic government controlled by the people, and better living conditions for all Chinese people.

Part F

Answers will vary. Students' paragraphs should include at least some of these ideas: **33.** Similarities between them include that both took away rights of the people, both used secret police, and both were Communists. The differences were thatStalin killed many more Russians, Lenin became a leader because of a political takeover, and Stalin became a leader because the Communist Party appointed him. **34.** The Weimar Republic was the government set up after Kaiser William II was forced to step down. The Nazi Party, led by Hitler, opposed the Weimar Republic. When Hitler tried to overthrow the Weimar Republic the first time, he was jailed. The Weimar Republic became less popular during the depression. The Nazi Party and Hitler gained support.

Chapter 26 Mastery Test B

Part A

1. C 2. D 3. A 4. B 5. A

Part B

6. censored 7. Reichstag 8. Great Depression 9. purged
10. militia 11. democratic 12. inflation 13. swastika
14. Bolsheviks 15. gestapo

Part C

16. I 17. B 18. F 19. D 20. A 21. J 22. C 23. H 24. G 25. E

Part D

26. Lenin 27. Nicholas II 28. Chiang Kai-shek 29. Stalin
30. Hideki Tojo

Part E

Answers will vary. Students should support their answers with at least some of the following facts: **31.** The Reds, the Bolsheviks, and the Whites, the non-Communists, fought in the Russian Civil War. The Whites defeated the Reds, but millions died, factories closed, and there was nothing to trade. **32.** Sun Yat-sen supported nationalism and democracy. He opposed imperialism.

Part F

Answers will vary. Students' paragraphs should include at least some of these ideas: **33.** Under Stalin's rule, Russian became a powerful industrialized nation, and health care and education improved. But Stalin had millions of people killed because they opposed what the government was doing. In Stalin's totalitarian state, conditions were poor and people lived in fear of Stalin's secret police. People had no rights. **34.** Adolf Hitler became the Nazi leader in the 1920s. Hitler and the Nazis tried to take over the German government in 1923 but failed. Hitler was arrested and jailed. While Hitler was in prison, he came up with a plan to make Germany a powerful nation. In the 1930s, many Germans supported Hitler, who was then out of prison, because he opposed Communism. The Nazis became the largest political party in Germany and Hitler grew more popular. In 1933, Hitler became head of the German government.

Chapter 27 Mastery Test A

Part A

1. B 2. C 3. A 4. B 5. D

Part B

6. Great Britain 7. Germany 8. Stalingrad 9. superpowers
10. Hiroshima 11. Austria 12. nationalism 13. dictatorships
14. Iron Curtain 15. United Nations

Part C

16. H 17. F 18. C 19. I 20. A 21. J 22. B 23. D 24. E 25. G

Part D

26. D-Day is the day the Allies invaded France in 1944. **27.** V-E Day is the name for the Allied victory in Europe. **28.** V-J Day is the name for the Allied victory in Japan. **29.** President Truman approved the use of the first atomic bomb. **30.** Possible Answers: El Alamein, Stalingrad, Midway were important battles of World War II.

Part E

Answers will vary. Students should support their answers with at least some of the following facts: **31.** The Axis Powers included Italy, Germany, and Japan. The Allied Powers included France and Britain. **32.** Germany, Italy, and Japan wanted to conquer and take over the land and resources of other countries. This imperialistic attitude led to WWII.

Part F

Answers will vary. Students' paragraphs should include at least some of these ideas: **33.** Jews were treated badly. All Jews working in the German government lost their jobs. All Jews had to wear a yellow star on their clothes. Jews were moved to ghettos to live while Jewish businesses and synagogues were destroyed. Jews were loaded into cattle cars and taken to concentration camps where many were put to death. **34.** Allied troops crossed into Germany's western border at the same time that Soviet forces marched toward Berlin from the East. The two groups met at the Elbe River and captured Berlin. This ended the war in Europe. The war in the Pacific ended after the United States dropped the atomic bomb on Nagasaki.

Chapter 27 Mastery Test B

Part A

1. D **2.** B **3.** A **4.** D **5.** A

Part B

6. Maginot Line **7.** blitzkrieg **8.** Munich Pact **9.** satellite
10. arsenal **11.** genocide **12.** concentration camps **13.** guerilla
14. Allied Powers **15.** kamikaze

Part C

16. Japan bombed Pearl Harbor, Hawaii to hurt the U.S. Navy.
17. President Roosevelt of the United States developed the Lend-Lease program. **18.** A refugee is a person who is forced to flee from his or her country. **19.** The economy of the United States was not destroyed after World War II. **20.** A front is the place where armies meet and fight.

Part D

21. D **22.** C **23.** H **24.** I **25.** E **26.** A **27.** G **28.** B **29.** F **30.** J

Part E

Answers will vary. Students should support their answers with at least some of the following facts: **31.** Great Britain and France wanted to avoid war. These countries followed a policy of appeasement when the Axis countries began invading other countries. **32.** Germany invaded and conquered France. German troops conquered Denmark, Norway, the Netherlands, Luxembourg, and Belgium.

Part F: Answers will vary. Students' paragraphs should include at least some of these ideas: **33.** Hitler believed that the German people were the "master race" and that all other people were inferior. Hitler believed that the Jews were to blame for Germany's problems. Hitler had a plan to murder all the Jews of Europe. This plan was called the "Final Solution." The Holocaust was Hitler's plan for achieving the Final Solution. During the Holocaust, Jews were taken to concentration camps where many were killed. **34.** Italians voted to set up a republic in their country. Germany was divided into four zones. Each zone was controlled by Britain, France, the Soviet Union, or the United States. Eventually the western zones became the Federal Republic of Germany, or West Germany. The eastern zones became the German Democratic Republic, or East Germany.

Chapter 28 Mastery Test A

Part A

1. D **2.** C **3.** B **4.** D **5.** A

Part B

6. H **7.** G **8.** D **9.** A **10.** I **11.** E **12.** F **13.** B **14.** C **15.** J

Part C

16. Economic and social problems helped cause the collapse of the Soviet Union. The Soviet Union was made of people who spoke many different languages. The Soviet republics wanted independence, and this led to the end of the Soviet Union.
17. President Truman wanted to stop the spread of Communism. The effort that the United States put into the Berlin Airlift showed that the United States did not want the Communists to control any more European land. The United States had a strong interest in preventing the Soviet Union from taking over all of Berlin. **18.** The Hungarian government allowed its citizens to have some freedom of speech and freedom to assemble. In 1989, Hungarian soldiers cut down the fence between Austria and Hungary. (Austria was a democratic nation.) This created a "hole" in the Iron Curtain. As the first country in Eastern Europe to allow people to freely travel to a Western nation, Hungary provided a gateway for those who wanted to escape Communism. Thousands of people from East Germany, Poland, and Czechoslovakia moved through Hungary to freedom in the West. **19.** Workers in a shipyard in Gdansk, Poland, went on strike because they wanted better working conditions. They formed a union called Solidarity, and they wanted the government to recognize their union as legal. The union's members worked for years to bring about reform. Poland held free elections in 1989, and Solidarity won a huge victory. **20.** The euro is the form of currency used in the countries of the European Union.

Part D

21. latitude **22.** Chechnya **23.** NATO **24.** Yugoslavia **25.** KGB

Part E

Answers will vary. Students should support their answer with at least some of these facts: **26.** The cold war was caused by a rivalry between the two superpowers. The cold war was the result of a conflict of ideas between the United States and the Soviet Union. The cold war used words, ideas, and propaganda as weapons. The United States wanted democracies to be strong and not be taken over by the Communists. The United States did not want the Communists to control any more land in Europe. **27.** The Soviet Union, which had suffered from economic and social problems, no longer existed after 1991. The policy of glasnost encouraged some people to want an independent country of their own. Between 1988 and 1990, people in Soviet Georgia, Latvia, Estonia, Moldavia, Uzbekistan, Azerbaijan, and Lithuania demanded independence. Other people wanted to escape Communism. Thousands of people from East Germany, Poland, and Czechoslovakia moved through Hungary to freedom in the West. The Ukraine voted for independence on December 1, 1991, and other Soviet republics followed. Mikhail Gorbachev tried to stop the breakup of the Soviet Union, but he could not. The Soviet flag was lowered from the Kremlin on December 25, 1991.

Part F

Answers will vary. Students' paragraphs should include at least some of these ideas: **28.** In 1990, the republics of Croatia, Bosnia-Herzegovina, Slovenia, and Macedonia began to push for independence. Slobodan Milosevic, who became the leader of the Serbian republic, opposed this idea. Milosevic made war against other republics. Milosevic used a policy of "ethnic cleansing" to force Bosnian Muslims out of their homes. Nearly 250,000 Bosnians were killed. Milosevic began a war in Kosovo, where he tried to force non-Serbs out. In 1999, NATO began air strikes against Yugoslavia, hoping to get Milosevic to stop his attacks in Kosovo. Eventually, Yugoslav leaders took their forces out of Kosovo. Milosevic was put on trial for war crimes, but he died during the trial. Yugoslavia no longer exists because all of its former parts are now independent countries. **29.** The Korean War was a result of the cold war. After World War II, Soviet forces took over the northern part of Korea, and American forces took over the southern part. On June 25, 1950, Communist troops crossed the 38th parallel of latitude and moved into South Korea. The UN Security Council voted to send aid to South Korea to stop the troops. The Korean War put China and the Soviet Union on one side, and the United Nations forces (supported largely by the United States) on the other side. The opposing sides signed an armistice in 1953. The border between the Koreas did not change much as a result of the war. The Korean War was important because it showed that the UN could stop an attack on a member nation; that China could hold its own in a war that did not involve atomic weapons; and that the cold war between the two superpowers would continue. Today, the United States continues to support South Korea. North Korea remains Communist.

Chapter 28 Mastery Test B

Part A

1. A **2.** B **3.** B **4.** D **5.** C

Part B

6. I **7.** A **8.** G **9.** H **10.** D **11.** F **12.** B **13.** E **14.** C **15.** J

Part C

16. Propaganda is one-sided information meant to change people's thinking. **17.** Mikhail Gorbachev wanted to rebuild the Soviet economy by introducing perestroika, a policy that encouraged factories to produce the goods people wanted. **18.** The Marshall Plan, or European Recovery Program, was the American plan to rebuild Europe after World War II. **19.** After the Korean War ended, South Korea eventually became an industrial powerhouse in Asia. The United States has supported South Korea since 1953.
20. Slobodan Milosevic began a war in Kosovo, a small province of Serbia. Milosevic wanted to force non-Serbs out of the area. NATO began air strikes on Yugoslavia in 1999 in an effort to make Milosevic stop his attacks in Kosovo.

Part D

21. coup **22.** independence **23.** glasnost **24.** cold war **25.** Warsaw Pact

Part E

Answers will vary. Students should support their answer with at least some of these facts: **26.** The Truman Doctrine was a plan to give economic and military help to nations threatened by an outside power. The United States used the Truman Doctrine to try to stop the spread of Communism. The Truman Doctrine helped Greece and Turkey defeat the Communists. The Truman Doctrine was part of the cold war, which was the war of ideas between the United States and the Soviet Union after World War II. The United States did not want the Communists to gain any more land in Europe. This is why the United States participated in the Berlin Airlift, which prevented the Soviet Union from taking control of all of Berlin.
27. Economic and social problems contributed to the rejection of Communism in Eastern Europe. Another factor was the desire of various groups to have their own independent countries. The Soviet Union once contained more than 100 different ethnic groups, and the people spoke 112 different languages. The spirit of glasnost encouraged some groups to demand independence. Between 1988 and 1990, people in Soviet Georgia, Latvia, Estonia, Moldavia, Uzbekistan, Azerbaijan, and Lithuania demanded independence. Other people wanted to escape Communism, too. Thousands of people from East Germany, Poland, and Czechoslovakia moved through Hungary to freedom in the West. The Ukraine voted for independence on December 1, 1991, and other Soviet republics followed. Many people who fled from Communism wanted to live in a democracy.

Part F

Answers will vary. Students' paragraphs should include at least some of these ideas: **28.** After World War II, Britain, France, the United States, and the Soviet Union agreed that each would control a part of Berlin. In June 1948, the Soviets tried to take over all of Berlin by starving the people there. The Soviets set up a blockade. American and British planes carried food and fuel to the people of Berlin. The planes delivered more than two million tons of supplies. The Berlin Airlift was a success, and the Soviets stopped the blockade in May 1949. The Berlin Airlift showed that the Western powers would not let the Communists control any more European land. The West was determined to stop the spread of Communism. **29.** This statement means that people could escape from Communism by passing through Hungary. The Hungarian government allowed its citizens to have some freedom of speech and freedom to assemble. In 1989, Hungarian soldiers cut down the fence between Austria and Hungary. (Austria was a democratic nation.) This created a "hole" in the Iron Curtain. As the first country in Eastern Europe to allow people to freely travel to a Western nation, Hungary provided a gateway for those who wanted to escape Communism. Thousands of people from East Germany, Poland, and Czechoslovakia moved through Hungary to freedom in the West.

Chapter 29 Mastery Test A

Part A

1. A **2.** C **3.** D **4.** B **5.** A

Part B

6. African National Congress **7.** legalize **8.** terrorist **9.** passive resistance **10.** election **11.** apartheid **12.** Vietnamization **13.** demonstrate **14.** persecute **15.** African Nationalism

Part C

16. F **17.** I **18.** D **19.** C **20.** H **21.** G **22.** E **23.** A **24.** B **25.** J

Part D

26. Palestine **27.** India **28.** China **29.** Vietnam **30.** South Africa

Part E

Answers will vary. Students should support their answers with at least some of the following facts: **31.** Apartheid is a policy that sets blacks and other nonwhite people apart from white people. Apartheid was the official policy of South Africa from 1948 until F. W. de Klerk became president. **32.** The two groups that fought in China's civil war were the Communists and the Nationalists. The Communist group was led by Mao Zedong. The Nationalist group was led by Chiang Kai-shek.

Part F

Answers will vary. Students' paragraphs should include at least some of these ideas: **33.** Ho Chi Minh and his followers wanted the French to leave Vietnam. They agreed to divide Vietnam into two areas, a Communist area and a non-Communist area. The two areas were supposed to have an election to choose how to unite their country. The election never happened. North Vietnam tried to take over South Vietnam. The United States began sending military advisers to South Vietnam in the early 1960s to help battle the Communists. **34.** Palestine was the home of the Jewish people more than 2,000 years ago, but war and other troubles forced many Jews to move to other countries. Many Jews had trouble in these countries, too. The Jewish people wanted to return to their homeland in Palestine, but Palestine had been the home of Palestinian Arabs for many generations. In 1947, the UN divided Palestine into a Jewish state and an Arab state. The Arab nations surrounding Palestine protested the division. They attacked Israel in 1948. Israel defeated the Arabs but since then Israelis and Palestinians continue to battle against each other.

Chapter 29 Mastery Test B

Part A

1. B 2. C 3. D 4. A 5. B

Part B

6. Kwame Nkrumah 7. Nelson Mandela 8. F.W. de Klerk 9. David Ben-Gurion 10. Mohandas Gandhi 11. Mao Zedong 12. Ho Chi Minh 13. Bishop Desmond Tutu 14. Chiang Kai-shek 15. Yitzhak Rabin

Part C

16. A 17. F 18. I 19. G 20. E 21. C 22. J 23. D 24. H 25. B

Part D

26. Gandhi faced the problem of religious differences in trying to unite India. 27. In 1948, David Ben-Gurion announced the new nation of Israel. 28. Guerilla warfare uses surprise attacks. 29. The PLO wanted to regain their homeland from Israel. 30. France ruled Vietnam until 1954.

Part E

Answers will vary. Students should support their answers with at least some of the following facts: 31. African Nationalism is the struggle of native Africans to be economically and politically independent. African Nationalism allowed African nations to break free from European rulers and rule themselves. 32. At the end of the Chinese civil war, Mao Zedong and the Communists took control of China. Chiang Kai-shek and his followers fled to the island of Taiwan.

Part F

Answers will vary. Students' paragraphs should include at least some of these ideas: 33. Japan had conquered Indochina during World War II. Ho Chi Mind fought against the Japanese. After the war, the French controlled many lands in Indochina and Ho Chi Minh did not want Vietnam to be a French colony. Ho Chi Minh and his Communist followers fought against the French between 1946 and 1954. In 1954, Ho Chi Minh and the French agreed to divide Vietnam into two areas—North and South Vietnam. An election was supposed to be held so that the people could eventually choose how to unite North and South Vietnam. The election never took place, and North Vietnam started a guerilla war to make all of Vietnam a Communist nation. 34. The caste system prevented India from being a true democracy. The caste system did not give equal rights to all people. In the caste system, some people had more rights than others. Gandhi did away with the caste system. The other difficulty was the religious differences in India. Most Indians were Hindus, but a minority were Muslims. The Muslims wanted their own nation. The differences between the Hindus and the Muslims led to violence and, eventually, the assassination of Gandhi.

Chapter 30 Mastery Test A

Part A

1. C 2. A 3. D 4. C 5. B

Part B

6. C 7. A 8. F 9. D 10. H 11. G 12. I 13. J 14. B 15. E

Part C

16. Some of the causes of famine in Africa are droughts, rapid population growth, a lack of fertilizer and pesticides, an emphasis on industry over agriculture, and armed conflicts. 17. In November 1979, some Iranians took over the U.S. embassy in Iran. They made 52 Americans hostages and held them for almost 15 months. Eventually, the hostages were released. 18. The United States suspected that Iraq was behind the attack on the World Trade Center on September 11, 2001. The United States decided to attack Iraq because government leaders believed that Iraq supported terrorism. They believed that Saddam Hussein had weapons of mass destruction. They also believed Hussein had taken away the basic rights of the Iraqi people, and they believed that Iraq was a threat to the world. 19. Japan's government works with large companies to promote industrial growth. The Japanese government owns the Bank of Japan, which loans a lot of money to companies.
20. Poverty is widespread in Latin America. A few landowners often control a large percentage of the land that can be farmed. Campesinos are demanding land reform because they want large farms to be broken up and divided among the poor.

Part D

21. fertilizer 22. urbanization 23. migrant 24. canal 25. trade

Part E

Answers will vary. Students should support their answer with at least some of these facts: 26. The AIDS epidemic has affected Africa's economy in many ways. The death of farmers has reduced the food production. Also, a great deal of human resources must be devoted to caring for orphans and elderly people. Some children cannot attend school because they must care for sick relatives, and many of the countries are poor, so the cost of caring for AIDS patients puts a strain on an already weak economy. Some countries are so poor that they cannot provide much medical care for AIDS patients. 27. There is no trade between the United States and Cuba because the United States set up an embargo. Fidel Castro took over Cuba in 1959. The United States has been at odds with Cuba over the years because Castro became a dictator who would not allow free elections or a free press. Another reason is that Castro took over U.S.-owned businesses. He has been an anti-American leader. Also, the Soviet Union began building missile sites in Cuba in 1962.

Part F

Answers will vary. Students' paragraphs should include at least some of these ideas: **28.** In 1989, Chinese students went on a hunger strike in Tiananmen Square, which is located in China's capital city, Beijing. The protestors wanted a democratic government. More than a million people went out on the streets to call for change. The protests were televised around the world. On June 4, 1989, soldiers marched into the square and killed hundreds of protestors. Other protestors were put in jail, tortured, or killed. The Tiananmen Square massacre has put a strain on relations between China and the West. The United States and other countries have called for more human rights in China. **29.** Terrorist groups have made it hard for there to be lasting peace in parts of the Middle East. Terrorist groups like Hamas have used suicide bombings to try to stop the peace process. There has been tension between Israel and Syria because Israel believes that Syria should control Hezbollah, an organization that Israel believes sponsors terrorism. The peace process between Israelis and Palestinians has been disrupted by terrorism. In 2006, an Israeli soldier was kidnapped by Hezbollah, and Israel invaded Lebanon to try to rescue the soldier. The Iranians who took 52 Americans hostage in 1979 did a terrorist act that has caused a great strain on relations between Iran and the United States. Iran has been accused of supporting terrorist groups like Hezbollah in Lebanon. Prior to the U.S. attack on Iraq, President George W. Bush said that Iraq supported terrorism and that Iraq's leader, Saddam Hussein, cooperated with al Qaeda, a terrorist group led by Osama bin Laden. Acts of terrorism happened in Iraq after U.S. troops arrived there.

Chapter 30 Mastery Test B

Part A

1. B **2.** C **3.** A **4.** C **5.** D

Part B

6. D **7.** J **8.** B **9.** A **10.** G **11.** E **12.** F **13.** I **14.** H **15.** C

Part C

16. An embargo is an act that stops all trade. **17.** In 1989, the Chinese students who protested in Tiananmen Square wanted a democratic government. More than a million people went out on the streets to call for change. **18.** A war with Iran had left Iraq with a weakened economy and huge debts. Iraq owed money to Kuwait. Iraq invaded Kuwait in an effort to take over its rich oil fields. This led to the Persian Gulf War. **19.** A terrorist act is an act of violence, such as a kidnapping, a suicide bombing, or the taking of hostages. Organizations that have been accused of doing terrorist acts include Hamas, Hezbollah, and al Qaeda. **20.** Rapid urbanization in Africa has led to large numbers of migrants moving to cities, and this has put a strain on city services. Urbanization has led to the development of slums. People live in crowded areas with no electricity, running water, or sewers.

Part D

21. Shah **22.** economy **23.** attack **24.** embassy **25.** hostage

Part E

Answers will vary. Students should support their answer with at least some of these facts: **26.** Japan has the second largest economy in the world. Japan's government works with large companies to plan and promote industrial growth. The Japanese government owns the Bank of Japan, which loans a lot of money to companies. Many Japanese workers are well-educated, highly skilled employees who can work together easily to make products quickly and at a low cost. **27.** The problem of poverty in Latin America could be solved by reducing the gap between the extremely poor and the extremely wealthy. A few landowners often control a large percentage of the land that can be farmed. For example, in Paraguay, a few big landowners control 80 percent of the land that can be farmed. Campesinos are demanding land reform because they want large farms to be broken up and divided among the poor. The governments in Latin American countries could develop a plan that would pay landowners a fair price for farmland, which would then be distributed among poor workers. Another solution for poverty would be to develop a profitable mixture of agriculture and industry so that countries would not be as dependent upon the export of natural resources (such as oil, tin, copper, iron ore, and bauxite) for a large percentage of a nation's income.

Part F

Answers will vary. Students' paragraphs should include at least some of these ideas: **28.** Part of the reason for the history of conflict between Iran and Iraq has to do with the differences in language, culture, and religion between these two neighboring countries. The Iranian people are mainly Shiite Muslims. The Iraqi people are mainly Sunni Muslims. Iranians are Persians. Most Iraqis are Arabs. In 1980, Iraq invaded Iran, which led to a war that lasted eight years. A war with a neighboring country leaves bitter feelings on both sides. **29.** Some of the causes of famine in Africa are droughts, rapid population growth, a lack of fertilizer and pesticides, an emphasis on industry over agriculture, and armed conflicts. Civil wars have also damaged agriculture in many parts of Africa. The AIDS epidemic has resulted in the death of many farmers, which has reduced food production. Widespread poverty makes it difficult for farmers to find or purchase good farming equipment. Some farmers lack the fuel that is necessary for agriculture. Poverty can make it difficult to transport food to the people who need it.

Chapter 31 Mastery Test A

Part A

1. C **2.** A **3.** D **4.** A **5.** B

Part B

6. temperature **7.** pollutes **8.** village **9.** crops **10.** industries **11.** Thailand **12.** Japan **13.** renewable **14.** photoelectric **15.** fertilizers

Part C

16. H **17.** A **18.** C **19.** J **20.** D **21.** E **22.** B **23.** F **24.** I **25.** G

Part D

26. The World Wide Web is the network of information on the Internet. **27.** Nuclear energy provides most of the electricity in France. **28.** The word *international* describes things from around the world. **29.** Technology uses science to do practical things. **30.** The network that sends data is the electronic superhighway.

Part E

Answers will vary. Students should support their answers with at least some of the following facts: **31.** "Global village" is used to describe the change in the way that people view the world. Because of changes in technology, our Earth has become a place where all ideas, cultures, and traditions are shared around the world. The word "global" is used to describe the earth. The term "village" is used to describe a place where people share ideas and traditions, work and live together. People in a village know all other people in the village. **32.** The future will bring promises and problems. Problems include things such as disease, natural disasters, terrorism, wars, more pollution, and global warming. Promises include things such as new treatments for diseases, new technologies, human rights for all, and an improved standard of living for all people.

Part F

Answers will vary. Students' paragraphs should include at least some of these ideas: **33.** After the attacks of September 11, security increased near public places where large groups of people gather. The Department of Homeland Security was set up to help prevent future terrorist attacks. People around the world have become more aware of each other and of any suspicious behavior. The Patriot Act is a law passed in the United States that allows the government to check the background of people in the country. **34.** In free-market economies, manufacturers satisfy the wants and needs of consumers, and the government lets factories produce what they like. Most of the successful free-market countries are in the Northern Hemisphere. In developing countries, the economy is still developing, and most people do subsistence farming. That is, they grow crops mostly for their own use and do not sell what they grow. More than half of the people in the world live in developing countries.

Chapter 31 Mastery Test B

Part A

1. C **2.** A **3.** C **4.** B **5.** D

Part B

6. recession **7.** nuclear energy **8.** fossil fuels **9.** World Bank **10.** global **11.** Internet **12.** environment **13.** mass communication **14.** subsistence **15.** Pollution

Part C

16. I **17.** G **18.** C **19.** A **20.** D **21.** J **22.** E **23.** H **24.** F **25.** B

Part D

26. The World Wide Web is the network of information on the Internet. **27.** The Internet is the term used to describe the international computer network. **28.** The word "international" describes something that happens around the world **29.** Lasers, computers, and the space shuttle are examples of technology. **30.** The electronic superhighway sends data from phones, TVs, and computers.

Part E

31. Answers will vary. Students should support their answers with at least some of the following facts: The Internet and the World Wide Web have made it possible for businesses and individuals from anywhere in the world to communicate with each other. The Internet links the whole world electronically. **32.** Answers will vary. Students should support their answers with at least some of the following facts: Ideally, the world food supply grows at least at the same rate as the world population. Today, however, the world food supply is growing at about 1 percent a year. The world population is growing at about 1.5 percent per year. This means that there is not enough food to feed all the people in our world.

Part F

Answers will vary. Students' paragraphs should include at least some of these ideas: **33.** Operation Iraqi Freedom was the name given to the invasion of Baghdad, the capital of Iraq. Operation Iraqi Freedom involved troops from the United States, Great Britain, and some smaller nations. President George Bush thought that Iraq was hiding weapons of mass destruction. He also wanted to stop Saddam Hussein's tyranny in Iraq. Saddam Hussein was captured and executed. No weapons of mass destruction were ever found. Troops in Iraq are still trying to help Iraqis establish a democratic government in Iraq. **34.** The recession was the economic slowdown caused by the collapse of the money supply of Thailand in 1997. As a result, banks and businesses went bankrupt throughout Southeast Asia. People in Japan lost their jobs. U.S. companies lost money because people in other nations had no money to buy goods. Some blame multinational corporations for the recession.

Unit Mastery Tests

Unit 1 Mastery Test Answers

Part A

1. C 2. D 3. B 4. C 5. D

Part B

6. A 7. C 8. E 9. G 10. B 11. F 12. D

Part C

13. strong walls 14. geography 15. warlike 16. Toltec 17. Old

Part D

18. tribunes 19. emperors 20. decline

Part E

21. Answers will vary. Students should support their answers with at least some of the following facts: The pyramids were built as tombs for Egypt's dead rulers; Egyptians believed that their rulers continued to rule after death, so they wanted to provide a place for their bodies. 22. Answers will vary. Students should support their answers with at least some of the following facts: Hohokam, Mogollon, and Anasazi are the early southwestern cultures; Hohokam contributions—canals, Snaketown; Mogollon contributions—Rock Art, kivas; Anasazi contributions—master builders, cliff dwellings, pueblos, obsidian mirrors, Chaco Canyon. 23. Answers will vary. We use geometry and pulleys and levers. We base our science on the physics, biology, astronomy, and medicine that started during the Hellenistic Age. 24. Answers will vary. Students' paragraphs should include at least some of these ideas: Julius Caesar was part of the First Triumvirate; Caesar challenged the power of the Roman senate; eventually Caesar had more power than the Roman senate; Caesar passed laws against crime; Caesar forgave old enemies and made them government officials; Caesar made the Roman calendar more accurate; the senate made Caesar dictator for life; some senators were afraid that Caesar wanted to be king, which would end the republic; the fearful senators assassinated Caesar to "save the republic."

Unit 2 Mastery Test Answers

Part A

1. C 2. C 3. D 4. A 5. A

Part B

6. B 7. E 8. C 9. G 10. A 11. D 12. F

Part C

13. Answers will vary. Students should support their answer with at least some of these facts: The Crusades were fought over control of Palestine, or the Holy Land. For 400 years, Muslims had allowed Christian pilgrims to visit the Holy Land, but then another group of Muslims took control of Palestine. Pope Urban II called for a crusade against the Muslims. Crusaders believed that they were following God's orders in these battles. 14. The Mongols were responsible for the destruction of Kiev. 15. Mali took control of important trade routes. 16. Answers will vary. Students should support their answer with at least some of these facts: The emperors thought that the people who lived in other countries were barbarians. They wanted to keep China free from the influences of uncivilized people.

Part D

17. Acre 18. Islamic 19. Songhai 20. gunpowder

Part E

21. Answers will vary: I wouldn't go to school or know anything about history or art or where buildings came from. I wouldn't be able to read or write. It would be dangerous to travel. 22. Answers will vary. Students should support their answers with at least some of the following facts: Muslim doctors studied medicine carefully; Arab astronomers figured out that the earth is round and that it is about 25,000 miles around.

Part F

23. Answers will vary. Students' paragraphs should include at least some of these ideas: Like Christianity, Judaism, and Islam, Shinto is a religion based on a set of beliefs. Unlike those religions, however, Shinto has no holy books. In Christianity, Judaism, and Islam, followers worship one all-powerful God. Shinto followers, however, worship thousands of gods and spirits. The goddess of the sun is the most important Shinto entity. Shinto followers believe that kami, or spirits, control the forces of nature. 24. Answers will vary. Students should support their answer with at least some of these facts: Until about 1100, most churches looked like Roman buildings. These Romanesque churches had rounded arches, think walls, and narrow openings for windows, so they were dark and gloomy. Around 1200, the Gothic style started, with its narrow ribs of stone to support the roof, flying buttresses to hold up the walls, and pointed arches, which drew the eyes upward. Two examples of Gothic architecture in France are the cathedral of Notre Dame and the Rheims Cathedral.

Unit 3 Mastery Test Answers

Part A

1. A 2. C 3. A 4. D 5. D

Part B

6. A 7. B 8. A 9. F 10. D 11. C 12. E

Part C

13. Florence became wealthy by producing wool. 14. Answers will vary. Students should support their answer with at least some of these facts: Catholic priests were not allowed to marry, but Lutheran ministers could. Also, Lutheran ministers did not perform the same rituals as priests because the Lutheran Church got rid of most of the ceremonies of the Catholic Church. 15. The Habeas Corpus Act said that the government has to charge someone with a crime before putting the person in prison. 16. The Tories were people who supported a strong monarchy in England.

Part D

17. peasants 18. beliefs 19. East Indies 20. Dias

Part E

21. Answers will vary. Students should support their answers with at least some of the following facts: As a result of the Black Death, the population decreased; with fewer people, fewer taxes could be paid; less food was needed so the price of food dropped; farmers made less money; many people left the cities and fled to the country.
22. Answers will vary: The Bible had been the source of truth for scholars before the Middle Ages. The new ideas based on personal observation or experiments threatened the authority of the church.

Part F

23. Answers will vary. Students' paragraphs should include at least some of these ideas: After the Spanish conquered the Aztec and Inca Empires, Spanish conquistadores controlled large areas of land. To make money off the land, the landowners needed farmworkers and miners to work on their land. The Spanish forced American Indians to do the work for them. Within 100 years, the Indian population went from 20 million to 4 million. After the efforts of Bartolomé de las Casas, Spain started to import Africans to the Americas. This was the beginning of African slavery in the Americas. **24.** Answers will vary. Students' paragraphs should include at least some of these ideas: The reign of Louis XIV was good for France because he reorganized and expanded the army; the nobility was weakened; beautiful churches and palaces were built; and art and music spread. Louis XIV's reign was bad for France because the taxpayers had to pay for his love of beautiful things, such as the grand palace at Versailles; and because he fought too many wars, which were paid for by taxpayers, and which drained the French treasury. At the end of his life, Louis XIV urged his grandson to keep peace, saying, "I have been too fond of war."

Unit 4 Mastery Test Answers
Part A
1. D 2. C 3. C 4. B 5. D
Part B
6. B 7. D 8. A 9. C 10. B 11. F 12. E
Part C
13. Haydn is known as the "father of the symphony." **14.** In April 1775, the first shots of the American Revolutionary War were fired at Lexington after British troops had marched to Concord to seize colonial weapons. The minutemen killed one third of the "redcoats" as they marched back to Boston. **15.** To exile means to send someone away from his or her home country and to order this person not to come back.
Part D
16. Jacobins **17.** industrialized **18.** Simón Bolívar **19.** steel **20.** legislature
Part E
21. Answers will vary: In the past, people had learned about nature from the Bible or Aristotle. Galileo had done experiments. Newton used mathematics and reason to figure out how nature works.
22. Answers will vary. Students should support their answers with at least some of the following facts: Benefits—produced many goods for many people, city populations grew; Problems—conditions for workers were bad at first, bigger cities had more garbage, bad water, and bad sanitation.

Part F

23. Answers will vary. Students' paragraphs should include at least some of these ideas: It took 11 years form Mexico to become independent; Father Hidalgo organized the Indians to form an army; the army rebelled against the Spanish landowners; in 1811, Hidalgo and his army marched to Mexico City; Hidalgo was executed by the Spanish in Mexico City; Father Morelos continued Father Hidalgo's fight; by 1813, native Indians controlled most of the land outside the major cities of Mexico; in 1815, Creole soldiers captured and executed Morelos because they didn't want Mexico to be ruled by peasants; in 1821, Creole leaders revolted against Spain and made Mexico independent. **24.** Answers will vary. Students' paragraphs should include at least some of these ideas: Napoleon's failures were the invasion and retreat from Russia, his defeat in 1814, and his defeat at Waterloo. These were important events, but they were not as great as Napoleon's accomplishments. Napoleon was a natural leader; he was a smart military leader whose soldiers liked fighting for him; he conquered most of Europe; he had tremendous confidence and ambition; he ended the Holy Roman Empire; after his defeat in March 1814, he escaped from exile on Elba and returned to France to become a hero again; his Code of Napoleon made every man in France equal before the law; and he helped spread the ideas of liberty and equality throughout Europe.

Unit 5 Mastery Test Answers
Part A
1. D 2. A 3. B 4. D 5. B
Part B
6. B 7. E 8. C 9. F 10. D 11. A
Part C
12. Heritage is made up of the traditions that are passed down from ancestors to their descendents. **13.** Prussia's military victories over Denmark in 1864, Austria in 1866, and France in 1871 contributed to the movement for a unified Germany. **14.** Europeans did not respect the culture, religion, language, and customs of native people in Africa and Asia. Europeans tried to force them to change their way of life. Europeans viewed them as uncivilized, ignorant, and in need of help. **15.** European nations forced China to give them special trade rights. China was divided into spheres of influence so that a nation like Great Britain could benefit without competing with a nation like France, which had its own sphere of influence. Chinese rulers had no say in this European-controlled trade. **16.** In 1848, Sardinia declared war on Austria.
Part D
17. France **18.** country **19.** Africa **20.** Europe

21. Answers will vary. Students should support their answer with at least some of these facts: Otto von Bismarck lied to the newspapers about a meeting he had with a French ambassador. His comment caused such a strong reaction that it helped start the Franco-Prussian War. Prussia won this war in 1871, and France had to give up Alsace and Lorraine. These territories contained France's richest coal and iron fields. **22.** Answers will vary. Students should support their answer with at least some of these facts: Historians call Giuseppe Garibaldi the "sword" because of his great military feats. He led an army of Italian nationalists on an invasion of Sicily in May 1860. Garibaldi and his "Red Shirts" swept through Sicily and marched northward toward Rome. His troops and Sardinian troops teamed up to unite almost all of Italy. **23.** Answers will vary. Students should support their answer with at least some of these facts: Imperialism occurs when a powerful nation controls a weaker colony. Industrialization helped spread imperialism. Factory owners wanted natural resources and raw materials from colonies. Manufacturers also wanted markets for their goods. Each major nation let its colonies buy only those goods manufactured in the mother country. **24.** Answers will vary. Students' paragraphs should include at least some of these ideas: This expression means that British colonies were so spread out around the world that it was always daylight somewhere in Britain's empire. Britain took control of India, Afghanistan, South Africa, Burma (now Myanmar), Ceylon, Malaya, and Singapore, as well as areas that are now Sudan, Nigeria, Ghana, Kenya, and Uganda. Britain took control of the Suez Canal, and Egypt became a protectorate.

Unit 6 Mastery Test Answers

Part A

1. D **2.** D **3.** B **4.** C **5.** B

Part B

6. A **7.** E **8.** C **9.** F **10.** B **11.** D

Part C

12. Under socialism, the government owns all the land, industries, and transportation. Under this political and economic theory, the government controls the economy of a nation. **13.** Poison gas was dangerous because the wind could shift and blow the deadly gas back to the troops who were using it. **14.** A minority is a small group of like people within a larger group. **15.** The United States' economy was not destroyed as a result of World War II.

Part D

16. Russians **17.** Sun Yat-sen **18.** collective farm **19.** nationalism **20.** Iron Curtain

Part E

Answers will vary. Students should support their answer with at least some of these facts: **21.** World War I was the most important cause of the Russian Revolution of 1917. Millions of Russians were killed, wounded, or taken prisoner. Russians had to live with very little food, fuel, and other necessary supplies. Russians became very angry with Czar Nicholas II, and they wanted a more democratic form of government. Things were going very poorly for the people of Russia, and many people thought that socialism would solve the country's problems. **22.** The social effects of World War I were widespread because it was a total war that affected cities, farms, factories, and civilians. A generation was lost in the war. France lost one out of every five men between the ages of 20 and 44. Many soldiers who had fought in the war came home wounded. Cities and farms lay in ruins, and many people were unemployed.

Part F

Answers will vary. Students' paragraphs should include at least some of these ideas: **23.** Lenin—started the Communist Party, the class system was removed, people had to give up religion, formed a powerful dictatorship that controlled the government and the economy, used a secret police to control the people. Stalin—set up Five-Year Plan, set up collective farms, killed millions of farmers and their families, set up a totalitarian state, used secret police, industrialized the Soviet Union, improved health care and education. **24.** Hitler believed that the German people were the "master race" and that all other people were inferior. Hitler believed that the Jews were to blame for Germany's problems. Hitler had a plan to murder all the Jews of Europe, which was called the "Final Solution." The Holocaust was Hitler's plan for achieving the Final Solution. During the Holocaust, Jews were taken to concentration camps where many were killed.

Part A

1. B **2.** A **3.** D **4.** B **5.** B

Part B

6. D **7.** E **8.** A **9.** C **10.** B **11.** D

Part C

12. Economic and social problems helped cause the collapse of the Soviet Union. The Soviet Union was made of people who spoke many different languages. The Soviet republics wanted independence, and this led to the end of the Soviet Union.

13. The PLO wanted to regain their homeland from Israel.

14. Japan's government works with large companies to promote industrial growth. The Japanese government owns the Bank of Japan, which loans a lot of money to companies. **15.** Some of the causes of famine in Africa are droughts, rapid population growth, a lack of fertilizer and pesticides, an emphasis on industry over agriculture, and armed conflicts.

Part D

16. Chechnya **17.** Vietnam **18.** urbanization **19.** temperature **20.** crops

Part E

21. Answers will vary. Students should support their answers with at least some of the following facts: At the end of the Chinese civil war, Mao Zedong and the Communists took control of China. Chiang Kai-shek and his followers fled to the island of Taiwan.

22. Answers will vary. Students should support their answer with at least some of these facts: There is no trade between the United States and Cuba because the United States set up an embargo. Fidel Castro took over Cuba in 1959. The United States has been at odds with Cuba over the years because Castro became a dictator who would not allow free elections or a free press; because Castro took over U.S.-owned businesses; because Castro has been an anti-American leader; and because the Soviet Union began building missile sites in Cuba in 1962.

Part F

23. Answers will vary. Students' paragraphs should include at least some of these ideas: After the attacks of September 11, security increased near public places where large groups of people gather. The Department of Homeland Security was set up to help prevent future terrorist attacks. People around the world have become more aware of each other and of any suspicious behavior. The Patriot Act is a law passed in the United States that allows the government to check the background of people in the country.

24. Answers will vary. Students' paragraphs should include at least some of these ideas: This statement means that people could escape from Communism by passing through Hungary. The Hungarian government allowed its citizens to have some freedom of speech and freedom to assemble. In 1989, Hungarian soldiers cut down the fence between Austria and Hungary. (Austria was a democratic nation.) This created a "hole" in the Iron Curtain. As the first country in Eastern Europe to allow people to freely travel to a Western nation, Hungary provided a gateway for those who wanted to escape Communism. Thousands of people from East Germany, Poland, and Czechoslovakia moved through Hungary to freedom in the West.

Midterm Mastery Test

Part A

1. B **2.** D **3.** C **4.** A **5.** D **6.** A **7.** C **8.** D **9.** B **10.** A

Part B

11. artifacts **12.** Mesopotamia **13.** Athens **14.** Augustus Caesar **15.** Muslims **16.** Battle of Hastings **17.** gold **18.** Michelangelo **19.** Huguenots **20.** Whig

Part C

21. People in Sumer lived better than prehistoric humans. All citizens owned their own farm or house. Women had legal rights, and slaves could set up a business, borrow money, and buy their freedom. Children had to obey and could be sold into slavery.

22. The Shang Dynasty developed Chinese writing and put all of China under a single ruler. That made it easier for later dynasties to rule and gave them time to do and invent other things.

23. Romans built sewers, which are underground pipes used to carry away dirty water and human waste. Sewers reduce the spread of disease because dirty water can contain germs that cause people to get sick. Aqueducts transported water to places where it was needed. **24.** The Hajj is a pilgrimage to Mecca. **25.** Frederick the Great expanded Prussia's territory by invading Silesia and taking it away from Austria.

Part D

26. D **27.** C **28.** B **29.** H **30.** E **31.** F **32.** A **33.** G **34.** J **35.** O **36.** L **37.** I **38.** M **39.** K **40.** N

Part E

Answers will vary. Students should support their answers with at least some of the following facts: **41.** The Assyrian rebels were already disobeying so they were probably happy when the empire fell. The Assyrians treated captured people very badly.

42. Philosophers might spend too much time thinking about things and never get anything done. Leaders should be thinkers, but they should also be doers.

Part F

Answers will vary. Students' paragraphs should include at least some of these ideas: **43.** King Henry VIII wanted to end his marriage to Catherine, but the Catholic Church did not allow divorce. Henry asked Pope Clement VII to annul the marriage. Catherine was opposed to this, so she asked her nephew, Charles V, to influence the pope's decision. The pope refused to annul the marriage. Henry secretly wed Anne Boleyn anyway. Henry appointed a new archbishop of Canterbury, who said that the marriage to Catherine was not legal. In 1534, Parliament made Henry the head of the Church of England, or Anglican Church. Henry took control of all lands the Catholic Church owned in England. **44.** After the Spanish conquered the Aztec and Inca Empires, Spanish conquistadores controlled large areas of land. To make money off the land, the landowners needed farm workers and miners to work on their land. The Spanish forced American Indians to do the work for them. Within 100 years, the Indian population went from 20 million to 4 million. After the efforts of Bartolomé de las Casas, Spain started to import Africans to the Americas. This was the beginning of African slavery in the Americas.

Final Mastery Test

Part A

1. anthropologists 2. Confucius 3. Hohokam 4. scholars
5. religious 6. boycott 7. iron 8. Miguel Hidalgo 9. siege
10. China 11. Lenin 12. Versailles 13. Berlin Wall
14. Nelson Mandela 15. NAFTA

Part B

16. B 17. D 18. B 19. C 20. A 21. C 22. C 23. A 24. A
25. B 26. D 27. B 28. D 29. A 30. A

Part C

31. H 32. B 33. E 34. F 35. A 36. C 37. D 38. G 39. O
40. L 41. N 42. M 43. I 44. J 45. K

Part D

46. Roman art contained imperfections such as wrinkles and broken noses. This differed from Greek art, which celebrated perfection and idealized beauty. 47. Ghana, Mali, and Songhai became powerful West African empires between 400 and 1586 A.D.
48. Jabir's discoveries led to chemistry. 49. The word *science* comes from the Latin word that means "to know." 50. The conquistadors killed many of the Incas and captured their leader, Atahualpa.
51. A nation needs workers and natural resources to become industrialized. 52. The Reds, the Bolsheviks, fought the Whites, the non-Communists, in the Russian Civil War. 53. Disease and war are two things the United Nations tries to prevent. 54. The Internet is the international computer network. 55. North and South Vietnam united into one Communist country.

Part E

56. culture 57. Fertile Crescent 58. Reason 59. Napoleon
60. Simón Bolívar 61. Myanmar 62. Serbs 63. fascist party
64. Marshall Plan 65. Thailand

Part F

Answers will vary. Students should support their answers with at least some of the following facts: 66. We do not know how Upper and Lower Egypt were united. One story is that Menes, the god-king, conquered Lower Egypt and built his capital where Upper Egypt and Lower Egypt meet. 67. The French set up settlements along the Great Lakes and the Mississippi River.

Part G

Answers will vary. Students' paragraphs should include at least some of these ideas: 68. Militarism is a nation's warlike policy or practice. Otto von Bismarck, the prime minister of Prussia, believed that war was a means for solving problems. He forced the Prussian parliament to give him money to build a strong army. Prussia defeated Denmark in 1864, Austria in 1866, and France in 1871. France had to give up Alsace and Lorraine. All these military victories contributed to the movement for a unified Germany. William I became the first kaiser of Germany. This German empire is called the Second Reich. 69. The recession was the economic slowdown caused by the collapse of the money supply of Thailand in 1997. As a result, banks and businesses went bankrupt throughout Southeast Asia. People in Japan lost their jobs. U.S. companies lost money because people in other nations had no money to buy goods. Some blame multinational corporations for the recession.

Scoring Rubric for Short-Response Items on the last page of Mastery Tests

2 points— The student demonstrates a solid understanding of the content by providing:

- a complete set of accurate facts that support the answer
- a clearly stated answer to the question

1 point— The student demonstrates a partial understanding of the content by providing *one* of the following:

- a complete set of accurate facts that support the answer
- a clearly stated answer to the question

0 points— The student fails to demonstrate understanding of the content by doing *one* of the following:

- includes no facts or incorrect facts, and fails to provide a clearly stated answer
- provides no answer at all

Scoring Rubric for Essay Items on the last page of Mastery Tests

3 points— The student demonstrates a solid understanding of the content by providing:

- a complete set of accurate facts that support the answer
- a clearly stated answer to the essay's primary question
- a standard essay response (topic sentence, body, conclusion)

2 points— The student demonstrates a good understanding of the content by providing *two* of the following:

- a complete set of accurate facts that support the answer
- a clearly stated answer to the essay's primary question
- a standard essay response (topic sentence, body, conclusion)

1 point— The student demonstrates a partial understanding of the content by providing *one* of the following:

- a complete set of accurate facts that support the answer
- a clearly stated answer to the essay's primary question
- a standard essay response (topic sentence, body, conclusion)

0 points— The student fails to demonstrate understanding of the content by doing *one* of the following:

- includes no facts or incorrect facts, fails to answer the essay's primary question, and fails to include a standard essay response (topic sentence, body, conclusion)
- provides no answer at all

Teacher Questionnaire

Attention Teachers! As publishers of *World History,*
we would like your help in making this textbook more valuable to you.
Please take a few minutes to fill out this survey. Your feedback will
help us to better serve you and your students.

1. What is your position and major area of responsibility?

    _____

    _____

2. Briefly describe your setting:

    _____ regular education _____ special education _____ adult basic education

    _____ community college _____ university _____ other _____

3. The enrollment in your classroom includes students with the following
    (check all that apply):

    _____ at risk for failure _____ low reading ability _____ behavior problems

    _____ learning disabilities _____ ESL _____ other _____

4. Grade level of your students:

5. Racial/ethnic groups represented in your classes (check all that apply):

    _____ African American _____ Asian _____ Caucasian _____ Hispanic

    _____ American Indian _____ other

6. School location:

    _____ urban _____ suburban _____ rural _____ other _____

7. What reaction did your students have to the materials? Include comments
    about the cover design, lesson format, illustrations, etc.

    _____

    _____

    _____

8. What features in the student text helped your students the most?

    _____

    _____

    _____

9. What features in the student text helped your students the least? Please include suggestions for changing these to make the text more relevant.

_____

_____

10. How did you use the Teacher's Edition and support materials, and what features did you find to be the most helpful?

_____

_____

11. What activity from the program did your students benefit from the most? Please briefly explain.

_____

_____

_____

12. Optional: Share an activity that you used to teach history content that enhanced the learning and motivation of your students.

_____

_____

_____

Several activities will be selected to be included in future editions. Please include your name, address, and phone number so we may contact you for permission and possible payment.

Thank you!

▼ fold in thirds and tape shut at the top   ▼

Name: _____

School: _____

Address: _____

City/State/ZIP: _____

Phone: _____

BUSINESS REPLY MAIL
FIRST-CLASS MAIL   PERMIT NO. 3046   ST PAUL, MN

POSTAGE WILL BE PAID BY ADDRESSEE

PEARSON
AGS Globe

PEARSON AGS GLOBE   ATTN: Textbook Product Manager
DEPT 3171
5910 RICE CREEK PKWY STE 1000
ST PAUL MN 55126-9802